West's Law School
Advisory Board

CRIMINAL LAW AND THE REGULATION OF VICE

By

Franklin E. Zimring

William G. Simon Professor of Law and
Wolfen Distinguished Scholar
University of California, Berkeley

Bernard E. Harcourt

Julius Kreeger Professor of Law and Criminology
The University of Chicago

AMERICAN CASEBOOK SERIES®

THOMSON
WEST

Mat #40501755

© 2007 Thomson/West
      610 Opperman Drive
      St. Paul, MN 55123
      1–800–328–9352

Printed in the United States of America

ISBN: 978–0–314–16952–5

 *TEXT IS PRINTED ON 10% POST CONSUMER RECYCLED PAPER*

Preface

The principles and problems of the substantive criminal law have a prominent but quite limited role in the curriculum of the modern American law school. The course in substantive criminal law is one of the star attractions in the standard first year program, but that is not merely the beginning of course work on substantive principles, it is the end as well. There will be one or more courses on criminal procedure, courses on evidence and trial practice and perhaps a course on the criminal justice system. Some schools offer courses in the jurisdictional and procedural aspects of federal criminal law. But the issues of substance on criteria for selecting behaviors properly to be prohibited and punished in the modern state are considered in the first course one takes on the subject or not at all.

These materials were created as an effort to construct a second course in the principles of modern criminal law, an offering that could be characterized as advanced criminal law. The idea was to build on the foundation of case analysis and statutory issues that is provided in the first course but to add the materials of modern history, legal philosophy and social science. To build an advanced course, we wanted to consider interesting topics where policies were changing rapidly.

There are two attractive candidates in the borderlands of current criminal law for an advanced course. One is the area variously called organizational, corporate, or white-collar crime. This is a complicated and important cluster of questions that richly deserves a sustained treatment in a law school classroom, and many but not all of its central concerns fit closely with the principles of substantive criminal law. It is also an area where regulatory and criminal law efforts require coordination. So a modern course in white collar or organizational crime spans both regulatory and criminal concerns in areas such as the environment, securities and consumer protection.

The second natural area for advanced work in substantive criminal law involves a central debate over the last two centuries: the harm principle of John Stuart Mill and the response of James Fitzjames Stephen in the nineteenth century produced a lively debate between Lord Devlin and H.L.A. Hart in the twentieth century and a rich literature on harm and the costs of prohibition in a wide variety of behaviors traditionally governed by criminal statute but subject to a wide variety of swift changes in the twentieth century. Traditionally regarded as vice offenses, behaviors such as pornography and prostitution, non-marital and nontraditional sexual conduct, recreational drug taking, gambling and alcohol control have been the subject of a wide variety of legal changes throughout the twentieth century. Alcohol was first the subject of national prohibition in the United States then its repeal. Gambling and pornography were decriminalized in the United States and most of the developed world in the generation after 1970. But the criminal prohibition of narcotics and other recreational drugs was intensified dramatically in the 1980s in the United States. Other traditional vice behaviors such as prostitution have not yet been the subject of extensive legal or regulatory change. Are these traditional topics of the police vice squad one type of criminal law question or many very different topics? Is there one dominant trend over time in the legal regulation of these behaviors or several crosscurrents? Is there a single thread of principle that is observable through the wide variety of traditional "vice" crimes? Do these principles also apply to modern topics like handgun control and drunk driving? These are the cutting edge issues we confront in the materials we have organized in this book.

And the modern discussions of sexual conduct, pornography, drugs and gambling are also a crossroads for the humanities and social sciences. The relevant literature on the topics of this class includes philosophy, history, economics, criminology, sociology and psychology. One set of important questions is whether the criminal law should play a dominant, secondary or minor role in governmental policy toward the behaviors we consider and why. A second question is what other domains of governmental involvement are potential substitutes for the policy of criminal courts? Or do we mean it when we say that some of this conduct is not the business of the public law at all?

The topics discussed in the chapters that follow are frontier areas for legal policy in both the twentieth and twenty-first centuries.

Authors' Note

A variety of people and institutions helped us produce this volume. Our earliest and largest debt is to Gordon Hawkins, a philosopher and senior fellow at the Earl Warren Legal Institute from 1984 to 2001, who launched this project in 1996 and put together the first draft of Chapter 1. Professor Hawkins was the inspiration for this venture. The Boalt Hall Fund of the University of California, Berkeley supported the preparation of these materials through the Criminal Justice Research Program. Toni Mendicino at the Institute for Legal Research produced the volume and kept us organized. Karen Chin provided the substantial administrative support this kind of effort requires. Judith Randle, a doctoral student in Jurisprudence and Social Policy at Berkeley helped to assemble the materials in Chapters 3 and 7 while Jeffrey Bergman at the University of Chicago Law School helped with Gambling and sections of Chapters 2, 6, and 7. Aaron Blumenthal, a Berkeley undergraduate helped with the index. Tim Chevalier coordinated permissions and was indispensable in preparing a properly formatted electronic version of the final manuscript. Bonnie Karlen at Thompson West helped launch the project and Kathleen Vandergon supervised the production process with care and good humor.

We hope the final product merits this epic assistance.

FRANKLIN E. ZIMRING
BERNARD E. HARCOURT

*

Acknowledgments

Bingham, Nicole, *Nevada Sex Trade: A Gamble for the Workers,* 10 Yale J. L. & Feminism 69–99 (1998). © by the Yale Journal of Law & Feminism, Inc. Reprinted by permission.

Boudreaux, Donald and A.C. Pritchard, *The Price of Prohibition,* 36 Ariz. L. Rev. 1–10 (Spring 1994). © The Arizona Law Review, Donald J. Boudreaux, Professor of Economics, George Mason University and A.C. Pritchard, Professor of Law, University of Michigan. Reprinted by permission.

Cattelino, Jessica R., *"From Bingo Halls to Billions": Tribal Gaming and Indigenous Sovereignty, with Notes from Seminole Country,* 46 Am. Stud. 3/4: 171–188 (Fall–Winter 2005). © by American Studies. Reprinted by permission.

Cattelino, Jessica R., *Indian Gaming in the United States,* in the Handbook of North American Indians, Vol. 2, Contemporary Issues, Garrick Bailey, vol. ed., W.C. Sturtevant, general editor. Published by the Smithsonian Institution, Washington D.C. (forthcoming). Reprinted by permission of the author.

Conant, Michael, *Federalism, the Mann Act, and the Imperative to Decriminalize Prostitution,* 5 Cornell J. L. & Pub. Pol'y 99 (Winter 1996). © by the Cornell Journal of Law and Public Policy. Reprinted by permission.

Devlin, Baron Patrick, Morals and the Criminal Law, 14 *The Proceedings of the British Academy* 129–151 (1932). © by The British Academy. Reprinted by permission.

Farrior, Stephanie, *The International Law on Trafficking in Women and Children for Prostitution: Making it Live Up to its Potential,* 10 Harv. Hum. Rts. J. 213–255 (Spring 1997). © by the Harvard Human Rights Journal. Reprinted by permission.

Flowers, R. Barri, *The Sex Trade Industry's Worldwide Exploitation of Children* 575 Annals Am. Acad. Pol. & Soc. Sci., 147–157 (May 2001). © by the Annals of the American Academy of Political and Social Science. Reprinted by permission of Sage Publications, Inc.

Gouvin, Eric, *Drunk Driving and the Alcoholic Offender: A New Approach to an Old Problem,* 12 Am. J. L. and Med. 99–130 (1986). © 1987 by the American Journal of Law and Medicine, Inc. and the Boston University School of Law. Reprinted by permission.

Hamm, Richard, Shaping the Eighteenth Amendment: Temperance, Reform, Legal Culture, and the Polity, 1880–1920 (excerpt) (1995). © by the University of North Carolina Press. Reprinted by permission.

Harcourt, Bernard, *Revisiting the Legal Enforcement of Morality: The Collapse of the Harm Principle*, 90 J. of Crim. L. & Criminology 109–194 (1999). © by Northwestern University School of Law. Reprinted by special permission of Northwestern University School of Law, *The Journal of Criminal Law and Criminology.*

Harcourt, Bernard, *You Are Entering a Gay and Lesbian Free Zone: on the Radical Dissents of Justice Scalia and Other (Post-)Queers [Raising Questions about Lawrence, Sex Wars, and the Criminal Law]*, 94 J. of Crim. L. and Criminology 503–549 (2004). © by Northwestern University School of Law. Reprinted by special permission of Northwestern University School of Law, *The Journal of Criminal Law and Criminology.*

Harris, Donald, *The Concept of State Power Under the Twenty-First Amendment*, 40 Tenn. L. Rev. 465–495 (1973). © by The Tennessee Law Review Association, Inc. and Donald Harris. The full text of this article was published originally at 40 Tenn. L. Rev. 465 (1973) and this edited version is used here by permission of Donald Harris and the Tennessee Law Review Association, Inc.

Hart, H.L.A., Law, Liberty, and Morality, 1, 4–6, 13–16, 18–20, 30–33, 69, 75–78, 79, 81–83 (1963). © 1963 by the Board of Trustees of the Leland Stanford Jr. University. Reprinted by permission of Stanford University Press.

Hawkins, Gordon and Franklin E. Zimring, Pornography in a Free Society 20–29, 74–108, 175–197 (1988). © by Cambridge University Press. Reprinted by permission.

Kadish, Sanford, *The Crisis of Overcriminalization*, 374 Annals of the American Academy of Political and Social Science; Combating Crime 157–170 (November 1967). © by The Annals of the American Academy of Political and Social Science. Reprinted by permission of Sage Publications, Inc.

Kindt, John Warren, *Legalized Gambling Activities: The Issues Involving Market Saturation*, 15 N. Ill. U. L. Rev. 271–306 (Spring 1995). © by the Northern Illinois University Law Review. Reprinted by permission.

MacKinnon, Catherine A., *Not a Moral Issue*, 2 Yale L. & Pol'y Rev. 2:321–345 (1984). © by the Yale Law & Policy Review. Reprinted by permission.

MacKinnon, Catherine A., Only Words 22–41 (1993). © 1993 by Catharine MacKinnon. Reprinted by permission of the author and Harvard University Press, Cambridge, Mass.

Martz, Stephanie, McDonald, Daniel, *Regulating Sexually Oriented Businesses: The Regulatory Uncertainties of a "Regime of Prohibition by Indirection" and the Obscenity Doctrine's Communal Solution*, 1997

B. Y. U. L. Rev. 339 (1997). © by Brigham Young University Law Review. Reprinted by permission.

Morris, Norval and Gordon Hawkins, The Honest Politician's Guide to Crime Control, 2–28 (1970). © The University of Chicago Press. Reprinted by permission.

Murdoch, Joyce and Deb Price, Courting Justice: Gay Men and Lesbians v. The Supreme Court, 337–344 (2001). © by Basic Books. Reprinted by permission from The Perseus Book Group.

Nagel, Ernest, *The Enforcement of Morals,* 3 The Humanist 20–27 (1968). © by The Humanist. Reprinted by permission of the American Humanist Association.

Packer, Herbert, *The Pornography Caper,* 51 Commentary 72–77 (1971). © by Commentary. Reprinted by permission of Commentary, February 1971; all rights reserved.

Pearl, Julie, *The Highest Paying Customers: America's Cities and the Costs of Prostitution Control,* 38 Hastings L. J. 769 (1987). © 1987 by the University of California, Hastings College of the Law. Reprinted by permission.

Quigley, John, *The Dilemma of Prostitution Law Reform: Lessons from the Soviet Russian Experiment,* 29 Am. Crim. L. Rev. 1197–1234 (1992). © 1992 by the publisher, the American Criminal Law Review, Georgetown University Law Center. Reprinted by permission.

Removing the Incentive to Act Corruptly, or, Teaching an Old Dog New Tricks, 13 J. L. & Politics 453–492 (Spring 1997). © by the Journal of Law & Politics. Reprinted by permission.

Richards, David A. J., *Commercial Sex and the Rights of the Person: A Moral Argument for the Decriminalization of Prostitution,* 127 Univ. of Pa. L. Rev. 1195, 1203–1214 (1979). © by the University of Pennsylvania Law Review. Reprinted by permission of William S. Hein & Co., Inc.

Rychlak, Ronald, *Lotteries, Revenues and Social Costs: A Historical Examination of State-Sponsored Gambling,* 34 B. C. L. Rev. 11–81 (Spring 1993). © 1992 by Ronald J. Rychlak. Reprinted by permission.

Stigler, Stephen M., Casanova's Lottery (March 6, 2003), available at http://www.uchicago.edu/docs/education/record/pdfs/37-4.pdf. Reprinted by permission of the author.

Stout, Lynn, *Why the Law Hates Speculators: Regulation and Private Orderings in the Market for OTC Derivatives,* 48 Duke L. J. 701–786 (1999). © 1999 by Duke Law Journal. Reprinted by permission of the author and Duke Law Journal.

Stremler, Alexandra Bongard, *Sex for Money and the Morning After: Listening to Women and the Feminist Voice in Prostitution Discourse,* 7 J.

Law. & Pub. Pol'y 189–204 (1994–1995). © by the University of Florida Journal of Law & Public Policy. Reprinted by permission.

Sunstein, Cass, *What Did Lawrence Hold? Of Autonomy, Desuetude, Sexuality, and Marriage,* 27 Sup. Ct. Rev. (2004). © by the University of Chicago Press. Reprinted by permission.

The Wolfenden Committee, The Wolfenden Report: Report of the Committee on Homosexual Offenses and Prostitution (1963). © by Stein and Day. Permission not required.

Zhao, Victor, Alyshea Austern, Shaudy Danaye-Elmi, Brian Hill, David Gearey, Jenny Maldonaldo, Mary McKinney, Brad Russo, Andrew Sherman, Sean Williams, Tim Karpoff, Ranjit Hakim, Allen McKenzie, Gabriel Galloway, Naria Kim, Carl LeSueur, Anne Mullins, Angela Ramey, Deidra Ritcherson and Tamer Tullgren, Opinion, *Chicago Casino: Worth a Crapshoot? University of Chicago Law Students Debate the Merits,* Chic. Sun-Times, p. 18 (June 19, 2004). © by the Chicago Sun-Times, Inc. Reprinted by permission of the authors.

Summary of Contents

Table of Contents

*

Table of Cases

The principal cases are in bold type. Cases cited or discussed in the text are roman type. References are to pages. Cases cited in principal cases and within other quoted materials are not included.

---

*

CRIMINAL LAW AND THE REGULATION OF VICE

*

Chapter 1

PRINCIPLE AND POLICY

A. THE ENFORCEMENT OF MORALS

THE HART–DEVLIN DEBATE

from Bernard E. Harcourt, *The Collapse of the Harm Principle,* 90 Journal
of Criminal Law and Criminology 109, 120–131 (1999).

The harm principle traces back to John Stuart Mill's essay *On
Liberty* (1859). Mill succinctly stated the principle in a now-famous
passage in the opening pages of the essay:

> The object of this essay is to assert one very simple principle, as
> entitled to govern absolutely the dealings of society with the individ-
> ual in the way of compulsion and control...

> That principle is that the sole end for which mankind are
> warranted, individually or collectively, in interfering with the liberty
> of action of any of their number is self-protection. That the only
> purpose for which power can be rightfully exercised over any mem-
> ber of a civilized community, against his will, is to prevent harm to
> others.

Though simple at first blush, the harm principle actually was far
more complicated than it looked, and, over the course of the essay, it
took on many nuances. The argument in fact became more complex with
each restatement. In Mill's short essay, the harm principle metamor-
phosed from a simple inquiry into harm, to a more complex analysis of
interests (self-regarding and other regarding interests), and eventually to
a quasi-legal determination of rights. In his final restatement of the
harm principle, Mill ultimately defined the concept of harm on the basis
of recognized or legal rights. Mill wrote:

> Though society is not founded on a contract, ... the fact of
> living in society renders it indispensable that each should be bound
> to observe a certain line of conduct toward the rest. This conduct
> consists, first, in not injuring the interests of one another, *or rather
> certain interests which, either by express legal provision or by tacit
> understanding, ought to be considered as rights*; and secondly, in

1

each person's bearing his share (to be fixed on some equitable principle) of the labors and sacrifices incurred for defending the society or its members from injury and molestation.

As Mill explained elsewhere, the notion of rights embodied in this final restatement rested on a modified utilitarian calculus grounded on the permanent interests of man as a progressive being.

In Mill's writings, then, the original, simple harm principle evolved into a more cumbersome principle. Mill nevertheless applied the principle and justified, on its basis, a large number of regulations and prohibitions. The harm principle, in Mill's own hands, produced a blueprint for a highly regulated society: a society that regulated the sale of potential instruments of crime, that taxed the sale of alcohol and regulated the public consumption of alcohol, that regulated education and even procreation, and that prohibited public intoxication and indecency.

Beginning at least in the 1950s, liberal theorists, most prominently Professors H.L.A. Hart and Joel Feinberg, returned to Mill's original, simple statement of the harm principle. The context was the debate over the legal enforcement of morality. In England, this debate was reignited by the recommendation of the Committee on Homosexual Offences and Prostitution (the "Wolfenden Report") that private homosexual acts between consenting adults no longer be criminalized. In the United States, the debate was reignited by the Supreme Court's struggle over the definition and treatment of obscenity and the drafting of the Model Penal Code. In both countries, the debate was fueled by the perception among liberal theorists that legal moralist principles were experiencing a rejuvenation and were threatening to encroach on liberalism. More than anyone else, Lord Patrick Devlin catalyzed this perceived threat. In his Maccabaean Lecture, delivered to the British Academy in 1959, Lord Devlin argued that purportedly immoral activities, like homosexuality and prostitution, should remain criminal offenses. Lord Devlin published his lecture and other essays under the title *The Enforcement of Morals*, and Devlin soon became associated with the principle of legal moralism—the principle that moral offenses should be regulated *because* they are immoral.

The Hart–Devlin exchange structured the debate over the legal enforcement of morality, and thus there emerged, in the 1960s, a pairing of two familiar arguments—the harm principle and legal moralism. All the participants at the time recognized, naturally, that this structure was a recurrence of a very similar pairing of arguments that had set the contours of the debate a hundred years earlier. The Hart–Devlin debate replicated, in many ways, the earlier debate between Mill and another famous British jurist, Lord James Fitzjames Stephen. In 1873, in a book entitled *Liberty, Equality, Fraternity*, Lord Stephen had published a scathing attack on Mill's essay and strenuously advocated legal moralism. Stephen described his argument as "absolutely inconsistent with and contradictory to Mr. Mill's." Stephen's argument, like Mill's, was best captured in a now-famous passage: "[T]here are acts of wickedness

so gross and outrageous that, self-protection apart, they must be prevented as far as possible at any cost to the offender, and punished, if
they occur, with exemplary severity.''

Professor Hart immediately underscored the similar structure of the
emerging debate. ''Though a century divides these two legal writers,''
Hart observed, referring to Lords Stephen and Devlin, ''the similarity in
the general tone and sometimes in the detail of their arguments is very
great.'' In his defense, Devlin responded that at the time he delivered
the Maccabaean lecture he ''did not then know that the same ground
had already been covered by Mr. Justice Stephen....'' Nevertheless,
Devlin conceded that there was ''great similarity between [Lord Stephen's] view and mine on the principles that should affect the use of the
criminal law for the enforcement of morals.'' Devlin also noted the
similarity between Hart, Mill, and the Wolfenden Report. Referring to
the Wolfenden Report, Devlin observed that ''this use of the [harm]
principle is, as Professor Hart observed, 'strikingly similar' to Mill's
doctrine.''

BARON PATRICK DEVLIN—MORALS AND THE CRIMINAL LAW

from The Enforcement of Morals—Oxford University Press (1965).

What is the connexion between crime and sin and to what extent, if
at all, should the criminal law of England concern itself with the
enforcement of morals and punish sin or immorality as such?

The statements of principle in the Wolfenden Report provide an
admirable and modern starting-point for such an inquiry.... Early in
the Report the Committee put forward:

> Our own formulation of the function of the criminal law so far as it
> concerns the subjects of this enquiry. In this field, its function, as we
> see it, is to preserve public order and decency, to protect the citizen
> from what is offensive or injurious, and to provide sufficient safe-
> guards against exploitation and corruption of others, particularly
> those who are specially vulnerable because they are young, weak in
> body or mind, inexperienced, or in a state of special physical, official
> or economic dependence.

> It is not, in our view, the function of the law to intervene in the
> private lives of citizens, or to seek to enforce any particular pattern
> of behaviour, further than is necessary to carry out the purposes we
> have outlined.

The Committee preface their most important recommendation that
homosexual behaviour between consenting adults in private should no
longer be a criminal offence, [by stating the argument] which we believe
to be decisive, namely, the importance which society and the law ought
to give to individual freedom of choice and action in matters of private
morality. Unless a deliberate attempt is to be made by society, acting
through the agency of the law, to equate the sphere of crime with that of

sin, there must remain a realm of private morality and immorality which is, in brief and crude terms, not the law's business. To say this is not to condone or encourage private immorality.

Similar statements of principle are set out in the chapters of the Report which deal with prostitution. No case can be sustained, the Report says, for attempting to make prostitution itself illegal. The Committee refer to the general reasons already given and add: "We are agreed that private immorality should not be the concern of the criminal law except in the special circumstances therein mentioned." They quote with approval the report of the Street Offences Committee, which says: "As a general proposition it will be universally accepted that the law is not concerned with private morals or with ethical sanctions." It will be observed that the emphasis is on private immorality. By this is meant immorality which is not offensive or injurious to the public in the ways defined or described in the first passage which I quoted. In other words, no act of immorality should be made a criminal offence unless it is accompanied by some other feature such as indecency, corruption, or exploitation. This is clearly brought out in relation to prostitution: "It is not the duty of the law to concern itself with immorality as such... it should confine itself to those activities which offend against public order and decency or expose the ordinary citizen to what is offensive or injurious."

These statements of principle are naturally restricted to the subject-matter of the Report. But they are made in general terms and there seems to be no reason why, if they are valid, they should not be applied to the criminal law in general. They separate very decisively crime from sin, the divine law from the secular, and the moral from the criminal. They do not signify any lack of support for the law, moral or criminal, and they do not represent an attitude that can be called either religious or irreligious. There are many schools of thought among those who may think that morals are not the law's business....

I think it is clear that the criminal law as we know it is based upon moral principle. In a number of crimes its function is simply to enforce a moral principle and nothing else. The law, both criminal and civil, claims to be able to speak about morality and immorality generally. Where does it get its authority to do this and how does it settle the moral principles which it enforces? Undoubtedly, as a matter of history, it derived both from Christian teaching. But I think that the strict logician is right when he says that the law can no longer rely on doctrines in which citizens are entitled to disbelieve. It is necessary therefore to look for some other source.

In jurisprudence, as I have said, everything is thrown open to discussion and, in the belief that they cover the whole field, I have framed three interrogatories addressed to myself to answer:

1. Has society the right to pass judgement at all on matters of morals? Ought there, in other words, to be a public morality, or are morals always a matter for private judgement?

2. If society has the right to pass judgement, has it also the right to use the weapon of the law to enforce it?

3. If so, ought it to use that weapon in all cases or only in some; and if only in some, on what principles should it distinguish?

I shall begin with the first interrogatory and consider what is meant by the right of society to pass a moral judgement, that is, a judgement about what is good and what is evil. The fact that a majority of people may disapprove of a practice does not of itself make it a matter for society as a whole. Nine men out of ten may disapprove of what the tenth man is doing and still say that it is not their business. There is a case for a collective judgement (as distinct from a large number of individual opinions which sensible people may even refrain from pronouncing at all if it is upon somebody else's private affairs) only if society is affected. Without a collective judgement there can be no case at all for intervention. . . .

What makes a society of any sort is community of ideas, not only political ideas but also ideas about the way its members should behave and govern their lives; these latter ideas are its morals. Every society has a moral structure as well as a political one: or rather, since that might suggest two independent systems, I should say that the structure of every society is made up both of politics and morals. Take, for example, the institution of marriage. Whether a man should be allowed to take more than one wife is something about which every society has to make up its mind one way or the other. In England we believe in the Christian idea of marriage and therefore adopt monogamy as a moral principle. Consequently the Christian institution of marriage has become the basis of family life and so part of the structure of our society. It is there not because it is Christian. It has got there because it is Christian, but it remains there because it is built into the house in which we live and could not be removed without bringing it down. The great majority of those who live in this country accept it because it is the Christian idea of marriage and for them the only true one. But a non-Christian is bound by it, not because it is part of Christianity but because, rightly or wrongly, it has been adopted by the society in which he lives. It would be useless for him to stage a debate designed to prove that polygamy was theologically more correct and socially preferable; if he wants to live in the house, he must accept it as built in the way in which it is.

We see this more clearly if we think of ideas or institutions that are purely political. Society cannot tolerate rebellion; it will not allow argument about the rightness of the cause. Historians a century later may say that the rebels were right and the Government was wrong and a percipient and conscientious subject of the State may think so at the time. But it is not a matter which can be left to individual judgement.

The institution of marriage is a good example for my purpose because it bridges the division, if there is one, between politics and morals. Marriage is part of the structure of our society and it is also the basis of a moral code which condemns fornication and adultery. The institution of marriage would be gravely threatened if individual judgements were permitted about the morality of adultery; on these points there must be a public morality. But public morality is not to be confined to those moral principles which support institutions such as marriage. People do not think of monogamy as something which has to be supported because our society has chosen to organize itself upon it; they think of it as something that is good in itself and offering a good way of life and that it is for that reason that our society has adopted it. I return to the statement that I have already made, that society means a community of ideas; without shared ideas on politics, morals, and ethics no society can exist. Each one of us has ideas about what is good and what is evil; they cannot be kept private from the society in which we live. If men and women try to create a society in which there is no fundamental agreement about good and evil they will fail; if, having based it on common agreement, the agreement goes, the society will disintegrate. For society is not something that is kept together physically; it is held by the invisible bonds of common thought. If the bonds were too far relaxed the members would drift apart. A common morality is part of the bondage. The bondage is part of the price of society; and mankind, which needs society, must pay its price....

You may think that I have taken far too long in contending that there is such a thing as public morality, a proposition which most people would readily accept, and may have left myself too little time to discuss the next question which to many minds may cause greater difficulty: to what extent should society use the law to enforce its moral judgements? But I believe that the answer to the first question determines the way in which the second should be approached and may indeed very nearly dictate the answer to the second question. If society has no right to make judgements on morals, the law must find some special justification for entering the field of morality: if homosexuality and prostitution are not in themselves wrong, then the onus is very clearly on the lawgiver who wants to frame a law against certain aspects of them to justify the exceptional treatment. But if society has the right to make a judgement and has it on the basis that a recognized morality is as necessary to society as, say, a recognized government, then society may use the law to preserve morality in the same way as it uses it to safeguard anything else that is essential to its existence. If therefore the first proposition is securely established with all its implications, society has a prima facie right to legislate against immorality as such....

Prostitution is not in itself illegal and the Committee do not think that it ought to be made so. If prostitution is private immorality and not the law's business, what concern has the law with the ponce or the brothel-keeper or the householder who permits habitual prostitution? The Report recommends that the laws which make these activities criminal offences should be maintained or strengthened and brings them (so far as it goes into principle; with regard to brothels it says simply that the law rightly frowns on them) under the head of exploitation. There may be cases of exploitation in this trade, as there are or used to be in many others, but in general a ponce exploits a prostitute no more than an impresario exploits an actress. The Report finds that "the great majority of prostitutes are women whose psychological makeup is such that they choose this life because they find in it a style of living which is to them easier, freer and more profitable than would be provided by any other occupation. . . . In the main the association between prostitute and ponce is voluntary and operates to mutual advantage." The Committee would agree that this could not be called exploitation in the ordinary sense. They say: "It is in our view an over-simplification to think that those who live on the earnings of prostitution are exploiting the prostitute as such. What they are really exploiting is the whole complex of the relationship between prostitute and customer; they are, in effect, exploiting the human weaknesses which cause the customer to seek the prostitute and the prostitute to meet the demand."

All sexual immorality involves the exploitation of human weaknesses. The prostitute exploits the lust of her customers and the customer the moral weakness of the prostitute. If the exploitation of human weaknesses is considered to create a special circumstance, there is virtually no field of morality which can be defined in such a way as to exclude the law.

I think, therefore, that it is not possible to set theoretical limits to the power of the State to legislate against immorality. It is not possible to settle in advance exceptions to the general rule or to define inflexibly areas of morality into which the law is in no circumstances to be allowed to enter. Society is entitled by means of its laws to protect itself from dangers, whether from within or without. Here again I think that the political parallel is legitimate. The law of treason is directed against aiding the king's enemies and against sedition from within. The justification for this is that established government is necessary for the existence of society and therefore its safety against violent overthrow must be secured. But an established morality is as necessary as good government to the welfare of society: Societies disintegrate from within more frequently than they are broken up by external pressures. There is disintegration when no common morality is observed and history shows that the loosening of moral bonds is often the first stage of disintegration, so that society is justified in taking the same steps to preserve its moral code as it does to preserve its government and other essential institutions. The suppression of vice is as much the law's business as the suppression of subversive activities; it is no more possible to define a sphere of private morality than it is to define one of private subversive activity. It is wrong to talk of private morality or of the law not being concerned with immorality as such or to try to set rigid bounds to the part which the law may play in the suppression of vice. There are no theoretical limits to the power of the State to legislate against treason and sedition, and likewise I think there can be no theoretical limits to legislation against immorality. You may argue that if a man's sins affect only himself it cannot be the concern of society. If he chooses to get drunk every night in the privacy of his own home, is any one except himself the worse for it? But suppose a quarter or a half of the population got drunk every night, what sort of society would it be? You cannot set a theoretical limit to the number of people who can get drunk before society is entitled to legislate against drunkenness. The same may be said of gambling. The Royal Commission on Betting, Lotteries, and Gaming took as their test the character of the citizen as a member of society. They said: "Our concern with the ethical significance of gambling is confined to the effect which it may have on the character of the gambler as a member of society. If we were convinced that whatever the degree of gambling this effect must be harmful we should be inclined to think that it was the duty of the state to restrict gambling to the greatest extent practicable!"

In what circumstances the State should exercise its power is the third of the interrogatories I have framed. But before I get to it I must raise a point which might have been brought up in any one of the three. How are the moral judgements of society to be ascertained? By leaving it until now, I can ask it in the more limited form that is now sufficient for my purpose. How is the law-maker to ascertain the moral judgements of society? It is surely not enough that they should be reached by the opinion of the majority; it would be too much to require the individual assent of every citizen. English law has evolved and regularly uses a standard which does not depend on the counting of heads. It is that of the reasonable man. He is not to be confused with the rational man. He is not expected to reason about anything and his judgement may be largely a matter of feeling. It is the viewpoint of the man in the street— or to use an archaism familiar to all lawyers—the man in the Clapham omnibus. He might also be called the right-minded man. For my purpose I should like to call him the man in the jury box, for the moral judgement of society must be something about which any twelve men or women drawn at random might after discussion be expected to be unanimous. This was the standard the judges applied in the days before Parliament was as active as it is now and when they laid down rules of public policy. They did not think of themselves as making law but simply as stating principles which every right-minded person would accept as valid. It is what Pollock called "practical morality", which is based not on theological or philosophical foundations but "in the mass of continuous experience half-consciously or unconsciously accumulated and embodied in the morality of common sense". He called it also "a certain way of thinking on questions of morality which we expect to find in a reasonable civilized man or a reasonable Englishman, taken at random".

Immorality then, for the purpose of the law, is what every right-minded person is presumed to consider to be immoral. Any immorality is capable of affecting society injuriously and in effect to a greater or lesser extent it usually does; this is what gives the law its *locus standi*. It cannot be shut out. But—and this brings me to the third question—the individual has a *locus standi* too; he cannot be expected to surrender to the judgement of society the whole conduct of his life. It is the old and familiar question of striking a balance between the rights and interests of society and those of the individual. This is something which the law is constantly doing in matters large and small. . . .

[I]t is possible to make general statements of principle which it may be thought the legislature should bear in mind when it is considering the enactment of laws enforcing morals.

I believe that most people would agree upon the chief of these elastic principles. There must be toleration of the maximum individual freedom that is consistent with the integrity of society. . . . Nothing should be punished by the law that does not lie beyond the limits of tolerance. It is not nearly enough to say that a majority dislike a practice; there must be a real feeling of reprobation. Those who are dissatisfied with the present law on homosexuality often say that the opponents of reform are swayed simply by disgust. If that were so it would be wrong, but I do not think one can ignore disgust if it is deeply felt and not manufactured. Its presence is a good indication that the bounds of toleration are being reached. Not everything is to be tolerated. No society can do without intolerance, indignation, and disgust; they are the forces behind the moral law, and indeed it can be argued that if they or something like them are not present, the feelings of society cannot be weighty enough to deprive the individual of freedom of choice. I suppose that there is hardly anyone nowadays who would not be disgusted by the thought of deliberate cruelty to animals. No one proposes to relegate that or any other form of sadism to the realm of private morality or to allow it to be practised in public or in private. It would be possible no doubt to point out that until a comparatively short while ago nobody thought very much of cruelty to animals and also that pity and kindliness and the unwillingness to inflict pain are virtues more generally esteemed now than they have ever been in the past. But matters of this sort are not determined by rational argument. Every moral judgement, unless it claims a divine source, is simply a feeling that no right-minded man could behave in any other way without admitting that he was doing wrong. It is the power of a common sense and not the power of reason that is behind the judgements of society. But before a society can put a practice beyond the limits of tolerance there must be a deliberate judgement that the practice is injurious to society. There is, for example, a general abhorrence of homosexuality. We should ask ourselves in the first instance whether, looking at it calmly and dispassionately, we regard it as a vice so abominable that its mere presence is an offence. If that is the genuine feeling of the society in which we live, I do not see how society can be denied the right to eradicate it. Our feeling may not be so intense as that. We may feel about it that, if confined, it is tolerable, but that if it spread it might be gravely injurious; it is in this way that most societies look upon fornication, seeing it as a natural weakness which must be kept within bounds but which cannot be rooted out. It becomes then a question of balance, the danger to society in one scale and the extent of the restriction in the other. On this sort of point the value of an investigation by such a body as the Wolfenden Committee and of its conclusions is manifest.

The limits of tolerance shift. This is supplementary to what I have been saying but of sufficient importance in itself to deserve statement as a separate principle which law-makers have to bear in mind. I suppose that moral standards do not shift; so far as they come from divine revelation they do not, and I am willing to assume that the moral judgements made by a society always remain good for that society. But the extent to which society will tolerate—I mean tolerate, not approve—departures from moral standards varies from generation to generation. It may be that over-all tolerance is always increasing. The pressure of the human mind, always seeking greater freedom of thought, is outwards against the bonds of society forcing their gradual relaxation. It may be that history is a tale of contraction and expansion and that all developed societies are on their way to dissolution. I must not speak of things I do not know; and anyway as a practical matter no society is willing to make provision for its own decay. I return therefore to the simple and observable fact that in matters of morals the limits of tolerance shift. . . .

A third elastic principle must be advanced more tentatively. It is that as far as possible privacy should be respected. This is not an idea that has ever been made explicit in the criminal law. Acts or words done or said in public or in private are all brought within its scope without distinction in principle. But there goes with this a strong reluctance on the part of judges and legislators to sanction invasions of privacy in the detection of crime. The police have no more right to trespass than the ordinary citizen has; there is no general right of search; to this extent an Englishman's home is still his castle. The Government is extremely careful in the exercise even of those powers which it claims to be undisputed. Telephone tapping and interference with the mails afford a good illustration of this. A Committee of three Privy Councillors who recently inquired into these activities found that the Home Secretary and his predecessors had already formulated strict rules governing the exercise of these powers and the Committee were able to recommend that they should be continued to be exercised substantially on the same terms. But they reported that the power was "regarded with general disfavour". . . .

The last and the biggest thing to be remembered is that the law is concerned with the minimum and not with the maximum; there is much in the Sermon on the Mount that would be out of place in the Ten Commandments. We all recognize the gap between the moral law and the law of the land. No man is worth much who regulates his conduct with the sole object of escaping punishment, and every worthy society sets for its members standards which are above those of the law. . . .

This then is how I believe my third interrogatory should be answered—not by the formulation of hard and fast rules, but by a judgement in each case taking into account the sort of factors I have been mentioning. The line that divides the criminal law from the moral is not determinable by the application of any clear-cut principle. It is like a line that divides land and sea, a coastline of irregularities and indentations.

There are gaps and promontories, such as adultery and fornication, which the law has for centuries left substantially untouched. Adultery of the sort that breaks up marriage seems to me to be just as harmful to the social fabric as homosexuality or bigamy. The only ground for putting it outside the criminal law is that a law which made it a crime would be too difficult to enforce; it is too generally regarded as a human weakness not suitably punished by imprisonment. All that the law can do with fornication is to act against its worst manifestations; there is a general abhorrence of the commercialization of vice, and that sentiment gives strength to the law against brothels and immoral earnings. There is no logic to be found in this. The boundary between the criminal law and the moral law is fixed by balancing in the case of each particular crime the pros and cons of legal enforcement in accordance with the sort of considerations I have been outlining. The fact that adultery, fornication, and lesbianism are untouched by the criminal law does not prove that homosexuality ought not to be touched. The error of jurisprudence in the Wolfenden Report is caused by the search for some single principle to explain the division between crime and sin. The Report finds it in the principle that the criminal law exists for the protection of individuals; on this principle fornication in private between consenting adults is outside the law and thus it becomes logically indefensible to bring homosexuality between consenting adults in private within it. But the true principle is that the law exists for the protection of society. It does not discharge its function by protecting the individual from injury, annoyance, corruption, and exploitation; the law must protect also the institutions and the community of ideas, political and moral, without which people cannot live together. Society cannot ignore the morality of the individual any more than it can his loyalty; it flourishes on both and without either it dies. . . .

I return now to the main thread of my argument and summarize it. Society cannot live without morals. Its morals are those standards of conduct which the reasonable man approves. A rational man, who is also a good man, may have other standards. If he has no standards at all he is not a good man and need not be further considered. If he has standards, they may be very different; he may, for example, not disapprove of homosexuality or abortion. In that case he will not share in the common morality; but that should not make him deny that it is a social necessity. A rebel may be rational in thinking that he is right but he is irrational if he thinks that society can leave him free to rebel.

A man who concedes that morality is necessary to society must support the use of those instruments without which morality cannot be maintained. The two instruments are those of teaching, which is doctrine, and of enforcement, which is the law. If morals could be taught simply on the basis that they are necessary to society, there would be no social need for religion; it could be left as a purely personal affair. But morality cannot be taught in that way. Loyalty is not taught in that way either. No society has yet solved the problem of how to teach morality without religion. So the law must base itself on Christian morals and to the limit of its ability enforce them, not simply because they are the morals of most of us, nor simply because they are the morals which are taught by the established Church—on these points the law recognizes the right to dissent—but for the compelling reason that without the help of Christian teaching the law will fail.

NOTE: FROM DEVLIN TO HART

from Bernard E. Harcourt, *The Collapse of the Harm Principle,* 90 Journal of Criminal Law and Criminology 109, 120–131 (1999).

In contrast to Lord James Fitzjames Stephen's straightforward legal moralist argument, Lord Devlin's argument in *The Enforcement of Morality* was susceptible to competing interpretations. Devlin's argument played on the ambivalence in the notion of harm—at times courting the idea of social harm, at other times aligning more closely with the legal moralism of his predecessor. As a result, there developed at least two interpretations of Devlin's argument: the first relied on public harm, the second on legal moralism. Professors H.L.A. Hart and Joel Feinberg labeled these two versions, respectively, the moderate thesis and the extreme thesis.

In large part, the source of the ambiguity stemmed from the fact that Lord Devlin himself defined public morality *in terms of harm to society.* In several key passages, Devlin strongly suggested that public morality necessarily encompassed conduct that affected society as a whole. Devlin wrote that "[t]here is a case for a collective [moral] judgement ... *only if society is affected.*" "[B]efore a society can put a practice beyond the limits of tolerance," Devlin emphasized, "there must be a deliberate judgement that the practice is *injurious to society.*" In these and numerous other passages, Devlin made clear that public morality would necessarily involve injury to society, and that the injury was precisely "what gives the law its *locus standi.*" This overlap of harm and morality significantly exacerbated the ambiguity in the debate, and the struggle for the meaning of harm.

The overlap fragmented Devlin's argument. Under the moderate interpretation, Devlin appeared to be arguing that morality should be enforced in order to protect society from the danger of disintegration— an argument that relied on harm. On this view, the only difference between Hart and Devlin was that Hart focused on harm to the individual, whereas Devlin focused on harm to society as a whole. It was precisely on this ground that Devlin criticized the Wolfenden Report: "The error of jurisprudence in the Wolfenden Report is caused by the search for some single principle to explain the division between crime and sin. The Report finds it in the principle that the criminal law exists *for the protection of individuals* ... But the true principle is that the law exists *for the protection of society.*"

One obvious flaw in the moderate interpretation was that Devlin never defined the causal mechanism of social harm. Though Devlin repeatedly referred to "social disintegration," he failed to articulate the pathway of harm. As a result, there developed, again, a number of competing interpretations of the causal mechanism—which, in part, replicated the ambiguities in the conception of harm.

Another major problem with the moderate interpretation was that Devlin ignored completely the empirical dimension of the public harm claim ... This empirical gap in Devlin's harm argument was terribly damaging, and, as a result, a second, more extreme reading of Devlin emerged. Under the second interpretation, referred to as the extreme thesis, Devlin argued that morality should be enforced for the sake of morality *tout court*: morality for morality's sake. If Devlin's claim (that private acts of immorality present a danger to society) was not intended to be an empirical claim, then Devlin perhaps equated morality with society.

Under the more extreme reading, Devlin's argument was much closer to the earlier statement of legal moralism in Lord Stephen's book, *Liberty, Equality, Fraternity*. Certain key passages in Devlin's writings supported this reading, especially the concluding sentence of the Maccabaean lecture:

> So the law must base itself on Christian morals and to the limit of its ability enforce them, not simply because they are the morals of most of us, nor simply because they are the morals which are taught by the established Church—on these points the law recognizes the right to dissent—*but for the compelling reason that without the help of Christian teaching the law will fail.*

These were ominous and somewhat bewildering words. "Christian morals." "The law will fail." To what extent was this a prediction of actual social harm or a traditional argument about legal moralism? Could they even be distinguished anymore? Was legal moralism, in reality, a harm argument? In which direction was Devlin going?

Unsure, Hart and other liberal theorists returned to Mill's essay *On Liberty* and to the original, simple statement of the harm principle. In *Law, Liberty, and Morality*, a set of lectures delivered at Stanford University in 1962 in response to Lord Devlin, Hart rehearsed Mill's harm principle, but carefully pared the argument down to its original, simple, and succinct statement.

H.L.A. HART—LAW, LIBERTY, MORALITY

Stanford University Press (1963).

I.

The Legal Enforcement of Morality

These lectures are concerned with one question about the relations between law and morals.... It concerns the legal enforcement of morality and has been formulated in many different ways: Is the fact that certain conduct is by common standards immoral sufficient to justify making that conduct punishable by law? Is it morally permissible to enforce morality as such? Ought immorality as such to be a crime?

To this question John Stuart Mill gave an emphatic negative answer in his essay *On Liberty* one hundred years ago, and the famous sentence in which he frames this answer expresses the central doctrine of his essay. He said, "The only purpose for which power can rightfully be exercised over any member of a civilised community against his will is to prevent harm to others." And to identify the many different things which he intended to exclude, he added, "His own good either physical or moral is not a sufficient warrant. He cannot rightfully be compelled to do or forbear because it will be better for him to do so, because it will make him happier, because in the opinions of others, to do so would be wise or even right."

This doctrine, Mill tells us, is to apply to human beings only "in the maturity of their faculties": it is not to apply to children or to backward societies. Even so, it has been the object of much academic criticism on two different, and indeed inconsistent, grounds. Some critics have urged that the line which Mill attempts to draw between actions with which the law may interfere and those with which it may not is illusory. "No man is an island"; and in an organised society it is impossible to identify classes of actions which harm no one or no one but the individual who does them. Other critics have admitted that such a division of actions may be made, but insist that it is merely dogmatic on Mill's part to limit legal coercion to the class of actions which harm others. There are good reasons, so these critics claim, for compelling conformity to social morality and for punishing deviations from it even when these do not harm others.

I shall consider this dispute mainly in relation to the special topic of sexual morality where it seems *prima facie* plausible that there are actions immoral by accepted standards and yet not harmful to others. But to prevent misunderstanding I wish to enter a *caveat*; I do not propose to defend all that Mill said; for I myself think there may be grounds justifying the legal coercion of the individual other than the prevention of harm to others. But on the narrower issue relevant to the enforcement of morality Mill seems to me to be right. It is of course possible simply to assert that the legal enforcement by society of its accepted morality needs no argument to justify it, because it is a morality which is enforced. But Mill's critics have not fallen back upon this brute assertion. They have in fact advanced many different arguments to justify the enforcement of morality, but these all, as I shall attempt to show, rest on unwarranted assumptions as to matters of fact, or on certain evaluations whose plausibility, due in large measure to ambiguity or vagueness or inaccuracy of statement, dwindles (even if it does not altogether vanish) when exposed to critical scrutiny....

Prostitution and Homosexuality

Much dissatisfaction has for long been felt in England with the criminal law relating to both prostitution and homosexuality, and in

1954 the committee well known as the Wolfenden Committee was appointed to consider the state of the law. This committee reported in September 1957 and recommended certain changes in the law on both topics. As to homosexuality they recommended by a majority of 12 to 1 that homosexual practices between consenting adults in private should no longer be a crime; as to prostitution they unanimously recommended that, though it should not itself be made illegal, legislation should be passed "to drive it off the streets" on the ground that public soliciting was an offensive nuisance to ordinary citizens. The government eventually introduced legislation to give effect to the Committee's recommendations concerning prostitution but not to that concerning homosexuality, and attempts by private members to introduce legislation modifying the law on this subject have so far failed.

What concerns us here is less the fate of the Wolfenden Committee's recommendations than the principles by which these were supported. These are strikingly similar to those expounded by Mill in his essay *On Liberty*. . . . [The] conception of the positive functions of the criminal law was the Committee's main ground for its recommendation concerning prostitution that legislation should be passed to suppress the offensive public manifestations of prostitution, but not to make prostitution itself illegal. Its recommendation that the law against homosexual practices between consenting adults in private should be relaxed was based on the principle stated simply in section 61 of the Report as follows: "There must remain a realm of private morality and immorality which is, in brief and crude terms, not the law's business."

It is perhaps clear from the foregoing that Mill's principles are still very much alive in the criticism of law, whatever their theoretical deficiencies may be. But twice in one hundred years they have been challenged by two masters of the Common Law. The first of these was the great Victorian judge and historian of the Criminal Law, James Fitzjames Stephen. His criticism of Mill is to be found in the sombre and impressive book *Liberty, Equality, Fraternity*, which he wrote as a direct reply to Mill's essay *On Liberty*. It is evident from the tone of this book that Stephen thought he had found crushing arguments against Mill and had demonstrated that the law might justifiably enforce morality as such or, as he said, that the law should be "a persecution of the grosser forms of vice." Nearly a century later, on the publication of the Wolfenden Committee's report, Lord Devlin, now a member of the House of Lords and a most distinguished writer on the criminal law, in his essay on *The Enforcement of Morals* took as his target the Report's contention "that there must be a realm of morality and immorality which is not the law's business" and argued in opposition to it that "the suppression of vice is as much the law's business as the suppression of subversive activities."

Though a century divides these two legal writers, the similarity in the general tone and sometimes in the detail of their arguments is very great. I shall devote the remainder of these lectures to an examination of them. I do this because, though their arguments are at points confused, they certainly still deserve the compliment of rational opposition. They are not only admirably stocked with concrete examples, but they express the considered views of skilled, sophisticated lawyers experienced in the administration of the criminal law. Views such as theirs are still quite widely held especially by lawyers both in England and in this country; it may indeed be that they are more popular, in both countries, than Mill's doctrine of Liberty. . . .

Lord Devlin bases his affirmative answer to the question on the quite general principle that it is permissible for any society to take the steps needed to preserve its own existence as an organized society, and he thinks that immorality—even private sexual immorality—may, like treason, be something which jeopardizes a society's existence. Of course many of us may doubt this general principle, and not merely the suggested analogy with treason. We might wish to argue that whether or not a society is justified in taking steps to preserve itself must depend both on what sort of society it is and what the steps to be taken are. If a society were mainly devoted to the cruel persecution of a racial or religious minority, or if the steps to be taken included hideous tortures, it is arguable that what Lord Devlin terms the "disintegration" of such a society would be morally better than its continued existence, and steps ought not to be taken to preserve it. Nonetheless Lord Devlin's principle that a society may take the steps required to preserve its organized existence is not itself tendered as an item of English popular morality, deriving its cogency from its status as part of our institutions. He puts it forward as a principle, rationally acceptable, to be used in the evaluation or criticism of social institutions generally. And it is surely clear that anyone who holds the question whether a society has the "right" to enforce morality, or whether it is morally permissible for any society to enforce its morality by law, to be discussable at all, must be prepared to deploy some such general principles of critical morality. In asking the question, we are assuming the legitimacy of a standpoint which permits criticism of the institutions of any society, in the light of general principles and knowledge of the facts.

To make this point clear, I would revive the terminology much favoured by the Utilitarians of the last century, which distinguished "positive morality," the morality actually accepted and shared by a given social group, from the general moral principles used in the criticism of actual social institutions including positive morality. We may call such general principles "critical morality" and say that our question is one of critical morality about the legal enforcement of positive morality.

II.

Paternalism and the Enforcement of Morality

I shall start with an example stressed by Lord Devlin. He points out that, subject to certain exceptions such as rape, the criminal law has never admitted the consent of the victim as a defence. It is not a defence to a charge of murder or a deliberate assault, and this is why euthanasia or mercy killing terminating a man's life at his own request is still murder. This is a rule of criminal law which many now would wish to retain, though they would also wish to object to the legal punishment of offences against positive morality which harm no one. Lord Devlin thinks that these attitudes are inconsistent, for he asserts of the rule under discussion, "There is only one explanation," and this is that "there are certain standards of behaviour or moral principles which society requires to be observed." Among these are the sanctity of human life and presumably (since the rule applies to assaults) the physical integrity of the person. So in the case of this rule and a number of others Lord Devlin claims that the "function" of the criminal law is "to enforce a moral principle and nothing else."

But this argument is not really cogent, for Lord Devlin's statement that "there is only one explanation" is simply not true. The rules excluding the victim's consent as a defence to charges of murder or assault may perfectly well be explained as a piece of paternalism, designed to protect individuals against themselves.... Lord Devlin says of the attitude of the criminal law to the victim's consent that if the law existed for the protection of the individual there would be no reason why he should avail himself of it if he did not want it. But paternalism—the protection of people against themselves—is a perfectly coherent policy. Indeed, it seems very strange in mid-twentieth century to insist upon this, for the wane of laissez faire since Mill's day is one of the commonplaces of social history, and instances of paternalism now abound in our law, criminal and civil. The supply of drugs or narcotics, even to adults, except under medical prescription is punishable by the criminal law, and it would seem very dogmatic to say of the law creating this offence that "there is only one explanation," namely, that the law was concerned not with the protection of the would-be purchasers against themselves, but only with the punishment of the seller for his immorality. If, as seems obvious, paternalism is a possible explanation of such laws, it is also possible in the case of the rule excluding the consent of the victim as a defence to a charge of assault. In neither case are we forced to conclude with Lord Devlin that the law's "function" is "to enforce a moral principle and nothing else."

In Chapter 5 of his essay Mill carried his protests against paternalism to lengths that may now appear to us fantastic. He cites the example of restrictions of the sale of drugs, and criticises them as interferences with the liberty of the would-be purchaser rather than with that of the seller.... Certainly a modification in Mill's principles is required, if they are to accommodate the rule of criminal law under discussion or other instances of paternalism. But the modified principles would not abandon the objection to the use of the criminal law merely to enforce positive morality. They would only have to provide that harming others is something we may still seek to prevent by use of the criminal law, even when the victims consent to or assist in the acts which are harmful to them. The neglect of the distinction between paternalism and what I have termed legal moralism is important as a form of a more general error. It is too often assumed that if a law is not designed to protect one man from another its only rationale can be that it is designed to punish moral wickedness or, in Lord Devlin's words, "to enforce a moral principle." Thus it is often urged that statutes punishing cruelty to animals can only be explained in that way. But it is certainly intelligible, both as an account of the original motives inspiring such legislation and as the specification of an aim widely held to be worth pursuing, to say that the law is here concerned with the suffering, albeit only of animals, rather than with the immorality of torturing them. Certainly no one who supports this use of the criminal law is thereby bound in consistency to admit that the law may punish forms of immorality which involve no suffering to any sentient being.

The Preservation of Morality and Moral Conservatism

This . . . brings us to what is really the central issue in [the extreme version of Lord Devlin's] thesis. Let us suppose, contrary to much evidence, that Stephen's picture of society and its moral mechanisms is a realistic one: that there really is a moral code in sexual matters supported by an overwhelming majority and that they are deeply disturbed when it is infringed even by adults in private; that the punishment of offenders really does sustain the sense that the conduct is immoral and without their punishment the prevalent morality would change in a permissive direction. The central question is: Can anything or nothing be said to support the claim that the prevention of this change and the maintenance of the moral *status quo* in a society's morality are values sufficient to offset the cost in human misery which legal enforcement entails? Is it simply a blank assertion, or does it rest on any critical principles connecting what is said to be of value here with other things of value? . . .

Th[e] distinction between the use of coercion to enforce morality and other methods which we in fact use to preserve it, such as argument, advice, and exhortation, is both very important and much neglected in discussions of the present topic. Stephen, in his arguments against Mill, seems most of the time to forget or to ignore these other methods and the great importance which Mill attached to them. For he frequently argues as if Mill's doctrine of liberty meant that men must never express any convictions concerning the conduct of their fellow citizens if that conduct is not harmful to others. It is true that Mill believed that "the state or the public" is not warranted *for the purposes of repression or punishment"* in deciding that such conduct is good or bad. But it is not true that he thought that concerning such conduct or "the experiments in living" which it represents "no one else has anything to say to it. Nor did he think that society could draw a line where education ends and perfect moral indifference begins." In making these ill-founded criticisms Stephen not only misunderstood and so misrepresented Mill, but he showed how narrowly he himself conceived of morality and the processes by which it is sustained. For Mill's concern throughout his essay is to restrict the use of coercion, not to promote moral indifference. It is true he includes in the coercion or "constraint" of which he disapproves not only legal enforcement of morality but also other peremptory forms of social pressure such as moral blame and demands for conformity. But it is a disastrous misunderstanding of morality to think that where we cannot use coercion in its support we must be silent and indifferent. In Chapter 4 of his essay Mill takes great pains to show the other resources which we have and should use . . .

Discussion, advice, argument—all these, since they leave the individual "the final judge," may according to Mill be used in a society where freedom is properly respected. We may even "obtrude" on another "considerations to aid his judgment and exhortations to strengthen his will." We may in extreme cases "warn" him of our adverse judgment or feelings of distaste and contempt. We may avoid his company and caution others against it. Many might think that Mill here comes perilously near to sanctioning coercion even though he regards these things as "strictly inseparable from the unfavourable judgments of others and never to be inflicted for the sake of punishment." But if he erred in that direction, it is certainly clear that he recognised the important truth that in morality we are not forced to choose between deliberate coercion and indifference.

Moral Populism and Democracy

Mill's essay *On Liberty*, like Tocqueville's book *Democracy in America*, was a powerful plea for a clearheaded appreciation of the dangers that accompany the benefits of democratic rule. The greatest of the dangers, in their view, was not that in fact the majority might use their power to oppress a minority, but that, with the spread of democratic ideas, it might come to be thought unobjectionable that they should do so. For Mill, these dangers were part of the price to be paid for all that is so valuable in democratic government. He thought the price certainly worth paying; but he was much concerned to remind the supporters of democracy of the danger and the need for vigilance. . . .

[Devlin and Stephen's] central mistake is a failure to distinguish the acceptable principle that political power is best entrusted to the majority from the unacceptable claim that what the majority do with that power is beyond criticism and must never be resisted. No one can be a democrat who does not accept the first of these, but no democrat need accept the second. Mill and many others have combined a belief in a democracy as the best—or least harmful—form of rule with the passionate conviction that there are many things which not even a democratic government may do. This combination of attitudes makes good sense, because, though a democrat is committed to the belief that democracy is better than other forms of government, he is not committed to the belief that it is perfect or infallible or never to be resisted. To support this last conclusion we need a further premise, going far beyond the simple assertion that it is better to entrust political power to the majority than to a selected class. This further premise must be some variant, secular or otherwise, of the identification of *vox populi* with *vox Dei*. One variant, which has been frequently referred to in these lectures, is the view that positive morality supported by an overwhelming moral majority is immune from criticism....

Whatever other arguments there may be for the enforcement of morality, no one should think even when popular morality is supported by an "overwhelming majority" or marked by widespread "intolerance, indignation, and disgust" that loyalty to democratic principles requires him to admit that its imposition on a minority is justified.

Conclusion

I hope that these three lectures are clear enough and short enough to make a detailed summary unnecessary. Instead I shall say a word in conclusion about the method of argument which I have followed. I have from the beginning assumed that anyone who raises, or is willing to debate, the question whether it is justifiable to enforce morality, accepts the view that the actual institutions of any society, including its positive morality, are open to criticism. Hence the proposition that it is justifiable to enforce morality is, like its negation, a thesis of critical morality requiring for its support some general critical principle. It cannot be established or refuted simply by pointing to the actual practices or morality of a particular society or societies. Lord Devlin, whose thesis I termed the moderate thesis, seems to accept this position, but I have argued that the general critical principle which he deploys, namely, that a society has the right to take any step necessary for its preservation, is inadequate for his purpose. There is no evidence that the preservation of a society requires the enforcement of its morality "as such." His position only appears to escape this criticism by a confused definition of what a society is.

I have also assumed from the beginning that anyone who regards this question as open to discussion necessarily accepts the critical principle, central to all morality, that human misery and the restriction of freedom are evils; for that is why the legal enforcement of morality calls for justification. I then endeavoured to extricate, and to free from ambiguity of statement, the general principles underlying several varieties of the more extreme thesis that the enforcement of morality or its preservation from change were valuable apart from their beneficial consequences in preserving society. These principles in fact invite us to consider as values, for the sake of which we should restrict human freedom and inflict the misery of punishment on human beings, things which seem to belong to the prehistory of morality and to be quite hostile to its general spirit. They include mere outward conformity to moral rules induced simply by fear; the gratification of feelings of hatred for the wrongdoer or his "retributory" punishment, even where there has been no victim to be avenged or to call for justice; the infliction of punishment as a symbol or expression of moral condemnation: the mere insulation from change of any social morality however repressive or barbarous. No doubt I have not *proved* these things not to be values worth their price in human suffering and loss of freedom; it may be enough to have shown what it is that is offered for the price.

NOTE: HART–DEVLIN'S IMMEDIATE AFTER–EFFECT

from Bernard E. Harcourt, *The Collapse of the Harm Principle,* 90 Journal
of Criminal Law and Criminology 109, 131–134 (1999).

Gradually, over the course of the 1960s, '70s, and '80s, Mill's harm principle began to dominate the legal philosophic debate over the enforcement of morality. Harm became a critical principle used to police the line between law and morality within Anglo–American philosophy of law. Most prominent theorists who participated in the debate either relied on the harm principle or made favorable reference to the argument. Professor Ronald Dworkin engaged the Hart–Devlin debate in an article first published in the *Yale Law Journal* in 1966 entitled *Lord Devlin and the Enforcement of Morals.* Professor Louis Henkin similarly joined the debate, with specific reference to the question of obscenity. . . .

Over time, the harm principle essentially prevailed in the legal philosophic debate over the legal enforcement of morality. From one end of the spectrum to the other, there arose a consensus that Hart had carried the day. At the liberal end of the spectrum, Professor Ronald Dworkin reported that Devlin's argument "was widely attacked" and that his thesis was, ultimately, "very implausible." On the other end of the spectrum, Professor Robert George would report that "many . . . perhaps even most [commentators] think that Hart carried the day. . . ." Professor Jeffrie Murphy—who is today a skeptic of the harm principle— captured well the prevailing consensus. "I believed, along with most of the people with whom I talked about legal philosophy," Murphy wrote, "that legal moralism had been properly killed off, that liberalism had once again been vindicated against the forces of superstition and oppression, and that legal philosophy could now move on to new and more important topics."

This is not to suggest that the controversy simply disappeared from philosophic circles. There were attempts to rehabilitate Devlin's position. There were even attempts to radicalize Devlin's argument. And still today, Devlin has supporters. In fact, in 1999, Professor Gerald Dworkin published a provocative essay entitled *Devlin Was Right*. In the essay, Dworkin sides with Devlin "in believing that there is no principled line following the contours of the distinction between immoral and harmful conduct such that only grounds referring to the latter may be invoked to justify criminalization."

As the harm principle began to dominate the legal philosophic debate, the principle also began to dominate criminal law scholarship and legal rhetoric. Most of the leading criminal law scholars either adopted the harm principle or incorporated it in their writings. Herbert Packer, in his famous book published in 1968, entitled *The Limits of the Criminal Sanction*, included the harm principle in his list of limiting criteria that justified the criminal sanction. Although Packer did not focus primarily on the harm principle—focusing instead on the effectiveness and social consequences of policing certain activities—he did incorporate it into his work and argued that "[t]he harm to others formula seems to me to have ... uses that justify its inclusion in a list of limiting criteria for invocation of the criminal sanction."

The harm principle featured prominently in criminal law treatises and casebooks. Most casebooks reproduced for law students the Hart–Devlin debate. One of the most popular casebooks, Professors Monrad Paulsen and Sanford Kadish's first edition of *Criminal Law and Its Processes*, published in 1962, started off on page one with the debate over Devlin's Maccabaean lecture. It extracted a lengthy portion of the lecture, as well as Hart's preliminary response published in the *Listener*. Later editions of the popular casebook would excerpt Devlin's lecture, describe Hart's response in *Law, Liberty and Morality,* and refer the law student to Feinberg's four-volume treatise. Professors Rollin Perkins and Ronald Boyce, in their treatise, *Criminal Law*, emphasized that the genus of crime is harm. Crime, they explained, is "any social harm defined and made punishable by law." Professor Paul Robinson, in his popular treatise, *Criminal Law*, refers first and foremost to societal harm in discussing the definition of criminal conduct. Robinson cites exclusively Joel Feinberg's treatise, *The Moral Limits of the Criminal Law*.

The harm principle also permeated the rhetoric of the criminal law itself. This was reflected most clearly in the drafting of the Model Penal Code by the American Law Institute, which was begun in 1952 and completed in 1962. Professor Herbert Wechsler, the chief reporter and intellectual father of the Model Penal Code, strongly endorsed harm as the guiding principle of criminal liability. As early as 1955, Wechsler wrote: "All would agree, I think, that there is no defensible foundation for declaring conduct criminal unless it injures or threatens to injure an important human interest...." In his scholarly writings, Wechsler consistently emphasized the harm principle: conduct "is not deemed to be a proper subject of a penal prohibition" unless it "unjustifiably and inexcusably inflicts or threatens substantial harm...." This was, Wechsler emphasized, "a declaration designed to be given weight in the interpretation of the [Model Penal] Code."

The language of the Model Penal Code reflected this emphasis on the harm principle. In the preliminary article, Section 1.02, the drafters addressed the purposes of criminal law and stated, as the very first principle, the objective "to forbid and prevent conduct that unjustifiably and inexcusably inflicts or threatens substantial harm to individual or public interests." In the Explanatory Note attached to the final draft, the drafters referred to this harm principle as the "major goal" of the provisions governing the definition of crimes—in contrast to the other four stated purposes which are referred to as "subsidiary themes." The Comment to the preliminary article refers to the harm principle as "the dominant preventive purpose of the penal law." It emphasizes that the harm principle "reflect[s] inherent and important limitations on the just and prudent use of penal sanctions as a measure of control." Substantially similar provisions regarding the harm principle were enacted in Alabama, Alaska, Delaware, Florida, Georgia, Nebraska, New Jersey, New York, Oregon, Pennsylvania, Tennessee, Texas, and Washington, among other states.[1]

The harm principle was also reflected in the definition of crimes, especially moral offenses and public decency crimes. "The Model Penal Code does not attempt to enforce private morality," the drafters explained. "Thus, none of the provisions contained in Article 251 purports to regulate sexual behavior generally." Professor Wechsler emphasized that:

> Private sexual relations, whether heterosexual or homosexual, are excluded from the scope of criminality, unless children are victimized or there is coercion or other imposition. Penal sanctions also are withdrawn from fornication and adultery, contrary to the law of many states. Prostitution would continue to be penalized, primarily because of its relationship to organized crime in the United States, but major sanctions would be reserved for those who exploit prostitutes for their own gain.

With regard to each moral offense, the drafters specifically discussed harm. In the case of prostitution, the drafters retained the criminal sanction specifically because of the potential harm in the spread of syphilis and gonorrhea. "Of special importance to the continuation of penal repression," the drafters emphasized, "was the perceived relationship between prostitution and venereal disease." In the case of consensual homosexual activity, the drafters rejected criminal responsibility on the ground of lack of harm. The drafters canvassed the moral grounds for sanctioning sodomy, but ultimately rejected them because of the "absence of harm to the secular interests of the community occasioned by atypical sexuality between consenting adults." With regard to obscenity, the drafters paid special attention to the relationship between obscene materials and overt misbehavior. The drafters noted that "in another era, spiritual error may have been a sufficient ground for penal repression, but in an age of many faiths and none, society tends to look to more objective criteria to determine what is harmful." Even the proposed definition of public drunkenness incorporated the harm (and offense) principles. In the Model Penal Code, the offense of public intoxication "differs from prior law principally in requiring that the person be under the influence of alcohol or other drug 'to the degree that he may endanger himself or other persons or property, or annoy persons in his vicinity.'"

---

1. *See* ALA. CODE § 13A–1–3(1) (1994); ALASKA STAT. § 11.81.100(1) (1998); DEL. CODE ANN. tit. 11, § 201(1) (1995); FLA. STAT. ANN. § 775.012(1) (West 1992); GA. CODE ANN. § 26–102(1) (1998); NEB. REV. STAT. § 28–102(1) (1998); N. J. STAT. ANN. § 2C:1–2(a)(1) (West 1998); N. Y. PENAL LAW § 1.05(1) (McKinney 1998); OR. REV. STAT. § 161.025(1)(b) (1992); 18 PA. CONS. STAT. ANN. § 104(1) (West 1998); TENN. CODE. ANN. § 39–11–101(1) (1997); TEX. PENAL CODE ANN. § 1.02 (West 1994); WASH. REV. CODE ANN. § 9A.04.020(1)(a) (West 1998). *See generally* MODEL PENAL CODE, OFFICIAL DRAFT AND EXPLANATORY NOTES, *supra* note 97, at 17 n.4.

From philosophy of law to substantive criminal law, the harm principle permeated the debate during the 1960s and 1970s. As evidenced by the writings of Professors Hart and Feinberg in the legal philosophic debate, and of Professor Wechsler and the drafters of the Model Penal Code in the substantive criminal law debate, the harm principle became an important discursive principle used to draw the line between law and morality.

ERNEST NAGEL—THE ENFORCEMENT OF MORALS
The Humanist 3:20–27 (1968).

1

An adequate account of the different ways in which moral principles enter into the development, the operation, and the evaluation of legal systems would require an examination of a broad spectrum of difficult issues. Such an account is certainly not a task to which a relatively short paper can do justice, and the present paper is not an attempt to do the impossible. I am therefore restricting myself in it almost entirely to but one issue that arises in considering the relation of law to morality—to the question whether there is a sharply delimited domain of human conduct that is by its very nature excluded from justifiable legal control, and in particular whether a society is ever warranted in using the law to enforce what are held to be widely accepted moral rules. The question has a long ancestry in discussions of moral and political theory, and is closely related to issues raised in historical doctrines of natural law and inalienable rights. However, the question can be examined without reference to natural law theory, and in any case it is not simply of antiquarian interest, but is of vital interest to humanist writers. It is also directly relevant to a number of currently debated social problems, among others to problems created by changing attitudes toward euthanasia, obscenity, and deviant sexual practices; and it received considerable attention in recent years from legislators, judges, sociologists, and psychologists, as well as from philosophers and writers on jurisprudence.

Many current philosophical and jurisprudential discussions of the question I want to consider take as their point of departure a challenging essay by Lord Patrick Devlin—a distinguished British judge, who was for many years a Justice of the High Court, Queen's Bench, and subsequently a Lord of Appeal in Ordinary. Devlin's essay, entitled "The Enforcement of Morals" and published in 1959, tried to show that a fundamental principle to which many moral theorists subscribe and which had been recently invoked in support of certain recommendations for amending the English criminal law, is untenable—for reasons I will presently mention. Devlin's views have found some defenders, but have also been the subject of much severe criticism. Since my paper is for the most part a commentary on the main points in dispute between Devlin and his critics—especially H. L. A. Hart in the latter's *Law, Liberty, and Morality* (1963)—I must describe briefly the problem to which Devlin's essay was addressed, and the context in which the debate over his views has its locus.

In 1954, in response to widespread criticism of the provisions of the English criminal law dealing with prostitution and homosexual practices, a committee was appointed, headed by Sir John Wolfenden, to look into the matter and to recommend needed changes in the law. The Report of the Committee was issued in 1957, and proposed a number of modifications, in the existing law relating to various kinds of sexual offenses. The factual findings and the detailed proposals of the Committee are not pertinent here. What is of interest is that the Wolfenden Committee based its recommendations on the view that

> ... the function of the criminal law ... is to preserve public order and decency, to protect the citizen from what is offensive or injurious, and to provide sufficient safeguards against exploitation and corruption of others, particularly those who are specially vulnerable because they are young, weak in body or mind, inexperienced, or in a state of special physical, official or economic dependence.

> It is not the function of the law [the report went on] to intervene in the private lives of citizens, or to seek to enforce any pattern of behavior, further than is necessary to carry out the purposes we have outlined.

Moreover, in recommending that solicitation of the young should continue to be punishable by law, but that "homosexual behavior between consenting adults should no longer be a criminal offence," the Wolfenden Report offered what it called a "decisive" reason, namely:

> the importance which society and the law ought to give to individual freedom of choice and action in matters of private morality. Unless a deliberate attempt is to be made by society, acting through the agency of the law, to equate the sphere of crime with that of sin, *there must remain a realm of private morality and immorality which is, in brief and crude terms, not the law's business.* To say this is not to condone or encourage private immorality.[76]

Some of the Report's proposals were eventually adopted by Parliament. However, it is not my aim to examine either the merits of these recommendations or the recent history of English legislation. The question I do want to discuss is the adequacy of the general principle underlying the specific proposals of the Wolfenden Committee—that there is a realm of conduct which, irrespective of its morality or immorality, is not the law's business and by its very nature falls outside the legitimate concerns of the law. It is this principle that Devlin challenged on grounds that I will presently describe, even though he eventually expressed himself as being in agreement with some of the Report's specific recommendations; and it is largely to a critique of Devlin's stand on this principle that Hart's own book previously mentioned is devoted.

---

76. Patrick Devlin, *The Enforcement of Morals* (New York: Oxford University Press, 1965), pp. 2–3 [my italics]. All references to Devlin are to this book.

However, as the Wolfenden Report explicitly notes, the principle is stated by it only in brief and crude terms, without any attempt to articulate it clearly or to give supporting reasons for it. But there is little doubt that in its statement of the principle the Report was invoking the far more inclusive political doctrine which John Stuart Mill expounded at some length in his classic essay *On Liberty* (1859), and was simply applying that doctrine to the particular problem of the legal regulation of sexual practices. Accordingly, since both Devlin and Hart make constant reference to Mill's views on individual liberty, and since I want to discuss the principle espoused by the Wolfenden Committee when it is stated in its most general and influential form, it is desirable to quote the passage in which Mill expressed the central idea of his political philosophy. Mill declared that

> ... The sole end for which mankind is warranted, individually or collectively, in interfering with the liberty of action of any of their number is sell-protection. That the only purpose for which power can be rightfully exercised over any member of a civilized community, against his will, is to prevent harm to others. His own good, whether physical or moral, is not a sufficient warrant. He cannot rightfully be compelled to do or forbear because it will be better for him to do so, because it will make him happier, because, in the opinion of others, to do so would be wise, or even right. These are good reasons for remonstrating with him, or reasoning with him or persuading him, or entreating him, but not for compelling him, or visiting him with any evil in case he do otherwise. To justify that, the conduct from which it is desired to deter him must be calculated to produce evil to someone else. The only part of the conduct of anyone, for which he is amenable to society, is that which concerns others. In the part which merely concerns himself, his independence is, of right, absolute.[77]

Mill thus advanced a comprehensive rule for determining the limits of warranted interference with men's conduct through the use of any agency of social control and compulsion—not only through the operation of the law, whether civil or criminal, but also through other institutions, such as religious organizations, economic associations, or more temporary groups that may be formed to achieve particular ends. But in any event, the rule appears to provide a firm support for the recommendations of the Wolfenden Report, for on the face of it the general principle Mill enunciates excludes the use of the machinery of the law to enforce what the Report calls "private morality."

Nevertheless, the principle is not as determinate as it is often alleged to be; and it is debatable whether, in view of the complications involved in attempts to apply it to concrete cases, it suffices to define categorically a realm of conduct that is inherently outside the scope of the law. I propose to enter into this debate, by reviewing some of the

---

77. J. S. Mill, *Utilitarianism, Liberty, and Representative Government* (New York: Dutton, 1950, Everyman's Library edition), p. 73.

problems confronting a doctrine such as Mill's that seeks to circumscribe the area of conduct into which no measure of social control can be justifiably introduced. I am afraid that little if anything I have to say will be unfamiliar, for the problems have been repeatedly canvassed; nor do I have a neat resolution for the controversy over the legal enforcement of morals, for if I am right there can be no wholesale answer to the question. But I hope that by distinguishing several issues that are often confounded, I will succeed in placing the controversy in clearer light.

2

Mill offers two formulations—a broader and a narrower one—for his principle to distinguish between conduct that does and conduct that does not fall within the scope of permissible social control. 1. According to the broad formulation, a person's actions are matters for legitimate social scrutiny only if they are of "concern" to others, but not if they "merely concern himself." On this criterion for deciding on the justifiability of social control, the relevant question to ask is not whether an action is performed in private (e.g., within the walls of a man's home) or in public, but whether it has consequences that in some way may affect other men. However, as has often been noted, there are few if any actions, even when done in private, which can be guaranteed to have no effects whatsoever on others than the actors themselves, so that on this formulation of the principle the domain of conduct that is reserved for the exercise of individual liberty is at best extremely narrow.

2. In point of fact, it is not upon this broad formulation of his principle that Mill relies, but on the narrower one according to which no adult member of a civilized community can be rightfully compelled to perform or to desist from performing an act, unless the action or the failure to perform it is likely to produce *harm* or *evil* to others. But it takes little to see that even on this narrower injunction relatively few human actions are in principle excluded from social regulation. For example, a successful courtship may bring joy to a lover but acute anguish to his rival; the acclaim won by a musician or a scientist may produce self-destructive feelings of inferiority in those who do not achieve such distinction; and the vigorous expression of heterodox opinions may cause severe distress in those hearing them. Mill himself was fully aware of this, and qualified his principle by excluding from the class of actions he regarded as "harmful to others" (in the sense that they are subject to social control) many actions which, though they may affect others adversely by causing them physical or mental pain, he designated as merely "inconveniences"; and he maintained that society should tolerate such inconveniences, without attempting to control the actions that are their source, on the ground that this is the price men must be prepared to pay for the enjoyment of individual liberty.

However, the actions mentioned by Mill as productive of inconveniences only, rather than of serious evils that warrant social intervention, are in some instances highly idiosyncratic; but they frequently also reflect attitudes and standards of conduct that were held by many other men of Mill's time and station in life. Thus, he saw in the prohibition of the sale of alcoholic beverages an infringement of personal liberty, despite the social evils that excessive consumption of alcohol may produce; and he maintained that though a person attempting to cross an unsafe bridge should be warned of the risk he is incurring, no public official would be warranted in forcibly preventing the person from exposing himself to danger. But Mill also believed that society is justified in compelling parents to educate their young; that society is warranted in forbidding marriages between individuals who cannot prove that they have the means to support a family; and that contracts between persons should be prohibited, even if no one else is affected by the agreements, when the parties bind themselves to abide by some arrangement for an indefinite number of years, if not in perpetuity, without the power to revoke the agreement. On the other hand, though Mill had no doubt that society must tolerate fornication and gambling, he evaded answering the question whether a person should be free to be a pimp or a gambling-house keeper.

I do not believe it is possible to state a firm rule underlying Mill's selection of conduct for inclusion in the category of actions whose consequences for others are merely annoying inconveniences, rather than serious evils that justify the adoption of some form of social regulation. Indeed, it is obvious that his principle for demarcating a realm of behavior which is exempt from social control excludes virtually *nothing* from the scope of justifiable legal enactment—*unless* some agreement is first reached on what to count as "harm or evil to others." But two points are no less clear: (1) an explication of what is to be understood as harmful to others (in the sense of warranting some type of social control), cannot escape reference to some more or less explicit and comprehensive system of moral and social assumptions—more fully articulated than Mill's, whether or not the moral theory involved in the explication is one about which reasonable men may differ; and (2) even when agreement on general moral principles can be taken for granted, it may be difficult to decide whether a given type of conduct is indeed harmful to others, especially if the circumstances under which the actions take place may vary considerably, or if the number of individuals who engage in them should increase. Each point merits brief comment.

1. There are various categories of behavior whose harmful character (as distinct from its mere inconvenience to others) is in general not disputed in our society—for example, actions resulting in physical injury to others, or in depriving them of their possessions (as in theft); and no elaborate moral theory is usually invoked in justifying legal measures designed to prevent such actions. Nevertheless, the point needs stressing that though in a given society certain kinds of conduct seem unquestionably harmful, the classification of such conduct as harmful may, and frequently does, involve far-reaching assumptions about the public weal—assumptions which may be modified for a variety of reasons, and which may not be operative in other societies. This is evident when we reflect that even in our own society not all actions resulting in physical injury to others, or in depriving others of their possessions, are held to be harmful in the sense here relevant. Thus the infliction of physical injury on others in duels or feuds currently counts as action that is harmful, but the infliction of such injury is not so regarded when it occurs in boxing contests, in acts of self-defense, or in many though not in all surgical operations. Moral assumptions and considerations of social policy surely control this classification of such conduct; and there have been societies in which those actions have been classified differently.

Again, it is pertinent to ask in the case of alleged theft, whether the article taken from a person "really" belonged to him. But the question is not settled by ascertaining whether the article had been in the person's actual possession—even when we limit ourselves to those relatively simple cases in which it makes sense to suppose that the articles under consideration can literally be in someone's physical possession. For in the context in which the question is being asked, the relevant answer to it is that the article is (or is not) his *property*. However, as is now widely recognized, the notion of property is a *legal* category, whose meaning and content are defined by some system of laws, and generally vary with different societies. Thus, a piece of land or a painting is a man's property, and not simply something in his possession, if he acquired the item in ways prescribed by the laws of the land. Similarly, a song composed by a musician is his property, only if there are copyright laws which grant him certain rights in it; it is his property only during the period of the copyright, but not after it has run its course; and if the copyright laws are changed, the status of the song as property is also altered. Accordingly, whether an action is a case of theft, and hence liable to legal sanctions, depends on whether the article taken from a man or used without his consent is indeed his property. In consequence, to justify the use of any form of social duress for compelling a man to abstain from theft, one must in the end justify the social policy, and therefore the moral commitments, underlying the laws that determine what is to count as property.

Let me cite one further example. Suppose that one individual promises another to perform an action in return for some favor, and assume that if the promise is breached the person to whom it was given suffers a loss, but leaving it open whether or not anybody else does so. Is such a breach of promise a harmful action, or only an inconvenience? There are many promises whose breach is ignored by the laws of our society, even when the breach is the source of great inconvenience to others than the parties to the agreement—for example, in return for the use of a colleague's car, a promise to coach his son for an important examination. But there are also many promises whose breaking society does not ignore, and the legal institution of contract is a social technique for the enforcement of promissory agreements. On the other hand, complete freedom of contract is not an unmixed blessing, as Mill recognized; and there are a variety of contractual arrangements that are forbidden in many societies—for example, in our society no one is permitted to sell himself into slavery. Accordingly, society does not intervene into a large class of promises, even when their consequences affect others than those making them, but regulates other kinds of promises even when their results do not appear to impinge directly on those not party to them. Moreover, in placing restrictions on the freedom to contract, society seeks through the instrumentalities of the law to achieve what is assumed to be a greater social good, often in the form of establishing more equitable conditions for the exercise of individual liberty than could be achieved without the regulation of what at first blush seem to be purely "private transactions." As Morris R. Cohen observed, contract law has a function not entirely dissimilar from that of criminal law—for both seek to standardize conduct by penalizing departures from certain norms whose validation involves moral considerations.

In short, attempts such as Mill's to delimit *a priori* a realm of conduct that is exempt from social regulation presuppose a fairly detailed moral philosophy that articulates what actions are to count as harmful to others. But the discussion thus far has also suggested that unless individual freedom (as the maximum non-interference with individual conduct) is taken as an inalienable and absolute right, which must never be compromised or curtailed for the sake of satisfying other human needs (such as security from physical want or the development of human excellence), there appear to be no determinate and fixed limits to the scope of justifiable legal regulation of conduct.

2. I will return to this observation, but will now comment on the second point mentioned earlier. Given some explication of the notion of "harm (or evil) to others," the question whether a certain form of conduct is indeed harmful can be settled only by an empirical study of its consequences—it cannot be resolved by appeal to uncriticized custom or by considering that conduct in isolation from the enormously complex field of human relations in which it may actually be embedded. Now it may in principle be always possible to find reliable answers to such questions, and frequently such answers are undoubtedly available; but it is also the case that in a large number of instances adequate answers are difficult to obtain. Thus, to mention a trivial example, it appears quite certain in the light of current physical and biological knowledge that the kind of clothing a man wears, especially in the privacy of his home, has no "harmful" consequences for others—although in this connection some geneticists have raised (but as far I know not resolved) the question whether the kind of clothing men wear affects the mutation rate of genes, and therefore the character of the gene stock in inbreeding human populations. On the other hand, while there are reasons to believe that were artificial insemination practiced with the full consent of both parties to a marriage, no undesirable consequences would ensue either for those directly involved or for anyone else, no one can say today with any surety what effects the practice might have on the institution of the family or on current systems of property relations, if the practice were to become widespread. More generally, one should not ignore the truism that men's actions have unintended consequences; and Hegel was at least partly correct in his claim that the owl of Minerva spreads its wings only when the dusk begins to fall.

These comments must not be construed to mean that no deliberate changes in policies of social control in respect to some type of conduct should ever be made, until thoroughly competent knowledge becomes available concerning the likely consequences for others of the proposed policy change. For the desired knowledge can often be acquired only if the change is instituted; and refusal to make a change in the absence of fully adequate knowledge of its consequences is itself a policy decision, whose own likely effects may also be unknown to us. The conclusion that does emerge from these observations is that the distinction between conduct which is merely of concern to the actors (and hence, according to Mill, should be excluded from the scope of the law), and conduct that affects others adversely (and hence may be a proper subject for social regulation), cannot be drawn precisely or once for all, and may require repeated revision as conditions change and our funded knowledge grows.

3

In the light of these reflections, I want now to examine the grounds on which Lord Devlin defends the thesis that under certain conditions the enforcement of morals through the agency of criminal law is justifiable. Devlin bases his argument on the premise that a society is constituted not only by individuals with certain more or less concordant habits of behavior which they exhibit despite differences in personal aims, but also by a "community of ideas"—and in particular moral ideas "about the way its members *should* behave and govern their lives."[78] The shared convictions of a community concerning what is the "right" mode of conduct in such matters as marriage or the protection of life and property make up what he calls the "public morality" or the "moral structure" of a society. And according to him, every threat to the moral order of a society is a threat to the continued existence of the society itself. But since on this view "society has the right to make a judgment [on morals], and has it on the basis that a recognized morality is as necessary to society as . . . a recognized government," Devlin concludes that "society may use the law to preserve morality in the same way as it uses it to safeguard anything else that is essential to its existence" (p. 11). To be sure, he believes that "there must be toleration of the maximum individual freedom that is consistent with the integrity of society" (p. 16), and also recognizes that "the extent to which society will tolerate . . . departures from moral standards varies from generation to generation" (p. 18). He nevertheless maintains that if in the collective but deliberate judgment of society some practice, even though it is carried on in private, would be gravely injurious to the moral order were it to become widespread, then society may well be justified *as a matter of general principle* in outlawing that "immoral" conduct—just as it is

78.   Devlin, *op. cit.*, p. 9 [my italics].

justified in taking steps to preserve its government by enacting laws against treason (p. 13).

In my opinion, Devlin makes out a strong case for the impossibility of constructing a firm and enduring boundary between conduct that is a matter for individual conscience or private morality, and conduct that properly belongs to the domain of public concern. On the other hand, although I also think that his argument for the conclusion that under certain conditions the state may be justified in using the criminal law to enforce rules of public morality is *formally* sound, the conclusion rests on premises whose content is unclear and whose merits appear to me doubtful. Let me mention some of my difficulties.

1. In the first place, while Devlin seems to me to be on firm ground in claiming that every social system involves a community of certain ideas among its members, he does not explain what is to be understood by the "preservation" or "destruction" of a social order (as distinct from the persistence or collapse of its form of government), or just how one is to distinguish between the supposition that a social order has been *destroyed* and the supposition that there has been only a *change* in some pervasive pattern of institutionalized behavior. Much talk about societies continues to be based on the model which compares them to living organisms, and there is a point to the analogy. But the analogy is misleading if it leads us to assume that a society can die or flourish in the same sense that a biological organism does. Thus, an organism is usually defined to be a living one, if its so-called "vital functions"—such as respiration or assimilation of food—are being maintained, and to be dead when these processes no longer continue. In the case of societies, there are also processes (such as the maintenance of the food supply or the education of the young) that are sometimes compared with biological vital functions; and a society could therefore be said to have perished when these processes have ceased or, in the extreme instance, when its members have been permanently dispersed or have died without leaving any progeny. But with the possible exception of this extreme case, there appears to be no general agreement on the activities that *define* what it is for a society to be destroyed, rather than to be undergoing some alteration in its modes of organizing human conduct. It is therefore difficult to know what Devlin is asserting when he says that a given society fails or succeeds in preserving itself.

2. But secondly, Devlin does not establish his claim that any *specific tenet* of public morality—that is, any concrete moral conviction most members of a community ostensibly share about how men should behave and govern their lives in connection with some determinate activity, such as the conviction that marriages should be monogamous or that animals should not be mistreated—is *actually included* in the community of ideas whose maintenance he thinks is *indispensable* for the preservation of a social order. There is considerable evidence for believing that members of a given community do have in common a variety of more or less general ideas and attitudes as to what are the proper ways in which men should conduct themselves—for example, in many societies if not in all, most men expect others to have some regard for the sanctity of the lives of fellow members in their society, to comply with current laws or customs and the rules for changing them, or to make allowances for differences in the conduct of others because of differences in age and capacity. Moreover, it is quite plausible to hold that human societies would be impossible without the existence of a community of such general moral ideas. Indeed, given the biological makeup of men, their common desire to live and to procreate, and their dependence on the services rendered by others, it would be surprising if this were not so. But however this may be, and assuming that the notion of what it is for a society to be destroyed has been clarified, neither logic nor history appears to support the supposition that the violation of any *specific* moral standards prescribed by public morality may threaten the life of a social order.

An example may help to make the point clearer. Assume for the sake of the argument that no society can exist if it does not have *some* form of private property and if its members do not in the main believe that *some* ways of acquiring private property are morally justifiable. On this assumption, the preservation of a given society therefore requires the preservation of the conviction among its members that private owner- ship is morally warranted. But suppose further that in a particular society slavery is legal during a certain period, that during this period most of its members think it is entirely moral to own human beings as articles of private property, but that because of widespread protests against the institution of slavery the conviction that the institution is moral becomes seriously weakened. However, it does not follow from the basic premise of the argument that a weakening of *this* particular conviction is a threat to the social order—for on that premise, a neces- sary condition for the preservation of society is not the continued commitment to the morality of *human slavery*, but rather the continued commitment to the justifiability of *private property* in some form; and it is evident that this latter commitment is entirely compatible with the rejection of the former one.

Moreover, it is difficult to find in the historical record unquestiona- ble instances in which a society collapsed because some one specific tenet of public morality had been extensively violated in actual practice, or because widely held beliefs in such a tenet had been seriously weakened. Human societies do not appear to be such fragile systems that they cannot survive a successful challenge to some established norm of conduct, nor are they such rigid structures that they are unable to accommodate their institutions to deviations from customary patterns of behavior and approved moral standards. Thus, since the end of the eighteenth century there have been radical transformations in the U.S. not only in commonly held ideas about the morality of numerous forms of private property but also in ideas about the morality of various kinds of individual conduct—including sexual practices, the treatment of chil- dren by parents, and personal attitudes toward members of minority groups. On the face of it, at any rate, the society (or societies) occupying the territory of the U.S. during this period has adjusted itself to these changes in public morality. Or ought one to say that because of these changes in what were at various times deeply felt moral beliefs, American society has failed to preserve itself? In the absence of an unambiguous characterization of what constitutes the American social order and what is essential for its continuing existence, the question can be answered to suit one's preference. But if this is so, Devlin's major premise is either unproven (so that it cannot serve as a reason for accepting his conclusion), or the premise is so indeterminate in its content that a conclusion different from the one he reaches can also be drawn from it. There is therefore only a farfetched analogy at best between violations of public morality and treasonable actions—for there is, no clear sense in which a social order is alleged to be capable of destruction by the former, while the downfall of established political authority can sometimes be correctly attributed to the latter. Accordingly, to build a case for the enforcement of morals on this analogy, as Devlin in effect does, is to build it on insubstantial foundations.

3. There are two other related assumptions in Devlin's argument that require brief notice ... (a) Although he recognizes that public morality is subject to change, he appears to have no doubt that there is a quite definite community of moral ideas among members of a society during a given period. Moreover, he believes that the content of this morality can be ascertained without inordinate difficulty; and I, he suggests that for the purposes of the law, immorality is what any so-called "right-minded person" or "man in the Clapham omnibus," any jury of twelve men or women selected at random, is presumed to consider to be immoral.

However, neither assumption seems to me plausible. There have been communities in the past, and there are still some in the present, which were exposed to but a single intellectual and moral tradition, and were unaccustomed to the exchange and criticism of ideas on diverse subjects; and for such communities, the notion of a public morality which directs the energies of men into definite channels makes good sense. But in large urban societies such as our own, in which divergent ideals of life (often based on new scientific discoveries) are widely discussed, and technological advances in medicine as well as industry create opportunities for developing novel patterns of behavior, men differ widely in what they take to be moral conduct, and are in some measure tolerant of moral ideals which they do not themselves espouse. It is by no means evident whether in such pluralistic societies the notion of a public morality as Devlin conceives it is strictly applicable. For example, he declares that "The Institution of marriage would be gravely threatened if individual judgments were permitted about the morality of adultery; on [this matter] there must be a public morality" (p. 10). But there is reason to believe that Devlin overestimates the extent of current agreement on the immorality of extramarital relations and, as recent discussions of proposed reforms of divorce laws suggest, it is by no means certain that there is a real consensus on the immorality of adultery upon which the persistence of the institution of marriage is alleged to be contingent. Moreover, the educative and transformation function of the law must not be ignored. For while the effectiveness of a legal system undoubtedly depends on the support it receives from the prevailing moral convictions of a community, the law does not simply *reflect* those convictions, but is in turn frequently an agency for *modifying* accepted moral standards. The supposition that even during a relatively brief period there is a determinate and clearly identifiable public morality is not a realistic picture of modern societies.

(b) Devlin's recommendation on how to ascertain the content of public morality is certainly simple. But is it also sound? If the moral convictions of members of contemporary societies are as diverse and divergent as I have suggested they are, what reason is there to suppose that the unanimous judgment of a dozen individuals drawn at random to serve on a jury is representative of the moral standards (for what may be to them an unfamiliar type of conduct) that are entertained throughout the society? Moreover, since on Devlin's view actions judged to be criminal because they are held to be immoral are actions which threaten the safety of the social order, why should we assume that twelve "right-minded persons" in a jury box—who presumably have no specialized training for evaluating the effects on others of some form of deviant behavior, nor the opportunity to undertake a careful study of what is already known about them—are more qualified to make competent judgments on what may be complex moral issues, than they are to pass on the significance of a scientific idea or on the merits of a surgical technique? To be sure, Devlin does not intend, as some commentators accuse him of doing, that the snap decisions of unreflective morality based on mere feelings of dislike and indignation are to be the ground on which a practice is to be made criminal. Thus he declares that "before a society can put a practice beyond the limits of tolerance [and hence make it a criminal offense], there must be a *deliberate* judgment that the practice is injurious to society" (p. 17, my italics). Nor does he maintain, as some critics have suggested, that "the arm of the law" should always be used to enforce society's judgment as to what is immoral—on the contrary, he presents a number of important prudential considerations which severely restrict the use of the criminal law to eradicate such immoral behavior. But except for the suggestion that a reliable symptom of practices that could destroy a social order is whether they generate in all members of a jury (and inferentially, in a majority of "right-minded persons" in the community) strong feelings of reprobation and intoler-ance (p. 17), he gives no reasons for supposing that the "deliberate judgments" he has emphasized as essential can be obtained by the procedure he recommends for ascertaining whether some conduct is detrimental to the social order; and he does not even discuss obvious alternatives to his proposal, such as the use of special commissions like the Wolfenden Committee itself to determine whether a practice does indeed have adverse consequences for society.

In short, while Mill's attempt to delimit a category of conduct which is permanently immune to legal as well as other forms of social control seems to me unsuccessful, I also think the difficulties I have been surveying make inconclusive Devlin's argument that the use of the criminal law to enforce moral standards for so-called "private conduct" is justifiable, if it is essential for preserving the integrity of society.

4

However, Devlin has been criticized by Professor Hart and others for disavowing Mill's doctrine on the justifiable limits of interference with an individual's freedom, and especially for dissenting from Mill's view that it is never warranted to compel a person to do or refrain from doing an action merely for the sake of his own welfare. I want therefore to examine briefly the main line of Hart's defense of Mill.

There are a variety of practices which are illegal in many countries, though on the face of it only the parties directly involved in their performance are affected by them. I have already noted that Mill himself approved a number of such laws; but despite the doubtful consistency of his doing so, he offered no clear rationale for them. On the other hand, Devlin maintains that the existence of such laws can be explained only on the assumption that they illustrate society's efforts "to enforce a moral principle and nothing else."[79] But Hart rejects this interpretation, and in his discussion of several examples of such laws, he proposes what he claims to be a different one. I will comment on his views as he presents them in the context of two examples.

1. Bigamy is a crime in many countries. Why should it be made a criminal offense, especially since in most jurisdictions a married man is doing nothing illegal if, while his legal spouse is alive, he lives with another woman and appears in public with her as husband and wife— *unless* he also goes through a marriage ceremony with her? Hart denies that the law is justified as an attempt "to enforce private morality as such"; and after expressing, some sympathy for the view that the law might be "accepted as an attempt to protect religious feelings from offence by a public act desecrating the ceremony" of marriage, he declares that on this view "the bigamist is punished neither as irreligious nor as immoral but as a *nuisance*. For the law is then concerned with the *offensiveness to others* of his public conduct, not with the immorality of his *private conduct*."[80] However, as Devlin has been quick to note, a marriage ceremony can be performed in the privacy of some civil servant's office, with no one but the celebrants and their intimate friends any the wiser; and it is therefore difficult to make sense of Hart's suggestion that the bigamist is being punished for the offense created by a public act, if there was no such offense because the bigamous marriage ceremony was in fact performed in private. But however this may be, there is a more fundamental point to be made. Hart is begging the

79. H. L. A. Hart, *Law, Liberty, and Morality* (Stanford, Cal.: Stanford University Press, 1963), p. 7.   **80.** *Ibid.*, p. 41 [my italics].

question if he assumes that to judge an action to be a nuisance (or offensive) to others, is always independent of any judgment of its morality. If bigamous marriages and other kinds of public conduct are crimes in the U.S. because they are offensive to others in America, they are in fact not offensive to members of other cultures in which Puritanical conceptions of moral behavior are not widespread; and such examples make it difficult to deny that some conduct is regarded as a nuisance to others, just because those others regard the conduct as immoral. Accordingly, if bigamy is a crime because it is a nuisance to others, it does not follow without further argument that the bigamist is not punished because he is judged by society to be immoral, but for some other reason. This further argument Hart does not supply; but without it, he has not presented a clear alternative to the claim that in the case of bigamy at any rate the law is being used to enforce morals.

2.   Hart's second example is as follows. With some exceptions such as rape, the criminal law does not permit, and has never permitted, the consent of the victim in a case involving physical injury to be used as an argument for the defense. But if one person makes a pact with a second to be beaten or even be killed, and the second one does as he promised, why should he be liable to punishment by society, if the parties to the agreement were of sane mind when they made it, both entered into it voluntarily, and no one else was injured by the transaction? (Incidentally, the example is not as grotesque as it may seem—it states the situation covered by current laws forbidding voluntary euthanasia.) To punish the defendant in this case is in direct conflict with Mill's explicit injunction that the law must never be used to interfere with an individual's freedom to make his "private" arrangements as he thinks best, even though as others see the matter his best interests are not served by his actions. Can this rule of law be justified? Devlin thinks it can, but only in one way; and he offers the justification that will by now be familiar, namely, that "there are certain standards of behavior or moral principles which society requires to be observed; and the breach of them is an offence not merely against the person who is injured but against society as a whole."[81] On the other hand, Hart denies this claim. How then does he justify this rule of law? He maintains that "The rules excluding the victim's consent as a defence to charges of murder or assault may perfectly well be explained as a piece of *paternalism*, designed to protect individuals against themselves."[82] In consequence, he finds fault with Devlin for failing to distinguish between what Hart calls "legal moralism" (the doctrine he attributes to Devlin and which justifies the use of the law to enforce positive morality), and "legal paternalism" (the doctrine which justifies using the law to protect people against themselves). According to Hart, Mill's principle of liberty excludes legal moralism. But while in general he aligns himself with Mill's principle, he believes that if it is to accommodate such rules of law as the one under discussion, the principle must be amended; and although he does not

---

81. Devlin, *op. cit.*, pp. 6–7.   **82.** Hart, *op. cit.*, p. 31 [my italics].

present a formulation of the revised principle, he suggests that the amended form must be consonant with legal paternalism.

However, Hart does little to make clear just how legal moralism differs from legal paternalism, and that it is not a distinction without difference. He suggests that while a legal moralist justifies a law regulating actions that are allegedly not harmful to others, on the ground that its aim is to enforce morality "as such"—whatever the phrase "as such" may signify—a legal paternalist who endorses the law will justify it on the ground that it seeks to protect people against themselves. But is there a substantive difference here? Can there be a rule of law that is compatible with legal moralism, but which is necessarily excluded by legal paternalism? Could not any law that is said to be simply an attempt to enforce morality be also construed as an attempt to protect men against themselves? Thus, Hart argues that the English law making the sale of narcotics a criminal offense is not concerned with punishing the seller for his immorality, as legal moralists claim, but with protecting the would-be purchaser.[83] But could not a legal paternalist offer an analogous support for any law endorsed by a legal moralist? And conversely, in endorsing the narcotics law on the ground that it punishes the seller for his immorality, the legal moralist can maintain that the seller is immoral because he makes available to others an article that is harmful to its users.

Hart also defends the distinction between legal paternalism and legal moralism by claiming that the former is a sounder moral policy than the latter. For according to him, the conceptions of men's best interests that legal paternalism seeks to enforce are the products of what he calls "critical morality," while the conceptions legal moralism would enforce are the creatures of blind custom and unexamined tradition. If there is this difference, it is undoubtedly an important one. But even if there is, Hart's claim presupposes that the distinction between legal moralism and legal paternalism has already been established; and it assumes without argument that there is a unique system of critical morality which underlies the proposals of legal paternalism, and that this system is a sound one. It is plain, however, that many systems of critical morality have been developed, and that their conceptions of what is to men's best interests do not always agree. There is certainly no consensus even among deeply reflective men as to which system of critical morality is the most adequate one, so that legal paternalists are likely to differ among themselves as well as with legal moralists as to the rules that should guide men's conduct. It surely does not follow that because legal paternalism is based on a critical morality, its proposals for regulating men's actions are necessarily sounder than the proposals of legal moralists.

But however this may be, if legal paternalism is a justifiable policy in the law—as Hart appears to hold—its adoption as a principle of legislation destroys the possibility of establishing a permanent division

83. *Ibid.*, p. 32.

between conduct that is only of private concern and conduct that is of legitimate public interest. Adoption of the policy certainly permits the introduction of legal controls at which Mill would have been aghast.

5

I have taken much time to belabor the simple point that Mill's principle is not an adequate guide to legal and other forms of social control of men's behavior. My excuse for doing so is that the principle is still very much alive in current discussions of legal and social philosophy, as the controversy between Devlin and his critics makes evident. Moreover, though the limitations of Mill's views on liberty have been often noted, they stress an important component in a reasonable ideal of human life—a component that needs to be stressed, if it is not to be swept aside by more insistent demands directed to realizing other human aspirations. But while I think Mill overdid the stress, how the ideal of individual freedom can be adjusted to competing aspirations is to me a question of perennial interest.

Like Tocqueville, Mill feared some of the leveling tendencies in modern democracies, and was apprehensive of the intolerance that custom-bound and unenlightened majorities can exhibit toward new ideas, fresh sensibilities, and intellectual as well as artistic excellence. He prized these achievements above all else, and believed they are indissolubly linked with the possession of maximum individual freedom that is compatible with life in society as he knew it. He therefore sought to secure the continuance of these achievements; and his principle of liberty was not only an expression of his conception of the human good, but also a protective wall to safeguard its pursuit.

As in the case of other political philosophers who saw in the pursuit of a multiplicity of objectives a danger to the realization of what they prized highly, Mill thus made individual freedom an absolute good to which he formally subordinated all other objectives—though his actual evaluations of social practices and his recommendations of changes in them are not always consonant with his formal principle. However, the elevation of individual liberty to the rank of the supreme good is clearly arbitrary. Most men do not cherish personal freedom above all else, even after prolonged and careful reflection; and in any case, they prize other things as well—indeed, sometimes as indispensable to a satisfactory and well-ordered life—such as health, some measure of worldly success and security, friendship and family, achievement and recognition by one's peers, or influence in the affairs of men. Moreover, maximum personal freedom is in general neither a necessary condition for the realization of all other legitimate objectives, nor is it compatible with some of them.

Accordingly, since many different interests, some of which may be conflicting ones, must be recognized in dealing with social problems, and since no one interest dominates the others permanently and in all contexts, it does not seem possible to set fixed limits to justifiable legal control of men's conduct. On the other hand, though it is frequently claimed that a compromise must be effected between the interests involved in a given problem, how the compromise should be made and in conformity with what rules, are questions to which I know no satisfactory answer. To be sure, broad rules have been proposed for dealing with this issue—for example, that the domain of personal freedom should be diminished as little as possible, or that the compromise should be so made as to maximize the expected social utility. But the proposed rules are vague and do not carry us very far. For in the absence of effective techniques for assessing the relative importance (or the utilities) of the various interests involved in the problem, it is not clear how the rules are to be applied; and despite the development of modern decision theory, there is no prospect that the needed techniques will soon be available.

There is then no general answer to the question whether certain categories of actions should be legally controlled and whether certain standards of conduct should be legally enforced. The question can be resolved only case by case, and though the proposed answers cannot be guaranteed to be the best ones possible, they are often the best ones available. And I cannot do better by way of a conclusion to this reflection than to quote a brief passage from Learned Hand:

> We shall never get along in matters of large public interest, if we proceed by generalization, indeed, if you insist, by principles, put forward as applicable in all circumstances.... The only way that public affairs can be successfully managed is by treating each case by itself; even so, the trouble is far from ended. We must ask what a proposed measure will do in fact, how all the people whom it touches react and respond to it? ... Then—and this the more difficult part—one must make a choice between the values that will be affected, for there are substantially always conflicts of group interest.[84]

Notes and Questions

1. How would H.L.A. Hart define the term "morals"? How would Patrick Devlin?

2. Do we know whether Lord Devlin would support criminal sanctions against homosexual behavior in Great Britain? What method would he use to determine whether a criminal sanction makes sense? What data would he need to reach a conclusion?

3. Does Lord Devlin take a position about the justification of criminal prohibitions on narcotics, alcohol, pornography or gambling? In Lord Devlin's view, does the fact that all these behaviors have a moral dimension mean that the case for or against criminal prohibition involves the same sort of considerations and the same preferred outcome?

84. Learned Hand, *The Spirit of Liberty* (New York: Alfred A. Knopf, Inc., 1960), pp. 172–73.

4. Why does H.L.A. Hart think that homosexuality and drugs are different categories of behavior when discussing the wisdom of paternalism? Compare Professor Hart with John Stuart Mill's *On Liberty* ([1859] 1961:147). A classic early parallel to the Hart–Devlin debate can be found in Mill's *On Liberty* (1859) and James Fitzjames Stephens' *Liberty, Equality, Fraternity* (1873).

5. Professor Hart distinguishes between criminal prohibitions based on moralistic judgments, of which he disapproves, and criminal prohibitions based on paternalistic judgments, some of which might be justified. Homosexuality provides an example of a moralistic judgment; narcotics provide an example of paternalistic prohibitions that may not be objectionable. Does this mean that Professor Hart does not believe that criminal prohibition on the consumption of substances like marijuana is based on moral judgments? Or does Hart argue that there is a palpable harm apart from moral wrongdoing that is associated with narcotics?

    If that is his argument, is he also asserting that there is no secular harm involved in the practices associated with homosexual conduct? Is Hart's distinction between behaviors that are harmful (whether to the self or others) and behaviors that cause no harm other than offending the community's sense of propriety? If so, who has the burden of proof on the issue of whether a behavior generates secular harm: the prohibitionist or the advocate of decriminalization?

6. Professor Nagel criticizes Professor Hart's distinction between moralistic and paternalistic control. Do you agree with his critique? Nagel concludes that determining the proper scope of the criminal law can only be done on a case-by-case basis. Do you agree with that? What sort of considerations should be balanced when making case-by-case determination regarding pornography, gambling or the possession of cocaine? When a criminal prohibition is already in place, who should have the burden of proof when making a case-by-case determination about whether the law should continue? Is Professor Nagel's case-by-case determination simply another description of "cost-benefit" analysis? Would Professor Nagel approve of the approach taken by Professor Kadish in the next section? What about Morris and Hawkins?

B. THE MODERN CONCEPTION OF VICTIMLESS CRIME

SANFORD H. KADISH—THE CRISIS OF OVERCRIMINALIZATION

Annals of the American Academy of Political and
Social Science, Vol. 374, Combating Crime.
(Nov., 1967), pp. 157–170.

Since the last war there have been striking achievements in reform of the substantive criminal law. Largely under the impetus of the American Law Institute's Model Penal Code, a number of states have completed revisions of their criminal codes, and still more are in the process. The importance of this reform for criminal justice cannot be overstated.

But there is a significant feature of substantive law-revision which these reforms have succeeded in reaching only in part. By and large, these efforts have dealt with offenses entailing substantial harm to persons, property, and the state, against which the criminal law is generally accepted as the last and necessary resort. But American criminal law typically has extended the criminal sanction well beyond these fundamental offenses to include very different kinds of behavior, kinds which threaten far less serious harms, or else highly intangible ones about which there is no genuine consensus, or even no harms at all. The existence of these crimes and attempts at their eradication raise problems of inestimable importance for the criminal law. Indeed, it is fair to say that until these problems of overcriminalization are systematically examined and effectively dealt with, some of the most besetting problems of criminal-law administration are bound to continue.

Chapter VIII of *Task Force Report: The Courts*, of the President's Commission on Law Enforcement and Administration of Justice, is an attempt to deal with some of these problems.[85] The Executive Director has chosen to reveal my own hand in its preparation,[86] and I could hardly come now either to praise it or to bury it. Still, it may be said that the controversial character of these issues, and the need to achieve consensus among nineteen Commissioners of highly differing backgrounds and orientation, quite understandably required some reduction in scope and muting in tone and conclusion of my original draft. I note this not in complaint. Indeed, that these distinguished citizens, who, as a group, can scarcely be charged with being immoderate or visionary, were prepared to raise substantial reservations concerning the overextension of the criminal law is itself an event of significance. Still, this special issue of THE ANNALS provides an opportunity to present, free of the restraints of the need for consensus, a number of observations and conclusions which appeared to me compelling in thinking about these matters for the Commission. I do this not to disown Chapter VIII, but to add to it. Indeed, I have not hesitated to make use of its substance, and occasionally its phrasing, where desirable, in the interest of making this statement self-contained. In short, whereas Chapter VIII is a version of my original draft, this article is my own version of Chapter VIII, though compressed as far as possible in keeping with the admirable ANNALS policy of brevity.

The subjects raising the central issue of overcriminalization cut a wide swathe through the laws of most jurisdictions. In the process of revising the California criminal law, we encountered a mass of crimes outside the Penal Code, matching the Penal Code itself in volume, and authorizing criminal convictions for such offenses as failure by a school principal to use required textbooks,[87] failure of a teacher to carry first-

85. U.S. PRESIDENT'S COMMISSION ON LAW ENFORCEMENT AND ADMINISTRATION OF JUSTICE, TASK FORCE REPORT: THE COURTS 97–107 (1967). This commission will be referred to herein as the National Crime Commission.

86. *Idem* at 2.

87. CALIF. EDUCATION CODE § 9255.

aid kits on field trips,[88] gambling on the result of an election,[89] giving private commercial performances by a state-supported band,[90] and allowing waste of an artesian well by the landowner.[91] Then there are the criminal laws, enforced by state police forces, which have been the primary means used to deal with the death and injury toll of the automobile. Indications are that this response may ultimately do more harm than good by blocking off politically harder, but more likely, remedial alternatives.[92] Problematic also has been the use of criminal sanctions to enforce economic regulatory measures, a matter which I have dealt with elsewhere.[93] And there are other instances as well. In this piece I want to comment on the problems of overcriminalization in just three kinds of situations, in each of which the costs paid primarily affect the day-to-day business of law enforcement are the situations in which the criminal law is used: (1) to declare or enforce public standards of private morality, (2) as a means of providing social services in default of other public agencies, and (3) as a disingenuous means of permitting police to do indirectly what the law forbids them to do directly.

ENFORCEMENT OF MORALS

The use of the criminal law to prohibit moral deviancy among consenting adults has been a recurring subject of jurisprudential debate. Stephens in the last century[94] and Lord Devlin in this century have urged the legitimacy of criminal intervention on the ground that "society cannot ignore the morality of the individual any more than it can his loyalty; it flourishes on both and without either it dies."[95] The contrary view, vigorously espoused by John Stuart Mill in the nineteenth century,[96] and by H. L. A. Hart[97] and many others in recent years, is, in the words of the Wolfenden Report:

> Unless a deliberate attempt is to be made by society, acting through the agency of the law, to equate the sphere of crime with that of sin, there must remain a realm of private morality and immorality which is, in brief and crude terms, not the law's business.[98]

It is not my purpose here to mediate or resolve that dispute. My objective is to call attention to matters of the hardest concreteness and practicality, which should be of as much concern in reaching final

88. Idem at § 11955,

89. CALIF. ELECTIONS CODE § 29003.

90. CALIF. GOVERNMENT CODE § 6650.

91. CALIF. WATER CODE § 307.

92. See the telling account of Moynihan, *The War Against the Automobile*, The Public Interest, No. 3 (Spring 1966), especially at 21 *et seq.*

93. Kadish, *Some Observations on the Use of Criminal Sanctions in Enforcing Economic Regulations*, 30 U. CHI. L. REV. 423 (1963).

94. J.F. STEPHENS, LIBERTY, FRATERNITY AND EQUALITY (1873).

95. DEVLIN, THE ENFORCEMENT OF MORALS 23 (1959).

96. J.S. MILL, ON LIBERTY (1859).

97. H.L.A. HART, LAW, LIBERTY AND MORALITY (1963).

98. GREAT BRITAIN COMMITTEE ON HOMOSEXUAL OFFENSES AND PROSTITUTION, REPORT, COMMAND No. 247 (1957) (Wolfenden Report), Paras. 61 and 62.

judgment to a Devlin as to the staunchest libertarian; namely, the adverse consequences to effective law enforcement of attempting to achieve conformity with private moral standards through use of the criminal law.

SEX OFFENSES

The classic instance of the use of the criminal law purely to enforce a moral code is the laws prohibiting extramarital and abnormal sexual intercourse between a man and a woman. Whether or not Kinsey's judgment is accurate that 95 per cent of the population are made potential criminals by these laws,[99] no one doubts that their standard of sexual conduct is not adhered to by vast numbers in the community, including the otherwise most respectable (and, most especially, the police themselves)[100] nor is it disputed that there is no effort to enforce these laws. The traditional function of the criminal law, therefore—to curtail socially threatening behavior through the threat of punishment and the incapacitation and rehabilitation of offenders—is quite beside the point. Thurman Arnold surely had it right when he observed that these laws "are unenforced because we want to continue our conduct, and unrepealed because we want to preserve our morals."[101]

But law enforcement pays a price for using the criminal law in this way. First, the moral message communicated by the law is contradicted by the total absence of enforcement; for while the public sees the conduct condemned in words, it also sees in the dramatic absence of prosecutions that it is not condemned in deed. Moral adjurations vulnerable to a charge of hypocrisy are self-defeating no less in law than elsewhere. Second, the spectacle of nullification of the legislature's solemn commands is an unhealthy influence on law enforcement generally. It tends to breed a cynicism and an indifference to the criminal-law processes which augment tendencies toward disrespect for those who make and enforce the law, a disrespect which is already widely in evidence. In addition:

> Dead letter laws, far from promoting a sense of security, which is the main function of the penal law, actually impair that security by holding the threat of prosecution over the heads of people whom we have no intention to punish.[102]

Finally, these laws invite discriminatory enforcement against persons selected for prosecution on grounds unrelated to the evil against which these laws are purportedly addressed grounds, whether those grounds be "the prodding of some reform group, a newspaper-generated hysteria over some local sex crime, a vice drive which is put on by the

99. KINSEY, POMEROY, and MARTIN, SEXUAL BEHAVIOR IN THE HUMAN MALE 392 (1948).

100. See SKOLNICK, JUSTICE WITHOUT TRIAL (1966), chap. iii.

101. THURMAN ARNOLD, SYMBOLS OF GOVERNMENT 160 (1936).

102. MODEL PENAL CODE § 207.11, comments at 111 (Tent. Draft No. 9, 1959).

local authorities to distract attention from defects in their administration of the city government."[103]

The criminalization of consensual adult homosexuality represents another attempt to legislate private morality. It raises somewhat different problems from heterosexual offenses, in that there are some attempts at enforcement. The central questions are whether the criminal law is an effective way of discouraging this conduct and how wasteful or costly it is.

Despite the fact that homosexual practices are condemned as criminal in virtually all states, usually as a felony with substantial punishment, and despite sporadic efforts at enforcement in certain situations, there is little evidence that the criminal law has discouraged the practice to any substantial degree. The Kinsey Report as well as other studies suggest a wide incidence of homosexuality throughout the country. One major reason for the ineffectiveness of these laws is that the private and consensual nature of the conduct precludes the attainment of any substantial deterrent efficacy through law enforcement. There are no complainants, and only the indiscreet have reasons for fear. Another reason is the irrelevance of the threat of punishment. Homosexuality involves not so much a choice to act wickedly as the seeking of normal sexual fulfillment in abnormal ways (though not abnormal to the individual) preferred by the individual for reasons deeply rooted in his development as a personality. Moreover, in view of the character of prison environments, putting the homosexual defendant into the prison system is, as observed recently by a United States District Judge, "a little like throwing Bre'r Rabbit into the briarpatch."[104]

On the other hand, the use of the criminal law has been attended by grave consequences. A commonly noted consequence is the enhanced opportunities created for extortionary threats of exposure and prosecution. Certainly, incidents of this kind have been reported often enough to raise genuine concern.[105] But, of more significance for the administration of justice, enforcement efforts by police have created problems both for them and for the community. Opportunities for enforcement are limited by the private and consensual character of the behavior. Only a small and insignificant manifestation of homosexuality is amenable to enforcement. This is that which takes place, either in the solicitation or the act, in public places. Even in these circumstances, it is not usual for persons to act openly. To obtain evidence, police are obliged to resort to behavior which tends to degrade and demean both themselves personally and law enforcement as an institution.[106] However one may deplore homosexual

103. KINSEY, MARTIN, and GEBHARD, SEXUAL BEHAVIOR IN THE HUMAN FEMALE 392 (1953).

104. Chief Judge Craven in Perkins v. North Carolina, 234 F. Supp. 333, 339 (W.D.N.C. 1964).

105. As recently as August 1966 a nationwide extortion ring was uncovered which used blackmail of homosexuals to extort millions of dollars from thousands of victims, many of whom were prominent personalities in entertainment, business, education, and government. Time, August 26, 1966, p. 14.

106. See Project, *The Consenting Adult Homosexual and the Law: An Empirical Study of Enforcement in Los Angeles County*, 13 U.C.L.A. LAW REV. 643 (1966).

conduct, no one can lightly accept a criminal law which requires for its enforcement that officers of the law sit concealed in ceilings, their eyes fixed to "peepholes," searching for criminal sexuality in the lavatories below;[107] or that they loiter suggestively around public toilets or in corridors hopefully awaiting a sexual advance.[108] Such conduct corrupts both citizenry and police and reduces the moral authority of the criminal law, especially among those portions of the citizenry—the poor and subcultural—who are particularly liable to be treated in an arbitrary fashion. The complaint of the critical that the police have more important things to do with their time is amply attested by the several volumes of the National Crime Commission's reports.

The offense of prostitution creates similar problems. Although there are social harms beyond private immorality in commercialized sex— spread of venereal disease, exploitation of the young, and the affront of public solicitation, for example—the blunt use of the criminal prohibition has proven ineffective and costly. Prostitution has endured in all civilizations; indeed, few institutions have proven as hardy. The inevitable conditions of social life unfailingly produce the supply to meet the ever-present demand. As the Wolfenden Report observed: "There are limits to the degree of discouragement which the criminal law can properly exercise towards a woman who has deliberately decided to live her life in this way, or a man who has deliberately chosen to use her services."[109] The more so, one may add, in a country where it has been estimated that over two-thirds of white males alone will have experience with prostitutes during their lives.[110] The costs, on the other hand, of making the effort are similar to those entailed in enforcing the homosexual laws— diversion of police resources; encouragement of use of illegal means of police control (which, in the case of prostitution, take the form of knowingly unlawful harassment arrests to remove suspected prostitutes from the streets;[111] and various entrapment devices, as only means of obtaining confessions);[112] degradation of the image of law enforcement; discriminatory enforcement against the poor; and official corruption.

107. See Bielicki v. Superior Court, 57 Cal.2d 602, 371 P.2d 288 (1962); Britt v. Superior Court, 58 Cal.2d 469, 374 P.2d 817 (1962); Smayda v. United States, 352 F.2d 251 (9th Cir. 1965).

108. See Project, *supra*, note 22, at 690–691: "The decoy method is utilized by undercover officers who 'operate' by intentionally providing homosexuals with the opportunity to make a proscribed solicitation.... The decoy's modus operandi at a public restroom may be to loiter inside engaging a suspect in friendly conversation, using handwashing or urinal facilities, or even occupying a commode for long periods of time. If the suspect makes a lewd solicitation or touching, the decoy will usually suggest going elsewhere to consummate the act and the arrest will be made outside of the restroom. When a street area is a known rendezvous location for homosexuals and male prostitutes, the decoy will operate by loitering on the street or by using a car to approach the suspect. In bars frequented by homosexuals, the decoy will order a drink and engage in friendly conversation with a suspect. Enforcement in bathhouses may necessitate operation by nude and semi-nude decoys."

109. *Supra*, note 14 at 247.

110. Kinsey, *supra*, note 15 at 597.

111. LAFAVE, ARREST: THE DECISION TO TAKE A SUSPECT INTO CUSTODY 450 (1965).

112. Skolnick, *supra*, note 16 at 100.

To the extent that spread of venereal disease, corruption of the young, and public affront are the objects of prostitution controls, it would require little ingenuity to devise modes of social control short of the blanket criminalization of prostitution which would at the same time prove more effective and less costly for law enforcement. Apparently, the driving force behind prostitution laws is principally the conviction that prostitution is immoral. Only the judgment that the use of the criminal law for verbal vindication of our morals is more important than its use to protect life and property can support the preservation of these laws as they are.

ABORTION

The criminal prohibition of abortions is occasionally defended on the ground that it is necessary to protect the mother against the adverse psychological effects of such operations. There seems little doubt, however, that these laws serve to augment rather than to reduce the danger. The criminal penalty has given rise to a black market of illegal abortionists who stand ready to run the risk of imprisonment in order to earn the high fees produced by the law's discouragement of legitimate physicians. As a consequence, abortions are performed in kitchens and private rooms instead of in properly equipped hospitals, and often by unqualified amateurs rather than by licensed physicians. A relatively simple and nondangerous operation on patients strongly desirous of avoiding parenthood is therefore converted into a surreptitious, degrading, and traumatic experience in which the risk to the mental and physical well-being of the woman is many times increased. Indeed, the evidence is irresistible that thousands of lives are needlessly lost yearly at the hands of illegal abortionists.[113]

It is plain, therefore, that the primary force behind retention of the abortion laws is belief that it is immoral. One of the serious moral objections is based on the view that the unborn foetus, even in its early stages of development, has an independent claim to life equivalent to that of a developed human being. Even those holding this judgment, however, can scarcely ignore the hard fact that abortion laws do not work to stop abortion, except for those too poor and ignorant to avail themselves of black-market alternatives, and that the consequence of their retention is probably to sacrifice more lives of mothers than the total number of fetuses saved by the abortion laws.

While there are no reliable figures on the number of illegal abortions, estimates have ranged from a hundred thousand to a million and a half yearly.[114] Among the factors responsible for this widespread nullification predominate. The first is that there is no general consensus on

---

113. See the sobering testimony of the Assistant Chief of the Division of Preventive Medical Services of the State Department of Public Health, before the California Assembly Interim Committee on Criminal Procedure, July 20, 1964, quoted in TASK FORCE REPORT: THE COURTS, supra, note 1 at 5.

114. See the sources in MODEL PENAL CODE, § 207.11, Comments at 147 (Tent. Draft No. 9, 1959).

the legitimacy of the moral claim on behalf of the foetus. While it is vigorously asserted by some portions of the community, it is as vigorously denied by others of equal honesty and respectability. In democratic societies, fortunately, the coercive sanctions of the criminal law prove unacceptable and unworkable as a means of settling clashes of sharply divided moralities. Second, the demand for abortions, by both married and unmarried women, is urgent and widespread, arising out of natural and understandable motives manifesting no threat to other persons or property. As with most morals offenses, therefore, sympathy for the offender combines with an unsettled moral climate to preclude any real possibility of enforcement.

GAMBLING AND NARCOTICS

Laws against gambling and narcotics present serious problems for law enforcement. Despite arrests, prosecutions and convictions, and increasingly severe penalties, the conduct seems only to flourish. The irrepressible demand for gambling and drugs, like the demand for alcohol during Prohibition days, survives the condemnation of the criminal law. Whether or not the criminal restriction operates paradoxically, as some have thought, to make the conduct more attractive, it is clear that the prohibitions have not substantially eliminated the demand.

Nor have the laws and enforcement efforts suppressed sources of supply. No one with an urge to gamble in any fair-sized city of this country has far to go to place an illegal bet. And in the case of narcotics, illicit suppliers enter the market to seek the profits made available by the persistence of the demand and the criminal law's reduction of legitimate sources of supply, while "pusher"-addicts distribute narcotics as a means of fulfilling their own needs. Risk of conviction, even of long terms of imprisonment, appears to have little effect. Partly, this is because the immediate and compelling need of the "pusher"-addict for narcotics precludes any real attention to the distant prospect of conviction and imprisonment. For large-scale suppliers, who may not be addicts, the very process of criminalization and punishment serves to raise the stakes—while the risk becomes greater, so do the prospects of reward[115] In addition, experience has demonstrated that convictions are difficult to obtain against large, nonaddict, organized dealers.

Our indiscriminate policy of using the criminal law against selling what people insist on buying has spawned large-scale, organized systems, often of national scope, comprising an integration of the stages of production and distribution of the illicit product on a continuous and thoroughly business-like basis. Not only are these organizations especially difficult for law enforcement to deal with; they have the unpleasant quality of producing other crimes as well because, after the fashion of legitimate business, they tend to extend and diversify their operations. After repeal of Prohibition, racketeering organizations moved into the illegal drug market. Organizations which purvey drugs and supply gam-

115. Packer, The Crime Tariff, 33 AMERICAN SCHOLAR 551 (1964).

bling find it profitable to move into loan-sharking and labor racketeering. To enhance their effectiveness, these organized systems engage in satellite forms of crime, of which bribery and corruption of local government are the most far-reaching in their consequences.[116] Hence the irony that, in some measure, crime is encouraged and successful modes of criminality are produced by the criminal law itself.

Another significant cost of our policy is that the intractable difficulties of enforcement, produced by the consensual character of the illegal conduct and the typically organized methods of operation, have driven enforcement agencies to excesses in pursuit of evidence. These are not only undesirable in themselves, but have evoked a counterreaction in the courts in the form of restrictions upon the use of evidence designed to discourage these police practices. One need look no farther than the decisions of the United States Supreme Court. The two leading decisions on entrapment were produced by overreaching undercover agents in gambling[117] and narcotics prosecutions,[118] respectively. Decisions involving the admissibility of evidence arising out of illegal arrests have, for the most part, been rendered in gambling, alcohol, and narcotics prosecutions.[119] Legal restraints upon unlawful search and seizure have largely grown out of litigation over the last five decades concerning a variety of forms of physical intrusion by police in the course of obtaining evidence of violations of these same laws.[120] The same is true with respect to the developing law of wire-tapping, bugging, and other forms of electronic interception.[121] Indeed, no single phenomenon is more responsible for the whole pattern of judicial restraints upon methods of law enforcement than the unfortunate experience with enforcing these laws against vice.

There is, finally, a cost of inestimable importance, one which tends to be a product of virtually all the misuses of the criminal law discussed in this paper. That is the substantial diversion of police, prosecutorial, and judicial time, personnel, and resources. At a time when the volume of crime is steadily increasing, the burden on law-enforcement agencies is becoming more and more onerous, and massive efforts are being considered to deal more effectively with threats to the public of danger-

116. For a detailed description, see U.S. PRESIDENT'S COMMISSION ON LAW ENFORCEMENT AND ADMINISTRATION OF JUSTICE, TASK FORCE REPORT: ORGANIZED CRIME (1967).

117. Sorrells v. U.S., 287 U.S. 435 (1932).

118. Sherman v. U.S., 356 U.S. 369 (1958).

119. E.g., Johnson v. U.S. 333 U.S. 10 (1948) (narcotics); Draper v. U.S. 358 U.S. 307 (1959) (narcotics) ; Beck v. Ohio, 379 U.S. 89 (1964) (gambling).

120. E.g., Carroll v. U.S., 267 U.S. 132 (1925) (prohibition) ; Agnello v. U.S., 269 U.S. 20 (1925) (narcotics) ; Marron v. U.S., 275 U.S. 192 (1927) (prohibition) ; Go–Bart Co. v. U.S., 282 U.S. 344 (1931) (narcotics);

Lefkowitz v. U.S., 285 U.S. 452 (1932) (prohibition); Johnson v. U.S., 333 U.S. 10 (1948) (narcotics) ; Rochin v. California, 342 U.S. 165 (1952) (narcotics); Jones v. U.S., 362 U.S. 257 (1960) (narcotics) ; Wong Sun v. U.S., 371 U.S. 471 (1963) (narcotics) ; Ker v. California, 374 U.S. 23 (1963) (narcotics).

121. E.g., Olmstead v. U.S., 277 U.S. 438 (1928) (prohibition); Nardone v. U.S., 302 U.S. 379 (1938), 308 U.S. 338 (1939) (smuggled alcohol); On Lee v. U.S., 343 U.S. 747 (1952) (narcotics); Irvine v. California, 347 U.S. 128 (1954) (gambling); Benanti v. U.S. 355 U.S. 96 (1957) (illicit alcohol); Silverman v. U.S., 365 U.S. 505 (1961) (gambling).

ous and threatening conduct, releasing enforcement resources from the obligation to enforce the vice laws must be taken seriously. Indeed, in view of the minimal effectiveness of enforcement measures in dealing with vice crimes and the tangible costs and disadvantages of that effort, the case for this rediversion of resources to more profitable purposes becomes command. It seems fair to say that in few areas of the criminal law have we paid so much for so little.

One might, even so, quite reasonably take the position that gambling and narcotics are formidable social evils and that it would be dogmatic to insist that the criminal law should in no circumstances be used as one way, among others, of dealing with them. The exploitation of the weakness of vulnerable people, in the case of gambling, often results in economic loss and personal dislocations of substantial proportions. And the major physical and emotional hardships imposed by narcotics add even more serious evils. Still, such a view would scarcely excuse perpetuating the pattern of indiscriminate criminalization. There are obvious ways at least to mitigate the problems deed; for example, by narrowing the scope of criminality. In the case of gambling, there is an overwhelming case for abandoning the traditional approach of sweeping all forms of gambling within the scope of the prohibition, while relying on the discretion of police and prosecutor to exempt private gambling and charitable and religious fund-raising enterprises.[122] At least, the evil of delegating discretion in such magnitude as to abandon law can be remedied by a more careful legislative definition of precisely the form of gambling conduct which the legislature means to bring within the criminal sanction. In the case of narcotics, our legislatures have tended indiscriminately to treat all narcotics as creative of the same dangers despite the strong evidence that some drugs, particularly marijuana, present evils of such limited character that elimination of the criminal prohibition is plainly indicated.[123] In short, there is much of value that could be done even if the whole dose of repeal were too much to swallow.

PROVISION OF SOCIAL SERVICES

In a number of instances which, taken together, consume a significant portion of law-enforcement resources, the criminal law is used neither to protect against serious misbehavior through the medium of crime and punishment nor to confirm standards of private morality, but rather to provide social services to needy segments of the community. The drunk, the deserted mother, and the creditor have been the chief

---

122. The Model Anti–Gambling Act deliberately overgeneralizes the prohibition in this way even though recognizing "that it is un realistic to promulgate a law literally aimed at making a criminal offense of the friendly election bet, the private, social card game among friends, etc.," on the ground that "it is imperative to confront the professional gambler with a statutory facade that is wholly devoid of loopholes." 2 ABA COMM'N ON ORGANIZED CRIME, OR-GANIZED CRIME AND LAW ENFORCEMENT 74–78 (1953).

123. See the review of the evidence in the papers of Messrs. Blum and Rosenthal in U.S. PRESIDENT'S COMMISSION ON LAW ENFORCEMENT AND ADMINISTRATION OF JUSTICE, TASK FORCE REPORT: NARCOTICS AND DRUG ABUSE (1967), especially at pp. 24–26, 126 131.

beneficiaries. In each instance, the gains have been dubious in view of the toll exacted on effective law enforcement.

The Drunk

Using the criminal law to protect against offensive public behavior, whether by drunken or sober persons, is not the issue here. The trouble arises out of the use of laws against public drunkenness to deal with the inert, stuporous drunk in the public streets and alleyways, who constitutes a danger to himself and an ugly inconvenience to others. Staggering numbers of these drunks are fed daily into the criminal machinery. Indeed, more arrests are made than for any other crime—35 to 40 per cent of all reported arrests. Not only does the use of the criminal law, therefore, divert substantial law-enforcement resources away from genuinely threatening conduct, but the whole criminal justice system is denigrated by the need to process massive numbers of pathetic and impoverished people through clumsy and inappropriate procedures. Hearings and trials degenerate into a mockery of the forms of due process, with mass appearances, guilt assumed, and defendants unrepresented. Even if the social and personal problems of drunkenness were, in some measure, helped by this effort, these costs would make the investment doubtful. In fact, however, apart from a very temporary cleaning of the streets by the police, the effort is notoriously unsuccessful. Poverty, rootlessness, and personal inadequacy, which are at the bottom of alcoholism, are scarcely deterrable by the threat of criminal conviction. And rehabilitation in the human warehouses of our city jails is unthinkable.

In view of the detailed accounting of the experience with using the criminal law to deal with the public drunk and the suggestions of alternative civil remedies in the article in this issue by Mr. Stern[124] and in the report of the Crime Commission,[125] the matter need not be further pursued here. But it should be said that no single experience so dramatically exemplifies the misuse of the criminal law.

The Creditor and the Deserted Mother

The bad-check laws and the family-nonsupport laws are two other instances in which the criminal law is used in practice to provide social services; in these cases, to assist a merchant in obtaining payment and to assist needy families in obtaining support from a deserting spouse. The issue for legislative choice is straightforward: Is it ultimately worthwhile to employ the resources of police, prosecutors, and the criminal process generally in order to supplement civil remedies, even though such use entails a diversion of law-enforcement energies from more threatening criminal conduct?

124. See the article by Gerald Stern in this issue of THE ANNALS, 147–156.

125. See U.S. PRESIDENT'S COMMISSION ON LAW ENFORCEMENT AND ADMINISTRATION OF JUSTICE, TASK FORCE REPORT: DRUNKENNESS (1967).

Checks, of course, can be instruments of serious fraud for which it is proper to employ the sanctions of the criminal law. However, the typical bad-check laws provide for serious punishment as well for the person who draws a check on his account knowing that at the time it has insufficient funds to cover the check. Usually, the intent to defraud is presumed in these cases. Merchants, of course, are aware of the risk of accepting payment in checks, but expectedly prefer not to discourage sales. The effect of the insufficient-fund bad-check laws, is to enable them to make use of the resources of the criminal law to reduce what, in a sense, are voluntarily assumed business risks. If not, the usual practice is to discourage prosecution and instead to assume the role of free collection agencies for the merchants.[126]

The cost to law enforcement is, again, the diversion of resources from genuine threatening criminality. It is not clear that it is anything but habit which keeps states from narrowing their bad-check laws to exclude the occasional bad-check writer where there is no proof of intent to defraud. This would make it more difficult for merchants to obtain payment, but it is hard to see why it would not be preferable to conserve precious law-enforcement resources at the far lesser cost of requiring the merchant to choose between being more conservative in accepting checks and assuming the risk as a business loss.

Nonsupport complaints by wives against deserting husbands are handled similarly. The objective of law-enforcement personnel—the probation officer, a deputy in the prosecutor's office, a welfare agency—is not to invoke the criminal process to punish or rehabilitate a wrongdoer, but to obtain needed support for the family.[127] Instead, jailing the father is the least likely means of obtaining it. As in the bad-check cases, the chief effect on law-enforcement officers is that this duty amounts to still another diversion from their main business. Unlike the bad-check cases, however, here the criminal process is being used to provide a service which, indisputably, the state has an obligation to provide. It is apparent from the economic status of those usually involved that the service amounts to the equivalent of legal aid for needy families, although the service is a useful one, it makes little sense to provide it through the already overburdened processes. Although the obligation is performed by police and prosecutors with some success, it is done reluctantly and usually less effectively than by a civil agency especially designed to handle the service. In addition, it is performed at a sacrifice to those primary functions of protecting the public against dangerous and threat which only the criminal law can perform.

AVOIDING RESTRAINTS ON LAW ENFORCEMENT

Another costly misuse of the substantive criminal law is exemplified in the disorderly conduct and vagrancy laws. These laws are not crimes

126. AMERICAN BAR FOUNDATION, PILOT PROJECT REPORT ON THE ADMINISTRATION OF CRIMINAL JUSTICE IN THE UNITED STATES, Vol. III, 570 (1959); LaFave, *supra,* note 27 at 118;

Frank Miller and Frank Remington, *Procedures Before Trial,* 335 THE ANNALS, 111, 114 (1962).

127. *Ibid.*

which define serious misconduct which the law seeks to prevent through conviction and punishment. Instead, they serve as delegations of discretion to the police to act in ways which formally we decline to extend to them because it would be inconsistent with certain fundamental principles with respect to the administration of criminal justice. The disorderly–conduct laws constitute, in effect, a grant of authority to the police to intervene in a great range of minor conduct, difficult or impossible legally to specify in advance, in which the police find it desirable to act. The vagrancy laws similarly delegate an authority to hold a suspect, whom police could not hold under the law of arrest, for purposes of investigation and interrogation.

Disorderly-conduct statutes vary widely. They usually proscribe such conduct as riot, breach of the peace, unlawful assembly, disturbing the peace, and similar conduct in terms so general and imprecise as to offer the police, a broad freedom to decide what conduct to treat as criminal. A New York Court of Appeals Judge observed of that state's disorderly-conduct statute:

"It is obviously one of those dragnet laws designed to cover newly invented crimes, or existing crimes that cannot be readily classified or defined."[128] In examining disorderly-conduct convictions, the Model Penal Code found that the statutes have been used to proscribe obscenity in a sermon, swearing in a public park, illicit sexual activity, picketing the home of a nonstriking employee, picketing the United Nations, obstructing law enforcement, a shouting preacher whose "Amen" and "Glory Hallelujah" could be heard six blocks away, and talking back and otherwise using loud and offensive language to a policeman.[129] But the reported decisions give only a remote hint of the use of these laws since convictions are appealed only in a minute percentage of the cases.[130] In fact, arrests for disorderly conduct exceed those of arrests for any other crime except drunkenness—in 1965, a half-million arrests out of a total of five million were made for disorderly conduct.[131]

Vagrancy-type laws define criminality in terms of a person's status or a set of circumstances. Often, no disorderly conduct need be committed at all. The usual components of the offense include living in idleness without employment and having no visible means of support; roaming, wandering or loitering; begging; being a common prostitute, drunkard, or gambler; and sleeping outdoors or in a residential building without permission. Beginning in feudal days, when these laws had their beginning, they have been pressed into a great variety of services. Today, they are widely and regularly used by police as a basis for arresting, searching, questioning, or detaining persons (who otherwise could not legally be subjected to such interventions) because of suspicion that they have

128. People v. Tylkoff, 212 N.Y. 197, 201, 105 N.E.2d 835, 836 (1914).

129. MODEL PENAL CODE, § 250.1, Comments at 2 et seq. (Tent. Draft No. 13, 1961).

130. See Adlerberg and Chetow, *Disorderly Conduct in New York Penal Law Section 722,* 25 BROOKLYN L. REV. 46 (1958).

131. U.S. FBI, UNIFORM CRIME REPORTS 108 (1965)

committed or may commit a crime or for other police purposes, including cleaning the streets of undesirables, harassing persons believed to be engaged in crime, and investigating uncleared offenses. The story has been told in a number of descriptive studies in recent years.[132]

Both the disorderly-conduct and vagrancy laws, therefore, constitute a powerful weapon in the hands of police in the day-to-day policing of urban communities. Since "penalties involved are generally minor, and defendants are usually from the lowest economic and social levels,"[133] they have proved largely immune from the restraints of appellate surveillance and public criticism. A weighing of the long-term costs of use of these laws against their immediate benefit to law enforcement suggests the wisdom of either scrapping them or at least substantially narrowing their scope.

The chief vice of these laws is that they constitute wholesale abandonment of the basic principle of legality upon which law enforcement in a democratic community must rest—close control over the exercise of the delegated authority to employ official force through the medium of carefully defined laws and judicial and administrative accountability. If I may, in the circumstances, take the liberty of quoting the language of Chapter VIII:

> The practical costs of this departure from principle are significant. One of its consequences is to communicate to the people who tend to be the object of these laws the idea that law enforcement is not a regularized, authoritative procedure, but largely a matter of arbitrary behavior by the authorities. The application of these laws often tends to discriminate against the poor and subcultural groups in the population. It is unjust to structure law enforcement in such a way that poverty itself becomes a crime. And it is costly for society when the law arouses the feelings associated with these laws in the ghetto—a sense of persecution and helplessness before official power and hostility to police and other authority that may tend to generate the very conditions of criminality society is seeking to extirpate.[134]

I would only add that police conduct undertaken under color of these laws produces the typical resentment associated with what is perceived as double-dealing. There is, after all, what can reasonably be taken for hypocrisy in formally adhering to the constitutional, statutory, and judicial restrictions upon the power of the police to arrest, search, and otherwise intervene in the affairs of citizens on the streets, while actually authorizing disregard of those limitations, principally against

132. Note, *Use of Vagrancy–Type Laws for Arrest and Detention of Suspicious Persons*, 59 YALE L. J. 1351 (1950); Foote, *Vagrancy-Type Law and Its Administration*, 104 U. PA. L. REV. 603 (1956); Justice Douglas, *Vagrancy and Arrest on Suspicion*, 70 YALE L. J. 1 (1960); LaFave, *supra*, note 27 at 87–88, 151–152, 343–363. See N.Y. Law Revision Commission Report 591 (1935): "The underlying purpose [of vagrancy laws] is to relieve the police of the necessity of proving that criminals have committed or are planning to commit specific crimes."

133. MODEL PENAL CODE, *supra*, note 44 at 2

134. TASK FORCE REPORT: COURTS, *supra*, note 1 at 103–104.

the poor and disadvantaged, though the subterfuge of disorderly-conduct and vagrancy laws.

The proper legislative task is to identify precisely the powers which we want the police to have and to provide by law that they shall have these powers in the circumstances defined. Amending the law of attempt to make criminality commence earlier in the stages of preparation than now generally is the case would help to some degree. More substantial moves in this direction are exemplified in the attempts to authorize stopping and questioning short of arrest such as those of the New York "Stop and Frisk" law and the proposals of the American Law Institute's Model Pre–Arraignment Code. Unfortunately, however, the future is not bright. Increasingly, in recent years, the Supreme Court has been imposing constitutional restraints upon powers which the police and most legislatures strongly believe the police should have. If anything, therefore, the temptation to invent subterfuge devices has increased. This is another of the unfortunate consequences of the tension between the police and the courts. But until law enforcement comes to yield less grudgingly to the law's restraints in the process of imposing its restraints upon others, the problem will long be with us.

CONCLUDING REMARKS

The plain sense that the criminal law is a highly specialized tool of social control, useful for certain purposes but not for others; that when improperly used it is capable of producing more evil than good; that the decision to criminalize any particular behavior must follow only after an assessment and balancing of gains and losses—this obvious injunction of rationality has been noted widely for over 250 years, from Jeremy Bentham[135] to the National Crime Commission,[136] and by the moralistic philosophers[137] as well as the utilitarian ones[138] And those whose daily business is the administration of the criminal law have, on occasion, exhibited acute awareness of the folly of departing from it.[139] The need for restraint seems to be recognized by those who deal with the criminal laws, but not by those who make them or by the general public which lives under them. One hopes that attempts to set out the facts and to particularize the perils of overcriminalization may ultimately affect the decisions of the legislatures. But past experience gives little cause for optimism.

Perhaps part of the explanation of the lack of success is the inherent limitation of any rational appeal against a course of conduct which is

135. BENTHAM, PRINCIPLES OF MORALS AND LEGISLATION 281–288 (Harrison ed., 1948).

136. See *supra*, note 1.

137. DEVLIN, THE ENFORCEMENT OF MORALS 17 (1959). It is noteworthy that, as a practical matter, Lord Devlin became convinced of the undesirability of continuing to consider consenting homosexuality a crime. See Dworkin, *Lord Devlin*

and the Enforcement of Morals, 75 YALE L. J. 986, 987 n.4 (1966).

138. E.g., H.L.A. HART, THE MORALITY OF THE CRIMINAL LAW, chap. ii (1964).

139. See the quotation from the statement of a representative of the FBI before the National Crime Commission, *supra*, note 1 at 107.

moved by powerful irrational drives. Explaining to legislatures why it does more harm than good to criminalize drunkenness or homosexuality, for example, has as little effect (and for the same reasons) as explaining to alcoholics or homosexuals that their behavior does them more harm than good. It may be that the best hope for the future lies in efforts to understand more subtly and comprehensively than we do now the dynamics of the legislative (and, it must be added, popular) drive to criminalize. The sociologists, the social psychologists, the political scientists, the survey research people, and, no doubt, others will have to be conscripted for any effort of this kind. A number of studies have already appeared which have revealed illuminating insights into the process of conversion of popular indignation into legislative designation of deviancy,[140] the nature of the competitive struggles among rival moralities, and the use of the criminal law to solidify and manifest victory.[141] We also have a degree of understanding of the effect of representative political processes on the choice of sanctions and the dynamics of law enforcement by the police.[142] Perhaps by further substantial research along these lines—research which would put the process of overcriminalization by popularly elected legislators itself under the microscope—we will understand better the societal forces which have unfailingly produced it.[143] Understanding, of course, is not control, and control may prove as hopeless with it as without it. But scientific progress over the past one hundred years has dramatized the control over the physical environment which comes from knowledge of its forces. It may prove possible to exert in like manner at least some measure of control over the social environment. It is an alternative worth pursuing.

NORVAL MORRIS AND GORDON HAWKINS—THE OVERREACH OF THE CRIMINAL LAW

From *The Honest Politician's Guide to Crime Control*
(The University of Chicago Press, 1970).

The first principle of our cure for crime is this: we must strip off the moralistic excrescences on our criminal justice system so that it may concentrate on the essential. The prime function of the criminal law is to protect our persons and our property; these purposes are now engulfed in a mass of other distracting, inefficiently performed, legislative duties. When the criminal law invades the spheres of private morality and social welfare, it exceeds its proper limits at the cost of neglecting its primary

140. H.S. BECKER, OUTSIDERS: STUDIES IN THE SOCIOLOGY OF DEVIANCE (1963); Kai Erikson, Sociology of Deviance, in SOCIAL PROBLEMS 457 (J. Simpson ed., 1965).

141. GUSFIELD, SYMBOLIC CRUSADE: STATUS POLITICS AND THE AMERICAN TEMPERANCE MOVEMENT (1963); Joseph Gusfield, The Symbolic Process in Deviance Designation (Ms. 1967).

142. Westley, Violence and the Police, 59 AMER. J. SOCIOLOGY 34 (1953); Skolnick, *supra*, note 12.

143. Under a Ford Foundation grant for a Program of Criminal Law and Social Policy, the Earl Warren Legal Center and the Center for the Study of Law and Society of the University of California (Berkeley) are at tempting to undertake studies of this kind.

tasks, This unwarranted extension is expensive, ineffective, and crimino-genic.

For the criminal law at least, man has an inalienable right to go to hell in his own fashion, provided he does not directly injure the person or property of another on the way. The criminal law is an inefficient instrument for imposing the good life on others. These principles we take as self-evident, though we shall soon consider some of the consequences of their neglect. They must receive priority of attention in our cure for crime since only when they are applied will we have both the resources and the clarity of purpose to deal with the serious problems of crime—injury to the person, fear in the streets, burglaries, muggings, and the larger incursions on our property rights.

Hence, our first series of dictatorial ukases deals with law reform. They are not an academic refashioning of minutiae of the law; they are rather a determined return to the proper, more modest and realistic role of the criminal law. It is fortunate that we have dictatorial powers, since this type of law reform is distasteful to politicians and probably commands less than majority popular support. Politicians rely heavily on the criminal law and like to invoke criminal sanctions in connection with most social problems, if only to indicate their moral fervor and political virtue. They take little interest in the consequences of the invocation. Moreover, support for the removal of a sanction is often interpreted as support for the behavior previously punished; if you vote for the legalization of consensual adult homosexual conduct you must be either a faggot or a homosexual fellow traveler. Few votes are so gained. Likewise, the public often cherishes criminal sanctions as an expression of their virtuous inclinations as distinct from the squalid realities of their lives.

It is necessary, however, if we are to be serious about the crime problem, to clear the ground of action of the criminal law. This is essential to the police, to the courts, and to the correctional agencies. They must deal only with those problems and those people for whom their services and their capacities are appropriate; not those who are merely being sacrificed to prejudice and taboos. Public sacrifice, throwing virgins off the rocks, to reinforce the group superego, to placate the ancient gods, is not the job of the criminal justice system.

We provide, initially, a bare statement of our program; the rationale follows.

A. **Drunkenness.** Public drunkenness shall cease to be a criminal offense.

B. **Narcotics and drug abuse.** Neither the acquisition, purchase, possession, nor the use of any drug will be a criminal offense. The sale of some drugs other than by a licensed chemist (druggist) and on prescription will be criminally proscribed: proof of possession of excessive quantities may be evidence of a sale or of intent to sell.

C. **Gambling.** No form of gambling will be prohibited by the criminal law; certain fraudulent and cheating gambling practices will remain criminal.

D. **Disorderly conduct and vagrancy.** Disorderly conduct and vagrancy laws will be replaced by laws precisely stipulating the conduct proscribed and defining the circumstances in which the police should intervene.

E. **Abortion.** Abortion performed by a qualified medical practitioner in a registered hospital shall cease to be a criminal offense.

F. **Sexual behavior.** Sexual activities between consenting adults in private will not be subject to the criminal law.

Adultery, fornication, illicit cohabitation, statutory rape and carnal knowledge, bigamy, incest, sodomy, bestiality, homosexuality, prostitution, pornography, and obscenity: In all of these the role of the criminal law is excessive.

G. **Juvenile delinquency.** The juvenile court should retain jurisdiction only over conduct by children which would be criminal were they adult.

The last ukase—the removal of, in effect, half the jurisdiction of the juvenile courts—will be discussed in a later chapter. It is mentioned here as an important part of the law-reform component of our cure for crime, encompassing one-sixth of all "criminal" cases. Our rationale of the other planks in our legislative program follows and culminates in an eighth ukase.

The consequences of our program for adults emerge from the statistics. There are six million nontraffic arrests of adults per year in the United States. Counting most conservatively, the reforms listed above account for three million of those arrests. Indeed, the report of the President's Commission on Law Enforcement and the Administration of justice (hereafter referred to as the President's Crime Commission) states, "Almost half of all arrests are on charges of drunkenness, disorderly conduct, vagrancy, gambling, and minor sexual deviations." The consequent reduction of pressure on police, courts, and correctional services would have a massive impact on the criminal justice system.

"We may start with the obvious observation that not every standard of conduct that is fit to be observed is also fit to be enforced." Ernst Freund's words define the theme of this chapter. There are two senses in which the criminal law causes crime. It is the formal cause of crime. If we had no criminal law we would have no crime. It is also an efficient cause of crime in that some of our criminal laws foster, encourage, sustain, and protect crime—in particular, organized crime. It is therefore necessary to begin with the question of what constitutes and what ought to constitute a crime? Or to put it another way: when should we use the criminal law in an effort to regulate human conduct?

This is not the place to make a contribution to a classic debate between John Stuart Mill and Sir James Fitzjames Stephen in the nineteenth century and between Professor H. L. A. Hart and Lord Devlin in recent years. We are broadly in agreement with the definition of the proper sphere of the criminal law given by Mill in his essay *On Liberty*:

> The principle is, that the sole end for which mankind are warranted, individually or collectively, in interfering with the liberty of action of any of their members is self-protection. That the only purpose for which power can be rightfully exercised over any member of a civilized community against his win, is to prevent harm to others. His own good, either physical or moral, is not a sufficient warrant, he cannot rightfully he compelled to do or forbear because it would be better for him to do so, because it will make him happier, because in the opinion of others, to do so would be wise or even right.

The function, as we see it, of the criminal law is to protect the citizens, person and property, and to prevent the exploitation or corruption of the young and others in need of special care or protection. We think it improper, impolitic, and usually socially harmful for the law to intervene or attempt to regulate the private moral conduct of the citizen. In this country we have a highly moralistic criminal law and a long tradition of using it as an instrument for coercing men toward virtue. It is a singularly inept instrument for that purpose. It is also an unduly costly one, both in terms of harm done and in terms of the neglect of the proper tasks of law enforcement.

Most of our legislation concerning drunkenness, narcotics, gambling, and sexual behavior and a good deal of it concerning juvenile delinquency is wholly misguided. It is based on an exaggerated conception of the capacity of the criminal law to influence men. We incur enormous collateral disadvantage costs for that exaggeration and we overload our criminal justice system to a degree which renders it grossly defective as a means of protection in the areas where we really need protection—from violence, incursions into our homes, and depredations of our property.

The present "overreach" of the criminal law contributes to the crime problem in the following ways, which will be more fully documented as we deal with particular areas of that overreach:

1. Where the supply of goods or services is concerned, such as narcotics, gambling, and prostitution, the criminal law operates as a "crime tariff" which makes the supply of such goods and services profitable for the criminal by driving up prices and at the same time discourages competition by those who might enter the market were it legal.

2. This leads to the development of large-scale organized criminal groups which, as in the field of legitimate business, tend to extend and diversify their operations, thus financing and promoting other criminal activity.

3. The high prices which criminal prohibition and law enforcement help to maintain have a secondary criminogenic effect in cases where demand is inelastic, as for narcotics, by causing persons to resort to crime in order to obtain the money to pay those prices.

4. The proscription of a particular form of behavior (e.g., homosexuality, prostitution, drug addiction) by the criminal law drives those who engage or participate in it into association with those engaged in other criminal activities and leads to the growth of an extensive criminal subculture which is subversive of social order generally. It also leads, in the case of drug addiction, to endowing that pathological condition with the romantic glamour of a rebellion against authority or of some sort of elitist enterprise.

5. The expenditure of police and criminal justice resources involved in attempting to enforce statutes in relation to sexual behavior, drug taking, gambling, and other matters of private morality seriously depletes the time, energy, and manpower available for dealing with the types of crime involving violence and stealing which are the primary concern of the criminal justice system. This diversion and overextension of resources results both in failure to deal adequately with current serious crime and, because of the increased chances of impunity, in encouraging further crime.

6. These crimes lack victims, in the sense of complainants asking for the protection of the criminal law. Where such complainants are absent it is particularly difficult for the police to enforce the law. Bribery tends to nourish; political corruption of the police is invited. It is peculiarly with reference to these victimless crimes that the police are led to employ illegal means of law enforcement.

It follows therefore that any plan to deal with crime in America must first of all face this problem of the overreach of the criminal law, state clearly the nature of its priorities in regard to the use of the criminal sanction, and indicate what kinds of immoral or antisocial conduct should be removed from the current calendar of crime.

DRUNKENNESS

One of every three arrests in America—over two million each year—is for the offense of public drunkenness; more than twice the number of arrests in the combined total for all of the seven serious crimes which the FBI takes as its index crimes (willful homicide, forcible rape, aggravated assault, robbery, burglary, theft of $50 or over, and motor vehicle theft). The cost of handling each drunkenness case involving police, court, and correctional time has been estimated at $50 per arrest. We thus reach a conservative national estimate of annual expenditure for the handling of drunkenness offenders (excluding expenditure for treatment or prevention) of $100 million. In addition, the great volume of these arrests places an enormous burden on the criminal justice system; it overloads the police, clogs the courts, and crowds the jails.

The extent to which drunkenness offenses interfere with other police activities varies from city to city, but in the majority of cities it involves a substantial diversion of resources from serious crime, Thus, in Washington, D.C., during a nine-month period, it was found that 44 percent of the arrests made by the special tactical police force unit used "to combat serious crime" was for drunkenness. A similar situation exists in relation to correctional systems. In one city it was reported that 95 percent of short-term prisoners were drunkenness offenders. One-half of the entire misdemeanant population consists of drunkenness offenders. Yet the criminal justice system is effective neither in deterring drunkenness nor in meeting the problems of the chronic offenders who form a large proportion of those arrested for drunkenness. All that the system appears to accomplish is the temporary removal from view of an unseemly public spectacle.

We think that the use of the police, the courts, and the prisons on this scale to handle unseemliness at a time when one-third of Americans are afraid to walk alone at night in their own neighborhoods is so ludicrously inept and disproportionate that we need no more than point it out to justify the removal of drunkenness from the criminal justice system. This is not to say that if a person while drunk causes damage to property, steals, or assaults another person he should not be arrested under the appropriate statutes dealing with malicious damage, theft, or assault. But there should always be some specific kind of offensive conduct in addition to drunkenness before the criminal law is invoked.

It is sometimes argued that we have a choice between the criminal law model and the medical model, in the treatment of drunkenness. And there is a considerable literature which deals with the dangers of medical authoritarianism. To us this is a false dichotomy; our choice need not be so narrowly restricted. A social welfare model may, in the present state of medical knowledge, be preferable to either the criminal law or the medical model.

For the police lockups, courts, and jails we would substitute community-owned overnight houses capable of bedding down insensible or exhausted drunks. For the police and the paddy wagons we would substitute minibuses, each with a woman driver and two men knowledgeable of the local community in which the minibus will move. A woman is preferred to a man as the driver-radio-operator because it is our experience that the presence of a woman has an ameliorative effect on the behavior of males, even drunken males.

The minibus would tour the skid row area, picking up the fallen drunks and offering to help the weaving, near-to-falling drunks. If there be a protest or resistance by a drunk, cowardice and withdrawal must control our team's actions; if there be assaults or other crimes, a police transceiver will call those who will attend to it; if there be unconsciousness or drunken consent, the minibus will deliver the body to the overnight house.

If there be talk by the drunk the next day of treatment for his social or alcoholic problem, let him be referred, or preferably taken, to whatever social assistance and alcoholic treatment facilities are available. Indeed, let such assistance be offered if he fails to mention them; but let them never be coercively pressed.

The saving effected by abolishing the costly-and pointless business of processing drunkenness cases through the criminal justice system would vastly exceed the cost of providing such facilities and treatment programs for those willing to accept them.

Such a system may be less effective than a medical detoxification model of the type now operating in New York and Saint Louis, but it is clearly cheaper and more humane than our present processes and does not distract the criminal justice system from its proper and important social functions.

NARCOTICS AND DRUG ABUSE

As in the case of drunkenness, so in regard to the use of other drugs, the invocation of the criminal process is wholly inappropriate. Yet at present, although drug addiction itself is not a crime in America, the practical effect of federal and state laws is to define the addict as a criminal. According to FBI arrest data, 162,177 arrests for violations of the narcotic drug laws were made in 1968. As the President's Crime Commission report puts it, " ... the addict lives in almost perpetual violation of one or several criminal laws." Neither the acquisition nor the purchase nor the possession nor the use of drugs should be a criminal offense. This elimination of criminal prosecution provisions should apply to the narcotics (opiate; synthetic opiates, and cocaine), marihuana, hallucinogens, amphetamines, tranquilizers, barbiturates., and the volatile intoxicants.

Those who support the present laws and the traditional methods of enforcement commonly claim a causal connection between dying use and crime. Yet leaving aside crime to raise funds to support the inflated costs of purchasing legally proscribed drugs, the evidence of a causal connection between drug use and crime is slight and suspect.

As with alcohol, the fact that drugs not only release inhibition but also suppress function is commonly ignored. They may well inhibit more crime than they facilitate; heroin for example has a calming depressant effect, and the "drug crazed sex fiend" of popular journalism has no counterpart in reality although the myth dies hard. The prototypal headline, "Addict Rapes Widow" is misleading—the truth would be "Addict Nods While Widow Burns."

There seems to be no doubt, however, that the policy of criminalization and the operations of criminal justice agencies in this field have in themselves been criminogenic without measurably diminishing the extent of the drug problem or reducing the supply of narcotics entering the country. There is substantial evidence that organized criminals engaged in drug traffic have made and continue to make high profits. There is evidence, too, that criminalization of the distribution of drugs has caused much collateral crime with drug addicts, "to support their habits," as the President's Crime Commission puts it, "stealing millions of dollars worth of property every year and contributing to the public's fear of robbery and burglary."

The one certain way totally to destroy the criminal organizations engaged in the narcotics trade and to abolish addict crime would be to remove the controls and make narcotics freely available to addicts. As Harvard economist Thomas C. Schelling puts it. If narcotics were not illegal, there could be no black market and no monopoly profits, and the interest in "pushing" it would probably be not much greater than the pharmaceutical interest in pills to reduce the symptoms of common colds.

We do not propose the abolition of all controls over the importation, manufacture, and distribution of drugs, nor the abolition of penalties against those unauthorized persons who trade in drugs for profit; but we are convinced that if addiction were treated as a medical matter this would undercut the illicit traffic and largely eliminate the profit incentive supporting that traffic. The British approach to this problem, which involves the maintenance of strict control over the supply of drugs but leaves the treatment of addicts (including maintenance doses to addicts) in the hands of the medical profession, has resulted in a situation where no serious drug problem exists.

Certain difficulties in the British approach have recently emerged. Heroin addiction has increased with immigration of groups having larger addict subcultures within them and for other reasons. But though the increase, stated as a percentage, seems great, it starts from a base so very much smaller than that in the United States that the figures showing increase misstate the problem. It remains a problem of little social significance. Further, the outlets for medical prescription and administration of drugs need to be better controlled to avoid the development of a black market. But these are details in a scheme of incomparably sounder structure than we have evolved in this country.

With regard to marihuana, it is necessary to say something further. At present marihuana is equated, in law, with the opiates although its use does not lead to physical dependence nor does tolerance and the desired dose increase over time. Further, the risks of crime, accident, suicide, and physical or psychological illness are less than those associated with alcohol.

At the moment the law, by treating marihuana as equivalent to opiates, may well foster the belief that there is no difference between them. Yet as marihuana can be relatively easily obtained in most states and found not to have the dramatically deleterious effects advertised, graduation to the use of heroin, which is addictive and harmful, could be stimulated by this policy. Worse still, because marihuana is bulky and detection is thereby facilitated, youthful experimenters are encouraged to move to dangerous and addictive drugs which arc more easily concealed. As with alcohol, controls relating to the sale or other disposition of the drug to minors are necessary, but that is all.

One of the principal advantages of the decriminalization and the pathologization of addiction is that the "image" of drug taking as an act of adventurous daring conferring status on the taker as a bold challenger of authority, convention, and the Establishment will be destroyed. With punitive laws and the brunt of law enforcement falling heavily on the user and the addict rather than on traffickers, we have created a persecuted minority with its own self-sustaining myths and ideology. The alcoholic, on the other hand, is nowhere seen as a heroic figure in our culture but quite commonly as a person to be pitied and treated as sick. Consequently, no addict subculture with a morale-enhancing, self-justifying ideology and recruitment process has developed in this area.

Gambling

Gambling is the greatest source of revenue for organized crime, Estimates of the size of the criminal revenue from gambling in the United States vary from $7 to $50 billion, which means that it is huge but nobody knows how huge. Because statutes in every state, except Nevada, prohibit various forms of gambling, criminals operate behind the protection of a crime tariff which guarantees the absence of legitimate competition. This has led to the development of a powerful and influential vested interest opposed to the legalization of gambling.

Despite sporadic prosecution, the laws prohibiting gambling are poorly enforced and there is widespread disregard for the law. We do not face a choice between abolishing or legalizing gambling; the choice is between leaving gambling and the vast profits which accrue from it in the hands of criminals or citizens taking it over and running it for the benefit of society or, by licensing and taxation measures, controlling it.

The position regarding betting on horse races is highly irrational. In many states those who attend races are allowed to bet on horses and a portion of the money wagered is paid as a tax to the state treasury. Yet it is illegal to accept off-track wagers. But as most people cannot find time to go to the track, such wagers are placed on a scale far exceeding the legitimate ones. The President's Crime Commission cites "estimates by experts" which state that the total involved in off-track betting "is at least two or three times as great" as the total of $5 billion involved in legal betting at race tracks. Yet of the sum of from $10 to $15 billion wagered off-track, nothing at all is forfeit to the state treasury.

It has proved impossible to enforce the laws against betting, and all attempts to make the laws effective have failed. In this situation a major step toward insuring rational and socially beneficial control of gambling would be the institution of state lotteries, such as operate in New

Hampshire and New York. More than twenty-five governments, from the Kenyan, which makes $42,000 a year, to the Spanish, which makes $70 million, run national lotteries. Norway, Sweden, France, and Australia all have such lotteries with a substantial levy on gross revenue going to state treasuries.

In addition to the provision of state lotteries, off-track betting can be controlled by the establishment of state-run betting shops as in Australia. Insofar as gambling is harmful, the harm can at least be reduced by fixing limits to wagers and other measures of control. As for other forms of gambling, the Nevada solution whereby the state tax commission administers gambling by supervising a license system under which all applicants have to be cleared by the commission and state, county, and city taxes and license fees represent a substantial revenue—has operated with success for many years. The infiltration of organized criminals has been blocked by screening all applicants for criminal records. The tax commission employs inspectors and has held hearings and revoked several licenses. The principal lesson to be learned from Nevada is that gambling can be kept clean and does not have to be run by criminals.

DISORDERLY CONDUCT AND VAGRANCY

According to the Uniform Crime Reports, there were nearly six hundred thousand arrests for disorderly conduct in 1968. This represents more arrests than for any other crime except drunkenness. Disorderly conduct statutes vary in their formulation, and the conduct dealt with as disorderly includes a wide variety of petty misbehavior including much that is harmless, although annoying, and not properly subject to criminal control.

Criminal codes and statutes should prohibit specific, carefully defined, serious misconduct so that the police can concentrate on enforcing the law in that context. Disorderly conduct statutes allow the police very wide discretion in deciding what conduct to treat as criminal and are conducive to inefficiency, open to abuse, and bad for police-public relations.

Similar considerations apply to vagrancy. It is a criminal offense in all states, with over ninety-nine thousand arrests in 1968. Here, however, it is not a question of more rigorously defining the type of behavior to be prohibited but rather of entirely abandoning the vagrancy concept. The commentary to the American Law Institute's Model Penal Code states: "If disorderly conduct statutes are troublesome because they require so little in the way of misbehavior, the vagrancy statutes offer the astounding spectacle of criminality with no misbehavior at all." And the fact is that those statutes, which frequently make it an offense for any person to wander about without being able to give a "good account of himself," burden defendants with a presumption of criminality and constitute a license for arbitrary arrest without a warrant.

Vagrancy laws are widely used to provide the police with justification for arresting, searching, questioning, and detaining persons whom they suspect may have committed or may commit a crime. They are also used, according to the President's Crime Commission task force report on the courts, "by the police to clean the streets of undesirables, to harass persons believed to be engaged in crime and to investigate uncleared offenses." These laws often make possible the conviction of persons without proof of antisocial behavior or intention and in general confer unbounded discretion on the police.

In our view the police need authority to stop any person whom they reasonably suspect is committing, has committed, or is about to commit a crime and to demand his name, address, and an explanation of his behavior—to stop and frisk, now clearly constitutionally permissible. The police need such powers of inquiry to control crime and to protect themselves in dealing with persons encountered in suspicious circumstances, and they should have these powers without having to resort to the subterfuge of vagrancy arrest.

As for such behavior as begging, which is included in many vagrancy statutes, we agree with the American Law Institute's Model Penal Code commentary that "municipalities may properly regulate the use of sidewalks to safeguard against annoying and importunate mendicants and merchants; but such legislation does not belong in the penal code."

ABORTION

It is estimated that a million abortions are performed every year in America and that criminal abortion is the third most remunerative criminal enterprise in the United States—following gambling and narcotics. The arrest rate is certainly less than one per thousand abortions performed. No other felony is as free from punishment as illegal abortion, particularly when it is performed by a medical practitioner.

Nevertheless it would be incorrect to say that the laws relating to abortion have no effect on behavior. The commentary to the American Law Institute's Model Penal Code states that "experience has shown that hundreds of thousands of women, married as well as unmarried, will continue to procure abortions ... in ways that endanger their lives and subject them to exploitation and degradation. We cannot regard with equanimity a legal pattern which condemns thousands of women to needless death at the hands of criminal abortionists. This is a stiff price to pay for the effort to repress abortion."

The principal effect of the abortion laws appears to be that whereas women of higher socioeconomic status can usually receive competent and even legal termination of pregnancy—"therapeutic abortion on psychiatric grounds"—those less fortunately placed are forced to resort to the backstreet abortion with its grim train of consequential shame, misery, morbidity, and death. It is a law for the poor.

Abortion may be sinful or immoral, but it is not the function of the law to enforce the whole of morality, It is difficult to understand what religious or moral principle, what divine or human purpose, is served by compelling underprivileged women to undergo pregnancy for the full term and to bear unsought and frequently unwanted children or to risk sickness or death at the hands of incompetent and frequently lecherous and importunate abortionists. No doubt the fact that the price of maintaining this principle is paid almost exclusively by the poor has delayed its critical examination.

We, as criminologists, have a professional reason for advocating a rational approach to abortion legislation. We have been impressed by observation in many countries of the disproportionate number of unwanted children we find in orphanages, reformatories, correctional institutions for youth, and on through the correctional treadmill to institutions for habitual criminals. We believe that the single factor most highly correlated with persistent delinquency and crime would be, if properly tested, being unwanted.

The principle which is most often invoked in this connection is that designated by the phrase "the sanctity of life." It is ironical that in defense of the sanctity of life we pursue a policy which tends toward the maximization of maternal mortality. The highest mortality rates occur in cases of illegal abortion, followed next by cases of confinement (i.e., parturition after at least twenty-eight weeks of pregnancy) and finally by cases of legal abortion where the rate in some countries is as low as 0.01 percent. Thus by confining legal abortion to a minimum so that for the vast majority the alternatives are either confinement or illegal abortion, we ensure that the incidence of maternal mortality is maximized.

The sanctity of life is often also taken to refer to the life of "the unborn child." Yet the use of this expression is as if we referred to the reader as "an adult fetus." To say that a fertilized ovum or an embryo is a human being and therefore entitled to the full protection of the law is a prejudicial abuse of language. Nor do those who take this position ever maintain it consistently, for they never embrace the logical corollary which is that all abortive operations are murders and should be so treated in law.

For our part, in view of the fact that human reproduction is a continuum, such questions as "When does life begin?" are unanswerable, except perhaps in metaphysical or theological terms. Nevertheless it is quite practicable to draw objective distinctions between abortion, infanticide, and homicide; and in terms of these well-recognized distinctions we say that abortion should not be regarded as criminal as long as the woman desires its performance. We see no reason to regard some other arbitrarily selected point prior to parturition, in what is a continuous process, as having any particular significance.

In regard to this problem we adopt what Professor Glanville Williams calls "the short and simple solution" of permitting abortions to be conducted by qualified legal practitioners in certified hospitals when requested by the pregnant woman. We believe that the woman herself should have the full right to decide whether she will go through with the pregnancy or not, although there should be formal provisions to ensure that she is protected from undue pressure from other persons and that her request represents what she on some advised reflection really wants. In short, we regard the total legalization of abortion performed by a licensed physician as the answer. We see no advantage to be gained by a protracted piecemeal approach in this area.

SEXUAL BEHAVIOR

With the possible exception of sixteenth-century Geneva under John Calvin, America has the most moralistic criminal law that the world has yet witnessed. One area in which this moralism is most extensively reflected is that of sexual behavior. In all states the criminal law is used in an egregiously wide-ranging and largely ineffectual attempt to regulate the sexual relationships and activities of citizens. Indeed, it is as if the sex offense laws were designed to provide an enormous legislative chastity belt encompassing the whole population and proscribing everything but solitary and joyless masturbation and "normal coitus" inside wedlock.

It is proper for the criminal law to seek to protect children from the sexual depredations of adults, and adults and children from the use of force, the threat of force, and certain types of fraud in sexual relationships. Further, there is some justification for the use of the criminal law to suppress such kinds of public sexual activity or open sexual solicitation as are widely felt to constitute a nuisance or an affront to decency. But beyond this, in a post-Kinsey and post-Johnson and Masters age, we recognize that the criminal law is largely both unenforceable and ineffective, and we think that in some areas the law itself constitutes a public nuisance. We shall deal with some of the principal areas of conduct from which the criminal law should be withdrawn in whole or in part; types of behavior which although at present adjudged criminal are more properly regarded as matters of private morals.

ADULTERY, FORNICATION, AND ILLICIT COHABITATION

Extramarital intercourse is punishable in the majority of states with penalties ranging from a $10 fine for fornication to five years' imprisonment and a $1,000 fine for adultery. Mercifully, prosecutions are rare. The vast disparity between the number of divorces on the ground of adultery and the minute number of prosecutions for that offense reveals that enforcement is deliberately kept at a microscopic level.

A situation of this kind constitutes a double threat to society. In the first place it provides opportunities for victimization and discriminatory enforcement often provoked by jealousies. In the second place the promulgation of a code of sexual behavior unrelated to actuality (according to Kinsey, 95 percent of the male population is criminal by statutory standards), and its enforcement on a derisory scale, and in arbitrary fashion, cannot but provoke contempt and resentment.

It is one thing to retain laws which, because of difficulty of detection, cannot be rigorously enforced, quite another to preserve those which are not seriously intended to be applied. At a time when it is of considerable importance that the law should mean what it says, anything likely to make citizens take it less than seriously can only be harmful. It is at least a reasonable assumption that anything which provokes cynicism, contempt, derision, indifference, resentment, and hostility toward the law and law enforcement agencies is likely to have undesirable repercussions on behavior. At this time it seems unwise to incur the risk of such costs and for no discernible gain.

STATUTORY RAPE OR CARNAL KNOWLEDGE

Sexual intercourse with a willing female under the statutory age of consent is sometimes referred to as carnal knowledge, sometimes as statutory rape. It is usually a felony. The statutory age of consent varies from ten years of age (in Florida, South Dakota, and New Mexico) to eighteen years of age (in New York and thirteen other states) and, in Tennessee, twenty-one years of age. Such variations must confuse the divining rod of the natural lawyer! The maximum penalties range from death (in fifteen states) to ten years' imprisonment (in New York). In general these penalties are exceeded only by those for murder and equaled only by those for forcible rape and kidnapping. In North Carolina and Washington sexual intercourse between an adult female and a male under the age of consent is also statutory rape on the part of the female, but in general, as one textbook puts it, "the criminality of statutory rape seeks to protect the purity of young girls."

A great deal of statutory rape legislation is totally unrealistic in a number of respects. Most age limits were fixed at a time when physical maturity was attained later than it is now. Furthermore, nowadays teenage girls are far more knowledgeable and sophisticated than the law appears to recognize, and the assumption that in cases of consensual intercourse the male is necessarily the initiator and the female always plays a passive, bewildered role is unlikely to correspond closely to reality. Moreover, even if the male genuinely believes, on reasonable grounds, that the girl is over the age of consent, he has, except in California, no defense to a charge of statutory rape; it is thus clear that not only rationality but also justice is sacrificed in the pursuit of purity.

The offense of statutory rape should clearly be abolished and since in all such cases the girl has given her consent—otherwise it would be rape, viking rape not statutory rape—the man's offense should be that of intercourse with a minor. In our view, the function of the law in relation to sexual behavior of this nature should be restricted to providing protection for the immature in cases where there is significant disparity of age between the male and the female.

An abuse of a relation of trust or dependency should be regarded as an aggravating circumstance. This need would be adequately met if the age of consent were fixed at sixteen. The accused should be acquitted if he can establish that he reasonably believed the girl to be past her sixteenth birthday, It should be added that we are speaking of adult criminal liability here; that is, we are not talking about problems of sexual experimentation by youths and criminal liability within whatever is the juvenile court age in any jurisdiction.

BIGAMY

Bigamy, the triumph of hope over experience, is contracting a second marriage during the existence of a prior marriage and is a statutory crime. It does not constitute a serious part of the crime problem. We mention it only as an interesting example of the legal stigmatization and punishment of conduct which may (as when both parties are aware of the previous marriage, which is the general situation) harm no one although it offends some religious and moral codes. It may be that a certain amount of wrath on the part of the Deity is engendered but his appeasement is no longer regarded as a function of the criminal law. The bigamous marriage itself is legally a nullity.

In many cases the only antisocial consequences of bigamy are the falsification of state records and the waste of time of the celebrating officer. This problem would be better handled by penalties for false declarations in relation to ceremonies of marriage. Sanctions are to be found in all criminal codes for giving false information in relation to official processes, and deceiving the woman would be an aggravating circumstance relevant to sentencing. If necessary, the maximum punishment for such false declarations could be statutorily increased.

The great value of such a low-key approach to a practical problem is that it avoids the trails of ecclesiastical glory that accompany the crime of bigamy at present. Commonly all that is involved in bigamy is, as Glanville Williams puts it, "a pathetic attempt to give a veneer of respectability to what is in law an adulterous association," and prosecution serves no purpose and achieves no object other than increasing the sum of human misery.

One Australian judge, impressed with this analysis, in sentencing a convicted bigamist upbraided him thus: "Wretched man! Not only have you and this young lady deceived your friends. Worse, you have thrown Her Majesty's records into confusion."

INCEST

Incest is sexual intercourse between persons related within prohibited degrees which vary widely. In some societies the interpretation of incest is so broad as to exclude half the available population. In America, a number of states prohibit the marriage of first cousins and few if any permit the marriage of those more closely related than that.

Incest is an ecclesiastical offense. In England it did not become a criminal offense until 1908. In America it has also generally been made a crime by statute and usually includes affinity (i.e., relationship by marriage) as well as consanguinity.

The statutory prohibition of marrying one's deceased brother's wife was designed to reduce fratricide, suggesting a somewhat cynical estimate of the nature of brotherly love. By contrast, marrying one's deceased sister's husband is generally not proscribed, revealing the law's gallant misjudgment of female determination. In some gentler societies it is thought admirable and is sometimes obligatory, to assume matrimonial responsibilities for one's brother's widow and children.

Although incest figures prominently in the literature of psychoanalysis, all available evidence indicates that it is rare, and certainly prosecutions for it are exceptional. We mention it here merely as an example of the law trying to enforce morality, for where both parties are adult and commit incest with full consent, no other purpose is served. Insofar as children need protection from adults, or force or the threat of force is involved, protection is already provided by other statutes. Incest between consenting adults in private is not a proper subject for the criminal law.

SODOMY AND CRIMES AGAINST NATURE

Statutes concerning sodomy and crimes against nature include within their scope such sexual behavior as bestiality, both homosexual and heterosexual, anal and oral copulation, and mutual masturbation. These laws receive only capricious and sporadic enforcement, usually, although not exclusively, in regard to such relations outside marriage, Obviously laws of this kind are peculiarly liable to abuse because of the wide discretion involved.

No social interests whatsoever are protected by desultory attempts to impose upon persons adherence to patterns of sexual behavior arbitrarily selected from the great variety which forms our mammalian heritage. Bestiality would be more properly dealt with under statutes relating to cruelty to animals where any cruelty is involved; otherwise, there is no reason to include it within the criminal law.

HOMOSEXUAL ACTS

Homosexual offenses are treated under such tides as sodomy, buggery, perverse or unnatural acts, and crimes against nature; homosexual practices are condemned as criminal in all states but Illinois, usually as a felony. Penalties vary enormously. A consensual homosexual act which is legal in Illinois is a misdemeanor in New York and can he punished as a felony by life imprisonment in some states. The Kinsey report states: "There appears to be no other major culture in the world in which public opinion and the statute law so severely penalize homosexual relationships as they do in the United States today."

Our primacy in this field is purchased at a considerable price. Although the Kinsey report maintains that "perhaps the major portion of the male population, has at least some homosexual experience between adolescence and old age," only a small minority are ever prosecuted and convicted. Yet the law in this area, while not significantly controlling the incidence of the proscribed behavior, not only increases unhappiness by humiliating and demoralizing an arbitrarily selected sample of persons every year and threatening numberless others, but at the same time encourages corruption of both the police and others who discover such relationships by providing opportunities for blackmail and extortion.

As far as the police are concerned, a great deal has been written both about corruption in this area and the degrading use of entrapment and decoy methods employed in order to enforce the law. It seems to us that the employment of tight-panted police officers to invite homosexual advances or to spy upon public toilets in the hope of detecting deviant behavior, at a time when police solutions of serious crimes are steadily declining and, to cite one example, less than one-third of robbery crimes are cleared by arrest, is a perversion of public policy both maleficent in itself and calculated to inspire contempt and ridicule.

In brief, our attitude to the function of the law in regard to homosexual behavior is the same as in regard to heterosexual behavior. Apart from providing protection for the young and immature; protection against violence, the threat of violence, and fraud; and protection against affronts to public order arid decency, the criminal law should not trespass in this area. If all the law enforcement agents involved in ineffectual efforts to control buggery were to be diverted to an attempt to improve the current 20 percent clearance rate for burglary it is unlikely that there would be an immediate fall in the burglary rate. But it is utterly unlikely that there would be an increase in buggery for peoples' sexual proclivities and patterns are among the least labile of their responses, as the almost total failure of "cures" and treatment programs for homosexuals should have taught us. And in the long run such a strategic redeployment of resources could riot but be beneficial to society.

PROSTITUTION

According to Kinsey almost 70 percent of the total white male population of the United States has some experience with prostitutes. But many of them have never had more than a single experience, and relations with female prostitutes represent a very small part of the total sexual outlet of the male population. It would appear that the incidence and importance of prostitution in this country have been greatly exaggerated in the literature, much of which seems to be the product of a prurient interest in the subject. In fact, professional prostitution is said by some authorities to be declining as a result of increasing sexual permissiveness which eliminates some of the need for such outlets. The Uniform Crime Report shows 42,338 arrests for "prostitution and commercialized vice" in 1968 but many arrests of prostitutes are included in the four hundred thousand yearly arrests for "disorderly conduct," so that the figures cannot be regarded as a meaningful index.

Prostitution is commonly statutorily defined as the indiscriminate offer by a female of her body for sexual intercourse or other lewdness for the purpose of gain and is a criminal offense in all states. The penalties most commonly imposed are fines or short prison sentences.

At one time it was widely believed that most prostitutes were unfortunate women who had been "driven" to a life of prostitution by poverty, bad upbringing, seduction at an early age, or broken marriages, but some research sponsored by the British Social Biology Council suggests that in the majority of cases this way of life is chosen because it offers greater ease, freedom, and profit than available alternatives. There is no evidence that the incidence of neurosis or psychological abnormality is greater among prostitutes than among housewives.

Prostitution is an ancient and enduring institution which has survived centuries of attack and condemnation, and there is no doubt that it fulfills a social function. It is often asserted that prostitution provides an outlet for sexual impulses which might otherwise be expressed in rape or other kinds of sexual crime. No research has been done in this area but the notion has a certain plausibility. It is undeniable, however, that prostitutes are sought out by some men who, because of a physical deformity, psychological inadequacy, or (in the case of foreigners and immigrants) unfamiliarity with the language and customs, find great difficulty in obtaining sexual partners. The Kinsey report states that prostitutes provide a sexual outlet for many persons who without this "would become even more serious social problems than they already are."

The costs of attempting to enforce our prostitution laws have been admirably summarized by Professor Sanford Kadish

> ... diversion of police resources; encouragement of use of illegal means of police control (which, in the case of prostitution, take the form of knowingly unlawful harassment arrests to remove suspected prostitutes from the streets; and various entrapment devices, usually the only means of obtaining convictions); degradation of the image of law enforcement; discriminatory enforcement against the poor; and official corruption.

Once again it is our view that the use of law enforcement resources in this way, in a fruitless effort to promote moral virtue, is wasteful and socially injurious. Insofar as prostitution itself is responsible for social harms like the spread of venereal disease, regular compulsory medical inspection would provide better protection than our present haphazard enforcement policies. Moreover, all the evidence indicates that it is ordinary free promiscuity which is more largely responsible for the spread of venereal disease. Insofar as public solicitation constitutes an affront to some persons' susceptibilities, it would be perfectly possible (as has been done in some German cities) for municipal regulation to confine the activities of prostitutes to certain prescribed areas. As in many cases they are already largely confined in this way for purely commercial reasons, this would create few enforcement problems.

With regard to the pimp, procurer, and brothel keeper or operator we face a problem about which John Stuart Mill was for once somewhat equivocal. Thus he says, "Fornication, for example, must be tolerated, and so must gambling; but should a person be free to be a pimp or to keep a gambling house?" In his view "there are arguments on both sides." But he concludes by saying that he "will not venture to decide" whether there is sufficient justification for "the moral anomaly of punishing the accessory, when the principal is (and must be) allowed to go free; of fining or imprisoning the procurer, but not the fornicator."

Currently the punishment of those who live on immoral earnings is often justified on the ground that the pimp may exploit the prostitute, On balance we incline to the view that the criminal law is improperly used in this area. There is no evidence that exploitation is in fact a serious problem.

In this connection the Wolfenden committee states; "Such evidence as we have been able to obtain on this matter suggests that the arrangement between the prostitute and the man she lives with is usually brought about at the instance of the woman and it seems to stem from a need on the part of the prostitute for some element of stability in the background of her life.... We have no doubt that behind the trade of prostitution there lies a variety of commercial interests.... The evidence submitted to us, however, has disclosed nothing in the nature of 'organized vice' in which the prostitute is an unwilling victim coerced by a vile exploiter." The President's Crime Commission task force report on organized crime states that in America prostitution plays "a small and declining role in organized crime's operations." Apparently it "is difficult to organize and discipline is hard to maintain."

It is relevant here to mention also the call girl who caters to a more exclusive clientele than the ordinary prostitute. These girls are largely immune to the law. Possibly this is because, as Harold Greenwald says in his social and psychoanalytic study *The Call Girl*, "to arrest one call girl generally requires the services of a number of highly trained men for many days and involves expensive wire-tapping equipment." It may also be that there is a certain reluctance on the part of law enforcement agencies to invade privacy on the social levels where these girls operate. However that may be, it can only be to the benefit of society if the highly trained men and expensive equipment employed in this field are diverted to dealing with crime which really injures and frightens the public.

PORNOGRAPHY AND OBSCENITY

The law relating to obscenity has remained virtually the same since 1873, although it has lately been interpreted more liberally. On the whole, sparing and only occasional use has been made of the legal sanctions in recent years although their minatory force cannot be and is not disregarded. The only consequence of censorship for which there is any solid evidence is that a number of works of literature and art have had their circulation severely restricted,

It is still confidently asserted in many quarters that exposure to erotica and pornography leads to moral degeneration and sex crime. But the exhaustive Kinsey Institute study of 15,000 sex offenders found no evidence that pornography was a causal factor in the offenses, Indeed, their findings suggest that it may rather be inability to secure fantasy release of impulse by means of pornography which distinguishes sex offenders from other people. If prurience can find satisfaction by reading books or looking at pictures, it is difficult to conceive anything less harmful to society. It is those who cannot achieve satisfaction in this way who may constitute a danger.

If controls are felt to be necessary in this area, we think that they should be limited to providing "protection" for the "immature" and preventing affronts to public decency. The former might be partially met—no more can be expected—by prohibiting the sale of pornography to minors; the latter, by the prohibition of the public display of pornographic material in the streets.

Other Areas: Moral and Social Welfare

There are a number of other areas in which we feel that the criminal law's interference in matters of morals is unwarranted. Fond as we are of Blackstone's justification for the rule treating suicide as a felony—"the suicide is guilty of evading the prerogative of the Almighty, and rushing into his immediate presence uncalled for"—we do not think it the proper function of the law to enforce ancient eschatological doctrines. Therefore, in those few states which still treat attempted suicide as a crime and the larger number where the altruistic abetment of suicide is a crime and the survivor of a genuine suicide pact is guilty of murder, we submit that the law goes beyond its proper sphere. We are not impressed by the argument that the police must have power to prevent a suicide from killing himself and that only the criminal prohibition of attempted suicide can provide that power. As Glanville Williams says, "So far as is known, no inconvenience has been felt to arise from the absence of specific powers in those American jurisdictions that do not punish attempted suicide." But if it is felt to be necessary, it would be perfectly possible to enact legislation allowing any person some right of interposition to prevent a suicide without resorting to the criminal law.

Some years ago the American Bar Foundation conducted a pilot survey of the administration of criminal justice in the United States which was designed to identify some causes of "breakdown, delay and ineffectiveness" in the systems which administer criminal justice in the United States. The report of that study indicates two other areas in which it is evident that the resources of the criminal justice system are employed to perform tasks which have no relevance to the crime problem and should be handled by other agencies. In the first place a large number of states have special statutes dealing with the issuance of worthless checks; that is, checks which have the genuine signature of the drawer but are drawn upon a bank in which he has neither sufficient funds nor any arrangement for payment. A considerable amount of police time is involved in investigating and processing these cases. In our view the conduct involved should be regarded as unethical rather than criminal (except where there is a genuine attempt to defraud) and should be handled by debt-collecting agencies and through the civil rather than the criminal process.

An analogous case is that of failure to support one's family. Nonsupport is commonly prosecuted under disorderly conduct statutes as a misdemeanor although the conviction and the imprisonment of the offender mean that he is thus legally prevented from fulfilling the obligation which lie is being punished for neglecting. There is no doubt that the invoking of the criminal process may ultimately become necessary in some cases. But to employ the police and prosecutors to pursue husbands who are errant in this way is not only a wasteful use of their time but also exceedingly maladroit, For matters of this kind are clearly the province of welfare or social service agencies equipped to handle family problems. In this connection the President's Crime Commission task force report on the courts is clearly right when it says that insofar as using the criminal process serves to provide legal aid to indigent families, "the explicit provision of more legal aid services for civil proceedings is plainly preferable." Certainly the use of the police as agents of both social and moral welfare and crime control represents a confusion of purposes which inevitably results in neither being adequately fulfilled.

CONCLUSION: SOME OBJECTIONS AND THE EIGHTH UKASE

We are of the opinion that if the employment of the criminal justice system's resources were to be curtailed and restricted along the lines we have suggested in the seven major fields of action indicated, and the means thus made available were devoted to protecting the public from serious crime, such a redeployment would result in a substantial accession of strength to law enforcement which would help appreciably to reduce the crime problem to manageable proportions.

We recognize, however, that so radical a program as that proposed may be regarded by some as unacceptable and that it could justifiably be said that we have so far ignored a number of legitimate objections to the repeal of criminal laws. Thus Rupert Cross in his admirable paper "Unmaking Criminal Laws" says, "In general the criminal law has selected as proper subjects for its attention those parts of the moral law which are suitable for enforcement by the infliction of punishment following upon a judicial enquiry, and in general the criminal law disregards those parts of the moral law which are unsuitable for enforcement in this way."

He goes on to say that "whenever the repeal of a criminal law is mooted, it is proper to ask" a number of questions, which he lists as follows:

> Would the repeal of the relevant law lead to an increase in the prohibited practice? Would it weaken the moral condemnation of that practice? Is the prohibited practice harmful to other individuals? Is it actually or potentially harmful to society? Is the practice

strenuously condemned by public opinion? And, is the criminal sanction effective?

We agree that these are all in some degree relevant questions. They are not, however, questions to which it is possible to give categorical answers in every case. And even if answers can be given it is by no means clear what the practical implications of any particular answer or combination of answers might be. Indeed, it is evident that if one accepts Mill's doctrine that "the only purpose for which power can rightfully be exercised over any member of a civilized community against his will is to prevent harm to others," then the crucial question in this context must be: Is the prohibited conduct harmful to other individuals or to society? If the answer to that question is negative, then questions about whether a repeal of the relevant law might lead to an increase in the prohibited conduct or weaken moral condemnation of it are otiose.

It should be clear, then, that in the light of our definition of the function of the criminal law, in terms of the protection of the lives and property of citizens and the preservation of public order and decency, the sort of restrictions on the use of the criminal sanction we have proposed are not only unobjectionable but desirable. Moreover, we have suggested that even those who do not accept our definition must face the question whether the collateral social costs of endeavoring to preserve the particular prohibitions we have discussed are not excessive.

We have argued that they are excessive, not only in terms of human suffering and the loss of freedom, but also in that in many cases the attempt to use the criminal law to prohibit the supply of goods and services which are constantly demanded by millions of Americans is one of the most powerful criminogenic forces in our society. By enabling criminals to make vast profits from such sources as gambling and narcotics; by maximizing opportunities for bribery and corruption; by attempting to enforce standards which do not command either the respect or compliance of citizens in general; by these and in a variety of other ways, we both encourage disrespect for the law and stimulate the expansion of both individual and organized crime to an extent unparalleled in any other country in the world.

We are not writing for the law technician; we therefore ask you to accept our eighth ukase largely on trust:

8. A Standing Law Revision Committee. Every legislature must establish a Standing Criminal Law Revision Committee charged with the task of constant consideration of the fitness and adequacy of the criminal law sanctions to social needs.

Our present criminal law is a product of a series of historical accidents, emotional overreactions, and the comforting political habit of adding a punishment to every legislative proposition.

The American Law Institute in its Model Penal Code blazed a path of codification in this country which had earlier been traced by Sir James Fitzjames Stephen in England and Lord Macaulay in India. That Occam's razor should be brought to bear on the jungle of criminal sanctions none will doubt; that the steps toward consolidation, codification, and constant critical observation of the body of the criminal law are suitable steps in this direction few will controvert. All movements toward codification have rapidly revealed the facility with which the deadwood of the criminal law may be chopped away and sanctions designed comprehensible to the interested layman, clear even to the potential criminal, and more suited to our regulatory purposes than our present criminal law jungle. The American Law Institute's Model Penal Code, emulated in the Illinois Code of 1961 and being followed to a greater or lesser extent by the present codification efforts in several states of this country, provides an excellent model but this is not a task that can be done once and then left. It needs continuing attention.

The complete reform and rationalization of the criminal law is a long-term task. Our immediate concern in the present context is to increase its effectiveness by reducing its overreach. In the President's Crime Commission task force report on the courts it is said:. "Only when the load of law enforcement has been lightened by stripping away those responsibilities for which it is not suited will we begin to make the criminal law a more effective instrument of social protection." This primary phase of our program is designed precisely to achieve that end, by that method.

Herbert Packer's *The Limits of the Criminal Sanction* (Stanford University Press. 1968), published after this chapter was written, is a comprehensive and, since we heartily agree with him, wise study of the issues discussed in this chapter.

Notes and Questions

1. There is an important distinction to be drawn between persons who object to criminal law regulation of some arguably victimless behavior on principle and those opposed to it on pragmatic grounds. The outstanding example of principled objection to the criminal prohibition of victimless behavior is John Stuart Mill's *On Liberty*. Pragmatic objections are more narrowly drawn arguments that *this* prohibition in *that* particular context involves more costs to society than benefits.

It might be useful to review the readings in Parts A and B in this chapter in order to classify the authors in terms of whether their positions are governed by principled or pragmatic judgments. If Lord Devlin would oppose a criminal prohibition on adultery for example, would his opposition be based on principled or on pragmatic consideration? What about Professor Hart? Do you believe that Professor Nagel is a pragmatist on these questions? If so, what considerations led him to his pragmatic stance? Are Professor Kadish's objections principled or pragmatic? Is the Morris and Hawkins position principled or pragmatic?

2. Both Sanford Kadish and Norval Morris are professors of criminal law who agree that the prohibition and prosecution of victimless behavior are harmful to the criminal law and the criminal justice system. One question to consider is whether criminal law specialists have a distorted

perception of the costs and benefits of the prohibition of victimless crimes because of their special concern with the welfare of the criminal justice system. What kinds of professionals might in a similar vein be predisposed to support the enforcement of the laws against victimless behavior? School teachers? Police? Clergy?

C. FIVE APPROACHES TO THE DEFINITION OF VICTIMLESS CRIME

1. HARM TO OTHERS: JOHN STUART MILL

The object of this essay is to assert one very simple principle ... that the only purpose for which power can be rightfully exercised over any member of a civilized community, against his will, is *to prevent harm to others*... His own good, either physically or moral, is not a sufficient warrant. He cannot rightfully be compelled to do or forbear because it will be better for him to do so, because it will make him happier, because, in the opinions of others, to do so would be wise, or even right. There are good reasons for remonstrating with him, or reasoning with him, or persuading him, or entreating him, but not for compelling him, or visiting him with any evil, in case he do otherwise. To justify that, the conduct from which it is desired to deter him must be calculated to produce evil to some one else. The only part of the conduct of any one, but which he is amenable to society, is that which concerns others. In the part which merely concerns himself, his independence is, of right, absolute. Over himself, over his own body and mind, the individual is sovereign.[144]

How does the following differ from Mill?:

... *in all cases the idea of crime* has involved the idea of *some definite, gross undeniable injury to some one.* In our own country this is now and has been from the earliest times perfectly well established.[145]

Criminal law ... can be applied **only** to definite overt *acts or omissions ... which acts or omissions inflict definite evils* either on specific persons or on the community at large.[146]

A. As you review the various definitions in these materials, there are three separate questions that should be addressed for each:

    1. The Definitional Standard

    2. The Methodology of Classification

    3. The Policy Implications of Classification

144. John Stuart Mill, *On Liberty*, Chapter 1 Introductory, in Marshall Cohen, ed., *The Philosophy of John Stuart Mill*, 1967, pp. 196–197.

145. Stephen Fitzjames, *A History of the Criminal Law of England*, Volume II, 1883, p. 78.

146. Ibid., pp. 78–79.

For Mill, the distinction of importance in this definition (question a) is between behaviors that cause harm to other people and those that do not. The methodology for classifying a behavior (question b) is thus to determine whether a particular behavior causes harm to a person other than the actor. The policy implication (question c) if the conclusion on harm is "no" is that the behavior should not be criminal.

B. Which of the three issues discussed in question one above causes the most problems for Mill's theorem: the standard, the classification, or the implications of finding no harm?

C. Is the Stephen standard the same as that of Mill? The conclusions Stephen reaches on what qualifies as harm to others to justify a criminal prohibition are quite different.[147]

D. How would the standards set forth by John Stuart Mill classify the following behaviors?:

   • Possession or use of cocaine.

   • Possession of a handgun—a concealable firearm that dominates the crime statistics, but no more than one in ten handguns are used in assaults, robberies, or suicide attempts.

   • Prostitution and pornography.

   • Gambling.

   • Cigarette smoking.

   • Auto theft.

   • Riding a motorcycle without wearing a helmet.

   • Physical assaults or killings where the victim consents.

E. Make a list of behaviors prohibited by criminal law but that you believe do not threaten harm to others.

F. Harm and the Issue of Risk.

   Consider the following problem:

   Smith consumes five martinis at a social occasion over a period of three hours. When he reaches his automobile to drive fifteen miles back to his residence, his blood alcohol content is in excess of the 0.15 legal limit for driving while intoxicated. He drives home passing 300–400 automobiles going in the opposite direction and overtakes three or four cars proceeding in the same direction as he is traveling. Two pedestrians including Jones cross the street in front of Smith without incident.

   There are two alternative ways in which to analyze these events from the perspective of "harm to others," as that concept is used by John Stuart Mill. One alternative is to restrict the notion of harm to palpable bad incidents that result from particular human actions. By this standard, Smith has caused no harm by his driving under the influence of alcohol. The second perspective considers behaviors that generate the

147. Vide Stephen, The Doctrine of Liberty in its Application to Morals, in R.J. White, ed., *Liberty, Equality & Fraternity*, 1967, pp. 135–178.

risk of harm to others as the moral equivalent of human actions that actually do cause harm. On this interpretation, because operating a motor vehicle while under the influence of as much alcohol as Smith had consumed is many times more likely to cause an automobile accident, the behavior of people who drive under the influence of alcohol should be regarded as the moral equivalent of causing harm to others because their behavior increases the risk of harm to others. Which approach is superior?

If you regard the risk of an accident as the moral equivalent of harm to others, in the case of Smith's drunk driving, would you distinguish that case from the following problem:

Assume that a person who habitually uses drugs or alcohol is three or four times more likely than a nonuser to engage in predatory criminal behavior such as burglary or robbery. If it is correct to assume that drinking alcohol or using drugs causes increased chances of subsequent property crimes, would it be correct to regard the alcohol drinking or the drug use as causing harm to others because of the increased rates of burglary and robbery that result? Need the chance of burglary or robbery be higher than five or ten percent to justify your conclusion? Or is it sufficient that the relative risk of burglary or robbery is increased even if its absolute magnitude is low?

If all behaviors that increase the risk of eventual harm should be regarded as themselves harmful, how important is John Stuart Mill's limitation as a restraint on the overreach of the criminal law?

G. Harm and Inchoate Crime. The law provides for criminal punishment for those who agree to the commission of crime with others or attempt to commit crimes themselves, whether or not the crime intended is ever completed. The technical term for offenses of this sort is "inchoate crimes."[148] If Smith and Jones agree to blow up the World Trade Center in New York with high explosives, but the planned explosion never takes place, they may be prosecuted for criminal conspiracy if an overt act towards commission of the offense is committed by either of them or they can be convicted of attempt if with intent that the offense be committed either of them takes substantial steps towards commission of the bombing. Merely because the explosion does not happen, is conspiracy with the intent to commit bombing a victimless crime?[149] Is an unsuccessful criminal attempt the same kind of victimless behavior as homosexual conduct between consenting adults?

H. Risk and Intention. What is the difference between inchoate crime which punishes behavior like attempted murder and criminal prohibition of behavior like loitering that pose a risk to the community that some of the loiterers will become criminally active? Is loitering a victimless crime?

148. Vide Model Penal Code.   **149.** Vide Meier and Geis, *Victimless Crime?*, 1997, p. 9.

Loitering and vagrancy can be thought of as behaviors that pose a risk of further criminal harm by the loiterer and the vagrant. To what extent is the risk that the loiterer will become a thief similar to the risk that a driver under the influence of alcohol will be involved in an accident? If the distinction between drunk driving and loitering is that criminal acts by the loiterer require an independent criminal intention from that of loitering, while no further criminal intention is necessary for a high risk of harm to exist in the case of drink driving is the criminal offense of carrying a concealed handgun more like drunk driving or more like loitering?

2. A CRIMINAL JUSTICE APPROACH

The present "overreach" of the criminal law ... The expenditure of police and criminal justice resources in attempting to enforce statutes in relation to sexual behavior, drug-taking, gambling, and other matters of private morality ... *these crimes lack victims in the sense of complainants asking for the protection of the criminal law.*[150]

It is peculiarly with reference to **these victimless crimes** that the police are led to employ illegal means of law enforcement....[151]

It follows therefore that any plan to deal with crime in America must first of all face this problem of *the overreach of the criminal law.*[152]

Most of our legislation concerning drunkenness, narcotics, gambling, and sexual behavior and a good deal concerning juvenile delinquency is wholly misguided.[153]

To the same effect:

Victimless crimes, i.e., offenses that do not result in anyone's feeling that he has been injured so as to impel him to bring the offense to the attention of the authorities.[154]

A. Recall the three separate questions that should be addressed for each:

a. The Definitional Standard

b. The Methodology of Classification

c. The Policy Implications of Classification

The distinction of importance in this definition (question a) is between behaviors where there is a complaining witness and those without. The methodology for classifying a behavior (question b) is thus to determine whether a particular behavior has a complaining witness. What are the policy implications of this finding?

150. Norval Morris and Gordon Hawkins, *Victimless Crime*, 1970, p. 6.

151. Ibid., p. 6.

152. (Ibid., p. 6).

153. (Ibid., p. 5)

154. Herbert Packer, *The Limits of the Criminal Sanction*, 1968, p. 151.

B.   Which of the three issues discussed in question a above causes the most problems for the Morris and Hawkins theorem: the standard, the classification, or the implications of finding no harm?

C.   Why do Morris and Hawkins and Packer put emphasis on a complaining witness?

D.   How is the Morris and Hawkins definition different from Mill?

E.   How would the standards set forth by Morris and Hawkins classify the following behaviors?

- Possession or use of cocaine?

- Possession of a handgun—a concealable firearm that dominates the crime statistics, but no more than one in ten handguns are used in assaults, robberies, or suicide attempts.

- Prostitution and pornography

- Gambling

- Cigarette smoking

- Auto theft

- Riding a motorcycle without wearing a helmet

- Physical assaults or killings where the victim consents

F.   Make a list of all the behaviors prohibited by criminal laws that lack a complaining witness.

3. MARKET DEFINITIONS: VICTIMLESS CRIME

... *Crimes without victims*—the meaning and significance of that phrase. It refers essentially to the willing exchange, among adults, of strongly demanded, but legally proscribed goods or services.[155]

... the marijuana smokers, the homosexuals, the abortionist and his client, and the "runner" and the persons wagering—though all are violating criminal statutes—are in each instance committing acts, which, in terms of the common understanding of the term, *do not have victims.*[156]

A.   How do these definitions differ from Mill's? From that of Morris and Hawkins?

B.   How would this standard classify the following behaviors?

- Possession or use of cocaine?

- Possession of a handgun—a concealable firearm that dominates the crime statistics, but no more than one in ten handguns are used in assaults, robberies, or suicide attempts.

- Prostitution and pornography

- Gambling

155. Edwin Schur, *Crimes Without Victims*, 1965, p. 169; emphasis added.

156. Gilbert Geis, *Not the Law's Business*, 1972, p. 2; emphasis added.

- Cigarette smoking
- Auto theft
- Riding a motorcycle without wearing a helmet
- Physical assaults or killings where the victim consents

C. What policy consequences should flow from classifying a behavior as victimless for Schur?

4. THE ENFORCEMENT OF MORALS AS VICTIMLESS CRIME

H.L.A. Hart has asked,

"Ought immorality as such be a crime?" *Crimes without victims* involve attempts to legislate morality for its own sake ... certain laws are indeed designed merely to legislate morality.[157]

The use of the criminal law to prohibit moral deviancy among consenting adults has been a recurring subject of jurisprudential debate. Stephens in the last century and Lord Devlin in this century have urged the legitimacy of criminal intervention on the ground that "society cannot ignore the morality of the individual any more than it can his loyalty; it flourishes on both and without either it dies."[158]

A. Recall the three separate questions developed earlier in this unit for a definitional approach to victimless crime:

- The Definitional Standard
- The Methodology of Classification
- The Policy Implications of Classification

What is the definition of "morals?" How does one determine whether a prohibition involves "the enforcement of morals?" Or is the issue whether a criminal prohibition involves *only* the enforcement of morals? Is this a reference back to the harm to others question?

B. How would this standard classify the following behaviors?:

- Possession or use of cocaine
- Possession of a handgun—a concealable firearm that dominates the crime statistics, but no more than one in ten handguns are used in assaults, robberies, or suicide attempts.
- Prostitution and pornography
- Gambling
- Cigarette smoking
- Auto theft
- Riding a motorcycle without wearing a helmet
- Physical assaults or killings where the victim consents

157. Edwin Schur, *Crimes Without Victims: Deviant Behavior and Public Policy*, 1995, p. 169; emphasis added.

158. Sanford Kadish, The Crisis of Overcriminalization, *The Annals of the American Academy of Political and Social Science* 374:159, 1967.

5.   VICTIMLESS CRIME AND VICE

The following is from "An Introduction to Vice" by Philip J. Cook:

This symposium is about the legal response to drug abuse, gambling, pornography, and sex outside of marriage. "Vice" is commonly used as a generic term for these activities; the police vice squads concern themselves primarily with these matters, for example. One feature that distinguishes vice crimes from other concerns of the criminal law is their allure: In Jerome Skolnick's words, vice "implies pleasure and popularity, as well as wickedness." The vices addressed in this symposium are as old as civilization, yet they are of intense modern day concern. Some of the most prominent news stories of 1987 were about vice: illicit sex by a presidential candidate, and by a television preacher; marijuana use by a nominee to the Supreme Court; cocaine dealing by Wall Street brokers; and the growth of commercial gambling through the state lotteries. Above all, there was the AIDS epidemic, claiming 50,000 victims in the United States and spreading rapidly due primarily to homosexual promiscuity and junkies sharing needles. This symposium does not lack for motivation or vivid points of reference.

A.   To what extent is "vice," as so conceived, the same as the Mill definition of a crime without victims? As Morris and Hawkins? As Schur?

B.   Is possession of a handgun where this is prohibited by law a vice? Is sexual harassment vice? Is bribery vice? If not, how can these activities be distinguished from Professor Cooks' examples of generic vices?

C.   Which is the better term: vice or victimless crime? Why?

D.   Is cigarette smoking a vice? Drinking alcohol? What about gambling in states where it is legal? Does this mean that vice is a category of social behavior, and criminalization is one legal status that can be attached to it? Are all victimless crimes also vices?

D.   CHILDREN AS A POLICY ISSUE

1.   CHILDREN, JOHN STUART MILL, AND THE ISSUE OF HARM

The most famous exception to the principle that harm to oneself cannot justify governmental coercion is immaturity, in Mill's formulation:

It is, perhaps, hardly necessary to say that this doctrine is meant to apply only to human beings in the maturity of their faculties. We are not speaking of children, or of young persons below the age which the law may fix as that of manhood or womanhood. Those who are still in a state to require being taken care of by others, must be protected against their own action as well as external injury.[159]

A.   Any harm the immature actor might do to him or herself can justify criminal prohibition attaching to the behavior if it involves a child. But since the child is presumably the victim under these circumstances, would Mill approve of the punishment of children because of the harm that they risk to themselves? Is not this blaming the victim?

B.   Can a criminal prohibition on all persons engaging in behavior be justified because the general prohibition on a behavior more effectively protects children than would allowing adults free access to that behavior? If the harm to children justifies a criminal prohibition, why not extend that prohibition as far as necessary to adults so that the children may be more effectively protected? Or is that "bootstrapping?" The harm principle announced by Mill certainly allows us to prohibit children under eighteen years of age from smoking. But what if we find tobacco available to all the adults who want it increases the rate at which children can obtain and smoke cigarettes? Is not the additional harm to child smokers sufficiently palpable so that outlawing cigarettes for everybody does not violate Mill's principle? If not, why not?

Under the narrower reading of Mill's childhood exception, there would be justification for laws that remove the rights of minors to use cigarette vending machines. Under a broader reading, the harm that cigarette vending machines may do to children could be used to justify total prohibition. If this broader interpretation is persuasive, what sorts of behavior that might potentially injure children would the state be obliged to allow to adults?

2.   THE CHILD AS UNCOMPLAINING WITNESS

A.   Under the Morris and Hawkins definition of victimless crime (Section C.2 *supra*), is it a victimless crime when a twelve-year-old child purchases cigarettes from a vending machine intended exclusively for adults? Do Morris and Hawkins argue for the legalization of all childhood smoking because the behavior lacks a "complaining witness?"

Or is a parent or guardian who objects to the sale of cigarettes to minors a "complaining witness" in the Morris and Hawkins sense? As far as Morris and Hawkins are concerned, what is the difference between underage smoking when an adult might complain and sexual practices between consenting adults that offend third parties and provoke them to complain to the police?

B.   If the consent of children means that pederasty, drug sales, and other behavior generally regarded as harmful to children lack a "complaining witness" in the Morris and Hawkins sense, how good

---

159.   (Mill, 1967, p. 197).

is that criterion as a guide to criminal justice policy? Should all behaviors that lack a complaining witness be removed from the criminal law statutes or just some behaviors that meet this criterion? If only some behaviors that are victimless in this sense should be removed from the list of criminal prohibitions, by what standard do we select which such crimes should be stricken and which should be retained?

3. THE CHILD AS WILLING BUYER

A.   Is the child who wishes to buy pornography, cigarettes, drugs, and alcohol seeking "a willing exchange" in the sense that Gilbert Geis used that expression[160] Or does immaturity remove the capacity of an individual to be regarded as sufficiently competent to know his or her own mind? Does the fact that the customer is immature make him or her, in any significant psychological sense, an unwilling buyer or quite the reverse? Is the willing seller/willing buyer criterion for the existence of a victimless crime a behavioral or moral judgment?

B.   If the correct interpretation of "willing buyer" includes enthusiastic but misguided children, of what use is that criterion for drawing the line between behavior that is the proper subject of a criminal sanction and behavior that is not? If immature children should not be viewed as "unwilling," how would one define the term "unwilling" as it is used in this formulation? If willing seller/willing buyer does not apply when immaturity is present, how does this standard differ from the harm to self/harm to others standard?

4. ENFORCEMENT OF MORALS

Is the enforcement of morals permissible in the view of H.L.A. Hart when the target group is children?

5. THE STAGES AND BOUNDARIES OF CHILDHOOD

The Mill definition quoted above is typical in that it includes in the childhood category all of those younger than the legal age of majority. Usually this will range from birth to the age of eighteen—a considerable span in human development. Presumably children acquire judgment and maturity as they progress from quite young ages to their mid-teens. Should this mean less regulation for older than for younger children?

If self-harm is a permissible basis of prohibition for adolescents because of their immaturity, why not prohibit self-harming behavior in adults as long as it seems plausible to suppose that anyone willing to engage in such behavior is immature for that reason? If nobody in his right mind would take an intravenous injection of heroin, why not prohibit the practice on the grounds that only the immature would behave in this fashion? Is the presumption that anyone who would inject heroin is immature more defensible or less defensible than the presump-

160. Vide Geis, 1972, p. 2.

tion that all persons who are seventeen years of age are immature? If age is a weaker proxy for immaturity than the willingness to make foolish decisions, are these still reasons to regard prohibiting behavior to children as less offensive than prohibiting behavior to everyone?

6. THE REGULATION OF ADOLESCENCE

A. A long list of age-related duties and prohibitions is an important part of the legal system in the United States and in most Western democracies. Children within a specific age range must attend school and obey their parents. Children under specific ages cannot purchase alcoholic beverages or cigarettes, drive automobiles, or be found after specified hours of the night in public places. Laws regulating the behavior of children and adolescents have generated a specialized vocabulary: e.g., "curfew," "truancy," "child beyond control," "minor in need of supervision," and "contributing to the delinquency of a minor." The general category of behavior required of or prohibited to minors is usually referred to as "status offenses"; and young persons brought before a juvenile court for such offenses are called "status offenders." In the original jurisprudence of the juvenile court, minors who committed such offenses could receive the same treatment by a juvenile court as juveniles found guilty of automobile theft or assault. Are such status offenses victimless crimes?

B. Why do you think cities pass curfew ordinances? Is the only harm that concerns the authorities that which may befall an unsupervised teenager who stays out too late?

C. One major element of juvenile justice reform legislation since the mid–1960s has been the reduction in the amount of state power that can be used in responding to status offenders. Many states now prohibit judges from ordering secure custodial confinement for minors who violate age-related prohibitions relating to truancy, curfew violation, and parental disobedience.[161] The usual rationale for the decriminalization of status offenses is that harsh sanctions for juveniles do more harm than good. How does that differ from the rationale for abolishing victimless crime?

E. SECULAR HARM AND MODERN CRIMINAL JUSTICE POLICY

BERNARD E. HARCOURT—THE COLLAPSE OF THE HARM PRINCIPLE
90 Journal of Criminal Law and Criminology 109–194 (1999).

INTRODUCTION

In November 1998, fourteen neighborhoods in Chicago voted to shut down their liquor stores, bars, and lounges, and four more neighborhoods voted to close down specific taverns. Three additional liquor

---

161. Vide Franklin Zimring, *The Changing Legal World of Adolescence,* Chapter 5, 1982.

establishments were voted shut in February 1999. Along with the fourteen other neighborhoods that passed dry votes in 1996 and those that went dry right after Prohibition, to date more than fifteen percent of Chicago has voted itself dry. The closures affect alcohol-related businesses, like liquor stores and bars, but do not restrict drinking in the privacy of one's home. The legal mechanism is an arcane 1933 "vote yourself dry" law, enacted at the time of the repeal of Prohibition, and amended by the state legislature in 1995.

Chicago's temperance movement reflects a fascinating development in the legal enforcement of morality. Instead of arguing about morals, the proponents of enforcement are talking about individual and social harms in contexts where, thirty years ago, the harm principle would have precluded regulation or prohibition. Chicago is a case on point. The closures are part of Mayor Richard Daley's campaign to *revitalize* neighborhoods. The campaign focuses on the *harms* that liquor-related businesses produce in a neighborhood, *not* on the morality or immorality of drinking. "People are voting for their pocketbook, for home values, for church, children and seniors," Mayor Daley is reported to have said. "This is a quality of life issue, not an attempt to impose prohibition."

A similar shift in justification is evident in a wide range of debates over the regulation or prohibition of activities that have traditionally been associated with moral offense—from prostitution and pornography, to loitering and drug use, to homosexual and heterosexual conduct. In a wide array of contexts, the proponents of regulation and prohibition have turned away from arguments based on *morality*, and turned instead to *harm* arguments. In New York City, for example, Mayor Rudolph Giuliani has implemented a policy of zero-tolerance toward quality-of-life offenses, and has vigorously enforced laws against public drinking, public urination, illegal peddling, squeegee solicitation, panhandling, prostitution, loitering, graffiti spraying, and turnstile jumping. According to Mayor Giuliani, aggressive enforcement of these laws is necessary to combat serious crime—murders and robberies—because minor disorderly offenses contribute causally to serious crime. The justification for the enforcement policy is the *harms* that the activities cause, *not* their immorality. "[I]f a climate of disorder and lack of mutual respect is allowed to take root," Mayor Giuliani argues, "incidence of other, more serious antisocial behavior *will increase....* [M]urder and graffiti are two vastly different crimes. But they are part of the same continuum...."

Similarly, in the pornography debate, Professor Catharine MacKinnon has proposed influential administrative and judicial measures to regulate pornographic material. Her enforcement proposals, again, are *not* based on the immorality of pornography. Instead, the principal justification is the *multiple harms* that pornography and commercial sex cause women. "[T]he evidence of the harm of such material," Mac-

Kinnon explains, "shows that these materials change attitudes and impel behaviors in ways that are unique in their extent and devastating in their consequences."[162] MacKinnon's provocative discourse, and her vivid descriptions of injury, violence, erections, and rape, are all about *harm*. In a similar vein, the recent crack-down on commercial sex establishments—peep shows, strip clubs, adult book and video stores—in New York City has been justified in the name of tourism, crime rates, and property value, *not* morality. As Mayor Giuliani explains, the campaign to shut down pornography businesses "will allow people to restore and maintain their neighborhoods, and protect generations of New Yorkers against . . . the destabilization that [sex shops] cause."

A similar development has taken place in the debate over homosexuality. In the 1980s, the AIDS epidemic became the *harm* that justified legal intervention. When San Francisco and New York City moved to close gay bathhouses in the mid–1980s, the argument was not about the *immorality* of homosexual conduct. Instead, the debate was about the *harm* associated with the potential spread of AIDS at gay bathhouses. Former New York State Governor Mario Cuomo, who endorsed the strict regulation of gay bathhouses and threatened to close down non-compliant establishments, emphasized *harm*, stating: "We know certain sexual behavior can be fatal. We must eliminate public establishments which profit from activities that foster this deadly disease." The same argument about harm has been used to justify the regulation of sexual practices among military personnel infected with the HIV virus.

In fact, the focus on harm has become so pervasive that the concept of harm, today, is setting the very terms of contemporary debate. This is illustrated well, again, in the pornography context. In response to MacKinnon's proposal to regulate pornography, Professor Judith Butler has argued, in her recent book, *Excitable Speech: A Politics of the Performative*, that the very etiology of pornography's harm suggests a different remedy. Butler's argument, in effect, is that the *harm to women* caused by pornography is not constitutive, but allows for a spatial and temporal gap within which personal resistance can be mounted. Similarly, in striking down MacKinnon's proposed ordinance in Indianapolis, Judge Frank Easterbrook acknowledged the harm that pornography causes women. According to Easterbrook, it is precisely the *harm* of pornography that "simply demonstrates the power of pornography as speech,"[163] and requires protected status under the First Amendment. Harm, not morality, structures the debate.

This is illustrated also in the ongoing controversy over the legalization of marijuana and other psychoactive drugs. In response to a wave of enforcement of anti-drug policies in the 1980s—a wave of enforcement that was justified because of the *harms* associated with drug use and the illicit drug trade—the movement for drug policy reform has increasingly turned to the argument of *"harm reduction."* Whereas thirty years ago

162. MacKinnon, Only Words, at 37.

163. American Booksellers Ass'n, Inc. v. Hudnut, 771 F.2d 323, 329 (7th Cir. 1985).

the opponents of criminalization talked about marijuana use as a "victimless crime"—as *not* causing harm to others—the opponents of criminalization now emphasize the *harms* associated with the war on drugs. Ethan Nadelmann, the director of an influential drug reform policy center in New York City, and other reformers have carefully crafted and employed the term "harm reduction". Their focus is on designing policies that will reduce the overall harm associated with drug use *and* drug interdiction policies. Nadelmann's main argument is that we must "[a]ccept that drug use is here to stay and that we have no choice but to learn to live with drugs so that *they cause the least possible harm.*"[164] Again, harm, not morality, now structures the debate.

A RECENT DEVELOPMENT IN THE DEBATE OVER
THE LEGAL ENFORCEMENT OF MORALITY

As we approach the end of the twentieth century, we are witnessing a remarkable development in the debate over the legal enforcement of morality. The harm principle is effectively collapsing under the weight of its own success. Claims of harm have become so pervasive that the harm principle has become meaningless: the harm principle no longer serves the function of a *critical principle* because non-trivial harm arguments permeate the debate. Today, the issue is no longer *whether* a moral offense causes harm, but rather what type and what amount of harms the challenged conduct causes, and how the harms compare. On those issues, the harm principle is silent. This is a radical departure from the liberal theoretic, progressive discourse of the 1960s.

More formally, in the writings of John Stuart Mill, H.L.A. Hart and Joel Feinberg, the harm principle acted as a *necessary but not sufficient* condition for legal enforcement. The harm principle was used to *exclude* certain categories of activities from legal enforcement (*necessary condition*), but it did not determine what to *include* (*but not sufficient condition*), insofar as practical, constitutional or other factors weighed into the ultimate decision whether to regulate a moral offense. Today, although the harm principle formally remains a *necessary but not sufficient* condition, harm is no longer in fact a *necessary* condition because non-trivial harm arguments are being made about practically every moral offense. As a result, today, we no longer focus on the existence or non-existence of harm. Instead, we focus on the types of harm, the amounts of harms, and the balance of harms. As to these questions, the harm principle offers no guidance. It does not tell us how to compare harms. It served only as a threshold determination, and that threshold is being satisfied in most categories of moral offense. As a result, the harm principle no longer acts today as a *limiting principle* on the legal enforcement of morality.

The collapse of the harm principle has significantly altered the map of liberal legal and political theory in the debate over the legal enforce-

164. Ethan A. Nadelmann, *Learning to*   at A21.
Live With Drugs, WASH. POST, Nov. 2, 1999,

ment of morality. To be sure, the liberal criteria themselves have not changed. As in the 1960s, it is still possible today to define "liberalism," in the specific context of the legal enforcement of morality, on the basis of the same three criteria, namely (1) that it is a justifiable reason to limit an individual's freedom of action if their action causes harm to other persons (the harm principle), (2) that it is also a justifiable reason to limit someone's activities in order to prevent serious offense to other persons (the offense principle), and (3) that it is generally not a justifiable reason to limit harmless conduct on the ground that it is immoral. The criteria are the same today.

But the map of liberalism has changed. In the 1960s and '70s, liberalism was predominantly progressive in relation to moral offenses: liberal theory was dominated by progressives, like H.L.A. Hart, Joel Feinberg, and Ronald Dworkin, who were favorably inclined, by and large, toward the relaxation of sexual morality in the area of homosexuality, fornication, and pornography. In the 1960s and '70s, liberalism was opposed, chiefly, by moral conservatives, like Lord Patrick Devlin, who were theoretically illiberal insofar as they espoused legal moralist principles. Today, liberalism is the domain of progressives *and* conservatives. Conservatives have adopted the harm principle, and increasingly are making harm arguments. As a result, liberal theory itself is no longer formally opposed. Liberal theory has colonized moral conservatism and, it would appear, is being colonized by conservatives in return. The net effect is the emergence of what I will call conservative liberalism. The change can be represented in the following figure:

Figure 1: The Emergence of Conservative Liberalism

1960s

Liberal Theory		*Illiberal Theory*
Harm Principle		Legal Moralism
H.L.A. Hart		Lord Devlin
Progressive		Conservative
	1990s	
	Liberal Theory	
	Harm Principle	
Progressive		Conservative

The emergence of conservative liberalism represents the ironic culmination of a long debate between liberal theorists and their critics. It is ironic because it symbolizes a victory for both sides. Liberal theory prevails in the sense that the harm principle is hegemonic—if only in theory. The critics of 1960s liberalism prevail in the sense that morality gets enforced—if only under a liberal regime.

In this article, I explore the emergence of conservative liberalism and the effective collapse of the harm principle. My goal is to bridge, on the one hand, the legal and political theoretic discussion of the harm principle and, on the other, the actual arguments being made by activists, lawyers, academics, judges, politicians, and cultural critics. The project is to demonstrate how debates in the philosophy of law influence legal and political rhetoric, and how the latter, in turn, impact philosophical principle. It is a project about legal rhetoric, or more precisely about the interplay between legal philosophic and practical legal rhetoric. In this sense, the project is a study in legal semiotics.

THE RISE OF THE HARM PRINCIPLE

[In this part, the article begins by tracing the intellectual history of the harm principle from John Stuart Mill's essay *On Liberty*, to H.L.A. Hart's writings in the 1950s, to the Hart–Devlin debate and Hart's lectures *Law, Liberty, and Morality*, as well as Joel Feinberg's multi-volume treatise on *The Moral Limits of the Criminal Law*, the first and most important volume of which was entitled *Harm to Others*. The article then explores how the harm principle triumphed over legal moralism in Anglo–American jurisprudence and American criminal law.]

THE TRIUMPH OF THE HARM PRINCIPLE

Gradually, over the course of the 1960s, '70s, and '80s, Mill's famous sentence began to dominate the legal philosophic debate over the enforcement of morality. Harm became *the* critical principle used to police the line between law and morality within Anglo–American philosophy of law. Most prominent theorists who participated in the debate either relied on the harm principle or made favorable reference to the argument. Professor Ronald Dworkin engaged the Hart–Devlin debate in an article first published in the *Yale Law Journal* in 1966 entitled *Lord Devlin and the Enforcement of Morals*. Although Dworkin focused on the implications for democratic theory—arguing that legislators must ultimately decide whether the community has expressed a reasoned moral position about purportedly immoral activities—Dworkin presented the harm principle as a leading response in the debate. Professor Louis Henkin similarly joined the debate, with specific reference to the question of obscenity. Although Henkin, like Dworkin, took a different approach to the question—emphasizing the constitutional dimensions of laws enforcing claims of morality that have their roots in religious principles—Henkin also sided with Hart against Devlin. "By my hypotheses," Henkin noted in conclusion, "the United States would be a polity nearer the heart of Professor Hart, and of John Stuart Mill."[165]

From philosophy of law to substantive criminal law, the harm principle permeated the debate during the 1960s and 1970s. As evidenced by the writings of Professors Hart and Feinberg in the legal philosophic debate, and of Professor Wechsler and the drafters of the Model Penal Code in the substantive criminal law debate, the harm principle became the dominant discursive principle used to draw the line between law and morality. The decision to embrace Mill's original, simple statement of the harm principle was a powerful rhetorical move.

---

165. Louis Henkin, *Morals and The Constitution: The Sin of Obscenity*, 63 Co-   LUM. L. REV. 391, 413 (1963).

Devlin's writings had fragmented the conservative position by conflating harm and morality—by defining public morality in terms of social harm—and had significantly ambiguated the conception of harm at the heart of the debate. The liberal response reclaimed the conception of harm. It simplified and pared it back down to the mere idea of "harm." It bracketed out the competing normative dimensions of harm. And it offered a bright-line rule. A rule that was simple to apply. A rule that was simply applied.

THE EMERGENCE OF CONSERVATIVE LIBERALISM

During the course of the last two decades, the proponents of legal enforcement have increasingly deployed the rhetoric of harm. Armed with social science studies, with empirical data and with anecdotal evidence, the proponents of regulation and prohibition have shed the 1960s rhetoric of legal moralism and adopted, instead, the harm principle. Whether they have been motivated by moral conviction or by sincere adherence to the harm principle, the result is the same: the harm principle has undergone an ideological shift—or, what Professor Balkin would call "ideological drift"—from its progressive origins.

Today, the harm principle is being used increasingly by conservatives who justify laws against prostitution, pornography, public drinking, drugs and loitering, as well as regulation of homosexual and heterosexual conduct, on the basis of *harm to others*. The conservative harm arguments are powerful. By endorsing the harm principle and simultaneously making harm arguments, the proponents of legal enforcement have disarmed the progressive position and the traditional progressive reliance on the harm principle. This has significantly changed the structure of the debate over the legal enforcement of morality.

In this part, I will discuss a number of illustrations from a variety of different contemporary debates. The purpose of these illustrations is to show significant examples of the conservative deployment of harm arguments—significant in the sense that these particular arguments have been taken seriously in contemporary debates. My purpose here is not to prove that these conservative harm arguments have been accepted by everyone, nor even by a majority of the participants in the debates. Nor is it my intention to prove that these conservative harm arguments have resulted in a higher level of actual enforcement. Again, larger social, political, cultural and historical factors may also, and more significantly, influence the actual regulation or prohibition of conduct. My focus in this Article is on changes in justification, and these changes themselves may not necessarily produce different enforcement. They do, however, have a significant impact on the way we think, argue and debate practices like prostitution, drug use, drinking and homosexuality, as well as other conduct that has traditionally been viewed as morally offensive.

PORNOGRAPHY AND HARM

In the mid–1980s, Professor Joel Feinberg discussed the feminist critique of pornography and suggested that the proper liberal position would be to leave open the possibility of regulating pornography if empirical evidence of harm developed. Feinberg intimated that further empirical research regarding some types of pornography might demonstrate harm. "In that case," Feinberg wrote, "a liberal should have no hesitation in using the criminal law to prevent the harm." Feinberg cautioned, however, that "in the meantime, the *appropriate liberal response* should be a kind of uneasy skepticism about the harmful effects of pornography on third-party victims, conjoined with increasingly energetic use of 'further speech or expression' against the cult of macho, 'effectively to combat the harm.' "[173]

Things are different today. The "appropriate liberal response" to pornography today, I would suggest, is the free speech argument—not the harm principle. Proponents of the regulation and prohibition of pornography have skillfully employed the harm argument in support of their own position, and thereby undercut the earlier progressive response. Professor Catharine MacKinnon, perhaps more than anyone else, has focused the debate on the harm to women caused by pornography and her work has emphasized at least three types of harm emanating from pornography.

[In this section, the article traces the MacKinnon debates over pornography and demonstrates how the argument of harm has infiltrated American legal and political rhetoric. It explores how MacKinnon's focus on harm also has influenced the responses of her main opponents—Judge Frank Easterbrook, who struck down the Indianapolis ordinance in *American Booksellers Association, Inc. v. Hudnut*, and Professor Judith Butler, whose recent book, *Excitable Speech: A Politics of the Performative*, take issue with MacKinnon's approach.]

In the specific context of the pornography debate then, MacKinnon's use of the harm argument has produced an ideological shift in the harm principle. In contrast to an earlier period when the harm principle was employed by progressives to justify limits on the regulation of pornography, the principle is no longer an effective response to conservative proposals to regulate. To the contrary, the conservatives have essentially taken over the harm principle: harm has become the principal argument for state intervention, as illustrated and, in this particular case, at least temporarily implemented, in Indianapolis and New York City. Easterbrook and Butler's responses to MacKinnon reflect how destabilizing this ideological shift has been. These contemporary responses essentially discard the harm principle in favor of free speech and strategic arguments about political effectiveness. Most tellingly, these contemporary responses *incorporate harm* into their own arguments to bolster their position—in the case of free speech, to show the very power of speech, and in the case of political strategy, to demonstrate the need for political resistance, rather than state intervention. The result is an entirely

---

173. 2 JOEL FEINBERG, THE MORAL LIMITS   (1985).
OF THE CRIMINAL LAW: OFFENSE TO OTHERS 157

different structure in the debate over the legal enforcement of morality: a structure of competing harm claims with no internal mechanism to resolve them.

Prostitution and Harm

Traditionally, prostitution presented a hard case for the progressives. It implicated all three safe harbors in the harm principle: consent, privacy, and supposedly self-regarding conduct. The private act of consensual, heterosexual fornication was, after all, the paradigm activity protected by the harm principle. What then distinguished a private act of consensual, heterosexual prostitution?

In sharp contrast, the last two decades have witnessed a distinct shift in the debate over prostitution. The proponents of regulation or prohibition, instead of arguing about morality or offense, have turned to the harm argument, and thereby disarmed the traditional progressive position. This shift is the result again, at least in part, of Catharine MacKinnon's writings, but what has also transformed the debate over prostitution is the "broken windows" theory of crime prevention, first articulated in James Q. Wilson and George L. Kelling's article, *Broken Windows*, in the *Atlantic Monthly* in 1982. Under the broken windows argument, the potential harm to society in prostitution is not so much the harm to women, but rather the likelihood of increased serious criminal activity. The broken windows hypothesis provides that, if prostitution and other minor disorderly conduct in a neighborhood go unattended, serious crime will increase in that neighborhood. Disorder, such as prostitution, brings about increased criminal activity. According to the broken windows argument, prostitution causes harm to society by causing more violent crimes.

The conception of harm at the heart of the *Broken Windows* essay— in conjunction with MacKinnon's harm argument—has significantly altered the structure of the debate over the enforcement of laws against prostitution. The contemporary proponents of regulation or prohibition have changed the equation of harm, undercut the earlier progressive argument, and neutralized the harm principle: the principle is no longer an effective argument because it is silent once a threshold of harm has been met. The conservative claims of harm have, in essence, disarmed the 1960s progressive position.

Homosexual Conduct and Harm

The case of homosexual conduct is particularly interesting because here, it seemed, legal moralism was still strong. In 1986, the United States Supreme Court adopted legal moralism for purposes of rational basis review under the Fourteenth Amendment to the United States Constitution. In *Bowers v. Hardwick*, Justice White, writing for the Court, specifically said that moral sentiments provided a rational basis for enforcing Georgia's criminal ban on homosexual sodomy. In other words, morality alone justified limiting the liberty of homosexuals. In the case of the debate over the enforcement of laws regulating homosexuality, then, it appeared that legal moralism remained strong and that, as a result, there was no real need for the proponents of regulation to turn to harm arguments to justify regulation or prohibition.

The tragic advent of the AIDS epidemic, however, changed things. The threat of AIDS became the harm that justified increased regulation. So much so, in fact, that today harm arguments appear to play at least an equal role with legal moralist arguments in the debate over the regulation of homosexual conduct. This became immediately apparent in the debate over the closing of gay bathhouses at the time of the outbreak of the AIDS epidemic. The issue of closing gay bathhouses—and thereby regulating homosexual activity—first arose in San Francisco in 1984. With approximately 475 men in San Francisco diagnosed with AIDS, the director of public health announced that the city would prohibit sexual contacts in gay bathhouses and close down any establishment that did not comply with the new prohibition. Six months later, the public health director ordered the closure of fourteen gay bathhouses and clubs. The bathhouses were allowed to reopen in November 1985 under strict court-ordered guidelines regulating sexual contacts. Those regulations "ordered operators to hire employees to monitor patrons; ordered doors removed from private cubicles; and required the bathhouses to expel patrons seen engaging in 'high-risk sexual activity.'"

What is important, for present purposes, is that the justification offered by the proponents of regulation was harm, not morality. The justification was the potential threat of the spread of AIDS. The director of public health accused the establishments of "fostering disease and death" by allowing high-risk sexual contacts. In other words, the city officials relied on harm arguments, rather than legal moralism, *even though* legal moralism may have been sufficient as a legal matter.

DRUG USE AND HARM

The structure of the debate over the criminalization of the use of psychoactive drugs has also changed significantly since the 1960s. The early progressive argument that the use of marijuana was a "victimless crime" was countered in the late 1970s and 1980s by a campaign against drug use that emphasized the *harms to society,* and justified an all-out war on drugs. The proponents of legal enforcement—in this case modeled on military enforcement—forcefully deployed the harm argument. Here, again, the harm principle experienced an ideological shift from its progressive origins: today, the debate over drug use pits conservative harm arguments against new progressive arguments about "harm reduction." As a result, today, both conservatives and progressives are making harm arguments. The debate is over which harms are worse. In that debate, the harm principle is silent.

OTHER ILLUSTRATIONS OF CONSERVATIVE HARM ARGUMENTS

Debates over fornication and adultery are two other areas of sexual morality where proponents of regulation have, in certain discrete instances, turned to harm arguments. But there are numerous other illustrations of the increased proliferation of conservative harm arguments. . .

THE COLLAPSE OF THE HARM PRINCIPLE

THE RELATIVE IMPORTANCE OF HARMS

Pornography, prostitution, disorderly conduct, homosexuality, intoxication, drug use, and fornication: with regard to each of these, the proponents of legal enforcement are now deploying the harm argument in support of a conservative agenda. The arguments are powerful. It is hard to respond adequately to the harm to women caused by pornography and prostitution, to the threat of the spread of AIDS caused by high-risk activities like homosexual and heterosexual fornication, or to the neighborhood decline and loss of property value associated with prostitutes, smut shops, and liquor establishments. The harm arguments are particularly compelling when the conception of harm has been pared down to its bare bones and brackets out other normative values.

The proliferation of harm arguments in the debate over the legal enforcement of morality has effectively collapsed the harm principle. Harm to others is no longer today a *limiting* principle. It no longer *excludes* categories of moral offenses from the scope of the law. It is no longer a *necessary (but not sufficient) condition*, because there are so many non-trivial harm arguments. Instead of focusing on whether certain conduct causes harm, today the debates center on the types of harm, the amounts of harm, and our willingness, as a society, to bear the harms. And the harm principle is silent on those questions.

The harm principle is silent in the sense that it does not determine whether a non-trivial harm justifies restrictions on liberty, nor does it determine how to compare or weigh competing claims of harms. It was never intended to be a *sufficient* condition. It does not address the comparative importance of harms. Joel Feinberg's thorough discussion of the harm principle recognized this important fact. In discussing the relative importance of harms, Feinberg admitted that "[i]t is impossible to prepare a detailed manual with the exact 'weights' of all human interests, the degree to which they are advanced or thwarted by all possible actions and activities, duly discounted by objective improbabilities mathematically designated." Thus, Feinberg concluded, "in the end, it is the legislator himself, using his own fallible judgment rather than spurious formulas and 'measurements,' who must compare conflicting interests and judge which are the more important."

Feinberg proposed a three-prong test to determine the relative importance of harms:

> Relative importance is a function of three different respects in which opposed interests can be compared:
>
> I. how "vital" they are in the interest networks of their possessors;
>
> II. the degree to which they are reinforced by other interests, private and public;

III.   their inherent moral quality.

But what are the inherent moral qualities of interests affected by claims of harm? And how could the harm principle tell us what those inherent moral qualities are? In the end, it can not. The harm principle itself—the simple notion of harm—does not address the relative importance of harms. Once non-trivial harm arguments have been made, we inevitably must look beyond the harm principle. We must look beyond the traditional structure of the debate over the legal enforcement of morality. We must access larger debates in ethics, law and politics—debates about power, autonomy, identity, human flourishing, equality, freedom and other interests and values *that give meaning to the claim that an identifiable harm matters*. In this sense, the proliferation of conservative harm arguments and the collapse of the harm principle has fundamentally altered the structure of the future debate over the legal enforcement of morals.

A Skeptical Response

At this point, some readers of this Article may respond that the discussion here—especially the emphasis on rhetorical structure and legal semiotics—is misleading. A skeptical reader might respond: Truth is, the harm principle is still right today and the structure of the debate has not really changed. What we have witnessed, over the past two decades, is not the *collapse* of the harm principle, but rather the natural *evolution* of a useful analytic principle. What we need to do is to continue to *refine* the harm principle to better address these claims of harm. The harm principle is fully capable of dealing with these conservative harm arguments.

This skeptical response could take either of two forms. The first variant of the argument is that the harm principle remains a serviceable distinction and functions entirely properly today. Progressive thinkers in the 1960s and 1970s were simply wrong to suggest that pornography, prostitution, or drinking were harmless. In fact, they do cause certain harms and therefore may be legally regulated. Still, there are other activities generally considered to be morally questionable that are nonetheless protected by the harm principle. These include, for instance, masturbation or non-fraudulent lying. Many people might consider these acts immoral, but very few would argue that they should be regulated by the state because of their harm.

A second version of the argument is that the harm principle is still a useful critical principle in theory, but that it has been distorted in practice. The new evidence of harm is simply misleading. We should continue to use the harm principle, but we must do a better job at policing the facts. We should subject the empirical evidence to more rigorous scrutiny.

I suspect that many opponents of Professor MacKinnon's argument would respond in this way. Judge Easterbrook in fact flirts with this response in the *Hudnut* decision, when he writes in the margin:

The social science studies are very difficult to interpret, however, and they conflict. Because much of the effect of speech comes through a process of socialization, it is difficult to measure incremental benefits and injuries caused by particular speech. Several psychologists have found, for example, that those who see violent, sexually explicit films tend to have more violent thoughts. But how often does this lead to actual violence? National commissions on obscenity here, in the United Kingdom, and in Canada have found that it is not possible to demonstrate a direct link between obscenity and rape or exhibitionism.[174]

This footnote is intended, at the very least, to undermine our confidence in the causal connection underlying MacKinnon's harm argument. Similarly, my previous article on the broken windows theory, *Reflecting on the Subject*, could be interpreted as an attempt to police the harm argument underlying the broken windows hypothesis. The quantitative analysis, in particular the replication of Wesley Skogan's study on disorder and crime, could be seen as an effort to prove that the harm allegedly associated with disorder has not been established. The article as a whole could be read as an attempt to police the facts.

Alternatively, it could be argued that the theories of harm—not the facts—are wrong. The harm alleged by MacKinnon or by the broken windows theory relies on an intervening actor—the rapist, the sexist male, or the armed robber—and therefore should not be imputed to the original conduct, viewing pornography or loitering. In other words, the argument would go, it is not pornography or disorder that causes serious crime, it is serious criminals; therefore, the challenged conduct does not cause harm to others, and should not be regulated. This argument is somewhat similar to the "perpetrator theories" advanced by opponents of gun control, or more popularly the argument that guns don't kill people, people kill people.

Under both versions of the argument, the central point is that the harm principle continues to be a useful analytic principle and that it is simply undergoing a natural process of evolution. Like any other analytic principle, it is only clear and easy when it is first articulated. It becomes more cumbersome as it is applied in an increasing number of cases. At present, it may have a temporary conservative tilt, but over the long run, it will even out politically and continue to be a useful and fair way to draw the line between law and morality. In other words, the structure of the debate may be undergoing change, but the harm principle will nevertheless remain at its core: the harm principle has *not* collapsed.

THE NORMATIVE DIMENSIONS OF HARM

The problem with the skeptical response is that it ignores the hidden normative dimensions of harm and their crucial role in the

174. American Booksellers Ass'n, Inc. v.   1985).
Hudnut, 771 F.2d 323, 329 n.2 (7th Cir.

application of the harm principle. Those hidden normative dimensions are what do the work in the harm principle, not the abstract, simple notion of harm. They *limit* claims of harm. They *exclude* harm arguments. In contrast, the abstract, simple idea of harm—bracketing out any other normative value—is broad enough to include most, if not all, of the harms alleged by contemporary proponents of regulation and prohibition. It is sufficiently robust to include the incitement to rape, the negative effects on women's sexuality, the stimulus to rob, the possible spread of AIDS, or the diminution in property values. In each of these cases, the strength of the abstract claim of harm will depend on normative assessments of pornography, male dominance, disorder, crime, or sexual freedom. Depending on those assessments, harm may be easier or harder to prove. But experience suggests that some harm attaches to most human activities, and especially to conduct that traditionally has been associated with moral offense. The very fact that society views these activities with opprobrium itself *generates harms*. Thus, even if we set aside the notion of legal rhetoric, the skeptical response is not persuasive.

Looking at the historical shifts in the debate through the lens of legal semiotics, however, offers an important insight: the ideological shift of the harm principle over the past twenty years reflects a natural tilt in the original, simple harm principle—*a natural tilt that favors a finding of harm*. By returning to the original, simple statement of the harm principle in the 1960s, the progressives opened the door to the proliferation of harm arguments and brought about the collapse of the harm principle.

This risk was always present. Critics of Mills had warned that most, if not all, human activity could be deemed to cause harm to others, and that "no man is an island." Mill acknowledged this criticism. So did Hart and Feinberg. They each tried to shield the harm principle from this criticism. What I would suggest, though, is that they were only able to hold the line on harm—to give the conception of harm a critical edge—by deploying *other* normative principles. In all three cases, there were competing normative values lurking behind their definition of harm, and limiting the scope of the harm principle.[175] In Mill, the supplemental normative principle was the notion of human self-development; in Hart, it was an emphasis on preventing human suffering; and in Feinberg, it was the concern for consistency and equal treatment.

With hindsight, the proliferation of harm arguments could have been predicted. The notion of harm, standing alone, was not the only critical principle at play in Mill, Hart, or Feinberg. Yet the original, simple statement of the harm principle attempted to bracket out normative values other than harm. By paring the harm principle back to its

---

175. In this regard, I agree with Professor Gerald Dworkin's suggestion, in his recent essay *Devlin Was Right*, that if one examines closely the category of harm "one reaches the conclusion that the term itself is a normative one. Not every setback to a person's interests counts as harmful for the purposes of justifying coercion. Only those that are 'wrongs' count." Dworkin, at 930.

original formulation, progressive theorists actually undermined its critical potential.

HARM IN MILL, HART AND FEINBERG

We saw earlier, in the discussion of Mill's essay *On Liberty*, that Mill's treatment of harm led him to an analysis of legal or recognized rights. Mill referred to these interests as "certain interests which, either by express legal provision or by tacit understanding, ought to be considered as rights." Mill explained that a right, in order to be cognizable, must relate in some way to utility. But, he emphasized, not just any kind of utility. "I regard utility as the ultimate appeal on all ethical questions," Mill famously wrote, "but it must be utility in the largest sense, grounded on the permanent interests of man as a progressive being." For Mill, the utilitarian calculus had to be defined in terms of human self-development.

In Mill's writings, then, the conception of harm was tied to that of human flourishing. The harm principle was supplemented by a principle of utility in the interest of "man as a progressive being." And it resulted in a surprisingly regulated society. Mill envisioned a society that regulated the sale of potential instruments of crime, alcohol consumption, education, and even procreation. In his essay dedicated to liberty, Mill even endorsed laws forbidding marriage among the poor in order to effectively limit the number of children that poor couples could have.

Mill did not perceive that these numerous regulations would infringe on the self-development of humankind, because the regulations promoted the interests of a more noble and artistic self. Restrictions on activities like drinking did not present a threat to human self-development, but rather promoted a healthier and more noble society. The normative work—the critical principle—was being done by the concept of human self-development—by the idea that human beings should become "a noble and beautiful object of contemplation," and that human life should become "rich, diversified, and animating, furnishing more abundant alignment to high thoughts and elevating feelings, and strengthening the tie which binds every individual to the race, by making the race infinitely better worth belonging to." In the end, Mill's harm principle was not simply about harm. It was also, importantly, about human flourishing.

H.L.A. Hart's writings betray, similarly, an important added normative dimension to harm. In Hart's case, though, the emphasis was not so much on human self-development, but rather on an abhorrence for human suffering. In this regard, Hart's writings are similar to those of Ronald Dworkin, who also emphasized, in the context of regulating homosexuality, the "miseries of frustration and persecution."

Central to Hart's writings is a concern about human misery. This concern recurred throughout his debate with Devlin. Human suffering made an appearance at almost every pivotal juncture. Hart repeatedly referred to the "cost of human suffering" that attends the enforcement of morality—"the misery and sacrifice of freedom," "the cost in human misery." In fact, Hart vigorously opposed the legal enforcement of morality precisely because it inflicted so much human suffering. He opposed the regulation of homosexuality because it "demand[s] the repression of powerful instincts with which personal happiness is intimately connected" (43). Hart attacked Devlin for his underlying retributiveness. Hart wrote:

> Notwithstanding the eminence of its legal advocates, this justification of punishment, especially when applied to conduct not harmful to others, seems to rest on a strange amalgam of ideas. It represents as a value to be pursued at the cost of human suffering the bare expression of moral condemnation, and treats the infliction of suffering as a uniquely appropriate or "emphatic" mode of expression. But is this really intelligible? Is the mere expression of moral condemnation a thing of value in itself to be pursued at this cost? The idea that we may punish offenders against a moral code, not to prevent harm or suffering or even the repetition of the offence but simply as a means of venting or emphatically expressing moral condemnation, is uncomfortably close to human sacrifice as an expression of religious worship. (65–66)

Hart's emphasis was on the human aspects of human suffering. His focus was on individual pain.

Hart suggested, at one point in his lectures, that anyone engaged in the debate over the legal enforcement of morality must accept "the critical principle, central to all morality, that human misery and the restriction of freedom are evils" (82). Otherwise, Hart explained, the legal enforcement of morality would not call for justification (65–66). Of course, the restriction of freedom was not itself a critical principle since the very purpose of a critical principle was to find proper limits on freedom. But the question of human misery certainly was, at least for Hart. Human misery was the added normative dimension to harm that, in Hart's writings, reined in the harm principle.

Joel Feinberg, more so than Mill or Hart, explicitly acknowledged the multiple normative dimensions of harm. In *Harm to Others*, Feinberg conceded that "harm is a very complex concept *with hidden normative dimensions* . . . ." (214). Feinberg defined harm in a way that incorporated these normative dimensions, and he emphasized in particular the protection of personal autonomy and the equal respect for persons. Feinberg explained that "the harm principle . . . protects personal autonomy and the moral value of 'respect for persons' that is associated with it; it incorporates nonarbitrary interest-ranking principles and principles of fairness regulating competitions; it 'enforces' the moral principles that protect individual projects that are necessary for human fulfillment."

There is considerable debate over the normative ingredients in Feinberg's definition of harm and in his liberal position, and I do not intend to resolve that question here. Instead, I will return to Feinberg's earlier writings on legal reasoning and his emphasis on consistency and equal treatment of similar cases, and suggest that those writings corroborate the value of "respect for persons" that is expressly stated in *The Moral Limits*. In those earlier writings, Feinberg advocates a type of moral reasoning, similar to legal reasoning, that involves an analysis and consideration, back and forth, between principle and outcome. Feinberg described this method of analysis as follows:

> The best way to defend one's selection of principles is to show to which positions they commit one on such issues as censorship of literature, "moral offenses," and compulsory social security programs. General principles arise in the course of deliberations over particular problems, especially in the efforts to defend one's judgments by showing that they are consistent with what has gone before. If a principle commits one to an antecedently unacceptable judgment, then one has to modify or supplement the principle in a way that does the least damage to the harmony of one's particular and general opinions taken as a group. On the other hand, when a solid, well-entrenched principle entails a change in a particular judgment, the overriding claims of consistency may require that the judgment be adjusted. This sort of dialectic is similar to the reasonings that are prevalent in law courts.[176]

What is doing much of the normative work in Feinberg's writing, then, is a type of legal reasoning based on consistency, equal treatment of similarly situated persons, analogy, and harmony. The harm principle itself does not dictate any specific resolution with regard to specified moral offenses—it is rather consistency and equal treatment, and, of course, fundamental commitments on issues such as "censorship of literature, 'morals offenses,' and compulsory social security programs."

H.L.A. Hart's return to the original, simple statement of the harm principle reflected a desire for a bright-line rule that would draw a clean distinction between law and morality. But the simple harm principle bracketed out other important normative dimensions. It excluded Mill's discussion of human flourishing and Hart's abhorrence for human suffering. It eliminated the very principles that reined in the harm principle and actually gave the harm analysis its critical edge. The predictable result was a proliferation of harm arguments and a struggle over the meaning of harm. The very simplicity of the harm principle may explain why harm became universal and how the struggle over the meaning of harm eventually collapsed the harm principle.

CONCLUSION

During the past two decades, the proponents of regulation and prohibition of a wide range of human activities—activities that have traditionally been associated with moral offense—have turned to the

---

176. Feinberg, *Moral Enforcement and the Harm Principle* (from SOCIAL PHILOSOPHY (1973)), *reprinted in* ETHICS AND PUBLIC POLICY 291 (Tom L. Beauchamp ed., 1975), at 287.

harm argument. Catharine MacKinnon has focused on the multiple harms to women and women's sexuality caused by pornography. The broken windows theory of crime prevention has emphasized how minor crimes, like prostitution and loitering, cause major crimes, neighborhood decline, and urban decay. The harm associated with the spread of AIDS has been used to justify increased regulation of homosexual and hetero-sexual conduct The new temperance movement in Chicago and the quality-of-life initiative in New York City have focused on the harmful effect of liquor establishments and public drunks on neighborhoods and property values. The debate on drugs has focused on the harms caused by drug use and the harms cause by the war on drugs.

The proliferation of conservative harm arguments has produced an ideological shift in the harm principle from its progressive origins. This shift has significantly changed the structure of the debate over the legal enforcement of morality. The original pairing of the harm and legal moralist arguments in the nineteenth century offered two competing ways to resolve a dispute. Legal moralists could argue that the immorali-ty of the offense was sufficient to enforce a prohibition, and the propo-nents of the harm principle could argue that the lack of harm precluded legal enforcement. Similarly, in the 1960s and 1970s, when the debate was structured by the predominance of the harm principle over legal moralism, there were still two competing ways of resolving a dispute—even if there was a certain disequilibrium in the relative rhetorical force of the competing solutions.

The proliferation of conservative harm arguments has changed all that. Today the debate is characterized by a cacophony of competing harm arguments without any way to resolve them. There is no longer an argument within the structure of the debate to resolve the competing claims of harm. The original harm principle was never equipped to determine the relative importance of harms. Once a non-trivial harm argument has been made, the harm principle itself offers no further guidance. It is silent on how to weigh the harms, balance the harms, or judge the harms. With regard to those questions, we need to look beyond the original harm principle and the traditional debate over the legal enforcement of morality.

It may be wrong, however, to decry this development. The collapse of the harm principle may ultimately be beneficial. It may help us realize that there is probably harm in most human activities and, in most cases, on both sides of the equation—on the side of the persons harmed by the purported moral offense, but also on the side of the actor whose conduct is restricted by the legal enforcement of morality. By highlighting the harm on both sides of the equation, the collapse of the harm principle may help us make more informed arguments, and reach more informed conclusions. It may force us to address the other normative dimensions lurking beneath the conception of harm. It may force us to carefully analyze the harm to others, as well as the harm to the purportedly immoral actor, remembering that the punishment itself may affect, positively or negatively, the subject of punishment, our assessment of harm, and society as a whole. Moreover, it may change the way that we think about remedies. Instead of broad prohibitions that affect entire categories of moral offenses, we may instead develop more nuanced remedies that address particular harms. In sum, the collapse of the harm principle may bring about a richer structure for future debates over the legal enforcement of morals.

Notes and Questions

1. Why does Harcourt title his essay "The Collapse of the Harm Principle" instead of "The Triumph of the Harm Principle" or "The Proliferation of the Harm Principle"?

2. John Stewart Mill advanced at least two arguments. The first was that the presence of secular harm to persons other than the offender should be a necessary condition for criminal prohibition. The second argument was that the use of his first principle would drastically reduce the number of criminal offenses. The ubiquitous nature of harm debates in current discourse suggests that Mill's first argument has carried the day. But is the use of harm criteria decisive in many debates about whether criminal sanctions should continue?

3. Harcourt shows a proliferation of claims that many vice behaviors like drugs, pornography, prostitution, etc., cause harm to others, and he seems to suggest that claims of harm are distinctively recent. Is this true? To what extent do you think that most categories of vice crime were always vulnerable to harm claims?

4. Has the intensification of harm discourse been associated with greater or lesser criminal law coverage in pornography, drugs, adult sexual conduct and gambling? What does this tell us about the fate of harm principle in the modern marketplace of ideas?

Chapter 2

SODOMY, SEXUAL AUTONOMY AND SEXUAL ORIENTATION

A. THE ROAD TO *LAWRENCE*

GRISWOLD v. CONNECTICUT

Supreme Court of the United States, 1965.
381 U.S. 479.

Mr. Justice Douglas delivered the opinion of the Court.

Appellant Griswold is Executive Director of the Planned Parenthood League of Connecticut. Appellant Buxton is a licensed physician and a professor at the Yale Medical School who served as Medical Director for the League at its Center in New Haven—a center open and operating from November 1 to November 10, 1961, when appellants were arrested.

They gave information, instruction, and medical advice to married persons as to the means of preventing conception. They examined the wife and prescribed the best contraceptive device or material for her use. Fees were usually charged, although some couples were serviced free.

The statutes whose constitutionality is involved in this appeal are §§ 53–32 and 54–196 of the General Statutes of Connecticut (1958 rev.). The former provides:

"Any person who uses any drug, medicinal article or instrument for the purpose of preventing conception shall be fined not less than fifty dollars or imprisoned not less than sixty days nor more than one year or be both fined and imprisoned."

Section 54–196 provides:

"Any person who assists, abets, counsels, causes, hires or commands another to commit any offense may be prosecuted and punished as if he were the principal offender."

The appellants were found guilty as accessories and fined $100 each, against the claim that the accessory statute as so applied violated the

107

Fourteenth Amendment. The Appellate Division of the Circuit Court affirmed. The Supreme Court of Errors affirmed that judgment. * * *

Coming to the merits, we are met with a wide range of questions that implicate the Due Process Clause of the Fourteenth Amendment. Overtones of some arguments suggest that Lochner v. New York, 198 U.S. 45, should be our guide. But we decline that invitation * * * We do not sit as a super-legislature to determine the wisdom, need, and propriety of laws that touch economic problems, business affairs, or social conditions. This law, however, operates directly on an intimate relation of husband and wife and their physician's role in one aspect of that relation.

The association of people is not mentioned in the Constitution nor in the Bill of Rights. The right to educate a child in a school of the parents' choice—whether public or private or parochial—is also not mentioned. Nor is the right to study any particular subject or any foreign language. Yet the First Amendment has been construed to include certain of those rights.

By Pierce v. Society of Sisters, supra, the right to educate one's children as one chooses is made applicable to the States by the force of the First and Fourteenth Amendments. By Meyer v. Nebraska, supra, the same dignity is given the right to study the German language in a private school. In other words, the State may not, consistently with the spirit of the First Amendment, contract the spectrum of available knowledge. The right of freedom of speech and press includes not only the right to utter or to print, but the right to distribute, the right to receive, the right to read (Martin v. Struthers, 319 U.S. 141, 143) and freedom of inquiry, freedom of thought, and freedom to teach (see Wieman v. Updegraff, 344 U.S. 183, 195)—indeed the freedom of the entire university community. Sweezy v. New Hampshire, 354 U.S. 234, 249–250, 261–263; Barenblatt v. United States, 360 U.S. 109, 112; Baggett v. Bullitt, 377 U.S. 360, 369. Without those peripheral rights the specific rights would be less secure. And so we reaffirm the principle of the Pierce and the Meyer cases.

In NAACP v. Alabama, 357 U.S. 449, 462, we protected the "freedom to associate and privacy in one's associations," noting that freedom of association was a peripheral First Amendment right. Disclosure of membership lists of a constitutionally valid association, we held, was invalid "as entailing the likelihood of a substantial restraint upon the exercise by petitioner's members of their right to freedom of association." Ibid. In other words, the First Amendment has a penumbra where privacy is protected from governmental intrusion. In like context, we have protected forms of "association" that are not political in the customary sense but pertain to the social, legal, and economic benefit of the members. NAACP v. Button, 371 U.S. 415, 430–431. In Schware v. Board of Bar Examiners, 353 U.S. 232, we held it not permissible to bar a lawyer from practice, because he had once been a member of the Communist Party. The man's "association with that Party" was not shown to be "anything more than a political faith in a political party" (id., at 244) and was not action of a kind proving bad moral character. Id., at 245–246.

Those cases involved more than the "right of assembly"—a right that extends to all irrespective of their race or ideology. De Jonge v. Oregon, 299 U.S. 353. The right of "association," like the right of belief (Board of Education v. Barnette, 319 U.S. 624), is more than the right to attend a meeting; it includes the right to express one's attitudes or philosophies by membership in a group or by affiliation with it or by other lawful means. Association in that context is a form of expression of opinion; and while it is not expressly included in the First Amendment its existence is necessary in making the express guarantees fully meaningful.

The foregoing cases suggest that specific guarantees in the Bill of Rights have penumbras, formed by emanations from those guarantees that help give them life and substance. See Poe v. Ullman, 367 U.S. 497, 516–522 (dissenting opinion). Various guarantees create zones of privacy. The right of association contained in the penumbra of the First Amendment is one, as we have seen. The Third Amendment in its prohibition against the quartering of soldiers "in any house" in time of peace without the consent of the owner is another facet of that privacy. The Fourth Amendment explicitly affirms the "right of the people to be secure in their persons, houses, papers, and effects, against unreasonable searches and seizures." The Fifth Amendment in its Self–Incrimination Clause enables the citizen to create a zone of privacy which government may not force him to surrender to his detriment. The Ninth Amendment provides: "The enumeration in the Constitution, of certain rights, shall not be construed to deny or disparage others retained by the people."

The Fourth and Fifth Amendments were described in Boyd v. United States, 116 U.S. 616, 630, as protection against all governmental invasions "of the sanctity of a man's home and the privacies of life." We recently referred in Mapp v. Ohio, 367 U.S. 643, 656, to the Fourth Amendment as creating a "right to privacy, no less important than any other right carefully and particularly reserved to the people." See Beaney, The Constitutional Right to Privacy, 1962 Sup. Ct. Rev. 212; Griswold, The Right to be Let Alone, 55 Nw. U. L. Rev. 216 (1960).

     * * *

The present case, then, concerns a relationship lying within the zone of privacy created by several fundamental constitutional guarantees. And it concerns a law which, in forbidding the use of contraceptives rather than regulating their manufacture or sale, seeks to achieve its goals by means having a maximum destructive impact upon that relationship. Such a law cannot stand in light of the familiar principle, so often applied by this Court, that a "governmental purpose to control or prevent activities constitutionally subject to state regulation may not be achieved by means which sweep unnecessarily broadly and thereby invade the area of protected freedoms." NAACP v. Alabama, 377 U.S.

288, 307. Would we allow the police to search the sacred precincts of marital bedrooms for telltale signs of the use of contraceptives? The very idea is repulsive to the notions of privacy surrounding the marriage relationship.

We deal with a right of privacy older than the Bill of Rights—older than our political parties, older than our school system. Marriage is a coming together for better or for worse, hopefully enduring, and intimate to the degree of being sacred. It is an association that promotes a way of life, not causes; a harmony in living, not political faiths; a bilateral loyalty, not commercial or social projects. Yet it is an association for as noble a purpose as any involved in our prior decisions.

Reversed.

Mr. Justice Goldberg, whom The Chief Justice and Mr. Justice Brennan join, concurring.

I agree with the Court that Connecticut's birth-control law unconstitutionally intrudes upon the right of marital privacy, and I join in its opinion and judgment. Although I have not accepted the view that "due process" as used in the Fourteenth Amendment incorporates all of the first eight Amendments, I do agree that the concept of liberty protects those personal rights that are fundamental, and is not confined to the specific terms of the Bill of Rights. My conclusion that the concept of liberty is not so restricted and that it embraces the right of marital privacy though that right is not mentioned explicitly in the Constitution is supported both by numerous decisions of this Court, referred to in the Court's opinion, and by the language and history of the Ninth Amendment. In reaching the conclusion that the right of marital privacy is protected, as being within the protected penumbra of specific guarantees of the Bill of Rights, the Court refers to the Ninth Amendment, ante, at 484. I add these words to emphasize the relevance of that Amendment to the Court's holding.

The Court stated many years ago that the Due Process Clause protects those liberties that are "so rooted in the traditions and conscience of our people as to be ranked as fundamental." Snyder v. Massachusetts, 291 U.S. 97, 105. * * *

This Court, in a series of decisions, has held that the Fourteenth Amendment absorbs and applies to the States those specifics of the first eight amendments which express fundamental personal rights. The language and history of the Ninth Amendment reveal that the Framers of the Constitution believed that there are additional fundamental rights, protected from governmental infringement, which exist alongside those fundamental rights specifically mentioned in the first eight constitutional amendments.

The Ninth Amendment reads, "The enumeration in the Constitution, of certain rights, shall not be construed to deny or disparage others retained by the people." * * * It was proffered to quiet expressed fears that a bill of specifically enumerated rights could not be sufficiently broad to cover all essential rights and that the specific mention of certain rights would be interpreted as a denial that others were protected.

In presenting the proposed Amendment, Madison said:

"It has been objected also against a bill of rights, that, by enumerating particular exceptions to the grant of power, it would disparage those rights which were not placed in that enumeration; and it might follow by implication, that those rights which were not singled out, were intended to be assigned into the hands of the General Government, and were consequently insecure. This is one of the most plausible arguments I have ever heard urged against the admission of a bill of rights into this system; but, I conceive, that it may be guarded against. I have attempted it, as gentlemen may see by turning to the last clause of the fourth resolution [the Ninth Amendment]." I Annals of Congress 439 (Gales and Seaton ed. 1834).

These statements of Madison and Story make clear that the Framers did not intend that the first eight amendments be construed to exhaust the basic and fundamental rights which the Constitution guaranteed to the people.

I agree fully with the Court that, applying these tests, the right of privacy is a fundamental personal right, emanating "from the totality of the constitutional scheme under which we live." Id., at 521. Mr. Justice Brandeis, dissenting in Olmstead v. United States, 277 U.S. 438, 478, comprehensively summarized the principles underlying the Constitution's guarantees of privacy:

"The protection guaranteed by the [Fourth and Fifth] Amendments is much broader in scope. The makers of our Constitution undertook to secure conditions favorable to the pursuit of happiness. They recognized the significance of man's spiritual nature, of his feelings and of his intellect. They knew that only a part of the pain, pleasure and satisfactions of life are to be found in material things. They sought to protect Americans in their beliefs, their thoughts, their emotions and their sensations. They conferred, as against the Government, the right to be let alone—the most comprehensive of rights and the right most valued by civilized men."

The Connecticut statutes here involved deal with a particularly important and sensitive area of privacy—that of the marital relation and the marital home. * * * In sum, I believe that the right of privacy in the marital relation is fundamental and basic—a personal right "retained by the people" within the meaning of the Ninth Amendment. Connecticut cannot constitutionally abridge this fundamental right, which is protected by the Fourteenth Amendment from infringement by the States. I agree with the Court that petitioners' convictions must therefore be reversed.

MR. JUSTICE HARLAN, concurring in the judgment.

I fully agree with the judgment of reversal, but find myself unable to join the Court's opinion. The reason is that it seems to me to evince an approach to this case very much like that taken by my Brothers Black and Stewart in dissent, namely: the Due Process Clause of the Fourteenth Amendment does not touch this Connecticut statute unless the enactment is found to violate some right assured by the letter or penumbra of the Bill of Rights.

In other words, what I find implicit in the Court's opinion is that the "incorporation" doctrine may be used to restrict the reach of Fourteenth Amendment Due Process. For me this is just as unacceptable constitutional doctrine as is the use of the "incorporation" approach to impose upon the States all the requirements of the Bill of Rights as found in the provisions of the first eight amendments and in the decisions of this Court interpreting them.

In my view, the proper constitutional inquiry in this case is whether this Connecticut statute infringes the Due Process Clause of the Fourteenth Amendment because the enactment violates basic values "implicit in the concept of ordered liberty," Palko v. Connecticut, 302 U.S. 319, 325. For reasons stated at length in my dissenting opinion in Poe v. Ullman, supra, I believe that it does. While the relevant inquiry may be aided by resort to one or more of the provisions of the Bill of Rights, it is not dependent on them or any of their radiations. The Due Process Clause of the Fourteenth Amendment stands, in my opinion, on its own bottom.

MR. JUSTICE BLACK, with whom MR. JUSTICE STEWART joins, dissenting.

I agree with my Brother Stewart's dissenting opinion. And like him I do not to any extent whatever base my view that this Connecticut law is constitutional on a belief that the law is wise or that its policy is a good one. In order that there may be no room at all to doubt why I vote as I do, I feel constrained to add that the law is every bit as offensive to me as it is to my Brethren of the majority and my Brothers Harlan, White and Goldberg who, reciting reasons why it is offensive to them, hold it unconstitutional. There is no single one of the graphic and eloquent strictures and criticisms fired at the policy of this Connecticut law either by the Court's opinion or by those of my concurring Brethren to which I cannot subscribe—except their conclusion that the evil qualities they see in the law make it unconstitutional.

Had the doctor defendant here, or even the nondoctor defendant, been convicted for doing nothing more than expressing opinions to persons coming to the clinic that certain contraceptive devices, medicines or practices would do them good and would be desirable, or for telling people how devices could be used, I can think of no reasons at this time why their expressions of views would not be protected by the First and Fourteenth Amendments, which guarantee freedom of speech. But speech is one thing; conduct and physical activities are quite another. The two defendants here were active participants in an organization which gave physical examinations to women, advised them what kind of contraceptive devices or medicines would most likely be satisfactory for them, and then supplied the devices themselves, all for a graduated scale of fees, based on the family income. Thus these defendants admittedly engaged with others in a planned course of conduct to help people violate the Connecticut law. Merely because some speech was used in carrying on that conduct—just as in ordinary life some speech accompanies most kinds of conduct—we are not in my view justified in holding that the First Amendment forbids the State to punish their conduct. Strongly as I desire to protect all First Amendment freedoms, I am unable to stretch the Amendment so as to afford protection to the conduct of these defendants in violating the Connecticut law. What would be the constitutional fate of the law if hereafter applied to punish nothing but speech is, as I have said, quite another matter.

The Court talks about a constitutional "right of privacy" as though there is some constitutional provision or provisions forbidding any law ever to be passed which might abridge the "privacy" of individuals. But there is not. There are, of course, guarantees in certain specific constitutional provisions which are designed in part to protect privacy at certain times and places with respect to certain activities. Such, for example, is the Fourth Amendment's guarantee against "unreasonable searches and seizures." But I think it belittles that Amendment to talk about it as though it protects nothing but "privacy." To treat it that way is to give it a niggardly interpretation, not the kind of liberal reading I think any Bill of Rights provision should be given. The average man would very likely not have his feelings soothed any more by having his property seized openly than by having it seized privately and by stealth. He simply wants his property left alone. And a person can be just as much, if not more, irritated, annoyed and injured by an unceremonious public arrest by a policeman as he is by a seizure in the privacy of his office or home. * * *

I realize that many good and able men have eloquently spoken and written, sometimes in rhapsodical strains, about the duty of this Court to keep the Constitution in tune with the times. The idea is that the Constitution must be changed from time to time and that this Court is charged with a duty to make those changes. For myself, I must with all deference reject that philosophy. The Constitution makers knew the need for change and provided for it. Amendments suggested by the people's elected representatives can be submitted to the people or their selected agents for ratification. That method of change was good for our Fathers, and being somewhat old-fashioned I must add it is good enough for me. And so, I cannot rely on the Due Process Clause or the Ninth Amendment or any mysterious and uncertain natural law concept as a reason for striking down this state law. The Due Process Clause with an "arbitrary and capricious" or "shocking to the conscience" formula was liberally used by this Court to strike down economic legislation in the early decades of this century, threatening, many people thought, the tranquility and stability of the Nation. See, e. g., Lochner v. New York, 198 U.S. 45. That formula, based on subjective considerations of "natural justice," is no less dangerous when used to enforce this Court's views about personal rights than those about economic rights. I had thought that we had laid that formula, as a means for striking down state legislation, to rest once and for all. * * *

So far as I am concerned, Connecticut's law as applied here is not forbidden by any provision of the Federal Constitution as that Constitution was written, and I would therefore affirm.

Mr. Justice Stewart, whom Mr. Justice Black joins, dissenting.

Since 1879 Connecticut has had on its books a law which forbids the use of contraceptives by anyone. I think this is an uncommonly silly law. As a practical matter, the law is obviously unenforceable, except in the oblique context of the present case. As a philosophical matter, I believe the use of contraceptives in the relationship of marriage should be left to personal and private choice, based upon each individual's moral, ethical, and religious beliefs. As a matter of social policy, I think professional counsel about methods of birth control should be available to all, so that each individual's choice can be meaningfully made. But we are not asked in this case to say whether we think this law is unwise, or even asinine. We are asked to hold that it violates the United States Constitution. And that I cannot do.

In the course of its opinion the Court refers to no less than six Amendments to the Constitution: the First, the Third, the Fourth, the Fifth, the Ninth, and the Fourteenth. But the Court does not say which of these Amendments, if any, it thinks is infringed by this Connecticut law.

We are told that the Due Process Clause of the Fourteenth Amendment is not, as such, the "guide" in this case. With that much I agree. [A]s the Court says, the day has long passed since the Due Process Clause was regarded as a proper instrument for determining "the wisdom, need, and propriety" of state laws. My Brothers Harlan and White to the contrary, "we have returned to the original constitutional proposition that courts do not substitute their social and economic beliefs for the judgment of legislative bodies, who are elected to pass laws." Ferguson v. Skrupa, supra, at 730.

As to the First, Third, Fourth, and Fifth Amendments, I can find nothing in any of them to invalidate this Connecticut law, even assuming that all those Amendments are fully applicable against the States. It has not even been argued that this is a law "respecting an establishment of religion, or prohibiting the free exercise thereof." And surely, unless the solemn process of constitutional adjudication is to descend to the level of a play on words, there is not involved here any abridgment of "the freedom of speech, or of the press; or the right of the people peaceably to assemble, and to petition the Government for a redress of grievances." No soldier has been quartered in any house. There has been no search, and no seizure. Nobody has been compelled to be a witness against himself.

The Court also quotes the Ninth Amendment, and my Brother Goldberg's concurring opinion relies heavily upon it. But to say that the

Ninth Amendment has anything to do with this case is to turn somersaults with history. The Ninth Amendment, like its companion the Tenth, which this Court held "states but a truism that all is retained which has not been surrendered," United States v. Darby, 312 U.S. 100, 124, was framed by James Madison and adopted by the States simply to make clear that the adoption of the Bill of Rights did not alter the plan that the Federal Government was to be a government of express and limited powers, and that all rights and powers not delegated to it were retained by the people and the individual States. Until today no member of this Court has ever suggested that the Ninth Amendment meant anything else, and the idea that a federal court could ever use the Ninth Amendment to annul a law passed by the elected representatives of the people of the State of Connecticut would have caused James Madison no little wonder.

What provision of the Constitution, then, does make this state law invalid? The Court says it is the right of privacy "created by several fundamental constitutional guarantees." With all deference, I can find no such general right of privacy in the Bill of Rights, in any other part of the Constitution, or in any case ever before decided by this Court.[1]

At the oral argument in this case we were told that the Connecticut law does not "conform to current community standards." But it is not the function of this Court to decide cases on the basis of community standards. We are here to decide cases "agreeably to the Constitution and laws of the United States." It is the essence of judicial duty to subordinate our own personal views, our own ideas of what legislation is wise and what is not. If, as I should surely hope, the law before us does not reflect the standards of the people of Connecticut, the people of Connecticut can freely exercise their true Ninth and Tenth Amendment rights to persuade their elected representatives to repeal it. That is the constitutional way to take this law off the books.

Notes and Questions

1. What is the difference between the right to privacy and notions of freedom or autonomy?

2. The Griswold opinion was novel in two respects—the topic that received constitutional protection and the methodology used by Justice Douglas in finding constitutional protection. The methodology received most initial scholarly scrutiny, not all of it critical. See Charles Black, Structure and Relationship in Constitutional Law (1965).

3. What areas of behavior are covered by the liberty interests recognized in Griswold? Only whether to conceive a child? If so, then married couples could always avoid pregnancy by abstaining from sexual intercourse. So striking down state prohibition of contraception must be based on a substantive right to decide to have sexual relations without risking pregnancy. Is this right best regarded as a right to privacy in matters concerning

---

1. The Court does not say how far the new constitutional right of privacy announced today extends. I suppose, however, that even after today a State can constitutionally still punish at least some offenses which are not committed in public.

sexual relations and reproduction or a right to autonomy in making such decisions?

4. What aspects of sex and reproduction argue for allocation of power to individuals or married couples rather than governments? What is the government's interest in such matters? How important are decisions about sexual behavior and reproduction to individuals and married couples?

5. Can rights be conferred to married couples or must they be conferred individuals in a marriage? Are Griswold rights to decide about sex and reproduction also found in individuals who are not married? See Eisenstadt v. Baird, 405 U.S. 438 (1971). If governments can prohibit sexual intercourse to unmarried individuals, can't they also deny them access to contraceptives which could only be used in criminal activity? But what is the state interest in regulating the sexual behavior of unmarried adults? How would Professor Hart and Lord Devlin address that question? Even if it is proper to forbid sex to the unmarried, would that justify state efforts to forbid contraception?

6. If sexual autonomy is recognized in individuals, whether single or married, what limits can the state place on sexual behavior? Can heterosexual sodomy be prohibited (genital contacts with anal and oral cavities)? Homosexual sodomy? Sex with minors?

7. If the state cannot prohibit the use of contraceptive devices, what about efforts to terminate pregnancies once conception has occurred? See Roe v. Wade, 410 U.S. 113 (1973). What would Professor Hart and Lord Devlin say about this?

BOWERS v. HARDWICK

Supreme Court of the United States, 1986.
478 U.S. 186.

JUSTICE WHITE delivered the opinion of the Court.

In August 1982, respondent Hardwick (hereafter respondent) was charged with violating the Georgia statute criminalizing sodomy[2] by committing that act with another adult male in the bedroom of respondent's home. After a preliminary hearing, the District Attorney decided not to present the matter to the grand jury unless further evidence developed.

Respondent then brought suit in the Federal District Court, challenging the constitutionality of the statute insofar as it criminalized consensual sodomy.[3] He asserted that he was a practicing homosexual,

---

2. Georgia Code Ann. § 16–6–2 (1984) provides, in pertinent part, as follows:

"(a) A person commits the offense of sodomy when he performs or submits to any sexual act involving the sex organs of one person and the mouth or anus of another. . . .

"(b) A person convicted of the offense of sodomy shall be punished by imprisonment for not less than one nor more than 20 years. . . . "

3. John and Mary Doe were also plaintiffs in the action. They alleged that they wished to engage in sexual activity proscribed by § 16–6–2 in the privacy of their home, App. 3, and that they had been "chilled and deterred" from engaging in such activity by both the existence of the statute and Hardwick's arrest. Id., at 5. The District Court held, however, that because they had neither sustained, nor were in immediate danger of sustaining, any di-

that the Georgia sodomy statute, as administered by the defendants, placed him in imminent danger of arrest, and that the statute for several reasons violates the Federal Constitution. The District Court granted the defendants' motion to dismiss for failure to state a claim.

A divided panel of the Court of Appeals for the Eleventh Circuit reversed. [The court held] that the Georgia statute violated respondent's fundamental rights because his homosexual activity is a private and intimate association that is beyond the reach of state regulation by reason of the Ninth Amendment and the Due Process Clause of the Fourteenth Amendment. The case was remanded for trial, at which, to prevail, the State would have to prove that the statute is supported by a compelling interest and is the most narrowly drawn means of achieving that end.

Because other Courts of Appeals have arrived at judgments contrary to that of the Eleventh Circuit in this case, we granted the Attorney General's petition for certiorari questioning the holding that the sodomy statute violates the fundamental rights of homosexuals. We agree with petitioner that the Court of Appeals erred, and hence reverse its judgment.

This case does not require a judgment on whether laws against sodomy between consenting adults in general, or between homosexuals in particular, are wise or desirable. It raises no question about the right or propriety of state legislative decisions to repeal their laws that criminalize homosexual sodomy, or of state-court decisions invalidating those laws on state constitutional grounds. The issue presented is whether the Federal Constitution confers a fundamental right upon homosexuals to engage in sodomy and hence invalidates the laws of the many States that still make such conduct illegal and have done so for a very long time. The case also calls for some judgment about the limits of the Court's role in carrying out its constitutional mandate.

We first register our disagreement with the Court of Appeals and with respondent that the Court's prior cases have construed the Constitution to confer a right of privacy that extends to homosexual sodomy and for all intents and purposes have decided this case. The reach of this line of cases was sketched in Carey v. Population Services International, 431 U.S. 678, 685 (1977). Pierce v. Society of Sisters, 268 U.S. 510 (1925), and Meyer v. Nebraska, 262 U.S. 390 (1923), were described as dealing with child rearing and education; Prince v. Massachusetts, 321 U.S. 158 (1944), with family relationships; Skinner v. Oklahoma ex rel. Williamson, 316 U.S. 535 (1942), with procreation; Loving v. Virginia,

rect injury from the enforcement of the statute, they did not have proper standing to maintain the action. *Id.*, at 18. The Court of Appeals affirmed the District Court's judgment dismissing the Does' claim for lack of standing, 760 F.2d 1202, 1206–1207 (CA11 1985), and the Does do not challenge that holding in this Court.

The only claim properly before the Court, therefore, is Hardwick's challenge to the Georgia statute as applied to consensual homosexual sodomy. We express no opinion on the constitutionality of the Georgia statute as applied to other acts of sodomy.

388 U.S. 1 (1967), with marriage; Griswold v. Connecticut, supra, and Eisenstadt v. Baird, supra, with contraception; and Roe v. Wade, 410 U.S. 113 (1973), with abortion. The latter three cases were interpreted as construing the Due Process Clause of the Fourteenth Amendment to confer a fundamental individual right to decide whether or not to beget or bear a child. Carey v. Population Services International, supra, at 688–689.

Accepting the decisions in these cases and the above description of them, we think it evident that none of the rights announced in those cases bears any resemblance to the claimed constitutional right of homosexuals to engage in acts of sodomy that is asserted in this case. No connection between family, marriage, or procreation on the one hand and homosexual activity on the other has been demonstrated, either by the Court of Appeals or by respondent. Moreover, any claim that these cases nevertheless stand for the proposition that any kind of private sexual conduct between consenting adults is constitutionally insulated from state proscription is unsupportable. Indeed, the Court's opinion in Carey twice asserted that the privacy right, which the Griswold line of cases found to be one of the protections provided by the Due Process Clause, did not reach so far. 431 U.S., at 688, n. 5, 694, n. 17.

Precedent aside, however, respondent would have us announce, as the Court of Appeals did, a fundamental right to engage in homosexual sodomy. This we are quite unwilling to do. It is true that despite the language of the Due Process Clauses of the Fifth and Fourteenth Amendments, which appears to focus only on the processes by which life, liberty, or property is taken, the cases are legion in which those Clauses have been interpreted to have substantive content, subsuming rights that to a great extent are immune from federal or state regulation or proscription. Among such cases are those recognizing rights that have little or no textual support in the constitutional language. Meyer, Prince, and Pierce fall in this category, as do the privacy cases from Griswold to Carey.

Striving to assure itself and the public that announcing rights not readily identifiable in the Constitution's text involves much more than the imposition of the Justices' own choice of values on the States and the Federal Government, the Court has sought to identify the nature of the rights qualifying for heightened judicial protection. In Palko v. Connecticut, 302 U.S. 319, 325, 326 (1937), it was said that this category includes those fundamental liberties that are "implicit in the concept of ordered liberty," such that "neither liberty nor justice would exist if [they] were sacrificed." A different description of fundamental liberties appeared in Moore v. East Cleveland, 431 U.S. 494, 503 (1977) (opinion of POWELL, J.), where they are characterized as those liberties that are "deeply rooted in this Nation's history and tradition." Id., at 503 (POWELL, J.). See also Griswold v. Connecticut, 381 U.S., at 506.

It is obvious to us that neither of these formulations would extend a fundamental right to homosexuals to engage in acts of consensual sodomy. Proscriptions against that conduct have ancient roots. Sodomy was a criminal offense at common law and was forbidden by the laws of the original 13 States when they ratified the Bill of Rights. In 1868, when the Fourteenth Amendment was ratified, all but 5 of the 37 States in the Union had criminal sodomy laws. In fact, until 1961, all 50 States outlawed sodomy, and today, 24 States and the District of Columbia continue to provide criminal penalties for sodomy performed in private and between consenting adults. Against this background, to claim that a right to engage in such conduct is "deeply rooted in this Nation's history and tradition" or "implicit in the concept of ordered liberty" is, at best, facetious.

Nor are we inclined to take a more expansive view of our authority to discover new fundamental rights imbedded in the Due Process Clause. The Court is most vulnerable and comes nearest to illegitimacy when it deals with judge-made constitutional law having little or no cognizable roots in the language or design of the Constitution. That this is so was painfully demonstrated by the face-off between the Executive and the Court in the 1930's, which resulted in the repudiation of much of the substantive gloss that the Court had placed on the Due Process Clauses of the Fifth and Fourteenth Amendments. There should be, therefore, great resistance to expand the substantive reach of those Clauses, particularly if it requires redefining the category of rights deemed to be fundamental. Otherwise, the Judiciary necessarily takes to itself further authority to govern the country without express constitutional authority. The claimed right pressed on us today falls far short of overcoming this resistance.

Respondent, however, asserts that the result should be different where the homosexual conduct occurs in the privacy of the home. He relies on Stanley v. Georgia, 394 U.S. 557 (1969), where the Court held that the First Amendment prevents conviction for possessing and reading obscene material in the privacy of one's home: "If the First Amendment means anything, it means that a State has no business telling a man, sitting alone in his house, what books he may read or what films he may watch." Id., at 565.

Stanley did protect conduct that would not have been protected outside the home, and it partially prevented the enforcement of state obscenity laws; but the decision was firmly grounded in the First Amendment. The right pressed upon us here has no similar support in the text of the Constitution, and it does not qualify for recognition under the prevailing principles for construing the Fourteenth Amendment. Its limits are also difficult to discern. Plainly enough, otherwise illegal conduct is not always immunized whenever it occurs in the home. Victimless crimes, such as the possession and use of illegal drugs, do not escape the law where they are committed at home. Stanley itself recognized that its holding offered no protection for the possession in the home of drugs, firearms, or stolen goods. Id., at 568, n. 11. And if respondent's submission is limited to the voluntary sexual conduct between consenting adults, it would be difficult, except by fiat, to limit the claimed right to homosexual conduct while leaving exposed to prosecution adultery, incest, and other sexual crimes even though they are committed in the home. We are unwilling to start down that road.

Even if the conduct at issue here is not a fundamental right, respondent asserts that there must be a rational basis for the law and that there is none in this case other than the presumed belief of a majority of the electorate in Georgia that homosexual sodomy is immoral and unacceptable. This is said to be an inadequate rationale to support the law. The law, however, is constantly based on notions of morality, and if all laws representing essentially moral choices are to be invalidated under the Due Process Clause, the courts will be very busy indeed. Even respondent makes no such claim, but insists that majority sentiments about the morality of homosexuality should be declared inadequate. We do not agree, and are unpersuaded that the sodomy laws of some 25 States should be invalidated on this basis.

Accordingly, the judgment of the Court of Appeals is

Reversed.

CHIEF JUSTICE BURGER, concurring.

I join the Court's opinion, but I write separately to underscore my view that in constitutional terms there is no such thing as a fundamental right to commit homosexual sodomy.

As the Court notes, ante, at 192, the proscriptions against sodomy have very "ancient roots." Decisions of individuals relating to homosexual conduct have been subject to state intervention throughout the history of Western civilization. Condemnation of those practices is firmly rooted in Judeao–Christian moral and ethical standards. Homosexual sodomy was a capital crime under Roman law. See Code Theod. 9.7.6; Code Just. 9.9.31. See also D. Bailey, Homosexuality and the Western Christian Tradition 70–81 (1975). During the English Reformation when powers of the ecclesiastical courts were transferred to the King's Courts, the first English statute criminalizing sodomy was passed. 25 Hen. VIII, ch. 6. Blackstone described "the infamous crime against nature" as an offense of "deeper malignity" than rape, a heinous act "the very mention of which is a disgrace to human nature," and "a crime not fit to be named." 4 W. Blackstone, Commentaries *215. The common law of England, including its prohibition of sodomy, became the received law of Georgia and the other Colonies. In 1816 the Georgia Legislature passed the statute at issue here, and that statute has been continuously in force in one form or another since that time. To hold that the act of homosexual sodomy is somehow protected as a fundamental right would be to cast aside millennia of moral teaching.

This is essentially not a question of personal "preferences" but rather of the legislative authority of the State. I find nothing in the Constitution depriving a State of the power to enact the statute challenged here.

JUSTICE POWELL, concurring.

I join the opinion of the Court. I agree with the Court that there is no fundamental right—i. e., no substantive right under the Due Process Clause—such as that claimed by respondent Hardwick, and found to exist by the Court of Appeals. This is not to suggest, however, that respondent may not be protected by the Eighth Amendment of the Constitution. The Georgia statute at issue in this case, Ga. Code Ann. § 16–6–2 (1984), authorizes a court to imprison a person for up to 20 years for a single private, consensual act of sodomy. In my view, a prison sentence for such conduct—certainly a sentence of long duration—would create a serious Eighth Amendment issue. Under the Georgia statute a single act of sodomy, even in the private setting of a home, is a felony comparable in terms of the possible sentence imposed to serious felonies such as aggravated battery, § 16–5–24, first-degree arson, § 16–7–60, and robbery, § 16–8–40.[4]

In this case, however, respondent has not been tried, much less convicted and sentenced.[5] Moreover, respondent has not raised the Eighth Amendment issue below. For these reasons this constitutional argument is not before us.

JUSTICE BLACKMUN, with whom JUSTICE BRENNAN, JUSTICE MARSHALL, and JUSTICE STEVENS join, dissenting.

This case is no more about "a fundamental right to engage in homosexual sodomy," as the Court purports to declare, ante, at 191, than Stanley v. Georgia, 394 U.S. 557 (1969), was about a fundamental right to watch obscene movies, or Katz v. United States, 389 U.S. 347

---

4. Among those States that continue to make sodomy a crime, Georgia authorizes one of the longest possible sentences. See Ala. Code § 13A–6–65(a)(3) (1982) (1-year maximum); Ariz. Rev. Stat. Ann. §§ 13–1411, 13–1412 (West Supp. 1985) (30 days); Ark. Stat. Ann. § 41–1813 (1977) (1-year maximum); D. C. Code § 22–3502 (1981) (10-year maximum); Fla. Stat. § 800.02 (1985) (60-day maximum); Ga. Code Ann. § 16–6–2 (1984) (1 to 20 years); Idaho Code § 18–6605 (1979) (5-year minimum); Kan. Stat. Ann. § 21–3505 (Supp. 1985) (6-month maximum); Ky. Rev. Stat. § 510.100 (1985) (90 days to 12 months); La. Rev. Stat. Ann. § 14:89 (West 1986) (5-year maximum); Md. Ann. Code, Art. 27, §§ 553–554 (1982) (10-year maximum); Mich. Comp. Laws § 750.158 (1968) (15-year maximum); Minn. Stat. § 609.293 (1984) (1-year maximum); Miss. Code Ann. § 97–29–59 (1973) (10-year maximum); Mo. Rev. Stat. § 566.090 (Supp. 1984) (1-year maximum); Mont. Code Ann. § 45–5–505 (1985) (10-year maximum); Nev. Rev. Stat. § 201.190 (1985) (6-year maximum); N. C. Gen. Stat. § 14–177 (1981) (10-year maximum); Okla. Stat., Tit. 21, § 886 (1981) (10-year maximum); R. I. Gen. Laws § 11–10–1 (1981) (7 to 20 years); S. C. Code § 16–15–120 (1985) (5-year maximum);

Tenn. Code Ann. § 39–2–612 (1982) (5 to 15 years); Tex. Penal Code Ann. § 21.06 (1974) ($200 maximum fine); Utah Code Ann. § 76–5–403 (1978) (6-month maximum); Va. Code § 18.2–361 (1982) (5-year maximum).

5. It was conceded at oral argument that, prior to the complaint against respondent Hardwick, there had been no reported decision involving prosecution for private homosexual sodomy under this statute for several decades. See Thompson v. Aldredge, 187 Ga. 467, 200 S. E. 799 (1939). Moreover, the State has declined to present the criminal charge against Hardwick to a grand jury, and this is a suit for declaratory judgment brought by respondents challenging the validity of the statute. The history of nonenforcement suggests the moribund character today of laws criminalizing this type of private, consensual conduct. Some 26 States have repealed similar statutes. But the constitutional validity of the Georgia statute was put in issue by respondents, and for the reasons stated by the Court, I cannot say that conduct condemned for hundreds of years has now become a fundamental right.

(1967), was about a fundamental right to place interstate bets from a telephone booth. Rather, this case is about "the most comprehensive of rights and the right most valued by civilized men," namely, "the right to be let alone." Olmstead v. United States, 277 U.S. 438, 478 (1928) (Brandeis, J., dissenting).

The statute at issue, Ga. Code Ann. § 16–6–2 (1984), denies individuals the right to decide for themselves whether to engage in particular forms of private, consensual sexual activity. The Court concludes that § 16–6–2 is valid essentially because "the laws of ... many States ... still make such conduct illegal and have done so for a very long time." Ante, at 190. But the fact that the moral judgments expressed by statutes like § 16–6–2 may be " 'natural and familiar ... ought not to conclude our judgment upon the question whether statutes embodying them conflict with the Constitution of the United States.' " Roe v. Wade, 410 U.S. 113, 117 (1973), quoting Lochner v. New York, 198 U.S. 45, 76 (1905) (Holmes, J., dissenting). Like Justice Holmes, I believe that "[it] is revolting to have no better reason for a rule of law than that so it was laid down in the time of Henry IV. It is still more revolting if the grounds upon which it was laid down have vanished long since, and the rule simply persists from blind imitation of the past." Holmes, The Path of the Law, 10 Harv. L. Rev. 457, 469 (1897). I believe we must analyze respondent Hardwick's claim in the light of the values that underlie the constitutional right to privacy. If that right means anything, it means that, before Georgia can prosecute its citizens for making choices about the most intimate aspects of their lives, it must do more than assert that the choice they have made is an " 'abominable crime not fit to be named among Christians.' " Herring v. State, 119 Ga. 709, 721, 46 S. E. 876, 882 (1904).

I

In its haste to reverse the Court of Appeals and hold that the Constitution does not "[confer] a fundamental right upon homosexuals to engage in sodomy," ante, at 190, the Court relegates the actual statute being challenged to a footnote and ignores the procedural posture of the case before it. A fair reading of the statute and of the complaint clearly reveals that the majority has distorted the question this case presents.

First, the Court's almost obsessive focus on homosexual activity is particularly hard to justify in light of the broad language Georgia has used. Unlike the Court, the Georgia Legislature has not proceeded on the assumption that homosexuals are so different from other citizens that their lives may be controlled in a way that would not be tolerated if it limited the choices of those other citizens. Rather, Georgia has provided that "[a] person commits the offense of sodomy when he performs or submits to any sexual act involving the sex organs of one person and the mouth or anus of another." Ga. Code Ann. § 16–6–2(a) (1984). The sex or status of the persons who engage in the act is irrelevant as a matter of state law. In fact, to the extent I can discern a legislative purpose for Georgia's 1968 enactment of § 16–6–2, that purpose seems to have been to broaden the coverage of the law to reach heterosexual as well as homosexual activity.[6] I therefore see no basis for the Court's decision to treat this case as an "as applied" challenge to § 16–6–2, or for Georgia's attempt, both in its brief and at oral argument, to defend § 16–6–2 solely on the grounds that it prohibits homosexual activity. Michael Hardwick's standing may rest in significant part on Georgia's apparent willingness to enforce against homosexuals a law it seems not to have any desire to enforce against heterosexuals. But his claim that § 16–6–2 involves an unconstitutional intrusion into his privacy and his right of intimate association does not depend in any way on his sexual orientation.

Second, I disagree with the Court's refusal to consider whether § 16–6–2 runs afoul of the Eighth or Ninth Amendments or the Equal Protection Clause of the Fourteenth Amendment. Respondent's complaint expressly invoked the Ninth Amendment, see App. 6, and he relied heavily before this Court on Griswold v. Connecticut, 381 U.S. 479, 484 (1965), which identifies that Amendment as one of the specific constitutional provisions giving "life and substance" to our understanding of privacy. More importantly, the procedural posture of the case requires that we affirm the Court of Appeals' judgment if there is any ground on which respondent may be entitled to relief. * * * Thus, even if respondent did not advance claims based on the Eighth or Ninth Amendments, or on the Equal Protection Clause, his complaint should not be dismissed if any of those provisions could entitle him to relief. I need not reach either the Eighth Amendment or the Equal Protection Clause issues because I believe that Hardwick has stated a cognizable claim that § 16–6–2 interferes with constitutionally protected interests in privacy and freedom of intimate association. But neither the Eighth Amendment nor the Equal Protection Clause is so clearly irrelevant that a claim resting on either provision should be peremptorily dismissed. The Court's cramped reading of the issue before it makes for a short opinion, but it does little to make for a persuasive one.

II

"Our cases long have recognized that the Constitution embodies a promise that a certain private sphere of individual liberty will be kept largely beyond the reach of government." Thornburgh v. American College of Obstetricians & Gynecologists, 476 U.S. 747, 772 (1986). In construing the right to privacy, the Court has proceeded along two

---

6. Until 1968, Georgia defined sodomy as "the carnal knowledge and connection against the order of nature, by man with man, or in the same unnatural manner with woman." Ga. Crim. Code § 26–5901 (1933). In Thompson v. Aldredge, 187 Ga. 467, 200 S. E. 799 (1939), the Georgia Supreme Court held that § 26–5901 did not prohibit lesbian activity. And in Riley v. Garrett, 219 Ga. 345, 133 S. E. 2d 367 (1963), the Georgia Supreme Court held that § 26–5901 did not prohibit heterosexual cunnilingus. Georgia passed the act-specific statute currently in force "perhaps in response to the restrictive court decisions such as Riley," Note, The Crimes Against Nature, 16 J. Pub. L. 159, 167, n. 47 (1967).

somewhat distinct, albeit complementary, lines. First, it has recognized a privacy interest with reference to certain decisions that are properly for the individual to make. Second, it has recognized a privacy interest with reference to certain places without regard for the particular activities in which the individuals who occupy them are engaged. The case before us implicates both the decisional and the spatial aspects of the right to privacy. * * *

III

The Court's failure to comprehend the magnitude of the liberty interests at stake in this case leads it to slight the question whether petitioner, on behalf of the State, has justified Georgia's infringement on these interests. I believe that neither of the two general justifications for § 16–6–2 that petitioner has advanced warrants dismissing respondent's challenge for failure to state a claim.

First, petitioner asserts that the acts made criminal by the statute may have serious adverse consequences for "the general public health and welfare," such as spreading communicable diseases or fostering other criminal activity. Brief for Petitioner 37. Inasmuch as this case was dismissed by the District Court on the pleadings, it is not surprising that the record before us is barren of any evidence to support petitioner's claim. In light of the state of the record, I see no justification for the Court's attempt to equate the private, consensual sexual activity at issue here with the "possession in the home of drugs, firearms, or stolen goods," ante, at 195, to which Stanley refused to extend its protection. 394 U.S., at 568, n. 11. None of the behavior so mentioned in Stanley can properly be viewed as "[victimless]," ante, at 195: drugs and weapons are inherently dangerous, and for property to be "stolen," someone must have been wrongfully deprived of it. Nothing in the record before the Court provides any justification for finding the activity forbidden by § 16–6–2 to be physically dangerous, either to the persons engaged in it or to others.[7]

The core of petitioner's defense of § 16–6–2, however, is that respondent and others who engage in the conduct prohibited by § 16–6–2

7. Although I do not think it necessary to decide today issues that are not even remotely before us, it does seem to me that a court could find simple, analytically sound distinctions between certain private, consensual sexual conduct, on the one hand, and adultery and incest (the only two vaguely specific "sexual crimes" to which the majority points, ante, at 196), on the other. For example, marriage, in addition to its spiritual aspects, is a civil contract that entitles the contracting parties to a variety of governmentally provided benefits. A State might define the contractual commitment necessary to become eligible for these benefits to include a commitment of fidelity and then punish individuals for breaching that contract. Moreover, a State might conclude that adultery is likely to injure third persons, in particular, spouses and children of persons who engage in extramarital affairs. With respect to incest, a court might well agree with respondent that the nature of familial relationships renders true consent to incestuous activity sufficiently problematical that a blanket prohibition of such activity is warranted. See Tr. of Oral Arg. 21–22. Notably, the Court makes no effort to explain why it has chosen to group private, consensual homosexual activity with adultery and incest rather than with private, consensual heterosexual activity by unmarried persons or, indeed, with oral or anal sex within marriage.

interfere with Georgia's exercise of the " 'right of the Nation and of the States to maintain a decent society,' " Paris Adult Theatre I v. Slaton, 413 U.S., at 59–60, quoting Jacobellis v. Ohio, 378 U.S. 184, 199 (1964) (Warren, C. J., dissenting). Essentially, petitioner argues, and the Court agrees, that the fact that the acts described in § 16–6–2 "for hundreds of years, if not thousands, have been uniformly condemned as immoral" is a sufficient reason to permit a State to ban them today. Brief for Petitioner 19; see ante, at 190, 192–194, 196.

I cannot agree that either the length of time a majority has held its convictions or the passions with which it defends them can withdraw legislation from this Court's scrutiny. As Justice Jackson wrote so eloquently for the Court in West Virginia Board of Education v. Barnette, 319 U.S. 624, 641–642 (1943), "we apply the limitations of the Constitution with no fear that freedom to be intellectually and spiritually diverse or even contrary will disintegrate the social organization.... [Freedom] to differ is not limited to things that do not matter much. That would be a mere shadow of freedom. The test of its substance is the right to differ as to things that touch the heart of the existing order." It is precisely because the issue raised by this case touches the heart of what makes individuals what they are that we should be especially sensitive to the rights of those whose choices upset the majority.

The assertion that "traditional Judeo–Christian values proscribe" the conduct involved, Brief for Petitioner 20, cannot provide an adequate justification for § 16–6–2. That certain, but by no means all, religious groups condemn the behavior at issue gives the State no license to impose their judgments on the entire citizenry. The legitimacy of secular legislation depends instead on whether the State can advance some justification for its law beyond its conformity to religious doctrine. Thus, far from buttressing his case, petitioner's invocation of Leviticus, Romans, St. Thomas Aquinas, and sodomy's heretical status during the Middle Ages undermines his suggestion that § 16–6–2 represents a legitimate use of secular coercive power. A State can no more punish private behavior because of religious intolerance than it can punish such behavior because of racial animus. "The Constitution cannot control such prejudices, but neither can it tolerate them. Private biases may be outside the reach of the law, but the law cannot, directly or indirectly, give them effect." Palmore v. Sidoti, 466 U.S. 429, 433 (1984). No matter how uncomfortable a certain group may make the majority of this Court, we have held that "[mere] public intolerance or animosity cannot constitutionally justify the deprivation of a person's physical liberty." O'Connor v. Donaldson, 422 U.S. 563, 575 (1975).

Nor can § 16–6–2 be justified as a "morally neutral" exercise of Georgia's power to "protect the public environment," Paris Adult Theatre I, 413 U.S., at 68–69. Certainly, some private behavior can affect the fabric of society as a whole. Reasonable people may differ about whether particular sexual acts are moral or immoral, but "we have ample evidence for believing that people will not abandon morality, will not think any better of murder, cruelty and dishonesty, merely because some private sexual practice which they abominate is not punished by the law." H. L. A. Hart, Immorality and Treason, reprinted in The Law as Literature 220, 225 (L. Blom–Cooper ed. 1961). Petitioner and the Court fail to see the difference between laws that protect public sensibilities and those that enforce private morality. Statutes banning public sexual activity are entirely consistent with protecting the individual's liberty interest in decisions concerning sexual relations: the same recognition that those decisions are intensely private which justifies protecting them from governmental interference can justify protecting individuals from unwilling exposure to the sexual activities of others. But the mere fact that intimate behavior may be punished when it takes place in public cannot dictate how States can regulate intimate behavior that occurs in intimate places.

IV

It took but three years for the Court to see the error in its analysis in Minersville School District v. Gobitis, 310 U.S. 586 (1940), and to recognize that the threat to national cohesion posed by a refusal to salute the flag was vastly outweighed by the threat to those same values posed by compelling such a salute. See West Virginia Board of Education v. Barnette, 319 U.S. 624 (1943). I can only hope that here, too, the Court soon will reconsider its analysis and conclude that depriving individuals of the right to choose for themselves how to conduct their intimate relationships poses a far greater threat to the values most deeply rooted in our Nation's history than tolerance of nonconformity could ever do. Because I think the Court today betrays those values, I dissent.

JUSTICE STEVENS, with whom JUSTICE BRENNAN and JUSTICE MARSHALL join, dissenting.

Like the statute that is challenged in this case, the rationale of the Court's opinion applies equally to the prohibited conduct regardless of whether the parties who engage in it are married or unmarried, or are of the same or different sexes. Sodomy was condemned as an odious and sinful type of behavior during the formative period of the common law. That condemnation was equally damning for heterosexual and homosexual sodomy. Moreover, it provided no special exemption for married couples. The license to cohabit and to produce legitimate offspring simply did not include any permission to engage in sexual conduct that was considered a "crime against nature."

The history of the Georgia statute before us clearly reveals this traditional prohibition of heterosexual, as well as homosexual, sodomy. Indeed, at one point in the 20th century, Georgia's law was construed to permit certain sexual conduct between homosexual women even though such conduct was prohibited between heterosexuals. The history of the statutes cited by the majority as proof for the proposition that sodomy is not constitutionally protected, similarly reveals a prohibition on heterosexual, as well as homosexual, sodomy.

Because the Georgia statute expresses the traditional view that sodomy is an immoral kind of conduct regardless of the identity of the persons who engage in it, I believe that a proper analysis of its constitutionality requires consideration of two questions: First, may a State totally prohibit the described conduct by means of a neutral law applying without exception to all persons subject to its jurisdiction? If not, may the State save the statute by announcing that it will only enforce the law against homosexuals? The two questions merit separate discussion.

I

Our prior cases make two propositions abundantly clear. First, the fact that the governing majority in a State has traditionally viewed a particular practice as immoral is not a sufficient reason for upholding a law prohibiting the practice; neither history nor tradition could save a law prohibiting miscegenation from constitutional attack. Second, individual decisions by married persons, concerning the intimacies of their physical relationship, even when not intended to produce offspring, are a form of "liberty" protected by the Due Process Clause of the Fourteenth Amendment. Griswold v. Connecticut, 381 U.S. 479 (1965). Moreover, this protection extends to intimate choices by unmarried as well as married persons. Carey v. Population Services International, 431 U.S. 678 (1977); Eisenstadt v. Baird, 405 U.S. 438 (1972).

In consideration of claims of this kind, the Court has emphasized the individual interest in privacy, but its decisions have actually been animated by an even more fundamental concern. As I wrote some years ago:

> "These cases do not deal with the individual's interest in protection from unwarranted public attention, comment, or exploitation. They deal, rather, with the individual's right to make certain unusually important decisions that will affect his own, or his family's, destiny. The Court has referred to such decisions as implicating 'basic values,' as being 'fundamental,' and as being dignified by history and tradition. The character of the Court's language in these cases brings to mind the origins of the American heritage of freedom—the abiding interest in individual liberty that makes certain state intrusions on the citizen's right to decide how he will live his own life intolerable. Guided by history, our tradition of respect for the dignity of individual choice in matters of conscience and the restraints implicit in the federal system, federal judges have accepted the responsibility for recognition and protection of these rights in appropriate cases." Fitzgerald v. Porter Memorial Hospital, 523 F.2d 716, 719–720 (CA7 1975) (footnotes omitted), cert. denied, 425 U.S. 916 (1976).

Society has every right to encourage its individual members to follow particular traditions in expressing affection for one another and in gratifying their personal desires. It, of course, may prohibit an individual from imposing his will on another to satisfy his own selfish interests. It also may prevent an individual from interfering with, or violating, a legally sanctioned and protected relationship, such as marriage. And it may explain the relative advantages and disadvantages of different forms of intimate expression. But when individual married couples are isolated from observation by others, the way in which they voluntarily choose to conduct their intimate relations is a matter for them—not the State—to decide. The essential "liberty" that animated the development of the law in cases like Griswold, Eisenstadt, and Carey surely embraces the right to engage in nonreproductive, sexual conduct that others may consider offensive or immoral.

Paradoxical as it may seem, our prior cases thus establish that a State may not prohibit sodomy within "the sacred precincts of marital bedrooms," Griswold, 381 U.S., at 485, or, indeed, between unmarried heterosexual adults. Eisenstadt, 405 U.S., at 453. In all events, it is perfectly clear that the State of Georgia may not totally prohibit the conduct proscribed by § 16–6–2 of the Georgia Criminal Code.

II

If the Georgia statute cannot be enforced as it is written—if the conduct it seeks to prohibit is a protected form of liberty for the vast majority of Georgia's citizens—the State must assume the burden of justifying a selective application of its law. Either the persons to whom Georgia seeks to apply its statute do not have the same interest in "liberty" that others have, or there must be a reason why the State may be permitted to apply a generally applicable law to certain persons that it does not apply to others.

The first possibility is plainly unacceptable. Although the meaning of the principle that "all men are created equal" is not always clear, it surely must mean that every free citizen has the same interest in "liberty" that the members of the majority share. From the standpoint of the individual, the homosexual and the heterosexual have the same interest in deciding how he will live his own life, and, more narrowly, how he will conduct himself in his personal and voluntary associations with his companions. State intrusion into the private conduct of either is equally burdensome.

The second possibility is similarly unacceptable. A policy of selective application must be supported by a neutral and legitimate interest— something more substantial than a habitual dislike for, or ignorance about, the disfavored group. Neither the State nor the Court has identified any such interest in this case. The Court has posited as a justification for the Georgia statute "the presumed belief of a majority of the electorate in Georgia that homosexual sodomy is immoral and unacceptable." Ante, at 196. But the Georgia electorate has expressed no such belief—instead, its representatives enacted a law that presumably reflects the belief that all sodomy is immoral and unacceptable. Unless the Court is prepared to conclude that such a law is constitutional, it may not rely on the work product of the Georgia Legislature to support its holding. For the Georgia statute does not single out homosexuals as a separate class meriting special disfavored treatment.

Nor, indeed, does the Georgia prosecutor even believe that all homosexuals who violate this statute should be punished. This conclusion is evident from the fact that the respondent in this very case has formally acknowledged in his complaint and in court that he has engaged, and intends to continue to engage, in the prohibited conduct, yet the State has elected not to process criminal charges against him. As JUSTICE POWELL points out, moreover, Georgia's prohibition on private, consensual sodomy has not been enforced for decades. The record of nonenforcement, in this case and in the last several decades, belies the Attorney General's representations about the importance of the State's selective application of its generally applicable law.

Both the Georgia statute and the Georgia prosecutor thus completely fail to provide the Court with any support for the conclusion that homosexual sodomy, simpliciter, is considered unacceptable conduct in that State, and that the burden of justifying a selective application of the generally applicable law has been met.

III

The Court orders the dismissal of respondent's complaint even though the State's statute prohibits all sodomy; even though that prohibition is concededly unconstitutional with respect to heterosexuals; and even though the State's post hoc explanations for selective application are belied by the State's own actions. At the very least, I think it clear at this early stage of the litigation that respondent has alleged a constitutional claim sufficient to withstand a motion to dismiss.

I respectfully dissent.

Notes

To understand more fully the real story behind the 5 to 4 opinions in *Bowers*, it is important to peek into the Justices' chambers and explore the relationship between the judges and their clerks. This is especially true in the case of Justice Powell, who changed his mind several times during the opinion-writing process and may have been influenced heavily by a clerk. The following chapter chronicles the history of the Bowers decision.

COURTING JUSTICE: GAY MEN AND LESBIANS v. THE SUPREME COURT

Joyce Murdoch and Deb Price (New York: Basic Books 2001).

A LONG, SECRET STRUGGLE OVER A "FRIVOLOUS" CASE

The decent, fundamentally good-hearted man who cast the decisive vote in Hardwick agonized over that ruling long after it was handed down. Publicly, Justice Powell played down the case's importance. Privately, he sought to make peace with his anti-gay vote by concocting new justifications for it. His post-ruling mental tug-of-war with himself began in August 1986 as he told the American Bar Association, "The case may not be as significant as press reports suggest." Sodomy laws are "moribund and rarely enforced," he claimed.

Three years after his 1987 retirement, Powell publicly confessed that he'd "probably made a mistake" in Hardwick. After Powell branded his vote a mistake, he told a Washington Post reporter, "So far as I'm concerned it's just part of my past and not very important. I don't supposed I've devoted half an hour" to thinking about it since the ruling.

An inch-thick legal-sized file that stayed in the retired justice's Supreme Court office after most of his court papers had been shipped to the Washington and Lee University law library puts the lie to Powell's claims. Powell's extensive, handwritten notes and post-retirement memos reveal that he kept rearguing the case with himself, kept fighting with Blackmun's dissent and counted the ruling among the court's most important privacy decisions.

Hardwick was among the cases the retired Powell reviewed most thoroughly in 1988 and 1989 before lecturing at the University of Virginia and Washington and Lee. Girding himself for a March 1988 seminar on due process, Powell wrote two memos, totaling 11 pages, analyzing the case. "I will be grilled as to how Hardwick can be reconciled with Roe v. Wade, and to a lesser extent with the City of East Cleveland [Powell's extended-family zoning decision]," Powell's first memo said. Powell reminded himself to ask law students: "What does 'sodomy' contribute to family life?"

Powell also had clerk Bob Werner produce a due process memo focused on Hardwick. Werner found some merit in White's majority decision but ultimately sided with the dissent—spurring Powell to respond "No." To Werner's repeated assertion that homosexual sodomy was victimless, Powell three times wrote "AIDS" in the margin—though the disease had not been among his reasons for siding with White. Powell wrote that the "sanctity of the home," family and history didn't support a sodomy-rights decision. When Werner declared "sexual intimacy ... is important to the development of the human personality," Powell, aghast, wrote "sodomy!?!!"

Powell's second memo concluded by citing the language in Harlan's classic Poe v. Ullman dissent that listed "homosexuality" among activities "the state forbids altogether."

Powell counted the times that Blackmun's dissent had irked him by mentioning "family" and "home." Beside its mention of "family life," Powell hostilely asked, "what family?" Powell saw "no limiting principle" in Blackmun's "right to be let alone." Next to Blackmun's eloquent statement about the threat posed by intolerance, Powell wrote "error" and "history is contrary."

In a handwritten outline of key points for his seminar, Powell showed a male and biblical bias by characterizing the court's contraceptive decisions as establishing a "right to beget." In reference to sodomy he wrote, "AIDS (blood transfusions). There are victims—innocent ones."

Yet in reviewing Chief Justice Burger's contention that knocking down sodomy laws would "cast aside millennia of moral teaching," Powell circled "moral" and put a question mark beside it. Powell wrote, "Not a question of morality w/ [with] me."

Nowhere in his class preparation notes does Powell conclude his Hardwick vote was an error. The closest he came was in a margin note on a copy of White's ruling. Powell said, "DC [district court] found no standing. I should have done this." That district court assessment, of course, had applied only to the married couple who had tried to join the case.

When Powell discussed Hardwick during his 1988–89 seminars, he didn't call his vote a mistake. However, on October 18, 1990—four years after Hardwick branded gay Americans second class—he told students at New York University's law school, "I think I probably made a mistake in that one." That almost unprecedented admission of error by a former justice was triggered, he said, by a question about "any decision I made I had doubts about in retrospect." The 83–year-old Powell was in Manhattan to deliver the school's annual James Madison lecture. Among the guests—invited because of her Powell connection—was a lesbian former clerk. With a pained laugh, she recalls feeling, "Too bad you didn't think of this years ago."

A few days after calling his vote a mistake, Powell inadvertently rubbed salt in gay Americans' wounds by saying, "That case was not a major case, and one of the reasons I voted the way I did was the case was a frivolous case" filed "just to see what the court would do."

Powell somewhat disingenuously explained his change of heart to *The National Law Journal* by saying, "When I had the opportunity to reread the opinions a few months later, I thought the dissent had the better of the arguments." Powell's explanation was misleading because his high-profile switch has effectively cast his vote in concrete months before Blackmun's dissent was even drafted. Blackmun never had a real chance to win Powell's support by making "the better of the arguments."

Later, in a letter to Tribe, Powell said, "I did think the case was frivolous as the Georgia statute had not been enforced since 1935. The court should not have granted *certiorari*." The damage done by *Hardwick*, of course, could not be undone by a flip-flopping retired justice's change of heart. "There are numerous people in America who wouldn't have gone to jail if Justice Powell had come to his enlightenment earlier," William B. Rubenstein pointed out while director of the ACLU's gay-rights project.

The Powell clerks most upset by Powell's *Hardwick* vote got little satisfaction from his saying that he'd been wrong. Rather, they say, it deepened their feelings of inadequacy because it meant that Powell must have been reachable, that his anti-gay vote had never been chiseled in stone. Three of Powell's four 1985–86 clerks—Cabell Chinnis, Ann Coughlin and William Stuntz—readily admit to nagging guilt feelings.

Gay-friendly liberal Ann Coughlin regrets having taken herself out of the running for handling *Hardwick*, which ended up in the hands of ideological conservative Michael Mosman. She says, "I didn't know why Bill or Cabell didn't end up being the clerk in charge of *Bowers v. Hardwick*, but I know why I didn't. It's because I thought there's no way I could talk about sex with [Powell].... I felt it would potentially backfire if I, as a woman, were to come forward and try to educate him.... When we think about these failures in our lives.... for me, the failure was to think, 'Well, I can't have an explicit conversation with him about sex.'"

William Stuntz, who had wanted Powell to find a way to disarm sodomy laws without proclaiming a new fundamental right, sees the *Hardwick* ruling as a "very sad result." He says,

> In one sense, Tribe blew it. The clerks blew it.... Had we given [Powell] the right argument the case would have come out differently. I don't think Tribe can be fairly blamed for that. I don't think we can be fairly blamed for that. We were 27–year-olds.... I feel guilty about it on some level, but I don't think we can fairly be blamed for fumbling around in the dark and not seizing on the right argument. Of course, Powell bears responsibility. It's his vote. But it's a job in which these decisions are made much more quickly than one might assume from reading the files.... He is juggling lots of things. He's a very old man. He's very tired. And I don't think he can be fairly blamed for what amounts to failure of judgment on his part.

The passage of time hasn't caused Mosman to feel guilty, he says. The uneasiness evident in his voice when he discusses the decision is, he explains, a result of the clumsy way the court grappled with sodomy. "Everybody—Blackmun, White and Burger's letter—they're all throwing around social science statistics and perceived wisdoms they're picking up who knows where. It's a crummy way to decide an issue. I think we were all just in there using bad tools to decide an important question," he contends.

In describing the struggle over Hardwick, Powell biographer John Jeffries Jr. wrote, "Never before had Powell faced an issue for which he was by instinct and experience so uniquely unprepared." Yet if Powell had never before faced sodomy and homosexuality, he had largely himself to blame. More than two dozen homosexual cases—some involving long prison terms for sodomy—had come before the court since he had taken his oath of office in early 1972. Actually reading the court documents filed in those cases would give anyone a fairly thorough understanding of how sodomy laws are used to stigmatize and legally discriminate against a whole class of Americans, including undeniably outstanding teachers and sailors. Powell left that reading to his clerks. Powell usually had as little as possible to do with those cases.

Though Powell had done his best to duck homosexual issues, he was, as his clerks were well aware, a compassionate man capable of understanding the human toll exacted by rigid attempts to control sexuality. Powell's steadfast support for abortion rights was partially grounded in a panicked phone call he'd received from his 19–year-old office boy while working in his Richmond law firm. The distraught teenager's pregnant lover had died as he tried to help her illegally abort her fetus. Not only was a woman dead because abortion was outlawed, Powell's young assistant could have been sent to prison.

Especially after Powell declared that he'd made a mistake in Hardwick, his long line of gay clerks was plagued by questions about whether one or more of them should have come out to him before his 1986 vote. Could they have made him better prepared to wrestle with Hardwick? Could they have helped him see that the human toll of sodomy laws?

Not surprisingly, Cabell Chinnis is the ex-clerk most bedeviled by unanswerable questions. "I wish I knew why he changed his vote because then maybe I would be able to say to myself, 'Cabell, anything else you could have done wouldn't have made a difference.' ... It's the not knowing that really kills you," Chinnis said before war-gaming a series of "what if" scenarios over lunch in 1998.

What if he or Coughlin had handled the case? What if he had invited Powell to lunch and come out to him? What if he had hosted a dinner in which, one by one, gay Powell clerks had risen and said, "Justice Powell, I am a homosexual. This is my partner. We've been together four years." Or, "Justice Powell, I'm a lesbian. I want to be judged on my work and my character not my sexual orientation. I don't want to have to live in fear."

What if Chinnis had done something overt and it had backfired? "I never thought of that," he gasped in horror. "I really think I would have wanted to slit my wrists."

Other ex-clerks also wonder what would have happened if they'd told the grandfatherly Powell they were gay. A clerk from the mid–1980s said, "It's hard to imagine having a conversation like that with your grandfather.... He's a great grandfather, but he was still a grandparent." A gay Powell clerk from the 1982–83 term said, "I wondered what I would have done if I had been clerking at the time [of Hardwick]. And in my best moments, I'd like to think I would have gone into the justice and said, 'Hey, justice—'. [Y]ou don't lobby judges. You know, you don't say, 'Hey, my mother owns a lot of Shell Oil Company.' ... On the other hand, if in fact having some experience with being gay ... would help the judge, maybe you would tell him."

A lesbian whose Powell clerkship preceded Hardwick remembers thinking at the time the case came up "that Ann Coughlin and Bill Stuntz were such good people and such decent people that the appeal on behalf of humanity was going to get made." She thought it wouldn't be necessary for gay clerks to out themselves. Powell's anti-gay vote shifted her perspective. She says, "Maybe it would have made a difference if all the gay clerks came out to him because I think some of us were his favorites. But on the other hand, that would have been such an inappropriate thing to do. You just can't do that—try to direct somebody's decision in a pending case with information that is totally outside of the record and really should be irrelevant."

None of Powell's gay clerks ever came out to him, according to his administrative assistant Sally Smith, who kept tabs on virtually every interaction Powell had from 1962 until his death in 1999. A couple of years after Hardwick, Smith tried to talk to Powell about the fact that Cabell Chinnis was gay. "I saw it was not going anywhere. He was polite. He didn't tell me to shut up. It was just something he wouldn't deal with," she recalls.

Well into his retirement years, Powell told his lone clerk for that year that he didn't know that he'd ever had a gay clerk. The clerk, who happened to be gay, responded, "Considering the numbers, surely you have." Powell just chuckled. John Jeffries's 1994 Powell biography mentions that the justice had a gay clerk during *Hardwick's* term. Powell claimed never to have read the book, though his wife read portions aloud to him and Smith caught him peeking at it.

In 1995, Ronald Carr, a gay man who'd clerked for Powell in 1974–75, died of AIDS at 49. He was the first Powell clerk to die. Powell knew the cause of death but ignored it. "He just didn't want to face certain issues, and he didn't," Smith observes. Powell's court papers are archived at the Washington and Lee University law library in Lexington, Virginia. The library bulletin board includes announcements from the law school's gay student group. No one could attend law school at Powell's alma mater today and remain oblivious to gay people.

Though Powell labeled Hardwick "frivolous" because he'd been told sodomy laws weren't enforced, prosecutions continued. For example, a Georgia man was sentenced in 1988 to five years in prison for sodomy. James Moseley had successfully defended himself against a charge of raping his estranged wife by persuading the jury they had had consensual oral sex. He later said he hadn't realized he was admitting to criminal behavior. He had thought sodomy laws applied only to homosexuals. He served 18 months, and the conviction was used to deny him visitation rights to see his children.

Many gay-rights attorneys did their best to avoid the hostile Supreme Court after Hardwick. Focusing on state courts, state constitutions and state legislatures, they slowly chipped away at sodomy laws. In overturning Kentucky's same-sex sodomy law, that state's top court declared, "We need not sympathize, agree with or even understand the sexual preference of homosexuals in order to recognize their right to equal treatment before the bar of justice."

When Hardwick was handed down, 24 states, the District of Columbia and the military had sodomy laws. In 2000, they still existed in 18 states and the military. Gay-rights attorneys' most gratifying breakthrough came in 1998, when the Georgia Supreme Court struck down that state's notorious law. "We cannot think of any other activity that reasonable persons would rank as more private and more deserving of protection from governmental interference than consensual, private, adult sexual activity.... [S]uch activity is at the heart of the Georgia Constitution's protection of the right to privacy," Chief Justice Robert Benham declared, overturning the conviction of a man serving a five-year sentence for heterosexual sodomy in his own home.

Michael Hardwick didn't live to see his challenge to the Georgia law vindicated. He died of AIDS at his sister's home in Gainesville, Florida, on June 13, 1991. He was 37.

Notes and Questions

1. Moral disgust: Lord Devlin discusses the role of disgust in the debate over homosexuality, suggesting that "No society can do without intolerance, indignation, and disgust." (p. 17). Read the passage from his lecture on "Morals and the Criminal Law" attached, and react.

2. What if a minority feels disgust but not the majority? What do we do then? What if it is a larger minority than the homosexual population? Does that become a moral foundation for using the criminal law?

BARON PATRICK DEVLIN—MORALS AND THE CRIMINAL LAW

from *The Enforcement of Morals* (Oxford University Press, 1965).

I do not think that one can talk sensibly of a public and private morality any more than one can of a public or private highway. Morality is a sphere in which there is a public interest and a private interest, often in conflict, and the problem is to reconcile the two. This does not mean that it is impossible to put forward any general statements about how in our society the balance ought to be struck. Such statements cannot of their nature be rigid or precise; they would not be designed to circumscribe the operation of the lawmaking power but to guide those who have to apply it. While every decision which a court of law makes when it balances the public against the private interest is an ad hoc decision, the cases contain statements of principle to which the court should have regard when it reaches its decision. In the same way it is possible to make general statements of principle which it may be thought the legislature should bear in mind when it is considering the enactment of laws enforcing morals.

I believe that most people would agree upon the chief of these elastic principles. There must be toleration of the maximum individual freedom that is consistent with the integrity of society. It cannot be said that this is a principle that runs all through the criminal law. Much of the criminal law that is regulatory in character—the part of it that deals with *malum prohibitum* rather than *malum in se*—is based upon the opposite principle, that is, that the choice of the individual must give way to the convenience of the many. But in all matters of conscience the principle I have stated is generally held to prevail. It is not confined to thought and speech; it extends to action, as is shown by the recognition of the right to conscientious objection in war-time; this example shows also that conscience will be respected even in times of national danger. The principle appears to me to be peculiarly appropriate to all questions of morals. Nothing should be punished by the law that does not lie beyond the limits of tolerance. It is not nearly enough to say that a majority dislike a practice; there must be a real feeling of reprobation. Those who are dissatisfied with the present law on homosexuality often say that the opponents of reform are swayed simply by disgust. If that were so it would be wrong, but I do not think one can ignore disgust if it is deeply felt and not manufactured. Its presence is a good indication that the bounds of toleration are being reached. Not everything is to be tolerated. No society can do without intolerance, indignation, and disgust;[8] they are the forces behind the moral law, and indeed it can be argued that if they or something like them are not present, the feelings of society cannot be weighty enough to deprive the individual of freedom of choice. I suppose that there is hardly anyone nowadays who would not be disgusted by the thought of deliberate cruelty to animals. No one proposes to relegate that or any other form of sadism to the realm of private morality or to allow it to be practised in public or in private. It would be possible no doubt to point out that until a comparatively short while ago nobody thought very much of cruelty to animals and also that pity and kindliness and the unwillingness to inflict pain are virtues more generally esteemed now than they have ever been in the past. But matters of this sort are not determined by rational argument. Every moral judgement, unless it claims a divine source, is simply a feeling that no right-minded man could behave in any other way without admitting that he was doing wrong. It is the power of a common sense and not the power of reason that is behind the judgements of society. But before a society can put a practice beyond the limits of tolerance there must be a deliberate judgement that the practice is injurious to society. There is, for example, a general abhorrence of homosexuality. We should ask ourselves in the first instance whether, looking at it calmly and dispassionately, we regard it as a vice so abominable that its mere presence is an offence. If that is the genuine feeling of the society in which we live, I do not see how society can be denied the right to eradicate it. Our feeling may not be so intense as that. We may feel about it that, if confined, it is tolerable, but that if it spread it might be gravely injurious; it is in this way that most societies look upon fornication, seeing it as a natural weakness which must be kept within bounds but which cannot be rooted out. It becomes then a question of balance, the danger to society in one scale and the extent of the restriction in the other. On this sort of point the value of an investigation by such a body as the Wolfenden Committee and of its conclusions is manifest.

8. These words which have been much criticized, are considered again in the Preface at p. viii.

The limits of tolerance shift. This is supplementary to what I have been saying but of sufficient importance in itself to deserve statement as a separate principle which law-makers have to bear in mind. I suppose that moral standards do not shift; so far as they come from divine revelation they do not, and I am willing to assume that the moral judgements made by a society always remain good for that society. But the extent to which society will tolerate—I mean tolerate, not approve— departures from moral standards varies from generation to generation. It may be that over-all tolerance is always increasing. The pressure of the human mind, always seeking greater freedom of thought, is outwards against the bonds of society forcing their gradual relaxation. It may be that history is a tale of contraction and expansion and that all developed societies are on their way to dissolution. I must not speak of things I do not know; and anyway as a practical matter no society is willing to make provision for its own decay. I return therefore to the simple and observable fact that in matters of morals the limits of tolerance shift. Laws, especially those which are based on morals, are less easily moved. It follows as another good working principle that in any new matter of morals the law should be slow to act. By the next generation the swell of indignation may have abated and the law be left without the strong backing which it needs. But it is then difficult to alter the law without giving the impression that moral judgement is being weakened. This is now one of the factors that is strongly militating against any alteration to the law on homosexuality.

A third elastic principle must be advanced more tentatively. It is that as far as possible privacy should be respected. This is not an idea that has ever been made explicit in the criminal law. Acts or words done or said in public or in private are all brought within its scope without distinction in principle. But there goes with this a strong reluctance on the part of judges and legislators to sanction invasions of privacy in the detection of crime. The police have no more right to trespass than the ordinary citizen has; there is no general right of search; to this extent an Englishman's home is still his castle. The Government is extremely careful in the exercise even of those powers which it claims to be undisputed. Telephone tapping and interference with the mails afford a good illustration of this. A Committee of three Privy Councillors who recently inquired into these activities found that the Home Secretary and his predecessors had already formulated strict rules governing the exercise of these powers and the Committee were able to recommend that they should be continued to be exercised substantially on the same terms. But they reported that the power was "regarded with general disfavour."

This indicates a general sentiment that the right to privacy is something to be put in the balance against the enforcement of the law. Ought the same sort of consideration to play any part in the formation of the law? Clearly only in a very limited number of cases. When the help of the law is invoked by an injured citizen, privacy must be irrelevant; the individual cannot ask that his right to privacy should be measured against injury criminally done to another. But when all who are involved in the deed are consenting parties and the injury is done to morals, the public interest in the moral order can be balanced against the claims of privacy. The restriction on police powers of investigation goes further than the affording of a parallel; it means that the detection of crime committed in private and when there is no complaint is bound to be rather haphazard and this is an additional reason for moderation. These considerations do not justify the exclusion of all private immorality from the scope of the law. I think that, as I have already suggested, the test of "private behaviour" should be substituted for "private morality" and the influence of the factor should be reduced from that of a definite limitation to that of a matter to be taken into account. Since the gravity of the crime is also a proper consideration, a distinction might well be made in the case of homosexuality between the lesser acts of indecency and the full offence, which on the principles of the Wolfenden Report it would be illogical to do.

B. A NEW RIGHT

LAWRENCE v. TEXAS

Supreme Court of the United States, 2003.
539 U.S. 558.

JUSTICE KENNEDY delivered the opinion of the Court.

Liberty protects the person from unwarranted government intrusions into a dwelling or other private places. In our tradition the State is not omnipresent in the home. And there are other spheres of our lives and existence, outside the home, where the State should not be a dominant presence. Freedom extends beyond spatial bounds. Liberty presumes an autonomy of self that includes freedom of thought, belief, expression, and certain intimate conduct. The instant case involves liberty of the person both in its spatial and more transcendent dimensions.

I

The question before the Court is the validity of a Texas statute making it a crime for two persons of the same sex to engage in certain intimate sexual conduct.

In Houston, Texas, officers of the Harris County Police Department were dispatched to a private residence in response to a reported weapons disturbance. They entered an apartment where one of the petitioners, John Geddes Lawrence, resided. The right of the police to enter does not seem to have been questioned. The officers observed Lawrence and another man, Tyron Garner, engaging in a sexual act. The two petitioners were arrested, held in custody over night, and charged and convicted before a Justice of the Peace.

The complaints described their crime as "deviate sexual intercourse, namely anal sex, with a member of the same sex (man)." The applicable state law is Tex. Penal Code Ann. § 21.06(a) (2003). It provides: "A person commits an offense if he engages in deviate sexual intercourse with another individual of the same sex." The statute defines "[d]eviate sexual intercourse" as follows:

"(A) any contact between any part of the genitals of one person and the mouth or anus of another person; or

"(B) the penetration of the genitals or the anus of another person with an object." § 21.01(1).

The petitioners exercised their right to a trial *de novo* in Harris County Criminal Court. They challenged the statute as a violation of the Equal Protection Clause of the Fourteenth Amendment and of a like provision of the Texas Constitution. Tex. Const., Art. 1, § 3a. Those contentions were rejected. The petitioners, having entered a plea of *nolo contendere*, were each fined $200 and assessed court costs of $141.25.

The Court of Appeals for the Texas Fourteenth District considered the petitioners' federal constitutional arguments under both the Equal Protection and Due Process Clauses of the Fourteenth Amendment. After hearing the case en banc the court, in a divided opinion, rejected the constitutional arguments and affirmed the convictions. The majority opinion indicates that the Court of Appeals considered our decision in *Bowers v. Hardwick*, 478 U.S. 186, 92 L. Ed. 2d 140, 106 S. Ct. 2841 (1986), to be controlling on the federal due process aspect of the case. *Bowers* then being authoritative, this was proper.

We granted certiorari to consider three questions:

"1. Whether Petitioners' criminal convictions under the Texas Homosexual Conduct" law—which criminalizes sexual intimacy by same-sex couples, but not identical behavior by different-sex couples—violate the Fourteenth Amendment guarantee of equal protection of laws?

"2. Whether Petitioners' criminal convictions for adult consensual sexual intimacy in the home violate their vital interests in liberty and privacy protected by the Due Process Clause of the Fourteenth Amendment?

"3. Whether *Bowers v. Hardwick* should be overruled?"

The petitioners were adults at the time of the alleged offense. Their conduct was in private and consensual.

II

We conclude the case should be resolved by determining whether the petitioners were free as adults to engage in the private conduct in the exercise of their liberty under the Due Process Clause of the Fourteenth Amendment to the Constitution. For this inquiry we deem it necessary to reconsider the Court's holding in *Bowers*.

* * *

In *Griswold* the Court invalidated a state law prohibiting the use of drugs or devices of contraception and counseling or aiding and abetting the use of contraceptives. The Court described the protected interest as a right to privacy and placed emphasis on the marriage relation and the protected space of the marital bedroom.

After *Griswold* it was established that the right to make certain decisions regarding sexual conduct extends beyond the marital relationship. In *Eisenstadt* v. *Baird*, the Court invalidated a law prohibiting the distribution of contraceptives to unmarried persons. The case was decided under the Equal Protection Clause, *id.*, at 454; but with respect to unmarried persons, the Court went on to state the fundamental proposition that the law impaired the exercise of their personal rights.

* * *

The opinions in *Griswold* and *Eisenstadt* were part of the background for the decision in *Roe* v. *Wade*. As is well known, the case involved a challenge to the Texas law prohibiting abortions, but the laws of other States were affected as well. Although the Court held the woman's rights were not absolute, her right to elect an abortion did have real and substantial protection as an exercise of her liberty under the Due Process Clause. The Court cited cases that protect spatial freedom and cases that go well beyond it. *Roe* recognized the right of a woman to make certain fundamental decisions affecting her destiny and confirmed once more that the protection of liberty under the Due Process Clause has a substantive dimension of fundamental significance in defining the rights of the person.

In *Carey v. Population Services Int'l*, the Court confronted a New York law forbidding sale or distribution of contraceptive devices to persons under 16 years of age. Although there was no single opinion for the Court, the law was invalidated. Both *Eisenstadt* and *Carey*, as well as the holding and rationale in *Roe*, confirmed that the reasoning of *Griswold* could not be confined to the protection of rights of married adults. This was the state of the law with respect to some of the most relevant cases when the Court considered *Bowers v. Hardwick*.

The facts in *Bowers* had some similarities to the instant case. A police officer, whose right to enter seems not to have been in question, observed Hardwick, in his own bedroom, engaging in intimate sexual conduct with another adult male. The conduct was in violation of a Georgia statute making it a criminal offense to engage in sodomy. One difference between the two cases is that the Georgia statute prohibited the conduct whether or not the participants were of the same sex, while the Texas statute, as we have seen, applies only to participants of the same sex. Hardwick was not prosecuted, but he brought an action in federal court to declare the state statute invalid. He alleged he was a practicing homosexual and that the criminal prohibition violated rights guaranteed to him by the Constitution. The Court * * * sustained the Georgia law. * * *

The Court began its substantive discussion in *Bowers* as follows: "The issue presented is whether the Federal Constitution confers a fundamental right upon homosexuals to engage in sodomy and hence invalidates the laws of the many States that still make such conduct illegal and have done so for a very long time." *Id.*, at 190, 92 L.Ed.2d 140, 106 S.Ct. 2841. That statement, we now conclude, discloses the Court's own failure to appreciate the extent of the liberty at stake. To say that the issue in *Bowers* was simply the right to engage in certain sexual conduct demeans the claim the individual put forward, just as it would demean a married couple were it to be said marriage is simply about the right to have sexual intercourse. The laws involved in *Bowers* and here are, to be sure, statutes that purport to do no more than prohibit a particular sexual act. Their penalties and purposes, though, have more far-reaching consequences, touching upon the most private human conduct, sexual behavior, and in the most private of places, the home. The statutes do seek to control a personal relationship that, whether or not entitled to formal recognition in the law, is within the liberty of persons to choose without being punished as criminals.

This, as a general rule, should counsel against attempts by the State, or a court, to define the meaning of the relationship or to set its boundaries absent injury to a person or abuse of an institution the law protects. It suffices for us to acknowledge that adults may choose to enter upon this relationship in the confines of their homes and their own private lives and still retain their dignity as free persons. When sexuality finds overt expression in intimate conduct with another person, the conduct can be but one element in a personal bond that is more enduring. The liberty protected by the Constitution allows homosexual persons the right to make this choice.

Having misapprehended the claim of liberty there presented to it, and thus stating the claim to be whether there is a fundamental right to engage in consensual sodomy, the *Bowers* Court said: "Proscriptions against that conduct have ancient roots." *Id.*, at 192. * * *

At the outset it should be noted that there is no longstanding history in this country of laws directed at homosexual conduct as a distinct matter. Beginning in colonial times there were prohibitions of sodomy derived from the English criminal laws passed in the first instance by the Reformation Parliament of 1533. The English prohibition was understood to include relations between men and women as well as relations between men and men. Nineteenth-century commentators similarly read American sodomy, buggery, and crime-against-nature statutes as criminalizing certain relations between men and women and between men and men. The absence of legal prohibitions focusing on homosexual conduct may be explained in part by noting that according to some scholars the concept of the homosexual as a distinct category of person did not emerge until the late 19th century. Thus early American sodomy laws were not directed at homosexuals as such but instead sought to prohibit nonprocreative sexual activity more generally. This does not suggest approval of homosexual conduct. It does tend to show that this particular form of conduct was not thought of as a separate category from like conduct between heterosexual persons.

Laws prohibiting sodomy do not seem to have been enforced against consenting adults acting in private. * * * Instead * * *, 19th-century sodomy prosecutions typically involved relations between men and minor girls or minor boys, relations between adults involving force, relations between adults implicating disparity in status, or relations between men and animals.

To the extent that there were any prosecutions for the acts in question, 19th-century evidence rules imposed a burden that would make a conviction more difficult to obtain even taking into account the problems always inherent in prosecuting consensual acts committed in private. Under then-prevailing standards, a man could not be convicted of sodomy based upon testimony of a consenting partner, because the partner was considered an accomplice. A partner's testimony, however, was admissible if he or she had not consented to the act or was a minor, and therefore incapable of consent. See, *e.g.*, F. Wharton, Criminal Law 443 (2d ed. 1852); 1 F. Wharton, Criminal Law 512 (8th ed. 1880). The rule may explain in part the infrequency of these prosecutions. In all events that infrequency makes it difficult to say that society approved of a rigorous and systematic punishment of the consensual acts committed in private and by adults. The longstanding criminal prohibition of homosexual sodomy upon which the *Bowers* decision placed such reliance is as consistent with a general condemnation of nonprocreative sex as it is with an established tradition of prosecuting acts because of their homosexual character.

* * * [F]ar from possessing "ancient roots," *Bowers*, 478 U.S., at 192, American laws targeting same-sex couples did not develop until the last third of the 20th century. The reported decisions concerning the prosecution of consensual, homosexual sodomy between adults for the years 1880–1995 are not always clear in the details, but a significant number involved conduct in a public place.

It was not until the 1970's that any State singled out same-sex relations for criminal prosecution, and only nine States have done so. * * * Over the course of the last decades, States with same-sex prohibitions have moved toward abolishing them.

In summary, the historical grounds relied upon in *Bowers* are more complex than the majority opinion and the concurring opinion by Chief Justice Burger indicate. Their historical premises are not without doubt and, at the very least, are overstated.

It must be acknowledged, of course, that the Court in *Bowers* was making the broader point that for centuries there have been powerful voices to condemn homosexual conduct as immoral. The condemnation has been shaped by religious beliefs, conceptions of right and acceptable behavior, and respect for the traditional family. For many persons these are not trivial concerns but profound and deep convictions accepted as ethical and moral principles to which they aspire and which thus determine the course of their lives. These considerations do not answer the question before us, however. The issue is whether the majority may use the power of the State to enforce these views on the whole society through operation of the criminal law. * * *

[W]e think that our laws and traditions in the past half century are of most relevance here. These references show an emerging awareness that liberty gives substantial protection to adult persons in deciding how to conduct their private lives in matters pertaining to sex. "[H]istory and tradition are the starting point but not in all cases the ending point of the substantive due process inquiry."

This emerging recognition should have been apparent when *Bowers* was decided. In 1955 the American Law Institute promulgated the Model Penal Code and made clear that it did not recommend or provide for "criminal penalties for consensual sexual relations conducted in private." In *Bowers* the Court referred to the fact that before 1961 all 50 States had outlawed sodomy, and that at the time of the Court's decision 24 States and the District of Columbia had sodomy laws. Justice Powell pointed out that these prohibitions often were being ignored, however.

The sweeping references by Chief Justice Burger to the history of Western civilization and to Judeo–Christian moral and ethical standards did not take account of other authorities pointing in an opposite direction. A committee advising the British Parliament recommended in 1957 repeal of laws punishing homosexual conduct. The Wolfenden Report: Report of the Committee on Homosexual Offenses and Prostitution (1963). Parliament enacted the substance of those recommendations 10 years later. Sexual Offences Act 1967, § 1.

Of even more importance, almost five years before *Bowers* was decided the European Court of Human Rights considered a case with parallels to *Bowers* and to today's case. An adult male resident in Northern Ireland alleged he was a practicing homosexual who desired to engage in consensual homosexual conduct. The laws of Northern Ireland forbade him that right. He alleged that he had been questioned, his home had been searched, and he feared criminal prosecution. The court held that the laws proscribing the conduct were invalid under the European Convention on Human Rights. *Dudgeon v. United Kingdom*, 45 Eur. Ct. H. R. (1981) & ¶ 52. Authoritative in all countries that are members of the Council of Europe (21 nations then, 45 nations now), the decision is at odds with the premise in Bowers that the claim put forward was insubstantial in our Western civilization.

In our own constitutional system the deficiencies in *Bowers* became even more apparent in the years following its announcement. The 25 States with laws prohibiting the relevant conduct referenced in the *Bowers* decision are reduced now to 13, of which 4 enforce their laws only against homosexual conduct. In those States where sodomy is still proscribed, whether for same-sex or heterosexual conduct, there is a pattern of nonenforcement with respect to consenting adults acting in private. The State of Texas admitted in 1994 that as of that date it had not prosecuted anyone under those circumstances.

Two principal cases decided after *Bowers* cast its holding into even more doubt. In *Planned Parenthood of Southeastern Pa. v. Casey*, 505 U.S. 833, the Court reaffirmed the substantive force of the liberty protected by the Due Process Clause. The Casey decision again confirmed that our laws and tradition afford constitutional protection to personal decisions relating to marriage, procreation, contraception, family relationships, child rearing, and education. *Id.,* at 851. In explaining the respect the Constitution demands for the autonomy of the person in making these choices, we stated as follows:

> "These matters, involving the most intimate and personal choices a person may make in a lifetime, choices central to personal dignity and autonomy, are central to the liberty protected by the Fourteenth Amendment. At the heart of liberty is the right to define one's own concept of existence, of meaning, of the universe, and of the mystery of human life. Beliefs about these matters could not define the attributes of personhood were they formed under compulsion of the State." *Ibid*.

Persons in a homosexual relationship may seek autonomy for these purposes, just as heterosexual persons do. The decision in *Bowers* would deny them this right.

The second post-*Bowers* case of principal relevance is *Romer v. Evans*, 517 U.S. 620. There the Court struck down class-based legislation directed at homosexuals as a violation of the Equal Protection Clause. *Romer* invalidated an amendment to Colorado's constitution which named as a solitary class persons who were homosexuals, lesbians, or bisexual either by "orientation, conduct, practices or relationships," and deprived them of protection under state antidiscrimination laws. We concluded that the provision was "born of animosity toward the class of persons affected" and further that it had no rational relation to a legitimate governmental purpose. *Id.,* at 634.

As an alternative argument in this case, counsel for the petitioners and some *amici* contend that *Romer* provides the basis for declaring the Texas statute invalid under the Equal Protection Clause. That is a tenable argument, but we conclude the instant case requires us to address whether *Bowers* itself has continuing validity. Were we to hold the statute invalid under the Equal Protection Clause some might question whether a prohibition would be valid if drawn differently, say, to prohibit the conduct both between same-sex and different-sex participants.

* * * When homosexual conduct is made criminal by the law of the State, that declaration in and of itself is an invitation to subject homosexual persons to discrimination both in the public and in the private spheres. The central holding of *Bowers* has been brought in question by this case, and it should be addressed. Its continuance as precedent demeans the lives of homosexual persons.

The stigma this criminal statute imposes, moreover, is not trivial. The offense, to be sure, is but a class C misdemeanor, a minor offense in the Texas legal system. Still, it remains a criminal offense with all that imports for the dignity of the persons charged. The petitioners will bear on their record the history of their criminal convictions. Just this Term we rejected various challenges to state laws requiring the registration of sex offenders. We are advised that if Texas convicted an adult for private, consensual homosexual conduct under the statute here in question the convicted person would come within the registration laws of a least four States were he or she to be subject to their jurisdiction. This underscores the consequential nature of the punishment and the state-sponsored condemnation attendant to the criminal prohibition. Furthermore, the Texas criminal conviction carries with it the other collateral consequences always following a conviction, such as notations on job application forms, to mention but one example.

* * *

To the extent *Bowers* relied on values we share with a wider civilization, it should be noted that the reasoning and holding in *Bowers* have been rejected elsewhere. The European Court of Human Rights has followed not *Bowers* but its own decision in *Dudgeon v. United Kingdom*. Other nations, too, have taken action consistent with an affirmation of the protected right of homosexual adults to engage in intimate, consensual conduct. See Brief for Mary Robinson et al. as *Amici Curiae* 11–12. The right the petitioners seek in this case has been accepted as an integral part of human freedom in many other countries. There has been no showing that in this country the governmental interest in circumscribing personal choice is somehow more legitimate or urgent.

The doctrine of *stare decisis* is essential to the respect accorded to the judgments of the Court and to the stability of the law. It is not, however, an inexorable command. In *Casey* we noted that when a Court is asked to overrule a precedent recognizing a constitutional liberty interest, individual or societal reliance on the existence of that liberty cautions with particular strength against reversing course. The holding in *Bowers*, however, has not induced detrimental reliance comparable to some instances where recognized individual rights are involved. Indeed, there has been no individual or societal reliance on *Bowers* of the sort that could counsel against overturning its holding once there are compelling reasons to do so. *Bowers* itself causes uncertainty, for the precedents before and after its issuance contradict its central holding.

The rationale of *Bowers* does not withstand careful analysis. In his dissenting opinion in *Bowers* Justice Stevens came to these conclusions:

"Our prior cases make two propositions abundantly clear. First, the fact that the governing majority in a State has traditionally viewed a particular practice as immoral is not a sufficient reason for upholding a law prohibiting the practice; neither history nor tradition could save a law prohibiting miscegenation from constitutional attack. Second, individual decisions by married persons, concerning the intimacies of their physical relationship, even when not intended to produce offspring, are a form of "liberty" protected by the Due Process Clause of the Fourteenth Amendment. Moreover, this protection extends to intimate choices by unmarried as well as married persons." 478 U.S., at 216.

Justice Stevens' analysis, in our view, should have been controlling in *Bowers* and should control here.

Bowers was not correct when it was decided, and it is not correct today. It ought not to remain binding precedent. *Bowers v. Hardwick* should be and now is overruled.

The present case does not involve minors. It does not involve persons who might be injured or coerced or who are situated in relationships where consent might not easily be refused. It does not involve public conduct or prostitution. It does not involve whether the government must give formal recognition to any relationship that homosexual persons seek to enter. The case does involve two adults who, with full and mutual consent from each other, engaged in sexual practices common to a homosexual lifestyle. The petitioners are entitled to respect for their private lives. The State cannot demean their existence or control their destiny by making their private sexual conduct a crime. Their right to liberty under the Due Process Clause gives them the full right to engage in their conduct without intervention of the government. "It is a promise of the Constitution that there is a realm of personal liberty which the government may not enter." *Casey, supra*, at 847. The Texas statute furthers no legitimate state interest which can justify its intrusion into the personal and private life of the individual.

Had those who drew and ratified the Due Process Clauses of the Fifth Amendment or the Fourteenth Amendment known the components of liberty in its manifold possibilities, they might have been more specific. They did not presume to have this insight. They knew times can blind us to certain truths and later generations can see that laws once thought necessary and proper in fact serve only to oppress. As the Constitution endures, persons in every generation can invoke its principles in their own search for greater freedom.

The judgment of the Court of Appeals for the Texas Fourteenth District is reversed, and the case is remanded for further proceedings not inconsistent with this opinion.

It is so ordered.

Justice O'Connor, concurring in the judgment.

The Court today overrules *Bowers v. Hardwick*. I joined *Bowers*, and do not join the Court in overruling it. Nevertheless, I agree with the Court that Texas' statute banning same-sex sodomy is unconstitutional. Rather than relying on the substantive component of the Fourteenth Amendment's Due Process Clause, as the Court does, I base my conclusion on the Fourteenth Amendment's Equal Protection Clause.

The Equal Protection Clause of the Fourteenth Amendment "is essentially a direction that all persons similarly situated should be treated alike." *Cleburne v. Cleburne Living Center, Inc.*, 473 U.S. 432, 439. Under our rational basis standard of review, "legislation is presumed to be valid and will be sustained if the classification drawn by the statute is rationally related to a legitimate state interest." *Cleburne v. Cleburne Living Center, supra*, at 440.

Laws such as economic or tax legislation that are scrutinized under rational basis review normally pass constitutional muster, since "the Constitution presumes that even improvident decisions will eventually be rectified by the democratic processes." *Cleburne v. Cleburne Living Center, supra*, at 440. We have consistently held, however, that some objectives, such as "a bare ... desire to harm a politically unpopular group," are not legitimate state interests. *Department of Agriculture v. Moreno, supra*, at 534, 37 L.Ed.2d 782, 93 S.Ct. 2821. When a law exhibits such a desire to harm a politically unpopular group, we have applied a more searching form of rational basis review to strike down such laws under the Equal Protection Clause.

We have been most likely to apply rational basis review to hold a law unconstitutional under the Equal Protection Clause where, as here, the challenged legislation inhibits personal relationships. In *Department of Agriculture v. Moreno*, for example, we held that a law preventing those households containing an individual unrelated to any other member of the household from receiving food stamps violated equal protection because the purpose of the law was to " 'discriminate against hippies.' " In *Eisenstadt* v. *Baird*, we refused to sanction a law that discriminated between married and unmarried persons by prohibiting the distribution of contraceptives to single persons. Likewise, in *Cleburne v. Cleburne Living Center, supra*, we held that it was irrational for a State to require a home for the mentally disabled to obtain a special use permit when other residences—like fraternity houses and apartment buildings—did not have to obtain such a permit. And in *Romer v. Evans*, we disallowed a state statute that "impos[ed] a broad and undifferentiated disability on a single named group"—specifically, homosexuals. The dissent apparently agrees that if these cases have *stare decisis* effect, Texas' sodomy law would not pass scrutiny under the Equal Protection Clause, regardless of the type of rational basis review that we apply.

The statute at issue here makes sodomy a crime only if a person "engages in deviate sexual intercourse with another individual of the same sex." Tex. Penal Code Ann. § 21.06(a) (2003). Sodomy between opposite-sex partners, however, is not a crime in Texas. That is, Texas treats the same conduct differently based solely on the participants. Those harmed by this law are people who have a same-sex sexual orientation and thus are more likely to engage in behavior prohibited by § 21.06.

The Texas statute makes homosexuals unequal in the eyes of the law by making particular conduct—and only that conduct—subject to criminal sanction. It appears that prosecutions under Texas' sodomy law are rare. This case shows, however, that prosecutions under § 21.06 *do* occur. And while the penalty imposed on petitioners in this case was relatively minor, the consequences of conviction are not. As the Court notes, see *ante*, at 15, petitioners' convictions, if upheld, would disqualify them from or restrict their ability to engage in a variety of professions, including medicine, athletic training, and interior design. Indeed, were petitioners to move to one of four States, their convictions would require them to register as sex offenders to local law enforcement.

And the effect of Texas' sodomy law is not just limited to the threat of prosecution or consequence of conviction. Texas' sodomy law brands all homosexuals as criminals, thereby making it more difficult for homosexuals to be treated in the same manner as everyone else.

Texas attempts to justify its law, and the effects of the law, by arguing that the statute satisfies rational basis review because it furthers the legitimate governmental interest of the promotion of morality. In *Bowers*, we held that a state law criminalizing sodomy as applied to homosexual couples did not violate substantive due process. We rejected the argument that no rational basis existed to justify the law, pointing to the government's interest in promoting morality. The only question in front of the Court in *Bowers* was whether the substantive component of the Due Process Clause protected a right to engage in homosexual sodomy. *Bowers* did not hold that moral disapproval of a group is a rational basis under the Equal Protection Clause to criminalize homosexual sodomy when heterosexual sodomy is not punished.

This case raises a different issue than *Bowers*: whether, under the Equal Protection Clause, moral disapproval is a legitimate state interest to justify by itself a statute that bans homosexual sodomy, but not heterosexual sodomy. It is not. Moral disapproval of this group, like a bare desire to harm the group, is an interest that is insufficient to satisfy rational basis review under the Equal Protection Clause. Indeed, we have never held that moral disapproval, without any other asserted state interest, is a sufficient rationale under the Equal Protection Clause to justify a law that discriminates among groups of persons.* * *

Moral disapproval of a group cannot be a legitimate governmental interest under the Equal Protection Clause because legal classifications must not be "drawn for the purpose of disadvantaging the group burdened by the law." *Romer*, at 633. Texas' invocation of moral disapproval as a legitimate state interest proves nothing more than Texas' desire to criminalize homosexual sodomy. But the Equal Protection Clause prevents a State from creating "a classification of persons undertaken for its own sake." *Id.*, at 635. And because Texas so rarely enforces its sodomy law as applied to private, consensual acts, the law serves more as a statement of dislike and disapproval against homosexuals than as a tool to stop criminal behavior. The Texas sodomy law "raise[s] the inevitable inference that the disadvantage imposed is born of animosity toward the class of persons affected." *Id.*, at 634.

Texas argues, however, that the sodomy law does not discriminate against homosexual persons. Instead, the State maintains that the law discriminates only against homosexual conduct. While it is true that the law applies only to conduct, the conduct targeted by this law is conduct that is closely correlated with being homosexual. Under such circumstances, Texas' sodomy law is targeted at more than conduct. It is instead directed toward gay persons as a class.* * *

A State can of course assign certain consequences to a violation of its criminal law. But the State cannot single out one identifiable class of citizens for punishment that does not apply to everyone else, with moral disapproval as the only asserted state interest for the law. The Texas sodomy statute subjects homosexuals to "a lifelong penalty and stigma. A legislative classification that threatens the creation of an underclass ... cannot be reconciled with" the Equal Protection Clause. *Plyler v. Doe*, 457 U.S. at 239 (Powell, J., concurring).

* * *

That this law as applied to private, consensual conduct is unconstitutional under the Equal Protection Clause does not mean that other laws distinguishing between heterosexuals and homosexuals would similarly fail under rational basis review. Texas cannot assert any legitimate state interest here, such as national security or preserving the traditional institution of marriage. Unlike the moral disapproval of same-sex relations—the asserted state interest in this case—other reasons exist to promote the institution of marriage beyond mere moral disapproval of an excluded group.

A law branding one class of persons as criminal solely based on the State's moral disapproval of that class and the conduct associated with that class runs contrary to the values of the Constitution and the Equal Protection Clause, under any standard of review. I therefore concur in the Court's judgment that Texas' sodomy law banning "deviate sexual intercourse" between consenting adults of the same sex, but not between consenting adults of different sexes, is unconstitutional.

JUSTICE SCALIA, with whom THE CHIEF JUSTICE and JUSTICE THOMAS join, dissenting.

* * *

Most of * * * today's opinion has no relevance to its actual holding—that the Texas statute "furthers no legitimate state interest which can justify" its application to petitioners under rational-basis review. *Ante*, at 18 (overruling *Bowers* to the extent it sustained Georgia's anti-sodomy statute under the rational-basis test). Though there is discussion of "fundamental proposition[s]," and "fundamental decisions," nowhere does the Court's opinion declare that homosexual sodomy is a "fundamental right" under the Due Process Clause; nor does it subject the Texas law to the standard of review that would be appropriate (strict scrutiny) if homosexual sodomy were a "fundamental right." Thus, while overruling the *outcome* of *Bowers*, the Court leaves strangely untouched its central legal conclusion: "[R]espondent would have us announce . . . a fundamental right to engage in homosexual sodomy. This we are quite unwilling to do.". Instead the Court simply describes petitioners' conduct as "an exercise of their liberty"—which it undoubtedly is—and proceeds to apply an unheard-of form of rational-basis review that will have far-reaching implications beyond this case.

I

I begin with the Court's surprising readiness to reconsider a decision rendered a mere 17 years ago in *Bowers v. Hardwick.* I do not myself believe in rigid adherence to *stare decisis* in constitutional cases; but I do believe that we should be consistent rather than manipulative in invoking the doctrine. Today's opinions in support of reversal do not bother to distinguish—or indeed, even bother to mention—the paean to *stare decisis* coauthored by three Members of today's majority in *Planned Parenthood v. Casey.* There, when *stare decisis* meant preservation of judicially invented abortion rights, the widespread criticism of *Roe* was strong reason to *reaffirm* it. * * *

Today, however, the widespread opposition to *Bowers,* a decision resolving an issue as "intensely divisive" as the issue in *Roe,* is offered as a reason in favor of *overruling* it. * * *

Today's approach to *stare decisis* invites us to overrule an erroneously decided precedent (including an "intensely divisive" decision) *if:* (1) its foundations have been "eroded" by subsequent decisions, (2) it has been subject to "substantial and continuing" criticism, and (3) it has not induced "individual or societal reliance" that counsels against overturning. The problem is that *Roe* itself—which today's majority surely has no disposition to overrule—satisfies these conditions to at least the same degree as *Bowers.*

(1) * * *

I do not quarrel with the Court's claim that *Romer v. Evans,* 517 U.S. 620 "eroded" the "foundations" of *Bowers'* rational-basis holding. See *Romer, supra,* at 640–643 (*Scalia,* J., dissenting). But *Roe* and *Casey* have been equally "eroded" by *Washington v. Glucksberg,* 521 U.S. 702, 721 (1997), which held that only fundamental rights which are " 'deeply rooted in this Nation's history and tradition' " qualify for anything other than rational basis scrutiny under the doctrine of "substantive due process." *Roe* and *Casey,* of course, subjected the restriction of abortion to heightened scrutiny without even attempting to establish that the freedom to abort *was* rooted in this Nation's tradition.

(2) *Bowers,* the Court says, has been subject to "substantial and continuing [criticism], disapproving of its reasoning in all respects, not just as to its historical assumptions." * * * Of course, *Roe* too (and by extension *Casey*) had been (and still is) subject to unrelenting criticism. * * *

(3) That leaves, to distinguish the rock-solid, unamendable disposition of *Roe* from the readily overrulable *Bowers*, only the third factor. "[T]here has been," the Court says, "no individual or societal reliance on *Bowers* of the sort that could counsel against overturning its holding...." It seems to me that the "societal reliance" on the principles confirmed in *Bowers* and discarded today has been overwhelming. Countless judicial decisions and legislative enactments have relied on the ancient proposition that a governing majority's belief that certain sexual behavior is "immoral and unacceptable" constitutes a rational basis for regulation. * * * State laws against bigamy, same-sex marriage, adult incest, prostitution, masturbation, adultery, fornication, bestiality, and obscenity are * * * sustainable only in light of *Bowers'* validation of laws based on moral choices. Every single one of these laws is called into question by today's decision; the Court makes no effort to cabin the scope of its decision to exclude them from its holding. The impossibility of distinguishing homosexuality from other traditional "morals" offenses is precisely why *Bowers* rejected the rational-basis challenge. "The law," it said, "is constantly based on notions of morality, and if all laws representing essentially moral choices are to be invalidated under the Due Process Clause, the courts will be very busy indeed."

What a massive disruption of the current social order, therefore, the overruling of *Bowers* entails. Not so the overruling of *Roe*, which would simply have restored the regime that existed for centuries before 1973, in which the permissibility of and restrictions upon abortion were determined legislatively State-by-State. *Casey*, however, chose to base its *stare decisis* determination on a different "sort" of reliance. "[P]eople," it said, "have organized intimate relationships and made choices that define their views of themselves and their places in society, in reliance on the availability of abortion in the event that contraception should fail." 505 U.S., at 856. This falsely assumes that the consequence of overruling *Roe* would have been to make abortion unlawful. It would not; it would merely have *permitted* the States to do so. Many States would unquestionably have declined to prohibit abortion, and others would not have prohibited it within six months (after which the most significant reliance interests would have expired). Even for persons in States other than these, the choice would not have been between abortion and childbirth, but between abortion nearby and abortion in a neighboring State.

To tell the truth, it does not surprise me, and should surprise no one, that the Court has chosen today to revise the standards of *stare decisis* set forth in *Casey*. It has thereby exposed *Casey*'s extraordinary deference to precedent for the result-oriented expedient that it is.

II

Having decided that it need not adhere to *stare decisis*, the Court still must establish that *Bowers* was wrongly decided and that the Texas statute, as applied to petitioners, is unconstitutional.

Texas Penal Code Ann. § 21.06(a) (2003) undoubtedly imposes constraints on liberty. So do laws prohibiting prostitution, recreational use of heroin, and, for that matter, working more than 60 hours per week in a bakery. But there is no right to "liberty" under the Due Process Clause, though today's opinion repeatedly makes that claim. The Fourteenth Amendment *expressly allows* States to deprive their citizens of "liberty," *so long as "due process of law" is provided.* * * *

Our opinions applying the doctrine known as "substantive due process" hold that the Due Process Clause prohibits States from infringing *fundamental* liberty interests, unless the infringement is narrowly tailored to serve a compelling state interest. *Washington v. Glucksberg,* 521 U.S. At 721. We have held repeatedly, in cases the Court today does not overrule, that *only* fundamental rights qualify for this so-called "heightened scrutiny" protection—that is, rights which are " 'deeply rooted in this Nation's history and tradition,' " *ibid.* All other liberty interests may be abridged or abrogated pursuant to a validly enacted state law if that law is rationally related to a legitimate state interest.

Bowers held, first, that criminal prohibitions of homosexual sodomy are not subject to heightened scrutiny because they do not implicate a "fundamental right" under the Due Process Clause, 478 U.S., at 191–194. * * * *Bowers* concluded that a right to engage in homosexual sodomy was not " 'deeply rooted in this Nation's history and tradition,' " *id.,* at 192.

The Court today does not overrule this holding. Not once does it describe homosexual sodomy as a "fundamental right" or a "fundamental liberty interest," nor does it subject the Texas statute to strict scrutiny. Instead, having failed to establish that the right to homosexual sodomy is " 'deeply rooted in this Nation's history and tradition,' " the Court concludes that the application of Texas's statute to petitioners' conduct fails the rational-basis test, and overrules *Bowers'* holding to the contrary. * * *

I shall address that rational-basis holding presently. First, however, I address some aspersions that the Court casts upon *Bowers'* conclusion that homosexual sodomy is not a "fundamental right"—even though, as I have said, the Court does not have the boldness to reverse that conclusion.

III

The Court's description of "the state of the law" at the time of *Bowers* only confirms that Bowers was right. The Court points to *Griswold v. Connecticut,* 381 U.S. 479. But that case *expressly disclaimed* any reliance on the doctrine of "substantive due process," and grounded the so-called "right to privacy" in penumbras of constitutional provisions *other than* the Due Process Clause. *Eisenstadt v. Baird,* 405 U.S. 438, likewise had nothing to do with "substantive due process"; it invalidated a Massachusetts law prohibiting the distribution of contraceptives to unmarried persons solely on the basis of the Equal Protection

Clause. Of course *Eisenstadt* contains well known dictum relating to the "right to privacy," but this referred to the right recognized in *Griswold*—a right penumbral to the *specific* guarantees in the Bill of Rights, and not a "substantive due process" right.

Roe v. Wade recognized that the right to abort an unborn child was a "fundamental right" protected by the Due Process Clause. 410 US, at 155. The *Roe* Court, however, made no attempt to establish that this right was " 'deeply rooted in this Nation's history and tradition' "; instead, it based its conclusion that "the Fourteenth Amendment's concept of personal liberty . . . is broad enough to encompass a woman's decision whether or not to terminate her pregnancy" on its own normative judgment that anti-abortion laws were undesirable. See *id.,* at 153. We have since rejected *Roe's* holding that regulations of abortion must be narrowly tailored to serve a compelling state interest, see *Planned Parenthood v. Casey*, 505 U.S., at 876 (joint opinion of O'CONNOR, KENNEDY, and SOUTER, JJ.); id., at 951–953 (REHNQUIST, C. J., concurring in judgment in part and dissenting in part)—and thus, by logical implication, *Roe's* holding that the right to abort an unborn child is a "fundamental right."

After discussing the history of antisodomy laws, the Court proclaims that, "it should be noted that there is no longstanding history in this country of laws directed at homosexual conduct as a distinct matter." This observation in no way casts into doubt the "definitive [historical] conclusion," on which *Bowers* relied: that our Nation has a longstanding history of laws prohibiting *sodomy in general*—regardless of whether it was performed by same-sex or opposite-sex couples.* * *

It is (as *Bowers* recognized) entirely irrelevant whether the laws in our long national tradition criminalizing homosexual sodomy were "directed at homosexual conduct as a distinct matter." Whether homosexual sodomy was prohibited by a law targeted at same-sex sexual relations or by a more general law prohibiting both homosexual and heterosexual sodomy, the only relevant point is that it was criminalized—which suffices to establish that homosexual sodomy is not a right "deeply rooted in our Nation's history and tradition." The Court today agrees that homosexual sodomy was criminalized and thus does not dispute the facts on which *Bowers actually* relied.

Next the Court makes the claim, again unsupported by any citations, that "[l]aws prohibiting sodomy do not seem to have been enforced against consenting adults acting in private." The key qualifier here is "acting in private"—since the Court admits that sodomy laws *were* enforced against consenting adults (although the Court contends that prosecutions were "infrequent"). I do not know what "acting in private" means; surely consensual sodomy, like heterosexual intercourse, is rarely performed on stage. If all the Court means by "acting in private" is "on private premises, with the doors closed and windows covered," it is entirely unsurprising that evidence of enforcement would be hard to come by. (Imagine the circumstances that would enable a search warrant to be obtained for a residence on the ground that there was probable cause to believe that consensual sodomy was then and there occurring.) Surely that lack of evidence would not sustain the proposition that consensual sodomy on private premises with the doors closed and windows covered was regarded as a "fundamental right," even though all other consensual sodomy was criminalized. There are 203 prosecutions for consensual, adult homosexual sodomy reported in the West Reporting system and official state reporters from the years 1880–1995. See W. Eskridge, Gaylaw: Challenging the Apartheid of the Closet 375 (1999) (hereinafter Gaylaw). There are also records of 20 sodomy prosecutions and 4 executions during the colonial period. J. Katz, Gay/Lesbian Almanac 29, 58, 663 (1983). *Bowers'* conclusion that homosexual sodomy is not a fundamental right "deeply rooted in this Nation's history and tradition" is utterly unassailable.

Realizing that fact, the Court instead says: "[W]e think that our laws and traditions in the past half century are of most relevance here. These references show *an emerging awareness* that liberty gives substantial protection to adult persons in deciding how to conduct their private lives *in matters pertaining to sex*" (emphasis added). Apart from the fact that such an "emerging awareness" does not establish a "fundamental right," the statement is factually false. States continue to prosecute all sorts of crimes by adults "in matters pertaining to sex": prostitution, adult incest, adultery, obscenity, and child pornography. Sodomy laws, too, have been enforced "in the past half century," in which there have been 134 reported cases involving prosecutions for consensual, adult, homosexual sodomy. Gaylaw 375.* * *

In any event, an "emerging awareness" is by definition not "deeply rooted in this Nation's history and tradition[s]," as we have said "fundamental right" status requires. Constitutional entitlements do not spring into existence because some States choose to lessen or eliminate criminal sanctions on certain behavior. * * *

IV

I turn now to the ground on which the Court squarely rests its holding: the contention that there is no rational basis for the law here under attack. This proposition is so out of accord with our jurisprudence—indeed, with the jurisprudence of *any* society we know—that it requires little discussion.

The Texas statute undeniably seeks to further the belief of its citizens that certain forms of sexual behavior are "immoral and unacceptable," *Bowers, supra*, at 196—the same interest furthered by criminal laws against fornication, bigamy, adultery, adult incest, bestiality, and obscenity. *Bowers* held that this *was* a legitimate state interest. The Court today reaches the opposite conclusion. The Texas statute, it says, "furthers *no legitimate state interest* which can justify its intrusion into the personal and private life of the individual," (emphasis added). The Court embraces instead Justice Stevens' declaration in his *Bowers* dissent, that "the fact that the governing majority in a State has traditionally viewed a particular practice as immoral is not a sufficient reason for upholding a law prohibiting the practice." This effectively decrees the end of all morals legislation. If, as the Court asserts, the promotion of majoritarian sexual morality is not even a *legitimate* state interest, none of the above-mentioned laws can survive rational-basis review.

V

Finally, I turn to petitioners' equal-protection challenge, which no Member of the Court save *Justice O'Connor* embraces: On its face § 21.06(a) applies equally to all persons. Men and women, heterosexuals and homosexuals, are all subject to its prohibition of deviate sexual intercourse with someone of the same sex. To be sure, § 21.06 does distinguish between the sexes insofar as concerns the partner with whom the sexual acts are performed: men can violate the law only with other men, and women only with other women. But this cannot itself be a denial of equal protection, since it is precisely the same distinction regarding partner that is drawn in state laws prohibiting marriage with someone of the same sex while permitting marriage with someone of the opposite sex.

The objection is made, however, that the antimiscegenation laws invalidated in *Loving v. Virginia*, 388 U.S. 1, 8, similarly were applicable to whites and blacks alike, and only distinguished between the races insofar as the partner was concerned. In *Loving*, however, we correctly applied heightened scrutiny, rather than the usual rational-basis review, because the Virginia statute was "designed to maintain White Supremacy." *Id.*, at 6, 11. A racially discriminatory purpose is always sufficient to subject a law to strict scrutiny, even a facially neutral law that makes no mention of race. No purpose to discriminate against men or women as a class can be gleaned from the Texas law, so rational-basis review applies. That review is readily satisfied here by the same rational basis that satisfied it in *Bowers*—society's belief that certain forms of sexual behavior are "immoral and unacceptable," 478 U.S., at 196. This is the same justification that supports many other laws regulating sexual behavior that make a distinction based upon the identity of the partner—for example, laws against adultery, fornication, and adult incest, and laws refusing to recognize homosexual marriage.

Justice O'Connor argues that the discrimination in this law which must be justified is not its discrimination with regard to the sex of the partner but its discrimination with regard to the sexual proclivity of the principal actor. * * *

Of course the same could be said of any law. A law against public nudity targets "the conduct that is closely correlated with being a nudist," and hence "is targeted at more than conduct"; it is "directed toward nudists as a class." But be that as it may. Even if the Texas law *does* deny equal protection to "homosexuals as a class," that denial *still* does not need to be justified by anything more than a rational basis, which our cases show is satisfied by the enforcement of traditional notions of sexual morality.

Justice O'Connor simply decrees application of "a more searching form of rational basis review" to the Texas statute. The cases she cites do not recognize such a standard, and reach their conclusions only after finding, as required by conventional rational-basis analysis, that no conceivable legitimate state interest supports the classification at issue. Nor does *Justice O'Connor* explain precisely what her "more searching form" of rational-basis review consists of. It must at least mean, however, that laws exhibiting " 'a ... desire to harm a politically unpopular group,' " are invalid *even though* there may be a conceivable rational basis to support them.

This reasoning leaves on pretty shaky grounds state laws limiting marriage to opposite-sex couples. *Justice O'Connor* seeks to preserve them by the conclusory statement that "preserving the traditional institution of marriage" is a legitimate state interest. But "preserving the traditional institution of marriage" is just a kinder way of describing the State's *moral disapproval* of same-sex couples. Texas's interest in § 21.06 could be recast in similarly euphemistic terms: "preserving the traditional sexual mores of our society." In the jurisprudence *Justice O'Connor* has seemingly created, judges can validate laws by characterizing them as "preserving the traditions of society" (good); or invalidate them by characterizing them as "expressing moral disapproval" (bad).

      *   *   *

Today's opinion is the product of a Court, which is the product of a law-profession culture, that has largely signed on to the so-called homosexual agenda, by which I mean the agenda promoted by some homosexual activists directed at eliminating the moral opprobrium that has traditionally attached to homosexual conduct. * * *

One of the most revealing statements in today's opinion is the Court's grim warning that the criminalization of homosexual conduct is "an invitation to subject homosexual persons to discrimination both in the public and in the private spheres." It is clear from this that the Court has taken sides in the culture war, departing from its role of assuring, as neutral observer, that the democratic rules of engagement are observed. Many Americans do not want persons who openly engage in homosexual conduct as partners in their business, as scoutmasters for their children, as teachers in their children's schools, or as boarders in their home. They view this as protecting themselves and their families from a lifestyle that they believe to be immoral and destructive. The Court views it as "discrimination" which it is the function of our judgments to deter. So imbued is the Court with the law profession's anti-anti-homosexual culture, that it is seemingly unaware that the attitudes of that culture are not obviously "mainstream"; that in most States what the Court calls "discrimination" against those who engage in homosexual acts is perfectly legal; that proposals to ban such "discrimination" under Title VII have repeatedly been rejected by Congress, see Employment Non–Discrimination Act of 1994, S. 2238, 103d Cong., 2d Sess. (1994); Civil Rights Amendments, H. R. 5452, 94th Cong., 1st Sess. (1975); that in some cases such "discrimination" is *mandated* by federal statute, see 10 U. S. C. § 654(b)(1) (mandating discharge from the armed forces of any service member who engages in or intends to engage in homosexual acts); and that in some cases such "discrimination" is a constitutional right, see *Boy Scouts of America v. Dale*, 530 U.S. 640, 147 L.Ed.2d 554, 120 S.Ct. 2446 (2000).

Let me be clear that I have nothing against homosexuals, or any other group, promoting their agenda through normal democratic means. Social perceptions of sexual and other morality change over time, and every group has the right to persuade its fellow citizens that its view of such matters is the best. That homosexuals have achieved some success in that enterprise is attested to by the fact that Texas is one of the few remaining States that criminalize private, consensual homosexual acts. But persuading one's fellow citizens is one thing, and imposing one's views in absence of democratic majority will is something else. I would no more *require* a State to criminalize homosexual acts—or, for that matter, display any moral disapprobation of them—than I would *forbid* it to do so. What Texas has chosen to do is well within the range of traditional democratic action, and its hand should not be stayed through the invention of a brand-new "constitutional right" by a Court that is impatient of democratic change. It is indeed true that "later generations can see that laws once thought necessary and proper in fact serve only to oppress," and when that happens, later generations can repeal those laws. But it is the premise of our system that those judgments are to be made by the people, and not imposed by a governing caste that knows best.

One of the benefits of leaving regulation of this matter to the people rather than to the courts is that the people, unlike judges, need not carry things to their logical conclusion. The people may feel that their disapprobation of homosexual conduct is strong enough to disallow homosexual marriage, but not strong enough to criminalize private homosexual acts—and may legislate accordingly. The Court today pretends that it possesses a similar freedom of action, so that that we need not fear judicial imposition of homosexual marriage, as has recently occurred in Canada. At the end of its opinion—after having laid waste the foundations of our rational-basis jurisprudence—the Court says that the present case "does not involve whether the government must give formal recognition to any relationship that homosexual persons seek to enter." Do not believe it. More illuminating than this bald, unreasoned disclaimer is the progression of thought displayed by an earlier passage in the Court's opinion, which notes the constitutional protections afforded to "personal decisions relating to *marriage*, procreation, contraception, family relationships, child rearing, and education," and then declares that "[p]ersons in a homosexual relationship may seek autonomy for these purposes, just as heterosexual persons do." *Ante,* at 13 (emphasis added). Today's opinion dismantles the structure of constitutional law that has permitted a distinction to be made between heterosexual and homosexual unions, insofar as formal recognition in marriage is concerned. If moral disapprobation of homosexual conduct is "no legitimate state interest" for purposes of proscribing that conduct, and if, as the Court coos (casting aside all pretense of neutrality), "[w]hen sexuality finds overt expression in intimate conduct with another person, the conduct can be but one element in a personal bond that is more enduring,"; what justification could there possibly be for denying the benefits of marriage to homosexual couples exercising "[t]he liberty protected by the Constitution," *ibid.*? Surely not the encouragement of procreation, since the sterile and the elderly are allowed to marry. This case "does not involve" the issue of homosexual marriage only if one entertains the belief that principle and logic have nothing to do with the decisions of this Court. Many will hope that, as the Court comfortingly assures us, this is so.

The matters appropriate for this Court's resolution are only three: Texas's prohibition of sodomy neither infringes a "fundamental right" (which the Court does not dispute), nor is unsupported by a rational relation to what the Constitution considers a legitimate state interest, nor denies the equal protection of the laws. I dissent.

JUSTICE THOMAS, dissenting.

I join JUSTICE SCALIA's dissenting opinion. I write separately to note that the law before the Court today "is ... uncommonly silly." *Griswold v. Connecticut*, 381 U.S. 479, 527 (STEWART, J., dissenting). If I were a member of the Texas Legislature, I would vote to repeal it. Punishing someone for expressing his sexual preference through noncommercial consensual conduct with another adult does not appear to be a worthy way to expend valuable law enforcement resources.

Notwithstanding this, I recognize that as a member of this Court I am not empowered to help petitioners and others similarly situated. My duty, rather, is to "decide cases 'agreeably to the Constitution and laws of the United States.' " *Id.*, at 530. And, just like Justice Stewart, I "can find [neither in the Bill of Rights nor any other part of the Constitution a] general right of privacy," *ibid.*, or as the Court terms it today, the "liberty of the person both in its spatial and more transcendent dimensions."

Notes and Questions

1. Does Justice Kennedy consider a homosexual orientation to be a lifestyle choice or an aspect of personal identity more permanent? How important does Justice Kennedy believe the sexual relations of two homosexual adults are to them? How important to government?

2. Justice Scalia asserts:

"State laws against bigamy, same-sex marriage, adult incest, prostitution, masturbation, adultery, fornication, bestiality and obscenity are sustainable only in light of *Bowers'* validation of laws based on moral choices. Every single one of these laws is called into question by today's decision..."

Does *Lawrence* undermine state laws against masturbation? State laws against adultery? What about laws against gambling and cocaine use and possession?

3.   Justice White in *Bowers* and Justice Scalia dissenting in *Lawrence* assert that the issue is whether "homosexual sodomy" is a fundamental right. What other descriptive terms for the interests the parties seek to protect might be based on precedents such as *Griswold v. Connecticut* and *Eisenstadt v. Baird*?

4.   While the legislative trend all over the developed world was toward decriminalization of sodomy, the *Lawrence* decision imposed a rights-based prohibition on state regulation as a result of judicial action. What elements of the sexual conduct at issue here separate the personal interests at stake from decisions about alcohol and psychoactive drugs, from gambling, and from commercial sex?

C.   IN SEARCH OF MEANINGS AND LIMITS

CASS SUNSTEIN—WHAT DID LAWRENCE HOLD? OF AUTONOMY, DESUETUDE, SEXUALITY, AND MARRIAGE

2003 Supreme Court Review 27 (2004).

In 1900, Mr. Dooley famously said that "no matter whether th' constitution follows th' flag or not, th' supreme court follows th' ilection returns." The Court doesn't really do that. But members of the Supreme Court live in society, and they are inevitably influenced by what society appears to think. My principal suggestion here is that the Court's remarkable decision in *Lawrence v. Texas* represents judicial invalidation of a law that had become hopelessly out of touch with existing social convictions. So understood, *Lawrence,* like *Griswold,* reflects a distinctly American variation on the old English idea of desuetude. Put too simply, the basic idea is that when constitutionally important interests are at stake, due process principles requiring fair notice, and banning arbitrary action, are violated if criminal prosecution is brought on the basis of moral judgments lacking public support, as exemplified by exceedingly rare enforcement activity. On this reading, *Lawrence* had a great deal to do with procedural due process, rather than the clause's substantive sibling.

In *Griswold,* it will be recalled, the Court invalidated a Connecticut law forbidding married people to use contraceptives—a law that was ludicrously inconsistent with public convictions in Connecticut and throughout the nation. *Griswold* was decided in the midst of a substantial national rethinking of issues of sex and morality. Whatever the outcome of that rethinking, it was clear, by 1965, that reasonable people would no longer support bans on the use of contraceptives within marriage. In this respect, *Griswold* was quite similar to *Reed v. Reed.*

There the Court struck down an Idaho statute giving a preference to men over women in the administration of estates of decedents who had died intestate—a law that was unquestionably a holdover from views about sex roles that were widely regarded as obsolete. *Reed* was decided in the midst of a substantial rethinking of gender roles; whatever the outcome of that rethinking, it was clear, by 1971, that a flat presumption in favor of men over women in employment would no longer be acceptable in principle. *Lawrence* belongs in the same family. In the area of sexual orientation, America is in the midst of a civil rights revolution—one that has moved, in an extraordinarily short time, toward delegitimating prejudice against and hatred for homosexuals. *Lawrence* was made possible by that revolution, of which it is now a significant part.

In making this argument, my principal goal is not to evaluate *Lawrence*, but instead to obtain an understanding of its scope and of its relationship to other apparently dramatic decisions in the Court's past. But even if my argument is correct, it must be acknowledged that the Court's remarkably opaque opinion has three principal strands. Each of those strands supports a different understanding of the Court's holding and the principle that supports it.

1. *Autonomy.* A tempting reading of *Lawrence* is straightforward: *A criminal prohibition on sodomy is unconstitutional because it intrudes on private sexual conduct that does not harm third parties.* On this view, the Court has endorsed a quite general principle: *Without a compelling justification, the state cannot interfere with consensual sexual behavior, at least if that behavior is noncommercial.* On this view, consensual sexual behavior counts as a fundamental right for purposes of the Due Process Clause. The state is forbidden to intrude into the domain of consensual sexual behavior unless it can show that its intrusion is the least restrictive means of achieving a compelling state interest—a showing that will be impossible to make, at least most of the time.

2. *Rational basis.* An alternative reading of *Lawrence*, also quite broad, would take the Court to have held, not that sexual behavior counts as a fundamental right requiring compelling justification, but that *the criminal prohibition on sodomy is unconstitutional because it is not supported by a legitimate state interest.* The principle here is that *the government cannot interfere with consensual sexual behavior if it is attempting to do so for only moral reasons, unaccompanied by a risk of actual harm.* The implications of this reading are not so different from those of the first; both are strongly Millian in nature. But the two readings are nonetheless different, because the second depends not on the fundamental nature of the right to engage in sexual activity, but instead on the absence of even plausibly legitimate grounds for interfering with that right in the context of consensual sodomy. On this reading, *Lawrence* is rooted in an unusual form of "rational basis" review that would doom a great deal of legislation.

3. *Desuetude, American style.* A narrower reading of *Lawrence,* my emphasis here, would take the following form: *The criminal prohibition on sodomy is unconstitutional because it intrudes on private sexual conduct without having significant moral grounding in existing public commitments.* If this is the Court's holding, it is undergirded by a more general principle: *Without a strong justification, the state cannot bring the criminal law to bear on consensual sexual behavior if enforcement of the relevant law can no longer claim to have significant moral support in the enforcing state or the nation as a whole.* This aspect of the opinion is connected to the old idea of desuetude. It suggests that, at least in some circumstances, involving certain kinds of human interests, a criminal law cannot be enforced if it has lost public support.

It should be clear that while all three principles are potentially broad, the first and the second are the most far-reaching. And there is actually a fourth understanding of the opinion, one that cannot be characterized as the Court's holding, but one that is perhaps a subtext:

4. *Equality. Sodomy laws are unconstitutional because they demean the lives of gays and lesbians and thus offend the Constitution's equality principle.* The underlying principle is that at least as a general rule, *there is no legitimate basis for treating homosexuals differently from heterosexuals.* On this view, *Lawrence* is really a case about the social subordination of gays and lesbians, whatever the rhetoric about sexual freedom in general. *Lawrence's* words sound in due process, but much of its music involves equal protection.

Each of the four ideas can be found in *Lawrence,* a claim that I hope to establish here. But I want to draw special attention to the third, which is, I believe, central to the Court's own analysis, and a key to the development of substantive due process over the past decades. In fact something like a desuetude principle is part and parcel of the *Lawrence* Court's treatment of the state's interest, showing why that interest counts as inadequate, and also of the Court's explanation of why the case cannot be distinguished from *Griswold* and its successors. When the Court asserts the absence of a "legitimate state interest which can justify its intrusion into the personal and private life of an individual," it is best understood to be saying that the moral claim that underlies the intrusion has become hopelessly anachronistic. And the anachronistic nature of that moral claim has everything to do with the Court's rejection, not of moral claims in general, but of the particular moral claim that underlies criminal prohibitions on same-sex sodomy.

Lawrence might be read broadly as an effort to enact some version of John Stuart Mill's *On Liberty,* requiring respect for individual choices (at least with respect to sex) unless there is some kind of harm to others. But it is reasonable to understand the Court's decision more narrowly, as a ruling that forbids invocation of generally unenforced criminal law on the basis of a moral justification that has become anachronistic—at least when a constitutionally important interest is involved and when the absence of significant enforcement activity can be explained only by reference to the anachronistic nature of the relevant moral justification. This reading also helps clarify what made the decision possible and its fate. If I am correct, *Lawrence* was possible not because the Court reached, all on its own, an ambitious and novel view of the nature of constitutional liberty, or because it attempted to read a controversial view of autonomy into the Due Process Clause. The decision was possible only because of the ludicrously poor fit between the sodomy prohibition and the society in which the justices live. And if I am correct, *Lawrence* will have broad implications only if and to the extent that those broad implications receive general public support. For example, the Supreme Court may or may not read *Lawrence* to require states to recognize gay and lesbian marriages. But if and when it does so, it will be following public opinion, not leading it. Political and social change was a precondition for *Lawrence,* whose future reach will depend on the nature and extent of that change.

While I will spend most of my time on the Court's due process ruling, my own view is that the proper course in *Lawrence* was sketched by Justice O'Connor in her concurring opinion. Rather than invalidating the Texas statute on grounds of substantive due process, the Court should have invoked the Equal Protection Clause to strike down, as irrational, the state's decision to ban homosexual sodomy but not heterosexual sodomy. In important respects, this approach would have been more cautious than the Court's own. It would have had the large advantage of making it unnecessary to overrule any precedent. At the same time, an equal protection ruling would have recognized the fact, established by the Court's opinions, that the Equal Protection Clause does not build on long-standing traditions, but instead rejects them insofar as they attempt to devalue or humiliate certain social groups. The problem in *Lawrence* is not adequately understood without reference to the social subordination of gays and lesbians, not least through the use of the criminal law. Hence Justice O'Connor's approach suggests, lightly to be sure, the plausibility of rationale (4) above, a rationale that seems to me essentially correct. And if states are required to punish heterosexual sodomy if they are attempting to punish homosexual sodomy, I believe that it is quite implausible to think that any form of sodomy would be subject to criminal prosecution; political safeguards are far too strong to permit significant numbers of arrests and prosecutions of heterosexuals for engaging in conduct that is quite widespread.

For all these reasons, invalidation on equal protection grounds would have been preferable to the substantive due process route. But if the Due Process Clause is to be invoked, the idea of desuetude provides a method for understanding, disciplining, and narrowing what the Court did. This reading of *Lawrence* prevents the opinion from being a simple invocation of "liberty"; it also helps explain what made the *Lawrence* decision conceivable from a generally conservative Supreme Court. Best of all, it has considerable independent appeal.

THE COURT'S DILEMMA

The *Lawrence* Court had three options. It could have invalidated the Texas statute under the Equal Protection Clause. It could have invalidated the law on due process grounds. Or it could have upheld the law against both challenges. As we will see, the Court faced a serious difficulty in *Lawrence:* a majority believed, in my view correctly, that the Texas statute had to be invalidated—but any rationale for invalidation would inevitably raise serious doubts about practices, including the ban on same-sex marriages, that the majority did not want to question. For the majority, a central problem was to develop a rationale that would strike down the Texas statute without producing an unintended revolution in the law. Let us investigate the Court's options in light of preexisting law.

A. *Equal Protection*

1. *Heightened scrutiny.* The Equal Protection Clause might have been used to strike down the Texas statute under decisions calling for "heightened scrutiny" of laws that discriminate against traditionally disadvantaged groups. The paradigm examples of such groups are, of course, African–Americans and women. Perhaps laws discriminating against gays and lesbians should be subject to similarly skeptical judicial scrutiny. To say the least, the Court has not laid down a clear test for deciding when such scrutiny will be applied; instead it has pointed to a series of considerations, including a history of discrimination, a circumstance of immutability, and political powerlessness. Probably the best way of making sense of the doctrine is to say that heightened scrutiny is applied when the relevant discrimination is peculiarly likely to reflect prejudice and hostility rather than legitimate interests. In the context of race, for example, the problem is not that skin color is immutable, but that discrimination against African–Americans is usually based on illicit considerations; heightened scrutiny is a way of testing whether other, legitimate, public-spirited justifications can actually be brought forward in defense of the relevant law. In principle, discrimination against homosexuals can easily be understood in analogous terms. Suppose, for example, that a school forbids homosexuals from becoming teachers, In both cases, prejudice is especially likely to be at work. If heightened scrutiny were applied, a ban on same-sex sodomy would be extremely difficult to defend.

As a matter of precedent, the problem is that the Court has never suggested that gays and lesbians are entitled to heightened scrutiny. In fact it has been extremely reluctant to expand the class of groups so entitled—ruling, for example, that rational basis review applies to discrimination against handicapped people These are not decisive problems, to be sure; a ruling that required heightened scrutiny is not foreclosed by existing decisions. But such a ruling would certainly be an innovation.

An alternative route to heightened scrutiny would be to contend that discrimination against homosexuals *is* a kind of discrimination on the basis of sex. Here it might be suggested that if a law punishes same-sex sodomy, it is punishing people who would not be punished if their gender were different. But this view raises a number of complexities. It would also seem to have broad implications, essentially treating all discrimination against gays and lesbians as indistinguishable from, because literally identical to, discrimination against women.

2. *Rationality review.* When rational basis review is applied, statutes are almost always upheld under the Equal Protection Clause. But three cases provided a plausible backdrop for the plaintiffs' challenge in *Lawrence.* Taken together, the three cases suggest that a bare "desire to harm a politically unpopular group" is constitutionally unacceptable. Texas's prohibition of homosexual sodomy, not affecting heterosexual sodomy, could be challenged as reflecting such a bare desire.

The problem in *United States Department of Agriculture v. Moreno* arose from Congress's decision to exclude from the food stamp program any household containing an individual who was unrelated to any other member of the household. Thus the statute required that any household receiving food stamps must consist solely of "related" individuals. The Court invalidated the statute. The Court noted that the legislative history suggested a congressional desire to exclude "hippies" and "hippie communes." To this the Court said: "If the constitutional conception of 'equal protection of the laws' means anything, it must at the very least mean that a bare congressional desire to harm a politically unpopular group cannot constitute a legitimate governmental interest...." This idea was extended in the *Cleburne* case, in which the plaintiffs challenged a city's denial of a special use permit for the operation of a group home for the mentally retarded. Applying rational basis review, the Court admonished that "mere negative attitudes, or fear, unsubstantiated by factors which are properly cognizable in a zoning proceeding, are not permissible bases for" unequal treatment. Thus the Court concluded that the discriminatory action under review was based "on an irrational prejudice." And in *Romer v. Evans,* the Court struck down a Colorado law forbidding localities from including gays and lesbians within the protection of laws prohibiting discrimination. The Court held that the law violated rational basis review because it was based not on a legitimate public purpose but on a form of "animus"—with the apparent suggestion that statutes rooted in "animus" represent core offenses of the equal protection guarantee. The Court said that the law stands (and falls) as "a status-based classification of persons undertaken for its own sake."

An equal protection ruling in *Lawrence,* based on these cases, would have had a great deal of appeal. It would have made it unnecessary for the Court to reconsider *Bowers v. Hardwick.* It would have built carefully on *Romer v. Evans.* In these ways, such a ruling would have been narrow, simply converting the *Moreno–Cleburne–Romer* trilogy into the *Moreno–Cleburne–Romer–Lawrence* quartet. On the other hand, it is not clear that such a ruling would have had more limited consequences than a due process ruling. An invalidation of the line between homosexual and heterosexual sodomy would have raised questions about a host of other discriminatory practices. Is the state permitted not to recognize gay marriages? To discriminate against homosexuals in its employment practices? Is the federal government permitted to maintain its "don't ask, don't tell" policy in the military context? If the Court wanted to cabin the reach of its ruling, and not to create anything like a revolution in the law, these were important (and difficult) questions to answer.

B.   *Due Process*

The modern story of substantive due process begins in 1965, when the Court invalidated a Connecticut law forbidding the use of contraceptives by married people. After that decision, the Court decided a set of cases protecting certain choices involving sex, reproduction, the family, and other areas that appeared to be intimate and private. The cases turned out to be quite unruly, and there was no clear line between what was protected and what was not.

A possible view would be that since *Bowers,* or at least since *Washington v. Glucksberg,* the Court has said something like this: "Thus far, but no further!" Since 1985, the Court has been extremely reluctant to use the idea of substantive due process to strike down legislation, and before *Lawrence,* the Court seemed unwilling to add to the list even if the logic of the prior cases suggested that it ought to do so reflects not approval of that decision, and much less a willingness to extend its logic, but a kind of temporal dividing line between permissible and prohibited uses of substantive due process. In other words, the continuing validity of *Roe* suggests not that the Court will try to follow the logic of the privacy cases, but that the Court will refuse to overrule its precedents while also failing to build on their logic.

If we sought to bring more principled order to the Court's decisions, we might invoke the Court's own words and insist that any asserted right must have a strong foundation in Anglo–American traditions. This was the limiting principle invoked in both *Bowers* and *Glucksberg.* In *Bowers,* the Court, quoting Justice Powell, emphasized the need to ask whether the relevant liberties "are 'deeply rooted in this Nation's history and tradition.'" In *Glucksberg,* the Court said that "the development of this Court's substantive-due-process jurisprudence ... has been ... carefully refined by concrete examples involving fundamental rights found to be deeply rooted in our legal tradition." The Court stressed that this historical test tended "to rein in the subjective elements" and to avoid "the need for complex balancing of competing interests in every case." The historical approach might have the advantage of disciplining judicial discretion, but it has the disadvantage of fitting extremely poorly with some of the cases. It is not at all clear, for example, that the right to choose abortion has a strong foundation in tradition. Nonetheless, it would hardly be implausible, before *Lawrence v. Texas,* to argue that henceforth, the line between protected and unprotected interests would turn largely on history—and for that reason, *Lawrence* could well have been resolved favorably to the state.

WHAT THE COURT DID

A. *Substantive Due Process Reborn*

The heart of the Court's opinion in *Lawrence* began with a dramatic reading of precedent, stating, for the first time in the Court's history, that the Constitution recognizes a right to make sexual choices free from state control. Putting *Griswold* together with *Eisenstadt,* the Court said that "the right to make certain decisions regarding sexual conduct extends beyond the marital relationship." Taken by itself, this statement equivocates between two readings: the state may not punish sexual activity through the particular *means* of threatening unwanted pregnancy; or the state may not punish sexual activity at all. The first reading would fit with the Court's previous holdings. But the *Lawrence* Court clearly endorsed the broader reading. In speaking of homosexual activity in particular, the Court said that the government was seeking "to control a personal relationship that, whether or not entitled to formal recognition in the law, is within the liberty of persons to choose without being punished as criminals." Thus the Court suggested that the state could not intrude on sexual liberty "absent injury to a person or abuse of an institution the law protects." Here, then, is the foundation for a reading of *Lawrence* as rooted in a general principle of sexual autonomy.

The Court then turned from its precedents to an investigation of the suggestion in *Bowers* that prohibitions on same-sex sodomy "have ancient roots." Rejecting that conclusion, the Court emphasized the complexity of American traditions on this count. In a lengthy discussion, the Court undermined the suggestion that there has been an unbroken path of hostility to same-sex sodomy. But the Court freely conceded that there is no history of accepting that practice; it did not contend that traditions affirmatively support a constitutional right to sexual freedom in that domain. On the contrary, and in a dramatic departure from both *Bowers* and *Glucksberg,* the Court said that long-standing traditions were not decisive. Current convictions were important, not old ones. "We think that our laws and traditions in the past half century are of most relevance here." Hence the Court stressed an "emerging recognition that liberty gives substantial protection to adult persons in deciding how to conduct their private lives in matters pertaining to sex."

The Court added that it had issued two decisions casting the holding of *Hardwick* "into even more doubt." In *Casey,* the Court had reaffirmed not only *Roe* but also its commitment to substantive due process, emphasizing "that our laws and traditions afford constitutional protection to personal decisions relating to marriage, procreation, contraception, family relationships, child rearing, and education." Thus the Court read *Casey* as an endorsement of the ideas underlying *Roe,* and not simply as a refusal to reject a decision on which the nation had come to rely. And in *Romer v. Evans,* the Court struck down a law "born of animosity toward the class of persons affected." These decisions made *Bowers* decreasingly plausible.

The Court acknowledged that the plaintiff's equal protection challenge, based on *Romer,* was "tenable." But the Court said that "the instant case requires us to address whether *Bowers* itself has continuing validity." (This is remarkable because the instant case "required" no such thing; it would have been fully possible to resolve the case without addressing *Bowers.*) The Court explained that if the Texas statute were invalidated on equal protection grounds, it would remain unclear whether a state could forbid both same-sex and different-sex sodomy. The Court added that when "homosexual conduct is made criminal by the law of the State, that declaration in and of itself is an invitation to subject homosexual persons to discrimination both in the public and in the private spheres." In the Court's view, the continued validity of *Bowers* "demeans the lives of homosexual persons." Here the Court emphasized the stigma imposed by the law, coming not only from the fact that the act is a misdemeanor but also because of "all that imports for the dignity of the persons charged." The collateral consequences of the criminal conviction could not be avoided.

At this point the Court emphasized that *Bowers* had been eroded not only by *Casey* and *Romer,* but also by independent sources. * * * Stare decisis was relevant but not conclusive, for the *Bowers* decision did not produce detrimental reliance "comparable to some instances where recognized individual rights are involved." The Court concluded that "*Bowers* was not correct when it was decided, and it is not correct today."

The Court was aware of the potential breadth of its ruling, and it took steps to clarify its scope. "The present case does not involve minors. It does not involve persons who might be injured or coerced or who are situated in relationships where consent might not easily be refused. It does not involve public conduct or prostitution. It does not involve whether the government must give formal recognition to any relationship that homosexual persons seek to enter." What was involved instead was "full and mutual consent" to engage in "sexual practices common to a homosexual lifestyle ... The State cannot demean their existence or control their destiny by making their private sexual conduct a crime." In a closing word, the Court said that the Texas law "furthers no legitimate state interest which can justify its intrusion into the personal and private life of the individual."

B.   Other Voices

I will return to the complexities in the opinion shortly. For the moment, let us explore the views of the three other justices who wrote in *Lawrence.*

1.   *Equal protection and Justice O'Connor.* Justice O'Connor rejected the Court's due process holding and urged the equal protection route. Building on the *Moreno–Cleburne–Romer* trilogy, she contended that when a law is based on "a desire to harm a politically unpopular group," the Court has applied "a more searching form of rational basis review."

She added that invalidation, via rational basis review, is more likely when the challenged legislation "inhibits personal relationships."

To be sure, Texas had justified its law as a means of promoting morality, and that kind of justification had been found sufficient in *Bowers,* which Justice O'Connor did not seek to disturb. But *Bowers* was decided under the Due Process Clause. *Lawrence* was different, because it presented the not-yet-decided question "whether, under the Equal Protection Clause, moral disapproval is a legitimate state interest to justify by itself a statute that bans homosexual sodomy, but not heterosexual sodomy." She concluded that it is not. Under rational basis review, moral disapproval is not a sufficient basis for discriminating among groups of persons. "Texas' invocation of moral disapproval as a legitimate state interest proves nothing more than Texas' desire to criminalize homosexual sodomy." And because the law is enforced so infrequently, "the law serves more as a statement of dislike and disapproval than as a tool to stop criminal behavior."

Aware of the potentially broad implications of the equal protection argument, Justice O'Connor urged that her analysis would not doom all distinctions between homosexuals and heterosexuals. With her eye firmly on the military and on family law, she said that "Texas cannot assert any legitimate state interest here, such as national security or preserving the traditional institution of marriage." In the latter context, "other reasons exist to promote the institution of marriage beyond mere moral disapproval of an excluded group."

2. *Scalia, the slippery slope, and "a massive disruption of the current social order."* Justice Scalia's argument had three elements. First, he chastised the Court for what he saw as its palpable inconsistency on the issue of stare decisis. Invoking stare decisis, the Court had refused to overrule *Roe,* a nineteen-year-old ruling, in its *Casey* decision in 1992. The same Court was now willing to overrule *Bowers,* decided seventeen years previously. Justice Scalia saw no justification for the differential treatment. Second, Justice Scalia urged that the Court's ruling would have extremely large implications. "State laws against bigamy, same-sex marriage, adult incest, prostitution, masturbation, adultery, fornication, bestiality, and obscenity" can be upheld "only in light of Bowers' validation of laws based on moral choices. Every single one of these laws is called into question by today's decision." The Court's decision therefore entails "a massive disruption of the current social order" (something that could not have been said about a decision to overrule *Roe*). Thus Justice Scalia urged that the Court's opinion "dismantles the structure of constitutional law that has permitted a distinction to be made between heterosexual and homosexual unions, insofar as formal recognition in marriage is concerned."

Justice Scalia's third argument involved the proper interpretation of the Constitution in principle. After doubting that the Due Process Clause is a substantive safeguard at all, he urged that as it has developed, the idea of substantive due process has been disciplined by asking whether the relevant rights are "deeply rooted in this Nation's history and tradition." Justice Scalia questioned the idea that there is an "emerging awareness" that consensual homosexual activity should be protected; but his more basic objection was that any emerging awareness was irrelevant to the decision. "Constitutional entitlements do not spring into existence because some States choose to lessen or eliminate criminal sanctions on certain behavior." Justice Scalia saw the Court as holding that the moral views underlying the Texas statute did not provide a legitimate basis for it. Here his objection was exceedingly simple: "This effectively decrees the end of all morals legislation." With respect to equal protection, Justice Scalia urged that a rational basis was what was required, and that as for due process purposes, "the enforcement of traditional notions of sexual morality" provided the rational basis.

3. *Thomas and the uncommonly silly law.* Justice Thomas's short dissenting opinion emphasizes that as a member of the Texas legislature, he would vote to repeal the relevant law. "Punishing someone for expressing his sexual preference through noncommercial consensual conduct with another adult does not appear to be a worthy way to expend valuable law enforcement resources." Invoking Justice Stewart's concurrence in *Griswold,* he contended that the law is "uncommonly silly,"

INTERPRETIVE PUZZLES

I will suggest that *Lawrence* is best understood as responsive to what the Court saw as an emerging national awareness, reflected in a pattern of nonenforcement, that it is illegitimate to punish people because of homosexual conduct—and that the decision therefore embodies a kind of American-style desuetude. But to support this suggestion, it will be necessary to unpack the Court's opaque opinion, which raises a number of puzzles. Let us begin with the simplest.

A. *A Fundamental Right or Rational Basis Review?*

Was *Lawrence* based on rational basis review, or instead on something else? It is astonishing but true that this question is exceedingly difficult to answer.

If the Court had attempted to write a conventional due process opinion, it would have taken one of two routes. First, the Court might have said that the right to engage in consensual sexual activity qualifies as fundamental, so that the government may not interfere with that right unless it has a compelling justification. Second, the Court might have said that whether or not the relevant right qualifies as fundamental, the state cannot interfere with it, simply because it lacks a legitimate reason to justify the interference. But the Court said neither, at least not in plain terms. The Court did not unambiguously identify any "fundamental interest" on the part of the plaintiffs that would support its ruling. In fact it did not use the "fundamental interest" formulation at any point in its analysis. Moreover, the Court did not say that the Texas statute lacked a "rational basis." In fact it did not use the "rational basis" formulation at any point in its analysis. Much of the opacity of the Court's opinion stems from its failure to specify what kind of review it was applying to the Texas statute. The conventional doctrinal categories and terms are simply missing.

To be sure, the Court did end its opinion with a reference to the absence of any "legitimate interest" on the state's part. Justice Scalia seized on this point to urge that the Court issued a rational basis opinion after all—a characterization to which the Court (revealingly?) does not specifically object. Thus Justice Scalia contends that much of the Court's opinion "has no relevance to its actual holding," which was that the statute failed rational basis review. Justice Scalia's reading cannot be said to be senseless; it is not demonstrably wrong. But I believe that it is incorrect, and that in the end the Court's opinion treats the underlying right as a fundamental one. Begin with the most relevant part of the Court's opinion:

> The petitioners are entitled to respect for their private lives. The State cannot demean their existence or control their destiny by making their private sexual conduct a crime. Their right to liberty under the Due Process Clause gives them the full right to engage in their conduct without intervention of the government. "It is a promise of the Constitution that there is a realm of personal liberty which the government may not enter." The Texas statute furthers no legitimate state interest which can justify its intrusion into the personal and private life of the individual.

The Court immediately follows its reference to "no legitimate state interest" with the phrase, "which can justify its intrusion into the personal and private life of the individual." on "control [of] their destiny," suggests that the interest involved is not an ordinary one—and that the Court is demanding something more than a rational basis. The same point is strongly suggested by the Court's reference, in this paragraph, to *Casey,* which of course involved a fundamental right, not a rational basis test.

But there is a more basic reason for seeing the Court's opinion as finding the relevant interest to be fundamental. The Court begins with an effort to assimilate the issue in *Lawrence* to the issues in *Griswold, Eisenstadt, Roe, Carey,* and *Casey*—all of which are now taken, by the Court, to suggest a fundamental right in the domain of sex and reproduction. Hence the Court refers to "the right to make certain decisions regarding sexual conduct," to the individual's interest in making "certain fundamental decisions affecting her destiny," and to the "emerging awareness that liberty gives substantial protection to adult persons in deciding how to conduct their private lives in matters pertaining to sex." These statements would be unintelligible if *Lawrence* were based solely on rational basis review. Indeed, much of the Court's opinion would be dicta. In the end, *Lawrence* is not plausibly a rational basis decision.

An alternative reading is that the Court deliberately refused to specify its "tier" of analysis because it was rejecting the idea of tiers altogether. Perhaps the Court was signaling its adoption of a kind of sliding scale, matching the strength of the interest to the demand for state justification, without formally requiring identification of a fundamental right. And, indeed, some of the Court's decisions do suggest a partial collapse of the traditional tiers approach to judicial review. For many years, Justice Marshall complained of the rigidity of the usual tiers, urging a more open-ended form of balancing. Justice Marshall's views appeared to fall on deaf ears. But perhaps *Lawrence* reflects some appreciation of the difficulties in fitting all cases within the traditional framework. This is not a wholly implausible reading, but it would be quite surprising if the Court meant to adopt a sliding scale of analysis without saying so. The more natural interpretation is simpler: The Court's assimilation of the *Lawrence* problem to that in *Griswold* and its successors suggests that a fundamental right was involved.

B.   *Autonomy Simpliciter, or Desuetude–Informed Autonomy?*

But why, exactly, does the relevant interest count as a fundamental one? There are two possibilities. The first is that the right to engage in consensual sex counts, simply as a matter of principle, as part of the liberty that the Due Process Clause substantively protects. On this view, in *Lawrence* the Court accepted, to this extent, John Stuart Mill's view in *On Liberty,* holding that the government may not interfere with (certain) private choices unless there is harm to others. The second and narrower idea is that this particular *kind* of sex—homosexual sex between consenting adults—counts as fundamental. It does so because of major changes in social values in the last half-century. On this view, *Lawrence* finds a fundamental right as a result of existing public convictions, with which the Texas statute cannot be squared, simply because sodomy prosecutions are so hopelessly out of step with them.

Lawrence could be read in either way. But the second interpretation is far more plausible. A simple autonomy reading would have consequences that the Court did not likely intend. As Justice Scalia suggests, it would raise, even more than the first, serious doubts about prohibitions on adult incest, prostitution, adultery, fornication, bestiality, and obscenity. (I do not mention his suggestion that the Court has questioned laws forbidding masturbation, for one reason: There are no laws forbidding masturbation!) Now it might be possible, even under the autonomy reading, to justify most or all of those prohibitions on the ground that they counteract concrete harms, sufficient to support the intrusion on a presumptively protected right. (I return to this question below.) And cases involving commercial activity probably must be analyzed in a way that gives the government more room to maneuver. But it would be surprising if *Lawrence* were understood to require a careful inquiry into the adequacy of government justifications for banning (say) adult incest and bestiality.

In any case, a simple autonomy reading would make the Court's apparently pivotal discussion of "emerging awareness" into an irrelevancy. Recall that the Court rejected *Bowers* in large part by pointing to a range of indications that bans on homosexual sodomy have become out of step with existing values. Hence two factors were emphasized in the Court's ruling: only thirteen states prohibited sodomy; and the sodomy laws were rarely enforced, through criminal prosecution, even in those states. It does appear that the Court was responding to, and requiring, an evolution in public opinion—something like a broad consensus that the practice at issue should not be punished.

These points suggest that the Court's decision was less about sexual autonomy, as a freestanding idea, and closer to a kind of due process variation on the old common law idea of desuetude. According to that concept, laws that are hardly ever enforced are said, by courts, to have lapsed, simply because they lack public support. The rationale here is that unenforced laws lack support in public convictions, and they may not be brought to bear, in what will inevitably be an unpredictable and essentially arbitrary way, against private citizens. Most American courts do not accept that idea in express terms. But long ago, Alexander Bickel invoked the notion of desuetude to help account for *Griswold*. The simple idea is that the ban on use of contraceptives by married people had become hopelessly out of touch with existing convictions—so much so that the ban could rarely if ever be invoked as a basis for actual prosecutions. The public would not accept a situation in which married people were actually convicted of that crime. In those circumstances, the statutory ban was a recipe for arbitrary and even discriminatory action, in a way that does violence to democratic ideals and even the rule of law. It does violence to democratic ideals because a law plainly lacking public support is nonetheless invoked to regulate private conduct. It violates the rule of law because a measure of this kind lacks, in practice, the kind of generality and predictability on which the rule of law depends.

If anything, a ban on sodomy is even worse than the Connecticut law struck down in *Griswold*. Such a ban is used, not for frequent arrests or convictions, but for rare and unpredictable harassment by the police. An advantage of this reading is that it mutes the apparent roots of *Lawrence* in substantive due process. The idea of desuetude is, in a sense, a procedural one. There is a procedural problem: a lack of fair notice combined with denial of equal treatment, a problem that is inevitable in a system in which criminal prosecutions are rare and episodic. In fact, the idea of desuetude forbids criminal punishment not in spite of public values but in their service—a claim that the *Lawrence* Court makes explicitly.

Of course this interpretation of *Lawrence* raises its own problems; a desuetude-informed reading is far from simple and straightforward. The decision should not be read to say that each and every criminal statute becomes unenforceable if it is rarely enforced; that reading would be far too broad. (It could, for example, endanger laws forbidding domestic violence or marital rape in jurisdictions in which enforcement is rare.) At a minimum, it is also necessary to say that the rarity of enforcement is a product of the anachronistic nature of the moral judgment that underlies it. Building on this idea, the notion of desuetude might be applied whenever a criminal statute is rarely invoked *because* the public no longer supports the moral argument that lies behind it. Let us call this the broad version of the basic idea. But it is true that the Court is not well equipped to say when statutes are anachronistic, and any use of desuetude, under the Due Process Clause, is likely to be limited to certain interests that have a threshold of importance. Thus *Lawrence* must be understood as involving another, less ambitious version of the idea, suggesting that when those interests are implicated, the state may not rely on a justification that has lost public support. Let us call this the narrow version of the idea.

Because of its modesty, the narrow version is obviously preferable; the Court should not be read to have gone as far as the broad version suggests. But there is an evident problem with the narrow version. For it to operate, we must have an antecedent way, to some extent independent of public convictions, to determine whether an interest has some kind of constitutional status. Without that independent way, the narrow version dissolves into the broader one: Any interest on which the public no longer wants to intrude becomes a fundamental one by definition. (Is this true of the right to use marijuana within the home? Of the right of sixteen-year-olds to drink alcohol within the home?) In the end, the *Lawrence* Court must have concluded that as a matter of principle, the right to engage in same-sex relations had a special status in light of the Court's precedents taken along with emerging public convictions—and that the moral arguments that supported the ban were no longer sufficient to justify it.

In this sense, the "emerging public awareness" emphasized by the Court operated at two levels. First, it served to discredit the particular moral justification for the law, in a conventional use of the idea of desuetude. Second, it helped to inform the Court's judgment that the interest at stake could not be distinguished, in principle, from those involved in *Griswold, Eisenstadt, Carey,* and *Roe.* Hence some idea about autonomy is an inescapable part of the analysis. This second use of public convictions is not a use of the idea of desuetude; but it does belong in the same family. There are a number of complexities here, and I shall return to them shortly.

C. *The Dog That Barked Very Quietly: Equal Protection*

Lawrence was rooted in the Due Process Clause, not the Equal Protection Clause. But it defies belief to say that it is not, in a sense, an equal protection ruling. Everyone knows that the case was about sexual orientation. When Justice Scalia urges that the Court "has largely signed on to the so-called homosexual agenda," he is correct in an important sense: The Court was not willing to legitimate, or to deem legitimate, "the moral opprobrium that has traditionally attached to homosexual conduct." I have questioned Justice Scalia's broader suggestion that the Court meant to say that a moral position, unaccompanied by convincing evidence of tangible harm, is an illegitimate basis for law. The Court was concerned not to excise moral grounds from law, but instead to excise a *particular* moral ground, that is, the moral ground that underlies criminal prohibitions on same-sex relationships. The Court's judgment to this effect had a great deal to do with considerations of equality.

It is not hard to find support for this claim in the Court's opinion. In many places, the Court suggested that equality, and a particular sort of moral claim, were pivotal to the outcome. Consider this suggestion: "Persons in a homosexual relationship may seek autonomy ... just as heterosexual persons do." Or this: "When homosexual conduct is made criminal by the law of the State, that declaration in and of itself is an invitation to subject homosexual persons to discrimination in both the public and in the private spheres." Or this: "Adults may choose to enter upon this relationship ... and still retain their dignity as free persons ... The liberty protected by the Constitution allows homosexual persons the right to make this choice." Now delete, from the sentences just quoted, the word "homosexual," and replace it with the word "adulterous," or "bigamous," or "incestuous." Somehow the sentences do not work. The Court's due process decision was powerfully influenced by a claim of equality.

D. *What Lawrence Did, With an Evaluation*

If we emphasize the *Lawrence* Court's reliance on "emerging awareness," we will see the decision as most closely analogous to *Griswold* and *Reed*. When the Court held that married people could not be prohibited from using contraceptives, it was using the Due Process Clause to forbid the invocation of a law that could not be fit with current values. When the Court began to invalidate sex discrimination of the most arbitrary kinds, it was not making a revolution on its own. *Lawrence* is in the same spirit. To the extent that the *Lawrence* Court treated homosexual sodomy as equivalent, in principle, to opposite-sex relationships, it was responding to the fact that with respect to the invocation of the criminal law, the American public had come to the same conclusion. To the extent that the Court held that no legitimate state interest justified the ban on same-sex relationships, it was acting in the service of widely held convictions. Judges do not interpret the Constitution to please majorities. But widespread social convictions are likely to influence anyone who lives in society. Judges live in society. *Lawrence* is a testimonial to this process of influence.

If *Lawrence* is understood in these terms, should it be applauded or deplored? I do not intend to answer that question fully here. An obvious issue is: Compared to what? I do believe that Justice O'Connor's equal protection approach would have been better and simpler—better because of its fit with precedent, simpler because it is analytically in the same line with *Moreno, Cleburne,* and *Romer.* But what of the other alternatives? I have urged that if *Lawrence* is a kind of American-style desuetude, it can claim to be rooted in a form of procedural due process. A law of the sort that the Court invalidated is a violation of the rule of law; it does not provide fair notice; and it invites arbitrary and unpredictable enforcement, of just the sort that occurred in the case itself. Such a law also lacks a democratic pedigree. It is able to persist only because it is enforced so rarely.

1. *Specifying desuetude, American-style: National outliers or rare enforcement?* If a desuetude-type rationale is accepted, it is necessary to know when, exactly, it will be triggered. We can imagine many possibilities. The *Lawrence* Court emphasized two separate points: few states now forbid consensual sodomy; and even in states in which a ban is in place, prosecution is rare. The first point stresses the problem of states-as-outliers; the second is a more standard point about intrajurisdictional desuetude. In *Lawrence* itself, the two points marched hand-in-hand, but they could easily be pulled apart. A law might fit with existing social values in one state, but those values might be rejected in the rest of the union. This would not be a simple case of desuetude, because the statute would, by hypothesis, receive support within the relevant state. By contrast, a state-specific analysis, based on more conventional ideas about desuetude, would emphasize the ideas of fair notice and arbitrariness and suggest that at least when certain interests are involved, a state may not bring the criminal law to bear when the values that underlie those laws are now anachronistic in that very state. Certainly the standard desuetude idea cannot be invoked in a state in which the law in question is actively enforced. For the Supreme Court, the easiest cases are *Lawrence* and *Griswold:* those in which the relevant values lack support both in the enforcing state and in the nation as a whole. My emphasis here is not on national outliers, but on the fact that in Texas itself, the sodomy statute, hardly ever enforced, created problems of both unpredictability and arbitrariness.

2. *Too little?* But for many defenders of the outcome in *Lawrence,* this interpretation will give the plaintiffs far too little. One obvious alternative is a more critical approach to conventional morality. Such an approach would not define liberty by identifying society's "emerging awareness" as if it were a kind of brute fact for judicial use, but would instead attempt to define the idea of liberty, and the legitimacy of intrusions on it, by reference to an evaluative account that is independent of whatever views now happen to prevail. For those who prefer this more critical approach, the problem with a desuetude-type interpretation is that it would allow states to have sodomy laws, or adultery laws, or fornication laws, so long as those laws are taken seriously and actually brought to bear against the citizenry. Wouldn't that situation be worse rather than better?

In fact it is possible to understand the Court's opinion in this more critical and evaluative way. Certainly the Court's use of the word "awareness" suggests that it believes the emerging view to be worth attention not merely because it is emerging but also because it is right.

Consider too the Court's suggest that the framers "knew times can blind us to certain *truths* and later generations can see that laws once thought necessary and proper *in fact* serve only to oppress." Perhaps we might build on the Court's reference to "truths" and what happens "in fact" to suggest its endorsement of a more independent and critical approach to public convictions.

But a more critical approach, from the Court, should not be accepted so readily. Let us agree that if the Court's judgments on the appropriate content of liberty were reliable, then a more critical approach would have much to be said in its favor. But even those who endorse that approach might agree that *Lawrence,* read in the way that I have suggested, has the advantage of comparative modesty—and that it does not foreclose use of the critical approach for the future. And for those who endorse the critical approach, there are reasons for caution. The first is the simple risk of judicial error. Unmoored from public convictions, there is a risk that the Court's conception of liberty will be confused or indefensible. (Recall *Dred Scott v. Sandford*) The second problem is the danger of unintended bad consequences. Even if the Court has the right conception of liberty, it may not do much good by insisting on it when the nation strongly disagrees. If the Court had held, in 1980, that the Due Process Clause requires states to recognize same-sex marriage, it would (in my view) have been responding to the right conception of liberty. But it would undoubtedly have produced a large-scale social backlash, and very likely a constitutional amendment, that would have made same-sex marriage impossible. The simple point is that judicial impositions may do little good and considerable harm, even from the standpoint of the causes that the Court hopes to promote. To be sure, these points are cautionary notes and no more. But at the very least, they suggest that where the Court is in a position to choose, a desuetude-type ruling, building on widespread convictions, has considerable advantages over a ruling that is based on the Court's own conception of autonomy.

3. *Too much?* Of course *Lawrence,* read in the way I have suggested, might be criticized from other directions. Perhaps a better alternative is Thayerism: An approach that would uphold any intrusion on liberty unless it lacks even a minimally rational basis. This approach might be defended on the ground that a judicial judgment about emerging public convictions is not very reliable, and certainly less so than the evidence provided by actual legislation. If there is a serious risk in judicial efforts, why not require people to resort to their political remedies? I believe that the idea of desuetude provides a partial answer. If legislation is infrequently enforced, most citizens can treat it as effectively dead. They have nothing to worry about. At least in clear cases, it seems plausible, and inoffensive to democratic values, to use the Due Process Clause to forbid criminal prosecutions in cases of this kind. Both *Griswold* and *Lawrence* are defining examples.

But perhaps the Court would have done better, in *Lawrence,* to continue on the path marked out by *Bowers* and *Glucksberg,* and hence to uphold any intrusion on liberty unless it runs afoul of Anglo–American traditions. Due process traditionalism might be supported on the ground that federal judges are not especially good at evaluating our practices, and that if a practice has endured there is good reason to support it, if only because many people have endorsed it, or at least not seen fit to change it. When the Court has urged that fundamental interests should be so defined by reference to traditions, it has done so on the ground that traditionalism helps to cabin judicial discretion and to minimize the risk of judicial error. Constitutional traditionalism therefore makes decisions simpler at the same time that it makes them less likely to go wrong. If economic terminology is thought to be helpful here, the use of traditions by imperfect human beings might not be perfect, but it is the best way to go because it minimizes both "decision costs," taken as the burdens of deciding what to do, and "error costs," taken as the problems introduced by making mistakes.

A central question is whether tradition-bound judges will make more or fewer errors than judges who depart from traditions and pay a great deal of attention to conventional morality. At least some of those who are skeptical about substantive due process might endorse traditionalism as a possible source of law, but also conclude that it is proper for the Court to strike down statutes that lack support in popular convictions. In other words, the desuetude-type approach of the *Lawrence* Court might be a modest, cautious supplement to due process traditionalism, rooted in similar concerns. Indeed, a desuetude-type approach has the advantage of underlining the procedural features of procedural due process. As we have seen, a statute like that invalidated in *Lawrence* fails to provide predictability, and it is a recipe for arbitrary enforcement. The Court's refusal to permit criminal convictions, under these circumstances, is not radically inconsistent with democratic ideals. In a sense, it helps to vindicate them.

4.   *Coherence, optimal deterrence, and expressive condemnation.* Another response is possible, one that would raise questions about the coherence of any approach that draws on the idea of desuetude. For governments, there is a trade-off between the magnitude and the frequency of punishment. A government might decide to lessen the deterrent signal simply by scaling back enforcement. In the context of conduct that a state would like to deter, but not greatly, the sensible strategy might be to maintain a prohibition but to enforce it rarely. It is easy to imagine a city taking this approach with respect to nonflagrant speeding (driving, say, ten miles over the speed limit), or certain parking offenses (giving tickets rarely in certain places, for example), or certain alcohol or drug offenses (rarely arresting or convicting teenagers for use of alcohol, or infrequently arresting or convicting people for marijuana use). In fact countless prohibitions are rarely enforced. Is this situation unconstitutional? Why is a state banned from making this particular trade-off between severity and

probability of sanction? If the desuetude idea is about absence of fair notice and discriminatory enforcement, shouldn't the Court strike down any statute that suffers from these defects, including those that not only have lost popularity, but also those that never had sufficient support to be a basis for frequent enforcement? In any case, the *ex ante* deterrent effect of a rarely enforced law, including the sodomy law in Texas, applies equally to all those subject to it. Isn't this *ex ante* equality a sufficient response to the objection of unpredictability?

To answer this objection, it is necessary to be more specific about the due process ruling in *Lawrence.* We could imagine many possible situations of rare or nonexistent enforcement, and these do not ordinarily raise constitutional problems. For example, the conduct might itself be unobjectionable, but prohibited to get at related conduct (as, perhaps, in the case of certain gambling, outlawed because it invites organized crime). Alternatively, the conduct might be mostly objectionable, but banned as a way of enforcing a prohibition on a subset of it (as in the case of sodomy laws used to punish nonconsensual sex). Or the conduct might be mostly objectionable, but a subset of it is unpunished, because it is close to the line (as in driving slightly over the speed limit). Or the conduct might be objectionable, but problems in obtaining witnesses and evidence are formidable (as, perhaps, in the cases of domestic violence and more obviously marital rape).

The problem with the Texas sodomy law was not only the fact that it was enforced rarely; infrequent enforcement stemmed from the particular fact that the moral claim that underlay it could no longer claim public support. The same cannot be said in the examples just described; in those cases, there is public ambivalence about arrest and conviction, but not because of a widespread belief that the prohibition is outmoded or rooted in values that no longer deserve support. But *Lawrence* does not depend on this factor alone. It is also important that the interest at stake is similar, in principle, to those protected by earlier cases. In these circumstances, the state is required to produce, by way of justification, something other than a moral position that no longer fits with public convictions. To be sure, the effect of a rarely enforced law is similar to that of a lottery, and in that respect there is a degree of *ex ante* equality. But that's the problem. Criminal punishments should not operate like lotteries. People are punished *ex post*, not *ex ante*, and it is the *ex post* randomness that supports the Court's ruling, at least in the light of the particular interest involved.

Consider a final argument. One purpose of the criminal law is to impose expressive condemnation. For some conduct, the social judgment is in favor of expressive condemnation but opposed to much in the way of actual prosecution. As examples, consider laws forbidding adultery or the consumption of alcohol by sixteen-year-olds. Rare enforcement reflects a belief that the law, operating in conjunction with social norms, will deter misconduct optimally—and that criminal prosecution would be too heavy-handed, at least in most cases. Does it follow, from *Lawrence,* that states are forbidden from adopting the strategy of expressive condemnation with rare prosecution? Why isn't that strategy the most sensible one in some circumstances? The answer is that when certain interests are involved, states are indeed forbidden from following that strategy, and the reason has to do with the lack of fair notice and the inevitability of randomness. As I have emphasized, these are the conventional (procedural) concerns of the Due Process Clause.

IV. Implications

What are the implications of *Lawrence?* Because of the opacity of the Court's opinion, this is not an easy question to answer. In the fullness of time, it is imaginable that *Lawrence* will be a sport, a decision with no descendants, one in which the Court struck down a law that shocked its conscience but that proved unable to generate further doctrine. But it is no less imaginable that *Lawrence* will turn out to have broad consequences for regulation of sexual relationships, in a way that vindicates a quite general interest in sexual autonomy. *Bowers* had stopped a number of potential doctrinal innovations here; *Bowers* is no longer good law. And it is wholly imaginable that *Lawrence* will draw into question many forms of discrimination against gays and lesbians. If my basic argument is correct, the eventual path of the law will have a great deal to do with public convictions over time. My guess is that *Lawrence* will have some of the features of *Reed v. Reed:* it will inaugurate a set of judgments, from lower courts and the Court itself, that go, in case-by-case fashion, toward eliminating the most arbitrary and senseless restrictions on liberty and equality. I am concerned in this section with the logic of the Court's opinion and with its bearing on issues that the Court did not resolve.

A. Sex

Justice Scalia urged that *Lawrence* decrees an end to "morals" legislation, and in the aftermath of the decision, it is natural to wonder about the constitutionality of laws forbidding sexual harassment, prostitution, adultery, fornication, obscenity, polygamy, and incest. Before *Lawrence,* such laws seemed quite secure. The Court had made clear that substantive due process would be used only to protect rights well recognized by tradition; and in any event the privacy cases had originally been defined with close reference to reproduction and its control, not to sex itself. But after *Lawrence,* it would be possible to contend that many statutory restrictions impose unconstitutional barriers to consensual sexual activity. And in each of these cases, it would be possible to urge both that the relevant right is a fundamental one and that the state lacks a legitimate basis for interfering with consensual activity. Let us see how the underlying issues might be assessed.

1. *Coercion.* The easiest cases involve coercion. In such cases, the predicate for *Lawrence*—consent—is absent. If consensual sex is not involved, there is no fundamental right that would require the state to provide a compelling justification. And for the same reason, the

state has a perfectly legitimate, even compelling, reason to impose a restriction. In cases of sexual harassment, coercion of one or another sort is generally involved, and hence a legal ban is perfectly acceptable. The same is true for many and indeed most cases involving incest, which involve minors unable to give legal consent. The interest in preventing coerced sex is sufficient.

But somewhat harder cases are imaginable even here. Suppose, for example, that under a public university's sexual harassment policy, a teacher and a graduate student are banned from having a consensual relationship, even though the teacher is not (and will not be) in a supervisory position over the student. Or suppose that the incestuous relations are between adults—first cousins, let us say. In an "as applied" challenge, these would be genuinely difficult after *Lawrence*. If real consent is found in either case, a fundamental right might well be involved. But it would be possible to defend the broad sexual harassment prohibition as a way of reducing risks and introducing clarity for all. And it would be possible to defend the ban on incest among adults as a way of eliminating certain psychological pressures and protecting any children who might result from medical risk. In neither case can it be said that the prohibitions run afoul of some emerging national awareness. These are far weaker cases for invalidation than *Lawrence,* but some of the underlying logic of the case seems to raise doubts in imaginable applications.

2.   *Commerce.* Other easy cases involve commerce. In the case of prostitution, it is hard to urge that a fundamental right is involved. Under *Lawrence,* commercial sex is to be treated differently. The outcome is easy; but the analysis is not. Why the sharp distinction between commercial and noncommercial sex? Why are sexual relations unprotected, or less protected, if dollars are exchanged? Books, after all, are protected, whether they are given away or sold. Part of the analysis here might be that commercial sex should not be treated more protectively than any other kind of commercial interaction, now subject to rational basis review. But if sexual relationships have a special constitutional status, this distinction is far from obvious. The more basic claim must be that special constitutional status attaches to sexual intimacy, not to sexual relationships, and that intimacy in the relevant sense is not involved when sex is exchanged for cash. Hence no fundamental right is involved. To be sure, this argument is not entirely convincing. Many sexual relationships (including many that fall within the category protected by *Lawrence*) do not involve intimacy (except by definition). But perhaps the Court can be said to be suggesting that noncommercial sex involves intimacy frequently enough to justify protection of the overall class, whereas the opposite is true of sex-for-money.

But what justification does the state have for forbidding prostitution? It is probably sufficient here to point to the adverse effects of prostitution on the lives of prostitutes; the risk of exploitation (and worse) is real and serious. Nor are moral justifications, pointing to the corrosive effects of prostitution on sexuality and sex equality, ruled off-limits by *Lawrence.* I am not taking a position on the complex and disputed question whether and how prostitution should be outlawed. My suggestion is only that under rational basis review, restrictions on prostitution are easily defensible. The ban on the sale of obscenity should be understood in similar terms; the use of obscenity raises different issues, but here too *Lawrence* is best taken not to affect existing law.

3. *Without coercion and without commerce.* For the state, the most serious problems, post-*Lawrence,* come in cases challenging restrictions on genuinely consensual and noncommercial practices. Begin with what might seem an intermediate case: bans on sexual devices. Following the previous discussion, we should distinguish here between sale on the one hand and use on the other. On one view, the state could ban the sale itself, urging that it is attempting to regulate a commercial enterprise, and that it is permitted to do so in light of the commercial-noncommercial distinction just made. But even this is not entirely clear. And could the state make it a crime for people to *use* such devices? The right to do so might well fall within the protection of fundamental interests. In any case, what is the state's justification for banning such use? It is easy to imagine an as-applied challenge, in which a married couple (or for that matter an unmarried one, or for that matter a single person) attacks a ban on either the sale or the use of sexual devices with reference to *Griswold* itself.

The difference is that in *Griswold,* the ban on use of contraceptives was an effort to prevent nonprocreative sex, whereas in the hypothetical case, the state is banning devices that are designed to increase sexual pleasure. But why, exactly, would it seek to do that? Is there something wrong with certain sources of sexual pleasure within constitutionally protected relationships? Perhaps the answer would be affirmative if real harms were involved, as for example through some (hardly all) sadomasochistic practices. Almost certainly the state could justify a prohibition on the public display of such devices. But we are not now speaking of these questions. At first glance, individuals have a fundamental interest here, and the state seems to lack a legitimate basis for intruding on that interest.

If there were laws forbidding masturbation, *Lawrence* would indeed raise extremely serious questions about them. But, as I have noted, there are no such laws. What about laws forbidding fornication, understood to mean nonadulterous sex outside of marriage? *Lawrence* creates serious doubts, simply because coercion and consent are not present. In any case, there seems to be an emerging social awareness that fornication is not a proper basis for criminal punishment. And with respect to consenting adults, it is not easy to produce a legitimate ground for interfering with nonadulterous sex. As I have noted, fully consensual incest is a somewhat harder case. In the case of adult brothers and sisters, it might be urged that the goal is to prevent harms to any children who might result, or psychological difficulties that would predictably produce and accompany any such relationships. Certainly the ban on sexual relations within the family cannot be said to be anachronistic. There is no "emerging public awareness" that such relations should be accepted. But imagine, for example, that sex is banned among first cousins, in circumstances in which any harms are highly speculative. Rational basis review would be satisfied. But *Lawrence* does not apply rational basis review, and in some applications, the ruling would seem to throw legal prohibitions on incest into considerable doubt.

The most difficult cases involve laws forbidding adultery. We could also imagine cases in which government takes adverse employment action against those involved in adulterous relationships. Here, as in other contexts, it would be possible to urge that a consensual relationship is involved, one with which the state may not interfere on purely moral grounds. On the other hand, it is possible to justify prohibitions on adultery by reference to harms to third parties: children, in many cases, and the betrayed spouse, in many more cases. The adultery laws can be seen as an effort to protect the marital relationship, involving persons and interests, including those of children, that are harmed if adultery occurs. Marriage can and usually is understood as an exchange of commitments, which have individual and social value; and a prohibition on adultery, moral and legal, operates in the service of those commitments. If rational basis review is involved, prohibitions on adultery should certainly be acceptable—except, perhaps, in cases in which the married couple has agreed to nonexclusivity (in which case criminal prosecution would be especially surprising).

The difficulty here is that in the context of adultery, criminal prosecutions are extremely unusual, at least as rare as criminal prosecutions for sodomy. There is a good argument that criminal prosecutions, in this context, are inconsistent with emerging social values. This is not because adultery is thought to be morally acceptable; it is not. It is because adultery is not thought to be a proper basis for the use of the criminal law. Perhaps it could be said that *Lawrence* turned at least in part on the Court's evident desire to ensure against practices that would "demean[] the lives of homosexual persons." It is not plausible to say that the Court should take special steps to ensure against practices that would "demean the lives of" adulterers. But in the end, it is not so easy to distinguish an adultery prosecution from the sodomy prosecution forbidden in *Lawrence.*

B. *Sexual Orientation, Employment, and Marriage*

1. *Employment.* May a public employer discharge or punish an employee because of his sexual orientation or because of homosexual acts? Before *Lawrence,* the lower courts were divided on the issue. The logic of *Bowers* supported the decisions upholding such discharges, at least against due process challenges. And it was possible to urge that because homosexual activity is not protected by the Constitution, government employees are permitted to discriminate against those who engage in that activity. At first glance, however, *Lawrence*

resolves that question the other way. A public employer is not permitted to discharge an employee because she has exercised a constitutional right (an oversimplification to which I shall return). If an employee has converted to Catholicism, or voted for a Republican, she may not be adversely affected for that reason. So too if an employee has exercised a right protected by the Due Process Clause. A state may not refuse to hire a secretary who has used contraception or had an abortion. Under *Lawrence,* government may not refuse to hire people who have engaged in same-sex relations. It could perhaps be argued that a criminal punishment is worse than a civil disability, and hence that the prohibition on criminal prosecution does not entail an equivalent prohibition on adverse employment actions. But the cases just described should be sufficient response to that argument.

Most cases of adverse employment action, prompted by homosexual activity, are easy after *Lawrence.* But there are some possible rejoinders. One would emphasize the reading I have stressed here: *Lawrence* turned not simply on a finding of a fundamental right, but more importantly on the Court's conclusion that the Texas criminal statute was no longer supported by public convictions. If desuetude is involved, then perhaps employment discrimination is permitted even if criminal prosecution is not. This argument is not at all implausible or incoherent. If we emphasize the idea of desuetude, then a moral judgment might be permissible for use in the employment context even if it cannot be invoked as a basis for criminal prosecution. A narrow reading of *Lawrence,* then, would suggest that the Due Process Clause forbids criminal punishment of sexual conduct not violative of existing moral convictions, but that there is no barrier to judgments, by government employers, that gays and lesbians should not be employed. But this approach reads *Lawrence* a bit too finely; it would be most surprising if the Court were to permit states not to hire, or to fire, people for engaging in the conduct that the Court held to be protected. The Court is best read to have found a fundamental interest, although desuetude-type ideas played a role in its judgment; and if so, states may not refuse to hire people who have engaged in the relevant behavior. In fact, a mild extension of the Court's own use of emerging convictions would suggest that the moral judgments that underlie the Texas statute may not be used for either criminal or civil disability.

Another response would emphasize that on occasion, the government may indeed refuse to hire people for engaging in constitutionally protected activity. The President is permitted to refuse to employ, as Secretary of State, someone who has publicly criticized his policies; so too, a public university is almost certainly allowed not to hire, or even to fire, an admissions officer who has said that women should not go to college, or that it is best for African–Americans to attend vocational school. In such cases, the university can claim, plausibly, that it is not trying to censor anyone, or to punish them for exercising a constitutional right, but instead to accomplish the substantive task that it has set for itself. An admissions officer is not likely to be effective if he is on record as supporting race or sex discrimination. Might discrimination against gays and lesbians be similarly justified? This is not entirely unimaginable in some contexts, but in general, it is hard to see how the justification could be made convincing. Unless the state is to capitulate to private prejudice, as it is generally forbidden from doing, it cannot easily invoke a distinct, employment-related reason to discriminate on the basis of sexual orientation.

It also follows that the "don't ask, don't tell" policy, in the military setting, is under new pressure. It is no longer possible to defend that policy simply by citing *Bowers.* If the policy is to be upheld, it is because courts should give great deference to military judgments, applying a form of rational basis review to them. I believe that federal courts are not likely to interfere with military judgments here, and that there is good reason for a general posture of deference to such judgments. In principle, however, it is extremely difficult to defend "don't ask, don't tell" against constitutional challenge, and this appears to be one of the exceedingly rare settings in which judicial interference with military judgments is probably justified.

2. Marriage. Of course the largest issue is the fate of same-sex marriage. Under *Lawrence,* must states recognize such marriages? I have suggested that *Lawrence* is akin to *Griswold;* but *Griswold* led to *Roe.* Perhaps *Lawrence* will lead to its own *Roe,* in the form of a requirement that states allow gays and lesbians, not less than heterosexuals, to marry.

The issue is exceedingly complex. At first glance, *Lawrence* has nothing at all to do with same-sex marriage. It involved sodomy prosecutions, brought under anachronistic laws, and the due process challenge to those prosecutions need not draw into doubt the still-universal practice of defining marriage to involve one man and one woman. In any case, the most natural challenge to laws rejecting such marriages is rooted in the Equal Protection Clause; and *Lawrence* said nothing about the Equal Protection Clause (perhaps because it sought to avoid the marriage issue). To the extent that the Court was emphasizing an "emerging awareness," its decision does not touch prohibitions on same-sex marriage—and will not do so unless and until such prohibitions seem as outmoded as bans on homosexual sodomy do today. Existing practice suggests universal opposition to same-sex marriage, and polling evidence suggests that most Americans support existing practice.

But under current law, the issue cannot be disposed of so readily. In *Loving v. Virginia,* the Court struck down a ban on racial intermarriage on two grounds. The first is the familiar equal protection ground, seeing that ban as a form of racial discrimination. But in a separate ruling, the Court also held that the ban violated the Due Process Clause. In the Court's words, "the freedom to marry has long been recognized as one of the vital personal rights essential to the orderly pursuit of happiness by free men." It added that "marriage is one of the 'basic civil rights of man,' fundamental to our very existence and survival.'' The *Loving* Court's due process ruling was not free from ambiguity; the problem of racial discrimination played a large role. But subsequent cases confirm that the right to marry counts as fundamental for due process purposes—and is sufficient by itself to take the analysis into the domain of heightened scrutiny.

In *Zablocki v. Redhail,* the Court struck down a Wisconsin law forbidding people under child support obligations to remarry unless they had obtained a judicial determination that they had met those obligations and that their children were not likely to become public charges. The Court insisted that ''the right to marry is of fundamental importance for all individuals,'' and that ''the decision to marry has been placed on the same level of importance as decisions relating to procreation, childbirth, child rearing, and family relationships.'' The Court said that it would uphold ''reasonable regulations that do not significantly interfere with decisions to enter into the marital relationship.'' But any direct and substantial interference with the right to marry would be strictly scrutinized. In a concurring opinion, Justice Stevens underlined the point, urging that the Constitution would cast serious doubt on any ''classification which determines who may lawfully enter into the marriage relationship.''

In this light, a prohibition on same-sex marriage is not so easy to defend in the aftermath of *Lawrence.* Under the Court's decisions, a fundamental right does seem to be involved, one on which the state can intrude only by pointing to a countervailing interest that is not merely legitimate but also compelling. In the context of same-sex marriage, what might that interest be? What sorts of social harms would follow from recognizing marriages between people of the same sex? It is conventional to argue that the refusal to recognize same-sex marriage is a way of protecting the marital institution itself. But this is very puzzling; how do same-sex marriages threaten the institution of marriage? Or perhaps the state can legitimately reserve the idea of marriage to men and women for expressive reasons. Perhaps the state can urge that it does not want to give the same expressive support to same-sex unions as to opposite-sex unions. But why not? As compared to a ban on same-sex marriages, a prohibition on adultery seems easy to justify. Such a prohibition is likely, in numerous cases, to protect one or even both spouses, and to protect children besides. If, as I have suggested, *Lawrence* draws prohibitions on adultery into some doubt, it would seem to raise extremely serious questions about prohibitions on same-sex marriage.

But perhaps criminal punishment is special. Perhaps such punishment is quite different from, and to be assessed more skeptically than, a statute that confers the benefits of marriage on some but not to all. Perhaps *Lawrence* forbids the state from using the heavy artillery of the criminal law—but without raising questions about civil rights and civil duties. It would not be at all implausible to say that the *Lawrence* Court was responsive to the assortment of disabilities associated with criminal punishment—a set of disabilities that might be thought unique. But *Loving* and *Zablocki* themselves raise questions for this kind of distinction. Neither case involved a criminal prohibition. Both applied careful judicial scrutiny to laws saying that certain people could not enter into the marital relationship.

Perhaps we should read *Loving* and *Zablocki* more narrowly. Notwithstanding the Court's rhetoric, it is quite doubtful that the Court really meant to raise serious questions about *all* state laws dictating who may enter into a marital relationship. People are not permitted to marry dogs or cats or cars. They are banned from marrying their first cousins or their aunts. They cannot marry two people, or three, or twenty. Must these restrictions be justified by showing that they are the least restrictive means of achieving a compelling state interest? If so, at least some of them would be in serious trouble. Perhaps the ban on incestuous marriages could be defended by pointing to the risk of coercion and the danger to any children who would result. But as we have seen, it is easy to imagine some cases in which any such defense would be weak—as, for example, where the would-be spouses are both adults and do not plan to have children. Perhaps bans on polygamy could be defended by pointing to the risk of exploitation, especially of the women involved. But we might doubt whether *Loving* and *Zablocki* should be read to require a careful judicial inquiry into that question.

A possible opinion would urge that by deeming the right to marry fundamental, the Court did not mean to suggest that it would strictly scrutinize any law that departed from the traditional idea that a marriage is between (one) woman and (one) man. It meant only to say that when a man and a woman seek to marry, the state must have good reasons for putting significant barriers in their path. This rationale has the advantage of fitting with both *Loving* and *Zablocki*. The problem is that it seems somewhat arbitrary and opportunistic. Why, exactly, should a marriage be defined in this way? Why, in any case, should the definition be such as to allow the state not to recognize same-sex marriages?

It is not at all easy to answer this question. True, the slippery slope problems are serious if it is said that the state must justify, in compelling terms, any limitation on the right to marry. For this reason the idea that there is any such right is deeply puzzling. But in my view, the major difference between *Lawrence* and a ban on same-sex marriage is that the sodomy law no longer fits with widespread public convictions, whereas the public does not (yet) support same-sex marriages. If we rely heavily on the desuetude-type passages of the Court's opinion, then it would be possible to sketch an opinion upholding the ban on same-sex marriages while also invalidating any state law that punishes consensual sodomy. Such an opinion would read *Loving* and *Zablocki* in the narrow way just suggested, with reference to slippery slope problems, and conclude that a rational basis is all that is required for a law that restricts the institution of marriage to one woman and one man. This opinion would certainly be plausible. The problem is a general one with any approach that relies on public convictions: they might not be principled. The public might have gone this far, and no further; but there may be no good reason for it not to have gone further. It is not easy to identify a principled distinction, aside from public convictions, between what the Court did in *Lawrence* and what a court would do in striking down a state's failure to recognize same-sex marriages.

CONCLUSION

The *Lawrence* decision is susceptible to two broad readings. The Court's ruling could easily be seen as a recognition of the constitutionally fundamental character of sexual liberty, disabling the state from controlling the acts of consenting adults without an extremely powerful justification. Alternatively, it could be seen as a rational basis holding with a strong Millian foundation—a holding that invalidates "morals" legislation, requiring harm to third parties whenever government is regulating private sexual conduct. In practice, these two readings would not be terribly far apart; they would use different doctrinal avenues to similar results.

I have suggested the possibility of a third and narrower reading, one that stresses, as the Court did, that a criminal ban on sodomy is hopelessly out of accord with contemporary convictions. Thus understood, the due process holding of *Lawrence* is genuinely procedural. It asserts a constitutional objection to statutes that are rarely enforced and that interfere with important human interests without anything like a justification in contemporary values. Such statutes are a recipe for unpredictable and discriminatory enforcement practices; they do violence to both democratic values and the rule of law. I have stressed the roots of *Lawrence* in a narrow, American-style version of the idea of desuetude—not because the broader readings are entirely implausible, but because the Court would have been extremely unlikely to rule as it did if not for its perception that the Texas law could not claim a plausible foundation in widely shared moral commitments. I believe that an equal protection ruling, of the sort sketched by Justice O'Connor, would have been preferable, not least because it would have emphasized what should be clear to all: The problem in *Lawrence* had everything to with the social subordination of gays and lesbians. But a due process ruling, understood in the relatively narrow terms outlined here, has considerable appeal.

What is the reach of *Lawrence?* Restrictions on sex that is nonconsensual or commercial are surely valid. By contrast, laws forbidding fornication (defined as extramarital but nonadulterous sex) are surely invalid. The Constitution probably forbids government from punishing, either criminally or civilly, those who have used sexual devices. The state is almost certainly banned from discriminating against those who have engaged in homosexual conduct, at least outside of certain specialized contexts (most notably the military). In some applications, bans on incest and adultery could be subject to serious constitutional challenge.

The hardest cases involve the failure to recognize same-sex marriages. If *Lawrence* is put together with *Loving* and *Zablocki,* it would seem plausible to say that the government would have to produce a compelling justification for refusing to recognize such marriages, and compelling justifications are not easy to find. If we emphasize an equality rationale, the subtext of *Lawrence,* then bans on same-sex marriages are in serious constitutional trouble. On the other hand, the ban on same-sex marriages cannot, at this point in time, be regarded as an anachronism, or as conspicuously out of touch with emerging social values; on the contrary, the ban on same-sex marriage continues to have widespread public support. In any case, there are strong prudential reasons for the Court to hesitate in this domain and to allow democratic processes much room to maneuver. The marriage issue, more than any other, will test the question whether *Lawrence* is this generation's *Griswold*—or the start of something far more ambitious.

BERNARD E. HARCOURT—YOU ARE ENTERING A GAY AND LESBIAN FREE ZONE: ON THE RADICAL DISSENTS OF JUSTICE SCALIA AND OTHER (POST-)QUEERS

94 Journal of Criminal Law and Criminology 503—549 (2004).

The most renowned substantive criminal law decision of the October 2002 Term, *Lawrence v. Texas,* will go down in history as a critical turning point in criminal law debates over the proper scope of the penal sanction. For the first time in the history of American criminal law, the United States Supreme Court has declared that a supermajoritarian moral belief does not necessarily provide a rational basis for criminalizing conventionally deviant conduct. The Court's ruling is the *coup de grâce* to legal moralism administered after a prolonged, brutish, tedious, and debilitating struggle against liberal legalism in its various criminal law representations. Henceforth—or at least until further notice—majoritarian morality no longer automatically trumps liberal argument (whether consequentialist or deontological) in defining the reasonable and permissible contours of the penal code. Justice Byron White's infamous declaration in *Bowers v. Hardwick* that the criminal law is constantly, and may properly be, "based on notions of morality" no longer stands. Instead, Justice John Paul Stevens's contrary statement from his dissent in *Bowers* is elevated, in block quote, to supreme law of the land: "the fact that the governing majority in a State has traditionally viewed a particular practice as immoral is not a sufficient reason for upholding a law prohibiting the practice." With much pomp and circumstance, the majority in *Lawrence* inters legal moralism and crowns liberal legalism. As a matter of federal due process, courts reviewing penal legislation must now deploy *some other principle* to distinguish between permissible and impermissible majoritarian moral opprobrium.

What that other principle will consist of is not clear. Justice Anthony Kennedy's opinion for the majority in *Lawrence* offers a dizzying array of possibilities, ranging from the watered-down harm principle of the American Law Institute's Model Penal Code, to evolving standards of morality as reflected in the history of state legislative enactments (and repeal) of sodomy provisions, to the critical commentary of reputedly conservative American academic judges such as Charles Fried and Richard Posner, to international law decisions of the European Court of Human Rights, to the 1957 British Wolfenden Report of the Committee on Homosexual Offenses and Prostitution, to the *Romer v. Evans* equal protection anti-animosity principle, to state judicial resistance to the *Bowers* ruling, to conceptions of privacy, notions of dignity, or what Cass Sunstein refers to as "an American version of desuetude." The result is a rhetorical smorgasbord of legal authority, a judicial *mélange* of bibliographic references. As Mary Anne Case observes, the *Lawrence* opinion points to a "this" and "that" of ambiguous referents—it is, in Case's words, an opinion that "starts its readers off with this and in the end may deliver that instead."

Justice Kennedy's pastiche in *Lawrence* is, at a legal theoretical level, incoherent, and under normal circumstances—in many other cases—would be internally contradictory. As a jurisprudential matter, utilitarian welfare maximizing or harm calculations are anathema to a deontological human rights paradigm, which in turn is in tension with jurisdictional bean-counting. These different rules of decision have little in common except, of course, when they converge on the same result, which is apparently the case here—or at least, it is the case for decriminalizing homosexual sodomy. The theoretical incoherence and rhetorical overkill of Justice Kennedy's opinion lends credence to Justice Antonin Scalia's incendiary dissent in *Lawrence,* specifically to the idea that the majority's holding is no technical knock-out victory for liberal legalism, but rather a politically or culturally partisan decision.

To Justice Scalia, the majority in *Lawrence* simply took sides in our contemporary culture wars over the sexual and moral fabric of American society. The *Lawrence* ruling, Justice Scalia declares, is a partisan outcome that aligns the court with the pro-gay faction in large part because of a law profession that is biased in favor of gay men and lesbian women. "It is clear from this [decision] that the Court has taken sides in the culture war, departing from its role of assuring, as neutral observer, that the democratic rules of engagement are observed," Justice Scalia writes. "Today's opinion is the product of a Court, which is the product of a law-profession culture, that has largely signed on to the so-called homosexual agenda. . . . " These are fighting words—a battle cry, a call to arms in our contemporary culture wars—and according to the Associated Press, Justice Scalia has continued to wage war outside the courthouse. Several months after the *Lawrence* decision, Justice Scalia reportedly ridiculed the majority's ruling in a speech to the Intercollegiate Studies Institute, reading from Justice Kennedy's opinion with "a mocking tone," and deriding the majority for imposing, in his words, "the latest academic understanding of liberal political theory."

Despite the vitriolic tone, Justice Scalia's dissent is remarkably insightful—in certain respects prescient—in situating the *Lawrence* decision in its proper social and political context, and it offers a useful heuristic to help interpret the result. The fact is, there is today a war of sexual projects that is being fought on American soil, and the federal courts, including the United States Supreme Court, are inextricably caught up in the ongoing battles. But what is missing in Justice Scalia's critique are the important nuances and subtleties that shape these contemporary sex wars, that make them so fascinating and so unpredictable—and that both resignify and ambiguate the purported gay victory in *Lawrence*.

The heart of the problem is that Justice Scalia incorrectly models our contemporary culture wars on two-sided military conflict—specifically on a war between, on the one hand, liberal homosexual activists who are promoting a pro-gay-rights agenda and the law profession with its "anti-anti-homosexual culture," and, on the other hand, mainstream anti-homosexual attitudes represented by those "[m]any Americans [who] do not want persons who openly engage in homosexual conduct as partners in their business, as scoutmasters for their children, as teachers in their children's schools, or as boarders in their home." This two-party model does not—and cannot—begin to capture the complex social, political, and sexual dynamics of our contemporary sex wars. While it is true, of course, that everyone, if pushed to the limit, is either "for" or "against" the legalization of homosexual relations—just as everyone, again if pushed to the limit, is either "for" or "against" abortion, "for" or "against" the death penalty, "for" or "against" gun control—it is necessary to focus not simply on the ultimate polarity but rather on the much wider range of sexual projects in order to begin to understand the unexpected alliances, unanticipated tipping points, and surprising truces that characterize our sex wars. Instead of two-sided military conflict, the model should approximate more fluid and shifting patterns of temporary equilibria in a continually interrupted, jarred, and hence moving medium.

Our present sexual landscape in the United States—and in the West more generally—is marked by a multiplicity of sexual projects, at times ambiguous and fluid, at other times rigid, doctrinaire, even fascistic; sometimes overlapping or allied, at other times in tense conflict; some militant and hard, others nurturing, warm, even embracing; some exclusionary, some missionary. The battle lines are drawn not only over the sex of sexual partners—that's the least of it—but over multiple dimensions of promiscuity, monogamy, child custody, sadomasochism, commitment, "fisting,"[9] public sex, female-to-male sex change operations (and male-to-female), "barebacking" and "bug chasing,"[10] importuning, "role-

---

9. The practice of inserting a fist and forearm into the anus or vagina.

10. The practice among some men of engaging in unprotected same-gender anal

sex or of actively seeking to be infected with HIV.

playing,"[11] "piercing" and "cutting," "packing,"[12] "fancying,"[13] marrying, childbearing, adopting, pornography, and sexual assault—to name just a few. The very definitions of heterosexual, homosexual, bi-, trans-, poly-, metro-, pomo-sexual, lesbian, queer—again, to name just a few—are fought over,[14] even whether the labels themselves should be abandoned. The academy, the courts, the media and public sphere have witnessed an explosion of sexual projects and related discourses of sexuality.

If a male worker on an all-man oil rig is held down by his fellow guy workers while they deliberately put their penises up against his body, if he is threatened with same-sex rape, is he the victim of sexual harassment under Title VII, as Justice Scalia writing for a unanimous court makes possible in *Oncale v. Sundowner Offshore Services, Inc.,*[15] or should the lower federal court reread the factual allegations in a manner that ambiguates sexual desire, as Janet Halley, professor at Harvard Law School, ingeniously and provocatively suggests in *Sexuality Harassment*?[16] Could it be, as Halley writes, that the alleged victim in *Oncale* "performs a feminine man to signal his willingness to be mastered," that "the other guys comply with a big display of masculinity," so that " 'man fucks woman' but with a twist that undoes the capacity of the male/female model to underwrite [the plaintiff Oncale] as a victim"? Could it be, as Halley suggests, that in reality it is the plaintiff alleging sexual harassment who may be attacking his fellow guy workers "by invoking the remarkable powers of the federal court to restore his social position as heterosexual?" And would we really want the average juror or Justice Scalia using their common sense to resolve these questions? (For the skeptical or unaccustomed reader, try mapping this on the rape allegations of the concierge of the Lodge & Spa at Cordillera Colorado against NBA superstar Kobe Bryant, and keep in mind that, shortly before Bryant's appearance in court, a *USA Today*/CNN/Gallup poll revealed that forty-one percent of white respondents and sixty-eight percent of African American respondents believed her allegations probably untrue). Notice in the debate over *Oncale* how a gay-friendly judicial

---

11. For example, the femme/butch debates among lesbian women.

12. The practice among some women of "the wearing of a dildo down the trouser leg to suggest the existence of a penis." SHEILA JEFFREYS, UNPACKING QUEER POLITICS 1 (Cambridge UK: Polity Press, 2003).

13. "Fancying" is "attraction based simply on physical appearance" and triggered significant debate as to whether it is objectifying, racist, "ableist," and reflects "a construction of sexuality which was hostile to women's interests." SHEILA JEFFREYS, THE LESBIAN HERESY: A FEMINIST PERSPECTIVE ON THE LESBIAN SEXUAL REVOLUTION, at xii (Melbourne, Australia: Spinifex Press, 1993).

14. Not to mention "post-queer" (referring to younger more radical queers who

are positioning themselves in opposition to assimilationist queer politics) and "breeder" (referring to heterosexuals with children, and meant to connote that the childbearing and child-raising capabilities of heterosexuals are privileged over those of homosexual couples). *See* CHERRY SMYTH, LESBIANS TALK QUEER NOTIONS 57 (London: Scarlet Press, 1992).

15. 523 U.S. 75 (1998). In *Oncale*, the Court held that this may amount to sex discrimination under Title VII on a theory of same-sex sexual harassment. *Id.* at 75.

16. Janet Halley, *Sexuality Harassment*, *in* LEFT LEGALISM/LEFT CRITIQUE 80 (Wendy Brown & Janet Halley eds.) (Durham, NC: Duke University Press, 2002).

opinion that has the potential of protecting gay men and lesbians from same-sex sexual harassment, a decision supported by the liberal pro-gay-rights forces, a ruling that promotes the "so-called homosexual agenda" and that is authored, ironically, by Justice Scalia himself, is attacked as potentially encroaching on same-gender sexual advances and sexuality more generally from a gay-friendly theoretic perspective that challenges the homosexual (as well as heterosexual) identity.

If four men nail the heads of their penises to a butcher block with stainless steel needles while being photographed by an editor of a gay newsmagazine, *The Advocate*, are they manifesting an unhealthy psychotic internalization of their oppression as homosexual men, as Sheila Jeffreys, professor of political science at the University of Melbourne, suggests, or are they instead performing a valuable and cathartic gay male initiation ritual that helps overcome the stigma of unmanliness associated with gay male sex? Are they, in the words of Jeffreys, "act[ing] out upon their bodies the woman-hating and gay-hating of the societies they inhabit"? Or are similar acts of sadomasochism, instead, as Leo Bersani reports, "passionate, erotic, growthful, consensual, sometimes fearful, exorcism, reclamation, joyful, intense, boundary-breaking, trust building, loving, unbelievably great sex, often funny, creative, spiritual, integrating, a development of inner power as strength." Within the gay-friendly community—within the community of scholars and activists whose agenda is, in the words of Justice Scalia, "directed at eliminating the moral opprobrium that has traditionally attached to homosexual conduct"—where do we look for an answer to this question? In gay male studies, in queer theory, in lesbian feminist writings? And is it really true, as Jeffreys contends, that "the political agenda of queer politics is damaging to the interests of lesbians, women in general, and to marginalized and vulnerable constituencies of gay men"?

If a male transvestite marries a male-to-female transsexual who has undergone sexual-reassignment surgery, is he entitled to an annulment of the marriage because his wife was a man and has refused to consummate the marriage?[17] Is homosexual public sex good or bad for gay politics? Is John Rechy, author of *The Sexual Outlaw*, right when he argues that promiscuous gay males are "the shock troops of the sexual revolution," that the "streets are the battleground," that "the revolution is the sexhunt," and that "a radical statement is made each time a man has sex with another on a street"? These types of questions—and the debates they engender—reflect a proliferation of sexual projects in contemporary Western culture that fractures Justice Scalia's simple two-sided military conflict model, undercuts the very coherence of an expression like "homosexual agenda" or "anti-homosexual agenda," and complexifies the symbolic meaning of a decision like *Lawrence*.

In order to properly understand *Lawrence*—and other sex and cultural wars—we need a much finer grained understanding of sexual

---

17. This is the legal question in *Corbett v. Corbett*, a British case from 1970. *See*   Corbett v. Corbett, 2 W.L.R. 1306 (P.D.A. 1970).

projects and of the fragmentation of those projects. In the *Lawrence* litigation, the surprising coalitions, the telling alliances, the strange bedfellows were most clearly visible on the libertarian side—with amicus briefs filed in support of John Lawrence by Republican groups, Baptist ministers and representatives of twenty-eight other religious organizations, a conservative think-tank, the American Bar Association, the American Psychiatric and Psychological Associations, and the National Organization of Women, in addition to the usual suspects, such as the American Civil Liberties Union (ACLU) and ACLU of Texas, Amnesty International, and gay-rights organizations. To be sure, the cornucopia of *amicus* briefs reflects strategy and lobbying on the part of John Lawrence's lawyers. But, more important, it reflects the kind of political coalition-formation that produced the result in *Lawrence*. The same kind of fragmented politics occur on both sides of sex wars on most issues— same-sex marriage, public sex, sadomasochism, for example. And it is what will account for the outcomes there too.

The ruling in *Lawrence* simply does not lend itself to facile, dichotomous interest-group political interpretation. The result in *Lawrence* does not symbolize primarily an endorsement of homosexuality or an embrace of a "homosexual agenda." What it reflects much more is a curious and fascinating alliance between liberal pro-gay-rights advocates, conservative social libertarians, Republican gay men and lesbian women, and pro-sex traditional liberal heterosexuals, among others. The loudest message that *Lawrence* conveys is: "what two consenting mature adults do in their own bedroom (as long as they are not hurting anyone) is none of the government's business." The symbolic message of *Lawrence* is not "We're on board with homosexuals," it sounds more of "We're against surveillance in adult bedrooms."

More important, the result in *Lawrence* is not unambiguously pro-gay. The fracturing of sexual projects in the West also means, paradoxically, that the *Lawrence* decision does not so simply or unambiguously advance the interests of all self-identified gay men, lesbian women, queers, liberal (pro-gay) heterosexuals, or others who are gay-friendly yet reject sexual labels. The problem is not just the potential backlash against gay men and lesbian women that may follow the *Lawrence* decision. The rub is that the proliferation of sexual projects makes it far too simplistic today to think about a decision such as *Lawrence* in dichotomous terms—as either "good" or "bad" for "homosexuals." Who wins and who loses depends on a much closer parsing of sexual projects. Justice Scalia is only partly right: the decision does favor the liberal pro-gay-rights position and in this sense is gay-friendly. But it may, possibly, ill-serve the interests of many others who oppose the dominance of what Judith Butler refers to as "the defining institutions of phallogocentrism and compulsory heterosexuality."[18] There may be more to be gained from resisting a criminal stigma where—or so long as, or on the condition

18. *See* Judith Butler, Gender Trouble: (New York: Routledge, 1990).
Feminism and the Subversion of Identity, at ix

that—criminal enforcement and accompanying punishments are in fact *de minimis,* than there is to be lost in the normalization of conventional deviance.

This Article probes the fragmentation of sexual projects in the West and its implications for the sex wars and the penal law. It is intended as a guide or manual for the interpretation of the result in *Lawrence* and future sex battles. Its goal is to help make sense of the dynamic interactions that give rise to a political resolution such as *Lawrence.* In this interpretive process, Justice Scalia's incendiary dissent is perhaps the most helpful starting point. Justice Scalia in *Lawrence* has begun to put his finger on cultural conflict. This Article builds on Justice Scalia's radical dissent to tap the real pulse of the sex wars. Part I focuses on the fracturing of sexual projects and demonstrates that it is, today, far too simplistic—in fact profoundly counterproductive—to describe the culture wars as a two-party conflict or to talk about a "homosexual agenda." In the *Lawrence* litigation, this point was brought home in the surprising coalition opposing the Texas statute. The question this raises is, what kinds of fissures split the gay community? What would it sound like to argue from a gay-friendly perspective against the ruling in *Lawrence?* Part II explores this question and develops through a pastiche of radical statements a politics that embraces the marginal, even criminal desire to transgress for the sake of transgression, that thrives on rebellion against hegemonic legal regimes. With this in place, Part III reconstructs Justice Scalia's radical dissent and sharpens it to produce a keener interpretive framework to understand the result in *Lawrence* and future sex wars. Justice Scalia is right that there is a culture war and that the courts are inextricably involved in those wars. He is also right that the court is shaped by the legal profession and that their decisions are largely shaped by the law profession culture. This culture—and the legal academy that reproduces it—are by and large more tolerant of homosexuality than other sectors of society, such as listeners of talk radio or leaders of organized religions, but also than other trade or professional networks, such as, most probably, police or corrections officers, electricians, or perhaps corporate executives. The decision in *Lawrence* is the product of this law profession culture, and, at least on the surface, is gay-friendly—it favors the interests of liberal pro-gay-rights advocates. But it does not necessarily promote the interests of all the gay-friendly. It is here that the Foreword probes *Lawrence*—dark side and all.

I.

Casually inspect a contemporary high school lunch room, a college or university campus, a youth clothing store. Open the pages of a staid alumni magazine. The sexual projects are, literally, all over the map—on both sides of the traditional divides. They are wide and varied—in fact, far more varied than a two-party model would suggest. This, from a cover feature on Professor Robert George, a highly distinguished and conservative professor of politics and jurisprudence at Princeton University, in the staid pages of the *Princeton Alumni Weekly:*

[According to Professor Robert George,] "Good" sex is genital sex between spouses, while "bad" (i.e., immoral) sex is defined as sex between unmarried partners, masturbation, or sex between spouses other than the genital-to-genital variety. He writes in *The Clash of Orthodoxies*, "The plain fact is that the genitals of men and women are reproductive organs all of the time—even during periods of sterility.... Insofar as the point or object of sexual intercourse is marital union, the partners achieve the desired unity (i.e., become 'two-in-one-flesh') precisely insofar as they mate ... or, if you will, perform the type of act—the only type of act—upon which the gift of a child may supervene."

George explains in greater detail in *The Clash of Orthodoxies* that "masturbatory and sodomitical acts, by their nature, instrumentalize the bodies of those choosing to engage in them in a way that cannot but damage their integrity as persons." This accounts, George contends, for the "self-alienating and disintegrating qualities of masturbatory and sodomitical sex."

Contrast George—specifically on the question of homosexual sodomy—with Judge Richard Posner. Posner's sexual project is to treat sex from a morally indifferent, purely economic perspective.[19] Posner views the homosexual life as an unhappier one than the heterosexual, and for this reason does not wish homosexuality on anyone. Yet he favors decriminalization. His argument takes three steps. First, approximately 2.5 percent of the American population is predominantly or exclusively homosexual and thus legal discrimination imposes a significant aggregate cost. Second, homosexual orientation is more innate than chosen and thus decriminalization is unlikely to increase the number of homosexuals. Third, the homosexual has a less happy life than the heterosexual—stemming primarily from the biological difficulties associated with childbearing and the resulting disruption of family life—and there is no reason to add to their misery. Posner writes:

> If I am correct that even in a tolerant society the male homosexual's lot is likely to be a less happy one on average than that of his heterosexual counterpart, still this is no reason in itself to strew legal or other social obstacles in the path of the homosexual. On the contrary, *in itself* it is a reason to remove those obstacles in order to alleviate gratuitous suffering. It becomes a reason for repression only if repression can change homosexual preference, incipient or settled, into heterosexual preference at acceptable cost and thereby make persons who would otherwise become or remain homosexuals happier. There is no reason to think that repression, psychotherapy, behavior modification, or any other technique of law or medicine can

19. Posner develops in his work, *Sex and Reason*, an economic theory of sexuality that, as a descriptive matter, embraces a rational choice perspective on sexual behavior and, from a normative perspective, adopts a libertarian position on sexual regulation—"not to be confused," Posner emphasizes, "with either libertine or modern liberal." RICHARD POSNER, SEX AND REASON 3 (Cambridge MA: Harvard University Press, 1992).

do so in a large enough number of cases to warrant the costs, not least to the "unconverted" homosexual, that legal and social discrimination imposes.

Posner concludes that "the sodomy laws ought to be repealed." Though Posner agrees with the result in *Lawrence,* he deplores the majority's reasoning. The homosexual sodomy laws are rarely enforced and do little harm, he emphasizes. Although the country may not have been ready for a pro-gay decision in 1986 at the time of *Bowers v. Hardwick,* Posner believes that, by 2003, seventeen years later, "the climate of opinion had changed sufficiently that the court could get away with invalidating the sodomy laws as underenforced, irrational, and a gratuitous insult to homosexuals."

Where does Posner, who does not wish homosexuality on anyone, yet supports the result in *Lawrence,* fit in Scalia's two-party model? How about the Cato Institute, a conservative or classical liberal or libertarian or market liberal think tank—notice the identity problems here too—which retained William Eskridge, professor at Yale Law School and author of one of the leading liberal pro-gay-rights texts, as counsel of record for its intervention in the *Lawrence* litigation? How about the many self-identified conservatives who think homosexuality is immoral and who clearly "do not want persons who openly engage in homosexual conduct as partners in their business, as scoutmasters for their children, as teachers in their children's schools, or as boarders in their home," yet who support the *Lawrence* decision? As one of these many self-identified conservatives writes on www.intellectualconservative.com:

> Of course most of the displeasure among Conservatives over the Supreme Court ruling stems from our belief that Homosexuality is abnormal and morally wrong. And yes it is wrong; it is sinful, and I strongly believe it is abnormal. Yet when it occurs between two, or three, or more consenting adults, in the privacy of their homes it is not my business. It is not your business. And certainly none of the government's business.

The fact is, there are a lot of people who do not want homosexuals around them, yet who do not support the criminalization of homosexual sodomy. Where do we place their sexual projects?

What about "metrosexuals," whose sexual project is ambiguously parasitic on the marginalization and taboo of homosexuality? "Metrosexuals" refer somewhat imprecisely to generally heterosexual practicing males—sometimes hyper-heterosexual—who share aesthetic sensibilities with the more traditional stereotype of the gay male. This definition of metrosexual is sketchy precisely because the thrust of the metrosexual identity—like so many others today—is to ambiguate sexuality. According to William Safire of *The New York Times,* quoting Mark Simpson who coined the term, "[h]e might be officially gay, straight or bisexual, but this is utterly immaterial, because he has clearly taken himself as his own love object and pleasure as his sexual preference." (The iconic figure of the metrosexual is the British soccer superstar, David Beckham, who reportedly wears nail polish, sports designer clothes, braids his hair, poses for gay magazines, and has a well-publicized hyper-heterosexual relationship with a member of the Spice Girls). In seeking to ambiguate sexuality, the metrosexual is not only *not* afraid of being called or perceived as homosexual, he thrives off the taboo that contributes to the mystique of being gay. Cultural critics have made the analogy to the way that "white suburban teenagers have long cribbed from hip-hop culture, as a way of distinguishing themselves from the pack." It is the criminalization of drugs and guns, and the marginalization of black rap culture that makes hip hop, in part, attractive to white suburban youths. The metrosexual too flirts with the danger of outlaw status. Where then do we fit the "metrosexual" in a two-party model?

At the other end of the political spectrum, how do we categorize the radical anti-assimilationist queer activists who embrace a marginalized status? How about the "lesbian outlaw" whose "status as outlaw is, for many lesbians, one important source of the satisfaction to be gained from lesbianism"? What about the homosexual public-sex activist "living fully at the very edge, triumphant over the threats, repression, persecution, prosecution, attacks, denunciations, hatred that have tried powerfully to crush him from the beginning of 'civilization' "? What about Gay Shame, a queer activist group based in San Francisco whose web motto is "Don't be devoured by the consumerist monster of 'Gay Pride'—Stop the monster of assimilation, before it's too late." Listen carefully to how Gay Shame describes itself:

> GAY SHAME IS THE VIRUS IN THE SYSTEM. We are a radical alternative to the gay mainstream and the increasingly complacent left. We seek nothing less than a new queer activism that addresses issues of race, class, gender, and sexuality to counter the self-serving 'values' of the gay mainstream. We are dedicated to fighting the rabid assimilationist monster of corporate gay 'culture' with a devastating mobilization of queer brilliance. Gay Shame is a celebration of resistance: all are welcome.

Under the rubric "Queercore," other radicals draw the line even more sharply. Queercore refers to "the punky, anti-assimilationist, transgressive movement on the fringe of lesbian and gay culture." It has produced a number of "zines"—e.g. "personal little xeroxed rags," "a kind of popular press"—and has annual conventions that are far from conventional, even by queer terms. This, from a 1991 editorial by Johnny Noxema and Rex Boy, the editors of the Toronto zine *BIMBOX*:

> You are entering a gay and lesbian-free zone.... Effective immediately, BIMBOX is at war against lesbians and gays. A war in which modern queer boys and queer girls are united against the prehistoric thinking and demented self-serving politics of the above-mentioned scum. BIMBOX hereby renounces its past use of the term lesbian and/or gay in a positive manner. This is a civil war against the ultimate evil, and consequently we must identify us and them in no uncertain terms.... So, dear lesbian woman or gay man to whom

perhaps BIMBOX has been inappropriately posted ... prepare to pay dearly for the way you and your kind have fucked things up.

The internal critique of gay culture is vitriolic. It verges on the violent—at least, verbally—as evidenced by this other pronouncement in *BIMBOX*: "We will not tolerate any form of lesbian and gay philosophy. We will not tolerate their voluntary assimilation into heterosexual culture.... *[I]f we see lesbians and gays being assaulted on the streets, we will not intervene, we will join in.* ... Effective immediately, [we are] at war with lesbians and gays." This does sound like a culture war, but surely it defies a two-party model.

What about "queer punk," a new music trend that cultivates anti-assimilation? These bands, with names like The Skin Jobs and The Rotten Fruits, are out to turn the queer left upside down. They "tear our current notions of gay pride to shreds" with lyrics like: "Don't imitate, stop trying to fit in. If everyone looked like everyone, then tell me 'Just who would you fuck?' And when the kids go 'We're gonna burn your rainbow and we're having fun!' Yeah! We don't need you, we don't care." Queer punk provokes its audiences with anti-assimilationist harangues, singing the virtues of promiscuity and rebellion. Here are The Rotten Fruits from their song, "Fuck Media Faggots": "I don't want to be 'Queer as Folk,' My life is no HBO joke.... Fuck Media Faggots, they don't care. Fuck Media Faggots, they won't dare."

Where do these groups and others like them—the Whores of Babylon (Queers Fighting Religious Intolerance), SISSY (Schools Information Services on Sexuality), or PUSSY (Perverts Undermining State Scrutiny)—fit in the picture? Does embracing an anti-assimilationist, radical pro-difference, pro-marginalization position constitute part of the "so-called homosexual agenda"?

We live in a post-identity politics—a politics where formerly cohesive identities have fragmented to the point that it is no longer possible to talk of a "homosexual agenda"—"so-called" or otherwise. The "homosexual agenda" is fractured along multiple dimensions, including, classically, the political. So some self-identified gay men and lesbian women oppose the liberal pro-gay-rights project from the right, contesting the need for broad anti-discrimination laws based on sexual orientation. Bruce Bawer, editor of *Beyond Queer: Challenging Gay Left Orthodoxy*, Andrew Sullivan and others offer what Bawer calls "a new gay paradigm:" the main thrust (though it comes in different variations) is to seek an end to all public or state-sanctioned forms of discrimination and to leave the rest alone. "No cures or re-educations; no wrenching civil litigation; no political imposition of tolerance;" Andrew Sullivan writes, "merely a political attempt to enshrine formal civil equality, in the hope that eventually the private sphere will reflect this public civility." Within internal discussions on the right, it is acceptable to argue for social assimilation *through sexual restraint*. As John Berresford writes:

> Among ourselves, we must be willing to talk about morals, to impose them on ourselves, and to do so conspicuously. As long as our

primary image is one of gleeful promiscuity . . . we will be ostra-cized. Until we start imposing honesty, fidelity, and emotion on our lives—in other words, until we are willing to talk about moral standards—we will make little real progress in social acceptance.

Other self-identified gay men, lesbian women, and queer theorists oppose the gay-rights-project from the left, challenging the very notion of sexual identities. Janet Halley's critique of the same-sex harassment protection in *Oncale,* discussed earlier, represents one variation. For Halley, the queer project "emphasizes the fictional status of sex, gender, and sexual orientation identity, and . . . affirms rather than abhors sexuality, 'dark side' and all." It "regards the homosexual/heterosexual distinction with skepticism and even resentment, arguing that it is historically contingent and is itself oppressive." From this perspective, it is the gay-friendly construction of homosexuality that is problematic and reflects a deep chasm between anti-discrimination approaches and a more radical questioning of sexuality—a conflict "not simply between older 'gay' assimilationists . . . and 'queers' asserting their 'queerness'. Rather it is between those who think of the politics of sexuality as a matter of securing minority rights and those who are contesting the overall validity and authenticity of the epistemology of sexuality itself."

In research exploring the dominant sexual ideologies in lesbian, gay, bisexual, and transgender (LGBT) communities published in the *Journal of Homosexuality* in 2003, the authors identify two "prominent sexual 'ideological types' "—assimilationist and radical. These positions are familiar, especially in the context of the same-sex marriage debates. But the truth is, each one of these positions comes in multiple flavors. Within the assimilationist position, there are dignity strands, but there are also moralist strands. So too in the radical position, where there is a wide range of positions. In the gay-marriage context, for instance, there are arguments against the institution of marriage per se, arguments against the resulting exclusion of marriage laws, as well as more strategic arguments against marriage *for gays.* And these tensions have been present for a long time. The different variations are themselves different ideologies. The two ideal types form a spectrum, not a dichotomous pair. There are, in effect, moral assimilationists, incremental assimilations, strategic assimilationists, among others, as well as radical anti-assimila-tionists, libertarian radicals, and separatists—a whole plethora of gay-friendly ideologies in the identified LGBT community.

Even within a single narrower community—the lesbian community, for example—there are recurring, sharp, often caustic conflicts. In fact, from a historical perspective, what may be most characteristic of lesbian cultural discourse and activism is its constant need to transgress—*itself.* Lesbian feminists of the 1970s—Adrienne Rich, Sheila Jeffries, Mary Daly, among others—reacted against the patriarchal elements that they perceived in lesbianism, especially the role-playing butch/femme identi-ties that pervaded the lesbian underworld of the 1950s and 60s, and turned toward a more separatist approach. This sparked, in the 1980s, a reaction to what women saw as an "anti-sex" attitude and a turn to

S/M—to "a new politics of outlawry, of sexual deviance." As Emma Healey tells it, the 1990s "saw a new orthodoxy that trumpeted S/M sexuality while at the same time decrying anything vanilla." This new lesbian ideology was more willing to ally itself with gay men, giving rise to queer politics. This in turn engendered a rebirth of the lesbian feminist movement. In essays such as *Queer Straights*, critics railed against the new politics of queer as a regression to patriarchy and heterosexuality:

> [T]he 'in your face radicalism' which is claimed to be the most important signifier of queer, is, in the end, hard to distinguish from plain old liberalism; queer's 'shocking' tactics constitute little more than a plea to be included in straight society, rather than a demand that we change it.

The bottom line is that, today, the "lesbian agenda" would be a meaningless term: it would be necessary to distinguish between "lesbian feminists," "lesbians who are also feminists," "radical lesbians" or "lesbian separatists," "heterofeminists," queer theorists, post-queer theorists, "libertarian lesbians," among others, to properly define a political intervention. Monique Wittig famously remarked that "Lesbians are not women." By this, I take it, she meant that the interests of lesbians do not coincide with those of lesbian feminists. Perhaps a more accurate statement would be, "Lesbians are not."

The point is that to refer to a "homosexual agenda" is as meaningless as to talk about an "American sexual agenda," an "American criminal law agenda," or for that matter an anti-"homosexual agenda." The internal positions vary widely. Even the more specific concept of a "homosexual agenda ... directed at eliminating the moral opprobrium that has traditionally attached to homosexual conduct" is incoherent. This agenda ranges from homosexual public-sex activism—from engaging in homosexual sex *in public*—to embracing sexual restraint and moral puritanism. How the myriad sexual projects compare is complex and it is what makes the sex wars unpredictable. It is not a war between homosexual activists (and their *companions de route*) against mainstream heterosexual Americans who don't want to be around gay and lesbians. It is a complex, multi-party conflict that affects conceptions of the self, relations to others, eroticism, sexual practices, etc. As one commentator writes in the *Daily Targum*, the Rutgers University paper, on the topic of same-sex marriage:

> The media has constructed a binary opposition between all Queers along with their straight alliances, and the conservative Christian Right's wish for the state to prohibit the sanctioning of homosexual sins. But, as a radical, a lesbian and a feminist, my opposition to [normalizing homosexual relations] does not fall into these dichotomous categories.

Sexuality is so central to each individual that every person has a sexual project—by which I mean a position on how others should act sexually, an *other regarding* ideology of sexual practice. These sexual projects may or may not be related to one's own sexual practices—some may actively engage in one type of practice only, yet firmly believe that others should (or should be allowed) to engage in other practices. (Sexual projects may also include complete *indifference* to the practices of others). What is important is not the sexual practices that the individual personally engages in, nor the bottom line dichotomous "pro" or "against" position on homosexuality or the morality of any particular sex act. They may vary widely as between individuals who engage in very similar sexual acts—in fact, whether two persons engage in similar or different sex acts tells us very little about how their sexual projects compare. What matters is the ideology that surrounds other-regarding sexual views. Are they, for instance, based on a libertarian impulse, a libertine penchant, a pro-sex attitude, morality, religion, or other grounds? This matters because it will determine the future shape of coalitions and conflict in other sex wars in the criminal law and elsewhere.

The proliferation and fracturing of sexual projects destabilizes simple dichotomies. In the more technical terms of Arrow's Theorem, the fractiousness creates a multidimensional political voting model that may make it difficult to predict how coalitions will form or whether they will remain stable in future sex wars in criminal law and elsewhere. So, for instance, the alliances that formed in the *Lawrence* context become unstable in the same-sex marriage debates, where anti-marriage libertarians and gays may ally with conservative legal moralists to overcome the pro gay-rights and liberal coalition. This is precisely what makes the sex wars so unpredictable, and why we need to engage in a far more nuanced analysis of the different sexual projects to understand how they result in coalitions, alliances, and ultimately victories or losses. It also implies, paradoxically, that we need to attend more carefully to fractiousness in the gay-friendly camp of the *Lawrence* decision.

II.

What would it sound like to ambiguate the result in *Lawrence* from a gay-friendly perspective? In her review in *Artforum* of the Diane Arbus exhibition *Revelations*, Judith Butler probes the curious relationship between generations of prohibitory norms. Diane Arbus, in her photographs, rebelled against the prevailing norms of bourgeois society that erased the stigmatized body from view—the prohibitory norms that hid the physically or mentally handicapped from the public gaze. Arbus's photographs are renowned for their many disturbing representations of the deviant—a veritable freak show of deformed bodies, dwarves, muscle men, and the mentally ill. Her photographs exposed oddity, buried in everyday portraits. *The Human Pincushion, Ronald C. Harrison, N.J.* (1962) depicts the proud, perhaps defiant, bare chested, tattooed Mr. Harrison with three-inch pins sticking through his throat, forehead, cheeks, lips, arms and chest. The photographs are "fascinated by human distortions, playing on spectacle, pandering to the unseemly desire to gawk at what might seem aberrant, to peer, to invade."

In their time, Arbus's photographs challenged the prohibitory norm of surface aesthetics. Today, however, the photographs trigger a different prohibitory norm—the norm against objectifying the deviant, against gawking at the stigmatized body. "We are not supposed to make into visual spectacles human bodies that are stigmatized within public life or to treat them as objects available for visual consumption." Few are willing to pander to the desire to gawk. Yet the more modern prohibition against gazing at the formerly prohibited reproduces its own desire. As Judith Butler explains,

> [O]ne finds oneself wanting to see what one "should not" enjoy seeing, and now partly to test the thesis that these photos are nothing but specularization or objectification. One does not, from a critical perspective, want to accept such a blanket judgment without first seeing for oneself, so the desire to "see for oneself" is instigated by the newer prohibition as well. There is in Arbus—and in the discomfort with her work—always that struggle: a certain solicitation to see what one should not see.

Is it the original prohibition that accounts for our fascination today? Are the photographs more irresistible because of the redoubled prohibition, like some kind of return of the repressed? Does the desire to see what we should not see make the seeing all that more intriguing? Would there be any fascination with seeing at all if there had not been the original prohibition? Does our present fascination require a former prohibition?

The notorious debates over "camp"—an older, equally ambiguated, and highly contested term of sexual identity—reflect much of this subtle interaction between norm and prohibition. For some cultural critics, camp could only exist *against* the norm. In his response to Susan Sontag's essay, "Notes on 'Camp,'" Andrew Britton proposed that camp could simply not exist without the conventions of masculinity. Although camp may define itself precisely in opposition to those conventions of masculinity, it depends on their continuing to exist. "The camp gay man declares," Britton states, " 'Masculinity is an oppressive convention to which I refuse to conform'; but his non-conformity depends at every point on the preservation of the convention he ostensibly rejects—in this case, a general acceptance of what constitutes 'a man.' " The rejection of the norm, Britton suggests, requires the norm. Role-playing demands the foil. "Camp behavior is only recognisable as a deviation from an implied norm, and without that norm it would cease to exist, it would lack definition. It does not, and cannot, propose for a moment a radical critique of the norm itself." This is so because the camp identity, according to Britton, plays off the convention.

Part of the vitality of camp, then, is the transgression. "Camp requires the *frisson* of transgression, the sense of perversity in relation to bourgeois norms which characterises the degeneration of the Romantic impulse in the second half of the nineteenth century, and which culminates in England with Aestheticism and in France with the *déca-*

dence," Britton writes. "Camp is a house-trained version of the aristo-cratic, anarchistic ethic of transgression, a breach of decorum which no longer even shocks, and which has gone to confirm the existence of a special category of person—the male homosexual." This idea of *frisson* harks back to Jean Genet—and, before him, to the Surrealist, André Breton. Genet's romanticization of the delinquency of homosexuality—of homosexual rape in *Querelle*—did not aspire to decriminalization. As Jean–Paul Sartre writes in his study of Genet, *Saint Genet*, "Genet does not want to change anything at all. Do not count on him to criticize institutions. He needs them, as Prometheus needs his vulture."

Part of what may be going on is the erotic attraction to the utterly deviant—but only part. There is far more to desire than the erotic, and the biological dimensions of homosexuality undermine any simple associ-ation between sexual orientation and the appeal of deviance. Yet there may well be an erotic dimension to the prohibited. Sheila Jeffreys quotes a delicious passage from Sarah Schulman's novel, *After Dolores*, where a character says:

> It's too easy to be gay today in New York City. I come from those times when sexual excitement could only be in hidden places. Sweet women had to put themselves in constant danger to make love to me. All my erotic life is concerned with intrigue and secrets. You can't understand that these days, not at all. Lesbians will never be that sexy again.

Lesbians will never be that sexy again. To what extent does the erotic derive from the forbidden? *Glamour* magazine reports having conducted, in partnership with MensHealth.com, a survey of 2793 men to explore issues of sexual practices. One question they asked was "Why are men so fixated on having anal sex?" (Who knew?) Forty-seven percent of the respondents answered "because it's taboo." (Twenty-two percent chose "because it feels great," and thirty-one percent "because it's an accomplishment just talking her into it.") Does the taboo really account for the erotic practice? And is the practice really erotic if it is brought on by taboo, or is it some other kind of desire? Chicago public radio reports an increase in rates of sexually transmitted diseases. One explanation is a lot more experimenting with bisexual relations among teenagers in part because of the stigma of same-sex intercourse. Survey data from the period 1988 to 1998 suggests an increase in the percentage of people with same-sex partners, despite constant levels of "exclusively" homosexual men and women. The survey data—from the General Social Surveys conducted by the National Opinion Research Center at the University of Chicago over the period 1988 to 1998—revealed between a doubling and tripling of the likelihood of having a same-gender sex partner over the period (though the number remained low in 1998, 4.1 percent for men and 2.8 percent for women). The increase could not be attributed to changing demographics, increased urbanization or edu-cational attainment, or racial or ethnic shifts in the population. Is the increase due to greater social acceptance of homosexual relations or to the taboo associated with same-sex relations?

Think of unsafe sex among gay men in urban areas—what is known as "barebacking," a term used to describe unprotected anal sex. Or even more troubling, "bug chasing," the practice of some gay men of actively trying to acquire HIV through unprotected same-gender sex. A recent documentary by filmmaker Louise Hogarth, *The Gift*, documents the new development. The title derives "from the term 'gift givers,' or HIV-positive men who give 'the gift' of HIV infection." In the documentary, "a soft-spoken, Midwestern college youth named Doug Hitzel tearfully recalls what drove him to become a 'bug chaser'—an HIV-negative man who seeks to be infected with the virus that causes AIDS." The attraction to danger and to deviance must play a role in these practices.

Criminality, prohibition, danger—seduction. As Jack Katz powerfully demonstrates in *Seductions of Crime,* the thrill of breaking the law can produce an emotional high. Katz describes in compelling detail the thrill-seeking of some of his students who shoplift. He shows, through their own words, how merchandise in stores become so much more irresistible *because* they are forbidden.

> There we were, in the most lucrative department Mervyn's had to offer.... Once my eyes caught sight of the beautiful white and blue necklaces alongside the counter, a spark inside me was once again ignited.... Those exquisite puka necklaces were calling out to me, "Take me! Wear me! I can be yours!"

It is the criminality of shoplifting that makes the jewelry so attractive, the theft so thrilling, and the object so compelling. One student explains: "Every time I would drop something into my bag, my heart would be pounding and I could feel this tremendous excitement, a sort of 'rush,' go through me." Another student reports, "The experience was almost orgasmic for me. There was a build-up of tension as I contemplated the danger of the forbidden act, then a rush of excitement at the moment of committing the crime, and finally a delicious sense of release." Yet another recalls: "It's really funny being 23 years old now and in writing this, I can't stop feeling how thrilling it was, certainly a feeling much like the anticipation of sex."

The same prohibition helps make guns so seductive to detained youths, gangsta-rap so exciting for suburban youths, and pink underwear so attractive to adults. Pink underwear? Sheriff Arpaio of Maricopa County, Arizona, started issuing pink boxers to his jail inmates in order to stem vandalism of underwear stock—Arpaio reported losing more than $40,000 worth of purloined underwear in a nine-month period in 1995. The pink boxers became such a phenomenon, that Arpaio started selling the pink boxers on the free market for $10 per boxers. According to the *Phoenix New Times* writing in 1995, "Souvenir versions of the boxer shorts have become all the rage. Volunteers in the 2,500–member Sheriff's Posse have sold 3,000 pairs of pink skivvies, grossing $30,000" in 1995 alone.

But there is more to homosexual erotic attraction than the forbidden, and there must also be more to the forbidden than erotic attraction.

There is something else, something deeper about the attraction of deviance, about the urge to resist hegemonic power, about the felt need to "question authority," about the desire to "subvert the dominant paradigm." How do these emotions, desires, urges, personalities depend on, relate to, derive from prohibitory norms? Sheila Jeffreys writes about "the lesbian romance with outlaw status." She suggests that "[t]he lesbian's status as outlaw is, for many lesbians, one important source of the satisfaction to be gained from lesbianism.... [L]esbianism offers the glamour and excitement of outlawry." As Ruby Rich explains,

> For many women, the drive toward lesbianism was not only sexual but also a will to be the outlaw, the same drive that moved other subcultures, like the Beats, to cross to the 'wrong' side of the tracks, if only metaphorically. Thus, there was a very real sense of loss associated with the hard-won respectability: a loss of taboo and with it eroticism.

In fact, some of these critics argue that, as lesbianism became more acceptable, the appeal of the outlaw led to "outlaw sexuality"—sadomasochism. "Where once outlawry could be assured simply by adoption of lesbian sexuality and lifestyle it seems that the apparently greater social possibilities gained for lesbians by lesbian liberation have made things too easy," thus leading to the new "sexual outlaw" lesbians engaging in S/M. "A political movement of sexual outlawry has developed in the eighties amongst lesbians of which the glamourising of prostitution is but one part. The new lesbian politics of transgression is an offshoot of an older tradition in gay male culture and politics."

The outlaw impulse, Jeffreys suggests, is tied closely to the attraction to the lesbian bar and bar culture—places that are often described as "dingy" or "decadent." "Lesbian bars," at least in London, "have traditionally been sited in cellars or basements with backed up toilets, crush, smoke, and terrible food," likely in order to escape the attention of homophobes. In part, what may account for this attraction is, Jeffreys suggests,

> nostalgie de la boue, an expression coined in the end of century decadence of the 1890s to denote a fascination with 'low-life' amongst the bourgeoisie. This fascination was acted out by middle-class straight men mainly through consorting with prostitutes in London bars.... Oscar Wilde was fascinated with his favourite version of boue i.e. use of young working class male prostitutes and drugs and not just in practice but in art. In *The Picture of Dorian Gray* Wilde painted a romantically decadent picture of the opium den.

The opium den of the late nineteenth century plays an equally mystical role in the work of Charles Baudelaire. The forbidden, the haunting pleasures of escape, the fascination with *spleen*, run through *Les Fleurs du Mal*. The romanticized Bohemian life of the late nineteenth century cohabited parasitically alongside, within, and against the dominant bourgeois society. It fed off the moral and legal opprobrium of the bourgeoisie. It needed bourgeois society in the same way that camp needs masculinity.

Perhaps the best way to understand the constitutive dimensions of deviance is to listen carefully to the more radical activists today—the second wave of more militant, radical, younger queer activists, sometimes called "post-queer," Queercore, or pomo-queer. What do they seek from deviance? In the introduction to their edited volume, *PomoSexuals*, Carol Queen and Lawrence Schimel write:

> Pomosexuality lives in the space in which all other non-binary forms of sexual and gender identity reside—a boundary-free zone in which fences are crossed for the fun of it, or simply because some of us can't be fenced in. It challenges either/or categorizations in favor of largely unmapped possibility and the intense charge that comes with transgression. It acknowledges the pleasure of that transgression, as well as the need to transgress limits that do not make room for all of us.

Writing about Queercore, Dennis Cooper suggests:

> Based on everything I've read, heard, interpreted, and felt, they are disappointed that so many lesbians and gays have accepted the heterosexual model of normalcy, reiterating all of society's mistakes in Disneyesque ghettos like West Hollywood, the Castro, the Village. The new queers accept that assimilation [is] irreversible for much of lesbian/gay culture at this point. So they're trying to construct an alternate culture in and around it. They don't pretend for a moment that they can alter the dominant culture—gay or straight. They don't want to. All they really want is to be taken seriously. And left alone.

Left alone. Could that possibly mean left alone while leaving in place the legal prohibition against homosexual relations?

In the U.K., there developed a group called "Homocult-perverters of culture" based in Manchester in the early 1990s that positioned itself in opposition to the queer activist group OutRage as "too queer to be OutRaged." In their poster, they declare that the terms "lesbian and gay" describe:

> Persils fucked up by privilege who wish to blend with sick society rather than change it.... OutRage is a cosy sham. You can only be outraged by what surprises you. It's no surprise to common queers that there is no justice for us. We are not outraged. WE ARE DEFIANT.

This defiance is a form of radical critique that goes beyond mere reform. It aims instead at "radical social change: change which strikes at the 'root,' at the 'source,' at the 'structural foundations' of the social 'system,' pushing change forward towards transformation of the social totality rather than mere reformation of even conservation of this existing system." There are more theorized statements of this position— or perhaps less radical positions that nevertheless seek more than reform. Cathy Cohen expresses this position in her article *Punks, Bulld-aggers, and Welfare Queens: The Radical Potential of Queer Politics?*, where she too laments the failed potential of queer politics. She argues that "a truly radical or transformative politics has not resulted from queer activism," in large part because "instead of destabilizing the assumed categories and binaries of sexual identity, queer politics has served to reinforce simple dichotomies between heterosexual and every-thing 'queer.' " What has been left unchallenged is "an understanding of the ways in which power informs and constitutes privileged and margin-alized subjects on both sides of this dichotomy." Cohen argues for a "new politics":

> I envision a politics where one's relation to power, and not some homogenized identity, is privileged in determining one's political comrades. I'm talking about a politics where the *nonnormative* and *marginal* position of punks, bulldaggers, and welfare queens, for example, is the basis for progressive transformative coalition work. Thus, if there is any truly radical potential to be found in the idea of queerness and the practice of queer politics, it would seem to be located in its ability to create a space in opposition to dominant norms, a space where transformational political work can begin.

The thrust of this "new politics" is opposition to dominant norms by all those "who stand on the outside of the dominant constructed norm of state-sanctioned white middle-and upper-class heterosexuality." It focus-es on a close analysis of "the intersection of systems of oppression." It proposes a more expansive understanding of political coalitions that embraces other marginalized identities based on race, class, etc. It is a politics different from liberal or civil rights—frameworks that are inef-fective at confronting homophobia, Cohen argues. Civil rights, Cohen asserts, "do not change the social order in dramatic ways; they change only the privileges of the group asserting those rights." The reason is that civil rights movements seek only access to the dominant framework, they do not challenge the framework of rights. But it is that framework of rights—not the lack of civil rights—that produces the systematic homophobia. It is "the nature and construction of the political, legal, economic, sexual, racial and family systems within which we live."

The problem, of course, is that Cohen simply substitutes "white middle-and upper-class heterosexual" for "heterosexual," without in any way problematizing the category, the idea of class, or the concept of heterosexuality itself. It seems that the more theorized the expression of the radical position, the less well it captures the positive underbelly of deviance. There has to be something more than simple class or identity warfare. There must exist a space for a genuine non-assimilationist, non-reformist, nihilist, hedonistic appreciation of marginalization.

Perhaps the best or only way to express this politics, then, is through a pastiche of post-queer venom. It has something to do with *"the intense charge that comes with transgression and the pleasure of that transgression."* It involves *"an alternate culture in and around it, to be taken seriously, and left alone."* It is a *"boundary-free zone in which fences are crossed for the fun of it, or simply because some of us can't be fenced in. It challenges either/or categorizations in favor of largely unmapped possibility."* It is nostalgic, transgressive, full of hope and hopeless at the same time. It is a politics of *spleen*—an expression that refers back and captures the uncomfortable co-dependence of nineteenth-century Bohemia on bourgeois law and society.

I have endeavored here to explore the constitutive, dark side of the penal sanction. There are, of course, other friendly but skeptical accounts of *Lawrence*—but they only scratch the surface. There is the backlash argument—the incrementalist argument against *Lawrence*-type litigation. Some pro-gay activists warn that the *Lawrence* decision may scare many away from the prospect of gay marriage or create a more hostile environment for gay men and lesbian women. And of course, there have been a number of judicial decisions rendered since *Lawrence*, as well as polling data, that flame these debates. With each new ruling, with each new poll, there are loud waves of "I told you so" rolling through the legal academy—on both sides of the debate. The Eleventh Circuit upheld Florida's adoption laws which preclude adoption by any person who engages in homosexual activity. A Kansas court of appeals upheld a disparate sentencing scheme that punishes far more severely an older teenager when he engages in sex with a same-sex younger teenager as opposed to a different-sex younger teenager. The Massachusetts Supreme Judicial Court, in two separate decisions, has required same-sex *marriage*, not just civil union. And the polling data reflect a backlash in public opinion regarding both whether homosexual relations should be legal—the *Lawrence* issue—and whether the state should allow same-sex marriage—at least in the short term.

But the backlash critique—whether right or wrong—still aspires to the elimination of criminal sodomy laws. It is a strategic argument, not an outlaw argument. The same is true of the other friendly but skeptical critique, the accommodation argument—namely the idea that civil rights litigation never really challenges the anti-gay norms. These arguments all aspire to a liberation ideal that does not necessarily embrace deviance. I have sought instead to explore the positive side of the deviant impulse.

III.

With all this in place, it may be possible to reconstruct Justice Scalia's incendiary dissent, to tweak it so that it reflects more accurately the nuances and subtleties of our contemporary sex wars. To begin, Justice Scalia is certainly right that there is a culture war in this country that encompasses, among other things, the trilogy of sexuality, family, and morality/religion—what I would call a war of sexual projects. Justice Scalia is also right that the Supreme Court partakes in the culture wars in *Lawrence*. The Court's engagement, however, is by no means new or a departure from some neutral role as arbiter of the democratic rules of engagement. The Supreme Court has been a central player in these culture wars since at least the mid-twentieth century. There is a rich tradition of gay-rights cases going back to the 1950s. Joyce Murdoch and Deb Price chronicle the history of Supreme Court cases affecting the rights of gay men and lesbian women in their excellent book, *Courting Justice: Gay Men and Lesbians v. the Supreme Court*. They trace the start of the gay-rights lineage of cases back to *ONE v. Olesen*, a 1957 Supreme Court ruling on the censorship, on obscenity grounds, of the nation's first homosexual publication, *ONE*—where the court ruled in favor of the gay publication and imposed the same standard of obscenity on homosexual as heterosexual material. Murdoch and Prince chronicle over eighteen cases decided on the merits—and list in an appendix over eighty cases including important certiorari denials—that dealt with homosexuality. These included cases addressing the deportation of immigrants for homosexuality, employment discrimination against homosexuals, the right of teachers to advocate gay rights issues, and the use of the term "Olympics" for the Gay Olympic Games, as well as the more well-known recent cases involving the exclusion of a gay group from Boston's St. Patrick's Day Parade, Colorado's anti-gay Amendment 2, and the Boy Scouts of America's exclusion of gays. Moreover, the court has addressed the issue of homosexual sodomy on several previous occasions, including *Wade v. Buchanan* in 1971, *Wainwright v. Stone* in 1973, *Doe v. City of Richmond* in 1976, *New York v. Uplinger* in 1984, and, of course, *Bowers v. Hardwick* in 1986. Several of the justices had dealt with homosexuality cases as well before acceding to the Supreme Court. Justice Kennedy, for instance, while serving on the Ninth Circuit, had ruled in five cases involving homosexual issues and had written the decision in a case upholding Navy regulations that banned homosexuals.

Moreover, the justices themselves actively partake in the culture wars, not only through their written opinions, but also and importantly through their speeches. Justice Scalia is notorious for making provocative statements in speeches. As noted earlier, he has taken the fight over homosexual sodomy beyond the courthouse. He has also made comments about other cultural conflicts, including the controversy over the Pledge of Allegiance which has caused him to recuse himself from hearing that case. Justice Scalia is very much of a cultural warrior, and he is, of course, not alone. Justices O'Connor and Ginsburg have made politically-engaged comments about the death penalty, and Justices Kennedy and Breyer about mandatory minimum sentencing.

To be sure, in his dissenting opinion Justice Scalia maintains that the court only participates in the culture wars when it "depart[s] from its role of assuring, as neutral observer, that the democratic rules of engagement are observed." Justice Scalia contends, in the sodomy context, that finding a federal constitutional right *is* partaking in the culture war, but leaving it to the democratic process is *not*. It is not entirely clear whether Justice Scalia is being completely sincere in this respect, given that much of his dissenting opinion is turned over to arguing that *Roe v. Wade* should be overruled—in other words, given that he too, like the majority which he criticizes, is playing fast and loose with the standard of *stare decisis*. But if sincere, then Justice Scalia's argument definitely needs to be tweaked because it fundamentally misunderstands the concept of "war" and fails to appreciate that *any* decision about the rule of decision to apply in the sodomy context—whether to accept legal moralism or impose a harm principle—represents a judicial choice. In this respect, Toni Massaro is right: "The Court in *Lawrence* did step into a cultural fray, to be sure. But no matter how the Court resolved *Lawrence*, it would have been engaged in that fray...."

The ultimate decision about which rule to follow is itself a choice and is never neutral. Justice Scalia misses a basic existentialist insight. *Bowers* itself was not neutral: the decision to let morality simpliciter satisfy rational basis review—without a showing of harm—is itself a loaded choice. It requires *continuing* to buy into legal moralism. It is not *dictated*. Instead it reaffirms. The same is true of adopting or reaffirming a harm principle. Requiring a showing of harm in order to satisfy rational basis review is not a neutral act. It may well be the case that, for many years, majoritarian morality was a valid basis for penal prohibition. But each time the court decided to keep it that way, the court had the option of changing the decisional rule, of inching toward a harm principle. Every time it chose not to, it *chose* not to. To suggest that the court would *not* engage in the culture war by leaving the democratic process to its own devices is blinking reality.

Moreover, in this culture war, the very rules of war are at stake. The court is not an outside observer overseeing the sex wars. The court is not a referee, because it is precisely the rules of the game that are being fought over. The rule whether there is foul play—whether a party, like the state, has overreached or gone off-sides—is up for grabs. Justice Scalia is, in effect, mixing metaphors and in the process, forgetting that this is a war, not a refereed game. The way to think about this conflict is not in terms of a formal game with established rules where the court is there to make sure that the game is being played properly. The way to think about this is in war terms: there are no rules, there is no arbiter, there is no referee. And when a case is filed in federal court, the federal courts inextricably takes sides. They have no option not to participate. Dismissing the claim under Rule 12(b)(6) is no more neutral than ruling on the merits of the constitutional argument. Granting certiorari, denying certiorari—these are not neutral acts.

Next, Justice Scalia is undoubtedly right that the majority's decision in *Lawrence* is indeed shaped by the legal-professional complex within which the Supreme Court exists and operates. In claiming that the decision "is the product of a law-profession culture," Justice Scalia is making an accurate statement. In identifying the legal academy as an important institution in shaping the legal-professional complex, Justice Scalia is also right. And in claiming that the law-profession culture "has largely signed on to the so-called homosexual agenda," Justice Scalia is, to be sure, painting with a broad brush, perhaps too broad a brush, but there is nevertheless a grain of truth in what he says. The legal-professional structure that most closely touches the Supreme Court—

namely, the elite legal academy that produces not only most of the justices, but also most of their law clerks, most of the constitutional commentators, and many of the regular oral advocates—tends to be liberal, equal-rights-oriented and, at least superficially, gay friendly. But it is a far stretch from this to say that the law profession has "signed on" to the pro-gay-rights position. A more fair characterization is that, despite patches of extreme to mild homophobia, the legal profession may be slightly more tolerant of gays and lesbians than other identifiable sectors of society. It would be difficult—though fascinating—to get more precise than that and to calibrate exactly how gay-friendly the legal profession is compared to the medical profession, the psychiatric profession, the ministry, commercial bankers or accountants.

Justice Scalia is right that the Court and its members are deeply embedded in a network of institutions, social networks, practices and discourses that shape the way that they reason, deliberate and judge; the way that they write opinions and express themselves; and the way that they reproduce law clerks and lawyers. The justices themselves are the product of the elite American legal academy, sporting law degrees from Harvard, Stanford, Yale, Columbia, and Northwestern. Many of the justices were faculty members at elite law schools before acceding to the bench. Justice Scalia, for instance, was a professor at the University of Chicago, and the University of Virginia before that, and in that capacity, was himself at least indirectly associated with the American Association of Law Schools. Justice Ginsburg was a law professor at Columbia Law School, Justice Breyer a professor at Harvard Law School, and Justice Stevens taught as well at Northwestern and the University of Chicago. Their closest employees—their elbow clerks with whom they spend the most time—are hand-picked from an elite group of top-ranking law students from the country's elite law schools. From 1997 through 2003, Justice Scalia has hired at least six Harvard Law grads, five University of Chicago Law grads, two from Columbia, two from Notre Dame, and one each from Yale, Stanford, Boalt, New York University, Michigan, Northwestern and Penn. Justice Scalia is certainly not alone. During the 2001 and 2002 Terms alone, the nine justices hired a combined total of seventeen Harvard law graduates, eleven Yale law graduates, nine University of Chicago law graduates, five from Columbia, three each from Stanford and New York University, and another twenty-one graduates from an assortment of elite law schools. Most of the justices are on speaking circuits that take them frequently back to law schools, and naturally they socialize with elite Washington, D.C. lawyers. Justice Scalia, for instance, is a regular at what has been called "one of Washington's most exclusive poker games," which includes the Chief Justice, William Rehnquist, and elite D.C. lawyers such as Robert S. Bennett (the personal attorney to President Bill Clinton and numerous other cabinet members, such as former defense secretary Caspar Weinberger) and Leonard Garment (counselor to President Richard Nixon).

In addition, beginning in the early-to mid–1990s, gay and lesbian law clerks and former law clerks began coming out to their justices in part as an effort to normalize homosexual relations at the Supreme Court. Bill Araiza, law clerk to Justice Souter during the 1991–92 Term, reportedly was committed to coming out to any justice who hired him, wanting to make sure that the justice did not, reportedly in his own words, "walk away thinking he's never met a gay person." So, in spring 1992, Araiza told Justice Souter "very bluntly" that he was gay. Professor Chai Feldblum of Georgetown University, who clerked for Justice Blackmun during the 1986–87 Term, recounts coming out to Justice Blackmun in 1992, reportedly coaxing herself in the following terms: "Come on, Chai. You know he really likes you. You know it makes a difference when people know someone who's gay. You should *do* it." According to Murdoch and Price, "Feldblum was one of a number of current and former gay clerks who by the early 1990s were coming out to justices." Michael Conley and J. Paul Oetken were openly gay when they clerked for Justice Blackmun in 1990–91 and 1993–94 respectively, referring openly to their respective partners as "boyfriend" or "partner." In fact, by 1998, Justice Blackmun included in his list of "office family" members the same-sex partners of Feldblum, Conley, Oetken and Al Lauber. According to Murdoch and Price, "some [gay and/or lesbian clerks] have taken their partners to court reunions." At least one justice has had a male law clerk who has had a child in a same-sex relationship and has included the child among the chamber's "grand clerks."

Murdoch and Price report that, going back to the mid 1950s, "We found 22 gay former Supreme Court clerks—18 gay men and four lesbians. . . . (Another gay man and a lesbian clerked for appeals court judges who later became justices)." However, practically all of those clerks were closeted during their clerkships, and the prevalence of closeted gay law clerks does not guarantee a gay-friendly vote—Justice Powell's notorious swing vote in *Hardwick* is testament to that. As Murdoch and Price emphasize, "[t]he impact of gay Supreme Court clerks has been very muted until very recent years because clerks tended to come out only after the justice for whom they'd worked had left the court."

The role of gay and lesbian clerks—closeted or open—may be offset by the role of more conservative chamber colleagues. The *Hardwick* case is a notorious case study. Justice Powell was the swing vote—the fifth vote that would decide the case—and originally voted for Michael Hardwick. That term, Justice Powell had four clerks: Carter Cabell Chinnis Jr., a self-identified gay man who was in the closet at the time of his clerkship, a graduate of Yale Law School, and now a partner in a leading law firm, Mayer, Brown, Rowe, and Maw, in Washington, D.C.; Michael Mosman, a conservative Mormon from Idaho, married at the time with three children, a graduate of Brigham Young University's law school, recently appointed by President George W. Bush to the federal district court in Portland, Oregon; Anne Coughlin, a graduate of New York University School of Law, now professor of law at the University of Virginia; and William Stuntz, a graduate of the University of Virginia

School of Law, now professor at Harvard Law School. (Note, the knowl-edge/power dimensions should be obvious even to the uninitiated read-er).

Justice Powell assigned the case to Michael Mosman, his more conservative, Mormon clerk. Much controversy surrounds the exact role of Mosman still today. It was in fact raised during his confirmation for federal district court in Oregon. What is known is that Mosman wrote a twelve-page bench memo for Powell dated March 29, 1986, which Powell received on the Saturday before oral argument. In the bench memo, Mosman argued against Michael Hardwick on due process grounds: "The right to privacy calls for the greatest judicial restraint, invalidating only those laws that impinge on those values that are basic to our country," Mosman wrote. "I do not think that this case involves any such values. I recommend reversal [of the Eleventh Circuit decision]." "Personal sexu-al freedom is a newcomer among our national values," Mosman empha-sized, "and may well be, as discussed earlier, a temporary national mood that fades." On the memo in the Powell archives, a hand-written note reads: "Well written as usual. Mike would find no fundamental right." In a memo received by Justice Powell on April 1, 1986, in response to Justice Powell's suggestion to Mosman that there may be room for protection of "homosexual relationships that resemble marriage," Mos-man wrote to Justice Powell:

> I think this is not a good approach, for several reasons.... [T]he kind of marriage that our society has traditionally protected is heterosexual, not homosexual. It would be bootstrapping to say that marriage is protected because of our history and tradition, and then add that homosexual relationships are protected because they "re-semble" marriage.

Justice Powell originally voted, in conference after oral argument, to affirm Judge Johnson's Eleventh Circuit decision for Michael Hardwick. He based his decision at the time on the Eighth Amendment, along the lines of *Robinson v. California*: it would be cruel and unusual to punish someone for being gay. The opinion writing was assigned to Justice Blackmun by Justice Stevens, with Justices Powell, Brennan, and Mar-shall in majority. By letter dated April 3, 1986, Chief Justice Burger lobbied Powell to change his vote, declaring that "[t]his case presents for me the most far reaching issue of those 30 years [that I have sat on the bench]." Whether influenced or not by Chief Justice Burger's letter, Justice Powell switched his vote pre-draft and joined Chief Justice Burger, who now assigned the majority opinion to Justice White. Mos-man may also have had a role in convincing Justice Powell to join Justice White's opinion and minimize his concurrence. The extent of Mosman's influence on Justice Powell will never be known. What is clear, though, is that Justice Powell's actions were not the product of gay clerks or gay-leaning law schools.

Nevertheless, it is probably fair to say that, by and large, within legal academic and law profession circles, homosexuality became relative-

ly more tolerated over the decade or decades preceding *Lawrence*—or, at
the very least, that the centrists on the Supreme Court have become
more gay-friendly. The decision in *Hardwick* itself was a close call—
closer than we tend to think. Had Justice Powell not changed his vote,
Justice White's opinion would have been the dissent. But *Lawrence* was
much less of a close call. From *Hardwick* to *Lawrence*, the court
composition changed significantly. Justices Rehnquist, Stevens, and
O'Connor were the only justices who sat on both cases. The new justices
included Justices Scalia, Kennedy, Souter, Thomas, Ginsburg, and Breyer. If you stack them up against each other, substituting relatively
comparable political ideologies on homosexual sodomy, the game card
would look something like the following:

Hardwick pro-gay		Lawrence pro-gay		Hardwick pro-state		Lawrence pro-state
Stevens	→	Stevens		Rehnquist	→	Rehnquist
Blackmun	→	Souter		Burger	→	Scalia
Brennan	→	Ginsburg		White	→	Thomas
Marshall	→	Breyer				
		O'Connor	←	O'Connor		
		Kennedy	←	Powell		

Hardwick may have been a close call, but *Lawrence,* it turns out,
was not: a strong five-person majority with a change in vote by Justice
O'Connor (on other grounds). The additional votes of Justices Kennedy
and Souter—liberal replacements on this issue—made all the difference.
If you eliminate the extremes at both ends of the political spectrum—
Justices Stevens, Brennan, Marshall, Ginsburg and Breyer at one end,
and Justices Rehnquist, Burger, White, Scalia and Thomas at the other—then the court's center has moved to the left on gay-rights issues. It
was composed of Justices Blackmun, O'Connor and Powell in *Hardwick*.
It is now composed of Justices O'Connor, Kennedy and Souter—clearly a
more gay-friendly center court.

None of this is to suggest that the legal profession or the court is
overly sensitive to gay issues. To the contrary, at every turn there are
significant disadvantages in terms of contacts and opportunities. Justice
Scalia, after all, is not going duck hunting with Evan Wolfson, the
former director of the marriage project at Lambda. And there are
recurring incidents of homophobia and prejudice. This is still a court
that is lead by a Chief Justice who, in 1978, "publicly compared homosexuality to a contagious disease requiring a quarantine." But still, it is
an institutional and practice milieu that has come to some form of
negotiated existence that tolerates and in some cases affirmatively
protects the interests of gay men and lesbian women more than other
social networks.

Justice Scalia's last point—that the six-member majority in *Lawrence* largely signs on to the liberal pro-gay-rights agenda, defined as the

project to eliminate the moral opprobrium attached to homosexual practices—requires the most reworking. On the surface, it is right. The *Lawrence* decision is gay-friendly. Spending the night in jail and leaving the station house with a criminal arrest for a consensual intimate act is, from a gay-friendly perspective, abhorrent. Insofar as the criminal law shapes the society that we live in and distributes status, power, and wealth, the *Lawrence* decision helps to neutralize material harms to gay men and lesbian women. The consequences of criminalization and marginalization are material: homosexual partners may not get health benefits, testamentary succession rights, or an opportunity to adopt the child they are raising. As Nan Hunter emphasizes,

> [s]odomy laws have functioned as the lynchpin for denial of employment, housing and custody or visitation rights; even when we have proved that there was no nexus between homosexuality and job skills or parenting ability, we have had the courts throw the 'habitual criminal' label at us as a reason to deny relief.

In this sense, gay men and lesbian women won a major battle. But in order to understand how *Lawrence* happened and what it tells us about future sex wars, it is critical to dispense with the notion of a "homosexual agenda" and to explore, instead, the proliferation of sexual projects in contemporary society, to examine the surprising alliances that form on sex matters, and to reconsider all the different interests at stake. This may lead us, in the process, to revisit exactly who won and who lost in *Lawrence*.

IV.

In the end, the politics of *spleen* may be fundamentally unstable in the criminal law context. Maybe the penal sanction, punishment, and state coercion change everything. After all, who in their right mind would want to live in fear of criminal prosecution? And even if they did, how on earth would they justify imposing that fear on others? That would be *utterly* deviant. Perhaps the politics of *spleen*, in reality, is nothing more than a coping mechanism—a way of making the best of a terrible situation. The Warsaw ghetto, some might say, may also have had positive, constitutive effects—so what? Or maybe the politics of *spleen*, by definition, simply cannot *willingly* embrace the prohibition. It may be internally incoherent to *choose* criminalization, to *will* the oppression: the transgressive impulse may not allow for the prohibition norm to be self-inflicted. In this sense, the politics of *spleen* may be unspeakable—and for that reason, unspoken.[20]

But this leaves me with a nagging sense that the discourse of equality, of justice, of non-discrimination against gay men and lesbian women serves to render more palatable a gradual extension of the traditional heterosexual-marriage model. The surface discourse on *Law-*

---

20. In all my extensive research, I have not identified one academic or activist willing to advance, in writing, a gay-friendly position opposed to *Lawrence* that embraces the criminalization of homosexual sodomy.

rence is that gays were repressed, coerced, punished for their sexual orientation, and that the larger society has now liberated gays from the oppression of the homophobic state sanction. The question is, has society instead simply made the world safe for the heterosexual-married-with-children model? Under the cover of a discourse of justice, have we not reshaped our institutions and practices in a hetero-mono mold? Instead of liberating homosexual relations, perhaps the law has figured out a better way to administer, to manage, to shape gays. Thomas Grey points in this direction in his marvelous essay, *Eros, Civilization and the Burger Court*:

> For [the gay community] to be governed effectively, it must be recognized as legitimate. Perhaps something like marriage will have to be recognized for homosexual couples, not because *they* need it for their happiness (though they may), but because *society* needs it to avoid the insecurity and instability generated by the existence in its midst of a permanent and influential subculture outside the law.

Could that possibly be right? Some part of it? Some fraction? It is hard to know. What is clear, though, is that if it is right, then we do need to probe further, to dig deeper, to explore, again, the politics of *spleen*.

Notes and Questions

1. Does *Lawrence* mean that laws against fornication (traditionally defined as heterosexual intercourse between two unmarried individuals) are also unconstitutional?

2. What is the effect of *Lawrence* on laws against solicitation and importuning?

3. These materials on the regulation of sexuality are all about notions of individual autonomy and the importance of sexual expression to individual life. In this sense, they raise important questions about sexual identity and its role in creating the self. Notice that this is nowhere in the Hart–Devlin debate and as we will see, it is nowhere in Chapter 3 on drugs. What is it about sexuality that triggers these identity issues—when other similar contexts do not seem to?

Chapter 3

ILLICIT DRUGS

A. INTRODUCTION

The institutions of criminal justice are more prevalent in the area of illicit drugs than in any other of the categories usually regarded as vice crime. The drug phenomenon in the late 20th century was by far the most important domain of vice control in all Western developed nations, whether we measure this by police effort, arrests, persons imprisoned, or economic impact. Only in the era of prohibition of alcohol in the United States did narcotics control take a secondary position in crime and criminal justice priority.

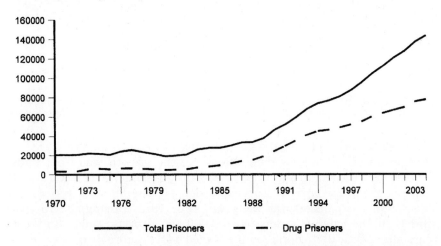

Figure 1: U.S. Federal Prison Population: Total Prisoners and Drug Prisoners, 1970-2004

But however distinctive drug control is in most nations at most times, the recent history of the United States represents a singular chapter in the history of criminal justice. With respect to most traditional vice crimes, the generation after 1970 was a period of declining penal enforcement or stability. Drugs and drug control were the exception: the period after 1985 was a period of explosive growth. Beginning in 1985 with public and political concern about crack cocaine, a multi-front "war

217

on drugs" was launched in the United States that both expanded the total punishment system and increased the share of total prison space attributable to drugs. The explosion of criminal law response to drugs after 1985 in the United States was both unprecedented in the history of vice control and unexplained as part of recent American history.

Figure 1[1] begins this story by tracing the total sentenced population of the federal prison system and the number of federal prisoners whose most serious offense was a drug offense. Figure 3.will show the percentage of total sentenced federal prisoners whose most serious offense was drug crime. The federal prisons hold only a small share of state and federal prisoners, but have a larger proportion of their population committed for drug offenses.

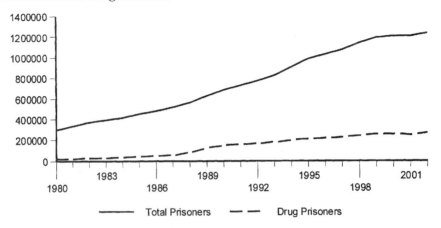

Figure 2: U.S. State Prison Population: Total Prisoners and Drug Prisoners, 1980-2002

Between 1970 and 2000, the total number of sentenced federal prisoners expanded from 20,686 to 112,329, or just over 400%. This expansion masks a stark difference between drug and non-drug offenders: for all non-drug cases, the population grew from 17,302 to 48,431, or 180% in 30 years, but for drug offenders, the growth was from under 4,000 to over 63,000, about 1,800%. The drug offender expansion was 10 times as great as the non-drug expansion for the 30 year period. The heart of that expansion was the years after 1985. During the 15 years after 1970, the federal system added 6,000 new drug prisoners. In the 15 years after 1985, the federal prisons added 44,407 more drug prisoners— more than seven times the volume of new drug prisoners added in the previous 15 years. As Figure 3 will show, the percentage of sentenced prisoners in the system who were classified as drug offenders went from under a fifth of all prisoners to well over half.

The bulk of all sentenced prisoners in the United States are in state prisons, and the traditional share of state prisoners in on drug charges is lower than in federal prisons. In 1980, for example, when 24% of all

---

1. Source: U.S. Department of Justice, Federal Bureau of Prisons [Online]. Available: http://www.bop.gov/fact0598.html [Sept. 9, 2003]; and data provided by the U.S. Department of Justice, Federal Bureau of Prisons.

sentenced federal prisoners were drug offenders, the parallel estimate from the state system was 6%, but that 6% share was 19,000 prisoners, four times as many as confined drug offenders in the federal system. Figure 2 shows the annual growth in drug and non-drug prisoners in state prisons since 1980.[2]

The aggregate growth of the U.S. state prison population between 1980 and 2000 was 309%, from just under 300,000 to just over 1.2 million. Again, however, the aggregate growth figure hides an important distinction between drug and non-drug imprisonment: in 20 years, non-drug prisoners more than tripled, from 275,000 to 952,000, but the drug prisoners grew twelve-fold. The share of drug offenders in state prisons grew from under 7% to over 21%, as is shown in Figure 3.[3] And the number of persons in prison for drug crimes in 2002 was greater than the total number of persons in prison for all crimes in the United States in 1980 (335,000 drug offenders in 2002 versus 315,000 total prisoners in 1980).

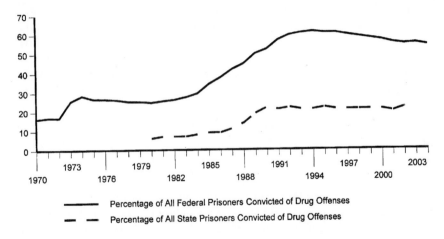

Figure 3: Percentage of Prisoners Convicted of Drug Offenses, U.S. Federal and State Prisons

Three features of the statistics on drugs and prison deserve special mention. The first is that the legal and political processes that increase prison populations responded quickly and on a major scale to the drug concerns of the mid–1980s. Rates of imprisonment were already going up, but the jump start in federal and state drug offender populations was quick and large. None of the hydraulic processes to abate pressure toward penal action, to make the bark of the criminal law louder than its

2. Bureau of Justice Statistics; filename: corrtyp.csv; data source(s): Correctional Populations in the United States, 1997, and Prisoners in 2004.

3. Sources: U.S. Department of Justice, Federal Bureau of Prisons [Online]. Available: http://www.bop.gov/fact0598.html

[Sept. 9, 2003]; and data provided by the U.S. Department of Justice, Federal Bureau of Prisons; Bureau of Justice Statistics; filename: corrtyp.csv; data source(s): Correctional Populations in the United States, 1997, and Prisoners in 2004.

bite, were evident in the drug war era. Almost immediately, the compound growth rate in state prison drug offender populations reached 20%. So there was little friction or initial resistance in the mid–1980s in passing from panic to action.

The second evident feature of the growth in drug prisoners is that it did not, apparently, come at the expense of growth in other types of prisoners, except perhaps in the federal system. The growth in state non-drug prisoners between 1980 and 2000 was 246%, which would have been the highest growth rate for 20 years in history *without* the added boost of twelve-fold growth in drug prisoners. There is no evidence that failure to punish other sorts of offenders in the state systems could have been an opportunity cost of the explosion in drug punishment. The more selective federal criminal justice system may have restrained the growth in non-drug cases because the non-drug prison population only increased 180% in 30 years, a much smaller non-drug increase than the states generated in 20 years, and one-tenth the growth of federal drug prisoners. It is hard to imagine a good comparison to test the drug drain hypothesis, but it seems easier to imagine a diversion of federal prison beds from non-drug to drug offenders than to imagine an even larger non-drug prisoner growth for U.S. rates after 1980 in state prisons if the drug prisoner boom hadn't happened. So most of the huge expansion in drug prisoners did not detract from the growth in other types of incarceration.

This means that most—if not all—of the expansion in drug prisoners after 1985 was also a net addition to the total scale of imprisonment in the United States. What would have been just under a tripling of U.S. imprisonment in just over two decades became instead a quadrupling!

The third obvious feature of the epic growth of drug imprisonments in the United States is the lack of *any* tendency toward regression once the peak period of concern has passed. The growth rate of federal drug prisoners slowed down somewhat in the mid–1990s, but there was no spike in prison populations followed by a drop or regression toward longer-term averages. In the seven years between 1988 and 1995, state drug prisoners grew from 79,000 to 212,000, or 169%. During the seven years after 1995, the total for drug prisoners only grew another 24%, or less than one-sixth the percentage of increase during 1988–1995. A tripling of federal drug prisoners in the seven years after 1988 moderated to a 51% growth rate in the seven years after 1995. But the growth process continued in each case, indicating forward momentum rather than a regression toward more typical historical norms. The all-time record high for drug imprisonment in the time series data in Figures 1 and 2 came in the last year in the series. Each year seems to set a new all-time high for drug incarceration.

The Elasticity of Drug Enforcement

Many of the characteristics that Morris and Hawkins mention in their analysis of victimless crime were mentioned in Chapter 1. Because drug sales and possessions lack a victim in the Morris and Hawkins sense of a complaining witness, law enforcement receives little routine information on drug offenses. Thus, the level of drug arrests and drug punishments will vary in direct proportion to the proactive priorities and efforts of police and prosecutors. Because of that, the rapid escalation in drug punishment in the 1980s is easier to explain and to distinguish from enforcement efforts for offenses like homicide and robbery. But what of the continual increase in imprisonment after the peak in public pressure and anxiety in the early 1990s?

Notes and Questions

1. Why the panic around crack cocaine in the United States in the mid–1980s?

2. How would one measure the costs and benefits of such a massive law enforcement campaign as the post–1985 war on drugs in the United States?

3. How are drugs different from alcohol? From pornography? From gambling?

4. What, if anything, can the drug control adventures in the United States after 1985 teach us about policy toward alcohol or gambling?

5. What, if anything, can recent experience with gambling and alcohol teach us about the options available for drug control?

6. Should different types of illegal drugs generate different types of control strategies and costs?

B.   IDEOLOGY AND DRUG CONTROL POLICY

Introduction

This first selection of materials presents two governmental efforts to outline and justify a national drug control strategy in the United States. The first *National Drug Control Strategy* was published in 1989, during a period of high public concern and rapid governmental expansion of drug control efforts at all levels. William Bennett wrote the 14–page introduction that is reproduced in this section, as close to an official rationale for drug policy in 1989 as can be found.

The second document in the section is an analysis of the 1989 drug control statement that attempts to provide an ideological context for considering the assumptions and priorities of the 1989 National Strategy with other ideologies of drug control.

The third and final installment in this section is the 2006 edition of the *National Drug Control Strategy,* the same type of publication from the same office that produced the 1989 report. This later document is interesting in its own right but also provides important contrasts with the priorities and rhetoric of the 1989 report.

WILLIAM BENNETT—NATIONAL DRUG CONTROL STRATEGY (EXCERPT)

U.S. Office of National Drug Control Policy (1989).

Insofar as this crisis is the product of individual choices to take or refuse drugs, it has been—and continues to be—a crisis of national character, affecting and affected by the myriad social structures and agencies that help shape individual American lives: our families, our schools, our churches and community organizations, even our broadest messages to one another through popular culture and the media. At least in part, NIDA's most recent Household Survey is proof that grassroots America can meet the challenge of drugs, and meet it well.

Not so long ago, drug use was an activity widely thought of as harmless fun or isolated self-indulgence. Today it is seen—just as widely, and far more accurately—to be a personal, social, medical, and economic catastrophe. In less than a decade, parents, educators, students, clergy, and local leaders across the country have changed and hardened American opinion about drugs. The effectiveness of their activism is now largely vindicated. Despite the persistent widespread availability of illegal drugs, many millions of Americans who once used them regularly appear to have recently given them up altogether. Many others—young people for the most part—have been successfully induced not to try drugs in the first place.

What, then, accounts for the intensifying drug-related chaos that we see every day in our newspapers and on television? One word explains much of it. That word is *crack*.

COCAINE IN OUR CITIES

For all its welcome good news, the NIDA Household Survey also brings us terrible proof that our current drug epidemic has far from run its course. Estimated "frequent" use of cocaine in any form (measured by the number of survey respondents who report ingesting that drug one or more times each week, and calculated as a percentage of the total cocaine-using population) has doubled since 1985. Not coincidentally, 1985 was the first year in which crack became an almost ubiquitous feature of American inner-city life. It is an inexpensive, extremely potent, fast-acting derivative of cocaine with a limited-duration "high" that encourages compulsive use. It is, in fact, the most dangerous and quickly addictive drug known to man.

Crack is responsible for the fact that vast patches of the American urban landscape are rapidly deteriorating beyond effective control by civil authorities. Crack is responsible for the explosion in recent drug-related medical emergencies—a 28–fold increase in hospital admissions involving smoked cocaine since 1984. Crack use is increasingly responsible for the continued marketing success enjoyed by a huge international cocaine trafficking industry, with all its consequential evils. And crack use is spreading—like a plague.

We seem to be witnessing a common and tragic phenomenon of drug-use epidemiology. Interest in a given illegal substance often begins first among a particular—usually elite—segment of the population. It is next picked up and spread more broadly through so-called "casual use" in the mainstream middle class. After a time, the drug's dangers are made widely known through public health advisories or painful personal experience, and mainstream use then drops sharply. But the drug continues to slide further down the socio-economic scale, and its chronic or addictive use eventually becomes concentrated among the most vulnerable of our citizens: young, disadvantaged, inner-city residents.

So it is now with cocaine. We must be extremely careful with our new statistics, of course, lest they limit and distort either public thinking about the drug problem or public policy that such thinking will do much to shape. Demographics are not destiny. In 1985, a current cocaine user was likely to be white, male, a high-school graduate, employed full-time, and living in a small metropolitan area or suburb in the western United States. Except that he has now moved to the Northeast, the profile of this "median" current cocaine user remains, the profile of this "median" current cocaine user remains essentially unchanged today.

No inevitable link exists between urban life—however disadvantaged—and drug use. The majority of American city residents—rich or poor; male or female; black, white, or Hispanic; well-or poorly-educated—do not take drugs. And far too many Americans outside our cities do. Our drug problem remains acute, it remains national in scope and size, and it continues to involve drugs of every sort. No effective anti-drug campaign can ignore our current epidemic's full complexity.

Nevertheless, the epidemiological trend is unmistakable. We are now fighting two drug wars, not just one. The first and easiest is against "casual" use of drugs by many Americans, and we are winning it. The other, much more difficult war is against addiction to cocaine. And on this second front, increasingly located in our cities, we are losing—badly.

Few American communities can afford to assume they are immune to cocaine. The drug black market has proved itself remarkably flexible and creative. Crack is an innovation in cocaine retailing that takes uncanny advantage of the nation's changing drug use patterns. And because it is so horribly seductive and "new," it threatens to reverse the current trend and send a fresh wave of cocaine use back out of our cities and into the country at large. Indeed, to some extent at least, it is happening already: almost every week, our newspapers report a new first sighting of crack—in the rural South or in some midwestern suburb, for example.

What's more, as we guard against crack's spread, we must begin to prepare ourselves for what may well come after it. Almost every stimulant epidemic in history has ignited a sedative epidemic in its wake, as users begin employing chemical "downs" to modulate the peaks and valleys of addiction. With cocaine, the sedative of choice has traditionally been heroin. And here, too, the drug market has shown a genius for innovation. In the past year or so, a cheap, powerful, and instantly intoxicating form of smokable heroin—which obviates the need for intravenous needles—has begun to appear on our streets.

For now, however, our most intense and immediate problem is inner-city crack use. It is an acid that is fast corroding the hopes and possibilities of an entire generation of disadvantaged young people. They need help. Their neighborhoods need help. A decent and responsible America must fully mobilize to provide it.

THINKING ABOUT DRUGS AND PUBLIC POLICY

What, generally speaking, should we do? What's the best way to fight drugs and drug-use? It is a broad and complicated-question. It is also a question the United States has struggled with inconclusively for many decades.

Facing understandable public outrage and alarm over the terrible consequences of widespread drug use, Federal, State, and local governments have repeatedly sought to concentrate dramatic responsive action against one or another point on the drug-problem continuum: first through law enforcement; later through a combination of education and treatment efforts; and most recently through heavy emphasis on interdiction of imported drugs at our borders.

Conceived largely as an end in itself, each of these national initiatives has succeeded—in a limited but worthy sphere. We have had, in slow succession, more law enforcement, more education and treatment, and more interdiction. But through it all, undeniably, our national drug problem has persisted. Until late July, convincing evidence of dramatic forward progress was painfully scarce. Indeed, until late July, most evidence continued to suggest that the United States was at best only just beginning to recover from the worst epidemic of illegal drug use in its history—more severe than the heroin scare of the late 1960s and early 1970s; far more severe, in fact, than any ever experienced by an industrialized nation.

The new Household Survey changes our picture of the drug problem a bit, making it more precise and comprehensible. But it does not change the lesson that must be learned from all our many years of experience in the fight. That lesson is clear and simple: no single tactic—pursued alone or to the detriment of other possible and valuable initiatives—can work to contain or reduce drug use. No single tactic can justly claim credit for recent reductions in most use of most drugs by most Americans. And no single tactic will now get us out of our appalling, deepening crisis of cocaine addiction.

Unfortunately, however, the search for such a tactic still consumes the bulk of American public energy and debate about drugs. Two radically opposed strains of thought are principally at issue in this unavailing search. Each, interestingly enough, casts unfair aspersions on the skill and utility of our law enforcement agencies and their officers—the first by complaining that law enforcement doesn't work at all and should be junked; the second by complaining that law enforcement doesn't work enough and should be the focus of all our future effort. Each of these positions, in turn, is incomplete and therefore misguided.

Most Americans correctly view drugs as a personal tragedy for those who use them. Most Americans are eager to provide drug users with the medical attention that can help them stop, and young people with the social and educational training that can help prevent them from starting in the first place. Neither goal is a primary concern of law enforcement. So does it then follow that we should undertake a massive shift of emphasis away from drug enforcement and toward, instead, treatment for addicts and counseling for students?

Some people think so. Consider the argument in its starkest and most extreme form. Hardly a week goes by these days in which some serious forum or other—a national news magazine, for example, or the opinion page of a major newspaper, or a scholarly conference or television panel discussion—fails to give solemn consideration to the advocacy of wholesale drug legalization. Legalization's proponents generally say something like this: Enforcing our many laws against drugs is a terribly expensive and difficult business. Were we to repeal those laws, drug-related crime would vanish, and the time and money saved in reduced law enforcement could be more effectively spent on health care for addicts, and on preventive instruction for the rest of us.

Exactly how under this scenario we could convincingly warn potential new users about the evils of drugs—having just made them legally acceptable—is not entirely clear. Nor is it clear how an already overburdened treatment system could possibly respond to what candid legalization proponents themselves admit would probably be a sharply increased rate of overall drug use. The cost of drugs—measured in purchase price, the time it takes to search them out, and the risks involved due to unreliable "quality" and legal sanction—is a key predictor of drug use. Cheaper, easier-to-get, and "better" legalized drugs would likely mean more drug users and more frequent drug use.

And would legalization actually reduce crime? Crimes committed by addicts to pay for their habits might theoretically decline a bit. But since addicts use drugs—especially cocaine—as often as they can, less expensive drugs might just as well mean more frequent purchases and a still-constant need for cash-producing burglaries and robberies. What's more, since cocaine use is known to produce dangerous behavioral side-effects—paranoia, irritability, and quick resort to violence on minimal provocation—legalization might also entail an increase in more serious crime by addicts.

Drug traffickers, by contrast, are involved in crime for profit alone. An average gram of cocaine now sells for $60 to $80. The free-market price would be roughly 5 percent of that—$3 or $4. If legalized drug sales were heavily regulated and taxed to restrict availability and maximize government revenue, then a gram of cocaine might sell for $30 or $40. In that case, criminal organizations could still undercut legal prices and turn a substantial profit. In truth, to destroy the cocaine black market entirely, we would probably have to make the drug legally available at not much more than $10 a gram. And then an average dose of cocaine would cost about 50 cents—well within the lunch-money budget of the average American elementary school student.

In short, legalizing drugs would be an unqualified national disaster. In fact, *any* significant relaxation of drug enforcement—for whatever reason, however well-intentioned—would promise more use, more crime, and more trouble for desperately needed treatment and education efforts.

None of this is to suggest that stronger and better coordinated law enforcement *alone* is an answer to the drug problem, though this view, too, has its many adherents. In the teeth of a crisis—especially one which has for so long appeared to spiral wildly out of control—we naturally look for villains. We need not look far; there are plenty of them. Anyone who sells drugs—and (to a great if poorly understood extent) anyone who uses them—is involved in an international criminal enterprise that is killing thousands of Americans each year. For the worst and most brutal drug gangsters, the death penalty is an appropriate sentence of honest justice. And for the multitude of crimes associated with trafficking and use, many of the other tough and coherently punitive anti-drug measures proposed in recent years have their place and should be employed.

We should be tough on drugs—much tougher than we are now. Our badly imbalanced criminal justice system, already groaning under the weight of current drug cases, should be rationalized and significantly expanded. But we cannot afford to delude ourselves that drug use is an exclusively criminal issue. Whatever else it does, drug use degrades human character, and a purposeful, self-governing society ignores its people's character at great peril. Drug users make inattentive parents, bad neighbors, poor students, and unreliable employees—quite apart from their common involvement in criminal activity. Legal sanctions may help to deter drug use, and they can be used to direct some drug users to needed treatment. But locking up millions of drug users will not by itself make them healthy and responsible citizens.

Few people better understand this fact, and the limitations of drug enforcement that it implies, than our drug enforcement officers themselves. They are regularly showered with criticism. They are said to waste time and energy in petty bureaucratic disputes and "turf battles." When they are actually in the field risking their lives in a fight whose odds are heavily stacked against them, their every misstep and failure—however small—is nevertheless routinely held up to political and journalistic ridicule.

We do them a grave injustice. Jealousy and bickering among Federal, State, and local drug agencies make for interesting gossip, to be sure.

But the plain truth is that they are not the norm. And when interagency cooperation does occasionally break down, it can usually be traced either to the overriding spirit and energy of our front-line drug enforcement officers—which we should be extremely reluctant to restrict within formal and arbitrary lines—or, more basically, to a failure of coherent policymaking in Washington.

In the too-long absence of any real national consensus about the proper overarching goal of American drug policy, the only available measure of drug enforcement success has been statistical: so many thousands of arrests, so many tons of marijuana seized, so many acres of opium poppy and coca plants destroyed. In this kind of policy vacuum, some degree of competition over "body counts" among involved enforcement agencies is almost inevitable. The real miracle is that intramural rivalries have been so relatively restrained and insignificant.

No doubt Federal, State, and local drug enforcement can and should be made tougher, more extensive, more efficient. This report offers a number of major proposals to accomplish just that. But, again, stronger and better coordinated drug enforcement alone is not the answer. It is a means to an end. It should not become the end itself.

We must be tough. We must be humane. And we must pursue change—in some cases, sweeping change. But before it can begin, we must get smart about the drug problem—smarter than we have been in the past.

First, we must come to terms with the drug problem in its essence: use itself. Worthy efforts to alleviate the symptoms of epidemic drug abuse—crime and disease, for example—must continue unabated. But a largely ad-hoc attack on the holes in our dike can have only an indirect and minimal effect on the flood itself. By the same token, we must avoid the easy temptation to blame our troubles first on those chronic problems of social environment—like poverty and racism—which help to breed and spread the contagion of drug use. We have been fighting such social ills for decades; that fight, too, must continue unabated. But we need not—and cannot—sit back and wait for that fight to be won for good. Too many lives will be lost in the interim. The simple problem with drugs is painfully obvious: too many Americans still use them. And so the highest priority of our drug policy must be a stubborn determination further to reduce the overall level of drug use nationwide—experimental first use, "casual" use, regular use, and addiction alike.

That said, we must be scrupulously honest about the difficulties we face—about what we can reasonably hope to accomplish, and when. People take drugs for many complicated reasons that we do not yet fully understand. But most drug users share an attitude toward their drugs that we would do well to acknowledge openly: at least at first, they find drugs intensely pleasurable. It is a hollow, degrading, and deceptive pleasure, of course, and pursuing it is an appallingly self-destructive impulse. But self-destructive behavior is a human flaw that has always been with us and always will–And drug addiction is a particularly tenacious form of self-destruction, one which its victims very often cannot simply *choose* to correct on their own.

Last fall, an important and valuable piece of omnibus Federal drug legislation was enacted, "The Anti–Drug Abuse Act of 1988." Among its several hundred provisions was a declaration that it would be the policy of the United States Government to "create a Drug–Free America by 1995." That is an admirable goal. It is already a reality for the vast majority of Americans who have never taken an illegal drug. And government has a solemn obligation to keep those Americans—and their children after them—safe and secure from the poison of drug trafficking and drug use.

But government also has an obligation to tell the truth and act accordingly. There is no quick fix or magic bullet for individual dissipation, and policymakers should not pretend that we are on the verge of discovering one for drugs. The continued search for a single "answer" to our troubles with drugs—in law enforcement, in education and treatment, in border interdiction, or somewhere else—is a bad idea. We have bounced back and forth in emphasis this way for too long. It has not worked well. And it will hold us back in the near-and long-term future, by diverting our attention from new and serious work that can and must be done *right now*.

The United States has a broad array of tools at its disposal, in government and out, each of which—in proper combination with the others—can and does have a significant effect on the shape and size of our drug problem. We must use them all. We must have what we have never had before: a comprehensive, fully integrated national drug control strategy. It must proceed from a proper understanding of all that we do and do not know about drugs. It must take calm and intelligent measure of the strengths and limitations of specific available drug control initiatives. And it must then begin to intensify and calibrate them so that the number of Americans who still use cocaine and other illegal drugs, to the entire nation's horrible disadvantage, is—more and more as time goes by—dramatically reduced.

DRUG USE: SOURCE AND SPREAD

Drug use takes a number of distinct forms. There are those who take a given drug just a few times—or only once—and, for whatever reason, never take it again. Others take drugs occasionally, but can and do stop, either voluntarily or under some compulsion. There may be a small number of people who use drugs regularly—even frequently—but whose lives nevertheless go on for the most part unimpeded. But there remain a large number of Americans whose involvement with drugs develops into a full-fledged addiction—a craving so intense that life becomes reduced to a sadly repetitive cycle of searching for drugs, using them, and searching for them some more.

After many years of research, we still have no reliable way to predict which drug users will follow which patterns of use, and we are just beginning to understand why some users become addicts and others do not. But we do know a good deal about how drug use begins; how it spreads from individual to individual; what addicts are like and how they behave; and what factors influence the drug marketplace in which critical transactions between dealers and users are carried out—all of which should help us decide how further to contain, prevent, treat, and reduce the prevalence of drug use nationwide.

Drug use usually starts early, in the first few years of adolescence. But notwithstanding popular mythology about shadowy, raincoated pushers corrupting young innocents on school playgrounds, children almost never *purchase* their first drug experience. Generally speaking, drug dealers still make most of their money from known, regular customers, and they still—all things being equal—prefer to avoid the risk of selling their wares to strangers, however young. Similarly, new and novice users themselves are typically reluctant to accept an unfamiliar substance from an unfamiliar face. In fact, young people rarely make *any* independent effort to seek out drugs for the first time. They don't have to; use ordinarily begins through simple personal contact with other users. Where drugs are concerned, as with so much else, young people respond most immediately and directly to the blandishments of peer pressure. And so first use invariably involves the free and enthusiastic offer of a drug by a friend.

This friend—or "carrier," in epidemiological terms—is seldom a hard-core addict. In the terminal stage of an uninterrupted drug use career, the addict is almost completely present-minded—preoccupied with finding and taking his drug; other planning and organizational skills have largely deserted him. He very often cannot maintain anything resembling a normal family or work life. Some addicts may attempt to become dealers to earn money, but most fail at this work, too, since they lack sufficient self-control to avoid consuming their own sales inventory. What's more, an addict's active enthusiasm for his drug's euphoric high or soothing low tends significantly to recede over time; for biochemical reasons, that high or low becomes increasingly difficult to reproduce (except at risk of a lethal overdose), and drug taking becomes a mostly defensive effort to head off the unpleasant psychological effects of a "crash"—or the intensely painful physical effects of actual withdrawal.

In short, the bottomed-out addict is a mess. He makes the worse possible advertisement for new drug use. And he is not likely to have much remaining peer contact with non-users in any case, as he isolates himself in the world of addicts and dealers necessary to maintain his habit. Simply put, a true addict's drug use is not very contagious.

The non-addicted casual or regular user, however, is a very different story. He is likely to have a still-intact family, social, and work life. He is likely still to "enjoy" his drug for the pleasure it offers. And he is thus much more willing and able to proselytize his drug use—by action or example—among his remaining non-user peers, friends, and acquaintances. A non-addict's drug use, in other words, is highly contagious.

And casual or regular use—whether ongoing or brand new—may always lead to addiction; again, we have no accurate way to predict its eventual trajectory.

These facts about drug use phenomenology are both a problem and an advantage for any intelligent national drug control campaign. Unfortunately, they mean that those specifically addict-directed efforts of law enforcement and treatment—though urgently required for neighborhood safety and reasons of simple compassion—will remain difficult, time-consuming, and labor intensive, and will promise to reduce the number of American drug users only, for the most part, on a one-by-one, case-by-case basis. They also mean that non-addicted casual and regular use remains a grave issue of national concern, despite NIDA's report of recent dramatic declines in its prevalence. Non-addicted users still comprise the vast bulk of our drug-involved population. There are many millions of them. And each represents a potential agent of infection for the non-users in his personal ambit.

But there is good news, too. Though compared to addiction, non-addicted drug behavior is the more common and contagious form, it is also more susceptible to change and improvement. The same general techniques employed to slow and mixed effect with addicts may achieve markedly better results with non-addicts. Casual and regular drug users are much more easily induced to enter treatment, for example, and they are much more likely to reduce or cease their use as a result of it.

In fact, all the basic mechanisms we use against illegal drugs—to raise their price; to restrict their availability; to intensify legal and social sanctions for their sale, purchase, and use; and to otherwise depress general demand for them—have a more immediate and positive behavioral effect on non-addicts than on addicts. And in the search for long-term solutions to epidemic drug use, this fact works to our benefit. Any additional short-term reduction in the number of American casual or regular drug users will be a good in itself, of course. But because it is their kind of drug use that is most contagious, any further reduction in the non-addicted drug user population will also promise still greater future reductions in the number of Americans who are recruited to join their dangerous ranks.

Demand, Supply, and Strategy

It is commonly and correctly assumed that the extent of our problem with drug use can be described in terms borrowed from classical economics; that is, as a largely market function influenced by the variable "supply" of drug sellers and the variable "demand" of drug buyers. So far, so good. But it is just as commonly—and *incorrectly*—assumed that each of our many weapons against drug use can be successfully applied only to one or the other side of the supply/demand equation.

Supply reduction, by these lights, involves overseas crop eradication and associated foreign policy initiatives; interdiction of foreign-manufactured drugs at our national borders; and domestic law enforcement. For its part in this calculus, demand reduction is thought to involve medical or other treatment for current drug users; education about the dangers of drugs and techniques to resist them; and various interdisciplinary, community-based prevention efforts. Demand reduction, then, is understood to be exclusively "therapeutic," and seeks to help those in trouble—or those likely to get in trouble in the future. Supply reduction, by contrast, is understood to be exclusively "punitive," and seeks to bring stern sanctions to bear against those who grow, refine, smuggle, or distribute illegal drugs.

This division of anti-drug strategy into two rigidly independent—even opposed—tactical camps may do a good job of mirroring conflicting public sentiment about the need to be hard-headed or tenderhearted. But it makes a poor guide to policymaking and funding decisions about the drug problem, because—as the preceding pages should already have suggested—it does not do a good job of reflecting either the complicated reality of the drug market or the actual effect specific anti-drug initiatives can and do have on that market.

Granted, overseas and border activities against drugs work primarily to reduce supply. But they can have an important, radiating effect on demand, as well, because they make the purchase of certain imported drugs more difficult—and therefore less likely. In much the same way, drug treatment and education work *primarily* to reduce demand, but in so doing they may encourage suppliers to scale back production and distribution in an effort to sustain consistent profits.

Domestic law enforcement is a special case. The sale and purchase of drugs are both illegal. And so our criminal justice system is obliged to ensure that neither aspect of the drug marketplace is left unpenalized and therefore undeterred. In fact, a paramount target of law enforcement activity—especially at the local level—must be the disruption of those street markets for drugs-in which retail demand and supply finally meet in a combustible mix. So it stands to reason that properly conceived law enforcement cannot be meaningfully assigned to any uniquely demand-or supply-side role.

The proposed national strategy outlined in this report takes pains to avoid the artificial and counter-productive distinctions so often drawn among the various fronts necessary to a successful fight against epidemic drug use. Instead it seeks to draw each of them into full participation in a coherent, integrated, and much improved program. The next five chapters, taken together, describe a coordinated and balanced plan of attack involving all basic anti-drug initiatives and agencies: our criminal justice system; our drug treatment system; our collection of education, workplace, public awareness, and community prevention campaigns; our international policies and activities; and our efforts to interdict smuggled drugs before they cross our borders. Two subsequent chapters discuss a research and intelligence agenda designed to support and sustain this overall strategy. And Appendix A offers a series of quantified goals and measures of success—each of which this strategy, if fully implemented, can reasonably be expected to achieve.

No attempt should be made to disguise the fact that significant new resources will be required to pay for the many proposals advanced in this report. And no attempt is made here to deny that the Federal government has a major role to play in providing them. Last February, this Administration requested nearly $717 million in new drug budget authority for Fiscal Year 1990. Now, after six months of careful study, we have identified an immediate need for $1.478 billion more. With this report, the Administration is requesting FY 1990 drug budget authority totalling $7.864 billion—the largest single-year dollar increase in history. A detailed Federal implementation plan—and the budget tables to accompany it—are included in Appendix B.

Appendix C provides a package of recommended State anti-drug legislation. Appendix D discusses possible Federal designations of high intensity drug trafficking areas, as mandated in the "Anti–Drug Abuse Act of 1988." And Appendix E proposes a plan for improved automatic data processing and information management among involved Federal drug agencies, also mandated in the 1988 Act.

FRANKLIN E. ZIMRING AND GORDON HAWKINS— IDEOLOGY AND POLICY

From *The Search for Rational Drug Control* (Cambridge University Press, 1992).

IDEOLOGY AND POLICY: A LOOK AT THE NATIONAL DRUG CONTROL STRATEGY

The National Drug Control Strategy, published in September 1989, is not, in several respects, an ordinary government document. Rather, it is a government report that is meant to be read—it is only ninety pages long, excluding appendices, with a fourteen-page introduction personally written by then-"drug czar" William Bennett that seeks to build a rhetorical and philosophical foundation for a multifaceted campaign against drug abuse. The goal is a comprehensive program involving not only national, state and local government but also employers, community groups, and the private sector. Budgetary figures and projections by fiscal year—usually the mother's milk of government planning documents—are relegated to the appendices of the white-on-red-covered document with the presidential seal on the cover. Indeed, the report is intended to serve as a manifesto for a long-term drug control strategy in the United States. By grounding its proposals in strategic rather than merely tactical considerations, this document helps illuminate the basic premises on which public policy is to be based.

Analysis of the *National Drug Control Strategy* is a window into the three competing schools of thought that divide those in our midst who support some version of a war on drug abuse. We aim in this chapter to illustrate the powerful role of ideology in drug policy choice in the United States, with a special emphasis on the ideological stance that dominates the current government program. After a brief description of the contents of the Bennett report, we outline three contrasting approaches to drug control—the generalist, the legalist, and the specifist modes. We then contrast each of these three schools of thought in relation to four issues of drug policy. We show how the Bennett drug program fits squarely in the legalist framework. The final section discusses the implications of adopting a hard-line legalist perspective on the degree of power that the government should be permitted to exercise and the theoretical justification for exercising such power.

I. *The National Strategy*

In his letter to the speaker of the House of Representatives and the president of the Senate laying out his administration's 1989 drug control strategy, President George Bush described it as "a comprehensive blueprint for new directions and effort" focused on "the scourge of drugs." The national strategy proposed in the report takes the form of a "plan of attack" (Office of National Drug Control Policy, 1989, p. 13), outlined in five chapters dealing with the criminal justice system, public awareness and community prevention campaigns, international policies, and activities and efforts to interdict smuggled drugs.

Two further chapters discuss a research and intelligence agenda. These are followed by a number of appendices describing various quantified goals and measures of success; a federal implementation plan with budget tables; a package of recommended state antidrug legislation; possible federal designations of high-intensity drug-trafficking areas, as mandated in the Anti–Drug Abuse Act of 1988; and a proposed plan for improved automatic data processing and information management among the involved federal drug agencies.

The introduction by William Bennett, then the director of the Office of National Drug Policy, which prefaces the report, begins by reporting some "very good news." According to the most recent National Survey on Drug Abuse conducted by the National Institute on Drug Abuse (NIDA), there had been a "dramatic and startling" decline in the use of illegal drugs, in that the estimated number of Americans using any illegal drug dropped 37 percent, from 23 million in 1985 to 14.5 million in 1988. Moreover, use of the two most common illegal substances— marijuana and cocaine—had fallen by 36 and 48 percent in that period.

According to Mr. Bennett, this good news is "difficult to square with common sense perceptions." Americans, he states, have "good reason" for being convinced "that drugs represent the gravest present threat to our national well-being," for there is a wealth of other evidence that "suggests that our drug problem is getting worse, not better." The only specific evidence he actually cites is related to an increase in drug-related emergency hospital admissions between 1985 and 1988. But Bennett asserts that the "fear of drugs and attendant crime are at our all-time high"; "reports of bystander deaths ... continue to climb"; "drug trafficking, distribution, and sales in America have become a vast, economically debilitating black market"; "drugs have become a major concern of U.S. foreign policy"; and that in every state in America, "drugs are cheap, and ... available to almost anyone who wants them" (Office of National Drug Control Policy, 1989, pp. 1–2).

What is called "the intensifying drug-related chaos" is said to be largely explained by crack, which "is an inexpensive, extremely potent, fast-acting derivative of cocaine .. And crack use is spreading—like a plague." "Our most intense and immediate problem is inner-city crack use." Nevertheless, it also appears to be spreading "into the country at large ... almost every week, our newspapers report a new first sighting of crack—in the rural South or in some midwestern suburb, for example." America is faced with an "appalling, deepening crisis of cocaine addiction" (Office of National Drug Control Policy, 1989, pp. 3–5).

But although cocaine use in the form of crack is defined as the principal current problem, the "drug problem ... continues to involve drugs of every sort." Moreover, "anyone who sells drugs—and (to a great if poorly understood extent) anyone who uses them—is involved in an international criminal enterprise that is killing thousands of Americans each year." It follows that "we should be tough on drugs—much tougher than we are now" and "we should be extremely reluctant to restrict [drug enforcement officers] within formal and arbitrary lines" (Office of National Drug Control Policy, 1989, pp. 4, 7–8).

In short, the United States is facing "the worst epidemic of illegal drug use in its history—more severe than the heroin scare of the late 1960s and early 1970s; far more severe, in fact, than any ever experienced by an industrialized nation." Indeed, the suggestion that this should be met by a "shift of emphasis away from drug enforcement and toward instead treatment for addicts" and that the "money saved in reduced law enforcement could be more effectively spent on health care for addicts and on preventive instruction of the rest of us" is mentioned only to be peremptorily dismissed: "Any significant relaxation of drug enforcement—for whatever reason, however well-intentioned—would promise more use, more crime, and more trouble for desperately needed treatment and education efforts" (Office of National Drug Control Policy, 1989, pp. 5, 6, 7; emphasis in original).

It follows from this analysis of the problem that faced with "a crisis—especially one which has for so long appeared to spiral wildly out of control ... tough and coherently punitive anti-drug measures ... should be employed." The "essence" of the drug problem is the "use itself," and the "highest priority of our drug policy" must be an attack on "drug use nationwide—experimental first use, 'casual' use, regular use, and addiction alike." Moreover, the focus of the attack must not be on drug addicts but on non-addicted users of whom there are many millions, each of whom is "highly contagious" and represents "a potential agent of infection" (Office of National Drug Control Policy, 1989, pp. 7, 8, 11; emphasis in original).

It is acknowledged that "locking up millions of drug users will not by itself make them healthy and responsible citizens." But while "the search for longterm solutions" continues, "short-term reduction in the number of American casual and regular users will be a good in itself," and "because it is their kind of drug use that is most contagious ... [it] will also promise still greater future reductions in the number of Americans who are recruited to join their dangerous ranks" (Office of National Drug Control Policy, 1989, pp. 7, 12).

The antidrug strategy document outlined in the five chapters immediately following this introduction discusses, in varying degrees of detail, the practical steps required to implement the policy that it proposes. The first chapter, "The Criminal Justice System," sets the tone in the first paragraph: "We declare clearly and emphatically that there is no such thing as innocent drug use." The criminal justice system, it is said, has suffered too long from the policies of "those who enthusiastically endorse plans for more parole officers but balk when it comes to planning new prisons" (Office of National Drug Control Policy, 1989, pp. 17, 32). It is evident that if "the war against illegal drug use" is waged along the lines indicated, planning new prisons may well need to be given priority as a part of the significant expansion foreshadowed in the introduction (Office of National Drug Control Policy, 1989, p. 7). Both "more police" and "more prisons" are said to be necessary (Office of National Drug Control Policy, 1989, p. 24). The estimated cost of the "many proposals advanced in this report" is considerable, involving a FY 1990 federal drug budget totaling $7.864 billion, "the largest single-year dollar increase in history" (Office of National Drug Control Policy, 1989, p. 13).

Four aspects of this national strategy document challenge us to examine the ideological roots of these policy prescriptions: First, the nature of the drug problem is never precisely defined. Not one sentence in a 153–page report is devoted to defining the terms drug or drug problem. Implicitly, therefore, all illegal drugs seem to be included, with alcohol and tobacco evidently excluded. Also apparently excluded are barbiturates, amphetamines, and other substances that are frequently obtained both legally and illegally for abusive use.

A second significant element of the report is its novel treatment of all levels of drug use as equally troublesome and threatening. The memorable phrase is "experimental first use, casual use, regular use, and addiction alike" (Office of National Drug Control Policy, 1989, p. 8; emphasis added).

The third striking feature of the report is the way in which all types of drugs—that is, illegal drugs—seem to be regarded as equally pernicious. Although the use of crack cocaine is described as "our most intense and immediate problem" (Office of National Drug Control Policy, 1989, p. 4), there is nowhere any suggestion of choosing priorities for the resource allocation in waging the war on drugs. "The highest priority" is said to be simply "to reduce the overall level of drug use nationwide" (Office of National Drug Control Policy, 1989, p. 8).

Table 1: Distinguishing features of three approaches to drug control policy

	Generalist	Specifist	Legalist
Which drugs are problematic?	Licit and illicit	Licit and illicit	Illicit only
Are all drugs defined as equally problematic?	Yes	No	Yes
Is drug taking or its harmful consequences the primary problem?	Harmful consequences	Harmful consequences	Drug taking

Finally, one of the most extraordinary features of this report is the characterization of the effort to control drugs as essentially a struggle between good and evil. "Drug use is a moral problem" (Office of National Drug Control Policy, 1989, p. 53; emphasis added). The report divides the United States into two parts. On the one hand are drug use and drug users representing the forces of evil, and on the other hand is "the vast majority of Americans who have never taken an illegal drug" (Office of National Drug Control Policy, 1989, p. 9), together with their government, representing the forces of good.

In this chapter, we shall describe the view of the drug problem presented in the *National Drug Control Strategy* as reflecting a legalist position, and we shall contrast that approach with two alternative schools of thought regarding drug control policy.

II. *Three Schools of Thought*

We have found it helpful to distinguish among three schools of thought when sorting through contemporary discussion of drug control policy. All three approaches support some version of a "war on drugs" and thus can be contrasted with approaches that urge the across-the-board decriminalization of drugs considered in Chapter 4. But the policies supported differ as a function of different, perspectives on why drugs constitute a societal problem.

PUBLIC HEALTH GENERALISM

The public health perspective is principally concerned with reducing the harmful consequences produced by the consumption of psychoactive substances: problems such as health costs, time off from work, family problems, and a shortened life span. The public health generalist worries about these consequences no matter whether the drugs that produce them are legal or illegal. Usually the generalist believes that many different drugs produce the same type and extent of dependency costs and that in this respect most drugs have been created equal.

Thus, patterns of morbidity and mortality, rather than the statute book, are the standard used by the public health school to judge policy toward drugs. The presumption seems to be that most of the abusable substances can cause nearly equal harm. The proponents of this view commonly see the drug abuser as the victim of a disease, even if the user is generally viewed with the mixed feelings that we tend to reserve for those who suffer from self-inflicted wounds.

LEGALISM

The principal concern of the legalist school is the threat that illegal drugs represent to the established order and political authority structure. In this view, it is the consumption of the prohibited substance rather than any secondary consequences that might ensue that is the heart of the matter. The taking of drugs prohibited by the government is an act of rebellion, of defiance of lawful authority, that threatens the social fabric.

From this perspective, all illegal drugs are similar to one another and quite different from drugs that are not prohibited. For the legalist, the harms and injuries that result from alcohol consumption are beside the point, because those who ingest alcohol are not affiliating themselves with enemies of the government. For similar reasons, the legalist regards as irrelevant any claim that a particular prohibited substance is nontoxic. If the harm lies in the rebellious nature of ingestion, then the chemical properties of the substance ingested are of little significance. According to this account, drug taking is a species of treason. That it might not harm the user—who is in effect a declared enemy of the state—is of no comfort to the legalist.

COST-BENEFIT SPECIFISM

The distinctive feature of cost-benefit specifism is the belief that all drugs of abuse have not been created equal. Specifists agree with public health generalists that drugs of abuse generate substantial individual and social costs, and they count those costs in the same way as the generalists do. They see drug policy as requiring a balance between the costs of abuse and the likelihood of reducing them by means of legal prohibition, and the manifold costs of enforcing those prohibitive laws. In regard to such a delicate balance, the specifist school insists that judgments about the appropriateness of drug prohibitions should be made one at a time, rather than with sweeping generalization, and that they should also be tied to the social context in which particular drugs are used.

Table 1 contrasts the three schools of thought in regard to their answers to three key questions: Which drugs are problematic? Are all drugs equally troublesome? Is the primary importance of the drug problem the consequences that flow from drug abuse or the drug taking itself? As this table illustrates, the legalist sees only illegal drugs as the problem, whereas both the generalist and the specifist see the drug problem as including legal substances as well. Both the generalist and the legalist think that most drugs, as they define them, are equally harmful, but each has a different definition of the term *drug*. Finally, the legalist sees drug taking itself as the major harm to be combated, and the other two schools are more concerned about the harmful effects of drug taking.

The public health generalist approach is the dominant viewpoint of the medical community that deals with the assessment and treatment of substance dependency. It is this "all drugs are created equal" philosophy that has led to the creation of treatment programs in which all drugs— from alcohol to cocaine to heroin to diet pills—are dealt with in the same type of twenty-eight-day inpatient programs. This "one size fits all" treatment design is a good example of a generalist approach to drugs of abuse. Prominent spokespersons for this approach include Lester Grinspoon of Harvard University and Arnold Trebach of American University. The cost-benefit specifists include a number of scholars of the criminal justice system whose expertise is drugs. The most prominent modern proponent of this viewpoint is the late John Kaplan of Stanford University, who balanced a call for the decriminalization of marijuana with the subsequent endorsement of the continued prohibition of heroin and cocaine (compare Kaplan, 1970, with Kaplan, 1983, 1988).

The legalist perspective is the dominant orientation of the law enforcement community in the United States, including the extensive specialized policy enforcement networks that have grown up around drug control. The *National Drug Control Strategy* is the charter of the legalist perspective on drugs and their control in modern American life.

This tripartite scheme cannot claim to cover every possible basis for supporting an antidrug campaign, and there are doubtless also variations and shadings of opinion among adherents to the three schools that the basic outline overlooks. Still, a surprisingly large proportion of U.S. attitudes toward illegal drugs is found in the generalist, specifist, and legalist rubrics, and as the next two sections illustrate, the essential orientation that the observer brings to these issues determines much concerning what policies will be supported.

III.   *Three Views of Drug Programs*

The general orientations discussed in Section II explain not only the shape of the proposals in the *National Drug Control Strategy* but also the character of much of the criticism that has been directed at them. This can be shown in a survey of the attitudes of the three schools of thought toward four different potential elements of a drug control strategy: supply reduction, treatment programs, prevention and drug education, and decriminalization.

Supply Reduction

As the *National Drug Control Strategy* makes clear, the legalist perspective puts great stock in programs to reduce the supply of illegal drugs in the United States by means of interdiction and domestic law enforcement efforts. The logic of such support is straightforward: If a reduced supply results in a net decrease in the consumption of illegal drugs, the legalist will count the policy as a success.

The public health generalist sees the effort to reduce the supply of prohibited drugs as necessarily futile because nonprohibited drugs will still be available to inflict the same amount of damage. For example, diverting an abuser from cocaine to alcohol or amphetamines through supply reduction efforts directed at cocaine would create no net benefit for the generalist, but it would represent a total victory for the legalist. Both the legalist and the generalist believe that all drugs are created equal, but the legalist's definition of drugs includes only the illegal ones (hence the "victory" in our example), and the generalist's definition is much broader.

The hallmark of the specifist approach is that not all drugs are created equal. The specifist believes that in a social context some drugs are so much more destructive to the user and to the community that the costs of selective criminal prohibition can be justified. Because the possession of only these drugs should be made criminal, the diversion of users from illegal to legal drugs, such as from cocaine to alcohol, should reduce the aggregate social cost of drug use. Thus, the specifist would support the beneficial potential of supply reduction strategies only as long as the dividing line between legal and illegal drugs is correctly drawn. The specifist would expect the diversion from illegal to legal drugs to result in decreases in morbidity and mortality. Unlike the legalist, these benefits are the reason that the specifist supports supply reduction.

TREATMENT

In regard to drug treatment, it is the legalist who is the most suspicious of treatment interventions. The specifist and the generalist would invest larger resources in treatment, but for different reasons. Once the *National Drug Control Strategy* has defined drug use as a moral problem, and one involving a majority of nonaddicted and willful participants, it is hard to imagine a treatment regime suited to the task of their moral rehabilitation. In fact, the conception of drug treatment in this report is a regimen in which the participants are forced or frightened into treatment programs and threatened into abstinence during and after treatment. This radical restructuring of the treatment enterprise is necessary to fit the legalist conception of how drug users can be changed into a conception of treatment and rehabilitation.

For the specifist, drug treatment competes on an equal footing for resources with supply reduction and other countermeasures. The specifist is particularly anxious to target high-risk, active users for treatment because these persons impose the highest per-person social costs, through crime and needle-sharing disease (Kaplan, 1983, p. 230).

The specifist perspective is also particularly well suited to the substitution of relatively benign drugs for more harmful ones. Thus the "lesser of two evils" approach that maintains heroin addicts on methadone makes sense to a specifist because this approach emphasizes loss reduction rather than victory over rebellion or the notion of a disease requiring a cure.

For similar reasons, the specifist is also likely to be sympathetic to supplying syringes to intravenous drug users as a policy of loss reduction, but the legalist might not see this as leading to moral improvement. The legalist is not highly motivated to protect drug abusers from bad consequences.

If treatment might be an attractive option to the specifist, it is the only hope for, the public health generalist, because reducing the supply of dangerous drugs is impossible as long as alcohol and tranquilizers are widely available.

The generalist assumes that destructive drugs are widely available to the population and that the appropriate public policy is to treat those who become pathologically involved with psychoactive substances. Just as the legalist believes that the medical dimensions of drug use are of little consequence, the generalist feels that any capacity of the system to turn users from one drug of abuse to another makes little difference in personal or social cost. Only the specifist can choose between treatment and supply reduction without a strong initial bias.

PREVENTION AND EDUCATION

Drug prevention and education seem to represent as close to a point of consensus as there is in the current drug control debate. But the consensus support for primary prevention does not extend to the content of drug education messages, and the absence of any strong group of skeptics may also lead to an unquestioned investment in antidrug messages that are not effective.

The legalist, specifist, and public health generalist all support drug abuse prevention campaigns, but the sort of campaign that each would favor differs. The legalist endorses antidrug propaganda messages, distrusting pure informational campaigns. The legalist is less concerned about fact content than either the specifist or generalist is. The legalist drug message to children is that illegal drugs are a bad thing and that drug takers are bad people. For the legalist, the most important target audience of these messages are those who have never taken illegal drugs and who are thus to be reinforced and congratulated. Because this view seeks to divide the population into good people (who never try drugs) and bad people (who do), there is no room on the prevention pulpit for either discussion of the continuity between licit and illicit drugs or for distinctions among different illicit drugs. Preaching against alcohol abuse may be problematic from this perspective because it blurs the sharp distinction between legal and illegal drugs that lies at the heart of the legalist brief.

The public health campaign stresses information and a high-priority target audience of those who probably will experiment with at least one illegal drug in their substance career. Information about potential misuse of both legal and illegal drugs is important to minimizing the deleterious impact of substance abuse. The generalist tries to build a course on drugs into a broader life skills or health education curriculum, whereas the legalist wants a freestanding course on the perils of illegal street drugs. The legalist wants antidrug sermons delivered to the young, and one function of such sermons is preaching for the benefit of the converted. The generalist wishes questions from the audience and factual answers to them. The conflict in these two agendas is obvious.

But the legalist agenda for drug education may clash even more clearly with the specifist program, because the specifist hopes that public programs can distinguish among illicit drugs in order to provide special warnings for the most dangerous drugs. A specifist might believe that a credible campaign against needle sharing or injectable heroin should issue from a source that does not overstate the dangers of marijuana, particularly if most of the persons in the audience at high risk for heroin use have acquired or will acquire firsthand experience with marijuana.

This sort of approach is rejected by the legalist because it comes close to condoning drug abuse and fails to chastise those who have used an illegal drug. From the legalist perspective, this undermines the gospel of absolute abstention from illicit drugs and tends to demoralize the faithful never-users who are the most important target audience of the legalist appeal.

DECRIMINALIZATION

The contrast among the schools of thought regarding the function of decriminalizing currently prohibited drugs concerns both substance and tone. Both the generalist and specifist wish to approach questions of change in the criminal law concerning drugs with a dispassionate and pragmatic tone. In part because many of them come from criminal justice specialties, specifists tend to regard the scope of criminal prohibitions as a more important drug control topic than do generalists, with the latter group more skeptical that the number of prohibited substances or the substances on that list will have a large impact on the size of the substance abuse problem in the social system. Unless a society attempts to impose a general ban on mood-affecting substances, the profile of licit versus illicit substances should not matter much. Whereas it is an article of the specifist credo that where the law draws the line can have an effect that is significant enough to warrant the continual rethinking of the scope and justification of the criminal law. Accordingly, specifists invest much more time and energy than do generalists in discussing changing boundaries in the criminal law.

Rethinking is the last thing that legalists wish to encourage in regard to the scope of criminal prohibition, and they vehemently oppose decriminalization proposals. For the legalists, the proponents of decriminalization are the fellow travelers of the 1990s. Indeed, the legalists characterize proposals to decriminalize as "stupid" and "irrational," and they portray their purveyors as "naive," with the same sinister undertones to the adjective that used to be aimed at those who were accused of communist sympathies.

The *National Drug Control Strategy* amply illustrates the tone and substance of the legalist approach to this issue. The report speaks not of decriminalization but of what is called *legalization,* and it seems to suggest that a legalization process would represent a governmental seal of approval for drug abuse. "Exactly how under this scenario we would convincingly warn potential new users about the evils of drugs—having just made them legally acceptable—is not entirely clear" (Office of National Drug Control Policy, 1989, p. 6). The text of the report is unqualified in its condemnation of any decriminalization of any drug— "it would be an unqualified national disaster"—in rhetorical terms that could well have been used to oppose the repeal of alcohol prohibition ("would promise more use, more crime, and more trouble for desperately needed treatment and education efforts") (Office of National Drug Control Policy, 1989, p. 7).

The reason that the decriminalization of any currently illegal drug is anathema to the legalist position is that the vindication of state authority is the central value to be upheld in this version of the drug war. Changing the law thus would be literally surrendering to the enemy, by admitting that state authority has been inappropriately directed at drug users. The central inflexibility is that there is no way to change the terms of the criminal law regarding drugs without admitting defeat in the power struggle between good and evil that is the essence of this account of drug use and abuse. Thus, there can be no such thing as an unjust drug law, or the whole fabric of the legalist position would unravel. It is not that decriminalization might lead to bad things; it is, in itself, the bad consequence that the legalist most fears.

IV. A legalist manifesto

The legalist pedigree of the *National Drug Control Strategy* explains many of the curious features of the document that we have noted. Only illegal drugs are the concern of this strategy, and all illegal drugs are considered the natural enemy in the drug war. The subject of the war on drugs is therefore not defined because it is regarded as obvious: All, and only, illegal psychoactive substances are the target. What a drug is, is thus a question of the content of the criminal law at a given time.

On the question of whether the principal concern is drug use or the social and health consequences of drug use, the report is unambiguous:

> First, we must come to terms with the drug problem in its essence: use itself. Worthy efforts to alleviate the symptoms of epidemic drug abuse—crime and disease, for example—must continue unabated. But a largely ad-hoc attack on the holes in our dike can have only an indirect and minimal effect on the flood itself. (Office of National Drug Control Policy, 1989, p. 8)

If crime and disease are only "the symptoms," what is the problem? Here the report is not explicit, but the inclusion of all illegal drugs and the failure to discuss the abuse of legal drugs implicitly makes the priority the threat posed to the government's authority. After calling the creation of "a Drug–Free America" an "admirable goal," the report goes on to say that "it is already a reality for the vast majority of Americans who have never taken an illegal drug" (Office of National Drug Control Policy, 1989, p. 9). By its own terms, this announcement includes some alcoholics and Valium users as members of "a Drug–Free America."

Indeed, the only concern with alcohol expressed in the report appears much later:

> Though the legislated mandate of the Office of National Drug Control Policy excludes alcohol (since it is not a controlled substance under the law), it must be recognized that alcohol is still the most widely abused substance in America. *It is illegal for young people to purchase or consume alcohol.* Prevention programs must obviously take this fact into account. (Office of National Drug Control Policy, 1989, p. 48; emphasis added)

The choice of language in this passage speaks volumes: Even though alcohol is "the most widely abused *substance* [emphasis added] in America," it is not a drug viewed in the perspective of the *National Drug Control Strategy*. And the report seems not to be uncomfortable with this limited mandate for the Office of National Drug Control Policy, for nowhere is it suggested that the office's restricted jurisdiction is inappropriate or should be expanded.

Two other aspects of the *National Drug Control Strategy* make sense only in light of its legalist orientation. First, the report makes the same policy recommendations for all drugs. With respect to enforcement priority, the policy toward the casual user, treatment, and drug testing, the presumption is that all (illegal) drugs are created equal. This is so even though the report paints very different portraits of the threat posed by various drugs. For example, crack cocaine "is, in fact, the most dangerous and quickly addictive drug known to man" (Office of National Drug Control Policy, 1989, p. 3). Marijuana is worthy of prohibition mostly because it is a "gateway drug" leading to the use of more dangerous drugs (Office of National Drug Control Policy, 1989, p. 55). Some drugs apparently may be, in George Orwell's words, "more equal than others," but the priority and strategy are the same for each of these drugs and for all other illegal substances.

This lack of priorities is related to seeing the central harm of drug taking as defiance of the law. Whatever else their effects, all illegal drugs are equally illegal and, on that account, are worthy of equivalent treatment. While deploring the special costs of crack cocaine, then, a legalist advocate can never forget that all illegal drugs carry the same imperative for suppression. So the legalist must simultaneously argue that crack cocaine is the worst drug in human history and also that marijuana is just as bad as crack cocaine.

Another legalist sentiment animates the need to seek out and punish casual, nonaddicted drug users, and this is the most novel element in the *National Drug Control Strategy*. The justification for targeting casual users is that they present "a *highly* contagious" example to potential drug users (Office of National Drug Control Policy, 1989, p. 11; emphasis in the original). But the enforcement of laws against this group can also be justified because according to the legalist view, their deliberate infraction of the law is the central harm, the essential drug problem. That these persons are neither addicted nor collaterally criminal makes them even more dangerous role models. That is, their defiance of the legal authority of the state is more blameworthy and dangerous than that of addicts driven by their craving, for the addicts' "drug use is not very contagious" because they are "a mess" and make "the worst possible advertisement for new drug use" (Office of National Drug Control Policy, 1989, p. 11). It is the nonaddicted drug users who are most conspicuously thumbing their noses at the state authority. Both the priority of the nonaddicted users and the passion with which it is argued are salient aspects of the legalist perspective.

Indeed, it is hard to find departures from legalist priorities in the *National Drug Control Strategy*. Even when the report supports policies that do not flow from legalist premises, the qualifications that it imposes on them confirm the need to state all elements of drug control policy in the legalist mode. In this connection, the report's handling of the issue of drug treatment provides a significant example of the powerful influence of the legalist bias on the specific policies proposed in the *National Drug Control Strategy*.

As we noted in the last section, legalists do not place much stock in spending scarce resources on programs of drug treatment. Part of the reason is their distrust of medical models. But the legalists also view drug users as social and political enemies, and treatment programs therefore seem to represent a way of giving aid and comfort to the enemy, never a popular category of wartime expenditure. It is thus not surprising that the legalists prefer to invest resources in punishment and interdiction efforts. Yet this legalist document supports the expansion of treatment programs at an annual cost of over $600 million. Does this represent a deviation from legalist orthodoxy? Hardly. The drug treatment establishment contemplated in this document is permeated with the legalistic distrust of comfort to the drug users. Because the efficacy and patriotism of treatment programs are distrusted, their rigorous evaluation is required (Office of National Drug Control Policy, 1989, p. 102). But there is no such strict accountability for law enforcement efforts, education programs, or interdiction. The report also calls for mandatory treatment with confinement sanctions for treatment failures. It is thus the legalistic gloss of treatment-as-punishment that makes treatment initiatives palatable in the *National Drug Control Strategy*.

A final and striking example of the priorities of legalism can be found in the list of quantified objectives, at the back of the report, for reducing the extent of the drug problem. Nine quantified goals are presented, with eight of the nine relating to reducing drug availability or drug use. Only one, decreasing the number of drug-related hospital

emergency room admissions, concerns the lessening of harmful consequences that flow from drug abuse. The report mentions lower domestic
marijuana production as one of its nine specific goals. But fewer
drug:overdose deaths in the United States or fewer babies born drug
addicted are not among the quantified objects of the national drug
control policy as presented in the *National Drug Control Strategy.*

V. *Legacies of Legalism*

It is important to consider some of the collateral consequences of a
legalist emphasis for drug policy. In this section, we shall examine the
impact of a legalist emphasis on a constitutional constraint on drug
control policy, on the relationship between drug users and government-
sponsored helping programs, and on the impact of government policy on
how drug users respond to public opinion polls.

The state's motivation for action can carry implications for the kind
of power that will be allowed in a limited government with constitutional
constraints. In the coming years, the courts will face a substantial
number of novel constitutional questions as new techniques for compulsory testing and for treatment for the purpose of controlling drugs
become state policy. There are two respects in which a policy that
emphasizes hostility to the drug user may be more strictly scrutinized
for excesses of government power than would be the case for policies
apparently motivated by the impulse to help. Procedures like civil
commitment, traditionally justified more as compulsory assistance than
as punitive isolation, may not be permitted when introduced as part of a
legalist crusade against dangerously immoral drug users. If the medical
model does not fit the apparent motives of state power, the exercise of
that power may be more sharply curtailed. If the government's stance
toward the targets of the program is unmitigated hostility, a constitutional court might conclude that the only legitimate arena for such
warfare is the criminal justice system.

There is a second way in which the martial character of a drug war
may limit the degrees of power exercised on its behalf. The courts are
traditionally more vigilant in providing right-to-privacy and search-and-
seizure limits in criminal law than in government intrusions that are
justified for reasons of public health. The reason for this distinction may
he a feeling that the government should be allowed more latitude when
it is acting only, or principally, for the benefit of those citizens that it is
inspecting. Also, the courts may feel that the offending citizen turned up
in a public health search has less to lose than does the prototypical
criminal defendant. Thus, for instance, the U.S. Supreme Court has been
more amenable to inspections without probable cause made by health
and building inspectors than to those made by police searching for the
fruits of crime. Which analogy the judiciary applies to drug control
strategies may be a function of the announced or imputed motive of the
strategy.

Consider a program of universal, compulsory urine testing for drugs in secondary schools, patterned after the program currently in use in the U.S. military. The justification for such a program could not be based on the express or implicit consent of the schoolchildren or of their parents because education is compulsory. Thus, one key justification for military and employer drug test regimes would be absent. Yet the potential for identifying drug users would be more than substantial. How might a court resolve the novel constitutional question relating to such a program?

The point we wish to emphasize here is that the orientation of the government program could be a decisive factor in determining whether the program violated constitutional standards. A credible claim for public health justification based on finding out whether students are using any of a wide spectrum of legal and illegal substances and referring them to treatment and support programs that are avowedly nonpunitive might pass constitutional muster, whereas a drug-testing program aimed at suspending and expelling those with urine testing positive for illegal drugs could be viewed as overreaching either Fourth Amendment standards or the government's obligation to protect the young. In this way, ironically, a moral crusade on legalist premises may have to proceed from a narrower power base than would government programs with a more benign orientation to drug users.

A not-unrelated set of problems concerns the orientation of employer "employee assistance programs" that have been established to discover and facilitate the treatment of employees with alcohol and drug abuse problems. The mixed motives of such programs have always been inherent in the employer—employee relationship. Unlike drug and alcohol screening programs that operate before the establishment of such employment relationships, programs that involve workers with established employment relationships have usually been premised on employee entitlement. Yet an unmitigated legalist stance could drive a wedge between the perceived interests of employers and those of employees with a use history of those drugs targeted by legalist antidrug programs. Employees might well distrust the benign intentions of companies toward drug users. So might labor unions and employee associations, despite the upbeat narrative history provided by the *National Drug Control Strategy*: "As drugs have become more prevalent in the workplace, many corporations have begun to use drug testing as a means of identifying employees *in need of assistance*" (Office of National Drug Control Policy, 1989, p. 56; emphasis added).

In the view of the *National Drug Control Strategy*, the role of the employee assistance program is a combination of assistance and deterrence, in which the program simultaneously keeps "the workplace safe and productive by identifying those employees" using drugs and helps drug-using employees "by referring them to treatment, counseling, and rehabilitation." The *National Drug Control Strategy* favors a federal policy in which such programs are required to take punitive action in response to an employee found to be using illegal drugs (Office of National Drug Control Policy, 1989, pp. 5657).

One problem with deputizing employee assistance programs to deter and ferret out drug use is the damage to the credentials of such programs as helping agencies for employees with drug and alcohol problems, at which they feel they can get confidential assistance. If employees attempt to conceal drug and alcohol problems, the resulting delays in treatment referral will have negative effects on workplace safety. And these could be compounded by the unwillingness of fellow employees to refer drinking or drug-using colleagues to an employer agency that has come to resemble a drug enforcement office. Finally, the attempt to keep alcohol and illegal drug policies on a separate track might well fail, and so one casualty of militant antidrug employer programs could be early intervention and treatment efforts for alcohol.

The way in which punitive orientations might discourage candidates from seeking treatment or their fellow employees from using the employee assistance program is nowhere considered in the document under review, and it is the lack of consideration rather than any substantive choices made in the report that concerns us here. The transformation of every institution relating to drugs in society into a branch of the criminal enforcement enterprise could have manifold effects that need more attention than has been provided in the *National Drug Control Strategy*.

One final example of the potential effects of a sustained legalist emphasis concerns the sensitivity of public opinion that the report uses to keep score for its nine quantified two-and ten-year objectives. No fewer than five of these benchmarks involve trends over time in survey responses of the population. One of the measures is the trend in student attitudes toward drug use, and four of the targets pertain to lowering the percentage of the population who tell the poll taker that they have taken illegal drugs in the previous month.

With the success or failure of a coordinated national campaign hinging on trends over time in survey responses, it is a matter of some concern that a campaign to censure and stigmatize drug use might reduce the willingness of citizens to respond candidly to strangers who ask whether they have ingested cocaine or other illegal drugs in the past thirty days. The more harshly focused a government campaign is, the more impact such a campaign can be expected to have on the respondents' candor about their drug use: The danger, then, is that of an antidrug campaign appearing to succeed because increasing proportions of the population conceal personal drug use from survey researchers. Yet even this artifact represents a substantial achievement for the dedicated legalist, because such a campaign would certainly reduce open defiance of the drug laws, even if it had zero impact on the levels of illegal drug use or the health and economic consequences that are associated with drug use.

Whereas the public health generalist and the specifist would regard any decrease in public support for drug taking or opinion poll reporting of illegal drug taking as illusory achievements unless they reflected real declines in the ingestion of drugs, the legalist would view such a trend as meaning that a growing segment of the population acknowledged the immorality of illegal drug taking. That the fear of consequences produced this acknowledgment is not the sort of thing that would offend legalist sensibility in the least. Nor would the fact that such a victory would be only symbolic be at all discouraging, because from the legalist perspective, symbolic adherence to legal definitions of right and wrong behavior is the most significant issue.

But this mode of analysis leads us to an important puzzle and a significant worry. The puzzle is that from a legalist perspective the late 1980s was by no means a peak period for illegal drugs as a national problem. The percentage of Americans who reported current use of illegal drugs did drop from double to single digits in the past decade, and this is, in the words of the *National Drug Control Strategy*, "very good news," whether or not the illegal drug use itself declined by any such margin. Some of the other social indicators that concern people—overdose deaths, AIDS infection, crack babies, and the like—seem to be viewed by the legalists more as the wages of sin than as indices of the seriousness of the drug threat to the law-abiding population. Why, then, was 1989 a more problematic period than the late 1960s or early 1970s? After all, from the legalist perspective, the more benign the social reputation of an illegal drug is, the larger its threat to the antidrug stance of the legal order will be. If drug takers are suffering more harmful consequences, so much the better for the deterrence of others.

Our worry is that many legalists saw the cocaine situation of the late 1980s as an opportunity rather than as an emergency. Drugs in the 1990s are a highly attractive target of authoritarian opportunity when compared with other issues and other time periods. Public support for extreme governmental responses to drugs is higher than for authoritarian countermeasures to any other social problem. In this sense, what the general public perceives as a drug emergency is a special opportunity to institutionalize the judgments and tactics of the legalist school. Indeed, the special opportunity for legalists may have arisen only because of the declining popularity of drugs among the general population. Just as the anti-Left witch hunts of the 1950s took place when the Left's popularity was waning, the lessened public support of drug use may be more of a cause of the legalist crusade against drugs than a consequence of it. The climate of opinion of the 1990s may thus be seen by the legalist as an opportunity to take revenge on earlier errors of permissiveness in American drug policy.

One problem with all this is its essential lack of relation to the public health costs of substance abuse in the United States of the 1990s. The lower priority accorded to illness, debility, and death in the legalist drug scheme is a matter of some concern when conflicting goals compete for scarce public resources, as is the warping effect produced by an overemphasis on punishment in treatment and rehabilitation processes. But the largest concern about ideological overkill in the current debate should be reserved for the potential exploitation of the drug problem as a rallying point for authoritarian sentiments in American society and government.

THE WHITE HOUSE—NATIONAL DRUG CONTROL STRATEGY

February 2006.

INTRODUCTION

When President George W. Bush took office in 2001, drug use had risen to unacceptably high levels. Over the past decade, drug use by young people had nearly doubled, as measured by those who reported having used drugs in the past month: 11 percent of young people had used drugs in the past month in 1991, and 19 percent had done so in 2001. Indeed, in 2000, over half of all 12th graders in the United States had used an illicit drug at least once in his or her life before graduation.

Determined to fight this trend, the President set aggressive goals to reduce drug use in the United States, including reducing youth drug use by 10 percent in two years. That goal has been met and exceeded.

To achieve the goal of reducing drug use, the President set out an ambitious, balanced strategy that focuses on three primary elements: stopping drug use before it starts, healing drug users, and disrupting the market for illicit drugs.

The President's strategy is producing results. According to the latest University of Michigan *Monitoring the Future* survey of youth drug use that was released in December 2005, overall teen drug use has declined significantly since the President took office. Current use of illicit drugs by 8th, 10th, and 12th graders combined has dropped 19 percent since 2001. This translates into nearly 700,000 fewer young people using illicit drugs.

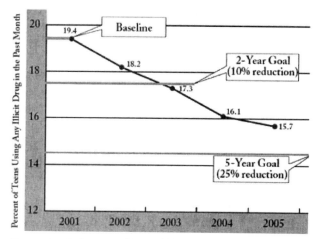

*Illustration 1: Progress Toward Two- and Five-Year Goals
Current Use of Any Illicit Drug Continues to Decline*

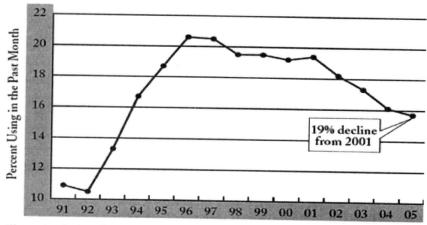

Illustration 2: Any Illicit Drug Use by 8th, 10th, and 12th Graders Combined

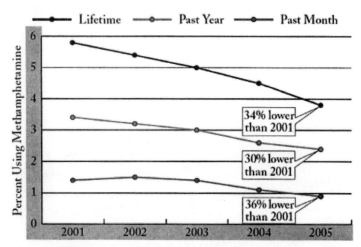

Illustration 3: Methamphetamine Use Among 8th, 10th, and 12th Graders Combined, 2001 to 2005

The survey reports other positive trends for this age group:

● The use of methamphetamine by 8th, 10th, and 12th graders combined has dropped by approximately one-third since 2001. The declines were 34 percent for lifetime use, 30 percent for past-year use, and 36 percent for past-month use.

● Steroid use has dropped dramatically among young people since 2001, particularly in the past year. According to the survey, the use of steroids by 8th, 10th, and 12th graders was down 38 percent for lifetime use, 37 percent for past-year use, and 30 percent for past-month use.

● Although marijuana remains the most commonly used illicit drug among teens, usage rates are declining. Since 2001, marijuana use among 8th, 10th, and 12th graders combined dropped 13 percent for lifetime use, 15 percent for past-year use, and 19 percent for past-month use. Current use of marijuana decreased 28 percent (from 9.2 percent among 8th graders to 6.6 percent) and 23 percent among 10th graders (from 19.8 percent to 15.2 percent).

● There has been a steep decline in LSD use since 2001. Current use of LSD dropped approximately 50 percent among 8th graders (from 1.0 percent to 0.5 percent), 60 percent among 10th graders (from 1.5 percent to 0.6 percent), and 70 percent among 12th graders (from 2.3 percent to 0.7 percent).

● Use of Ecstasy (MDMA) has declined by nearly two thirds since 2001. Current use dropped 66 percent among 8th graders (from 1.8 percent to 0.6 percent), 61 percent among 10th graders (from 2.6 percent to 1.0 percent), and approximately 64 percent among 12th graders (from 2.8 percent to 1.0 percent).

● The use of certain other club drugs has also decreased, including rohypnol, GHB, and ketamine.

• In addition, consumption of alcohol and cigarettes by minors is down, including the rate of young people reporting being drunk.

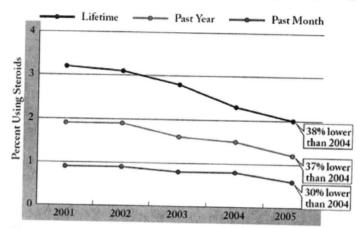

Illustration 4: Methamphetamine Use Among 8th, 10th, and 12th Graders Combined, 2001 to 2005

The President's strategy has an impressive record of accomplishment, but important work remains to be done. *Monitoring the Future* reports that cocaine and heroin use, while low, has remained stable. And prescription drug abuse remains troubling. Oxycontin, a prescription drug used as a painkiller, is the only drug for which the survey reports an increase in use across all three age groups: past-year use increased from 2.7 percent in 2002 to 3.4 percent in 2005, a 26 percent increase. (The survey began monitoring this drug in 2002.) And, despite the declines in use of many other drugs reported in the most recent survey, overall illicit drug use remains too high among America's young people.

This year's *National Drug Control Strategy* seeks to build on the progress that has already been made by outlining a balanced, integrated plan aimed at achieving the President's goal of reducing drug use. Each pillar of the strategy is crucial, and each sustains the others. The three components are outlined in the following chapters.

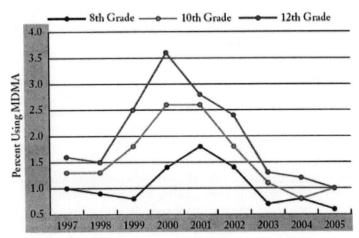

Illustration 5: Past Month Use of MDMA (Ecstasy), by Grade

The first chapter, Stopping Drug Use Before It Starts, outlines the Administration's work to prevent the initiation of drug use. An integral part of this effort is the new "Above the Influence" initiative by the White House Office of National Drug Control Policy (ONDCP)—National Youth Anti–Drug Media Campaign—and the Partnership for a Drug Free America. This initiative, which consists of television advertisements and interactive web-based outreach, calls on young people to be true to themselves by remaining "above the influence."

The second chapter, Healing America's Drug Users, highlights initiatives that treat drug users. Key initiatives include the President's Access to Recovery program, which expands treatment options, and drug courts, which seek to rehabilitate offenders with substance abuse problems.

The third chapter, Disrupting Drug Markets, outlines the Administration's work at home and abroad to disrupt the availability of illicit drugs, through source country efforts, interdiction programs, and investigative operations. We are attacking market vulnerabilities in the illegal drug trade and applying pressure to reduce profits and raise the risks of drug trafficking.

As in past years, this year's *National Drug Control Strategy* highlights the good work faith-based and community organizations are doing to combat the scourge of illicit drugs in their own communities. The Strategy seeks to harness these efforts, and the work of state and local officials, so that Americans work together to reach the President's goal of reducing overall drug use.

MAJOR CITIES DRUG INITIATIVE

ONDCP began the *Major Cities Drug Initiative* to channel the efforts of communities to combat drug abuse in the areas that need it most. Drug use harms communities everywhere, but America's large cities are particularly hard hit. A recent survey showed that large metropolitan areas in the United States have the highest rates of current illicit drug use. Targeting drugs in these cities can bring about a significant decline in the Nation's drug problem.

In 2003, the *Major Cities Drug Initiative* was launched in 25 of the Nation's largest metropolitan areas. Drawing on the resources and dedication of local officials who are on the front lines of combating drug problems in their neighborhoods, this initiative brings together Federal, state, and local officials working in drug prevention, treatment and law enforcement to identify the unique challenges drugs pose to each community.

ONDCP helps broker these relationships and promotes the development of local drug control strategies by bringing stakeholders together, offering information on current drug use, and developing inventories of Federal, state, and local resources for prevention, treatment and law enforcement. In the two years since the start of the *Major Cities Drug Initiative*, there have been important achievements in developing better approaches to reducing drug use. For example, Miami and Baltimore have developed city-wide drug control strategies, while Washington, DC, and Denver have strengthened and rewritten their existing strategies. ONDCP is working with other large cities to develop their own local strategies.

To assist cities in learning best practices, ONDCP published *Cities Without Drugs: The Major Cities Guide to Reducing Substance Abuse in Your Community*, which helps cities learn valuable lessons from one another.

Additionally, ONDCP has facilitated city-to-city dialogue, provided training and technical assistance, and brokered improved relationships between cities and their Federal partners using diverse venues including summits, video and audio teleconferences, and leadership meetings. ONDCP has worked in conjunction with the US Conference of Mayors and the National League of Cities to convene and facilitate mini-summits for mayors and their policy staff. Representatives from several cities have been linked via video and audio teleconferences on a variety of issues relating to the drug problem, including prostitution and addiction, community health and epidemiology, and building better community coalitions.

Stopping Drug Use Before It Starts—Education and Community Action

When President Bush took office, drug use had been on the rise over much of the previous decade and had reached unacceptably high levels. The Administration set out a bold agenda to counter these trends, and the Nation is seeing results: drug use is down, particularly by young people.

At the heart of the Administration's success in reducing drug use is a change in perceptions about the acceptability of using illicit substances. Education programs and outreach activities, backed up by scientific studies, have worked to spread the word that illicit substance use can be harmful to a person's health and wellbeing, as well as a detriment to society as a whole. Drug addiction can also be seen as a threat to individual freedom in that it can reduce people to a single, destructive desire. Given the harmful effects of substance abuse, the *National Drug Control Strategy* has made healing drug users a priority—a testament to the fact that America is the land of second chances.

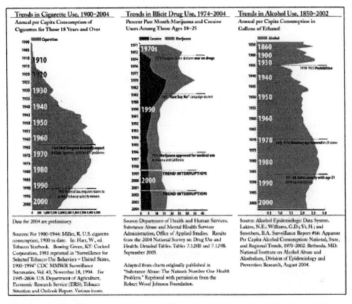

Illustration 6: The three charts above show Trends in Cigarette Use, 1900–2004 (left), Trend in Illicit Drug Use, 1974–2004 (middle), and Trends in Alcohol Use, 1850–2002 (right)

The greatest pressure on young people to start using drugs does not come from drug pushers but from their peers. It is, therefore, important to continue to educate young people about the dangers of drug use and build a cultural norm that views illicit drug use as unacceptable. This culture, and the attitudes that support it, works as a bulwark against the spread of drug use.

Attitudes start at home—and parents and caregivers play the most influential roles in the lives of children. Children who have parents and caregivers who are engaged, loving, and supportive are more likely to grow up to be healthy, productive adults. Engaging young people directly about drug use has been shown to reduce the chances of drug initiation. Also, research shows that if teens can make it to adulthood without experimenting with drugs, they are far less likely to begin using drugs later in life. The community also plays an important role in establishing a culture that promotes healthy choices. Through their actions and attitudes toward drug use, teachers, coaches, faith leaders, employers, and community organizations show young people how to lead their lives. If these role models treat drug use as a rite of passage, young people will take the cue and experiment with dangerous, addictive substances. On the other hand, if they highlight the dangers of drug use and set out clear guidance that drug use is not tolerable, then they help build a culture that promotes drug free lives.

Trends in cigarette, illicit drug and alcohol use illustrate this point. The use of these substances has ebbed and flowed, reflecting cultural changes regarding perceptions of risk and the social acceptability of substance use, as well as the impact of effective policies that affect the availability of, and demand for, harmful substances (see chart above). As substance abuse became socially acceptable in the 1970s, use increased. Likewise, when social norms changed and people became more aware of the dangers of substance abuse, use declined.

The Bush Administration has worked to change a culture of acceptance of drug use by providing information about the dangers of drugs to users and the costs to society. The Administration is working with parents, faith leaders, and community organizations to help young people make the decision to avoid illicit substances. Last year, First Lady Laura Bush launched the *Helping America's Youth Initiative*, which is intended to help young people avoid risky behavior. At the Helping America's Youth conference in October 2005, Mrs. Bush and five members of the President's Cabinet were joined by more than 600 parents, caregivers, civic leaders, faith-based and community service providers, researchers, and other interested parties to highlight the challenges young people face and identify ways to help young people grow to live successful, productive lives.

To help bolster cooperation among Federal, state, local, and non-governmental sectors, the Bush Administration launched the Strategic Prevention Framework (SPF). The framework develops data-driven comprehensive strategies that effectively reduce factors that put communities at risk for drug abuse, while strengthening protective factors that can result in healthy outcomes for individuals of all ages—particularly our Nation's youth.

The framework creates an infrastructure that ties together prevention efforts at Federal, state, and local levels and within communities. Each participating state develops a prevention strategy that is tailored to local needs and works to implement new policies, programs, and practices that leverage existing community resources while working to build new ones. The framework has two primary components: an evidenced-based five-step planning process to guide the development of a comprehensive prevention strategy and a data-driven methodology that states and communities can use to plan and implement strategies that best serve their communities. Since the framework was announced in October 2004, the Substance Abuse and Mental Health Services Administration (SAMHSA) has awarded 26 SPF State Incentive Grants.

This SPF program is built on the idea that states and local organizations are in the best position to identify the challenges they face and to take action to overcome them. Indeed, communities across the country have formed local anti-drug community coalitions that coordinate prevention and intervention efforts. These coalitions bring together community leaders and professionals in health care, law enforcement, and education to provide local, grassroots solutions to the challenges drug and alcohol abuse pose to their neighborhoods. Coalitions work to develop a model for all sectors to work together to change community norms and send the same no-use messages to young people. The Administration supports the efforts of many of these coalitions by providing $79.2 million in the President's FY 2007 Budget through the Drug Free Communities (DFC) program. Through the establishment of community coalitions, the DFC program is designed to complement the development and implementation of the SPF in communities across America.

Currently, there are over 700 funded DFC coalitions, which exist in every state and form the backbone of the Nation's community prevention system. Under this program, each grantee receives up to $100,000 annually for up to five years to develop a comprehensive community plan to address substance abuse problems.

Drug use is a particular concern for those who are leaving prison, and the Administration is supporting local organizations that help prisoners transition to independent, drug-and crime-free life outside prison walls. Recently, 30 organizations were awarded grants as part of a proposed four-year, $300 million initiative that the President announced in his 2004 State of the Union Address.

Parents, caregivers, and community leaders play an important role in promoting healthy decisions, but ultimately young people must choose for themselves to stay away from drugs. Recognizing this, ONDCP's National Youth Anti–Drug Media Campaign, working with the Partnership for a Drug–Free America, launched a new advertising and online campaign for teens ages 14–16 that encourages them to live "above the influence" and to reject the use of illicit drugs and other negative pressures.

Above the Influence, launched in November 2005, features a series of television, print, and web-based interactive advertisements that tap into the power teens gain when they resist negative influences that compromise their values and aspirations.

Teens in high school today face competing pressures that can contribute to risky behaviors. These behaviors are positioned as "under the influence," and the brand calls on teens to rise above them. The aim of this new campaign is to speak directly to the aspirations of young people. Staying away from drugs is not just what their parents and caregivers want for them—it is a way to be true to themselves and their potential.

Promoting a culture that supports healthy, drug free choices requires providing disincentives to using drugs as well. Screening for drugs is an important way to send the message that drug use is unacceptable—in the workplace, in schools, or as a condition for participating in extracurricular activities (see *Student Testing to Maintain Safe Schools*). Screening for drug use gives young people an "out" to say no to drugs. If they want to play on the volleyball team and know that they will be tested as members of the team, they can cite their desire to play as a reason not to use drugs when pressured by a peer.

In addition to creating a culture of disapproval toward drugs, drug testing also achieves three public health goals: it deters young people from initiating drug use; it identifies those who have initiated drug use so that parents and counselors can intervene early; and it helps identify those who have a dependency on drugs so that they can be referred for treatment.

Many schools across the country have instituted student testing as a way to maintain drug free schools and ensure that students who use drugs get the help they need. In his 2004 State of the Union Address, President Bush announced a new initiative to support communities that want to include drug screening as part of their efforts to maintain drug free schools. The program is optional—communities must apply for the grants—and it is not tied in any way to Federal education funding. Furthermore, testing cannot result in referral to law enforcement agencies or adversely affect the student's progress in academic programs. Instead, the program is designed to help students make healthy choices and provide support for those who may have become addicted to illicit drugs. As the President said in his 2004 State of the Union Address, "The aim here is not to punish children, but to send them this message: We love you, and we don't want to lose you."

Illustration 7: Student Drug Testing Sites

        * Department of Education grantees
        ** School districts and private schools that identified themselves as conducting student drug testing in a 2003 survey conducted by the Office of National Drug Control Policy.
        ** Schools that were identified in media reports as conducting student drug testing.

Recognizing the vital role that student drug-testing programs can play in reducing drug use in our Nation's schools, the Administration has hosted a series of student drug-testing summits nationwide. These summits are designed to equip community leaders and local school officials with the tools they need to construct a successful student drug-testing program. Summit attendees learn from national and regional experts in the field about current technology, research, and legal issues surrounding the program and receive practical advice from those who have run successful programs and found innovative ways to fund them. The Administration will build on these successes and host several more summits in 2006.

Screening for drug use in school also helps prepare students for the workforce. Students must prepare for being part of a workforce that is increasingly insistent on maintaining a drug free environment. Employers cite safety, absenteeism, and health-related problems as key reasons why positive tests can result in serious sanctions for employees. Student testing prepares young people for this reality.

For adults, drug screening helps prevent initiation of use by sending a clear message that in order to work, one must be drug free. Furthermore, because the vast majority of American adults work, and most of these workers are parents, the workplace is an effective setting for prevention messages that have the power to spread exponentially to America's families, schools, and communities. Perhaps most importantly, drug screening also keeps people who use drugs away from positions that can affect the safety of others, such as operating public transportation vehicles or caring for children and the elderly.

In all cases, the purpose of screening is twofold: send the message that drug use is unacceptable, and identify those who use drugs so they can receive appropriate intervention and treatment.

HEALING AMERICA'S DRUG USERS

The previous chapter outlines the Administration's work to prevent drug use before it starts. Recognizing that despite prevention efforts, some people will choose to begin using drugs, and many of them will become addicted, the Administration has made intervention and treatment a priority.

Indeed, 19.1 million Americans have used at least one illicit substance in the past month. Intervention and treatment are therefore key components to the President's drug control strategy. Both aim to accomplish two important goals: stem the use of illicit drugs, while providing help to those who have become addicted.

Adopting a public health understanding of drug use and addiction provides important insights into what is a preventable and treatable disease. Drug use is a learned behavior most often transmitted by peers who are non-dependent users and have yet to show the negative effects of using illicit substances. The consequences of drug use are often delayed and therefore not always apparent, so current users can appear to live normal, productive lives before the effects of use take hold. During this "honeymoon period," the user may convey the impression that drug use is not dangerous, and subsequently others with whom they interact may likewise choose to use drugs. In this sense, the so-called "casual" drug user is a critical vector in the spread of this behavior.

The Administration's prevention efforts, described in the previous chapter, work to curb the spread of drug use by building a culture that rejects drugs. This effort is built on education, outreach, and intervention programs and relies on the individual to make an informed decision.

However, even the best prevention efforts can be undermined by young people witnessing seemingly consequence-free drug use. Therefore, intervening with users who are in early stages of use is important both to ensure that the user does not develop dependency and to interrupt the transmission of this behavior to others.

The Administration is focused on expanding intervention programs and increasing the options for treatment. Intervention programs focus on users who are on the verge of developing serious problems. Focusing on this nexus is cost effective and limits the spread of drug use by individuals who are in the early stages of use before the negative effects of continued use and addiction begin to fester.

A key priority of this Administration has been to make drug screening and intervention programs part of the Nation's existing network of health, education, law enforcement, and counseling providers. This requires training professionals to screen for drug use, identify users, and refer the users for treatment.

The programs vary widely, and the Administration is evaluating each to identify best practices, which can then be replicated. In one program, new students in a local community college must fill out a survey before opening their school email accounts. The interactive survey takes them through a line of questioning that helps them identify potential substance abuse problems. Students who may have a problem are referred to counselors who can do a more thorough evaluation in person. This program is built on a body of research showing that simply by asking questions regarding unhealthy behaviors and conducting a brief intervention, patients are more likely to avoid the behavior in the future and seek help if they believe they have a problem.

In other programs, emergency medical professionals are given training in how to screen for drug use through verbal questioning and identifying physical signs of drug use. Individuals can then be more accurately diagnosed because the underlying pathology that brings patients to the emergency room may be linked to illicit substance use. Identified users are then referred to intervention and treatment services as needed.

Expanding intervention programs requires including drug screening and intervention training for medical students and for physicians already in practice. The Administration held a medical education conference with leading health professionals in December 2004 to expand the intervention programs of the Nation's existing health service providers. This effort will continue in partnership with the medical community.

For those who have become drug dependent, the Administration is working to expand treatment options across the country. The President's

Access to Recovery Program offers vouchers so that people can choose a program that works for them. Access to Recovery expands the choices to include faith-based providers, because a person's faith can play an important role in the healing process. The President's program is now in 14 states and one tribal organization and is working to provide services to the more than 125,000 people who seek treatment each year, but are not able to obtain it, in part, because they cannot afford it. Indeed, getting users into treatment is also cost effective. One study of treatment programs found that every dollar spent on treatment saves nearly $7.50 in costs associated with crime and lost productivity.

As part of the President's efforts to expand choice and individual empowerment in Federal assistance programs, the Administration will offer incentives to encourage states to provide a wider array of innovative treatment options by voluntarily using their Substance Abuse Block Grant funds for drug-treatment and recovery support service vouchers. Building on the successful model of the President's Access to Recovery program, distribution of block grant funds through a voucher system will promote innovative drug and alcohol treatment and recovery programs, provide a wider array of treatment provider options, and introduce into the system greater accountability and flexibility.

Another important program to help drug users who have been involved in crime is the use of drug courts. Drug courts are an innovative approach to helping drug offenders achieve a drug-and crime-free life (see *Drug Courts per State, 2005*). Drug courts use the power of the courts and the support of family, friends, and counselors to bring people to the path of recovery and to help them achieve drug free lives. This mix of incentives and sanctions has been found to be effective at reducing recidivism. Data show that within the first year of release, 43.5 percent of drug offenders are rearrested, whereas only 16.4 percent of drug court graduates are rearrested.

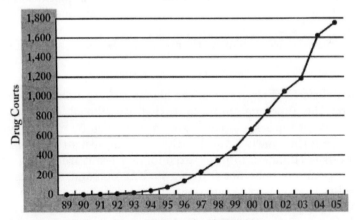

Illustration 8: Drug Courts Nationwide, 1989–2005

Methamphetamine is a dangerous and highly addictive drug that poses complex challenges for drug control. Of particular note is the problem of production. Because the drug can be manufactured in homes or vehicles and the precursor chemicals used to make it can be purchased from retail stores, the consequences of methamphetamine go beyond merely using this toxic drug. Indeed, the production of methamphetamine poses, in itself, a challenge for communities. Dangerous chemicals used in the manufacturing of the drug can cause harm to those in the vicinity of the producer. Cognizant of the nature of this synthetic drug threat, the Bush Administration is working closely with state and local authorities to combat methamphetamine use and production.

A key element to fighting methamphetamine production is striking a balance in the regulation of precursor chemicals such as *pseudoephedrine*, which are used to manufacture the drug. This balance aims to allow for the use of legitimate products that contain *pseudoephedrine*, such as cold medicine, while preventing methamphetamine cooks from diverting the chemical for illegitimate uses. The Bush Administration has urged Congress to enact legislation that would limit the amount of *pseudoephedrine* for retail sale to what could be used for individual, legitimate medical purposes. However, diversion of *pseudoephedrine* can also occur when bulk shipments are imported into the United States. To ensure that the drug is not rerouted away from legitimate businesses and consumers, the Administration is working with other countries to improve the flow of information to the US Drug Enforcement Administration (DEA) about bulk shipments of this chemical.

These and other actions to combat methamphetamine are part of the Administration's Synthetic Action Plan, announced in October 2004. The Action Plan was the first step in developing a coordinated, strategic response to the problem of synthetic drugs like methamphetamine. The plan set out more than 40 recommendations for Federal, state, and local action aimed at preventing the illicit use of methamphetamine and other synthetic drugs. Most of these recommendations have been implemented or are in the process of being implemented. The Administration is in the process of developing and releasing a strategic document—a subset of this National Strategy—that details next steps for addressing the problem of synthetic drugs like methamphetamine over the coming years.

DISRUPTING DRUG MARKETS

The policies and programs of the *National Drug Control Strategy* are guided by the fundamental insight that the illegal drug trade is a market, and both users and traffickers are affected by market dynamics. By disrupting this market, the US Government seeks to undermine the ability of drug suppliers to meet, expand, and profit from drug demand. When drug supply does not fully meet drug demand, changes in drug price and purity support prevention efforts by making initiation to drug use more difficult. They also contribute to treatment efforts by eroding the abilities of users to sustain their habits.

An increasingly diverse body of scientific evidence underscores the significance of drug price and purity to the habits of drug users. Youth surveys have demonstrated the strong inverse relationship between cocaine use and price. Emergency department admissions data and arrestee urinalysis results for both cocaine and heroin also reveal a strong correlation between use and price. Additional studies indicate that decreases in heroin purity and increases in heroin price are linked to increases in methadone program enrollments and dose requirements. The sensitivity of users to drug price and purity is a durable relationship that can be influenced to help achieve America's national drug control goals.

Drug control programs focused on market disruption attempt to reduce the profits and raise the risks involved in drug trafficking. The desired result is a reduced incentive for traffickers or would-be traffickers to enter or remain in the illicit trade. Moreover, these programs generate and exacerbate the challenges involved in the drug trade by forcing traffickers to take additional steps, identify new accomplices, and choose new methods of operation that increase the cost, risk, and complexity of smuggling drugs. The US Government and its international partners focus on eradicating drug crops, interdicting drug production and movement, and attacking drug trafficking organizations with support from critical information and intelligence activities.

Combining these drug control tools into effective market-disruption campaigns requires an understanding of the operation and organization of illicit drug markets. Applying concepts used to analyze legal markets can be helpful. Similar to many lawful agricultural industries, the illicit drug industry is composed of business sectors focused on functions such as cultivation, production, transportation, distribution, and finance. Damaging these large business sectors often requires a deliberate and extended application of resources to overcome the resilience generated by multiple organizations operating in a single functional area.

Sometimes market disruptions can be achieved by rolling up trafficking organizations operating within a particular business sector. For example, law enforcement efforts targeting major Colombian cocaine transporters in 1999 resulted in the disruption of organizations responsible for smuggling 20–30 tons of cocaine each month. The dramatic impact of similar initiatives focused on major Dutch MDMA (Ecstasy) transporters is reflected in the 80 percent decline in US seizures of Ecstasy tablets shipped from abroad from 2001 to 2004. In other instances, eliminating a critical element of a business sector may be more effective. For example, between 1995 and 1999, the Peruvian coca cultivation sector was devastated by the interdiction of airplanes carrying coca to Colombia for processing into cocaine.

The illicit drug industry can also be viewed as a series of segments in a supply chain extending from fields abroad to streets at home. This segmented market view is based on the transfer of drug ownership from one organization to another in each segment. In the past, a single drug cartel owned the drug that it trafficked from its cultivation and production all the way to its wholesale distribution. Now, many large trafficking organizations specialize in specific segments of the supply chain, such as cultivation, production, transportation from source country to US border areas, and smuggling across the border into the United States. By participating in only one market segment, traffickers can concentrate their expertise and connections while limiting their overall risk.

This segmented market view is perhaps most relevant to the cocaine industry, where unified Colombian cartels have been replaced by looser networks of Colombian and Mexican trafficking organizations. Separate Colombian organizations may handle the cultivation, production, and initial offshore movement segments of the cocaine supply chain. Mexican organizations then coordinate the remaining transportation and distribution segments required for the cocaine to reach US streets. In each exchange between traffickers, ownership of the product is transferred in a manner that ensures that the supplier will be compensated regardless of the final disposition of the cocaine.

The characteristics of each market segment enable us to identify areas where our market disruption resources can be used most effectively. Returning to the cocaine industry example, an analysis of the initial offshore movement segment of the cocaine supply chain reveals ample opportunities for market disruption. Colombian cocaine transporters must make arrangements for coastal departure points, suitable speedboats and fishing vessels, and the requisite crews and fuel. They must also coordinate drug storage, refueling, and product exchange. These unique skills take time and effort to replace when successful interdiction and investigation initiatives remove these transporters from the supply chain.

Armed with a better understanding of the different market segments, the United States can strategically target vulnerabilities and optimize impact on the market. Relatively short-term disruptions of drug markets caused by events such as the removal of a key drug trafficker can lead to significant challenges in the drug trade because of the importance of relationships and routines. However, combining sustained, focused operations on drug-market segments can yield more substantial changes in drug availability, price, and purity that support the reductions in drug use that are the ultimate goal of the *National Drug Control Strategy*.

We are beginning to see the results of our market disruption strategy in the United States. Cocaine price and purity at the retail level have reversed a three year trend of increasing purity and decreasing price. Continued declines in the potential production of cocaine in South America and record worldwide cocaine seizures have gradually reduced global supply. Worldwide seizures of cocaine, for example, reached record levels of more than 400 metric tons annually in 2003 and 2004. These unprecedented removals of cocaine from global distribution, combined with the diminished ability of the source countries to replenish worldwide supply, is beginning to have an effect in the United States. Between February and September 2005, retail cocaine purity dropped by 15 percent. Retail cocaine prices increased during the same period, suggesting the beginnings of a disruption of the cocaine market.

Not only are we now seeing positive changes in the domestic cocaine market, we are also achieving results with heroin. Expanded aerial eradication efforts, supported by the State Department's airwing, have inflicted substantial damage to the Colombian opium poppy cultivation sector, leading to a 68 percent reduction in cultivation from 2001 to 2004. Upgraded security screening at US airports has led to increased seizures of Colombian heroin, from 15 percent of available heroin in 2001 to 23 percent of available heroin in 2002. (Available heroin is the net amount of heroin available to the United States; it is Colombian potential production of heroin less the seizures of heroin in Colombia.) As a result of these and many other law enforcement efforts, the retail purity of Colombian heroin dropped by 22 percent, and the retail price increased by 33 percent from 2003 to 2004.

Regardless of the time and expense involved, market disruption yields several additional benefits. It contributes to the Global War on Terrorism, severing the links between drug traffickers and terrorist organizations in countries such as Afghanistan and Colombia, among others. It renders support to allies such as the courageous administration of President Alvaro Uribe in Colombia. Market disruption initiatives remove some of the most violent criminals from society, from kingpins such as the remnants of the Cali Cartel to common thugs such as the vicious MS–13 street gang. This Strategy outlines how the efforts of the United States and its allies are working to disrupt the drug markets that threaten our society while furthering broader goals both at home and abroad.

PROGRESS IN THE ANDEAN RIDGE

The Andean Ridge is the sole supplier of the world's cocaine and a provider of the heroin consumed in the United States. Although Colombia is the predominant source of both illicit drugs, any plan targeting cocaine and heroin production must consider the latent capacity within Bolivia and Peru. Drug production and trafficking in Ecuador and Venezuela must also be considered. The Administration's Andean Counterdrug Initiative (ACI) addresses all of these concerns and is yielding promising results. President Uribe and the Government of Colombia are firmly committed to countering the threat that drug trafficking poses to Colombia, the Western Hemisphere, and the world. Colombia and the United States are solid partners in a combined strategy of eradication, interdiction, and organizational attack.

In 2004, Colombia sprayed more than 131,000 hectares of coca and manually eradicated another 10,279 hectares. The Government of Colombia reported spraying more than 138,000 hectares of coca and manually eradicating more than 31,000 hectares in 2005. These efforts have reduced cultivation by one-third since 2001 and reduced potential pure cocaine production from 700 metric tons in 2001 to 430 metric tons in 2004.

Although substantial progress has been made in eradication, tactics must continually be adjusted as traffickers try to adapt to the Government of Colombia's massive eradication campaign (see *Increasing Colombian Coca Aerial Eradication*). In fact, the shrinking and dispersal of coca fields, the systematic use of seedbeds, and countermeasures designed to make plots harder to find from the air may require additional spray planes to continue to reduce Colombian coca production. It has already required increased aerial spray and manual eradication operations. The Department of State has received authorization to spend $30 million in FY 2006 to buy and refurbish spray aircraft for Colombia under the Critical Flight Safety Program. The State Department will receive additional funding in FY 2007 to continue this crucial safety upgrade that will bolster a much-needed aerial eradication capability in Colombia.

Reports from the field indicate that the narcotraffickers are focusing their cultivation efforts in areas that are difficult to identify from the air because of bad weather, such as Nariño. With that in mind, the Government of Colombia, with our assistance, began additional spray operations late last year in Nariño and increased manual eradication operations in eastern Colombia and the national parks where additional, previously undetected coca has been planted.

The attack on opium poppy has been just as relentless (see *Decline of Potential Production of Pure Colombian Heroin*). In 2004, Colombia sprayed 3,060 hectares of poppy and manually eradicated another 1,253. In 2005, Colombia sprayed more than 1,600 hectares of poppy and manually eradicated 496 hectares. Poppy cultivation has decreased by two-thirds since 2001, and potential pure heroin production decreased to 3.8 metric tons from 11.4 metric tons in 2001. These efforts have contributed greatly to the significant reductions in heroin purity that has taken place in the United States over the past two years.

Colombia is also aggressively pursuing the movement of illicit drugs throughout its national territory and is seizing record quantities of cocaine, coca base, heroin, and precursor chemicals. Contributing to Colombia's success has been the Air Bridge Denial program. In 2005, this program resulted in seven interdictions, five impounded aircraft, the destruction of two aircraft, and the seizure of 1.5 metric tons of cocaine in Colombia. Additionally, three aircraft and 2.1 metric tons of cocaine were impounded in neighboring countries after coordination between host nations and JIATF–South. In 2004, the program resulted in the destruction of 13 aircraft, damage to one aircraft, and impounding three aircraft.

Colombian security forces, reaping the benefits of US law enforcement training and assistance, report the seizure of more than 200 metric tons of cocaine and coca base in 2005—setting an impressive single-year record. Additionally, security forces destroyed more than 130 cocaine

HCl labs, preventing a significant amount of cocaine from being produced. In one significant operation in May 2005, Counternarcotics Police and Navy personnel captured 15 metric tons of cocaine along the Mira River in southern Nariño. The cocaine was packaged and ready to be loaded onto several trafficker speedboats that would have moved it through the eastern Pacific to eventual delivery points along the Mexican–Central American corridor.

Interdiction programs have benefited from the Government of Colombia's commitment to extend its presence and establish the rule of law throughout the country. This has restricted the movement of narcotraffickers and denied them operating space. By the end of 2005, public security forces such as the High Mountain Battalions and the Mobile Brigades will have grown from 1 to 7 and from 7 to 15, respectively. Additionally, 54 rural police (Carabineros) squadrons were in place by the end of 2005, up from 25 squadrons in 2002. Furthermore, for the first time in history, all 1,098 Colombian municipalities have a National Police presence.

Finally, the Colombian military has continued implementation of its Plan Patriota (Plan Patriot) in the south-central part of the country—the general area of what was formerly a Revolutionary Armed Forces of Colombia (FARC) demilitarized zone. This operation has reduced the number of transportation corridors that the FARC used to move illicit drugs from the growing areas to the coast. This successful disruption of the transportation of illicit drugs has diminished the FARC's income from drugs over the past year. It also weakened a vicious terrorist organization that for decades attempted to violently overthrow Colombia's democratically elected government.

The commitment of the Government of Colombia to attack powerful drug traffickers and extradite them to the United States is unparalleled (see *Extraditions from Colombia*). In 2005, Colombia extradited several key narcotraffickers, including a former Consolidated Priority Organizations Target (CPOT), Elias Cobos Muñoz; FARC logistics leader, Omaira Rojas Cabrera; and former head of the Cali Cartel, Miguel Rodríguez Orejuela. In December 2004, the Government of Colombia extradited the other Cali Cartel leader, Gilberto Rodriguez Orejuela, as well as a key FARC leader, Ricardo Palmera.

Colombia has also been aggressive in attacking the three designated foreign terrorist organizations in Colombia—the FARC, the United Self–Defense Forces/Group of Colombia (AUC), and the National Liberation Army (ELN)—which are all deeply involved in drug trafficking. However, President Uribe has also been willing to engage in a peace process with any terrorist organization that is willing to end violence and negotiate a peace agreement. In July 2005, Uribe signed the Justice and Peace Law, designed to provide the framework for members of the illegal armed groups to demobilize and reenter Colombian society. It is intended to apply to all illegal armed groups including the FARC and the ELN, as well as the AUC, if they also enter a peace process. The AUC entered into a cease-fire agreement with the government in 2003 and began demobilizing its organization. More than 20,000 AUC personnel had demobilized collectively as of January 31, 2006. The ELN has been engaged in exploratory talks concerning a possible peace process with the Colombian Government.

The United States and Colombia must work to secure and extend the success of the Andean Counterdrug Initiative and Plan Colombia by aggressively countering trafficker responses to the success of ongoing eradication, interdiction, and organizational attack programs. Increased aerial eradication capability is necessary to attack replanting efforts more swiftly. Additional focus must be placed on identifying new cultivation of coca and opium poppy, particularly in more remote areas. The United States will also support Colombia in coordinated efforts to increase interdiction pressure against drug-movement corridors within Colombia and to target the most vulnerable segments of the Colombian supply chain through organizational attack.

Peru and Bolivia remain the second and third largest producers of cocaine, with Peru producing 145 metric tons and Bolivia some 70 metric tons of pure cocaine in 2004. The United States has been and, to the extent possible, intends to continue working with these two countries in eventually reducing their illicit coca cultivation while creating an inhospitable environment for those considering reentry into cultivation, cocaine production, and transportation of the illicit product.

These countries continue to eradicate coca, attacking its spread into new areas. Both Peru and Bolivia have pressed their eradication campaigns in the face of organized opposition, and their success is evident by the strident objections and attempts to derail the eradication efforts by narcotrafficker groups.

Peru and Bolivia are interdicting record levels of cocaine and precursor chemicals in the traditional growing areas, creating logistical jams in the pipeline from the coca field to the HCl lab. Finally, these governments have been creating an environment that respects the rule of law by increasing the number of counterdrug prosecutors, developing laws that punish the white-collar dimensions of narcotrafficking (such as money laundering), and improving the efficiency of police units. The United States will work with Peru and Bolivia in these efforts as part of the broader Andean Counterdrug Initiative to ensure that drug trafficking does not experience a resurgence in these countries.

TARGETING METHAMPHETAMINE AND OTHER SYNTHETICS

Since the early 1990s, and especially over the past few years, the illicit use of synthetic drugs such as methamphetamine and otherwise-legal prescription drugs has become a severe and troubling problem, both at the national level and in affected communities. The most devastating of these synthetic drugs has been methamphetamine, but in some areas, so-called club drugs such as Ecstasy have also become a major concern.

The abuse of prescription drugs, including OxyContin (oxycodone), has become the second most prevalent form of drug abuse.

In response to these developments, in October 2004, the Federal Government released the *National Synthetic Drugs Action Plan*, the first comprehensive national plan to address the problems of synthetic and pharmaceutical drug trafficking and abuse. The Action Plan outlines current Federal and state efforts in the areas of prevention, treatment, regulation, and law enforcement and made concrete recommendations for enhancing government efforts to reduce synthetic drug abuse. These efforts will be outlined in a separate document that will describe the Administration's plan for affecting the illicit market for synthetic drugs during the next 24 months.

Attacking the Domestic Methamphetamine and Precursor Threat

In the past decade and a half, methamphetamine use has gradually spread eastward across the United States. Between 1992 and 2002, the treatment admission rate for methamphetamine/amphetamine has increased from 10 to 52 admissions per 100,000 population age 12 or older (an increase of over 500 percent). Additionally, between 2000 and 2004, the positive drug-testing rates among the general US workforce for methamphetamine/amphetamine increased from 0.25 percent to 0.52 percent of all tests (an increase of more than 200 percent). Although the spread of methamphetamine use is troubling, there is a significant bright spot in youth use rates since the President took office. Methamphetamine use rates have dropped by almost one-third among 8th, 10th and 12th graders since 2001 (as addressed in the Introduction).

In response to the increased threat from methamphetamine, US law enforcement agencies have increased their efforts both domestically and internationally to stem the flow of methamphetamine and the precursors that are used to produce it. States have also taken decisive action with dramatic results. Within the past year, 35 states have passed legislation to impose new regulations on the retail sale of the methamphetamine precursor pseudoephedrine. Because the challenges vary from state to state, these restrictions vary by state in their severity and content. States with the strictest pseudoephedrine laws have seen significant reductions in the seizure of small toxic labs. For example, 662 labs were seized in Oklahoma in 2003 (see *Reduced Methamphetamine Lab Seizures in Oklahoma*). After instituting strict laws controlling pseudoephedrine in March 2004, lab seizures in Oklahoma dropped by 38 percent to 409 labs in 2004, and only 62 labs were reported seized in Oklahoma during the first six months of 2005. Iowa has had similar results, with 503 labs seized in 2003, 463 labs seized in 2004 (an 8 percent drop), and only 120 reported labs seized during the first six months of 2005 (see *Reduced Methamphetamine Lab Seizures in Iowa*). As other states have adopted similar restrictions, methamphetamine lab seizures have declined nationally, with 10,182 lab seizures in 2003 to 9,851 lab seizures in 2004. Additionally, the number of seized "super-labs" (labs capable of producing more than 10 pounds of methamphetamine per production run) has declined from 245 in 2001 to 55 in 2004—a 77 percent decrease (see *Reduced Methamphetamine Superlab Seizures*).

Federal efforts have also had a dramatic effect on the fight against methamphetamine. ONDCP's High Intensity Drug Trafficking Area (HIDTA) program has 96 initiatives that are specifically focused on methamphetamine—the largest number of initiatives focused on any single drug. In addition, DEA has taken steps to counter the methamphetamine threat. In 2005, DEA streamlined its Mobile Enforcement Teams (MET) program, which provides investigative support to state and local authorities, and focused it on methamphetamine trafficking. DEA also conducted Operation Wildfire, a sweep operation conducted with state and local law enforcement partners in more than 200 cities across the United States that resulted in 427 arrests and the seizure of more than 208 pounds of methamphetamine. Additional Operation Wildfire seizures included 56 clandestine methamphetamine laboratories, more than 200,000 pseudoephedrine tablets, 300 pounds of pseudoephedrine powder, more than 224,000 ephedrine tablets, 123 weapons, 28 vehicles, and $255,000 in US currency. Further, 30 drug-endangered children (DEC) were removed from methamphetamine-contaminated environments.

Decreasing the number of domestic labs not only reduces methamphetamine production and the environmental damage caused by the production process but also reduces the threat that these labs pose to families and children. According to the El Paso Intelligence Center, 14,260 methamphetamine lab-related incidents occurred during calendar year 2003. At 1,442 of the lab incidents during FY 2003, at least one child was present. The labs affected more than 3,000 children, including children who were residing at the labs but may not have been present at the time of the seizure and children who were visiting the site. Nearly 1,300 incidents involved a child being exposed to toxic chemicals.

In October 2003, ONDCP launched a national DEC initiative to assist with coordination among existing state programs that help rehabilitate children who have been affected by methamphetamine. The initiative also created a standardized training program to extend programming to states where such initiatives do not yet exist. Previously, the Department of Justice's Office of Community Oriented Policing Services (COPS) awarded $2,124,000 to be used for programs helping children as part of the COPS Methamphetamine Initiative.

ATTACKING INTERNATIONAL METHAMPHETAMINE AND PRECURSOR THREATS

Although a great deal of law enforcement resources have been dedicated to fighting the spread of methamphetamine domestically, much of the success in disrupting the methamphetamine market will continue to rely on our ability to work with other countries to reduce the flow of methamphetamine and its precursors—principally pseudoephedrine and ephedrine—into the United States.

Over the past few years, increasing production of methamphetamine within Mexico has been indicated by increased seizures at the US southwest border (see *Increased Southwest Border Methamphetamine Seizures*), reports of additional methamphetamine lab seizures within Mexico, and reports from state and local law enforcement throughout the United States concerning the influx of out-of-state methamphetamine within their jurisdictions. Although this is a significant and growing threat, Mexico has taken some important steps.

Through its Federal Commission for the Protection Against Sanitary Risks (COFEPRIS), Mexico is implementing several important wholesale and retail controls on pseudoephedrine in cooperation with the pharmaceutical industry and is considering others. In addition, Mexico recently imposed a policy limiting imports of pseudoephedrine and ephedrine to manufacturers only. Wholesale distributors are barred from importing raw pseudoephedrine and ephedrine. Furthermore, importers can import shipments of no more than 3,000 kilograms at a time. Mexico also has begun imposing import quotas tied to estimates of national needs after a study revealed a significant excess of pseudoephedrine imports over Mexico's estimated lawful needs.

With US support, Mexico is training and equipping methamphetamine-focused law enforcement teams to combat the spread of methamphetamine production in Mexico. DEA is providing laboratory cleanup and investigation training for Mexican law enforcement elements.

These teams have already identified and destroyed several large methamphetamine laboratories and many small-scale labs. Additionally, Mexican authorities have seized nearly 50 million methamphetamine precursor pills since December 2000.

Canada, like Mexico, is aiding us in the fight against trafficking and diversion. Canada has taken numerous steps over the past few years to prevent the diversion of pseudoephedrine and ephedrine through increased control of imports and exports. From 2000 to 2004, lawful pseudoephedrine imports into Canada fell from just over 500 to less than 50 metric tons. Additionally, from 2003 to 2004, lawful ephedrine imports fell from 19 to 7 metric tons, and overall pseudoephedrine and methamphetamine seizures have dropped over the past year. These reduced precursor imports into Canada resulted in sharp declines in the amounts of pseudoephedrine and ephedrine diverted into the United States for the manufacture of methamphetamine.

In addition to working with Mexico and Canada on this issue, the United States continues to work with the primary producing and exporting countries for bulk ephedrine and pseudoephedrine—China, the Czech Republic, Germany, and India (see *Foreign Sources of Methamphetamine Precursors: Pseudoephedrine or Ephedrine*). The United States is also collaborating with the wider international community to reach arrangements that will impede the diversion of these precursors to methamphetamine labs. For example, the DEA and its Mexican counterparts recently obtained a commitment from Hong Kong not to ship chemicals to the

United States, Mexico, or Panama until receiving an import permit or equivalent documentation and notifying the receiving country.

The United States is very interested in reaching these types of prenotification agreements with India and China, as well for all shipment of pseudoephedrine and ephedrine regardless of destination country. This type of export transparency is solely intended to reduce diversion and illicit demand for both products. The United States and Mexico are also working to gain broader international support for prenotification of international shipments of combination tablets containing pseudoephedrine through multilateral bodies such as the Organization of American States and the Project Prism initiative convened by the United Nations International Narcotics Control Board.

REDUCING PRESCRIPTION DRUG ABUSE

The rise in the nonmedical use of prescription drugs listed as controlled substances has created a new challenge not only for traditional organizations involved in reducing drug use (e.g., law enforcement, treatment providers, and prevention specialists) but also for the medical and pharmaceutical community. The nature of this problem poses he deceptively simple question: How do individuals who abuse prescription drugs get them? Data of this sort are hard to obtain, but experience suggests that it largely occurs in six ways (in no particular order): illegal purchases without a prescription over the Internet; so-called doctor shopping; theft or other diversion directly from pharmacies; unscrupulous doctors who—knowingly at worst, carelessly at best—overprescribe medications; traditional street-level drug dealing; and receiving prescription drugs for no cost from family and friends. The illegal use of pharmaceuticals is one of the fastest growing forms of drug abuse.

The Administration's strategy in this area focuses on preventing diversion and getting users into treatment where necessary. For example, one of the programs meeting with some success at the state level is the prescription-drug monitoring program (PDMP), which helps provide doctors, pharmacists, and, when appropriate, law enforcement with information about patient prescriptions. As of October 2005, a total of 25 states have operational PDMPs or are in the process of implementing them. To give a specific example of where PDMPs can help, an individual struggling with an addiction to Vicodin might go to five doctors to complain of back pain and receive five separate prescriptions for the drug, which could then be filled at five separate pharmacies. States with PDMPs help prevent doctors and pharmacists from becoming unwitting accessories to the abuse of these prescription drugs by showing information on other prescriptions given to, or filled by, the individual within the preceding weeks or months. In addition, identifying the abuser can help medical professionals recommend appropriate treatment.

PDMPs assist states in identifying diversion trends as they emerge. Analysis of PDMP data assists law enforcement in the identification of doctor shoppers and overprescribers. In addition, the information collected and analyzed by a state PDMP may be used to assist in identifying patients whose drug usage is increasing and who may benefit from a referral for treatment, to assist health care professionals in making appropriate treatment decisions for their patients, and to assist pharmacists in providing appropriate pharmaceutical care.

In 2003, Virginia implemented a limited PDMP in the southwestern portion of the state to address the growing abuse of oxycodone and other prescription drugs. Virginia's limited PDMP monitored schedule II controlled substances in one state-defined health district. The database now contains close to 500,000 prescriptions, and more than 1,000 requests for data have been processed. Virginia's limited PDMP was so successful in addressing diversion that legislation was passed in 2005 to extend the program to the entire state beginning in FY 2006. The program will capture data for all schedule II–IV prescriptions.

One of the Nation's flagship PDMAs is Kentucky's All Schedules Prescription Electronic Reporting program, or KASPER. The program is fully electronic. Within 16 days of filling a prescription, pharmacists must input the information into the KASPER database. KASPER covers drugs listed under schedules II–V. Physicians may request patient information from the KASPER system. Law enforcement agencies can receive information from KASPER for an active investigation. The KASPER system is entirely web based. During this past legislative session, Kentucky's PDMP received approval to bring in an expert consultant to focus on enhancing the data-collection side of the program. The goal was to make the entire system operate in real time.

Meanwhile, another source of prescription-drug diversion is the Internet, which is populated with thousands of sites that offer pharmaceutical controlled substances. Some Internet pharmacies operate within the law and accepted medical practice, providing a valuable service to consumers with a legitimate medical need for prescription drugs. However, the DEA has investigated cases where unscrupulous doctors have operated "pill mills" that essentially sell prescriptions or drugs after cursory or nonexistent medical examinations, sometimes making use of pharmaceuticals that have been smuggled into the United States.

The problem, of course, is one of safety and effectiveness: otherwise-legal prescription drugs can be distributed over the Internet with no medical exam, tests, or follow-up care nd no guarantees of safety and effectiveness or assurance of safe handling, storage, or shipping.

In response to this challenge, DEA will continue to work closely with the FDA to identify, investigate, and target online pharmacies operating outside the bounds of the law and legitimate medical practice. For example, in 2005, DEA announced the culmination of *Operation CY-BERx*, an investigation that targeted major alleged pharmaceutical drug traffickers. The ringleaders of this group are believed to have operated more than 4,600 rogue Internet pharmacy websites, shipping prescription drugs—without a prescription—to the doors of many US citizens. To further assist in the identification and targeting of these rogue websites,

DEA launched a toll-free international hotline (1–877–RX–ABUSE) for anonymous reporting on the illegal sale and abuse of controlled substances.

INTELLIGENCE AND ORGANIZATIONAL ATTACK

Effective implementation of the Nation's market disruption strategy poses new challenges for law enforcement and foreign intelligence capabilities. Market disruption requires a broad understanding of the global operations of the illicit-drug industry, from cultivation and production through transportation and distribution until it is marketed and consumed. Our counterdrug intelligence system can assist the market disruption effort in three critical ways. First, counterdrug intelligence can help identify the structure and components of the drug market and collect information in support of law enforcement efforts to attack and disrupt the market. Second, intelligence helps US Government officials locate strategic vulnerabilities within various drug markets that can be targeted by counterdrug initiatives. Third, counterdrug intelligence provides critical information to help US officials evaluate the success of counterdrug programs that target drug markets. Real-time detailed information about market indicators helps counterdrug authorities determine whether an initiative had the desired effect on the market.

Of these three priorities, perhaps none is more important than providing real-time intelligence and information about drug markets. To evaluate the success of counterdrug programs, policy makers need detailed information about the market's reaction to any counterdrug initiative. Not only does this information help counterdrug authorities gauge the success of a specific initiative, but it helps government officials formulate-future initiatives based on the resulting impact on the market. Critical information that helps evaluate changes in illicit drug markets includes the price and purity of drugs throughout the distribution chain, a transport crew's wages, overall costs of various types of transport operations, and required amount of deposit for a drug trafficker to purchase bulk quantities of drugs.

Often during the course of an investigation of a specific trafficker, critical operational information related to other traffickers and their operations is uncovered. To disrupt the illicit drug market on a national basis, this information must be extracted from open case files, pushed upward for further analysis and dissemination, fused with other national intelligence, and used to drive counterdrug operations.

Such exacting systemic requirements can only be met by establishing intelligence structures and protocols for the rapid sharing of critical information. The counterdrug intelligence structure is evolving rapidly to better meet the shifting drug trafficking threat and to adjust to substantial changes in the structure of the US Government. Narcotics specific intelligence initiatives are refocusing to ensure that our assets and capabilities are used to maximum effect.

Drug control agencies are leveraging their enforcement and intelligence capabilities against CPOTs—Consolidated Priority Organizations Targets—considered the highest level of criminal organizations in the drug trade. Efforts to disrupt and dismantle CPOT organizations are primarily accomplished through multiagency investigations coordinated by Organized Crime Drug Enforcement Task Force (OCDETF) agencies. Of the 45 CPOTs identified in FY 2005, 39 (87 percent) have been successfully indicted and 15 (33 percent) have been arrested. In three years, we have dismantled 20 organizations while severely disrupting an additional 11. The heads of 36 CPOT organizations—nearly 51 percent of the total CPOTs—have been arrested. In addition, in the past three years, the US Government has identified 70 major trafficking organizations, 13 of which have links to terrorist organizations, and added them to the CPOT list.

The OCDETF Fusion Center (OFC), when it reaches its initial operating capability in 2006, will significantly enhance law enforcement's ability to "connect the dots" and increase the flow of investigative information to the field. OFC is an intelligence center designed to collect, store, and analyze relevant all-source drug and related financial investigative information. The center will support multijurisdictional investigations focused on the disruption and dismantlement of significant drug trafficking and money-laundering enterprises. OFC, which is composed of nine agencies, is developing a comprehensive data warehouse that will give access to investigative drug and financial information to OCDETF member agencies and other intelligence centers. Analysts at the center will use sophisticated link analysis tools to comprehensively analyze information and develop intelligence products and leads that can be used by OCDETF member agencies.

US law enforcement has recognized that predictive intelligence is the key to effective and efficient targeting and enforcement. Intelligence improvements are part of DEA-wide efforts to use intelligence to identify strategic targets whose arrest will have a maximum effect on the drug market. Expanded intelligence capabilities generate predictive intelligence, identifying trends and vulnerabilities against which limited enforcement resources can be directed. DEA's intelligence program provides dedicated analytical support to DEA investigations, programs, and operations worldwide. Significant initiatives include using DEA reports officers to extract information from DEA case files and disseminating that information by cable to the intelligence community, implementing a centralized collection management system that will determine collection priorities and task collection assets and identify collection gaps, and expanding career management and training opportunities for analysts.

DEA used enhanced intelligence capabilities in the execution of *Operation All Inclusive* in Central America. *Operation All Inclusive* was a multiagency US Government and host country effort that involved predictive intelligence modeling, thorough analytic assessment of trafficker vulnerabilities, and unprecedented intelligence sharing, planning, and operational collaboration. Overall, this cooperative, interagency effort had a significant effect. Intelligence clearly identified the disruption of maritime transportation operations. *Operation All Inclusive* contributed to drug seizures, including many in the Transit Zone by Joint Interagency Task Force South (JIATF–South), and $15.2 million in bulk currency shipments.

DEA is refocusing El Paso Intelligence Center (EPIC) capabilities to enhance its efforts at predictive intelligence. EPIC is composed of 15 Federal agencies, which combine their intelligence and databases to provide wide-ranging investigative support. EPIC maintains several state-of-the-art programs that support law enforcement operations along the southwest border. Technological advances in information sharing in the past two years and EPIC's 24/7 watch operation gives law enforcement tactical information related to the border 24 hours a day. EPIC is also developing its Open Connectivity Project that will provide its Federal, state, and local partners with online access to EPIC's research and analytical products, around the clock support, and National Seizure System data. The project will be highly secure, thus enabling law enforcement agencies to coordinate joint operations and investigations safely and enhancing officer/personnel safety. It will also provide analysts with sophisticated Geospatial Information System technology.

A critical need to facilitate information sharing through electronic connectivity and automation continues to exist among Federal, state, local, and tribal law enforcement agencies. To meet this challenge, DEA, HIDTA, and their state and local partners have created an interagency committee to develop a National Virtual Pointer System (NVPS). NVPS connects existing Federal, state, local, and tribal law enforcement investigative systems to eliminate the possibility that multiple law enforcement organizations' activities could conflict in investigating and arresting the same criminal or criminal organization and allows for sharing of vital intelligence about the target. NVPS enables participating agencies to exchange target information through a single point of entry using a "sensitive but unclassified" network. NVPS established a single format for information sharing that lets participating systems communicate with many dissimilar systems.

Another effort to coordinate law enforcement efforts is *COBIJA*, which means "blanket" in Spanish. *COBIJA* is a coordinated planning effort managed by the Arizona Partnership of the Southwest Border HIDTA to synchronize local, tribal, state, and Federal highway interdiction operations through planning, information sharing, and intelligence generation. It establishes a mechanism that enhances operational coordination/cooperation and information/intelligence sharing throughout the United States. For example, *COBIJA* provides intelligence to field enforcement personnel to disrupt/dismantle smuggling routes/organizations, criminal enterprise activities, and other potential threats. The *COBIJA* planning effort has three components: an operational planning conference (attended by local, state, tribal, and Federal law enforcement task force participants) where agencies develop coordinated interdiction operations plans; an operational period, where dates are determined by an intelligence analysis process (and are usually two to six weeks long); and an after-action review process, where every participant has the opportunity to share lessons learned. The last *COBIJA* meeting took place in spring 2005 where more than 600 law enforcement personnel representing 45 states attended and provided written coordinated highway interdiction plans that resulted in 5,000 seizure incidents, $37 million seized, more than 500,000 pounds of illicit drugs seized, and 7,000 subjects arrested. Efforts are under way to regionalize this concept in selected areas of the United States, enhancing *COBIJA's* focus on regional drug threats.

FINANCIAL ATTACK

The lure of making large sums of cash is the main motivation that drives drug trafficking. In our local communities, young adults begin selling narcotics because they see it as a quick way to earn a lot of money. Foreign drug traffickers ruthlessly fight their way to the top of criminal organizations for the monetary rewards and the power that it buys. In addition, numerous foreign terrorist organizations worldwide finance their terrorist operations through drug trafficking.

Because the drug trade is a profit-making business, a balance of cost versus reward and risk comes into play. Upsetting this balance offers the possibility of damaging the entire drug trade. Without sufficient funds, drug trafficking organizations' efforts to produce, purchase, and distribute drugs are seriously impaired. Major drug trafficking organizations have significant expenses that must be paid regardless of the income generated. Not being able to promptly pay these expenses will undermine a drug trafficking organization's ability to continue its business. Lack of money also diminishes organizations' ability to corrupt local and national governments and influence others.

Federal agencies are strategically refocusing their resources to attack the financial infrastructure of drug trafficking organizations. A strong ally in this attack is the financial sector of our economy, which has been effectively keeping most illegal funds out of our banking system. Drug trafficking organizations are being forced to ship narcotics proceeds in bulk to foreign countries rather than deposit the funds directly into the US banking system. The bulk and weight of the illicit proceeds that must be returned to the trafficking organizations vastly outweigh the drugs themselves and represent a significant vulnerability of drug trafficking organizations. Drug trafficking organizations are also resorting to the Colombian Black Market Peso Exchange to move their drug proceeds to Colombia. The United States is working with the Colombian Government along with the financial sector to disrupt and dismantle this system, as well as with Mexican authorities to seize bulk cash smuggled into Mexico.

To accomplish this strategy, the OFC, as referenced in the intelligence section above, is being established. Within the next year, the OFC should be fully operational and capable of analyzing massive amounts of intelligence concerning the financial operations of drug trafficking organizations. In addition, DEA has initiated Financial Investigative Teams (FITs) in all domestic field division offices to attack drug finances. Internationally, DEA has initiated FITs in Colombia and Thailand and increased the number of agents who specialize in financial investigations in Mexico. DEA, ICE, and Customs and Border Protection (CBP) agents are training and working with vetted units in many foreign countries to intercept both narcotics and narcotics money. Internal Revenue Service Criminal Investigations Division (IRS–CID) and DEA have initiated a joint Wire Remitter Project to identify illegal money that is transmitted by wire service businesses. Identifying the sender and recipient of illegal funds will help us better understand and target the illegal financial infrastructure of drug trafficking organizations.

ICE, IRS–CID, and DEA have initiated Bulk Currency Initiatives to identify, intercept, and seize narcotics proceeds. Federal law enforcement agencies working together with state and local law enforcement in Operations Pipeline, Convoy, and Jetway continue to show improvements in attacking the bulk currency and monetary instrument shipments of drug trafficking organizations. DEA has exploited the intelligence gleaned from drug and bulk currency interdictions to identify, investigate, and dismantle five drug and currency transportation organizations linked to CPOT organizations. In the future, ICE and CBP intend to expand their use of dedicated outbound currency interdiction teams to sharply increase border-area cash seizures.

The United States is making progress in disrupting the market by seizing the profits of drug trafficking. During 2002, law enforcement agencies seized more than $696.3 million just in currency and monetary instruments that were destined for foreign drug trafficking organizations.

In 2004, that amount increased to more than $785.7 million, not including the value of assets seized or currency seized by state and local law enforcement. The new initiatives highlighted above will substantially increase the seizure of trafficker assets and further disrupt the operation of drug trafficking organizations.

Transit Zone Interdiction

Transit Zone interdiction accounted for the removal of hundreds of tons of cocaine from the market in 2005 (see *Increasing Transit Zone Cocaine Seizures*). Large seizures denied traffickers significant profits from selling bulk quantities of cocaine. They also prevented millions of dollars in illegal proceeds from returning to Colombia.

For the third straight year, joint service, interagency, and multinational forces in the Transit Zone, under the able coordination of JIATF–South, seized and disrupted a record amount of cocaine (see *Making a Difference in the Transit Zone*). Transit Zone seizures and disruptions in 2005 amounted to 254 metric tons, compared to 219 metric tons in 2004 and 176 metric tons in 2003. In 2005, JIATF–South and allies air and maritime assets interdicted an impressive 66 go-fasts and 49 fishing vessels loaded with cocaine. During August 2005 alone, JIATF–South removed 45 metric tons of cocaine destined for US markets, stopping seven smuggler go-fasts, a similar number of trafficker fishing vessels, and two motor vessels.

Key to these successes is the collection and dissemination of actionable intelligence regarding maritime cocaine shipments. Operation Panama Express, an OCDETF initiative managed jointly by FBI, DEA, ICE, Coast Guard, and JIATF–South has greatly expanded interdiction-related intelligence. Since its inception in February 2000, Operation Panama Express has directly contributed to the seizure of more than 480 metric tons of cocaine and the arrest of over 1,000 individuals.

As expected, drug traffickers attempted to adapt to US interdiction efforts. Trafficker fishing-vessel operations moved farther out in the Pacific, in the area of the Galapagos Islands, and Ecuador was used more often as a logistical hub for cocaine deliveries. Traffickers continued to launch cocaine-laden speedboats from the Colombian north coast to points along Central America and Mexico and increased their use of fishing vessels in the Caribbean.

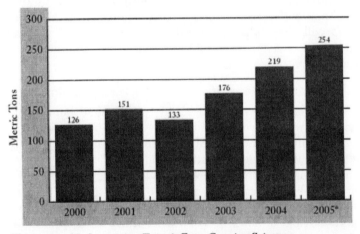

Illustration 19: Increasing Transit Zone Cocaine Seizures

JIATF–South, which integrates the interdiction efforts of US law enforcement and intelligence agencies with the Department of Defense, was a model of interagency coordination and efficiency in 2005. Of particular significance is JIATF–South's close working relationship with numerous allied countries—11 countries from South America and Europe have liaison officers at JIATF–South—which is critical for the synchronization of regional operations. As a result, allies such as the United Kingdom, the Netherlands, Spain, and France also seized record-breaking amounts of European-bound cocaine in the eastern Caribbean and the Atlantic Ocean in 2005—68 metric tons of cocaine, compared to 38 metric tons in 2004.

Transit Zone interdiction is a team effort that relies on the successful execution of several steps in an interdiction continuum, including the collection and dissemination of actionable intelligence, the detection and monitoring of suspect vessels, and the physical interdiction of those vessels. A key player in the interdiction continuum, and one of the principal factors behind the record-breaking cocaine seizures, is the US Coast Guard's employment of armed helicopters, commonly referred to as HITRON (Helicopter Interdiction Tactical Squadron). Flying at 140 knots, these helicopters easily outrun the fastest trafficker speedboat. Armed with laser-sighted .50–caliber sniper rifles, they are capable of convincing even the most desperate smuggling crew that it is in their best interest to surrender. In FY 2005, HITRON interdicted 30 trafficker speedboats, 12 of them at night, capturing an impressive 50 metric tons of cocaine. These results should further improve as the United Kingdom, using US Coast Guard tactics, training, and procedures, has recently implemented Airborne Use of Force (AUF) capabilities and the US Navy prepares to employ armed helicopters against drug traffickers in 2006.

Record seizures are hurting traffickers, eroding their profits and destabilizing the transportation sector of the cocaine industry. However, as long as fishing-vessel and speedboat drug deliveries are still getting past our defenses in the Transit Zone, more work has to be done. As the traffickers modify their strategy, we will continue to adapt and forge new initiatives that will have an even greater impact on the illicit drug market. We will also continue working with our partner nations in the Source and Transit Zones to build their own capacity to detect, monitor, and interdict narcotics.

MEXICO AND THE SOUTHWEST BORDER CHALLENGE

The harsh climate, vast geography, and sparse population of the American southwest have long challenged law enforcement along the roughly 2,000–mile border with Mexico. In addition to the 33 legitimate crossing points, the border includes hundreds of miles of open desert, rugged mountains, and the Rio Grande River, providing an ideal environment for cross-border criminal activity. Drug traffickers exploit the border in two directions, smuggling drugs from Mexico into the United States and moving billions of dollars in illicit drug profits from the United States back into Mexico. This trafficking is conducted by using hidden compartments in cars and trucks, tunnels and aqueducts, backpackers on foot, lightweight aircraft and gliders, all-terrain vehicles, package delivery services, motorized launches, and even rafts floating across the Rio Grande. The same transportation networks that smuggle drugs across the border are also capable of bringing terrorists or weapons of mass destruction into our Nation.

Because the US Government's counterdrug, counterterror, and immigration enforcement missions are interrelated, improved counterdrug efforts will also enhance border security. In February 2005, the Homeland Security Advisor directed the development of a strategy to address the drug threat to the southwest border. Interagency efforts, at the time of this writing, are culminating in a coordinated *National Southwest Border Counternarcotics Strategy* that will identify key strategic objectives and provide specific recommendations to address the illicit narcotics threat and significantly improve overall interdiction efforts along the southwest border.

Most illicit drugs that enter the United States are smuggled across the US–Mexican border. Mexico produces the most heroin and foreign-sourced marijuana in the Western Hemisphere and is the primary transit route for US-bound cocaine. Mexican drug trafficking organizations are also increasingly involved in the production of methamphetamine consumed in the United States. Responding to this challenge requires intense effort by both the United States and Mexico.

During the presidency of Vicente Fox, Mexico has demonstrated its commitment to countering the drug threat through its large-scale opium poppy and marijuana eradication programs. The Mexican Army and the Attorney General's Office conduct eradication operations, and these programs consistently kill at least 80 percent of the opium poppy and marijuana crop each year.

This commitment to effective eradication is clearly reflected in its impact on Mexican opium poppy cultivation. In 2004, Mexico eradicated nearly 16,000 hectares of opium poppy, causing cultivation to drop 27 percent, from 4,800 hectares in 2003 to 3,500 hectares in 2004. Potential heroin production in Mexico fell by 25 percent over the same period, from 12 metric tons in 2003 to 9 metric tons in 2004.

Mexico's commitment to eradication has reduced the country's marijuana cultivation (see *Mexican Annual Marijuana Eradication Totals*). As a result of the eradication of 30,836 hectares of marijuana in 2004, marijuana cultivation fell 23 percent, from 7,500 hectares in 2003 to 5,800 hectares in 2004. Marijuana potential production, although still high by historical standards, fell from 13,400 metric tons in 2003 to an estimated 10,400 metric tons in 2004. As of November 2005, the Mexican Government reported that it had eradicated 30,883 hectares. The impact of these eradication efforts is amplified by the roughly 2,000 additional metric tons of marijuana that Mexico seizes annually.

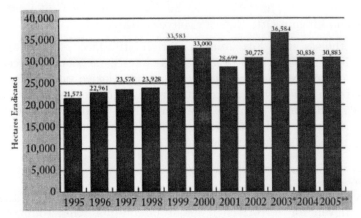

Illustration 20: Mexican Annual Marijuana Eradication Totals

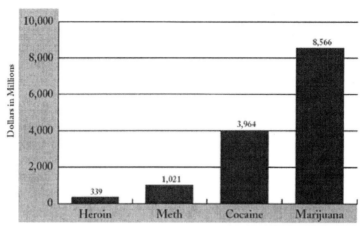

Illustration 21: Estimated Revenue for Mexican Drug Trafficking
Organizations

Mexico's efforts against marijuana trafficking cause damage to an extremely profitable business. The US Government estimates that Mexican traffickers receive more than $13.8 billion in revenue from illicit-drug sales to the United States; 61 percent of that revenue, or $8.5 billion, is directly tied to marijuana export sales. Marijuana has become the primary revenue source for Mexican drug trafficking organizations, eclipsing the potential revenue from cocaine, heroin, and methamphetamine combined (see *Estimated Revenue for Mexican Drug Trafficking Organizations*).

Mexico has also improved the investigative and analytic capabilities of its premier Federal law enforcement institutions. The Federal Investigative Agency (AFI) and the National Center for Analysis, Planning, and Intelligence Against Organized Crime (CENAPI) of the Attorney General's Office are more capable than they were before the Fox Administration. This progress was apparent in 2004, with the capture of five senior members of the Arellano Felix Organization, a senior operator of the Ismael Zambada Organization, two lieutenants of the Gulf Cartel, and Guatemalan kingpin Otto Roberto Herrera–García.

Nonetheless, the Fox Administration still faces significant challenges. Mexican trafficking organizations have generated unprecedented violence, especially in border cities. Although Mexico has attempted an array of initiatives, it has yet to extradite a major active drug trafficker to the United States. To help overcome these challenges, the United States and Mexico will continue to work to address our shared problem with drug production and trafficking.

BUILDING AFGHANISTAN'S FUTURE

The United States is working to ensure that Afghanistan is never again a haven for terrorists, a major opium-producing country, or a source of instability or oppression.

The production and trafficking of narcotics in Afghanistan is a threat to the stability of both Afghanistan and the surrounding region. Recent estimates from the United Nations Office on Drugs and Crime indicate that 87 percent of the world's illegal opiates are produced in Afghanistan. In addition to all the other nefarious and debilitating consequences of opium poppy cultivation in Afghanistan, robust drug production contributes to an environment of corruption and of political and economic instability that can foster insurgent and terrorist organizations, thus threatening the democratically elected Afghan Government. Unchecked trafficking and production of narcotics threatens to undermine all of the other achievements that the United States and our allies are working towards in the region. The continued support of counternarcotics efforts must remain an important part of overall US policy in Afghanistan.

The strategy for attacking the economic basis of the drug trade in Afghanistan reinforces other priorities in the US Global War on Terror. We are committed to a counternarcotics strategy that aims to enhance stability in this fledgling democracy by attacking a source of financial and political support for terrorist organizations that threaten the United States and our allies. Our strategic objectives are to (1) build Afghan institutional capacity to sustain the battle against narcotics; (2) assist Afghan authorities to arrest, prosecute, and punish drug traffickers and corrupt Afghan officials; (3) increase the risk and provide economic alternatives to the illegal narcotics trade; and (4) support Afghan Government efforts to make the narcotics trade culturally unacceptable.

Eliminating the entrenched drug trade and drug-funded corruption requires a long-term and sustained effort, to which Afghanistan President Hamid Karzai has pledged his complete support and commitment. This effort calls for US and other foreign assistance to eliminate this serious threat to both Afghanistan and the international community. Toward this end, working with the Governments of Afghanistan and the United Kingdom, the lead nation for coordinating international counternarcotics support in Afghanistan, we have developed a comprehensive and integrated strategy based on a five-pillar program designed to meet the challenge of narcotics production and trafficking on several fronts. The Public Information pillar aims at galvanizing the Afghan populace to reject opium poppy cultivation and trade. The Alternative Livelihoods pillar, spearheaded by the US Agency for International Development (USAID), seeks to establish economic alternatives to poppy cultivation (see text box: *USAID Alternative Livelihood* Program). The Poppy Elimination Program pillar centers on preventing poppy planting and eradicating fields when prevention is unsuccessful. Our Interdiction pillar seeks to build Afghan capacity to destroy drug labs, seize precursor chemical and opiates, and arrest major traffickers. The Justice Reform pillar assists the Afghan Government in building its capacity to arrest, prosecute, and punish traffickers and corrupt officials.

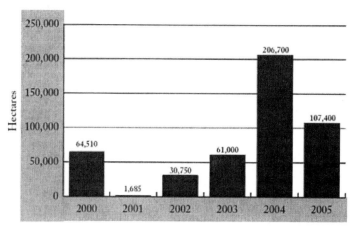

*Illustration 22: Opium Poppy Cultivation in Afghanistan from 2000–
2005*

Opium poppy cultivation in Afghanistan fell 48 percent from 2004
levels to 107,000 hectares in 2005. Potential opium production was
estimated at 4,475 metric tons, a 10 percent decrease from 2004. The
decrease in potential opium production was lower than the decrease in
opium poppy cultivation because exceptionally good precipitation and
minimal disease problems contributed to a rebound in opium yields. If
the entire opium crop were processed, production results would equate
to a potential 526 metric tons of heroin. Cultivation levels appear to have
declined in 2005 primarily due to decisions by farmers to grow less poppy
rather than through substantial eradication programs.

Although we are encouraged by the decline in poppy cultivation in
2005, we remain vigilant and determined to rid Afghanistan of the
scourge of the opium trade. The overall scope of the drug threat in
Afghanistan remains unacceptably high. Building on these results will
continue to require enormous political and administrative efforts, and we
look forward to working with the Government of Afghanistan to
strengthen its ability to combat this dangerous threat.

The United States is also working closely with the United Kingdom
to help give Afghan farmers real economic alternatives, support the
Afghan central government and governors to discourage cultivation and
eradicate poppy fields, strengthen Afghan drug law enforcement, and
help Afghanistan establish interdiction programs. The US Government
is also working with our Afghan counterparts to build civic institutions
and raise public awareness about the serious harm that drugs inflict.

ROBERT J. MacCOUN—TOWARD A PSYCHOLOGY
OF HARM REDUCTION

American Psychologist—November 1988.

During the 1980s, a grassroots movement called *harm reduction* (or
harm minimization) emerged in Amsterdam, Rotterdam, and Liverpool
as a response to pervasive drug-related public health problems(Heather,

Wodak, Nadelmann, & O'Hare, 1993). The movement gradually spread to many other European cities, eventually influencing the policies of several nations(MacCoun, Saiger, Kahan, & Reuter, 1993). Harm reduction is not yet a well-developed approach. Rather, it is a set of programs that share certain public health goals and assumptions. Central among them is the belief that it is possible to modify the behavior of drug users, and the conditions in which they use, in order to reduce many of the most serious risks that drugs pose to public health and safety. Examples of specific harm reduction interventions for drug use include needle and syringe exchange, low-threshold methadone maintenance, "safe use "educational campaigns, and the use of treatment as an alternative to incarceration for convicted drug offenders.

THE ENDS OF DRUG CONTROL

Table lists and briefly defines six overlapping drug control strategies. The first two have dominated the American drug policy debate, centered on the appropriate balance between *supply reduction* (interdiction, source country control, domestic drug law enforcement) and *demand reduction* (treatment, prevention) in the federal budget. But despite their disagreements, demand-side and supply-side advocates share a common allegiance to what might be called the use reduction paradigm—the view that the highest, if not the exclusive, goal of drug policy should be to reduce (and hopefully eliminate) psychoactive drug use. In both practice and rhetoric, use reduction usually means *prevalence reduction*. That is, the goal has been to reduce the total number of users by discouraging initiation on the part of nonusers, and by promoting abstinence for current users. Table introduces three newer terms—*quantity reduction, micro harm reduction,* and *macro harm reduction*—that are described in more detail below. These terms add more jargon to an already jargon-laden domain, but I hope to show that they make it possible to think more strategically about options for effective drug control.

The harm reduction critique of the enforcement-oriented U.S. drug strategy is twofold. First, prevalence-reduction policies have failed to eliminate drug use, leaving its harms largely intact. Second, these harsh enforcement policies are themselves a *source* of many drug-related harms, either directly or by exacerbating the harmful consequences of drug use (Nadelmann, 1989). Although many drug-related harms result from the psychopharmacologic effects of drug consumption, many others are mostly attributable to drug prohibition and its enforcement (MacCoun, Reuter, & Schelling, 1996). These harms would be greatly reduced, if not eliminated, under a regime of legal availability. The acknowledgment that prohibition is a source of harm does not imply that legalizing drugs would necessarily lead to a net reduction in harm; as we shall see, much depends on the effects of legal change on levels of drug use (MacCoun, 1993; MacCoun & Reuter, 1997).But by almost exclusively relying on use reduction—especially drug law enforcement—as an indirect means of reducing harm, we are foregoing opportunities to reduce harm directly. We are even increasing some harms in the process.

AMERICAN RESISTANCE TO HARM REDUCTION

With remarkable consistency, the U.S. government has aggressively resisted harm reduction (Kirp & Bayer,1993; Reuter & MacCoun, 1995). For example, there are probably more than 1 million injecting drug users in this country, and injection drug use accounts for about one third of all AIDS cases. Though the evidence is not unanimous, a considerable body of evidence demonstrates that needle exchange programs can bring about significant reductions in HIV transmission (Des Jarlais, Friedman, & Ward, 1993; General Accounting Office, 1993; Hurley, Jolley, & Kaldor, 1997; Lurie & Reingold, 1993).[4] Lurie and Drucker (1997) recently estimated that between 4,394 and 9,666 HIV infections could have been prevented in the United States between 1987 and 1995 if a national needle exchange program had been in place. Yet there are fewer than 100 needle exchange programs operating in the United States. Why? Because prescription laws, paraphernalia laws, and local "drug-free zone" ordinances ban needle exchange programs in most of the country. Indeed, almost half of the existing programs are operating under an illicit or quasi-legal status. Despite the fact that these programs have been endorsed by the Centers for Disease Control, the National Academy of Sciences, and various leading medical journals and health organizations, drug policy officials in the federal government and most state governments have actively opposed needle exchange. In 1998, Department of Health and Human Services (DHHS) Secretary Donna Shalala publicly endorsed needle exchange on scientific grounds,but subsequently announced that the administration had decided that federal funding of needle exchanges would be unwise. A *Washington Post* story claimed that DHHS officials had arranged her press conference in the mistaken belief that the President would support needle exchange funding; Secretary Shalala's memo of talking points announcing his support was reported to say "the evidence is airtight" and "from the beginning of this effort, it has been about science, science, science" (J. F. Harris & Goldstein, 1998).

Our almost exclusive emphasis on use reduction rather than harm reduction probably has many causes(Reuter & MacCoun, 1995). One is the fear that harm reduction is a Trojan horse for the drug legalization movement (e.g., McCaffrey, 1998). Another factor might be that whereas harm reduction focuses on harms to users, drug-related violence and

---

4. This finding is not universal; participation in needle exchanges was associated with elevated HIV risk in recent studies in Vancouver(Strathdee et al., 1997) and Montreal (Bruneau et al., 1997), though the authors caution that this association might reflect features that distinguish these evaluations from others in the literature; for example, they were conducted at the peak of the HIV epidemic, their clients were heavily involved in cocaine injection, and the number of needles dispersed fell well short of the amount needed to prevent needle sharing(Bruneau & Schechter, 1998). A broader comparison of 81 U.S. cities estimated a 5.9% increase in HIV seroprevalence in 52 cities without needle exchange, and a 5.8% decrease in 29 cities with needle exchange during the period 1988 to 1993 (Hurley, Jolley, & Kaldor, 1997).

other harms to nonusers are more salient in the United States than in Europe. In addition, prevalence is more readily measurable than harms, and few harm-reduction programs, with the notable exception of needle exchange, have been rigorously evaluated—though political opposition to harm reduction is itself a major cause of the lack of relevant data. But other objections involve beliefs about behavior. For example, it may seem only logical that reducing use is the best way to reduce harm. But this logic holds only if the elimination of drug use is nearly complete, and if efforts to reduce use do not themselves cause harm. Unfortunately, many prevalence-reduction policies often fail on one or both counts. Although it is true that abstinence from drugs (or teenage sex, or drinking among alcoholics) is "100% effective" at reducing harm, the key policy question is whether we are 100% effective at convincing people to become abstinent. Finally, the most frequent objection to harm reduction is the claim that harm reduction programs will "send the wrong message."The logic by which harm reduction "sends the wrong message" is rarely articulated in any detail, suggesting that for its proponents, the proposition is self-evident. It seems likely that harm-reduction advocates will continue to face opposition in the United States until they successfully address this concern.

Harm Reduction in Other Policy Domains

Strategy	Goal
Supply reduction	Reduce total supply of drugs
Demand reduction	Reduce total demand for drugs
Prevalence reduction	Reduce total number of drug users
Quantity reduction	Reduce total quantity consumed
Micro harm reduction	Reduce average harm per use of drugs
Macro harm reduction	Reduce total drug-related harm

Table 2: Overlapping Drug Control Strategies

The tension between preventing a behavior and reducing the harmfulness of that behavior is not unique to the debate about illicit drugs. Table 2 lists some intriguing parallels in other contemporary American policy debates. Despite many superficial differences, each domain involves a behavior that poses risks to both the actor and others. And each raises the question about the relative efficacy of policies that aim to reduce the harmful consequences of a risky behavior (harm reduction) versus policies designed to discourage the behavior itself (prevalence or quantity reduction).

The first row of Table 3—safety standards for consumer products—is notable for its relative lack of controversy outside of the halls of Congress. Even though these safety regulations clearly have a harm-reduction rationale-albeit one generally not recognized as such—recent Congressional efforts to scale them back have received a remarkably lukewarm public response. But in the other domains listed in Table 3, a debate centers on the fear that an intervention to reduce harm—harm reduction in spirit if not in name—will in some way "send the wrong message," encouraging the risky behavior. The parallels to drugs are particularly striking for the topic of condom distribution in schools (and to a lesser degree,sex education). Advocates argue that condom distribution is needed to reduce the risks of unplanned pregnancies and sexually transmitted diseases, whereas opponents vociferously argue that distribution programs and other safe sex interventions actually promote sexual activity (Mauldon & Luker, 1996). On the other hand, recent U.S. debates about welfare and immigration benefits may seem to have little to do with concepts like risk regulation or harm reduction. But at an abstract level, the issues are similar. Assertions are made that policies designed to mitigate the harmful consequences of being unemployed,or of immigrating to the United States, actually encourage people to become (or remain) unemployed, or to immigrate to the United States. Aside from brief excursions into the lessons of motor vehicle safety standards and tobacco and alcohol policy, this article focuses almost exclusively on harm reduction for illicit drugs. But it seems possible that the analysis might provide insights for other domains of risk reduction— in part because my arguments were often informed by those literatures but also because it seems unlikely that the underlying behavioral questions are unique to the drug domain.

Policy	Risky behavior	Harms that policy tries to reduce
Mandated safety standards for motor vehicles, toys, sports equipment, food, pharmaceuticals, and so on	Driving, participation in sports, consumption of products, and so on	Physical illness, injury, death
Needle exchange	Intravenous drug use	HIV transmission
Teaching of controlled drinking skills	Drinking by diagnosed alcoholics	Social, psychological, and physical harms of alcohol abuse
School condom programs	Unprotected sexual contact among teens	Sexually transmitted diseases, unwanted pregnancies
Welfare	Becoming or remaining unemployed	Poor quality of life (housing, health, education), especially for children
Provision of benefits for illegal immigrants	Illegal immigration to the United States	Poor quality of life (housing, health, education), especially for children

Table 3: Policies Aimed at Reducing Harms Associated with Risky Behaviors

OVERVIEW

The remainder of this article explores critics' concerns about harm reduction. This article does not attempt a comprehensive review of the evaluation literature on harm reduction or on the specifics of interventions at the clinical level (see Des Jarlais, Friedman, & Ward, 1993;

Heather et al., 1993). Instead, the article has four goals:(a) to demonstrate the value of distinguishing microlevel harm from macrolevel harm, and prevalence of a behavior from the quantity or frequency of that behavior; (b)to identify potential trade-offs between prevalence reduction,quantity reduction, and micro harm reduction; (c)to explore some nonconsequentialist psychological bases for opposition to harm reduction; and (d) to offer some tentative suggestions for successfully integrating harm reduction into our national drug control strategy. The next section examines two different senses in which harm reduction might "send the wrong message," either directly through its rhetorical effects or indirectly by making drug use less risky. I offer a theoretical framework for integrating prevalence-reduction and harm-reduction policies. I believe it offers a way of thinking about harm reduction that might reduce some of the barriers to a more flexible public health orientation to U.S. drug policy. But not necessarily. The tone of the harm-reduction debate suggests that attitudes toward drug policies—on both sides—are influenced by deeply rooted and strongly felt symbolic factors that are largely independent of concerns about policy effectiveness per se. These factors are explored in a later section.

USE REDUCTION AND HARM REDUCTION: AN INTEGRATIVE FRAMEWORK
MICRO VERSUS MACRO HARM REDUCTION

The efficacy of harm reduction depends on behavioral responses to policy interventions. In explaining this point, it is important to make a distinction between levels of analysis that is sometimes obscured in the harm-reduction literature. Let me begin with a truism that is largely overlooked in the harm-reduction debate: *Total Harm =Average Harm per Use x Total Use*, where total use is a function of the number of users and the quantity each user consumes, and average harm per use is a function of two vectors of specific drug-related harms, one involving harms to users (e.g., overdoses, addiction, AIDS) and the other involving harms to nonusers (e.g., HIV transmission, criminal victimization; MacCoun & Caulkins, 1996; Reuter & MacCoun, 1995).

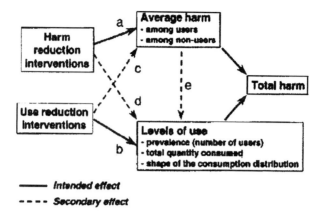

Figure 4: Use Reduction and Harm Reduction: An Integrative Framework

Figure 4 depicts this relationship graphically using a causal path diagram. Links *a* and *b* depict the intended effects of harm-reduction and use-reduction policies, respectively. Links *c, d,* and *e* depict the ancillary harmful effects—unintended and often unanticipated—these policies might have. Link c denotes the unintended harms caused by prohibiting a risky behavior (e.g., the lack of clean needles, lack of drug quality control, violence associated with illicit markets, inflated prices that encourage income-generating crime, and so on; Nadelmann, 1989). This category of unintended harms is of central concern to any assessment of alternative legal regimes for drug control (MacCoun, Reuter, & Schelling, 1996). But here I focus on a second set of unintended consequences,those resulting from harm-reduction policies, to see whether objections to harm reduction have merit. If a harm-reduction strategy reduces harm per incident but leads to increases in drug use (links *d* and *e),* the policy might still achieve *net* harm reduction; on the other hand,a sufficiently large increase in use could actually result in an *increase* in total harm. There are two potential mechanisms for such an unintended consequence, one direct and one indirect. For reasons to be explained, link *d* can be conceptualized as the direct rhetorical effect (if any) of harm reduction on total use; link *e* is an indirect *compensatory behavior* effect. Either might be interpreted as "sending the wrong message."

Direct Version: Does Harm Reduction Literally Send the Wrong Message?

The rhetorical hypothesis is that irrespective of their effectiveness in reducing harms, harm-reduction programs literally communicate messages that encourage drug use. As noted earlier, those who espouse this rhetorical hypothesis rarely explain how it is supposed to work. The most plausible interpretation is that without intending to do so, harm reduction sends tacit messages that are construed as approval or at least the absence of strong disapproval—of drug consumption.

If harm reduction service providers *intend* to send a message, it is something like this: "We view drugs as harmful. We discourage you from using them, and we are eager to help you to quit if you've started. But if you will not quit using drugs, we can help you to use them less harmfully." Is that the only message? Psycholinguistic theory and research do suggest that people readily draw additional inferences that are *pragmatically implied* by an actor's conduct, regardless of whether those inferences were intended, or even endorsed, by the actor (R.J. Harris & Monaco, 1978; Wyer & Gruenfeld, 1995).Thus if we provide heroin users with clean needles, they might infer that we don't expect them to quit using heroin—if we did, why give them needles? Arguably, this perception could undermine their motivation to quit.

But would users infer that we believe heroin use is good, or at least "not bad"? It is not obvious how harm reduction might actually imply *endorsement* of drug use. Ultimately, whether any such rhetorical effects occur is an empirical question. It would be useful to assess the kinds of unintended inferences that users and nonusers draw from harm-reduction messages, and from the mere existence of harm-reduction programs. But in the absence of such evidence, the rhetorical hypothesis that harm reduction conveys approval of drug use is purely speculative.

Moreover, it is difficult to reconcile this notion with the secondary prevention and treatment efforts that frequently accompany actual harm-reduction interventions. Through such efforts, users are informed that their behavior is dangerous to themselves and others and that assistance and support are available to help them if they wish to quit drug use. Braithwaite's (1989) research on *reintegrative shaming* indicates that it is possible simultaneously to send a social message that certain acts are socially unacceptable while still helping the actors to repair their lives. Braithwaite suggests that this approach is integral to Japanese culture, but it is also reflected in the Christian tradition of "hating the sin but loving the sinner."

INDIRECT VERSION: DOES A REDUCTION IN HARM MAKE DRUGS MORE ATTRACTIVE?

Even if no one took harm reduction to imply government endorsement of drugs, harm reduction might still influence levels of drug use indirectly through its intended effect, that is, by reducing the riskiness of drug use. This is a second interpretation of "sending the wrong message." Though there are ample grounds for being skeptical of a pure "rational-choice" analysis of drug use (MacCoun, 1993), the notion that reductions in risk might influence drug use is certainly plausible and would be consistent with a growing body of evidence of compensatory behavioral responses to safety interventions. Thus we should be mindful of potential trade-offs between harm reduction and use reduction.

Risk assessors have known for some time that engineers tend to overestimate the benefits of technological improvements in the safety of traffic signals, automobiles, cigarettes, and other products. The reason is that engineers often fail to anticipate that technological improvements lead to changes in behavior. When technological innovations successfully reduce the probability of harm given unsafe conduct, they make that conduct less risky. And if the perceived risks were motivating actors to behave somewhat self-protectively, a reduction in risk should lead them to take fewer precautions than before, raising the probability of their unsafe conduct to a higher level. This notion has been variously labeled *compensatory behavior, risk compensation, offsetting behavior*, or in its most extreme form, risk *homeostasis*—a term that implies efforts to maintain a constant level of risk (Wilde, 1982). Although some find this general idea counterintuitive, one economist has noted that, on reflection, it is hardly surprising that "soldiers walk more gingerly when crossing minefields than when crossing wheat fields," and "circus performers take fewer chances when practicing without nets" (Hemenway, 1988).

Compensatory behavioral responses to risk reduction have been identified in a variety of settings. For example, everything else being equal, drivers have responded to seat belts and other improvements in the safety of automobiles by driving faster and more recklessly than they would in a less safe vehicle (Chirinko & Harper, 1993). Similarly, filters and low-tar tobacco each reduce the harmfulness per unit of tobacco, yet numerous studies have demonstrated that smokers compensate by smoking more cigarettes, inhaling more deeply, or blocking the filter vents (Hughes, 1995). In both domains,some of the safety gains brought about by a reduction in the probability of harm given unsafe conduct have been offset by increases in the probability of that conduct. Though early correlational studies were criticized on methodological grounds, the compensatory behavioral hypothesis has received important support from recent controlled laboratory experiments (Stetzer & Hofman, 1996).

The compensatory behavioral mechanism suggests that if reductions in average drug-related harm were to motivate sufficiently large increases in drug use, micro harm reduction would actually increase macro harm. Blower and McLean (1994) offer a similar argument based on epidemiological simulations that suggest that an HIV vaccine, unless perfectly prophylactic, could actually exacerbate the San Francisco AIDS epidemic, provided that individuals behaved less cautiously in response to their increased sense of safety. But to date, research on compensatory responses to risk reduction provides little evidence that behavioral responses produce net increases in harm, or even the constant level of harm predicted by the "homeostatic" version of the theory. Instead, most studies find that when programs reduce the probability of harm given unsafe conduct, any increases in the probability of that conduct are slight, reducing but not eliminating the gains in safety (Chirinko & Harper, 1993; Hughes, 1995; Stetzer & Hofman, 1996). As a result, in our terms, micro harm reduction produces macro harm reduction.

Do Drug Interventions Achieve Macro Harm Reduction?

It is impossible to calculate total drug harm in any literal fashion, or to rigorously compare total harm across alternative policy regimes (Mac-Coun, Reuter, & Schelling, 1996). Many of the harms are difficult to quantify, and observers will differ in their weighting of the various types of harm. Thus at the strategic level of national policy formation, macro harm reduction is not a rigid analytical test but rather a heuristic principle: Are we reducing drug harms, and reducing drug use in ways that do not increase drug harm? But at the level of specific interventions, macro reduction of *specific* harms is a realistic evaluation criterion, as illustrated by the compensatory behavioral research just cited. Unfortunately, few drug policy programs are evaluated with respect to both use reduction and harm reduction. Prevention and treatment programs are generally evaluated with respect to changes in abstinence or relapse rates, whereas harm reduction evaluators tend to assess changes in crime, morbidity, and mortality rates. As a result, researchers are unable to determine whether many programs achieve macro harm reduction.

The empirical literature on needle exchange is a notable and exemplary exception. There is now a fairly sizable body of evidence that needle exchange programs produce little or no measurable increase in injecting drug use (Lurie & Reingold, 1993; Watters, Estilo, Clark, & Lorvick, 1994). Because it significantly reduces average harm, needle exchange provides both micro and macro harm reduction. But the empirical success record for needle exchange does not constitute blanket support for the harm reduction movement. Each intervention must be assessed empirically on its own terms.

Let me offer a few cautionary tales. One harm reduction intervention that has been tried and rejected is the "zone of tolerance" approach tried by Zurich officials in the Platzspitz—or, as the American press labeled it, "Needle Park." By allowing injecting drug users to congregate openly in this public park, and to shoot up without police interference, city officials were able to make clean needles and other health interventions readily available at the time and place of drug use. Even sympathetic observers agree that these benefits were ultimately offset by increases in local crime rates and in the prevalence of hard drug use in the city (Grob, 1992). Another example involves bongs and water pipes. Though these devices have been touted as a means of reducing the health risks of marijuana smoking, a recent test found that they actually increase the quantity of tars ingested. The apparent reason harkens back to the compensatory behavioral mechanism. Water pipes filter out more THC than tar, so users smoke more to achieve the same high, thereby increasing their risk (Gieringer, 1996). The Zurich case and the bong study suggest that harm-reduction strategies can fail, but it is important to note that neither failure resulted from increasing rates of *initiation* to drug use. In the Zurich case, the prevalence of drug use rose because the park attracted users from other Swiss cities and neighboring countries. Arguably, the program might have been successful had other European cities adopted the idea simultaneously. In the bong case, the filtering benefits were offset by increases in consumption levels among users, but I am unaware of any evidence that bongs and water pipes have ever encouraged nonusers to start smoking marijuana.

One can imagine hypothetical examples of how a harm-reduction strategy might plausibly attract new users. For example, from a public health perspective, we are better off if current heroin injectors switch to smoking their drug. Imagine a public information campaign designed to highlight the relative health benefits of smoking. If some fraction of nonusers have resisted heroin because of an aversion to needles (for anecdotal evidence, see Bennetto, 1998), our campaign might indeed end up encouraging some of them to take up heroin smoking, despite our best intentions. Of course, no one has seriously proposed such a campaign. But the example demonstrates that concerns about increased use are plausible in principle.

QUANTITY REDUCTION AS A MIDDLE GROUND?

As noted earlier, American drug policy rhetoric is dominated by concerns about the number of users, drawing a bright line between "users" and "nonusers." This is illustrated by our national drug indicator data. Most available measures of drug use are *prevalence* oriented: rates of lifetime use, use in the past year, or use in the past month. But drug-related harms may well be more sensitive to changes in the *total quantity consumed* than to changes in the total number of users. One million occasional drug users may pose fewer crime and health problems than 100,000 frequent users. Our nation's recent cocaine problems provide an illustration. After significant reductions in casual use in the 1980s, total consumption has become increasingly concentrated among a smaller number of heavy users. At an individual level, these heavy users are at much greater risk than casual users with respect to acute and chronic illness, accidents, job-and family-related problems, and participation in criminal activities. Thus although cocaine prevalence has declined, total cocaine consumption and its related harms have remained relatively stable (Everingham & Rydell, 1994).

This suggests that *quantity reduction* (reducing consumption levels) holds particular promise as a macro harm reduction strategy. Quantity reduction occupies a point halfway between prevalence reduction and micro harm reduction. Like prevalence reduction, quantity reduction targets use levels rather than harm levels. But like harm reduction, quantity reduction is based on the premise that when use cannot be prevented, we might at least be able to mitigate its harms.

What is less clear is the optimal targeting strategy for quantity reduction. Consider the distribution of users across consumption levels, which for most psychoactive drugs (licit and illicit) is positively skewed, with a long right tail indicating a small fraction of very heavy users. One strategy is to target those heaviest users—to "pull in" the right tail of the distribution. The marginal gains in risk reduction should be greatest at the right tall, and only a small fraction of users need be targeted.

This approach has received considerable attention—and notoriety—in the alcohol field under the rubric "controlled drinking." Few public health experts dispute the notion that problem drinkers are better off drinking lightly than drinking heavily. But there has been an extraordinary furor surrounding the notion of controlled drinking as a treatment goal. The evidence suggests that (a) although abstinence-based treatment programs experience high relapse rates, many of the relapsing clients successfully reduce their drinking to relatively problem free levels; (b) it is possible to teach controlled drinking skills to many, but not all, problem drinkers; (c) we cannot yet predict which problem drinkers will be able to control their drinking at moderate levels; and (d) most treated problem drinkers fail to achieve either abstinence or controlled levels of drinking (Marlatt, Larimer, Baer, & Quigley, 1993). But opponents assert that, irrespective of any benefits to be derived from controlled drinking, the very notion undermines the goal of abstinence and discourages drinkers from achieving it. The small-scale studies conducted to date do not support that claim, but the evidence is not yet decisive.

In addition to the abstinence-moderation debate, a second quantity-reduction debate has emerged among alcohol experts. Are problem drinkers even the appropriate intervention target? An alternative quantity-reduction strategy targets the middle of the alcohol consumption distribution. For some years, many experts have argued that the total social costs of alcohol might be better reduced by lowering average consumption levels rather than concentrating on the most problematic drinkers at the right tail (Rose, 1992; Skog, 1993). If so—and this is a matter of ongoing debate in the pages of *Addiction* and other journals—broad-based efforts to reduce total drug use might indeed be the best way to achieve total harm reduction, at least for alcohol consumption. The controversy here has been more purely technical and less emotional than the controlled drinking debate, in part because few people still champion the notion of abstinence for casual drinkers. Many Americans seem quite willing to accept the notion of "nonproblem" alcohol consumption yet reject the notion of "nonproblem" marijuana or cocaine consumption.

In fact, the viability of "lower-risk" drug consumption, and the relative efficacy of the "pull in the tail" and the "lower the average" strategies, will depend on a variety of factors. One factor is the degree of skew of the consumption distribution: The greater the probability mass in the right tail, the greater the efficacy of targeting heavy users. A second is the dose-response curve for risks, which is usually S-shaped for those drug-risk combinations that have been studied. (We know a great deal more about dose-response functions for health and public safety risks involving licit drugs than for comparable risks involving illicit drugs.) When this function is very steep, even moderate consumption levels are very risky, making the "shift-the-distribution" strategy more efficacious. A third factor involves the possibility that individuals with a higher propensity for danger self-select higher consumption levels. The latter effect will spuriously inflate the quantity-risk relationship. To the extent that this effect predominates, convincing right-tail users to cut back may yield fewer benefits than anticipated.

The Public Acceptability of Harm Reduction

Whereas American citizens and policymakers have embraced drug strategies that promote prevalence reduction, harm reduction and some forms of quantity reduction are often greeted with considerable hostility—when they are not ignored altogether. In this section, I offer a number of hypotheses about this negative reaction. The opposition to harm reduction surely has multiple causes, so these explanations are not mutually exclusive. They vary along a continuum ranging from *consequentialist* to *symbolic* grounds for opposition. Many people probably hold both kinds of views. Harm reduction opponents might be placed along this continuum based on their responses to the following hypothetical questions:

1. If new evidence suggested that needle exchange (or some other harm-reduction strategy) reduced total harm, would you still be opposed?

2. If the answer is "yes": If new evidence suggested a reduction in harm, with *no increase in use*, would you still be opposed?

3. If the answer is "yes": Would you be opposed to drug use even if it were made completely harmless? Those who would say "no" to the first question are pragmatic or consequentialist in their opposition to harm reduction.

Those who say "yes" to the third question are at the other extreme; for them, drug use is intrinsically immoral, irrespective of its consequences—what philosophers call a deontological stance. Those who would support harm reduction only if there were no increase in drug use fall somewhere in between. Their views might reflect a complex mix of instrumental and symbolic concerns.

Consequentialist Grounds

The consequentialist grounds for opposing harm reduction are the easiest to describe. They are characterized primarily by the belief that harm reduction will be counterproductive, either by failing to reduce average harm or by increasing drug use enough to increase total harm. Those who oppose harm reduction on truly consequentialist grounds should change their mind and support it if the best available facts suggest that an intervention reduces harm without producing offsetting increases in use. In recent years, the favorable evidence for needle exchange has received increasing publicity in the mass media. This media coverage may explain why a 1996 poll found that 66% of Americans endorsed needle exchange as a means of preventing AIDS—a dramatic increase over earlier surveys (The Henry J. Kaiser Family

Foundation, 1996). Of course, this may be an over-optimistic reading of the impact of empirical research (MacCoun, 1998). Program evaluations rarely yield unequivocal verdicts; even when effects are statistically reliable, they are usually open to multiple interpretations. Expert consensus on the effects of high-profile policy interventions is rare, even when the accumulated body of research is large. And the vehemence of the opposition to harm reduction suggests that attitudes toward these interventions are based on something more than purely instrumental beliefs about the effectiveness of alternative drug policies.

Attitudes toward the death penalty are instructive in this regard. Attitude research indicates that many citizens overtly endorse a *deterrence* rationale for the death penalty, believing that "it will prevent crimes." Yet most do not change their views when asked how they would feel if there were unequivocal evidence that execution provided no marginal deterrence above and beyond life imprisonment. The evidence suggests that ostensibly instrumental views are actually masking deeper retributive motives (Ellsworth & Gross, 1994). As a result, support for capital punishment is relatively impervious to research findings (Lord, Ross, & Lepper, 1979).

The nonconsequentialist grounds for opposing harm reduction are more complex than the consequentialist grounds. There are a number of distinct psychological processes that might play a role in shaping these views.[5]

The Need for Predictability and Control

Harmonious social relations require a minimal, level of predictability because we must routinely relinquish control to other people—automobile drivers, surgeons, airline pilots, our children's teachers, and so on. The notion that others are using drugs can be threatening because it suggests that they've lost some self-control. Although harm reduction can minimize the consequences of diminished control, it may be more reassuring to believe that others are completely abstinent. When we are unable to control aversive stimuli, any signal that helps us to anticipate danger will significantly reduce our anxiety (Miller, 1980). Perhaps the belief that others are abstinent from drugs works like a "safety signal" to free us from worrying about their conduct.

Our fears about others are augmented by a robust bias in risk perceptions. Most people—adults as well as adolescents—perceive themselves to be less vulnerable than the average person to risks of injury or harm (e.g., Weinstein & Klein, 1995). An apparent corollary is that most of us believe we are surrounded by people less cautious or skillful than ourselves. We may think we can control our own use of intoxicants (most of us feel that way about alcohol), but we find it harder to believe that others will do the same. Indeed, this might explain why a sizable

5. Note that these psychological accounts by themselves do not constitute evidence for or against the wisdom of opposition to harm reduction, nor are they meant to imply that such views are somehow pathological.

minority of regular cannabis users opposes the complete legalization of that drug (Erickson, 1989).

AVERSION TO MAKING VALUE TRADE-OFFS

Our attitudes toward public policy involve more than simple judgments about effectiveness and outcomes. They are symbolic expressions of our core values. Unfortunately, most difficult social problems bring core values into conflict. Drug problems are no exception; they bring personal liberty into conflict with public safety, compassion into conflict with moral accountability. Contemplating harm reduction brings these conflicts into strong relief. According to Tetlock's *value pluralism model* acknowledging such conflicts is psychologically aversive, and so many people avoid explicit trade-off reasoning, preferring simpler mental strategies (Tetlock, Peterson, & Lerner, 1996). The easiest is to deny that there is a conflict, by ignoring one value or the other. If that doesn't work, we may adopt a simple "lexicographic" ranking. Many of us engage in complex multidimensional trade-off reasoning only when we can't avoid it, as when the conflicting values are each too salient to dismiss or ignore.

In a recent content analysis of op-ed essays debating the reform of drug laws, my colleagues and I found that legalizers and decriminalizers (all of whom were harm reduction advocates, though the converse is not necessarily true) used significantly more complex arguments than prohibitionists (MacCoun, Kahan, Gillespie, & Rhee, 1993). The reform advocates were less likely to view the drug problem in terms of a simple good-bad dichotomy; they identified multiple dimensions to the problem and were more likely to acknowledge trade-offs and counterarguments to their own position. It may be hard to persuade others to acknowledge the full complexity of harm-reduction logic unless the values that support it become more salient in drug policy discourse.

THE PROPRIETY OF HELPING DRUG USERS

Of course, there is little basis for value conflict if one feels that drug users should suffer harm when they use drugs. There are a number of reasons why some people might hold this view. One is authoritarianism, a complex trait defined as a chronic tendency to cope with anxiety by expressing hostility toward outgroup members; intolerance of unconventional behavior; and submissive, unquestioning support of authority figures. Authoritarianism is strongly correlated with support for punitive drug policies (Peterson, Doty, & Winter, 1993). Indeed, several items from the Right Wing Authoritarianism Scale—a leading research instrument for measuring this trait—seem to equate authoritarianism with opposition to harm reduction interventions almost by definition (Christie, 1991). According to Item 7, "The facts on crime, sexual immorality, and the recent public disorders all show we have to crack down harder on deviant groups and troublemakers if we are going to save our moral standards and preserve law and order." Item 12 states, "Being kind to loafers or criminals will only encourage them to take advantage of your weakness, so it's best to use a firm, tough hand when dealing with them." And authoritarians are more likely to disagree with Item 19: "The courts are right in being easy on drug offenders. Punishment would not do any good in cases like these."

But scoring high in authoritarianism is probably not a prerequisite for hostility toward drug users. There is a general antagonism to hard drug users among U.S. citizens, partly stemming from the strong association between drugs and street violence in American cities. It is much easier to see harshness as the appropriate response in the United States than in Europe, where drug use is more likely to be perceived as a health problem. Race and social distance may play a role here as well; arguably, Americans were more tolerant of drug users in the 1970s, when the mass media's prototypical drug user was an Anglo–American student in a college dorm instead of a young African American man on a city street corner (Kirp & Bayer, 1993). As a result, Americans have supported (or at least tolerated) sentencing policies that tend to disproportionately burden minority and poor offenders relative to those who are Anglo–American or middle class (Tonry, 1995).

But irrespective of race and class, the mere fact that someone uses drugs will often be sufficient to categorize them as "the other," particularly if we don't already know them. Citizens with a friend or family member who is an addict may embrace micro harm reduction, whatever its aggregate consequences, but those who don't know any addicts may prefer a strategy of isolation and containment.

Even in the absence of malice, many people may feel that addicts should suffer the consequences of their actions. Addiction is widely viewed as a voluntary state, regardless of many experts' views to the contrary (Weiner, Perry, & Magnusson, 1988). Many Americans, especially conservatives, are unwilling to extend help to actors who are responsible for their own suffering; such actors are seen as undeserving (Skitka & Tetlock, 1993). The retributive view that bad acts require punishment is deeply rooted in the Judeo–Christian tradition, particularly in Protestant fundamentalist traditions. In light of the possibility that opposition to harm reduction traces back to our nation's strong Puritan and Calvinist roots, it is quite ironic that the Dutch and the Swiss have championed such an approach in Europe.

DISGUST AND IMPURITY

A final ground for opposing harm reduction might be the vague, spontaneous, and nonrational sense that drug use defiles the purity of the body and hence that anything that comes in contact with drug users becomes disgusting through a process of contagion. Stated so bluntly, this may sound utterly implausible; such concepts are quite alien to Western moral discourse. Nevertheless, this kind of thinking is quite explicit in other cultures, and anthropologists argue that it often lurks below the surface of our own moral judgments (Douglas, 1966; Haidt, Koller, & Dias, 1993).I know of no direct evidence that such reactions influence attitudes toward drug policy, but the hypothesis is testable in principle and worthy of further investigation.

CONCLUSION

In this article, I have tried to take a frank look at the arguments against harm reduction, and I have suggested that, like most policy interventions, the approach has potential pitfalls. Not every harm-reduction intervention will be successful, and some might even increase aggregate harm. We are still woefully ignorant about the complex interplay between formal drug policies and informal social and self-control factors (MacCoun, 1993). Still, the evidence to date on harm reduction is encouraging(as the success of needle exchange programs makes clear), and I believe that we have much to gain by integrating harm-reduction interventions and goals into our national drug control strategy. I conclude by offering five hypotheses about how harm reduction might be more successful—successful both in reducing aggregate harm and in attracting and retaining a viable level of political support.

1. Harm-reduction interventions should have the greatest political viability when they can demonstrate a reduction in average harm—especially harms that affect nonusers—without increasing drug use levels. Interventions that lead to increases in drug use are likely to encounter stiff opposition, even if they yield demonstrable net reductions in aggregate harm. Thus, harm-reduction interventions need to be rigorously evaluated with respect to four types of outcome: effects on targeted harms, "side effects" on untargeted harms (especially harms to nonusers), effects on participants' subsequent use levels, and effects on local nonparticipants' use levels.

2. Because the compensatory behavioral mechanism is triggered by perceived changes in risk, harm-reduction efforts seem least likely to increase drug use when those harms being reduced were already significantly underestimated, discounted, or ignored by users and potential users (see Wilde, 1982). At one extreme, if perceptions of risk are serious enough, few people will use the drug in the first place. (Witness the almost complete disappearance of absinthe after its dangers became apparent in the late 19th century.) At the other extreme, those who are either ignorant of, or indifferent to, a drug's risks, seem unlikely to escalate their use when an intervention lowers those risks.

3. Similarly, interventions involving safe-use information or risk-reducing paraphernalia should be less likely to increase total use, and hence be more politically viable, when they are highly salient for heavy users but largely invisible to potential initiates to drug use. Maintenance interventions,which provide drugs or drug substitutes for addicts, should be less likely to encourage use if the program has few barriers to entry for heavy users but high barriers to entry for casual users. (The risk of these

targeting strategies is that new initiates may fail to obtain the benefits of the interventions.)

4. Reducing users' consumption levels should generally provide harm reduction, an important strategy for achieving use reduction when heavy users refuse to become abstinent.

5. Whenever feasible, harm-reduction interventions should be coupled with credible primary and secondary prevention efforts, as well as low-threshold access to treatment.

This last point is a truism among many harm-reduction providers. Still, a few in the harm-reduction movement are uncomfortable with the notion that harm-reduction programs should urge users to stop their drug use. Some take that position on libertarian grounds, but others associate traditional use-reduction efforts with dishonesty ("reefer madness"), hypocrisy ("what about alcohol and tobacco?"), or an apparent willingness to jeopardize user health (e.g., the U.S. decision to spray Mexican marijuana crops with paraquat in the 1970s). But harm reduction advocates who categorically reject the opposition risk undermining their own cause. Americans who oppose harm reduction are unlikely to change their views until they feel their fears have been taken seriously.

Notes and Questions

1. If the 1989 National Strategy was based on strict legalist priorities— only illegal drugs were a concern, all illegal drugs were of equal concern, and drug use rather than the problems that it might cause is the central problem—what is the ideology and what are the important priorities of the 2006 National Strategy?

2. A number of programs and target behaviors are featured in the 2006 report that do not receive positive attention in the 1989 analysis. There is an entire chapter on drug treatment. Prescription drug abuse is featured in Chapter 3, although the substances involved are not themselves unlawful, and Chapter 1 begins with trends in cigarette use by adults and per capita alcohol consumption (2006 Strategy, p. 5). Does this mean that the federal government has adopted a public health generalist ideology?

3. Is the 2006 report in any clear disagreement with the 1989 report? Is the 2006 report less punitive in its approach than the 1989 report?

4. Does the 2006 report treat all illicit drugs as equal problems? Does the 2006 report prefer treatment to punishment or punishment to treatment?

5. Are there any current anti-drug programs or law enforcement efforts that the 2006 report does not support? Does the 2006 report indicate any priorities for federal action or resources? If the correct term for the report is "all-inclusive" or "all-embracing," what is the political objective of this kind of approach?

6. Does the shift from the emphasis of the 1989 report to that of the 2006 report carry any implications for the number of persons imprisoned for drug offenses or the length of their sentences?

7. Is Professor MacCoun's *Psychology of Harm Reduction* another ideology of drug control or simply a way of classifying policy choices?

8. Is harm reduction consistent with the emphasis in public health approaches to drug control? Is harm reduction consistent with the priorities of legalist approaches to drug control?

C. THE LEGALIZATION DEBATE

ETHAN NADELMANN—THE CASE FOR LEGALIZATION
The Public Interest (1988; 92: pp. 3–17).

INTRODUCTION

What can be done about the "drug problem"? Despite frequent proclamations of war and dramatic increases in government funding and resources in recent years, there are many indications that the problem is not going away and may even be growing worse. During the past year alone, more than thirty million Americans violated the drug laws on literally billions of occasions. Drug-treatment programs in many cities are turning people away for lack of space and funding. In Washington, D.C., drug-related killings, largely of one drug dealer by another, are held responsible for a doubling in the homicide rate over the past year. In New York and elsewhere, courts and prisons are clogged with a virtually limitless supply of drug-law violators. In large cities and small towns alike, corruption of policemen and other criminal-justice officials by drug traffickers is rampant.

President Reagan and the First Lady are not alone in supporting increasingly repressive and expensive anti-drug measures, and in believing that the war against drugs can be won. Indeed, no "war" proclaimed by an American leader during the past forty years has garnered such sweeping bipartisan support; on this issue, liberals and conservatives are often indistinguishable. The fiercest disputes are not over objectives or even broad strategies, but over turf and tactics. Democratic politicians push for the appointment of a "drug czar" to oversee all drug policy, and blame the Administration for applying sufficient pressure and sanctions against the foreign drug-producing countries. Republicans try to gain the upper hand by daring Democrats to support more widespread drug testing, increasingly powerful law-enforcement measures, and the death penalty for various drug-related offenses. But on the more fundamental issues of what this war is about, and what strategies are most likely to be successful in the long run, no real debate-much less vocal dissent-can be heard.

If there were a serious public debate on this issue, far more attention would be given to one policy option that has just begun to be seriously considered, but which may well prove more successful than anything currently being implemented or proposed: Legalization. Politicians and public officials remain hesitant even to mention the word, except to dismiss it contemptuously as a capitulation to the drug traffickers. Most Americans perceive drug legalization as an invitation to drug-infested anarchy. Even the civil-liberties groups shy away from this issue, limiting their input primarily to the drug-testing debate. The minority communities in the ghetto, for whom repealing the drug laws would promise the greatest benefits, fail to recognize the costs of our drug-prohibition policies. And the typical middle-class American, who hopes only that his children will not succumb to drug abuse, tends to favor any measures that he believes will make illegal drugs less accessible to them. Yet when one seriously compares the advantages and disadvantages of the legalization strategy with those of current and planned policies, abundant evidence suggests that legalization may well be the optimal strategy for tackling the drug problem.

Interestingly, public support for repealing the drug-prohibition has traditionally come primarily from the conservative end of the political spectrum: Milton Friedman, Ernest van den Haag, William F. Buckley, and the editors of the Economist have all supported it. Less vocal support comes from many liberals, politicians among them, who are disturbed by the infringements on individual liberty posed by the drug laws. There is also a significant constituency in favor of repeal, found especially among criminal justice officials, intelligence analysts, military interdictors, and criminal-justice scholars who have spent a considerable amount of time thinking about the problem. More often than not, however, job-security considerations, combined with an awareness that they can do little to change official policies, ensure that their views remain discreet and off the record.

During the spring of 1988, however, legalization suddenly began to be seriously considered as a policy option; the pros and cons of legalization were discussed on the front pages of leading newspapers and news magazines, and were debated on national television programs. Although the argument for legalization was not new, two factors seem to have been primarily responsible for the blitz of media coverage: an intellectual rationale for legalization-the first provided in decades-appeared in my article in the Spring issue of Foreign Policy magazine; more importantly, political legitimacy was subsequently bestowed upon the legalization option when Baltimore Mayor Kurt Schmoke, speaking to the National Conference of Mayors, noted the potential benefits of drug legalization and asked that the merits of legalization be debated in congressional hearings.

The idea of legalizing drugs was quickly denounced by most politicians across the political spectrum; nevertheless, the case for legalization appealed to many Americans. The prominent media coverage lent an aura of respectability to arguments that just a month earlier had seemed to be beyond the political pale. Despite the tendency of many journalists to caricature the legalization argument, at long last the issue had been joined. Various politicians, law-enforcement officials, health experts, and scholars came out in favor of drug legalization-or at least wanted to debate the matter seriously. On Capitol Hill, three or four congressmen seconded the call for a debate. According to some congressional staffers, two dozen additional legislators would have wanted to debate the issue, had the question arisen after rather than before the upcoming elections. Unable to oppose a mere hearing on the issue, Congressman Charles Rangel, chairman of the House Select Committee on Narcotics, declared his willingness to convene his committee in Baltimore to consider the legalization option.

There is, of course, no single legalization strategy. At one extreme is the libertarian vision of virtually no government restraints on the production and sale of drugs or any psychoactive substances, except perhaps around the fringes, such as prohibiting sales to children. At the other extreme is total government control over the production and sale of these goods. In between lies a strategy that may prove more successful than anything yet tried in stemming the problems of drug abuse and drug-related violence, corruption, sickness, and suffering. It is one in which government makes most of the substances that are now banned legally available to competent adults, exercises strong regulatory powers over all large-scale production and sale of drugs, makes drug-treatment programs available to all who need them, and offers honest drug-education programs to children. This strategy, it is worth noting, would also result in a net benefit to public treasuries of at least ten billion dollars a year, and perhaps much more.

There are three reasons why it is important to think about legalization scenarios, even though most Americans remain hostile to the idea. First, current drug-control policies have failed, are failing, and will continue to fail, in good part because they are fundamentally flawed. Second, many drug-control efforts are not only failing, also proving highly costly and counter-productive; indeed, many of the drug-related evils that Americans identify as part and parcel of the "drug problem" are in fact caused by our drug prohibition policies. Third, there is good reason to believe that repealing many of the drug laws would not lead, as many people , to a dramatic rise in drug abuse. In this essay I expand on each these reasons for considering the legalization option. Government efforts to deal with the drug problem will succeed only if the rhetoric and crusading mentality that now dominate drug policy are replaced by reasoned and logical analysis.

Why Current Drug Policies Fail

Most proposals for dealing with the drug problem today reflect a desire to point the finger at those most removed from one's home area of expertise. New York Mayor Ed Koch, Florida Congressman Larry Smith, and Harlem Congressman Charles Rangel, who recognize government's inability to deal with the drug problem in cities, are among the most vocal supporters of punishing foreign drug-producing countries and stepping up interdiction efforts. Foreign leaders and U. S. State Department and drug-enforcement offices stationed abroad, on the other hand, who understand all too well why it is impossible to crack down successfully on illicit drug production outside the United States, are the most vigorous advocates of domestic enforcement and demand-reduction efforts within United States. In between, those agencies charged with drug interdiction, from the Coast Guard and U.S. Customs Services to U.S. military, know that they will never succeed in capturing more than a small percentage of the illicit drugs being smuggled into the United States. Not surprisingly, they point their fingers in both directions. The solution, they promise, lies in greater source-control efforts abroad and greater demand-reduction efforts at home.

Trying to pass the buck is always understandable. But in each of these cases, the officials are half right and half wrong-half right in recognizing that they can do little to affect their end of the drug problem, given the suppositions and constraints of current drug-control strategies; half wrong (if we assume that their finger-pointing is sincere) in expecting that the solution lies elsewhere. It would be wrong, however, to assume that the public posturing of many officials reflects their real views. Many of them privately acknowledge the futility of all current drug-control strategies, and wonder whether radically different options, such as legalization, might not prove more successful in dealing with the drug problem. The political climate pervading this issue is such, however, that merely to ask that alternatives to current policies be considered is to incur a great political risk.

By most accounts, the dramatic increase in drug-enforcement efforts over the past few years has had little effect on the illicit drug market in the United States. The mere existence of drug-prohibition laws, combined with a minimal level of law-enforcement resources, is sufficient to maintain the price of illicit drugs at a level significantly higher than it would be if there were no such laws. Drug laws and enforcement also reduce the availability of illicit drugs, most notably in parts of the United States where demand is relatively limited to begin with. Theoretically, increases in drug-enforcement efforts should result in reduced availability, higher prices, and lower purity of illegal drugs. That is, in fact, what has happened to the domestic marijuana market (in at least the first two respects). But in general the illegal drug market has not responded as intended to the substantial increases in federal, state, and local drug-enforcement efforts.

Cocaine has sold for about a hundred dollars a gram at the retail level since the beginning of the 1980s. The average purity of that gram, however, has increased from 12 to 60 percent. Moreover, a growing number of users are turning to "crack," a potent derivative of cocaine that can be smoked; it is widely sold in ghetto neighborhoods now for five to ten dollars per vial. Needless to say, both crack and the 60 percent pure cocaine pose much greater threats to users than did the relatively benign powder available eight years ago. Similarly, the retail price of heroin has remained relatively constant even as the average purity has risen from 3.9 percent in 1983 to 6.1 percent in 1986. Throughout the southwestern part of the United States, a particularly potent form of heroin known as "black tar" has become increasingly prevalent. And in many cities, a powerful synthetic opiate, Dilaudid, is beginning to compete with heroin as the preferred opiate. The growing number of heroin-related hospital emergencies and deaths is directly related to these developments.

All of these trends suggest that drug-enforcement efforts are not succeeding and may even be backfiring. There are numerous indications, for instance, that a growing number of marijuana dealers in both the producer countries and the United States are switching to cocaine dealing, motivated both by the promise of greater profits by government drug-enforcement efforts that place a premium minimizing the bulk of the illicit product (in order to avoid detection). It is possible, of course, that some of these trends would be even more severe in the absence of drug laws and enforcement. At the same time, it is worth observing that the increases in the potency of illegal drugs have coincided with decreases in the potency of legal substances. Motivated in good part by health concerns, cigarette smokers are turning increasingly to lower-tar and-nicotine tobacco products, alcohol drinkers from hard liquor to wine and beer, and even coffee drinkers from regular to decaffeinated coffee. This trend may well have less to do with the nature of substances than with their legal status. It is quite possible, for instance, that the subculture of illicit-drug use creates a bias or incentive in favor of riskier behavior and more powerful psychoactive effects. If this is the case, legalization might well succeed in reversing today's trend toward more potent drugs and more dangerous methods of consumption.

The most "successful" drug-enforcement operations are those that succeed in identifying and destroying an entire drug-trafficking organization. Such operations can send dozens of people to jail and earn the government millions of dollars in asset forfeitures. Yet these operations have virtually no effect on the availability or price of illegal drugs throughout much of the United States. During the past years, some urban police departments have devoted significant power and financial resources to intensive crackdowns on street drug dealing in particular neighborhoods. Code-named Open Pressure Point, Operation Clean Sweep, and so on, these massive police efforts have led to hundreds, even thousands, of arrests of low-level dealers and drug users, and have helped improve the quality of life in the targeted neighborhoods. In most cases, however, drug dealers have adapted relatively easily by moving their operations to nearby neighborhoods. In the final analysis, the principal accomplishment of most domestic drug-enforcement efforts is not to reduce the supply or availability of illegal drugs, or even to raise their price; it is to punish the drug dealers who are apprehended, and cause minor disruptions in established drug markets.

The Failure of International Drug Control

Many drug-enforcement officials and urban leaders recognize the futility of domestic drug-enforcement efforts and place their hopes in international control efforts. Yet these too are doomed to fail-for numerous reasons. First, marijuana and opium can be grown almost anywhere, and the coca plant, from which cocaine is derived, is increasingly being cultivated successfully in areas that were once considered inhospitable environments. Wherever drug eradication efforts succeed, other regions and countries are quick to fill the void; for example, Colombian marijuana growers rapidly expanded production following successful eradication efforts in Mexico during the mid–1970s. Today, Mexican growers are rapidly taking advantage of recent Colombian government successes in eradicating marijuana in the Guajira peninsula. Meanwhile, Jamaicans and Central Americans from Panama to Belize, as well as a growing assortment of Asians and Africans, do what they can to sell their own marijuana in American markets. And within the United States, domestic marijuana production is believed to be a multi-billion-dollar industry, supplying between 15 and 50 percent of the American market.

This push-down/pop-up factor also characterizes the international heroin market. At various points during the past two decades, Turkey, Mexico, Southeast Asia (Burma, Thailand, and Laos), and Southwest Asia (Pakistan, Afghanistan, and Iran) have each served as the principal source of heroin imported into the United States. During the early 1970s, Mexican producers rapidly filled the void created by the Turkish government's successful opium-control measures. Although a successful eradication program during the latter part of the 1970s reduced Mexico's share of the U.S. market from a peak of 87 percent in 1975, it has since retained at least a one-third share in each year. Southwest Asian producers, who had played no role in supplying the American market as late as 1976, were able to supply over half the American market four years later. Today, increasing evidence indicates that drug traffickers are bringing unprecedented quantities of Southeast Asian heroin into the United States.

So far, the push-down/pop-up factor has played little role in the international cocaine market, for the simple reason that no government has yet pushed down in a significant way. Unlike marijuana, opium-eradication efforts, in which aerial spraying of herbicides plays a prominent role, coca-eradication efforts are still conducted manually. The long anticipated development and approval of an environmentally safe herbicide to destroy coca plants may produce an unprecedented push-down factor into the market. But even in the absence of such government pressures, coca growing has expanded rapidly during the past decade within Bolivia and Peru, and has expanded outward into Colombia, Brazil, Ecuador, Venezuela, and elsewhere. Moreover, once eradication efforts do begin, coca growers can be expected to adopt many of the same "guerrilla farming" methods adopted by marijuana and opium growers to camouflage and protect their crops from eradication efforts.

Beyond the push-down/pop-up factor, international source-control efforts face a variety of other obstacles. In many countries, governments with limited resources lack the ability to crack down drug production in the hinterlands and other poorly policed regions. In some countries, ranging from Colombia and Peru to Burma and Thailand, leftist insurgencies are involved in drug production for either financial or political profit, and may play an important role in hampering government drug-control efforts. With respect to all three of the illicit crops, poor peasants with no comparable opportunities to earn as much money growing legitimate produce are prominently involved in the illicit business. In some cases, the illicit crop is part of a traditional, indigenous culture. Even where it is not, peasants typically perceive little or nothing immoral about taking advantage of the opportunity to grow the illicit crops. Indeed, from their perspective their moral obligation is not to protect the foolish American consumer of their produce but to provide for their families' welfare. And even among those who do perceive participation in the illicit drug market as somewhat unethical, the temptations held out by the drug traffickers often prove overwhelming.

No illicit drug is as difficult to keep out of the United States as heroin. The absence of geographical limitations on where it can be cultivated is just one minor obstacle. American heroin users consume an estimated six tons of heroin each year. The sixty tons of opium required to produce that heroin represent just 2–3 percent of the estimated 2–3,000 tons of illicit opium produced during each of the past few years. Even if eradication efforts combined with what often proves to be the opium growers' principal nemesis-bad weather-were to eliminate three-fourths of that production in one year, the U.S. market would still require just 10 percent of the remaining crop. Since U.S. consumers are able and willing to pay more than any others, the chances are good that they would still obtain their heroin. In any event, the prospects for such a radical reduction in illicit opium production are scanty indeed.

As Peter Reuter argues elsewhere in these pages, interdiction, like source control, is largely unable to keep illicit drugs out of the United States. Moreover, the past twenty years' experience has demonstrated that even dramatic increases in interdiction and source-control efforts have little or no effect on the price and purity of drugs. The few small successes, such as the destruction of the Turkish-opium "French Connection" in the early 1970s, and the crackdown on Mexican marijuana and heroin in the late 1970s, were exceptions to the rule. The elusive goal of international drug control since then has been to replicate those unusual successes. It is a strategy that is destined to fail, however, as long as millions of Americans continue to demand the illicit substances that foreigners are willing and able to supply.

THE COSTS OF PROHIBITION

The fact that drug-prohibition laws and policies cannot eradicate or even significantly reduce drug abuse is not necessarily a reason to repeal them. They do, after all, succeed in deterring many people from trying drugs, and they clearly reduce the availability and significantly increase the price of illegal drugs. These accomplishments alone might warrant retaining the drug laws, were it not for the fact that these same laws are also responsible for much of what Americans identify as the "drug problem." Here the analogies to alcohol and tobacco are worth noting. There is little question that we could reduce the health costs associated with use and abuse of alcohol and tobacco if we were to criminalize their production, sale, and possession. But no one believes that we could eliminate their use and abuse, that we could create an "alcohol-free" or "tobacco-free" country. Nor do most Americans believe that criminalizing the alcohol and tobacco markets would be a good idea. Their opposition stems largely from two beliefs: that adult Americans have the right to choose what substances they will consume and what risks they will take; and that the costs of trying to coerce so many Americans to abstain from those substances would be enormous. It was the strength of these two beliefs that ultimately led to the repeal of Prohibition, and it is partly due to memories of that experience that criminalizing either alcohol or tobacco has little support today.

Consider the potential consequences of criminalizing the production, sale, and possession of all tobacco products. On the positive side, the number of people smoking tobacco would almost certainly decline, as would the health costs associated with tobacco consumption. Although the "forbidden fruit" syndrome would attract some people to cigarette smoking who would not otherwise have smoked, many more would likely be deterred by the criminal sanction, the moral standing of the law, the higher cost and unreliable quality of the illicit tobacco, and the difficulties involved in acquiring it. Non-smokers would rarely if ever be bothered by the irritating habits of their fellow citizens. The anti-tobacco laws would discourage some people from ever starting to smoke, and would induce others to quit.

On the negative side, however, millions of Americans, including both tobacco addicts and recreational users, would no doubt defy the law, generating a massive underground market and billions in profits for organized criminals. Although some tobacco farmers would find other work, thousands more would become outlaws and continue to produce their crops covertly. Throughout Latin America, farmers and gangsters would rejoice at the opportunity to earn untold sums of gringo greenbacks, even as U.S. diplomats pressured foreign governments to cooperate with U.S. laws. Within the United States, government helicopters would spray herbicides on illicit tobacco fields; people would be rewarded by the government for informing on their tobacco-growing, -selling, and -smoking neighbors; urine tests would be employed to identify violators of the anti-tobacco laws; and a Tobacco Enforcement Administration (the T.E.A.) would employ undercover agents, informants, and wiretaps to uncover tobacco-law violators. Municipal, state, and federal judicial systems would be clogged with tobacco traffickers and "abusers." "Tobacco-related murders" would increase dramatically as criminal organizations competed with one another for turf and markets. Smoking would become an act of youthful rebellion, and no doubt some users would begin to experiment with more concentrated, potent, and dangerous forms of tobacco. Tobacco-related corruption would infect all levels of government, and respect for the law would decline noticeably. Government expenditures on tobacco-law enforcement would climb rapidly into the billions of dollars, even as budget balancers longingly recalled the almost ten billion dollars per year in tobacco taxes earned by the federal and state governments prior to prohibition. Finally, the State of North Carolina might even secede again from the Union.

This seemingly far-fetched tobacco-prohibition scenario is little more than an extrapolation based on the current situation with respect to marijuana, cocaine, and heroin. In many ways, our predicament resembles what actually happened during Prohibition. Prior to Prohibition, most Americans hoped that alcohol could be effectively banned by passing laws against its production and supply. During the early years of Prohibition, when drinking declined but millions of Americans nonetheless continued to drink, Prohibition's supporters placed their faith in tougher laws and more police and jails. After a few more years, however, increasing numbers of Americans began to realize that laws and policemen were unable to eliminate the smugglers, bootleggers, and illicit producers, as long as tens of millions of Americans continued to want to buy alcohol. At the same time, they saw that more laws and policemen seemed to generate more violence and corruption, more crowded courts and jails, wider disrespect for government and the law, and more power and profits for the gangsters. Repeal of Prohibition came to be seen not as a capitulation to Al Capone and his ilk, but as a means of both putting the bootleggers out of business and eliminating most of the costs associated with the prohibition laws.

Today, Americans are faced with a dilemma similar to that confronted by our forebears sixty years ago. Demand for illicit drugs shows some signs of abating, but no signs of declining significantly. Moreover, there are substantial reasons to doubt that tougher laws and policing have played an important role in reducing consumption. Supply, meanwhile, has not abated at all. Availability of illicit drugs, except for marijuana in some locales, remains high. Prices are dropping, even as potency increases. And the number of drug producers, smugglers, and dealers remains sizable, even as jails and prisons fill to overflowing. As was the case during Prohibition, the principal beneficiaries of current drug policies are the new and old organized-crime gangs. The principal victims, on the other hand, are not the drug dealers, but the tens of millions of Americans who are worse off in one way or another as a consequence of the existence and failure of the drug-prohibition laws.

All public policies create beneficiaries and victims, both intended and unintended. When a public policy results in a disproportionate magnitude of unintended victims, there is good reason to reevaluate the assumptions and design of the policy. In the case of drug prohibition policies, the intended beneficiaries are those individuals who would become drug abusers but for the existence and enforcement of the drug laws. The intended victims are those who traffic in rugs and suffer the legal consequences. The unintended beneficiaries' conversely, are the drug producers and traffickers who profit handsomely from the illegality of the market, while avoiding arrest by the authorities and the violence perpetrated by criminals. The unintended victims of drug prohibition policies are rarely recognized as such, however. Viewed narrowly, they are the 30 million Americans who use illegal drugs, thereby risking loss of their jobs, imprisonment, and the damage done to health by ingesting illegally produced drugs; viewed broadly, they are all Americans, who pay the substantial costs of our present ill-considered policies, both as taxpayers and as the potential victims of crime. These unintended victims are generally thought to be victimized by the unintended beneficiaries (i.e., the drug dealers), when in fact it is the drug-prohibition policies themselves that are primarily responsible for their plight.

If law-enforcement efforts could succeed in significantly reducing either the supply of illicit drugs or the demand for them, we would probably have little need to seek alternative drug-control policies. But since those efforts have repeatedly failed to make much of a difference and show little indication of working better in the future, at this point we must focus greater attention on their costs. Unlike the demand and supply of illicit drugs, which have remained relatively indifferent to legislative initiatives, the costs of drug-enforcement measures can be affected—quite dramatically—by legislative measures. What tougher criminal sanctions and more police have failed to accomplish, in terms of reducing drug-related violence, corruption, death, and social decay, may well be better accomplished by legislative repeal of the drug laws, and adoption of less punitive but more effective measures to prevent and treat substance abuse.

Costs to the Taxpayer

Since 1981, federal expenditures on drug enforcement have more than tripled-from less than one billion dollars a year to three billion. According to the National Drug Enforcement Board, the annual budgets of the Drug Enforcement Administration (DEA) and the Coast Guard have each risen during the past seven years from about $220 million to roughly $500 million. During the same period, FBI resources devoted to drug enforcement increased from $8 million a year to over $100 million; U.S. Marshals resources from $26 million to about $80 million; U.S. Attorney resources from $20 million to about $100 million; State Department resources from $35 million to $100 million; U.S. Customs resources from $180 million to over $400 million; and Bureau of Prison resources from $77 million to about $300 million. Expenditures on drug control by the military and the intelligence agencies are more difficult to calculate, although by all accounts they have increased by at least the same magnitude, and now total hundreds of millions of dollars per year. Even greater are the expenditures at lower levels of government. In a 1987 study for the U.S. Customs Service by Wharton Econometrics, state and local police were estimated to have devoted 18 percent of their total investigative resources, or close to five billion dollars, to drug-enforcement activities in 1986. This represented a 19 percent increase over the previous year's expenditures. All told, 1987 expenditures on all aspects of drug enforcement, from drug eradication in foreign countries to imprisonment of drug users and dealers in the United States, totaled at least ten billion dollars.

Of course, even ten billion dollars a year pales in comparison with expenditures on military defense. Of greater concern than the actual expenditures, however, has been the diversion of limited resources—including the time and energy of judges, prosecutors, and law-enforcement agents, as well as scarce prison space—from the prosecution and punishment of criminal activities that harm far more innocent victims than do violations of the drug laws. Drug-law violators account for approximately 10 percent of the roughly 800,000 inmates in state prisons and local jails, and more than one-third of the 44,000 federal prison inmates. These proportions are expected to increase in coming years, even as total prison populations continue to rise dramatically. (The total number of state and federal prison inmates in 1975 was under 250,000; in 1980 it was 350,000; and in 1987 it was 575,000. The projected total for 2000 is one million.) Among the 40,000 inmates in New York State prisons, drug-law violations surpassed first-degree robbery in 1987 as the number one cause of incarceration, accounting for 20 percent of the total prison population. The U.S. Sentencing Commission has estimated that, largely as a consequence of the Anti–Drug Abuse Act passed by Congress in 1986, the proportion of federal inmates incarcerated for drug violations will rise from one-third of the 44,000 prisoners sentenced to federal-prison terms today to one-half of the 100,000 to 150,000 federal prisoners anticipated in fifteen years. The direct costs of building and maintaining enough prisons to house this growing population are rising at an astronomical rate. The opportunity costs, in terms of alternative social expenditures foregone and other types of criminals not imprisoned, are even greater. (It should be emphasized that the numbers cited do not include the many inmates sentenced for "drug-related" crimes such as acts of violence committed by drug dealers, typically against one another, and robberies committed to earn the money needed to pay for illegal drugs.)

During each of the last few years, police made about 750,000 for violations of the drug laws. Slightly more than three-quarters of these have not been for manufacturing or dealing drugs, but solely for possession of an illicit drug, typically marijuana. (Those arrested, it is worth noting, represent little more than 2 percent of the thirty million Americans estimated to have used an illegal drug during the past year.) On the one hand, this has clogged urban criminal-justice systems: in New York City, drug-law violations last year accounted for more than 40 percent of all felony indictments-up from 25 percent in 1985; in Washington, D.C., the figure was more than 50 percent. On the other hand, it has distracted criminal-justice officials from concentrating greater resources on violent offenses and property crimes. In many cities, law enforcement has become virtually synonymous with drug enforcement.

Drug laws typically have two effects on the market in illicit drugs. The first is to restrict the general availability and accessibility of illicit drugs, especially in locales where underground drug markets are small and isolated from the community. The second is increase, often significantly, the price of illicit drugs to consumers. Since the costs of producing most illicit drugs are not much different from the costs of alcohol, tobacco, and coffee, most of the price paid for illicit substances is in effect a value-added tax created by their criminalization, which is enforced and supplemented by the law-enforcement establishment, but collected by the drug traffickers. A report by Wharton Econometrics for the President's Commission on Organized Crime identified the sale of illicit drugs as the source of more than half of all organized crime revenues in 1986, with the marijuana and heroin business each providing over seven billion, and the cocaine business over thirteen billion. By contrast, revenues from cigarette bootlegging, which persists principally because of differences among states in their cigarette-tax rates, were estimated at 290 million dollars. If the marijuana, cocaine, and heroin markets were legal, state and federal governments would collect billions of dollars annually in tax revenues. Instead, they expend billions on what amounts to a subsidy of organized crime and unorganized criminals.

DRUGS AND CRIME

The drug/crime connection is one that continues to resist coherent analysis, both because cause and effect are so difficult to distinguish and because the role of the drug-prohibition laws in causing and labeling "drug-related crime" is so often ignored. There are four possible connections between drugs and crime, at least three of which would be much diminished if the drug-prohibition laws were repealed. First, producing, selling, buying, and consuming strictly controlled and banned substances is itself a crime that occurs billions of times each year in the United States alone. In the absence of drug-prohibition laws, these activities would obviously cease to be crimes. Selling drugs to children would, of course, continue to be criminal, and other evasions of government regulation of a legal market would continue to be prosecuted; but by and large the drug/crime connection that now accounts for all of the criminal-justice costs noted above would be severed.

Second, many illicit-drug users commit crimes such as robbery and burglary, as well as drug dealing, prostitution, and numbers running, to earn enough money to purchase the relatively high-priced illicit drugs. Unlike the millions of alcoholics who can support their habits for relatively modest amounts, many cocaine and heroin addicts spend hundreds and even thousands of dollars a week. If the drugs to which they are addicted were significantly cheaper-which would be the case if they were legalized-the number of crimes committed by drug addicts to pay for their habits would, in all likelihood, decline dramatically. Even if a legal-drug policy included the imposition of relatively high consumption taxes in order to discourage consumption, drug prices would probably still be lower than they are today.

The third drug/crime connection is the commission of crimes-violent crimes in particular-by people under the influence of illicit drugs. This connection seems to have the greatest impact upon the popular imagination. Clearly, some drugs do "cause" some people to commit crimes by reducing normal inhibitions, unleashing aggressive and other antisocial tendencies, and lessening the sense of responsibility. Cocaine, particularly in the form of crack, has gained such a reputation in recent years, just as heroin did in the 1960s and 1970s, and marijuana did in the years before that. Crack's reputation for inspiring violent behavior may or may not be more deserved than those of marijuana and heroin; reliable evidence is not yet available. No illicit drug, however, is as widely associated with violent behavior as alcohol. According to Justice Department statistics, 54 percent of all jail inmates convicted of violent crimes in 1983 reported having used alcohol just prior to committing their offense. The impact of drug legalization on this drug/crime connection is the most difficult to predict. Much would depend on overall rates of drug abuse and changes in the nature of consumption, both of which are impossible to predict. It is worth noting, however, that a shift in consumption from alcohol to marijuana would almost certainly contribute to a decline in violent behavior.

The fourth drug/crime link is the violent, intimidating, and corrupting behavior of the drug traffickers. Illegal markets tend to breed violence not only because they attract criminally-minded individuals, but also because participants in the market have no resort to legal institutions to resolve their disputes. During Prohibition, violent struggles between bootlegging gangs and hijackings of booze-laden trucks and sea vessels were frequent and notorious occurrences. Today's equivalents are the booby traps that surround some marijuana fields, the pirates of the Caribbean looking to rip off drug-laden vessels en route to the shores of the United States, and the machinegun battles and executions carried out by drug lords—all of which occasionally kill innocent people. Most law-enforcement officials agree that the dramatic increases in urban murder rates during the past few years can be explained almost entirely by the rise in drug-dealer killings.

Perhaps the most unfortunate victims of the drug-prohibition policies have been the law-abiding residents of America's ghettos. These policies have largely proven futile in deterring large numbers of ghetto dwellers from becoming drug abusers, but they do account for much of what ghetto residents identify as the drug problem. In many neighborhoods, it often seems to be the aggressive gun-toting drug dealers who upset lawabiding residents far more than the addicts nodding out in doorways. Other residents, however, perceive the drug dealers as heroes and successful role models. In impoverished neighborhoods, they often stand out as symbols of success to children who see no other options. At the same time, the increasingly harsh criminal penalties imposed on adult drug dealers have led to the widespread recruitment of juveniles by drug traffickers. Formerly, children started dealing drugs only after they had been using them for a while; today the sequence is often reversed: many children start using illegal drugs now only after working for drug dealers. And the juvenile-justice system offers no realistic options for dealing with this growing problem.

The conspicuous failure of law-enforcement agencies to deal with this drug/crime connection is probably most responsible for the demoralization of neighborhoods and police departments alike. Intensive police crackdowns in urban neighborhoods do little more than chase the menace a short distance away to infect new areas. By contrast, legalization of the drug market would drive the drug-dealing business off the streets and out of the apartment buildings, and into legal, government-regulated, taxpaying stores. It would also force many of the gun-toting dealers out of business, and would convert others into legitimate businessmen. Some, of course, would turn to other types of criminal activities, just as some of the bootleggers did following Prohibition's repeal. Gone, however, would be the unparalleled financial temptations that lure so many people from all sectors of society into the drug-dealing business.

THE COSTS OF CORRUPTION

All vice-control efforts are particularly susceptible to corruption, but none so much as drug enforcement. When police accept bribes from drug dealers, no victim exists to complain to the authorities. Even when police extort money and drugs from traffickers and dealers, the latter are in no position to report the corrupt officers. What makes drug enforcement especially vulnerable to corruption are the tremendous amounts of money involved in the business. Today many law-enforcement officials believe that police corruption is more pervasive than at any time since Prohibition. In Miami, dozens of law-enforcement officials have been charged with accepting bribes, stealing from drug dealers, and even dealing drugs themselves. Throughout many small towns and rural communities in Georgia, where drug smugglers en route from Mexico, the Caribbean, and Latin America drop their loads of cocaine and marijuana, dozens of sheriffs have been implicated in drug-related corruption. In New York, drug-related corruption in one Brooklyn police precinct has generated the city s most far-reaching police corruption scandal since the l960s. More than a hundred cases of drug-related corruption are now prosecuted each year in state and federal courts. Every one of the federal law-enforcement agencies charged with drug-enforcement responsibilities has seen an agent implicated in drug-related corruption.

It is not difficult to explain the growing pervasiveness of drug-related corruption. The financial temptations are enormous relative required. Many police officers are demoralized by the scope of the drug traffic, their sense that maybe citizens are indifferent, and the fact that many sectors of society do not even appreciate their efforts—as well as the fact that many drug dealers who are arrested do not remain in prison. Some police also recognize that that enforcing the drug laws does not protect the victims from predators so much as it regulates an illicit market that cannot be suppressed, but can be kept underground. In every respect, the analogy to prohibition is apt. Repealing the drug-prohibition laws would dramatically reduce police corruption. By contrast the measures being proposed to deal with the growing problem, including better funding and more aggressive internal investigations, offer relatively little promise.

Among the most difficult costs to evaluate are those that relate to the widespread defiance of the drug-prohibition laws: the effects of labeling as criminals the tens of millions of people who use drugs illicitly, subjecting them to the risks of criminal sanction, and obliging many of these same people to enter into relationships with drug dealers (who may be criminals in many more senses of the word) in order to purchase their drugs; the cynicism that such laws generate toward other laws and the law in general; and the sense of hostility and suspicion that many otherwise law-abiding individuals feel toward law-enforcement officials. It was costs such as these that strongly influenced many of Prohibition's more conservative opponents.

PHYSICAL AND MORAL COSTS

Perhaps the most paradoxical consequence of the drug laws is tremendous harm they cause to the millions of drug users who not been deterred from using illicit drugs in the first place. Nothing resembling an underground Food and Drug Administration arisen to impose quality control on the illegal-drug market provide users with accurate information on the drugs they consume. Imagine that Americans could not tell whether a bottle of wine contained 6 percent, 30 percent, or 90 percent alcohol, whether or an aspirin tablet contained 5 or 500 grams of aspirin. Imagine, too, that no controls existed to prevent winemakers from selling their product with methanol and other dangerous impurities that vineyards and tobacco fields were fertilized with harmful substances by ignorant growers and sprayed with poisonous herbicides by government agents. Fewer people would use such substances, but more of those who did would get sick. Some would die.

The above scenario describes, of course, the current state of the illicit drug market. Many marijuana smokers are worse off for having smoked cannabis that was grown with dangerous fertilizers, sprayed with the herbicide paraquat, or mixed with more dangerous substances. Consumers of heroin and the various synthetic substances sold on the street face even severer consequences, including fatal overdoses and poisonings from unexpectedly potent or impure drug supplies. More often than not, the quality of a drug addict's life depends greatly upon his or her access to reliable supplies. Drug-enforcement operations that succeed in temporarily disrupting supply networks are thus a double-edged sword: they encourage some addicts to seek admission into drug-treatment programs, but they oblige others to seek out new and hence less reliable suppliers; the result is that more, not fewer, drug-related emergencies and deaths occur.

Today, over 50 percent of all people with AIDS in New York City, New Jersey, and many other parts of the country, as well as the vast majority of AIDS-infected heterosexuals throughout the country, have contracted the disease directly or indirectly through illegal intravenous drug use. Reports have emerged of drug dealers beginning to provide clean syringes together with their illegal drugs. But even as other governments around the world actively attempt to limit the spread of AIDS by and among drug users by instituting free syringe-exchange programs, state and municipal governments in the United States resist following suit, arguing that to do so would "encourage" or "condone" the use of illegal drugs. Only in January 1988 did New York City approve such a program on a very limited and experimental basis. At the same time, drug treatment programs remain notoriously underfunded, turning away tens of thousands of addicts seeking help, even as billions of dollars more are spent to arrest, prosecute, and imprison illegal drug sellers and users. In what may represent a sign of shifting priorities, the President's Commission on AIDS, in its March 1988 report, emphasized the importance of making drug-treatment programs available to all in need of them. In all likelihood, however, the criminal justice agencies will continue to receive the greatest share of drug control funds.

Most Americans perceive the drug problem as a moral issue and draw a moral distinction between use of the illicit drugs and use of alcohol and tobacco. Yet when one subjects this distinction to reasonable analysis, it quickly disintegrates. The most consistent moral perspective of those who favor drug laws is that of the Mormons and Puritans, who regard as immoral any intake of substances to alter one's state of consciousness or otherwise cause pleasure: they not only the illicit drugs and alcohol, but also tobacco, caffeine, even chocolate. The vast majority of Americans are so consistent with respect to the propriety of their pleasures. Yet once one acknowledges that there is nothing immoral about drinking alcohol or smoking tobacco for non-medicinal purposes, it is difficult to condemn the consumption of marijuana, cocaine, and other substances on moral grounds. The "moral" condemnation of some substances and not others proves to be little more than a prejudice in favor of some drugs and against others.

The same false distinction is drawn with respect to those who provide psychoactive substances to users and abusers alike. If degrees of morality were measured by the levels of harm caused by one's products, the "traffickers" in tobacco and alcohol would be vilified as the evil of all substance purveyors. That they are perceived as respected members of our community, while providers of more dangerous illicit substances are punished with long prison sentences, says much about the prejudices of most Americans with respect to psychoactive substances, but little about the morality or immorality of their activities.

Much of the same is true of gun salesmen. Most of the consumers of products use them safely; a minority, however, end up shooting themselves or someone else. Can we hold the gun salesman morally culpable for the harm that probably would not have occurred but for his existence? Most people say no, except perhaps the salesman clearly knew that his product would be used to commit a crime. Yet in the case of those who sell illicit substances to willing customers, the providers are deemed not only legally guilty but also morally reprehensible. The law does not require any demonstration that the dealer knew of a specific harm to follow; indeed, it does not require any evidence at all of harm having resulted from the sale. Rather, the law is predicated on the assumption that harm will inevitably follow. Despite the patent falsity of that assumption, it persist as the underlying justification for the drug laws.

Although a valid moral distinction cannot be drawn between the licit and the illicit psychoactive substances, one can point to a different kind of moral justification for the drug laws: they arguably reflect paternalistic obligation to protect those in danger of succumbing to their own weaknesses. If drugs were legally available, most people would either abstain from using them or would use them responsibly and in moderation. A minority without self-restraint, however, would end up harming themselves if the substances were more readily available. Therefore, the majority has a moral obligation to deny itself legal access to certain substances because of the plight of the minority. This obligation is presumably greatest when children are included among the minority.

At least in principle, this argument seems to provide the strongest moral justification for the drug laws. But ultimately the moral quality of laws must be judged not by how those laws are intended to work in principle, but by how they function in practice. When laws intended to serve a moral end inflict great damage on innocent parties, we must rethink our moral position.

Because drug-law violations do not create victims with an interest in notifying the police, drug-enforcement agents rely heavily on undercover operations, electronic surveillance, and information provided by informants. These techniques are indispensable to effective law enforcement, but they are also among the least palatable investigative methods employed by the police. The same is true of drug testing: it may be useful and even necessary for determining liability in accidents, but it also threatens and undermines the right of privacy to which many Americans believe they are entitled. There are good reasons for requiring that such measures be used sparingly.

Equally disturbing are the increasingly vocal calls for people to inform not only on drug dealers but also on neighbors, friends, and even family members who use illicit drugs. Government calls on people not only to "just say no," but also to report those who have not heeded the message. Intolerance of illicit-drug use and users is heralded not only as an indispensable ingredient in the war against drugs, but also as a mark of good citizenship. Certainly every society requires citizens to assist in the enforcement of criminal laws. But societies-particularly democratic and pluralistic ones-also rely strongly on an ethic of tolerance toward those who are different but do no harm to others. Overzealous enforcement of the drug laws risks undermining that ethic, and encouraging the creation of a society of informants. This results in an immorality that is far more dangerous in its own way than that associated with the use of illicit drugs.

THE BENEFITS OF LEGALIZATION

Repealing the drug-prohibition laws promises tremendous advantages. Between reduced government expenditures on enforcing drug laws and new tax revenue from legal drug production and sales, public treasuries would enjoy a net benefit of at least ten billion dollars year, and possibly much more. The quality of urban life would rise significantly. Homicide rates would decline. So would robbery and burglary rates. Organized criminal groups, particularly newer ones that have yet to diversify out of drugs, would be dealt a devastating setback. The police, prosecutors, and courts would focus their resources on combating the types of crimes that we cannot walk away from. More ghetto residents would turn their backs on criminal careers and seek out legitimate opportunities instead. And the health and quality of life of many drug users—and drug abusers—would improve significantly.

All the benefits of legalization would be for naught, however, if millions more Americans were to become drug abusers. Our experience with alcohol and tobacco provides ample warnings. Today, alcohol is consumed by 140 million Americans and tobacco by 50 million. All of the health costs associated with abuse of the illicit drugs pale in comparison with those resulting from tobacco and alcohol abuse. In 1986, for example, alcohol was identified as a contributing factor in 10 percent of work-related injuries, 40 percent of the suicide attempts, and about 40 percent of the approximately 46,000 annual traffic deaths in 1983. An estimated eighteen million Americans are reported to be either alcoholics or alcohol abusers. The cost of alcohol abuse to American society is estimated at over 100 billion dollars annually. Alcohol has been identified as the direct cause of 80,000 to 100,000 deaths annually, and as a contributing factor in an additional 100,000 deaths. The health costs of tobacco use are of similar magnitude. In the United States alone, an estimated 320,000 people die prematurely each year as a consequence of their consumption of tobacco. By comparison, the National Council on Alcoholism reported that only 3,562 people were known have died in 1985 from use of all illegal drugs combined. Even if we assume that thousands more deaths were related in one way or another to illicit drug abuse but not reported as such, we are still left the conclusion that all of the health costs of marijuana, and, and heroin combined amount to only a small fraction of those caused by tobacco and alcohol.

Most Americans are just beginning to recognize the extensive costs of alcohol and tobacco abuse. At the same time, they seem to believe that there is something fundamentally different about alcohol and tobacco that supports the legal distinction between those two substances, on the one hand, and the illicit ones, on the other. The most common distinction is based on the assumption that the illicit drugs are more dangerous than the licit ones. Cocaine, heroin, the various hallucinogens, and (to a lesser extent) marijuana are widely perceived as, in the words of the President's Commission on Organized Crime, "inherently destructive to mind and body." They are also believed to be more addictive and more likely to cause dangerous and violent behavior than alcohol and tobacco.

All use of illicit drugs is therefore thought to be abusive; in other words, the distinction between use and abuse of psychoactive substances that most people recognize with respect to alcohol is not acknowledged with respect to the illicit substances. Most Americans make the fallacious assumption that the government would not criminalize certain psychoactive substances if they were not in fact dangerous. They then jump to the conclusion that any use of those substances is a form of abuse. The government, in its effort to discourage people from using illicit drugs, has encouraged and perpetuated these misconceptions-not only in its rhetoric but also in its purportedly educational materials. Only by reading between the lines can one discern the fact that the vast majority of Americans who have used illicit drugs have done so in moderation, that relatively few have suffered negative short-term consequences and that few are likely to suffer long-term harm.

The evidence is most persuasive with respect to marijuana. U.S. drug-enforcement and health agencies do not even report figures on marijuana-related deaths, apparently because so few occur. Although there are good health reasons for children, pregnant women, and some others not to smoke marijuana, there still appears to be little evidence that occasional marijuana consumption does much harm. Certainly, it is not healthy to inhale marijuana smoke into one's lungs; indeed, the National Institute on Drug Abuse (NIDA) has declared that "marijuana smoke contains more cancer-causing agents than is found in tobacco smoke." On the other hand, the number of joints smoked by all but a very small percentage of marijuana smokers is a tiny fraction of the twenty cigarettes a day smoked by the average cigarette smoker; indeed, the average may be closer to one or two joints a week than one or two a day. Note that NIDA defines a "heavy" marijuana smoker as one who consumes at least two joints "daily." A heavy tobacco smoker, by contrast, smokes about forty cigarettes a day.

Nor is marijuana strongly identified as a dependence-causing substance. A 1982 survey of marijuana use by young adults (eighteen to twenty-five years old) found that 64 percent had tried marijuana at least once, that 42 percent had used it at least ten times, that 27 percent had smoked in the last month. It also found that 21 percent had passed through a period during which they smoked "frequently" (defined as twenty or more days per month), but that only one-third of those currently smoked "daily" and only one-fifth (about 4 percent of all young adults) could be described as heavy daily users (averaging two or more joints per day). This suggests that daily marijuana use is typically a phase through which people pass, after which their use becomes more moderate.

Marijuana has also been attacked as the "gateway drug" that leads people to the use of even more dangerous illegal drugs. It is true that people who have smoked marijuana are more likely than people who have not to try, use, and abuse other illicit substances. is also true that people who have smoked tobacco or drunk alcohol more likely than those who have not to experiment with illicit drugs and to become substance abusers. The reasons are obvious enough. Familiarity with smoking cigarettes, for instance, removes one of the major barriers to smoking marijuana, which is the experience of inhaling smoke into one's lungs. Similarly, familiarity with ring one's state of consciousness by consuming psychoactive stances such as alcohol or marijuana decreases the fear and increases the curiosity regarding other substances and "highs." But the evidence also indicates that there is nothing inevitable about the process. The great majority of people who have smoked marijuana do not become substance abusers of either legal or illegal substances. At the same time, it is certainly true that many of those who do become substance abusers after using marijuana would have become abusers even if they had never smoked a joint in their life.

DEALING WITH DRUGS' DANGERS

The dangers associated with cocaine, heroin, the hallucinogens, and other illicit substances are greater than those posed by marijuana, but not nearly so great as many people seem to think. Consider the case of cocaine. In 1986 NIDA reported that over 20 million Americans had tried cocaine, that 12.2 million had consumed it at least once during 1985, and that nearly 5.8 million had used it with the past month. Among those between the ages of eighteen and twenty-five, 8.2 million had tried cocaine, 5.3 million had used it within the past year, 2.5 million had used it within the past month, and 250,000 had used it weekly. Extrapolation might suggest that a quarter of a million young Americans are potential problem users. But one could also conclude that only 3 percent of those between the ages of eighteen and twenty-five who had ever tried the drug fell into that category, and that only 10 percent of those who had used cocaine monthly were at risk. (The NIDA survey did not, it should be noted, include people residing in military or student dormitories, prison inmates, or the homeless.)

All of this is not to deny that cocaine is a potentially dangerous drug, especially when it is injected, smoked in the form of crack, or consumed in tandem with other powerful substances. Clearly, tens of thousands of Americans have suffered severely from their abuse of cocaine, and a tiny fraction have died. But there is also overwhelming evidence that most users of cocaine do not get into trouble with the drug. So much of the media attention has focused on the small percentage of cocaine users who become addicted that the popular perception of how most people use cocaine has become badly distorted. In one survey of high school seniors' drug use, the researchers questioned recent cocaine users, asking whether they had ever tried to stop using cocaine and found that they couldn't. Only 3.8 percent responded affirmatively, in contrast to the almost 7 percent of marijuana smokers who said they had tried to stop and found they couldn't, and the 18 percent of cigarette smokers who answered similarly. Although a similar survey of adult users would probably reveal a higher proportion of cocaine addicts, evidence such as this suggests that only a small percentage of people who use cocaine end up having a problem with it. In this respect, most people differ from monkeys, who have demonstrated in experiments that they will starve themselves to death if provided with unlimited cocaine.

With respect to the hallucinogens such as LSD and psilocybic mushrooms, their potential for addiction is virtually nil. The dangers arise primarily from using them irresponsibly on individual occasions. Although many of those who have used one or another of the hallucinogens have experienced "bad trips," others have reported positive experiences, and very few have suffered any long-term harm.

Perhaps no drugs are regarded with as much horror as the opiates, and in particular heroin, which is a concentrated form of morphine. As with most drugs, heroin can be eaten, snorted, smoked, or injected. Most Americans, unfortunately, prefer injection. There is no question that heroin is potentially highly addictive, perhaps as addictive as nicotine. But despite the popular association of heroin use with the most down-and-out inhabitants of urban ghettos, heroin does relatively little physical harm to the human body. Consumed occasional or regular basis under sanitary conditions, its side effect, apart from addiction itself, is constipation. That is one reason why many doctors in early twentieth-century America rate addiction as preferable to alcoholism, and prescribed the as treatment for the latter when abstinence did not seem a option.

It is important to think about the illicit drugs in the same way talk about alcohol and tobacco. Like tobacco, many of the illicit substances are highly addictive, but can be consumed on a regular or decades without any demonstrable harm. Like alcohol, the substances can be, and are, used by most consumers in moderation, with little in the way of harmful effects; but like alcohol also lend themselves to abuse by a minority of users who become addicted or otherwise harm themselves or others as a consequence. And as is the case with both the legal substances, the active effects of the various illegal drugs vary greatly from one person to another. To be sure, the pharmacology of the substance is important, as is its purity and the manner in which it is needed. But much also depends upon not only the physiology and psychology of the consumer, but also his expectations regarding the drug, his social milieu, and the broader cultural environment—what Harvard University psychiatrist Norman Zinberg has called the "set and setting" of the drug. It is factors such as these that change dramatically, albeit in indeterminate ways, were the drugs made legally available.

CAN LEGALIZATION WORK?

It is thus impossible to predict whether legalization would lead to greater levels of drug abuse, and exact costs comparable to that of alcohol and tobacco abuse. The lessons that can be drawn from other societies are mixed. China's experience with the British pushers of the nineteenth century, when millions became led to the drug, offers one worst-case scenario. The devastation many native American tribes by alcohol presents another. On the other hand, the legal availability of opium and cannabis in Asian societies did not result in large addict populations until recently. Indeed, in many countries U.S.-inspired opium bans imposed during the past few decades have paradoxically contributed to dramatic increases in heroin consumption among Asian youth. In the United States, the decriminalization of marijuana by about a dozen states during the 1970s did not lead to increases in marijuana consumption. In the Netherlands, which went even further in decriminalizing cannabis during the 1970s, consumption has actually declined significantly. The policy has succeeded, as the government intended, in making drug use boring. Finally, late nineteenth-century America was a society in which there were almost no drug laws or even drug regulations-but levels of drug use then were about what they are today. Drug abuse was considered a serious problem, but the criminal-justice system was not regarded as part of the solution.

There are, however, reasons to believe that none of the currently illicit substances would become as popular as alcohol or tobacco, even if they were legalized. Alcohol has long been the principal intoxicant in most societies, including many in which other substances have been legally available. Presumably, its diverse properties account for its popularity-it quenches thirst, goes well with food, and promotes appetite as well as sociability. The popularity of tobacco probably stems not just from its powerful addictive qualities, but from the fact that its psychoactive effects are sufficiently subtle that cigarettes can be integrated with most other human activities. The illicit substances do not share these qualities to the same extent, nor is it likely that they would acquire them if they were legalized. Moreover, none of the illicit substances can compete with alcohol's special place in American culture and history.

An additional advantage of the illicit drugs is that none of them appears to be as insidious as either alcohol or tobacco. Consumed in their more benign forms, few of the illicit substances are as damaging to the human body over the long term as alcohol and tobacco, and none is as strongly linked with violent behavior as alcohol. On the other hand, much of the damage caused today by illegal drugs stems from their consumption in particularly dangerous ways. There is good reason to doubt that many Americans would inject cocaine or heroin into their veins even if given the chance to do so legally. And just as the dramatic growth in the heroin-consuming population during the 1960s leveled off for reasons apparently having little to do with law enforcement, so we can expect a leveling-off—which may already have begun—in the number of people smoking crack. The logic of legalization thus depends upon two assumptions: that most illegal drugs are not so dangerous as is commonly believed; and that the drugs and methods of consumption that are most risky are unlikely to prove appealing to many people, precisely because they are so obviously dangerous.

Perhaps the most reassuring reason for believing that repeal of the drug-prohibition laws will not lead to tremendous increases in drug-abuse levels is the fact that we have learned something from our past experiences with alcohol and tobacco abuse. We now , for instance, that consumption taxes are an effective method of limiting consumption rates. We also know that restrictions and bans on advertising, as well as a campaign of negative advertising, can make a difference. The same is true of other government measures including restrictions on time and place of sale, prohibition of consumption in public places, packaging requirements, mandated adjustments in insurance policies, crackdowns on driving while under the influence, and laws holding bartenders and hosts responsible for the drinking of customers and guests. There is even some evidence that government-sponsored education programs about the dangers of cigarette smoking have deterred many children from beginning to smoke.

Clearly it is possible to avoid repeating the mistakes of the past in designing an effective plan for legalization. We know more about legal drugs now than we knew about alcohol when Prohibition repealed, or about tobacco when the anti-tobacco laws were red by many states in the early years of this century. Moreover, we can and must avoid having effective drug-control policies undermined by powerful lobbies like those that now protect the interests of alcohol and tobacco producers. We are also in a far better position than we were sixty years ago to prevent organized criminals from finding and creating new opportunities when their most lucrative source of income dries up.

It is important to stress what legalization is not. It is not a capitulation to the drug dealers—but rather a means to put them out of business. It is not an endorsement of drug use—but rather a recognition of the rights of adult Americans to make their own choices of the fear of criminal sanctions. It is not a repudiation of the "just say no" approach-but rather an appeal to government to provide assistance and positive inducements, not criminal penalties and a repressive measures, in support of that approach. It is not even a call for the elimination of the criminal-justice system from drug regulation—but rather a proposal for the redirection of its efforts and attention.

There is no question that legalization is a risky policy, since it may lead to an increase in the number of people who abuse drugs. But that is a risk—not a certainty. At the same time, current drug control policies are falling and new proposals promise only to be more costly and more repressive. We know that repealing the drug prohibition laws would eliminate or greatly reduce many of the ills that people commonly identify as part and parcel of the "drug problem." Yet legalization is repeatedly and vociferously dismissed, without any attempt to evaluate it openly and objectively. The past twenty years have demonstrated that a drug policy shaped by exaggerated rhetoric designed to arouse fear has only led to our current disaster. Unless we are willing to honestly evaluate our options, including various legalization strategies, we will run a still greater risk: we may never find the best solution for our drug problems.

Note

Read carefully the language of Ethan Nadelmann's essay and notice the date. The text was written in 1988, several years before the turn to a "harm reduction" approach to discussing drugs. Contrast that language with the following passage from a *Washington Post* editorial, also by Ethan Nadelmann, titled *Learning to Live With Drugs* and published on November 2, 1999:

> Pointing to the harms that flow from our prohibitionist policies is not the same as advocating drug legalization, however. The more sensible and realistic approach today would be one based on the principles of "harm reduction." It's a policy that seeks to reduce the negative consequences of both drug use and drug prohibition, acknowledging that both are likely to persist for the foreseeable future.

What do you think accounts for the change in rhetoric from "legalization" to "harm reduction"?

In the debate over "harm reduction," the costs and benefits of both drug enforcement and the war on drugs need to be evaluated. Courts are in a difficult position to assess these costs and benefits rigorously and often simply assume that drug enforcement is cost-effective.

So, for instance, in *Edmond v. City of Indianapolis*, 183 F.3d 659 (7th Cir. 1999), aff'd 531 U.S. 32 (2000), Chief Judge Richard Posner reviews the constitutionality of police road1blocks intended to detect drug contraband set up by the Indianapolis police department in 1998. Over the course of the program, 1,161 vehicles were stopped. The stops produced 55 drug-related arrests and 49 non-drug related arrests (for offenses such as driving with an expired driver's license), resulting in a 4.74 percent drug-arrest hit rate and an overall hit rate of 8.96 percent. The roadblocks were perceived as successful in detecting illicit drug and other criminal violations. Chief Judge Posner repeatedly refers to the resulting hit rate as "high" and adds that it is "vastly higher than, for example, the probability of a hit as a result of the screening of embarking passengers and their luggage at airports." *Id*. at 662. Although there is no factual basis in the record, Posner goes on to state that "the deterrence of drug offenses produced *by these hits* advances the strong national, state, and local policy of discouraging the illegal use of controlled substances." *Id*. (emphasis added). This is relatively typical in judicial assessment of the costs and benefits of drug enforcement.

Incidentally, it is worth noting that the 0.0474 drug hit rate in Indianapolis—or, for that matter, the 0.0896 overall hit rate including minor traffic violations—is not really that high. Hit rates from other law enforcement interventions have been far greater. For example, the Maryland state patrol between January 1995 and January 1999 achieved drug hit rates along Maryland's I–95 corridor of 32% with regard to white drivers and 34% with regard to African–American drivers.[1] In Missouri for the year 2001, police traffic stops achieved drug hit rates of 19.7, 12.3 and 9.8 percent respectively for whites, African–Americans, and Hispanics.[2] A 1982 Department of Justice study of airport searches using a drug-courier profile reported 49 successful searches based on 96 total searches, for a hit rate of 51.04%.[3] A

1. Bernard E. Harcourt, *Rethinking Racial Profiling: A Critique of the Economics, Civil Liberties, and Constitutional Literature, and of Criminal Profiling More Generally*, 71 The University of Chicago Law Review, 1275, 1292 (2004).

2. *Id*. at 1293.

3. Bernard E. Harcourt, *Against Prediction: Profiling, Policing and Punishing in an Actuarial Age* (2007).

government report analyzing New York City stop-and-frisks, prepared in 1999, revealed average hit rates (stop-to-arrest) of approximately 13.7 percent in situations found to present reasonable suspicion.[4] In the abstract, devoid of any comparative evidence about search success rates in other contexts, the 4.74 percent drug hit rate may well seem "high;" however, that may be an artifact of judicial decision-making with no data, a perennial problem in constitutional criminal procedure.[5]

JOHN KAPLAN—TAKING DRUGS SERIOUSLY

The Public Interest, 92:32–50, 1988.

It would be difficult to deny that the efforts and resources expended in our attempt to prevent the production of heroin and cocaine in other countries, and to keep out of the United States those drugs that are produced, have passed the point of diminishing returns. The outcry over drugs in the newspapers and on the political hustings, and a look at what is occurring in many public-housing projects and in the large lower-class black and Hispanic neighborhoods of our central cities, should be enough to convince sober observers that our present drugs policies have simply not been successful enough.

Of course, there are politicians who still argue that our drug problems can be substantially improved by further attempts to push the Colombian, Mexican, Burmese and other governments toward greater efforts. But with the military and internal strength they have at their disposal, they are doing about as well as one could expect.

Nor is the related demand to increase the use of our army or navy to stop drug smuggling a more likely source of improvement. The ingenuity of smugglers, the tremendous volume of legitimate trade, and the huge number of individuals crossing our borders make it impracticable to achieve the kind of increases in the interdiction rate that would make heroin and cocaine significantly less available or more expensive in the United States.

The problem, then, for those who realize that our present efforts have bogged down, is what to do. In this respect, drug policy must proceed by elimination. None of the policy options is attractive. All involve great costs—either in expenditures on law enforcement or in damage to public health. Since no option is without severe disadvantages, we can aim only to choose the policy that is least bad.

At one level, the simplest solution would be simply to get out of the way, legalize heroin and cocaine, and allow their sale as we do alcohol's. Until recently, this was rarely advocated in print, though for years one

4. Tracey L. Meares and Bernard E. Harcourt, *Foreword: Transparent Adjudication and Social Science Research in Constitutional Criminal Procedure*, 90 Journal of Criminal Law and Criminology 733 (2000).

5. For an argument proposing increased use of social science evidence in constitutional criminal procedure, *see* Tracey L. Meares and Bernard E. Harcourt, *Foreword: Transparent Adjudication and Social Science Research in Constitutional Criminal Procedure*, 90 Journal of Criminal Law and Criminology 733 (2000).

would hear such recommendations in private conversation with intellectuals. Now, however, the legalization movement is becoming respectable, and even popular.

A Repeal of Drug Prohibition?

Probably the central problem with the solution of legalization is that it ignores basic pharmacology. There is such a thing as a dangerous drug, and both heroin and cocaine undoubtedly fall into this category. It is here, of course, that the alcohol analogy is usually brought up. The analogy is indeed suggestive, because alcohol is by any standard a dangerous drug as well. And when we repealed Prohibition, we replaced a legal ban on alcohol similar to that now imposed on heroin and cocaine with a system of legal, controlled sale, presumably much like that contemplated for heroin and cocaine. There is no doubt that legalization has attractions. When Prohibition was repealed, the enormous inflow of profits to organized crime and the large-scale corruption of public officials caused by the illegal alcohol traffic dropped sharply. And the large number of civil-liberties violations by Prohibition agents ceased as well.

Several factors, however, made the repeal of Prohibition a much better social decision than would be the case with heroin or cocaine. Hard as it is to believe, the social cost of maintaining Prohibition was not only greater than that which heroin and cocaine currently impose upon us, it was even greater than that imposed by what is now our greatest drug problem—alcohol. Although the addict criminality caused by the high price of heroin and cocaine seems to have had no counterpart in the case of alcohol, the strain on our institutions was far greater. Corruption in the United States during Prohibition approximated that which we now associate with many Third World countries. It is true that the heroin and cocaine trades have corrupted many local police, some prosecutors, and a few local judges. During Prohibition, however, things were much worse. Federal judges, federal and state prosecutors, and countless politicians—from congressmen and state governors to mayors, city councilmen, and chiefs of police—were in the pay of bootleggers.

Part of the difference is due to the passage of time. Wave upon wave of reform has made our government a far more honest one in the last fifty years. Perhaps more important is the fact that both before and during Prohibition, alcohol use was common among all social classes and in virtually every area of the nation, and had a much better "image" than heroin and cocaine do today. A society where many people in all walks of life considered themselves drinkers made this activity far more respectable than the use of "hard drugs" is today. And, of course, when an activity is more socially acceptable, it becomes easier for government agents to accept bribes and favors to allow it to continue.

The strain and social costs attributed to Prohibition were not the only factors justifying the legalization of alcohol. The majority of drinkers enjoyed the use of alcohol without any harm to themselves or society.

In a sense, the legalization of alcohol represented the willingness of these drinkers to shoulder their share of the social costs of legalized alcohol.

Nonetheless, the example of alcohol control illustrates a basic rule concerning all attempts to minimize the damage caused by habit-forming and destructive drugs. The principle also applies to a number of consensual (somewhat inaccurately called "victimless") crimes, such as gambling and prostitution. When one of these behaviors is made criminal, its enforcement is not particularly effective; it saddles the criminal-justice system with huge costs; it feeds organized crime gangs; it causes official corruption; and it leads to large numbers of violations of civil liberties. Finally, the law does not really solve the problems of those engaging in the activity.

On the other hand, the legalization of the behavior produces an increase in the behavior, which can produce a public-health problem of enormous magnitude. Prohibition, for example, despite its faults—including the fact that it was not strictly enforced—did lower the amount of drinking in the United States. The comparative figures for cirrhosis of the liver demonstrate this clearly. With the repeal of Prohibition, both the number of drinkers and their per capita consumption of alcohol gradually but substantially increased, leading eventually to one of our major public-health problems—alcoholism. According to most estimates, alcoholism results in somewhere between 50,000 and 200,000 deaths per year. And regardless of whether the yearly social cost of alcoholism amounts to forty billion dollars or one hundred and ten billion dollars (two frequently cited figures), no one would deny that the social cost of alcohol use far exceeds that of all illegal drugs together. The issue then is not whether we were correct in legalizing alcohol or tobacco (I would strongly argue that we were), but what we should do about the drugs that were currently illegal.

A Prescription System?

Of course, criminalization and legalization are not the only possibilities. We are probably correct in using a prescription system for valium, for example, which is quite a dangerous drug—but also a useful one. When heroin addicts in England consisted overwhelmingly of middle-aged, middle-class men and women who had become addicted during the course of medical treatment, a prescription system was successfully used to dispense the drug. (Sale without a prescription was a rather serious crime.) However, when an increasingly higher percentage of those addicted came to be more like American addicts—lower-class, criminal, and thrill-seeking—the "British system" was abandoned. England stopped using the prescription system for more than a tiny and diminishing number of addicts, adopted instead a legal-control method much like that used in the United States.

In any event, no one seems to be arguing for a prescription system to control our major illegal drugs. If marijuana, cocaine, and heroin have legitimate medical uses (and the possibility that heroin is better than morphine at relieving intractable pain is the subject of heated debate, with most of the evidence apparently arguing against its superiority), then a prescription system seems most suitable. In fact, this is already being done: we allow prescriptions for medical use of cocaine and THC, the major active ingredient in marijuana.

Though we can regard heroin addiction itself as a disease, and hence a possible candidate for a prescription system, the problems in making such a system work seem insurmountable, as the British have discovered. The sizable pool of non-addicted heroin users forms a ready market for diverted prescribed heroin; the ranks of the addicted would thus swell. (It is impossible for a physician to determine how much heroin an addict really "needs", since this amount varies enormously over time.) Moreover, another drug—methadone—that is available by prescription (although only under certain conditions) is seen, both in the United States and in Britain, as much preferable to heroin for the medical treatment of heroin addiction.

The most important reason, however, why a prescription system for marijuana, cocaine, or heroin is just as inappropriate as it would be for alcohol and tobacco is that people generally use these drugs because they want to, and not to cure their ailments. We may be able to treat them and convince them not to use these drugs, but providing these drugs through prescriptions is not the way to do it.

If the choice for each of the "recreational" drugs is between criminalization and some kind of legalization, then it must be made on a drug-by-drug basis, as was the case with alcohol and tobacco (and coffee, for that matter), taking into account such variables as the pharmacological makeup of each drug and the cost of attempting to suppress it.

This is not an issue to be decided by John Stuart Mill's "simple principle"—that is, by letting each person decide for himself. No nation in the world follows his rule regarding self-harming conduct, and the rule is probably unworkable in a complex, industrial society—particularly one that is a welfare state. Mill's principle, moreover, seems singularly inappropriate when it is applied to a habit-forming, psychoactive drug that alters the user's perspective as to postponement of gratification and his desire for the drug itself.

No Surrender?

On the other hand, certain arguments against legalization are even less impressive. Mill's principle, after all, is on the whole a rather sensible injunction to government, which tends—almost by reflex—to attempt to forbid any activity that it regards as harmful, immoral, or deviant. Far less sensible is the idea, advanced by Jesse Jackson and echoed by A.M. Rosenthal of the *New York Times*, that "you do not win a war by surrendering." Obviously, surrender is sometimes the better course. We did it with alcohol, and, if we go back further, we did it in many states with tobacco. (And in the international arena both we, in

Vietnam, and the Soviet Union, in Afghanistan, seem to have improved our respective positions by abandoning a war.)

The non-pragmatic, no-surrender arguments are often coupled with warnings about the consequences of legalization. Such arguments, however, are insubstantial—particularly when compared with the serious arguments with which we should be grappling. Take Rosenthal's *Times* argument: "How can we continue to fight against alcoholism and tobacco addiction," asks Rosenthal, "if we suddenly say that other drugs—even more dangerous—should be made available?" This is not persuasive. First, virtually every scientist who has looked at the issue would acknowledge that one of the illegal drugs—marijuana—is certainly no more dangerous than alcohol. Second, the argument is a *non sequitur*. Legalizing drugs thought to be more dangerous than alcohol and tobacco might well make it even easier to convince alcohol and tobacco users that legalization does not guarantee that these drugs are safe. The educational message of treating what are patently dangerous drugs the same way we treat alcohol might be valuable for yet another reason. Many people still fail to understand that, by virtually any definition, alcohol is a drug. Treating alcohol the same way we treat cocaine and heroin might help drive this point home to many drinkers.

A similar fallacy lies behind a more common and somewhat more general argument—that legalization of a formerly illegal drug "sends the wrong message" to the public, implying that the drug is safe. The fact is that when Prohibition was enacted alcohol was regarded as dangerous, and Prohibition was not repealed because we changed our minds and decided that alcohol was safe. We all grew up believing that tobacco was habit-forming and stunted one's growth, at the very least. People who chose to drink and smoke did not do so because they believed that no one could be hurt by such behavior or that the government gave them its blessing. The simple increase in availability seems to account for all the increase in drug use when a drug is legalized. After all, those who use dangerous drugs that the public condemns tend not to be highly aware of the nuances of governmental messages.

As a result, the issue boils down to a careful weighing of the costs of criminalization of each drug against the public-health costs we could expect if that drug were to become legally available.

I will not consider the case of marijuana. It is the most used of the three major illegal drugs (although its use has decreased considerably in the last decade); but at present marijuana is also the least socially costly of the illegal drugs, in addition to being the drug that has been most effectively interdicted (because of its relatively large bulk). Finally, marijuana is the drug that promises the lowest public-health costs if legalized.

Various commentators have considered the social costs of marijuana's criminalization and the projected public-health costs of legalization. And though they have been shouted down by parent groups and those who seek their votes, these commentators, by and large, have leaned toward legalization. The report of the National Academy of Sciences Committee on Substance Abuse and Habitual Behavior made a rather conservative recommendation: it merely asserted that "the current policies directed at controlling the supply of marijuana should be seriously reconsidered."

Nor need we devote any attention to LSD, mescaline, PCP, or any number of other illegal drugs here; for the illegal status of these drugs has not created a significant social problem.

Needless to say, this is not the case with heroin and cocaine. The costs of restricting supply of these drugs are substantial. Since space does not permit discussions of both heroin and cocaine, I will discuss only the anticipated costs of legalizing cocaine. First, a reasonable calculation of the public-health costs of heroin legalization, based on our admittedly inadequate information, already exists.[6]

THE CASE OF COCAINE

At a minimum, it is clear that anyone advocating the legalization of cocaine would have to make a serious estimate of how many more people would use the drug after it was legalized; how many of these users would become dependent on the drug; and how much harm this would cause them and society. Instead, there has been no serious discussion of all this. Moreover, no one has seriously considered the impact of a "new" drug upon a culture that has yet to develop patterns of self-control with respect to its use; by contrast, we should recall that over many generations our culture has developed a variety of informal controls over alcohol use, which allow most people to lessen the harm that alcohol does both to them in particular and society in general. Societies not accustomed to alcohol, however, such as England prior to the "gin epidemic" of that late seventeenth and early eighteenth centuries, and many Native American and Eskimo cultures, have experienced a public-health catastrophe of huge proportions as a result of the introduction of distilled spirits.

Nor have the advocates of the legalization of cocaine considered how we would be able to prevent teenagers from gaining access to the now legal drug. Many people assume that legalization of a drug would affect only adults, since, as with alcohol, we would make it illegal to sell the drug to minors. The problem, however, is that legal access for adults makes a drug *de facto* available to the young. This has been the experience with alcohol and tobacco. Cocaine is far less bulky and more concealable than alcohol, and its use does not leave the telltale aroma of smoke; thus it would be even more difficult to keep away from minors.

Yet another problem is the possibility of changes in public consciousness and values. Such changes can make use of a drug less dangerous, but they can also greatly augment its dangers. There are many examples

6. See my *The Hardest Drug: Heroin and Public Policy* (University of Chicago   Press, 1983).

of changes in public consciousness, entirely apart from governmental action, that have influenced drug use. The use of tobacco, alcohol, and marijuana seems to have dropped in the last several years, just as jogging and low-fat diets have increased, all as a consequence of the nation's greater fixation on health. Unfortunately, we cannot guarantee that such cultural trends will continue, or even that they will not be reversed, as has often happened in the past.

Youth culture, moreover, seems to be subject to dramatic fluctuations. The rapid changes in styles of dress, hair, music, and entertainment among the young have bewildered their elders for generations; and the appearance of a charismatic proselytizer for cocaine (as Timothy Leary was for LSD and marijuana) could change youth attitudes toward cocaine. Such a cultural change, even if only temporary, could present us with a permanent problem of large numbers of young people who became drug-dependent during the period of the drug's "window of acceptability."

Consider the case of heroin. Though most people have not noticed, the epidemic of heroin use stopped about ten years ago. Each year, the average age of heroin addicts goes up by about a year. Nevertheless, the last heroin epidemic has left us with an endemic problem of about 500,000 addicts who impose large social costs upon us.

The Dangers of Cocaine

This is not to say that problems like these cannot be solved, or that more careful thought and research might not satisfy us. As far as we now know, however, there is no particular cause for comfort. The pharmacological nature of cocaine, in fact, is especially worrisome. We need not list all the serious negative effects cocaine may have on its users, since an impressive list of such effects can be drawn up for any of the psychoactive drugs. The problem is to determine just how prevalent these effects would be if the drug were legalized.

With cocaine, we do not have to consider the relatively rare stoppages of the heart muscle, or the incidence of strokes; the common effects of cocaine are the most appropriate reasons for concern. The most important fact about cocaine is that it is an extremely attractive drug. In the 1950s a double-blind experiment on the "enjoyability" of a number of injected drugs was undertaken with twenty normal volunteers. Although fewer than half of the subjects found heroin or morphine euphoric, fully 90 percent liked an amphetamine (which is a pharmacological relative of cocaine), giving it by far the highest "pleasure score."

Probably related to its "pleasure score" is the fact that cocaine is the most "reinforcing" drug known to us. Animal studies corroborate the reports of many human users. Over the past four decades, self-administration equipment has been developed that permits animals to "work" for supplies of a drug and to administer all they want. It turns out that opiates such as heroin lie somewhere between alcohol and cocaine in their reinforcing power. Alcohol seems relatively unattractive;

it is quite difficult to get most animals to drink alcohol, and unless they are already addicted, monkeys and many other animals will go to some length to avoid ingesting alcohol. Virtually all monkeys, however, will continue injecting themselves with opiates until they become addicted, and even non-addicted animals will perform considerable amounts of work to "earn" their injections. But cocaine is the most impressive drug in this respect: animals will do enormous amounts of work to earn their cocaine shots. Indeed, if permitted, they will hit at their levers again and again to gain their reward of cocaine, neglecting food or rest until they die of debilitation.

This problem is exacerbated by several other properties of cocaine. Along with amphetamines, it is one of the few drugs that can improve one's mental and physical performance of a task. In fact, this improvement is limited to performance under conditions of fatigue, and the improvement is only temporary. Nonetheless, there will be many occasions during work, athletics or studies when an individual will be willing to mortgage his future for a little more energy and mental clarity. Moreover—and in this respect unlike amphetamines—cocaine not only produces an alert high, but also subsequently causes a noticeable low, a kind of depression after its relatively short term course has been run. This rather unusual effect results in the urge to use the drug again, both to re-create the past enjoyable high and to fight off the present dysphoric low.

The damage wrought by heavy cocaine use in terms of psychiatric symptoms and general debilitation is now widely known. What is less appreciated are the more subtle changes that regular cocaine use can cause. Unlike alcohol and heroin, cocaine use can easily be integrated with everyday activities. Its use can be quite inconspicuous, and, like cigarette smoking, can accompany a host of everyday activities. Cocaine use makes one feel good, then highly competent, then nearly omnipotent. It is easy to see why the use of such a drug would be damaging in a complex, mechanized, and interdependent society such as ours.

Nor should we take much comfort from the fact that most of those who use cocaine today have not become dependent upon the drug. As long as the drug is expensive and relatively difficult to procure, most of its users will be able to avoid dependence. When the drug is easily available, however, we can expect the temptations toward use to increase considerably.

We can see this by doing a quick calculation. Once the non-financial cost of cocaine (that is, inconvenience and criminal danger to the user) is greatly reduced by legalization, the drug's financial cost looms as the dominating one. At present, a gram of cocaine sells for about $80–$100. Its cost of production is certainly less than three dollars. Presumably, legalized cocaine would be taxed as heavily as possible, though the cost including tax would have to be sufficiently low, so as to make bootlegging unprofitable. Profits in today's cocaine trade are so huge, though, that it is hard to believe that we could keep the retail price of a gram of cocaine above $20. (Keep in mind that the bootlegger, who tries only to cheat the government out of its tax receipts, is treated much more leniently by both the criminal-justice system and society than in the universally maligned drug pusher.) When one considers that there are about fifty "hits" of cocaine in a gram, one is startled by the realization that at $20 per gram the cost of a hit will be only forty cents—a figure well within the budget of almost all grade-school children. Nor is the specter of very young children destroyed by the use of cocaine in any way unrealistic; there are ten-year-old cocaine addicts in the streets of Bogota today.

It is true that if the number of those dependent upon cocaine merely doubled, we would arguably be well ahead of the game, considering the large costs imposed by treating those users as criminals. But what if there was a fifty-fold increase in the number of those dependent on cocaine? We simply cannot guarantee that such a situation would not come to pass; since we cannot do so, it is the height of irresponsibility to advocate risking the future of the nation.

If all this is not enough to convince reasonably prudent people that legalizing cocaine is too risky a course, we can also consider the consequences of taking a risk and being wrong. After all, if we had legalized cocaine five years ago, we would not have known how easy it is to make cocaine into "crack", universally considered to be a much more habit-forming and dangerous form of the drug. If we legalize cocaine now, how long should we wait before deciding whether we made a mistake? And if we decided that we had, how would we go about recriminalizing the drug? By then, substantial inventories of legal cocaine would have been introduced to the drug. And once a drug has been made legally available, it is very difficult to prohibit it. This consideration helps to explain why Prohibition failed, and also explains why almost no one advocates the criminalization of tobacco.

FINDING A SOLUTION

The problem, then, is what we can do about the present situation. Several factors have made our drug policy politically tolerable up to now. First, it has protected most of middle-class American from the kind of continuous exposure to the use of drugs (and encouragement favoring their use) that are most likely to lead to the problems of drug abuse; such exposure and encouragement characterize the underclass areas in which drug use is endemic. Second, although drug enforcement has been expensive, it would have been even more expensive to do more. Third, we have continued to entertain hopes that we could solve our drug problem on the cheap, either by pressuring other nations to prevent the production of illegal drugs or by keeping drugs from being smuggled into the United States.

If we were to choose to take our drug problem more seriously, it is not clear what we could do. According to public-opinion polls, education is currently the most popular method for dealing with our drug problem.

A recent Gallup Poll showed that 47 percent of Americans believe it is the best antidrug strategy. (Thirty-six percent favor interdiction, and 6 percent favor drug treatment.)

Our research shows that it is doubtful that education can do much to lower the level of drug abuse, however. Newspaper advertising campaigns to discourage alcohol abuse and drug use have been shown to be ineffective. We have had experience with temperance campaigns, but as far as we can tell, most young people do not appear to pay much attention to them. Nor do school-based programs seem to be able to reduce alcohol and drug abuse.

This is predictable. Young people are notoriously resistant to their elders' efforts to get them to live less risky, more forward-looking lives. Well into adolescence, they tend to retain what psychiatrists refer to as "remnants of infantile omnipotence." Moreover, entirely apart from the question of risk, young people often take pleasure in things that adults tell them are bad. They are constantly told that they should avoid things (like sex or junk food) that they enjoy. At best they tend to disregard such advice—when they do not actually seek out occasions to disobey their elders' counsel. Indeed, the real mystery is how we have managed to convince significant numbers of youths in inner-city school systems— more than 50 percent of whose students drop out of school, despite a massive publicity campaign to the contrary—to avoid taking drugs, since at least in the beginning they would find drug use so enjoyable.

Nevertheless, one kind of drug education does show some promise. Several small-scale experiments have attempted to use peers to teach young students techniques by which they can refuse cigarettes if they want to. They learn, for instance, what to say when others offer them cigarettes or even exert social pressure on them to smoke; this approach has produced significant decreases in the initiation of cigarette use. Such programs are still quite rare, however, and whether we can duplicate them on a large scale with respect to cocaine and heroin, in the neighborhoods that most need them, is by no means clear. At the very least, we need years of research before we can develop programs that can be trusted to do more good than harm.

The charm of education, nonetheless, is seductive. Compared with other means of coping with illegal drugs, it is cheap and seems humane, because it does not require the coercion of our fellow citizens. In this regard, it is similar to bringing pressure upon foreign nations to prevent the production of illegal drugs. Indeed, education may well become the "crop substitution" of the nineties—that is, the supposed panacea for all drug problems.

Conceivably, we will decided simply to continue our present policies. We can spend a great deal on education programs; we can assign the military the task of sealing our borders against drugs; we can seize yachts or fishing boats when passengers or workers have abandoned marijuana cigarettes on them; we can legislate capital punishment for drug-related killings (as when drug dealers murder one another). But by adopting such a course of action, we would only be making an emphatic statement that we were taking the drug problem seriously; we would not really be acting seriously. For to act in this manner would in effect be to choose to keep putting up with our problem.

For most middle-class Americans, the use of heroin and cocaine is not a major threat. Heroin never was a threat; and although cocaine was very popular with some wealthy users—the conventional wisdom held that they were heavily overrepresented in advertising, entertainment, and professional sports—and its use significantly harmed the lives of many middle-class youths, much of the damage has already been done. Today, cocaine—especially in the form of "crack"—is increasingly becoming a drug of the lower classes. It is true that all of us suffer from the intimate connection between these drugs and predatory crime, and in more indirect ways from the enormous dislocation and damage done to lower-class neighborhoods by the sale and use of these drugs. Nonetheless, we learned to live with problems like these many years ago. Indeed, it seems that the public gets really excited about the drug problem only when someone from the middle class is killed in a gang shoot-out.

In an ideal world, the best way to reduce the damage done by illegal drugs would be to convince everyone not to use them. In this world, however, we will probably have to reconcile ourselves to using some coercion. On the other hand, once we give up on finding an inexpensive solution, we may take the problem seriously and apply more careful thought and more resources to the job.

SUPPLY-SIDE ENFORCEMENT

So long as we are unable to suppress the sale of drugs, we will be remitting large parts of our cities to the terrorization of innocent people, drug-related killings, and the brutalization that comes from constant exposure to the use of drugs. Perhaps equally demoralizing is the sight of the large number of teenage drug lords who own Jaguars or Ferraris before they are old enough to have driver's licenses. Nonetheless, we can accomplish much more than we have in the past.

Apart from our efforts in other countries and at the borders, the major thrust of enforcement within the United States has been the attempt to break up large-scale drug rings, arrest small-scale dealers when they sell drugs outside the areas in which drug use is endemic, and punish users when they commit other crimes. In recent years local police have stepped up their efforts to restrain street-level selling, and private employers have exerted greater efforts to apprehend their workers' "connection," and to weed out illegal drug users from their work force. The result has been a slow but steady loss of ground for law-enforcement agencies.

One cannot say that careful thought and greatly augmented law-enforcement resources will solve our drug problem. There are large number of sellers arranged hierarchically within the United States as part of loose but fairly sizable organizations, taking the drug from its importation into the United States through smaller wholesalers down to the small-scale sellers who provide the drug to users. Unfortunately, we cannot expect to achieve much of a reduction in the number of drug suppliers, even if we jail a sizable percentage of them. The high profits at every level of the drug trade guarantee a huge reservoir of individuals prepared to take the places of those who have been imprisoned. At each level in the distribution scheme there are more than enough competitors; and even at the lowest ranks, those who do minor jobs for the sellers (such as acting as lookouts for the police) seem ready to enter the business.

On the other hand, pressure upon the retailing of heroin and cocaine is not necessarily an unattractive option. In fact, it is probably the major governmental means of restraining drug use in the United States today. The number of locations in which an ordinary middle-class individual can buy heroin and cocaine is not very large. In most of the country, cocaine is not widely available to most people. Heroin is less so. A major task of law-enforcement resources is to increase that area of drug unavailability. At the very least, the police should act immediately to suppress the open-air drug markets that spring up whenever the police are distracted by other duties. In most of our urban areas, greater efforts could drive much of the dealing indoors, where a large percentage of potential customers are afraid to go.

At least for the foreseeable future, it is hard to imagine the police being able to do more than gradually drive the dealing back into the public-housing projects and other relatively small areas in which the police are unable to maintain a presence. Nonetheless, increases in law-enforcement efforts at the retail level may lower the availability of heroin and cocaine to large numbers of people without creating a need to involve ourselves in the most hard-core drug-trafficking areas, in which the police would have to maintain a virtual army of occupation.

Apart from the difficulty of policing the hard-core drug areas, the most important constraint upon our ability to suppress the sale of drugs is the cost of incarceration space. Our prisons and jails are full, and despite a massive and continuing effort to provide the infrastructure to imprison more and more lawbreakers, the demand threatens to permanently outrun the supply. Drug sales, moreover, are especially difficult and expensive to restrain through imprisonment. The deterrence we expect from the legal threat is in large part neutralized by the high profits at all levels of the drug trade. And incapacitation, the other major restraint provided by imprisonment, is weakened by the fact that the skills necessary to participate in the drug trade are not at all scarce.

Although we must allocate a large percentage of prison space to the incarceration of drug dealers if we are able to make headway, there are other methods that can help. At the higher levels of the drug trade, the forfeiture of assets has proven quite successful. We cannot show that the threat has caused any drug dealers to get out of the business, but at the margin it should have that effect; depriving sellers of working capital makes their reentry into the industry quite difficult. At the very least, it assuages our sense of justice, as well as providing additional resources with which to further enforcement. It is likely that we can go a great deal lower in the drug-trade hierarchy before forfeiture is no longer worthwhile. It will require a little more ingenuity by the police and cooperation from the agencies of the criminal-justice system before we can strike at the pocketbook of the small-scale seller, but it can be done—and to good effect.

Demand-Side Enforcement

While pressure on the small-scale sale of drugs represents an attempt to influence drug supply, it also has an impact on drug demand— perhaps a greater one. The buyer who does not reside in an area of heavy drug sales must not only come up with the money to pay for the drugs; he may also have to search longer to make a purchase and worry more about the danger of being robbed or assaulted. He may also be more conspicuous to the police. To some extent, we can take advantage of this problem faced by drug buyers by using a relatively inexpensive means of lessening the number of those who are willing to obtain their supplies from the areas of heavy drug dealing. On a few occasions police have seized the automobiles of those who drove them to purchase drugs. This is not only inexpensive, but also far less brutal than imprisoning otherwise law-abiding drug users—and it may have more of an impact. This should be a regular feature of all drug enforcement.

Probably the most important aspect of the attack on drugs is the attempt to lower the amount of predatory crime that drug use engenders. We know, for example, that those who use illegal drugs commit a substantial proportion of our urban burglaries, robberies, and thefts. A number of studies have demonstrated that the criminality rate of those using heroin daily—that is, those who were addicted—was about seven times as great as the criminality rate of the same people when they were using the drug only sporadically or temporarily not using it at all.

Newer studies have shown an even higher correlation between criminality and drug use, and have implicated cocaine as well. Urinalysis of those arrested for crimes in 1986 has revealed that a staggering percentage of those apprehended had recently used cocaine or heroin. In the District of Columbia, 74 percent of non-drug-felony arrestees tested positive for at least one illegal drug other than marijuana. (No one has alleged that marijuana use helps to cause predatory crime, in part because the drug is cheap, in part because it has a tranquilizing effect.) In New York City the figure was 72 percent; in Chicago, 60 percent; and in Los Angeles, 58 percent. It turns out that in large cities about 70 percent of those arrested for robbery, weapons offenses, and larceny tested positive for heroin, cocaine, or (in the few cities where use is common) PCP.

The data on urinalysis suggest an obvious course of action. We must institutionalize routine urinalysis for those arrested for any of the typical crimes arising out of drug use. Then we must act on this information by making maintenance of a urine clean of cocaine, heroin, and PCP a requirement for all those who are released on bail or, after conviction, are placed on probation or released on parole.

A positive urine sample must reliably and immediately mean a return to jail. It is far more important that the enforcement of these rules be consistent than that the jail terms be long. We do not have the jail space that would be needed to provide long terms for this type of offense. And if we try, our efforts will backfire: we will deprive the system of the consistency necessary to get the message through to drug users. But a properly implemented system of imprisonment can make possible a more lasting cure for drug dependency.

This kind of regimen is not without disadvantages. There will inevitably be a dispute over whether we can demand "clean" urine before releasing someone on bail. On the other hand, our jurisprudence tells us that bail is to be used only to guarantee the presence of the accused at judicial proceedings, and there is no firm evidence that drug users are less likely than others to show up in court. On the other hand, more recent precedent seems to allow consideration of the danger to the community if an arrestee is released on bail, and those who use illegal drugs are, on average, much more likely to commit crimes after they have been freed.

Such a system of mandatory urinalysis will also require more money. Parts of the criminal-justice system will simply not give up— even temporarily—the funds they already have and need, even though doing so may help to save money in the long run. The jails are already full, and in many cases under court order not to exceed their present population. Even at two days per failed urinalysis, the increased demand upon those institutions will be substantial. And the maintenance of such a system will require the police to go looking for those who miss urinalysis appointments, a burden that may initially be only partially compensated for by the lower criminality of those now compelled to be drug-free.

Furthermore, the inexpensive urine test, which costs only about $5, but is less than completely accurate, will have to be supplemented by a system in which an arrestee who was confident that he had not used an illegal drug could simply file an affidavit to that effect and be tested by a more expensive and foolproof method (costing about $70). Although there will have to be some sanction for a false affidavit, expensive prosecutions for perjury will not be necessary to deter such conduct (though it is hard to imagine a simpler case to prosecute). The judge, in revoking bail or probation, can simply revoke it for longer.

Then there are the privacy concerns. It should be noted that urinalysis for those who have been arrested involves far fewer restraints on the citizen's right to privacy than the usual attempt to require urinalysis of government employees or members of other large groups, who, as individuals, give us no reason to suspect their drug use. (Nor is it nearly so expensive.) Our statistics on the drug use of those arrested for street crimes already single them out. And apart from the use of urinalysis in the bail decision, there are no real constitutional doubts. If there is a good reason, those arrested for drunken driving, for example, may constitutionally be subjected to blood, urine, or breath analysis, and those released on bail or, after conviction, on probation or parole, forfeit even more of their privacy. They are subject not only to intrusive searches but also to various restrictions on their autonomy. Very few of the restrictions on the privacy and autonomy of defendants in the criminal-justice system make as much practical sense as requiring urinalysis in order to monitor their drug use.

THE PROGNOSIS

What, then, could we expect from the institutionalization of such a regimen? Many of those using drugs will find themselves constantly in and out of jail. Some would simply decide that enough is enough and clean themselves up. We do know that this can occur when the consequences are immediate and certain enough. Nonetheless, in most cases we will have to rely upon drug treatment to prevent the urinalysis system from becoming a huge, inhumane, and expensive revolving-door operation. While it is true that the most reliable and cost-effective drug treatment—methadone maintenance—is helpful only with heroin addicts, there are other therapies that are more cost-effective than permitting the drug abuser to continue untreated; and it is likely that requiring urinalysis will help persuade drug users to undergo treatment.

Indeed, probably the most foolish aspect of our antidrug posture has been the starvation of drug treatment. In many cities there is a months-long wait for those who want to enter a drug-treatment program; this is a serious problem, considering that the desire to reform is often ephemeral, and disappears if it cannot be acted upon at once. Part of the reluctance to invest in drug treatment stems from the moralistic view that it is wrong to spend resources on making life better for criminals; part stems from the (incorrect) belief that treatment does not work. Treatment is difficult; it is frustrating; and it does not always work. But it is cost-effective—and far more so than its only substitute, imprisonment. A necessary component of any serious effort to lower the social costs of illegal drug use, therefore, is a massive increase in funds for drug treatment.

Another fact about drug treatment is also quite important. Although many believe that compulsory treatment is ineffective, this does not appear to be the case. Virtually everyone undergoing drug treatment is in one way or another forced to do so. Indeed, like many alcoholics, who simply want to become social drinkers again and escape the social, psychological, and physical effects of overindulgence, most drug users do not wish to be abstinent, but rather to return to the early days of their more casual drug use. Nonetheless, one of the effects that those dependent on cocaine and heroin may most wish to escape is the pressure of the criminal-justice system. And a criminal-justice system that makes use of urinalysis will be more effective in driving them into—and keeping them in—treatment.

The approach I am recommending may have another important effect. For years, the drug-producing nations have argued that the United States must share the blame for the drug problem: if they cannot control the production of illegal drugs, neither can we control our consumption. We may now be able to have some success. Those users who are both criminals and drug consumers appear to be not merely a random selection of drug users; they tend, rather, to be the heaviest users. Thus it is likely that these heavy users consume a disproportionate percentage of the illegal drug supply. This should not be surprising: the heaviest-drinking 10 percent of all drinkers drink well over half the total quantity of alcohol—and our evidence, though less conclusive, points in the same direction with regard to illegal drugs. Indeed, the "J curve" seems to be a constant in human behavior: 15 percent of health-insurance users use 90 percent of the resources; 6 percent of Philadelphia's youths commit over 50 percent of its crimes; and 10 percent of Stanford Law School's students file 90 percent of the petitions to be excused from one requirement or another.

As a result, those users we will be focusing on will be those who do the most to support the illegal market. On average, each seller is supported by three heavy users. If we can bring their use under control—in addition to decreasing the number of predatory crimes—we may finally be able to deal a major blow to the illegal retail-distribution networks. We may also create a sizable cohort of former drug users who can help discourage drug use. If the zeal of the convert in this area is as strong as it seems to be in others—think of ex-smokers, for example—we may reap unanticipated and sizable dividends from our efforts. For decades we have attempted to get at the sellers as a way of preventing use; now we may have the means to get at the users as a means of restraining sales.

I do not mean to suggest that we will be able to solve the problem easily. For the foreseeable future we will have a serious drug problem, but we can lessen it considerably if we have the will. Where will the money necessary to accomplish this come from? The additional resources we need for law enforcement and drug treatment will come from the federal government, or they will not come at all. Whether the resources will come is simply a question of whether we have finally begun to take our drug problem seriously. It will be interesting to find out.

U.S. DEPARTMENT OF JUSTICE—SPEAKING OUT AGAINST DRUG LEGALIZATION

Drug Enforcement Agency web site—
http://www.dea.gov/demand/speakout/index.html

SUMMARY OF THE TOP TEN FACTS ON LEGALIZATION

Fact 1: We have made significant progress in fighting drug use and drug trafficking in America. Now is not the time to abandon our efforts.

The Legalization Lobby claims that the fight against drugs cannot be won. However, overall drug use is down by more than a third in the last twenty years, while cocaine use has dropped by an astounding 70 percent. Ninety-five percent of Americans do not use drugs. This is success by any standards.

Fact 2: A balanced approach of prevention, enforcement, and treatment is the key in the fight against drugs.

A successful drug policy must apply a balanced approach of prevention, enforcement and treatment. All three aspects are crucial. For those who end up hooked on drugs, there are innovative programs, like Drug Treatment Courts, that offer non-violent users the option of seeking treatment. Drug Treatment Courts provide court supervision, unlike voluntary treatment centers.

Fact 3: Illegal drugs are illegal because they are harmful.

There is a growing misconception that some illegal drugs can be taken safely. For example, savvy drug dealers have learned how to market drugs like Ecstasy to youth. Some in the Legalization Lobby even claim such drugs have medical value, despite the lack of conclusive scientific evidence.

Fact 4: Smoked marijuana is not scientifically approved medicine. Marinol, the legal version of medical marijuana, is approved by science.

According to the Institute of Medicine, there is no future in smoked marijuana as medicine. However, the prescription drug Marinol—a legal and safe version of medical marijuana which isolates the active ingredient of THC—has been studied and approved by the Food & Drug Administration as safe medicine. The difference is that you have to get a prescription for Marinol from a licensed physician. You can't buy it on a street corner, and you don't smoke it.

Fact 5: Drug control spending is a minor portion of the U.S. budget. Compared to the social costs of drug abuse and addiction, government spending on drug control is minimal.

The Legalization Lobby claims that the United States has wasted billions of dollars in its anti-drug efforts. But for those kids saved from drug addiction, this is hardly wasted dollars. Moreover, our fight against drug abuse and addiction is an ongoing struggle that should be treated like any other social problem. Would we give up on education or poverty simply because we haven't eliminated all problems? Compared to the social costs of drug abuse and addiction—whether in taxpayer dollars or in pain and suffering—government spending on drug control is minimal.

Fact 6: Legalization of drugs will lead to increased use and increased levels of addiction. Legalization has been tried before, and failed miserably.

Legalization has been tried before—and failed miserably. Alaska's experiment with Legalization in the 1970s led to the state's teens using marijuana at more than twice the rate of other youths nationally. This led Alaska's residents to vote to re-criminalize marijuana in 1990.

Fact 7: Crime, violence, and drug use go hand-in-hand.

Crime, violence and drug use go hand in hand. Six times as many homicides are committed by people under the influence of drugs, as by those who are looking for money to buy drugs. Most drug crimes aren't committed by people trying to pay for drugs; they're committed by people on drugs.

Fact 8: Alcohol has caused significant health, social, and crime problems in this country, and legalized drugs would only make the situation worse.

The Legalization Lobby claims drugs are no more dangerous than alcohol. But drunk driving is one of the primary killers of Americans. Do we want our bus drivers, nurses, and airline pilots to be able to take drugs one evening, and operate freely at work the next day? Do we want to add to the destruction by making drugged driving another primary killer?

Fact 9: Europe's more liberal drug policies are not the right model for America.

The Legalization Lobby claims that the "European Model" of the drug problem is successful. However, since legalization of marijuana in Holland, heroin addiction levels have tripled. And Needle Park seems like a poor model for America.

Fact 10: Most non-violent drug users get treatment, not jail time.

The Legalization Lobby claims that America's prisons are filling up with users. Truth is, only about 5 percent of inmates in federal prison are there because of simple possession. Most drug criminals are in jail—even on possession charges—because they have plea-bargained down from major trafficking offences or more violent drug crimes.

Crime, violence, and drug use go hand-in-hand.

> *Fact 1: We have made significant progress in fighting*
> *drug use and drug trafficking in America. Now*
> *is not the time to abandon our efforts.*

Demand Reduction

Legalization advocates claim that the fight against drugs has not been won and is, in fact, unconquerable. They frequently state that people still take drugs, drugs are widely available, and that efforts to change this are futile. They contend that legalization is the only workable alternative.

The facts are to the contrary to such pessimism. On the demand side, the U.S. has reduced casual use, chronic use and addiction, and prevented others from even starting using drugs. Overall drug use in the United States is down by more than a third since the late 1970s. That's 9.5 million people fewer using illegal drugs. We've reduced cocaine use by an astounding 70% during the last 15 years. That's 4.1 million fewer people using cocaine.

Almost two-thirds of teens say their schools are drug-free, according to a new survey of teen drug use conducted by The National Center on Addiction and Substance Abuse (CASA) at Columbia University. This is the first time in the seven-year history of the study that a majority of public school students report drug-free schools.

The good news continues. According to the 2001–2002 PRIDE survey, student drug use has reached the lowest level in nine years. According to the author of the study, "following 9/11, Americans seemed to refocus on family, community, spirituality, and nation." These statistics show that U.S. efforts to educate kids about the dangers of drugs is making an impact. Like smoking cigarettes, drug use is gaining a stigma which is the best cure for this problem, as it was in the 1980s, when government, business, the media and other national institutions came together to do something about the growing problem of drugs and drug-related violence. This is a trend we should encourage—not send the opposite message of greater acceptance of drug use.

The crack cocaine epidemic of the 1980s and early 1990s has diminished greatly in scope. And we've reduced the number of chronic heroin users over the last decade. In addition, the number of new marijuana users and cocaine users continues to steadily decrease.

The number of new heroin users dropped from 156,000 in 1976 to 104,000 in 1999, a reduction of 33 percent.

Of course, drug policy also has an impact on general crime. In a 2001 study, the British Home Office found violent crime and property crime increased in the late 1990s in every wealthy country except the United States. Our murder rate is too high, and we have much to learn from those with greater success—but this reduction is due in part to a reduction in drug use.

There is still much progress to make. There are still far too many people using cocaine, heroin and other illegal drugs. In addition, there are emerging drug threats like Ecstasy and methamphetamine. But the fact is that our current policies balancing prevention, enforcement, and treatment have kept drug usage outside the scope of acceptable behavior in the U.S.

To put things in perspective, less than 5 percent of the population uses illegal drugs of any kind. Think about that: More than 95 percent of

Americans do not use drugs. How could anyone but the most hardened pessimist call this a losing struggle?

Supply Reduction

There have been many successes on the supply side of the drug fight, as well. For example, Customs officials have made major seizures along the U.S.–Mexico border during a six-month period after September 11th, seizing almost twice as much as the same period in 2001. At one port in Texas, seizures of methamphetamine are up 425% and heroin by 172%. Enforcement makes a difference—traffickers' costs go up with these kinds of seizures.

Purity levels of Colombian cocaine are declining too, according to an analysis of samples seized from traffickers and bought from street dealers in the United States. The purity has declined by nine percent, from 86 percent in 1998, to 78 percent in 2001. There are a number of possible reasons for this decline in purity, including DEA supply reduction efforts in South America.

One DEA program, Operation Purple, involves 28 countries and targets the illegal diversion of chemicals used in processing cocaine and other illicit drugs. DEA's labs have discovered that the oxidation levels for cocaine have been greatly reduced, suggesting that Operation Purple is having a detrimental impact on the production of cocaine.

Another likely cause is that traffickers are diluting their cocaine to offset the higher costs associated with payoffs to insurgent and paramilitary groups in Colombia. The third possible cause is that cocaine traffickers simply don't have the product to simultaneously satisfy their market in the United States and their rapidly growing market in Europe. As a result, they are cutting the product to try to satisfy both.

Whatever the final reasons for the decline in drug purity, it is good news for the American public. It means less potent and deadly drugs are hitting the streets, and dealers are making less profits—that is, unless they raise their own prices, which helps price more and more Americans out of the market.

Purity levels have also been reduced on methamphetamine by controls on chemicals necessary for its manufacture. The average purity of seized methamphetamine samples dropped from 72 percent in 1994 to 40 percent in 2001.

The trafficking organizations that sell drugs are finding that their profession has become a lot more costly. In the mid–1990s, the DEA helped dismantle Burma's Shan United Army, at the time the world's largest heroin trafficking organization, which in two years helped reduce the amount of Southeast Asian heroin in the United States from 63 percent of the market to 17 percent of the market. In the mid–1990s, the DEA helped disrupt the Cali cartel, which had been responsible for much of the world's cocaine.

Progress does not come overnight. America has had a long, dark struggle with drugs. It's not a war we've been fighting for 20 years.

We've been fighting it for 120 years. In 1880, many drugs, including opium and cocaine, were legal. We didn't know their harms, but we soon learned. We saw the highest level of drug use ever in our nation, per capita. There were over 400,000 opium addicts in our nation. That's twice as many per capita as there are today. And like today, we saw rising crime with that drug abuse. But we fought those problems by passing and enforcing tough laws and by educating the public about the dangers of these drugs. And this vigilance worked—by World War II, drug use was reduced to the very margins of society. And that's just where we want to keep it. With a 95 percent success rate—bolstered by an effective, three-pronged strategy combining education/ prevention, enforcement, and treatment—we shouldn't give up now.

> Fact 2: A balanced approach of prevention, enforcement, and treatment is the key in the fight against drugs.

Over the years, some people have advocated a policy that focuses narrowly on controlling the supply of drugs. Others have said that society should rely on treatment alone. Still others say that prevention is the only viable solution. As the 2002 National Drug Strategy observes, "What the nation needs is an honest effort to integrate these strategies."

Drug treatment courts are a good example of this new balanced approach to fighting drug abuse and addiction in this country. These courts are given a special responsibility to handle cases involving drug-addicted offenders through an extensive supervision and treatment program. Drug court programs use the varied experience and skills of a wide variety of law enforcement and treatment professionals: judges, prosecutors, defense counsels, substance abuse treatment specialists, probation officers, law enforcement and correctional personnel, educational and vocational experts, community leaders and others—all focused on one goal: to help cure addicts of their addiction, and to keep them cured.

Drug treatment courts are working. Researchers estimate that more than 50 percent of defendants convicted of drug possession will return to criminal behavior within two to three years. Those who graduate from drug treatment courts have far lower rates of recidivism, ranging from 2 to 20 percent. That's very impressive when you consider that; for addicts who enter a treatment program voluntarily, 80 to 90 percent leave by the end of the first year. Among such dropouts, relapse within a year is generally the rule.

What makes drug treatment courts so different? Graduates are held accountable for sticking with the program. Unlike other, purely voluntary treatment programs, the addict—who has a physical need for drugs—can't simply quit treatment whenever he or she feels like it.

Law enforcement plays an important role in the drug treatment court program. It is especially important in the beginning of the process because it often triggers treatment for people who need it. Most people do not volunteer for drug treatment. It is more often an outside motivator, like an arrest, that gets—and keeps—people in treatment. And it is important for judges to keep people in incarceration if treatment fails.

There are already more than 123,000 people who use heroin at least once a month, and 1.7 million who use cocaine at least once a month. For them, treatment is the answer. But for most Americans, particularly the young, the solution lies in prevention, which in turn is largely a matter of education and enforcement, which aims at keeping drug pushers away from children and teenagers.

The role of strong drug enforcement has been analyzed by R. E. Peterson. He has broken down the past four decades into two periods. The first period, from 1960 to1980, was an era of permissive drug laws. During this era, drug incarceration rates fell almost 80 percent. Drug use among teens, meanwhile, climbed by more than 500 percent. The second period, from 1980 to 1995, was an era of stronger drug laws. During this era, drug use by teens dropped by more than a third.

Enforcement of our laws creates risks that discourage drug use. Charles Van Deventer, a young writer in Los Angeles, wrote about this phenomenon in an article in Newsweek. He said that from his experience as a casual user—and he believes his experience with illegal drugs is "by far the most common"—drugs aren't nearly as easy to buy as some critics would like people to believe. Being illegal, they are too expensive, their quality is too unpredictable, and their purchase entails too many risks. "The more barriers there are," he said, "be they the cops or the hassle or the fear of dying, the less likely you are to get addicted. . . . The road to addiction was just bumpy enough," he concluded, "that I chose not to go down it. In this sense, we are winning the war on drugs just by fighting them."

The element of risk, created by strong drug enforcement policies, raises the price of drugs, and therefore lowers the demand. A research paper, Marijuana and Youth, funded by the Robert Wood Johnson Foundation, concludes that changes in the price of marijuana "contributed significantly to the trends in youth marijuana use between 1982 and 1998, particularly Powder Cocaine. during the contraction in use from 1982 to 1992." That contraction was a product of many factors, including a concerted effort among federal agencies to disrupt domestic production and distribution; these factors contributed to a doubling of the street price of marijuana in the space of a year.

The 2002 National Drug Control Strategy states that drug control policy has just two elements: modifying individual behavior to discourage and reduce drug use and addiction, and disrupting the market for illegal drugs. Those two elements call for a balanced approach to drug control, one that uses prevention, enforcement, and treatment in a coordinated policy. This is a simple strategy and an effective one. The enforcement side of the fight against drugs, then, is an integrated part of the overall strategy.

Fact 3: Illegal drugs are illegal because they are harmful.

There is a growing misconception that some illegal drugs can be taken safely—with many advocates of legalization going so far as to suggest it can serve as medicine to heal anything from headaches to bipolar diseases. Today's drug dealers are savvy businessmen. They know how to market to kids. They imprint Ecstasy pills with cartoon characters and designer logos. They promote parties as safe and alcohol-free. Meanwhile, the drugs can flow easier than water. Many young people believe the new "club drugs," such as Ecstasy, are safe, and tablet testing at raves has only fueled this misconception.

Because of the new marketing tactics of drug promoters, and because of a major decline in drug use in the 1990s, there is a growing perception among young people today that drugs are harmless. A decade ago, for example, 79 percent of 12th graders thought regular marijuana use was harmful; only 58 percent do so today. Because peer pressure is so important in inducing kids to experiment with drugs, the way kids perceive the risks of drug use is critical. There always have been, and there continues to be, real health risks in using illicit drugs.

Drug use can be deadly, far more deadly than alcohol. Although alcohol is used by seven times as many people as drugs, the number of deaths induced by those substances are not far apart. According to the Centers for Disease Control and Prevention (CDC), during 2000, there were 15,852 drug-induced deaths; only slightly less than the 18,539 alcohol-induced deaths.

Ecstasy has rapidly become a favorite drug among young party goers in the U.S. and Europe, and it is now being used within the mainstream as well. According to the 2001 National Household Survey on Drug Abuse, Ecstasy use tripled among Americans between 1998 and 2001. Many people believe, incorrectly, that this synthetic drug is safer than cocaine and heroin. In fact, the drug is addictive and can be deadly. The drug often results in severe dehydration and heat stroke in the user, since it has the effect of "short-circuiting" the body's temperature signals to the brain. Ecstasy can heat your body up to temperatures as high as 117 degrees. Ecstasy can cause hypothermia, muscle breakdown, seizures, stroke, kidney and cardiovascular system failure, as well as permanent brain damage during repetitive use, and sometimes death. The psychological effects of Ecstasy include confusion, depression, anxiety, sleeplessness, drug craving, and paranoia.

The misconception about the safety of club drugs, like Ecstasy, is often fueled by some governments' attempts to reduce the harm of mixing drugs. Some foreign governments and private organizations in the U.S. have established Ecstasy testing at rave parties. Once the drug is tested, it is returned to the partygoers. This process leads partygoers to believe that the government has declared their pill safe to consume. But the danger of Ecstasy is the drug itself—not simply its purity level.

Cocaine is a powerfully addictive drug. Compulsive cocaine use seems to develop more rapidly when the substance is smoked rather than snorted. A tolerance to the cocaine high may be developed, and many addicts report that they fail to achieve as much pleasure as they did from their first cocaine exposure.

Physical effects of cocaine use include constricted blood vessels and increased temperature, heart rate, and blood pressure. Users may also experience feelings of restlessness, irritability, and anxiety. Cocaine-related deaths are often the result of cardiac arrest or seizures followed by respiratory arrest. Cocaine continues to be the most frequently mentioned illicit substance in U.S. emergency departments, present in Coca plant. 30 percent of the emergency department drug episodes during 2001.

Drug legalization advocates in the United States single out marijuana as a different kind of drug, unlike cocaine, heroin, and methamphetamine. They say it's less dangerous. Several European countries have lowered the classification of marijuana. However, as many people are realizing, marijuana is not as harmless as some would have them believe. Marijuana is far more powerful than it used to be. In 2000, there were six times as many emergency room mentions of marijuana use as there were in 1990, despite the fact that the number of people using marijuana is roughly the same. In 1999, a record 225,000 Americans entered substance abuse treatment primarily for marijuana dependence, second only to heroin—and not by much.

At a time of great public pressure to curtail tobacco because of its effects on health, advocates of legalization are promoting the use of marijuana. Yet, according to the National Institute on Drug Abuse, "Studies show that someone who smokes five joints per week may be taking in as many cancer-causing chemicals as someone who smokes a full pack of cigarettes every day." Marijuana contains more than 400 chemicals, including the most harmful substances found in tobacco smoke. For example, smoking one marijuana cigarette deposits about four times more tar into the lungs than a filtered tobacco cigarette.

Those are the long-term effects of marijuana. The short-term effects are also harmful. They include: memory loss, distorted perception, trouble with thinking and problem solving, loss of motor skills, decrease in muscle strength, increased heart rate, and anxiety. Marijuana impacts young people's mental development, their ability to concentrate in school, and their motivation and initiative to reach goals. And marijuana affects people of all ages: Harvard University researchers report that the risk of a heart attack is five times higher than usual in the hour after smoking marijuana.

Fact 4. Smoked marijuana is not scientifically approved medicine. Marinol, the legal version of medical marijuana, is approved by science.

Medical marijuana already exists. It's called Marinol.

A pharmaceutical product, Marinol, is widely available through prescription. It comes in the form of a pill and is also being studied by researchers for suitability via other delivery methods, such as an inhaler or patch. The active ingredient of Marinol is synthetic THC, which has been found to relieve the nausea and vomiting associated with chemotherapy for cancer patients and to assist with loss of appetite with AIDS patients.

Unlike smoked marijuana—which contains more than 400 different chemicals, including most of the hazardous chemicals found in tobacco smoke—Marinol has been studied and approved by the medical community and the Food and Drug Administration (FDA), the nation's watchdog over unsafe and harmful food and drug products. Since the passage of the 1906 Pure Food and Drug Act, any drug that is marketed in the United States must undergo rigorous scientific testing. The approval process mandated by this act ensures that claims of safety and therapeutic value are supported by clinical evidence and keeps unsafe, ineffective, and dangerous drugs off the market.

Morphine, for example, has proven to be a medically valuable drug, but the FDA does not endorse the smoking of opium or heroin. Instead, scientists have extracted active ingredients from opium, which are sold Marinol container as pharmaceutical products for domestic like morphine, codeine, distribution. hydrocodone or oxycodone. In a similar vein, the FDA has not approved smoking marijuana for medicinal purposes, but has approved the active ingredient-THC-in the form of scientifically regulated Marinol.

The DEA helped facilitate the research on Marinol. The National Cancer Institute approached the DEA in the early 1980s regarding their study of THC's in relieving nausea and vomiting. As a result, the DEA facilitated the registration and provided regulatory support and guidance for the study. California, researchers are studying the potential use of marijuana and its ingredients on conditions such as multiple sclerosis and pain. At this time, however, neither the medical community nor the scientific community has found sufficient data to conclude that smoked marijuana is the best approach to dealing with these important medical issues.

The most comprehensive, scientifically rigorous review of studies of smoked marijuana was conducted by the Institute of Medicine, an organization chartered by the National Academy of Sciences. In a report released in 1999, the Institute did not recommend the use of smoked marijuana, but did conclude that active ingredients in marijuana could be isolated and developed into a variety of pharmaceuticals, such as Marinol.

In the meantime, the DEA is working with pain management groups, such as Last Acts, to make sure that those who need access to safe, effective pain medication can get the best medication available.

Fact 5: Drug control spending is a minor portion of the U.S. budget. Compared to the social costs of drug abuse and addiction, government spending on drug control is minimal.

Legalization advocates claim that the United States has spent billions of dollars to control drug production, trafficking, and use, with few, if any, positive results. As shown in previous chapters, the results of the American drug strategy have been positive indeed—with a 95 percent rate of Americans who do *not* use drugs. If the number of drug abusers doubled or tripled, the social costs would be enormous.

Social Costs

In the year 2000, drug abuse cost American society an estimated $160 billion. More important were the concrete drug losses that are imperfectly symbolized by those billions of dollars—the destruction of lives, the damage of addiction, fatalities from car accidents, illness, and lost opportunities and dreams.

Legalization would result in skyrocketing costs that would illness is inextricably linked with drug abuse. In be paid by American taxpayers and consumers. Philadelphia, nearly half of the VA's mental patients Legalization would significantly increase drug use and abused drugs. The Centers for Disease Control and addiction—and all the social costs that go with it. With the Prevention has estimated that 36 percent of new HIV removal of the social and legal sanctions against drugs, cases are directly or indirectly linked to injecting drug many experts estimate the user population would at least users. double. For example, a 1994 article in the New England Journal of Medicine stated that it was probable, that if cocaine were legalized, the number of cocaine addicts in that year to America would increase from 2 million to at least 20 million.

Drug abuse drives some of America's most costly social problems— including domestic violence, child abuse, chronic mental illness, the spread of AIDS, and homelessness. Drug treatment costs, hospitalization for long-term drug-related disease, and treatment of the consequences of family violence burden our already strapped health care system. In 2000, there were more than 600,000 hospital emergency department drug episodes in the United States. Health care costs for drug abuse alone were about $15 billion.

Drug abuse among the homeless has been conservatively estimated at better than 50 percent. Chronic mental illness is inextricably linked with drug abuse. In Philadelphia, nearly half of the VA's mental patients abuse drugs. The Centers for Disease Control and Prevention has estimated that 36 percent of new HIV cases are directly or indirectly linked to injecting drug users.

In 1998, Americans spent $67 billion for illegal drugs, a sum of money greater than the amount spent on illegal drugs were devoted instead to finance public higher education in the United States.

If the money spent on illegal drugs were devoted instead to public higher education, for example, public colleges would have the financial ability to accommodate twice as many students as they already do.

In addition, legalization—and the increased addiction it would spawn—would result in lost workforce productivity—and the unpredictable damage that it would cause to the American economy. The latest drug use surveys show that about 75% of adults who reported current illicit drug use—which means they've used drugs once in the past month—are employed, either full or part-time. In 2000, productivity losses due to drug abuse cost the economy $110 billion. Drug use by workers leads not only to more unexcused absences and higher turnover, also presents an enormous safety problem in the workplace. Studies have confirmed what common sense dictates: Employees who abuse drugs are more likely than other workers to injure themselves or coworkers and they cause 40% of all industrial fatalities. They were more likely to have worked for three or more employers and to have voluntarily left an employer in the past year.

Legalization would also result in a huge increase in the number of traffic accidents and fatalities. Drugs are already responsible for a significant number of accidents. Marijuana, for example, impairs the ability of drivers to maintain concentration and show good judgment. A study by the National Institute on Drug Abuse surveyed 6,000 teenage drivers. It studied those who drove more than six times a month after using marijuana. The study found that they were about two-and-a-half times more likely to be involved in a traffic accident than those who didn't smoke before driving.

Legalizers fail to mention the hidden consequences of legalization.

Will the right to use drugs imply a right to the access to drugs? One of the arguments for legalization is that it will end the need for drug trafficking cartels. If so, who will distribute drugs? Government employees? The local supermarket? The college bookstore? In view of the huge settlement agreed to by the tobacco companies, what marketer would want the potential liability for selling a product as harmful as cocaine or heroin—or even marijuana?

Advocates also argue that legalization will lower prices. But that raises a dilemma: If the price of drugs is low, many more people will be able to afford them and the demand for drugs will explode. For example, the cost of cocaine production is now as low as $3 per gram. At a market price of, say, $10 a gram, cocaine could retail for as little as ten cents a hit. That means a young person could buy six hits of cocaine for the price of a candy bar. On the other hand, if legal drugs are priced too high, through excise taxes, for example, illegal traffickers will be able to undercut it.

Advocates of legalization also argue that the legal market could be limited to those above a certain age level, as it is for alcohol and cigarettes. Those under the age limits would not be five times permitted to buy drugs at authorized outlets. But teenagers today have found many ways to circumvent the age restrictions, whether by using false identification or by buying liquor and cigarettes from older friends. According to the 2001 National Household Survey on Drug Abuse, approximately 10.1 million young people aged 12–20 reported past month alcohol use (28.5 percent of this age group). Of these, nearly 6.8 million (19 percent) were binge drinkers. With drugs, teenagers would have an additional outlet: the highly organized illegal trafficking networks that exist today and that would undoubtedly concentrate their marketing efforts on young people to make up for the legalization. business they lost to legal outlets.

Costs to the Taxpayer

The claim that money allegedly saved from giving up on the drug problem could be better spent on education and social problems is readily disputed. When compared to the amount of funding that is spent on other national priorities, federal drug control spending is minimal. For example, in 2002, the amount of money spent by the federal government on drug control was less than $19 billion in its entirety. And unlike critics of American drug policy would have you believe, all of those funds did not go to enforcement policy only. Those funds were used for treatment, education and prevention, as well as enforcement. Within that budget, the amount of money Congress appropriated for the Drug Enforcement Administration was roughly $1.6 billion, a sum that the Defense Department runs through about every day-and-a-half or two days.

In FY 2002, the total federal drug budget was $11.5 billion.

By contrast, our country spent about $650 billion, in total, in 2000 on our nation's educational system. And most of us would agree that it was money well spent, even if our educational system isn't perfect. Education is a long-term social concern, with new problems that arise with every new generation. The same can be said of drug abuse and addiction. Yet nobody suggests that we should give up on our children's education. Why, then, would we give up on helping to keep them off drugs and out of addiction?

Even if drug abuse had not dropped as much as it has in the last 20 years—by more than a third—the alternative to spending money on controlling drugs would be disastrous. If the relatively modest outlays in the last 20 years—by more than a third—the alternative to spending money on controlling drugs would be disastrous. If the relatively modest outlays of federal dollars were not made, drug abuse and the attendant social costs ($160 billion in 2000) would be far greater.

Federal Drug Budget FY–2002 (billions) Drug Control DEA Budget source: 2003 National Drug Control Strategy $11.5 $1.6

On the surface, advocates of legalization present an appealing, but simplistic, argument that by legalizing drugs we can move vast sums of money from enforcing drug laws to solving society's ills. But as in education and drug addiction, vast societal problems can't be solved overnight. It takes time, focus, persistence—and resources.

Legalization advocates fail to note the skyrocketing social and welfare costs, not to mention the misery and addiction, that would accompany outright legalization of drugs.

Legalizers also fail to mention that, unless drugs are made available to children, law enforcement will still be needed to deal with the sale of drugs to minors. In other words, a vast black market will still exist. Since young people are often the primary target of pushers, many of the criminal organizations that now profit from illegal drugs would continue to do so.

Furthermore, it is reasonable to assume that the health and societal costs of drug legalization would also increase exponentially. Drug treatment costs, hospitalization for long-term drug-related diseases, and treatment of family violence would also place additional demands on our already overburdened health system. More taxes would have to be raised to pay for an American health care system already bursting at the seams.

Criminal justice costs would likely increase if drugs were legalized. It is quite likely that violent crime would significantly increase with greater accessibility to dangerous drugs—whether the drugs themselves are legal or not. According to a 1991 Justice Department study, six times as many homicides are committed by people under the influence of drugs as by those who are looking for money to buy drugs. More taxes would have to be raised to pay for additional personnel in law enforcement, which is already overburdened by crimes and traffic fatalities associated with alcohol. Law enforcement is already challenged by significant alcohol-related crimes. More users would probably result in the commission of additional crimes, causing incarceration costs to increase as well.

Fact 6: Legalization of Drugs will Lead to Increased Use and Increased Levels of Addiction. Legalization has been tried before, and failed miserably.

Legalization proponents claim, absurdly, that making illegal drugs legal would not cause more of these substances to be consumed, nor would addiction increase. They claim that many people can use drugs in moderation and that many would choose not to use drugs, just as many abstain from alcohol and tobacco now. Yet how much misery can already be attributed to alcoholism and smoking? Is the answer to just add more misery and addiction?

It's clear from history that periods of lax controls are accompanied by more drug abuse and that periods of tight controls are accompanied by less drug abuse.

During the 19th Century, morphine was legally refined from opium and hailed as a miracle drug. Many soldiers on both sides of the Civil War who were given morphine for their wounds became addicted to it, and this increased level of addiction continued throughout the nineteenth century and into the twentieth. In 1880, many drugs, including opium and cocaine, were legal—and, like some drugs today, seen as benign medicine not requiring a doctor's care and oversight. Addiction skyrocketed. There were over 400,000 opium addicts in the U.S. That is twice as many per capita as there are today.

By 1900, about one American in 200 was either a cocaine or opium addict. Among the reforms of this era was the Federal Pure Food and Drug Act of 1906, which required manufacturers of patent medicines to reveal the contents of the drugs they sold. In this way, Americans learned which of their medicines contained heavy doses of cocaine and opiates—drugs they had now learned to avoid.

Specific federal drug legislation and oversight began with the 1914 Harrison Act, the first broad anti-drug law in the United States. Enforcement of this law contributed to a significant decline in narcotic addiction in the United States. Addiction in the United States eventually fell to its lowest level during World War II, when the number of addicts is estimated to have been somewhere between 20,000 and 40,000. Many addicts, faced with disappearing supplies, were forced to give up their drug habits.

What was virtually a drug-free society in the war years remained much the same way in the years that followed. In the mid–1950s, the Federal Bureau of Narcotics estimated the total number of addicts nationwide at somewhere between 50,000 to 60,000. The former chief medical examiner of New York City, Dr. Milton Halpern, said in 1970 that the number of New Yorkers who died from drug addiction in 1950 was 17. By comparison, in 1999, the New York City medical examiner reported 729 deaths involving drug abuse.

The Alaska Experiment and Other Failed Legalization Ventures

The consequences of legalization became evident when the Alaska Supreme Court ruled in 1975 that the state could not interfere with an adult's possession of marijuana for personal consumption in the home. The court's ruling became a green light for marijuana use. Although the ruling was limited to persons 19 and over, teens were among those increasingly using marijuana. According to a 1988 University of Alaska study, the state's 12 to 17–year-olds used marijuana at more than twice the national average for their age group. Alaska's residents voted in 1990 to recriminalize possession of marijuana, demonstrating their belief that increased use was too high a price to pay.

By 1979, after 11 states decriminalized marijuana and the Carter administration had considered federal decriminalization, marijuana use shot up among teenagers. That year, almost 51 percent of 12th graders reported they used marijuana in the last 12 months. By 1992, with tougher laws and increased attention to the risks of drug abuse, that figure had been reduced to 22 percent, a 57 percent decline.

Other countries have also had this experience. The Netherlands has had its own troubles with increased use of cannabis products. From 1984 to 1996, the Dutch liberalized the use of cannabis. Surveys reveal that lifetime prevalence of cannabis in Holland increased consistently and sharply. For the age group 18–20, the increase is from 15 percent in 1984 to 44 percent in 1996.

The Netherlands is not alone. Switzerland, with some of the most liberal drug policies in Europe, experimented with what became known as Needle Park. Needle Park became the Mecca for drug addicts throughout Europe, an area where addicts could come to openly purchase drugs and inject heroin without police intervention or control. The rapid decline in the neighborhood surrounding Needle Park, with increased crime and violence, led authorities to finally close Needle Park in 1992.

The British have also had their own failed experiments with liberalizing drug laws. England's experience shows that use and addiction increase with "harm reduction" policy. Great Britain allowed doctors to prescribe heroin to addicts, resulting in an explosion of heroin use, and by the mid–1980s, known addiction rates were increasing by about 30 percent a year.

The relationship between legalization and increased use becomes evident by considering two current "legal drugs," tobacco and alcohol. The number of users of these "legal drugs" is far greater than the number of users of illegal drugs. The numbers were explored by the 2001 National Household Survey on Drug Abuse. Roughly 109 million Americans used alcohol at least once a month. About 66 million Americans used tobacco at the same rate. But less than 16 million Americans used illegal drugs at least once a month.

It's clear that there is a relationship between legalization and increasing drug use, and that legalization would result in an unacceptably high number of drug-addicted Americans.

When legalizers suggest that easy access to drugs *won't* contribute to greater levels of addiction, they aren't being candid. The question isn't whether legalization will increase addiction levels—it will—it's whether we care or not. The compassionate response is to do everything possible to prevent the destruction of addiction, not make it easier.

Fact 7: Crime, Violence, and Drug Use Go Hand–In–Hand

Proponents of legalization have many theories regarding the connection between drugs and violence. Some dispute the connection between drugs and violence, claiming that drug use is a victimless crime and users are putting only themselves in harm's way and therefore have the right to use drugs. Other proponents of legalization contend that if drugs were legalized, crime and violence would decrease, believing that it is the illegal nature of drug production, trafficking, and use that fuels crime and violence, rather than the violent and irrational behavior that drugs themselves prompt.

Yet, under a legalization scenario, a black market for drugs would still exist. And it would be a vast black market. If drugs were legal for those over 18 or 21, there would be a market for everyone under that age. People under the age of 21 consume the majority of illegal drugs, and so an illegal market and organized crime to supply it would remain—along with the organized crime that profits from it. After Prohibition ended, did the organized crime in our country go down? No. It continues today in a variety of other criminal enterprises. Legalization would not put the cartels out of business; cartels would simply look to other illegal endeavors.

If only marijuana were legalized, drug traffickers would continue to traffic in heroin and cocaine. In either case, traffic-related violence would not be ended by legalization.

If only marijuana, cocaine, and heroin were legalized, there would still be a market for PCP and methamphetamine. Where do legalizers want to draw the line? Or do they support legalizing *all* drugs, no matter how addictive and dangerous?

In addition, any government agency assigned to distribute drugs under a legalization scenario would, for safety purposes, most likely not distribute the most potent drug. The drugs may also be more expensive because of bureaucratic costs of operating such a distribution system. Therefore, until 100 percent pure drugs are given away to anyone, at any age, a black market will remain.

The greatest weakness in the logic of legalizers is that the violence associated with drugs is simply a product of drug trafficking. That is, if drugs were legal, then most drug crime would end. But most violent crime is committed not because people want to buy drugs, but because people are *on* drugs. Drug use changes behavior and exacerbates criminal activity, and there is ample scientific evidence that demonstrates the links between drugs, violence, and crime. Drugs often cause people to do things they wouldn't do if they were rational and free of the influence of drugs.

Six times as many homicides are committed by people under the influence of drugs as by those who are looking for money to buy drugs.

According to the 1999 Arrestee Drug Abuse Monitoring (ADAM) study, more than half of arrestees for violent crimes test positive for drugs at the time of their arrest.

For experts in the field of crime, violence, and drug abuse, there is no doubt that there is a connection between drug use and violence. As Joseph A. Califano, Jr., of the National Center on Addiction and Substance Abuse at Columbia University stated, "Drugs like marijuana, heroin and cocaine are not dangerous because they are illegal; they are illegal because they are dangerous."

There are numerous statistics, from a wide variety of sources, illustrating the connection between drugs and violence. The propensity for violence against law enforcement officers, coworkers, family members, or simply people encountered on the street by drug abusers is a matter of record.

A 1997 FBI study of violence against law enforcement officers found that 24 percent of the assailants were under the influence of drugs at the time they attacked the officers and that 72 percent of the assailants had a history of drug law violations.

Many scientific studies also support the connection between drug use and crime. One study investigated state prisoners who had five or more convictions. These are hardened criminals. It found that four out of every five of them used drugs regularly.

Numerous episodes of workplace violence have also been attributed to illegal drugs. A two-year independent postal commission study looked into 29 incidents resulting in 34 deaths of postal employees from 1986 to 1999. "Most perpetrators (20 of 34) either had a known history of substance abuse or were known to be under the influence of alcohol or illicit drugs at the time of the homicide. The number is likely higher because investigations in most other cases were inconclusive."

According to the 1998 National Household Survey on Drug Abuse, teenage drug users are five times far more likely to attack someone than those who don't use drugs. About 20 percent of the 12–17 year olds reporting use of an illegal drug in the past year attacked someone with the intent to seriously hurt them, compared to 4.3 percent of the non-drug users.

As we see in most cases, the violence associated with drug use escalates and, in many instances, results in increased homicide rates. A 1994 Journal of the American Medical Association article reported that cocaine use was linked to high rates of homicide in New York City.

As these studies, and others, prove—violence is the hallmark of drug abuse. Drug users are not only harming themselves, but as we can see, they are harming anyone who may have the misfortune of crossing their path. Dr. Mitchell Rosenthal, head of Phoenix House, a major drug treatment center, has pointed out that, "there are a substantial number of abusers who cross the line from permissible self-destruction to become 'driven' people who are 'out of control' and put others in danger of their risk-taking, violence, abuse, or HIV infection."

It is impossible to claim drug use is victimless crime or deny the relationship between drugs and violence, especially when looking at an Office of National Drug Control Policy (ONDCP) estimate for 1995, which estimates there were almost 53,000 drug-related deaths in that year alone, compared to 58,000 American lives lost in eight and a half years in the Vietnam War. The assertions dismissing the connection between drugs and violence by legalization proponents are simply not true. Drug use, legal or not, is not a victimless crime; it is a crime that destroys communities, families, and lives.

Fact 8: Alcohol has caused Significant Health, Social, and Crime Problems in this Country, and Legalized Drugs would only make the Situation Worse.

Drugs are far more addictive than alcohol. According to Dr. Mitchell Rosenthal, director of Phoenix House, only 10 percent of drinkers become alcoholics, while up to 75 percent of regular illicit drug users become addicted.

Even accepting, for the sake of argument, the analogy of the legalizers, alcohol use in the U.S. has taken a tremendous physical and social toll on Americans. Legalization proponents would have the problems multiplied by greatly adding to the class of drug-addicted Americans. To put it in perspective, less than 5 percent of the population uses illegal drugs of any kind. That's less than 16 million regular users of all illegal drugs compared to 66 million tobacco users and over 100 million alcohol users.

According to the Centers for Disease Control and Prevention (CDC), during 2000, there were 15,852 drug-induced deaths; only slightly less than the 18,539 alcohol-induced deaths. Yet the personal costs of drug use are far higher. According to a 1995 article by Dr. Robert L. DuPont, an expert on drug abuse, the health-related costs per person is more than twice as high for drugs as it is for alcohol: $1,742 for users of illegal drugs and $798 for users of alcohol. Legalization of drugs would compound the problems in the already overburdened health care, social service, and criminal justice systems. And it would demand a staggering new tax burden on the public to pay for the costs. The cost to families affected by addiction is incalculable.

If private companies were to handle distribution—as is done with alcohol—the American consumer can expect a blizzard of profit-driven advertising encouraging drug use, just as we now face with alcohol advertising. If the government were to distribute drugs, either the taxpayer would have to pay for its production and distribution, or the government would be forced to market the drugs to earn the funds necessary to stay in business. Furthermore, the very act of official government distribution of drugs would send a message that drug use is safe. After all, it's the U.S. Government that's handing it out, right?

Alcohol, a "legal drug," is already abused by people in almost every age and socio-economic group. According to the 2001 National Household Survey on Drug Abuse, approximately 10.1 million young people aged 12–20 reported past month alcohol use (28.5 percent of this age group). Of these, nearly 6.8 million (19 percent) were binge drinkers. American society can expect even more destructive statistics if drug use were to be made legal and acceptable.

If drugs were widely available under legalization, they would no doubt be easily obtained by young people, despite age restrictions. According to the 2001 National Household Survey on Drug Abuse, almost half (109 million) of Americans aged 12 or older were current drinkers, while an estimated 15.9 million or 7.1% were current illicit drug users.

The cost of drug and alcohol abuse is not all monetary. In 2001 more than 17,000 people were killed and approximately 275,000 people were injured in alcohol-related crashes. According to the National Highway Transportation Safety Administration, approximately three out of every ten Americans will be involved in an alcohol-related crash at some time in their lives.

Fact 9: Europe's More Liberal Drug Policies Are Not the Right Model for America.

Over the past decade, European drug policy has gone through some dramatic changes toward greater liberalization. The Netherlands, considered to have led the way in the liberalization of drug policy, is only one of a number of West European countries to relax penalties for marijuana possession. Now several European nations are looking to relax penalties on all drugs—including cocaine and heroin—as Portugal did in July 2001, when minor possession of all drugs was decriminalized.

There is no uniform drug policy in Europe. Some countries have liberalized their laws, while others have instituted strict drug control policies. Which means that the so-called "European Model" is a misnomer. Like America, the various countries of Europe are looking for new ways to combat the worldwide problem of drug abuse.

The Netherlands has led Europe in the liberalization of drug policy. "Coffee shops" began to emerge throughout the Netherlands in 1976, offering marijuana products for sale. Possession and sale of marijuana are not legal, but coffee shops are permitted to operate and sell marijuana under certain restrictions, including a limit of no more than 5 grams sold to a person at any one time, no alcohol or hard drugs, no minors, and no advertising. In the Netherlands, it is illegal to sell or possess marijuana products. So coffee shop operators must purchase their marijuana products from illegal drug trafficking organizations.

Apparently, there has been some public dissatisfaction with the government's policy. Recently the Dutch government began considering scaling back the quantity of marijuana available in coffee shops from 5 to 3 grams.

Furthermore, drug abuse has increased in the Netherlands. From 1984 to 1996, marijuana use among 18–25 year olds in Holland increased twofold. Since legalization of marijuana, heroin addiction levels in Holland have tripled and perhaps even quadrupled by some estimates.

The increasing use of marijuana is responsible for more than increased crime. It has widespread social implications as well. The head of Holland's best-known drug abuse rehabilitation center has described what the new drug culture has created: The strong form of marijuana that most of the young people smoke, he says, produces "a chronically passive individual—someone who is lazy, who doesn't want to take initiatives, doesn't want to be active—the kid who'd prefer to lie in bed with a joint in the morning rather than getting up and doing something."

Marijuana is not the only illegal drug to find a home in the Netherlands. The club drug commonly referred to as Ecstasy (3, 4–methylenedioxy-methamphetamine or MDMA) also has strong roots in the Netherlands. The majority of the world's Ecstasy is produced in clandestine laboratories in the Netherlands and, to a lesser extent, Belgium.

The growing Ecstasy problem in Europe, and the Netherlands' pivotal role in Ecstasy production, has led the Dutch government to look once again to law enforcement. In May 2001, the government announced a "Five Year Offensive against the Production, Trade, and Consumption of Synthetic Drugs." The offensive focuses on more cooperation among the enforcement agencies with the Unit Synthetic Drugs playing a pivotal role.

Recognizing that the government needs to take firm action to deal with the increasing levels of addiction, in April 2001, the Dutch government established the Penal Care Facility for Addicts. Like American Drug Treatment Courts, this facility is designed to detain and treat addicts (of any drug) who repeatedly commit crimes and have failed voluntary treatment facilities. Offenders may be held in this facility for up to two years, during which time they will go through a three-phase program. The first phase focuses on detoxification, while the second and third phases focus on training for social reintegration.

The United Kingdom has also experimented with the relaxation of drug laws. Until the mid–1960s, British physicians were allowed to prescribe heroin to certain classes of addicts. According to political scientist James Q. Wilson, "a youthful drug culture emerged with a demand for drugs far different from that of the older addicts." Many addicts chose to boycott the program and continued to get their heroin from illicit drug distributors. The British Government's experiment with controlled heroin distribution, says Wilson, resulted in, at a minimum, a 30–fold increase in the number of addicts in ten years.

Switzerland has some of the most liberal drug policies in Europe. In late 1980s, Zurich experimented with what became known as Needle Park, where addicts could openly purchase drugs and inject heroin without police intervention. Zurich became the hub for drug addicts across Europe, until the experiment was ended, and "Needle Park" was shut down.

Many proponents of drug legalization or decriminalization claim that drug use will be reduced if drugs were legalized. However, history has not shown this assertion to be true. According to an October 2000 CNN report, marijuana, the illegal drug most often decriminalized, is "continuing to spread in the European Union, with one in five people across the 15–state bloc having tried it at least once."

It's not just marijuana use that is increasing in Europe. According to the 2001 Annual Report on the State of the Drugs Problem in the European Union, there is a Europe-wide increase in cocaine use. The report also cites a new trend of mixing "base/crack" cocaine with tobacco in a joint at nightspots. With the increase in use, Europe is also seeing an increase in the number of drug users seeking treatment for cocaine use.

Drug policy also has an impact on general crime. In a 2001 study, the British Home Office found violent crime and property crime increased in the late 1990s in every wealthy country except the United States.

Not all of Europe has been swept up in the trend to liberalize drug laws. Sweden, Finland, and Greece have the strictest policies against drugs in Europe. Sweden's zero-tolerance policy is widely supported within the country and among the various political parties. Drug use is relatively low in the Scandinavian countries.

In April 1994, a number of European cities signed a resolution titled "European Cities Against Drugs," commonly known as the Stockholm resolution. It states: "The demands to legalize illicit drugs should be seen against the background of current problems, which have led to a feeling of helplessness. For many, the only way to cope is to try to administer the current situation. But the answer does not lie in making harmful drugs more accessible, cheaper, and socially acceptable. Attempts to do this have not proved successful. By making them legal, society will signal that it has resigned to the acceptance of drug abuse. The signatories to this resolution therefore want to make their position clear by rejecting the proposals to legalize illicit drugs."

Fact 10: Most non-violent drug users get treatment, not just jail time.

There is a myth in this country that U.S. prisons are filled with drug users. This assertion is simply not true. Actually, only 5 percent of inmates in federal prison on drug charges are incarcerated for drug possession. In our state prisons, it's somewhat higher—about 27% of drug offenders. In New York, which has received criticism from some because of its tough Rockefeller drug laws, it is estimated that 97% of drug felons sentenced to prison were charged with sale or intent to sell, not simply possession. In fact, first time drug offenders, even sellers, typically do not go to prison.

Most cases of simple drug possession are simply not prosecuted, unless people have been arrested repeatedly for using drugs. In 1999, for example, only 2.5 percent of the federal cases argued in District Courts involved simple drug possession. Even the small number of possession charges is likely to give an inflated impression of the numbers. It is likely that a significant percentage of those in prison on possession charges were people who were originally arrested for trafficking or another more serious drug crime but plea-bargained down to a simple possession charge.

The Michigan Department of Corrections just finished a study of their inmate population. They discovered that out of 47,000 inmates, only 15 people were incarcerated on first-time drug possession charges. (500 are incarcerated on drug possession charges, but 485 are there on multiple charges or pled down.)

In Wisconsin the numbers are even lower, with only 10 persons incarcerated on drug possession charges. (769 are incarcerated on drug possession charges, but 512 of those entered prison through some type of revocation, leaving 247 entering prison on a "new sentence." Eliminating those who had also been sentenced on trafficking and/or non-drug related charges; the total of new drug possession sentences came to 10.)

Policy Shift to Treatment

There has been a shift in the U.S. criminal justice system to provide treatment for non-violent drug users with addiction problems, rather than incarceration. The criminal justice system actually serves as the largest referral source for drug treatment programs.

Any successful treatment program must also require accountability from its participants. Drug treatment courts are a good example of combining treatment with such accountability. These courts are given a special responsibility to handle cases involving drug-addicted offenders through an extensive supervision and treatment program. Drug treatment court programs use the varied experience and skills of a wide variety of law enforcement and treatment professionals: judges, prosecutors, defense counsels, substance abuse treatment specialists, probation officers, law enforcement and correctional personnel, educational and vocational experts, community leaders and others—all focused on one goal: to help cure addicts of their addiction, and to keep them cured.

Drug treatment courts are working. Researchers estimate that more than 50 percent of defendants convicted of drug possession will return to criminal behavior within two to three years. Those who graduate from drug treatment courts have far lower rates of recidivism, ranging from 2 to 20 percent.

What makes drug treatment courts so different? Graduates are held accountable to the program. Unlike purely voluntary treatment programs, the addict—who has a physical need for drugs—can't simply quit treatment whenever he or she feels like it.

Many state governments are also taking the opportunity to divert non-violent drug offenders from prison in the hopes of offering treatment and rehabilitation outside the penal facility. In New York, prosecutors currently divert over 7,000 convicted drug felons from prison each year. Many enter treatment programs.

States throughout the Midwest are also establishing programs to divert drug offenders from prison and aid in their recovery. In Indiana, 64 of the 92 counties offer community corrections programs to rehabilitate and keep first time non-violent offenders, including nonviolent drug offenders, out of prison. Nonviolent drug offenders participating in the community corrections program are required to attend a treatment program as part of their rehabilitation.

In July of 2002, the Ohio Judicial Conference conducted a survey of a select group of judges. The results from the survey demonstrated that judges "offer treatment to virtually 100 percent of first-time drug offenders and over 95 percent of second-time drug offenders." According to the survey, these percentages are accurate throughout the state, no matter the jurisdiction or county size. The Ohio Judicial Conference went a step further, reviewing pre-sentence investigations and records, which demonstrated that "99 percent of offenders sentenced to prison had one or more prior felony convictions or multiple charges."

The assertion that U.S. prisons are filled with drug users is simply untrue. As this evidence shows, more and more minor drug offenders are referred to treatment centers in an effort to reduce the possibility of recidivism and help drug users get help for their substance abuse problems. The drug treatment court program and several other programs set up throughout the United States have been reducing the number of minor drug offenses that actually end up in the penal system. The reality is that you have to work pretty darn hard to end up in jail on drug possession charges.

FRANKLIN E. ZIMRING AND GORDON HAWKINS— THE WRONG QUESTION: CRITICAL NOTES ON THE DECRIMINALIZATION DEBATE

From *The Search for Rational Drug Control* (Cambridge University Press, 1992).

This chapter is both a summary and a critique of the current debate about decriminalization of drugs in the United States. Section I begins by rehearsing the arguments in favor of decriminalization advanced in the mid-nineteenth century by John Stuart Mill in *On Liberty* and the late nineteenth-century critique of that argument advanced by James Fitzjames Stephen, "the most powerful and penetrating of the contemporary critics of John Stuart Mill" (Quinton, 1978, p. 87). The Mill— Stephen exchange seems to us to exhaust most of the arguments currently employed in what we call the "polar debate" about drug decriminalization in the United States, a debate in which both sides believe that the only significant question is whether drugs should be prohibited by the criminal law.

Section II adds the two important new wrinkles present in the late twentieth-century continuation of the Mill–Stephen exchange as it related to drugs. These new points of emphasis, both prominent in the work of John Kaplan, are the significant role of the costs of maintaining a criminal prohibition in the calculus of policy and the likelihood that separate cost-benefit analyses for each of a wide variety of drugs will produce differing conclusions for different drugs.

Section III restates the decriminalization debate as a clash of presumptions in which those who favor decriminalization argue that when the facts are uncertain, government should presume that a policy that enhances liberty will best serve the public good, and those who support continuation of the criminal sanction contend that in uncertainty it is safest to presume that a continuation of current policy will maximize the public welfare. This conservative presumption explains why those who favor continuing prohibition do not also support extending prohibition to current licit substances. Preferring known to unknown evils is a legitimate technique of policy analysis in the drug area, and there is value in seeing the decriminalization debate as a competition of two presumptions, each with significant support in the American political tradition.

Section IV outlines our critique of the polar debate, which we find unfortunate in two respects. First, it emphasizes the question of whether the criminal law should be used in drug control when almost always the more important questions concern how, rather than whether, the criminal law will be used to control drugs. Second, the polar debate involves what we shall call "trickle-down" methods of policy determination. Both sides in the decriminalization debate think that the details of correct policy can work themselves out once the broad strokes of criminal justice policy are in place. It is assumed that the details of effective drug control can be inferred once the right answers to broad policy questions have been determined. But it is more plausible, we believe, to invest in a process of "trickle-up" policy analysis in which priority problems are identified and resources are allocated in real-world settings to particular problems.

I. John Stuart Mill and James Fitzjames Stephen

"In discussing drug control and freedom," Bakalar and Grinspoon observed, "it still makes sense to start with John Stuart Mill's essay *On Liberty*" (Bakalar and Grinspoon, 1984, p. 1). It does indeed make sense because Mill was particularly concerned about drug control laws, and his statement of the way in which they infringed on human liberty is a model of forceful argument. Writing in the 1850s at the time of America's first experiment with prohibition, he wrote:

Under the name of preventing intemperance the people of ... nearly half of the United States, have been interdicted by law from making any use whatever of fermented drinks, except for medical purposes: for prohibition of their sale is in fact, as it is intended to be, prohibition of their use.

Mill described this development as a "gross usurpation upon the liberty of private life" and an "important example of illegitimate interference with the rightful liberty of the individual" (Mill, 1859/1910, pp. 143–5).

"No person," Mill wrote, "ought to be punished simply for being drunk" (Mill, 1859/1910, p. 138). He also objected to taxes designed to limit consumption: "To tax stimulants for the sole purpose of making them more difficult to be obtained is a measure differing only in degree from their entire prohibition" (Mill, 1859/1910, p. 156). He was opposed to laws requiring the certificate of a medical practitioner for the purchase of dangerous drugs, for this, he asserted, "would make it sometimes impossible, always expensive" to obtain them. Although he did allow that "such a precaution, for example, as that of labelling a drug with some word expressive of its dangerous character, may be enforced without violation of liberty," because "the buyer cannot wish not to know that the thing he possesses has poisonous qualities" (Mill, 1859/1910, p. 152).

The basic principle underlying Mill's attitude toward drug control was stated in an often-quoted passage:

That the sole end for which mankind are warranted, individually or collectively, in interfering with the liberty of action of any of their members is self-protection. That the only purpose for which power can be rightfully exercised over any member of a civilized community against his will, is to prevent harm to others. His own good, either physical or moral, is not a sufficient warrant, he cannot rightfully be compelled to do or forbear because it would be better for him to do so, because it will make him happier, because, in the opinion of others, to do so would be wise or even right. (Mill, 1859/1910, pp. 72–3)

Less often cited are four qualifications that Mill placed on this principle that may be regarded as significant in relation to drug control. The first concerns children and young persons, a topic we shall cover in a later chapter. "It is, perhaps, hardly necessary to say," Mill added, "that this doctrine is meant to apply only to human beings in the maturity of their faculties" (Mill, 1859/1910, p. 73). Indeed, he thought that an important reason that society should not have "the power to issue commands and enforce obedience in the personal concerns of [adult] individuals" was that it "has had absolute power over them during all the early portion of their existence; it has had the whole period of childhood and nonage in which to try whether it could make them capable of rational conduct in life" (Mill, 1859/1910, p. 139).

With regard to this exception, one of Mill's more cogent critics, John Kaplan, argued that "Mill's exception for the young is unpersuasive," in that making a drug "available to adults would render completely unenforceable any effort to prevent the young from having access to the drug." "The median age for first heroin use is currently less than nineteen," Kaplan pointed out,

> and it is quite likely that giving adults freer access to the drug would considerably increase the number of users younger than this. That at least would be the natural conclusion we might derive from our experience with alcohol and tobacco, where our laws attempting to keep these drugs from the young have been rendered notoriously ineffective by their complete availability to adults.

And he suggested that Mill might have "countenanced a law making the drug unavailable to all on the ground that this was the only way of protecting youth" (Kaplan, 1983, p. 104).

This suggestion itself is unpersuasive, however, for two reasons. First, Mill, who was adamantly opposed to the prohibition of alcohol and other drugs, cannot have been unaware that giving adults free access to them raised some problems for anyone attempting to keep them from the young. Second, acceptance of the principle that the protection of children justified restrictions of this nature on adults would, in large measure, reduce adults to the status of children, and, to use Mill's own words, "there is no violation of liberty which it would not justify" (Mill, 1859/1910, p. 146). As a matter of fact, Mill did not think that prohibition was a feasible policy even for adults, and he noted that in America "the impracticality of executing the law has caused its repeal in several of the States which had adopted it" (Mill, 1859/ 1910, p. 145). But his objection to it was based on the more fundamental ground that the prohibition movement represented acceptance of a "doctrine [that] ascribes to all mankind a vested interest in each other's moral, intellectual, and even physical perfection, to be defined by each claimant according to his own standard." He viewed this as "monstrous," particularly because "there are many who consider as an injury to themselves any conduct which they have a distaste for, and resent it as an outrage to their feelings" (Mill, 1859/1910, pp. 140, 146).

The second exception to his principle related to "backward states of society in which the race itself may be considered as in its nonage." Despotism, Mill contended, "is a legitimate mode of government in dealing with barbarians" (Mill, 1859/1910, p. 73). As we shall see, Mill's most notable contemporary critic, James Fitzjames Stephen, regarded this exception as constituting a fatal flaw in Mill's argument, for in Stephen's view even in advanced, civilized communities there was "an enormous mass" of people who in relevant respects were effectively barbarians (Stephen, 1873/1967, p. 72).

The third exception to Mill's principle that is relevant to drug control relates to what he called "the right inherent in society, to ward off crimes against itself by antecedent precautions." This, he said, implied "obvious limitations to the maxim, that purely self-regarding misconduct cannot properly be meddled with in the way of prevention or punishment." In particular, he stated that although

> drunkenness, for example, in ordinary cases, is not a fit subject for legislative interference; ... I should deem it perfectly legitimate that a person, who had once been convicted of any act of violence to others under the influence of drink, should be placed under a special legal restriction, personal to himself; that if he were afterwards found drunk, he should be liable to a penalty, and that if when in that state he committed another offence, the punishment to which he would be liable for that other offence, should be increased in severity. The making himself drunk, in a person whom drunkenness excites to do harm to others, is a crime against others. (Mill, 1859/ 1910, p. 153)

We should note parenthetically here that over a century later, the British Committee on Mentally Abnormal Offenders proposed that an offense of "dangerous intoxication" should be punished by one year's imprisonment for a first offense and three years for a second or subsequent offense. The committee, however, did not go so far as Mill, who thought that intoxication alone should incur a penalty in the case of those previously convicted of violence while drunk. Rather, the commission's recommendation was intended to apply to people who, having become violent while intoxicated, might otherwise avoid conviction on the ground that they had lacked the intent necessary for the alleged offense (Great Britain, Home Office, 1975, pp. 235–7).

This third exception to Mill's principle might at first glance seem to be contrary to both his general commitment to individual liberty and his particular concern with the preventive function of government as "liable to be abused to the prejudice of liberty." For in that connection he observed that "there is hardly any part of the legitimate freedom of action of a human being which would not admit of being represented, and fairly too, as increasing the facilities for some form or other of delinquency" (Mill, 1859/1910, p. 151). In fact, however, there is no contradiction, for approval of using the criminal law to deal coercively or punitively with persons who under the influence of a drug commit crimes that harm others in no way conflicts with the principle that it should not be used against those whose conduct does no direct harm to others.

The fourth and final exception to Mill's principle pertains to the possibility of an individual selling himself into slavery, which, according to Mill, the state had a right to prevent:

> The ground for thus limiting [an individual's] power of voluntarily disposing of his own lot in life is apparent, and is very clearly seen in this extreme case. The reason for not interfering unless for the sake of others, with a person's voluntary acts, is consideration for his liberty. But by selling himself for a slave, he abdicates his liberty; he forgoes any future use of it, beyond that single act. He therefore defeats, in his own case, the very purpose which is the justification of allowing him to dispose of himself. He is no longer free; but is thenceforth in a position which has no longer the presumption in its favor, that would be afforded by his voluntarily remaining in it. The principle of freedom cannot require that he should be free not to be free. It is not freedom, to be allowed to alienate his freedom. These reasons, the force of which is so conspicuous in this peculiar case, are evidently of far wider application. (Mill, 1859/1910, pp. 157–8)

John Kaplan raised the question whether this "far wider application" might permit the government to prohibit heroin on the ground that heroin addiction is a species of slavery to which the user is at risk (Kaplan, 1983, p. 106). But it seems unlikely that Mill would have accepted this. First, Mill had nothing to say about acts that might involve only *some risk* of slavery, and the use of heroin involves merely some risk of addiction. Second, Mill cannot have been unaware of both alcohol and opiate addiction, and yet he made no mention of them in this context. Incidentally, Thomas De Quincey's widely acclaimed *Confessions of an English Opium Eater* first appeared in 1821, thirty-eight years before the publication of Mill's *On Liberty*.

However one may interpret the various limits on the application of his central principle, there is no doubt about either Mill's essential position or the relevance of his ideas to America today. In fact, in contemporary America, as in nineteenth-century England, "there are many who consider as an injury to themselves any conduct which they have a distaste for, and resent it as an outrage to their feelings" (Mill, 1859/1910, p. 140). Nor is this peculiar to America. Indeed, Mill himself stated that "it is not difficult to show, by abundant instances, that to extend the bounds of what may be called moral police, until it encroaches on the most unquestionably legitimate liberty of the individual, *is one of the most universal of all human propensities*" (Mill, 1859/1910, pp. 140–1; emphasis added). Mill went on to give numerous instances of the way in which the public in his own and other countries "improperly invests its own preferences with the character of moral laws," prohibition in America being only one such example.

But Mill did regard America as providing a singularly striking example of a country in which the government and the public upheld "the pretension that no person shall enjoy any pleasure which they think wrong." There was, he noted, "in the modern world" a strong tendency toward a democratic constitution of society accompanied by popular political institutions. Moreover, he pointed out that "in the country where this tendency is most completely realised—where both society and the government are most democratic—the United States—the feeling of the majority, . . . operates as a tolerably effectual sumptuary law." And when public opinion did not provide a sufficient sanction, it was accepted that there was "an unlimited right in the public . . . to prohibit by law everything which it thinks wrong" (Mill, 1859/1910, pp. 143–4).

What Mill saw as characteristic of America in the early nineteenth century remains true in the late twentieth century. Mill's statement that "the individual is not accountable to society for his actions, in so far as these concern the interests of no person but himself" (Mill, 1859/1910, p. 149) is no more generally accepted as a fundamental principle today than it was in 1859. Gore Vidal may have exaggerated when he said that the American people are "devoted to the idea of sin and its punishment" (Vidal, 1972, p. 375). But it is certainly true that "in this country we have a highly moralistic criminal law and a long tradition of using it as an instrument for coercing men toward virtue" (Morris and Hawkins, 1970, p. 5). Now, as then, it is probable that a great many Americans would echo Thomas Carlyle's angry reaction to Mill's essay: "As if," he said, "it were a sin to control, or coerce into better methods, human swine in any way; . . . Ach Gott im Himmel!" (Packe, 1954, p. 405).

If it makes sense when discussing drug control and freedom to start with John Stuart Mill's essay *On Liberty*, it makes equally good sense to follow that with his most formidable contemporary critic's *Liberty, Equality and Fraternity*. One of the things that makes Stephen's critique formidable is that he shared Mill's basic assumptions. As Anthony Quinton put it, Stephen's assumptions "were simply a more firmly held version of Mill's own first principles. He criticized Mill's deduction from utilitarian principles from the inside." Like Mill, Stephen did not regard the ideals of the French revolutionary formula, which he took for his title, as natural rights. Rather, he saw them as "valuable only to the extent that they contribute to the overriding end of the general happiness and, in Stephen's view, they did so only in a very qualified fashion" (Quinton, 1978, pp. 87–8).

When Stephen's book appeared, Mill had only a few more months to live, but he is on record as having said that Stephen "does not know what he is arguing against" (White, 1967, p. 1). Stephen, however, was quite clear that he was arguing against what he called Mill's "religious dogma of liberty" (Stephen, 1873/1967, p. 54). In what has been called "the finest exposition of conservative thought in the latter half of the nineteenth century" (Barker, 1915, p. 172), displaying that "certain brutal directness of mind" (Quinton, 1978, p. 87) that characterized all his polemical writings, Stephen subjected that "dogma" to vigorous criticism.

In particular, Stephen was sharply critical of Mill's statement that

> as soon as mankind have attained the capacity for being guided to their own improvement by conviction or persuasion (a period long since reached in all nations with whom we need here concern ourselves), compulsion either in the direct form, or in that of pains and penalties for noncompliance, is no longer admissible as a means to their own good, and is justifiable only for the security of others. (Mill, 1859/1910, pp. 73–4)

This, said Stephen, represented an exception or qualification to Mill's libertarian principle that reduced his doctrine either to an empty commonplace that no one would dispute or to an unproved and incredible assertion about the state of human society.

> Either then the exception means only that superior wisdom is not in every case a reason why one man should control another—which is a mere commonplace—or else it means that in all the countries which we are accustomed to call civilised the mass of adults are so well acquainted with their own interests and so much disposed to pursue them that no compulsion or restraint put upon any of them by any others for the purpose of promoting their interests can really promote them. No one can doubt the importance of this assertion, but where is the proof of it? (Stephen, 1873/1967, pp. 67–8)

Stephen noted that Mill had allowed that compulsion was justified as a means of dealing with barbarians, "provided the end be their improvement, and the means justified by actually effecting that end," because "liberty as a principle has no application to any state of things anterior to the time when mankind have become capable of being improved by free and equal discussion" (Mill, 1859/1910, p. 73). But he interpreted Mill as believing that "there is a period now generally reached all over Europe and America, at which discussion takes the place of compulsion, and in which people when they know what is good for them generally do it. When this period is reached, compulsion may be laid aside" (Stephen, 1873/1967, p. 69).

> To this, I should say that no such period has as yet been reached anywhere, and that there is no prospect of its being reached anywhere within any assignable time. Where, in the very most advanced and civilised communities, will you find any class of persons whose views or whose conduct on subjects on which they are interested are

regulated even in the main by the results of free discussion . . . of ten thousand people who get drunk is there one who could say with truth that he did so because he had been brought to think in full deliberation and after free discussion that it was wise to get drunk? (Stephen, 1873/1967, p. 69)

In Stephen's view, the idea that "in all nations with whom we need here concern ourselves" the period had long since been reached in which mankind had "attained the capacity of being guided to their own improvement by conviction or persuasion" was nonsensical.

Stephen not only saw no objection to people's being coerced for their own good but also regarded it as necessary. "Men are so constructed," he asserted,

that whatever theory as to goodness and badness we choose to adopt, there are and always will be in the world an enormous mass of bad and indifferent people—people who deliberately do all sorts of things which they ought not to do, and leave undone all sorts of things which they ought to do. Estimate the proportion of men and women who are selfish, sensual, frivolous, idle, absolutely common-place and wrapped up in the smallest of petty routines, and consider how far the freest of free discussion is likely to improve them. The only way by which it is practically possible to act upon them at all is by compulsion or restraint . . . the utmost conceivable liberty which could be bestowed upon them would not in the least degree tend to improve them. (Stephen, 1878/1967, pp. 72–3)

It is somewhat ironic that Mill, who had attacked English judges for their "extraordinary want of knowledge of human nature and life, which continually astonishes us in English lawyers" (Mill, 1859/1910, p. 126), was here in effect being told by an English judge that his own knowledge of human nature and life was defective. And Stephen took the view of human nature being what it was, it was necessary for society to use the criminal law to enforce society's moral code, whether or not breaches of it caused harm to others. "Criminal law in this country," he said, "is actually applied to the suppression of vice and so to the promotion of virtue to a very considerable extent; and I say this is right." In his view, the criminal law was "in the nature of a persecution of the grosser forms of vice," and he saw nothing wrong with that, because "the object of promoting virtue and preventing vice must be admitted to be a good one." It was therefore necessary "to put a restraint upon vice, not to such an extent merely as is necessary for definite self-protection, but generally on the ground that vice is a bad thing from which men ought by appropriate means to restrain each other" (Stephen, 1873/1967, pp. 143, 150, 152), and among those appropriate means he included the criminal law.

Stephen complained that in Mill's essay "there is hardly anything . . . which can properly be called proof as distinguished from enunciation or assertion" (Stephen, 1873/1967, p. 56; see also pp. 67, 74). And it is true that the principles enunciated by Mill are not supported by any proof; in fact they are not amenable to proof or logical demonstration. When they have read all the arguments in the debate on law and morals initiated by Mill, some readers may feel, with Herbert Packer, that "there is, perhaps, not much further to be said about it" (Packer, 1968, p. 251). But Stephen's case against Mill was not directed at Mill's principles so much as at their application in the real world, and in this connection some modern commentators have, tacitly at least, supported Stephen.

Thus in our own time, the notion that Mill's knowledge of human nature was deficient was echoed by H. L. A. Hart, who stated:

> Underlying Mill's extreme fear of paternalism there perhaps is a conception of what a normal human being is like which now seems not to correspond to the facts. Mill, in fact, endows him with too much of the psychology of a middle-aged man whose desires are relatively fixed, not liable to be artificially stimulated by external influences; who knows what he wants and what gives him satisfaction or happiness; and who pursues these things when he can. (Hart, 1963, p. 33)

Hart maintains that Mill carried his protests against paternalism "to lengths that may now appear to us fantastic." In particular, Hart cited Mill's criticism of restrictions on the sale on drugs as interfering with the liberty of the would-be purchaser:

> No doubt if we no longer sympathise with this criticism this is due, in part, to a general decline in the belief that individuals know their own interests best, and to an increased awareness of a great range of factors which diminish the significance to be attached to an apparently free choice or to consent.

In this connection, Hart took the view that "a modification in Mill's principles is required." Such a modification, he argued, need not abandon Mill's objection to the use of the criminal law to enforce morality. It would "only have to provide that harming others is something we may still seek to prevent by the use of the criminal law, even when the victims consent to or assist in the acts which are harmful to them" (Hart, 1963, pp. 32–33). But it is clear that acceptance of this modification of Mill's principle provides a rationale for a drug prohibition policy directed at traffickers and purveyors, if not consumers.

John Kaplan was another critic of Mill who appeared to disagree with Mill's "conception of what a normal human being is like." He observed: "It almost seems to be the nature of man to regard some types of predominantly self-harming conduct as, for one reason or another, the proper subject of official prohibition." He asserted that "the great majority of us do not agree with Mill's principle to begin with. Indeed, no modern state (or, so far as is known, any premodern state) has ever followed Mill's principle with respect to all activities." Kaplan then cited, as an example of "confrontation between Mill's principle and our nation's actions," the laws in about half of the American states requiring that motorcyclists wear protective helmets, although a helmetless cyclist does not pose any threat or cause any harm to others. In this case, the justification for the law is that helmetless cyclists expose all of us to the risk that we as taxpayers may, in the case of an accident, have to pay for expensive hospital treatment and, if they have families, to provide public assistance for them (Kaplan, 1983, pp. 106–7).

As with Stephen, it is the application of Mill's doctrine to the real world that Kaplan questioned. Thus he prefaced his discussion of the likely costs of legalizing cocaine by noting that the question is one that cannot be decided by reference to John Stuart Mill's "simple principle." Mill's rule regarding self-harming conduct, Kaplan believed, is "probably unworkable in a complex, industrial society—particularly one that is a welfare state," and moreover it "seems singularly inappropriate when it is applied to a habit-forming, psychoactive drug that alters the user's perspective as to postponement of gratification and his desire for the drug itself" (Kaplan, 1988, p. 36).

II.   CONTEMPORARY POLARITY

A survey of current opinion shows that the general terms of the decriminalization debate have not changed much at all. Most of the commentary we observe at the end of the twentieth century owes a great debt (most often unacknowledged) to the Mill—Stephen exchange. But sampling the current arguments of a wide variety of contemporary writers has value beyond making this basic point. Our canvas reveals a split among political conservatives between the Stephen-style prohibitionism of the *National Drug Control Strategy* and the laissez-faire sentiments regarding Mill's principles expressed by Milton Friedman and William Buckley. The texture and style of these general sentiments can be contrasted with the cost—benefit rhetoric of specific policy analyses as practiced by John Kaplan.

For Legalization

Although many critics have said that "we will never return to the social and intellectual conditions that made possible Mill's opposition to all drug laws" (Bakalar and Grinspoon, 1984, p. 69), there are today a number of intellectual descendants of Mill who have reaffirmed his basic principle that adults should be free to live their lives in their own way as long as their conduct is not directly hurtful to others (though others may think it foolish, perverse, or wrong). Some of them also reinforce Mill's concern with the "mischief of the legal penalties" (Mill, 1859/1910, p. 92) by enumerating the excessive collateral social costs of endeavoring to preserve various prohibitions. These writers are arguing, in effect, that the changing social conditions since Mill's day have not made irrelevant his opposition to drug laws but, instead, have provided powerful, prudent reasons for supporting his principled objection to them.

Many of these critics, however, see the crucial question as being not so much a matter of the collateral disadvantage costs or harmful side effects of prohibitions but, rather, a question, in Mill's words, of "the proper limits of what may be called the functions of the police; how far liberty may be legitimately invaded" (Mill, 1859/1910, p. 152). Thomas Szasz, for example, like Mill himself, is primarily concerned with the moral or ethical aspects of drug control in a free society dedicated to individual liberty. But unlike Mill, who declared "I forego any advantage which could be derived to my argument from the idea of abstract right" (Mill, 1859/1910, p. 74), Szasz maintains that we should regard "the freedom of choosing our diets and drugs as fundamental rights" (Szasz, 1987, p. 342).

Economist Milton Friedman is another authority who believes that we have no right in respect of adults

> to use the machinery of government to prevent an individual from becoming an alcoholic or a drug addict.... Reason with the potential addict, yes. Tell him the consequences, yes. Pray for and with him, yes. But I believe that we have no right to use force, directly or indirectly to prevent a fellow man from committing suicide, let alone from drinking alcohol or taking drugs. (Friedman, 1987, p. 135)

The correspondence with Mill's words is so close as to be almost paraphrastic. In such cases, wrote Mill, there may be "good reasons for remonstrating with him, or reasoning with him, or persuading him, or entreating him, but not for compelling him, or visiting him with any evil in case he do otherwise" (Mill, 1859/1910, p. 73).

Another opponent of drug prohibition laws, Gore Vidal, sees Mill's admission that a precaution such as "labeling the drug with some word expressive of its dangerous character may be enforced without violation of liberty" (Mill, 1859/1910, p. 152) as providing a solution to all the problems of drug addiction:

> It is possible to stop most drug addiction in the United States within a very short time. Simply make all drugs available and sell them at cost. Label each drug with a precise description of what effect—good and bad—the drug will have on the taker ... it seems most unlikely that any reasonably sane person will become a drug addict if he knows in advance what addiction is going to be like. (Vidal, 1972, pp. 373–4).

Not all the opponents of drug prohibition laws, however, have emphasized questions of liberty. Ronald Hamowy summarized some of the arguments offered in recent years "by a host of writers calling for repeal of our drug laws" as follows:

> Complete abandonment of all prohibitory laws ... the decriminalization of marijuana, cocaine, and the opiates would halt the current massive drain of public funds and the substantial suffering brought about through attempts to enforce these unenforceable laws. Evidence indicates that legalization would do much to reduce the current crime-rate and thus contribute to restoring the safety of our city streets. It would reduce the amount of government corruption, which is partly a function of the immense fortunes that are constantly made in the drug trade, and it would play a large part in

decreasing the profits that flow to organized crime. (Hamowy, 1987, p. 32)

Herbert Packer—who thought that "a clearer case of misapplication of the criminal sanction" than its use to enforce a policy of suppressing drug abuse "could not be imagined"—noted a number of other socially harmful effects of this misapplication:

> A disturbingly large number of undesirable police practices—unconstitutional searches and seizures, entrapment, electronic surveillance—have become habitual because of the great difficulty that attends the detection of narcotics offences.... The burden of enforcement has fallen primarily on the urban poor, especially Negroes and Mexican–Americans.... Research on the causes, effects and cures of drug use has been stultified ... A large and well entrenched enforcement bureaucracy has developed a vested interest in the status quo, and has effectively thwarted all but the most marginal reforms. (Packer, 1968, pp. 332–3)

Ernest van den Haag argued that from the history of the prohibition of alcohol in America "one may infer a general principle. In a democracy one can regulate, but one cannot effectively prohibit, sumptuary activities desired by a substantial segment of the population. Unenforceable attempts to prohibit certain substances will cause more harm than good." Van den Haag, who describes himself as not a "libertarian ideologue" but, rather, as "a strong political conservative," stated that his "argument for the legalization of marijuana, cocaine and heroin rests on the fact that their prohibition can be no more effective than the prohibition of alcohol." Those drugs, he asserted, "must be made as legal as alcohol is" (van den Haag, 1985).

William Buckley is another conservative who, although a one-time opponent of legalization in regard to heroin, now believes that "the accumulated evidence draws me away from my own opposition on the purely empirical grounds that what we now have is a drug problem plus a crime problem plus a problem of a huge export of capital to the dope-producing countries." Buckley also derides the possibility of making prohibition more effective: "Maybe we should breed 50 million drug-trained dogs to sniff at everyone getting off a boat or an airplane; what a great idea!" He advocates "legalization followed by a dramatic educational effort in which the services of all civic-minded, and some less than civic minded, resources are mobilized" (Buckley, 1985; p. All).

Milton Friedman, whose opposition to drug prohibition we noted earlier, also supplemented his libertarian case against it by reference to the social costs of prohibition. He argued that even if it were ethically justified, "considerations of expediency make that policy most unwise." Prohibition, he observed, is "an attempted cure that makes matters worse—for both the addict and the rest of us." Not only are addicts driven to crime to finance their addiction, but also "the harm to us from the addiction of others arises almost wholly from the fact that drugs are illegal" (Friedman, 1987, pp. 1356).

Those who advocate legalization tend to emphasize the social' and fiscal costs of prohibition and the benefits of legalization as though legalization were, if not a wholly costless policy at least, unlikely to involve any serious costs. Friedman, for example, pointed out that "legalizing drugs might increase the number of addicts, but it is not clear that it would." And he went on to say that if controls were removed and drugs were made legally available, not only would they lose the attractiveness that "forbidden fruit" has, but also the drug pushers would be put out of business because "any possible profit from such inhumane activity would disappear" (Friedman, 1987, p. 136). The latter point was also made by another economist, Thomas Schelling, when serving as a consultant to the 1967 President's Commission on Law Enforcement and Administration of Justice: "If narcotics were not illegal, there could be no black market and no monopoly profits, and the interest in 'pushing' them would probably be not much greater than the pharmaceutical interest in pills to reduce the symptoms of common colds" (Schelling, 1967, p. 124).

One advocate of legalization who has paid more than parenthetic attention to the probable costs of that policy is Ethan Nadelmann, who acknowledged that "all the benefits of legalization would be for naught, however, if millions more Americans were to become drug abusers" (Nadelmann, 1988, p. 24). But he maintains that there are "reasons to believe that none of the current illicit substances would become as popular as alcohol or tobacco, even if they were legalized." In particular, he asserted that "none of the illicit substances can compete with alcohol's special place in American culture and history."

There is good reason to doubt that many Americans would inject cocaine or heroin into their veins even if given the chance to do so legally ... the drugs and methods of consumption that are most risky are unlikely to prove appealing to many people, precisely because they are so obviously dangerous.

Nadelmann does not deny that legalization might lead to an increased consumption of the illicit drugs in their more benign forms. In his view, however, because in those forms they are less damaging to the human body than alcohol or tobacco and less strongly linked with violent behavior than alcohol, this does not invalidate "the logic of legalization" (Nadelmann, 1988, pp. 28–29).

For John Stuart Mill, drug prohibition represented an intolerable infringement of the moral and political principles of a free society. In our time, much greater emphasis is placed by opponents of prohibition on the social costs that such a policy is thought to entail. "Essentially," said Thomas Schelling, "the question is whether the goal of somewhat reducing the consumption of narcotics ... or anything else that is forced by law into the black market, is or is not outweighed by the costs to society of creating a criminal industry" (Schelling, 1967, p. 125). Those who favor legalization are doubtful about the extent to which consumption of the proscribed substances would be lessened by prohibition, and they even contend that consumption of them in their more harmful forms is frequently increased. They argue also that such reduction as may be achieved is always outweighed by its social costs, including the criminalization of consumers, the corruption of law enforcement, and the increase in organized crime.

For Prohibition

Section 6201 of the Anti–Drug Abuse Act of 1988 states categorically that "(1) proposals to combat sale and use of illicit drugs by legalization should be rejected; and (2) consideration should be given only to proposals to attack directly the supply of, and demand for, illicit drugs" (Criminal Law Reporter, 1988, p. 3011; emphasis added). This legislative interdiction of considering the repeal of drug prohibition laws has had little effect on either those who favor legalization or those who oppose it. In regard to those who oppose it, it is probably because those who favor the status quo—and prohibition in regard to drugs has been the status quo in America since 1914—rarely feel the need to defend it unless it happens to be threatened, and it has never been seriously threatened.

This is certainly true at the present time when the policy of prohibition is largely unquestioned and the "war on drugs" appears to enjoy wide public support. As Ethan Nadelmann put it:

> No "war" proclaimed by an American leader during the past forty years has garnered such sweeping bipartisan support; on this issue, liberals and conservatives are often indistinguishable. The fiercest disputes are not over objectives or even broad strategies, but over turf and tactics ... on the fundamental issues of what this war is about, and what strategies are most likely to prove successful in the long run, no real debate—much less vocal dissent—can be heard.

As for legalization: "Politicians and public officials remain hesitant even to mention the word, except to dismiss it contemptuously as a capitulation to drug traffickers. Most Americans perceive drug legalization as an invitation to drug-infested anarchy. Even the civil liberties groups shy away from this issue" (Nadelmann, 1988, pp. 3–4). It may be true, as Nadelmann asserted, that there is "a significant silent constituency in favour of repeal, found especially among criminal justice officials, intelligence analysts, military interdictors, and criminal justice scholars who have spent a considerable amount of time thinking about the problem." It may also be true that for many individuals in those categories, "job-security considerations, combined with an awareness that they can do little to change official policies, ensure that their views remain discreet and off the record" (Nadelmann, 1988, pp. 4–5). Insofar as those assertions are correct, they may explain why drug prohibition laws are not seen as needing justification. Silent constituencies do not require audible responses, and off-the-record views call for no on-the-record rebuttals.

An important exception to what might otherwise almost seem to be a conspiracy of silence can be found in the writings of James Q. Wilson, who in 1972 was appointed chairman of the National Advisory Council for Drug Abuse Prevention by President Nixon, with "marching orders ... to figure out how to win the war on heroin" (Wilson, 1990a, p. 21). Wilson specifically takes issue with advocates of legalization like Milton Friedman and Ethan Nadelmann and provides a rationale for drug prohibition and a defense of its political legitimacy. Just as those who advocate legalization emphasize the costs of prohibition, those who favor prohibition tend to stress the costs of legalization. Thus, Wilson summarized his views as follows: "I believe that the moral and welfare costs of heavy drug use are so large that society should bear the heavy burden of law enforcement, and its associated corruption and criminality, for the sake of keeping the number of people regularly using heroin and crack as small as possible" (Wilson, 1990b, p. 527).

The distinction between moral and welfare costs reflects the distinction between those libertarians who are concerned primarily with the moral costs and those who are more concerned with the economic, social, and fiscal costs of prohibition. Wilson pointed out that the costs of legalizing drugs are "difficult to measure, in part because they are to a large degree moral." His account of this aspect of drug use as a problem is in total accord with James Fitzjames Stephen's view of the proper role of the criminal law in ensuring "the suppression of vice" and "the promotion of virtue" (Stephen, 1873/ 1967, pp. 143, 150, 152). According to Wilson,

> The moral reason for attempting to discourage drug use is that the heavy consumption of certain drugs is destructive of human character. These drugs—principally heroin, cocaine, and crack—are, for many people, powerfully reinforcing. The pleasure or oblivion they produce leads many users to devote their lives to seeking pleasure or oblivion and to do so almost regardless of the cost in ordinary human virtues, such as temperance, fidelity, duty, and sympathy. (Wilson, 1990b, p. 523)

Society, Wilson believes, has an "obligation to form and sustain the character of its citizenry." In regard to "libertarians [who] would leave all adults free to choose their own habits and seek their own destiny so long as their behavior did not cause any direct or palpable harm to others," Wilson maintains that "government, as the agent for society, is responsible for helping instill certain qualities in its citizens" (Wilson, 1990b, p. 524). The use of drugs can "destroy the user's essential humanity" and "corrodes those natural sentiments of sympathy and duty that constitute our human nature and make possible our social life." In short, "dependency on certain mind-altering drugs is a moral issue and their illegality rests in part on their immorality ... legalizing them undercuts, if it does not eliminate altogether, the moral message" (Wilson, 1990a, p. 26).

One of the principal advantages "of making certain drugs illegal and enforcing the laws against their possession," according to Wilson, "is that these actions reinforce the social condemnation of drug use and the social praise accorded temperate behavior." They help "alter the moral climate so that drug use is regarded as loathsome" and help also "in shaping the ethos within which standards of personal conduct are defined" (Wilson, 1990b, pp. 542–3).

But Wilson is concerned not only with what he called "the tangible but real moral costs" (Wilson, 1990b, p. 527) of legalization but also with the social costs that he believes are underrated by those he referred to as "academic essayists and cocktail-party pundits." If the legalizers prevail,

> then we will have consigned millions of people, hundreds of thousands of infants, and hundreds of neighborhoods to a life of oblivion and disease. To the lives and families destroyed by alcohol we will have added countless more destroyed by cocaine, heroin, PCP, and whatever else a basement scientist can invent. (Wilson, 1990a, p. 28)

Even if we decided that government

> should only regulate behavior that hurt other people, we would still have to decide what to do about drug-dependent people because such dependency does in fact hurt other people . . . these users are not likely to be healthy people, productive workers, good parents, reliable neighbors, attentive students, or safe drivers. Moreover, some people are directly harmed by drugs that they have not freely chosen to use. The babies of drug-dependent women suffer because of their mothers' habits. We all pay for drug abuse in lowered productivity, more accidents, higher insurance premiums, bigger welfare costs, and less effective classrooms. (Wilson, 1990b, p. 524)

Apart from Wilson's essay on the subject, the strongest defense of current drug prohibition policies may be found in the Office of National Drug Control Policy's *National Drug Control Strategy*. Although possibly somewhat more strident in tone than Wilson's writing is, the rationale for prohibition provided in the latter document is essentially the same as his, and most of the differences are matters of emphasis.

The only apparent substantial disagreement relates to the effectiveness of drug prohibition as presently administered. According to Wilson, "Though drugs are sold openly on the streets of some communities, for most people they are hard to find" (Wilson, 1990b, p. 525). Whereas in the *National Drug Control Strategy* it is said that "here in the United States, in every State—in our cities, in our suburbs, in our rural communities . . . drugs are available to almost anyone who wants them" (Office of National Drug Control Policy, 1989, p. 2). But despite the disagreement about the availability of drugs and, by implication, about the current effectiveness of drug law enforcement activities, there is no dispute about the need for drug prohibition or about the nature of its justification.

Like Wilson, the authors of the *National Drug Control Strategy* see drug use as primarily "a moral problem." Although "people take drugs for many complicated reasons that we do not yet fully understand," for "most drug users" it is the result of "a human flaw" that leads them to pursue what is "a hollow, degrading and deceptive pleasure." It is necessary to take "a firm moral stand that using drugs is wrong and should be resisted." A person's "first line of defense against drugs is his own moral compass" (Office of National Drug Control Policy, 1989, pp. 9, 48, 50, 53).

Unfortunately, too many citizens appear to have defective moral compasses, and so America faces "a crisis of national character." Although "this crisis is the product of individual choices," it is not a matter that can be left to individuals, for "a purposeful, self-governing society ignores its people's character at great peril." It is necessary, therefore, for the state, by such means as "tough and coherently punitive anti-drug measures," a "significantly expanded . . . criminal justice system," and "the creation of more prison space," to ensure that "the number of Americans who still use cocaine and other illegal drugs, to the entire nation's horrible disadvantage, is . . . dramatically reduced" (Office of National Drug Control Policy, 1989, pp. 2, 7, 9, 26).

It cannot be said that the current debate about drug decriminalization has produced any particularly novel or illuminating insights into the issues of political principle or practice at stake. On the one hand, there is the libertarian's almost ritual invocation of Mill's assertion of the individual's right to do what he likes with his own body, providing that he does no harm to others. On the other hand, Stephen's assertion of the legitimacy of using the criminal law to regulate individual conduct, whether or not breaches of it cause harm to others, is re-echoed. On the conceptual level, the solution to "the drug problem" is viewed, for the most part, as a matter of choosing between diametrically opposed alternative expedients.

Specifism

A notable exception to such oversimplification may be found in the writings of John Kaplan, who recognized that whether or not John Stuart Mill's understanding of human nature was more or less accurate than that of Fitzjames Stephen or H. L. A. Hart, the fact is that the world he lived in—early nineteenth-century England—was very different from late twentieth-century America. Moreover, America in the 1990s bears little resemblance to America in the 1890s when today's illicit drugs were freely available. Thus, Kaplan made the point, in relation to the possibility of making heroin freely available, that we should hesitate "to extrapolate from our past experience in a predominantly rural, relatively crime-free, free-enterprise society to our present urban, crime-ridden, partially-welfare state." There was

> no turning back the clock. If we made heroin available today, it would be made available under very different conditions, with social variables such as the purpose and meaning of use and the availability of group support all very much changed. Even the drug would be different. Before the Harrison Act, the problem was opium or

morphine drunk in tonics and medicines. Today it is injectable heroin. (Kaplan, 1983, p. 112)

Kaplan regarded the rehearsal of past pieties as largely irrelevant to present problems. Mill's principle regarding self-harming conduct might have been "correct for early Victorian England," but today it was best viewed "as a very wise admonition to restraint in an exceedingly complex and emotion laden area" (Kaplan, 1983, p. 106).

Two features distinguish Kaplan's approach to problems in the drug area from that of most other scholars. The first is his emphasis on what Herbert Packer called "the practical or 'social cost-accounting' aspects of the criminal process" (Packer, 1968, p. 266). The Kaplan analysis places special emphasis on the costs of administering a criminal prohibition. The premise of this kind of cost-accounting approach is that

> every law that seeks to control human behavior entails social costs, as well as social benefits and that laws should be chosen to maximise the excess of benefits over costs. The clear implication is that, at the least, we should choose controls that entail more benefits than costs—or we should have no controls at all. (Bartels, 1973, p. 441)

Kaplan—in his first book on drug policy, in the first chapter on marijuana, which he then saw as "the key problem in the drug area"— put it as follows: "The wisdom of a law should be determined in pragmatic terms by weighing the costs it imposes upon society against the benefits it brings. The purpose of this book is to apply this principle to the laws criminalizing marijuana" (Kaplan, 1970, pp. x, 18).

This emphasis on cost—benefit analysis rather than the ideological or political aspects of drug policy is a feature of all Kaplan's writing on drugs. His book on heroin was, in his own description of it, "devoted to examination of the costs and benefits of different policies toward heroin" (Kaplan, 1983, p. 237). In his last contribution to the debate on drug policy in regard to cocaine, he stated once again that "the issue boils down to a careful weighing of the costs of criminalization of each drug against the public-health costs we could expect if that drug were to become legally available" (Kaplan, 1988, p. 37).

The reference to "the criminalization of each drug" in that passage reflects the other feature of Kaplan's analysis of the problems in a criminal justice policy toward drugs: his rejection of the idea that psychoactive drugs represented a unitary social problem to which the solution must be either prohibition or decriminalization. "Criminalization and legalization," he maintained, "are not the only possibilities." More importantly, he added that "if the choice for each of the 'recreational' drugs is between criminalization and some kind of legalization, then *it must be made on a drug-by-drug basis*" (Kaplan, 1988, pp. 35, 36; emphasis added).

Kaplan's emphasis on the specificity of the problems presented by each of the psychoactive drugs and his close attention to such variables as the singular pharmacological makeup of each of them and the costs of attempting to suppress them contrasts sharply with the approach of James Q. Wilson. Wilson sees all illicit drugs as representing an equal threat to "the moral climate" and as indistinguishable items in the total of "tangible but real moral costs" of drug use (Wilson, 1990b, pp. 527, 542).

In regard to that kind of generalization, Kaplan, in his book on marijuana, demonstrated that objective analysis led to a very different conclusion. Before becoming a professor of criminal law, he had, as an assistant U.S. attorney, prosecuted many violators of the federal drug laws. He commented that "like many Americans of my generation, I cannot escape the feeling that drug use, aside from any harm it does, is somehow wrong." He found it "easy to understand how, under the historical and social conditions present in this country at the time, the emergence of a strange intoxicant such as marijuana might have been felt to justify the official and popular apprehension it received" (Kaplan, 1970, pp. x, xi). However, in 1966 as one of the reporters to the Joint Legislative Committee to Revise the Penal Code of the State of California, Kaplan was assigned the drug laws as his first major item of concern. After reading everything available on the drug laws and the drugs themselves and discussing the relevant issues with law enforcement officials and the natural and social scientists most concerned, he decided that the only way to achieve a rational solution to the problems of drug control was to subject each drug and the relevant legislation to a separate analysis.

Alcohol prohibition, he maintained, had taught us that "a law is in essence society's purchase of a package of social effects." Whether or not the law was a wise one depended on the answers to two crucial questions: "(1) What are the total social and financial costs attributable to the law, and (2) what are the benefits that flow from this outlay?" "The important thing to note is that all laws have their costs" (Kaplan, 1970, pp. 1–2). After a detailed analysis of all the factors entering into the costs and benefits of the marijuana laws, Kaplan concluded that in this case there was "an enormous disparity between the costs and benefits of the marijuana laws" and that "the social and financial costs directly and indirectly attributable to the criminalization of marijuana far outweigh the benefits of this policy." In the circumstances, he said, "the only responsible course of action . . . is a liberalization of the marijuana law so extensive as to constitute an abandonment of primary reliance on the criminal law in this area" (Kaplan, 1970, pp. xi, 311, 374).

There are, of course, many difficulties in this kind of analysis. It is impossible to quantify with any precision the costs of criminalization, and it is no easier to predict the consequences of removing prohibitory laws in regard to illicit drugs. As Robert J. Michaels pointed out, "Anyone wishing to predict the consequences of legalized opiates must first invest in some facts . . . we clearly need numerical data about the present situation, summarized into relevant conceptual categories." But he went on to say that although all statistics are imperfect, "those related to drug use are egregiously bad." In particular, while they are frequently circulated and quoted with alarm, figures on the number of users and the volume of crime for which they are responsible are meaningless political constructs. They are highly sensitive to the use of arbitrary assumptions and are dependent on surveys or registers whose methodology is questionable and whose coverage is poor. (Michaels, 1987, pp. 289, 290, 324–5)

In short, it seems as though none of the conditions for plausible prediction can be met, for to offer quantitative forecasts regarding the future in the absence of reliable data about the present is to infer from the unknown to the unknown. Kaplan acknowledged that "it is hard to measure with precision the costs of laws, especially the human costs" and that "aside from more or less intelligent guesses, we are usually uncertain of the benefits of laws" (Kaplan, 1970, pp. 1–2). But he did not agree that because existing estimates are unable to provide reliable quantitative predictions of the consequences of legalization, therefore nothing could be said or all conjecture must be futile. Moreover, it is significant that when Kaplan applied the same mode of analysis that he had used for marijuana to heroin and cocaine, he reached very different conclusions regarding the probable consequences of decriminalization. In regard to both heroin and cocaine he demonstrated that it is possible to show some of the likely features of a world in which those drugs were legal and freely available and, in particular, what costs such a policy might entail.

Kaplan acknowledged that as far as the free availability of heroin is concerned, "the predictions are quite uncertain and difficult." But he stated that if we are to decide the wisdom of a free availability policy, we have to "attempt to predict what our society would look like if such a policy were adopted." Accordingly, he considered "the two most relevant social variables." These, he said, were "how many people would use the drug in various use patterns, and how harmful would their use be for them and for society?" (Kaplan, 1983, pp. 111, 112).

In regard to the first of these variables, he argued that the "statement that opiate availability is a major determinant of use ... means that within wide limits, the more available opiates are, the higher the rate of use—and of addiction." As examples of this, he cited our experience with American ground troops in Vietnam, where heroin was cheaply and easily available, and some 14 percent became addicted to the drug, with considerably more being non-addicted users. He also brought up the fact that the medical profession, which has greater access to opiates than the rest of us do, had an addiction rate estimated at about twenty times that of the general population. Moreover, he gave reasons for thinking that neither the Vietnam experience nor the extent of use among members of the medical profession "provide[s] a ceiling on the use to be expected under free availability" (Kaplan, 1983, pp. 113–14).

Kaplan agreed with Ethan Nadelmann that there seemed to be a psychological barrier against using a hypodermic needle. But he pointed out that heroin could be either smoked in cigarettes or snorted and that of the users in Vietnam, who began by smoking or sniffing the drug, a good percentage went on to intravenous use. Kaplan then quoted from a study that suggested that many young people, "sustained apparently by peer encouragement and the promise of euphoria," took their first heroin intravenously, and so the psychological barrier might not be so formidable after all. In addition, he contended that the act of making heroin legally accessible might change the message we convey about the dangers of the drug and, indeed, could be taken to indicate that it was safe enough to try. In addition to this disadvantage inherent in the repeal of any drug prohibition, he noted another consequence of free availability, that it would accustom the population to moderate users and thus weaken the incorrect but "perhaps functional" belief that heroin use leads inevitably to addiction and serious social and health consequences.

As to the likelihood of increased addiction, Kaplan maintained that there was no reason for confidence that the availability of pure, cheap heroin would not lead to sizable increases in addiction. Certainly the little evidence that existed on the use of opiates under conditions of free availability (e.g., the medical profession and the American soldiers in Vietnam) provided no support for any hope of low addiction rates. Moreover, apart from its effect of increasing addiction, free availability would be likely to make addiction longer lasting and more difficult to cure, for the most important reasons that addicts give up heroin—the trouble and expense of maintaining a "habit," the fear of legal sanctions, and the inability to obtain good heroin—would be removed (Kaplan, 1983, pp. 112–26).

With regard to the second variable, the harmfulness of the increased use of heroin both for the users and for society, little is known about the consequences of addiction under conditions of easy access and, in particular, about the long-term health consequences of heroin use. In this connection, Kaplan noted that although tobacco use is recognized today as an important cause of sickness and death, this was not recognized until investigations were carried out "far more probing than those to which chronic use of heroin has been subjected." The long-term health consequences of heroin use may well constitute a major public health problem.

In addition, there is the possibility that the free availability of heroin might produce a widespread unwillingness or inability to work. If this were the case, it is possible that the lowering of productivity and increased welfare payments resulting from the use of heroin could impose even greater social costs than do our present efforts at its suppression. There are, Kaplan contended, reasons to believe that for many people addiction would be incompatible with productive work, and "one would have to be an incurable optimist to believe that heroin could be made freely available without a considerable degree of social dislocation" (Kaplan, 1983, pp. 126–46).

Kaplan's analysis of the anticipated costs of legalizing cocaine followed the same lines as did his calculation of the costs of legalizing heroin. In the case of cocaine, however, he noted that it was "far more prevalent than heroin [and] imposes greater social costs upon us—from the amount of money flowing into criminal syndicates to the number of users arrested for predatory crimes." In addition, he noted the widely held view at that time, that cocaine was the more benign of the two drugs, which, he said, was "probably mistaken."

Kaplan offered no estimate of how many more people would use cocaine after it was legalized but pointed out that it was an extremely attractive drug with the highest "pleasure score" and greatest "reinforcing power" of any drug known to us. Although most of those who used the drug had not become dependent, this was mainly because it was both expensive and difficult to procure. But if the drug were made easily available and cheap, and the inconvenience and criminal danger to the user was removed, we should anticipate a considerable increase in the damage—psychiatric symptoms and general debilitation—brought by heavy cocaine use.

There was, moreover, a considerable problem in regard to preventing teenagers from gaining access to cocaine, for legalization would make it, de facto, available to the young, as are alcohol and tobacco. And being less bulky and more easily concealable than alcohol is and creating no aroma of smoke, cocaine would be even more difficult to keep from minors. In addition, even if it were taxed as heavily as possible, the financial costs of cocaine would be greatly curtailed by legalization. Kaplan calculated that because the cost including tax would have to be sufficiently low to make bootlegging unprofitable, the cost of one "hit" would be lowered to "only forty cents—a figure well within the budget of almost all grade-school children" (Kaplan, 1988; p. 41).

As for adults, Kaplan argued that the serious negative effects of heavy cocaine use on its users would render it extremely damaging in a complex, mechanized, and interdependent society such as ours. And there was no guarantee that legalization would not produce a fiftyfold increase in the number of those dependent on cocaine. In such circumstances, he reminded his readers that "it is the height of irresponsibility to advocate risking the future of the nation." In an ideal world it might be that the best way to mitigate the damage done by illegal drugs would be to persuade everyone not to use them, but in the real world we have to use coercion (Kaplan, 1988, pp. 36–44).

However one evaluates John Kaplan's drug-by-drug analysis and projections, the method he employed was quite different from the rhetoric on both sides of the decriminalization debate. First, the unit of analysis in Kaplan's policy universe is the single psychoactive substance. By contrast, the principal protagonists in the decriminalization debate seem to agree that the appropriate unit of analysis is the fortuitous assortment of drugs that happen to be currently prohibited. The second distinction between the specifist approach and the main part of the decriminalization debate concerns the basis for choice between policies. Kaplan's criteria for policy choice are exclusively pragmatic and can thus render those choices disconfirmable by subsequent experience. In arguing as a strict pragmatist that the prohibition of a particular drug generates more benefits than costs, whereas the prohibition of another drug does not, the specifist holds to a standard that makes predictions about cost and benefit, in principle at least, testable against historical events.

Both sides of the decriminalization debate—and the tradition extends from Mill and Stephen on through to Nadelmann and Wilson—support their preferred policies for a mixture of moral and prudent reasons that make their proposals impossible to assess objectively and virtually incontestable. If the operative costs of either policy seem too steep, its proponents can always retreat to the moral high ground. At that level the claim that "adult Americans have the right to choose what substances they will consume and what risks they will take" (Nadelmann, 1988, p. 11) is countered by the claim "that society has [an] obligation to form and sustain the character of its citizenry" (Wilson, 1990b, p. 524). And there is nothing that can count decisively against either claim.

Whether the imponderable element is the responsibility of the government for character formation or the freedom of adults to choose their own habits and seek their own destiny, the admixture of those elements with others that are at least in principle measurable renders the claims of both parties logically unassailable. In this respect the prohibitionist and the libertarian are closer to common ground with each other than either of them is to the specifist. So it is possible to read the specifist analysis of drug policy as an implicit critique of both sides in the decriminalization debate, a critique that we shall seek to extend in the next two sections.

III. THE CLASH OF PRESUMPTIONS

Although the contending parties in the decriminalization debate disagree on a number of factual issues, the debate itself is not centered on factual matters. What fundamentally divides the disputants is the contrast between them in regard to assumptions about what kind of policy should be preferred when only incomplete information is available.

Those on John Stuart Mill's side in the debate hold to a presumption of liberty. They claim that in regard to drugs and drug control—about which knowledge is limited and the outcomes of policy options cannot be predicted with any certainty—it is prudent to choose the course of conduct that maximizes individual liberty and freedom of choice. They assume that adults are capable of making up their own minds rationally and that rates of drug addiction are unlikely to soar if decriminalization is put into effect. They assume also that the interests of children are unlikely to be irredeemably compromised by the abandonment of drug prohibitions.

The contrary presumption associated with those who support drug prohibition is not so much a presumption in favor of authority or social control but more a presumption in favor of social continuity and adherence to established customs and institutions. As Edmund Burke put it, "It is a presumption in favour of any settled scheme of government against any untried project" (Burke, 1803/1890, p. 146). We know of no one who has argued that in the absence of perfect knowledge, all psychoactive substances should be proscribed. Instead, the prohibitionists discuss the risks of decriminalization in ways that suggest that in the absence of any definitive proof to the contrary, it is prudent to preserve and maintain the governmental policies that have been developed and not to subject them to innovative change and thereby disturb a settled traditional scheme of things.

Adherence to the presumption of continuity means opposition to the decriminalization of any currently prohibited substance. But it does not afford support for initiatives directed at restricting the availability of drugs that are currently not prohibited. In the absence of complete information, it is considered prudent to maintain, for instance, the prohibition of marijuana. But the presumption in favor of social continuity provides no reason for imposing restrictions on substances like alcohol and tobacco, the sale and consumption of which are currently permitted. Those who accuse prohibitionists of being inconsistent in their attitudes toward alcohol and other psychoactive drugs fail to recognize the underlying consistency implicit in a preference for the status quo that is the fundamental basis of the prohibitionist position.

Recognition that the prohibitionist side of the decriminalization debate is grounded in a presumption in favor of continuity renders intelligible the limited scope of the prohibitionist case in regard to psychoactive drugs. Even as they recognize the damage done by alcohol, none of the prohibitionist spokespersons in the modern era see this as an argument for prohibiting alcohol. Instead, they contend that things would get even worse if yet more substances were added to the list of currently available psychoactive drugs; this point was made in James Q. Wilson's earlier cited admonition that legalization would mean that "to the lives and families destroyed by alcohol we will have added countless more destroyed by cocaine, heroin, PCP, and whatever else a basement scientist can invent" (Wilson, 1990a, p. 28).

Both the presumption in favor of liberty and the presumption in favor of continuity have deep roots in American culture. The sentimental enshrinement of personal liberty is reflected in all facets of American life, from the Declaration of Independence to much popular music. And the preference for preserving the status quo, and for known evils over those unknown, is reflected in such popular slogans as "if it ain't broke don't fix it" and "why trade a headache for an upset stomach."

The debate on drug decriminalization is a tug-of-war between these two powerful sentimental forces, with the presumption in favor of liberty invoked in support of removing criminal sanctions on drugs and the preference for continuity providing support for the current categorization of licit and illicit substances. This clash of presumptions in regard to drug decriminalization differs from arguments concerning alcohol prohibition because in the case of that "noble experiment" (Fisher, 1930), the prohibition involved never achieved the tenure and consequent venerability that could have led people to see it as a stable and continuous feature of an historically evolved, established tradition.

The need to choose between the presumptions of liberty and continuity creates some strange crosscuts in customary political alignments in the United States. Both William Buckley and William Bennett are identified as staunch political conservatives. Yet in the current decriminalization debate they are diametrically opposed to each other. This contraposition, however, is readily intelligible in terms of Buckley's preference for the presumption of liberty and in Bennett's preference for the presumption of continuity.

The conservative political tradition in the United States is unique in that it combines both libertarian and continuative principles or presumptions. But these presumptions are not invariably consonant, and so a potential for divisiveness in the conservative ranks is always present. Nor are political liberals immune to dissension in the drug decriminalization debate. The mainstream liberal tradition in American politics incorporates both a reverence for established customs and institutions and a powerful attachment to libertarian principles. In arguing that this clash of presumptions is the subtext in the decriminalization debate, we do not suggest that the combatants themselves would use this vocabulary to describe their differences or to explain what animates their disagreement. But it seems to us that an explanation in these terms is consistent with the positions adopted by both parties to the debate. At the same time it renders intelligible the somewhat incongruous assortments of political bedfellows that have emerged as public spokespersons for both decriminalization and prohibition.

IV. THE WRONG QUESTION

The debate about drug decriminalization is lively and educational, but it threatens to become a distraction when decriminalization becomes the focus of a discussion of drug control policy. As a policy centerpiece, the decriminalization debates are flawed because they pose the wrong central question and because they use inappropriate methods to identify and resolve priority problems in drug control policies.

From John Stuart Mill to the morning newspaper, the decriminalization debate is about whether or not the criminal law should be a major element in the government's efforts to control drugs. Yet a world in which the administration of the criminal law and governmental efforts to control drugs inhabit totally different policy spheres is not only unprecedented but also unimaginable. The key question is not whether criminal law should play a significant role in the control of drug behavior but how a criminal law of drug control should be constructed. In making this assertion, we do not take sides in the decriminalization debate: The criminal law of drug control would be substantial and multifaceted in the United States even if the decriminalization movement carried the day.

Even if the substantive goals of decriminalization could be achieved, the strong likelihood is that efforts at decriminalization would come by amending rather than repealing criminal laws and leaving the formal structure of prohibition intact. We need look no further than the more than a dozen experiments with marijuana in the American states and in Canada to discern a common pattern of reducing rather than abolishing penalties for possession of small quantities for personal use. This is the functional form of steps toward decriminalization for both symbolic and practical reasons. Retention of the criminal sanction not only pays lip service to the tradition of prohibition, but it also allows some selective enforcement of the laws against suspected traffickers, as well as a continued police enforcement presence.

Further, the administrative burden of decriminalization tends to increase the number and complexity of criminal law controls in drug markets. Reducing the criminal penalties for using drugs generally does not mean withdrawing substantial penalties for drug trafficking in the same substances. Even with formal decriminalization, the tax and administrative regulations that come with the change in the status of substances increase the criminal law controls. The most famous example of this was the aftermath of the repeal of alcohol prohibition in 1933. Within three years, the number of people in federal prisons, for violating the tax laws and other administrative regulations produced in the post-Prohibition period, was nearly equal to that serving sentences for violating the Prohibition regulations just before its repeal. In his 1934–5 report, the director of the Federal Bureau of Prisons spoke of the failure of the repeal of Prohibition to reduce the number of liquor violators, remarking that "penitentiary commitments for liquor are substantially the same as they were during Prohibition days" (U.S. Department of Justice, Bureau of Prisons, 1936, pp. 1–3).

The likelihood that criminal prohibition would remain on the books for drugs historically treated by such prohibitions would mean that these drugs would generate even more business for the criminal law even as reliance on prohibition was de-emphasized. In his statement of the case for "the repeal of drug prohibition laws," Ethan Nadelmann made it clear that it is not "a call for the elimination of the criminal justice system from drug regulation." An "effective plan for legalization" would involve not only "consumption taxes" but also "restrictions on time and place of sale, prohibition on consumption in public places, packaging requirements, mandated adjustments in insurance policies, crackdowns on driving under the influence" (Nadelmann, 1988, p. 30). In addition to taxes and administrative controls, any regime of decriminalization would include the prohibition of drug use for minors and significant criminal penalties for those who supply minors. So, no matter how far toward an emphasis on regulatory and taxing controls the law might push, the residual role for the criminal law would be substantial.

Further, if there are behavioral links between drug use and predatory criminal activity, these linkages must be addressed within the criminal law and the correctional system, no matter what the formal status of the substances themselves. Whether and to what extent the number of drug users sent to our prisons would be decreased by various regimes of decriminalization is an empirical question not yet able to be answered. If alcohol can be considered a precedent, the link between serious drug abuse and the prison system would remain strong.

But what kind of criminal law of drug control? Where should drug control rank among the many other responsibilities of the criminal justice system? Which drugs and which strategies of enforcement of the criminal law should receive priority? These are the questions that by its terms the decriminalization debate does not address, and they are also among the most important issues that policy planners must confront.

The "Trickle-Down" Fallacy

The broad strokes of the decriminalization debate are just as troublesome to us as is the fact that the wrong central question is addressed. Both sides in that debate assume the correctness of what we shall call "trickle-down" policy determinations, a process in which people assume that details such as strategies of law enforcement and levels of resource allocation will be worked out as a matter of course once the large and general questions have been settled. The propensity to avoid questions of detail is the major intellectual vice of the decriminalization debaters.

General conclusions about whether criminal prohibitions should be maintained provide very little guidance to how drug policy should be conducted, because we live in a world where drug control competes with many other problems for public resources, where many different substances are subject to prohibition and thus compete with one another for antidrug resources, where many different methods of combating drugs are alternative candidates for funds, and where the single-umbrella term *prohibition* describes a range of public policies that vary from the passive toleration of marijuana in many states to high-intensity police activity in anticrack and antiheroin campaigns elsewhere.

What we call the trickle-down fallacy has been the particular vice in recent years of those who maintain that for many drugs, criminal prohibitions should be continued. Many prohibitionists simply ignore the detailed questions of enforcement priority and strategy. For these participants, inattention to the particulars of policy is a sin of omission, regrettable because the general propositions of the debate on decriminalization are the only topics considered. But there are also prohibitionists who seem to argue that the conclusion that drugs should be prohibited can translate into specific policy choices. For these actors, the trickle-down fallacy is a sin of commission.

Illustrations of why specific policy cannot be deduced from a prohibitionist stance are not hard to find. First, there are many claims for police, court, and prison resources, and so drug control must compete with other social problems that also have been deemed worthy of criminal prohibition. Should the marginal dollar or prison cell go to an antidrug campaign this year, to child sex abuse, or to convenience-store robbery?

Second, certain drugs must compete with other drugs for enforcement resources. Should the new task force emphasize marijuana or crack cocaine? To spread the available resources evenly across all prohibited drugs requires the agreement that all drugs are equally deserving of criminal prohibition, and this is not a popular sentiment.

There is a third reason that drug control policy cannot be deduced from a prohibitionist stance. Many different drug control strategies compete with one another as alternative means of achieving the objectives of antidrug campaigns. Simply because heroin qualifies for the use of the criminal prohibition, this does not mean that an extra police officer is the best method available for spending $50,000 in public funds to combat heroin dependence. Prohibition means that police and methadone maintenance can compete for antiheroin resources, but it does not mean that the police have a preferred position in that competition.

Those who propose decriminalization have also ignored issues of detail, but their failure is somewhat more understandable in that they are advocating a radical structural change in the status quo. Still, as the history of alcohol control has shown, decriminalization does not make drugs a less compelling subject for government attention and resources. And the history of tobacco has shown us the importance of governmental choice and the complexity of the choice process even when criminal prohibition is absent. Thus, decriminalization may be part of a drug control policy, but it cannot be the whole of drug policy.

If we are correct in arguing that the particulars of governmental drug policy cannot simply trickle down from broad generalizations about the use of the criminal sanctions, where should drug policy guidance come from? The second part of this book is an argument for (and application of) what we shall be calling a "trickle-up" policy process, in which specific readings on the problems posed by particular substances, and experience with the effectiveness of different drug control strategies, feed into a larger policy-planning process. Ours is a preference for an explicit trial-and-error method. In this process, the debate over decriminalization is something of a preliminary to the choice of specific policies. As long as the dialogue about the wisdom of prohibition complements rather than displaces the policy-planning process, the public interest can be served.

Notes and Questions

1. When the discourse on drug legalization in this section is compared to the debate about the prohibition of sodomy, there is a clear difference in vocabulary and emphasis on *both* sides of the two debates. The drug debate is saturated with the rhetoric of costs and benefits on both sides. There is no emphasis on personal liberty in Prof. Nadelmann's three main headings, nor

(more expectably) does the other side of the debate emphasize the liberty of adults. Why are the issues of sexual and reproductive autonomy discussed in rights-based language instead of cost/benefit-based language? What accounts for the absence of emphasis on personal liberty?

2.   The DEA document is organized around ten "facts on legalization," and fact 8 concerns alcohol. Does the DEA support alcohol prohibition? Or is their argument that illicit drugs and alcohol call for different legal policies? What critical differences does their argument identify, and do they apply to all illegal drugs?

3.   Even if decriminalization were the desired final objective of a law reform process, how would its advocates begin to shift legal policies? What steps would they take toward ultimate disengagement of the criminal law (e.g., reducing maximum criminal penalties, controlling the volume and type of drug behavior investigated and targeted for arrests, keeping classes of drug offenders out of prison)?

4.   Do Zimring and Hawkins confuse ends and means when they argue that legalization is the wrong question? Or do they argue that the criminal law always will and should stop short of total disengagement from drug control?

D.   MEDICAL MARIJUANA

Introduction

One long and extraordinary chapter in the recent politics of drug control in the United States concerns efforts by state governments to allow medical use of marijuana by eligible citizens notwithstanding the unwillingness of the federal drug control authorities and the Federal Drug Administration to encourage or allow medical marijuana use. This controversy is an important case study in government control of narcotics but also a conflict that many observers believe has strategic significance in the broader debate on the criminal law and drug control. One indication of the wider strategic significance of the medical marijuana issue is the Drug Enforcement Administration's effort to headline the issue in its argument against legalization—placing the issue as 4th in the "top ten facts on legalization" to argue that "smoked marijuana is not scientifically approved medicine. Marinol, the legal version of medical marijuana, *is* approved by science" (see DEA, supra Chapter 3, section 2). What is the broader strategic importance of this question? Do the following materials provide insight on this question? If the medical marijuana issue is a proxy for the wider debate on decriminalization, which side is winning this battle and why?

THE ECONOMIST—REEFER MADNESS
April 27th 2006.

MARIJUANA IS MEDICALLY USEFUL, WHETHER POLITICIANS LIKE IT OR NOT

If cannabis were unknown, and bioprospectors were suddenly to find it in some remote mountain crevice, its discovery would no doubt be hailed as a medical breakthrough. Scientists would praise its potential for treating everything from pain to cancer, and marvel at its rich pharmacopoeia—many of whose chemicals mimic vital molecules in the human body. In reality, cannabis has been with humanity for thousands of years and is considered by many governments (notably America's) to be a dangerous drug without utility. Any suggestion that the plant might be medically useful is politically controversial, whatever the science says. It is in this context that, on April 20th, America's Food and Drug Administration (FDA) issued a statement saying that smoked marijuana has no accepted medical use in treatment in the United States.

The statement is curious in a number of ways. For one thing, it overlooks a report made in 1999 by the Institute of Medicine (IOM), part of the National Academy of Sciences, which came to a different conclusion. John Benson, a professor of medicine at the University of Nebraska who co-chaired the committee that drew up the report, found some sound scientific information that supports the medical use of marijuana for certain patients for short periods—even for smoked marijuana.

This is important, because one of the objections to marijuana is that, when burned, its smoke contains many of the harmful things found in tobacco smoke, such as carcinogenic tar, cyanide and carbon monoxide. Yet the IOM report supports what some patients suffering from multiple sclerosis, AIDS and cancer—and their doctors—have known for a long time. This is that the drug gives them medicinal benefits over and above the medications they are already receiving, and despite the fact that the smoke has risks. That is probably why several studies show that many doctors recommend smoking cannabis to their patients, even though they are unable to prescribe it. Patients then turn to the black market for their supply.

Another reason the FDA statement is odd is that it seems to lack common sense. Cannabis has been used as a medicinal plant for millennia. In fact, the American government actually supplied cannabis as a medicine for some time, before the scheme was shut down in the early 1990s. Today, cannabis is used all over the world, despite its illegality, to relieve pain and anxiety, to aid sleep, and to prevent seizures and muscle spasms. For example, two of its long-advocated benefits are that it suppresses vomiting and enhances appetite—qualities that AIDS patients and those on anti-cancer chemotherapy find useful. So useful, in fact, that the FDA has licensed a drug called Marinol, a synthetic version of one of the active ingredients of marijuana—delta-9-tetrahydrocannabinol (THC). Unfortunately, many users of Marinol complain that it gets them high (which isn't what they actually want) and is not nearly as effective, nor cheap, as the real weed itself.

This may be because Marinol is ingested into the stomach, meaning that it is metabolised before being absorbed. Or it may be because the medicinal benefits of cannabis come from the synergistic effect of the multiplicity of chemicals it contains.

JUST WHAT HAVE YOU BEEN SMOKING?

THC is the best known active ingredient of cannabis, but by no means the only one. At the last count, marijuana was known to contain nearly 70 different cannabinoids, as THC and its cousins are collectively known. These chemicals activate receptor molecules in the human body, particularly the cannabinoid receptors on the surfaces of some nerve cells in the brain, and stimulate changes in biochemical activity. But the details often remain vague—in particular, the details of which molecules are having which clinical effects.

More clinical research would help. In particular, the breeding of different varieties of cannabis, with different mixtures of cannabinoids, would enable researchers to find out whether one variety works better for, say, multiple sclerosis-related spasticity while another works for AIDS-related nerve pain. However, in the United States, this kind of work has been inhibited by marijuana's illegality and the unwillingness of the Drug Enforcement Administration (DEA) to license researchers to grow it for research.

Since 2001, for example, Lyle Craker, a researcher at the University of Massachusetts, has been trying to obtain a licence from the DEA to grow cannabis for use in clinical research. After years of prevarication, and pressure on the DEA to make a decision, Dr Craker's application was turned down in 2004. Today, the saga continues and a DEA judge (who presides over a quasi-judicial process within the agency) is hearing an appeal, which could come to a close this summer. Dr Craker says that his situation is like that described in Joseph Heller's novel, "Catch 22". "We can say that this has no medical benefit because no tests have been done, and then we refuse to let you do any tests. The US has gotten into a bind, it has made cannabis out to be such a villain that people blindly say 'no'."

Anjuli Verma, the advocacy director of the American Civil Liberties Union (ACLU), a group helping Dr Craker fight his appeal, says that even if the DEA judge rules in their favour, the agency's chief administrator can still decide whether to allow the application. And, as she points out, the DEA is a political organisation charged with enforcing the drug laws. So, she says, the ACLU is in this for the long haul, and is already prepared for another appeal—one that would be heard in a federal court in the normal judicial system.

Ms. Verma's view of the FDA's statement is that other arms of government are putting pressure on the agency to make a public pronouncement that conforms with drug ideology as promulgated by the White House, the DEA and a number of vocal anti-cannabis congressmen. In particular, the federal government has been rattled in recent years by the fact that eleven states have passed laws allowing the medical use of marijuana. In this context it is notable that the FDA's statement emphasises that it is smoked marijuana which has not gone through the process necessary to make it a prescription drug. (Nor would it be likely to, with all of the harmful things in the smoke.) The statement's emphasis on smoked marijuana is important because it leaves the door open for the agency to approve other methods of delivery.

HIGH HOPES

Donald Abrams, a professor of clinical medicine at the University of California, San Francisco, has been working on one such option. He is allowed by the National Institute on Drug Abuse (the only legal supplier of cannabis in the United States) to do research on a German nebuliser that heats cannabis to the point of vaporisation, where it releases its cannabinoids without any of the smoke of a spliff, and with fewer carcinogens.

That is encouraging. But it does not address the wider question of which cannabinoids are doing what. For that, researchers need to be able to do their own plant-breeding programmes.

In America, this is impossible. But it is happening in other countries. In 1997, for example, the British government asked Geoffrey Guy, the executive chairman and founder of GW Pharmaceuticals, to come up with a programme to develop cannabis into a pharmaceutical product.

In the intervening years, GW has assembled a "library" of more than 300 varieties of cannabis, and obtained plant-breeder's rights on between 30 and 40 of these. It has found the genes that control cannabinoid production and can specify within strict limits the seven or eight cannabinoids it is most interested in. And it knows how to crossbreed its strains to get the mixtures it wants.

Nor is this knowledge merely academic. Last year, GW gained approval in Canada for the use of its first drug, Sativex, which is an extract of cannabis sprayed under the tongue that is designed for the relief of neuropathic pain in multiple sclerosis. Sativex is also available to a more limited degree in Spain and Britain, and is in clinical trials for other uses, such as relieving the pain of rheumatoid arthritis.

At the start of this year, the company made the first step towards gaining regulatory approval for Sativex in America when the FDA accepted it as a legitimate candidate for clinical trials. But there is still a long way to go.

And that delay raises an important point. Once available, a well-formulated and scientifically tested drug should knock a herbal medicine into a cocked hat. No one would argue for chewing willow bark when aspirin is available. But, in the meantime, there is unmet medical need that, as the IOM report pointed out, could easily and cheaply be met—if the American government cared more about suffering and less about posturing.

Notes and Questions

1. By the end of 2000, "twenty-six states and the District of Columbia had laws enabling the user of marijuana for medical purposes under specific

circumstances" (Pacula et al., "State Medical Marijuana Laws: Understanding the Laws and their Limitations", *Journal of Public Health Policy* 2002).

2. Why have more than half of all U.S. states passed some forms of medical marijuana law? For proponents of these laws, is the conflict about pain medication or a conflict about marijuana policies? What about for the laws' opponents?

PROPOSITION 215: TEXT OF PROPOSED LAW

Voter Information Pamphlet, State of California.

This initiative measure is submitted to the people in accordance with the provisions of Article II, Section 8 of the Constitution.

This initiative measure adds a section to the Health and Safety Code; therefore, new provisions proposed to be added are printed in *italic type* to indicate that they are new.

Proposed Law

SECTION 1. Section 11362.5 is added to the Health and Safety Code, to read:

11362.5. (a) This section shall be known and may be cited as the Compassionate Use Act of 1996.

(b)(1) The people of the State of California hereby find and declare that the purposes of the Compassionate Use Act of 1996 are as follows:

(A) To ensure that seriously ill Californians have the right to obtain and use marijuana for medical purposes where that medical use is deemed appropriate and has been recommended by a physician who has determined that the person's health would benefit from the use of marijuana in the treatment of cancer, anorexia, AIDS, chronic pain, spasticity, glaucoma, arthritis, migraine, or any other illness for which marijuana provides relief.

(B) To ensure that patients and their primary caregivers who obtain and use marijuana for medical purposes upon the recommendation of a physician are not subject to criminal prosecution or sanction.

(C) To encourage the federal and state governments to implement a plan to provide for the safe and affordable distribution of marijuana to all patients in medical need of marijuana.

(2) Nothing in this section shall be construed to supersede legislation prohibiting persons from engaging in conduct that endangers others, nor to condone the diversion of marijuana for nonmedical purposes.

(c) Notwithstanding any other provision of law, no physician in this state shall be punished, or denied any right or privilege, for having recommended marijuana to a patient for medical purposes.

(d) Section 11357, relating to the possession of marijuana, and Section 11358, relating to the cultivation of marijuana, shall not apply to

MEDICAL MARIJUANA

a patient, or to a patient's primary caregiver, who possesses or cultivates marijuana for the personal medical purposes of the patient upon the written or oral recommendation or approval of a physician.

(e) For the purposes of this section, "primary caregiver" means the individual designated by the person exempted under this section who has consistently assumed responsibility for the housing, health, or safety of that person.

SEC. 2. If any provision of this measure or the application thereof to any person or circumstance is held invalid, that invalidity shall not affect other provisions or applications of the measure that can be given effect without the invalid provision or application, and to this end the provisions of this measure are severable.

Argument in Favor of Proposition 215

Arguments on this page are the opinions of the authors and have not been checked for accuracy by any official agency.

Proposition 215 Helps Terminally Ill Patients

Proposition 215 will allow seriously and terminally ill patients to legally use marijuana, if, and only if, they have the approval of a licensed physician.

We are physicians and nurses who have witnessed firsthand the medical benefits of marijuana. Yet today in California, medical use of marijuana is illegal. Doctors cannot prescribe marijuana, and terminally ill patients must break the law to use it.

Marijuana is not a cure, but it can help cancer patients. Most have severe reactions to the disease and chemotherapy—commonly, severe nausea and vomiting. One in three patients discontinues treatment despite a 50% chance of improvement. When standard anti-nausea drugs fail, marijuana often eases patients' nausea and permits continued treatment. It can be either smoked or baked into foods.

Marijuana Doesn't Just Help Cancer Patients

University doctors and researchers have found that marijuana is also effective in: lowering internal eye pressure associated with glaucoma, slowing the onset of blindness; reducing the pain of AIDS patients, and stimulating the appetites of those suffering malnutrition because of AIDS "wasting syndrome"; and alleviating muscle spasticity and chronic pain due to multiple sclerosis, epilepsy, and spinal cord injuries.

When one in five Americans will have cancer, and 20 million may develop glaucoma, shouldn't our government let physicians prescribe any medicine capable of relieving suffering?

The federal government stopped supplying marijuana to patients in 1991. Now it tells patients to take Marinol, a synthetic substitute for marijuana that can cost $30,000 a year and is often less reliable and less effective.

Marijuana is not magic. But often it is the only way to get relief. A Harvard University survey found that almost one-half of cancer doctors surveyed would prescribe marijuana to some of their patients if it were legal.

If Doctors Can Prescribe Morphine, Why Not Marijuana?

Today, physicians are allowed to prescribe powerful drugs like morphine and codeine. It doesn't make sense that they cannot prescribe marijuana, too.

Proposition 215 allows physicians to recommend marijuana in writing or verbally, but if the recommendation is verbal, the doctor can be required to verify it under oath. Proposition 215 would also protect patients from criminal penalties for marijuana, but ONLY if they have a doctor's recommendation for its use.

Marijuana Will Still Be Illegal for Non–Medical Use

Proposition 215 DOES NOT permit non-medical use of marijuana. Recreational use would still be against the law. Proposition 215 does not permit anyone to drive under the influence of marijuana.

Proposition 215 allows patients to cultivate their own marijuana simply because federal laws prevent the sale of marijuana, and a state initiative cannot overrule those laws.

Proposition 215 is based on legislation passed twice by both houses of the California Legislature with support from Democrats and Republicans. Each time, the legislation was vetoed by Governor Wilson.

Polls show that a majority of Californians support Proposition 215. Please join us to relieve suffering and protect your rights. VOTE YES ON PROPOSITION 215.

RICHARD J. COHEN, M.D. Consulting Medical Oncologist (Cancer Specialist), California–Pacific Medical Center, San Francisco

IVAN SILVERBERG, M.D. Medical Oncologist (Cancer Specialist), San Francisco

ANNA T. BOYCE, Registered Nurse, Orange County

Rebuttal to Argument in Favor of Proposition 215

Arguments on this page are the opinions of the authors and have not been checked for accuracy by any official agency.

AMERICAN CANCER SOCIETY SAYS: "... Marijuana is not a substitute for appropriate anti-nausea drugs for cancer chemotherapy and vomiting. [We] see no reason to support the legalization of marijuana for medical use."

Thousands of scientific studies document the harmful physical and psychological effects of smoking marijuana. It is not compassionate to give sick people a drug that will make them sicker.

Smoking Marijuana Is Not Approved by the FDA for Any Illness

Morphine and codeine are FDA approved drugs. The FDA has not approved smoking marijuana as a treatment for any illness.

Prescriptions for easily abused drugs such as morphine and codeine must be in writing, and in triplicate, with a copy sent to the Department of Justice so these dangerous drugs can be tracked and kept off the streets. Proposition 215 requires absolutely no written documentation of any kind to grow or smoke marijuana. It will create legal loopholes that would protect drug dealers and growers from prosecution.

PROPOSITION 215 IS MARIJUANA LEGALIZATION— NOT MEDICINE

- Federal laws prohibit the possession and cultivation of marijuana. Proposition 215 would encourage people to break federal law.
- Proposition 215 will make it legal for people to smoke marijuana in the workplace ... or in public places ... next to your children.

NOT ONE MAJOR DOCTOR'S ORGANIZATION, LAW ENFORCEMENT ASSOCIATION OR DRUG EDUCATION GROUP SUPPORTS PROPOSITION 215—IT'S A SCAM CONCOCTED AND FINANCED BY DRUG LEGALIZATION ADVOCATES! PLEASE VOTE NO.

SHERIFF BRAD GATES Past President, California State Sheriffs' Association

ERIC A. VOTH, M.D., F.A.C.P. Chairman, The International Drug Strategy Institute

GLENN LEVANT Executive Director, D.A.R.E. America

Argument Against Proposition 215

Arguments on this page are the opinions of the authors and have not been checked for accuracy by any official agency.

READ PROPOSITION 215 CAREFULLY * IT IS A CRUEL HOAX

The proponents of this deceptive and poorly written initiative want to exploit public compassion for the sick in order to legalize and legitimatize the widespread use of marijuana in California.

Proposition 215 DOES NOT restrict the use of marijuana to AIDS, cancer, glaucoma and other serious illnesses.

READ THE FINE PRINT. Proposition 215 legalizes marijuana use for "any other illness for which marijuana provides relief." This could include stress, headaches, upset stomach, insomnia, a stiff neck ... or just about anything.

NO WRITTEN PRESCRIPTION REQUIRED * EVEN CHILDREN COULD SMOKE POT LEGALLY!

Proposition 215 does not require a written prescription. Anyone with the "oral recommendation or approval by a physician" can grow, possess or smoke marijuana. No medical examination is required.

THERE IS NO AGE RESTRICTION. Even children can be legally permitted to grow, possess and use marijuana ... without parental consent.

NO FDA APPROVAL * NO CONSUMER PROTECTION

Consumers are protected from unsafe and impure drugs by the Food and Drug Administration (FDA). This initiative makes marijuana available to the public without FDA approval or regulation. Quality, purity and strength of the drug would be unregulated. There are no rules restricting the amount a person can smoke or how often they can smoke it.

THC, the active ingredient in marijuana, is already available by prescription as the FDA approved drug Marinol.

Responsible medical doctors wishing to treat AIDS patients, cancer patients and other sick people can prescribe Marinol right now. They don't need this initiative.

NATIONAL INSTITUTE OF HEALTH, MAJOR MEDICAL GROUPS SAY NO TO SMOKING MARIJUANA FOR MEDICINAL PURPOSES

The National Institute of Health conducted an extensive study on the medical use of marijuana in 1992 and concluded that smoking marijuana is not a safe or more effective treatment than Marinol or other FDA approved drugs for people with AIDS, cancer or glaucoma.

The American Medical Association, the American Cancer Society, the National Multiple Sclerosis Society, the American Glaucoma Society and other top medical groups have not accepted smoking marijuana for medical purposes.

LAW ENFORCEMENT AND DRUG PREVENTION LEADERS SAY NO TO PROPOSITION 215

- The California State Sheriffs Association
- The California District Attorneys Association
- The California Police Chiefs Association
- The California Narcotic Officers Association
- The California Peace Officers Association Attorney General Dan Lungren

say that Proposition 215 will provide new legal loopholes for drug dealers to avoid arrest and prosecution ...

- Californians for Drug–Free Youth
- The California D.A.R.E. Officers Association
- Drug Use Is Life Abuse
- Community Anti–Drug Coalition of America
- Drug Watch International

say that Proposition 215 will damage their efforts to convince young people to remain drug free. It sends our children the false message that marijuana is safe and healthy.

HOME GROWN POT * HAND ROLLED "JOINTS" * DOES THIS SOUND LIKE MEDICINE?

This initiative allows unlimited quantities of marijuana to be grown anywhere ... in backyards or near schoolyards without any regulation or restrictions. This is not responsible medicine. It is marijuana legalization.

VOTE NO ON PROPOSITION 215

JAMES P. FOX President, California District Attorneys Association

MICHAEL J. MEYERS, M.D. Medical Director, Drug and Alcohol Treatment Program, Brotman Medical Center, CA

SHARON ROSE Red Ribbon Coordinator, Californians for Drug–Free Youth, Inc.

Rebuttal to Argument Against Proposition 215

Arguments on this page are the opinions of the authors and have not been checked for accuracy by any official agency.

SAN FRANCISCO DISTRICT ATTORNEY TERENCE HALLINAN SAYS ...

Opponents aren't telling you that law enforcement officers are on both sides of Proposition 215. I support it because I don't want to send cancer patients to jail for using marijuana.

Proposition 215 does not allow "unlimited quantities of marijuana to be grown anywhere." It only allows marijuana to be grown for a patient's personal use. Police officers can still arrest anyone who grows too much, or tries to sell it.

Proposition 215 doesn't give kids the okay to use marijuana, either. Police officers can still arrest anyone for marijuana offenses. Proposition 215 simply gives those arrested a defense in court, if they can prove they used marijuana with a doctor's approval.

ASSEMBLYMAN JOHN VASCONCELLOS SAYS ...

Proposition 215 is based on a bill I sponsored in the California Legislature. It passed both houses with support from both parties, but was vetoed by Governor Wilson. If it were the kind of irresponsible legislation that opponents claim it was, it would not have received such widespread support.

CANCER SURVIVOR JAMES CANTER SAYS ...

Doctors and patients should decide what medicines are best. Ten years ago, I nearly died from testicular cancer that spread into my lungs.

Chemotherapy made me sick and nauseous. The standard drugs, like Marinol, didn't help.

Marijuana blocked the nausea. As a result, I was able to continue the chemotherapy treatments. Today I've beaten the cancer, and no longer smoke marijuana. I credit marijuana as part of the treatment that saved my life.

TERENCE HALLINAN San Francisco District Attorney

JOHN VASCONCELLOS Assemblyman, 22nd District Author, 1995 Medical Marijuana Bill

JAMES CANTER Cancer survivor, Santa Rosa

DESMOND MANDERSON—FORMALISM AND NARRATIVE IN LAW AND MEDICINE: THE DEBATE OVER MEDICAL MARIJUANA USE

Journal of Drug Issues. 1999. 29(1): 121–134.

INTRODUCING DICHOTOMIES

The '30s, saw films like "Marihuana: Weed of Madness." In the'50s, the U.S. Congress was told it was a drug that incited "many of our most sadistic, terrible crimes ... such as sex slayings" (Inglis 1975: 183; see also Bonnie and Whitebread 1970; Himmelstein 1983: 19–26; Helmer 1975). In the'70s, the New South Wales parliament heard that it was to blame for "a yielding to homosexual advance" (N.S.W. 1976–77–78: 7779–80). So much, apparently, has marijuana wrought.

In the '90s, the debate has been fought on slightly different grounds. Proposition 215 amended the Californian Constitution to permit the use of cannabis as a medicine, in particular in cases of glaucoma, and to combat wasting syndrome and as an anti-nausea agent in the treatment of some cancers, AIDS, and MS (Grinspoon and Bakalar 1993; Vinciguerra, Moore and Brennan 1988; Hepler and Frank 1971; Clifford 1983; Consroe, Wood, and Buchsbaum 1975). But to give full effect to this would require the rescheduling of cannabis under the federal Controlled Substances Act, 21 U.S.C. § 812(b). As a Schedule II drug it would no longer be prohibited in absolute terms. Like a host of substances including morphine, the barbiturates, and so on, it would finally be capable of medical prescription in appropriate cases.

This step has provoked astonishing resistance and hostility. Although such a proposal does not envisage decriminalization of personal or recreational use, let alone legalization, the issue serves as a proxy war for the drug reform debate as a whole. The fear of floodgates and dangerous precedents undergirds the debate. It may be, therefore, that it will be impossible to understand this small skirmish except by reference to the cold war on drugs and its political imperatives. In 1992, the head of the United States Public Health Service, James Masin, declared that we ought not prescribe marijuana to AIDS patients because, "crazed" by the high, they "would be more likely to practise unsafe sex" (The

Economist 1992). If this is what counts as reasoned argument from an alleged expert, then it may be futile to take the opposition to the medical use of marijuana as anything other than a strategic opposition to the forces of drug law reform in general.

Questions of politics have been well documented in this area. We are familiar with the ways in which a continuing atmosphere of drug crisis serves the political aspirations of politicians and protects the budgets and power of institutions (Himmelstein 1978; Dickson 1968; Musto 1973; King 1978). We are also familiar with analyses that focus on the ways in which drug laws come to symbolize a broad range of social fears and insecurities (Helmer 1975; Gusfield 1963; Becker 1963; Manderson 1995). These critiques, as important as they are, can give the impression that "drug politics" is corrupting rational public policy. On this reasoning, drug policy will change if only people begin to look at 'the facts' objectively. But we all understand our facts and develop our politics from a particular, and often deeply held, philosophical position. Knowledge of the 'real facts' will not change people's minds. At the heart of the debate over drug policy lies a philosophical disagreement which must also be confronted.

The debate over the medical use of marijuana reflects a conflict between private and public, individual and society. According to this argument, the free choice of individual drug users is to be overridden because of the unacceptable social costs of use. This is an argument to which I return in the last section of this essay. But there is a remarkable paradox here. Those who come out in support of public virtue here are typically the same people who elsewhere support the hegemony of the private sphere. They are, in most other respects, philosophical "liberals" in the grand tradition of John Locke, Adam Smith, and John Stuart Mill. In most Western countries, including the United States and Australia, this liberalism entails an established commitment to the free market and individual autonomy. Why, then, does this ideological orthodoxy not extend to questions like the use of drugs? Why in particular does a belief in the free market in medicines and the individual's right to the relief of pain—or the "pursuit of happiness"—not extend to the use of cannabis?

Individualism is an important philosophical commitment of modem liberalism. But there is another philosophical framework which operates here—that of formalism. In the following section, the concept of formalism is explained and explored as a fundamental tenet of "liberal" law and "liberal" medicine alike.

Formalism or Narrative

Formalism is the philosophy which expresses the orthodox understanding of law. Hans Kelsen's Pure Theory of Law is perhaps the manifesto of this doctrine. He aims to make of the craft of law a "legal science," "objectivist and universalistic." "The law is an order," he writes, "and therefore all legal problems must be set and solved as order problems" (Kelsen 1934, in Goodrich 1983:248). The key element of legal formalism is a judicial system committed to results whose objectivity is conclusively determined by a process uncontaminated by external forces. This is what the "rule of law" means. It is an ideal which makes sense the moment one understands law as a logical system whose operations are designed to produce not true judgments but valid ones (Hart 1961). From axiom to conclusion, formalism shows no particular interest in the truth or otherwise of any legal system's basic principles, and every interest in ensuring the logical validity of its conclusions. As Pierre Bourdieu explains (1990).

> [F]ormalization, understood both in the sense of logic or mathematics as well as in the juridical sense, is what enables you to go from a logic which is immersed in the particular case to a logic independent of the individual case.

The "purity" of the process is guaranteed by the invariant structure which produces each and every result and by the specialists who administer it. Provenance and expertise, therefore, are the twin essences of formalism.

In the late 19th century, Max Weber described the development of a formal legal order according to which (Goodrich 1983:248)

> "abstract" legal propositions are organized systematically ... ; judges are to apply the code using specific modes of professional logic; not only is all human action "ordered by law," but what law allows no other social force can deny.

For law this means: specific criteria for legal enactment; procedural safeguards; and a specialist judiciary and legal profession to interpret the law. Let us imagine that law is a sausage factory, transforming conflict into justice by the operation of some great mill. According to the broad understanding which I am terming formalism, the quality of its sweetmeats is not assured by inspecting the sausages it produces, but rather by the regular machine that grinds the meat, and the white-coated technicians who keep it oiled.

This idea of law is far more relevant to the judiciary than the legislature. Policy-making has never claimed to be removed from substantive values. But there too, we place increasing emphasis on democracy as a process, in parliament and at elections, without inquiring as to the quality of our participation in it. Likewise, the "free press" is judged according to whether there are formal constraints on speech without regard to what is actually said and by whom. Weber's insight was to perceive elements of this trend towards a process-oriented understanding of truth, throughout the social world. He characterized ours as a society advancing in every sphere towards a system of "formal rationality" in which provenance and expertise would be the sole criteria by which to judge the truth or justice of a result (Weber 1954). This has been true in medicine no less than in law. The professionalization of health care has been a striking and relentless development this century (Friedson 1970; Carr–Saunders 1928; Boreham 1986; Willis 1983; Starr 1982). This trend towards the science of medicine has been accompanied by an emphasis on medical research as a product of experimental laboratories. Increasingly, unless medical results are obtained in this way, they do not constitute proof of "good science." It is the process by which medical science advances—the provenance of its techniques, and the professional expertise of its practitioners—that guarantees the objectivity and validity of its results.

Nevertheless, there are alternatives to this formalism. Experiment can be distinguished from discovery: experiments are designed to achieve a result, while discoveries emerge from experience. Indeed, until the very recent past, this was the nature, at least in the first instance, of most medical knowledge. One observed the result of taking, say, arrowroot or willowbark, opium or cod-liver oil, and from the rough conjunction of these experiences, began to detect a pattern. The essence of this model of medical discovery is a respect for the narratives of people's lives. Medical learning derives directly from the stories of how the sick and the healthy felt and what they did about it.

In law too, formalism can be contrasted with narrative. A formal process, as Kelsen put it, subjects "individual phenomena" to an overriding "systemic context." A narrative approach is instead interested in clients' own ways of describing their problems, in their own words. Without finding a space in law to hear and accommodate individuals' own experiences of their lives, we may end up exchanging substantive justice for an empty form. The idea of narrative in law, like that in medicine, values experience over abstraction, and results over process.

Philosophical liberalism reveals a strong commitment to formalism. It is scepticism about the idea of objective truth which drives it in this direction. Unsure as to what an objective or truly rational result might be, this philosophy puts its faith instead in the procedure to answer the question for them (Mill 1857; Habermas 1971; Weinrib 1993). In short, liberal philosophy gives up on defining substantive justice and hopes to provide it as a by-product of the process of law; it gives up on defining substantive health and hopes to provide it as a by-product of the process of medicine.

Paradoxically, this move subjugates individualism to a system (Habermas 1996). There is a tension here within the philosophy of liberalism which the debate on the medical use of marijuana highlights well. The next section illustrates how the contrasting frameworks of formalism and narrative underlie the conflicting medical and legal approaches in this area. To demonstrate these differences, I analyze two important and contradictory decisions that form the background to the current debate on the medical use of marijuana. On the one hand, the 1988 Opinion by Judge Francis Young, Chief Administrative Law Judge of the Drug Enforcement Administration (DEA), categorically recommended that marijuana be transferred to Schedule II (In the matter of Marijuana Rescheduling Petition 1988: 67); on the other hand, the 1992 Final Order by the Administrator of the DEA, determined that "marijuana does not have a currently accepted medical use in treatment in the

United States" and consequently refused to remove it from Schedule I (Marijuana Rescheduling Petition 1992; Alliance for Cannabis Therapeutics v. DEA, et al. 1 1994).

TWO FRAMEWORKS OF LIBERALISM

A Formal Order

Neither the Final Order of 1992 by Administrator Bonner, nor the Final Order by the Deputy Administrator the following year (In the matter of Petition of Carl Eric Olsen 1993) betray even the slightest acknowledgment of Judge Young's earlier ruling, although the hearing he conducted had been specifically requested by the DEA as part of a tortuously protracted series of proceedings lasting twenty years in the effort by the National Association for the Reform of Marijuana Laws (NORML) to remove marijuana to Schedule II.

Legal formalism is a framework of exclusion. It aims to treat legal rules as "an internally coherent whole ... a single justification that coherently pervades the entire relationship" (Weinrib 1993). The "gapless," ordered law is fundamental to the formalist ideal (Goodrich 1983). Internal consistency, then, is the prime value of legal formalism. The DEA's Final Orders reflect this in their very silences: that which is incommensurable must be ignored, for the law as a structure cannot concede its incompleteness or imperfection. So the Administrator of the DEA acknowledges the existence of no dissent.

Along with the Order's tacit commitment to legal formalism goes an explicit commitment to medical formalism. The Administrator concluded that marijuana had no "currently accepted medical use in treatment" (Controlled Substances Act, 21 U.S.C. § 812 (b)(2)(B)). He used the following criteria (Marijuana Rescheduling Petition 1992):

   a. the drug's chemistry must be known and reproducible;
   b. there must be adequate safety studies;
   c. there must be adequate and well-controlled studies proving efficacy;
   d. the drug must be accepted by qualified experts; and (and!)
   e. the scientific evidence must be widely available.

These criteria clearly do not determine the "currently accepted medical use" of a drug. Rather, they determine whether that medical use is in fact able to be "proved" effective.

Provenance, as we have seen, is integral to the formalist idea of proof. Dr Gabriel Nahas, a prominent foe of drug law reform, contrasts "anecdotal claims" for the therapeutic properties of marijuana smoking with "scientific scrutiny." Here too, Nahas emphasizes the need to "verify" the evidence of marijuana treatment by "clinical investigations," and concludes that the results of those studies have been inconclusive (Nahas and Pace 1994). In this framework, then, as in that of the Administrator, "proof" requires expertise and clinical process, while the experiences of those who have used the drug as an anti-nausea treatment while undergoing chemotherapy, for example, are dismissed as "hearsay" (ibid.). "Hearsay" is the heresy against which the faith of formalism sets itself: it condemns all truth-claims untested by a formal procedure, such as a scientific experiment or the legal oath.

The language of expertise is justified by the formalists' understanding of a drug as a collection of dangerous chemicals. Nahas' emphasis on this point is again typical (ibid.):

Indeed, marijuana contains in addition to THC 60 other cannabinoids which modify absorption, availability and transformation of THC in the body, and which are also biologically active. Besides cannabinoids, 360 other compounds have been identified in the plant material...

In legal and medical formalism alike, the role of the expert is to corral and protect an unwitting public from phenomena which would, if left in the state of nature, run wild. According to this Hobbesian worldview (1928; 1946) we need laws because without regulation our natural morals drive us to anarchy; we need medicine because without regulation our natural chemicals would drive us to pathology.

The Final Order of the Administrator emphasizes both expertise and provenance. According to the Administrator, medical use is only "accepted" if it is constituted by scientific processes of analysis (a) and experimentation (b and c), and carried out by scientific experts (d and e). The Administrator here confirms that medical science is legitimate not because it is substantively true but because it is formally valid. Like a law, medicine claims our allegiance because of the authority that supports it, and the process that brings it forth. Like a law, medicine tames our wild experience.

A NARRATIVE OPINION

The 1988 Opinion rendered by Judge Young took a different tack. He ascertained whether a drug is "used in medical treatment" not by the use of expert studies and clinical trials, but rather by investigating the experiences of doctors and their patients (In the matter of marijuana Rescheduling Petition 1988:31). Here he specifically criticized the earlier work of the DEA:

By considering little else but scientific test results and reports the Administrator was making a determination as to whether or not, in his opinion, [it] ought to be accepted for medical use in treatment ... It is not for this Agency to tell doctors whether they should or should not accept a drug or substance for medical use. The statute directs the Administrator merely to ascertain whether, in fact, doctors have done so.

Young's reasoning focuses on the many doctors who in fact accept marijuana as a useful treatment, rather than the process or expertise behind that acceptance. The word "acceptance" implies that medical treatment is grounded in a social practice tested by long experience and empirical observation. Judge Young quotes, for example, the mother of a cancer-riddled child in San Diego (ibid.: 22):

> When your kid is riding a tricycle while his other hospital buddies are hooked up to IV needles, their heads hung over vomiting buckets, you don't need a federal agency to tell you marijuana is effective. The evidence is in front of you, so stark it cannot be ignored.

The very evidence which a formalist approach dismisses as mere "hearsay" is treated here, as the judge frequently insists, as "uncontroverted" (ibid.:9). It could hardly be otherwise: in a study of oncologists undertaken in 1992, almost half had recommended marijuana to their patients despite the risk of prosecution (The Economist 1992). The disjunction between the decisions of Young and Bonner therefore lies in what counts as medical proof.

The medical anti-formalism of the judge is at one with his legal structure. For the evidence discussed by Young is, and is presented as, a sequence of personal and subjective narratives (In the matter of marijuana Rescheduling Petition 1988: 17–18):

> The patient's doctor, when asked about it later, stated that many of his younger patients were smoking marijuana. Those who did so seemed to have less trouble with nausea and vomiting.... The marijuana was completely successful with this patient, who accepted it as effective in controlling his nausea and vomiting ... The patient resumed eating regular meals and regained lost weight, his mood improved markedly, he became more active and outgoing and began doing things together with his wife that he had not done since beginning chemotherapy.

Listen to this language: "seemed to have less trouble"; "accepted it as effective"—not provenance but history governs what counts as evidence. He "resumed eating regular meals"; he "regained lost weight"; he revived in outlook and activity—not objective expertise but subjective experience governs why the evidence matters. Medical evidence is understood as the collection of personal experience; legal evidence is a way of giving respect to the stories of other people's lives.

Behind formalism we saw at work a fear of the state of nature, and its subjection to the control of expert systems. It is a liberalism with its roots in Hobbes. Behind anti-formalism there is a faith in nature and a corresponding fear of experts. Theirs is a liberalism which echoes Jean–Jacques Rousseau. Here the individualism of liberalism is most evident. The narrativists put their trust in the natural, the personal and the subjective, and distrust the institutional, the systemic, and the objective. As Robert Randall says, "The question is: who is going to control individual's biology—large corporations, doctors and governments, or people themselves" (ibid.).

BEYOND DICHOTOMIES

Formalism and Narrative

The debate on the use of marijuana in the treatment of illness is not just a political struggle or a dispute about facts; it is also a conflict between two kinds of liberal values, formalism and narrative. This explains the paradox by which the rhetoric of individualism succumbs in this case to the demand for social control. Nevertheless, the dichotomy between formalism and narrative, between public and private, individual and community, is a false one. Both aspects are already present within the discourse of liberal philosophy. It is the movement from an either/or absolutism in relation to these paradigms that suggests, within the realm of philosophy as well as of politics, how to couch the logic of drug law reform.

Law and medicine, no matter how formalist the theory which sustains them, are actually valued only because of the power of certain narratives as to their origins and development (Berman 1975; Cover 1983; Fitzpatrick 1992). Formalism is not just a theory which derives from nowhere and for no good purpose. It takes its place as part of a story of "progress" and "civilization". If legal process is thought to be more valuable than what Weber calls "kadi justice" (Weber 1954), in which each case is considered on its individual merits without reference to abstract principles, that is only because we understand formalism within a larger narrative about the development of our society.

Formalism in both law and medicine claims the mantle of a tradition stretching back to Aristotle and Hippocrates, Justinian and Galen, Sir Edward Coke and Sir Isaac Newton: rationalize, order, neutralize, objectify (Kuhn 1962; Foucault 1973; Blomley 1994). Its legitimacy stems not just from its logic, but because the legal and scientific method it represents has grown as a process over two and a half thousand years in response to on-going questions of how we are to test and enforce propositions about the nature of the physical world on the one hand, and the social world on the other. Formalism, if nothing else, is about proof—scientific truth and legal truth, what counts as reality and what counts as justice—but the justification of its truth is actually a reading of history: the history of struggle and contention through which our society has endeavoured to come to terms with how best to understand and structure our social interactions.

Formalism is embedded in a narrative, which actually provides it with its values. This is a fundamental point to make. In consequence, empirical and experiential claims about pain and treatment made by those who support the medical use of marijuana, ought to be addressed in their own terms.

PUBLIC AND PRIVATE

At the very heart of this narrative about social development, at the very heart of orthodox Western values, lies not one but two related philosophical traditions. The analysis I have undertaken of the workings of liberal theory, therefore, brings us back finally to consider how to balance these two traditions. On the one hand, the liberalism of Locke and Mill, with its commitment to individual freedom established through autonomous private action; on the other hand, a theory of "republicanism," which, going back to Aristotle and most recently articulated by Hannah Arendt and Michael Sandel, is committed to the idea of citizenship in which members of a democracy actively participate in a distinct "public sphere" (Sandel 1996; Arendt 1958; Kymlicka 1991; Aristotle 1967). Liberalism says we ought to be free to make individual decisions about how we want to give meaning and pleasure to our lives. Republicanism says we are entitled to decide, as a society, what kinds of personal behaviour ought to be encouraged or not. Our role as a citizen is to participate in this debate as to values and to abide by its outcome. This is what it is to be a member of "the community." And it is clear that there is a strong belief that drug use, no matter its purpose, destroys the public sphere by creating users who, through hedonism or addiction, are no longer able to be citizens in this strong sense.

The medical prescription of marijuana is not about pleasure; it is about pain. Those who support medical use emphasize not only its efficacy in reducing pain, but that those who take it obtain no pleasure from it (Marijuana Rescheduling Petition 1988:47):

> At college in Florida, Rosenfeld was introduced to marijuana by classmates. He experimented with it recreationally. He never experienced a "high" or "buzz" or "floating sensation" from it. . . .It had been very difficult for him to sit for more than five or ten minutes at a time because of tumors in the backs of his legs. . . .He experimented further and found that his pain was reduced whenever he smoked marijuana.

Notice the construction of parallel experiments, the recreational one which fails and the medical one which succeeds. Proposition 215 defends the use of marijuana as a response to pain and not as a desire for pleasure.

For those who oppose medical use, however, public values trump private use, and the distinction between pain and pleasure is ultimately irrelevant. The danger of marijuana use—of any kind—is typically seen to be the way in which it undermines the public sphere, encouraging hedonism and alienation, or creating a so-called "amotivational syndrome" (Himmelstein 1983). There is, indeed, a similar symbolism in play in all social attitudes to drug use. The fear of addiction is that the user will withdraw from the public realm into a world of private self-absorption (Peele 1989; 1985). Utopia or dystopia, hell or paradise, no matter. Marijuana encourages an atomised community: liberalism without republicanism to balance it. Whether their drug use stems from pain or pleasure is, it turns out, of no account; both must be sacrificed to a greater social good.

Neither can this dichotomy between "public" and "private"—between, perhaps, republican citizenship and liberal autonomy—be long sustained. "Public" welfare and "private" autonomy are symbiotic. The philosopher Jurgen Habermas writes about the role of public discourse in securing private freedom, since our personal identity is formed not in abstract isolation but out of the community in which we live (Habermas

1996:784). But the opposite is equally true. The efficacy of public life depends on the ability of private individuals to act with freedom and autonomy in their own lives. The public sphere constructs private identity and vice versa. The desire to make of our society not just an agglomeration but a community is admirable and familiar. But without respecting individual autonomy, such a community will be fictitious.

The specific context of the medical use of marijuana directly shows us how private freedom is necessary for the public sphere. The experience of pain and suffering denies in a very physical sense any personal autonomy, while simultaneously precluding the possibility of public participation. Citizenship asks us to look outside of ourselves and ahead to the future. Be in pain, feel weak, throw up every time you eat: such abstractions cease to matter. Chronic or acute pain is an intensely isolating experience (Scarry 1985). Between the sick and the well lies a gauze screen. To have no relief from pain is to feel yourself removed, step by step, from the world of others whose concerns and interests, even whose conversation, seems to recede. Your life becomes a constant cycle of anticipation and recovery. Wait for the next jolt of pain, the next wave of nausea to come upon you. Recoil, pause, wait. Illness is a completely individual battle. The hospital ward knows no wider public than itself: it is a sphere bounded by physical existence, debilitated by physical exertion.

Pain is the point at which the two traditions unite. Freedom from pain is both essential to individual autonomy and the very precondition for public participation. It is only by the relief of pain that the sick can be released into the public realm again. Bill Shanteau, living with the final stages of colon cancer, articulates the social as well as the personal importance of effective pain management (San Jose Mercury News 1995):

> The point is marijuana is a major agent in keeping me interested in life. Besides restoring my appetite, it's like a hot tub for the brain.... It keeps me focused in the moment instead of sitting here thinking I'm dying tomorrow.

Prohibiting the medical use of marijuana militates against precisely the "republican" values which would, in any philosophical sense, underlie such a policy.

Beyond the dichotomy between formalism and narrative, one can at last hear the stories of those who suffer and those who have been helped. Beyond the dichotomy between public and private, the control of pain becomes not just a private benefit, but a public advantage. "Amotivational syndrome" articulates a genuine fear as to the development of a dysfunctional community. But pain is the greatest amotivational syndrome of all.

NOTES

Proposition 215 added section 11362.5 to the State of California Health and Safety Code, "(A) To ensure that seriously ill Californians have the right to obtain and use marijuana for medical purposes where that medical use is deemed appropriate and has been recommended by a physician who has determined that the person's health would benefit from the use of marijuana in the treatment of cancer, anorexia, AIDS, chronic pain, spasticity, glaucoma, arthritis, migraine, or any other illness for which marijuana provides relief. (B) To ensure that patients and their primary caregivers who obtain and use marijuana for medical purposes upon the recommendation of a physician are not subject to criminal prosecution or sanction."

REFERENCES

Alliance for Cannabis Therapeutics v. DEA, et al., 15 F.3d. 1131 (D.C. Cir. 1994).

Arendt, H. 1958 The Human Condition. Chicago: University of Chicago Press.

Aristotle 1967 The Politics. Harmondsworth: Penguin.

Becker, H. 1963 Outsiders: Studies in the Sociology of Deviance. New York: Free Press.

Blomley, N. K. 1994 Law, Space, and the Geographies of Power New York: The Guilford Press.

Bonnie, R. and C. Whitebread. 1970 The Forbidden Fruit and the Tree of Knowledge. Virginia Law Review 56:971.

Boreham, P. (ed.) 1986 The Professions in Australia. St. Lucia: University of Queensland Press.

Bourdieu, P. 1990 In Other Words: Essays Towards a Reflexive Sociology. Cambridge: Polity.

Carr–Saunders, A. M. 1928 Professions. Oxford: Clarendon Press.

Clifford 1983 THC for Tremor in Multiple Sclerosis. Ann. Neurology 18:669.

Consroe, Wood, and Buchsbaum 1975 Anticonvulsant Nature of Marijuana Smoking. JAMA 234:306. Controlled Substances Act (U.S.) 21 U.S.C. § 812(b)

Dickson, D. 1968 Bureaucracy and Morality: An Organization Perspective on a Moral Crusade. Social Problems 16:143.

Fitzpatrick, P. 1992 The Mythology of Modern Law. London: Routledge.

Foucault, M. 1973 The Order of Things. New York: Vintage Books.

Friedson, E. 1970 Professional Dominance. New York: Aldine.

Goodrich, P. 1983 The Rise of Legal Formalism Or the Defences of Legal Faith. Legal Studies 3:248.

Grinspoon, L. and Bakalar. 1993 Marijuana: The Forbidden Medicine. New Haven: Yale University Press.

Gusfield, J. 1963 Symbolic Crusade. Urbana: University of Illinois Press.

Habermas, J. 1971 Toward a Rational Society. London: Heinemann.

Habermas, J. 1996 Paradigms of Law. Cardozo Law Review 17:771–84.

Hart, H. L. A. 1961 The Concept of Law. Oxford: Clarendon Press.

Helmer, J. 1975 Drugs and Minority Oppression. New York: Seabury Press.

Hepler and Frank 1971 Marijuana Smoking and Intraocular Pressure. JAMA 217:1392.

Himmelstein, J. 1978 Drug Politics Theory. Journal of Drug Issues 8:37.

Himmelstein, J. 1983 From Killer Weed to Drop-out Drug. Contemporary Crises 13–38.

Hobbes, T. 1928 The Elements of the Law, Natural and Politic. Cambridge: Cambridge University Press.

Hobbes, T. 1946 Leviathan. Oxford: Blackwells.

Inglis, B. 1975 The Forbidden Game: A Social History of Drugs London: Routledge.

In the Matter of Marijuana Rescheduling Petition 1988 Docket No. 86–22, http:www.calyx.com/olsen/MEDICAL/YOUNG/young.html. In the Matter of Petition of Carl Eric Olsen, on remand from the U.S. Court of Appeals (D.C. Cir. 93–1109).

Kelsen, H. 1934–5 The Pure Theory of Law. Law Quarterly Review 50, 51.

King, R. 1978 The Drug Problem and the Idioms of War. Journal of Drug Issues 8: 221–31.

Kuhn, T. 1962 The Structure of Scientific Revolutions. Chicago: Chicago University Press.

Kymlicka, W. 1991 Liberalism Community and Culture. Oxford: Clarendon Press.

Manderson, D. 1995 Metamorphoses: Clashing Symbols in the Social Construction of Drugs. Journal of Drug Issues 25: 799–816.

Marijuana Rescheduling Petition, 57 Fed. Reg. 10499 (1992).

Mill, J. S. 1857 On Liberty.

Musto, D. 1973 The American Disease. New Haven: Yale University Press.

Nahas, G. and N. Pace 1994 Marijuana Smoking as Medicine: A Cruel Hoax. www.drctalk@drcnet.org.

New South Wales Parliamentary Debates

1976 25, 26, 27 (1976–1978) Eliz. 11 Ser. 3 Vol. 133, 7779–80.

Peele, S. 1985 The Meaning of Addiction. Lexington, Mass.: Lexington Books.

Peele, S. 1989 Diseasing of America: Addiction Treatment Out of Control. Boston: Houghton Mifflin Co., San Jose Mercury News, May 14 1995.

Sandel, M. 1997 Democracy's Discontent: America in Search of a Public Philosophy. Cambridge, Mass.: Belknap Press.

Scarry, E. 1985 The Body in Pain: The Making and Unmaking of the World. New York: Oxford University Press.

Starr, P. 1982 The Social Transformation of American Medicine. New York: Basic Books. The Economist, March 28–April 4 1992.

Vinciguerra, Moore and Brennan 1988 Inhalation Marijuana as an Anti-emetic for Cancer Chemotherapy. New York State Journal of Medicine 88:525.

Weber, M. 1954 Law in Economy and Society, trans. M. Rheinstein. Cambridge, Mass.: Harvard University Press.

Willis, E. 1983 Medical Dominance. Sydney: Allen and Unwin.

ROBERT F. DIEGELMAN, ACTING ASSISTANT ATTORNEY GENERAL, U.S. DEPARTMENT OF JUSTICE— LETTER TO MR. PAUL JONES

State Medical Marijuana Laws (Appendix V: Comments from the Department of Justice), GOA, 2002.

Dear Mr. Jones:

On August 26, 2002, the General Accounting Office (GAO) provided the Department of Justice (DOJ) copies of its draft report entitled "MEDICAL MARIJUANA: Early Experiences With Four States' Laws." While we note that the report fully describes the current status of the programs in the states reviewed, we are concerned that it fails to adequately address some of the serious difficulties associated with such programs. The DOJ believes the report does not adequately address, through any considered analysis, issues related to the 1) inherent conflict between state laws permitting the use of marijuana and federal laws that do not; 2) potential for facilitating illegal trafficking; 3) impact of such Laws on cooperation among federal, state, and local law enforcement; and 4) lack of data on the medicinal value of marijuana. Further, the GAO's continued use of the term "medical marijuana" Implicitly accepts the fact that there is a 1) proven medicinal value to marijuana and 2) legitimate exception to federal law for this use. Neither of these premises are true. Finally, we note that the GAO fails to consider what the existence of state "medical marijuana" Laws communicates. We believe such laws send society the wrong message.

CONFLICT BETWEEN LAWS

The most fundamental problem with the draft GAO report is that it fails to emphasize the fact that there is no federally recognized medicinal use of marijuana and thus possession or use of this substance is a federal crime. Further, the GAO fails to even mention that state laws purporting to approve marijuana for medical use undermine the closed system of distribution for controlled substances established by the Controlled Substances Act (CSA). The time-proven safeguards that have made the medical drug supply in the United States the safest in the world are lacking. State medical marijuana legislation does not and could not require the cultivators and distributors of marijuana to comply with the federal requirement that all manufacturers and distributors of Schedule I controlled Substances be registered with the Drug Enforcement Administration (DEA). The registration process and record-keeping requirements established by federal law and administered by DEA are critical components of DEA's effort to restrict abuse of marijuana and other controlled substances. In this regard, there is no analysis nor comparison of state controls of marijuana subject to state "medical marijuana" Laws with federal and state controls of other prescribed medicines covered by the CSA. The regulation of the production and distribution of prescribed medicines is a critical component in preventing the diversion of controlled substances that are properly prescribed for medical use. A comparison of DEA's controls of other legitimately prescribed controlled substances would highlight the lack of proper oversight of marijuana as a "medicine.": The registration process is also an important aspect of the United States Government's implementation of international drug control treaties. These treaties obligate the federal government to prohibit the cultivation of marijuana except by persons licensed by, and under the direct supervision of, the federal government. The treaties also obligate the federal government to control the distribution of marijuana. This is required even if the federal government determines that marijuana has an accepted medical use. Any state legislation purporting to authorize medical use of marijuana is inconsistent with the CSA as none of these state laws require the cultivation of marijuana that is federally licensed and supervised by the federal government. These state laws undermine the ability of the federal government to meet its obligations under international law. The GAO Draft Report makes no mention of this critical issue.

ABUSE OF STATE LAWS TO FACILITATE ILLEGAL DRUG TRAFFICKING

The GAO Draft Report does not mention that state "medical marijuana" Laws are routinely being abused to facilitate traditional illegal marijuana trafficking and use. Information acquired by DEA during its investigations of cannabis clubs would provide specific examples of this abuse. The report focuses exclusively on so-called medical use of marijuana and omits any mention of the abuse of state "medical marijuana" Laws. The report fails to reflect the underlying criminal arena in which marijuana is produced and consumed and the significant profitability that drives the marijuana market. Because of that factor, there is a blurred line between medical and illegal commercial markets. Further, some U.S. Attorney's Offices have indicated that in their district violent crimes associated with marijuana cultivation (such as homicides) create significant law enforcement and social issues. Without addressing the illegal production and diversion of marijuana, the GAO Draft Report provides an incomplete analysis of the impact of the "medical" Marijuana laws on the enforcement of drug control laws.

The passage of Proposition 215 in California and similar legislation in other states has created unfortunate circumstances for state and local law enforcement officers. The state initiatives also have provided legal loopholes for drug dealers and marijuana cultivators to avoid arrest and prosecution. This is due in part to California state government's lack of guidance as to the implementation of the law and their seeming unwillingness to enforce state drug laws against traffickers who claim to be involved with marijuana under the state "medical marijuana" Law. Further, those counties that have taken a public position on proposition 215 have contributed to the dilemma now being experienced by state and local law enforcement. The vague guidelines established throughout the counties in California sends a message to many that anyone who has a "recommendation" From a doctor is permitted to grow and possess certain (varying) amounts of marijuana.

Impact on Law Enforcement Operations and Cooperation: The GAO Draft Report states that "[s]ome of the federal law enforcement officials we interviewed indicated that the introduction of state 'medical marijuana' Laws has had little impact on their operations." This statement does not accurately reflect DEA's experience in addressing state "medical marijuana" Laws. One of the major effects of the states legislation is the worsening of relations between federal, state, and local law enforcement.

As a result of these circumstances the most significant issue that now appears to be occurring is the recognizable rift that the laws have created between state and local law enforcement and federal drug agents, who are mandated to enforce the federal law. There have been and undoubtedly will continue to be instances that occur in the affected states where local officers working joint investigations with DEA have been ordered or instructed not to seize contraband plants and/or marijuana by their district attorney or state's attorney office. In some cases, DEA has been required to obtain Federal warrants to seize marijuana being held by local police agencies to prevent the return of the marijuana to persons pursuant to State court orders. This conflict has lead to several heated incidences on the West Coast.

For example, in one recent case, where federal agents were cooperating with local officers to serve a state search warrant at a residence, the District Attorney of Butte County, California, advised a Butte County detective to arrest a DEA Special Agent if the agent confiscated six marijuana plants that were found during the operation. The District Attorney asserted that under California's "medical marijuana" Law the plants were lawfully possessed; however, such possession violates federal law. The plants were seized and submitted to the DEA laboratory for destruction without incident only after negotiations between the U.S.

Attorney, the District Attorney, and DEA representatives to resolve the issue. In another instance, the Oakland Police Department referred to the DEA a shooting incident involving the theft of a pound of marijuana because the city of Oakland prohibits its officers from pursuing any investigation of marijuana that may be claimed to be subject to the state "medical marijuana" Law. In this instance the "victim" Of the robbery was a marijuana recipient under the state "medical marijuana" Law who was attempting to sell the marijuana he had to his robbers. Such conflicts over individual mandates have required frequent intervention by DEA's Office of Chief Counsel and the DOJ due to the clear lack of a coordinated drug law enforcement policy.

Because state and local law enforcement cannot work on certain marijuana cases under these laws, federal seized asset sharing has been negatively impacted. In the state of Oregon, the state legislation prevents the federal government from sharing seized assets directly with state/local law enforcement entities in cases involving asset seizure without criminal prosecution initiated following marijuana grow seizures.

It is much more difficult for federal and state officials to prosecute marijuana cases where medicinal use can be claimed. There is growing local sentiment that because of these laws, federal law enforcement resources should not be devoted to marijuana prosecutions. This sentiment also manifests itself injury trials where prosecutors have jury nullification concerns (as a result of softened public attitudes towards marijuana).

In these states, the perception that marijuana is accepted by the public has significantly impacted law enforcement. According to Oregon State Police authorities, outlaw motorcycle gang members are now applying for marijuana caregiver status, believing that this will officially authorize their marijuana grow operations. Marijuana grow operations have always presented problems to law enforcement, and marijuana potentially subject to state "medical marijuana" Laws only serve to further confuse the general public on this drug. Public perception on this issue appears to be further softened as a result of strong marketing strategies by pro-legalization/medicinal use advocates. Groups supporting the legalization of marijuana in Alaska are now preparing new proposals to legalize all marijuana. The public confusion on this issue can be demonstrated by the fact that the voters in these states approved the medical use of marijuana but do not allow use in public places (Oregon) or in medical facilities, or nearby school grounds, recreation centers or youth centers (Alaska). This sends a mixed message to the public as no other medicines are restricted in this way.

Marijuana as Medicine

The GAO Draft Report's discussion of the debate over the medical value of marijuana is inadequate and does not present an accurate picture. The draft states that "[t]he potential medical value of marijuana has been a continuing debate." It fails to mention, however, that smoked marijuana has never been approved as medicine by the Food and Drug Administration (FDA) and has never been proven safe and effective in sound scientific studies. Further, at its 2001 Annual Meeting, the American Medical Association (AMA)adopted the following as its policy on the medicinal use of marijuana:

> "The AMA calls for further adequate and well-controlled studies of marijuana and related cannabinoids in patients who have serious conditions for which preclinical, anecdotal, or controlled evidence suggests possible efficacy and the application of such results to the understanding and treatment of disease; (2) The AMA recommends that marijuana be retained in Schedule I of the Controlled Substances Act pending the outcome of such studies. (3) The AMA urges the National Institutes of Health (NIH) to implement administrative procedures to facilitate grant applications and the conduct of well-designed clinical research into the medical utility of marijuana.... (4) The AMA believes that the NIH should use its resources and influence to support the development of a smoke-free inhaled delivery system for marijuana or delta–9–tetrahydrocannabinol (THC) to reduce the health hazards associated with the combustion and inhalation of marijuana.":

We also believe the GAO Draft Report should at least reference DEA final orders concerning petitions to reschedule marijuana published in 1992 and 2001. These reports contain a comprehensive explanation of the scientific and legal bases for keeping marijuana in Schedule 1.

In addition, the GAO Draft Report fails to mention that medical "marijuana" Is legally available in the prescription drug Marinol. A pharmaceutical product, Marinol is widely available by prescription. It comes in the form of a pill and is also being studied by researchers for suitability via other delivery methods, such as an inhaler or patch, The active ingredient in Marinol is synthetic THC, which has been found to relieve the nausea and vomiting associated with chemotherapy for cancer patients and to assist with loss of appetite with AIDS patients. Unlike smoked marijuana-which contains more than 400 different chemicals, including most of the hazardous chemicals found in tobacco smoke-Marinol has been studied and approved by the medical community and the FDA. Information about Marinol is necessary to understand the debate over medical use of marijuana.

There is no mention in the report on the prescription of Marinol in these states, or more specifically the doctors identified in the study, as compared to doctors not prescribing marijuana under state "medical marijuana" Laws versus their prescriptions authored for Marinol, if any. Although the information concerning the prescription of Marinol may not yet be available, it would be available through a longer term study by DEA Office of Diversion Control. It would be informative to determine if Marinol is sold in any quantity to pharmacies in these states by distributors for the manufacturer, both before and after state "medical marijuana" Legislation was passed.

As noted by the above comments, we believe that the report falls short by not adequately addressing these significant issues. I urge you will consider our concerns in preparing the final GAO report on this important subject.

UNITED STATES v. OAKLAND CANNABIS BUYERS' COOPERATIVE

Supreme Court of the United States, 2001.
532 U.S. 483.

Justice Thomas delivered the opinion of the Court. The Controlled Substances Act, 84 Stat. 1242, 21 U. S. C. 801 *et seq.*, prohibits the manufacture and distribution of various drugs, including marijuana. In this case, we must decide whether there is a medical necessity exception to these prohibitions. We hold that there is not.

I

In November 1996, California voters enacted an initiative measure entitled the Compassionate Use Act of 1996. Attempting "[t]o ensure that seriously ill Californians have the right to obtain and use marijuana for medical purposes," Cal. Health & Safety Code Ann. 11362.5 (West Supp. 2001), the statute creates an exception to California laws prohibiting the possession and cultivation of marijuana. These prohibitions no longer apply to a patient or his primary caregiver who possesses or cultivates marijuana for the patient's medical purposes upon the recommendation or approval of a physician. *Ibid.* In the wake of this voter initiative, several groups organized "medical cannabis dispensaries" to meet the needs of qualified patients. *United States v. Cannabis Cultivators Club,* 5 F.Supp.2d 1086, 1092 (N.D. Cal. 1998). Respondent Oakland Cannabis Buyers' Cooperative is one of these groups.

The Cooperative is a not-for-profit organization that operates in downtown Oakland. A physician serves as medical director, and registered nurses staff the Cooperative during business hours. To become a member, a patient must provide a written statement from a treating physician assenting to marijuana therapy and must submit to a screening interview. If accepted as a member, the patient receives an identification card entitling him to obtain marijuana from the Cooperative.

In January 1998, the United States sued the Cooperative and its executive director, respondent Jeffrey Jones (together, the Cooperative), in the United States District Court for the Northern District of California. Seeking to enjoin the Cooperative from distributing and manufacturing marijuana,[7] the United States argued that, whether or not the

7. The Government requested, and the District Court granted, an injunction that prohibited the possession of marijuana with the intent to manufacture and distribute, as well as the distribution and manufacture of marijuana. For simplicity, in this opinion,

Cooperative's activities are legal under California law, they violate federal law. Specifically, the Government argued that the Cooperative violated the Controlled Substances Act's prohibitions on distributing, manufacturing, and possessing with the intent to distribute or manufacture a controlled substance. 21 U. S. C. 841(a). Concluding that the Government had established a probability of success on the merits, the District Court granted a preliminary injunction. App. to Pet. for Cert. 39a–40a, 5 F.Supp.2d, at 1105.

The Cooperative did not appeal the injunction but instead openly violated it by distributing marijuana to numerous persons, App. to Pet. for Cert. at 21a–23a. To terminate these violations, the Government initiated contempt proceedings. In defense, the Cooperative contended that any distributions were medically necessary. Marijuana is the only drug, according to the Cooperative, that can alleviate the severe pain and other debilitating symptoms of the Cooperative's patients. *Id.*, at 29a. The District Court rejected this defense, however, after determining there was insufficient evidence that each recipient of marijuana was in actual danger of imminent harm without the drug. *Id.*, at 29a–32a. The District Court found the Cooperative in contempt and, at the Government's request, modified the preliminary injunction to empower the United States Marshal to seize the Cooperative's premises. *Id.*, at 37a. Although recognizing that "human suffering" could result, the District Court reasoned that a court's "equitable powers [do] not permit it to ignore federal law." *Ibid.* Three days later, the District Court summarily rejected a motion by the Cooperative to modify the injunction to permit distributions that are medically necessary.

The Cooperative appealed both the contempt order and the denial of the Cooperative's motion to modify. Before the Court of Appeals for the Ninth Circuit decided the case, however, the Cooperative voluntarily purged its contempt by promising the District Court that it would comply with the initial preliminary injunction. Consequently, the Court of Appeals determined that the appeal of the contempt order was moot. 190 F.3d 1109, 1112–1113 (1999).

The denial of the Cooperative's motion to modify the injunction, however, presented a live controversy that was appealable under 28 U. S. C. 1292(a)(1). Reaching the merits of this issue, the Court of Appeals reversed and remanded. According to the Court of Appeals, the medical necessity defense was a "legally cognizable defense" that likely would apply in the circumstances. 190 F.3d, at 1114. Moreover, the Court of Appeals reasoned, the District Court erroneously "believed that it had no discretion to issue an injunction that was more limited in scope than the Controlled Substances Act itself." *Id.*, at 1114–1115. Because, according to the Court of Appeals, district courts retain "broad equitable discretion" to fashion injunctive relief, the District Court could have, and should have, weighed the "public interest" and considered factors such

we refer to these activities collectively as distributing and manufacturing marijuana. The legal issues are the same for all of these activities.

as the serious harm in depriving patients of marijuana. *Ibid.* Remanding the case, the Court of Appeals instructed the District Court to consider "the criteria for a medical necessity exemption, and, should it modify the injunction, to set forth those criteria in the modification order." *Id.,* at 1115. Following these instructions, the District Court granted the Cooperative's motion to modify the injunction to incorporate a medical necessity defense.[8]

The United States petitioned for certiorari to review the Court of Appeals' decision that medical necessity is a legally cognizable defense to violations of the Controlled Substances Act. Because the decision raises significant questions as to the ability of the United States to enforce the Nation's drug laws, we granted certiorari. 531 U.S. 1010 (2000).

II

The Controlled Substances Act provides that, "[e]xcept as authorized by this subchapter, it shall be unlawful for any person knowingly or intentionally ... to manufacture, distribute, or dispense, or possess with intent to manufacture, distribute, or dispense, a controlled substance." 21 U. S. C. 841(a)(1). The subchapter, in turn, establishes exceptions. For marijuana (and other drugs that have been classified as "schedule I" controlled substances), there is but one express exception, and it is available only for Government-approved research projects, 823(f). Not conducting such a project, the Cooperative cannot, and indeed does not, claim this statutory exemption.

The Cooperative contends, however, that notwithstanding the apparently absolute language of 841(a), the statute is subject to additional, implied exceptions, one of which is medical necessity. According to the Cooperative, because necessity was a defense at common law, medical necessity should be read into the Controlled Substances Act. We disagree.

As an initial matter, we note that it is an open question whether federal courts ever have authority to recognize a necessity defense not

---

8. The amended preliminary injunction reaffirmed that the Cooperative is generally enjoined from manufacturing, distributing, and possessing with the intent to manufacture or distribute marijuana, but it carved out an exception for cases of medical necessity. Specifically, the District Court ordered that "[t]he foregoing injunction does not apply to the distribution of cannabis by [the Cooperative] to patient-members who (1) suffer from a serious medical condition, (2) will suffer imminent harm if the patient-member does not have access to cannabis, (3) need cannabis for the treatment of the patient-member's medical condition, or need cannabis to alleviate the medical condition or symptoms associated with the medical condition, and (4) have no reasonable legal alternative to cannabis for the effective treatment or alleviation of the patient-member's medical condition or symptoms associated with the medical condition because the patient-member has tried all other legal alternatives to cannabis and the alternatives have been ineffective in treating or alleviating the patient-member's medical condition or symptoms associated with the medical condition, or the alternatives result in side effects which the patient-member cannot reasonably tolerate." App. to Pet. for Cert. 16a–17a.

The United States appealed the District Court's order amending the preliminary injunction. At the Government's request, we stayed the order pending the appeal. 530 U.S. 1298 (2000). The Court of Appeals has postponed oral argument pending our decision in this case.

provided by statute. A necessity defense "traditionally covered the situation where physical forces beyond the actor's control rendered illegal conduct the lesser of two evils." *United States v. Bailey*, 444 U. S. 394, 410 (1980). Even at common law, the defense of necessity was somewhat controversial. See, *e.g.*, *Queen v. Dudley & Stephens*, 14 Q. B. 273 (1884). And under our constitutional system, in which federal crimes are defined by statute rather than by common law, see *United States v. Hudson,* 7 Cranch 32, 34 (1812), it is especially so. As we have stated: "Whether, as a policy matter, an exemption should be created is a question for legislative judgment, not judicial inference." *United States v. Rutherford*, 442 U. S. 544, 559 (1979). Nonetheless, we recognize that this Court has discussed the possibility of a necessity defense without altogether rejecting it. See, *e.g., Bailey, supra*, at 415.[9]

We need not decide, however, whether necessity can ever be a defense when the federal statute does not expressly provide for it. In this case, to resolve the question presented, we need only recognize that a medical necessity exception for marijuana is at odds with the terms of the Controlled Substances Act. The statute, to be sure, does not explicitly abrogate the defense.[10] But its provisions leave no doubt that the defense is unavailable.

Under any conception of legal necessity, one principle is clear: The defense cannot succeed when the legislature itself has made a "determination of values." 1 W. LaFave & A. Scott, Substantive Criminal Law 5.4, p. 629 (1986). In the case of the Controlled Substances Act, the statute reflects a determination that marijuana has no medical benefits worthy of an exception (outside the confines of a Government-approved research project). Whereas some other drugs can be dispensed and prescribed for medical use, see 21 U.S.C. 829, the same is not true for marijuana. Indeed, for purposes of the Controlled Substances Act, marijuana has "no currently accepted medical use" at all. § 812.

The structure of the Act supports this conclusion. The statute divides drugs into five schedules, depending in part on whether the particular drug has a currently accepted medical use. The Act then imposes restrictions on the manufacture and distribution of the sub-

---

9. The Cooperative is incorrect to suggest that Bailey has settled the question whether federal courts have authority to recognize a necessity defense not provided by statute. There, the Court rejected the necessity defense of a prisoner who contended that adverse prison conditions justified his prison escape. The Court held that the necessity defense is unavailable to prisoners, like Bailey, who fail to present evidence of a bona fide effort to surrender as soon as the claimed necessity had lost its coercive force. 444 U. S., at 415. It was not argued, and so there was no occasion to consider, whether the statute might be unable to bear any necessity defense at all. And although the Court noted that Congress "legislates against a background of Anglo–Saxon common law" and thus "may" have contemplated a necessity defense, the Court refused to "balanc[e] [the] harms," explaining that "we are construing an Act of Congress, not drafting it." *Id.*, at 415, n. 11.

10. We reject the Cooperative's intimation that elimination of the defense requires an "explici[t]" statement. Brief for Respondents 21. Considering that we have never held necessity to be a viable justification for violating a federal statute, see *supra*, at 5–6, and n. 3, and that such a defense would entail a social balancing that is better left to Congress, we decline to set the bar so high.

stance according to the schedule in which it has been placed. Schedule I is the most restrictive schedule.[11] The Attorney General can include a drug in schedule I only if the drug "has no currently accepted medical use in treatment in the United States," "has a high potential for abuse," and has "a lack of accepted safety for use . . . under medical supervision." 812(b)(1)(A)-(C). Under the statute, the Attorney General could not put marijuana into schedule I if marijuana had any accepted medical use.

The Cooperative points out, however, that the Attorney General did not place marijuana into schedule I. Congress put it there, and Congress was not required to find that a drug lacks an accepted medical use before including the drug in schedule I. We are not persuaded that this distinction has any significance to our inquiry. Under the Cooperative's logic, drugs that Congress places in schedule I could be distributed when medically necessary whereas drugs that the Attorney General places in schedule I could not. Nothing in the statute, however, suggests that there are two tiers of schedule I narcotics, with drugs in one tier more readily available than drugs in the other. On the contrary, the statute consistently treats all schedule I drugs alike. See, e.g., 823(a) (providing criteria for Attorney General to consider when determining whether to register an applicant to manufacture schedule I controlled substances), 823(b) (providing criteria for Attorney General to consider when determining whether to register an applicant to distribute schedule I controlled substances), 823(f) (providing procedures for becoming a government-approved research project), 826 (establishing production quotas for schedule I drugs). Moreover, the Cooperative offers no convincing explanation for why drugs that Congress placed on schedule I should be subject to fewer controls than the drugs that the Attorney General placed on the schedule. Indeed, the Cooperative argues that, in placing marijuana and other drugs on schedule I, Congress "wishe[d] to assert the most restrictive level of controls created by the [Controlled Substances Act]." Brief for Respondents 24. If marijuana should be subject to the most restrictive level of controls, it should not be treated any less restrictively than other schedule I drugs.

The Cooperative further argues that use of schedule I drugs generally—whether placed in schedule I by Congress or the Attorney General—can be medically necessary, notwithstanding that they have "no currently accepted medical use." According to the Cooperative, a drug may not yet have achieved general acceptance as a medical treatment but may nonetheless have medical benefits to a particular patient or class of patients. We decline to parse the statute in this manner. It is clear from the text of the Act that Congress has made a determination that marijuana has no medical benefits worthy of an exception. The statute expressly contemplates that many drugs "have a useful and legitimate medical purpose and are necessary to maintain the health and general

11. As noted, supra, at 5, the only express exception for schedule I drugs is the Government-approved research project, see

21 U. S. C. 823(f). Unlike drugs in other schedules, see 829, schedule I drugs cannot be dispensed under a prescription.

welfare of the American people," 801(1), but it includes no exception at all for any medical use of marijuana. Unwilling to view this omission as an accident, and unable in any event to override a legislative determination manifest in a statute, we reject the Cooperative's argument.[12]

Finally, the Cooperative contends that we should construe the Controlled Substances Act to include a medical necessity defense in order to avoid what it considers to be difficult constitutional questions. In particular, the Cooperative asserts that, shorn of a medical necessity defense, the statute exceeds Congress' Commerce Clause powers, violates the substantive due process rights of patients, and offends the fundamental liberties of the people under the Fifth, Ninth, and Tenth Amendments. As the Cooperative acknowledges, however, the canon of constitutional avoidance has no application in the absence of statutory ambiguity. Because we have no doubt that the Controlled Substances Act cannot bear a medical necessity defense to distributions of marijuana, we do not find guidance in this avoidance principle. Nor do we consider the underlying constitutional issues today. Because the Court of Appeals did not address these claims, we decline to do so in the first instance.

For these reasons, we hold that medical necessity is not a defense to manufacturing and distributing marijuana.[13] The Court of Appeals erred when it held that medical necessity is a "legally cognizable defense." 190 F.3d, at 1114. It further erred when it instructed the District Court on remand to consider "the criteria for a medical necessity exemption, and, should it modify the injunction, to set forth those criteria in the modification order." *Id.*, at 1115.

12. The Government argues that the 1998 "sense of the Congress" resolution, 112 Stat. 2681–760 to 2681–761, supports its position that Congress has foreclosed the medical necessity defense. Entitled "Not Legalizing Marijuana for Medicinal Use," the resolution declares that "Congress continues to support the existing Federal legal process for determining the safety and efficacy of drugs and opposes efforts to circumvent this process by legalizing marijuana, and other Schedule I drugs, for medicinal use without valid scientific evidence and the approval of the Food and Drug Administration." Because we conclude that the Controlled Substances Act cannot sustain the medical necessity defense, we need not consider whether the 1998 "sense of the Congress resolution" is additional evidence of a legislative determination to eliminate the defense.

13. Lest there be any confusion, we clarify that nothing in our analysis, or the statute, suggests that a distinction should be drawn between the prohibitions on manufacturing and distributing and the other prohibitions in the Controlled Substances

Act. Furthermore, the very point of our holding is that there is no medical necessity exception to the prohibitions at issue, even when the patient is "seriously ill" and lacks alternative avenues for relief. Indeed, it is the Cooperative's argument that its patients are "seriously ill," see, *e.g.*, Brief for Respondents 11, 13, 17, and lacking "alternatives," see, *e.g.*, *id.*, at 13. We reject the argument that these factors warrant a medical necessity exception. If we did not, we would be affirming instead of reversing the Court of Appeals.

Finally, we share *Justice Stevens*' concern for "showing respect for the sovereign States that comprise our Federal Union." *Post*, at 3 (opinion concurring in judgment). However, we are "construing an Act of Congress, not drafting it." *United States* v. *Bailey*, 444 U.S. 394, 415 , n. 11 (1980). Because federal courts interpret, rather than author, the federal criminal code, we are not at liberty to rewrite it. Nor are we passing today on a constitutional question, such as whether the Controlled Substances Act exceeds Congress' power under the Commerce Clause.

III

The Cooperative contends that, even if the Controlled Substances Act forecloses the medical necessity defense, there is an alternative ground for affirming the Court of Appeals. This case, the Cooperative reminds us, arises from a motion to modify an injunction to permit distributions that are medically necessary. According to the Cooperative, the Court of Appeals was correct that the District Court had "broad equitable discretion" to tailor the injunctive relief to account for medical necessity, irrespective of whether there is a legal defense of necessity in the statute. *Id.,* at 1114. To sustain the judgment below, the argument goes, we need only reaffirm that federal courts, in the exercise of their equity jurisdiction, have discretion to modify an injunction based upon a weighing of the public interest.[14]

We disagree. Although district courts whose equity powers have been properly invoked indeed have discretion in fashioning injunctive relief (in the absence of a statutory restriction), the Court of Appeals erred concerning the factors that the district courts may consider in exercising such discretion.

A

As an initial matter, the Cooperative is correct that, when district courts are properly acting as courts of equity, they have discretion unless a statute clearly provides otherwise. For "several hundred years," courts of equity have enjoyed "sound discretion" to consider the "necessities of the public interest" when fashioning injunctive relief. *Hecht Co. v. Bowles,* 321 U. S. 321, 329–330 (1944). See also *id.,* at 329 ("The essence of equity jurisdiction has been the power of the Chancellor to do equity and to mould each decree to the necessities of the particular case. Flexibility rather than rigidity has distinguished it"); *Weinberger v. Romero–Barcelo,* 456 U. S. 305, 312 (1982) ("In exercising their sound discretion, courts of equity should pay particular regard for the public consequences in employing the extraordinary remedy of injunction"). Such discretion is displaced only by a "clear and valid legislative command." *Porter v. Warner Holding Co.,* 328 U. S. 395, 398 (1946). See also *Romero–Barcelo, supra,* at 313 ("Of course, Congress may intervene and guide or control the exercise of the courts' discretion, but we do not lightly assume that Congress has intended to depart from established principles").

The Cooperative is also correct that the District Court in this case had discretion. The Controlled Substances Act vests district courts with jurisdiction to enjoin violations of the Act, 21 U. S. C. 882(a). But a "grant of jurisdiction to issue [equitable relief] hardly suggests an absolute duty to do so under any and all circumstances," *Hecht, supra,*

---

14. Notwithstanding Justice Stevens' concerns, *post,* at 4, it is appropriate for us to address this issue because this case arises from a motion to modify the injunction, because the Court of Appeals held that the District Court misconstrued its equitable discretion, and because the Cooperative offers this conclusion as an alternative ground for affirmance.

at 329 (emphasis omitted). Because the District Court's use of equitable power is not textually required by any "clear and valid legislative command," the court did not have to issue an injunction.

TVA v. Hill, 437 U. S. 153 (1978), does not support the Government's contention that the District Court lacked discretion in fashioning injunctive relief. In *Hill,* the Court held that the Endangered Species Act of 1973 required the District Court to enjoin completion of a dam, whose operation would either eradicate the known population of the snail darter or destroy its critical habitat. *Id.,* at 193–195. The District Court lacked discretion because an injunction was the "only means of ensuring compliance." *Romero-Barcelo, supra,* at 314 (explaining why the District Court in *Hill* lacked discretion). Congress' "order of priorities," as expressed in the statute, would be deprived of effect if the District Court could choose to deny injunctive relief. *Hill, supra,* at 194. In effect, the District Court had only a Hobson's choice. By contrast, with respect to the Controlled Substances Act, criminal enforcement is an alternative, and indeed the customary, means of ensuring compliance with the statute. Congress' resolution of the policy issues can be (and usually is) upheld without an injunction.

B

But the mere fact that the District Court had discretion does not suggest that the District Court, when evaluating the motion to modify the injunction, could consider any and all factors that might relate to the public interest or the conveniences of the parties, including the medical needs of the Cooperative's patients. On the contrary, a court sitting in equity cannot "ignore the judgment of Congress, deliberately expressed in legislation." *Virginian R. Co. v. Railway Employees,* 300 U. S. 515, 551 (1937). A district court cannot, for example, override Congress' policy choice, articulated in a statute, as to what behavior should be prohibited. "Once Congress, exercising its delegated powers, has decided the order of priorities in a given area, it is ... for the courts to enforce them when enforcement is sought." *Hill,* 437 U. S., at 194. Courts of equity cannot, in their discretion, reject the balance that Congress has struck in a statute. *Id.,* at 194–195. Their choice (unless there is statutory language to the contrary) is simply whether a particular means of enforcing the statute should be chosen over another permissible means; their choice is not whether enforcement is preferable to no enforcement at all.[15] Consequently, when a court of equity exercises its

---

15. *Hecht Co.* v. *Bowles,* 321 U. S. 321 (1944), for example, held that the District Court was not required to issue an injunction to restrain violations of the Emergency Price Control Act of 1942 and regulations thereunder when "some 'other order' might be more appropriate, or at least so appear to the court." *Id.,* at 328 (quoting statutory provision that enabled district court to issue an injunction, a restraining order, "or other order"). *Weinberger v. Romero–Barce-* lo, 456 U. S. 305 (1982), held that a District Court had discretion not to issue an injunction precluding the United States Navy from releasing ordnance into water, but to rely on other means of ensuring compliance, including ordering the Navy to obtain a permit. *Id.,* at 314–318. See also *Amoco Production Co. v. Gambell,* 480 U.S. 531, 544–546 (1987) (holding that a District Court did not err in declining to issue an

discretion, it may not consider the advantages and disadvantages of nonenforcement of the statute, but only the advantages and disadvantages of "employing the extraordinary remedy of injunction," *Romero-Barcelo*, 456 U. S., at 311 , over the other available methods of enforcement. Cf. *id.,* at 316 (referring to "discretion to rely on remedies other than an immediate prohibitory injunction") To the extent the district court considers the public interest and the conveniences of the parties, the court is limited to evaluating how such interest and conveniences are affected by the selection of an injunction over other enforcement mechanisms.

C

In this case, the Court of Appeals erred by considering relevant the evidence that some people have "serious medical conditions for whom the use of cannabis is necessary in order to treat or alleviate those conditions or their symptoms," that these people "will suffer serious harm if they are denied cannabis," and that "there is no legal alternative to cannabis for the effective treatment of their medical conditions." 190 F.3d, at 1115. As explained above, in the Controlled Substances Act, the balance already has been struck against a medical necessity exception. Because the statutory prohibitions cover even those who have what could be termed a medical necessity, the Act precludes consideration of this evidence. It was thus error for the Court of Appeals to instruct the District Court on remand to consider "the criteria for a medical necessity exemption, and, should it modify the injunction, to set forth those criteria in the modification order." *Ibid.*

* * *

The judgment of the Court of Appeals is reversed, and the case is remanded for further proceedings consistent with this opinion.

It is so ordered.

Justice Breyer took no part in the consideration or decision of this case.

Justice Stevens, with whom Justice Souter and Justice Ginsburg join, concurring in the judgment.

Lest the Court's narrow holding be lost in its broad dicta, let me restate it here: "[W]e hold that medical necessity is not a defense to *manufacturing* and *distributing* marijuana." *Ante,* at 10 (emphasis added). This confined holding is consistent with our grant of certiorari, which was limited to the question "[w]hether the Controlled Substances Act, 21 U. S. C. 801 *et seq.*, forecloses a medical necessity defense to the Act's prohibition against *manufacturing* and *distributing* marijuana, a Schedule I controlled substance." Pet. for Cert. (I) (emphasis added). And, at least with respect to distribution, this holding is consistent with

injunction to bar exploratory drilling on Alaskan public lands, because the district court's decision "did not undermine" the policy of the Alaska National Interest Lands Conservation Act, 16 U. S. C. 3120, and because the Secretary of the Interior had other means of meaningfully complying with the statute).

how the issue was raised and litigated below. As stated by the District Court, the question before it was "whether [respondents'] admitted *distribution* of marijuana for use by seriously ill persons upon a physician's recommendation violates federal law," and if so, whether such distribution "should be enjoined pursuant to the injunctive relief provisions of the federal Controlled Substances Act." *United States v. Cannabis Cultivators Club*, 5 F.Supp.2d 1086, 1091 (N.D. Cal. 1998) (emphasis added).

Accordingly, in the lower courts as well as here, respondents have raised the medical necessity defense as a justification for distributing marijuana to cooperative members, and it was in that context that the Ninth Circuit determined that respondents had "a legally cognizable defense." 190 F.3d 1109, 1114 (1999). The Court is surely correct to reverse that determination. Congress' classification of marijuana as a schedule I controlled substance—that is, one that cannot be distributed outside of approved research projects, see 21 U. S. C. 812, 823(f), 829—makes it clear that "the Controlled Substances Act cannot bear a medical necessity defense to *distributions* of marijuana," *ante*, at 10 (emphasis added).[16]

Apart from its limited holding, the Court takes two unwarranted and unfortunate excursions that prevent me from joining its opinion. First, the Court reaches beyond its holding, and beyond the facts of the case, by suggesting that the defense of necessity is unavailable for anyone under the Controlled Substances Act. *Ante*, at 6–9, 10, n. 7, 15. Because necessity was raised in this case as a defense to distribution, the Court need not venture an opinion on whether the defense is available to anyone other than distributors. Most notably, whether the defense might be available to a seriously ill patient for whom there is no alternative means of avoiding starvation or extraordinary suffering is a difficult issue that is not presented here.[17]

Second, the Court gratuitously casts doubt on "whether necessity can ever be a defense" to *any* federal statute that does not explicitly provide for it, calling such a defense into question by a misleading reference to its existence as an "open question." *Ante*, at 5, 6. By contrast, our precedent has expressed no doubt about the viability of the common-law defense, even in the context of federal criminal statutes

---

16. In any event, respondents do not fit the paradigm of a defendant who may assert necessity. The defense "traditionally covered the situation where physical forces beyond the actor's control rendered illegal conduct the lesser of two evils." *United States* v. *Bailey*, 444 U. S. 394, 410 (1980); see generally 1 W. LaFave & A. Scott, Substantive Criminal Law 5.4, pp. 627–640 (1986). Respondents, on the other hand, have not been forced to confront a choice of evils—violating federal law by distributing marijuana to seriously ill patients or letting those individuals suffer—but have thrust that choice upon themselves by electing to become distributors for such patients. Of course, respondents also cannot claim necessity based upon the choice of evils facing seriously ill patients, as that is not the same choice respondents face.

17. As a result, perhaps the most glaring example of the Court's dicta is its footnote 7, where it opines that "nothing in our analysis, or the statute, suggests that a distinction should be drawn between the prohibitions on manufacturing and distributing and the other prohibitions in the Controlled Substances Act." *Ante*, at 10, n. 7.

that do not provide for it in so many words. See, *e.g., United States v. Bailey,* 444 U. S. 394, 415 (1980) ("We therefore hold that, where a criminal defendant is charged with escape and claims that he is entitled to an instruction on the theory of duress or necessity, he must proffer evidence of a bona fide effort to surrender or return to custody as soon as the claimed duress or necessity had lost its coercive force"); *id.,* at 415, n. 11 ("Our principal difference with the dissent, therefore, is not as to the *existence* of such a defense but as to the importance of surrender as an element of it" (emphasis added)). Indeed, the Court's comment on the general availability of the necessity defense is completely unnecessary because the Government has made no such suggestion. Cf. Brief for Petitioner 17–18 (narrowly arguing that necessity defense cannot succeed if legislature has already "canvassed the issue" and precluded it for a particular statute (internal quotation marks omitted)). The Court's opinion on this point is pure dictum.

The overbroad language of the Court's opinion is especially unfortunate given the importance of showing respect for the sovereign States that comprise our Federal Union. That respect imposes a duty on federal courts, whenever possible, to avoid or minimize conflict between federal and state law, particularly in situations in which the citizens of a State have chosen to "serve as a laboratory" in the trial of "novel social and economic experiments without risk to the rest of the country." *New State Ice Co. v. Liebmann,* 285 U.S. 262, 311 (1932) (Brandeis, J., dissenting). In my view, this is such a case.[18] By passing Proposition 215, California voters have decided that seriously ill patients and their primary caregivers should be exempt from prosecution under state laws for cultivating and possessing marijuana if the patient's physician recommends using the drug for treatment.[19] This case does not call upon the Court to deprive *all* such patients of the benefit of the necessity defense to federal prosecution, when the case itself does not involve *any* such patients.

An additional point deserves emphasis. This case does not require us to rule on the scope of the District Court's discretion to enjoin, or to refuse to enjoin, the possession of marijuana or other potential violations of the Controlled Substances Act by a seriously ill patient for whom the drug may be a necessity. Whether it would be an abuse of discretion for the District Court to refuse to enjoin those sorts of violations, and whether the District Court may consider the availability of the necessity defense for that sort of violator, are questions that should be decided on

18. Cf. Feeney, Bush Backs States' Rights on Marijuana: He Opposes Medical Use But Favors Local Control, Dallas Morning News, Oct. 20, 1999, p. 6A, 1999 WL 28018944 (then-Governor Bush supporting state self-determination on medical marijuana use).

19. Since 1996, six other States—Alaska, Colorado, Maine, Nevada, Oregon, and Washington—have passed medical marijuana initiatives, and Hawaii has enacted a similar measure through its legislature. See Alaska Stat. Ann. 11.71.090, 17.37.010 to 17.37.080 (2000); Colo. Const., Art. XVIII, 14; Haw. Rev. Stat. 329–121 to 329–128 (Supp. 2000); Me. Rev. Stat. Ann., Tit. 22, 2383–B(5) (2000); Nev. Const., Art. 4, 38; Ore. Rev. Stat. 475.300 to 475.346 (1999); Wash. Rev. Code 69.51A.005 to 69.51A.902 (1997 and Supp. 2000–2001).

the authority of cases such as *Hecht Co. v. Bowles*, 321 U.S. 321 (1944), and *Weinberger v. Romero–Barcelo*, 456 U.S. 305 (1982), and that properly should be left "open" by this case.

I join the Court's judgment of reversal because I agree that a distributor of marijuana does not have a medical necessity defense under the Controlled Substances Act. I do not, however, join the dicta in the Court's opinion.

Notes and Questions

1. In any conflict between federal and state law, the supremacy clause of the constitution suggests that the federal law should prevail, at least where federal power to legislate is clear. So this case is about the nature of federal law where a conflict has been alleged between a federal drug statute and a federal criminal law defense of necessity.

2. The opinion mentions that marijuana is a Schedule I by congressional classification. Is this status justified by the potential for abuse? By the lack of any medical usage? What is the difference between plant marijuana and Marinol in psychoactive potential for abuse? In proven medical usage? Do you believe that marijuana should be in the very top tier of dangerous recreational drugs in the United States?

3. The obvious next step in the politics of medical marijuana would be an effort to alter the federal legislation. Why might that be more difficult than state-by-state medical marijuana laws?

4. There are at least two separate contests involved in the struggle over medical marijuana. The therapeutic uses of smoked marijuana (and also marijuana eaten as part of baked goods, the brownies of countercultural song and story) are as symptomatic relief for nausea and lack of appetite that are produced from diseases such as HIV and cancer or as byproducts of cancer treatment. Most of these patients are not deeply invested in the politics of control of other drugs but are politically quite active and symbolically the leading advocates for medical marijuana. There is no parallel "medical marijuana only" interest group on the prohibition side of the debate. The anti-medical marijuana interest groups all see the issue as part of a wider attack on criminal prohibition on drugs—DEA (see section 2), the White House Office of Drug Control, etc., and the Department of Justice. And much of the financial support for medical marijuana movement like California's Proposition 215 does come from persons and organizations broadly interested in liberalization of narcotics control and deeply opposed to the central assumptions of what Zimring and Hawkins called the "legalist drug control ideology."

Why is medical marijuana such an important battleground? One factor is the curious position of marijuana. Marijuana is the illegal drug that more U.S. citizens have tried than any other and the most frequently used illegal drug. It is also, from a specifist perspective, the least dangerous illicit drug–it does not cause overdose deaths, is not associated with violence, is not physically addictive and on a risk per use basis, has been compared favorably to alcohol. John Kaplan, the author of the analysis supporting the criminal status of cocaine reproduced in section 2 of this chapter reached the opposite conclusion about marijuana (see John Kaplan, Marijuana: The New Prohibition.)

But the wide use of marijuana and its relatively benign social reputation may calm the fears of a specifist, but will have the opposite effect on a legalist like William Bennett. The fact that so many citizens have tried this illegal drug makes it more, not less, dangerous from the legalist perspective. That most of these offenders are not addicted and suffer no obvious damage makes marijuana more of a threat if the central danger of illicit drugs is the defiance of government authority. So substantial hostility to marijuana is a necessary element of a legalist drug ideology.

This makes the battle over medical marijuana into a classic status conflict between decriminalizers and legalist supporters of drug prohibition. Opponents of legalistic prohibitions see medical marijuana as the weakest case in American public opinion for drug prohibition—the softest drug, and older and disabled users who pose no obvious threat to public safety. And a successful effort to roll back the criminal prohibition for medical marijuana will also undercut the legitimacy of other drug prohibitions: once the criminal classification can be challenged and overcome, the authority of government categories is no longer beyond question.

The cancer and AIDS patients were an advertising expert's dream to lead this crusade—they sought pain relief, not sensual pleasure; they were seriously ill and older instead of hippies; there was no hint of generational rebellion or disdain of authority.

This presented the legalist drug authorities with a serious dilemma. If they conceded the appropriateness of reclassifying marijuana, the legitimacy of governmental competence to judge the benefits and dangers of illicit drugs would be broadly undercut. This is a particular problem for a legalist, because the infallibility of the government on drugs is the major premise of the legalist position.

But if the legalists don't concede, they must fight an unpopular and uphill battle. It is little old ladies in pain versus the narcotics police in settings where very few negative effects have been evident in the lived history of medical marijuana.

That the legalist authorities have felt the necessity to stonewall medical marijuana is eloquent testimony to how seriously they regard the cost of any withdrawal from the standard criminal categories. That any adjustment from the criminal classification must be adamantly fought shows how dangerous any concession seems. This is the legalist Maginot Line.

But one of the ironies of the continuing conflict over medical marijuana is that victories like *United States v. Oakland Cannabis Buyers' Cooperative* may give continual help to the enemies of legalism. The larger the continuing importance of medical marijuana to the public awareness of drug control, the bigger the problem for the legalists.

The larger the concentration of federal power to frustrate the little old ladies and AIDS victims, the more persistent is the damage to legalist prestige. The great victory for the legalist defense of government authority would be the end of this dispute as an important element of the drug war.

The more medical marijuana persists as the public face of drug prohibition, the more problematic the legalist claim to authority.

E. TREATMENT vs. IMPRISONMENT FOR DRUG OFFENDERS—PROPOSITION 36 IN CALIFORNIA

Introduction

While medical marijuana is symbolically of substantial importance, it is an issue of peripheral importance to the intense involvement of the institutions of criminal justice—courts, jails, prisons. The initiative proposed and passed in California in 2000 was, by contrast, an attempt to use the initiative process and direct democracy to confront one of the centrally important features of drug control legalism in the United States—prison terms for the possession of illicit narcotics, particularly heroin and cocaine.

In an era when direct democracy was usually associated with punitive policies such as three strikes and you're out (see Zimring, Hawkins and Kamin 2001), the ballot initiative designed to replace imprisonment with community treatment for first time drug possession felons was passed in California in 2000. One interesting set of questions raised by this political history is what elements of attitude toward drug offenders and toward imprisonment made this political outcome possible. A second set of important questions concerns the impact of this policy on sanctions for drug offenses and for the general rate of imprisonment in California. We have seen the considerable upward elasticity of prison populations during the drug war after 1985. How substantial is the down side elasticity?

LISA RETTIG RYAN: PROPOSITION 36: DRUG TREATMENT DIVERSION PROGRAM: REHABILITATION OR DECRIMINALIZATION OF DRUG OFFENSES IN CALIFORNIA?

California Initiative Review, November 2000.

Executive Summary

States across the nation are looking at an array of sentencing alternatives to address prison population growth. Concerning non-violent drug addicts, some argue that spending state resources on incarceration is too costly and ineffective. Recognizing that the traditional approach of incarcerating nonviolent drug offenders has failed to reduce drug-related crime, many drug treatment professionals instead advocate the use of intensive, supervised rehabilitative treatment in order to break the cycle of drugs and criminality.

Californians will have the opportunity to vote on Proposition 36, titled The Substance Abuse and Crime Prevention Act (Act), in the November 2000 General Election. Proposition 36 will create a drug diversion program,which requires automatic probation and completion of an approved drug treatment program for those convicted of drug possession. Under the proposed measure, those convicted of non-violent drug possession offenses will be sent to community drug treatment centers, rather than jail or state prison. If a drug user successfully completes treatment,the court can effectively erase the offender's conviction.

Not every drug offender qualifies under the new drug diversion program. For example, offenders who refuse drug treatment or who possess a firearm while under the influence of certain drugs are not eligible to participate in the program. Moreover, offenders who enter the program and fail to successfully complete it will be sentenced to jail time. In support of the new drug diversion program, Proposition 36 provides $120 million to cover the costs of program placement, drug treatment and vocational training programs. The measure prohibits this funding from being used for drug testing purposes.

Proposition 36's $1 million signature gathering campaign was financed by billionaire George Soros and was organized by the same group that successfully campaigned for California's 1996 medical marijuana measure, Proposition 215. Not coincidentally, these are the same proponents who also backed the successful 1996 Arizona ballot measure, Proposition 200, to divert drug offenders from prison into drug treatment programs. Now, four years later, these reformists are attempting to bring drug diversion to California.

Arizona's drug diversion program provides a glimpse into some of the problems California will face by implementing Proposition 36. Like the Arizona law, Proposition 36 raises significant concerns due to the ambiguity of many of its provisions. The measure fails to answer questions regarding the oversight of drug treatment programs. It is also unclear where the necessary funding and personnel to implement the program will come from. Perhaps more importantly, Proposition 36 does not specify whether drug diversion will be available to juveniles or known drug dealers. While not posing any constitutional concerns, Proposition 36 is replete with ambiguous language and lacks substance in critical areas of implementation. If the voters approve this measure at the ballots in November, it is likely to end up in litigation, leaving the courts to interpret its meaning and applicability.

Proposition 36 has already generated a lot of attention and controversy. Its supporters argue that by attacking the core of the problem and treating the offender's addiction, criminality will be eliminated, thereby reducing crime rates. However, opponents, including many public safety groups, disagree and are concerned that crime rates will increase throughout the state. They claim that Proposition 36 does little to address how these addicts will be treated and provides no accountability to ensure that probationers are not continuing to use drugs. They fear this measure will only put more criminals back on the street. Whether or not the voters pass Proposition 36, drug rehabilitation advocates will continue to seek alternatives to incarceration for those arrested for drug offenses.

II. The Law

A. Existing Law

California state law generally makes it a crime to illegally possess, use, or be under the influence of specific drugs, including marijuana, cocaine, heroin, or methamphetamine, as well as certain medicines obtained without a physician's prescription. The law classifies some drug-related offenses as felonies and some as misdemeanors. Whether a drug-related crime is classified as a felony or misdemeanor, as well as the punishment imposed upon conviction, depends primarily upon the specific substance found to be in the offender's possession. (Cal. Health & Safety Code 11350 [West 2000].)

California courts currently provide drug treatment as a component of sentencing in various situations. (Cal. Penal Code 1203.096 [West 2000].) The court will recommend that the defendant participate in substance abuse counseling or an education program while imprisoned if the defendant was convicted on a drug-related offense. Furthermore, courts can require, as a condition of probation, that the defendant not use or be under the influence of any controlled substance and must submit to drug and substance abuse testing as directed by a probation officer. (Cal. Penal Code 1203.1ab [West 2000].)

Following release from prison into the community, nearly all offenders are required to serve a parole period under the supervision of state parole agents. Offenders who have not committed violent crimes, such as those imprisoned for felony drug possession, are subject to three years of parole supervision, but can be discharged from parole after one year if no parole violations are committed. (Cal. Health & Safety Code 11370 [West 2000].)

A parolee found to have committed a new crime while on parole, such as using or possessing an illegal drug, is subject to punishment in one of two ways. Such a parolee is either prosecuted on new criminal charges and returned to prison with a new sentence or parole is revoked and the parolee is returned to prison for up to a year by the Board of Prison Terms.

DRUG DIVERSION PROGRAMS

Drug Diversion Programs are not a new concept. Hundreds of drug courts have arisen across the country in the last ten years. California's first drug court originated in Alameda County in 1991. As of June 1999, there were 98 recorded drug courts in California alone. (Office of National Drug Control Policy, Drug Policy Information Clearinghouse, State of California Profile of Drug Indicators, 4 [July 2000].) Drug courts, unlike prisons, provide addicts with substance abuse treatment, education, and the resources to help them return to society with the skills necessary to lead a drug-free, productive life. The drug court model usually entails the following: judicial supervision of structured community-based treatment; timely identification of defendants in need of treatment and referral to treatment immediately after arrest; regular status hearings before judicial officers to monitor treatment progress and program compliance; and increasing defendant accountability through a series of graduated sanctions and rewards.

Unlike the programs envisioned under Proposition 36, however, the drug court system places drug-using offenders in a closely supervised program where they are ordered to submit to frequent drug testing and make regular appearances before a judge.

President Bill Clinton dramatically increased federal funding for drug courts after meeting former Dade County State Attorney General Janet Reno, who helped plan the nation's first drug court. Since the program's inception in 1995, the Drug Courts Program Office in the U.S. Department of Justice has bestowed approximately 500 grants totaling more than $100 million to help jurisdictions plan, implement, enhance and evaluate the more than 350 drug courts operating in the United States. (U.S. Department of Justice, Office of Justice Programs Press Release, Attorney General Reno Announces Funds To Continue Successful Drug Court Program [June 3, 1999].)

Part of the recent popularity of drug diversion programs is due to the apparent success in reducing recidivism. A 1998 study by the Office of Justice Programs found that drug courts cut recidivism for defendants accused of drug possession from an average of 45 percent, for those who do not go through drug court, to 4 percent for drug court graduates. (Drug Court Clearinghouse and Technical Assistance Project, U.S. Department of Justice, Looking at a Decade of Drug Courts [June 1998].)

Under current California law, each county's drug program administrator, in consultation with the court and the county probation department, establishes minimum requirements, criteria, and fees for the successful completion of drug diversion programs. The county board of supervisors must ultimately approve these requirements.* (*Cal. Penal Code 1211 [West 2000].) In order to receive funding, these local programs must satisfy the guidelines adopted by the state. (Cal. Health & Safety Code 11999.3. [West 2000].)

Federal Sentencing Guidelines

With the advent of the Federal Sentencing Guidelines, some argue that rehabilitation plays a secondary role, as compared with such sentencing rationales as deterrence and punishment. (See Sharon M. Bunzel, The Probation Officer and the Federal Sentencing Guidelines: Strange Philosophical Bedfellows, 104 Yale L.J. 933, 951 [1995].) However, rehabilitation remains a fundamental consideration within the federal sentencing process and probation is permitted under the Guidelines. (See 18 U.S.C. 3553(a)(2)(D) ["To provide the defendant with the needed educational or vocational training ... or other correctional treatment in the most effective manner"].)

Courts have even upheld pre-sentence rehabilitation. For instance, courts may delay a defendant's sentencing for more than a year to allow participation in drug treatment programs. (United States v. Maier, 975 F.2d 944, 948 [2d Cir. 1992].)

B. Changes Proposed by Proposition 36

Proposition 36 contains provisions similar to Arizona's drug diversion laws. Essentially, Proposition 36 modifies state sentencing laws, so that an offender convicted of a nonviolent drug possession offense will be sentenced to county probation supervision and participation in a drug treatment program, rather than subjected to incarceration in state prison or county jail.

The highlights of this initiative include:

TITLE, FINDINGS & DECLARATIONS, PURPOSE & INTENT—SECTIONS 1–3

The first three sections loosely describe the intent of "The Substance Abuse and Crime Prevention Act of 2000." The declarations highlight the Arizona initiative and finds "non-violent, drug dependent criminal offenders who received drug treatment are much less likely to abuse drugs and commit future crimes, and are likelier to live healthier, more stable and more productive lives." (Secretary of State, California Official Voter Information Guide, 66 [November, 2000] [hereinafter Guide].)

The underlying idea behind Proposition 36 is that jailing drug addicts does nothing to solve the actual problem—curing the drug addiction itself. The purpose of this measure, then, is to provide effective treatment to drug addicts, the goal being to reduce drug addiction and crime rates.

DEFINITIONS—SECTION 4

The measure would apply in cases of felony or misdemeanor criminal charges for being under the influence, possession or transportation for personal use of any controlled substance. It would not apply in cases involving possession for sale, production, or manufacturing of illegal drugs. The measure specifies the various types of drug programs the court can assign a convicted offender to: up to one year, with six additional months of aftercare. Participation in vocational training, family counseling, and literacy training can also be required. The measure provides that offenders who are reasonably able to do so may be required to help pay for their own drug treatment.

MANDATORY PROBATION—SECTION 5

The real heart of the initiative is in Section 5. Here, the initiative adds section 1210.1 to the California Penal Code to provide automatic probation for any person convicted of a non-violent drug possession offense. Participation and completion of an appropriate drug treatment program is required as a condition of probation.

This measure specifies that certain offenders will be excluded from its provisions and subjected to sentencing under existing criminal laws. Those excluded from Proposition 36's automatic probation include:

1. any offender who refuses drug treatment,

2. any offender who uses a firearm during his or her crime,

3. any offender who is convicted in the same court proceeding of another crime, and

4. any offender who repeatedly fails the drug treatment programs mandated under this measure.

Additionally, offenders who fail to comply with their drug treatment requirements or conditions of probation, or those who commit new crimes, will be subject to various specified sanctions by the court, including incarceration in jail or prison. In contrast, offenders who successfully complete treatment and comply with their conditions of probation can petition the court for dismissal of the charges and have the arrest removed from their criminal record.

PAROLEES—SECTION 6

Parole violators found to have committed a nonviolent drug possession offense or to have violated any drug-related condition of parole will generally remain on parole supervision and be placed in a county-established drug treatment program. The parolee will not be subjected to re-incarceration in state prison for the parole violation.

This initiative specifies that its provisions for diversion from prison will not apply to certain parolees, thus making them subject to imprisonment for parole violations in accordance with existing law. The excluded parolees are any who refuse drug treatment, who are found to have also committed another crime, or who have a prior conviction on their record for a crime classified as either violent or serious. Parolees who fail to comply with their drug treatment requirements or conditions of parole or those who commit new crimes will be subject to various specified sanctions, including reincarceration in state prison.

FUNDING APPROPRIATION—SECTION 7

Section 7 creates the Substance Abuse Treatment Trust Fund. The measure provides additional funding to counties to support the proposed expansion of drug treatment and probation supervision for non-violent drug possession offenders and related costs. After providing $60 million in 2000–2001, $120 million will be appropriated annually through 2005–2006 for these purposes.

The initiative directs that the funds be distributed to counties through the state Department of Alcohol and Drug Programs (DADP). The funds received by counties cannot be used for drug testing of offenders (a problem cited by the opponents), but can be used to fund vocational training, family counseling and literacy training under this

Act. The initiative authorizes DADP to contract for additional drug treatment whenever it determines that existing services are insufficient.

The initiative directs DADP to conduct an annual study to evaluate the effectiveness and fiscal impact of the measure. County governments will report specified information on the conduct of the drug treatment programs to DADP, and their expenditures will be subject to audits by the department.

EFFECTIVE DATE, AMENDMENTS & SEVERABILITY—SECTIONS 8, 9, 10

The initiative provides that the Act becomes effective July 1, 2001, and its provisions applied prospectively. Any amendments to the Act requires a two-thirds vote of the Legislature. In addition, if the courts determine that any part of the initiative is invalid or unconstitutional, the other provisions of the initiative should not be affected.

III. Drafting Issues

The drafters of Proposition 36 have the benefit of learning from the drafting errors and ambiguities surrounding the Arizona initiative. In the past few years, a number of issues related to the statutory interpretation of Proposition 200 have been litigated in Arizona courts. For example, Arizona courts have recently grappled with issues ranging from whether their initiative distinguished "possession" of drugs from "selling" to whether the initiative applied to juveniles. Since a neighboring state jurisdiction decided the following cases, California courts are not bound by their holdings. However, Arizona State court case law does serve as persuasive precedent.

DOES PROPOSITION 36 PROHIBIT INCARCERATION FOR VIOLATION OF PROBATION?

What happens when a defendant violates the provisions of probation under this initiative? In the event the defendant violates probation conditions, the Arizona initiative contains no limit on the number of times a court is required to modify the conditions of probation and expressly precludes the court from incarcerating the defendant. For example, after a defendant violated probation conditions twice, an Arizona court revoked probation and sentenced petitioner to a 2.5–year prison term. However, in State v. Thomas, the appellate court determined that the trial court was precluded from sentencing him to prison by A.R.S. 13–901.01, providing a violation of probation shall have new conditions of probation established by the court short of incarceration, enacted as part of Proposition 200. (State v. Thomas, 996 P.2d 113 [Ariz. App. Div. 2, 1999].) Proposition 36 seems to avoid this problem by expressly allowing incarceration if probation is revoked. (Guide at 67.)

Is the Initiative applicable to persons who commit a specified offense before the effective date of the Act, but are found guilty after the effective date?

Proposed Penal Code section 1210.1 states that any person "convicted" of a non-violent drug possession offense shall receive probation.

What if a defendant is arrested in June 2001 for a non-violent drug possession, but is not sentenced until August 2001? Assuming passage of Proposition 36, would the mandatory probation apply to said defendant?

Rationalizing that ex post facto laws are unconstitutional, (U.S. Const. art. I, sec. 9, cl. 3), an Arizona court held that a defendant was not eligible for probation when the offense was committed prior to passage of the initiative. (Baker v. Superior Court In and For County of Maricopa, 947 P.2d 910 [Ariz. App. Div. 1, 1997].) However, ex post facto prohibitions are intended to protect defendants from laws that change the punishment, and inflict a greater punishment, than the law annexed to the crime, when committed.

Proposition 36, Section 8 explicitly states that the provisions of this Act "shall become effective July 1, 2001, and its provisions shall be applied prospectively." (Guide at 69.) Unlike the defendant in Baker, consider a hypothetical defendant who commits an offense after passage of the initiative, but before the effective date of July 1, 2001. If the sentencing occurs after this effective date, will the defendant receive automatic parole? In Tapia v. Superior Court of Tulare City, the California Supreme Court held that where a provision clearly benefits the defendant, the provisions apply even to crimes committed before passage of Proposition 115, the "Crime Victims Justice Reform Act." (Tapia v. Superior Court of Tulare Cty., 53 Cal.3d 282, 301 [April 1, 1991].) Presumably, California courts can find that Proposition 36 allows for sentences benefiting defendants convicted of drug possession, not greater punishments; therefore, the court may apply this reasoning to defendants sentenced after July 1, 2001.

Does the Initiative Apply to Juveniles?

The question of whether mandatory probation for non-violent drug possession applies to juveniles was raised in Arizona. (In re Fernando C., 986 P.2d 901 [Ariz. App. Div. 2, 1999].) There the court held that the Arizona statute does not apply to juveniles. Although the minor conceded that the proper terminology categorizes him as having been "adjudicated" and not "convicted," he maintained that the ordinary meaning of the word "convicted" should be applied and that it extends to juvenile court proceedings. Additionally, the minor argued that Proposition 200 changed the justice system's approach to non-violent drug offenders and should apply to juvenile offenders, not just persons charged and tried as an adult.

Although there is no language in Proposition 36 to infer that juveniles were included within the Act's purview, a juvenile in California may make a similar claim should this initiative pass. Thus, it might be wise to insert clarifying language into Proposition 36 stating whether the initiative does or does not apply to juveniles.

Does the Initiative Allow Probation for Defendants Arrested for Production or Sale of Drugs?

It appears that the drafter's intent is to provide mandatory probation only to those convicted of possession. Those individuals participating in the chain of manufacturing and commercial distribution of a controlled substance are not the target audience of this measure. State law differentiates between felons convicted of possessing illegal drugs for personal use and those convicted of possessing illegal drugs for sale to another party. (Cal. Health & Safety Code 11350, 11351 [West 2000].)

As proposed in Proposition 36, Penal Code section 1210 (a) defines non-violent drug possession offense as not including "possession for sale, production, or manufacturing of any controlled substance." (Guide at 66.) By definition, someone convicted for selling would not be eligible for mandatory probation. However, a defendant found possessing a controlled substance who has one or two prior convictions for possession to sell, may be eligible for mandatory probation.

In Goddard v. Superior Court, the Arizona court allowed judicial discretion for such sentencing by holding that the drafters and voters had in fact distinguished possession for use from possession for sale: "An evident purpose of Proposition 200 was to preserve such a distinction and to make it plain that those who commercially traffic in controlled substances are not entitled to the benefits accorded those who possess for use. This does not mean, however, as Petitioner contends, that one who has committed two or more past offenses of possession for sale is entitled to mandatory probation." (Goddard v. Superior Court of Arizona, 956 P.2d 529, 532 [App. 1998].)

The difficulty in distinguishing between possession to sell versus personal use is heightened by ambiguities in the language of Proposition 36.

Will Vague Language Require Litigation?

Section 4 of the Proposition adds section 1210 to the Penal Code to define "non-violent drug possession offense" as the "unlawful possession, use, or transportation for personal use of any controlled substance identified (in specified code)." (Guide at 66.) It is unclear whose personal use the provision is discussing. Since all drugs are for someone's personal use, such vague language may require additional litigation to determine the true intent of the individual unlawfully possessing the drugs. Another problem arises in determining whether an individual was transporting the illegal substances for personal use or whether this person is in fact transporting the drugs for future sale. How will the court determine whether an individual is a drug dealer if he claims the drugs are for personal use only? The purpose of the initiative is to "treat" individuals with drug problems. The initiative vitiates this purpose if it provides only probation and treatment for drug dealers.

Subdivision (a) of proposed Penal Code section 1210.1 provides that the "trial judge *may* require any person convicted of a non-violent drug possession offense who is *reasonably able *to do so to contribute to the cost of their own placement in a drug treatment program." (Guide at 66.) How is "reasonably able" defined? Currently, defendants sent to DUI programs are required to pay for the cost of the program. Under this initiative, it appears that even those who are able to pay for those costs of the treatment "may" not have to pay.

In another Arizona decision, the court rejected the argument that the drafters of Proposition 200 intended it to apply to possession of drug paraphernalia. (State v. Holm, 985 P.2d 527, 529 [App. 1998].) The defendant's argument in Holm depended upon an incorrect contention that possession of drug paraphernalia was a lesser-included offense of possession of drugs. While Proposition 36 does not refer to drug paraphernalia in its definition of non-violent drug possession, it does expressly exclude possession of drug paraphernalia in the definition of "misdemeanor not related to the use of drugs." (Guide at 66.) Therefore, Proposition 36 appears to eliminate the ambiguity for possession of drug paraphernalia previously seen in Proposition 200.

IV. *Constitutional Analysis*

While the initiative process empowers the people to enact laws, initiative measures must still pass constitutional muster. "The voters may no more violate the Constitution by enacting a ballot measure than a legislative body may do so by enacting legislation." (Citizens Against Rent Control/Coalition for Fair Housing v. City of Berkeley, 454 U.S. 290, 295 [1981].) With this in mind, it is necessary to review whether Proposition 36 raises any constitutional violations.

DUE PROCESS

The constitutional right to due process of law guarantees that any sanction that deprives a defendant of life, liberty, or property must be implemented in a fair manner. (United States v. Salerno, 481 U.S. 739, 746 [1987].) Sentencing in the criminal justice system has changed dramatically in our nation's short history. The drug diversion program is but one example of alternatives to a typical prison sentence. Although some sentences focus solely on punishment, others look to rehabilitation as an appropriate sentence. Regardless of the judgment, compliance with procedures for minimum due process is imperative. Questions of due process are especially pertinent to Proposition 36 in relation to parole violations.

Although the Fourteenth Amendment provides the essential requirements of due process, two important U.S. Supreme Court decisions further clarified the bare necessities of due process for sentencing alternatives and violations. (Morrissey and Booher v. Brewer, Warden, et al., 408 U.S. 471 [1972]; Gagnon, Warden v. Scarpelli, 411 U.S. 778 [1973].) Morrissey held that the Due Process Clause of the 14th Amendment requires that a state afford an individual some opportunity to be heard prior to revoking his parole. Specifically, the Court held that a parolee is entitled to two hearings, one a preliminary hearing at the time of his arrest and detention to determine whether there is probable cause to believe that he has committed a violation of his parole, and the other a somewhat more comprehensive hearing prior to the final revocation decision. (Morrissey at 485.)

The following year, the Court extended this reasoning in Gagnon holding that a previously sentenced probationer is entitled to a hearing when his probation is revoked. Probation revocation, like parole revocation, is not a stage of a criminal prosecution, but does result in a loss of liberty. "Accordingly, we hold that a probationer, like a parolee, is entitled to a preliminary and a final revocation hearing, under the conditions specified in Morrissey v. Brewer." (Gagnon at 782.)

Sections 5(c)(2), 5(e) and Section 6 of Proposition 36 describe the potential for probation revocation. Regarding essential due process, all implemented sentencing reforms have some basic procedural requirements, whether codified or through the common law. Given the increasing size of the criminal justice system, probation, parole, intermediate punishment and rehabilitation will not be the last sentencing reforms seen. Proposition 36 appears to meet the minimal due process procedures necessary by requiring the appropriate revocation hearings.

EQUAL PROTECTION

The Fifth and Fourteenth Amendments to the Constitution guarantee to all citizens the equal protection of the laws. (U.S. Const. amend. V, XIV 1.) Under the terms of this initiative, criminal defendants who have committed similar non-violent drug possession offenses in the same jurisdiction may receive different treatment regarding their probation, depending on the circumstances surrounding the offense.

Specifically, proposed section 1210.1(b) of the Penal Code (Guide at 66.) will not permit mandatory probation for the non-violent drug possession offense of any defendant who had previously been convicted of one or more serious or violent felonies in violation of Penal Code sections 667.5(c) or 1192.7 (specifying the violent felonies, including rape, murder and kidnapping) within the past five years. (Cal. Penal Code 667.5(c), 1192.7 [West 2000].) Under current equal protection analysis, however, this differential treatment easily withstands constitutional scrutiny.

Although the Supreme Court has not addressed the issue, lower federal courts have held that differing treatment of defendants accused of committing the same crime is a constitutional exercise of prosecutorial discretion. These courts have held that prosecutors have discretion to file different charges against individuals who have committed the same offense. (Newman v. United States, 382 F.2d 479, 481–82 [D.C. Cir. 1967] [to require prosecutors to treat all offenses and offenders alike would be "an impossible task."].) This situation commonly occurs when a district attorney offers one codefendant a plea bargain in exchange for testimony against an accomplice, who is then convicted at trial. The same reasoning allows Proposition 36 to provide different treatment for the same non-violent drug offenses based on past arrests.

Proposition 36 also raises an equal protection issue regarding non-drug-related probation violations and drug-related probation violations. (Guide at 67.) This distinction presents the question of whether defendants can constitutionally receive different treatment based upon their status as a drug user. Since this classification does not involve either a suspect class, such as race, or a fundamental interest, such as liberty, a rational basis standard of equal protection review applies. (*See* San Antonio Independent School District v. Rodriguez, 411 U.S. 1 [1973].) To meet the low standard of rational basis review, the classification need only rationally further some legitimate, articulated state purpose . The distinction between drug related and non-drug related violations rationally furthers the legitimate state interest in decreasing drug use and punishing such drug use with rehabilitation rather than incarceration, as well as reducing the prison population. Based on this reasoning, the distinction meets the rational basis standard of equal protection review.

The initiative also provides for two different standards of review for any defendant unamenable to drug treatment for exceptions to the parole requirement versus parole revocation. Proposed Penal Code 1210.1 (b)(5) would exempt from the mandatory probation any person convicted of a non-violent drug possession offense found to be unamenable to any and all forms of available drug treatment by clear and convincing evidence. (Guide at 67.) Yet, the court could revoke probation under Penal Code 1210.1 (e)(3)(B) if the state proves by a preponderance of the evidence that the defendant is unamenable to drug treatment. (Id.) Clear and convincing evidence requires a greater showing of proof than the preponderance of the evidence standard, requiring that the thing to be proven is highly probable. (Black's Law Dictionary, Seventh Edition [1999].) Such a distinction should not violate any equal protection guarantees as they apply to two separate phases of the criminal procedure process.

SIXTH AMENDMENT SPEEDY TRIAL CLAIM

Some drug diversion programs currently work as a pre-sentence rehabilitation option. Defendants may choose to enroll in a drug diversion program before sentencing. Ideally, this accomplishes the court's ultimate objective in sentencing for drug use violations—deterrence. Although there is some question as to whether this violates an individual's Sixth Amendment right to a speedy trial, courts have held that no Sixth Amendment violation occurs where the sentencing court postponed sentencing at the request of the defendant to allow consideration of post-offense, pre-sentence rehabilitation. (U.S. v. Flowers 983 F.Supp. 159 [E.D.N.Y. 1997].) Proposition 36 provides for mandatory drug treatment participation as a requirement to receiving a probation sentence. Because the defendant is actually sentenced, no Sixth Amendment issues arise.

V. *Public Policy Considerations*

An organization called California Campaign for New Drug Policies (CCNDP) is leading the campaign in support of Proposition 36. An array of state legislators (all Democrats), Republican U.S. Senate candidate Tom Campbell, and organizations such as Minorities in Law Enforcement, California Association of Alcoholism and Drug Abuse Counselors, and California Women Lawyers have all endorsed the initiative. (CCNDP, Official Endorsers of the Substance and Crime Prevention Act.)

The opposition to Proposition 36 is organized by a group called Californians United Against Drug Abuse (CUADA). Many law enforcement and victims' rights organizations are opposing Proposition 36 including: the California Peace Officers' Association, Chief Probation Officers of California, California Narcotic Officers' Association, Victims and Friends United, and the California District Attorneys' Association. Both sides have raised public policy concerns in support of and in opposition to the measure.

DRUG ABUSE AS A HEALTH CONCERN

A common sentiment today, and the major impetus behind Proposition 36, is that drug addicts need treatment not incarceration. Most advocates of the treatment route view drug addiction as a health issue. California State Senate's President Pro Tempore, John Burton, is an outspoken advocate for the public policy view that we should treat drug abuses as health problems, not law enforcement problems. (Lynda Gledhill, Drug Offense Measure Makes Ballot, San Francisco Chronicle, June 1, 2000.) These advocates claim that the drug addict lacks control over the commission of the offense, thus they do not benefit from, nor are they deterred by, punishment through incarceration. The threat of imprisonment has no effect on a drug addict because the compulsions and threat of withdrawal that are elements of addiction far outweigh any consequences a drug addict may face for the commission of these acts.

Opponents of the initiative, however, note that the initiative fails to set minimum treatment standards. Further, the initiative prohibits the use of appropriated funds for treatment programs to be used for drug testing. Presumably, the programs envisioned under the initiative would be low-cost, outpatient settings without drug testing. The opposition argues that without intense monitoring of the drug user there would be little accountability to treat the drug/health problem effectively. CUADA charges "if the initiative backers were sincere about improving drug treatment in California, they would have asked health care professionals to help draft the initiative." (Californians United Against Drug Abuse handout, What California Health Care Professionals Need to Know [2000].)

ISSUES OF PUBLIC SAFETY, RECIDIVISM

Many people view a ban on jailing drug offenders as a dangerous experiment. Opponents claim that the initiative weakens anti-drug laws and undermines legitimate drug treatment programs. According to a 1997 U.S. Bureau of the Census survey, 32.6% of all state prison inmates reported they were under the influence of drugs at the time they committed the offense that resulted in their incarceration. (Fact Sheet from the Office of National Drug Control Policy, Bureau of Justice

Statistics, Substance Abuse and Treatment, State and Federal Prisoners, 1997, 3 [March 2000].) Supporters contend that many of those crimes would not have been committed had those individuals been treated and not been under the influence of drugs.

Opponents claim that the initiative prohibits all individuals—even dangerous and violent felons—from being incarcerated for possessing or being under the influence of drugs like crack, heroin, LSD and other serious substances. (*See* Letter of opposition from California Narcotic Officers' Association to Mr. Walt Allen, Chairman, Californian's United Against Drug Abuse [June 5, 2000] [on file with California Initiative Review].) Victims' rights organizations also worry that prohibiting incarceration for anyone possessing or being under the influence of drugs will increase crime rates. They contend that this initiative is "a step backward for the crime victim's movement." (*See* Letter of opposition from Victims and Friends United to Californian's United Against Drug Abuse [June 20, 2000] [on file with California Initiative Review].)

The National Association of Drug Court Professionals (NADCP) also argues that this initiative removes a judge's discretion in sentencing. (Jessie Seyfer, U.S. drug czar says state initiative would weaken drug courts' power, San Diego Union–Trib., June 3, 2000, at A–3.) Under this initiative, there is little recourse for those who relapse. Under current law, if an individual is sentenced through a drug court and then relapses, that person receives an automatic 36 hours in jail—a significant deterrent. Under this initiative, there would be little or no punishment for any such relapse. In fact, anyone caught with drugs after two treatment diversions will only be jailed for 30 days. The advocates counter that judges may set any range of probation conditions for drug offenders processed under the initiative, including weekly court appearances in addition to drug testing. Furthermore, the court may drop the offender out of the initiative's system and incarcerate that person for up to 16 months, as provided under current law. (California Campaign for New Drug Policies, Response to NADCP Press Release [June 1, 2000].)

The opposition also raises the concern that the protections are so great under the initiative that drug felons can continue to work as school bus drivers, teachers and airline pilots. Section five of the initiative effectively erases any record for those complying with probation requirements. Without knowledge of an employee's criminal history, many employers will be oblivious to the inherent risk of hiring a former drug abuser.

TREATMENT PROGRAMS OVERSIGHT

Proposition 36 raises serious public policy questions regarding the oversight and operation of the proposed drug treatment programs. The initiative fails to specify who will regulate treatment facilities or programs. Will the State be required to license and set minimum treatment requirements? What are the standards to be used in determining successful treatment? There is nothing in the initiative specifying any requirements that trained professionals operate the programs. Opponents contend that the initiative will encourage "fly-by-night" operators who are only interested in the money, not the treatment of drug abusers.

FISCAL CONSIDERATIONS

According to the Official Voter Information Guide, this initiative will result in an annual net savings of $100 million to $150 million to the state and about $40 million to local governments. (Guide at 25) The Guide also cites potential avoidance of one-time capital outlay costs to the state of $450 million to $550 million. (Id.) The initiative mandates $120,000,000 appropriated annually from the state General Fund to cover the costs of placing persons in and providing specified drug treatment and vocational training programs under this Act. (Guide at 69.) Are these costs easily absorbable in the state's General Fund, or will other programs have to be cut?

The advocates advance numerous findings related to the costs of incarceration versus treatment. According to the Sourcebook of Criminal Justice Statistics, the average cost to the taxpayers of California per inmate, per year is $23,406. (Bureau of Justice Statistics, Sourcebook of Criminal Justice Statistics [1997].) They claim that the initiative reduces the number of state prison beds needed for drug offenders by 10,000 to 12,000 within a few years. Logically, this reduces the need for additional capital outlay to pay for construction of additional state prisons. The California Campaign for New Drug Policies estimates "a one-time savings of between $475 million and $575 million in deferred or avoided prison construction." (CCNDP, California Taxpayers Fact Sheet [on file with California Initiative Review].) Yet, these savings do not take into consideration the costs associated with developing, training and running effective drug treatment programs. Furthermore, the opposition questions how much mandatory probation requirements will cost the courts in increased litigation and oversight.

OTHER STATES

States across the nation are developing innovative programs to deal with a burgeoning prison population and an ever-increasing drug addiction problem. California's Proposition 36 follows directly on the heels of Arizona's Proposition 200.

Other states are also trying their hand at drug treatment and rehabilitation as an alternative to incarceration. In Nevada, the state government is pushing to extend a heroin-user diversion program across the state. A nine-month evaluation of the pilot program has indicated that it is effectively detecting heroin use in its early stages and diverting the users into treatment. In Colorado, the Juvenile Offender Substance Abuse Treatment (JOSAT) Project was created to help the large number of juvenile offenders who abuse alcohol and other drugs. In addition, Idaho has begun a 4–week, 30 hours a week, coed program to provide intensive drug education and group treatment to incarcerated offenders. (Justice Research and Statistics Association, Programs in Correctional

Settings: Innovative State and Local Programs, (June 1998) [available at http://www.ncjrs.org/txtfiles/170088.txt].) Regardless of the outcome of Proposition 36, states will continue to seek options for alternatives in the sentencing and rehabilitation of our nation's drug users.

VI. *Conclusion*

Proposition 36 is an innovative, yet controversial, approach to addressing the drug problem in California. The initiative proposes to divert defendants and parolees charged with drug possession or drug use offenses away from prison or jail and into local substance abuse treatment programs. By providing rehabilitation instead of simple incarceration, the goal is to break the drug abuser's cycle of crime. California judges already have sentencing discretion to provide drug treatment as a part of a defendant's incarceration, or as part of the alternative sentencing of the Drug Court. Proposition 36 goes a step further, making parole automatic for non-violent drug possession and use offenses.

If the voters pass Proposition 36 in November 2000, there will undoubtedly be more questions than answers as California's law enforcement community grapples with implementing the initiative. Will "The Substance Abuse and Crime Prevention Act" reduce drug-related crime and preserve jail and prison space for violent offenders as the supporter's promise? Or, will the initiative threaten public safety and cost taxpayers millions of dollars in added public safety, court and drug abuse costs as the opposition warns?

Ultimately, passage of this initiative will depend on whether California voters support the idea of substance abuse treatment as an automatic alternative to incarceration or whether the voters believe that this initiative goes too far at the expense of public safety.

SCOTT EHLERS AND JASON ZIEDENBERG— PROPOSITION 36: FIVE YEARS LATER

Justice Policy Institute (April 2006).

"Of likely voters, 73 percent would vote for Proposition 36 today. Proposition 36 was passed by 61 percent of California voters in November of 2000."—Results of a Field Poll Corporation survey, May 2004

INTRODUCTION: CALIFORNIA'S CORRECTIONAL CHALLENGE, AND PROPOSITION 36

While the United States still carries the dubious distinction of leading the world in imprisonment,[2] recent changes to sentencing in a number of states may signal that the country is turning the corner. Since 2000, at least 25 states have implemented sentencing and correctional reforms. Seventeen states, including Michigan, Louisiana, Wash-

2. Walmsley, Roy. World Prison Population List. (February, 2005). London: International Center for Prison Studies.

ington, Texas, Kansas, and Mississippi, have rolled back mandatory minimum sentences or restructured other harsh penalties that were originally enacted to "get tough" on low-level or nonviolent offenders, especially those convicted of drug offenses.[3] Sixteen states, including Texas, Washington, Colorado, and Kentucky, have eased prison population pressures by shortening time served in prison, increasing the release rate, and sanctioning probation or parole violators without returning them to prison.[4]

These changes to sentencing policy may be having an impact: The latest federal prisoner survey shows that in 2004, 11 states saw declines in their prison populations, and the rate of state prison growth has fal en from 8.7 percent a decade ago to 1.4 percent today.[5]

California, with the nation's largest prison system, is struggling with corrections reforms. While prison population growth has leveled off (in 2004, the rate of growth was lower than the U.S. state average), the state has failed to implement the kinds of sentencing reform seen elsewhere, and there are signs that the state is returning to the prison building boom that defined the 1990s.

In California, in the last three years:

- The Three Strikes reform ballot initiative failed to be enacted: California's "Three Strikes" law, which doubles some sentences and imposes a 25–to-life sentence for a third felony offense, contributed to longer sentences for 42,000 prisoners.[6] In 2004, polls showed for most of the year that Californians were poised to vote in favor of an initiative to reform the law. At the encouragement of law enforcement groups, Governor Schwarzenegger put a million dollars of his own political action funds into radio and television advertisements against the initiative. The initiative was narrowly defeated.

- Parole reforms failed to be enacted: The Governor embraced the recommendations of an Independent Review Panel on California correctional practices, and sought to implement "a new parole model" providing alternatives to prison for faltering parole. In April 2005, the California Correctional Peace Officers Association and Crime Victims United in California ran television advertisements accusing the administration of implementing policies that

3. Greene, Judith. *Smart On Crime: Positive Trends in State–Level Sentencing and Corrections Policy* (2003). Washington, D.C.: Families Against Mandatory Minimums.

4. Ibid.

5. Beck, Allen and Harrison, Paige. *Prisoners* in 2004 [1994]. (2005). Washington, D.C.: Office of Justice Programs, Bureau of Justice Statistics.

6. "Second and Third Strikers in the Institution Population by Offense Category, Offense Group and Admission or Return Status as of September 30, 2003," Second and Third Strikers in the Institution Population, Data Analysis Unit, Estimates and Statistical Analysis Section, Offender Information Services Branch, California Department of Corrections (November 2003).

would put violent criminals back on the street. The administration ordered the parole reforms pulled.[7]

- The Governor proposed to build new prisons and fund jail expansion: In 2005, when the Kern Valley State Prison was opened, the administration was hailed for overseeing the "end of an era:" it was the fi rst time in two decades the state was not planning to build a new prison.[8] In 2006, however, part of the administration's push for $68 billion in public works bonds was geared to support the construction of two new prisons and 83,000 jail beds.[9]

In California, the polarized nature of state politics, and the relative strength of interest groups (including the state's law enforcement associations, victims rights groups, and the prison guards union) has meant that even while the people of the state favor more rehabilitative approaches, policy change has not been realized. According to a poll conducted by the Field Research Corporation in May 2004, well over half of Californians surveyed (56%) think that rehabilitating and educating offenders outside of prison would reduce the state's crime problem.[10] According to the survey, by an 8 to 1 margin, Californians favor using state funds for rehabilitation over an approach that just punishes people with a prison sentence.

The 2004 Field Research Corporation survey also shows growing public support for Proposition 36, the Substance Abuse and Crime Prevention Act (SACPA), which was enacted through initiative process with the support of 61 percent of California voters in November 2000. Whereas the baseline penalty for felony drug possession in California ranges from 16 months to 3 years,[11] Proposition 36 allows people convicted of first-and second-time drug possession the opportunity to receive substance abuse treatment instead of incarceration. Since the initiative began in 2001, $120 million in funds has been spent every year to fund treatment for thousands of people who would otherwise be incarcerated for a drug offense.

Through Proposition 36, one of the few correctional policy reforms fully implemented this decade, California joins New York, Maryland, Kansas, Washington, and many other states that have taken efforts to divert people arrested for drug offenses to drug treatment. Like every other California correctional reform, Proposition 36 has been controversial. And the debate continues today: while the Field Research poll showed that a larger proportion of Californians supported the initiative four years after it was passed, legislators have attempted to change the

7. "Back on track: state must resume parole reform," *The San Diego Union–Tribune*, June 11, 2005.

8. Barbassa, Juliana. "Opening of new prison marks end of era in California," *The Associated Press*, June 15, 2005.

9. Marelius, John "Schwarzenegger proposes huge public works program," *The San Diego Tribune*, January 6, 2006.

10. Krisberg, Barry, Craine, Jessica, Marchionna Susan. *Attitudes of Californians toward Effective Correctional Policies.* Oakland, California: National Center on Crime and Delinquency.

11. California penal code sections, 12010–12010.5

initiative by adding jail sanctions to the program—a change that could contribute to growing jail and correctional populations in the state.

Five years after the initiative officially came into effect, the Justice Policy Institute has analyzed leading correctional, crime, and expenditure data, and reviewed the literature on treatment efficacy to help put the policy debate around Proposition 36 in context. The data shows that Proposition 36 may have succeeded in its goal of reducing drug imprisonment, and moving drug-addicted people arrested for drug offenses into the treatment system in greater numbers. The report also echoes the findings of a recent University of California report that shows that the initiative is saving the state $2.50 for every dollar spent on the program, and represented a net savings to government of $173.3 million in the first year alone.[12]

Given that California's prison population is on the rise again,[13] California policymakers should careful y consider the impact Proposition 36 may have had on the state's troubled corrections system, and how the law may have improved the state's ability to treat drug addiction.

METHODOLOGY

This policy brief summarizes and analyzes data and findings from a variety of criminal justice agencies and research entities whose work is national in scope, including the National Archive of Criminal Justice Data, the Federal Bureau of Investigation's Uniform Crime Report, the U.S. Justice Department's National Institute of Justice, the Office of Justice Programs Bureau of Justice Statistics, and the Substance Abuse and Mental Health Services Administration. This report contains original analysis by the Justice Policy Institute of crime and imprisonment data from the California Department of Corrections Data Analysis Unit and the Office of the Attorney General, Criminal Justice Statistics Center, the California Department of Alcohol and Drug Programs, the California Department of Finance, the California State Controller, and the California Board of Corrections. Findings that report on state imprisonment trends outside of California either come from the Bureau of Justice Statistics, or from the corrections departments or equivalent state correctional statistics bureau of those states. The authors have also reviewed and summarized analyses published by researchers with the John Jay College of Criminal Justice in New York City, National Bureau of Economic Research, *the American Journal of Sociology,* and other scholarship on treatment efficacy, and research in the fields of corrections, economics, and social policy.

12. Longshore, Douglas et. al. *SACPA Cost Analysis Report (First and Second Years).* (2006). Los Angeles: UCLA Integrated Substance Abuse Programs.

13. On March 15th, 2006, there were 168,000 prisoners in California. "Weekly report of population as of midnight March 15, 2006." (March 20, 2006). Data Analysis Unit Department of Corrections and Rehabilitation—Estimates and Statistical Analysis Section State of California Offender Information Services Branch.

CHOOSING A BASELINE: 1999 OR 2000

Within the policy community reviewing these issues, there is a methodological challenge in determining the baseline year for judging the impact of Proposition 36. The measure appeared on the ballot on Nov. 7, 2000. While the initiative did not officially go into effect until July 1, 2001, various effects of its passage may have begun prior to then. For example, startup appropriation of funds to support drug treatment, and development of the state's treatment infrastructure, was required by the initiative within weeks of its passage.

The mere presence of Proposition 36 on the ballot, and the elevated public discussion of drug sentencing that it provoked, may have affected sentencing practices for much of the year 2000. After the measure was approved, some justice system actors reported that some defendants with drug possession cases had their trials and/or sentencing postponed from 2000 to 2001, so that, in sentencing, they would be able to take part in Proposition 36 treatment. Further evidence of some pre-enactment effects of Proposition 36 comes from data showing a decline in the number of prison inmates serving time for drug possession, a figure that, between June 2000 and December 2000. It is reasonable to infer that fewer drug offenders were added to the prison population in late 2000 than might otherwise have been added without Proposition 36.

Because there appear to have been some effects of Proposition 36 during parts of the year 2000, researchers believe that using 2000 as a baseline for five-year comparisons could underestimate the impact of the initiative. The year 1999 might, therefore, be preferable as a baseline year, because only in that year could there have been no effects from Proposition 36 being on the ballot or approved by voters. Rather than resolve the issue, JPI has elected to report 1999 and 2000 figures wherever available and possible, and use 2000 as the baseline comparative year for most of our discussion.

Finding 1: California's drug possession prison population
has fallen since Proposition 36 passed

"The People of the State of California hereby declare their purpose
and intent in enacting this Act to be as follows: To divert from
incarceration into community-based substance abuse treatment pro-
grams nonviolent defendants, probationers and parolees charged
with simple drug possession or drug use offenses."—from the declaration of the Substance Abuse and Crime Prevention Act, Proposition 36.

One of the goals of Proposition 36 was to divert nonviolent defendants, probationers, and parolees from incarceration into community-based substance abuse treatment programs.[14] Since the initiative was passed by California voters and came into effect, the number of drug

---

14. Substance Abuse and Crime Prevention Act, Section 3, *Purpose and Intent,*   Subsection a.

possession offenders in California's prisons has gone from 19,736 in December 2000 to 14,325 in December 2005, a reduction of 27.4 percent. While Proposition 36 did not officially go into effect until July 1, 2001, it is believed that the drug possession offender population may have begun falling between its passage in November 2000 and its official enactment date since some defendants delayed their cases so they could qualify for drug treatment instead of incarceration.

Along with a drop in the absolute number of people incarcerated for drug possession, California's rate of drug-possession incarceration per 100,000 residents also fell during the period. The rate of incarceration for drug possession offenses has gone from 89 per 100,000 California adults in December 2000 to 58 in December 2005, a 34.3 percent decrease.

The "static" prison population reviewed above measures the population of drug prisoners at a particular point in time. Prison populations are affected by the length of sentence, the number people leaving prison, the number of people admitted to prison on new felonies, and parolees who are returned to prison on a new prison term or returned for a parole violation. While the Department of Corrections does not publish data on the reasons why parolees are returned to prison for parole violations, it does publish data on prison admissions for new felony admissions and parole violators with a new prison term handed down by the courts.

While it is not known if Proposition 36 is wholly responsible for the drop in drug-possession prison admissions since its enactment, no other changes in public policy, population, or public behavior provide an explanation. It is also possible that Proposition 36 diverted even more people from prison than are indicated from the reduced prison admissions, since prison admissions may rise because of increases in the population of California as a whole.

DECLINING DRUG POSSESSION ADMISSIONS TO PRISON

In the past four years, drug-possession admissions to prison—including new felon admissions for new crimes and parole violators returned with a new term—have been, on average, 32 percent lower than the year 2000, when Proposition 36 passed. This does not include parole violators returned to custody without a new term, who made up 77 percent of the felon parolees returned to custody in 2004.[15] Proposition 36 has likely helped reduce the number of parole violators returned to custody without a new term, which has dropped 20 percent since 2000.[16]

Proposition 36 only affects sentencing of people without a history of violence who are convicted for *drug possession*, not drug dealers or traffickers. Available sentencing data in California does not break down felony drug convictions into possession and dealing offenses, but FBI

15. *Rate of Felon Parolees Returned to California Prisons: Calendar Year 2004,* California Department of Corrections, May 2005, p. 1.

16. Ibid.

statistics indicate that nearly 80 percent of felony drug arrests in the West are for possession,[17] and felony drug convictions in California likely follow this pattern. While adult felony drug convictions have risen since the passage of Proposition 36, sentences to prison have decreased by over 20 percent, probation with jail sentences have decreased over 21 percent, and probation sentences have increased almost 370 percent.

Finding 2: California's prison population has grown at a much slower pace than was projected since 2000, and the state incarceration rate has fallen

"The key to reforming the system lies in reducing the numbers."— Corrections Independent Review Panel for Reforming California's Youth and Adult Correctional System, June 30, 2004.

"This measure would result in savings to the state prison system. This is because as many as 24,000 nonviolent drug possession offenders per year would be diverted to drug treatment in the community instead of being sent to state prison."—Legislative Analysts Office assessment of Proposition 36.

California's overall prison population growth did not achieve the levels predicted by the California Department of Corrections. Prior to Proposition 36's passage, the Department of Corrections projected[18] that the prison population would be more than 180,000 by June 2005.[19] The actual prison population on June 30, 2005[20] was just over 164,000 and reached 166,000 at year-end.

The overall prison population increased by 7,900 between December 2000 and December 2005. The *rate of incarceration* (per 100,000 resident adults, age 18 to 69) has *decreased* more than 5 percent.[21] Using the Bureau of Justice[22] statistics standard for comparing state incarceration rates (residents of all ages incarcerated, per 100,000 residents of all

---

17. *Crime in the United States 2004: Uniform Crime Reports*, Federal Bureau of Investigation, Table 4.1, p. 278. Calculation based on drug arrests in the West, where 74.6 percent of drug arrests are for non-marijuana possession offenses (likely felonies), 59.3 percent of all drug arrests are for possession of drugs other than marijuana, and 15.3 percent of all drug arrests are for sales and manufacturing.

18. Readers should note that the departments' method of estimating prison population growth has recently come under scrutiny by legislators who worry that the projections are not accurate enough to predict the need for new prisons. The authors also note that while system ended 2005 with 166,000 prisoners, and was at 168,000 prisoners at mid-March, we follow the methodology of using June as the benchmark to correspond to when Proposition 36 first had an impact.

19. *Spring 2001 Population Projections*, California Department of Corrections, Table A, p. 4.

20. *Prison Census Data as of June 30, 2005*, California Department of Corrections and Rehabilitation, September 2005, Table 1.

21. *Prison Census Data*, December 31, 2000 to December 31, 2005, California Department of Corrections. Population estimates of adults aged 18–69 from *Crime in California 2004*, California Criminal Justice Statistics Center, Table 58, p. 165. The 2005 population estimate is based on the population rate increase from 2003 to 2004 (2.6%).

22. Beck, Allen and Harrison, Paige. *Prisoners in 2004* [2000]. (2005). Washington, D.C.: Office of Justice Programs, Bureau of Justice Statistics.

ages), California's incarceration rate declined 4 percent, while the overall U.S. incarceration rate rose slightly.

California's prison population is composed of a higher percentage of people convicted of crimes against persons than in 2000. The percentage of the population that was convicted of property offenses has increased very slightly, as did percentage of "other crimes." At year-end 2005, 21 percent of the prison population was incarcerated for drug offenses—down from 27.6 percent in 2000.

Persons convicted of "crimes against persons" accounted for more than 68 percent of the increase in the prison population since 2000. Property offenders accounted for just over 17 percent of the increase. "Drug crimes" is the only offense category that has decreased in the prison population since 2000: The drug crime imprisonment rate fell 27 percent, and the number of people imprisoned for drug crimes fell 20 percent.

Finding 3: Since 2000, California has seen a larger decline in drug possession imprisonment than the other 10 largest prison systems in the United States

As shown above, California has reduced its drug possession population since Proposition 36 was passed by the voters. To put this decline in context, the researchers surveyed the states with the largest prison populations. Of the ten largest systems, six have data on the proportion of their prison population incarcerated for drug possession.[23]

23. Florida Department of Corrections, Agency Annual Reports, Table: "Primary Offenses", p. 25. Fiscal Years 1999/2000-2004/2005. Online at: http:// www.dc.state. fl.us/pub/annual/; Georgia Department of Corrections, Monthly Reports, Table: "Inmate Statistical Profile: Primary Offense, detailed Offense Code", p. 76–77, May 2000–December 2005 reports. Online at: www.dcor.state.ga.us/CORRINFO/Research Reports/MonthlyStatistics.html Illinois Dept. of Corrections, Statistical Presentations, Table 3: "Prison Population by Offense Type", p. 10 and Figure 3: "Drug Offenders in Prison Population", p. 7. Calendar Years 2001–2004. Online at: www. idoc.state.il.us/subsections/reports/default. shtml; Louisiana Department of Corrections, Corrections Services, Statistics— Briefing Book, Fact Sheet: "Demographic Profiles of the Adult Correctional Population (Including DOC Evacuees)" and Table: "Population Trends—Raw Data, 1989–2015", Online at: http://www.corrections. state.la.us/Statistics/BB.htm; Louisiana Department of Corrections, Corrections Services, Quarterly Statistical Performance Report: October 2003–March 2005, Table: "1st Quarter 2005 Current Population by Offense by Offender Class, Adult Incarcera-

tion Report", p. 157, Online at: http://www. corrections.state.la.us/Statistics/PDF_ QSPR/C.pdf; J. Austin, JFA Institute, correspondence, February 6, 2006. Report: "Louisiana Department of Public Safety and Corrections, Ten–Year Adult Secure Population Projection 2004–2015: Update." Michigan Department of Corrections, Statistical Reports, Table Ca: "Year End Prison Population (Institutions and Camps), Calendar Years 1989–2003", p. C–16, and Table C1b: "Total Prisoner Population by Minimum Term Distribution—Drug Offenses," Calendar Years 1999–2003. Online at: www.michigan.gov/corrections/0,1607,7– 119–1441—,00.html; P.H. Korotkin, New York State Department of Correctional Services, correspondence, January 31, 2006. Tables: "Drug Offenders under Custody by at Close of Year, Calendar Years 1970–2005" and "Drug Felons under Custody by Felony Class, Sales/Possession, Predicate Sentence Status: December 31, 2005." Bellas, Mike, Bureau of Research Studies, Ohio Department of Rehabilitation and Correction, correspondence, February 2, 2006. Table: "Offenders with a Drug Offense as the Most Serious Offense: By Type of Drug Offense and Total Offenders, 1998 & 2001, 2002, 2003, 2004, & 2005." Burk, Kathleen,

Between 2000 and 2005, California reduced its drug possession prison population by over 5,400 prisoners. For the six states that keep statistics on drug possession prisoners, New York had the second-highest drop in the number of drug-possession prisoners, reducing its population by 329. With a 27 percent decline in five years, California also had the largest percentage drop in drug prisoners incarcerated for possession; Michigan, which saw a decline of 127 drug-possession prisoners, had the second-highest percentage drop. When comparing the percentage of the prison populations that are made up of drug-possession offenders, California also experienced a larger decline than the other six reporting states: In 2000, drug-possession offenders made up over 12 percent of California's prison population; in 2005, it had dropped to 8.5 percent, a drop of 31 percent.

While California's drug possession prison population was much higher than states like New York, Ohio, and Georgia in 2000, it is now fairly close to those states when compared to their prison populations as a whole. As previously mentioned, 8.5 percent of California's prison population was serving time for drug possession in 2005; in New York the percentage was 8.7 percent, and Georgia's was 7 percent. Ohio's drug possession prison population used to be relatively smaller than California's, but now more than 9 percent of Ohio's prison population is serving time for drug possession.

Despite these reductions, California has a long way to go before reducing its drug-possession prison population to levels like those achieved in states like Michigan, Pennsylvania, and even Florida. In that southern state, 4.4 percent of the prison population was serving time for drug possession as of June 30, 2005. While recent data is not available from Michigan, as of 2003, only 1.9 percent of that state's prison population was serving a sentence for drug possession. In Pennsylvania, less than one-half of one percent of that state's prisoners was serving a sentence for drug possession in 2005.

Compared to the 10 largest state prison systems, which together account for 53 percent of the people incarcerated in state prisons, California experienced the biggest numerical *possession of the six* drop in drug prisoners. In contrast to 2000, today California's drug prisoner population is *largest state prison* more in line with other big states. *systems reporting.* It is of note that New York had the largest drop in drug prisoners on a percentage basis, with more than a 32 percent drop in drug prisoners since 2000. While it is beyond the scope of this analysis to note the cause of the New York decline, in 2000 New York's Unified Court System developed a proposal to divert 10,000 defendants from prison or jail into treatment at a savings of $500 million a year in incarceration and other taxpayer costs.[24]

Pennsylvania Department of Corrections, correspondence, February 7, 2006. Table: "Drug Offenses 2000–2005". Hall, Karen, Texas Department of Criminal Justice, cor-respondence, January 27, 2006. Table: "TDCJ & Drug Offenders 2000–2005."

24. Holman, Barry, Beatty, Philip and Schiraldi, Vincent. *Poor Prescription: The*

Finding 4: California's violent crime rate has declined since 2000, at a rate higher than the national average

"Proponents claim Proposition 36 deals only with nonviolent drug users. In reality, it will allow an estimated 37,000 felony drug abusers to remain on our streets every year—many of them addicted to drugs that often ignite violent criminal behavior."—ballot argument against Proposition 36.[25]

Proposition 36 specifically excluded persons with violent crime histories from being eligible for diversion into drug treatment for a drug offense, except in cases where the person had been out of prison for five or more years prior to committing the drug offense. While there were concerns that the initiative would lead to an increase in violent crime, since the initiative's passage, violent crime has declined. Between 2000 and 2004, the national average violent crime rate dropped 8.1 percent, while California's violent crime rate dropped 11.2 percent. During the same period, California also went from having the 10th-highest violent crime rate in 2000 to the 11th-highest in 2004.

Finding 5: Since 2000, California has experience a larger increase in drug treatment clients than the rest of the country

During a time in which the state was gripped by a budget shortfall that drove politicians to trim education and public service spending, California experienced an increase in drug treatment spending, an increase in drug treatment clients, and an increase in the number of drug treatment facilities in California.

According to the California Department of Alcohol and Drug Programs (ADP), the agency responsible for licensing treatment centers in California, the number of drug programs in the state has increased:[26]

- In 2000, there were 1,061 drug treatment programs, including 663 licensed residential facilities and 398 certified outpatient programs. Three years after Proposition 36 passed, there were 1,766 programs—842 licensed residential facilities and 924 certified outpatient programs.

- The number of treatment sites has increased by 705, or 66 percent. The number of licensed residential facilities increased by 179, or 27 percent.

- Since 2000, the number of certified outpatient programs increased by 526, or 132 percent.

- Since 2000, the residential treatment bed capacity of the state increased by 4,229 beds, or 27.6 percent increase.

Costs of Imprisoning Drug Offenders in the United States. (2000). Washington, D.C. The Justice Policy Institute.

25. Downloaded from the website of the California Secretary of State, March 25, 2006, http://vote2000.ss.ca.gov/VoterGuide/pdf/36.pdf.

26. *Substance Abuse and Crime Prevention Act: Fourth Annual Report to the Legislature*, Department of Alcohol and Drug Programs, August 2005, Powerpoint presentation, slide 11 (forthcoming).

Using a different methodology[27] to report standardized changes in national treatment capacity between states, data from the National Survey of Substance Abuse Treatment Services (N–SSATS) also shows a significant change in the number of California treatment facilities. According to the N–SSATS, the number of substance abuse treatment facilities in California went from 1,413 in the year 2000 to 1,779 facilities in 2004 (a 25.9 percent increase). If you exclude California from the national totals, during the same time period, the number of treatment facilities in the rest of the United States *declined*, going from 12,015 to 11,675, *a reduction of 2.8 percent.*[28]

According to the federal survey, the number of substance abuse treatment clients in California increased from 104,657 in the year 2000 to 140,401 in 2004, a 34.1 percent increase. During the same period, the number of treatment clients in the rest of the United States went from 896,239 to 931,850, an increase of only 4 percent. California has contributed over half of the increase in the number of people accessing substance abuse treatment in the U.S. since 2000.

As mentioned, during a time in which the state was trimming funding to higher education, schools, and other public services, drug treatment spending in California experienced a significant increase. Comparing drug treatment expenditures in fiscal year 2004–5 to fiscal year 1999–2000, state substance abuse treatment funding has more than doubled. Under the cost-sharing Medical program, where federal dollars match state dollars spent on *California has* health care, $16 million more in federal dollars were spent since 1999–2000.

Finding 6: The available literature on drug courts and completion rates of Proposition 36 suggest their completion rates are comparable.

> *"There are other programs, including California's drug courts, which offer a far better chance of success."*—Bonnie Dumanis, San Diego District Attorney, in a press release issued by Senator Denise Moreno Ducheny, February 22, 2005.

One of the most controversial parts of the Proposition 36 debate has centered on the differences between the operational procedures of the initiative compared with drug courts. The primary difference between drug courts and Proposition 36 is that drug courts utilize jail time as punishment for treatment relapses ("jail sanctions"), require more court appearances by participants, and require more judicial training and involvement in the treatment process. Drug courts also have varying eligibility requirements, whereas Proposition 36 made eligibility for

---

27. The difference in the methodology between both systems is due to the different way different states count drug treatment facilities. The difference between the two methodologies for California are small.

28. *National Survey of Substance Abuse Treatment Services 2004*, Substance Abuse and Mental Health Services Administration, Table 6.2a. Online at: http://wwwdasis.samhsa.gov/04nssats/nssats04_tbl6.2a.htm.

treatment universal for all people convicted of drug offenses who did not have violent criminal convictions on their record.

In 2005, legislation (SB 803) was introduced that would make the initiative more like drug courts by allowing judges to jail defendants up to 21 days for relapsing, among other changes.[29] The bill's "purposes" language says these changes are needed because "[d]rug dependent criminal offenders who receive drug treatment are far more likely to complete the drug treatment program if they are monitored and supervised by courts that use the drug court model...."[30]

Completion Rates of Drug Courts, SACPA Participants, and Other Drug Treatment Populations

The research on drug court treatment completion rates was reviewed to determine if clients are "far more likely" to complete drug treatment under drug courts, compared with Proposition 36.

Completion rates for drug court participants are as varied as the evaluation studies performed on the programs. When comparing the various models of providing drug treatment through the criminal justice system, it appears that outcomes are similar. In 2005, the federal Government Accountability Office reviewed 16 program evaluations and found completion rates ranging from 27 percent to 66 percent.[31] A 2001 study of 10 California drug court evaluations found treatment completion rates ranging from 11 to 61 percent, with most at or below 38 percent.[32]

The latest evaluation shows Proposition 36 completion rates were 34.4 percent in year one, and 34.3 percent in year two. Overall, 41.6 percent of Proposition 36 clients completed treatment or made satisfactory progress.[33] On a county-by-county basis, completion rates have ranged from a low of 13 percent in Monterey County in 2001/2002, to 100 percent in Alpine county in both years that data is available. Twenty-seven counties had completion rates of 40 percent or higher (see graph, Proposition 36 completion rates by county).

All non-SACPA persons entering treatment through the criminal justice system in California had drug treatment completion rates of 36 percent in 2001/2002, and 37.5 percent in 2002/2003. Non-criminal justice clients completed treatment at rates of 29.8 percent and 30 percent.[34]

29. S.B. 803, Section 6, amending Section 1210.1(e)(3)(A) and (B)

30. S.B. 803, Section 1(c)(2)

31. *Adult Drug Courts: Evidence Indicates Recidivism Reductions and Mixed Results for Other Outcomes* , Government Accountability Office, February 2005, p. 62.

32. Joseph Guydish, et al, "Drug Court Effectiveness: A Review of California Evaluation Reports, 1995–1999," *Journal of Psychoactive Drugs*, vol. 33(4), Oct.–Dec. 2001, p. 374.

33. *Evaluation of the Substance Abuse and Crime Prevention Act: 2004 Report*, UCLA Integrated Substance Abuse Programs, July 22, 2005, p. 32.

34. Ibid, p. 33.

Finding 7: While the effectiveness of using incarceration to prevent drug use and treatment relapse is not clear, there is an impact of the increased use of incarceration through jail on individuals and communities.

"There is no evidence for the efficacy of jail sanctions. Although there is research evidence supportive of drug courts in general, the use of jail time as a 'sanction' to enforce treatment compliance is not supported."—The California Society of Addiction Medicine

"Unquestionably, policies leading to mass incarceration created a dangerous crisis in state prisons and county jails."—Barry Krisberg, president of the National Council on Crime and Delinquency, writing in the San Francisco Chronicle, February 28, 2006

One of the key policy issues surrounding the differences between Proposition 36 and drug courts concerns whether or not incarceration effectively reduces drug use or prevents relapse.

According to the California Society of Addiction Medicine, "There is no evidence for the efficacy of jail sanctions. Although there is research evidence supportive of drug courts in general, the use of jail time as a 'sanction' to enforce treatment compliance is not supported. *Drug courts around the nation have been using this tool for over 15 years, yet not a single study isolates the impact of jail sanctions in generating improved treatment outcomes.*"[35]

While the recent UCLA cost analysis of Proposition 36 suggests that jail sanctions (or residential drug treatment) may be appropriate for the 1.6 percent of the population they studied who are "high cost" offenders—people with five or more prior convictions—they are equivocal on the benefits of the approach: "The benefits of flash incarceration are not yet consistently confirmed in the research literature.... Importantly, the offender's perception of fair and impartial use of this sanction weighs heavily in determining the success attributable to this method."[36]

THE IMPACT OF JAIL INCARCERATION ON INDIVIDUALS AND COMMUNITIES

If jail sanctions were an effective way of ensuring that people would complete treatment, the policy would still need to be weighed against the costs of what is known to be the impact of incarceration on the individual and his or her community. As the state and country grapples with the impact of the overuse of incarceration, a growing body of research shows that imprisoning or jailing people carries with it negative consequence for the people incarcerated, their families, and communities. Expanding the use of jail sanctions for people in treatment could contribute to the growing costs of jails in county corrections budgets, worsen the mental health issues some recovering drug users carry,

35. "Proposition 36 Revisited," California Society of Addiction Medicine. Online at: http://www.csam-asam.org/prop36article.vp.html.

36. *SACPA Cost Analysis Report (First and Second Years).* (2006), p. 36.

contribute to unemployment, and expose people to a higher risk of suicide.

JAIL SANCTIONS COULD COST COUNTIES AND COMMUNITIES MILLIONS MORE
IN JAILS SPENDING—DRAINING FUNDS FROM OTHER LOCAL SERVICES

In 2003, 30 percent of California counties spent more than they took in from various sources of revenue. The growing price tag of jails strains county budgets, which are already struggling to fund everything from public hospitals to roads and local transportation infrastructure. Eighty percent of county spending in California is comprised of public protection spending (including policing, jails, juvenile detention, and court costs), public assistance spending (welfare, social services, and general relief), and health and sanitation expenditures.[37]

It is hard to know how many days Proposition 36 participants would spend in jail if the option was more readily available to judges. While judges would not have to use the maximum jail time that SB 803 allows—21 days—an analysis of a Santa Clara drug court suggests they might use the full term available under the law. A 1998 study of the Santa Clara drug court found that the average number of jail days served by persons completing the program was 51 days per person. The cost of incarceration was $3,417 above all other treatment, probation, and court supervision costs.[38] If the annual 36,000 people currently enrolled in Proposition 36 were to serve five days in jail at an average daily cost of $62.60, it could cost counties an additional $11.2 million per year. For ten days, the cost to California counties would be $22.5 million.

County spending on jails and corrections reached $3.3 billion of the $44 billion spent by counties in 2003—accounting for a third of the increase in county spending on public protection. While total county per capita spending increased by 27 percent, spending on public protection (a third of which is jail spending) rose by 45 percent.

Looking at a different period, between 1998 and 2003, spending on jails and corrections rose by about billion dollars ($2.3 to $3.2 billion). During that five-year period, spending on jails increased at three times the level of spending on roads and local transportation infrastructure ($420 million).

According to the latest available *Jail Profile Survey*, "on days when the statewide jail population is about average, it exceeds the number of beds by over 3,400 inmates." With California's jail populations is on the rise, it is worth noting the local jail population dilemma: for every drug-involved person put in a jail bed, either the county will have to come up the funds to pay for a larger jail, or someone must be released—decisions that impact public safety and local resources for other services.[39]

37. Counties Annual Report, Fiscal Year 2002–03 [1998–1999]. Sacramento, CA: California State Controllers.

38. *Santa Clara County Drug Treatment Court: Two Year Progress Report and Out-* *come Comparisons (March 1, 1996–March 31, 1998).*

39. *Jail Profile Survey: Annual Report 2004*, California Board of Corrections, p. 1.

JAIL INCARCERATION "TRAUMATIZES PERSONS WITH MENTAL ILLNESSES AND MAKES THEM WORSE"

On any given day, one-sixth of the detained jail population suffers from mental illness.[40] People who have co-occurring disorders in the domains of drug addiction and mental health can experience a psychological deterioration once jailed due to the interruption in treatment and medication, and environmental stressors. According to the National Association of Counties, jail *"traumatizes persons with mental illness and makes them worse."*[41] People with drug and mental health issues are in need of extra care from health department psychiatrists, who, according to NACO, have to work "twice as hard to get them back to where they were before they entered the jail."[42]

JAIL POPULATIONS EXPERIENCE HIGHER RATES OF SUICIDE DEATHS THAN THE GENERAL POPULATION

Researchers have found that the reaction of detained populations to conditions of jails can exacerbate mental health or conditions that increase the individual's propensity towards suicidal behavior. Researchers have found that newly jailed people experience fear of the unknown, distrust of the environment, isolation from family and significant others, shame and stigma of incarceration, a loss of stabilizing resources, and severe guilt or shame over the alleged offense. Current mental illness and prior history of suicidal behavior also intensify in the jail environment.[43] These conditions and stressors conspire to increase the suicide rate in jails, as compared to the general population. According to the correctional research arm of the U.S. Justice Department, suicide is the leading cause of death in jail. Compared with a U.S. suicide rate of 17 per 100,000 people, the Bureau of Justice Statistics researchers founds that the suicide rate in local jails is 47 per 100,000 people.[44]

JAIL MAY EXPOSE PEOPLE TO VARIOUS DISEASES

According to the National Commission on Correctional Health Care, jails are recognized as settings where society's infectious diseases are highly concentrated. "In particular, sexually transmitted diseases (STDs) may be more common in jail settings than in prisons, as ... rapid turnover and frequent movement of inmates makes jails difficult settings in which to quantify the prevalence of various diseases."[45] In 1996, 12–15 percent of all individuals diagnosed with Hepatitis B and approximately

40. Ditton, Paula M. "Mental Health and Treatment of Inmates and Probationers." US Department of Justice: Bureau of Justice Statistics. 1999.

41. Edwin S. Rosado, "Diverting the Mentally Ill from Jail." National Association of Counties Legislative Department. March 6, 2002.

42. Ibid.

43. Hayes, Lindsay. M, Blaauw, Eric. "Prison suicide: a special issue." (2002) *Cri-*

sis: The Journal of Crisis and Suicide Prevention, Volume 18, Number 4.

44. Mumola, Christopher J. *Suicide and Homicide in State and Local Jails.* (2005) Washington, DC: Office of Justice Programs, Bureau of Justice Statistics.

45. *The Health Status of Soon-to-Be-Released Inmate: A Report to Congress.* National Commission on Correctional Health Care. (2002). Chicago, Illinois: National Commission on Correctional Health Care.

30 percent of the 4.5 million individuals diagnosed with Hepatitis C, spent time in a correctional facility.[46] The HIV/AIDS prevalence in jails is four to six times higher than the national population.[47] In 1997, the infection rate for tuberculosis in jails was 17 times higher than the rate for the general population: That year, thirty-five percent of the people nationwide with tuberculosis were in prison or jail, and 566,000 people released from prison or jail (the majority from jail) tested positive for latent tuberculosis.[48]

Jail May Impact Future Employment

A small but growing number of studies show that jail has significant immediate and long-term negative employment and economic outcomes. Richard Freeman of the London School of Economics and Harvard University has found that jail reduces work time of young people over the next decade by 25–30 percent when compared with arrested youths who were not incarcerated. According to Freeman, *"Having been in jail is the recognized as settings single most important deterrent to employment"* with *"the effect of incarceration on employment years later ... substantial and significant."*[49] Using the National Longitudinal Survey of Youth, Bruce Western and Katherine Beckett found that, on average, youth who spent some time incarcerated in a jail experienced three weeks less work a year compared to youth who had no history of incarceration. The effect was larger for African–American youth, who experienced five weeks less work a year than those African-American youth who experienced no jail time. Further, the impact of incarceration on reduced annual employment did not significantly decay over time: fifteen years later, formerly incarcerated youth worked between three and five weeks less a year than youth who had never been incarcerated.[50]

Jail May Increase the Likelihood of Recidivism

The proliferation of alternatives to jail incarceration reinforces the fact that even short-term incarceration may aggravate recidivism. According to a 2003 review conducted by the Office of Legislative Analyst for the San Francisco Board of Supervisors, the city's alternative to jail had lower recidivism rates than people who were simply jailed. People released to home detention, work release programs, and residential program all faired better than the control group in jail: nearly two-thirds of all inmates who were released without an alternative to incarceration committed a repeat offense compared to the 33 percent recidivism rate of

46. Ibid.

47. "United States Marshals Service's Prisoner Medical Care." (2004). Office of the Inspector General. Report No. 04–14. February 2004.

48. Ibid.

49. Freeman, R.B. and Rodgers, W.M. *Area Economic Conditions and the Labor Market Outcomes of Young Men in the 1990s Expansion.* (1999) National Bureau of Economic Research.

50. Western, Bruce and Beckett, Katherine. "How Unregulated Is the U.S. Labor Market?: The Penal System as a Labor Market Institution." The American Journal of Sociology, 1999.

inmates who completed diversion programs such as home monitoring with ankle bracelets, residential drug treatment, and/or work-release.[51]

Jail May Impact the Families and Children of People Jailed

Increasing the use of jail through jail sanctions not only affects people sent to jail, but it affects their families and children as well and compounds the costs to communities. The California Research Bureau has reported that 97,000 children have parents who are detained in jail.[52] According to a Bureau of Justice Statistics report, 25 percent of children remain in their father's custody after their mother has been incarcerated, yet almost 90 percent of children remain in their mother's care upon the incarceration of their father.[53] When a woman is imprisoned, her child is displaced: ten percent of children with mothers incarcerated in state prison are in foster homes or agencies. *When the related expenses of placing children of women who are incarcerated in foster care is considered, the cost of imprisonment more than doubles.*[54] These collateral consequences to jail have a disproportionate impact on the African–American community, whose children are almost 9 times more likely than white children to have a parent incarcerated.[55]

The Increased Use of Jail Contributes to the Impact of "Mass Incarceration"

Relying on jail sanctions adds to all the impacts associated with having the highest incarceration rate in the world, and what a growing body of researchers contend are the "unintended consequences" of mass incarceration. At mid-year 2004, the nation's prisons and jails incarcerated more than 2.1 million persons, driving up the U.S. incarceration rate to more than 726 people per 100,000 residents.[56] California contributes its fair share to the nation's growing use of imprisonment: the state prisons and jails hold about a quarter of a million people, or 12 percent of the incarcerated population of the entire country.[57]

Researchers have begun documenting the impact of America's experiment with "mass incarceration." Groundbreaking research by Todd Clear of the John Jay College of Criminal Justice in New York City has shown that, rather than keeping communities safe, mass incarceration

51. Van de Water, Adam. "Legislative Analyst Report: Criminal Justice Offender Profile." City and County of San Francisco Board of Supervisors, 2003.

52. Simons, Charlene Wear, PhD. "Children of Incarcerated Parents." California Research Bureau, 2000.

53. "Women in Prisons," Bureau of Justice Statistics Special Report, 1990.

54. Lapidus, Lenora et. al. Caught in the Net: The Impact of Drug Policies on Women and Families. (2005). New York, New York: The Brennan Center for Justice at the New York University Law School.

55. "Incarcerated Parents and Their Children." Bureau of Justice Statistics Special Report, 2000.

56. Beck, Allen and Harrison, Jane. Prison and Jail Inmates at Midyear 2004. (2005). Office of Justice Programs, Bureau of Justice Statistics.

57. *Probation and Parole in the United States, 2003* (2004). Washington, D.C.: Office of Justice Programs, Bureau of Justice Statistics.

may undermine public safety.[58] Clear found that neighborhoods with the highest levels of incarceration in one year had higher-than-expected crime rates the following year (compared to other neighborhoods, and controlling for factors such as poverty, racial composition, and voluntary mobility). In other words, high levels of incarceration were associated with reduced safety in communities.

Clear also contends that mass incarceration may "backfire," both in terms of crime control and the local economy: "As an economic being, the person would spend money at or near his or her area of residence— typically an inner city. Incarceration displaces that economic activity."

The impact of mass incarceration in California and elsewhere, is concentrated in the African–American community. An analysis of the U.S. Census found that one out of 33 California African Americans was in jail or prison on April 1, 2000, compared with about one in every 122 Hispanics and one in every 205 whites.[59] One out of 17 African-American men in California was incarcerated on April 1, 2000, compared with one out of 114 white men being behind bars.

Since increased of use of jail could worsen the problem of mass incarceration, that policy needs to be weighed against the costs. Ernest M. Drucker, professor of epidemiology and social medicine and professor of psychiatry at Montefiore Medical Center and the Albert Einstein College of Medicine in New York says that "when this phenomenon [mass incarceration] occurs on a large scale and for an extended period of time, it may significantly damage the mental and physical health of individuals, families, and entire communities—and create or intensify the very social conditions that enable crime to flourish."[60]

Finding 8: Proposition 36 is saving the state
hundreds of millions of dollars.

"The People of the State of California hereby declare their purpose and intent in enacting this Act to be as follows: To halt the wasteful expenditure of hundreds of millions of dollars each year on the incarceration—and re-incarceration—of nonviolent drug users who would be better served by community-based treatment."—Proposition 36

To determine the fiscal impact of Proposition 36, a methodology would need to be designed to estimate what would have happened to prison and jail populations absent the initiative. Key questions that would need to be answered include:

58. Clear, Todd R, The Problem with "Addition by Subtraction": The Prison–Crime Relationship in Low-income Communities. As found in *Invisible Punishment The Collateral Consequences of Mass Imprisonment*. Mauer, Marc and Chesney-Lind, Meda, ed. 2002. The New Press, New York, NY.

59. McCormick, Erin. "One in 33 blacks was behind bars in April last year," *The San Francisco Chronicle*, August 9, 2001.

60. State of Black America: 2003. (2003). Washington, D.C.: The National Urban League.

- What ultimately happens to probationers and parolees after they enter the program?

- How many of the participants would have gone to prison, and how many people to jail, if Proposition 36 had not been in place? How long would people have served in prison or jail?

- How many participants would have received probation with or without Proposition 36?

- How many Proposition 36 participants had their probation revoked? Of those who were revoked, were they sentenced to jail or prison, and for how long?

These and many other variables must be considered when trying to determine the ballot initiative's costs or savings.

ESTIMATED SAVINGS DUE TO REDUCED ADMISSIONS TO CALIFORNIA'S PRISONS

The researchers felt the most accurate way to approximate the prison-related fiscal impact of Proposition 36 was to examine prison admissions for drug possession prior to the passage of the initiative and compare that to drug possession admissions after its passage. Assuming that no other major policy changes occurred in the criminal justice system that would have reduced or increased drug-possession prison admissions, this method should yield a reasonable estimate of how many fewer persons went to prison as a result of the initiative and the savings that accrued.

As the table below shows, 14,616 fewer people were admitted to California's prisons for drug-possession convictions between the years 2001 and 2004, as compared with the year 2000. As discussed in the methodology section, prison admissions for drug possession convictions for the year 2000 were likely lower because of sentencing postponements until the measure came into effect—something that would underestimate the impact of the initiative. Nevertheless, for the purposes of this analysis, prison admissions for the year 2000 were used as a baseline. The researchers assume that drug-possession prison admissions would have stayed flat at the 2000 level for the years 2001 to 2006, and would not have risen with increases in the general population.

Based on these figures, the reduction in prison admissions for drug possession for the year 2005 and half of 2006 (the end of the initiatives' funding, according to the ballot initiative language) was estimated using the average reduction in prison admissions for drug possession between 2001 and 2004. These estimated cost savings were entirely due to reduced prison admissions, and do not include any savings resulting from prison closures or avoidance of capital outlays for prison construction.

Given this model, JPI estimates that Proposition 36 saved the state more than $350 million from reduced prison admissions since its enactment. This estimate is based on a presumption that persons diverted from prison would have served the average prison sentence for drug possession, which was 1.48 years in 2004, and that the cost of incarceration is $34,150 per year, the average per inmate in 2005. It also takes into account the cost of treatment and probation under Proposition 36—$660 million over five years.

These estimates do not include any savings due to any reductions in parolees returned to prison without a new term (i.e. returned for a parole violation that isn't a new conviction). Returns to prison for these parolees has dropped 20 percent since 2000.

Savings Due to Reduced Jail Admissions

Unlike admissions to prison, admissions to jail are not categorized by offense category. To estimate jail savings, the researchers examined the court dispositions of adult felony drug convictions to see how Proposition 36 might have impacted the number of people convicted of drug possession who would have been sentenced to serve time in jail. All felony drug conviction dispositions were displayed in chart on the preceding page. The chart below calculates the total number of fewer "probation with jail" sentences that were handed out since 2000, when Proposition 36 passed. We assumed that all reductions in this sentencing category were due to the diversions to straight probation and treatment, as required by the initiative.

Below is the estimated cost-savings due to the reduced number of persons serving jail time pursuant to Proposition 36. From mid–2001 to mid–2006, it is estimated that the initiative wil have saved more than $62 million in jail costs, or about $12.5 million per year.

Savings Accrued by Avoiding Prison Construction Costs

"We estimate that the state will run out of bed space by as soon as 2001 and would need additional space for as many as 27,000 inmates by June 30, 2004. That is the equivalent of fi ve to six state-operated prisons carrying a one-time construction cost of $1.6 billion and annual ongoing operational costs of more than $500 million."—California Legislative Analyst's Office, February 16, 1999

Around the time Proposition 36 was placed on the ballot, there were discussions of building anywhere from two to six new prisons in California.[61] In its analysis of the impact of Proposition 36, the state Legislative Analyst predicted that the state would be able to "delay the construction of additional prison space" if Proposition 36 passed, saving the state between $475 and $575 million.[62] After the initiative passed, the Kern Valley State Prison, also known as Delano II, was built, though that prison had been approved for construction in 1999,[63] prior to Proposition

61. California Legislative Analyst's Office, "Analysis of the 1999–00 Budget Bill, Judiciary and Criminal Justice Chapter," February 16, 1999, p. D–68, Online at: http://www.lao.ca.gov/analysis_1999/crim_ justice/crim_just_anl99.pdf.

62. Legislative analyst's review of the Substance Abuse and Crime Prevention Act

of 2000, File No. SA 1999 RF 0040, Amendment No. 2–NS, December 6, 1999, p. 5.

63. "Critics say new state prison defi es logic," San Francisco Chronicle, January 5, 2004.

36's passage. Since only one prison has been built, it appears that the Legislative Analyst's prediction that California would be able to avoid or delay building a prison has come to fruition.

PRISON SAVINGS FROM CLOSING THE NORTHERN CALIFORNIA WOMEN'S FACILITY

In February 2003, the Northern California Women's Facility closed. When there were discussions about the prison's closure, a spokesperson from the California Department of Corrections said, "There are a lot of reasons the [prison] population is down ... but we think the biggest factor with the women's numbers is Proposition 36."[64] The Department of Corrections and then-Gov. Gray Davis' office estimated that the savings would amount to approximately $1 million for fiscal year 2002–3, and $10.2 million in future years.[65] By the end of fiscal year 2005–6, that will amount to $31.6 million.

ADDITIONAL SAVINGS

The cost savings that come from the expanded availability of treatment instead of incarceration are beyond the scope of this paper to quantify. These estimates do not include any savings due to reductions in parolees returned to prison without a new term (i.e. parolees returned for a parole violation that is not a new conviction). Returns to prison for these parolees has dropped by over 14,000, or 20 percent since 2000, but it was not possible to determine how many of these parolees were not returned because of the initiative.

Other outcomes have been reported from Proposition 36 participants that could reduce recidivism, increase tax revenues, and reduce government expenditures. These outcomes include:

- An estimated 60,000 people will have successfully completed drug treatment under SACPA by mid–2006.[66] It is not likely that these people would have had access to the drug treatment services made available by the initiative's annual $120 million appropriation.

- Employment increased 83 percent for Proposition 36 clients who completed treatment, and the average number of days worked more than doubled.[67]

64. "Changing Population Behind Bars: Major Drop in Women in State Prisons," San Francisco Chronicle, April 21, 2002.

65. "Women's prison in Stockton on chopping block," The [Stockton] Record, January 11, 2003; "Northern California Women's Prison Shut Down in Economy Move," News10 website, February 26, 2003, online at: http://www.news10.net/storyfull. asp?id=3738.

66. Calculation based on 34.4 percent of 30,469 first-year clients completing treatment (10,481), 34.3 percent of 35,947 second-year clients completing treatment (12,-330), 34 percent of 37,103 third-year clients completing treatment (12,615), and 34 per-

cent of 36,000 treatment clients in years four (12,240) and five (12,240). Source: *Evaluation of the Substance Abuse and Crime Prevention Act: 2002 Report*, UCLA Integrated Substance Abuse Programs, July 7, 2003, p. 5; *Evaluation of the Substance Abuse and Crime Prevention Act: 2003 Report*, UCLA Integrated Substance Abuse Programs, September 23, 2004, p. 9; Evaluation of the Substance Abuse and Crime Prevention Act: 2004 Report, UCLA Integrated Substance Abuse Programs, July 22, 2005, p. 32.

67. *Evaluation of the Substance Abuse and Crime Prevention Act: 2004 Report*,

• Drug use by Proposition 36 completers dropped by 71 percent and by 60 percent by persons who entered but did not complete treatment.[68]

CONCLUSION

"There are clear, evidenced-based pathways that could lead us out of the hole we have dug. But we need to stop digging. California may yet find its way to a rational correctional policy, but it will take public courage and truthfulness about what is not working."—Barry Krisberg, president of the National Council on Crime and Delinquency, writing about California correctional policy in the San Francisco Chronicle, February 28, 2006

In a state which continues to fail to live up to the public will to find better ways of increasing public safety rather than investing in prison expansion, Proposition 36, enacted by the voters of California, stands out against the discouraging failure to enact other corrections reforms. This analysis shows that since Proposition 36 passed, the state has reduced the number and rate of people incarcerated for drug crimes. Since 2000, there has been an increase in treatment funding, treatment capacity, and treatment clients. Fears that people diverted to drug treatment would engage in violent crime have not been witnessed in the violent crime rate. While the true extent of cost savings cannot be fully known, prisons that were expected to be built did not break ground, and a reasonable method for calculating the savings from reduced prisons and jail admissions for drug possession suggest the state saved hundreds of millions of dollars. A recent cost analysis on Proposition 36 by UCLA's Integrated Substance Abuse Programs found that the state saved at least $2.50 for every dollar spent on the program each year, $4 for every person who successfully completed treatment, and represented a net savings to government of $173.3 million in the first year of the program. The initiatives treatment outcomes compare favorably to other substance abuse treatment programs, both voluntary and those associated with the criminal justice system, but do not carry the impacts that jail sanctions and increased use of imprisonment have on individuals and communities.

Despite these findings, there are some indications that the criminal justice system is "backsliding" and sending increasingly higher numbers of drug possession offenders to prison. For the first time since the initiative was enacted, the drug possession prison population increased during one six-month period. From June 30 to December 31, 2005, the drug possession prison population increased by about 900 prisoners, from 13,457 to 14,325.[69] Drug possession admissions to prison are also on the rise: From their all-time low in 2002 of 6,456, prison admissions for

UCLA Integrated Substance Abuse Programs, July 22, 2005, p. 66–67.

68. Ibid, p. 66.

69. *Prison Census Data as of June 30, 2005*, California Department of Corrections and Rehabilitation, September 2005, Table 2; *Prison Census Data as of December 31, 2005*, California Department of Corrections and Rehabilitation, February 2006, Table 2.

drug possession proceeded to creep up in 2003, and hit 9,141 admissions in 2004.[70] Sentences to prison are also driving the *reforms*. drug-possession prison population higher: Adult felony drug sentences to prison hit a low of 10,416 in 2003 and went up to 11,606 in 2004.[71] While these admissions and sentences are lower than when the initiative was enacted, the trend right now is that drug possession admissions are on the rise.

Why are drug possession prison sentences, admissions, and the prison population rising? Part of the reason may be increased law enforcement efforts: from the year 2000 to 2004, felony drug arrests increased over 18 percent from 121, 909 to 144,437.[72] Another reason may be that drug offenders are being sent to prison for violating their terms of probation and parole under Proposition 36: over 23 percent of SACPA probationers had their probation revoked in the third year; 56 percent of SACPA parolees had their parole revoked in the 12–month period after referral to SACPA.[73]

How can the state of California build on the successes that Proposition 36 has achieved thus far?

One improvement would be to make Proposition 36 treatment more accessible to the target group of drug-involved individuals in the criminal justice system. According to the latest available data, about 66 percent of SACPA-eligible offenders did not participate in the program in its first year.[74] One reason may be that many of these people may be charged with low-level marijuana possession offenses who do not want or need to participate in the rigors of the initiative's treatment and probation. Or they may be other types of possession offenders who prefer lower-intensity drug diversion or jail time to the time commitment that Proposition 36 requires.

One way to continue to build on the trends shown here might include expanding treatment availability to drug-involved property offenders. Right now only people convicted of drug possession and drug involved nonviolent parolees are eligible. By expanding substance abuse treatment opportunities to people convicted of property offenses who are drug-involved, California could reap additional reductions in the prison population while reducing recidivism. While violent crime rates went down in California from 2000 to 2004, property crime rates rose slightly.[75] One way to get at the challenge of reducing property crime rates

70. *Characteristics of Felon New Admissions and Parole Violators Returned with a New Term*, calendar years 2002 to 2004, California Department of Corrections and Rehabilitation, Data Analysis Unit.

71. *Crime in California, 2004*, California Department of Justice, Criminal Justice Statistics Center, Table 41, p. 149.

72. *Crime in California, 2004*, California Department of Justice, Criminal Justice Statistics Center, Table 22, p. 121.

73. *Evaluation of the Substance Abuse and Crime Prevention Act: 2004 Report*, UCLA Integrated Substance Abuse Programs, July 22, 2005, p. v.

74. Ibid, p. 59.

75. Between 2000 and 2004, California's property crime rate rose 9.65 percent.

would be to make eligible those people for whom addiction is a core issue relating to their criminality.

Other suggested improvements by such organizations as the California Society of Addiction Medicine include:[76]

- Increase funding for drug treatment. According to county drug treatment administrators, $184 million per year is needed, and, adjusting for inflation, $140 million is needed to keep the level of funding equal to 2001.

- Improve matching treatment needs with services delivered.

- Improve coordination between the courts, assessment, probation, and treatment. Expand the use of methadone and buprenorphine for opiate-addicted patients.

- Require counties to focus more resources on substance abuse treatment instead of the criminal justice system.

Notes and Questions

1. Why did Proposition 36 buck the trend toward punishment in democratic tests of criminal justice policy? One reason why Proposition 36 was appealing was that it provided an alternative theory of crime prevention: drug treatment programs attempt to prevent drug crime by permanently removing drug dependency, by contrast with imprisonment, which prevents drug use only during the period of confinement. So drug treatment presents a counter-narrative to the story of incapacitation. A second reason why treatment is appealing is the limited potential of secure confinement to cure drug use. Imprisonment is designed to protect the drug user from himself, rather than to protect members of the community against offenders (unless there is also a pattern of crime with victims). So the criteria of Proposition 36 fit closely to the circumstances where the apparent value of incapacitation is lowest. In this sense, the "victimless nature" of the drug possession offense was part of the success of the Proposition 36 campaign.

2. What operational criteria should be used to judge the impact of Proposition 36 in California? One important question is the degree to which the new rules diverted offenders from prison to treatment programs. Counting the felons who enter the treatment track is not a measure of Proposition 36's impact, because many of those felons might have avoided prison without Proposition 36. The test is the drop (if any) in prison commitments of Proposition 36 eligible offenders. How good is the evidence as to whether Proposition 36 reduced drug imprisonment? How good is the evidence on the extent to which Proposition 36 kept drug offenders out of prison? Is the volume of diverted offenders as large as supporters anticipated? How might it be increased?

3. A second question is whether the community treatment track is more or less successful than prison in reducing the future drug involvement

76. "Proposition 36 Refunding (SB 803); CSAM Position: Oppose unless amended," California Society of Addiction Medicine. Online at: http://www. csam-asam.org/pdf/misc/Prop36_Summary.pdf.

of drug offenders. Should community treatment be regarded as a success if it reduces the cost of treatment while the rate of drug recidivism remains the same, or should treatment only be regarded as a success if it is more effective than imprisonment at reducing drug use?

4. Why don't efforts like Proposition 36 have as much impact in reducing drug imprisonment as the war on drugs had in increasing drug prisoners?

F.   WHAT HAPPENS NEXT?

What can be said of the future of drug control policy in the United States and the rest of the developed world? In the United States, we may consider two distinct issues about the future of policy: the direction of change, and the magnitude of change. Various trends suggest that there will be some moderation in the criminal law of drug control. The current level of drug imprisonment in the United States is at an all-time high, compared with other eras in the U.S. or with other nations. Some moderation can be expected in the proximate future, but how much? This is an issue of great importance to the future of imprisonment in the United States.

One of us has recently argued:

"The Downside Potential for Imprisonment"

The imprisonment trend shows unmistakable signs that the era of unmitigated growth in prison population is at or near an end. The growth rate in prison populations in the first years of the 21st century is smaller in percentage terms, which happens automatically when the base rate increases greatly. Moreover, the numbers of additional prisoners at the national level are more modest, and a number of states exhibit downward variations in recent years. The decades of consecutive growth in the imprisonment rate have already ended, and very soon, the 30–year string of uninterrupted growth in the number of prisoners will also end. But what will happen after this era of expansion?

The two most plausible alternatives are: (1) relative stability at a new high plateau of incarceration rates with prison numbers not growing much, where the rates of imprisonment established in the late 1990s are maintained, or (2) higher volatility with relatively wide swings in the rate of imprisonment and a larger downside potential. The key question is one of commonsense physics: do the large upward shifts signal any two-way volatility for the future? Do huge increases carry the potential for huge decreases?

My suspicion is that the politics of criminal justice is the determining feature of downward variability in current rates of imprisonment, and that there is little in the current political climate that suggests a large imminent downward potential for the prison population.

The most expansive period of recent prison growth was the six years after 1993 when the U.S. prison population grew by 139 per 100,000 during a period when the crime rate was falling. If it is true that "what goes up must come down'', then a corresponding decline of imprison-ment of 139 per 100,000 should be achievable in stable crime environ-ments. In reality, no nation ever has reduced a prison population by that much during a period of political stability. Even so, the upward variation was unprecedented. Why can't volatility work both ways?

The answer is the new politics of criminal justice. The political environment in which the United States expanded its prison system by more prisoners than the whole system had contained prior to 1981 will determine the political system in which future punishment policy will form. Crime and the fear of crime have both declined, but basic attitudes have not shifted, nor has there been any second-guessing about the current distribution of power in criminal justice. None of the legislative products of the most recent political era have been repealed.

The most likely result will be a relatively high plateau of rates of imprisonment, quite close to 1.6 million prisoner totals of 2005, with a slight decline in the rate of imprisonment due to the general population expanding while the prison and jail population remains relatively stable.

"If any large dents do come in prison populations, drug offenders are the most likely source of sharp policy shifts. But as long as the arguments for moderating punishment policy are focused on prison costs rather than crime policy, the most likely policies to push down rates of incarceration will involve a little less of everything rather that discrete cutbacks in specific categories. In a stable political environment, it is hard to imagine population drops larger than 10%, which is a significant number of prisoners but less than one-sixth of the one-generation increase and only about one-third of the increase generated during declining crime rates in the 1990s."

* * *

"When examining the link between recent history and likely future developments, there is reason for only modest hope. It is likely that the penal expansion of recent decades will abate, but unlikely that the current scale of mass incarceration will shrink back even to rates found during the early 1990s. The barriers to extensive decarceration are no less formidable for being political rather than structural: they concern attitudes and values rather than the institutional dynamics of criminal justice."

Is this plausible? If there is no immediate prospect for a reduction from 300,000 U.S. drug prisoners, what about long-term prospects? What might the process of reducing drug imprisonment look like?

Chapter 4

GAMBLING

A. INTRODUCTION

Three characteristics set gambling apart from other vice activities in developed nations. The first is the large financial scale of gambling. The President's Crime Commission in 1967 estimated that illegal gambling had a net economic impact ten times as great as illegal drugs. The second distinguishing feature of gambling is the extent of legal change in recent times. Widespread removal of criminal penalties is only the beginning of the story. Gambling is now a major state enterprise in jurisdictions with state lotteries: not merely an external business to be regulated by government, but a part of government. This suggests the third major shift in modern times: the removal of moral and social stigma. The history of gambling in the United States during the past four decades looks like a moral transformation of the activity. It challenges the veracity of this book's title: gambling may no longer be a vice!

Why these changes? Is this a permanent change? To what extent is the history of gambling in recent years a model for other vice behaviors?

THE NATIONAL GAMBLING IMPACT STUDY COMMISSION: FINAL REPORT, JUNE 1999

OVERVIEW

Today the vast majority of Americans either gamble recreationally and experience no measurable side effects related to their gambling, or they choose not to gamble at all. Regrettably, some of them gamble in ways that harm themselves, their families, and their communities. This Commission's research suggests that 86 percent of Americans report having gambled at least once during their lives. Sixty-eight percent of Americans report having gambled at least once in the past year. In 1998, people gambling in this country lost $50 billion in legal wagering, a figure that has increased every year for over two decades, and often at double-digit rates. And there is no end in sight: Every prediction that the gambling market was becoming saturated has proven to be premature.

IMPACT AND CONTROVERSY

A Moving Target

Gambling is an ephemeral subject, the study of it is frustrated by the apparently solid repeatedly slipping away. A good starting point is a recognition that the gambling "industry" is far from monolithic. Instead, it is composed of relatively discrete segments: Casinos (commercial and tribal), state-run lotteries, pari-mutuel wagering, sports wagering, charitable gambling, Internet gambling, stand-alone electronic gambling devices (EGD's) (such as video poker and video keno), and so forth. Each form of gambling can, in turn, be divided or aggregated into a variety of other groupings. For example, pari-mutuel wagering includes the subgroups of horse racing, dog racing, and jai alai. In addition, the terms "convenience gambling" and "retail gambling" have often been used to describe stand-alone slot machines, video keno, video poker, and other EGD's that have proliferated in bars, truck stops, convenience stores, and a variety of other locations across several states. This term may also be applied to many lottery games. (These groupings will be discussed in greater detail later in this report.) Each group has its own distinct set of issues, communities of interests, and balance sheets of assets and liabilities. For example, lotteries capture enormous revenues for state governments, ostensibly benefiting the general public in the form of enhanced services, such as education. But critics charge that the states knowingly target their poorest citizens, employing aggressive and misleading advertising to induce these individuals to gamble away their limited means. Casinos spark different discussions. In Atlantic City, the casinos have transformed the Boardwalk and provide employment for thousands of workers. But opponents point to the unredeemed blight only blocks away, made worse by elevated levels of crime that some attribute to the presence of gambling. And so-called convenience gambling may help marginal businesses survive, but at the cost of bringing a poorly regulated form of gambling into the hearts of communities. The Internet brings its own assortment of imponderable issues.

The terrain also is becoming more complicated. As gambling has expanded, it has continued to evolve. Technology and competitive pressures have joined to produce new forms, with the onset of the Internet promising to redefine the entire industry. The participants in the various debates are similarly varied. Even the designations "proponents" and "opponents" must be applied with care because opponents can include those opposed to all gambling, those content with the current extent of gambling but opposed to its expansion, those favoring one type of gambling but opposed to another, and those who simply want to keep gambling out of their particular community, the latter being less motivated by questions of probity than of zoning. Proponents can be similarly divided: Few people in the casino industry welcome the advent of gambling on the Internet, and the owners of racetracks are no friends of the state lotteries. Similarly, if polls are to be believed, a clear majority of Americans favor the continued legalization of gambling but a clear majority also opposes unlimited gambling, preferring continued regulation. Drawing the line on gambling has proven difficult; and, in fact, most lines in this area become blurred when examined closely. But governments are in business to draw lines, and draw them they do.

The Role of Government

The public has voted either by a statewide referendum and/or local option election for the establishment or continued operation of commercial casino gambling in 9 of 11 states where commercial casinos are permitted. Similarly, the public has approved state lotteries via the ballot box in 27 of 38 instances where lotteries have been enacted. Whatever the case, whether gambling is introduced by popular referendum or by the decision of elected officials, we must recognize the important role played by government in the industry's growth and development. Government decisions have influenced the expansion of gambling in America, and influencing those decisions is the principal objective of most of the public debates on this issue. Although some would argue that gambling is a business like any other and, consequently, should be treated as such, in fact it is almost universally regarded as something different, requiring special rules and treatment, and enhanced scrutiny by government and citizens alike. Even in the flagship state of Nevada, operation of a gambling enterprise is explicitly defined as a "privilege," an activity quite apart from running a restaurant, manufacturing furniture, or raising cotton. Unlike other businesses in which the market is the principal determinant, the shape and operation of legalized gambling has been largely a product of government decisions.

No Master Plan

To say that gambling has grown and taken shape in obeisance to government decisions does not imply that there was a well thought-out, overall plan. All too commonly, actual results have diverged from stated intentions, at times completely surprising the decisionmakers. There are many reasons for this awkward fact. In the U.S. federalist system, use of the term "government" can easily mislead: Far from a single actor with a clear-eyed vision and unified direction, it is in fact a mix of authorities, with functions and decisionmaking divided into many levels—federal, state, local, and others, including tribal. Each of these plays an active role in determining the shape of legalized gambling. The states have always had the primary responsibility for gambling decisions and almost certainly will continue to do so for the foreseeable future. Many states, however, have delegated considerable authority to local jurisdictions, often including such key decisions as whether or not gambling will be permitted in their communities. And the federal government plays an ever-greater role: Indian gambling sprang into being as a result of federal court decisions and congressional legislation; and even the states concede that only Washington has the potential to control gambling on the Internet. And almost none of the actors coordinate their decisions with one another. The federal government did not poll the states when it authorized Indian gambling within their borders, nor have Mississippi and Louisiana—nor, for that matter, any other state—seen fit to adopt a common approach to gambling. In fact, rivalry and competition for investment and revenues have been far more common factors in government decisionmaking regarding gambling than have any impulses toward joint planning. Those decisions generally have been reactive, driven more by pressures of the day than by an abstract debate about the public welfare. One of the most powerful motivations has been the pursuit of revenues. It is easy to understand the impetus: Faced with stiff public resistance to tax increases as well as incessant demands for increased or improved public services from the same citizens, tax revenues from gambling can easily be portrayed as a relatively painless method of resolving this dilemma. Some believe another contributing factor has been the increasing volume of political contributions from interests with an economic stake in virtually every place expansion is sought. Critics have asserted that this legislative pursuit of revenues has occurred at the expense of consideration of the public welfare, a serious charge indeed, albeit an unproveable one. But advocates have successfully deployed many other arguments for legalizing or expanding gambling: economic development for economically depressed areas, the general promotion of business for the investment and employment opportunities it can bring with it, undermining illegal gambling and the organized crime it supports, and so forth. There is even the eminently democratic motivation of responding to public demand: A number of election campaigns and referenda have been successfully waged on the issue of legalizing or expanding gambling.

1. SOME HISTORY

JEFFREY BERGMAN—THE HISTORICAL ROOTS OF GAMBLING LAW

Evidence of recreational gambling extends far back into human history: archaeologists have unearthed Sumerian dice from the 28th century B.C.; by 300 B.C., cities in India were employing government officials to oversee games of chance—and apparently for good reason, since "loaded dice" from the ancient world have been discovered as well. Despite its ubiquity, however, gambling has never enjoyed a good public reputation. Some scholars trace this to a deep-seated aversion to "unearned" wealth, and the idea that gambling is a waste of time and human faculties. Others point to religious convictions, especially the belief that luck or fortune is God's domain, and should not be "cheapened" with rolls of the dice or games of poker.

Whatever the underlying reason, throughout history gambling has been attacked nearly as often as it has flourished. Yet English law, and through it American law, has long recognized important distinctions between types of gambling, as well as types of gamblers. Most early anti-gambling efforts were focused on particular manifestations of the problem. During the First Crusade, for example, King Richard I noticed the amount of time his soldiers spent on gambling, and feared the effect this might have on the readiness of his army. He threatened any soldier caught gambling with execution. Later penalties would not be so harsh, but legislation to suppress or control gambling was passed in 1388, 1477, 1494, 1503, 1511, 1535, 1541, 1664, 1699, and 1710—much of it motivated by worry that time spent gambling was time not spent working, farming, or practicing in the local militia. These early anti-gambling measures were thus seen more as attempts to preserve public order than to prevent the harm to individuals which excessive gambling might cause. An influential early case, *The Case of the Monopolies*, validated this approach—here, the court held that while no game was illegal unless Parliament specifically banned it, the government's authority to do so for the sake of public morals was virtually unlimited. The basis of these regulations in the English class system was often explicit, as many of the laws exempted the nobility from punishment. Large-scale gambling had long been endemic to the English gentry, and stories were often told of noblemen wagering entire estates on a single throw of the dice. At the time, however, this difference of treatment was seen as beneficial: the common folk simply could not afford to take the same risks as the wealthy, and needed to be protected against temptation.

Rather than treating all gambling as a criminal activity to be punished, most of this English legislation concentrated on combating it indirectly. Various laws prohibited the keeping of public gambling houses—the forerunners to today's casinos—and attempts were made to ban private wagers above a certain size. Finally, the Statute of Anne, passed in 1710, declared that any debts incurred through gambling would be unenforceable in court. The principle thus established became central to later law: unless otherwise authorized, a gambling debt had no legal status, and "creditors" could not sue for their winnings if the "debtors" refused to pay.

Despite such attempts to fight unauthorized gambling, however, publicly-sponsored lotteries were relatively common, overseen either by the government itself, or more commonly by specially chartered organizations. The justification for these will seem surprisingly familiar to anyone today: lotteries were an easy way to raise revenue, and less likely to meet public opposition that explicit taxation. They were almost always tied to particular projects, like highways and educational institutions, rather than going towards general public revenues.

In colonial America and the early United States, authorized lotteries played a similar role. The Royal Virginia Company sold shares in a massive lottery to raise revenue for the colony. Although the legislatures of Massachusetts and other colonies passed anti-gambling laws very similar to England's, they also condoned lotteries to support everything from Harvard College to the Revolutionary War. These state-authorized lotteries in the United States rose and fell in three waves. The first ran from colonization until about 1820, when lotteries began to be seen (not for the last time) as too unsavory for government sponsorship. By 1840 only Missouri and Kentucky still permitted them. The second wave coincided with the Civil War, a period of massive and unexpected public need. The Union conducted a lottery to raise extra funds for the war, and most of the states, particularly in the defeated South, set up their own lotteries afterwards to support infrastructure repairs. These quickly became riddled with corruption, which eventually brought nearly all of them down. By far the most infamous case was that of the Louisiana Lottery, a large private corporation that sold tickets nationwide. Under the Lottery's charter, a portion of its proceeds went to public projects, and sales of its tickets funded the New Orleans waterworks. In 1893, however, it was revealed that the Lottery's managers had paid large bribes to state legislators, and the resulting public outcry led the state to revoke its charter, and Congress to pass the first federal gambling statute. Use of the mails to distribute lottery materials and selling tickets across state lines were both prohibited—prohibitions which remain in force today. Although the Louisiana Lottery tried to save itself by rechartering in Honduras, Congress reacted by further banning the importation of gambling-related materials. Most of the other public lotteries were destroyed by similar controversies, and large-scale gambling went into decline, outside of a few limited arenas, until New Hampshire authorized a lottery in 1964. This began the third wave of large public lotteries, which is said to continue today. Forty states and the District of Columbia now operate their own lotteries, and nearly all the states permit some form of gambling within their borders (only Hawaii and Utah still ban it entirely).

Importantly, for decades in the United States and through the end of the second wave of public lotteries, few doubted that gambling could only occur under the special dispensation of the state. In the seminal case of *Stone v. Mississippi*, the U.S. Supreme Court considered whether a Mississippi lottery chartered under an old state constitution could be simply shut down under a new one that disallowed all gambling. Freedom of contract, the court ruled, did not protect the lottery from such fundamental changes in the law. Gambling was within the state's power to regulate or ban as the public saw fit and, as the court said, "all agree that the legislature cannot bargain away the police power of the State."

Gambling, then, has a long history in Anglo–American law, and not always a consistent one. Yet many of the contours and principles of the law of gambling have remained surprisingly stable over time: public distaste for the activity and a sense that it threatens other civic purposes have been confronted by the reality of gambling's popularity. What seems at first to be a blatant contradiction—that attitudes would alternate between condemnation and actual government sponsorship—can be understood as a response to this tension. The methods adopted in early law, in turn, tended towards amelioration rather than retribution. Whether these attempts to recognize and control gambling were more successful than total criminalization would have been remains one of the open questions of gambling law.

2. EARLY LOTTERIES

Lotteries were used on the Continent and in the colonies as a way to raise revenue for public works projects. Here is an account of early lotteries in France, followed by a discussion of lotteries in Colonial America.

STEPHEN M. STIGLER—CASANOVA'S LOTTERY
Available at http://www.uchicago.edu/docs/education/record/pdfs/37–4.pdf

My aim today is to shed some light on th[e] history of lotteries through a little-known story involving a famous but little-known character, Giacomo Casanova. Casanova was born in Venice in 1725, and he died in Bohemia in 1798. The facts of his life come mainly from his multi-volume *Memoirs*, published many years after he died from manuscripts written in old age and left in Bohemia. The *Memoirs* are the basis of his reputation as a lover. Casanova made close and consequential contact with the circle of Parisians around Madame de Pompadour, including members of the finance ministry. In the early 1750s, Pompadour had been instrumental in organizing and beginning construction of the Ecole Militaire, a school destined to be the king's military school, the same school that thirty years later would train the young Napoleon. In 1756, the school was unfinished but already in financial difficulty, and Casanova was invited to discussions on projects to raise money for the school—we would now call it "development." He opportunistically joined in advancing and supporting a proposal for a lottery, along the lines of one he had seen succeed in Italy.

The lottery he proposed was of a type unknown in Paris, although it had been introduced in the city-state of Genoa in the 1620s. It was an early cousin of Illinois Lotto. In the late 1500s, Genoa was governed by a council of five, the members of the council being selected annually at random from a list of perhaps ninety nobles of the city. The citizens of Genoa took to placing bets on who would be selected—you could bet on any single noble being included in the council or, presumably, on a pair. In 1626, a Genoese entrepreneur had the bright idea that an election was unnecessary in order to have a wager, and he introduced the idea of a lottery where five numbers would be selected by choosing five tokens blindly from a set of ninety sequentially numbered tokens in a rotatable cage called a wheel of fortune, with bets accepted on the outcome. A distant relative to this type of lottery had been popular in China since the Second Han Dynasty (that's nine hundred years before Casanova), where it was called the Game of Thirty-six Animals, and it is conceivable that Marco Polo's travel reports played a role in this history, too. In any event, it was just such a lottery that Casanova advocated to rescue the Ecole Militaire from insolvency.

Casanova's lottery was simple in design: In its initial version, the player had an option of betting on a single number (an extrait), or on a pair of numbers (an ambe), or on a set of three numbers (a terne). The odds of winning varied with the bet and became increasingly unfavorable as the chances of winning became more remote. Later the number of bets available was expanded to reach a maximum of seven different bets, including specifying which place in the drawing a single number would occur (for example, "57" as the third of the 5 numbers drawn, an extrait déterminé), or which places a pair of numbers would occur (an ambe déterminé). They were also permitted to bet on a set of four numbers (a quaterne), or five (a quine). Like our modern lotto, the choice of numbers was up to the bettor. Unlike our modern lotto, there was a choice of bets, and all were priced and treated separately. At this distance in time it is difficult to understand the reception this idea received from Louis XV's state council. We might understand them being concerned that the French would not rise to the bait in sufficient numbers to produce much revenue. But even then the lottery should not lose money at those odds, and it could always be cancelled later, if need be. But instead, the council adopted a very conservative stance and worried about major loss.

There were two reasons for this concern. The first is that while this type of lottery was unknown in France, there was another type that was familiar in France, in England, and in America well before 1750, and that type had a mixed and troublesome history. In England it was called a "blanks lottery," and it was run as a sort of a raffle. A scheme of prizes was announced and a set number of tickets was offered for sale. For example, in one English blanks lottery, 13,500 tickets were offered for sale and 2,754 prizes would be awarded. After the sale, a long and complicated drawing was held. The 13,500 ticket stubs were placed in one large barrel, and in another barrel there were placed another 13,500 slips of paper. Of these, 2,754 were marked with prize amounts, and the remainder were blank. Over a period that generally lasted several weeks, two small boys from foundling homes, wearing the blue coats that were the uniforms of those homes, would draw successive tickets from the two barrels and pair them, awarding the lucky winner the prize or the unlucky holder a blank.

The problem with this type of lottery is that to be successful, all the tickets needed to be sold. The nominal price per ticket was £20, too large an amount for many people, and for this reason most tickets were divided into fractions as small as one-sixteenth. Selling that many tickets took a large sales force, which cut into the profits. Tickets were also traded privately during the drawing. Worse, speculators with no connection to the state started offering "insurance" on the tickets—a thinly veiled way of selling tickets they did not hold, but promised to pay off in the unlikely event of a win. With all this going on, there was always the possibility that the sales would fail.

The first such lottery in England was introduced by Queen Elizabeth in 1567 and was a colossal failure: Less than one twelfth of the tickets were sold, and the queen was forced to cut the prizes after the tickets were sold—not a good way to generate repeat business. In France there were other scandals. The great Voltaire made a fortune in the 1720s by recognizing a flaw in the pricing and sales system that permitted him to wager with certainty of winning. Of course many lotteries were successful. In America, Harvard, Princeton, Columbia, and Yale Universities financed building plans with the aid of lotteries. Still, with all of this background there was ample reason for the French state council to be worried. And there was one further problem. Unlike modern lotto where the large prizes are not guaranteed but rather are paid from a pari-mutuel pool and the state cannot lose, it was theoretically possible in Casanova's lottery that the king could lose, even lose big. If a handful of gamblers got lucky and hit a quaterne (paying 75,000 to 1) or a quine (paying 1,000,000 to 1), the week's receipts would go sharply into the red. No minister would relish the idea of delivering such news to the king.

A hearing was held. Casanova argued that the announcement that the lottery was backed by the king, and that the king stood prepared to lose up to a hundred million francs, would dazzle people and guarantee sales. The councilors were taken aback by this prospect, even when Casanova reassured them that before the Crown would lose a hundred million it would receive at least a hundred and fifty million. The reaction, according to Casanova's account, was still concern.

A councilor asked, "I am not the only person who has doubts on the subject. You must grant the possibility of the Crown losing an enormous sum at the first drawing?"

Casanova replied, "Certainly, sir, but between possibility and reality is all the region of the infinite. Indeed, I may say that it would be a great piece of good fortune if the Crown were to lose a large sum on the first drawing."

"A piece of bad fortune, you mean, surely?"

"A bad fortune to be desired," Casanova answered. He argued that the publicity would be invaluable and the odds would safeguard the Crown's wealth in the long run. He reminded them that all the insurance companies were rich. He offered to prove the soundness of the scheme before all the mathematicians in Europe.

A second hearing was held, and Casanova showed himself as adept in seducing the state council as he is believed to have been in other encounters. He answered all objections, and yet another three-hour session was held, one that included testimony by the philosophe Jean le Rond D'Alembert who, in addition to his other accomplishments as co-editor of the Encyclopédie, was a talented and supremely skeptical mathematician. As a result of all this, the project—with the financial backing of the Crown—was approved. Casanova was awarded a pension and six sales offices, five of which he sold for 2,000 francs each. He ran the sixth himself, on Rue St. Denis, with his valet as clerk. Casanova even carried tickets to sell to the salons he visited. His memoirs do not report that he combined sales with his romantic life, however. The state council should not have worried.

Casanova soon moved on, leaving the country for what we may euphemistically call "other pursuits," but his lottery was an enormous success. It held five drawings in 1758, its first year, and soon settled into a routine of monthly draws. Madame de Pompadour died in 1764, and Louis XV died in 1774, succeeded by his grandson Louis XVI. In those years the budget was in poor shape, and in September 1776, a month after Turgot was dismissed as finance minister, the new finance minister was looking for ways to bolster the French treasury. With the king's permission, he kidnapped the lottery from the Ecole Militaire and made it the "Loterie Royale de France." It was expanded: Drawings were increased to twice a month. By the 1780s there were regional Loterie sales offices in Lyon, Strasbourg, Brussels, and Bordeaux. When the Bastille fell in July 1789, the Loterie did not miss a draw. When Louis XVI was executed in January 1793, the Loterie did not miss a draw. When Marie Antoinette lost her head in October of that year, the Loterie did not miss a draw. Only in December of 1793, when the Committee of Public Safety and the Reign of Terror held sway, was the Loterie suppressed.

Casanova would have understood why. Without civil authority, public faith in payouts plummeted, and with it the receipts of the Loterie! But just four years later, order was restored and the needs of the French treasury inspired its reestablishment under the same rules as before. In 1801, the Loterie expanded further, to three drawings a month, and separate drawings were introduced at each of the four regional offices, for a total of fifteen drawings a month! Parisian gamblers could wager on any of these from Parisian offices, and others in France could wager on either their own region or on the Paris draws. By 1811, the Loterie ran more than 1,000 sales offices across France, and the net proceeds reached as high as 4 percent of the national budget—more than the contribution from postal or customs levies. There were technological and educational benefits as well—to convey the results of the drawings to and from Paris, an energetic communications network with carriages and riders was developed to all corners of France. And the Loterie probably did more for public awareness of—and education in—the calculus of probabilities than any other state effort, before or since.

The Loterie was a frequent topic of discussion in popular culture as well. A home version was marketed already in the 1780s as Loto–Dauphin, essentially a board game. The Loterie was celebrated in novels. And it was attacked by moralists. Nonetheless, it thrived until May of 1836 when the moralists won a significant victory and by law it was permanently suppressed, not to reappear until the twentieth century.

. . .

Why was the Loterie permanently suspended in May of 1836? It had been a phenomenal success. The only year it did not make a net profit for the state was 1814, when every army in Europe was crossing France.

In that year, the Paris drawings continued, but most other offices were closed for a few months and the office in Brussels moved permanently to Lille, since Brussels was no longer part of France. That year, the cost of administration overran proceeds, and the Loterie lost a third of a million francs, but the net profit over the first quarter of the nineteenth century was generally ten million or more per year.

True, there were voices through the 1820s accusing the Loterie of being a moral scourge upon the nation, that it took money from those least able to pay, for hopes that were false in ways they could never understand.

Indeed there was a long tradition to such sentiments. Already in 1776, Adam Smith had written in *The Wealth of Nations*, "That the chance of gain is naturally overvalued, we may learn from the universal success of lotteries." Smith did not suggest this tendency to overvalue was limited to any particular economic class, but later writers thought the poor were especially susceptible.

In 1819, Pierre Simon Laplace, one of the architects of the modern theory of probability, rose to address a governmental council. In that year the French finances were in excellent shape, and he urged the members to take advantage of the moment of diminished need and abolish the Loterie. Laplace argued, "The poor, excited by the desire for a better life and seduced by hopes whose unlikelihood it is beyond their capacity to appreciate, take to this game as if it were a necessity. They are attracted to the combinations that permit the greatest benefit, the same that we see are the least favorable." He further argued, anticipating Quetelet's idea of social determinism, that the tax was not really voluntary, as was generally believed:

"No doubt," he stated, "it is voluntary for each individual, but for the set of all individuals it is a necessity, just as their marriages, births, and all sorts of variable effects are necessary, and nearly the same each year when their number is large, just as the revenues from the Loterie are as constant as is agricultural production."

And he further claimed that the state's annual net profit of 10 to 12 million was offset by a hidden tax upon the poor of 40 to 50 million per year in lost investment. Many others spoke in similarly colored terms. In 1832, one French attorney wrote that "each day it becomes more urgent to put an end to this odious exploitation of the credulity and misery of the people." Was, then, the suspension of the Loterie in 1836 simply the result of a moral reawakening in France? Now, I happen to believe that in this one matter Adam Smith was wrong, that in all of these lotteries the true odds were widely known (even widely advertised) to all levels of society, and the hypothesis that their practical implications were misunderstood despite the years of active observation is untenable. But even if you accept the arguments that were presented by Smith and Laplace and others, the question remains: Those voices had been there from the beginning; why were they only heard in the 1830s? Now, my longitudinal survey of the Loterie provides some revealing evidence bearing on this question. The record of winners allows us to estimate the number of bettors. We can crudely estimate the average number of quaternes bet per sales office for each drawing, and this average decreased from around 200 in 1800 to around 30 in 1833. From 1810 to 1830 the number of quaternes bet in Paris decreased about 25 percent. In the regional Loteries the decrease was greater: In Lyon there was an over 40 percent decline. The public was losing their taste for the Loterie, and by 1836 this shifted the political balance. As the survey shows, the Loterie was never more than an urban phenomenon in a predominantly agricultural country. When profits were running high, the ears of agricultural France were deaf to the moralists' complaints, but when the urban public began to tire of the Loterie, the arguments became more convincing. The Loterie de France flourished for three-quarters of a century, with a brief hiatus in the 1790s. The persistent demand for the Loterie by a public increasingly well educated in probability shows an attraction to low-cost risk at the individual level that continues today in all societies. The Loterie prospered with the increasingly general knowledge of probability and without doubt contributed to that knowledge; it was a public laboratory for chance where students could see almost daily the application of the techniques they studied in secondary school and university. And education in probability prospered: The great growth in France in the publication of textbooks and treatises on probability dates from 1783 to the 1830s, the period of the Loterie.

The Loterie also serves as an example of the phenomenon of corporate risk aversion by the state. From the resistance Casanova encountered at the founding of the Loterie to the demise of the quine as an option after about 1803, the state was ever mindful of the fact that it always stood the chance of losing on its bets, millions on the quine and hundreds of thousands on the quaterne. No modern state lottery, whether lotto or sweepstakes, accepts such a risk. The odds were so strongly in favor of the state on these bets that it would seem foolish that they would worry, but against that there was always the specter of undiscovered fraud and the administrative manuals of the time show they took this possibility very seriously. It is plausible that this risk aversion, coupled with the slow secular decline in public interest as the Loterie became dated, contributed to the Loterie's demise.

This type of lottery (with a menu of bets and guaranteed fixed payoffs even for long-odds bets) was never widely adopted internationally—only in parts of Italy and Spain, in some German cities, in Vienna, and in France. According to my wretched little book, the payoffs in France were superior to the others; for example, in Germany they paid only 14 times on an bet on a single number and 60,000 times on a quaterne. The Loterie survived the revolution, but by 1836 it had run its course. Nonetheless it left its mark on succeeding generations' understanding of chance.

The reason for its success—the attraction of risk whether by gambling or speculation—was obvious to Casanova even if it can confound economists to this present day. Casanova wrote his memoirs in retirement in Bohemia, working as a librarian for a duke, but as he vividly recalled the passions of his youth, he wrote, "The passion for gambling was rooted in me; to live and to play were to me two identical things."

Casanova's lottery inadvertently produced the first scientifically conducted social survey, a curious example of what the late sociologist Robert K. Merton referred to as an "unanticipated consequence of social action." It is a survey that is very much with us today. The next time you read of a cook or professor winning a hundred million dollars in the Powerball Lottery, do not simply think of that cook or professor as a very lucky person. Rather, you are observing the latest scientific random selection in a survey that dates back nearly 250 years, a survey with a remarkably high cost per observation. And think of Casanova.

B. DEFINITIONS AND STATUTORY LAW

1. GAMBLING VERSUS INVESTMENT AND SPECULATION

LYNN STOUT—WHY THE LAW HATES SPECULATORS: REGULATION AND PRIVATE ORDERING IN THE MARKET FOR OTC DERIVATIVES

48 Duke Law Journal 701 (1999).

INTRODUCTION

The public disapproves of speculators. So, traditionally, does the law. Although hostility towards speculators is so deeply woven into our nation's legal fabric that it often goes unnoticed, a remarkable variety of laws discourages people from trying to profit from short-term price changes. Tax law, for example, favors those who hold assets for long periods over those who resell quickly. Both the common law of contract and the Commodity Exchange Act (CEA) prohibit certain types of speculative transactions outside the confines of a regulated futures exchange. Even in the stock market, an area of economic life many regard as synonymous with speculation, federal regulations limit speculators' ability to wager on market downturns by "selling short." Antispeculation rules are pervasive, appearing in statutes and in the common law, in doctrines ancient and new, and at the state and federal levels.

I. Antispeculation Rules in American Law

To some observers, the claim that the law discourages speculation at first may seem implausible. Speculative trading appears to be the order of the day on stock exchanges like the New York Stock Exchange, and on commodities futures exchanges like the Chicago Board of Trade, not to mention the burgeoning derivatives market. How then can the law be hostile to speculators?

The answer lies in recognizing that speculators' presence in such highly visible but limited arenas obscures their relative absence elsewhere. In theory, there is no need for speculators to limit themselves to trading corporate securities and those relatively few commodities contracts officially listed for trading on an organized futures exchange. They also could wager on the future prices of plastic surgery, narrow ties, Manhattan condos, popular television shows, and law school graduates. In practice, speculation in such goods and services is rare. The reason can be traced to a network of obscure but important legal doctrines that severely limit speculators' role in most markets.

One of the most fundamental of these doctrines is the common law requirement that speculators who want to wager on prices through futures and options agreements have to make and accept delivery of the goods and services they trade. Although few contemporary legal scholars seem aware of this rule, it persists in a variety of modern forms, most notably in insurance law and the Commodity Exchange Act. Its net effect is to confine speculation primarily to regulated commodities futures exchanges, which are exempt from the general rule, and to the corporate securities market, where delivery is relatively easy and inexpensive. Even in these markets, moreover, speculators who seek short-term profits must run an obstacle course of margin requirements, position limits, short sales restrictions, capital gains rules, and other technical regulations that have both the purpose and the effect of deterring speculative trading. The arcana of modern tax, securities, and commodities law provide a second important curb on speculation.

The net result is a legal system that works with surprising consistency to channel our nation's economic energy toward the actual production and distribution of goods and services, and away from the pursuit of short-term trading profits. In illustration, the discussion below considers some important examples of antispeculation rules drawn from both statutes and common law. These rules suggest a pattern of legal antipathy toward speculators that springs from the longstanding belief that speculation wreaks economic harm because it is nonproductive, distorts market prices, and impoverishes speculators themselves.

A. The Common Law Rule Against Difference Contracts

One of the earliest and most important examples of antispeculation law can be found in the common law doctrine that shall be referred to below as "the rule against difference contracts." Difference contracts were close cousins to futures (contracts for the sale of goods for future delivery) and options (agreements granting one party the right but not the obligation to buy or sell at a specified price at or before some predetermined future date). In a difference contract, however, the contracting parties would agree to perform not by actually delivering the good that was the subject of the contract, but by paying the difference between the contract price and the market price at the time of performance. Thus a "seller" who didn't own wheat and a "buyer" who didn't want wheat might have entered a difference contract for one ton of wheat at a contract price of $1,000 per ton, to be settled in six months. If at the end of six months the market price for wheat had risen to $1,200 per ton, the seller would pay the buyer $200. If the price had dropped to

$900 per ton, the buyer would pay the seller $100. In either case, no wheat would actually change hands.

The common law regarded difference contracts as legally unenforceable on grounds of public policy. As the United States Supreme Court described the rule in the 1884 case of Irwin v. Williar:

> "The generally accepted doctrine in this country is ... that a contract for the sale of goods to be delivered at a future day is valid, even though the seller has not the goods, nor any other means of getting them than to go into the market and buy them; but such a contract is only valid when the parties really intend and agree that the goods are to be delivered by the seller and the price to be paid by the buyer; and, if under guise of such a contract, the real intent be merely to speculate in the rise or fall of prices, and the goods are not to be delivered, but one party is to pay to the other the difference between the contract price and the market price of the goods at the date fixed for executing the contract, then the whole transaction constitutes nothing more than a wager, and is null and void."

This rule against "settling differences" offers a variety of useful insights into antispeculation law. First, it suggests a perceived link between speculation and gambling, a link that is considered again in Part III. Common law courts regarded speculation as a type of wagering rather than a useful form of economic commerce. Thus difference contracts, like private wagers, were declared legally unenforceable.

A second striking aspect of the rule is the strategy it employed to discourage speculation. In effect, the rule forced speculators who wanted their contracts to be enforceable to trade in the underlying "spot market," making and accepting delivery of the goods they bought and sold. The rule thus imposed a "tax" on speculators by requiring them to incur expenses that they could have avoided if difference agreements had been enforceable. For example, spot market speculators would incur substantial transportation expenses trading in commodities that were bulky (wheat), obstinate (livestock), or difficult to transfer securely (gold bullion). Requiring delivery also forced speculators to bear the costs and risks of "carrying" goods—storing, protecting, maintaining, even feeding and watering them—during the period between purchase and sale. Finally, the rule reduced speculators' liquidity by tying up their wealth in inventory. For some forms of property, these transaction costs would be relatively small: baseball cards and corporate stocks could each be spot traded relatively cheaply. In most markets, however, delivery greatly increased the cost of taking a speculative position. The rule against difference contracts thus raised a significant hurdle to speculation in most goods and services.

A third remarkable feature of the rule against difference contracts is that is was explicitly grounded in public policy. Some cases phrased this policy in moral terms, describing difference contracts as "tainted and poisoned" and "the source of great injury to morals." Other cases, however, justified the rule as necessary to temper speculation's supposedly pernicious economic consequences. In other words, speculation was thought to harm not just morals, but markets.

While generally refusing to enforce contracts of sale not intended to be settled by delivery, common law courts applied an exception in cases where one party to a difference contract could demonstrate that the contract served a legitimate hedging function. Such a party would have to show that at the time she entered the contract, she held an economic interest that would be damaged by the happening of the very same event that would allow her to profit under the contract. Thus, for example, a plaintiff seeking to enforce a difference agreement that allowed her to profit if wheat prices fell might demonstrate that she held a wheat inventory, the value of which would be damaged by a price decline. Because such a contract would offset a preexisting source of loss rather than creating an opportunity for gain, courts recharacterized these types of contracts as enforceable "indemnity" agreements.

The indemnity exception to the rule against difference contracts suggests that judges recognized that difference agreements could be used for insurance as well as for gambling. At the same time, the fact that the indemnity exception was an exception implies a judicial perception that many difference contracts didn't insure against a preexisting risk. In other words, risk hedging was perceived as the exception—not the rule—in difference contract trading.

The notion that some difference contracts served a useful hedging function while others did not also underlay the second important exception to the rule against difference contracts: the exception for exchange-traded futures. To finance theorists, any contract of sale for future delivery is a "future." In legal terminology, however, the word "future" is sometimes interpreted more narrowly to apply only to the highly standardized contracts for future delivery that are traded in "pits" on organized commodities exchanges such as the Chicago Board of Trade. Traders who buy exchange-traded futures are technically entitled to demand delivery. As a practical matter, however, most exchange-traded futures are settled through an "offset" process in which one party to the contract extinguishes her obligation by reentering the pit and purchasing a second, offsetting contract. Thus a trader obligated to sell 100 bushels of wheat on May 1 might offset her obligation by purchasing a contract to buy 100 bushels on May 1, absorbing the price difference as profit or loss.

C. Antispeculation Rules in Insurance Law: The Doctrines of Indemnity and Insurable Interest

The common law rule against difference contracts and the CEA both deter speculation in a similar fashion: by requiring speculators outside a regulated futures exchange to incur the costs associated with spot market delivery. This strategy, it turns out, is mirrored in insurance law. Two doctrines that lie at the heart of insurance—the requirement of insurable interest and the indemnity principle—have both evolved, in part, to prevent speculators from using insurance for speculation.

There are several different tests for determining whether a policyholder has an "insurable interest." As a general rule, however, courts refuse to enforce an insurance policy unless the policyholder can demonstrate that she would suffer some significant economic detriment if the insured property is destroyed. Thus, the owner of an automobile has an insurable interest in her car, and her bank also may be able to purchase a policy if it financed the purchase and holds a collateral interest in the vehicle. Neither the owner nor the bank, however, can purchase a policy on some third party's vehicle.

Even for policyholders who hold insurable interests, recovery will be limited by a second antispeculation rule: the indemnity principle. Under the indemnity rules, a policyholder cannot recover any amount exceeding the economic value of her interest in the insured property. An automobile owner whose car is destroyed can recover the fair market value of the vehicle, but can not recover three times that amount even if she has purchased and paid for three policies. Similarly, her bank can recover only the amount of its unpaid loan.

The doctrines of indemnity and insurable interest arose in the earliest days of insurance law and persist, often in statutory form, to this day. Both reflect an axiom of insurance so fundamental that it goes to very meaning of the word: insurance policies are to compensate for losses suffered—not to generate profits. Two evils are thought to flow from using insurance policies for gain. The first is "moral hazard," a picturesque phrase referring to the fear that insurance might tempt policyholders into not protecting adequately against losses, or even destroying insured property for profit. The second fundamental concern underlying the indemnity and insurable interest requirements, however, is the fear that speculators otherwise would use insurance policies to wager on the future.

Both early and modern insurance cases frequently cite the antispeculation function of the indemnity and insurable interest rules, as does academic commentary dating well into the mid-twentieth century. More recently, however, scholars have shown a curious reluctance to credit the traditional antispeculation rationale, instead emphasizing moral hazard as the rules' underlying foundation. The very structure of the indemnity and insurable interest rules nevertheless reveals that they are at least as much concerned with discouraging speculation as they are with avoiding moral hazard. In some situations, for example, the requirement of insurable interest actually magnifies moral hazard problems. Consider the case of an insurance company that sells policies against damage from earthquakes or hurricanes. No policyholder is likely to be able to alter the chances of such a natural disaster occurring. A property owner can, however, take steps to limit any resulting damage through such preventative measures as reinforcing brickwork or storing valuables securely. If moral hazard was insurance law's principal concern, it would make more sense to allow insurance companies to sell earthquake and hurricane policies to third parties than to property owners. Yet in the interest of discouraging speculation, the rules of insurable interest dictate exactly the opposite result.

E. Summary: The Prevalence of Antispeculation Law

"Antispeculation law" generally is not taught as a subject in the modern legal curriculum. Perhaps it ought to be, for hostility towards speculators appears to be a fundamental characteristic of American law. The rule against difference contracts, the CEA, the doctrines of indemnity and insurable interest, and the SEA's margin requirements and short sales restrictions each play important roles in deterring speculative trading. They are, however, only a few of the many legal doctrines that work to rein in speculators. A policy of discouraging speculative trafficking in legal claims lies at the heart of the doctrine of champerty, the common law prohibition against buying and selling lawsuits that survives in statutory form in most states. The Internal Revenue Code also deters speculation by limiting preferential capital gains treatment of income earned from the sale of assets to those held for some minimum period (under current law, one year). This discourages speculation in spot markets outside the CFTC's jurisdiction, including not only the spot market for corporate securities—already subject to the SEA's margin requirements and short sales restrictions—but also spot markets for fine art, real estate, and other tangible assets. Although modern observers often attribute the holding period requirement to concerns over inflation, income averaging, and "lock in" effects, legislative history indicates that Congress adopted the requirement to reward long-term "investment" while discouraging short-term "speculation."

Throughout most of the nineteenth and twentieth centuries, American judges and legislators appear to have followed a policy of actively and deliberately discouraging speculative transactions. Recent years have seen a curious development, however. Lawmakers' longstanding belief that speculation is harmful seems to be eroding. Although antispeculation rules remain a staple of American law, contemporary observers seem increasingly reluctant to subscribe to the notion that deterring speculation should be a goal of public policy. Thus academics routinely offer alternative justifications for such traditional antispeculation rules as the SEA (now described as a disclosure statute) or insurance law's indemnity principle (now explained as a response to moral hazard).

What explains this modern skepticism towards antispeculation laws? The answer may lie in economic theory's growing influence on legal thinking. Judges and legislators traditionally condemned speculators as nonproductive parasites whose trading destabilizes market prices and often brings financial ruin to speculators themselves. Contemporary economic theory, however, describes speculators in far more flattering terms.

2. DEFINITIONS

RONALD RYCHLAK—VIDEO GAMBLING DEVICES

37 UCLA L. Rev. 555, 556—557 (1990).

The word "gambling" is derived from the Middle English word "gamen"—to amuse oneself. Gambling is traditionally said to consist of three elements: consideration, chance, and reward–all of which must be present to constitute gambling.

Consideration is often the easiest element to prove. Consideration is the stake, wager, or bet that gamblers risk losing if they are unsuccessful. With a traditional slot machine, for example, consideration is the coin that the gambler inserts into the machine before pulling the arm that sets the reels in motion.

The element of chance is more difficult to establish. The Supreme Court of Montana, for instance, has decided that poker is a game of skill, "with one player pitting his skills and talents against those of the other players," while the Supreme Court of Ohio has held that it is a game of chance. This direct contradiction obviously reflects less on the comparative abilities of citizens of the two states than on the difficulty involved in labeling a particular endeavor as being dependent upon either chance or skill. As the Superior Court of Pennsylvania has noted:

"A peculiar combination of luck and skill is the sine qua non of almost all games common to modern life. It is hard to imagine a competition or a contest which does not depend in part on serendipity. It cannot be disputed that football, baseball and golf require substantial skill, training and finesse, yet the result of each game turns in part upon luck or chance."

Courts and commentators have adopted various tests to distinguish games of skill from games of chance. The English rule is that any degree of skill will remove a game from the prohibited classification of lottery. A well-known test in the United States asks whether the outcome of a game is largely determined by chance. Regardless of the test used, complex issues of proof will undoubtedly arise when attempting to define and distinguish between chance and skill.

In addition to the blurry distinction between games of chance and games of skill, the label "chance" itself is somewhat misleading. For instance, if the city of Chicago sponsors a ten-kilometer run, charging an entry fee and offering prizes to winners in various age categories, it is clearly operating a contest of skill, not chance. Although there is consideration (the entry fee) and a reward (prizes to the winners), the element of chance is not present. Thus, the city is not sponsoring a gambling operation. However, suppose two spectators place a side bet on who will win. Is the side bet gambling? The contest itself is dependent upon skill. Yet, if a person wagers on a "future contingent event not under his control or influence," the element of chance is present. The side bet would therefore be illegal under traditional gambling laws, which permit awards to skillful players, but prohibit awards based on chance or awards given to noncontestants in a game of skill. Hence, although a football game's outcome is decided by the skill of the players, it is nonetheless illegal to place a bet on the outcome.

The final element of gambling is reward. Typically, reward is easy to prove: the wager would never have been made if not for the hope of receiving a reward. Does a free replay on a pinball or video machine constitute a reward? The modern view is that it does not. However, when games are equipped so that free replays represent something else, such as a right to receive cash, the element of reward is present and the game is properly categorized as a gambling device.

3.   SIGNIFICANT STATUTES

As with most of American law, laws relating to gambling exist on both the federal and state level. Generally, most regulation and criminalization of gambling depends on state law, while federal law aims at keeping the activity within state boundaries—by criminalizing national lotteries and gambling operations that cross state lines.

Federal

18 USC § 1084 ("THE WIRE ACT"). TRANSMISSION OF WAGERING INFORMATION; PENALTIES

(a) Whoever being engaged in the business of betting or wagering knowingly uses a wire communication facility for the transmission in interstate or foreign commerce of bets or wagers or information assisting in the placing of bets or wagers on any sporting event or contest, or for the transmission of a wire communication which entitles the recipient to receive money or credit as a result of bets or wagers, or for information assisting in the placing of bets or wagers, shall be fined under this title or imprisoned not more than two years, or both.

(b) Nothing in this section shall be construed to prevent the transmission in interstate or foreign commerce of information for use in news reporting of sporting events or contests, or for the transmission of information assisting in the placing of bets or wagers on a sporting event or contest from a State or foreign country where betting on that sporting event or contest is legal into a State or foreign country in which such betting is legal.

18 USC § 1301. IMPORTING OR TRANSPORTING LOTTERY TICKETS

Whoever brings into the United States for the purpose of disposing of the same, or knowingly deposits with any express company or other common carrier for carriage, or carries in interstate or foreign commerce any paper, certificate, or instrument purporting to be or to represent a ticket, chance, share, or interest in or dependent upon the event of a lottery, gift enterprise, or similar scheme, offering prizes dependent in whole or in part upon lot or chance, or any advertisement of, or list of the prizes drawn or awarded by means of, any such lottery, gift enterprise, or similar scheme; or, being engaged in the business of procuring for a person in 1 State such a ticket, chance, share, or interest in a lottery, gift, enterprise or similar scheme conducted by another State (unless that business is permitted under an agreement between the States in question or appropriate authorities of those States), knowingly transmits in interstate or foreign commerce information to be used for the purpose of procuring such a ticket, chance, share, or interest; or knowingly takes or receives any such paper, certificate, instrument, advertisement, or list so brought, deposited, or transported, shall be fined under this title or imprisoned not more than two years, or both.

* * *

The states exercise a great deal of flexibility in charting their own courses on gambling law, with some still committed to general criminalization, and others turning toward greater legalization. Even states that permit gambling, though, often face other criminal challenges—like cheating, game-rigging, and outright fraud.

State

NEW YORK PENAL LAW § 225.00 (2006)

The following definitions are applicable to this article:

1. "Contest of chance" means any contest, game, gaming scheme or gaming devise in which the outcome depends in a material degree upon an element of chance, notwithstanding that skill of the contestants may also be a factor therein.

2. "Gambling." A person engages in gambling when he stakes or risks something of value upon the outcome of a contest of chance or a future contingent event not under his control or influence, upon an agreement or understanding that he will receive something of value in the event of a certain outcome.

3. "Slot machine" means a gambling device which, as a result of the insertion of a coin or other object, operates, either completely automatically or with the aid of some physical act by the player, in such manner that, depending upon elements of chance, it may eject something of value. A device so constructed, or readily adaptable or convertible to such use, is no less a slot machine because it is not in working order or because some mechanical act of manipulation or repair is required to accomplish its adaptation, conversion or workability. Nor is it any less a slot machine because, apart from its use or adaptability as such, it may also sell or deliver something of value on a basis other than chance. A machine which sells items of merchandise which are of equivalent value, is not a slot machine merely because such items differ from each other in composition, size, shape or color. A machine which awards free or extended play is not a slot machine merely because such free or extended play may constitute something of value provided that the outcome

depends in a material degree upon the skill of the player and not in a material degree upon an element of chance.

4. "Bookmaking" means advancing gambling activity by unlawfully accepting bets from members of the public as a business, rather than in a casual or personal fashion, upon the outcomes of future contingent events.

5. "Lottery" means an unlawful gambling scheme in which (a) the players pay or agree to pay something of value for chances, represented and differentiated by numbers or by combinations of numbers or by some other media, one or more of which chances are to be designated the winning ones; and (b) the winning chances are to be determined by a drawing or by some other method based upon the element of chance; and (c) the holders of the winning chances are to receive something of value provided, however, that in no event shall the provisions of this subdivision be construed to include a raffle as such term is defined in subdivision three-b of section one hundred eighty-six of the general municipal law.

6. "Policy" or "the numbers game" means a form of lottery in which the winning chances or plays are not determined upon the basis of a drawing or other act on the part of persons conducting or connected with the scheme, but upon the basis of the outcome or outcomes of a future contingent event or events otherwise unrelated to the particular scheme.

TEXAS PENAL CODE § 47.02 (2005)

(a) A person commits an offense if he:

(1) makes a bet on the partial or final result of a game or contest or on the performance of a participant in a game or contest;

(2) makes a bet on the result of any political nomination, appointment, or election or on the degree of success of any nominee, appointee, or candidate; or

(3) plays and bets for money or other thing of value at any game played with cards, dice, balls, or any other gambling device.

(b) It is a defense to prosecution under this section that:

(1) the actor engaged in gambling in a private place;

(2) no person received any economic benefit other than personal winnings; and

(3) except for the advantage of skill or luck, the risks of losing and the chances of winning were the same for all participants.

NEVADA REVISED STATUTES 465.015. DEFINITIONS.

As used in this chapter:

1. "Cheat" means to alter the elements of chance, method of selection or criteria which determine:

(a) The result of a game;

(b) The amount or frequency of payment in a game;

(c) The value of a wagering instrument; or

(d) The value of a wagering credit.

NEVADA REVISED STATUTES 465.070. FRAUDULENT ACTS.

It is unlawful for any person:

1. To alter or misrepresent the outcome of a game or other event on which wagers have been made after the outcome is made sure but before it is revealed to the players.

2. To place, increase or decrease a bet or to determine the course of play after acquiring knowledge, not available to all players, of the outcome of the game or any event that affects the outcome of the game or which is the subject of the bet or to aid anyone in acquiring such knowledge for the purpose of placing, increasing or decreasing a bet or determining the course of play contingent upon that event or outcome.

3. To claim, collect or take, or attempt to claim, collect or take, money or anything of value in or from a gambling game, with intent to defraud, without having made a wager contingent thereon, or to claim, collect or take an amount greater than the amount won.

4. Knowingly to entice or induce another to go to any place where a gambling game is being conducted or operated in violation of the provisions of this chapter, with the intent that the other person play or participate in that gambling game.

5. To place or increase a bet after acquiring knowledge of the outcome of the game or other event which is the subject of the bet, including past-posting and pressing bets.

6. To reduce the amount wagered or cancel the bet after acquiring knowledge of the outcome of the game or other event which is the subject of the bet, including pinching bets.

7. To manipulate, with the intent to cheat, any component of a gaming device in a manner contrary to the designed and normal operational purpose for the component, including, but not limited to, varying the pull of the handle of a slot machine, with knowledge that the manipulation affects the outcome of the game or with knowledge of any event that affects the outcome of the game.

8. To offer, promise or give anything of value to anyone for the purpose of influencing the outcome of a race, sporting event, contest or game upon which a wager may be made, or to place, increase or decrease a wager after acquiring knowledge, not available to the general public, that anyone has been offered, promised or given anything of value for the purpose of influencing the outcome of the race, sporting event, contest or game upon which the wager is placed, increased or decreased.

9. To change or alter the normal outcome of any game played on an interactive gaming system or the way in which the outcome is reported to any participant in the game.

4. A CASE STUDY IN LEGALIZATION: THE LINE BETWEEN CIVIL REGULATION AND CRIMINALIZATION IN INDIAN GAMING

JESSICA R. CATTELINO—INDIAN GAMING IN THE UNITED STATES

In *Handbook of North American Indians*, Smithsonian Institution, 2007.

The origins of tribal gaming were modest. On December 14, 1979, the Seminole Tribe of Florida opened the first tribally-operated high-stakes bingo hall in Native North America on the corner of State Road 7 and Stirling Road in Hollywood, Florida. Broward County sheriff Robert Butterworth promptly sought to close the bingo hall, arguing that it violated state gambling laws. The Seminole Tribe successfully defended gaming in the courts, winning a federal appellate court ruling that the relevant Florida state gaming regulations were civil, not criminal, and as such that the tribe, not the state, had jurisdiction over tribal gaming (658 F.2d 310 [5th Cir. 1981]). In 1987, the United States Supreme Court ruled similarly in *California v. Cabazon Band of Mission Indians* (480 U.S. 202 [1987]) that the tribal government could operate high-stakes card rooms. This ruling also drew a distinction between state gaming laws that were criminal/prohibitory and those that were civil/regulatory, affirming tribal governments' protection from the latter. Subsequently, tribal governments across the continent began to launch gaming operations. Ensuing pressures from states and other interests led Congress to enact the Indian Gaming Regulatory Act (IGRA) in 1988.

Federal gaming laws have shaped the history and status of tribal casinos, but the top-down perspective of federal law can blind observers to the origins and meanings of Indian gaming. The origin of tribal gaming in its current form, after all, was not with federal law but with tribal action. Tribes such as Florida Seminoles and Cabazons opened casinos as an assertion of their sovereignty-based right to operate and regulate on-reservation activities, but even more as a mechanism for reversing sustained and endemic reservation poverty. Decisions about whether and how to pursue gaming prompted Native communities to debate their pasts, futures, and values. Some tribal nations, including the Navajo, Onondaga, and Hopi Nations, rejected gaming, at least during the initial years, for diverse reasons that included fear of gambling's social consequences and philosophical, religious, and moral opposition to gambling. . . .

LEGAL FRAMEWORK

The Indian Gaming Regulatory Act of 1988 stated its purposes as threefold: first, to provide a statutory basis for tribal gaming in order to promote tribal economic development and governance; second, to author-ize regulation of tribal gaming; and third, to establish the National Indian Gaming Commission as the federal regulatory authority over tribal gaming (25 U.S.C. §§ 2701–2721).... The Act outlined three classes of tribal gaming, which became important as the bases for differing levels of regulation and the focal points of legal and political maneuvering. First, "class I gaming" refers to social games with prizes of minimal value or traditional forms of Indian gaming. "Class II gaming" includes bingo (paper and electronic) played for money and card games (excluding banking games like blackjack) not prohibited by the laws of the state, so long as they are played in conformity with state regulations. The most controversial is "class III gaming," which includes all forms of gaming, such as slot machines, that do not fall under class I or class II. Class I gaming is within the exclusive jurisdiction of Indian tribes, and class II gaming is also within tribal jurisdiction, but subject to provisions of IGRA. IGRA limited the use of class II and III tribal gaming revenues to: funding for tribal government operations; provi-sions for the general welfare of the tribe and its members; promotion of tribal economic development; donations to charity; and funding of local government agencies. A tribe pursuing class III gaming must enter into negotiations with the state for the purpose of entering into a tribal-state compact governing gaming activities, and this provision has been the focus of litigation, hard-ball politics, and debate about sovereignty and federalism. States are to negotiate in good faith, but this has not always occurred. IGRA originally specified that U.S. courts had jurisdiction over state failures to enter into good-faith negotiations, but in the important federalism case *Seminole Tribe v. Florida* (517 U.S. 44 [1996]) the U.S. Supreme Court ruled that under the Eleventh Amendment states were immune from suit by tribes in federal court unless a state had waived its sovereign immunity. Efforts to find a "Seminole fix" remained underway in 2006, with some tribes pursuing class III agreements directly with the Secretary of the Interior; this "fix" would place gaming negotiations at a nation-to-nation level between tribal governments and the U.S. federal government.

The National Indian Gaming Commission (NIGC), established by IGRA, is the independent federal agency that regulates tribal gaming. The NIGC conducts background investigations, limits the terms of tribal contracts with casino management companies, reviews tribal ordinances to ensure compliance with IGRA, and enacted and enforces a set of regulations entitled the "Minimum Internal Control Standards" (MICS). NIGC has the authority to fine and close tribal gaming operations.

CALIFORNIA v. CABAZON BAND OF MISSION INDIANS

Supreme Court of the United States, 1987.
480 U.S. 202.

JUSTICE WHITE delivered the opinion of the Court.

The Cabazon and Morongo Bands of Mission Indians, federally recognized Indian Tribes, occupy reservations in Riverside County, Cali-fornia. Each Band, pursuant to an ordinance approved by the Secretary of the Interior, conducts bingo games on its reservation. The Cabazon Band has also opened a card club at which draw poker and other card games are played. The games are open to the public and are played predominantly by non-Indians coming onto the reservations. The games are a major source of employment for tribal members, and the profits are the Tribes' sole source of income. The State of California seeks to apply to the two Tribes Cal. Penal Code Ann. § 326.5 (West Supp. 1987). That statute does not entirely prohibit the playing of bingo but permits it when the games are operated and staffed by members of designated charitable organizations who may not be paid for their services. Profits must be kept in special accounts and used only for charitable purposes; prizes may not exceed $250 per game. Asserting that the bingo games on the two reservations violated each of these restrictions, California insisted that the Tribes comply with state law. Riverside County also sought to apply its local Ordinance No. 558, regulating bingo, as well as its Ordinance No. 331, prohibiting the playing of draw poker and the other card games.

The Tribes sued the county in Federal District Court seeking a declaratory judgment that the county had no authority to apply its ordinances inside the reservations and an injunction against their enforcement. The State intervened, the facts were stipulated, and the District Court granted the Tribes' motion for summary judgment, holding that neither the State nor the county had any authority to enforce its gambling laws within the reservations. The Court of Appeals for the Ninth Circuit affirmed, 783 F.2d 900 (1986), the State and the county appealed, and we postponed jurisdiction to the hearing on the merits. 476 U.S. 1168.

I

The Court has consistently recognized that Indian tribes retain "attributes of sovereignty over both their members and their territory," *United States v. Mazurie*, 419 U.S. 544, 557 (1975), and that "tribal sovereignty is dependent on, and subordinate to, only the Federal Government, not the States," *Washington v. Confederated Tribes of Colville Indian Reservation*, 447 U.S. 134, 154 (1980). It is clear, however, that state laws may be applied to tribal Indians on their reservations if Congress has expressly so provided. Here, the State insists that Congress has twice given its express consent: first in Pub. L. 280 in 1953, 67 Stat. 588, as amended, 18 U. S. C. § 1162, 28 U. S. C. § 1360 (1982 ed. and Supp. III), and second in the Organized Crime Control Act in 1970, 84 Stat. 937, 18 U. S. C. § 1955. We disagree in both respects.

In Pub. L. 280, Congress expressly granted six States, including California, jurisdiction over specified areas of Indian country within the States and provided for the assumption of jurisdiction by other States. In § 2, California was granted broad criminal jurisdiction over offenses committed by or against Indians within all Indian country within the State. Section 4's grant of civil jurisdiction was more limited. In *Bryan v. Itasca County*, 426 U.S. 373 (1976), we interpreted § 4 to grant States jurisdiction over private civil litigation involving reservation Indians in state court, but not to grant general civil regulatory authority. Id., at 385, 388–390. We held, therefore, that Minnesota could not apply its personal property tax within the reservation. Congress' primary concern in enacting Pub. L. 280 was combating lawlessness on reservations. Id., at 379–380. The Act plainly was not intended to effect total assimilation of Indian tribes into mainstream American society. Id., at 387. We recognized that a grant to States of general civil regulatory power over Indian reservations would result in the destruction of tribal institutions and values. Accordingly, when a State seeks to enforce a law within an Indian reservation under the authority of Pub. L. 280, it must be determined whether the law is criminal in nature, and thus fully applicable to the reservation under § 2, or civil in nature, and applicable only as it may be relevant to private civil litigation in state court.

The Minnesota personal property tax at issue in *Bryan* was unquestionably civil in nature. The California bingo statute is not so easily categorized. California law permits bingo games to be conducted only by charitable and other specified organizations, and then only by their members who may not receive any wage or profit for doing so; prizes are limited and receipts are to be segregated and used only for charitable purposes. Violation of any of these provisions is a misdemeanor. California insists that these are criminal laws which Pub. L. 280 permits it to enforce on the reservations.

Following its earlier decision in [*Barona Group of Capitan Grande Band of Mission Indians, San Diego County, Cal. v. Duffy,*] 694 F.2d 1185 (1982), cert. denied, 461 U.S. 929 (1983), which also involved the applicability of § 326.5 of the California Penal Code to Indian reservations, the Court of Appeals rejected this submission. 783 F.2d, at 901–903. In Barona, applying what it thought to be the civil/criminal dichotomy drawn in *Bryan v. Itasca County*, the Court of Appeals drew a distinction between state "criminal/prohibitory" laws and state "civil/regulatory" laws: if the intent of a state law is generally to prohibit certain conduct, it falls within Pub. L. 280's grant of criminal jurisdiction, but if the state law generally permits the conduct at issue, subject to regulation, it must be classified as civil/regulatory and Pub. L. 280 does not authorize its enforcement on an Indian reservation. The shorthand test is whether the conduct at issue violates the State's public policy. Inquiring into the nature of § 326.5, the Court of Appeals held that it was regulatory rather than prohibitory. This was the analysis employed, with similar results, by the Court of Appeals for the Fifth Circuit in *Seminole Tribe of Florida v. Butterworth*, 658 F.2d 310 (1981), cert. denied, 455 U.S. 1020 (1982), which the Ninth Circuit found persuasive.

We are persuaded that the prohibitory/regulatory distinction is consistent with Bryan's construction of Pub. L. 280. It is not a bright-line rule, however; and as the Ninth Circuit itself observed, an argument of some weight may be made that the bingo statute is prohibitory rather than regulatory. But in the present case, the court reexamined the state law and reaffirmed its holding in Barona, and we are reluctant to disagree with that court's view of the nature and intent of the state law at issue here.

There is surely a fair basis for its conclusion. California does not prohibit all forms of gambling. California itself operates a state lottery, Cal. Govt. Code Ann. § 8880 et seq. (West Supp. 1987), and daily encourages its citizens to participate in this state-run gambling. California also permits parimutuel horse-race betting. Cal. Bus. & Prof. Code Ann. § § 19400–19667 (West 1964 and Supp. 1987). Although certain enumerated gambling games are prohibited under Cal. Penal Code Ann. § 330 (West Supp. 1987), games not enumerated, including the card games played in the Cabazon card club, are permissible. The Tribes assert that more than 400 card rooms similar to the Cabazon card club flourish in California, and the State does not dispute this fact. Brief for Appellees 47–48. Also, as the Court of Appeals noted, bingo is legally sponsored by many different organizations and is widely played in California. There is no effort to forbid the playing of bingo by any member of the public over the age of 18. Indeed, the permitted bingo games must be open to the general public. Nor is there any limit on the number of games which eligible organizations may operate, the receipts which they may obtain from the games, the number of games which a participant may play, or the amount of money which a participant may spend, either per game or in total. In light of the fact that California permits a substantial amount of gambling activity, including bingo, and actually promotes gambling through its state lottery, we must conclude that California regulates rather than prohibits gambling in general and bingo in particular.

California argues, however, that high stakes, unregulated bingo, the conduct which attracts organized crime, is a misdemeanor in California and may be prohibited on Indian reservations. But that an otherwise regulatory law is enforceable by criminal as well as civil means does not necessarily convert it into a criminal law within the meaning of Pub. L. 280. Otherwise, the distinction between § 2 and § 4 of that law could easily be avoided and total assimilation permitted. This view, adopted here and by the Fifth Circuit in the *Butterworth* case, we find persuasive. Accordingly, we conclude that [HN9] Pub. L. 280 does not authorize California to enforce Cal. Penal Code Ann. § 326.5 (West Supp. 1987) within the Cabazon and Morongo Reservations.

California and Riverside County also argue that the Organized Crime Control Act (OCCA) authorizes the application of their gambling laws to the tribal bingo enterprises. The OCCA makes certain violations of state and local gambling laws violations of federal law. The Court of Appeals rejected appellants' argument, relying on its earlier decisions in *United States v. Farris*, 624 F.2d 890 (CA9 1980), cert. denied, 449 U.S. 1111 (1981), and *Barona Group of Capitan Grande Band of Mission*

Indians, San Diego County, Cal. v. Duffy, 694 F.2d 1185 (1982). 783 F.2d, at 903. The court explained that whether a tribal activity is "a violation of the law of a state" within the meaning of OCCA depends on whether it violates the "public policy" of the State, the same test for application of state law under Pub. L. 280, and similarly concluded that bingo is not contrary to the public policy of California.

The Court of Appeals for the Sixth Circuit has rejected this view. *United States v. Dakota*, 796 F.2d 186 (1986). Since the OCCA standard is simply whether the gambling business is being operated in "violation of the law of a State," there is no basis for the regulatory/prohibitory distinction that it agreed is suitable in construing and applying Pub. L. 280. 796 F.2d, at 188. And because enforcement of OCCA is an exercise of federal rather than state authority, there is no danger of state encroachment on Indian tribal sovereignty. Ibid. This latter observation exposes the flaw in appellants' reliance on OCCA. That enactment is indeed a federal law that, among other things, defines certain federal crimes over which the district courts have exclusive jurisdiction. There is nothing in OCCA indicating that the States are to have any part in enforcing federal criminal laws or are authorized to make arrests on Indian reservations that in the absence of OCCA they could not affect. We are not informed of any federal efforts to employ OCCA to prosecute the playing of bingo on Indian reservations, although there are more than 100 such enterprises currently in operation, many of which have been in existence for several years, for the most part with the encouragement of the Federal Government. Whether or not, then, the Sixth Circuit is right and the Ninth Circuit wrong about the coverage of OCCA, a matter that we do not decide, there is no warrant for California to make arrests on reservations and thus, through OCCA, enforce its gambling laws against Indian tribes.

II

Because the state and county laws at issue here are imposed directly on the Tribes that operate the games, and are not expressly permitted by Congress, the Tribes argue that the judgment below should be affirmed without more. They rely on the statement in *McClanahan v. Arizona State Tax Comm'n*, 411 U.S. 164, 170–171 (1973), that " '[state] laws generally are not applicable to tribal Indians on an Indian reservation except where Congress has expressly provided that State laws shall apply' " (quoting United States Dept. of the Interior, Federal Indian Law 845 (1958)). Our cases, however, have not established an inflexible per se rule precluding state jurisdiction over tribes and tribal members in the absence of express congressional consent. "[Under] certain circumstances a State may validly assert authority over the activities of nonmembers on a reservation, and ... in exceptional circumstances a State may assert jurisdiction over the on-reservation activities of tribal members." *New Mexico v. Mescalero Apache Tribe*, 462 U.S. 324, 331–332 (1983) (footnotes omitted). Both *Moe v. Confederated Salish and Kootenai Tribes*, 425 U.S. 463 (1976), and *Washington v. Confederated*

Tribes of Colville Indian Reservation, 447 U.S. 134 (1980), are illustrative. In those decisions we held that, in the absence of express congressional permission, a State could require tribal smokeshops on Indian reservations to collect state sales tax from their non-Indian customers. Both cases involved nonmembers entering and purchasing tobacco products on the reservations involved. The State's interest in assuring the collection of sales taxes from non-Indians enjoying the off-reservation services of the State was sufficient to warrant the minimal burden imposed on the tribal smokeshop operators.

This case also involves a state burden on tribal Indians in the context of their dealings with non-Indians since the question is whether the State may prevent the Tribes from making available high stakes bingo games to non-Indians coming from outside the reservations. Decision in this case turns on whether state authority is pre-empted by the operation of federal law; and "[state] jurisdiction is pre-empted ... if it interferes or is incompatible with federal and tribal interests reflected in federal law, unless the state interests at stake are sufficient to justify the assertion of state authority." Mescalero, 462 U.S., at 333, 334. The inquiry is to proceed in light of traditional notions of Indian sovereignty and the congressional goal of Indian self-government, including its "overriding goal" of encouraging tribal self-sufficiency and economic development. Id., at 334–335. See also, *Iowa Mutual Insurance Co. v. LaPlante*, ante, p. 9; *White Mountain Apache Tribe v. Bracker*, 448 U.S. 136, 143 (1980).

These are important federal interests. They were reaffirmed by the President's 1983 Statement on Indian Policy. More specifically, the Department of the Interior, which has the primary responsibility for carrying out the Federal Government's trust obligations to Indian tribes, has sought to implement these policies by promoting tribal bingo enterprises. Under the Indian Financing Act of 1974, 25 U. S. C. § 1451 et seq. (1982 ed. and Supp. III), the Secretary of the Interior has made grants and has guaranteed loans for the purpose of constructing bingo facilities. See S. Rep. No. 99–493, p. 5 (1986); *Mashantucket Pequot Tribe v. McGuigan*, 626 F.Supp. 245, 246 (Conn. 1986). The Department of Housing and Urban Development and the Department of Health and Human Services have also provided financial assistance to develop tribal gaming enterprises. See S. Rep. No. 99–493, supra, at 5. Here, the Secretary of the Interior has approved tribal ordinances establishing and regulating the gaming activities involved. See H. R. Rep. No. 99–488, p. 10 (1986). The Secretary has also exercised his authority to review tribal bingo management contracts under 25 U. S. C. § 81, and has issued detailed guidelines governing that review. App. to Motion to Dismiss Appeal or Affirm Judgment 63a–70a.

These policies and actions, which demonstrate the Government's approval and active promotion of tribal bingo enterprises, are of particular relevance in this case. The Cabazon and Morongo Reservations contain no natural resources which can be exploited. The tribal games at present provide the sole source of revenues for the operation of the tribal governments and the provision of tribal services. They are also the major sources of employment on the reservations. Self-determination and economic development are not within reach if the Tribes cannot raise revenues and provide employment for their members. The Tribes' interests obviously parallel the federal interests.

California seeks to diminish the weight of these seemingly important tribal interests by asserting that the Tribes are merely marketing an exemption from state gambling laws. In *Washington v. Confederated Tribes of Colville Indian Reservation*, 447 U.S., at 155, we held that the State could tax cigarettes sold by tribal smokeshops to non-Indians, even though it would eliminate their competitive advantage and substantially reduce revenues used to provide tribal services, because the Tribes had no right "to market an exemption from state taxation to persons who would normally do their business elsewhere." We stated that "[it] is painfully apparent that the value marketed by the smokeshops to persons coming from outside is not generated on the reservations by activities in which the Tribes have a significant interest." Ibid. Here, however, the Tribes are not merely importing a product onto the reservations for immediate resale to non-Indians. They have built modern facilities which provide recreational opportunities and ancillary services to their patrons, who do not simply drive onto the reservations, make purchases and depart, but spend extended periods of time there enjoying the services the Tribes provide. The Tribes have a strong incentive to provide comfortable, clean, and attractive facilities and well-run games in order to increase attendance at the games. The tribal bingo enterprises are similar to the resort complex, featuring hunting and fishing, that the Mescalero Apache Tribe operates on its reservation through the "concerted and sustained" management of reservation land and wildlife resources. *New Mexico v. Mescalero Apache Tribe*, 462 U.S., at 341. The Mescalero project generates funds for essential tribal services and provides employment for tribal members. We there rejected the notion that the Tribe is merely marketing an exemption from state hunting and fishing regulations and concluded that New Mexico could not regulate on-reservation fishing and hunting by non-Indians. Ibid. Similarly, the Cabazon and Morongo Bands are generating value on the reservations through activities in which they have a substantial interest.

The State also relies on *Rice v. Rehner*, 463 U.S. 713 (1983), in which we held that California could require a tribal member and a federally licensed Indian trader operating a general store on a reservation to obtain a state license in order to sell liquor for off-premises consumption. But our decision there rested on the grounds that Congress had never recognized any sovereign tribal interest in regulating liquor traffic and that Congress, historically, had plainly anticipated that the States would exercise concurrent authority to regulate the use and distribution of liquor on Indian reservations. There is no such traditional federal view governing the outcome of this case, since, as we have explained, the current federal policy is to promote precisely what California seeks to prevent.

The sole interest asserted by the State to justify the imposition of its bingo laws on the Tribes is in preventing the infiltration of the tribal games by organized crime. To the extent that the State seeks to prevent any and all bingo games from being played on tribal lands while permitting regulated, off-reservation games, this asserted interest is irrelevant and the state and county laws are pre-empted. Even to the extent that the State and county seek to regulate short of prohibition, the laws are pre-empted. The State insists that the high stakes offered at tribal games are attractive to organized crime, whereas the controlled games authorized under California law are not. This is surely a legitimate concern, but we are unconvinced that it is sufficient to escape the pre-emptive force of federal and tribal interests apparent in this case. California does not allege any present criminal involvement in the Cabazon and Morongo enterprises, and the Ninth Circuit discerned none. 783 F.2d, at 904. An official of the Department of Justice has expressed some concern about tribal bingo operations, but far from any action being taken evidencing this concern—and surely the Federal Government has the authority to forbid Indian gambling enterprises—the prevailing federal policy continues to support these tribal enterprises, including those of the Tribes involved in this case.

We conclude that the State's interest in preventing the infiltration of the tribal bingo enterprises by organized crime does not justify state regulation of the tribal bingo enterprises in light of the compelling federal and tribal interests supporting them. State regulation would impermissibly infringe on tribal government, and this conclusion applies equally to the county's attempted regulation of the Cabazon card club. We therefore affirm the judgment of the Court of Appeals and remand the case for further proceedings consistent with this opinion.

C. THE DIFFERENT TYPES OF GAMBLING

There are at least three major types of commercial gambling, and in each case, they are the outgrowth of a different type of betting. The first consists of lotteries and have included over time numbers games, bingo, and other games of chance that depend on the drawing of numbers. There are, of course, non-monetary lotteries that are used regularly, such as for instance the military draft or course assignments. Cards, dice, and gaming machines represent a second type of gambling that has become associated, today, with casino gambling (and internet gambling). The third type is sports and events betting, which is somewhat unique in that it remains illegal under federal law. Though gambling on sporting events is as old as the sports themselves, it retains a stigma that other forms of gambling do not. Many argue that this is because of the corruption and "fixing" inevitably associated with such gambling, much of which has been very high-profile. The most infamous scandal involved the 1919 World Series, which eight members of the Chicago White Sox were discovered to have deliberately lost in exchange for large cash bribes. Though nothing this severe has emerged since, there have been plenty of smaller gambling-related scandals: in 1989, Pete Rose was permanently expelled from Major League Baseball after he was discovered placing bets on games in which he was involved; during the 90's, college athletes at Northwestern University, Arizona State University, and other schools were suspended and denied scholarships after being charged with accepting bribes to throw games.

D. THE SCALE OF GAMBLING

THE NATIONAL GAMBLING IMPACT STUDY COMMISSION—FINAL REPORT, JUNE 1999

[Chapter 2: Gambling in the United States].

LOTTERIES

Growth of Lotteries

Along with the lottery's rapid expansion, lottery revenues have increased dramatically over the years. In 1973 lotteries were found in 7 states and had total sales of $2 billion. In 1997 lotteries existed in 37 states and the District of Columbia and garnered $34 billion in sales, not counting electronic gambling devices (EGD's) sales. This rapid growth is a result of both the expansion of lotteries into new states and increased per capita sales, from $35 per capita in 1973 to $150 in 1997. In addition to expansion and increased per capita sales, technological advances have played a major role in lottery growth, especially on-line computer links between retail outlets and the central computer, which are required for the daily numbers games and lotto. Changing technologies also have allowed lotteries to branch out into new games enabling them to compete with casino-style gambling.

The Contradictory Role of State Governments

The lottery industry stands out in the gambling industry by virtue of several unique features. First, it is the most widespread form of gambling in the United States. It also is the only form of commercial gambling that a majority of adults report having played. Furthermore, the lottery industry is the only form of gambling in the United States that is a virtual government monopoly. State lotteries have the worst odds of any common form of gambling, but promise the greatest potential payoff to the winner in absolute terms, with prizes regularly amounting to tens of millions of dollars. One theme that emerged at the Commission hearings is the contradictory role of state government as an active promoter of lotteries while imposing a heavy "sin" tax on the lottery buyer. According to experts, states have "gone into business selling a popular consumer product, and they have carried on with Madison Avenue gusto and an unfettered dedication to the bottom line. The complete about-face from prohibition to promotion in one state after another is remarkable, to say the least." Lotteries are established and run exclusively by state governments and the government of the District of Columbia. Since the beginning of the wave of lotteries in the 1960's, state governments have seized on the lottery as a state-operated monopoly. State governments have become dependent on lottery sales as a source of revenue, and have tried to justify the money by earmarking it for good causes, such as education. The lotteries are used to finance various state programs and services. Of the 38 state lotteries, the revenue from only 10 go into their general funds. Of the remaining states, 16 earmark all or part of the lottery revenues for education, making that the most common use of lottery funds. For example, in Georgia lottery money is used for the HOPE Scholarship Program, which provides college scholarships, and for kindergarten education for 65,000 children. Georgia also sets aside several hundred thousand dollars of lottery profits for gambling treatment programs. Other uses range from the broad (parks and recreation, tax relief, and economic development) to the narrow (Mariner's Stadium in Washington and police and fireman pensions in Indiana).

CONVENIENCE GAMBLING AND STAND–ALONE ELECTRONIC GAMBLING DEVICES

The terms "convenience gaming" and "retail gaming" have been used to describe legal, standalone slot machines, video poker, video keno, and other EGD's that have proliferated in bars, truck stops, convenience stores, and a variety of other locations across several states. However, these terms do not adequately convey the range of locations at which EGD gambling takes place, nor do they describe the spectrum of laws and regulations that apply (or fail to apply) to EGD's. Some states, including Louisiana, Montana, and South Carolina, permit private sector businesses to operate EGD's; in other states, such as Oregon and California, this form of gambling is operated by the state lottery. In Nevada, slot machines can be found in many public locations, including airports and supermarkets. Montana was the first state after Nevada to legalize stand-alone EGD's, specifically video poker in bars. In California, video keno operated by the state lottery can be found in most traditional lottery outlets and in many other locations as well.

South Carolina, where video poker has been legal for 8 years, reports by far the largest number of legal, non-casino EGD's. In that state video poker machines, which can be played 24 hours a day excluding Sundays,15 operate in about 7,500 separate establishments, including bars, restaurants, gas stations, convenience stores, and "video game malls." Video poker machines started as arcade games where players could only win credits to replay the game, but in 1991, the South Carolina Supreme Court ruled that cash payoffs were legal if the money did not come directly from the gaming device. According to recent figures from the South Carolina Department of Revenue, EGD's in that state generated $2.5 billion in annual gross machine receipts (cash in) and paid prizes (cash out) to players of $1.8 billion, a payout rate of approximately 71 percent. Video poker licensing fees yielded $60 million during the most recent fiscal year. Although several states have legalized standalone EGD's, illegal and quasi-legal EGD's offering a similar if not identical gambling experience to legal EGD's are common in the bars and fraternal organizations of many other states, including West Virginia, New Jersey, Alabama, Illinois, and Texas. Quasi-legal EGD's are often referred to as "gray machines" because they exist in a gray area of the law. Typically, they are legal as long as no winnings are paid out—in fact, they are often labeled "For Amusement Only." In practice, however, winnings are not paid out directly by the machine, but are instead paid more or less surreptitiously by the establishment in either monetary or non-monetary forms.

ISSUES

One controversial feature of legal and illegal EGD's is their location. Because this form of gambling occurs in close proximity to residential areas and/or at consumer oriented sites, patrons regularly encounter them in the course of their day-to-day activities. Most other forms of gambling take place at gambling-oriented sites, such as casinos and racetracks, which patrons visit specifically for the purpose of gambling and other entertainment. EGD's proliferate rapidly because they can be purchased and installed quickly at existing sites with a relatively small capital investment. By contrast, casinos and racetracks require substantial capital investment and cannot be built overnight. This form of gambling creates few jobs and fewer good quality jobs, and it is not accompanied by any significant investment in the local economy. Opponents of convenience gambling argue that electronic gambling creates dependency and should not be widely available or legalized.

CASINOS

Before the beginning of this decade, legalized casinos operated in two jurisdictions: Nevada and Atlantic City. Casinos are now legalized in 28 states. With the multiplication of locations, there was a metamorphosis of the types of casinos. In addition to Las Vegas resort casinos, there are now nearly 100 riverboat and dockside casinos in six states and approximately 260 casinos on Indian reservations. The expansion of gambling to these new sites has been called the "most significant development" in the industry in the 1990s. Casinos are an important source of entertainment, jobs, and income. The largest casino markets are: Nevada, with 429 full-scale casinos, 1,978 slots-only locations, one Indian casino, and gross casino revenues for 1997 of $7.87 billion; New Jersey, with 14 casinos and gross casino revenues for 1997 of $3.9 billion; and Mississippi, with 29 state-regulated casinos, one Indian casino, and gross casino revenues for 1997 of $1.98 billion. The largest concentration of casinos are in urban areas, including Clark County and Las Vegas, with 211 casinos, 30.5 million visitors in 1997, and gross casino revenues for 1997 of $6.2 billion accounting for 79 percent of the Nevada market; Atlantic City, where all of New Jersey's 14 casinos are located, with 34.07 million visitors in 1997, and gross casino revenues for 1997 of $3.9 billion accounting for 100 percent of the New Jersey market; and Tunica County (Mississippi), with 10 casinos, approximately

17.4 million visitors in 1997 and gross casino revenues for 1997 of $933.3 million accounting for 47 percent of the Mississippi casino market. For many people, casinos symbolize the gambling industry. Hence, casino locations are often viewed as indicative of a community's embrace of the gambling industry.

Riverboat Casinos

Riverboat casinos are a relatively new, and uniquely American, phenomenon. Riverboat casinos began operating in Iowa in 1991, and quickly expanded throughout the Midwest. By 1998 there were over 40 riverboat casinos in operation in Illinois, Indiana, Missouri, Iowa, and nearly 50 riverboat and dockside casinos in Louisiana and Mississippi. In 1997 revenues for riverboats totaled $6.1 billion. The same year, riverboats paid over $1 billion in gambling privilege taxes. And growth has continued, with revenues up 11.3 percent from 1996 to 1997. With these original states now approaching saturation point, several state governments have decided to take a closer look at the record compiled so rapidly by this industry. Iowa, the pioneer state, recently legislated a 5–year moratorium on the expansion of casinos, in part to allow time to assess the impact to date; Indiana has established a commission to examine and report on the economic and social effects stemming from the state's experience with gambling.

Native American Tribal Gambling

Large-scale Indian casino gambling is barely a decade old. Most Native American tribal gambling started after 1987, when the United States Supreme Court issued a "landmark decision" in *California* v. *Cabazon Band of Mission Indians.* This decision, in effect, confirmed the inability of states to regulate commercial gambling on Indian reservations. In an effort to provide a regulatory framework for Indian gambling, Congress passed the *Indian Gaming Regulatory Act* (IGRA) in 1988. IGRA provides a statutory basis for the regulation of Indian gambling, specifying several mechanisms and procedures and including the requirement that the revenues from gambling be used to promote the economic development and welfare of tribes. For casino gambling— which IGRA terms "Class III" gambling—the legislation requires tribes to negotiate a compact with their respective states, a provision that has been a continuing source of controversy and which will be discussed at length later in this chapter. The result of those two developments was a rapid expansion of Indian gambling. From 1988, when IGRA was passed, to 1997, tribal gambling revenues grew more than thirty-fold, from $212 million to $6.7 billion. By comparison, the revenues from non-Indian casino gambling (hereinafter termed "commercial gambling") roughly doubled over the same period, from $9.6 billion to $20.5 billion in constant 1997 dollars. As was IGRA's intention, gambling revenues have proven to be a very important source of funding for many tribal governments, providing much-needed improvements in the health, education, and welfare of Native Americans on reservations across the

United States. Nevertheless, Indian gambling has not been a panacea for the many economic and social problems that Native Americans continue to face. More than two-thirds of Indian tribes do not participate in Indian gambling at all. Only a small percentage of Indian tribes operate gambling facilities on their reservations. According to the Bureau of Indian Affairs (BIA), there are 554 federally recognized tribes in the United States, with 1,652,897 members, or less than 1 percent of the U.S. population. Of these 554 tribes, 146 have Class III gambling facilities, operating under 196 tribal-state compacts. In 1988, approximately 70 Indian casinos and bingo halls were operating in a total of 16 states; in 1998, approximately 298 facilities were operating in a total of 31 states. For the majority of tribal governments that do run gambling facilities, the revenues have been modest yet nevertheless useful. Further, not all gambling tribes benefit equally. The 20 largest Indian gambling facilities account for 50.5 percent of total revenues, with the next 85 accounting for 41.2 percent.

PARI-MUTUEL WAGERING

The pari-mutuel industry, so called for the combining of wagers into a common pool, consists of horse racing, greyhound racing, and jai alai. Pari-mutuel wagering provides for winnings to be paid according to odds, which are determined by the combined amount wagered on each contestant within an event. The increased interest in racing and jai alai in the twentieth century is largely attributed to the rise in the pari-mutuel style of betting.

THE HORSE-RACING INDUSTRY

The largest sector within pari-mutuel gambling is the horse-racing industry. Today, several of the larger racing venues, such as Churchill Downs in Louisville, Kentucky, have been operational since the 1800's. Many economic and traditional aspects of the horse-racing industry stem from the agroindustrial sector. This base is responsible for the diversity of racing's economic impact. Beyond directly related occupations such as track operators, trainers, owners, breeders, and jockeys, the beneficiaries of the racing industry include veterinarians, stable owners, etc. The total employment for the horse-racing industry has been estimated at 119,000. Pari-mutuel wagering on horse racing is legal in 43 states, generating annual gross revenues of approximately $3.25 billion. While there are over 150 operational racetracks, most wagering takes place away from the venue of the originating race. Fueling this development is the availability of satellite broadcasting making it possible to simultaneously broadcast races either between racetracks or at Off–Track Betting sites (OTB), where no racing occurs at all. The simulcasts provide for larger betting pools by increasing patron access to numerous racetracks.

THE GREYHOUND INDUSTRY

The greyhound industry began in 1919 with the first track in Emeryville, California. Today there are 49 tracks operating in 15 states.

Greyhound racing is responsible for approximately 14 percent of the total handle of pari-mutuel betting. In 1996 the gross amount wagered in the greyhound industry totaled $2.3 billion with $505 million in revenues. The industry accounts for approximately 30,000 jobs directly related to the operation of the racetracks and other agricultural operations. Over the last decade, the greyhound industry has experienced significant financial decline, dropping $300,000 in handle annually.

Jai Alai

Jai alai, the smallest segment of the pari-mutuel industry, involves players hurling a hard ball against a wall and catching it with curved baskets in a venue called a "fronton." With a handle of approximately $275,000 annually, Jai alai accounts for less than 2 percent of the total handle among the three pari-mutuel sectors. Jai alai has experienced a dramatic decline in overall revenues over the last decade. Jai alai hit its peak in the early 1980's with over $600 million wagered annually. By 1996, the total amount wagered was less than $240 million.

Issues

The issues facing pari-mutuel wagering have changed dramatically in the last 30 years. Legalizing slot machines and other EGD's is a highly contentious issue throughout the pari-mutuel industry. Even with the increased availability to racing information and account wagering, the pari-mutuel industry is facing economic problems. Industry officials point to the expansion of different forms of gambling as the reason for the downward financial turn. They say that competing for gambling dollars is making it increasingly difficult to maintain wagering pools large enough to pay for the cost of running the races. In response, several members of the pari-mutuel industry have fought for and received the opportunity to provide for alternative forms of gambling at racetracks. Presently, several states—such as Delaware, Rhode Island, South Carolina and West Virginia—permit EGD's at the racing venues. Proponents of installing EGD's point to increased revenues raised at the racetracks from both the machines and from larger number of patrons betting on the actual races. Other states have fought off the battle for increasing forms of gambling at pari-mutuel venues and are looking for alternatives to keep the industry alive within their state. Recently, Maryland provided $10 million in subsidies to the state's ailing horseracing industry to stave off another round of campaigning to provide slot machines at racetracks.

Simulcasting and Account Wagering

In addition to EGD's and slot machines, the pari-mutuel industry is taking advantage of advances in communication technology and changes in regulations to expand gambling opportunities. In 1978, Congress passed the Interstate Horseracing Act (IHA), 15 U.S.C. Sec. 3001–3007, which extended authority for States and the pari-mutuel industry to provide regulated interstate wagering on races. The law allows the racing industry to create larger wagering pools by combining bets from sources beyond the originating track. To facilitate interstate wagering, the pari-mutuel industry uses satellite communications to instantaneously broadcast races, known as "simulcast" wagering. Even before passage of the IHA, wagering was available at off-track venues, commonly known as off-track betting (OTB) sites. In 1970, the New York legislature approved the first OTB operation. Since then, simulcast wagering has grown rapidly both in the United States and internationally. Presently, at least 38 States have authorized simulcast interstate wagering. Along with OTB sites, racetracks began offering telephone account wagering services to their patrons. Recent industry figures estimate that off-track and simulcast wagering constitute more than 77 percent of the total annual amount wagered on pari-mutuel races; in 1997 they accounted for $11.8 billion of the $15 billion industry total. In 1998 the amount wagered through telephone account wagering systems reached almost $550 million. Several companies are developing racing channels, which are offered either through basic cable or as a subscription-based channel.

Sports Wagering

Despite its popularity, sports wagering in America is illegal in all but two states. Nevada has 142 legal sports books that allow wagering on professional and amateur sports. Oregon runs a game called "Sports Action" that is associated with the Oregon Lottery and allows wagering on the outcome of pro football games. Outside of these two states, wagering on sports is illegal in the United States. According to Russell Guindon, Senior research analyst for Nevada's Gaming Control Board, sports wagering reached $2.3 billion in Nevada's legalized sports books in fiscal 1998. Nevada sports books took in $77.4 million in revenue on college and professional sports wagering. According to one major strip resort, betting on amateur events accounted for 33 percent of revenue.

Issues

This Commission heard testimony that sports wagering is a serious problem that has devastated families and careers. Sports wagering threatens the integrity of sports, it puts student athletes in a vulnerable position, it can put adolescent gamblers at risk for gambling problems, and it can devastate individuals and careers. There is considerable evidence that sports wagering is widespread on America's college campuses. Cedric Dempsey, executive director of the NCAA, asserts that "every campus has student bookies. We are also seeing an increase in the involvement of organized crime on sports wagering." Gambling rings have been uncovered at Michigan State, University of Maine, Rhode Island, Bryant, Northwestern, and Boston College, among many other institutions. While studies of college gambling are sparse, Lesieur has found in a survey of six colleges in five states that 23 percent of students gambled at least once a week. The same study found that between 6 and

8 percent of college students are "probable problem gamblers," which was defined in that study as having uncontrollable gambling habits.

INTERNET

Beginning with its introduction on the World Wide Web in the summer of 1995, Internet gambling is the newest medium offering games of chance. While projected earnings are open to subjective interpretations, the previously small number of operations has grown into an industry practically overnight. In May of 1998, there were approximately 90 on-line casinos, 39 lotteries, 8 bingo games, and 53 sports books. One year later, there are over 250 on-line casinos, 64 lotteries, 20 bingo games, and 139 sportsbooks providing gambling over the Internet. Sebastian Sinclair, a gambling industry analyst for Christiansen/Cummings Associates, estimates that Internet gambling revenues were $651 million for 1998, more than double the estimated $300 million from the previous year. A separate study conducted by Frost and Sullivan shows that the Internet gambling industry grew from $445.4 million in 1997 to $919.1 million in 1998. Both the Sinclair and the Frost and Sullivan studies estimate that revenues for Internet gambling doubled within 1 year. Several factors have contributed to the dramatic growth. First, Internet access has increased throughout the world, particularly in the United States. As interest in the Internet has increased, technologies that drive the Internet have continued to improve. Internet gamblers can participate instantaneously through improved software providing real-time audio and visual games and races. Additionally, the public's confidence in conducting financial transactions on-line has increased. Furthermore, a number of foreign governments, such as Australia and Antigua, are licensing Internet gambling operators within their borders.

Additional Notes

- Sports gambling has exploded in recent years. In 1983, approximately $8 billion was wagered; estimates for 1997 range between $80 and $380 billion (only about $2 billion of which was legal). (Dan McGraw, "The National Bet," U.S. News & World Report, April 7, 1997, at 50.)

- In 1996, according to Arthur Andersen, the casino industry employed some 300,000 people, and indirectly supported another 400,000 who held tourism- and hospitality-related jobs in casino-driven areas. (NGISC Final Report, at 6.) 2005 casino employment totals more than 350,000, with over $12.6 billion paid in wages. (AGA 2006 Survey.)

- An estimated 25 percent of Americans visited a casino at least once in 2005, and many did so more than once—there were 322 million total visits, up 3 million from the year before. Approximately 4 percent of Americans report gambling online, but the majority of those apparently do not know that doing so is illegal. (AGA 2006 Survey.)

- Tax rates vary widely by jurisdiction, but many states draw substantial public revenues from casino taxes: more than half of Nevada's state budget is drawn from gambling taxes; Illinois pulled in $512 million in gambling taxes in 2000. Total state and local taxes paid by casinos, exclusive of tribal operations, came to about $3.5 billion in 2000, and $4.9 billion in 2005. (AGA 2006 Survey.)

● The total amount of money gambled by Americans in 1996 has been estimated at $586 billion. If accurate, this would make gambling more popular than baseball, the movies, and Disneyland—combined. (Timothy O'Brien, Bad Bet: The Inside Story of the Glamour, Glitz, and Danger of America's Gambling Industry, Crown Business Press, 1998, at pg. 4.)

E.   THE INTERNET FRONTIER

THE NATIONAL GAMBLING IMPACT STUDY COMMISSION—FINAL REPORT, JUNE 1999

[Chapter 5: Internet Gambling].

THE EMERGENCE OF INTERNET GAMBLING

The increasing number of people who use the Internet and the growing consumer confidence in conducting on-line financial transactions have led to a greater number of people who are willing to engage in Internet gambling. Although the phenomenon is difficult to measure, all observers agree that the growth is rapid. Sebastian Sinclair, a research consultant for Christiansen/Cummings Associates, Inc., estimates that Internet gambling more than doubled from 1997 to 1998, the number of gamblers increasing from 6.9 million to 14.5 million and revenues from $300 million to $651 million. Other studies indicate similar rates of growth. One study, which looked at Internet gambling revenues and the revenues of companies that produce software for on-line gambling operators, concluded that the Internet gambling industry's revenues grew from $445.4 million in 1997 to $919.1 million in 1998. Although projections concerning the turbulent world of the Internet are notoriously inaccurate, virtually all observers assume the rapid growth of Internet gambling will continue. Sinclair estimates that Internet gambling revenues will reach $2.3 billion by 2001. *The Financial Times* and Smith Barney have estimated that the Internet gambling market will reach annual revenues of $10 billion in the beginning of the next millennium. Obviously, the numbers are greatly influenced by a number of hard-to-predict variables, the most important of which are regulatory measures undertaken by governments. Such efforts are unlikely to be uniform, however: Even as the U.S. Congress debates legislation to prohibit Internet gambling, several foreign governments have moved in the other direction and have licensed Internet gambling operations within their own borders, which Americans can access. Clearly, the politics of Internet gambling are evolving almost as quickly as the medium itself, and with a similar lack of common direction.

Types of Internet Gambling Sites

The most visible indicator of change is the proliferation of Internet gambling sites. At the present, a comprehensive inventory of the number of gambling sites is probably impossible to compile, given companies' constant entry into and exit from the market and the lack of any central registry. In December 1998, the online publication *Bloomberg News* reported that 800 gambling-related sites existed, 60 of which offered real-time betting. Reflecting the lack of sharp borders in this area, this estimate includes sites that provide information for all types of gambling, such as Web pages promoting tourism to large casinos. The Web site *Rolling Good Times* provides links to approximately 1,000 Internet sites that offer some form of betting. By itself, however, this number may be misleading, because many of those sites are segments within a single operation and many of the on-line gambling operations are merely subsidiaries of the same companies. Nevertheless, the number of sites can be expected to grow. Along with a burgeoning presence on the Internet, the design and pace of the on-line games have advanced dramatically over the past few years, as has their ease of use. Gambling sites now feature interactive games, broadcast races in real-time video, and walk customers through a virtual tour of the site, complete with colorful graphics and background music. Prior to gambling, most sites require people to fill out registration forms and to either purchase "chips" or set up accounts with a preset minimum amount. Payment is made using credit or debit cards, money transfers, or other forms of electronic payment, such as "smart cards" or "Cybercash." Once registered, the gambler has a full range of games from which to choose. Most Internet gambling sites offer casino-style gambling, such as blackjack, poker, slot machines, and roulette. Casino-style sites also often require gamblers to either download special software or ask for a CD–ROM, with the software to be sent to their home. Another form of gambling available on the Internet is sports gambling, which is receiving increasing media attention. The January 26, 1998, edition of *Sports Illustrated* highlighted the proliferation of Internet sports gambling sites, which increased from 2 in 1996 to more than 50 by 1998. As of February 1, 1999, *Rolling Good Times* had listed 110 sports-related Internet gambling sites. The rapid increase in sites likely is the result of the financial success of existing operations. According to National Football League estimates, the Internet sports-gambling market will reach $750 million by the end of 1999. For many reasons, gambling on sports via the Internet is increasingly financially successful. Unlike casino-style games, Internet sports books do not necessarily use highly complex Web sites that require bettors to download software in order to participate. Whereas casino-style games can generate concerns over the possibility of tampered results, the outcomes of sporting events are public knowledge and are assumed to be beyond the control of the site operator. The integrity of Internet sports wagering results is therefore less open to question.

In the United States, Powerball and Interlotto maintain Web sites, as does the Coeur d'Alene Native American Tribe in Idaho. In keeping with the borderless world of the Internet, however, many other sites have appeared outside of the United States. One of the largest Internet lotteries, called "One Billion Through Millions 2000," is a site launched by the Liechtenstein Principality under contract with the International Red Cross. The United Kingdom has an Internet site for its lottery, and other European government-sponsored lotteries also are exploring the option of providing lottery and bingo games on-line.

Candidates For Prohibition
Youth Gambling

Because the Internet can be used anonymously, the danger exists that access to Internet gambling will be abused by underage gamblers. In most instances, a would-be gambler merely has to fill out a registration form in order to play. Most sites rely on the registrant to disclose his or her correct age and make little or no attempt to verify the accuracy of the information. Underage gamblers can use their parents' credit cards or even their own credit and debit cards to register and set up accounts for use at Internet gambling sites. Concerns regarding underage gambling derive in part from this age group's familiarity with and frequent use of the Internet.

Pathological Gamblers

Pathological gamblers are another group susceptible to problems with Internet gambling. In addition to their accessibility, the high-speed instant gratification of Internet games and the high level of privacy they offer may exacerbate problem and pathological gambling. Access to the Internet is easy and inexpensive and can be conducted in the privacy of one's own home. Shielded from public scrutiny, pathological gamblers can traverse dozens of Web sites and gamble 24 hours a day. Experts in the field of pathological gambling have expressed concern over the potential abuse of this technology by problem and pathological gamblers. The director of the Harvard Medical School's Division on Addiction Studies, Dr. Howard J. Shaffer, likened the Internet to new delivery forms for addictive narcotics. He stated, "As smoking crack cocaine changed the cocaine experience, I think electronics is going to change the way gambling is experienced." Bernie Horn, the executive director of the National Coalition Against Legalized Gaming, testified before Congress that Internet gambling "magnifies the potential destructiveness of the addiction."

Criminal Use

The problems associated with anonymity extend beyond youth and pathological gambling. Lack of accountability also raises the potential for criminal activities, which can occur in several ways. First, there is the possibility of abuse by gambling operators. Most Internet service providers (ISPs) hosting Internet gambling operations are physically located offshore; as a result, operators can alter, move, or entirely remove sites within minutes. This mobility makes it possible for dishonest operators to take credit card numbers and money from deposited accounts and close down. Stories of unpaid gambling winnings often surface in news reports and among industry insiders. In fact, several Web sites now exist that provide analysis of the payout activity for Internet gambling operations. Second, computer hackers or gambling operators may tamper with gambling software to manipulate games to their benefit. Unlike the physical world of highly regulated resort-destination casinos, assessing the integrity of Internet operators is quite difficult. Background checks for licensing in foreign jurisdictions are seldom as thorough as they are in the United States. Furthermore, the global dispersion of Internet gambling operations makes the vigilant regulation of the algorithms of Internet games nearly impossible. Third, gambling on the Internet may provide an easy means for money laundering. Internet gambling provides anonymity, remote access, and encrypted data. To launder money, a person need only deposit money into an offshore account, use those funds to gamble, lose a small percent of the original funds, then cash out the remaining funds. Through the dual protection of encryption and anonymity, much of this activity can take place undetected.

Regulation or Prohibition?

State Efforts

Given the traditional responsibility of the states regarding gambling, many have been in the forefront of efforts to regulate or prohibit Internet gambling. Several states, including Louisiana, Texas, Illinois, and Nevada, have introduced and/or passed legislation specifically prohibiting Internet gambling. Florida has taken an active role, including cooperative efforts with Western Union, to stop the money-transfer service of 40 offshore sports books. Additionally, Florida's Office of the Attorney General mailed letters to media throughout the State advising them to "cease and desist" advertising for offshore sports books. A number of state attorneys general have initiated court action against Internet gambling owners and operators and have won several permanent injunctions; some companies have been ordered to dissolve, and their owners have been fined and sanctioned. But the impact has been limited: The large majority of Internet gambling sites, along with their owners and operators, are beyond the reach of the state attorneys general.

An Enhanced Federal Role at State Request

Given this and other experiences, several states have concluded that only the federal government has the potential to regulate or prohibit Internet gambling. To this end, the National Association of Attorneys General (NAAG) has called for an expansion in the language of the federal anti-wagering statute to prohibit Internet gambling and for federal-state cooperation on this issue.

Federal Efforts

The federal government has been active in the area of Internet gambling. Thus far, DOJ has investigated and brought charges against 22 Internet gambling operators on charges of violating the Wire Communications Act. All the defendants operated their businesses offshore and maintained that they were licensed by foreign governments. However, the defendants are U.S. citizens, some of whom were living in the United States at the time of their arrests. In a public statement following the charges, Attorney General Janet Reno announced, "The Internet is not an electronic sanctuary for illegal betting. To Internet betting operators everywhere, we have a simple message: 'You can't hide online and you can't hide offshore.'" Ongoing efforts aim to strengthen Federal regulation and prohibition of Internet gambling. Members in both chambers of Congress have introduced legislation to address Internet gambling. The Internet Gambling Prohibition Act, first introduced by Senator Kyl during the 105th Congress, provides for the prohibition of Internet gambling through amending the Wire Communications Act. As reintroduced during the 106th Congress, the bill would expand and/or clarify definitions within the statute to include the technology of the Internet and all forms of gambling.

Obstacles to Regulation

Although amending or creating new federal statutes to prohibit or regulate gambling on the Internet would provide law enforcement with greater authority to prosecute owners and operators, there are many ways of frustrating the efforts of regulators. The international nature of business is perhaps the most important facilitator of owners' and operators' ability to circumvent regulations. Currently, governments in 25 countries license or have passed legislation to permit Internet gambling operations. To effectively prohibit Internet gambling, the U.S. government would have to ensure that these licensed operators do not offer their services within U.S. borders, a proposition that poses a range of unanswered questions regarding feasibility. Efforts to prevent customers in the United States from accessing and using these sites may be easily circumvented. For example, the on-line registration process makes possible an initial screening of customers when they disclose the locations of bank accounts or credit card companies. Yet potential customers can take a number of steps to conceal their location within the United States. For example, patrons can establish offshore bank accounts and wire the money from those accounts to the Internet gambling site. In addition, patrons can mask their origins by first dialing an offshore ISP before logging onto a particular site, thereby creating the appearance of operating in a legal Internet gambling jurisdiction. Internet gambling operators also have several tools at their disposal for concealing their activity from law enforcement. Internet gambling operators can change the address of their Web site quickly and without cost, maintaining their easily identifiable domain name. Although Internet users typically key in a domain name to visit a particular site, the addresses of Web sites actually consist of a series of numbers. By changing its numerical address, the site may appear to remain in the exact place each time a user accesses the address, even though the site may have moved or may be one of several mirrored sites.

F. INDIAN GAMING

JESSICA R. CATTELINO—"FROM BINGO HALLS TO BILLIONS": TRIBAL GAMING AND INDIGENOUS SOVEREIGNTY, WITH NOTES FROM SEMINOLE COUNTRY

American Studies, 46:3/4 (Fall–Winter 2005): 171–188.

According to the National Indian Gaming Commission (NIGC), a federal regulatory body, in 2004 Indian gaming grossed $19.4 billion in revenues (National Indian Gaming Commission 2005). The National Indian Gaming Association (NIGA), a trade organization, put the figure at $18.5 billion, reporting that 19.5 million Americans visited Indian gaming facilities across twenty-eight states. Tribal government gaming comprised 23 percent of consumer spending on legal gambling in the United States in 2003 (National Indian Gaming Association 2004). The industry has grown rapidly from its modest birth in a small bingo hall on the intersection of Stirling Road and State Road 7 in Hollywood, Florida, where in 1979 Seminoles opened the first high-stakes gaming operation in Native North America. Not surprisingly, today's largest gaming operations are located near densely-populated urban areas: they include the Mashantucket Pequot and Mohegan casinos in Connecticut, the Shakopee Mdewakanton Sioux casino outside Minneapolis, the Seminole Hollywood Hard Rock casino near Fort Lauderdale and Miami, and numerous casinos operated by California tribes near Los Angeles and San Diego. Casinos have partially realigned the geography of power in Indian Country.

Too often, however, the history of Indian gaming is told as if it begins with a Congressional mandate or a judicial ruling, rather than with indigenous action. It is worth remembering that Seminoles opened Hollywood Bingo before any U.S. law on tribal gaming had been passed or any judge had issued a ruling on the matter. They did so as part of a long history of failed efforts to establish a secure economic base for the tribal government, as an attempt to alleviate ongoing poverty on their urban and rural reservations, and with the hope that more money could reduce individual and tribal government reliance on the Bureau of Indian Affairs (BIA) and other federal agencies. Seminoles, like other tribes, had rarely been able to convince banks and other lenders to invest on reservation land, which could not serve as collateral because of its federal trust status. Since their 1957 reorganization into a federally-recognized tribe (under the 1934 Indian Reorganization Act), Seminoles had participated in a string of BIA and public-private economic development projects (e.g., light manufacturing, cattle ranching, land leasing, and tourism), but these either had failed entirely or had brought only marginal profits.

Nor was gaming the first economic project to generate local controversy about its appropriateness for Indian people: as I discuss elsewhere, non-Indian concerns about Seminoles losing their authenticity and "selling out" swirled around earlier twentieth-century Seminole ventures in cattle, crafts, alligator wrestling, and cigarette sales (Cattelino 2004; see also West 1998). Tribal government gaming, then, was neither a "new buffalo" that mysteriously appeared to lead Indians out of poverty (Lane 1995) nor an unexpected "windfall"; instead, it was the result of sustained efforts by Indian people to fight poverty and reinforce their self-governance.

A brief outline of how Seminoles allocate casino profits and understand their effects [is useful here]. The Seminole Tribe of Florida, whose approximately 3,000 citizens live on six reservations in the swamps and suburbs of South Florida, turned a profit almost instantly after Hollywood Bingo's 1979 launch. By 2001 the Tribe's five casinos generated annual profits of over $300 million, making Seminole gaming unusually successful when compared to most tribal casino operations. Revenues have shot up since the 2004 opening of massive Hard Rock casino-resorts on the urban Tampa and Hollywood reservations. The democratically-elected Seminole Tribal Council distributes casino revenues, in accordance with annual budgetary and policy decisions, to a growing number of tribal programs and as per capita dividends to all tribal citizens.

The direct financial impact of casino revenues for the Seminole government and citizens is stunning. Prior to 1979, when Hollywood Bingo opened, The Seminole Tribe of Florida administered a budget of less than $2 million, almost all from federal grants. In 2001, by contrast, the tribe's annual budget exceeded $200 million, with over 95 percent of the funds coming from casino revenues. Seminole gaming employed nearly 2,000 people, only twenty of whom, mostly in management positions, were Seminoles; the tribe estimates that gaming contributed $65 million to the local economy that year. Yet gaming's "economic impact" cannot be measured by financial indicators alone, as all too many economists are trying to do. This single-generation shift from grinding poverty to economic security has enabled—and also forced—Seminoles to consider what kind of people and government they want to be. I understand these efforts as processes of valuation.

When I asked Seminoles whether and how gaming had affected their lives, they generally responded by praising the benefits brought by investments of casino income in tribal administration, cultural programs, and economic development. First, Seminole casinos fund a vast array of tribal government programs including health clinics, law enforcement, the K–12 Ahfachkee School and other education projects, and housing. Since gaming, the tribal government has expanded radically, with more than 1,300 tribal employees occupying several gleaming new office buildings by 2001. The tribal government also directs casino revenues toward political lobbying and legal defense of sovereignty-based rights. That Seminoles have been able to mobilize casino revenues toward self-governance and decreased reliance on the BIA is not only a consequence of gaming. Instead, archival and oral historical research showed that these were key motivations for pursuing gaming in the first place. Second, Seminoles also have devoted large sums to cultural production. In 1997 they opened the Ah–Tah–Thi–Ki Museum, and the tribe also funds craftwork, language classes, festivals, and other cultural programs. That there is a self-proclaimed Seminole "cultural renaissance" in the wake of casinos is a testament to Seminoles' valuation of distinct cultural practices, and many individuals expressed relief that decreased financial pressures freed up more time for cultural projects and practices. Still, the bureaucratization of culture and institutionalization of language education in the casino era have caused some Seminoles to worry that the strengthening of tribal cultural programs will undermine the matrilineal clan as the locus of cultural (re)production. The public display of Seminole cultural difference also has responded to casino critics and multicultural logics demanding that Seminoles and other indigenous groups perform culture as a condition of their recognition and legitimacy.

Third, Seminoles invested casino revenues in economic diversification, for example sugarcane, citrus, cattle ranching, an airplane manufacturer, and ecotourism at the Billie Swamp Safari. Less often publicized, and less understood by many tribal members, have been the Tribal Council's ventures in the financial sector: investment in other Indian casinos, a bank, casino boat, offshore reinsurance firm, and real estate. Economic diversification is not just a way for Seminoles to make money or protect assets; it is not just an "investment strategy" in the narrowest economistic terms. Diversification is also a matter of pride, politics, and nationalism. Being able to list off an array of tribal enterprises, as Seminoles often do, shows them to be and do more than casinos. It is common for tribal gaming advocates around the country to promote diversification, but often this presumes a particular model of "economic development," rather than asking what diversification *means* to people. For some Seminoles, diversification is a defense against being associated too closely with casinos or cigarette sales. For other Seminoles, it is a marker of governmental legitimacy, as Seminoles compare themselves to similar nations that "have an economy." Still others hope to distribute political power more evenly by supporting new projects and individual entrepreneurs, reducing reliance on gaming experts.

Fourth, Seminoles allocate monthly casino dividends to each tribal member, including minors, raising household incomes and reflecting localized processes whereby the redistribution of wealth enacts political leadership. Per capita dividends get a lot of play in press accounts of Indian gaming. Although per capita dividends sometimes are taken as evidence that Indians are getting "rich" off of casinos, they take particular meanings in relation to Seminole history and political norms. That is, cash distributions are not simply economic transfers, but are social decisions and historical markers. Many Seminoles draw a moral and civic contrast between dividends, which can modestly support most families, and the U.S. welfare benefits upon which they once relied. They are proud that dividends enable them to provide for their children, comparing the abundant food on their tables to prior reliance on U.S. government commodity foods, and they contrast their children's FUBU and DKNY designer clothes to the missionary hand-me-downs they once wore. There is a certain irony that many Seminoles now depend on *tribal*, not federal government, checks, in an extension and perhaps deepening in everyday Seminole life of modes and economies of governmentality (cf. Foucault 1991). But it matters *who* governs whom, and how. That these are Seminole checks, not U.S. checks, takes on historical significance against the backdrop of BIA control and prevalent anti-Indian racism that so often was couched in terms of welfare dependency. Moreover, per capita dividends reinforce longstanding norms and practices of political leadership that are grounded in the redistribution of wealth, as several Seminoles explained by comparing dividends to the redistributive rituals of the annual Green Corn Dance.

Of course, the rapid infusion of money into a relatively small community has not been entirely smooth. Internal disputes about how to use the money simmer, focused less on whether money is a good thing than upon the equity of its distribution. Gaming has exacerbated some political tensions, though Seminoles have not been burdened with the distinction between so-called "progressives" and "traditionalists" (the terms are problematic but widespread) that shape political division in some other tribes, nor have they faced the membership disputes so widely publicized among other Native groups in gaming's wake. Seminoles do indeed worry about how to raise their children under radically new economic conditions, how to teach them the value of work and bind them to a distinctly Seminole history and future. Like other parents, Seminoles complain about the effects of new technology and materialism. While these concerns are newly framed in terms of gaming wealth, they are not simply "about" money or gaming. Rather, discourses of "cultural loss" and concerns about children and the future operate as mechanisms for policing social reproduction and as reminders of collective obligation. Indeed, Seminole political divisions generally do not seem to be the "result" of gaming; rather, gaming has become the idiom through which pre-existing and emergent political and social differences are articulated. My observations are not intended to serve as a blanket apology for gaming-related conflict: rather, they suggest the need to analyze gaming narratives in Indian communities as complex social discourses. It also could prove fruitful to compare gaming tribes with other communities that experience single-generation transformations from poverty to economic security, and to single-commodity nation-states such as oil states.

It is beyond my capability and the available evidence to suggest patterns in how and why tribal gaming has taken the diverse forms and meanings across American Indian communities. For example, why have some tribes but not others struggled against the growth of problem gaming (often called "gambling addiction") among tribal members? But these variations should not be surprising. To assume otherwise—to suggest that a particular economic form would generate standardized sociopolitical practice across human groups so diverse as the peoples of Native North America—would homogenize indigenous difference and take a naïve approach to economic practice. Comparative analysis will advance scholarship and aid Native groups who seek to avoid social problems while benefiting from casino profits.

G. DEBATING GAMBLING

1. CLASSICAL STATEMENTS ON GAMBLING AND THE DE-BATE

KING WILLIAM III—PREAMBLE TO THE ACT FOR SUPPRESSING OF LOTTERIES (1699)

Whereas several evil-disposed persons, for divers years last past, have set up many mischievous and unlawful games, called lotteries...in most of the eminent towns and places in England...and have thereby most unjustly and fraudulently got themselves great sums of money from the children and servants of several gentlemen, traders and merchants, and from other unwary persons, to the utter ruin and impoverishment of many families, and to the reproach of the English laws and government, by color of several patents or grants under the great seal of England...which said grants or patents are against the common good, trade, welfare and peace of his Majesty's kingdoms: for remedy whereof be it enacted, adjudged and declared...That all such lotteries, and all other lotteries are common and public nuisances, and that all grants, patents and licenses for such lotteries, are void and against law.

ADAM SMITH—THE WEALTH OF NATIONS (1776)

Book I, Chapter X.

The over-weening conceit which the greater part of men have of their own abilities, is an ancient evil remarked by the philosophers and moralists of all ages. Their absurd presumption in their own good fortune, has been less taken notice of. It is, however, if possible, still more universal. There is no man living who, when in tolerable health and spirits, has not some share of it. The chance of gain is by every man more or less over-valued, and the chance of loss is by most men under-valued, and by scarce any man, who is in tolerable health and spirits, valued more than it is worth.

That the chance of gain is naturally over-valued, we may learn from the universal success of lotteries. The world neither ever saw, nor ever will see, a perfectly fair lottery; or one in which the whole gain compensated the whole loss; because the undertaker could make nothing by it. In the state lotteries the tickets are really not worth the price which is paid by the original subscribers, and yet commonly sell in the market for twenty, thirty, and sometimes forty per cent. advance. The vain hope of gaining some of the great prizes is the sole cause of this demand. The soberest people scarce look upon it as a folly to pay a small sum for the chance of gaining ten or twenty thousand pounds; though they know that even that small sum is perhaps twenty or thirty per cent. more than the chance is worth. In a lottery in which no prize exceeded twenty pounds, though in other respects it approached much nearer to a perfectly fair one than the common state lotteries, there would not be the same demand for tickets. In order to have a better chance for some of the great prizes, some people purchase several tickets, and others, small shares in a still greater number. There is not, however, a more certain proposition in mathematics, than that the more tickets you adventure upon, the more likely you are to be a loser. Adventure upon all the tickets in the lottery, and you lose for certain; and the greater the number of your tickets the nearer you approach to this certainty.

JOHN STUART MILL—ON LIBERTY (1859)
Chapter V: Applications.

Then, indeed, a new element of complication is introduced; namely, the existence of classes of persons with an interest opposed to what is considered as the public weal, and whose mode of living is grounded on the counteraction of it. Ought this to be interfered with, or not? Fornication, for example, must be tolerated, and so must gambling; but should a person be free to be a pimp, or to keep a gambling-house? The case is one of those which lie on the exact boundary line between two principles, and it is not at once apparent to which of the two it properly belongs. There are arguments on both sides. On the side of toleration it may be said, that the fact of following anything as an occupation, and living or profiting by the practice of it, cannot make that criminal which would otherwise be admissible; that the act should either be consistently permitted or consistently prohibited; that if the principles which we have hitherto defended are true, society has no business, as society, to decide anything to be wrong which concerns only the individual; that it cannot go beyond dissuasion, and that one person should be as free to persuade, as another to dissuade. In opposition to this it may be contended, that although the public, or the State, are not warranted in authoritatively deciding, for purposes of repression or punishment, that such or such conduct affecting only the interests of the individual is good or bad, they are fully justified in assuming, if they regard it as bad, that its being so or not is at least a disputable question: That, this being supposed, they cannot be acting wrongly in endeavoring to exclude the influence of solicitations which are not disinterested, of instigators who cannot possibly be impartial—who have a direct personal interest on one side, and that side the one which the State believes to be wrong, and who confessedly promote it for personal objects only. There can surely, it may be urged, be nothing lost, no sacrifice of good, by so ordering matters that persons shall make their election, either wisely or foolishly, on their own prompting, as free as possible from the arts of persons who stimulate their inclinations for interested purposes of their own. Thus (it may be said) though the statutes respecting unlawful games are utterly indefensible—though all persons should be free to gamble in their own or each other's houses, or in any place of meeting established by their own subscriptions, and open only to the members and their visitors—yet public gambling-houses should not be permitted. It is true that the prohibition is never effectual, and that whatever amount of tyrannical power is given to the police, gambling-houses can always be maintained under other pretences; but they may be compelled to conduct their operations with a certain degree of secrecy and mystery, so that nobody knows anything about them but those who seek them; and more than this, society ought not to aim at. There is considerable force in these arguments. I will not venture to decide whether they are sufficient to justify the moral anomaly of punishing the accessary, when the principal is (and must be) allowed to go free; of fining or imprisoning the procurer, but not the fornicator, the gambling-house keeper, but not the gambler.

2.   IDENTIFYING THE HARMS OF GAMBLING

(1) Gambling and Lotteries as a Regressive Tax

RONALD RYCHLAK—LOTTERIES, REVENUES AND SOCIAL COSTS: A HISTORICAL EXAMINATION OF STATE–SPONSORED GAMBLING

34 B.C. L. Rev. 11, Spring 1993.

1.   OPPOSITION IN THE 1800S

Until the early 1800s, there was little opposition to state-conducted lotteries. State regulation, including bonding of operators and supervision of receipts, quieted opponents. Churches usually benefited from lotteries, so they were not quick to condemn. As the country's dependence on lotteries increased, however, so did the opportunities for abuse. Serious lottery opposition began to mount in the early to mid–1800s as part of general social reform that included movements for temperance, peace, women's rights, educational reform, prison reform, and abolition of slavery. As one authority has noted:

> "In 1842, Democrats swept to power because of their opposition to lotteries. The lotteries in turn were portrayed merely as an adjunct to a corrupt monopolistic banking system dominated by the wealthy Whig power elite. The great moral fervor of the 1830's produced many reform movements. ... [A] class element [also] entered the picture. Lotteries, like corporations, made men wealthy without physical work. The poor, who worked hard for their fatback and beans, resented the state's approval of activities that made men wealthy without sweat. Thus, anti-lottery leaders were often enemies of all forms of speculation."

Lottery opposition focused on two primary concerns: social problems, such as the impact that lotteries had on the morality and work ethic of the people, and fraudulent operation.

a.   Social Problems

As the nation's financial institutions developed, and as state and federal governments became sufficiently stable and organized to collect taxes, the need for lotteries as a means of raising public funds diminished. With the development of taxation and public bonds as revenue sources, the primary remaining justification for using lotteries was that they provided a popular form of entertainment. That justification ignored the social problems associated with state-sponsored gambling. Close examination of these problems led to a flood of lottery criticism.

When early-nineteenth century Americans closely examined lotteries and compared them to other forms of generating revenue, the perception that lotteries were a voluntary tax paid only by the willing was gradually replaced by a belief that they actually imposed a highly regressive levy. The 1813 edition of the *Old Farmer's Almanac* cautioned that lotteries were the "path [that] leads down to the gloomy pits of ruin." An influential 1814 novel, *The Wonderful Advantage of Adventuring in the Lottery*, written by Reverend Samuel Wood, dramatized the personal problems associated with the lottery. The plot is essentially a morality play involving John Brown who, against his wife's wishes, decides to play the lottery. The lottery causes John to ignore and lose his job, turn to lying, lose his money, steal from his employer, consider suicide, fall in with the wrong crowd, turn to alcohol, take part in a highway robbery, and shoot and kill the victim. John is ultimately sentenced to death, and grief kills his wife. The judge at the end of the trial states:

> "I have never sat upon this bench after the drawing of the Lottery, but I had reason to think it had provided the ruin of many of the unhappy culprits who appeared before me. I would earnestly exhort the crowds that hear me to abhor the thought of adventuring in it, and to fly from it as from a plague, which will destroy domestic happiness and inward peace, and bring upon them every kind of distress."

John goes to his doom hoping that his fate will be a warning to others against playing the lottery. Popular publications gave similar cautions, referring to lotteries as "a vile tax on the needy and ignorant." Even children's books cautioned against the lottery.

Lotteries were also blamed for larger-scale social ills. In 1818, the Society for the Prevention of Pauperism in the City of New York published a report on the principal causes of poverty. It listed these four causes, in order: alcohol, lotteries, pawnbrokers and "the many charitable institutions in the city." A similar report on the city of Baltimore, issued three years later, listed alcohol, lotteries, prostitution and charitable institutions. Not surprisingly, both New York and Maryland acted to place more controls on lotteries before 1820.

As lotteries fell from grace, several politicians and civic groups began to condemn them. The Governor of Massachusetts, in an 1833 message to the legislature, explained:

> "The influence of such schemes of deception to allure the laborious poor from the path of honest industry, and to cheat them of their hard earned wages, to entice the young and the unreflecting from their fidelity, and betray them into a violation of their trust, and the

commission of heinous crimes, cannot be doubted, while the desolating and fatal effects upon the social relations of life, are scarcely less to be deplored."

An 1830 New York grand jury found that fifty-two lotteries per year (with prizes totaling $9,270,000) were being conducted, and that this had a pernicious effect upon morals, "creating a spirit of gambling which was productive of idleness, vicious habits, and the ruin of credit and character." This shift in perception foreshadowed the ultimate demise of the nineteenth century state-sponsored lottery.

(2) Gambling as Non–Productive Economic Activity

JOHN WARREN KINDT—LEGALIZED GAMBLING ACTIVITIES: THE ISSUES INVOLVING MARKET SATURATION

15 N. Ill. U. L. Rev. 271, Spring 1995.

In his classic book entitled Economics, Nobel–Prize laureate Paul Samuelson summarized the economics involved in gambling activities as follows:

"There is ... a substantial economic case to be made against gambling. First, it involves simply sterile transfers of money or goods between individuals, creating no new money or goods. Although it creates no output, gambling does nevertheless absorb time and resources. When pursued beyond the limits of recreation, where the main purpose after all is to 'kill' time, gambling subtracts from the national income. The second economic disadvantage of gambling is the fact that it tends to promote inequality and instability of incomes."

Furthermore, Professor Samuelson observed that "just as Malthus saw the law of diminishing returns as underlying his theory of population, so is the 'law of diminishing marginal utility' used by many economists to condemn professional gambling."

The concern of the legalized gambling interests over "market saturation" is largely a non-issue. From the governmental perspective, focusing on this issue misdirects the economic debate, because fears of market saturation are predicated upon the unwarranted assumption that legalized gambling operations constitute regional economic development—which they do not. In reality, legalized gambling operations consist primarily of a transfer of wealth from the many to the few—accompanied by the creation of new socio-economic negatives.

These issues should first be examined from the strategic governmental perspective. In this context, the inherently parasitic manner in which legalized gambling activities must apparently collect consumer dollars to survive is frequently described as "cannibalism" of the pre-existing economy—including the pre-existing tourist industry. In California and Nevada: Subsidy, Monopoly, and Competitive Effects of Legalized Gambling, the California Governor's Office of Planning and Research high-lighted in December of 1992 "the enormous subsidy that Californians provide to Nevada through their gambling patronage" and concluded that "Nevada derives an enormous competitive advantage from its monopoly on legal gambling." The report summarized that "gambling by Californians pumps nearly $3.8 billion per year into Nevada, and proba-bly adds about $8.8 billion—and 196,000 jobs—to the Nevada economy, counting the secondary employment it generates" and that this was "a direct transfer of income and wealth from California to Nevada every year." Thus, the Nevada economy appears to constitute a classic example of a legalized gambling economy "parasitically" draining or "cannibaliz-ing" another economy (primarily Southern California).

A summary of these concepts reveals that when compared to legal-ized gambling parlors, pre-existing entertainment activities in the Unit-ed States generally create and contribute to a positive economic cycle, and they do not leave behind the enormous social problems inherent in gambling economies. As previously mentioned, an exception appears to occur when a small gambling economy is subsidized by a large non-gambling economy (for example, Nevada vis-à-vis California). However, when viewed from the proper perspective, whether regional or strategic in scope, legalized gambling activities always drain the relevant economic base. For example, it was emphasized to the Illinois Senate Committee on riverboat gambling that "the money spent on riverboats will be drained off other portions of the Illinois economy." Similarly, "Iowa [erroneously] thought it would have a monopoly with its riverboat gambling, a parasitic casino industry growing fat off the Chicago mar-ket."

In an economic scenario, dollars spent in gambling parlors are often removed from circulation, and this process contributes to a negative economic impact. Most revenues to the legalized gambling organizations must necessarily be directed primarily into attracting new consumer markets or toward increased marketing efforts to keep "selling hope" to pre-existing gamblers. Gambling organizations argue that the industry is predicated upon policies which keep their dollars "in-house" and that gambling-oriented machines perform no useful task, and therefore na-tional, as well as local, productive capacity is better directed toward manufacturing appliances or other machines.

Once again, the net result according to Professor Jack Van Der Slik, who echoed the sentiments of much of the academic community, was that state-sanctioned "gambling produces no product, no new wealth, and so it makes no genuine contribution to economic development." Similarly, in 1989 Professor William Thompson cautioned that Illinois riverboat gambling would "not be a catalyst for general economic devel-opment." Of course, if the focus is only on a localized gambling area, such as Las Vegas, instead of the proper perspective on the overall region Las Vegas is draining, there can be the illusion of an overall positive economic impact.

Most insidious to traditional businesses and to the rest of the economy, practically all of the dollars flowing into gambling organizations are "reinvested" in more and newer and "harder" forms (i.e., "more thrilling" forms) of gambling, as well as their associated cluster services. This process tends continually to intensify the large socio-economic negatives (as well as the local positives) associated with legalized gambling activities. In other words, the truism "gambling begets gambling" appears accurate, and the gambling dollars are almost exclusively kept "in-house" despite the protestations of the gambling supporters to the contrary.

(3) Compulsive Gambling Disorders

THE NATIONAL GAMBLING IMPACT STUDY COMMISSION—FINAL REPORT, JUNE 1999

Chapter 4: Problem and Pathological Gambling.

PROBLEM AND PATHOLOGICAL GAMBLING

For millions of Americans, problem and pathological gambling is a serious consequence of legal and illegal gambling. Part of our challenge has been to pin down the exact number of individuals suffering from these disorders. Virtually every study varies in these estimations. For example, a Harvard University meta-analysis concluded that approximately 1.6 percent, or 3.2 million, of the American adult population are pathological gamblers. The combined rate of problem and pathological gambling in 17 states where surveys have been conducted ranges from 1.7 to 7.3 percent. In Oregon, the lifetime prevalence of problem and pathological gambling is 4.9 percent. Recent studies in Mississippi and Louisiana indicate that 7 percent of adults in these states have been classified as problem or pathological gamblers. The two principal studies sponsored by this Commission found that the prevalence of problem and pathological gambling in America is troubling. NRC estimates that, in a given year, approximately 1.8 million adults in the United States are pathological gamblers. NORC found that approximately 2.5 million adults are pathological gamblers. Another three million of the adult population are problem gamblers. Over 15 million Americans were identified as at-risk gamblers. About 148 million Americans are low-risk gamblers. Approximately 30 million Americans have never gambled at all. While some believe that lifetime prevalence rates are overstated, others believe that past year rates are understated. Reasonable people, including those with clinical expertise, disagree over the exact number of individuals suffering from gambling disorders and the relevance of "problem" versus "at-risk." While getting an exact number is important for scientists, policymakers and treatment providers, more important is the acknowledgement that a significant number of individuals are pathological, problem or at-risk gamblers. And it is time for the public and private sector to come together in a meaningful way to address these problems. The Commission is united in our concern for those currently suffering from problem gambling and our desire to prevent this problem in the future. The Commission also agrees that this should be a public-private partnership and that government at all levels should commit resources for research into the study and treatment of problem gambling.

General Impacts

THE NATIONAL GAMBLING IMPACT STUDY COMMISSION—FINAL REPORT, JUNE 1999

Chapter 7: Gambling's Impact on People and Places.

DETERMINING THE IMPACT OF GAMBLING

In attempting to determine the impact of gambling on people and places, the Commission offers a number of caveats for policymakers to consider. First, social and economic impacts are not as easily severable as policymakers would like. In fact, this is considered a false dichotomy for most individuals other than economists. Employment, for instance, is both an economic and a social benefit. Likewise, crime is both an economic and social cost. Secondly, as was noted in the overview to this chapter, it is extremely difficult to quantify social costs and benefits. Some economists suggest distinguishing between a "private" cost and benefit and a "social" cost and benefit. NRC also notes the confusion of "transfer effects" from "real effects." For instance, in an economic analysis of transfer effects, bankruptcy would not be considered to be a cost by economists because the dollars are merely transferred. Nor would a casino job necessarily be considered a true benefit, since other jobs may be available. While this may be true to economists, we know that bankruptcy is indeed a "cost" to the individuals and families involved, just as a good job is a tremendous benefit to that family. Just as only net economic and social benefits should be included on the positive side of legalized gambling's ledger, only net social and economic costs should be tallied on the negative side.

GROWTH AND EMPLOYMENT

A number of arguments have been advanced to promote gambling in an area or to demonstrate its positive impact. The most significant are associated with economic growth and employment. Unlike many industries, casino gambling creates full-time, entry-level jobs, which are badly needed in communities suffering from chronic unemployment and underemployment. In its analysis of 100 gambling and non-gambling communities, NORC found that in communities close to newly opened casinos, "unemployment rates, welfare outlays, and unemployment insurance decline by about one-seventh." Additionally, NORC found increased per capita income in the construction, hotel and lodging, and recreation and amusement industries. However, "no change is seen in overall per capita income as the increases noted above are offset by reductions in welfare and transfer payments as well as a drop-off in income from restaurants and bars ... " In other words, there were more jobs in the communities NORC studied after casino gambling was established than before. Although income in those communities stayed the same, more came from paychecks and less from government checks than before. The Commission also heard testimony quantifying job quality in the casino industry, and these data show that in terms of income, health insurance, and pension, casino jobs in the destination resorts of Las Vegas and Atlantic City are better than comparable service sector jobs. Within the casino industry, destination resorts tend to create more and better quality jobs than other kinds of casinos. In the Commission's casino survey conducted by NORC, the casinos that responded were divided into three groups: the top 25 casinos in terms of revenue; other commercial casinos; and, tribal casinos. Almost all of the casinos in the first group are destination resorts, and all but four are unionized. By contrast, a much smaller proportion of the other two groups are destination resorts. Moreover, fewer of the smaller commercial casinos and none of the tribal casinos are unionized. Annual salaries were, on average, $26,000 in the largest casinos, $20,500 in the smaller commercial casinos, and $18,000 in the tribal casinos. Employer contributions to employee health and retirement plans were also higher in the large casinos.

Native American Tribal Government Gambling

Tribal gambling accounted for $6.7 billion in revenues in 1997. "Two-hundred and eighty seven tribal gambling facilities operated, most of them small; the eight largest account for more than forty percent of all revenue." It is estimated that approximately 100,000 individuals are employed in Indian gambling facilities, but a breakdown of employees indicating how many are Indian is not generally available. While the social benefits to some tribes appear evident, information about economic benefits of Indian gambling cannot be factually proven, other than through estimates, because they have not been forthcoming with information they perceive to be "proprietary." One perceived economic benefit to both the tribes and the general population—reduction of the reliance upon taxpayer-funded federal assistance—has not manifested itself to date. For the most part, requests for federal assistance from tribes involved in gambling have continued. As an example, the Mashantucket Pequots, whose Foxwoods facility in Connecticut is the largest casino in the world and grosses more than $1 billion in annual revenues for the 550 tribal members, still received $1.5 million in low-income housing assistance in 1996 and continues to receive other federal funds. As of the writing of this report, the unemployment rate among Native Americans continues to hover around 50 percent.

A Careful Look at Economic Benefits

One indirect method to get a qualitative sense of the net effects of gambling is to look at its effect on property values. An increase in property values reflects growing attractiveness of a location. For example, if a new factory increases property values in a metropolitan area, but depresses them near its location, one can draw conclusions about the near-by and the broader impacts of the factory. This method has been applied to evaluate the effects of airports, waste disposal, and other public sector activities. It has also been used to estimate the consequences of casino gambling on the economy of a community. Needless to say, it is not a simple matter to extract the effect of any particular presumed cause on property values. One study that looked at counties that added casinos between 1991 and 1994 suggests several conclusions concerning the effect of gambling on property values. First, the counties that introduced gambling had relatively poor growth in property values before the introduction of gambling (compared to similar counties). The introduction of gambling increased the rate of growth of property values, making it similar to that in comparable counties that lacked casinos. The greatest effect of the introduction of gambling is on commercial property values, with residential property values not raised at all, perhaps even lowered by casino gambling. There is general agreement that legalized gambling has offered regulators the opportunity to locate gambling activities where incomes are depressed, thus providing, in some cases, an economic boost to needy people and places. So doing, however, has the negative consequence of placing the lure of gambling proximate to individuals with few financial resources.

Crime

Historically, there is a view that the introduction of legalized gambling will increase crime in a community. It is also claimed that legalized gambling reduces crime because it eliminates incentives for illegal gambling. Since the types of crime involved in each of these hypotheses are different, it is not surprising that proponents of both views are able to advance research to support their views. Some of the more thorough studies examine crime and pathological gambling. Not surprisingly, the findings reveal that many problem and pathological gamblers steal or commit other crimes to finance their habit. According to the National Research Council, "As access to money becomes more limited, gamblers often resort to crime in order to pay debts, appease bookies, maintain appearances, and garner more money to gamble." In Maryland, a report by the Attorney General's Office stated: "[c]asinos would bring a substantial increase in crime to our State. There would be more violent crime, more juvenile crime, more drug-and alcohol-related crime, more domestic violence and child abuse, and more organized crime. Casinos would bring us exactly what we do not need a lot more of all kinds of crime." Some commentators link crime to pathological gambling, where addicted gamblers steal or commit other crimes to finance their habit. In a survey of nearly 400 Gamblers Anonymous members, 57 percent admitted stealing to finance their gambling. Collectively they stole $30 million, for an average of $135,000 per individual. But beyond pathological gambling, tracing the relationship between crime and gambling has proven difficult. One problem is the scope of the studies being done:

some look at street crime alone, others include family crimes, still others may simply look at adolescent gambling, and others include white collar crime. Another problem is differentiating the effects of gambling from the effects of tourism in general. Nevada consistently has one of the highest crime rates in the nation. Several researchers suggest this is caused more by tourism than it is by the nature of the gambling industry. Is the crime surrounding an upscale Las Vegas resort similar to crime surrounding an amusement park? Are the volume and types of crimes comparable? Despite having few answers to these questions, policymakers continue to push or pull gambling based on a real or perceived, positive or negative, relationship between gambling and crime. The NORC study found that pathological gamblers had higher arrest and imprisonment rates than non-pathological gamblers. A third of problem and pathological gamblers had been arrested, compared to 10 percent of low-risk gamblers and 4 percent of non-gamblers. About 23 percent of pathological gamblers have been imprisoned, and so had 13 percent of problem gamblers.

FINANCIAL AND CREDIT ISSUES

The Commission found wide-spread perception among community leaders that indebtedness tends to increase with legalized gambling, as does youth crime, forgery and credit card theft, domestic violence, child neglect, problem gambling, and alcohol and drug offenses. One of the issues of most concern to this Commission is the ready availability of credit in and around casinos, which can lead to irresponsible gambling and problem and pathological gambling behavior. Forty to sixty percent of the cash wagered by individuals in casinos is not physically brought onto the premises. Each year casinos extend billions of dollars in loans to their customers in the form of credit markers. Additional sums are charged by casino customer on their credit cards as cash advances. Casinos charge fees for cash advances ranging from 3 percent to 10 percent or more. Nearly one in five (19.2 percent) of the identified pathological gamblers in the NORC survey reported filing bankruptcy. This compares to rates of 4.2 percent for non-gamblers and 5.5 percent for low-risk gamblers. Twenty-two percent of nearly 400 members of Gamblers Anonymous surveyed had declared bankruptcy.

LOCAL EFFECTS

Finally, while the national impact of gambling is significant, the greatest impact is felt at the local level. In some locales, gambling has been a critical component of community economic development strategies. For example, the Nevada Resort Association and the Nevada Commission on Tourism found that the gambling/hospitality industry created gross state-wide revenues of almost $8 billion in 1997; contributed $2.2 billion annually to federal, state and local taxes; paid taxes representing one-third of the state's general fund revenues forecast for 1997–99; generated about $36.5 million in county-level revenues in fiscal year 1997; directly employed 307,500 people and was directly and indirectly responsible for 60 percent of the state employment total; disbursed salaries of nearly $6 billion, representing one quarter of all wages paid statewide in 1996; added $10.3 billion to personal incomes; and contributed an estimated $30.6 billion to the state's business receipts, representing 63 percent of Nevada gross state product in 1995. Nevada, however, is unique. Roughly 85 percent of Nevada's gambling revenues come from out-of-state tourists. Thus, Nevada receives the economic benefits of the dollars lost to gambling, while the attendant social and economic impacts of unaffordable gambling losses are visited on the families and communities in the states from which those individuals come. Every other gambling venue in the United States is far more reliant on spending by citizens in a far more concentrated geographic area. In many cases, gambling operations are overwhelmingly dependent on spending by local citizens. For instance, a survey of 800 riverboat gamblers in Illinois found more than 85 percent lived within 50 miles of the casino in which they were gambling. In New Jersey, the gambling industry is also a significant factor in the local and state-wide economy. The New Jersey Casino Control Commission, in a report to this Commission, found that the gambling industry created gross casino gambling revenues of $3.79 billion in 1996; paid revenue taxes totaling $303.2 million in 1996; generated $717 million for redevelopment projects in Atlantic City (including investment in low and moderate income housing, historic restoration projects and nonprofit facility improvement) as well as an additional $69 million for projects state-wide since 1984 through contributions to the Casino Reinvestment Development Authority (CRDA); provided 50,000 full and part-time jobs with a payroll exceeding $1 billion before fringe benefits; contributed to the creation of another 48,000 indirect jobs with wages of almost $1 billion in 1994; spent $1.54 billion on goods and services with more than 3,400 companies in New Jersey and almost $2.5 billion with more than 8,000 companies across the United States in 1996; and expects to invest $5 billion or more for the development of casino hotel facilities during the next several years.

SUICIDE

According to the National Council on Problem Gambling, approximately one in five pathological gamblers attempts suicide. The Council further notes that the suicide rate among pathological gamblers is higher than for any other addictive disorder. A survey of nearly 400 Gamblers Anonymous members revealed that two-thirds had contemplated suicide, 47 percent had a definite plan to kill themselves, and 77 percent stated that they have wanted to die. University of California–San Diego sociologist Dr. David Phillips found that "visitors to and residents of gaming communities experience significantly elevated suicide levels." According to Phillips, Las Vegas "displays the highest levels of suicide in the nation, both for residents of Las Vegas and for visitors to that setting." In Atlantic City, Phillips found that "abnormally high suicide levels for visitors and residents appeared only after gambling casinos were opened." Visitor suicides account for 4.28 percent of all visitor deaths in

Las Vegas, 2.31 percent of visitor deaths in Reno, and 1.87 percent of visitor deaths in Atlantic City. Nationally, suicides account for an average of .97 percent of visitor deaths. A study commissioned by the American Gaming Association to counter Phillips' findings explains the suicide rates in Las Vegas not as a result of gambling but rather as a result of the city's geographic and demographic characteristics. University of California–Irvine Social Ecology professors Richard McCleary and Kenneth Chew, using different methodologies than Phillips, concluded that suicide rates in Las Vegas are comparable to other Western cities. They account for the high rates by analyzing the rapid growth of many Western cities, which results in a large population without established roots to a community. While these studies may account for the different rates, they both conclude that Las Vegas has the highest resident suicide rate in the nation.

DIVORCE

The Commission likewise heard abundant testimony and evidence that compulsive gambling introduces a greatly heightened level of stress and tension into marriages and families, often culminating in divorce and other manifestations of familial disharmony. In NORC's survey, 53.5 percent of identified pathological gamblers reported having been divorced, versus 18.2 percent of non-gamblers and 29.8 percent of low-risk gamblers. Further, NORC respondents representing two million adults identified a spouse's gambling as a significant factor in a prior divorce.

HOMELESSNESS

Individuals with gambling problems seem to constitute a higher percentage of the homeless population. The Atlantic City Rescue Mission reported to the Commission that 22 percent of its clients are homeless due to a gambling problem. A survey of homeless service providers in Chicago found that 33 percent considered gambling a contributing factor in the homelessness of people in their program. Again, whether this is caused by gambling or by other factors related to addictive behavior is unclear, but homelessness and gambling should be included in future research.

ABUSE AND NEGLECT

Family strife created by gambling problems also appears in the form of abuse, domestic violence or neglect. NRC cites two studies showing that between one quarter and one half of spouses of compulsive gamblers have been abused. Six of the 10 communities surveyed in NORC's case studies reported an increase in domestic violence relative to the advent of casinos. In its case studies of 10 casino communities, NORC reported, "Six communities had one or more respondents who said they had seen increases in child neglect, and attributed this increase at least in part to parents leaving their children alone at home or in casino lobbies and parking lots while they went to gamble." Respondents in these communities did not report noticeable increases in child abuse. NORC noted that the casino effect was not statistically significant for the infant mortality measure. The NRC, however, reported on two studies indicating between 10 and 17 percent of children of compulsive gamblers had been abused.

H. HARM REDUCTION

STEPHANIE MARTZ—LEGALIZED GAMBLING AND PUBLIC CORRUPTION: REMOVING THE INCENTIVE TO ACT CORRUPTLY, OR, TEACHING AN OLD DOG NEW TRICKS

13 J. L. & Politics 453 (Spring 1997).

The burgeoning corruption problem that has accompanied legalized gambling springs from the tense relationship between the two talismanic goals of legalized gambling: raising revenue and controlling crime. These public policy aims often find themselves at odds with one another, and sometimes have proven completely incompatible. Such conflict should not be surprising in light of the waste and expense associated with current methods of gambling regulation.

ADDRESSING THE CORRUPTION PROBLEM

Curbing gambling-related corruption on the legislative and administrative levels presents unusually difficult challenges to public policy makers. In order to deter public officials and gambling industry representatives from corruptly agreeing to award licenses outside of the regulatory and lawmaking processes, lawmakers need to revise not only anticorruption laws (on which this note will not focus), but also laws that directly regulate the primary activity of the gambling industry itself. Proposals along these lines might include: 1) increasing oversight through changes in the structure of the regulatory process; 2) shifting control of the legalization process from centralized state officials to local policy makers; and 3) taking away the gambling entrepreneur's monopoly profits. A combination of all three proposals would prove most effective in reducing the number and size of corrupt transactions in the legalization process.

CORRUPTION AND DETERRENCE: SOME BASIC PRINCIPLES

Although many of the U.S.'s biggest gambling companies are publicly traded and generally considered to be free of criminal influence, corrupt transactions still occur routinely between gambling entrepreneurs and malfeasant public officials. In fact, the sheer number of newsworthy anecdotes linking corruption and legalized gambling makes it appropriate to ask whether some degree of corruption is necessarily correlated with gambling activity. Assuming that the answer is "yes," this note continues by examining both the moral and the economic reasons for this connection.

Two issues inform the discussion. The first issue addresses the moral climate in which state-sponsored gambling usually operates: how do we control corruption in an industry or a state that typically has condoned it? In other words, how do we vitiate the motive to act corruptly, and create a motive to act honestly? The second issue addresses the same motive concern but uses an economic model. Assuming that gambling enterprises are rational actors, they will act corruptly "unless the probability and consequences of sanctions are high enough to deter them." A positivist approach of this type conveniently avoids describing desirable behavior, but instead defines the material incentives that encourage ideal behavior.

Increasing gambling regulation's oversight function

This note will continue to emphasize that eliminating entrenched, centralized bureaucracies—despite their efficiency—will reduce the incentive to give and accept bribes. Any kind of centralization increases the potential giver's willingness to pay because the transaction costs of reaching an optimum bribe price are reduced as centralization increases. Centralizing and organizing the power to allocate rights might increase the bribe price the receiver demands, thus having a possible deterrent effect on potential givers. However, decentralizing the power to influence a rights assignment will likely bring bribe prices down through competition. Such competition would enable officials to deter bribery through a fine structure primarily aimed at the receiver, relying on the fact that public officials would risk only so much for a relatively small bribe. However, without the expectation of a relatively certain and substantial expected penalty, even risk-neutral receivers of small bribes may be undeterred.

In addition to decentralization of regulation, increasing the specificity of regulations would help to deter corruption. Any growth in the government's role in allocating resources and rights can lead to an increase in corrupt transactions. However, we can drive the rate of bribery towards zero by reducing the amount of vagueness inherent in most gambling enabling statutes, thus giving high-level bureaucrats, the public, the press, and other enforcers a way to measure whether the guidelines are being circumvented. We can also reduce the incentives for bribery by restructuring a state's regulatory framework into a sequential model in which applicants for a gambling license "must have the portions of their petitions approved in a particular order." Applying these anti-discretionary principles to riverboat gambling, we arrive at one way to restructure gambling regulation's oversight function in order to curb corruption: enacting specific licensing standards for riverboats that enable an enforcer more easily to detect corrupt transactions. Some riverboat states have set limits on the number of licenses that the state may award; others have set betting and loss maximums, and some even require that riverboats actually "cruise." Most state legislatures, however, have delegated broad authority to gaming commissioners, appointed by the governor and entrusted with adopting riverboat regulations "in the public interest." Not surprisingly, gambling commissions have used this grant of authority to enact few specific rules of their own. The Missouri Gaming Commission, for example, gave itself the right to "waive any type of licensing requirement or procedure if it determines that the waiver is in the best interest of the public."

Vague gambling regulations such as these pave a smooth road for aspiring gambling licensees to pay off—or at least curry influence with—bureaucrats and elected officials. The concentration in state legislatures and governors' mansions of ultimate authority over gambling, together with vague regulations, account for the lion's share of corrupt illegal (and legal) transactions between officials and gambling entrepreneurs. This broad, poorly defined authority, designed to facilitate case-by-case determinations of license eligibility, gives legislators and members of the executive branch enormous leverage over gambling interests, allowing elected officials to arrange easily campaign contributions and bribes in exchange for exercising influence over agencies on behalf of their patrons. The most outlandish example of this occurred in 1993 in Louisiana, where members of the state's Riverboat Gaming Commission "flouted [even their] own [vague] guidelines," by giving "preliminary approval" to a list of riverboat operators who met no objective criteria, save for their status as "friends, relatives and supporters of the [Gov. Edwin Edwards]." The power to grant preliminary approval for licenses was not even a statutorily approved exercise of the commission's delegated powers.

SHIFTING GAMBLING CONTROL TO LOCAL AUTHORITIES

The pervasive argument against giving localities regulatory control over projects that pack enormous potential for economic growth is that local officials will be more likely than state-level legislators and bureaucrats to cave in to the demands of a lucrative new enterprise. Such an argument upends the notion that a locale's self-interest will insure a cleanly operated licensing system and instead avers that increased self-interest has a destructive affect on oversight. Recent gambling legalization efforts have yielded some sparse, anecdotal evidence in support of the contention that local officials may prove particularly vulnerable to corruption. In Illinois, for example, the mayor of a tiny Chicago suburb, "hoping against hope that the legislature increases the number of riverboat licenses," personally contributed $102,000 to state legislators' campaigns, hired a former Illinois governor as a lobbyist, and offered to build a river through his town, primarily because he and his family have business holdings that would stand to profit from riverboats. However, this is a tale of legal activities, and whatever it may say about local corruption, it says more about the dearth of laws regulating campaign contributions and conflicts-of-interest; Illinois, for example, has no limit on campaign contributions.

Presently, five of the six riverboat states—all except Louisiana—provide for some local control over gambling. Iowa, Missouri, and Indiana all require that a local referendum be held in the county or municipality where a riverboat proposes to dock before the state commission can license a riverboat for that location. Illinois requires that the governing body of a municipality approve a riverboat by majority vote. Adopting a veto model of local control, Mississippi presumes that a riverboat is legal unless a county decides to hold an anti-gambling referendum, which is triggered by a petition signed by 20 percent or 1,500 of a county's registered voters, whichever is fewer. As a trade-off, Mississippi allows communities to impose their own fees on local gambling operations, and takes only a small part of the total gambling revenue through licensing and operations fees imposed on cruise vessels.

Naturally, no amount of tinkering with licensing procedures will overcome a lack of individual honesty in immoral, self-aggrandizing politicians or a lack of civic-mindedness in apathetic voters. Nevertheless, some local, grass-roots-type movements have begun to challenge the miserly way in which states dole out supervisory and licensing powers, and the laxity with which the state's reserved powers are exercised. In Missouri, for example, a St. Louis alderman proposed two bills that would give the city more control over its prospective riverboat operators. One called for the aldermen to hold formal hearings (complete with subpoena power and witnesses testifying under oath) on the issue of local ownership in riverboat casino proposals. The second, largely aimed at eradicating the usefulness of "rent-a-citizens"—potential casino investors who were close to public officials—would ban city employees from going to work for riverboats within two years of leaving municipal employment. In Louisiana, where state-level corruption in distributing riverboat licenses (not to mention myriad other gambling-related licenses) is by far the worst in the country, and state power the most consolidated, the district attorneys in Orleans, Jefferson and East Baton Rouge parishes notified riverboat operators that they must begin cruising, as required by law, and cease their dockside operations. This move was prompted in part by political pressure from citizens who felt that docked riverboat gambling was too intrusive on their communities, and that state law enforcement authorities were blind to their concerns because of the revenues the boats were raking in.

CHANGING THE MONOPOLY STRUCTURE OF RIVERBOAT LICENSES

Licensing structures that reduce the value of any given, individual license should deter bribery by lessening its returns. Currently, the chief deterrent for firms considering bribing a public official to get a riverboat license is the (somewhat amorphous) calculation of moral costs. Given the general public's recent disinclination to legalize new forms of gambling, companies may prove responsive to the shaming effects of a bribery conviction, which could damage public relations campaigns in other jurisdictions. While raising fines might seem the most direct route to reducing the returns from bribery, such an analysis fails to consider that a rise in fines necessarily brings a rise in the state's fixed enforcement costs, ultimately reducing the overall expected fine. Thus either allowing the market to regulate the number of riverboat licenses or selling the licenses through a public auction will provide the most effective reduction in a gambling firm's incentive to bribe.

1. The Market Approach

If states granted riverboat licenses to all who qualified, market competition would only improve the "gambling product" and increase aggregate revenues for riverboats. A state opting for market regulation of the number of licenses might have to trade off a fraction of the generally accepted twenty percent tax rate on gross riverboat receipts in exchange for the lack of a protected market, but the overall increase in gambling revenue fostered by competition would compensate for the reduced tax rate. Furthermore, the externalized social costs of "buying" licenses would be reduced towards zero, and could be driven into state coffers in the form of a yearly licensing fee or initial entry cost.

2. The Auction Possibility

In assessing the merits of auctioning off monopoly rights to operate riverboats, we must first decide whether preserving an effective monopoly for boats is socially and economically desirable. Economic justifications for state-sponsored monopolies generally focus on protecting consumers from their own lack of information and bargaining power, and often tout the allegedly superior revenue-raising potential of monopolies.

Auctioning off monopoly franchises, but keeping the current market protections for riverboats, would eliminate waste. The auction process would assure that states and not individual politicians would get the market-clearing fee—up to the present value of monopoly profits discounted by the chance of getting the license—for the monopoly franchise. Currently, the vast difference between the sum of initial and yearly licensing fees for a riverboat—which in all states would be under $500,000 for the term of the license—and the millions of dollars of monopoly profits reaped from the enterprise is a windfall for gambling companies, and can be (and often is) used for lobbying, campaign contributions, and outright bribery.

CONCLUSION: CONFUSED GOALS AND INEFFICIENT REGULATION

The success of reforms such as changing the state's bureaucratic structure, increasing local authority, and letting the market regulate the value of riverboat licenses, thus depend on state legislators' collective resolve to tighten controls on gambling while ceding some regulatory power to localities. The task becomes more complicated if legislators and bureaucrats act for their own self-enrichment and voters are too apathetic to catch them at it. Gambling presents particularly difficult challenges in this regard because our policy goals in legalizing it are at odds and raise heretofore unanswered questions. Have we finally resolved to remove the moral opprobrium from gambling? Can gambling actually raise money for state coffers? Are politicians willing to regulate gambling in a manner that does not compromise the public trust in its elected officials? Creating incentives to abhor corruption, through economic and oversight-related reform, will reduce public corruption. The ultimate success of the effort, however, will turn on the degree to which responsible politicians and voters can respond in logical and creative ways to the varied pressures that a mixed capitalist system inevitably places on a democracy.

CHICAGO CASINO: WORTH A CRAPSHOOT? UNIVERSITY OF CHICAGO LAW STU-DENTS DEBATE THE MERITS

Chicago Sun–Times, June 19, 2004.

Pro

Mayor Daley proposes adding a spanking new facility to the downtown area that could potentially provide an unprecedented spark to Chicago's tourism industry. This new toy could add an estimated $250 million annually to the city's coffers.

What is the catch? This new entertainment option is a casino.

So why is "casino" such an unmentionable word? Is it because we don't like the idea of government operating an industry that's designed to prey on our shortcomings?

Illinois, along with 36 other states, runs a state lottery.

It allows racetrack betting and all kinds of charitable gambling.

Think the lottery is entirely too innocent and altogether different from casino gambling?

Think again.

The lottery pays out approximately 50 percent of what it takes in. Returns on casino games are well over 90 percent. A game like blackjack gives you nearly even odds against the house.

Is it because we don't like the people who gamble?

Perhaps we should take a look in the mirror first.

According to a government-funded study, 86 percent of Americans have gambled; 68 percent have gambled within the past year. More than a quarter of adult Americans gambled at a casino in 2001.

Gambling has become a normal American activity, simply another form of entertainment. And it is one of the few entertainment options that hold appeal for every rung of society.

Where else can you find the everyman rubbing shoulders with the wealthiest of the wealthy?

Is it because we think gambling is affiliated with organized crime?

Gambling's current affiliation with organized crime is one of the most commonly held misconceptions.

What better way to eliminate the vice elements from gambling than to allow the government to regulate?

Or is it that we just don't like gambling itself?

Gambling—just like going to the movies, or a bar, or a Steppenwolf show—is a form of entertainment that holds immense appeal for many folks. For a set amount of money, consenting adults get in return the opportunity of winning, the thrill of taking the risk, and the camaraderie of doing it with others in the same boat.

Once considered exotic, gambling has now rooted itself in main-stream culture. Just observe the wild commercial popularity of televised championship poker, a card game.

Besides, casino gambling already exists around the Chicago area. Places such as Gary, East Chicago and Hammond already attract a line of Chicagoans. Why not allow the city the opportunity to become the beneficiary of Chicagoans who are already willing to spend?

The fact is, casino gambling is surrounded by myths and treated differently than other forms of entertainment. We do not ban bars because some patrons are alcoholics.

And it's not a regressive tax: People with higher incomes visit casinos more. Only 22 percent of persons with incomes under $35,000 visited a casino in 2001, in contrast to about 35 percent of those with incomes over $95,000.

If Chicago decides to build a casino, why not build it right? Let's complement the casino with shopping venues, restaurants, perhaps even an amusement center for those under 21. Let's create a world-class entertainment venue. Let's emphasize table games over slot machines.

Let's provide jobs for the thousands of Chicagoans who need stable jobs in a booming industry. Let's provide access to Gamblers Anonymous in the casinos for those who need help. Let's have voluntary patron-tracking systems so casinos can identify and help those showing signs of gambling problems.

Let's pump the funds generated from gambling into improving our schools, our parks and our libraries.

Let's create a better future for this city, and let's do it sooner, rather than later.

Victor Zhao, Alyshea Austern, Shaudy Danaye–Elmi, Brian Hill, David Gearey, Jenny Maldonado, Mary McKinney, Brad Russo, Andrew Sherman and Sean Williams are students at the University of Chicago Law School studying gambling law as part of a course on Advanced Criminal Law

Con

Why would Mayor Daley want to corrupt this beautiful city with a casino—an institution with admittedly measurable benefits (an estimated $250 million in city tax revenue annually) but also incalculable costs?

The simple fact is, gambling disproportionately exploits the poor and vulnerable—and sends the wrong message. The majority of casino revenues are derived from slot machines, in fact, casinos make $7 out of every $10 on slots—and these machines are designed to target the less wealthy and the elderly, people who lack the disposable income to support the habits these machines encourage. Poor people lose a greater proportion of their income gambling.

Hooking first-time gamblers through glitz and glamour, or securing the lifelong devotion of the occasional off-track bettor by offering "better odds" or "stirring play" is preying on people's weaknesses. Of all things, this city should not be encouraging laziness, greed and a desire for material gain without work. Casino gambling is only going to promote compulsive addictions, bankruptcy and family disruption.

Many of us have lived in Chicago for only two or three years, and many of us will not make our lives here in the future. But in our short time in Chicago, we have come to love this city. We love it for the lake, its food, its culture and its people. We love it for its parks, its night life and its neighborhoods. In a perverse way, we even love it for its winters. Some of us are born and raised here and proud of our reputation for hard work. In many ways, Chicago is the anti-Vegas: The "get-rich-quick" mentality goes against what it means to be born and bred here.

We all know the arguments for casino gambling. "It brings jobs, revenue and tourism." "People already gamble, so we might as well get some taxes out of it." "It's a legitimate form of entertainment, no different than going to a movie or the theater." "It will boost the city's economy." "The extra revenue will make our schools better."

Many of these arguments are valid. True, a casino would bring Chicago new revenue, create jobs and attract tourists. But the taxes that a casino would generate would come from those of us least able to afford them. The jobs it would create would be low-paying ones that don't actually address the structural failings in our economy. And the tourists who would come to Chicago for a casino are not the ones we want to encourage.

Yes, many Americans gamble in some form, but not at casinos. They play in a friendly poker game or in a football pool Casino gambling draws a different crowd entirely. It's an institution of which can be said even its benefits are stained from their origin.

A casino may create some low-paying jobs, but it is not a tool of economic growth. It builds nothing creates nothing, and makes nothing because it is nothing—just an empty shell that houses a market in false hopes. Such a thing is untrue to the ideals that made Chicago the city that it is.

Daley announced that he liked the idea of casino gambling because he is worried about the burden of high property taxes in the city. It seems that Daley is shifting the tax burden from those with means to those without. Not only that, but the revenue stream is likely to be diverted to other projects. According to news accounts, only $60 million "may" go to education, museums and parks. How much will really end up in education is anyone's guess. Our guess: little.

Casinos make their money by preying on their players. They are built to keep the gamblers in and the real world out They bring problems of addiction, alcoholism and organized crime. It's bad enough that private casinos do this to their customers, but it's far worse that a city wants to do it to its citizens. The City of Chicago should continue to promote the cultural institutions and events that make Chicago stand head and shoulders above its peer cities. Let's find smarter ways to grow.

Tim Karpoff, Ranjit Hakim, Allen McKenzie, Gabriel Galloway, Naria Kim, Carl LeSueur, Anne Mullins, Angela Ramey, Deidra Ritcherson and Tamer Tullgren are students at the University of Chicago Law School in a course on Advanced Criminal Law.

I.   CONCLUDING NOTES AND QUESTIONS

1.   One definition of gambling would be playing any game for money. The financial context is essential to the activity although the reward for winning can be services or non-financial property. While prohibited commercial acts of sex also have a financial aspect, the money is essential there to the wrongfulness of the conduct but is not essential to interpersonal sexual relationships. In that sense, the material aspect of gambling seems more central to gambling as a social behavior than to the other behaviors considered in this volume. Or is the commercial context of prostitution so transformative as to be essential?

2.   The second remarkable financial aspect of gambling is its scale. The Gambling Impact Study Commission estimated the gross profit from gambling in the United States in 1997 at 50 billion dollars, which would be more than 100 billion in 2008.

The estimate for legal gambling is in range of 10% of recreational spending in the United States. No good estimates of current levels of illegal gambling are available, but the majority of sports betting and a large proportion of card playing are not counted in legal gambling.

3.   While there are obvious problems with estimating the volume of illegal gambling, the effort by the President's Crime Commission in 1965 provides some eye-opening contrasts. The method they used to estimate "the economic impact" of illegal gambling was the same "gross profit" amount used by the 1997 commission. The seven billion dollars gross profit from gambling for organized crime was almost twice as much as the total cost of all property crime and also 20 times the profit estimated for all narcotics (350 million in 1965 dollars)—see President's Commission on Law Enforcement and the Administration of Justice, *The Challenge of Crime in a Free Society*, p. 33, "Illegal Goods and Services." This total was also more than 30 times the gross profit of prostitution and 70 times the cost of tax fraud. Does the scale of illegal gambling in 1965 help to explain the expansion of legal gambling in the generation after 1965?

4.   The 50 billion dollar estimate of legal gambling in the United States by 1997 tells a story of massive legal change, a transformation of types of

gambling from illegal to legal in 47 of 50 states in the United States. To what extent can the last 50 years of experience with gambling serve as a useful model for study as decriminalization of narcotics or prostitution? What do we know about the impact of the legal status on the number of persons who gamble and the amount wagered? About the impact on crime, violence, bankruptcy and other social harms?

5. If the United States as a whole is one model of decriminalization, the state of Nevada is another. Gambling is more important to the economy and society there than would be the case in full national decriminalization, but doesn't that make Las Vegas an overstated model of decriminalization, one where both positive and negative impacts are clearly visible? What do we know of the differences between Las Vegas and Phoenix, Arizona that tell us of gambling effects? Are there negative gambling effects that might not be visible in Las Vegas? What and why?

6. Some gambling activities are organized around the prediction of events, and large economic incentives may produce efforts to influence events that generate gambling activity. Sports gambling is the most prominent form of event gambling, and "fixed" outcomes in horse racing, boxing, and college athletics have been not infrequent in U.S. history. Does legalization of event gambling increase or decrease the chances of such corruption? What aspects of events make them prone to corruption? What are the alternative methods of preventing this type of problem?

7. What potential exists to restrict either the scale of gambling or the types of gambling in the 21st century? Is the problem technical (the internet) or political (state gambling interests) or both? Some potential exists in internet gambling to regulate gambling access by restricting the payments system from allowing fund transfers. But has the moral transformation of gambling removed the moral basis for such restrictions?

Chapter 5

PORNOGRAPHY

A. INTRODUCTION

The explosive growth of publicly available pornography in the last third of the 20th century is almost parallel to the growth of non-criminal gambling. In a single generation, in most developed nations in the world, books and film went from the vice districts of big cities to business hotels and computer screens everywhere. But while the decriminalization of pornography involving adult subjects and objects was as extensive as gambling, the moral transformation of pornography in society and government is nowhere near as dramatic. No state government would sponsor an adult entertainment Web site as governments now support and advertise lotteries. And while the stars of pornographic films have achieved celebrity status, it is not a status free from taint. The moral legitimacy of pornography is contested. Is this merely a transitional status or a longstanding distinction between pornography and gambling? What legal and social consequences are likely if the social status of the practice and the industry remains marginal?

GORDON HAWKINS AND FRANKLIN E. ZIMRING—ON DEFINITIONS

From *Pornography in a Free Society* (Cambridge University Press, 1988).

It might seem obvious, although it has not always been recognized, that an essential preliminary to any discussion of the censorship or prohibition of pornographic material must be some attempt at the definition of pornography. It is not sufficient, although it has in the past been so regarded, to say "I think I can recognize it when I see it" (Allen, 1962:143) or "I know it when I see it" (*Jacobellis v. Ohio*, 378 U.S. 184, 197, [1964], Stewart, J., concurring).

Announcing that we will know "it" when we see it represents an evasion of definition. Even if by means of some kind of intuitive insight we were able instantly to recognize pornography, we would still not be able to say upon inspection what it is that is pornographic about pornography. And unless we can do this, although different observers might agree that a particular work was a piece of pornography, it would be impossible to tell what they were agreeing about. Even widespread agreement would provide no comprehension of the rationale underlying the classification.

Some years ago, a volume of *Law and Contemporary Problems* was devoted to the subject of "Obscenity and the Arts." The editor in his foreword to the volume said: "Assuming there is general agreement that obscenity should be suppressed, the basic problem of definition presents itself: What is obscene?" He then went on, without answering that question, to raise other questions about "the problem of control," the effectiveness of sanctions, and whether the "suppression of obscenity [would] perhaps give rise to even more noxious social evils?" (Shimm, 1955:532).

What is puzzling about this is the assumption of unanimity about the desirability of suppressing some unidentified phenomenon. Clearly the "basic problem of definition" should, if it was going to present itself at all, have had precedence. For unless we know what it is that ought to be suppressed, to say there is "general agreement" tells us nothing. Even if all know it when they see it and are united in agreeing that it should be suppressed, how do we know that the agreement is not totally illusory?

What about the U.S. Treasury Department official who judged photographs of the paintings on the ceiling of the Sistine Chapel to be obscene (Haight, 1978:12)? Then there was the "cultivated Chinese gentleman" who found the pronounced and regular rhythms of the Sousa march "The Stars and Stripes Forever" played by the Marine band "almost unbearably lascivious and suggestive of coitus" (La Barre, 1955:536). As Walter Allen says in an essay in a volume devoted to "original studies in the nature and definition of 'obscenity,'" "we find ourselves floundering in the morass of the subjective" (Allen, 1962:143). This may not matter very much in the context of literary or artistic discussion, but it is of crucial importance in relationship to policymaking.

The importance of such theoretical considerations and the emphasis on the necessity for definition received striking confirmation in the career of the Meese Commission. In this case, the failure to agree about what is pornographic about pornography meant that the commission could not for this reason properly evaluate the evidence on the impact of pornography. But this is to anticipate.

For purposes of exposition, we here set out seriatim the findings of the three commissions on the subject of definition of terms. This is done by identifying the different interpretations of the key terms—obscenity, pornography, and erotica—offered by each, as well as by indicating which term each commission regarded as central to its inquiries.

The Johnson Commission

The Johnson Commission deals with the question of definition summarily in the preface to its report, where it is noted that "the area of the Commission's study" had been "marked by enormous confusion over terminology." The area of the commission's study was described as "a wide range of explicit sexual depictions in pictorial and textual media." The commission explained its use of terms and defined the subject of its investigation in a brief footnote. As to obscenity, the report notes that "some people equate 'obscenity' with 'pornography' and apply both terms to any type of explicit sexual material." It goes on to say simply that "in the Commission's Report, the terms 'obscene' and 'obscenity' are used solely to refer to the legal concept of prohibited sexual materials" (U.S. Commission, 1970:3 n.4).

The emphasis given to the definition of pornography is one of the important contrasts between these three reports. The Johnson Commission, although the word "pornography" appears in the title of its report, deals with the term briefly and dismissively. Having noted that some people use the terms "obscenity" and "pornography" interchangeably, and others "intend differences of various degrees in their use of these terms," it concludes: "The term 'pornography' is not used at all in a descriptive context because it appears to have no legal significance and because it most often denotes subjective disapproval of certain materials rather than their content or effect" (ibid.).

The discussion regarding the use of the term "erotica" in these reports seems a matter chiefly of connotation. The Johnson Commission did not define erotica expressly, but by implication indicated that it should be regarded as identical or coextensive in sense and usage with "sexually explicit." Thus, "the Report uses the phrases 'explicit sexual materials,' 'sexually oriented material,' 'erotica,' or some variant thereof to refer to the subject matter of the Commission's investigations" (ibid.:3,4). It is notable that the report of the commission's Effects Panel, which takes up 125 pages of the commission's report, is entitled "The Impact of Erotica."

The Williams Committee

The Williams Committee Report states that "obscene" is a term that expresses certain reactions such as repulsion and disgust, or even outrage, that an object or work arouses "rather than telling one what kind of thing actually arouses those reactions." It deals at considerable length with the legal usage of the term but concludes that "we suspect that the word 'obscene' may now be worn out, and past any useful employment at all. It is certainly too exhausted to do any more work in the courts" (Home Office, 1979:103–104).

By contrast, the Williams Committee found that pornography was "a rather more objective expression referring to a certain kind of writing, pictures, etc." Pornography was defined as follows:

The term "pornography" always refers to a book, verse, painting, photograph, film or some such thing—what in general may be called a representation ... We take it that, as almost everyone understands the term, a pornographic representation is one that combines two features: it has a certain function or intention, to arouse its audience sexually, and also a certain content, explicit representations of sexual material (organs, postures, activity, etc.). A work has to have both this function and this content to be a piece of pornography. (ibid.:104)

For the Williams Report, the term "pornography" is regarded as central to its analysis. Although "pornography" appears neither in the title of the Williams Committee Report nor in its terms of reference, the word is used deliberately and repeatedly. Thus "in the course of Chapter 7, we have referred almost all discussions to pornography rather than to obscenity. This emphasis was deliberate" (Home Office, 1979:103). It may be added that in defining pornography as an objective expression rather than as denoting subjective approval or disapproval the Williams Committee enjoyed the support of both the *Oxford English Dictionary* and *Webster's New World Dictionary of the American Language.*

That the Williams Committee's definition is consonant with the dictionary definitions is, of course, not accidental. The expression "as almost everyone understands the term" refers to ordinary usage, and lexical definition is also derived from ordinary usage. In this connection, there is a distinction commonly recognized between what is called lexical definition and stipulative definition: the former referring to "the customary or dictionary meaning of a word" and the latter, to "establishing or announcing or choosing one's own meaning for a word" (Robinson, 1950:19; see also Morris, 1960:30–32). We mention this distinction here because, as we shall see in Chapter 6 when we come to deal with what has been called the "radical feminist critique" of pornography, it assumes some importance.

With regard to "erotica," the Williams Committee begins by noting that the term "erotic" is sometimes used as an alternative to "pornographic," being milder with regard to both the content and the intention. The content by this interpretation is described as being more allusive and less explicit, and what is intended is not strong sexual arousal but some lighter degree of sexual interest.

But the report adds that there is another interpretation of the term "erotica," "under which the erotic is what *expresses* sexual excitement rather than causes it—in the same way as a painting or a piece of music may express sadness without necessarily making its audience sad.... In this sense an erotic work will suggest or bring to mind feelings of sexual attraction or excitement. It may cause some such feelings as well and put the audience actually into that state, but if so that is a further effect" (Home Office, 1979: 105).

The Meese Commission

The Meese Commission report devotes some five pages to "Defining Our Central Terms." With regard to "obscenity," it is noted that the word "has taken on a legal usage." Accordingly:

> We will here use the words "obscene" and "obscenity" ... to refer to material that has been or would likely be found to be obscene in the context of a judicial proceeding employing applicable legal and constitutional standards. Thus, when we refer to obscene material, we need not necessarily be condemning that material, or urging prosecution, but we are drawing on the fact that such material could now be prosecuted without offending existing authoritative interpretation of the Constitution. (U.S. Department of Justice, 1986:230)

As to pornography the Meese Commission decided that "the appellation "pornography" is undoubtedly pejorative." The Williams Committee definition was criticized as not reflecting "modern usage." "To call something "pornographic" is plainly, in modern usage, to condemn it." Pornography, the report says, "seems to mean in practice any discussion or depiction of sex which the person using the word objects." Accordingly, the commission decided to try to minimize the use of the word "pornography" in this Report (ibid.:227–228).

Whereas the Johnson Commission used the term "erotica" freely and the Williams Committee found the term "erotic" helpful to mark "significant and useful distinctions" (Home Office 1979:105), the Meese Commission rejected it. The reference to the term "erotica" in that commission's report runs all follows:

> It seems clear to us that the term as actually used is the mirror image of the broadly condemnatory use of "pornography," being employed to describe sexually explicit materials of which the user of the term approves. For some the ... word "erotica" describes any sexually explicit material that contains neither violence nor subordination of women, for others the term refers to almost all sexually explicit material, and for still others only material containing generally accepted artistic value qualifies as erotica. In light of this disagreement, and in light of the tendency to use the term "erotica" as a conclusion rather than a description, we again choose to avoid the term wherever possible. (U.S. Department of Justice, 1986:230–231)

Key terms

With respect to what are regarded as key terms in its analysis, each commission follows a separate path. The American commissions use a legal definition of obscenity: material that could be prohibited under prevailing constitutional standards. The Williams Committee speaks of obscenity as expressive of the reactions of an audience, which conforms with the dictionary definitions. All three reports deal with the term in a conclusory fashion, and none of the reports identifies obscenity as a centrally important term in the inquiry.

For the Johnson Commission, "erotica" and "sexually explicit material" are used interchangeably as the most important terms. The problems of denoting what is sexually explicit are considered minimal, and for good reason. The Williams Committee considers the term "pornography" central and devotes substantial energy to its definition.

The Meese Commission rejects each term—"obscenity," "pornography," and "erotica"—as a central term with a fixed, formal, and approved definition. With each, reasons are given, although it is never suggested that none of the terms requires definition. It is hardly surprising that the commission., finds that "questions of terminology and definition have been recurring problems in our hearings and deliberations" (U.S. Department of Justice; 1986:227). The Meese Commission rejects the approach of the Williams Committee report in two respects. The specific definition of pornography is disputed, and the function of pornography as the central term in the inquiry is disavowed.

The Canadian Special Committee on Pornography and Prostitution, incidentally, thought that the Williams Committee definition encompassed "a great deal, if not most, of what the ordinary person would think of as pornography" but expressed "reservations about the definition for purposes of the criminal law." In the end, although "very conscious of our debt to those who have struggled with the question of the meaning of pornography," the committee decided that it would "not formulate our own precise working definition of pornography" (Canada, 1985:52, 54, 59). Later in the committee's report, however, we are told that "perhaps the most central issue of all which requires attention is that of defining what it is that makes material pornographic, and that the question of what pornography is ... needs careful and systematic consideration" (ibid:103). But although the term is used freely throughout the report, this "most central issue" somehow has escaped further attention.

THE TOWER OF BABEL

A panoramic view of the findings of the three commissions on the subject of definition of terms is presented in Table 2.1, where we have italicized the key terms.

The Babelish confusion of tongues in respect to definition offered by the three commissions can hardly be said to have done a great deal to alleviate "the enormous confusion over terminology" complained of in the Johnson Commission report.

CONCLUSION

Although all the terms employed in this context are commonly used with meanings that are equivocal and overlapping, there is no doubt, as the report of the Williams Committee pointed out, that "there are significant and useful distinctions to be made here, and these words can be helpfully used ... to mark those distinctions" (Home Office, 1979;105).

The most appropriate method for selecting the key terms to be employed in discussions of this matter is a process of elimination. It seems clear to us that the term "obscenity," which was rejected by all the commissions except in its "legal usage," and even in that context rejected by the Williams Committee, cannot serve to facilitate discussion or make any significant distinction. We add our own concurrence to the rare unanimity of the three reports on this issue.

Nor is the expression "explicit sexual materials," preferred by the Johnson Commission, much more satisfactory. It is itself explicit as to content—the representation of sexual material—but it denotes nothing in respect to function or intention, which is an essential conceptual element and the basis for special treatment of this category of material. To distinguish content and ignore the author's or artist's intention or purpose is to miss that aspect which is of central significance in this context. For we are not here concerned with textbooks of human biology or marriage guidance manuals that deal explicitly with sexual techniques.

With respect to "erotica", the two American commissions define the term only insofar as it refers to sexually explicit material. The Williams Committee distinguishes another interpretation of the term "erotic" as that which refers to material that *expresses* sexual excitement rather than arouses it. Assuming for the moment that such material may suggest or bring to mind feelings of sexual excitement without actually stimulating or causing such feelings, this distinction clearly rules out "erotica" as an appropriate key term for policy. We should be here concerned with provocative rather than evocative reference, and public policy concern relates to material that is both sexually explicit and has sexual arousal as its primary objective.

Thus, the most suitable and apposite term is evidently "pornography," and the Williams Committee definition of the concept of pornography brings out the essential fact that it is a category of both content and function: A "pornographic representation is one that combines two features: it has a certain function or intention, to arouse its audience sexually, and also a certain content, explicit representations of sexual material" (Home Office, 1979:104).

It seems clear that however a liberal Western democracy may decide to deal with pornography, any modern secular government will seek to permit sexually explicit communication to adults on the same basis as it permits communication about a wide variety of other topics. What seems to be of special concern to governments and communities is a combination of sexually explicit content and the sexual provocation, arousal, or excitation of an audience, from which it is assumed sexual activity will follow.

The Williams Committee's identification of "pornography" as the key term in the discussion of this matter and its definition of it are examples of the kind of work that should have made the task of later commissions considerably easier. That committee identified, we think, what is pornographic about pornography.

Having said that, we confront one of the puzzles of the Meese Commission report: that is, its failure to recognize the centrality of the concept of pornography and its rejection of the Williams Committee definition of the term as an example of "analytic purity" that does not reflect "modern usage" (U.S. Department of Justice, 1986:228). The result of this rejection was, as we document at length in Chapter 4, a profound muddle in relation to the issue of the effects of pornography.

It is remarkable that having adopted a definition of the word as a perjorative or derogatory term and having declared that it would "minimize that use of the word 'pornography' in this Report," the commission found itself unable to avoid its use. Indeed, it recurs constantly throughout the report.

Moreover, it is explained that "where we do use the term ... in this Report a reference to material as 'pornographic' means only that the material is predominantly sexually explicit and intended primarily for the purpose of sexual arousal." In the same context, but in relation to "hard core pornography," the report states:

> If we were forced to define the term "hard core pornography," we would probably note that it refers to the extreme form of what we defined as pornography, and thus would describe material that is sexually explicit to the extreme, intended virtually exclusively to arouse, and devoid of any other apparent content or purpose. (ibid.:228–229)

Thus having criticized the Williams Committee definition of "pornography" because of its "analytic purity" the commission then, for the purpose of exposition, adopted a definition virtually identical to its own rendering of the Williams Committee definition: "The Williams Committee in Great Britain several years ago ... defined pornography as a description or depiction of sex involving the dual characteristics of 1) sexual explicitness; and 2) intent to arouse sexually" (ibid.:228).

Table 2.1 *The Tower of Babel*

	Obscenity	Pornography	Erotica	Key term
Johnson Commission	"The terms *'obscene'* and *'obscenity'* are used solely to refer to the legal concept of prohibited sexual materials." (U.S. Commission, 1970:3 n. 4)	"The term *'pornography'* is not used... appears to have no legal significance... most often denotes subjective disapproval of certain materials rather than their content or effect." (U.S. Commission, 1970:3 n.4)	"The Report uses the phrases 'explicit sexual material,' *'erotica,'* or some variant thereof to refer to the subject matter of the Commission's investigations." (U.S. Commission, 1970:3 n.4)	Explicit sexual materials
Williams Committee	"*Obscene* is a term which expresses certain reactions such as repulsion or disgust... may now be past any useful employment... certainly too exhausted to do any more work in the courts." (Home Office, 1979:104)	"A *pornographic* representation combines two features: it has a certain function or intention, to arouse its audience sexually, and also a certain content, explicit representations of sexual materials (organs, postures, activity, etc.)" (Home Office, 1979:103)	"The *erotic* is what expresses sexual excitement rather than causes it ...an erotic work will suggest or bring to mind feelings of sexual attraction or excitement. It may cause some such feelings ...but if so that is a further effect." (Home Office, 1979:10)	Pornography
Meese Commission	"We will here use the words *'obscene'* and *'obscenity'* ...to refer to material that has been or would likely to be found to be obscene in the context of a judicial proceeding employing applicable legal and constitutional standards." (U.S. Department of Justice, 1986:230)	"*Pornography* seems to mean in practice any depiction of sex to which the person using the word objects.... We have tried to minimize the use of the word 'pornography' in this Report." (U.S. Department of Justice, 1986:227-228)	"The term *'erotica'* is employed to describe sexually explicit materials of which the user of the term approves. We again choose to avoid the term wherever possible." (U.S. Department of Justice, 1986:230-231)	No key term

What was the reason for this extraordinarily equivocal posture? Perhaps lawyerly caution about *proving* the elements of pornography identified in the Williams Committee definition, in a court of law, held back some members of the commission from wholehearted and explicit acceptance of that definition. For this was a commission that sought to avoid narrowing the boundaries of governmental control over sexually explicit communication. And the central issue that lay behind this effort was concern with *provocative* sexual communication.

How is it possible to prove that material was intended, or is likely, to trigger impulses to engage in sexual activity? Clearly, one can understand the attempt to avoid definitions that would place obstacles in the way of any expansion of control. Yet the sexually provocative aspect of pornography is absolutely necessary to its existence as a separate topic for governmental concern.

A subsidiary issue is whether the message sent must be intended as provocative for the communication to be regarded as pornography or whether sexual explicitness with the effect of arousing the audience is sufficient. The issue is confused somewhat by the tendency of those accused of pornographic communication to deny provocative intent, even when the circumstances strongly corroborate the awareness of provocation. Certainly if any special social or legal judgments are to be attached to pornography, we believe that the sender's knowledge of provocative impact or reckless disregard of the strong likelihood of such an effect should be required.

We have dealt at length with issues of definition because they matter, as we will see when we turn to the vigorously contested if muddled debate on the effects of pornography.

B. THE QUESTION OF HARM

GORDON HAWKINS AND FRANKLIN E. ZIMRING— PORNOGRAPHIC COMMUNICATION AND SOCIAL HARM: A REVIEW OF THE REVIEWS

From *Pornography in a Free Society* (Cambridge University Press, 1988).

The issue broadly stated is: What are the effects of pornographic communications on their audiences? But that is far too general a question, for the issues multiply when the questions become specific.

The kinds of audiences to be considered in assessing effects vary widely in many characteristics and almost certainly in regard to their responses to pornographic communication. Moreover, the kinds of effects that have been suggested are equally variable. Does pornography induce forcible rape? Does it provoke masturbation? And in addition to possible immediate behavioral consequences of pornographic communication, what about effects on attitudes and long-range behavior tendencies? As we shall see, the spectrum of possible effects discussed in the policy literature goes from extreme sexual violence to rather trivial shifts in attitude-questionnaire responses.

Two preliminary points need to be made before we commence analysis of research into the effects of pornographic communication and the conclusions drawn from it by pornography commissions. First, it would be utterly astounding if pornographic communication, a medium-sized industry in the Western world, had no impact at all on its audience. The billions of dollars expended on pornographic materials by willing consumers testify to the capacity of such material to have some effect on human states of consciousness. The question is thus not whether such materials have any effects but whether they have certain specific effects and what value, positive or negative, we associate with the occurrence of those specific effects.

The second reason why specificity is required in discussion of the impact of pornographic communication relates to the methodology and limitations of empirical social science. Different forms of pornographic communication, different audiences, and different attitudinal and behavioral characteristics of those audiences must be studied one or two at a time. This sort of incremental process of investigation provides a fragile basis for the kind of sweeping generalizations frequently advanced as social science in debates about pornography.

There are two senses in which analysis of the effects of pornographic communication is crucial to the determination of what government might do to regulate it. First, the high value placed on freedom of expression throughout the West places a presumption against regulation in the way of any regulatory scheme. Both the freedom to speak and freedom to hear can be seen as of primary importance in this context. The First Amendment of the Constitution of the United States which provides that "Congress shall make no law ... abridging the freedom of speech, or the press" is just one embodiment of a larger tradition of liberty that demands some indication of harmful effects—and thus inquiry into impact on behavior—before special regulation would be considered.

There is a second reason why investigation of the behavioral effects of pornographic communication is required. By definition, at least by the definition adopted here, pornography is oriented toward the stimulation of sexual arousal, To analyze its impact on conduct is thus especially appropriate, just as analogously we might wish to investigate the impact of political commercials on voting behavior or advertisements for food on the purchase and consumption of foodstuffs. Indeed, it would be absurd, having defined pornography in terms of its intent to arouse sexually, to fail to investigate its impact on behavior.

The Question of Harm: No, Maybe, and Yes

A comparison of the three commissions' reports on the issue of whether pornography causes palpable social harm reveals sharply contrasting postures in both approach and conclusion, as shown in Table 1. The Johnson Commission's evidential basis for reaching conclusions about harm was a series of commissioned psychological and sociological studies and a review of the available research. It came close to summarizing the available evidence as proof of a negative relationship between pornography and sex crime, The Williams Committee, by contrast, took an aggressively agnostic stance that was used to support many if not all of the same policy conclusions as the Johnson Commission without, however, relying on or endorsing the quality of the research.

Johnson Commission	"In sum empirical research designed to clarify the question has found no evidence to date that exposure to explicit sexual materials plays a significant role in the causation of delinquent or criminal behavior among youth or adults. The Commission cannot conclude that exposure to erotic materials is a factor in the causation of sex crimes or sex delinquency." (U.S. Commission, 1970:27)
Williams Committee	"It is not possible, in our view, to reach well based conclusions about what in this country has been the influence of pornography on sexual crime." (Home Office, 1979:80)
Meese Commission	"We have reached the conclusion, unanimously and confidently, that the available evidence strongly supports the hypothesis that substantial exposure to sexually violent materials as described here bear a causal relationship to antisocial acts of sexual violence and for some subgroups possible to unlawful acts of sexual violence." (U.S. Department of Justice, 1986:326)

Table 1: Behavioral effects: sex crime

In fact, on the question of the weight to be placed on existing research the sharpest contrast on one dimension is between the Johnson Commission and the Williams Committee rather than between the Johnson Commission and the Meese Commission. The Meese Commission, relying on a mixture of empirical studies and its own reading of softer empirical data, concluded that what it categorized as a particular subset of pornographic material—sexually violent material—probably caused sex crime. Only the Williams Committee rejected any confident conclusions from existing studies.

Two further points merit mention before examining the reports individually. First, it is important to note that these three efforts did not produce two directly opposed conclusions but rather three different approaches. It is not simply a matter of different preferences on the ultimate question of censorship predetermining conclusions on the available evidence. Both the Johnson Commission and the Williams Committee favored the unrestricted availability of most pornography for adults, but their treatment of, and reliance on, social science research and field experimental method was quite distinct.

	Benign effects	Rape	Aggression	Perversion
Johnson Commission	"Two studies found that a substantial number of married couples reported more agreeable and enhanced marital communication and an increased willingness to discuss sexual matters with each other after exposure to erotic stimuli." (U.S. Commission, 1970:25)	"The Commission cannot conclude that exposure to erotic materials is a factor in the causation of sex crimes." (U.S. Commission, 1970:27)		"In general, established patterns of sexual behavior were found to be very stable and not altered substantially by exposure to erotica." (U.S. Commission, 1970:25)
Williams Committee	"We also received evidence of how pornography had been of help in enabling married couples to overcome their sexual problems: ...More generally ....such material is also used in the clinical treatment of sexual dysfunction." (Home Office, 1979:88)	"We unhesitatingly reject the suggestion that the available statistical information for England and Wales lends any support at all to the argument that pornography acts as a stimulus to the commission of sexual violence." (Home Office, 1979:80)	"We consider that the only objective verdict must be one of 'not proven.' " (Home Office, 1979:68)	"All evidence points to the fact that material dealing with bizarre or perverted sexual activity appeals only to those with a pre-existing interest established by the experiences of early life...there is no evidence that exposure to such materials inculcates a taste for it." (Home Office, 1979:86-87)
Meese Commission	"If we take the entire potential rate of 'effects' which could occur as a result of exposure to sexually explicit materials, and if we take the commission of sex offenses to be one extreme of that continuum, then the other end might be represented by beneficial effects. Many have made an argument for such benefits. Public opinion data both in 1970 and 1985 show that a majority believe use of sexually explicit materials 'provide entertainment,' relieve people of the impulse to commit crimes, and improve marital relations... There are also two areas in which sexually explicit materials have been used for positive ends: the treatment of sexual dysfunctions and the diagnosis and treatment of some paraphilias." (U.S. Department of Justice, 1986:1028)	"We have reached the conclusion, unanimously and confidently, that the available evidence strongly supports the hypothesis that substantial exposure to sexually violent materials as described here bears a causal relationship to antisocial sets of sexual violence and, for some subgroups, possibly to unlawful acts of sexual violence." (U.S. Department of Justice, 1986:326)	"In both clinical and experimental settings, exposure to sexually violent materials has indicated an increase in the likelihood of aggression. More specifically the research which is described in much detail later in this Report, shows a causal relationship between exposure to material of this type and aggressive behavior towards women." (U.S. Department of Justice, 1986:324)	"It would be strange indeed if graphic representations of a form of behavior, especially in a form that almost exclusively portrays such behavior as desirable, did not have at least some effect on patterns of behavior." (U.S. Department of Justice, 1986:326)

Table 2: Behavior finding

Second, it would be a mistake to review these three clearly distinguishable approaches with a view to determining which was correct. Each assessment has significant weaknesses, which we discuss later in the chapter. In these matters, there are many different ways of making a mistake.

Nevertheless, with such sharp differences in the conclusions reached we should ask whether the evidentiary base assessed at the three different points in time—1968–70, 1977–79, and 1985–86—was significantly different. Our own answer to this question is that it was not. Although many more studies were available to the Meese Commission than to the Johnson Commission fifteen years earlier, the principal differences between those commissions relate not to the nature and extent of the evidence but to how the evidence was evaluated and weighed.

No new statistical studies of either the incidence of sex crimes in population areas or the behavior of sex offenders led to the Meese Commission's rejection of the Johnson Commission's conclusions. The new laboratory studies produced between 1970 and 1985 measured attitudes and the willingness to engage in behavior far removed from sex crime, The anecdotal evidence cited by the Meese Commission in 1986 was in abundant supply when the two earlier bodies took evidence.

The contrasting conclusions of the three commissions provide a remarkable instance of the role of social science in the formulation of public policy. Indeed, we have found no more striking example of the drawing of contrary conclusions from the evidence provided by social science research in any area of modern policy debate. We shall now examine how each commission reached its particular conclusion, before returning to a critique of the inferences they drew. Their respective findings are shown in Tables 4 and 3.

THE JOHNSON COMMISSION

The conclusion of the Johnson Commission regarding the effects of obscenity or pornography in relation to delinquent or criminal behavior was that in sum, "empirical research designed to clarify the question has found no evidence to date that exposure to explicit sexual materials plays a significant role in the causation of delinquent or criminal behavior among youth or adults. The Commission cannot conclude that exposure to erotic materials is a factor in the causation of sex crimes or sex delinquency" (U.S. Commission, 1970:27). This conclusion and the way in which it was reached met with widespread criticism.

	Toward women	Toward rape	Other
Johnson Commission	"One presumed consequence .. is that erotica transmits an inaccurate and uninformed conception of sexuality, and that the viewer or user will (a) develop a calloused and manipulative orientation toward women and (b) engage in behavior in which affection and sexuality are not well integrated. A recent survey shows that 41% of American males and 46% of females believe that 'sexual materials lead people to lose respect for women.' ...Recent experiments . . . suggest that such fears are probably unwarranted." (U.S. Commission, 1970:201)		"Exposure to erotic stimuli appears to have little or no effect on already established attitudinal commitments regarding either sexuality or sexual morality." (U.S. Commission, 1970:26)
Williams Committee	"Many of our women correspondents wanted the law to be invoked against the degradation of women in pornography; but the consensus of those parts of the women's movement from which we heard tended to attach greater importance to freedom of expression than to the need to suppress pornography." (Home Office, 1979:88)		"From everything we know of social attitudes, and have learnt in the course of our enquiries, our belief can only be that the role of pornography in influencing the state of society is a minor one. To think anything else, and in particular to regard pornography as having a crucial or even a significant effect on essential social values, is to get the problem of pornography out of proportion." (Home Office, 1979:95)
Meese Commission	"To the extent that these materials create or reinforce the view that women's function is disproportionately to satisfy the sexual needs of men, then the materials will have pervasive effects on the treatment of women in society. . . . We obviously cannot here explore fully all the forms in which women are discriminated against in contemporary society. Nor can we explore all the causes. But we feel confident in concluding that the view of women as available for sexual domination is one cause of that discrimination." (U.S. Department of Justice, 1986:334)	"The evidence is also strongly supportive of significant attitudinal changes on the part of those with substantial exposures to violent pornography. These attitudinal changes are numerous. Victims of rape and other forms of sexual violence are likely to be perceived by people so exposed as more responsible for the assault, as having suffered less injury, and as having been less degraded as a result of the experience. Similarly, people with-a substantial exposure to violent pornography are likely to see the rapist or other sexual offender as less responsible for the act and as deserving of less stringent punishment." (U.S. Department of Justice, 1986:326-327)	"These attitudinal changes have been shown experimentally to include a larger range of attitudes than those just discussed. The evidence also strongly supports the conclusion that substantial exposure to violent sexually explicit material leads to a greater acceptance of the 'rape myth' in its broader sense – that women enjoy being coerced into sexual activity, that they enjoy being physically hurt in a sexual context, and that as a result a man who forces himself on a women sexually is in fact merely acceding to the 'real' wishes of the woman, regardless of the extent to which she seems to be resisting. The myth is that a woman who says 'no' really means 'yes,' and that men art justified in acting on the assumption that the 'no' answer is indeed the 'yes' answer. We have little trouble concluding that this attitude is both pervasive and profoundly harmful, and that any stimulus reinforcing or increasing the incidence of this attitude is for that reason alone properly designated as harmful." (U.S. Department of Justice, 1986:327)

Table 3: Attitude

The Johnson Commission in statements of this kind and in its endorsement of the consultant and panel reports has been widely read as concluding that "exposure to erotic materials is" not "a factor in the causation of sex crimes or sex delinquency." Their report does go beyond the "not proven" posture of the Williams Committee by placing heavy emphasis on the lack of relationship reported in the various studies made and by citing that research with approval.

Yet in a strict sense there is no allegation in the Johnson Commission report that the negative proposition had been proved or was relied on to support the commissions' recommendations. Why, then, was the Johnson Commission regarded by observers, rightly in our view, as implying that there was strong evidence against a causal relation between pornography and sex crime, whereas the Williams Committee escaped this categorization, even while advocating similar social policy based on its conclusions about social harm?

The difference, we believe, reflects the contrast between a lawyer's manipulation of presumptions to determine an outcome and the social scientist's attempt to marshal empirical evidence in support of a policy argument. The Williams Committee put distance between its policy conclusions and the social science data. The Johnson Commission, more committed to the value of the research, gave the impression that it was relying on research evidence.

The Johnson Commission reviewed the evidence on the question of effects from a great variety of sources, including survey research among youths and adults, psychological studies of normal and criminal sex-offender adults and normal and delinquent adolescents, and studies based on crime statistics.

With very few exceptions, the evidence discussed at length by the Johnson Commission and the research conducted under its auspices focused on the relatively immediate physiological, psychological, and behavioral impact of pornographic communication. Both the immediate and long-term impact of such communication on sexual attitudes and sexual practices are notably absent from the Johnson Commission's research emphasis, although some survey responses concerned these topics; the question of the impact of pornographic communication on attitudes toward women and toward fraud and force in sexual behavior was not emphasized. Only one study was reported on the relationship between exposure to pornography and willingness to use ethically marginal seduction techniques such as alcohol and verbal manipulation. This study was interpreted as suggesting that exposure to pornography had a mild suppressive effect on the approval of the use of those techniques by those disposed to use them (U.S. Commission, 1970:201).

In a review of the Johnson Commission's report, Professor Herbert L. Packer wrote, "the most controversial portion of the Commission's Report is unquestionably the Panel Report on the 'Impact of Erotica.'" He criticized the commission for "relying so heavily and so misguidedly on the behavioral sciences," at the same time acknowledging "my bias that research is the opiate of behavioral scientists" (Packer, 1971:74, 76).

Professor Packer was not alone in being critical of the panel report. Indeed, the commission's report itself includes, in a dissenting statement by two commissioners (Morton A. Hill and Winfrey C. Link), a lengthy "Critique of Commission Behavioral Research" and an evaluation by Dr. Victor B. Cline ("University of Utah psychologist and specialist in social science research methodology and statistics"), who reported that "the empirical research studies ... reveal of great number of serious flaws, omissions, and grave shortcomings" (U.S. Commission, 1970:390).

Much of the criticism the report provoked was directed at what was called "the Commission's exclusive reliance upon statistical and 'behavioral science' techniques of analysis (and) the implicit claims that the Commission has made for the primacy of its behaviorist methodology over other ways of thinking about social problems and legal principles" (Clor, 1971:65, 76). Even James Q. Wilson, who judged that the research carried out "within the limited framework of each study, was on the whole quite unexceptionable," argued that "the weakness of the Obscenity Commission is that it relied too exclusively on social science research" (Wilson, 1971:61).

In his critique Professor Packer noted, in relation to the Effects Panel, that "of the six members of this Panel only one (Dean Lockhart, sitting ex officio) was not a behavioral scientist" (Packer, 1971:74). This was correct: the panel chairman, Otto N. Larsen, was professor of sociology at the University of Washington; G. William Jones taught communications at Southern Methodist University; Joseph T. Klapper was director of social research for CBS; Morris A. Lipton was teaching psychiatry and was director of research development at the University of South Carolina; and Marvin Wolfgang was director of the Center for Criminological Research at the University of Pennsylvania.

But this is hardly surprising. It may be true that contemporary social and behavioral science is subject to many "conceptual and methodological limitations" (Johnson, 1971:199), and that some questions about some of the effects of erotic materials may not be researchable. Yet it seems not unreasonable that a panel assigned to study social effects, in particular the causal relationship of such materials to antisocial behavior, should be composed of social and behavioral scientists.

Some of the considerable critical comment generated by this aspect of the Commission's work does not meet the "hope and expectation [for] careful appraisal of public policy in this emotionally charged area" expressed by the commission's chairman, William B. Lockhart (Boyd, 1970:453). A great deal of it seems to have been animated by the same spirit that led Billy Graham to declare the commission's report to be "one of the worst and most diabolical ever made by a presidential commission" and one that "no Christian or believing Jew could support" (Geyer, 1970:1339). Indeed, the dissenting statement filed by the sole appointee of President Nixon to the commission, which is included in the report, was accurately characterized by James Q. Wilson as "an intemperate unpleasantly *ad hominem* screed in which interesting and perhaps important objections are frequently obscured by a ranting tone" (Wilson, 1971:54).

The nature of the more serious criticism directed at the research conducted by the panel into the effects of exposure to erotic material was ably summarized by Professor Weldon T. Johnson, who was senior author of the panel's report, as follows: "Three issues have emerged. It has been argued that: a) the investigation of effects is irrelevant to dealing with the pornography problem; b) the actual effects of exposure to erotic materials are not measurable within the framework of social science research; and c) the effects, particularly the presumed pernicious effects, are obvious hut have not been recognized generally or in the Report" (Johnson, 1971:195). With regard to the first of these issues it seems unnecessary to add to Professor Johnson's own response. He points out that when the commission was established it was instructed to undertake "a thorough study which shall include a study of the causal relationship of such materials to antisocial behavior" (ibid.:195). He adds, moreover, that not only was the commission directed specifically to work in the area but also a commission-funded national survey found the question of the effect of erotic materials was "an important one in determining public attitudes" and "of general social concern" (ibid.:197– 198).

On the question of measurability of the effects of exposure to erotic materials and the various methodological criticisms of the commission's research program, it is hard to improve on the statement of a member of the Effects Panel, Joseph T. Klapper, which is included in the commission's report:

As a professional researcher in the behavioral sciences, I have long been aware that research answers complex questions only by a series of approximations. The pioneering research which the Commission has been able to accomplish in a two-year period is not and could not be either complete or flawless, not indeed could it have been so if five years had been available. The strengths and limitations of the research bearing on effects are stated at length in the Report of the Effects Panel. Given these imperfections the research is nevertheless remarkably consistent, and it does not establish a meaningful causal relationship between exposure to erotica and antisocial behavior. (U.S. Commission, 1970:373)

In a similar vein is the statement by the two psychiatrist members of the commission, Professor Morris A. Lipton and Dr. Edward D. Greenwood, one of whom (Lipton) was a member of the Effects Panel:

All research, and especially research in the behavioral sciences, initially produces imperfect results ... We would have welcomed evidence relating exposure to erotica to delinquency, crime, and antisocial behavior, for if such evidence existed we might have a simple solution to some of our most urgent problems. However, the work of the Commission has failed to uncover such evidence. Although the many and varied studies contracted for by the Commission may have flaws, they are remarkably uniform in the direction to which they point. This direction fails to establish a meaningful causal relationship or even significant correlation between exposure to erotica and immediate or delayed antisocial behavior among adults. To assert the contrary from the available evidence is not only to deny the facts, but also to delude the public by offering a spurious and simplistic answer to highly complex problems. (ibid.:380)

The strengths and limitations of the commission's research bearing on effects are, as Joseph Klapper pointed out, "stated at length in the Report of the Effects Panel." Moreover, although a number of reviews of the state of knowledge regarding the effects of pornography or sexually explicit material reflected in the scientific literature have been carried out since 1970, it remains true, as Maurice Yaffe pointed out in a review carried out for the Williams Committee, that "there does not appear to be any strong evidence that exposure to sexually explicit material triggers off antisocial sexual behavior" (Yaffe, 1978:242).

The verdict of the Williams Committee on the studies undertaken for the Johnson Commission is relevant:

> We noted that the American commission, in the light of all the studies undertaken for it, concluded that "empirical research has found no evidence to date that exposure to explicit sexual materials plays a significant role in the causation of delinquent or criminal behavior among youth or adults"; we noted also that this conclusion was criticized in a number of quarters as having been based on a partial examination of the evidence in which ambiguities and certain contraindications were ignored. Without ourselves entering into the controversy about the Commission's methods, we make the comment that the effect of reexamining the original studies in the light of a hostile critique of the Commission's conclusions, such as that put forward principally by Professor Victor Cline, is simply to make one adopt rather more caution in drawing inferences from the studies undertaken. (Home Office, 1979:66)

With regard to the criticism that the presumed pernicious effects were obvious but not recognized in the report because of its orientation toward behavioral science research, it is true that this was the established research orientation of at least six commissioners. But the senior author of the Effects Panel report seems to have had few illusions about the limitations on the utility of behavioral science research in policymaking. He claimed no more than that "behavioral science can contribute to some of the issues raised by the concern about pornography, and that potential contribution probably is in the clarification of logical and empirical assumptions underlying various policy strategies" (Johnson, 1971:217).

We would add here what can be called a conditional critique of the Johnson Commission's summary of the evidence, a critique that only applies forcefully if the commission's report is read as asserting that there is strong evidence against the proposition that pornography causes socially harmful behavior. Viewed in that light, the psychological experiments can be faulted on a number of grounds and the crude statistical time series studies on criminal statistics are of limited probative value.

The psychological experiments are early research, and although some of the studies reported in volumes 7 and g of the commission's technical reports are impressive, it is also the case that the number of studies, the range of groups, and the variety of types of communication studied are inadequate to sustain sweeping generalization. Frequently the research approach is applied to only one group without replication on another similar group or tests on differently constituted groups. Often only two groups, adults and younger persons, are the subject of experiments rather than special high-risk groups. No psychological experiments, as opposed to questionnaires, seem to have been employed with sex offenders in the commission's research.

A second problem with psychological research among normal populations is the insensitivity of such experiments to changes in low-incidence behavior. A study, such as the commission reports, of the impact of pornography on slightly fewer than two hundred people can statistically measure the impact of the stimulus only on the frequency of activities involving a substantial number of the audience. One can discover how many subjects are sexually aroused; how many of the sexually active had intercourse (if rates of sexual activity are high enough); and how many of the subjects masturbate (if the rate of that activity is high enough). But with respect to forcible rape, incest, or any other sexual practice allow statistical frequency among normal populations, a doubling or trebling of a very low rate of deviation is likely to be invisible.

A third problem with the research review of the Johnson Commission as proof of the negative of the harm hypothesis is the failure to examine separately the impact of all of the widely different types of pornography. Pornographic communications differ along a variety of dimensions: homosexual or heterosexual, the presence or absence of sadistic or masochistic themes, or material involving adults or children. Pornographic communications also vary in regard to additional affective content that does not strictly relate to sexual orientation: for example, and this is considered a crucial influence by the Meese Commission, heterosexual pornography can combine elements of force or violence. And the media of pornographic communication vary from the written word to the large screen. Finally, the contexts in which pornographic communication is projected and received may vary widely.

Of special significance in assessing die impact of pornography on the young is the nature of the peer group context in which pornography is usually consumed. This is a special case of the problem of external validity of sufficient importance to merit special mention in any commission report. Moreover, experimental interventions of the kind described in the Johnson Commission report do not provide opportunities to study the interactive effects of pornographic stimuli with other psychoactive stimuli—for instance, the combination of pornography with alcohol, or with deviant peer group pressure, or with both. It is not simply the inhibitions that are introduced by the observational apparatus of the experiment but also the way in which the experimental environment simplifies and distorts social realities that is troublesome in this context.

With such variation, a general conclusion of noneffect cannot be established on the basis of even one hundred experimental interventions unless variations in the character of the appeal, the medium of communication, and the context in which the message is received can be disregarded as being unimportant. The Johnson Commission did not assert that these differences were unimportant.

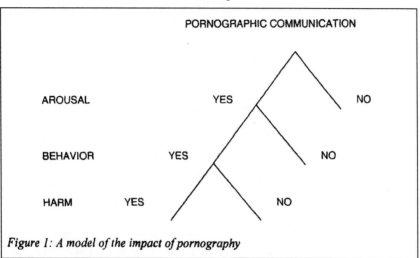

PORNOGRAPHIC COMMUNICATION

AROUSAL   YES   NO

BEHAVIOR   YES   NO

HARM   YES   NO

Figure 1: A model of the impact of pornography

The manipulation of aggregate crime statistics at the national level presents its own set of formidable barriers to inferences about the effects of pornography on sex crime. With respect to national aggregates—for example, the United States as a unit, or England and Wales—there are problems, both in measuring variations in the availability of pornography and in controlling for all the other changes that may occur with the passage of time, that may affect the incidence of crime, If sex crimes and street robbery both increase by similar amounts as pornography becomes more freely available, does this mean that pornography cannot be the cause of the increase in sex crimes? Or does it indicate that the increased availability of pornography along with other factors caused the increase in both types of offenses? Even the Danish studies, which are more specific as to time and more carefully controlled as to other factors, represent a relatively crude method of measuring the short-term impact of sharp changes in the availability of pornography.

All these considerations may not be strictly relevant to the conclusions actually drawn by the U.S. Commission on Obscenity and Pornography. But we highlight these problems in our discussion of the work of this first commission to indicate the problems encountered in regard to the work of each of the commissions considered here.

Moreover, there is one other respect in which the analysis of the Johnson Commission report provides a quite useful introduction to the assessment of the work of the subsequent commissions. As we read the report of the Johnson Commission's Effects Panel it appears that the commission adopted a single model for the relationship between pornographic communication and behavior that can be regarded as socially harmful.

Figure 1 is our attempt to depict the principal model for behavior effect investigated by the Johnson Commission. In this model, pornographic communication either produces a state of sexual arousal in the subject or it does not. If the subject does not experience sexual arousal the inquiry about pornography causing harm to the subject has concluded. If the pornographic communication has caused sexual arousal, the next question is whether the state of arousal and other effects of that communication are followed by behavior. If the state of arousal is not followed by behavior, the inquiry about the relationship between pornography and harm from that individual has concluded. If the state of arousal is followed by behavior, then a further bifurcation is required in the analysis between those behaviors considered harmless and those behaviors judged to be harmful. If the behavior is regarded as harmless, the subjects who so behave are excluded from the social harm analysis. Examples of such harmless behavior in the Johnson Commission report are masturbation (by those who already masturbate) and heterosexual intercourse (among those with an already established pattern of that activity). Examples of harmful behavior include sexual crimes such as child molestation and forcible rape. If these harmful behaviors follow pornographic stimulation, then the issue of whether the pornographic communication caused the behavior would need to be addressed.

Our suggestion that this model explains the pattern of analysis of pornographic communication followed by the Johnson Commission does not have obvious textual support in the commission's report. Figure 1 is our own invention, not that of the commission. But support for this interpretation may be found both in the nature of the questions that the commission staff regarded as necessary to research and in the sequence in which they are treated, as well as in those questions that were not regarded as significant research priorities. The sequence of questions in the Effects Panel analysis is: first, to study the existence and extent of sexual arousal; then, to study any behavior response to arousal; and finally, to classify the behavioral responses using both the respondents' and the commission's criteria for harmful and benign behavior.

Casual hypotheses outside that paradigm are not seen as important research questions by this commission. For example, individual subjects of pornographic communication who evince negative attitude changes with no immediate arousal or behavior response were not regarded as highly significant research interest to the Johnson Commission, as opposed to the high priority given this scenario by the Meese Commission. And variations in pornographic content that do not obviously affect the level of arousal seem to interest this commission less than those that obviously affect the level of arousal of particular subjects.

Adherence to this paradigm or pattern of investigation precluded study of the impact of pornographic communication on moral or cultural climate. For not only is the paradigm specific to the sequence of events hypothesized, it is also confined temporally and conceptually to a single proximate act or event.

One other aspect of this paradigm of the putative link between pornography and harm is significant. In investigating harm, the model emphasizes what is definitionally unique about pornography. The Williams committee definition of pornography, which we approve, refers to explicit representation of sexual material designed to produce sexual arousal. By concentrating attention on the immediate behavioral impact of that arousal to the exclusion of other possibilities, the Johnson Commission restricted the search for harmful effects of those special features which set pornography apart from other forms of communication.

THE WILLIAMS COMMITTEE

The Williams Committee uses its review of the social science research evidence en route to policy recommendations rather similar to those of the Johnson Commission, but in a way that renders it less vulnerable. Rather than rely on psychological and statistical evidence, the committee makes a point of underlining the methodological problems, ambiguities of interpretation, and the dangers of generalization we have been discussing. However, by merging a presumption against the regulation of consensual conduct in the absence of provable harm with a persistent verdict of "not proven" coming from its review of the social science research on harm, the Williams Committee finds existing research useful in support of its policy conclusions while keeping a comfortable distance from anything like asserting that the absence of harm from pornography has been established by evidence.

One explanation for this distinction relates to personnel. The Williams Committee was a group of lawyers and humanists availing themselves of social science evidence at their convenience rather than a group of social scientists committed in advance to the validity of their methods and the value of empirical studies. It was largely this commitment to social science that rendered the Johnson Commission less flexible in deciding how to reach its policy conclusions and therefore more vulnerable than Professor Williams and his colleagues.

The Williams Committee's discussion of the effects of pornography attempts to answer the question "whether pornography constitutes a class of publication to which, as such, there belongs a tendency to cause harms" (Home Office, 1971:60). The report deals first with the area where the harms alleged are of a definitely identifiable kind, in that the effects of the material are said to be kinds of behavior that are criminal. But it also deals with more impalpable social harms, which were not considered by the Johnson Commission, a neglect that occasioned considerable criticism (Clor, 1971; Packer, 1971; van den Haag, 1971; Wilson, 1971).

The Williams Committee based its approach on what it called "the harm condition," which is defined in its report as "that no conduct should be suppressed by law unless it *can be shown* to harm someone" (Home Office, 1979:50; emphasis added). As applied to its assigned task this meant that what, if anything, should be done about pornography should be determined by an investigation into the consequences of its existence or dissemination. It was for this reason that it reviewed the evidence supporting the view that certain kinds of behavior, particularly in the form of criminal offenses of a sexual nature, are either directly provoked by exposure to pornography or are more likely to occur in an atmosphere created by it.

The committee's review considered three kinds of evidence relating to this aspect of the harm alleged to he caused by the availability of pornography. First, it dealt with anecdotal and clinical evidence drawn from particular instances in which an association between crime and pornographic material had been observed and a causal connection was claimed, including in this category psychiatric evidence based on clinical experience. Second, it considered research studies involving experiments into, or observations of, human responses to pornographic material. Finally, it reviewed evidence drawn from statistical analysis of trends in known crime relative to the varying availability of pornography.

The committee's conclusions in relation to the first type of evidence was that "clinical opinion and our impression of the anecdotal evidence cohere: the cases in which a link between pornography and crime has been suggested are remarkably few." The report adds that stimuli which might have some relation to sexual deviation or the commission of offenses may be found all around us, including "even passages in the Bible," but "from our study of the anecdotal and clinical evidence . . there is very little indication that pornography figures very significantly among these stimuli" (ibid.:63–64).

In regard to research into the effects of exposure to pornographic or explicit sexual material, the committee notes that "serious reservations inevitably attach to research in this field." This is because there is considerable doubt about the extent to which correlation experiments in artificial conditions can be regarded as a reliable way of investigating complex behavior "even in many other species, let alone in human beings." In addition, criminal and antisocial behavior cannot for practical and ethical reasons be experimentally produced or controlled and observations are therefore confined to "some surrogate or related behavior" (ibid.:65).

Besides observations of behavior under experimental conditions, the committee also reviewed other evidence relating to sexual material, including retrospective personal history studies of exposure to the material; self-reports before and after experimental exposure; and physiological and biochemical measures of change in response to experimental exposure. The committee's report states that the reliability of studies that depend on retrospective surveys or self-reporting is highly suspect "and this is particularly true where they touch on highly personal and value-laden subjects such as sexual behavior." As to the studies of this nature carried out for the Johnson Commission, the report notes "the difficulty of deriving any lessons from them." The committee's general conclusion regarding the evidence from research studies is that "no clear impression emerges from the results of this work" and that "the only objective verdict must be one of 'not proven'." (ibid.:65–68)

Finally, in relation to this aspect of the harm said to be caused by pornography (that is, that people are more likely to be sexually assaulted as a result of its free availability), the committee examined in some detail the available statistical evidence regarding a possible link between pornography and sex crimes. The discussion deals principally with the available information, and the inferences that can be drawn from it, in respect of England and Wales and Denmark. Denmark was selected for attention in part because the Johnson Commission in reaching its conclusion on this question had relied on two technical reports dealing with the statistical relationship between the availability of erotic materials and the incidence of sex crimes in Copenhagen, Denmark, for the period 1958–69, which suggested that the legalization of pornography in 1967 had led to a reduction in sexual offenses.

The discussion is prefaced by a summary of the difficulties involved in "proving or even plausibly arguing for, causal relationships between general or diffuse social phenomena on a purely statistical basis." In this instance the imperfections of information about the incidence of sexual offenses and the absence of a reliable index of the availability of pornography, together with the fact that "the causes of crime undoubtedly are complex," are said to render any inference particularly hazardous (ibid.:69–71).

In regard to England and Wales, the committee's report deals with the case put to it that free availability of pornography could be linked to an increase in sexual offenses. After a detailed analysis of the available information the committee concluded:

> First, there is no firm information about the availability of pornography over the years, and there is no foundation to suggestions that have been made about particular times at which pornography became increasingly available. Second, the rising trend in sexual offenses generally, including rape and sexual assault, starting long before it is alleged pornography began to be widely available. Third, the increase in sexual offenses generally, and in rape and sexual assaults, has been significantly slower (though in the case of rape alone the difference is less significant) in the last twenty years than that in crime generally. Fourth, the contrast between the upward trend in crime generally and the greater stability in the number of rapes and sexual assaults has been most marked in the years from 1973 to 1977 (except in the case of rapes alone reported to the police in London where the increase is consistent with that in other forms of crime), when this period appears to have been the one when pornography was most available ... It is not possible, in our view, to reach well-based conclusions about what in this country has been the influence of pornography on sexual crime. But we unhesitatingly reject the suggestion that the available statistical information for

England and Wales lends any support at all to the argument that pornography acts as a stimulus to the commission of sexual violence. (ibid.:78, 80)

The committee dealt next with what it referred to as "something of a folk myth about the effect of the Danish liberalization [of the laws restricting pornography] on the incidence of sexual offenses" (ibid.:80). In this connection the committee paid particular attention to the work of Dr. Berl Kutchinsky, of the Institute of Criminal Science at the University of Copenhagen, who had carried out a preliminary study for the Johnson Commission in 1969.

Perhaps Dr. Kutchinsky's most striking data were that there had been a reduction of two-thirds in the number of sex offenses against children between 1967 and 1969, which was closely correlated with the increased availability of pornography. His explanation for this apparent relationship was that the literature concerning this type of offender indicates that those who interfere with children typically do so not because they are irresistibly attracted to children but as a substitute for a preferred relationship with a woman, which they found difficult to achieve; but if there was another substitute available in the form of pornography, then that served the purpose just as well. The fact that the reduction was most significant in offenses involving younger children and less so in relation to more "normal" offenses against older girls appeared to support the hypothesis.

On this the committee commented:

We recognize ... that Dr. Kutchinsky has identified a very dramatic reduction in reported offenses against children which coincided with the sudden upsurge in the availability of pornography and which, in consequence of the careful studies undertaken by Dr. Kutchinsky, cannot readily be explained by any other likely factor.

While Dr. Kutchinsky's explanation cannot be conclusive, we have to admit that it is plausible. (ibid.:84)

But it found that it was impossible to discern a significant trend in serious sex crimes, such as rape and attempted rape, that could be linked in any way with the free availability of pornography in Denmark since the late 1960s. The committee's general conclusion was:

While we were impressed by the thoroughness with which Dr. Kutchinsky had studied the situation and the restraint with which he sought to derive lessons from his findings, the fact remains that correlation studies are a weak research tool, partly because of the difficulties of measurement—which still exist in relation to both the availability of pornography and the incidence of offenses in Denmark, in spite of Dr. Kutchinsky's considerable efforts to overcome them—and partly because of the impossibility of translating a correlation into cause and effect. A common explanation of that correlation between two sets of social data is that each is affected by some third, possibly unknown, factor and no matter how strong a correlation, it can never, bearing in mind all the other factors and influences that are also present, "prove" anything. (ibid.:83–84)

Having dealt with the relationship between pornography and sex crimes, the committee next directed attention to "other kinds of consideration, including other concepts of harm which have been put to us" and which, it said, "are also important." In respect of many of these matters (for example, the effect of pornography on sexual behavior generally; the possibility that readers of pornography might be led into deviant sexual practices; the possibility that pornography could damage relationships and lead to marital breakdown) the committee found the evidence of detrimental effects too equivocal or too insubstantial to suggest that pornography was a significant cause of harm (ibid.:86–88).

On the question of the degradation of women, which is a feature of much pornography and is seen by some as demeaning in a way that could be regarded as socially harmful, the committee reported that "the consensus of those parts of the women's movement from which we heard tended to attach greater importance to freedom of expression than to the need to suppress pornography." With regard to the effects of pornography on children, "some of our expert witnesses" expressed "a certain caution about just how susceptible children were to such influences," although "most of our witnesses wished to see children and young persons protected." It was, however, "clear ... that no very definite answer can be given about the age at which the special protection of children is no longer necessary" (ibid.:88–89).

The committee also considered the question of the harm done to those said to be exploited in the production of pornography, both adults and children. It concluded that in the case of children, "there are strong arguments that the prevention of this harm requires the power to suppress the pornographic product as well as the original act." But in respect to adult participants, "we were not able to conclude that participation in these activities was a cause of harm" (ibid.:90–91).

Finally, the committee considered those alleged harms of a less definite and more pervasive kind that, as we have noted, concerned many critics of the Johnson Commission, such as "cultural pollution, moral deterioration, and the undermining of human compassion, social values, and basic institutions." In this connection the committee noted that although "technical innovations have offered new scope to the producer of pornography," the output of pornography in earlier times was very considerable; indeed, in England during the nineteenth century it "was prodigious."

The committee warned that the arguments about long-term effects on civilization and culture involved the danger "of citing as a cause something that is itself only an effect or part of a cultural and historical process." It concluded that while cultural artifacts play a role not only in reflecting but also in influencing social development, "from everything we know of social attitudes and have learnt in the course of our inquiries, our belief can only be that the role of pornography in influencing the state of society is a minor one" (ibid.:92–95).

It is difficult for us to accept at face value the idea that indeterminate behavioral science findings and a presumption in favor of freedom of expression were all that lay behind the deregulation proposals made by the Williams Committee, Indeed, it is rather as though the committee played a game of peek-a-boo with the social science research on pornography and harm, in which attempts to demonstrate harm—for example, by Dr. John Court—are excoriated and the substantial number of studies reviewed and discussed are relied on at least to set an upper boundary to the amount of palpable harm that pornography might cause; but this is not acknowledged as a basis for action by the committee.

One feature that makes this interpretation seem plausible is the contrast between the Williams Committee's recommendations for adults and for children. The behavioral science evidence on the link between pornography and harm to young or adolescent consumers is nothing if not indeterminate, yet the Williams Committee endorses restrictions designed to provide "special protection" for "young people" (ibid.:125–126). It seems that something more is operative here than John Stuart Mill's distinction between "human beings in the maturity of their faculties" and "those who are still in a state to require being taken care of by others" (Mill, 118591 1975:11). We suspect that the majority of the Williams Committee believed it was not likely that freely available pornography would significantly increase sex crime among adults. We further suspect that one important reason for this belief was the range of studies they scrutinized. So, to a limited extent this committee may have also indulged in the pleasures of behavioral science, but privately.

THE MEESE COMMISSION

The Meese Commission was ambivalent toward social and behavioral science research on the harmful effects of pornography. Although it argued that statistical evidence was not required to make the case for governmental control, at the same time it relied on social science evidence much more explicitly than did the Williams Committee, and some of its statements about what research establishes are considerably less qualified than those of either the Williams or Johnson report.

We will show that in addition to this ambivalence, the Meese Commission was hampered by persistent and crucial problems arising from its handling of the question of definition. It had no clear conception of what constitutes pornography to discipline its survey of behavioral effects.

The report of the Meese Commission states that "a central part of our mission has been to examine the question whether pornography is harmful" and it contains a chapter entitled "The Question of Harm." It is a relatively brief chapter, taking up only 52 of the report's 1,960 pages. Later in the report, however, a longer chapter of 134 pages entitled "Social and Behavioral Science Research Analysis" concludes with a "Summary of Commission Findings of Harm from Pornography." This analysis is described as "a sensitive, balanced, comprehensive, accurate, and current report on the state of the research. We have relied on it extensively, and we are proud to include it here" (U.S. Department of Justice, 1986:323).

The chapter on the question of harm indicates that the commission's conclusions were based on several varieties of evidence: anecdotal evidence from "people claiming to be victims of pornography" or from offenders claiming that their crimes were committed as a result of exposure to pornography; evidence provided by "clinical professionals"; evidence from experimental behavioral and social scientists and from other forms of social science. The advantages and disadvantages of the different types of evidence are discussed and it is noted that in reaching conclusions, "each of us has relied on different evidence from among the different categories of evidence" (ibid.:322).

The commission's conclusions about harm are presented under four headings: Sexually Violent Material; Nonviolent Materials Depicting Degradation, Domination, Subordination, or Humiliation; Nonviolent and Non–Degrading Materials; and Nudity. It is stressed that the conclusions regarding the consequences of material within a given subdivision relate not necessarily to all the material but rather to "most but not all of what might be within a given category" (ibid.:321).

The first category (Sexually Violent Material) is defined as "material featuring actual or unmistakably simulated or unmistakably threatened violence presented in sexually explicit fashion with a predominant focus on the sexually explicit violence." It is stated that "the most prevalent forms of pornography, as well as an increasing body of less sexually explicit material, fit this description" (ibid.:323). No evidence is cited for the assertion about the degree 01 prevalence of this type of pornography; nor is it explained how "less sexually explicit material" can come within the category of material defined by its "predominant focus on the sexually explicit."

In relation to this category of material it is claimed that the experimental and other evidence show "a causal relationship between exposure to material of this type and aggressive behavior towards women." It is acknowledged that finding a link between exposure to pornography and sexual violence, whether lawful or unlawful, required assumptions not found exclusively in the experimental evidence. But the commission found that those assumptions were "supported by the clinical evidence, as well as by much of the less scientific evidence [self-reports of offenders themselves are cited in a footnote]. They are also to all of us assumptions that are plainly justified by our common sense" (ibid.: 324–325).

In regard to the second category (Nonviolent Materials Depicting Degradation, Domination, Subordination, or Humiliation) the commission found that "effects similar although not as extensive as that involved with violent material can he identified ... with respect to material of this variety, our conclusions are substantially similar to those with respect to violent material." It is noted that in this case "there is less evidence causally linking the material with sexual aggression but ... the absence of evidence should by no means be taken to deny the existence of a causal link" (ibid.:330–331).

The commission's general conclusion about this type of material is:

On the basis of all the evidence we have considered, from all sources, and on the basis of our own insights and experiences, we believe we are justified in drawing the following conclusion: Over a large enough sample a population that believes that many women like to be raped, that believes that sexual violence or sexual coercion is often desired or appropriate, and that believes that sex offenders are less responsible for their acts will commit more acts of sexual violence or sexual coercion than would a population holding these beliefs to a lesser extent.

The third category (Nonviolent and Non–Degrading Materials), which comprises materials in which "the participants appear to be fully willing participants occupying substantially equal roles in a setting devoid of actual or apparent violence or pain," is said to be "quite small in terms of currently available materials." No evidence is cited in support of this statement; "but we are convinced that only a small amount of currently available highly sexually explicit material is neither violent nor degrading" (ibid.:335–336).

This is described as "our most controversial category" and members of the commission "disagree substantially about the effects of such materials." There were, however, areas of agreement: for example, "we are on the current state of the evidence persuaded that material of this type does not bear a causal relationship to rape and other acts of sexual violence." Again "we unanimously agree that the materials in this category in some settings and when used for some purposes can be harmful." Thus "we would unanimously take to be harmful to society a proliferation of billboards displaying [a] highly explicit photograph of a loving married couple engaged in mutually pleasurable and procreative vaginal intercourse" (ibid.:335–346). In this curious example, quite apart from the harm envisaged, it is not immediately obvious how the fact that the intercourse was, or was intended to be, "procreative" is relevant, or could be captured on film.

Finally, in regard to this type of material the commission refers to "perhaps the largest question, and for that reason the question we can hardly touch here ... the question of harm as it relates to the moral environment of a society." On this question, unlike the Williams Committee, the commission found it impossible to reach agreement. "We have talked about these issues, but we have not even attempted to resolve our differences because these differences are reflective of differences that are both fundamental and widespread in all societies" (ibid.:345–346).

The fourth category (Nudity) was also "the subject of some difference of opinion." None of the commission members thought that the human body or its portrayal was harmful, but "with respect to . . . more explicit materials, we were unable to reach complete agreement." The only example of more explicit material given, runs as follows: "Consider a woman shown in a reclining position with genitals displayed, wearing only red feathers and high heeled shoes, holding a gun and accompanied by a caption offering a direct invitation to sexual activity." Not everyone would find this alarming apparition provocative; nor is it a very good example of the nude (that is, completely unclothed). However, the commission concluded that "by and large we do not find the nudity that does not fit within any of the previous categories to be much cause for concern" (ibid.:347–349).

The attorney general's commission had neither the funding not-the ability under its mandate to conduct or commission original research. But it did provide, in its chapter entitled "Social and Behavior Science Research Analysis," a review of research conducted in the fifteen years since the Johnson Commission published its report in 1970. The major question that framed the research review was: "What are the effects of exposure to pornography and under what conditions and in what kinds of individuals are these effects manifested?" (ibid.:901).

The use of the term "pornography" here is curious in the light of the commission's earlier resolution "to minimize the use of the word 'pornography' in this Report." But in the preliminary observations on terminology in this chapter it is said that "we will simply avoid the usual definitional morass by using the term 'pornography' to refer to the range of sexually explicit materials used in the various studies reviewed here" (ibid.:228,902),

The review begins with an "overview" of the Johnson Commission and the Williams Committee research conclusions. It points out that since the Johnson Commission "the quantity and quality of research has been impressive [and] has provided a better insight into understanding the various conditions under which certain effects may or may not occur." It suggests that "the conclusion of the Williams Committee on the effects of viewing pornography" might be explicable and was not "surprising since much of the experimental work was published after 1978" (ibid.:905,909).

It is pointed out that methodological and technological advances have enhanced the reliability of research findings. More sophisticated statistical techniques have allowed for better data analysis, control, and interpretation. Instruments such as the penile plethysmograph and the vaginal photoplethysmograph now provide better measures of sexual arousal. In addition, "more recent studies have used, as stimulus materials: films, audio-tapes, videos, and material from various adult men's magazines, all easily available from outlets as diverse as the neighborhood video store, the corner newsstand, or the local adult bookstore" (ibid.:907).

The research review is set out under three headings: Public Attitudes Toward Pornography; Sex Offenders and Pornography; and Effects on the "Average Individual." It includes a brief note on "Other Effects of Sexually Explicit Materials," in which it is observed that looking at the entire potential range of effects that might occur as a result of exposure to sexually explicit materials, "if we take the commission of sex offenses to be one extreme of the continuum, then the other end might be represented by beneficial effects" (ibid.:1028). However, the amount of space devoted to possible beneficial effects (just over two pages) might not be an accurate measure of the importance the commission attached to this aspect. Although it was asked to "determine the nature, extent, and impact on society of pornography in the United States," the specific emphasis in its charter was on "the relationship between exposure to pornographic materials and antisocial behavior" (emphasis added).

The commission's review of the evidence regarding public attitudes toward pornography makes a comparison between survey and poll data findings for 1970 and 1985 in three areas: public exposure to sexually explicit materials; perception of the effects of pornography; and opinion on the regulation of pornography. In regard to public exposure the available data are highly unsatisfactory and comparable only in a limited way. This is in part because of variations in the questions asked and also because of changes in technology (widespread use of cable and home videos in 1985). Moreover, it is hard to know what to make of the responses of those who in 1970 said they had seen a pornographic movie in the previous year and mentioned such films as *Butch Cassidy and the Sundance Kid*, *The Graduate*, *Easy Rider*, and *Bonnie and Clyde*. The survey concludes that "the most frequent exposure to pornography is reported by adolescents between twelve to seventeen years" (ibid.:937).

With regard to perceptions of the effects of pornography, it is notable that "public opinion data both in 1970 and in 1985 show that a majority believe the use of sexually explicit materials provide entertainment, relieve people of the impulse to commit crimes, and improve marital relations" (ibid.:1028).

At the same time the "changes between 1970 and 1985 are most apparent in the increase in the numbers who perceive that exposure to these materials leads to loss of respect for, and the commission of sexual violence" against, women. It is notable that the 1985 questions referred to "sexually explicit magazines, movies, video cassettes, and books," whereas in 1970 they were framed in terms of "looking at or reading sexual materials" (ibid.:933, 937).

Opinions on the regulation of pornography in 1985 showed "a greater overall public tolerance for sexually explicit materials." Although a majority of both men and women were in favor of banning materials that depicted sexual violence, there is also a greater willingness to impose restrictions on theater showing and magazine publication of sexual activities than on home videos (ibid.:937).

The section on sex offenders and pornography deals with the evidence relating to the "common contention that exposure to pornography leads to the commission of sex offenses" by looking at the relationship between sexual-offense statistics and the availability of pornography; and also by examining interview data and experimental data derived from sex offenders.

In the summary of the commission's findings it is asserted that the social science evidence has "demonstrated" negative effects in respect of both the commission's first two categories of pornography: sexually violent material and nonviolent material depicting degradation, domination, subordination, or humiliation (ibid.:1034).

Unfortunately, if "to demonstrate" means what the dictionaries say (that is, "to prove" or "to establish as true"), then the social science evidence does not provide a demonstration of the commission's conclusions about harm. To take a specific example, it does not demonstrate the commission's conclusion "that substantial exposure to sexually violent materials as described here bears a causal relationship to antisocial acts of sexual violence and for some subgroups, possibly to unlawful acts of sexual violence" (ibid.:326).

The conclusions regarding this category of material are said to be based "primarily on evidence presented by professionals in the behavioral sciences," but the report adds that "we are each personally confident on the basis of our own knowledge and experiences that the conclusions are justified" (ibid.:329). In fact, the conclusion cited certainly cannot be derived from the behavioral science evidence, and at least two of the commissioners were not only welt aware of that but also indicate this in the commission's report.

Thus, in one of the individual commissioner statements coauthored by Dr. Judith Becker and Ellen Levine, it is said that the Commission sought to break down pornography into the various types of sexually explicit material available in our society. Unfortunately, social science research to date has not uniformly followed any such categorization and the attempt to force the available social science data to fit the Commission's categories is fruitless. The statement continues: "It is essential to state that the social science research has not been designed to evaluate the relationship between exposure to pornography and the commission of sexual crimes; therefore efforts to tease the current data into proof of a causal link between these acts simply cannot be accepted" (ibid.:203–204).

The striking contrast between the confident conclusions of the main body of the report and this skeptical statement is not, however, merely an isolated example of dissent, for it reflects an extraordinary feature that pervades the whole of the report. Throughout the report there is evident an almost schizophrenic dissociation between the research findings and their interpretation by the commission.

On the one hand many passages in the report evince a clear recognition of the inadequacy of the data provided by social science research and awareness of the need for caution in drawing inferences. Thus, in the chapter on the question of harm, "In many respects research is still at a fairly rudimentary stage, with few attempts to standardize categories of analysis, self-reporting questionnaires, types of stimulus materials, description of stimulus materials, measurement of effects, and related problems" (ibid.:349). Again, in the chapter on social and behavioral science research: "We also are sensitive to the limitations and strengths of specific research approaches and we have taken special efforts to review these briefly in each major section of this Chapter, if only to underscore the fact that our evaluation of the research recognizes these limitations" (ibid.:902).

Unfortunately, this sensitivity to the limitations of research appears to dissolve when specific examples are under consideration. Nowhere is this extraordinary disjunction between principle and practice better demonstrated than in the discussion of sex offenders and pornography. It is evident in the treatment of both aspects of research related to that topic which the commission considered.

The first aspect the commission chose to examine was the relationship between sexual offense statistics and the availability of pornography. In this regard the commission drew the conclusion that examination of aggregate social indicators of pornography availability and sexual-offense statistics showed there was a significant relationship between pornography and sexual offenses, which was widely interpreted as "pornography causes rape."

The principal study on which the commission's review of social science research based this conclusion was one carried out by Baron and Straus (1985) which involved a fifty-state correlational analysis of rape rates and circulation rates of adult magazines using aggregate circulation rates for eight magazines (*Chic, Club, Gallery, Genesis, Hustler, Oui, Playboy*, and *Penthouse*). This study is cited as evidence for what is described as "the sex magazine/rape rate relationship" (U.S. Department of justice, 1986:947).

One of the authors, Murray Straus, has since written to explain his research, stating, "I do not believe that this research demonstrates that pornography causes rape" (ibid.:206). Moreover, in the commission report itself, at the conclusion of a six-page discussion of "the relationship between these sexually explicit magazines' circulation rates and rape rates" (ibid.:947), there is a footnote stating that "Baron and Straus recently conducted additional analysis of their data" in which "the relationship between the sale of sex magazines and rape disappeared" (ibid.:950, 1112n). Yet this disappearing relationship is the crucial item in "the study on which the Commission has based its conclusion" (ibid.:206).

The other aspect of research related to sex offenders and pornography that the commission considered was that dealing with interview data from sex offenders and experimental laboratory studies. In regard to the former the report initially states that "the evidence from formal and informal studies of self-reports of offenders themselves supports the conclusion that the causal connection we identify relates to actual sexual offenses" (U.S. Department of Justice, 1986:325). Later in the report, however, it is acknowledged that "while self-reports of some offenders appear to implicate pornography in the commission of their sex offenses, the objective data of actual offenses committed ... show no significant differences between those who use pornography and those who don't" (ibid.:976).

In fact, the conclusion of the section dealing with evidence from sexual offenders runs as follows:

> While these figures are suggestive of the implication of pornography in the commission of sex crimes among some rapists and child molesters, the question still remains; is there a difference in the rates of offenses among those who use pornography versus those who don't? The only data available that directly address this issue suggest that these offenses occur regardless of the use of pornography by the offender. Those offenders who did not use pornography did not differ significantly from those who did in frequency of sex crimes committed, number of victims, ability to control deviant urges, and degree of violence used during commission of the sex crime. (ibid.:970)

In regard to experimental laboratory studies the commission claims that "clinical and experimental research ... shows a causal relationship between exposure to sexually violent material of this type and aggressive behavior toward women." "Sexual violence," it states, "is reported in the research to result from substantial exposure to sexually violent materials" (ibid.:324,326),

It hardly needs to be said that for both ethical and practical reasons laboratory experiments involving "exposure to sexually violent materials" followed by "sexual violence" on the part of experimental subjects have nowhere been carried out. Observations of behavior under experimental conditions can only be made on some proxy or substitute behavior. In other words, any relationship observed is one not between exposure to pornographic representations and behavior in the real world but between exposure to pornographic representation and another kind of artificial representation.

Moreover, the commission was well aware of, and explicitly acknowledged, both what the report refers to as "the problem of the ability to generalize the results [of experimental studies] outside the laboratory (what researchers call 'external validity')" and also "the problem of ..., the measures used to reflect 'antisocial behavior'" (ibid.:1007–1008). And at the conclusion of the survey of the evidence regarding effects on behaviors, in the final paragraph, in fact, there occur two sentences that have a ring of almost ingenuous honesty:

> After all, the question which social scientists must ultimately address—with both theoretical and pragmatic or public policy implications—is what types of effects have been demonstrated for what

classes of materials? Such investigations for some social scientists may have undesirable political or ideological implications but ignoring the issue also hampers our ability to explain the nature of effects more fully so as to provide for nonlegal policy strategies that are firmly anchored in social science findings. (ibid.:1021)

It is notable that there is no mention of the possibility that the results of such investigations might have some implications for the conclusions already arrived at, about which the commissioners were said to be "each personally confident on the basis of our own knowledge and experiences" (ibid.:329),

As we have seen, the major innovation of the Meese panel was a series of categories and a sustained critical analysis of the evidence relating to those categories.

The strongest conclusion of the commission was with respect to the category of what was called variously sexually violent material or violent sexually explicit material. The commission agreed unanimously that negative effects in both attitude and behavior have been consistently noted as resulting from this class of material. There was no finding of the Johnson Commission to compare with this class of material because violent pornography was not recognized by that commission as a separate category. However, since the Johnson Commission found no evidence that any pornography produced such behavioral effects, some clash is apparent. Part of the difference in conclusions may be explicable because this is one of two areas where the Meese Commission was relying on research conducted and published in the 1980s and unavailable to either of the two previous commissions.

At the outset it should be said that the behavioral effects attributed to stimuli that the Meese Commission classified as sexually violent material were laboratory simulations of, or substitutes for, aggressive behavior. Regarding evidence produced as to the negative effect of violent pornography, two special problems require sustained attention: one of definition and the other of attribution. The expression "violent pornography" contains two key terms, neither of which is clearly defined anywhere in the Meese Commission report.

		VIOLENCE	
		Yes	No
EXPLICIT SEX	Yes	xx	xx
	No		xx

Figure 2: Sex and violence

We have previously discussed the problem in relation to the definition of pornography. We add here the point that there is also no definition of violence. The sequence of studies relied on in the section is described as involving "violent sexually explicit materials" (U.S. Department of Justice, 1986:977) without any claim that the material is pornographic. One such study used as stimuli two films, Lina Wertmuller's *Swept Away* and Sam Peckinpah's *The Getaway* (ibid.:983), neither of which was considered pornographic anywhere in the Western world. And with respect to *Swept Away*, the characterization of that film as violent is at minimum controversial.

The "definitional" problem is that the commission created a separate category for special public policy treatment and yet did not define it. It is difficult to assess whether the studies they cite deal with material meeting the commission's criteria of violent pornography, because those criteria are never stated. It is also difficult to understand how one could test the hypothesis about the differential effects of violent pornography without being able to describe clearly what sort of stimulus should be used as an independent variable.

This problem is compounded by a special problem of attribution that exists because of the nature of the studies. A typical set of studies is described by the commission as follows:

> In a study designed to evaluate the effects of massive exposure to sexual violence and to further explore the components of the desensitization process, a series of four studies—all part of a Ph.D. dissertation—were conducted (Linz, 1985). College males were exposed to a series of "slasher films," all R-rated, using a formula of sexual explicitness juxtaposed with much blood and gore. A typical example is a scene from *Toolbox Murders* showing a naked woman taking a tub bath, masturbating, then being stalked and killed with a power drill by a masked male. Comparisons were also made among R-rated nonviolent films and X-rated nonviolent films, both of which included sexually explicit scenes (the former were of the teenage sex film variety)[1124]

Footnote 1124 tells us:

> The following films were used: R-rated nonviolent "teen sex" films: *Porky's, Fast Times at Ridgemont High, Private Lessons, Last American Virgin*, and *Hots*; X—rated nonviolent films: *Debbie Does Dallas, Health Spa, The Other Side of Julie, Indecent Exposure*, and *Fantasy*; R-rated "slasher" films: *Texas Chainsaw Massacre, Maniac, Toolbox Murders, Vice Squad*, and *I Spit On Your Grave*. (ibid.:986–987)

For present purposes, we put to one side questions about whether either *Porky's* or *Texas Chainsaw Massacre* constitute pornography. Let us further assume that the *Toolbox Murders* audience experiences sharply different behavioral effects from those of audiences exposed to nonviolent sex films and nonviolent not-so-sexual films. Is this evidence of the harmful effect of violent pornography? In one important sense the answer must be no; because we do not know whether harmful differential effects can he attributed to the sexual content of the communication or not.

Figure 2 shows both the experimental conditions present in the studies cited by the commission and the crucial missing connection. The three conditions checked off were listed by the commission's staff survey. But if violent cues produce the same harmful effects without sexually arousing content, then what is harmful about the communication is not pornographic and what is pornographic about the communication is not harmful. In yet another demonstration of noncoordination, the negative effect of nonpornographic violence is mentioned in the Part II section of the commission's report (ibid.:328–329) but not discussed in the longer and more detailed survey of research.

Two illustrations of this problem will help point up its importance. The reader will recall the sequence from Toolbox Murders which showed a naked woman taking a tub bath, masturbating, and then being stalked and killed with a power drill by a masked male. Assuming that we find negative effects on attitudes to women and simulated aggressive behavior following exposure, the question arises: How would the same sequence influence behavior if the woman did not masturbate and was fully clothed when impaled on the power drill?

This is not an academic point if the sole basis for restricting the availability of a communication is not causally related to its propensity to cause harm. If violence alone or in the context of sexual suggestion produces negative effects, then the special focus on pornography is pointless. It would be as though a commission of inquiry studying the effect of multiple Bloody Mary cocktails on human behavior recommended a governmental ban on the production and sale of tomato juice.

We might ask why a problem of this size and salience is not addressed in the lengthy survey of research. Our own view is that this was facilitated by a lack of sustained attention to the definition of pornography and thus to the characteristic that sets off pornographic communication from other forms of communication. And this is, in fact, only one of the difficulties generated and exacerbated by inattention to definitional detail, as we shall see later in this section.

The Meese Commission also places special, separate emphasis on the category of "Nonviolent Materials Depicting Degradation, Domination, Subordination, or Humiliation" (U.S. Department of Justice, 1986:329335). With respect to this category, the commission found evidence of a specific kind of effect: a change in attitude toward women, the use of force, and in the context of heterosexual encounters, "increased acceptance of the proposition that women like to be forced into sexual practices and that the woman who says 'no' really means 'yes'" (ibid.:332). The discussion of this category by the commission raises problems of definition and attribution that parallel the treatment of sexual violence. It also raises the perplexing issue of whether government action is justified when the harm produced by communications is an influence on attitudes or sentiments rather than a direct effect on conduct.

The problems of definition encountered in regard to this category are analogous to those discussed in relation to sexual violence. "Pornography" is still an undefined term. Because violence is also undefined the borderline between violence and nonviolence cannot be confidently delineated. And in this new category, a host of new terms are introduced and yet not defined: degradation, domination, subordination, and humiliation. The commission does state that "an enormous amount of the most sexually explicit material available, as well as much of the material that is somewhat less sexually explicit, is material that we would characterize as 'degrading' " (ibid.:331). But readers are not told what specific elements of currently available pornography render it degrading.

The problem of attribution is that depictions of relations between the sexes that would meet no one's definition of pornography might still produce negative effects in the form of attitude changes, changes as large as those produced by pornography. This cannot be known until pornographic and nonpornographic degradations of women are compared. Proposing special restrictions only on degrading communication that is also pornographic might again be like tolerating vodka while prohibiting tomato juice.

And there are special problems with arguments for the regulation of communication that see the social harm in changes in the attitude of audiences. Two elements of individual attitudes require special caution when considering issues of regulation: the distance of attitudes and sentiments from more palpable social harms and the closeness of toleration of differences in attitude and sentiment to the core value of free expression in a democratic society. Western legal thought in a diverse variety of areas distinguishes between prohibitable harms and what are usually called the attempt to influence mere attitudes or sentiments. This is seen throughout the criminal law and plays a central role in American constitutional law regarding the regulation of speech and written expression.

Problems with the regulation of wrongful thoughts and sentiments include the difficulty of making governmental judgments about the wrongfulness of sentiments in a plural society; the attenuated nexus between wrongful attitudes and wrongful conduct; and the difficulty of determining who among the population possesses an evil intent not yet manifest in overt behavior. But the difficulties involved in the regulation of attitudes and sentiments are not regarded as important in Western democracies because the attempt to alter attitudes and opinions is a central protected enterprise in those countries which place a high value on freedom of expression. We feel protected by the difficulty of a task that most of us believe should not be undertaken. Inefficiency is seen as a protector of civil liberty.

We shall return to these issues in the next chapter. For present purposes it is important to note that the special status of attitudes and sentiments would seem to require particular scrutiny of the link between attitudes and conduct when considering the negative effects of communication. No special scrutiny can be found in the Meese Commission's analysis.

The Meese Commission's next category is "sexually explicit materials that are not violent and are not degrading" (ibid.:335–347). This category, mystified two audiences: the commission's members and the report's readers. The problem the members of the commission had with it seems to center around the example of a "highly explicit photograph of a loving married couple engaged in mutually pleasurable and procreative vaginal intercourse" (ibid.:342). What seems to be special about the example is that it exemplifies this third category. Indeed, it is the only specific example of the category given anywhere in the report.

Two questions are to be asked about this example and thus about this category of material. Why should it be regarded as a subject for special treatment in a discussion of pornography? Why should there be a restriction of the availability of this kind of communication to a willing audience?

What distinguishes this from other sexually explicit materials the commission discussed is the absence of any intention on the part of the producers to inculcate bad attitudes in the audience to the communication. The situation described in a way that assures us that the couple represents a moda' positive, approved sexual behavior that every commission member could subscribe to. We take it that this is why the sexual intercourse has to be "procreative" as well as loving and pleasurable.

Why, then, should one consider the censorship of this type of model communication? Should not the intended behavioral message exempt this depiction from the restriction of sexually explicit material? The logical answer is that no distinction can be justified, for the behavioral model and the psychological and behavioral effects may be only distantly related one to another. The lady on the screen or in the photograph may be the wife of her sex partner but not of any man in the audience. Audience arousal therefore will occur in a whole separate set of contexts from that depicted on the screen. There is no reason to suppose that any person immediately aroused by observing the hypothesized scene would feel impelled to procreate. And there might be special problems if one of the depicted couple's children were to be sexually aroused by exposure to this particular depiction.

This category of material is invented in the Meese Commission analysis and distinguished by that commission's special emphasis on attitudes and values. "We are dealing in this category with 'pure' sex . . . material . . . not perceived as harmful for the messages it carries or the symbols it represents" (ibid.:336, 340). Even so, there is confusion between intended effects and effects likely to be produced.

The conceptual problems of the Meese Commission are also implicated in the discussion of the subject of nudity (ibid.:347–349). On this topic the report states, "We pause only briefly to mention the problem of mere nudity." The pause is too brief for the commission to get around to stating expressly what the subject of nudity is doing in the commission's report. The problem, as the commission saw it in connection with "portrayals of nudity," ass that "nudity without force, coercion, sexual activity, violence, or degradation" can have a "definite provocative element" (ibid.:348). What this suggests to us, above all else, is the need for a definition of pornography. Provocation to what, and the degree to which such provocation should be the subject of regulation, are topics that discussants are forced to regard as central if they pay attention to questions of definition.

What is there that is pornographic about pornography? Is any communication about sex pornographic? Or is it only communication about sex that creates harmful attitudes? What is the difference between harmful attitudes toward sex and harmful attitudes toward religious toleration and race relations? What is there about pornography that justifies separate analysis, and does this also justify special public policy?

SUMMARY

It remains for us to summarize our view of the work of the three commissions and to suggest a short list of research questions that are worthy of consideration.

The Johnson Commission was rendered vulnerable to criticism by two kinds of biases and failed to explore a variety of possible pornographic effects, such as impact on attitudes, that might in turn condition aggressive behavior. Nor did it attempt to justify its relatively narrow focus. The bias of this commission in favor of unrestricted access to adults has been frequently noted. But it was the commitment of the commission to the utility and quality of behavioral science research that rendered it most vulnerable to criticism.

The Williams Committee, by contrast, used presumptions against regulation (the "harm" principle) to remain more skeptical of research than the Johnson Commission while endorsing the deregulatory thrust of that earlier commission. The Meese Commission raised the possibility of new subcategories of pornographic communication and focused attention on the attitudinal impact of the material. This was an effort pervaded by definitional and conceptual confusion, political agendas, and some result orientation in its view of research.

When the work of the more recent commission is reviewed together with that of the two earlier bodies, two specific lines of research seem promising. First, there is laboratory research designed to test the link between (a) sexual pornography and (b) apparently problematic attitudes and laboratory behavioral responses, and (c) postadministration observed behavioral effects. Second, we noted that the research relied on by the Meese Commission compared what were called violent stimuli with some sexual content with nonviolent stimuli with sexual content. At minimum, comparison should be made between the impact of sexual pornography with violent themes and a combination of violence and sexual themes well short of pornography.

We should here make a point about the public-policy context of research methodology. Unless the American law relating to freedom of expression is to be substantially altered, special regulation of pornography will be confined to communication (this is the realm of prurient interest) that seeks to provoke through sexual arousal. It is therefore the combination of this high level of sexual appeal with violent themes that should be tested for its special impact. If it is violence alone or violence in the context of less provocative sexual themes that produce troublesome consequences, existing standards of freedom of expression will preclude special regulatory consequences.

But it is possible that high levels of intentional sexual arousal combined with specific cues in relation to violence and coercion have differentially negative impacts on subject behavior. If highly sexually arousing violent materials have a more troublesome impact than softcore sexuality with violence or nonviolent sexual provocation, then what is pornographic about violent pornography might be causally related to a palpable harm that would invite dialogue about regulation.

Currently we are light years away from any such conclusion. One reason for this is the lack of any evidence linking the kinds of attitudes studied in psychological experiments with behavioral harm such as criminal sexual aggression. The link between attitude and behavior should provoke much more research than it has to date.

HERBERT L. PACKER—THE PORNOGRAPHY CAPER
Commentary 51:72–77 (1971).

Presidential commissions, as Elizabeth B. Drew once put it in the Atlantic, are often "self-inflicted hotfoots." The tangled story of the Commission on Obscenity and Pornography serves as a paradigmatic example of the truth of this observation. After documenting that assertion, I shall try to come to grips with the substance of the Report and the data on which it rests. Finally, I want to explore a possible constitutional doctrine that could render moot legislative arguments about what kind of conduct to forbid.

My bias in this essay is that of a lawyer who believes pornography to be a nuisance rather than a menace. Effective legal controls for this nuisance I consider to be a worse nuisance than what they attempt to suppress. which a democratic, open society can ill afford.

I

The commission owes its existence to the initiative of Senator John McClellan (D., Ark.). He, joined by Senator Karl Mundt (D., S. Dak.) and others, introduced a resolution that found the traffic in obscenity and pornography to be "a matter of national concern." What John McClellan thinks is a matter of "national concern" clearly becomes just that. He steered his resolution through the Senate Judiciary Committee, through the House, and it became law as P.L. 90–100. This law directed the President to set up an advisory commission whose purpose was: "After a thorough study which shall include a study of the causal relationship of such materials to anti-social behavior, to recommend advisable, appropriate, effective, and constitutional means to deal effectively with such-traffic in obscenity and pornography." The Commission was further directed:

1. with the aid of leading constitutional law authorities, to analyze the laws pertaining to the control of obscenity and pornography; and to evaluate and recommend definitions of obscenity and pornography;

2. to ascertain the methods employed in the distribution of obscene and pornographic materials and to explore the nature and volume of traffic in such materials;

3. to study the effect of obscenity and pornography upon the public. and particularly minors, and its relationship to crime and other antisocial behavior; and

4. to recommend such legislative, administrative, or other advisable and appropriate action as the Commission deems necessary to regulate effectively the flow of such traffic, without in any way interfering with constitutional rights.

P.L. 90–100 became law in October 1967 and President Johnson appointed the Commission's members in January 1968. In July 1968 Congress funded the Commission and extended its tenure to provide two years for its studies.

I have no idea what backstairs maneuvers accompanied the selection of the members. The Commission at its first meeting in July 1968 elected William B. Lockhart as its chairman. Although it is most unusual for a Commission to elect its own chairman, Lockhart was a natural choice. He is dean of the University of Minnesota Law School. and a leading academic authority on obscenity laws. (It may or may not be a coincidence that the White House, on announcing the composition of the Committee in January, stated that Mr. Lockhart would be the chairman.)

The Commission set about its work quietly, eschewing public hearings and proceeding with the help of a carefully selected staff to commission, carry out, and review the studies that Congress had expected. The first public hint of trouble came in the late fall of 1969 when two members of the Commission—Commissioners Hill and Link—conducted "runaway-public hearings" in eight cities, contrary to the Commission's announced policy. These hearings, whose general tenor was strongly in favor of tightening legal controls, were extensively reported in the press.

As the time for publication of the Report drew close, a number of odd incidents occurred. The first was the publication of what purported to be the Commission's Report[1] which sounded very much like a Birchite document. Many people thought this document a parody. Among lawyers, it was thought to be a hoax perpetrated by law students. Although its provenance is unknown to me. one ought to compare this spurious document with the dissenting views expressed in the genuine report by Commissioners Hill and Link, who had conducted the "runaway" hearings. There is a marked similarity.

Then the text of the Report was prematurely "leaked" to the House Subcommittee on Postal Operations. The leak was made by an unidentified Commission member to Representative Robert Nix (D., Pa.), who on August 11 and 12 conducted hearings before the Subcommittee on the leaked report. The hearings were pretty much given over on the first day to a refutation of the as-yet-unpublished findings of the Commission. The star witness, Professor Victor B. Cline, of the University of Utah—who reappears as the dissenters' principal expert on the behavioral sciences—said:

> This review is limited by the fact that I don't have most of the original studies which are cited and used as evidence in coming to many of [the Commission's] conclusions.... Despite this, enough details are given and I am acquainted with some of the studies sufficiently to comment on them.

Professor Cline's sense of grievance is a bit hard to understand, since he was trying to refute an unpublished purloined Report.

President Nixon's sole appointee to the Commission—"Charles H. Keating, Jr., a Cincinnati lawyer and founder of Citizens for Decent Literature—"had been warning the President for about eleven months "not only that the pornographers will have taken a giant step toward winning the war but that your administration will receive the blame." The warning was quickly heeded. Ronald Ziegler, the President's flack, declared to reporters without being asked: The President has views at variance with those of the Report. Thus, before the Report was even submitted to him, the President dissociated himself from it.

The Associated Press also obtained a "leaked" version of the final report, which then became extensively publicized. As the controversy grew hotter, Commissioner Keating, Nixon's man on the Commission, filed suit to enjoin publication of the Report on the ground that the Commission had denied him sufficient time to prepare a dissent. He obtained a preliminary injunction. But, finally, Keating and Lockhart agreed that Keating could have until September 29 to file his dissent. Since the Report was scheduled to go to the President and Congress on September 30, had it been delayed beyond that date, it might never have been released. Mr. Keating met his deadline and the Government Printing Office printed just enough copies of the whole Report and the various dissents for the officials immediately involved. I have never seen the

---

1. The Obscenity Report. 130, pp. 35–95, distributed by Stein and Day. The copyright of this volume is held by Stein and Day and no indication of authorship is ever given. Stein and Day obviously owe us an explanation.

GPO Report, nor do I have any expectation of seeing it. Private enterprise rapidly filled the breach.[2]

Just seventeen days after the Commission's Report was made public, the Senate rejected it. On October 17, the Senate passed a condemnatory resolution introduced by Senator McClellan by a vote of 60 to 5; and President Nixon, in a statement released at the height of the 1970 campaign, denounced the document. There is no good reason to suppose that the President even glanced at the Report. Thus hundreds of thousands of dollars and thousands of man-hours later. the Commission's work had become a source of personal pain for many of its members and the occasion for national cries of shame.

II

What did the report say to outrage the Senate and the President at a time when the political wars were at their hottest? Just this: 1) "Extensive empirical investigation ... provides no evidence that exposure to or use of explicit sexual materials play a significant role in the causation of social or individual harms such as crime, delinquency, sexual or non-sexual deviancy or severe emotional disturbances." 2) "Public opinion in America does not support the imposition of legal prohibitions upon the right of adults to read or see explicit sexual materials." 3) "Therefore, the Commission recommends the repeal of [federal, state, and local] legislation" which prevents adults from getting access to what has previously been labeled "obscene."

The Commission also recommended that the states should enact legislation preventing the exposure of young persons to pictorial erotica—"by which textual material is to be excluded—"and prohibiting public displays of pictorial erotica. The Commission recommended that Congress legislate against unsolicited mail advertising. In fact, Congress has already done just that.[3] But, of course, these modest legislative proposals have not saved the Commission from attack on the repeal proposals just cited.

The Commission's Report, whose legislative recommendations take up only twenty-eight pages, is based on four reports prepared by panels of the Commission. These include: (a) a report on traffic and distribution of sexually-oriented materials in the United States; (b) a report on the impact of erotica; (c) a report on positive approaches: the development of healthy attitudes toward sexuality; and (d) a report on legal considerations relating to erotica. I shall comment only on the second panel report. All four consume over 400 pages in the Bantam edition. Another

2. The Report of the Commission on Obscenity and Pornography, Bantam Books (paperback). 720: Random House (hardcover edition).

3. The Senate on September 23, 1970, passed a bill providing specific language for labeling sexually-oriented advertising sent through the mails and permitting recipients of such mail to return it unopened at the sender's expense. A similar bill had previously been passed by the House. After the two bills have their language reconciled, the completed bill will be sent to the President for his signature.

175 pages are taken up primarily by the dissents of three members of the Commission.

Perhaps the best way of discussing the Commission's findings is to put them in the context of the bitter and venomously personal attacks of the dissenters. They were Morton A. Hill, S. J., president of Morality in Media, New York; the Rev. Winfrey C. Link. administrator of the McKendree Manor Methodist Retirement Home, Hermitage. Tennessee; and the aforementioned Charles H. Keating, Jr., appointed by the President. These several gentlemen—the dissent of Messrs. Hill and Link is concurred in by Mr. Keating, who then voices a disagreement of his own—open their dissent with the statement that: "The Commission's majority report is a Magna Carta for the pornographer." They quickly dispose of the Commission's empirical evidence with the observation that inquiry into effects is beside the point because the central question is whether and to what extent society may establish and maintain moral standards. I should have thought that the question was not that, but rather how society may do that. Precisely, the question is not (as the dissenters seem to think) a moral question but a functional question asking what laws enforced by what sanctions and involving what costs will enable society (meaning *our* society) to establish and maintain morals. Unfortunately, neither the Report nor the dissent illuminates that question. As I shall presently show, the Report fails just because it does not illuminate that question. However, since it is hard for the dissenters to keep reiterating their central proposition for 175 pages, they first attack the chairman, Dean Lockhart. and the Commission's General Counsel, Professor Paul Bender, both of whom they identify as members of the American Civil Liberties Union, whose subversive nature apparently (to the dissenters) requires no comment. They attack the Report of the Legal Panel which had summarized the state of the law with respect to obscenity. One would have to be a legal illiterate to accept the dissenters' attempt to frame a counter-Legal Report, consisting as it does of a mishmash of headnotes, quotations from legal encyclopedias, and excerpts from Supreme Court opinions (interspersed with ominous comments such as "Justice Fortas is no longer on the Court").

The Legal Panel Report is uninspired. It is a straight-faced but hopeless attempt to give some intellectual coherence to the Supreme Court's lucubrations on the subject. As I shall suggest below, this effort was misguided. Yet the Panel Report is as game an effort to summarize the bewildering state of constitutional law on obscenity as I have seen in print.

The most controversial portion of the Commission's Report is unquestionably the Panel Report on the "Impact of Erotica." Of the six members of this Panel only one (Dean Lockhart. sitting ex officio) was not a behavioral scientist.[4] Although the dissenters had opened their

4. The Panel chairman, Otto N. Larson, is professor of sociology at the University of Washington; G. William Jones teaches communications at Southern Methodist Univer-

attack by claiming that empirical studies were irrelevant, they here enlisted the support of Professor Cline to mount what is their most effective engagement against the Report. To me, it is odd that this Panel Report neglected to deal with the "aesthetic objections to erotica" (the Report's own term). Students of literature like George Steiner have dwelt on the pernicious effects of erotica not only on readers but also on the creators of what passes for "literature."[5] The gist of the "aesthetic" objection is that pornography corrupts taste, primarily the taste of those who seek to supply what the consumer wants. While I believe that writers like Steiner are profoundly right, it is hard to see what remedy laws can provide for the evils they discern. The Panel Report would have been strengthened had this been pointed out.

The "behavioral scientists" reached two conclusions from their empirical evidence: 1) Public opinion does not support legal efforts to prevent adult Americans from reading or seeing whatever they like; 2) it cannot be demonstrated that pornography causes crime or delinquency. Their conclusions are based on a review of the empirical literature, on analysis of crime statistics, and on research commissioned by the Panel.[6]

The Panel commissioned a very elaborate attitudinal study. This particular document comes down to the facts that (a) only 2 per cent of their interviewees spontaneously mentioned the prevalence of erotica as an important national problem. and that (b) most Americans think that erotica has undesirable effects on people's behavior, but that (c) when this attitude is more carefully examined it appears that with respect to the respondents own experience, socially desirable or neutral effects of exposure to erotica predominate. To give two examples of the variation between people's perception of the effects of erotica and their own experience the study reports as follows:

sity; Joseph T. Klapper is director of social research for CBS; Morris A. Lipton teaches psychiatry and is director of research development at the University of North Carolina; Marvin E. Wolfgang is director of the Center of Criminological Research at the University of Pennsylvania.

5. See Steiner, "Night Words: High Pornography and Human Privacy," reprinted in Hughes (ed.) Perspectives on Pornography. The essays by George P. Elliott and Ernest van den Haag in the same volume are marked by sensitivity to the same values as Steiner's.

6. The studies on which these conclusions rest are contained in the ten-volume Technical Reports of the Commission available from the Government Printing Office. While I have not yet tried to obtain these volumes, I won't conceal from the reader my conclusion that the game isn't worth the candle. While perusal of the Technical Report volumes might alter this conclusion, I leave to intending PELD's in sociology the task of examining the underlying data.

Effect	% who say it has effect	Effect on respondent	Effect on someone known to respondent	Effect on no one known
Provide info re sex	61%	24%	15%	22%
Lead to a breakdown of morals	56%	1%	13%	38%

They further report that 51 per cent of their sample would "be inclined to favor the availability" of erotica if it were "clearly demonstrated" that such material had no harmful effects while 79 per cent would oppose availability if it were shown that harmful effects occurred. Fifty-one per cent is a pretty slim majority, particularly considering the quoted qualifications.

Finally, the authors of the Panel Report state that people who identify harmful results are more likely to have seen less erotic material recently, to be less educated, older, and more conservative than ... whom? Than their "counterparts," we are told, whoever that may be. The complete study, including the ten volumes of Technical Reports, may supplement these data. Yet it is. at best, very poor strategy for a report to be as dogmatic and unsupported as this one appears to be. The attitudinal study that the Panel commissioned is a pretty damp firecracker.

Obviously, the empirical studies of effects are far more important than the public-opinion studies, since the latter fall if the former are weak. Citing Masters's and Johnson's *Human Sexual Response* as demonstrating that it is possible to measure human sexual arousal, the Panel Report moves on to an examination of behavioral responses to erotica. The Panel Report relies exclusively (with one exception) on second-hand studies. By second-hand I mean both people's asserted recollections of their previous exposure to erotica and their own statements about their arousal when experimentally exposed to erotica. These second-hand studies, which owe nothing to Masters and Johnson, are simply hearsay which the Panel analyzes for many tedious pages. The Commission appears to have sponsored only one study that may justly be called "experimental." That study sparked a controversy that made headlines.

The experiment, conducted at the University of North Carolina so outraged Congressman Nix that he devoted the second day of his hearings to raking the principal investigator—James L. Howard, assistant professor of psychiatry at the University of North Carolina Medical School—over the coals (at one point he gratuitously observed that had Dr. Howard not volunteered to testify. he would have been subpoenaed). Twenty-three male students had volunteered to participate in this experiment. While I cannot share Congressman Nix's sense of outrage, I tend to view the experiment as trivial and of doubtful relevance. By hooking up the subjects' penises to measuring devices (it is not reported whose ingenuity was responsible for devising the hardware, or perhaps, software)[7]—the principal investigator succeeded in demonstrating that over a three-week period the subjects became satiated with erotica. After a short layoff, their interest returned. Consequently, the study concluded triumphantly that the hypothesized satiation effect was confirmed, as anyone could have told the experimenters. This seems to me a good example of how rigor and triviality are related in empirical behavioral work. One may well conclude that, if the controversy had been foreseen, the Panel would probably not have commissioned this experiment. One may also wonder whether not commissioning it would have been a defeat for "behavioral science."

The culminating section of the Panel Report on Effects is entitled "Erotica and Antisocial and Criminal Behavior." This is where the behavioral approach stands or falls: as the Report plainly concedes, people's attitudes toward erotica depend on whether a harmful effect an be shown to exist. The Report claims that the existing research "provides no substantial basis for the belief that erotic materials constitute a primary or significant cause of the development of character defects or that they operate as a significant determinative factor in causing crime or delinquency."

As I have previously said, the Panel. Report is based on a review of the empirical literature, on an analysis of crime statistic, and on studies that the Panel had commissioned. That remains true of this culminating section of the Panel Report. It is terribly difficult to prove a negative. Burying the reader in a cloud of studies and in statistical analysis only compounds the difficulty. The statistical analysis is flawed because the Panel forgot to define "delinquency." If delinquency includes conduct that would not be criminal in an adult—like being a wayward child. or a child in need of correction—which the concept usually does include. then I fail to see how any amount of statistical analysis can possibly demonstrate anything whatever about the connection between X (which is undefined) and Y (exposure to erotica).

The studies, of which one comparing a group of convicted rapists with a matched group of non-sex offenders is typical,[8] tend to demonstrate almost nothing except that such studies prove nothing. We are told that this study shows:

> All subjects were asked at what age they first saw each of fifteen erotic depictions, and mean ages of first exposure were computed for

---

7. The experiment also measured urinary acid phosphatase and heart rate. Interest in erotica was measured by observing the time spent by the subjects in examining erotic material. In addition, the subjects each submitted to a variety of psychological tests and to three psychiatric interviews.

8. My assertion chat this study is "typical" should be checked against the Panel Report in the light of my bias that research is the opiate of behavioral scientists.

each of the two groups and each of the types of erotica. The data in Table 36 show that the mean age of first exposure of the rapists was one-half a year or more later than that of the matched nonsex offenders in reference to eight of the fifteen items and one-half a year or more earlier in reference to two. The biggest difference between the groups for which nonsex offenders had a mean age of first exposure of 14.95, and rapists a mean age of first exposure of 18.19. Rapists were also found to have a generally later mean age of first exposure to erotica than a nonmatched sample of college students and a lower age than a nonmatched sample of members of men's clubs.

Who needs it?

After 140 pages of examining "the data," the Panel Report on the Impact of Erotica finally sputters out with the observation that:

> . . . [I]t is obviously not possible, and never would be possible, to state that never on any occasion, under any conditions, did any erotic material ever contribute in any way to the likelihood of any individual committing a sex-crime. Indeed, no such statement could be made about any kind of nonerotic material.

Thanks a lot, fellows.

While the behavioral studies, which are the heart of the Effects Panel's case, prove almost nothing, the dissenters devote many pages to picking holes in the data which likewise prove almost nothing. They muster much material to support their assertion that erotica does cause criminal behavior. This material is worthless: it consists almost exclusively of anecdotal reports by police. While the proponents of the majority position have not succeeded in proving their case,-the dissenters may have inadvertently strengthened the case by resorting to halftruths, distortions, and, to paraphrase the old story about statistics, "damned lies." The most clearly disgusting passage in the entire report comes when Mr. Keating in his separate dissent prints the names and addresses of the leading distributors of pornography.[9] Mr. Keating is plainly guilty of aiding and abetting the distribution of pornography.

The predominantly behavioral tone of the Report strikes me as a disservice to the position that the majority espouses. Given the fact that the behavioral sciences have so little to say about the connection between erotica and people's behavior, a far better ploy. in my judgment, would have been to acknowledge this deficiency and simply to state the recommendations without attempting to justify them as resting on anything but the liberal. humane. and pluralistic values that presumably motivated the majority of the Commission. That course would have given the dissenters much less to snipe at and would have cost the Commission much less in money, time, and, finally, credibility. By relying so heavily and so misguidedly on the behavioral sciences, the Commission's Report

9. Let the interested reader find them himself.

suffers terribly in readability. The effort may have been very costly in all the respects just stated.

III

The violence of the Presidential and Congressional reaction, provoked by the Report's behavioral tone, guarantees that it will be consigned to at least temporary oblivion. At this stage in the nation's history there is no chance whatever that the recommendations of the Commission will be enacted into law. The contrary may very well happen. I would bet that we are quite likely to see a spate of even tougher laws passed against pornography than we now have, fueled at least in part by the controversy over the Report.

That prospect does not dismay me, since there is no reason to suppose that we are willing to support a vigorous campaign of law-enforcement against pornography. Such a campaign would involve costs in money, manpower, and invasions of privacy that we as a society are unwilling to pay. Passing laws costs a great deal. Given the dimensions of our present crime problem, rhetoric (passing tough laws) is the administration's only weapon.

I think that our present use of the First Amendment as a constitutional means of limiting the effect of anti-pornography laws is misguided. The Supreme Court has got itself into a box: it must either function as a Supreme Board of Censors and read every allegedly dirty book and watch every allegedly dirty movie that is attacked before it or give up the unequal struggle. Potter Stewart's famous quip that he doesn't know the meaning of hard-core pornography but that he knows it when he sees it is a perfect illustration of the Court's dilemma. In the end, if we stick with the First Amendment I would guess that the pressure of their other business will compel the Supreme Court to get out of the obscenity business and leave it to the local boards of censorship. As for reinterpreting the First Amendment, that seems naive. First, the Supreme Court is so heavily mired in its old decisions. (In *Roth v. United States*, 354 U.S. 476 [1957], the Court held that "obscenity is not within the area of constitutionally protected speech or press." This decision and its numerous progeny placed the Court in the dilemma to which I have referred. While the Court can distinguish Roth, how can it overrule that decision and still rely on the First Amendment?) Second, the Black–Douglas absolutist position that freedom of speech means just that is indefensible: libel and incitement to commit a crime, to say nothing of conspiracy, demonstrate that "speech is speech" can never mean that the First Amendment protects every form of speech.

In place of the First Amendment, I would suggest that the opponents of anti-pornography laws should rely instead on the doctrine of "substantive due process," which means simply that legislation which lacks a rational basis does not pass constitutional muster. "Substantive due process" is a doctrine that has been in bad odor for at least thirty-five years. It was used to strike down economic regulatory legislation.

Holmes and Brandeis had labeled the doctrine as an effort to read the economic predilections of justices like the Four Horsemen (MacReynolds, Van Devanter, Sutherland, and Butler) into the Constitution. And so it was. The effect of the great authority of Holmes and Brandeis, plus the effects of the changing views of constitutional law that their views induced the law schools to adopt, resulted in the present generation of judges and legal scholars becoming allergic to "substantive due process".[10] The reluctance strikes me as being counter-productive for the liberal spirit in 1971. After all, it is the choice of minorities to be pluralistic rather than economic regulation which is at stake when the state uses the ultimate weapon of the criminal sanction to suppress such things as pornography. The "Brandeis brief" (which Brandeis developed before he took his seat on the Supreme Court) was originally a weapon against "substantive due process." The Brandeis brief was originally used to marshal economic facts to sustain economic regulatory legislation by demonstrating its rationality, thus undermining the old-fashioned substantive due process. The same technique, I believe, can be used to show that it is irrational to enforce morals legislation that attempts to sup-press consensual transactions, like the sale of pornography. By mustering economic facts that demonstrate what a heavy price we pay in money and human resources, costs which could he allocated to more pressing social needs than the chimerical benefits of suppressing pornography, courts may eventually be brought to view morals legislation as irrational and, therefore, unconstitutional.

So far, the attack on morals legislation has had some limited successe[11] without the benefit of a Brandeis brief. A variety of constitutional pegs exists: the Religion Clause of the First Amendment,[12] the "cruel and unusual punishment" clause of the Eighth Amendment,[13] the Ninth Amendment.[14] But these *ad hoc* constitutional pegs are not good enough. The Supreme Court badly needs a unifying theory if the attack is to be truly successful. "Substantive due process" may well be that theory, if the Supreme Court can ever be led to overcome its "allergy" to it. Doctrinal purity—"not producing *ad hoc*, result-oriented decisions—" ought to be important to the Supreme Court. Doctrinal purity means essentially intellectual honesty. That seems to me to weigh the scales quite heavily in favor of "substantive due process."

10. The term "allergy" as referring to substantive due process was first used by Justice White. dissenting in Robinson v. California, 370 US. 660. 639 (1962).

11. *Stanley v, Georgia*, 394 U.S. 557 (1969) (prohibiting making the mere private possession of pornography criminal); *Griswold v. Connecticut*, 381 U.S. 479 (1965) (invalidating statute making the prescription of contraceptives illegal); *People v. Retails*, 80 Cal. Rptr. 354 (1969) (invalidating anti-abortion statute).

12. As Professor Louis Henkin has pointed out in a much-cited article. "Morals and the Constitution: The Sin of Obscenity," *Columbia Law Review*, LXIII, 39 (1953) among the constitutional clauses that may be mustered in aid of the battle is the Religion Clause of the First Amendment.

13. See *Robinson v. California*, 370 U.S. 660 (1962).

14. Cited, *inter alia* in support of the holding in *Griswold v. Connecticut*, 381 U.S. 479 (1965).

However the Supreme Court may resolve the "substantive due process" problem. I suspect that it is to courts rather than to legislatures that we must look to begin the process of reforming our substantive criminal law to bring our commitments into balance with our capacities.

CATHARINE A. MacKINNON—NOT A MORAL ISSUE
Yale Law and Policy Review 2:321–345 (1984) (excerpt).

A critique of pornography is to feminism what its defense is to male supremacy. Central to the institutionalization of male dominance, pornography cannot be reformed or suppressed or banned. It can only be changed. The legal doctrine of obscenity, the state's closest approximation to addressing the pornography question, has made the First Amendment into a barrier to this process. This is partly because the pornographers' lawyers have persuasively presented First Amendment absolutism, their advocacy position, as a legal fact, which it never has been. But they have gotten away with this (to the extent they have) it part because the abstractness of obscenity as a concept, situated with an equally abstract approach to freedom of speech embodied in First Amendment doctrine, has made the indistinguishability of the pornographers' speech from everyone else's speech, their freedom from our freedom, appear credible, appealing, necessary, nearly inevitably principled. To expose the absence of a critique of gender in this area of law is to expose both the enforced silence of women and the limits of liberalism.

... Pornography causes attitudes and behaviors of violence and discrimination which define the treatment and status of half of the population. To make the legal and philosophical consequences of this distinction clear, I will describe the feminist critique of pornography (I); then criticize the law of obscenity in terms of it (II); then discuss the criticism that pornography "dehumanizes" women (III) to distinguish the male morality of liberalism and obscenity law from a feminist political critique of pornography.

* * *

The law of obscenity, the state's primary approach to its version of the pornography question, has literally nothing in common with this feminist critique. Their obscenity is not our pornography. One commentator has said, "Obscenity is not suppressed primarily for the protection of others. Much of it is suppressed for the purity of the 'community.' Obscenity, at bottom, is not a crime. Obscenity is a sin." This is, on one level, literally accurate. Men are turned on by obscenity, including its suppression, the same way they are by sin. Animated by morality from the male standpoint, in which violation—of women and rules—is eroticized, obscenity law can be seen to proceed according to the interest of male power, robed in gender-neutral good and evil.

To define the pornographic as the "patently offensive" further misconstrues its harm. Pornography is not bad manners or poor choice of audience; obscenity is. Pornography is also not an idea; obscenity is. The legal fiction whereby the obscene is "not speech" has deceived few; it *has* effectively avoided the need to adjudicate pornography's social etiology. But obscenity law got one thing right: pornography is more act-like than thought-like. The fact that pornography, in a feminist view, furthers the idea of the sexual inferiority of women, a political idea, does not make the pornography itself a political idea. That one can express the idea a practice embodies does not make that practice into an idea. Pornography is not an idea an more than segregation is an idea, although both institutionalize the idea of the inferiority of one group to another. The law considers obscenity deviant, anti-social. If it causes harm, it causes anti-social *acts,* acts against the social order. In a feminist perspective, pornography is the essence of a sexist social order, *its* quintessential social act.

If pornography is an act of male supremacy, its harm is the harm of male supremacy made difficult to see because of its pervasiveness, potency, and success in making the world a pornographic place. Specifically, the harm cannot be discerned from the objective standpoint because it *is* so much of "what is." Women live in the world pornography creates. We live its lie as reality. As Naomi Scheman has said, "lies *are* what we have lived, not just what we have told, and no story about correspondence to what is real will enable us *to* distinguish the truth from the lie." So the issue is not what the harm of pornography is, but how the harm of pornography is to become visible. As compared with what? To the extent pornography succeeds in constructing social reality, it becomes *invisible as harm.* Any perception of the success, therefore the harm, of pornography, I will next argue, is precluded by liberalism and so has been defined out of the customary approach taken to, and dominant values underlying, the First Amendment.

The theory of the First Amendment under which most pornography is protected from governmental restriction proceeds from liberal assumptions which do not apply to the situation of women. First Amendment theory, like virtually all liberal legal theory, presumes the validity of the distinction between public and private: the "role of law [is] to mark and guard the line between the sphere of social power, organized in the form of the state, and the area of private right." On this basis, courts distinguish between obscenity in public (which can be regulated, even if attempts founder, some seemingly in part *because* the presentations are public) and the private possession of obscenity in the home. The problem is that not only the public but also the private *is* a "sphere of social power" of sexism. On paper and in life pornography is thrust upon unwilling women in their homes. The distinction between public and private does not cut the same for women as for men. It is men's right to inflict pornography upon women in private that is protected.

The liberal theory underlying First Amendment law further believes that free speech, including pornography, helps discover truth. Censorship restricts society to partial truths. So why are we now—with more pornography available than ever before—buried in all these lies? *Laissez faire* might be an adequate theory of the social preconditions for knowledge in a nonhierarchical society. But in a society of gender inequality the speech of the powerful impresses its view upon the world, concealing the truth of powerlessness under that despairing acquiescence which provides the appearance of consent and makes protest inaudible as well as rare. Pornography can invent women because it has the power to make its vision into reality, which then passes, objectively, for truth. So while the First Amendment supports pornography believing that consensus and progress is facilitated by allowing all views, however divergent and unorthodox, it fails to notice that pornography (like the racism, in which I include anti-Semitism, of the Nazis and the Klan) is not at all divergent or unorthodox. It is the ruling ideology. Feminism, the dissenting view, is suppressed by pornography. Thus, while defenders of pornography argue that allowing all speech, including pornography, frees the mind to fulfill itself, pornography freely enslaves women's minds and bodies inseparably, normalizing the terror that enforces silence from women's point of view.

To liberals, speech must never be sacrificed for other social goals. But liberalism has never understood that the free speech of men silences the free speech of women. It is the same social goal, just other people. This is what a real inequality, a real conflict, a real disparity in social power looks like. The law of the First Amendment comprehends that freedom of expression, in the abstract, is a system but fails to comprehend that sexism (and racism), in *the concrete,* are also systems. That pornography chills women's expression is difficult to demonstrate empirically because silence is not eloquent. Yet on no more of the same kind of evidence, the argument that suppressing pornography might chill legitimate speech has supported its protection.

First Amendment logic, like nearly all legal reasoning, has difficulty grasping harm that is not linearly caused in the "John hit Mary" sense. The idea is that words or pictures can only be harmful if they produce harm in a form that is considered an action. Words work in the province of attitudes, actions in the realm of behavior. Words cannot constitute harm in themselves—never mind libel, invasion of privacy, blackmail, bribery, conspiracy or most sexual harassment. But which is saying "kill" to a trained guard dog, a word or an act? Which is its training? How about a sign that reads "Whites only"? Is that the idea or the practice of segregation? Is a woman raped by an attitude or a behavior? Which is sexual arousal? It is difficult to avoid noticing that the ascendancy of the specific idea of causality used in obscenity law dates from around the time that it was first believed to be proved that it is impossible to prove that pornography causes harm. Instead of the more complex causality implicit in the above examples, the view became that pornography must cause harm like negligence causes car accidents or its effects are not cognizable as harm. The trouble with this individuated, atomistic, linear, isolated, tort-like—in a word, positivistic—conception of injury is that the way pornography targets and defines women for abuse and discrimination does not work like this. It does hurt individuals, just not *as* individuals in a one-at-a-time sense, but as members of the group "women." Harm is caused to one individual woman rather than another essentially like one number rather than another is caused in roulette. But on a group basis, as women, the selection process is absolutely selective and systematic. Its causality is essentially collective and totalistic and contextual. To reassert atomistic linear causality as a *sine qua non* of injury—you cannot be harmed unless you are harmed through this etiology—is to refuse to respond to the true nature of this specific kind of harm. Such refusals call for explanation. Morton Horowitz says that the issue of causality in tort law is "one of the pivotal ideas in a system of legal thought that sought to separate private law from politics and to insulate the legal system from the threat of redistribution." Perhaps causality in the pornography issue is an attempt to privatize the injury pornography does to women in order to insulate the same system from the threat of gender equality, also a form of redistribution.

Women are known to be brutally coerced into pornographic performances. But so far it is only with children, usually male children, that courts consider that the speech of pornographers was once someone else's *life*. Courts and commissions and legislatures and researchers have searched largely in vain for the injury of pornography in the mind of the (male) consumer or in "society," or in empirical correlations between variations in levels of "anti-social" acts and liberalization in obscenity laws. Speech can be regulated "in the interests of unwilling viewers, captive audiences, young children, and beleaguered neighborhoods," but the normal level of sexual force—force that is not seen as force because it is inflicted on women and called sex—has never been a policy issue. Until the last few years experimental research never approached the question of whether pornographic stimuli might support *sexual* aggression against women or whether violence might be sexually stimulating or have sexual sequelae. Only in the last few months are we beginning to learn the consequences for women of so-called consensual sexual depictions that show normal dominance and submission. We still don't know the impact of female-only nudity or of depictions of specific acts like penetration or of even mutual sex in a social context of gender inequality.

The most basic assumption underlying First Amendment adjudication is that, socially, speech is free. The First Amendment says, "Congress shall not abridge *the freedom of speech*." Free speech exists. The problem for government is to avoid constraining that which, if unconstrained by government, *is* free. This tends to presuppose that whole segments of the population are not systematically silenced *socially*, prior to government action. The place of pornography in the inequality of the sexes makes such a presupposition untenable and makes any approach to *our* freedom of expression so based worse than useless. For women, the urgent issue of freedom of speech is not primarily the avoidance of state intervention as such, but finding an affirmative means to get access to speech for those to whom it has been denied.

CATHARINE A. MacKINNON—DEFAMATION
AND DISCRIMINATION

From *Only Words* (Harvard University Press, 1993).

On the basis of its reality, Andrea Dworkin and I have proposed a law against pornography that defines it as graphic sexually explicit materials that subordinate women through pictures or words. This definition describes what is there, that is, what must be there for the materials to work as sex and to promote sexual abuse across a broad spectrum of consumers. This definition includes the harm of what pornography says—its function as defamation or hate speech—but defines it and it alone in terms of what it does—its role as subordination, as sex discrimination, including what it does through what it says. This definition is coterminous with the industry, from *Playboy*, in which women are objectified and presented dehumanized as sexual objects or things for use; through the torture of women and the sexualization of racism and the fetishization of women's body parts; to snuff films, in which actual murder is the ultimate sexual act, the reduction to the thing form of a human being and the silence of women literal and complete. Such material combines the graphic sexually explicit—graphically showing explicit sex—with activities like hurting, degrading, violating, and humiliating, that is, actively subordinating, treating unequally, as less than human, on the basis of sex. Pornography is not restricted here because of what it says. It is restricted through what it does. Neither is it protected because it says something, given what it does.

Now, in First Amendment terms, what is "content"—the "what it says" element—here? We are told by the Supreme Court that we cannot restrict speech because of what it says, but all restricted expression says something. Most recently, we have been told that obscenity and child pornography are content that can be regulated although what distinguishes child pornography is not its "particular literary theme." In other words, it has a message, but it does not do its harm through that message. So what, exactly, are the children who are hurt through the use of the materials hurt by?

Suppose that the sexually explicit has a content element: it contains a penis ramming into a vagina. Does that mean that a picture of this conveys the idea of a penis ramming into a vagina, or does the viewer see and experience a penis ramming into a vagina? If a man watches a penis ram into a vagina live, in the flesh, do we say he is watching the idea of a penis ramming into a vagina? How is the visual pornography different? When he then goes and rams his penis into a woman's vagina, is that because he has an idea, or because he has an erection? I am not saying his head is not attached to his body; I am saying his body is attached to his head.

The ideas pornography conveys, construed as "ideas" in the First Amendment sense, are the same as those in mainstream misogyny: male authority in a naturalized gender hierarchy, male possession of an objectified other. In this form, they do not make men hard. The erections and ejaculations come from providing a physical reality for sexual use, which is what pornography does. Pornography is often more sexually compelling than the realities it presents, more sexually real than reality. When the pimp does his job right, he has the woman exactly where the consumers want her. In the ultimate male bond, that between pimp and john, the trick is given the sense of absolute control, total access, power to take combined with the illusion that it is a fantasy, when the one who actually has that power is the pimp. For the consumer, the mediation provides the element of remove requisite for deniability. Pornography thus offers both types of generic sex: for those who want to wallow in filth without getting their hands dirty and for those who want to violate the pure and get only their hands wet.

None of this starts or stops as a thought or feeling. Pornography does not simply express or interpret experience; it substitutes for it. Beyond bringing a message from reality, it stands in for reality; it is existentially being there. This does not mean that there is no spin on the experience—far from it. To make visual pornography, and to live up to its imperatives, the world, namely women, must do what the pornographers want to "say". Pornography brings its conditions of production to the consumer: sexual dominance. As Creel Froman puts it, subordination is "doing someone else's language." Pornography makes the world a pornographic place through its making and use, establishing what women are said to exist as, are seen as, are treated as, constructing the social reality of what a woman is and can be in terms of what can be done to her, and what a man is in terms of doing it.

As society becomes saturated with pornography, what makes for sexual arousal, and the nature of sex itself in terms of the place of speech in it, change. What was words and pictures becomes, through masturbation, sex itself. As the industry expands, this becomes more and more the generic experience of sex. The woman in pornography becoming more and more the lived archetype for women's sexuality in men's, hence women's, experience. In other words, as the human becomes thing and the mutual becomes one-sided and the given becomes stolen and sold, objectification comes to define femininity, and one-sidedness comes to define mutuality, and force comes to define consent as pictures and words become the forms of possession and use through which women are actually possessed and used. In pornography, pictures and words are sex. At the same time, in the world pornography creates, sex is pictures and words. As sex becomes speech, speech becomes sex.

The denial that pornography is a real force comes in the guise of many mediating constructions. At most, it is said, pornography reflects or depicts or describes or represents subordination that happens elsewhere. The most common denial is that pornography is "fantasy?" Meaning it is unreal, or only an internal reality. For whom? The women in it may dissociate to survive, but it is happening to their bodies. The pornographer regularly uses the women personally and does not stop his business at fantasizing. The consumer masturbates to it, replays it in his head and onto the bodies of women he encounters or has sex with, lives it out on the women and children around him. Are the victims of snuff films fantasized to death?

Another common evasion is that pornography is "simulated." What can this mean? It always reminds me of calling rape with a bottle "artificial rape." In pornography, the penis is shown ramming up into the woman over and over; this is because it actually was rammed up into the woman over and over. In mainstream media, violence is done through special effects; in pornography, women shown being beaten and tortured report being beaten and tortured. Sometimes "simulated" seems to mean that the rapes are not really rapes but are part of the story, so the woman's refusal and resistance are acting. If it is acting, why does it matter what the actress is really feeling? We are told unendingly that the women in pornography are really enjoying themselves (but it's simulated?). Is the man's erection on screen "simulated" too? Is he "acting" too?

No pornography is "real" sex in the sense of shared intimacy; this may make it a lie, but it does not make it "simulated." Nor is it real in the sense that it happened as it appears. To look real to an observing camera, the sex acts have to be twisted open, stopped and restarted, positioned and repositioned, the come shot often executed by another actor entirely. The women regularly take drugs to get through it. This is not to say that none of this happens in sex that is not for pornography; rather that, as a defense of pornography, this sounds more like an indictment of sex.

One wonders why it is not said that the pleasure is simulated and the rape is real, rather than the other way around. The answer is that the consumer's pleasure requires that the scenario conform to the male rape fantasy, which requires him to abuse her and her to like it. Paying the woman to appear to resist and then surrender does not make the sex consensual; it makes pornography an arm of prostitution. The sex is not chosen for the sex. Money is the medium of force and provides the cover of consent.

The most elite denial of the harm is the one that holds that pornography is "representation," when a representation is a nonreality. Actual rape arranges reality; ritual torture frames and presents it. Does that make them "representations," and so not rape and torture? Is a rape a representation of a rape if someone is watching it? When is the rapist not watching it? Taking photographs is part of the ritual of some abusive sex, an act of taking, the possession involved. So is watching while doing it and watching the pictures later. The photos are trophies; looking at the photos is fetishism. Is nude dancing a "representation" of eroticism or is it eroticism, meaning a sex act? How is a live sex show different? In terms of what the men are doing sexually, an audience watching a gang rape in a movie is no different from an audience watching a gang rape that is reenacting a gang rape from a movie, or an audience watching any gang rape.

To say that pornography is categorically or functionally representation rather than sex simply creates a distanced world we can say is not the real world, a world that mixes reality with unreality, art and literature with everything else, as if life does not do the same thing. The effect is to license whatever is done there, creating a special aura of privilege and demarcating a sphere of protected freedom, no matter who is hurt. In this approach, there is no way to prohibit rape if pornography is protected. If, by contrast, representation is reality, as other theorists argue, then pornography is no less an act than the rape and torture it represents.

At stake in constructing pornography as "speech" is gaining constitutional protection for doing what pornography does: subordinating women through sex. This is not content as such, nor is it wholly other than content. Segregation is not the content of "help wanted—male" employment advertisements, nor is the harm of the segregation done without regard to the content of the ad. It is its function. Law's proper concern here is not with what speech says, but with what it does. The meaning *of* pornography in the sense of interpretation may be an interesting problem, but it is not this one. This problem is its meaning for women: what it does in and to our lives.

I am not saying that pornography is conduct and therefore not speech, or that it does things and therefore says nothing and is without meaning, or that all its harms are noncontent harms. In society, nothing is without meaning. Nothing has no content. Society is made of words, whose meanings the powerful control, or try to. At a certain point, when those who are hurt by them become real, some words are recognized as the acts that they are. Converging with this point from the action side, nothing that happens in society lacks ideas or says nothing, including rape and torture and sexual murder. This presumably does not make rape and murder protected expression, but, other than by simplistic categorization, speech theory never says why not. Similarly, every act of discrimination is done because of group membership, such as on the basis of sex or race or both, meaning done either with that conscious thought, perception, knowledge, or consequence. Indeed, discriminatory intent, a mental state, is required to prove discrimination under the Fourteenth Amendment. Does this "thought" make all that discrimination "speech"?

It is not new to observe that while the doctrinal distinction between speech and action is on one level obvious, on another level it makes little sense. In social inequality, it makes almost none. Discrimination does not divide into acts on one side and speech on the other. Speech acts. It makes no sense from the action side either. Acts speak. In the context of social inequality, so-called speech can be an exercise of power which constructs the social reality in which people live, from objectification to genocide. The words and images are either direct incidents of such acts, such as making pornography or requiring Jews to wear yellow stars, or are connected to them, whether immediately, linearly, and directly, or in more complicated and extended ways.

Together with all its material supports, authoritatively saying someone is inferior is largely how structures of status and differential treatment are demarcated and actualized. Words and images are how people are placed in hierarchies, how social stratification is made to seem inevitable and right, how feelings of inferiority and superiority are engendered, and how indifference to violence against those on the bottom is rationalized and normalized. Social supremacy is made, inside and between people, through making meanings. To unmake it, these meanings and their technologies have to be unmade.

A recent Supreme Court decision on nude dancing provides an example of the inextricability of expression with action in an unrecognized sex inequality setting. Chief Justice Rehnquist wrote, for the Court, that nude dancing can be regulated without violating the First Amendment because one can say the same thing by dancing in pasties and a G-string. No issues of women's inequality to men were raised in all the pondering of the First Amendment, although the dancers who were the parties to the case could not have been clearer that they were not expressing anything. In previous cases like this, no one has ever said what shoving dollar bills up women's vaginas expresses. As a result, the fact that the accessibility and exploitation of women through their use as sex is at once being said and done through presenting women dancing nude is not confronted. That women's inequality is simultaneously being expressed and exploited is never mentioned. Given the role of access to women's genitals in gender inequality, dancing in a G-string raises similar "themes" and does similar harms, but neither says nor does exactly the same thing.

Justice Souter, in a separate concurrence, got closer to reality when he said that nude dancing could be regulated because it is accompanied by rape and prostitution. These harms are exactly what is made worse by the difference between dancing in a G-string and pasties, and dancing in the nude. Yet he did not see that these harms are inextricable from, and occur exactly through, what nude dancing expresses. Unlike the majority, Justice Souter said that dancing in a G-string does not express the same "erotic message" as nude dancing. In other words, men are measurably more turned on by seeing women expose their sexual parts entirely to public view than almost entirely. Nobody said that expressing eroticism is speech-think for engaging in public sex. Justice Souter did say that the feeling nude dancing expresses "is eroticism." To express eroticism is to engage in eroticism, meaning to perform a sex act. To say it is to do it, and to do it is to say it. It is also to do the harm of it and to exacerbate harms surrounding it. In this context, unrecognized by law, it is to practice sex inequality as well as to express it.

The legal treatment of crossburning in another recent Supreme Court opinion provides yet another example of the incoherence of distinguishing speech from conduct in the inequality context. Crossburning is nothing but an act, yet it is pure expression, doing the harm it does solely through the message it conveys. Nobody weeps for the charred wood. By symbolically invoking the entire violent history of the Ku Klux

Klan, it says, "Blacks get out," thus engaging in terrorism and effectuating segregation. It carries the message of historic white indifference both to this message and to the imminent death for which it stands. Segregating transportation expressed (at a minimum) the view that African–Americans should ride separately from whites; it was not seen to raise thorny issues of symbolic expression. Ads for segregated housing are only words, yet they are widely prohibited outright as acts of segregation.

Like pornography, crossburning is seen by the Supreme Court to raise crucial expressive issues. Its function as an enforcer of segregation, instigator of lynch mobs, instiller of terror, and emblem of official impunity is transmuted into a discussion of specific "disfavored subjects." The burning cross is the discussion. The "subject" is race—discriminating on the basis of it, that is. The bland indifference to reality is underlined by the lack of a single mention of the Ku Klux Klan. Recognizing the content communicated, Justice Stevens nonetheless characterized the crossburning as "nothing more than a crude form of physical intimidation."

In this country, nothing has at once expressed racial hatred and effectuated racial subordination more effectively than the murder and hanging of a mutilated body, usually of a Black man. I guess this makes Black male bodies the subject of the discussion. Lynching expresses a clear point of view. Photographs were sometimes taken of the body and sold, to extend its message and the pleasure of viewing it. More discussion. Are these acts inexpressive and contentless? Are the pictures protected expression? Is a Black man's death made unreal by being photographed the way women's subordination is? Suppose lynchings were done to make pictures of lynchings. Should their racist content protect them as political speech, since they do their harm through conveying a political ideology? Is bigoted incitement to murder closer to protected speech than plain old incitement to murder? Does the lynching itself raise speech issues, since it is animated by a racist ideology? If the lynching includes rape, is it, too, potentially speech? A categorical no will not do here. Why, consistent with existing speech theory, are these activities not expressive? If expressive, why not protected?

Consider snuff pornography, in which women or children are killed to make a sex film. This is a film of a sexual murder in the process of being committed. Doing the murder is sex for those who do it. The climax is the moment of death. The intended consumer has a sexual experience watching it. Those who kill as and for sex are having sex through the murder; those who watch the film are having sex through watching the murder. A snuff film is not a discussion of the idea of sexual murder any more than the acts being filmed are. The film is not "about" sexual murder; it sexualizes murder. Is your first concern what a snuff film says about women and sex or what it does? Now, why is rape different?

Child pornography is exclusively a medium of pictures and words. The Supreme Court has referred to it as "pure speech." Civil libertarians and publishers argued to protect it as such. Child pornography conveys very effectively the idea that children enjoy having sex with adults, the feeling that this is liberating for the child. Yet child pornography is prohibited as child abuse, based on the use of children to make it. A recent Supreme Court case in passing extended this recognition of harm to other children downstream who are made to see and imitate the pictures. Possessing and distributing such pictures is punishable by imprisonment consistent with the First Amendment, despite the fact that private reading is thereby restricted. Harm like this may be what the Supreme Court left itself open to recognizing when it said, in guaranteeing the right to possess obscenity in private, that "compelling reasons may exist for overriding the right of the individual to possess" the prohibited materials.

The point here is that sex pictures are legally considered sex acts, based on what, in my terms, is abuse due to the fact of inequality between children and adults. For seeing the pictures as tantamount to acts, how, other than that sexuality socially defines women, is inequality among adults different?

Now compare the lynching photograph and the snuff film with a *Penthouse* spread of December 1984 in which Asian women are trussed and hung. One bound between her legs with a thick rope appears to be a child. All three express ideology. All had to be done to be made. All presumably convey something as well as provide entertainment. If used at work, this spread would create a hostile unequal working environment actionable under federal sex discrimination law. But there is no law against a hostile unequal living environment, so everywhere else it is protected speech.

Not long after this issue of *Penthouse* appeared, a little Asian girl was found strung up and sexually molested in North Carolina, dead. The murderer said he spent much of the day of the murder in an adult bookstore. Suppose he consumed the *Penthouse* and then went and killed the little girl. Such linear causality, an obsession of pornography's defenders, is not all that rare or difficult to prove. It is only one effect of pornography, but when one has that effect, is restricting those pictures "thought control," the judicial epithet used to invalidate our law against pornography? Would the girl's death be what *Penthouse* "said"? If she was killed because of its "content," should it be protected?

Should it matter: the evidence of the harm of such materials—from testimony of victims (called evidence, not anecdote, in court) to laboratory studies in which variables and predisposed men are controlled for, to social studies in which social reality is captured in all its messiness— shows that these materials change attitudes and impel behaviors in ways that are unique in their extent and devastating in their consequences. In human society, where no one does not live, the physical response to pornography is nearly a universal conditioned male reaction, whether they like or agree with what the materials say or not. There is a lot wider variation in men's conscious attitudes toward pornography than there is in their sexual responses to it.

There is no evidence that pornography does no harm; not even courts equivocate over its carnage anymore. The new insult is that the potency of pornography as idea is said to be proven by the harm it does, so it must be protected as speech. Having made real harm into the idea of harm, discrimination into defamation, courts tell us in essence that to the extent materials are defamatory, meaning they contain defamatory ideas, they are protected, even as they discriminate against women from objectification to murder.

"Every idea is an incitement," said Justice Holmes in a famous dissent in an early case on freedom of speech. Whether or not this is true to the same degree for every idea, it has come to mean that every incitement to action that has an idea behind it—especially a big idea, and misogyny is a very big idea—is to that degree First Amendment protected territory. This doctrine was originally created to protect from suppression the speech of communists, thought by some to threaten the security of the U.S. government. This experience is the crucible of the "speech" doctrine, its formative trauma, the evil of suppression of dissent that First Amendment law, through coming to terms with this debacle, has been designed to avoid. This is where we got the idea that we must protect ideas regardless of the mischief they do in the world, where the First Amendment got its operative idea of what an "idea" is.

Applying this paradigm for political speech to pornography requires placing, by analogy, sexually abused women relative to their abusers, in a position of power comparable to that of the U.S. government relative to those who advocated its overthrow. This is bizarre, given that risk of harm is the issue. Women are far more likely to be harmed through pornography than the U.S. government is to be overthrown by communists. Putting the pornographers in the posture of the excluded underdog, like communists, plays on the deep free speech tradition against laws that restrict criticizing the government. Need it be said, women are not the government? Pornography has to be done to women to be made; no government has to be overthrown to make communist speech. It is also interesting that whether or not forced sex is a good idea—pornography's so-called viewpoint on the subordination of women—is not supposed to be debatable to the same degree as is the organization of the economy. In theory, we have criminal laws against sexual abuse. We even have laws mandating sex equality.

Yet the First Amendment orthodoxy that came out of the communist cases is reflexively applied to pornography: if it is words and pictures, it expresses ideas. It does nothing. The only power to be feared as real is that of the government in restricting it. The speech is impotent. The analogy to communism has the realities reversed. Not only is pornography more than mere words, while the words of communism are only words. The power of pornography is more like the power of the state. It is backed by power at least as great, at least as unchecked, and at least as legitimated. At this point, indeed, its power is the power of the state. State power protects it, silencing those who are hurt by it and making sure they can do nothing about it.

Law is only words. It has content, yet we do not analyze law as the mere expression of ideas. When we object to a law—say, one that restricts speech—we do not say we are offended by it. We are scared or threatened or endangered by it. We look to the consequences of the law's enforcement as an accomplished fact and to the utterance of legal words as tantamount to imposing their reality. This becomes too obvious to mention not only because the First Amendment does not protect government speech but because law is backed by power, so its words are seen as acts. But so is pornography: the power of men over women, expressed through unequal sex, sanctioned both through and prior to state power. It makes no more sense to treat pornography as mere abstraction and representation than it does to treat law as simulation or fantasy. No one has suggested that our legal definition of pornography does what the pornography it describes in words does; nor that, if enacted in law, our ordinance would be only words.

As Andrea Dworkin has said, "pornography is the law for women." Like law, pornography does what it says. That pornography is reality is what silenced women have not been permitted to say for hundreds of years. Failing to face this in its simplicity leaves one defending abstraction at the cost of principle, obscuring this emergency because it is not like other emergencies, defending an idea of an "idea" while a practice of sexual abuse becomes a constitutional right. Until we face this, we will be left where Andrea Dworkin recognizes we are left at the end of *Intercourse*: with a violated child alone on the bed—this one wondering if she is lucky to be alive.

C. CHILDREN

GORDON HAWKINS AND FRANKLIN E. ZIMRING— PORNOGRAPHY AND CHILD PROTECTION

From *Pornography in a Free Society* (Cambridge University Press, 1988).

On one question commissions on pornography are simultaneously unanimous and unhelpful. It is generally agreed that children constitute a special case in relation to governmental policy on pornography. Yet, until the Meese Commission, little time or space was devoted to exploring the special character and requirements of policy toward children.

There is very little in the Johnson Commission's report, which notes that "a large majority of sex educators and counselors are of the opinion that most adolescents are interested in explicit sexual materials, and that this interest is a product of natural curiosity about sex" (U.S. Commission, 1970:29). The commission took "the view that parents should be free to make their own conclusions regarding the suitability of explicit sexual materials for their children" (U.S. Commission, 1970:57);

and, as we shall see, it appears to have regarded the use of children as the subjects of pornography as not a serious problem. Only about 4 out of 270 pages in the Williams Committee's report (Home Office, 1979:88–90, 123–124, 125–126, 131–132) deal with the topic of children as consumers of, or participants in, pornography.

The Meese Commission has two contributions on child pornography. A 14–page treatment of the problem in Part II of the report is followed in Part III by a 140–page listing of recommended law enforcement and victim aid responses (U.S. Department of Justice, 1986:405–418, 595–735). This long chapter will be discussed in the next section.

The Canadian Special Committee on Pornography and Prostitution proved to be no exception to the rule. Its report includes only 4 pages (out of a total of 753) devoted to discussion of "the issue of children or young people and pornography in Canada" (Canada, 1985:569–572). A further 45 pages detail the present state of the relevant laws in Canada and elsewhere and include proposals for changes in the law (Canada, 195:579–591, 601–603, 609–618, 627–650).

There is no doubt that the formulation of social policy regarding both exposure to, and involvement in the production of, pornographic material on the part of children evokes questions and raises issues that do not arise in connection with adults. Moreover, the tendency in recent years for Western democratic governments to deregulate the treatment of explicit sexual materials for adults does not diminish but rather increases the significance of issues involving children and pornography.

We begin our treatment of the topic with an analysis of the Meese Commission recommendations for legislative action on child pornography. We then consider, separately, the jurisprudential problems raised when children become the subjects in pornographic communications and when they are the target audience of pornography.

PAVED WITH GOOD INTENTIONS

The 16–page review of the problem of child pornography in Part II of the Meese Commission's report is, as noted, followed in Part III by a 140–page chapter on proposed law enforcement responses. It is as though a one-page diagnosis were followed by ten pages of prescription. And the prescription in this case consists mainly of penal folk remedies.

The commission proposes no fewer than forty-eight initiatives in this chapter, a majority of all the report's recommendations on all matters. Yet the chapter is a case study in the hazards of nonspecificity.

In one sense, the commission's agenda was a narrow one: They were only considering the problems of children participating in the production of pornography. While the terms "child" and "minor" are frequently used in the discussion of these forty-eight recommendations, it is only in the discussion of federal law that the appropriate age limit or age limits for the protection of children are discussed. The commission asserts that the expansion of the child pornography age standard from under age sixteen to under age eighteen in 1984 federal law was inadequate and suggests in its Recommendation 38 that Congress should enact legislation prohibiting producers of certain sexually explicit visual depictions from using performers under the age of twenty-one (U.S. Department of Justice, 1986:623). In fact, the "certain sexually explicit visual depictions" include all of the acts prohibited under current federal law except simulations. The commission never discusses how simulated sexual acts will be differentiated.

Presumably the twenty-one-year-old age boundary recommended for federal legislation is the commission's notion of the appropriate single age boundary for both federal and state criminal law. Certainly nothing in the discussion of Recommendation 38 is specifically federal about the justifications for the twenty-first birthday. The rationales provided for age twenty-one include the high levels of poverty associated with youths aged eighteen to twenty-one, higher rates of infant and maternal mortality associated with the pregnancies of women aged fifteen to nineteen, the greater risks that accompany abortions in late adolescence for white women, and the permanent stigma associated with adolescent participation in pornography: "The adolescent 'porn star' must always live in fear that the film or photograph will surface, once again wreaking havoc in his or her personal and professional life" (ibid.:627). The double standard of age eighteen for simulated sex and twenty-one for real sex is never justified in any detail. The economic issues and pregnancy risk just discussed might extend to some distinctions between real and simulated sex for vaginal intercourse, but certainly not for masturbation or oral—genital sex and some of the others specifically listed by the commission as to be prohibited.

Notwithstanding the lack of justification, this single age of the twenty-first birthday for actual sex seems to hold for the whole topic of child pornography in these recommendations.

There are several problems involved with taking the series of forty-eight recommendations by the Meese Commission seriously as policy analysis. We will here provide only some samples. First, the spirit of youth protection that informs Recommendation 38 does not extend evenly throughout the commission's recommendations, something that can be seen in Recommendation 37, the first of the child pornography proposals. The commission proposes that "Congress should enact a statute requiring the producers, retailers, or distributors of sexually explicit visual depictions to maintain records containing consent forms and proof of performers' ages" (ibid.:618). Under this provision, producers of pornography fulfill the proof requirement by obtaining a driver's license, birth certificate, or other verifiable or acceptable form of age documentation from each performer (ibid.:620, 464n). Forms will be filed at specific location listed in the opening or closing footage of the film and maintained for five years. Failure to comply with any of these requirements would be punishable *as a felony*. And producers would have the burden of verifying the actual age of the performer. These forms would be available for police inspection for up to five years after the release of the pornographic depiction. What will happen under the Freedom of Information Act to public requests for access to this data is not discussed.

Why this provision? The reason provided is: "The decision by [a] young performer to appear in pornographic materials has serious implications for his or her future personal life and career prospects. The existence of the material and its intermittent resurfacing may destroy employment prospects and threaten family stability" (ibid.:623). The only authority for this, other than the story in *Playgirl* of Sylvester Stallone's financial need and subsequent embarrassment at having appeared in a skin flick, are references to the Los Angeles Hearings testimony of Mild Garcia and the Washington, D.C., Hearings testimony of Tom (ibid.:623, 627).

Immaturity does not end at the twenty-first birthday, and the permanent record and impossibility of denial that are generated by this statutory proposal will place young performers over the age of twenty-one in increased risk of stigma all in the name of protecting starving eighteen-, nineteen-, and twenty-year-olds from employment in the production of pornography.

Further, by the commission's own admission, late adolescents who are denied employment in the pornographic representation of actual sex acts will seek employment either in the pornographic representation of simulated sex (if they are over eighteen) or through acts of prostitution, regarded, at least in the discussion of Recommendation 37, as a species of lesser harm.

The point we seek to make here is not that the commission was wrong in its judgment that larger stigma for twenty-one-year-old victims of pornography was outweighed by the protection it felt those under twenty-one would receive from its proposal. Nor do we think we are second-guessing a considered judgment by the commissioners that increasing the pressure for acts of prostitution by young offenders aged eighteen to twenty is preferable to allowing them to appear in pornographic films. We do not think these matters were ever seriously considered.

And the problems with these proposed changes pale in comparison to some of the consequences associated with the commission's use of a unified age standard of twenty-one for all child pornography other than simulation and thus presumably in all its state law recommendations. Perhaps the most stunning recommendation in the whole Meese Commission Report is Number 45: "State legislatures should amend laws, where necessary, to make the knowing possession of child pornography a felony" (ibid.:648).

Why should the knowing possession of a photograph involving a person under twenty-one engaged in sexual intercourse or masturbation become a felony under state law? No justification broad enough to cover all acts of what it defines as child pornography is given by the commission. The broadest justification offered is "the . . . use of [pornography by] pedophiles . . . for sexual arousal and gratification" (ibid.:648–649).

There are two problems with this as a justification for the commission's recommendations. First, it is unclear that the use of photographs by pedophiles while they masturbate should be considered harmful enough to generate eligibility for more than a year in the state penitentiary, the traditional criterion for felony status. Second, it is not clear that the only people to be sexually aroused by pornographic representations of persons under the age of twenty-one are pedophiles.

The age boundaries for child pornography were set by the commission at eighteen and twenty-one, not in relation to pedophilia but because of the economic circumstances, immaturity, and permanent stigma of late adolescents engaging in pornographic performances. Yet the jurisprudence of the commission's definition of child pornography, contained in its Recommendation 38, seems to have been forgotten eleven pages later when it seeks to educate states about the proper definition and penal treatment of possession of child pornography.

And that is just the beginning. In its Recommendation 53, the commission suggests that "state legislatures should amend or enact legislation, if necessary, to permit judges to impose a sentence of lifetime probation for convicted child pornographers and related offenders" (ibid.:670). If the felony of possession of child pornography is one of the "related offenses," and there is no indication that it is not, lifetime probation would be available for felons convicted of possession of pictures of persons under the age of twenty-one engaged in sexual intercourse or masturbation.

Are these people pedophiles? Does the commission mean to make all individuals in possession of such photographs eligible for lifetime probation? Were the commission members thinking of the age boundaries they recommended in Recommendation 38 when they made the lifetime probation recommendation? Indeed, is there any self-conscious coordination between the various proposals spread so widely and so thinly throughout this chapter? The problem of the right foot not knowing what the left foot is doing is particularly problematic when the organism being examined is a centipede.

What the Meese Commission calls "the horror of child pornography" calls for detail and rigor in the analysis of penal policy. This chapter is intended as a foundation for the more rigorous consideration of child welfare issues in the construction of government policy toward pornography.

The special nature of the problem posed for public policy regarding children and pornography does not lie on a single dimension. Children differ from adults in many respects, and we must distinguish the several issues that give this problem its unique and inconvenient character. Accordingly, this chapter is organized under five headings:

    1.   Children as subjects

2. Children as objects
3. Child pornography and social values
4. The criminal enforcement of child protection
5. The boundaries of childhood

CHILDREN AS SUBJECTS

No mainstream commentary we have seen takes exception to prohibiting the use of children in the production of commercial, or for that matter private, pornography; or to the use of the criminal law to enforce that prohibition. About what the Meese Commission referred to as "The Special Horror of Child Pornography" (U.S. Department of Justice, 1986:405), there is probably less dispute than in regard to any other issue in the pornography debate. There is disagreement about the nature and extent of the child pornography industry; but about its undesirability there appears to be, apart from the pedophile lobby, virtual unanimity.

The distinguishing characteristic of this particular pornographic genre has been described as being "that actual children are photographed while engaged in some form of sexual activity, either with adults or other children" (ibid.:405). The principal concern felt about this type of material relates not to the harmful effect it might have on consumers of the material, but to the possible harmful effects on the children participating in its production.

In this connection the Meese Commission reported that "none of us doubt that child pornography is extraordinarily harmful both to the children involved and to society, that dealing with child pornography in all its forms ought to be treated as a governmental priority of the greatest urgency, and that an aggressive law enforcement effort is an essential part of this urgent governmental priority" (ibid.:418). Professor Trevor Gibbens, who told the Williams Committee that "long-term damage to those involved was more doubtful than is widely assumed," did not, however, argue that "the use of children in pornography was anything but undesirable" (Home Office, 1979:90).

It may be that in regard to this type of material the Johnson Commission's finding in respect of erotic material in general, "that although substantial proportions of people are worried about the effects ... there is also considerable annoyance that such materials *merely exist*" (Johnson, 1971:219 n. 96), applies with peculiar force. Certainly there appears to be, as the Williams Committee noted, almost universal agreement that the protection for children provided by law, against sexual behavior which they are too young to properly consent to, should apply to participation in pornography (Home Office, 1979:90).

About the extent of the problem of child pornography, one of the Johnson Commission's technical reports, entitled "Commercial Traffic in Sexually Oriented Material in the United States (1969–1970)," stated that the producers of American stag films or blue movies "have avoided using pre-pubescent or pubescent children in their films"; and that although young males were used as models in "homosexual magazines," magazines "wholly composed of [nude] photos of young girls were unknown" (U.S. Commission, 1971–72, 3:100 n. 79, 188).

In 1978, however, it was claimed that child pornography was "one of the fastest growing industries in the United States." There were, it was said, "264 'kiddie porn mags' of the Lolita type produced each month ... 300,000 children under sixteen being involved in the commercial sex industry" (Eysenck and Nias, 1978:20–21). And in 1977 the Senate Judiciary Committee found that child pornography was "a large industry—representing millions of dollars in annual revenue—that operates on a nationwide scale" (U.S. Congress, Senate, 1977:6).

In 1986 child pornography was described in Harvard Women's Law Journal as one of the "major industries in this country" (Loken, 1986:133). Moreover, in 1986 the Meese Commission found that in addition to the "domestic commercial child pornography industry" there was "a commercial network for child pornography, consisting to a significant extent of foreign magazines"; and that "although the publication of these magazines is largely foreign, there is substantial evidence that the predominant portion of the recipients of and contributors to these magazines [is] American" (U.S. Department of Justice, 1986:408–409).

In no case was any real evidence cited in support of these assertions, and other observers have been skeptical. Berl Kutchinsky argues that "the numbers of children exploited by pornographers have probably been greatly exaggerated" and that "the market for child pornography is quite limited." Kutchinsky does not deny that child pornography, which "long existed as an obscure, rare, and expensive commodity," did after 1970 become more readily available. "In the mid–1970s," he says, "Danish, West German, and Dutch child pornography magazines featured Playboy-like centerfolds, contact advertisements, short stories in several languages, and articles advocating the legalization of 'child sexuality.' "

But he reports that concern about the child models involved led to widespread restrictive legislation so that by 1980 "there was hardly a single country in which child pornography could legally be reproduced and sold." The demand for it, he asserts, came from "a small, very much outcast sexual minority" (Kutchinsky, 1983:1080–1081). The Williams Committee reported in relation to child pornography that there was only a small area not covered by the law on sexual offenses and that "on the evidence we received, this area is even smaller in practice than it may appear on paper" (Home Office, 1979:88).

About the extent of this "Special Horror," the Meese Commission report provides no precise information. It states that "prior to the late 1970s, when awareness and concern about child pornography escalated dramatically, commercially produced and distributed child pornography was more prevalent than it is now." But about how "it is now" the report is indecisive. "We have little doubt that there is some distribution in the United States of commercially produced material, although the extremely clandestine nature of the distribution networks makes it difficult to assess the size of this trade" (U.S. Department of Justice, 1986:408–410).

According to the Meese Commission, "the greatest bulk of child pornography is produced by child abusers themselves in largely 'cottage industry' fashion." This "noncommercial use of and trade in noncommercially produced sexually explicit pictures of children" is said to be substantially larger than domestic commercial production. Efforts to deal with the problem will fail, it says, if the noncommercial side of the practice is underestimated (ibid.:409–410). But what would constitute either an underestimate or an overestimate is not indicated.

It should be remembered, however, that vagueness and imprecision characterize the commission's references to the extent not merely of child pornography but of all types of pornography. The commission was able to report that a particular category of pornographic materials was "the most prevalent" or "increasingly prevalent"; that "an enormous amount" of the material available had a certain character; and that a certain class of material was "as it stands a small class" (ibid.:323, 331, 347). But what these references might be intended to denote in more specific quantitative terms is never made clear.

Perhaps because the problem of child pornography is uncontroversial it has not been the subject of serious empirical study, logical analysis, or strategic planning. Possibly unanimity in condemnation led to the assumption that no detailed examination was necessary, and thus a considerable number of general statements float on top of an abundance of unexamined issues relating to the possible harms involved in children's participation in the production of pornographic material.

To begin with, two definitional issues of some importance require attention. Both the character of child pornography and the meaning of the term "child" in this context need to be defined. As to "child pornography" we here refer to the use of children in explicit sexual depictions designed to excite sexually at least some members of the adult population. This definition, which derives from the Williams Committee's discussion of pornography (Home Office, 1979:103–104), is in accordance with ordinary usage, but it raises the question of who should be considered a child for the purpose of public policy toward child pornography. The discussion of the Meese Commission proposals shows that this is not a matter of small importance and may explain some of the apparently conflicting statements made about the amount of child pornography in debate on the matter.

There are, in fact, three different definitions of childhood that may apply in the discussion of child pornography. In the first place the reference may be to the sexually immature, thus giving the concept an explicitly biological connotation. Second, the term "child" may be used to refer to preadolescents of those in the very early years of adolescence (e.g., fourteen or fifteen years of age), thus being defined in social rather than biological terms. Third, childhood may be defined in legal terms as referring to all those below the legal age of majority. We distinguish these three different uses of the term "child" not in order to nominate one of them as especially appropriate. More important to us is that the implications in terms of the population involved in child pornography vary considerably depending upon which definition is adopted.

Thus, the character and size of the audience attracted by child pornography involving the participation of eleven-year-olds are likely to be quite different from those of the audience attracted by pornography involving seventeen-year-olds; midadolescent subjects are likely to attract much larger audiences than more immature subjects. Such differences may explain some differences of opinion about the nature and extent of the child pornography problem.

The Meese Commission did advert to this matter parenthetically in a footnote where it states that "a significant amount of sexually explicit material involves children over the applicable age of majority who look somewhat younger" and that "in general this variety of material does not cater to the pedophile, but instead to those who prefer material with young-looking models." Because those who are used are not actually minors the commission reported that this type of publication "would not qualify as child pornography" (U.S. Department of Justice, 1986:405 70).

But differences in definition also bear on the different kinds of harm that may be specific to the participation of children in the production of pornography. In the first place, we may be concerned about children, however defined, participating in the production of pornography because it is reasonable to expect any harm experienced to be greater and qualitatively different from that which might be anticipated in the case of adults. Children may not be as resilient as adults and not as familiar with varieties of sexual behavior. They may suffer pains and experience special fears that would be less likely to affect more mature subjects. Obviously, the likelihood of these kinds of harm occurring will depend to a large extent on the category of children involved. Thus, Professor Trevor Gibbens told the Williams Committee "that young girls often had the ability to exploit what they saw as a 'good racket' and were quite capable of still growing up into well-adjusted women" (Home Office, 1979:90). But his statement is more likely to refer to sixteen-year-old than to nine-year-old girls.

In the second place, we may be concerned about children's participation in the production of pornography not simply because the harm that may come to them may be different from the harm that might afflict adults, but also because children lack the capacity to make mature judgments about the harm involved. In this connection it is emotional or psychological rather than physical immaturity that is the crucial consideration. Certainly it is this that provides the rationale underlying the prohibition of statutory rape and the prescription of minimum ages for marriage and for contractual consent. The relevant concerns here relate more to the social definitions of childhood than to those based on sexual maturity.

That this is not the exclusive basis for concern about children's participation in pornography can be demonstrated by reference to the implausibility of permitting the substitution of adult judgment for that of the child in this context. As to contractual capacity and also to the marriage of minors, we allow adults in a fiduciary relationship to give consent for a child. It is unlikely in the extreme that any Western state would permit adults to give effective consent to the participation of a minor ward in the production of pornography.

The harms so far discussed relate to those children who are participants in the production of pornography. But there is another way in which child pornography might threaten the welfare of children more generally. If the depiction of children in sexually provocative material led to an expansion of the number of persons desiring and seeking children as sex objects, this might lead to an increase in the risk of predation, which could expose children (who were strangers to the original transactions) to harm.

The nature of the harm that concerns us will have consequences in regard to the ways in which we might wish to regulate child pornography. For example, it has been noted that some of the sexually explicit material involved in the discussion of child pornography involves young adult actors (U.S. Department of Justice, 1986:405 n. 70). Public policy relating solely to the protection of child participants in pornographic production might not be concerned with materials in which the participants were adults in social or legal terms. But a policy designed to minimize the appeal of children as sexual objects should be concerned about the harmful impact of material involving childlike actors as well as that involving "real" children.

An analogous point can be made about enforcement priorities in relation to existing stocks of child pornography. A policy emphasizing the horrors and harms of today's children participating in the production of pornography would give relatively low priority to the clearing up of stocks of films, pictures, and postcards of years gone by. Indeed, assuming that the demand for child pornography, however defined, was relatively stable, one way to reduce or limit the demand for fresh pornographic material portraying children might be to tolerate the free availability of existing stocks. But concern that the use of this material might possibly increase the demand for children as sex objects would be more likely to inspire a policy of general prohibition and suppression in which the priority would be to reduce the total amount of such material available of whatever vintage.

In determining these different possibilities we operate far beyond any foundation in existing empirical knowledge or research. Yet one reason for the lack of knowledge and absence of research in relation to such matters is the failure to address questions at this level of specificity. The continued importance of this subtopic for the administration of the criminal law suggests that further attention should be paid to the child as participant in the production of pornography.

CHILDREN AS OBJECTS

It is almost universally agreed that the public-policy considerations that govern the regulation of the audiences of pornography are different when the audience consists of children. Although some of the same considerations that give rise to special concern when children are the subjects of pornography also apply here, the harms that attach to the child as a consumer of pornography are different and merit separate analysis.

In the case of pornography with children as the central subjects, the extent of the practice is, as we have seen, the subject of debate. But there can be no doubt that large numbers of children, particularly those in early and middle adolescence, make up part of the audience for pornography. Some studies of the characteristics of customers of movie theaters and bookstores that offer sexually explicit materials suggest that a substantial majority of customers are males in the twenty-eight-to sixty-year-old range (e.g., U.S. Commission, 1971–72, 4:231). But although middle-aged males may spend more money and be more visible consumers, there is no doubt that exposure to explicit sexual materials that the Johnson Commission found to be "widespread in adolescence" (U.S. Commission, 1970:21) in 1970 is no less extensive today. Part of the special appeal of pornography for young audiences is that it provides a source of information about sexual practice; and this is also a special concern of those who see children as vulnerable and susceptible to harm.

The Williams Committee heard a number of witnesses who saw ways in which pornography might be harmful to children as an audience and reported that "most of our witnesses wished to see children and young persons protected" (Home Office, 1979:88). In particular, Dr. Gallwey of the Portman Clinic thought that "a particular experience of exposure to pornography at a time of stress in the child's process of growing up, particularly when trying to evolve an understanding of aspects of life, could be very confusing to a child and, if in constellation with other disturbing factors, could tip the balance towards psychological damage." Dr. Hyatt Williams, by contrast, saw the danger "more in terms of pornography being used by an adult with a view, for example, to homosexual seduction than in relation to pornography being passed around among children" (ibid.:89).

On the other hand, the Williams Committee also reported: "We did hear from some of our expert witnesses a certain caution about just how susceptible children were to such influences ... and we heard no evidence of actual harm being caused to children. Some witnesses suspected that children would not take very much notice of pornography and that they might be more robust than was commonly assumed" (ibid.:88–89).

The Meese Commission took the view that the exposure of children even to those sexually explicit materials not violent and not degrading was harmful. "We all agree that at least much, probably most, and maybe even all material in this category . . . is harmful when it falls into the hands of children." The commission's report does not cite any expert evidence on this topic but asserts simply that "the near unanimity in society about the effects on children and on all society in exposing children to explicit sexuality in the form of even nonviolent and nondegrading pornographic materials makes a strong statement about the potential harms of this material, and we confidently agree with that longstanding societal judgment" (U.S. Department of Justice, 1986:343, 344–345).

In fact, there is no doubt that children lack both the maturity of judgment and the experiential background in relation to sex that may come with adulthood. Immaturity of judgment may be associated with vulnerability to the attraction of deviant life-styles, to perverse or misguided attitudes, to poor impulse controls, and to distorted values. Lack of an experiential background about sex, which can be an antidote to grandiose and distorted elements in pornographic material, may lead to psychological stress and confusion.

The distinction between immaturity of judgment and lack of experience has implications for the selection of appropriate means of preventing harms associated with exposing children to pornography. If the problem is seen as one of immaturity of judgment, then the only safeguard may be preclusion of the availability of pornography or the substitution of adult judgment as to what should be made available and at what ages. However, concern about childhood vulnerability because of lack of experience or background in the reality of human sexuality might be better addressed, as the Johnson Commission suggested, by increasing the availability of other sources of information, for example, providing "access to adequate information regarding sex, through appropriate sex education" (U.S. Commission, 1970:29), rather than attempting to block channels of pornographic communication.

Indeed, if lack of experience is the problem, the best antidote for the unusual, grandiose, and misleading features of currently available pornography might be realistic, anatomically correct, and humanistic sexually explicit communication. But if the central concern of those troubled about children as consumers of pornography is the sexual stimulation of the young, clearly a more appropriate policy would be aimed at the minimization of the amount of sexually arousing content in the diet of childhood America. The appropriate responses to innocence may thus operate at cross-purposes to the right method of dealing with immaturity.

In considering these different possibilities, the widely different concepts of childhood referred to in the previous section are not merely relevant but extraordinarily important. Public policy regarding childhood exposure to pornography must deal with children of four, seven, nine, and twelve years of age and, if social and legal definitions are applied, with those fourteen and seventeen years of age as well. Risks of different harms and harms of different magnitudes must attend these substantial age variations.

The Issue of Experiment

There are very few empirical data available on the question of children as consumers of pornography. Very little work has been done and there has been no attempt to expand research in this area in recent years. The Johnson Commission reported that "insufficient research is presently available on the effect of the exposure of children to sexually explicit materials ... strong ethical feelings against experimentally exposing children to sexually explicit material considerably reduced the possibility of gathering the necessary data and information regarding young persons" (U.S. Commission, 1970:57). Eysenck and Nias, in their survey of experimental and other research into the effects of exposure to violent and pornographic material, report numerous laboratory studies of violence-viewing with child subjects but remark that "children ... for ethical reasons, have not been involved in laboratory experiments on the effects of pornography" (Eysenck and Nias, 1978:162). The Williams Committee also noted that "for obvious reasons, children have not been involved in laboratory experiments on the effects of pornography" (Home Office, 1979:88).

Neither the Johnson Commission, nor Eysenck and Nias, nor the Williams Committee explain the nature of the "ethical" and "obvious" reasons that preclude the use of child subjects in experimental work or exposure to pornography. Nor does it seem indisputably obvious that the exposure of children to scenes of violence should be seen as perfectly acceptable while their exposure to portrayals of sexual acts must be regarded as unethical. Indeed, an argument could be made for a directly contrary conclusion.

Four hundred years ago, Montaigne remarked the curious paradox that "we boldly utter the words *kill, rob, betray*" but in regard to "the genital act ... we dare not speak of it without shame" (Montaigne, (1580–881 1946:739)). More recently, Gershon Legman in his study of censorship, Love and Death, asked: "Why this absurd contradiction? Is the creation of life really more reprehensible than its destruction?" (Legman, 1949:94).

In a similar vein, Geoffrey Gorer wrote:

I have never seen it seriously suggested that the literature of murder detective stories or crime stories—tended to deprave and corrupt, or would incite weak-minded or immature readers into carrying out in reality the activities described in the fantasies. On the contrary, the literature of murder is considered particularly "healthy" and desirable; and in England representatives of all the most respected professions have stated that detective stories are among their favourite reading. Musing about murder is apparently "healthy"; musing about sexual enjoyment is not. No one, it is apparently assumed, will commit a murder because he spends his leisure reading about other people committing murders; but there is a grave danger that people will commit illegal sexual acts because they read pornography. (Gorer, 1961:37)

Yet, although it may not be immediately self-evident, there are reasonable grounds for distinguishing the two types of material and for reluctance to involve children in experiments on the effects of pornography that do not apply in the case of depictions of violence. In the first place, few children today are not familiar, through the media, with the overt presentation of scenes of violence between real and fictional; and few are unable to distinguish between the real world and the fantastic portrayals of violence found in films and comic books. In the laboratory experiments in which they have been involved, they have not been presented with material significantly different from presentations with which they are already probably overly familiar.

Yet explicit portrayals of sexual acts are not as readily available to children, nor do children have a background of experience to enable them to distinguish between reality and fantasy. Dr. Hanna Segal, an expert witness before the Williams Committee, suggested that one of the principal ways in which exposure to pornographic material might be harmful to children derived from the fact that "children learn to overcome their sexual fantasies by looking at behavior in the real world," whereas if their view of the adult world via the medium of pornography confirmed those fantasies, "they were likely to become fixated by them" (Home Office, 1979:89).

With respect to the ethical issues regarding experimentation with children as consumers of pornography, we think that a distinction should be drawn between prepubescent and older children. The absence of experimentation makes some sense among age groups that have low exposure to pornography and do not seek out such materials on their own.

In age groups where exposure to pornography is higher, and where children frequently and successfully seek pornography on their own initiative, controlled experiments that pay careful attention to human subject issues seem justified by the importance of the issues and the less substantial prospect of great harm to the subjects.

Another dimension of this matter relates to the social context in which children receive sexual cues. This must be an important variable in determining the nature and amount of harm they are likely to suffer. The more importance society attaches to the kinds of harm children may suffer sexually, the more significant those harms tend to become. Thus, many of the traumas arising from the sexual abuse of children owe a great deal to the stigma attached by society to the acts involved: a stigma that, as in some cases of adult rape, is projected onto the victim.

Thus, one could argue that if adults were to treat the process of victimization in cases of child sexual abuse as less of a stigmatizing event and more as the kind of misfortune that is a not uncommon feature of life, and one that can be overcome, the experience might be less traumatic for many child victims. Analogously, a social context in which the existence of pornography is acknowledged and generally accepted by adult society might enable children to adjust more easily to their personal experience with it. We are unaware of any cross-cultural research that has addressed issues of this nature but such studies might provide valuable information.

Child Pornography and Social Values

There is another objection to child pornography that, while not decisive on public policy grounds, is important enough and distinctive enough to merit separate discussion. It can be argued that the portrayal of the sexual use of children tends to corrupt the moral values of a community in a way distinct from, and more troublesome than, either the social effects of pornography generally or even of the degradation of women that is associated with much pornography.

This "moral climate" point is distinguishable from concern about the advertisement of children as sexual objects increasing the amount of predation on children. For the toleration of the sexual use of children may have negative consequences quite apart from any increase in the rate of child sex victimization. And the notion that a society is corrupted by its toleration of child pornography can also be distinguished from the view that all pornography is morally corrupting. Although it has been asserted that everything which is pornographic is also exploitative, there seems to be no obvious reason why all explicit depictions of sexual activity designed to arouse the sexual appetites of an audience should necessarily involve exploitation.

With regard to the argument that pornography is of its nature degrading to the status of women (MacKinnon, 1987:158–162), the contrast between adult women and children as portrayed in pornography may be significant. Pornographic material that portrays the consent to, and pleasure in, sexual activity of female participants may be sheer fantasy and may degrade by suggesting that adult women might behave in ways they should not or do not behave. One may argue that pornography of this sort is inherently misleading in relation to the desires and intentions, actions and reactions, of women. The "central conceit" in the pornographic film Deep Throat, says Catharine MacKinnon, is "that we get pleasure in ways we do not" (MacKinnon, 1987:128). But as long as we are willing to grant women a capacity to consent, there is nothing inherently forcible and in *that* sense exploitative about the portrayal of adult women in pornography.

The child's lack of capacity to consent makes it possible to argue that all portrayals of the sexual use of children constitute an exploitation that is the moral equivalent of force, no matter if the child involved is pictured as enjoying participating in the pornographic fantasy. If we take seriously distinctions based on capacity to consent, the whole category of child pornography represents the celebration of exploitation.

The contrast between the use of adult women and children in pornography throws light on two other child pornography issues. One involves the definition of childhood that proponents of this view would employ, and the other relates to the question of whether actual children must be the subjects of sexual use for the pornography in question to be socially harmful.

As to the definition of "child," the recent history of the definition of children for the purpose of consent is not without irony. Of the three definitions of "child" just discussed, biological, social, and legal, the legal boundary between childhood and adulthood is both the most arbitrary basis for distinguishing the capacity to consent and also the most frequently used.

Almost no one would doubt that eight-, ten-, and eleven-year-olds lack a meaningful capacity for consent in relation to sex. The problem cases in the troubled career of the crime of statutory rape have involved "legal" children who were well into sexual maturity and possessed a substantial degree of sexual sophistication. In this way, the use of high-legal-age categories such as twenty-one tends to obscure a moral issue that is of considerable importance for younger children.

The "moral climate" problem is not an automatic justification for censorship. It bears repeating that a high regard for free expression counsels against attempts to prohibit communications merely because they foster bad attitudes. We live in a society that rightly tolerates the advocacy of racial discrimination and political violence, as long as no clear and present danger of the attitudes generated being manifested in conduct is the proximate consequence of the communication. Thus, prohibiting the portrayal of the sexual use of children should be based on the risk of child victimization rather than on concern about general community values.

It might not do, however, to regard the issue as resolved; as the Williams Committee put it in relation to children, "there is only a small area of pornographic activity which is not covered by the law on sexual offences" (Home Office, 1979:90). It may be the case that most of the sexual acts portrayed would be unlawful if the actors employed were children. But many less explicit poses by children may stimulate a pedophile audience. And the use of young-looking actors, makeup, and special effects raises questions of the celebration of exploitation that should not be ignored. To overlook them is to take a short cut that obscures an inquiry relevant to the special problem of child pornography.

CRIMINAL LAW ENFORCEMENT OF CHILD PROTECTION

We here discuss aspects of using the criminal law for child protection in an environment where pornographic communication by, for, and about adults is generally permitted. The topics dealt with include child pornography as victimless crime; the distinction between child consumption of, and participation in the production of, pornography as occasions for criminal law enforcement; the extent to which minors should be punished as part of a regulatory scheme; and the need for both the grading of offenses and the selection of appropriate penalties.

Child Pornography as Victimless Crime

There are two contrasting definitions of victimless crime, only one of which would include most instances of the involvement of children in pornography. The most common definition, derived from John Stuart Mill and according to which such crimes have no other victim than the perpetrator, who harms only himself (Mill, (1859) 1975:10–11), does not really apply in this context. Even if children consent to being used in, or exposed to, pornographic communication, their immaturity could nonetheless render them victims in Mill's sense.

But another concept of victimless crime defines it as referring to "crimes [that] lack victims, in the sense of complainants asking for the protection of the criminal law" (Morris and Hawkins, 1970:6). In light of this definition, all of the consumption of pornographic material by willing children, and a substantial amount of child participation in the production of pornography, would be victimless crime. Most children will not complain to the authorities. Law enforcement has to be proactive and organized on the traditional vice-squad model to enforce child-specific bans on consumption.

There are two further contemporary developments that hinder official attempts to restrict child pornography: the deregulation of adult pornography as an industry and the loosening of restrictions on midadolescents who run away from home and seek to live autonomous lives in the American city.

It is not merely that adult pornography has been decriminalized in America and many other Western countries that is the problem here; it has also been deregulated. There is little in the way of law enforcement presence in most "adult" bookstores or video-rental agencies. And in many cities there is a substantially reduced police presence, although still an important one, in bars, live sex shows, and the like.

In theory, the trend toward decriminalization of commercial sex could have resulted in more intensive regulation of the manufacture and sale of pornography. That argument is made by proponents of decriminalization of some forms of vice under the rubric of "it is impossible to regulate behavior that is prohibited" (Morris and Hawkins, 1977:21). In fact, however, the formal prohibition of commercial sex had already evolved into a de facto regulatory scheme in most American cities: a regulatory arrangement that might have made it easier to police special problems such as the exploitation of young children than when further deregulation took place.

Decriminalization has not led to the extensive development of non-criminal law regulation for two reasons: First, the classification of pornographic material as communication creates in the United States a strong presumption against any regulatory control as constituting censorship. Second, once the police are removed as an agency concerned with observing and regulating the commercial sex industry, there are no other public agencies with the incentive or the capacity to take their place. So that a more laissez-faire attitude toward some aspects of pornographic production and consumption by adults diminishes the will and ability of law enforcement to keep children and pornographic communication in separate worlds.

Just as it is more difficult to use traditional vice-control powers to regulate pornography as a way to protect children, it is also increasingly difficult to use the special legal classification of children and the quasi-parental power of the state over them to protect them from exposure to, or even participation in the production of, pornography.

Traditional powers to lock up status offenders, allegedly for their own good, allowed the police and juvenile courts considerable control over truants, runaways, vagrants, and the insubordinate, at least in theory. Removing the power to arbitrarily lock up the young also removed leverage on the part of the police to protect juveniles from real dangers. In effect, the decriminalization of status offenses has also led to the deregulation of youth.

The police, deprived of the power to lock children up, have often staged a strategic withdrawal; many no longer regard themselves as responsible for the welfare of fifteen- and sixteen-year-olds. Other public agencies lack the incentives and resources to fill the gap.

The withdrawal from the coercive regulation of adolescence can be justified because the costs of regulation—in dollars, in liberty, and, most importantly, in youth welfare—exceeded their benefits. But withdrawal of the use of coercive state power has not been costless. The dangers of exercising immature judgment on the streets of major urban areas, living in squalor, and risking disease and death are quite real (Zimring, 1982:61–75).

CONSUMPTION VERSUS PARTICIPATION

While the factors just described hinder law enforcement of both the consumption of, and participation in the production of, pornography by the young, the opportunities for enforcement and the prospects for effectiveness differ markedly in relation to these two aspects.

Put simply, the prospects for enforcing a ban on the consumption of pornography by adolescents who wish to do so are minimal. The prospects for enforcing criminal prohibition of child participation in commercial sex and newly produced pornography are much better, particularly for younger children. The prospects for restricting the availability of pornographic material involving children or childlike subjects come somewhere between these two poles.

With respect to children as pornography consumers, the task of keeping millions of pornographic communications out of the hands of millions of children seems hopeless. As we shall show, the severe punishment of the children if caught would be perverse. The notion of punishing only those who make available, or facilitate the availability of, pornography to other children is little better. Most who aid and abet minors in obtaining access to pornography are themselves minors. And many of the remainder are relatively blameless adults who would, in effect, be punished for their own use of pornography or for failing to effectively keep children away from materials intended for adult use.

The situation parallels the one pertaining to tobacco and alcohol. The decision to deregulate for adults guarantees a high level of availability for older children and adolescents. But the prospects for some forms of control are probably less discouraging than this analysis implies. Most of the children who cannot be denied access to pornography are the older and more enterprising young, whose exposure to pornography is less problematic than with the very young or the especially naive.

Further, the extremely limited amount of research available on the effects of pornography does not suggest any harm to children as consumers of pornography comparable to what might be expected from their direct participation in commercial sex. It seems likely that the best policy to adopt in restricting the consumption of pornography by children is a relatively relaxed one without the call for rigorous enforcement or publicized show prosecutions as an attempt to compensate for the futility of the overall effort.

Better prospects exist for enforcing the prohibition of child participation in the production of pornographic books and films, although there are limits. Children from midadolescence onward who are willing participants in the exercise are difficult to remove from the street and will usually be unavailable as complaining witnesses against their corrupters. Much of their participation in movies or employment as photographic models may be beyond the reach of law enforcement.

But the live-sex segment of the industry, particularly if it involves public display or the licensed sale of alcoholic beverages, is often the subject of police scrutiny. And police supervision of bars can make proprietors quite vigilant about age gradations. Whether this can be regarded as a wholly desirable youth-protection policy depends on the extent to which it diminishes the involvement of the young in the commercial sex business, rather than driving adolescents into less visible and less desirable branches of the industry.

For younger children, their appearance atone may operate as a red-flag warning that will reinforce regulatory powers. Purveyors of commercial sex are not unaware of the opprobrium attached to the employment of the young in this area, as well as likelihood of more intensive law enforcement and heavier penalties. Moreover, for very young children, the runaway population from which participants can be recruited is smaller.

The prohibition of the use of children in live displays in public places does not present major enforcement problems. Films, books, and magazines can also be confiscated, although never as fast as they can be reproduced. Yet the relative rarity of unambiguous child pornography, which the Meese Commission acknowledged (saying "there now appears to be comparatively little domestic commercial production of child pornography") (U.S. Department of Justice, 1986:409j), may not be so much due, as the commission thought, to the success of "major law enforcement initiatives" as to the fact that the demand for the product has never been as great or as elastic as the more vocal protesters against this "major horror" have believed.

The Punishment of Children

One issue highlighted by the consideration of child pornography as victimless crime is the extent to which it is appropriate to punish children for placing their own interests in jeopardy or for jeopardizing the interests of other children. In considering this question, it might also be useful to distinguish between punishing a child for engaging in self-jeopardization and punishing minors for the exploitation of other minors.

It is never appropriate to use either the criminal law or the delinquency jurisdiction of the juvenile court to punish minors severely solely because they put themselves at risk. To do so would be to make assumptions about personal responsibility in deciding punishments that are inconsistent with the ideas about responsibility that led to, and are inherent in, the definition of the offense. Lesser punishments may be predicated on partial responsibility. But secure confinement as punishment for self-jeopardy appears to us to be nonsensical.

If the punishment of minors for putting themselves at risk is unjustified, what about the exercise of state power based on the minor's need for protection rather than on the concept of blameworthiness? This was, and is, the basis of the "status offenses" jurisdiction of the juvenile court; and it has not been totally repudiated.

The problem is that substantial amounts of punishment have been imposed in the guise of nonpunitive child protection. And the one effective control on this tendency is the limitation, on child-protection grounds, of the degree of physical control that can be exercised over adolescent subjects. Long-term secure confinement should be restricted to cases involving the kind of extreme danger that justifies civil commitment. Short-term secure confinement might be permitted as a means of crisis intervention, but it involves the risk of misuse or manipulation by the police and the courts.

The problem of the minor who is responsible for the sexual exploitation of other minors is distinguishable from self-jeopardization, but not in an absolute fashion. The paradigm case of the sexual exploitation of children involves not only incapacity on the victim's part but the assumption of a greater capacity on the part of those responsible for the offense. Something of the same problem involved in punishing the child victim counsels against punishing one fifteen-year-old for exploiting the immaturity of another fifteen-year-old with respect to either commercial or noncommercial sexual practices.

The punishment of minors for the exploitation of other minors might be limited to cases where either physical force was used or there were clear differences in age or capacity. The punishment of a sixteen-year-old for the exploitation of a twelve-year-old is much more clearly justifiable than the punishment of two sixteen-year-olds for mutual exploitation. As a threshold matter, we should require some significant difference in capacity before permitting the punishment of one minor for the exploitation of another. Once that threshold is passed, moreover, an inquiry into the extent of the overreach would be relevant to the selection of the appropriate punishment in such cases.

The Criminal Jurisprudence of Child Pornography

The foregoing discussion of the punishment of children is just one of many specific issues that require consideration in relation to the use of criminal sanctions in regulating the involvement of children in pornography and commercial sex. A great many questions regarding the definition and gradation of sexual offenses involving children have received little attention and practically no critical scrutiny. It is almost as though child pornography were a homogeneous harm, so that there was no need to devote serious consideration to the definition of offenses in this area.

In fact, given the tendency for criminal prohibitions to be enacted with enthusiasm and buttressed with inflated penalty scales, the opposite is the case. It is essential that careful thought be given to issues of definition and gradation. Among the key issues are the following:

- Is a single grade of offense involving participation in the commercial sexual exploitation of a child sufficient? Or should a higher grade of offense be provided for cases involving younger children, with proportionately lesser penalties being provided for the exploitation of children closer to the borders of adult status? (See Zimring, 1982, 1987.)

- Should aggravated penalties be provided for cases involving the use of force?

- Should there be mitigation of punishment in cases involving the admittedly imperfect consent of minor victims? Or should the consent of a minor only warrant mitigation when the victim is an older child and when the victim and offender are relatively close in age and capacity?

- To what extent should the scale of a commercial child pornography operation be regarded as relevant to the moral blameworthiness of actors in it and the eligibility of offenders for larger penalties? The production of ten child-pornographic films may be regarded as more culpable than the production of one such film; but should the distribution of ten copies of the same film be regarded as more serious than the distribution of one or two? And if so, to what extent and why?

We cannot here even outline a complete jurisprudence of child pornography. Instead we wish to demonstrate that if this matter is to be taken seriously, such questions as these cannot be ignored. And some attempt to construct or formulate a principled basis for sentencing those who exploit children in this manner is a necessary feature of taking child pornography seriously.

On the Boundaries of Childhood

Just as we do not propose to offer a detailed jurisprudence for the sentencing of those convicted of the sexual exploitation of children, neither shall we attempt a definitive analysis of the appropriate age boundaries that should be prescribed in applying the criminal law to the sexual exploitation of children. Instead we offer two general guidelines that should govern the determination of those boundaries.

First, asking questions about the age at which children are sufficiently mature to make responsible decisions about participation in pornographic production is the wrong way to go about defining the boundaries for criminal prohibition. There is a sense in which no age is old enough for such decisions, and no child or young adult has the experience to make those decisions until he or she has made them. More importantly—and the victimless crime category is again instructive here—the point in adolescence at which criminal prohibitions cease to be useful is when they begin to do more harm than good. And that typically is long before the targets of predation reach anywhere near their full maturity.

Pornography and Child Protection

Second, it is clear that no single age boundary can usefully span the great variety of issues involved in the regulation of sexual communication and children. If exposure to pornographic material is to be made criminal, it should be so only in relation to young children, with the maximum age certainly no higher than thirteen or fourteen. Sexual conduct is quite different from sexual communication, and there is no reason why the criminal law should not prohibit sexual practices of adults with fourteen-or fifteen-year-olds even if such minors are over the age at which pornographic communication to them ceases to be criminal. Finally, there would be nothing wrong with a scheme of regulation that set the age of consent for participation in commercial sexual activity higher—say at eighteen years of age—than for noncommercial sexual conduct. We think this may be both compatible with, and justifiable in, a situation where a society has completely decriminalized participation in commercial sex by adults.

The specific age boundaries just suggested are, like all age boundaries, largely arbitrary, although the scheme itself both in the distinctions drawn and in the kind of gradation involved is not in itself arbitrary but based on empirical observation. Moreover, it is clearly at this level of specificity that any useful analysis of the problems presented in this chapter must proceed.

CONCLUSION

We do not intend this chapter as a final statement of the manifold issues of pornography and childhood. Our aim is to help build an agenda for discussion, analysis, and research. In an area known for passionate emotions and frequent political posturing, the need for detached policy assessments is not always obvious. But the case against government by sentiment has this important element: Child welfare is apt to suffer in the absence of reasoned discourse.

Notes and Questions

Decriminalization and the Availability of Pornographic Communication

1. One of the most dramatic trends toward decriminalization of pornographic communication occurred during the period from 1955 to 1980. All kinds of written materials and most kinds of pictorial materials that are designed to sexually arouse are now openly available in most industrialized nations. By the early 1980s, the "adult" bookstore, carrying books, pictures, videos and films that would have been clearly felonious in most countries before 1960, was nearly universal in major Western cities. The major exception to the decriminalization trend involved child pornography (a term whose definitions varied) and—in the United States—some forms of explicit sexual material that could be classified as obscene. While the verbal and conceptual difficulties attendant on distinguishing obscene and nonobscene pornography are of interest to lawyers and philosophers, the significant social fact is that "hard core" pornography is ubiquitously available in the Western democracies.

Several historical questions that can be asked about this revolutionary change:

    a. How and why did this dramatic liberalization occur?

    b. What can be concluded about the social importance of pornography from the rapid increase in legal availability in North America, Europe, and the British Commonwealth?

    c. How has the adult bookstore down the street changed information, attitudes, and behavior in relation to sex?

    d. How has legal availability altered exposure to pornography in different demographic and social groups?

Technological and legal changes interacted in the 1980s in ways that profoundly affected the distribution of explicit sexual materials. The video cassette and video cassette recorder quickly became the primary channel for viewing explicitly pornographic material, which relocated pornographic exposure from peepshows and theaters to living rooms. One consequence was that many "adult" theaters have disappeared from the American urban "combat zones" as explicit pornography has become home entertainment (see Zimring and Hawkins, 1988, Chapter 3). What do you think are some of the social effects of this change? If you have viewed any pornography, where did you see it?

2. The Meese Commission (discussed at length in the Zimring and Hawkins material) worked entirely within a period when pornography was shifting from public theater to private video performances and easily-copied pornographic videocassettes were proliferating. Yet the Commission did not consider the wholesale recriminalization of explicit sexual material to be practical. The Commission tried to use criminalization and regulatory strategies to expand the definitions of obscenity and child pornography without frontally assaulting the legal availability of pornography.

3. What would Sir Patrick Devlin have to say about the wide availability of explicit pornographic communication (see Chapter 1)? What would H.L.A. Hart believe? Is not the notorious line between available pornography and suppressible obscenity precisely the kind of distinction that Devlin's tests for the appropriate threshold of moral repugnance should produce? Could one say that nonobscene pornography could be defined as material that would give the man on the Clapham omnibus an erection while obscene material is that which would make him nauseated?

4. Does the central argument about pornography rely on distinguishing between harm to self and harm to others? Or does the liberalizer really argue that pornography does not harm adults? If pornography is harmless to adults, then is it also harmless to children? If not, why not?

5. What of the argument that the literary quality of pornography is so low that it harms its readers and ruins the market for good literature (see George Steiner, "Night Words", in *Perspectives on Pornography*, D.A. Hughes, ed., 1970)? Does this argument have implications about the harm of pornography? Is this an argument for banning all bad books, or for banning all bad books that potentially appeal to the public?

6. Note the linkage between pornographic materials that depend on sexual behavior occurring and policies relating to prostitution. Can one produce a pornographic motion picture without prostitution taking place? By contrast, pornographic materials that can be wholly imagined or simulated are not necessarily linked with prostitution policy. If prostitution is decriminalized, are there still persuasive reasons to prohibit some forms of pornography? If prostitution does remain criminal, are there persuasive reasons why portrayals of sexual activity on film for commercial gain should not be regarded as criminal?

7. The most extensively documented and most plausible effects of some forms of pornography relate to the attitude toward rape and the sexual exploitation of women on the part of males exposed to materials portraying sexual violence with approval. When sexually arousing communications also appear to approve of the use of force in sexual relations, this is associated with higher levels of what have been called "rape attitudes" on the part of some audience members. The approving portrayal of sexual violence may also affect attitudes in this way when the communication is not pornographic. Assume that higher levels of favorable attitudes toward sexual violence can be linked to greater evidence of actual sexual violence in individuals or communities. Would this effect on attitudes represent the kind of harm to others that John Stuart Mill would have regarded as a proper foundation for

a criminal sanction? If so, would the relationship between "violent pornography" and "rape attitudes" justify the prohibition of all pornography or only violent pornography? Would it also justify restrictions on nonpornographic communications that generate "rape attitudes"?

8. What if all or most pornography results in lower opinions of women or encourages male audience members to think of women solely as sex objects? Does this lowered regard for women constitute the kind of palpable harm that John Stuart Mill would have considered proper foundation for a criminal prohibition? Can attitudinal changes that lower esteem for women be distinguished from attitudinal changes that raise esteem for violence as a means of sexual gratification? Should this kind of "sexist speech" be governed by the same legal standards as the use of racial epithets and assaults on patriotism? (If so, then suppressing it is only justified if the speech act represents a "clear and present danger" to public order.)

9. Is the case for regarding pornography as a victimless crime weaker or stronger than the case for regarding the possession and use of heroin and cocaine as victimless crimes? The recent history of criminal justice policy in relation to adult pornography and to psychoactive drugs such as heroin and cocaine is a study in marked contrasts. After 1985, the resources devoted to and public support for the criminal prohibition of psychoactive drugs in the United States increased dramatically. (See Chapter 3.)

By contrast, the campaign against the evils of pornography exemplified by the Meese Commission remained a largely symbolic and rhetorical exercise. The number of people imprisoned for violating United States drug laws outnumbers the number imprisoned for non-child-related pornographic offenses by many hundreds to one. What might account for these divergent patterns? How likely is it that future changes in public opinion will lead to a "War on Pornography" equivalent in effort and practical effect to the recent American "War on Drugs"?

10. Compare and contrast the argument used to justify the possession and consumption of pornography as a victimless category of behavior with the argument for so regarding abortion. On a "harm to others" standard, which is the easier case to argue?

11. The publication of the Meese Commission's report was followed by a major U.S. effort at the federal level to arrest and imprison those who dealt, possessed, and used child pornography. What are the special harms of child pornography? Why do you think a crusade against child pornography might attract major support subsequent to a report that disapproved of *all* pornography but nevertheless did not recommend its prohibition?

12. Pornography is generally available in the United States of the early 21st century, and reported rapes have declined over the last generation. Is there a connection? (See D'Amato, Anthony, "Porn Up, Rape Down" (June 23, 2006). Northwestern Public Law Research Paper No. 913013, available at SSRN: http://ssrn.com/abstract=913013).

13. After a cluster of studies and debates in the late 1980s and early 1990s, the attention given to the link between pornography and social harm seems to have declined compared to the mid–1970s. Why?

Chapter 6

PROSTITUTION

A. INTRODUCTION

The half century after 1950 produced very large changes in criminal law and in levels of punishment for drugs, gambling, pornography, and sodomy, in the United States and in many developed nations. Prostitution seems an exception to this pattern of high activity. Both the law and levels of law enforcement have seemed much less volatile. While the Wolfenden Commission began this era considering prostitution as one of its two major topics, not much legal change can be found in Great Britain, the U.S., or in Western Europe. Why? How is prostitution different from gambling? From drugs? From pornography? What is likely to happen in the next 50 years? What should happen?

B. HISTORICAL PERSPECTIVES

DAVID A.J. RICHARDS—PROSTITUTION: ANTHROPOLOGICAL AND HISTORICAL PERSPECTIVES

From "Commercial Sex and the Rights of the Person: A Moral Argument for the Decriminalization of Prostitution." University of Pennsylvania Law Review 127:1203–1214 (1979).

For contemporary purposes, prostitution is usually defined in terms of "an individual who indiscriminately provides sexual relations in return for money payments." Older definitions strikingly omit the gender-neutral "individual" (or "person") and even the commercialism requirement. For example, one commentator defined it in 1951 as "the indiscriminate offer by a female of her body for the purpose of sexual intercourse or other lewdness." These twin omissions suggest that the traditional concern for prostitution was peculiarly associated with female sexuality—more particularly, with attitudes toward promiscuous unchastity in women—apart from any commercial aspects. Contemporary legal definitions attempt to modify the scope of prostitution. On the one hand, they enlarge the class of persons who may be prostitutes to include men in order to square anti-prostitution laws with emerging moral and constitutional norms of gender-neutral fairness in distributing governmental burdens and benefits. On the other hand, the commercialism requirement narrows the class of prostitutional sexual activities to indiscriminate "sexual relations in return for money payments," thus excluding mere sexual promiscuity or unchastity per se. Since enforcement patterns under even gender-neutral anti-prostitution statutes indicate that the continuing concern is largely with female sexuality, the total effect of the modern definitions has been to narrow the class of female sexual activities to which prostitution laws apply. A crucial concern has obviously been to exclude from the concept of prostitution forms of sexual relations which are not conventionally condemned today. There may be a commercial element to some marital sexual relations, for example; and there is not always a sharp line, perhaps, between the dinners and entertainment expenses in now conventional premarital sexual relations and the more formalized business transactions of the prostitute. In consequence, in order to draw the desired distinctions between the conventional and the impermissible, contemporary definitions place great weight on money payments for indiscriminate sex. The mark of the contemporary prostitute is indiscriminate availability for sexual relations with any willing buyer, in contrast to other forms of now widespread pre- and extramarital sexual relations.

The emergence of prostitution, within the terms of the modern definition, is generally associated with the development of urban civilization. It is misleading to interpret the anthropological cross-cultural data of patterns of promiscuity among primitive peoples as forms of prostitution, for such peoples often attached little value to virginity; furthermore, there is little evidence in this data of the existence of a class of women indiscriminately available to men for money. Rather, the patterns of sexual promiscuity in question represent highly selective choices, often spontaneous and mutually pleasurable with no commercial elements other than gift giving. The conditions of life in primitive society, with closely knit family and kin networks that regulate the behavior of the young in detail, do not lend themselves to the emergence of a rootless class of women who are available for anonymous indiscriminate sexual encounters for money. This phenomenon is historically associated with the emergence of large cities and the possibility of anonymity associated therewith.

The emergence of commercial prostitution in the modern sense appears to have been a development from the institution of temple prostitution that was a feature of religious life in the first high civilizations. Herodotus, for example, notes that women of ancient Babylonia, prior to marriage, were required to engage once in sexual intercourse as temple prostitutes with the first man who presented himself. The religious significance of temple prostitution is remote from us, but it probably was an institutionalized expression of primitive orgiastic communion with the divine forces of fertility, both sexual and agricultural. We know the appeasement and worship of these forces to have been at the core of the ancient Babylonian and Egyptian cosmological conceptions of the universal order.

Forms of temple prostitution continued to exist in ancient Greece, but commercial prostitution emerged as an independent empirical phenomenon, associated, for example, with the commercial life of Athens as a metropolitan seaport. Both the ancient Greeks and Romans regulated prostitution, not merely permitting it, but in some cases establishing state brothels. Prostitutes appear to have been divided into distinct classes, not unlike the still-familiar distinctions among streetwalkers, brothel prostitutes, and call girls. In ancient Greece and China, the highest classes of prostitutes appear to have enjoyed extraordinary intellectual and artistic advantages that women of their periods were, in general, not permitted. Nonetheless, it is probably a mistake to romanticize the life of the typical prostitute of these periods. Prostitutes were often slaves. While their conduct was not criminal, their activities were highly regulated, and their status as prostitutes deprived them of rights that other women enjoyed. Prostitutes were regarded as useful to the state in the context of two factors that appear empirically to be part of the standard causal background for the existence of prostitution: (1) toleration of male sexual experimentation but insistence on female virginity before marriage and fidelity in marriage, often combined with late marriage for men or lifelong bachelorhood, and (2) a class of women freed from traditional familial and clan restraints. The usefulness of prostitutes as an outlet for male sexual experimentation in such circumstances does not, of course, mean that they were esteemed or, with certain narrow exceptions, admired. On the contrary, we know that the ancient Greeks thought of women as of inferior moral worth intrinsically, their moral value deriving in large part from their role in nurturing the development of men, who were considered to have intrinsic moral worth. Prostitutes were regarded as of worth instrumentally in satisfying certain male needs much as Aristotle regarded slaves as valuable instruments and tools for their masters' uses. For the Romans, with their higher esteem for respectable women as such, prostitutes were held in general contempt although, again, they were thought to be instrumentally useful.

The history of prostitution under Christianity falls into two strikingly different periods: pre- and post-Reformation. In the pre-Reformation period, prostitution was perceived in the context of St. Augustine's classic conception that the only proper "genital commotion" is that consciously aimed at the reproduction of the species in marriage. Augustine argues that the only plausible explanation for the privacy associated with sexual experience is that humans experience sex as intrinsically degrading because it involves the radical loss of control over mental functions, experiences, sensations, and behavior. This perception of shame, in turn, is alleged to rest on the fact that the only proper form of sex is accompanied by the controlled marital intention to procreate. Augustine concludes that sexuality is intrinsically degrading because we tend to experience it without or independent of those intentions which alone can validate it. It follows from this view not only that certain rigidly defined kinds of intercourse in conventional marriage are alone moral, but that sexuality even within marriage is a natural object of continuing shame, for sexual drives generally operate quite independently of the will, let alone of the will to reproduce. In the Augustinian view, prostitution, as a form of extramarital sex, is, of course, immoral. For Augustine, however, sexuality in general is problematic: asexuality is obviously the preferred state, and sex even in marriage is validated only by its procreational intentions. This unsentimental view of marriage and the desire to protect it realistically led both St. Augustine and St. Thomas to argue for the toleration of prostitution on the ground that it best protected the marital procreational unit. Unmarried men, incapable of celibacy, would be tempted to seduce neither married women nor the virgins destined to be married, and married men, incapable of fidelity, would be tempted to seduce neither of the above nor to form more permanent liaisons that would threaten their dedication to the procreational unit. In the pre-Reformation period, as a consequence, prostitution, with a few notable exceptions, was tolerated.

Reformation thinkers, such as Luther, perceived prostitution in the context of attacks on the Catholic idealization of celibacy as the religiously preferable state and the corresponding greater emphasis on the status of companionate marriage in which all one's sexual and emotional needs were to be satisfied. Ideas of romantic love, which in the Middle Ages had been celebrated in secular literature in extramarital, often adulterous terms, were here explicitly absorbed into religious thought and vested by Luther and other Reformation thinkers in the marital unit alone. In consequence, Lutheran and Calvinist thought not only regarded prostitution as immoral, but, unlike the Catholic thinkers, urged its absolute legal prohibition, because prostitution violated the moral norm that all one's emotional needs were to be satisfied in marriage alone.

Calvinist thought, in the form of Puritanism, powerfully influenced popular attitudes toward and the legal treatment of prostitution in England and the United States. In England, Puritanism acted as a political force effectively prohibiting brothels for a short time. As an empirical phenomenon, prostitution flourished in England due to the concurrence of the two standard background causal factors noted earlier. During the Victorian period, a combination of religious forces and the first wave of British feminists, led by the redoubtable Josephine Butler, frontally attacked the toleration of prostitution and the double standard of sexual morality that they perceived to underlie it; men, like women, should be compelled to observe the same standards, which the reformers assumed to be chastity or sex in marriage alone. Among other things, these reformers secured the end of the brief British attempt at government licensing of prostitution, which was then common in Europe. Following the recommendations of the *Wolfenden Report*, prostitution is not itself a crime in England today, although public solicitation on the streets is prohibited. In consequence, commerce in sexual services in

England is largely negotiated through discreet advertisements in certain familiar locations and publications.

In the United States, Puritan ideas have had much deeper impact on the legal treatment of prostitution than in England. Calvinist ideas of companionate marriage, secularized by the combined influence of Calvinist preachers and female popular novelists, developed into a reigning theory of sentimental marriage in which the asexual and more intensely spiritual wife would purify and elevate the husband's coarser worldly nature. Drawing on these ideas, the first wave of American feminists, including Susan B. Anthony, viewed attaining the vote as a means to secure expression in American politics of the higher spiritual vision that was uniquely feminine. This vision took the form of "purity leagues" that frontally attacked first slavery, and then alcoholism and prostitution. The consequence of the latter attack was not merely the end of brief American experiments with licensing prostitution and the decisive rejection of the sometimes eloquent arguments of American proponents of licensing, but the criminalization throughout the nation of prostitution per se. Today, of the American states, only Nevada permits local communities to allow prostitution.

In continental Europe, the pattern of broad state toleration of prostitution was set in the early 1800's by the Napoleonic licensing of brothels. Licensing of prostitution continued throughout Europe into this century. Growing concern for the alleged "white slave trade" in women and girls led the League of Nations and later the United Nations to call for the abolition of licensed brothels, which were claimed to be the main sources of regular demand for the international commerce in women and girls. These international conventions, in conjunction with feminist arguments against the degree to which licensing unjustly regulated and stigmatized the lives of prostitutes, led to the abolition of state licensing in Europe. Although prostitution itself is not criminal in Europe, forms of solicitation and place of business are subject to various kinds of regulations.

C. MORALITY AND THE PROHIBITION OF PROSTITUTION

THE WOLFENDEN COMMITTEE—THE WOLFENDEN REPORT: REPORT OF THE COMMITTEE ON HOMOSEXUAL OFFENSES AND PROSTITUTION (EXCERPT)

New York: Stein and Day (1963).

GENERAL CONSIDERATIONS

By our terms of reference we are required to consider "the law and practice relating to offenses against the criminal law in connection with prostitution and solicitation for immoral purposes."

So far as our terms of reference relate to offenses in streets and public places, the problems were examined by an earlier Committee (the

Street Offenses Committee) set up in 1927 under the chairmanship of the late Lord Macmillan (then Mr. Hugh Macmillan, K.C.); and we have studied the report of that Committee(') in coming to our own conclusions.

It would have taken us beyond our terms of reference to investigate in detail the prevalence of prostitution or the reasons which lead women to adopt this manner of life. On the former point we have something to say below(') in connection with street offenses. On the latter point, we believe. that whatever may have been the case in the past, in these days, in this country at any rate, economic factors cannot account for it to any large or decisive extent. Economic pressure is no doubt a factor in some individual cases. So, in others, is a bad upbringing, seduction at an early age, or a broken marriage. But many women surmount such disasters without turning to a life of prostitution. It seems to us more likely that these are precipitating factors rather than determining causes, and that there must be some additional psychological element in the personality of the individual woman who becomes a prostitute. Our impression is that the great majority of prostitutes are women whose psychological make-up is such that they choose this life because they find in it a style of living which is to them easier, freer and more profitable than would be provided by any other occupation. As one of our women witnesses put it:

> Prostitution is a way of life consciously chosen because it suits a woman's personality in particular circumstances.

Prostitution in itself is not, in this country, an offense against the criminal law. Some of the activities of prostitutes are, and so are the activities of some others who are concerned in the activities of prostitutes. But it is not illegal for a woman to "offer her body to indiscriminate lewdness for hire," provided that she does not, in the course of doing so, commit any one of the specific acts which would bring her within the ambit of the law. Nor, it seems to us, can any case be sustained for attempting to make prostitution in itself illegal. We recognize that we are here, again, on the difficult borderland between law and morals, and that this is debatable ground. But, for the general reasons which we have outlined in Chapter II above, we are agreed that private immorality should not be the concern of the criminal law except in the special circumstances therein mentioned.

Prostitution is a social fact deplorable in the eyes of moralists, sociologists and, we believe, the great majority of ordinary people. But it has persisted in many civilizations throughout many centuries, and the failure of attempts to stamp it out by repressive legislation shows that it cannot be eradicated through the agency of the criminal law. It remains true that without a clientele for her services the prostitute could not survive, and that there are enough men who avail themselves of prostitutes to keep the trade alive. It also remains true that there are women who, even when there is no economic need to do so, choose this form of livelihood. For so long as these propositions continue to be true there will be prostitution, and no amount of legislation directed towards its abolition will abolish it.

It follows that there are limits to the degree of discouragement which the criminal law can properly exercise towards a woman who has deliberately decided to live her life in this way, or a man who has deliberately chosen to use her services. The criminal law, as the Street Offenses Committee plainly pointed out, "is not concerned with private morals or with ethical sanctions." This does not mean that society itself can be indifferent to these matters, for prostitution is an evil of which any society which claims to be civilized should seek to rid itself; but this end could be achieved only through measures directed to a better understanding of the nature and obligation of sexual relationships and to a raising of the social and moral outlook of society as a whole. In these matters, the work of the churches and of organizations concerned with mental health, moral welfare, family welfare, child and marriage guidance and similar matters should be given all possible encouragement. But until education and the moral sense of the community bring about a change of attitude towards the fact of prostitution, the law by itself cannot do so.

At the same time; the law has its place and function in this matter. We cannot do better than quote the words of the Street Offenses Committee:

> As a general proposition it will be universally accepted that the law is not concerned with private morals or with ethical sanctions. On the other hand, the law is plainly concerned with the outward conduct of citizens in so far as that conduct injuriously affects the rights of other citizens. Certain forms of conduct it has always been thought right to bring within the scope of the criminal law on account of the injury which they occasion to the public in general. It is within this category of offenses, if anywhere, that public solicitation for immoral purposes finds an appropriate place.

The statement very clearly represents our own approach and attitude to this part of our inquiry. We are concerned not with prostitution itself but with the manner in which the activities of prostitutes and those associated with them offend against public order and decency, expose the ordinary citizen to what is offensive or injurious, or involve the exploitation of others.

Notes and Questions

1. The Wolfenden Report addressed two issues: homosexuality and prostitution. With regard to homosexuality, the recommendation to decriminalize became the law of England in a short time. Since then, sexual relations between consenting adults have been decriminalized in many other countries as well.

With regard to prostitution, however, decriminalization was reflected less widely throughout the Western world. The exchange of money for sexual services is criminal in forty-nine of the fifty United States, throughout most of Europe, in the rest of the British Commonwealth, and in Britain half a century after the Wolfenden report, remains in the state the report describes.

Why do you suppose the scope of nonpecuniary sexual liberty has broadened so much more than the freedom to buy and sell sexual services?

2. The recent legal history of pornography and prostitution is another study in sharp contrasts. Pornographic communication (including film, video, and photographs of a wide variety of sexual acts) is available throughout the industrialized Western world. The criminal law prohibitions that until quite recently restricted the production, sale, display, and possession of pornography have been cut back in favor of a free market in the depiction of adults having sex. (Vide Gordon Hawkins and Franklin Zimring, *Pornography in a Free Society*, 1988, Chapter 3.) Under these circumstances, films of sexual behavior which are designed to provoke a customer to masturbate are not regulated by the criminal law, but some in-person sexual services are prohibited. What distinguishes these two forms of commercial sex?

Incidentally, the criminal prohibition of prostitution casts a legal shadow over the production of pornographic photographs, motion pictures, and video recordings. If the actors in a pornographic film are paid to copulate in front of the camera, are they not engaged in prostitution as defined by most statutes? If so, does not the sale of pornography involve being an accessory after the fact to prostitution (U.S. Department of Justice, *Attorney General's Commission on Pornography Final Report*, 1986:797–798, 831)? Beyond legal technicalities, what is the moral difference between the forms of sexual excitation and assistance generated by pornography and by prostitutes? Should live displays of nude and sexually provocative dancing be considered pornography or prostitution? What about massage parlors? What about lap dancing?

3. The legal status of prostitution may not changed much in the Western world, but the rhetorical character of writing about prostitutes and prostitution has changed a great deal. Stremler outlines some of the conflict in current feminist writing about prostitutes and prostitution (see pp. 654–58). Discourse about policy toward prostitution in the 1980s and 1990s was dominated by concepts and terms unknown to the Wolfenden Committee members. The last generation's hookers, streetwalkers, and tarts are often referred to as "sex workers" in contemporary writing. Whether the practice should be regarded as egregiously exploitational or relatively benign seems to depend on whether it is inherently subordinating to the female prostitute and a reinforcement of patriarchal domination.

It is commonly suggested that monogamous heterosexual marriage is a sole source contracted form of prostitution. Why the feminist ambivalence on decriminalizing what is the second leading cause of female arrests in the United States? Do some feminist critics find prostitution objectionable, but regard the abuse of prostitutes by the criminal justice system as also problematic? But if the behavior of prostitutes is voluntary, should not the criminal law prohibition be removed?

DAVID A.J. RICHARDS—COMMERCIAL SEX, HUMAN RIGHTS, AND MORAL IDEALS

From "Commercial Sex and the Rights of the Person: A Moral Argument
for the Decriminalization of Prostitution." *University of
Pennsylvania Law Review* 127:1203–1214 (1979).

So far, we have considered a number of negative arguments directed at showing why various moral arguments condemning commercial sex are mistaken. Let us now constructively consider the affirmative case for allowing commercial sex, that is, for the existence of rights of the person that include the right to engage in commercial sex. In this way, we can clarify the scope and limits of this right, and address in more systematic fashion the relation of this right to the personal ideals, frequently invoked previously, that the state allegedly has no right to enforce.

Let us reconsider the view of sexual autonomy that emerged in our discussion of romantic love and its relation to the contractarian analysis of human rights. We argued that human sexuality is marked by its powerful role in the imaginative life and general development of the person, and that the neutral theory of the good, expressive of the values of equal concern and respect for autonomy, required toleration of a number of different visions of the role of sexuality in human life. In the contractarian model, we express these ideas by saying that the choice in the original position is choice under uncertainty: rational people in the original position have no ways of predicting that they may end up in any given situation of life and they must decide only on the basis of facts capable of interpersonal empirical validation. By definition, none of the contractors knows his or her own age, sex, native talents, particular capacity for self-control, social or economic class or position, or the particular form of his or her personal desires. Each contractor will be concerned not to end up in a disadvantaged situation with no appeal to moral principles to denounce deprivations that may render life prospects bitter and mean. To avoid such consequences, the rational strategy in choosing the basic principles of justice would be the "maximin" strategy.

As we have suggested, the contractors in the original position would regard self-respect as the primary good. Accordingly, their aim would be to adopt principles that would ensure that people have the maximum chance of attaining self-respect. Sexual autonomy, the capacity to choose whether or how or with whom or on what terms one will have sexual relations, would be one crucial ingredient of this self-respect; it is one of the forms of personal competence in terms of which people self-critically decide, as free and rational agents, what kind of person they will be. Because contractors in the original position are assumed to be ignorant of specific identity and to take into account only those facts subject to general empirical validation, they may not appeal to special religious duties to procreate in order to override sexual liberty; nor may they appeal to any taste or distaste for certain forms of the physical expression of sexuality in order to override the interest in sexual autonomy;

nor may they appeal to concepts of love that illegitimately smuggle in covert premises or prejudices incompatible with respect for the myriad paths to sexual fulfillment. As we have seen, self-respect in the fulfillment and expression of one's sexuality is compatible with a number of modes. Sexual love is one of these modes; romantic love is one highly special form of it. But meaningful sexual fulfillment takes other forms as well. From the point of view of the original position and the values of equal concern and respect for autonomy that it expresses, there is no form of sexual expression that can be given preferred status, for a large and indeterminate class of forms of sexual intercourse is compatible with autonomous self-respect. Accordingly, subject to qualifying moral principles shortly to be discussed, the contractors would, in order to secure the values of sexual self-respect, agree to a principle of obligation and duty, defining correlative human rights, requiring that people be guaranteed the greatest equal liberty of autonomous sexual expression compatible with a like liberty for all.

The contractarian model would, of course, also yield qualifying moral principles relevant to understanding the limits of this human right. Thus, on contractarian grounds, one may easily derive principles forbidding killing or the infliction of harm or gratuitous cruelty. These principles would be accepted because they protect basic interests. Such moral principles are relevant to sexual expression; sexual partners should not inflict serious and irreparable bodily harm on one another, even if such harm is consensual. On the other hand, these principles would not justify prohibition of forms of consensual sexual conduct, including commercial sex, which are not harmful. Similarly, moral principles of fidelity can be derived from the original position, requiring that mutual undertakings, voluntarily and maturely entered into, be observed faithfully. Such principles, again, do not justify general prohibition of forms of consensual sexual conduct, or commercial sex in particular; they justify, at most, only specific constraints on breaches of fidelity, such as breach of contract, or fraud and deception. A principle of consideration can also be derived from the original position, requiring that persons not impose upon others unnecessary annoyance and disturbances. This principle would justify time, place, and manner restrictions on prostitution and its solicitation, but certainly not a complete prohibition.

In addition, the contractarian model justifies, as we have seen, a moral principle of paternalism in certain carefully delimited circumstances. This principle does not justify an absolute prohibition on consensual sexual conduct in general or commercial sex in particular. However, it is important to notice here that the imperative of sexual autonomy would not apply to persons presumably lacking rational capacities—young children, for example—since the value of autonomous sexual expression turns on the existence of developed capacities of rational choice. Accordingly, the sexual commerce of quite young children may be forbidden, just as sexual intercourse with and by them may be limited in various ways. One would need, of course, to determine the appropriate age of majority for those purposes based on available psychological data. The most that can be said here is that the principle of paternalism would not sustain an unrealistically old age at which sexual nonage is ended.

Finally, principles of distributive justice would be agreed to in the original position that would require a certain form of the distribution of wealth, property, status, and opportunity. Sometimes it is suggested that prostitution is appropriately criminalized in order to advance the more just distribution of the goods required by such principles of distributive justice, on the grounds that prostitution is mainly a temptation to the poor and a symptom of poverty. Of course, on grounds of distributive justice, people should have more equal job opportunities than they currently have. Certainly better job opportunities should, for example, be available to racial minorities and women. But it does not follow that high-income job opportunities that currently exist for poor people should, on grounds of justice, be ended. If one wishes responsibly to ameliorate the situation of racial minorities who are a disproportionate number of the women arrested for prostitution, decriminalization, not criminalization, is the just course, for it would remove the moral stigma and the consequent unjustified self-contempt that they experience, the various ancillary evils that criminalization fosters, and the uniquely degrading exposure to the American criminal justice system that their more advantaged call-girl sisters in large part avoid. In addition, responsible moral concern for whatever economic disadvantages streetwalkers suffer would take the form of regulations to ensure them economic fairness, including forms of union organization. Criminalization, in contrast, fosters the economic exploitation that it is fallaciously assumed to remedy.

To summarize, the principle of sexual autonomy does not apply to persons presumably lacking rational capacities, such as young children, nor does it validate the infliction of serious bodily harm. In addition, the liberty of sexual expression comports with the liberty of others to choose to be sexual partners. It follows, therefore, that there should be no moral objection on grounds of sexual autonomy to the reasonable regulation of consensual adult sex as regards time, manner, and place. For example, there is no objection to the reasonable regulation of the obtrusive solicitation of sexual relations. But the moral principles qualifying the principle of sexual autonomy do not justify any absolute prohibition of sexual autonomy of the kind that the criminalization of prostitution involves. Such criminal prohibitions flatly violate the rights of the person. These rights may not be abridged by vague appeals to public distaste that, if given the force of law, would dilute their moral force and transform them from a powerful vindication of autonomy into the empty and vapid idea that people be allowed to do that which gives rise to no strong objection. Majority attitudes by themselves, unsupported by defensible moral reasoning, cannot justify the deprivations of liberty of the criminal law. They are merely intractable prejudices that the state should circumscribe where necessary to protect the system of human rights, rather than elevate into law.

It is important to see the scope and limits of an argument grounded in human rights of the kind here presented. To say that a person has a human right to do "x" is a claim of political and legal morality which justifies the claim that certain conduct must be protected by the state from forms of coercive prohibition. But justifiably to assert the existence of such a right is not to conclude the question whether people should exercise these rights. This latter question is an issue of personal morality, the disposition of which may turn on considerations that have no proper place in questions of political and legal morality.

Consider, for example, the moral right to choose one's work. Often, we take highly critical attitudes to these choices, arguing, for example, that someone's choice is a waste of talent or a refusal to take risks with his or her life. Such arguments are often not simply prudential calculations of the best way rationally to realize the agent's ends, nor are they purely morally supererogatory, for we do not merely praise appropriate choices, but assign a species of moral blame for failing to act on these ideals or for acting on the wrong ideals. We may criticize, for example, ideals of competitive excellence on the grounds that they are elitist or in various ways inhumane, or we may challenge obsessive venality as crudely selfish. Such moral arguments are a central focus of civilized life, for they help us to cultivate our autonomy self-critically and to change our lives with reasonable integrity and sensitivity. However, while such arguments help us as individuals to decide how we should exercise our rights, they are often not relevant to discussions of whether we have these rights. We are frequently very clear that people unqualifiedly have rights that they should not exercise; when they do exercise these rights in ways we deem morally undesirable, we say or think they had the right to do the wrong thing. How are we to understand this important distinction, which we understand and apply throughout our everyday lives?

In order to explicate this distinction, we must note the fundamental difference between the kinds of questions addressed by questions of moral rights and issues of moral and human ideals. When we reflect on questions of human rights, we consider the general conditions that must be guaranteed to facilitate the exercise and development of human capacities for autonomy. Such rights define minimum boundary conditions, assuring people personal integrity and independence compatible with a like integrity and independence for all. Within the constraints established by these rights, broad latitude is given to persons to decide on their own how they will choose to exercise the independence that rights guarantee. When we consider how people should make these choices, we invoke consideration of various kinds, prudential and moral. One form of moral consideration is a moral ideal, which defines the particular form in which a person dedicates his or her self to lesser or greater service to others and on what terms. Such ideals often bear metaphorical analogies to the principles which define human rights, but they go well beyond them. Some of them are the supererogatory ideals of saints and heroes, which justify special praise when they are acted upon, but no blame when they are not. Others, not requiring excessive sacrifice of personal self-interest, define various ways in which one may render humane service beyond the rights owed others. Often we criticize and blame people for not including such moral ideals among their narrow and parochial ends and aspirations.

Criticism of the actions of others, based on such moral ideals, is importantly limited by two factors: first, mistakes are likely in the judgments of one person about the circumstances and ends of another; and second, the standards of value against which we judge issues of these kinds are vague and indeterminate. Issues of this kind are uniquely sensitive to personal idiosyncrasy and individual context. Often, one person's critical judgments of another in this area betray failures of imagination to understand the other's special relation to his or her own life, to appreciate the sacrifices a certain choice would require, or to assess with sensitivity the trade-offs among humane values. Such factors explain why moral arguments of these kinds are both so important to our lives and justify forms of critical blame, but, on the other hand, debar us from more extensive interference into the lives of others. Nothing can be more important than constantly cultivating and challenging our critical imaginations about whether we are living our lives as humanely as we can, but our respect for personal separateness and individuality restrains us from coercive interference.

To say, therefore, that people have a human right to engage in commercial sex is not to conclude the question whether everyone should exercise this right. For example, we have discussed certain ideals of romantic love that a person might justifiably invoke in refusing to engage in commercial sex. Certainly such ideals cannot justifiably be invoked to qualify our general rights of sexual autonomy, for sexual self-respect and fulfillment do not require conformity to this idea. Even in the purely personal sphere, as a personal moral ideal, romantic love may be criticized as sentimental, unrealistic, and lacking reciprocity. Nonetheless, a person, after careful purification of the ideal by criticism, may justifiably espouse a form of it as a moral ideal, regulate his or her life accordingly, and criticize others for not observing it and thus not being as humane in their sexual lives as they could be. Certainly, moral ideals like romantic love are of incalculable cultural and human importance. Indeed, in some views, the ideal of romantic love has humanely and pervasively tempered personal relationships not only of sexual partners but also more widely. On the other hand, legal enforcement of such an ideal imposes a personal ideal upon persons who may find it unfulfilling or even oppressive and exploitative.

D. A COMPARATIVE ANALYSIS

JOHN QUIGLEY—THE DILEMMA OF PROSTITUTION LAW REFORM: LESSONS FROM THE SOVIET RUSSIAN EXPERIMENT (EXCERPT)

American Criminal Law Review 29:1197–1234 (1992).

By the 1980s, many in the United States were calling for an end to the criminalization of prostitution. American writers criticized all three systems currently used in the world: criminalization, regulation, and decriminalization. These existing methods did nothing to address the causes of prostitution.

Many of the critics were drawn to the Marxist critique that women are forced into prostitution by economic circumstance. They shared the view of the French social theorist Simone de Beauvoir that a woman's decision to engage in prostitution "condemns a society in which this occupation is still one of those which seem the least repellent to many women." A body of feminist-oriented literature appeared and portrayed the prostitute as victim. This view gained increasing adherence as prostitution globalized and third world countries became the prostitution venue for a clientele from the developed world. The image of Japanese tour groups traveling to Bangkok, where poor young Thai women were their prostitutes, dramatically reinforced this position.

Notwithstanding other factors involved, the lack of economic alternatives for women would seem to be a significant factor in the decision of many women to engage in prostitution. In contemporary society, prostitution sets a woman apart and subjects her to the negative opinions of others. Most governments have not addressed these problems and have not made a serious effort to remedy the social ills that facilitate prostitution.

One approach that has been suggested, but not explored fully, is the provision of services for women in prostitution to help them establish themselves through education, health services, drug counseling, job placement, job training, or child care for their children. Proposals have been made for the United States, along lines that parallel the Soviet Russian approach of the 1920s. One writer calls for:

> a large-scale network of support and services, a network which recognizes the severity of the situation which women are leaving or escaping and brings together a range of support to respond to the needs of the whole person. Those needs will range from practical considerations like a meal and a place to sleep, to emotional support and caring, to realistic analysis of economic alternatives such as a job or educational program, to medical care, to intensive personal counseling. A network providing these and many other services would extend to many levels of operation, including outreach teams

or street workers, crisis hot lines and emergency store-front shelters, and long-term live-in centers.

Few countries have moved in this direction. Sweden set up a program in the 1970s to offer housing, jobs, and emotional counseling to prostitutes.

One factor that may make it difficult for a woman to leave prostitution is a history of abuse in her upbringing. If she has been abused physically or psychologically, or if she has been raised to think that she lacks self-worth, she may not possess the self-confidence to take the risk of change. Counseling coupled with other services may be needed.

Beyond factors specific to a particular woman, a societal attitude that denigrates the value of women's labor and of women's worth in general may contribute to a woman's willingness to engage in prostitution. This attitude may also foster society's willingness to allow prostitution and forego reforms that would free women from prostitution.

Soviet Russia introduced a new analysis of prostitution, arguing that the prostitute was a victim of economic circumstance and that prostitution could be eradicated by socio-economic reform. It put that theory into practice by eliminating the tsarist system of government-regulated brothels, establishing institutions to help prostitutes into a new life, and ensuring full employment for women.

Soviet Russia certainly did not eradicate prostitution, a fact cited to dispute the Marxist analysis of the causes of prostitution. Yet the lack of success in eradicating prostitution in Soviet Russia does not necessarily disprove the Marxist thesis. There was, as indicated, some success in Soviet Russia, but the country did not achieve the economic progress it sought.

Although the Soviet Russian approach of eradicating prostitution by attacking its causes has exercised considerable influence abroad, to date, most governments typically view prostitution as inevitable, and decide what penal or administrative policy to adopt to limit it.

The Soviet Russian approach still has much to recommend it. Governments that do nothing about the many women with no alternative to prostitution fail in their duty, as defined by contemporary human rights standards. While the enormity of the task may deter many governments, in a society that values human rights, it is not an unrealistic expectation for the government for the government to ensure that no woman need engage in prostitution to provide a living for herself or her dependents.

The Soviet Russian approach may be as important for showing the enormity of the task as it is for specific solutions. Perhaps the most important lesson is that the various legislative techniques used to regulate prostitution are not likely to eliminate it or even reduce its occurrence.

The overall solution that would seem most acceptable for the phenomenon of prostitution would run as follows. First, a society provides full employment, thereby ensuring that a woman has a choice of professions. Second, it eliminates the social attitude that stigmatizes women who engage in prostitution, even if they later enter other work. Third, society changes the commonly held negative attitude about prostitutes so that they are not seen as easy targets for violence and so that police deal more seriously with crimes of violence against them. Finally, in order to help women who want to leave prostitution, social services are made available.

If all of this were done, women would not be forced into prostitution. In this construct, there would be no need for criminal laws against the acts of the prostitute, the client, the procurer, or the brothel keeper, because their conduct would produce no significant social harm.

These goals may appear utopian. However, the difficulty of achieving perfection in social policy is no reason to forego the attempt. If the suggested ideal future situation is not achieved, perhaps something approximating it can be reached. Unless far-sighted goals are kept in view, public policy on prostitution will only produce results that will continue to draw justified criticism. The Soviet Russian government may not have found a solution, but it did identify the issues.

Notes and Comments

1. Professor Quigley places great stock in a system that provides social services and support to prostitutes who wish to quit. He also argues that making those services available should obviate the necessity for the criminal prohibition of prostitution. Do you agree? What about fifteen-year-old prostitutes?

2. Would H.L.A. Hart regard prostitution as more like drugs (subject to state prohibition on paternalistic grounds) or like non-commercial homosexual conduct (not the proper business of the criminal law)?

E. CURRENT DISCOURSE

1. THE SCALE OF PROSTITUTION

The precise scope of the prostitution industry, both within the United States and internationally, is the subject of much debate and even more uncertainty. As with any black market activity, researchers have found it difficult to make dependable numerical estimates. The number of minors engaged in prostitution has, however, been more actively studied. If the scope of this portion of the sex trade is any indication, the overall size is nothing short of staggering.

MICHAEL CONANT—FEDERALISM, THE MANN ACT, AND THE IMPERATIVE TO DECRIMINALIZE PROSTITUTION

5 Cornell J. L. & Pub. Pol'y 99 (Winter 1996).

The widespread existence of prostitution in industrial societies indicates that the demand for sexual services is very great. The earliest survey evidence was in the 1948 Kinsey Report. The survey estimated that three and a half to four per cent of total U.S. male sexual activity involved prostitutes. For unmarried males, three point seven per cent of total sexual activity for those in their late teens, over nine and a half percent for those between thirty and forty and over fifteen percent for those over forty involved prostitutes. The estimate for married males was that about one percent of sexual activity involved prostitutes. In the more recent period of sexual liberalism, demand for prostitutes seems to have declined. A 1991 survey of males aged twenty to thirty-nine reported that 6.7 per cent had at some time paid for sex. A recent major study of sexuality reported that 8.6 per cent of persons aged eighteen to fifty-nine had ever paid for sex, but in the twelve months of the study only 0.4 per cent responded that they had paid for sex.

As for the supply of female prostitutes, the key inducement to enter the industry is the perception that a prostitute can earn much more in this line of work than in alternate employment. Many commentators have suggested that the great majority of prostitutes are willing members of the profession and that only a small percentage are unwilling workers under the total control of pimps. Also, many drug addicts become prostitutes to finance their addiction.

In 1968, one survey estimated that there were 300,000 to 500,000 women and girls in the United States selling sexual services, full-time or part-time. This would be approximately 0.3 to 0.6 per cent of the female population ages fifteen to thirty-five. The gross revenues of these persons is estimated at approximately $20 billion. One commentator, Helen Reynolds, has explained the differences between different types of prostitutes and the estimated fees for each type. These types include streetwalkers, masseuses, escorts, bar prostitutes, call girls, and brothel inmates. The prices in the 1968 study ranged from as low as $10 for some streetwalkers to over $100 for some call girls. The possibility of moving up the hierarchy from streetwalker to call girl was slim. At the higher income levels, pimp involvement decreased and the danger of arrest declined. It was much more likely, in fact, that over time a prostitute would move down the income hierarchy. If drug problems increased, she might be less able to handle her affairs, fall under the control of a pimp, and find it necessary to move into a brothel.

It is impossible to estimate the extent to which illegality limits the supply of prostitutes. The general view is that prostitution is immoral because, contrary to marriage and similar emotional alliances, prostitution is the alienation of the body to the will of another and thus undermines the ultimate roots of the moral personality. It is thus reasonable to hypothesize that even if prostitution were legal, the number of prostitutes would not increase substantially. Even presuming that legalization would raise prostitutes' income because they would no longer need to share fees with madams, pimps, lawyers or corrupt police, this advantage would be offset in part by income taxes previously evaded and higher medical expenses under state health regulations. Hence there is no reason to infer that incomes would rise enough to encourage significant increase in entry into the profession.

R. BARRI FLOWERS—THE SEX TRADE INDUSTRY'S WORLDWIDE EXPLOITATION OF CHILDREN

575 Annals of the American Academy of Political
and Social Science 147 (May 2001).

In the early part of the twenty-first century, the ongoing issue of worldwide commercial child sex-ploitation through child prostitution, child pornography, and a flourishing sex trade industry shows little sign of abating. The literature is replete with research addressing various aspects of this tragedy (Bracey 1979; ECPAT 1996; Ennew et al. 1996; Flowers forthcoming; Truong 1982; Weisberg 1985). Much of the focus has been on child sexual exploitation in Southeast Asia, especially Thailand and the Philippines (Ennew 1986; Leuchtag 1995), South Asia, and countries such as India, Nepal, and Sri Lanka (Barry 1995; Flowers 1998; Hodgson 1994), and in the West, including Australia, Canada, the United States, and Western Europe (Densen–Gerber and Hutchinson 1978; Flowers 1994; James 1980; Johnson 1992). Less attention has been paid to the significant sex trade industry and exploited children in other parts of the world, such as Latin America, Africa, and Eastern Europe (Ennew et al. 1996; Horn-blower 1993; U.S. Department of Justice 1999). For example, recent years have seen an explosion in the child sex-for-sale market in Russia and other countries of the former Soviet bloc with the fall of Communism and rise of organized crime and poverty (Flowers 1998; Hornblower 1993; Leuchtag 1995).

In reality, there is still much that we do not know about the dimensions and dynamics of the world marketplace for child prostitution and child pornography. The very nature of the child sex trade, with its flesh peddling of minors by adults—sometimes in cooperation with the government or powerful organizations—makes it one that in many respects remains secretive, seedy, and hard to get accurate, conclusive information on. Yet there has been enough research and documentation to know that the proliferation of the sex trade industry globally has resulted in an increase in the prostitution and sexual exploitation of children. Millions of children ... are being targeted by flesh traders, pimps, gangs, organized crime syndicates, and promoters of tourism worldwide for a lucrative sex tourism business.... The growth of international prostitution is not only robbing its victims of innocence and any semblance of a normal life during or after prostitution but is also putting them at greater risk for exposure to crime, criminals, unfamiliar foreign countries and languages, and health problems, including the AIDS virus. (Flowers 1998, 176)

The gross violation of children's fundamental rights through commercial international sexual exploitation can be seen in every aspect of a sex industry that insists on profiting and benefiting through sexual gratification against those most vulnerable and least able to protect themselves (Melton 1991; Seng 1989; World Health Organization 1996). Only in continuing to address the crisis of prostituted children and other forms of child sexploitation and its impact on victims and society at large can we hope to avert an even greater tragedy.

INTERNATIONAL SCOPE OF CHILD SEXUAL EXPLOITATION

How big is the problem of child sexploitation globally? Many sources—including government and nongovernment organizations, researchers, and experts in the commercial sexual exploitation of children—have produced figures estimating its incidence and prevalence from country to country and internationally (Campagna and Poffenberger 1988; ECPAT 1996; Ennew et al. 1996; Flowers 1998; Smolenski 1995; U.S. Department of Justice 1999).

The clear indications are that the worldwide exploitation of children by the sex trade industry has reached numbers that merit serious attention and action, if not epidemic proportions. According to UNICEF, there are over 1 million child prostitutes in Asia alone (Flowers 1998). End Child Prostitution, Child Pornography and Trafficking of Children for Sexual Purposes (ECPAT) estimated that there are 800,000 child prostitutes in Thailand, 400,000 in India, and 60,000 in the Philippines (ECPAT 1996; Smolenski 1995). A 1991 conference of Southeast Asia women's groups reported that 30 million women and girls had been forced into prostitution since the mid–1970s (Leuchtag 1995).

Other figures on child prostitution are just as notable. Up to 500,000 children are being exploited in the sex trade industry in Brazil, while as many as 200,000 teenage prostitutes are plying their trade in Canada (Flowers 1998; Kotash 1994). In the United States, estimates of juvenile prostitutes range from the hundreds of thousands to 2 million selling their bodies on the streets (Flowers 1986, forthcoming; Smolenski 1995). Child sexual exploitation is also believed to be flourishing in Western Europe, Eastern Europe, and Africa (Flowers 1998; U.S. Department of Justice 1999).

Further examples of the global sexual exploitation of children were described in the ECPAT *Country Reports* (1996) and in the U.S. Department of Justice's *Prostitution of Children and Child Sex Tourism* (1999):

- In Cambodia, the Human Rights Vigilance reported that more than 3 in 10 sex workers in the country were between 13 and 17 years of age.

- In China, the *Peking People's Daily* reported that in Sichuan alone over 10,000 children and women are sold into sexual slavery annually.

- In Columbia, the Bogota Chamber of Commerce recently reported that child prostitution had increased five times in the preceding seven years.

- In Sri Lanka, an estimated 100,000 minors age 6 to 14 are being prostituted in child brothels, with 5,000 other children selling sexual favors in child sex tourism areas of the country.

- In Johannesburg, South Africa, black and white juveniles are reported to be prostitution-involved, while brothel prostitutes are often young females from Russia, Thailand, and Taiwan.

- In a 1995 *Asia Watch Report*, it was reported that around half of the 100,000 girl prostitutes working in Bombay came from Nepal. In Nepal, the number of girls under the age of 15 working for pimps or as brothel prostitutes was on the increase.

- In the 1995 *Human Rights Watch Report*, one in five brothel prostitutes in Bombay was reported to be a female under the age of 18.

- In Vietnam, as many as one in five prostitutes are under the age of 18. The rise in juvenile prostitution is attributed to a growing sex tourism industry in the country.

Given the wildly varying estimates, serious definitional and methodological differences, and a lack of worldwide studies, it is virtually impossible to measure the true global extent of the sexual exploitation of children (Ennew 1986; Flowers 1998; U.S. Department of Justice 1999). Many studies, for example, focus only on sexually exploited girls (James 1972; Newman and Caplan 1981); others focus on boy prostitutes (Cates 1989; Lloyd 1976; Snell 1995). There are other studies that do not sufficiently explain the differences between child prostitution and child sexual abuse (Joseph 1995). There are also differences in defining what constitutes a child or minor by age and in separating figures on children from figures on adults in the sex trade industry (Ennew et al. 1996).

Most studies of child sexploitation focus mainly on child prostitution without adequately accounting for the global danger of child pornography and the correlation between the two through child sex rings and the trafficking of children (Flowers 1994; Smolenski 1995; U. S. Department of Justice 1999). There is also the issue of illegal versus legal use of children for purposes of sexual exploitation. For example, in some countries, child prostitution is technically legal, making it difficult to separate what is outlawed from what is tolerated (Flowers 1998; Goodall 1995; Leuchtag 1995; Miller 1995). Perhaps the greatest limitation in assessing the true measure of international child sexual exploitation is the lack of cooperation between countries and researchers in gathering and quantifying data.

2. FEMINIST PERSPECTIVES

ALEXANDRA BONGARD STREMLER—SEX FOR MONEY AND THE MORNING AFTER: LISTENING TO WOMEN AND THE FEMINIST VOICE IN PROSTITUTION DISCOURSE

7 J. Law. & Pub. Pol'y 189.

II. TRADITIONAL LEGAL THOUGHT AND PROSTITUTION

The nature and legal status of prostitution creates unique problems for lawmakers and policy makers. United States' law generally criminalizes the solicitation of sexual services. Courts apply traditional constitutional and criminal analysis to prostitution case law. States regulate and prohibit prostitution through legislation based on health, safety, economics, ancillary crime prevention and community morality. Traditional legal arguments on the legal status of prostitution can be used both to refute and defend statutes based on these criteria.

Social morality, rather than concern for women's safety, has deemed prostitution illegal. Commentator Belinda Cooper calls this position the "conservative moral approach." Conservative moralists argue that virtuous women need protection from the innate sexual urges of men, and that society needs protection from the whores who engage in commercial sex. They blame the spread of sexually transmitted disease, drug use, crime and child pornography on the existence of prostitution. By eradicating prostitution, conservative moralists attempt to rid society of ancillary crime and other problems. Ingrained cultural beliefs about sexuality and the role of women justify convictions of prostitutes under the conservative moral analysis. Conservative moralists classify all women as either loving mothers or deviant whores; within this context, they define all women.

While case law often reflects the conservative moral approach, decisions and commentary contain traditional arguments favoring the decriminalization of prostitution. This school of thought favors legalization based on rights of self-determination. Shuster, for example, recommends a model statute for legal but regulated prostitution. Because liberal jurists rely on the individual's freedom of choice, Belinda Cooper refers to this school as the "liberal individual approach." Arguments from liberal individualists also include: freedom of contract, equal protection and the right to privacy and autonomy.

Traditional liberal arguments for legalization of prostitution compare prostitutes to wage laborers. Using a contractual analysis, prostitutes merely perform a service for payment. Some liberal individualists argue that there is an inherent male need for sex which creates a demand that women engaged in prostitution could, and should, be entitled to fulfill. They explain that legalizing and regulating this trade would not only protect prostitutes from exploitation but also provide legal economic opportunities.

In their arguments for individual rights, Shuster and the liberal individualists ignore the economic and social pressures which lead women into prostitution. Liberal individualists assume that prostitutes choose their vocation unconstrained by circumstance. They fail to acknowledge the absence of real equality between women and men before the law. While their arguments seem egalitarian, the liberal individualist response fails to protect women from the underlying inequities perpetuated by prostitution. Shuster contends that although women may initially be pressured into prostitution, they remain in it by choice.

Another liberal individualist argument involves equal protection violations against women prosecuted for solicitation. Those citing equal protection address discrimination in statutes both facially and as applied to individual women. Although many states have altered their prostitution statutes to criminalize both the solicitation and procurement of commercial sex, women continue to bear the burden of enforcement, prosecution and sentencing. In the publicized "Mayflower Madam" case, a New York attorney chose to defend a prostitution operation on the basis that women are disparately treated within the legal system. Criminal defense attorney Mark Denbeaux defended the Madam, Sidney Biddle Barrows, because of the systematic harassment by the state directed solely at the women defendants as opposed to their male clients. On the eve of the trial, Denbeaux said he would read aloud names from a client book at jury selection, which included many prominent members of the New York legal community. After this unconventional legal tactic, the attorney for the state agreed to fines and conditional discharge for Barrows. In this case, traditional legal alternatives failed women involved in prostitution. The case illustrates the inequity of the judicial system, and the extreme steps required for women in order to obtain justice. Since the case never reached trial, it has no precedential value. Nevertheless, it does demonstrate a small step toward equal justice for women involved in prostitution prosecution.

The Barrows case exemplifies why prostitution statutes need to be reconsidered and redirected. Selective enforcement places disproportionate blame on women. Equal protection arguments for decriminalization of prostitution focus on privacy and civil rights for all of those engaged in the practice. The means to a solution remain controversial. Some favor stricter enforcement against procurers of commercial sex, that is, equalizing the application of existing law. Others question whether evenhanded enforcement could realistically be expected given present entrenched stereotypes. Shuster's explains this inequality of enforcement:

> One reason for discriminatory law enforcement against female prostitutes is that they are considered expendable; few persons, other than perhaps their pimps, will miss them if they are incarcerated. To imprison, or otherwise stigmatize, the average male patron, on the other hand, usually involves disrupting a man's "respectable" employment, standing in the community, and even his marriage.

In his statement, Shuster clearly articulates an underlying premise of many legal concerns.

Publicity frequently accompanies the prosecution of prostitutes with high-profile clients. Although the male client's status fuels press coverage, my observation is that the media usually protects the identities of the men involved in the latest sex scandal. For example, in the summer of 1993, prosecutors hounded Heidi Fleiss, alleged Madam to the stars, yet the identities of her clients remained anonymous. While Heidi Fleiss and Sidney Biddle Barrows have become household names, it remains unlikely that the public will ever know the names of the men in their records.

Although high-profile prostitution cases bring the discussion into mainstream America, public concern rarely extends to prostitutes and their struggle to survive while living in poverty. Sex, glamour and fame generate material for tabloid news, not questions of legal justice and reform for women in prostitution. Reality for most prostitutes is not the glitz of the high-class hooker. Their reality is danger, crime and despair. "In these recesses you'll find no sequins, no lipstick, few small-town girls duped by pimps in Caddies. Just home-grown women like Starla with their tennis shoes, their unexceptional histories and an unshakable urge to be high." These women, trapped by poverty and prostitution, find virtually no support from the system, and many consider themselves to be the throwaways of our society. For some feminists opposed to prostitution, these women epitomize the victims of prostitution.

III. FEMINIST JURISPRUDENCE AND PROSTITUTION

Prostitution presents a complex problem for feminists. Feminist legal scholars who discuss prostitution account for the perspectives of women and prostitutes. They represent a broad spectrum of opinion, both favoring and opposing prostitution. While feminist scholars welcome this diversity, prostitution divides them along several lines.

In the view of feminists favoring the legalization of prostitution, women are empowered by prostitution. They argue that prostitution can provide women with economic freedom and control in the power struggle between women and men. Whereas, feminists opposed to legalization believe that women are victimized by prostitution. They argue that since prostitutes generally play the role of the dominated sexual partner, the expression of male power through paid subservience creates the ultimate form of subordination and danger.

Feminists who would permit prostitution with regulation or protection have been accused of perpetuating the patriarchal devaluation of women. They often side with traditional liberals. Feminists who oppose prostitution often find themselves aligned with political and religious conservatives. These groups rarely align on other issues affecting women. In fact, this alignment of liberal feminists with individualists, and radical feminists with conservative moralists, threatens feminist solidarity on other issues affecting women, such as sexual discrimination, domestic violence and abortion.

While liberal-individualist and conservative-moral responses lack adequate remedies for the harm created by prostitution, feminist thought has fared no better. Feminists also argue a range of alternatives from prohibition to legalization, but their concerns are different from those of liberal individualists or conservative moralists. For example, feminists favoring decriminalization of prostitution stress women's self-employment, rather than freedom of contract or individual rights to privacy. Feminists opposing decriminalization stress prostitution's objectification of women's bodies and sexuality, instead of the need to regulate community moral standards. Whether for or against legalization of prostitution, feminist analysis considers both its harm and benefit to women.

Few feminists favor complete legalization of prostitution, as they believe government approval would further entrench society's stereotypes of women. Even liberal individualists, who do support decriminalization, often advocate government regulation of prostitution. For example, Shuster advocates the regulation of prostitution for the protection of children and others traditionally deemed worthy. The liberal individualist view assumes that women choose prostitution from among a range of available career options, and therefore, such women are not in need of protection. The underlying assumption is that women should be available to men for their sexual gratification.

Feminists favoring decriminalization and regulation of prostitution do so on the grounds that it would protect the women involved from coercion and violence. They view decriminalization in the broader context of necessary social changes. They argue that the social stigma associated with prostitution might be reduced with recognition in society of the realities which force some women into prostitution. Also, they propose pay equity for work traditionally done by women and meaningful job training to ensure that women who choose to become prostitutes do so freely not because they have been forced to by economic necessity.

Some feminist writers find transitional answers for women's safety and self-determination in the decriminalization of prostitution. Prostitution is one of only a few unskilled jobs where women on average earn more than men. The opportunity for economic independence attracts women to prostitution. Shuster reports that between twelve to twenty percent of all women engage in prostitution at some point in their lives. Feminist commentators suggest that the figure is closer to twelve percent. Divorce and child-support delinquency contribute to the economic burdens suffered by many women. Whatever the causes that force women into prostitution, feminists explain that most women *remain* because of job flexibility and high pay.

Unlike the feminist view discussed above, Shuster fails to take into account the importance of the economic realities of women in any analysis of prostitution. In an effort to discount this importance, Shuster describes the societal devaluation of work done by women as complaints by prostitutes that their clients make more money than they do. This male-centered view trivializes the real problem of pay inequity between men and women to a squabble between disgruntled whores and their patrons. It analyzes prostitution in a vacuum rather than in society.

Shuster also addresses the relationship between prostitution and violence against women from the same simplistic perspective, acknowledging that violence against women exists, but contending that "since in American culture, women as a class are frequently mistreated, even if prostitution remains illegal, women will continue to be victimized in their other relationships." He adopts the traditional attitude of what has been will be and uses circular reasoning to reach his position. His analysis does not explore the possibility of safer and more reasonable choices for women. Even though prostitution and violence against women center around women, Shuster focuses his attention on the needs of the male clients. He states that "[legalized prostitution might] promote marital harmony by providing an approved emotional and sexual outlet to the hostile spouse." His position is carried to its most *illogical* conclusion in the following:

> The argument that prostitution should remain illegal because it promotes abuse carried to its logical extreme requires that because there are rapists, love should be illegal; because child abuse exists, people should not rear children; and because husbands beat wives, marriage should be disallowed.

In the United States, perceptions of women are often defined by pornography and prostitution. While many find prostitution merely offensive, others attribute the rise in acts of violence against women to it. Many crime reports link these activities to the increasing violence against women in our society.

> New York, 1993—Acting on information from Joel Rifkin, a confessed serial killer, police today dug up the badly decomposed body of a woman next to a highway in Southampton on eastern Long Island and found another in a shallow grave near John F. Kennedy International Airport. ... After the two arresting officers smelled and then found the decaying body of a woman in the back of the truck, Rifkin told police that he had slain 17 women—all prostitutes—over the last two years.

Safety for all women is a primary concern for feminists considering the prostitution dilemma. Those favoring legalization look to regulation as a means of protecting prostitutes from illness and physical violence. Currently, prostitutes do not receive legal protection for many reasons. Discrimination, fear of prosecution, and physical coercion limit access to justice. Prostitution activist and law professor, Margaret Baldwin, discusses the distinction between prostitutes and "other women." Especially in cases of domestic violence, rape and sexual harassment, other women separate themselves from prostitutes. According to Baldwin, other women may be victims of these crimes, but prostitutes may not.

Yet, women from all walks of life suffer from the same types of violence and abuse.

Addressing the connection between prostitution and abuse, feminist scholar, Catharine MacKinnon, places prostitution on a continuum with pornography, sexual abuse and rape. Citing frequent patterns of violence, MacKinnon explains that both sex and violence define power relationships between men and women. Her feminist analysis addresses the economic reality of pimping, and the devastating exploitation of prostitutes by men. Both economic and physical coercion lead women into prostitution and keep them there.

STEPHANIE FARRIOR—THE INTERNATIONAL LAW ON TRAFFICKING IN WOMEN AND CHILDREN FOR PROSTITUTION: MAKING IT LIVE UP TO ITS POTENTIAL
10 Harv. Hum. Rts. J. 213 (Spring 1997).

I. TREATY LAW MECHANISMS

A. Background

The International Agreement for the Suppression of the White Slave Traffic, adopted in 1904, was the first international treaty on trafficking in women. The title of the instrument shows that only the exploitation of white women was of enough concern to prompt treaty protection. The goal of the Agreement was to halt the sale of women into prostitution in Europe at a time when economic conditions were so dire that women were increasingly vulnerable to being forced into prostitution. The provisions of the Agreement were aimed at protecting the victims, not at punishing procurers. This approach proved ineffective, thereby prompting the adoption in 1910 of the International Convention for the Suppression of White Slave Traffic under which its thirteen signatories agreed to punish procurers.

After World War I, the League of Nations considered the worldwide problem of trafficking in women and children to be of such concern that the text of the Covenant of the League of Nations itself entrusted the League "with the general supervision over the execution of agreements with regard to the traffic in women and children and the traffic in opium and other dangerous drugs."

Under the League of Nations' auspices, two treaties were concluded that addressed trafficking. The first, adopted in 1921, sought to suppress such traffic using three approaches: prosecuting persons who trafficked in children, licensing and supervising employment agencies, and protecting immigrating and emigrating women and children. The second, adopted in 1933, required punishment of persons who trafficked in women of full age and declared that consent was not a defense to the crime of trafficking.

In 1949, the United Nations consolidated the four prior treaties, as well as a 1937 League of Nations draft, to produce the Convention for the Suppression of the Traffic in Persons and of the Exploitation of the Prostitution of Others.

B. The 1949 Convention for the Suppression of the Traffic in Persons and of the Exploitation of the Prostitution of Others

The 1949 Convention for the Suppression of the Traffic in Persons and of the Exploitation of the Prostitution of Others (1949 Convention) has done little to suppress trafficking. Although the Convention focuses on punishing procurers, persons exploiting prostitution, and brothel owners, its enforcement clauses are weak. It affords little protection of the rights of women who are trafficked and ignores the socio-economic causes of trafficking for prostitution. The 1949 Convention therefore takes a limited approach in its measures to stop trafficking.

1. States Parties' Obligations

States that have ratified the Convention "agree to punish any person who, to gratify the passions of another ... procures, entices or leads away, for purposes of prostitution, another person, even with the consent of that person; exploits the prostitution of another person, even with the consent of that person." Moreover, the 1949 Convention aims for the total abolition of brothels, and for the punishment of any person who keeps, manages, or knowingly finances a brothel. It does not require that the trafficking be conducted across international borders.

It is significant that the 1949 Convention does not condone the existence of brothels, even those regulated by the state. This total abolition approach resulted from U.N. studies showing that state regulation of brothels and prostitution sends a message that the state tolerates forced prostitution. The U.N. studies concluded that because brothels exist in part because of the supply of women provided through international trafficking, trafficking will not cease unless brothels are abolished.

Although the 1949 Convention takes an abolitionist approach with respect to brothels, it does not prohibit prostitution per se. The failure to prohibit prostitution has led the Coalition Against Trafficking in Women to describe the Convention as being of "limited value" because of the role prostitution plays in the subordination of women. Even if one does not oppose prostitution per se, one could find the 1949 Convention to be of limited value because it fails to take a rights-based approach to protecting trafficked women. The 1949 Convention does provide one limited procedural right that enables trafficked women to participate in proceedings against offenders; however, that right is available only if allowed by national law of the state party (Article 5).

According to the 1949 Convention, victims of trafficking are to be repatriated if they wish or if their "expulsion is ordered in conformity with law." Women without legal resident status in a country are likely to be expelled under the latter clause. Therefore, although repatriation is to take place "without prejudice to prosecution or other actions for violations" of the law, states are even less likely to pursue criminal prosecution against the pimps or brothel owner without the presence of the victims.

In a measure designed to address a conduit, but not a cause of prostitution, states parties agree to supervise "employment agencies in order to prevent" those seeking employment, especially women and children, "from being exposed to the danger of prostitution." States are to publicize warnings about the dangers of trafficking and to ensure supervision of airports, train stations, and other ports of entry and departure in order to prevent trafficking. They also agree to provide for the "rehabilitation and social adjustment" of the victims of prostitution, through "public and private educational, health, social, economic and other related services."

One weakness of the 1949 Convention lies in the potential conflict between two of its provisions. Article 12 declares that the Convention "does not affect the principle that the offences to which it refers shall in each State be defined, prosecuted and punished in conformity with its domestic law." This provision could create potential conflict with the removal of the defense of consent in Article 1. This deference to national law could be explained by the fact that in 1949, the notion of human rights as a matter of international concern was still relatively new in international law. Unease still existed within the U.N. about perceptions of undue interference in the domestic affairs of a state by intergovernmental organizations. The fact remains that the 1949 Convention's deference to national law undermines potential advances in human rights law, such as the advance of abolishing the defense of consent to being trafficked.

These weaknesses in the substantive provisions of the 1949 Convention are one reason that relatively few countries have ratified it. Sweden, for example, has stated that the 1949 Convention's "obsolescence" is the "main reason ... for Swedish uneasiness." Referring to the 1949 Convention's "old-fashioned spirit," the Swedish government stated that it "doubts that the Convention is an effective means of suppressing traffic in persons and of combating the problems arising from prostitution in today's society." Sweden has also raised concerns about a possible conflict between the right to privacy and certain obligations under the Convention, such as the Article 17 provision on informing authorities of the arrival of *prima facie* victims" of international traffic in persons.

2. Implementation and Enforcement Mechanisms

The 1949 Convention's enforcement mechanisms are weak. The Convention does require states parties to report annually to the U.N. Secretary–General those laws, regulations, and other measures which they have adopted to give effect to the Convention's provisions. In addition, the Secretary–General is directed to publish and send these communications to all U.N. members and non-member states that have been invited to ratify the Convention. That, however, is the extent of the Convention's implementation and enforcement mechanisms. No independent supervisory body exists with authority to question the reports of states parties, issue recommendations to the states based on those reports, or receive and act on petitions brought by victims of trafficking who allege that a state party has failed to try to eliminate trafficking. In 1974, however, the Economic and Social Council of the United Nations (ECOSOC) decided that states parties to the 1949 Convention should submit regular reports on the situation in their countries regarding slavery and trafficking to the U.N. Sub–Commission on Prevention of Discrimination and Protection of Minorities. The Sub–Commission's Working Group on Contemporary Forms of Slavery reviews these reports, but it is not empowered to take action on them.

C. The Slavery Convention of 1926

In addition to the trafficking treaties discussed above, anti-slavery treaties also cover trafficking for prostitution. The Slavery Convention of 1926 (1926 Convention) defines slavery as "the status or condition of a person over whom any or all of the powers attaching to the right of ownership are exercised." Victims of trafficking for prostitution would fit this definition. Under the 1926 Convention, states parties commit to "prevent and suppress the slave trade" and to bring about "the complete abolition of slavery in all its forms." They undertake to adopt the necessary measures in order that severe penalties may be imposed in respect of infractions of laws and regulations that give effect to the 1926 Convention's purposes.

The 1926 Convention's enforcement mechanisms suffer from many of the same weaknesses as those in the 1949 Convention discussed above. There is a very general reporting requirement, and no supervisory body is established by the treaty to monitor implementation and enforcement of its provisions. These weaknesses are only partially remedied by the 1974 ECOSOC resolution referred to above. Like the parties to the 1949 Convention, parties to the 1926 Slavery Convention are to submit regular reports on the measures they have taken to implement the treaty to the U.N. Sub–Commission on Prevention of Discrimination and Protection of Minorities.

D. The 1956 Supplementary Convention on the Abolition of Slavery, the Slave Trade, and Institutions and Practices Similar to Slavery

In 1956, the U.N. adopted a convention to supplement the 1926 Convention by including slavery-like practices and by bringing the 1926 Convention into the U.N. system. The 1956 Supplementary Convention on the Abolition of Slavery, the Slave Trade, and Institutions and Practices Similar to Slavery (1956 Convention) requires states parties to impose domestic criminal sanctions on individuals who engage in, among other things, selling women, turning children over for exploitation, and debt bondage schemes.

Unfortunately, the enforcement provisions of the 1956 Convention are as weak as those of the 1949 Trafficking Convention. States are to "co-operate with each other and with the United Nations to give effect to" the treaty provisions. The 1956 Convention contains a mild reporting mechanism similar to that of the 1926 Convention. States simply undertake to send the U.N. Secretary–General "copies of any laws, regulations and administrative measures enacted or put into effect to implement the provision of this Convention." The Secretary–General must then communicate the information received through this process to the states parties, as well as to ECOSOC for consideration regarding further recommendations that ECOSOC might make on abolishing slavery.

As with the treaties discussed above, the 1956 Convention contains no provisions for monitoring implementation, reviewing the information submitted by states and making recommendations, or receiving petitions alleging violations of the treaty. Beginning in 1974, however, states parties to the 1956 Convention were to submit regular reports regarding slavery and trafficking to the Sub–Commission on Prevention of Discrimination and Protection of Minorities. The Sub–Commission's Working Group reviews these reports along with those submitted by parties to the 1926 Convention and the 1949 Convention.

E. International Labor Organization Conventions

1. Obligations and Enforcement

Two International Labor Organization (ILO) conventions are applicable to trafficking for prostitution: the Forced Labor Convention (No. 29), adopted in 1930, and the 1957 Abolition of Forced Labor Convention (No. 105). Under both conventions, states parties undertake to eliminate and to penalize the practice of forced labor. "Forced labor" is defined in both conventions as "all work or service which is exacted from any person under the menace of any penalty and for which the said person has not offered himself voluntarily." This definition may be construed as applicable to persons who are trafficked. The ILO's Committee of Experts on the Application of Conventions and Recommendations has identified the use of children for prostitution as "one of the worst forms of forced labor." Consequently, the focus of the ILO's efforts in this area has been on trafficking in children.

Supervision and enforcement mechanisms under the ILO system include a reporting requirement as well as the provision of advisory services. Under the Constitution of the ILO, states parties must submit reports to the International Labor Office regarding the measures they have taken to give effect to any ILO conventions they have ratified. States must also submit copies of their reports to the organizations that represent employers and workers at the ILO. These organizations may make their own observations on states parties' implementation of ILO conventions, and states are to inform the ILO of any observations received. A periodic reporting mechanism also exists for ILO member states that have not ratified a particular ILO convention. These members must report to the Director–General of the International Labor Office "the position of [their] law and practice in regard to the matters dealt with" in ILO Conventions they have not ratified. Each year the

Director–General presents a summary of the reports communicated by states to the International Labor Conference.

A key player in the ILO's enforcement mechanism is the ILO Committee of Experts on the Application of Conventions and Recommendations. This Committee reviews states' reports, relevant laws, publications, and information contained in comments made by employers' and workers' organizations. Significantly, the Committee may issue "observations" on government reports to the state concerned and to the ILO Conference; make recommendations to the government on how better to comply with the Convention's provision; and make "direct requests" to governments for reply. The Committee may also initiate direct contacts with governments. In addition, member states, as well as employers' and workers' organizations, may file complaints or representations that a state is not in compliance with a convention it has ratified.

Technical support and advisory services comprise an important part of the ILO's work to end trafficking and forced prostitution. These services are provided in part by the ILO's International Program on the Elimination of Child Labour (IPEC), which includes in its mandate efforts to end child prostitution. IPEC seeks to find solutions to the problem of child labor through a range of programs that include conducting analyses of trafficking in specific sectors, helping to prepare a national program of action, mobilizing wide participation in the program, developing demonstration projects, and consulting on policy-making.

2. Role for Nongovernmental Organizations

The ILO has a unique tripartite structure in which representatives of governments, as well as worker and employer organizations, have decision-making authority. However, because only representatives of designated worker and employer organizations may participate fully with governments in decision-making, the role NGOs may play is somewhat limited. The complaint procedures are not available to individuals or human rights organizations. Human rights NGOs may, however, work in cooperation with the designated worker organizations, and have some influence through such interaction.

Professor Virginia Leary, a noted international labor law expert, has recommended that the ILO open up its procedures to greater participation by NGOs, at least informally, and that human rights NGOs "apply to the ILO Director–General to be placed on a list of organizations whose objectives are in harmony with the ILO," thereby entitling them "to receive notice of meetings, documentation, and, with special permission, to distribute documents and make oral interventions in some meetings." Thus far, the ILO has not adopted these recommendations.

F. International Covenant on Civil and Political Rights

1. States Parties' Obligations

Under the International Covenant on Civil and Political Rights (ICCPR), states parties have an obligation to protect people against being trafficked for prostitution. The ICCPR provides in Article 8(1) that "no one shall be held in slavery; slavery and the slave-trade in all their forms shall be prohibited." Notably, the clause does not limit its coverage to active state participation. By virtue of Article 2 of the Covenant, states violate their obligations under the Covenant if they fail to exercise due diligence to end slavery and the slave trade by private actors within their jurisdiction. Under Article 2, states parties obligate themselves to "ensure to all individuals within [their] territory the rights recognized" in the Covenant, and to do so without discrimination. Furthermore, Article 2 requires states parties "to ensure" to victims an "effective remedy" for a violation of their rights.

2. *Enforcement—Review of States' Reports*

Unlike the trafficking and slavery conventions, the ICCPR establishes an oversight body, the Human Rights Committee, to monitor states parties' compliance with the treaty's provisions. This Committee reviews the periodic reports that states parties are required to submit under Article 40 of the ICCPR, and issues comments on them. A review of the Committee's Annual Reports from 1977 through 1995 unearthed almost no references to trafficking at all. None of these references arose under examination of Article 8; instead, they are mentioned under "Protection of the family and children," or under "Non-discrimination equality of the sexes before the law and protection of family and children." One of these references appears in the Human Rights Committee's review of Spain's report. Committee members asked "what the authorities had done to put an end to the practice of traffic in women along the border with Portugal." The Spanish government representative replied that "he had no knowledge of any traffic in women along the border with Portugal, but recently a crime network selling people into prostitution had been unmasked." The only other reference to trafficking was made with respect to Peru. In examining Peru's report in 1994, Committee members "requested information concerning child prostitution and trafficking in women and children." The Committee's report reflects no response from Peru to these questions. None of the reports included a recommendation to the government in question to take more serious measures to end trafficking for prostitution. Moreover, the report on Japan, where trafficking for prostitution is known to be a serious problem, only briefly mentions child prostitution and does not mention trafficking at all.

3. *Enforcement—Individual Complaint Procedure*

Individuals who believe their rights under the ICCPR have been violated may submit a complaint to the Human Rights Committee, but only if the state in question has agreed to submit to the procedure by ratifying the First Optional Protocol to the ICCPR. The individual complaint mechanism has not yet been utilized by those seeking to end trafficking in women and children. This is unfortunate, for such complaints have the potential for pressing a state to take action against trafficking. Once the Human Rights Committee reviews a communication, along with any government comments on the case, the Committee determines whether the government has violated the Covenant. The Committee asks governments found to be in violation to inform it of what measures have been taken to remedy the situation.

G. Convention on the Elimination of All Forms of Discrimination Against Women

1. States Parties' Obligations

The Convention on the Elimination of All Forms of Discrimination Against Women (Women's Convention) is another treaty that may be used by NGOs to press governments to end trafficking for prostitution. Article 6 of the Convention requires states parties "to take all appropriate measures, including legislation, to suppress all forms of traffic in women and exploitation of prostitution of women." As with the ICCPR, the Women's Convention reaches private conduct. If a state takes inadequate measures, or no measures at all, to eliminate trafficking by either state or private actors, it violates its treaty obligations.

The Committee on the Elimination of Discrimination Against Women (CEDAW), established by the Women's Convention to monitor its implementation, has issued an analysis of Article 2. Although the Women's Convention does not define what measures are "appropriate" in Article 6, Article 2 sets out a general framework of steps that states parties must undertake. The Committee's analysis elaborates what states must do under each of the given tasks.

As of this writing, no procedure exists that would allow individual complaints alleging violation of the Convention's provisions. Such a protocol, however, has been proposed. At its 1996 session, the U.N. Commission on the Status of Women recommended to ECOSOC that it renew the mandate of the Working Group on the Elaboration of a Draft Optional Protocol to the Convention.

2. Enforcement—Review of States' Reports

Under Article 18 of the Women's Convention, states parties undertake to report periodically on the legislative, judicial, administrative and other measures they have taken to give effect to the Convention's provisions, and on the progress they have made. The first report is due within a year of the treaty's entry into force for a given state, and every four years thereafter.

Of all the human rights treaty bodies with some competence to examine trafficking, CEDAW has given the most attention to the matter, primarily, but not exclusively, under the Article 6 provision on trafficking. A review CEDAW reports from 1987 through 1995 reveals that the Committee paid significant attention to trafficking as it examined the periodic reports submitted by states parties. For example, the 1988 report examines two important issues on the subject: sex tourism in Thailand and the trafficking of women from developing countries in the United Kingdom.

3. Challenging Social and Cultural Stereotypes

Trafficking will not end until states take steps to modify cultures that allow women and girls to be viewed as commodities to be trafficked. The "appropriate measures" to stop trafficking required of governments in Article 6 should be read in conjunction with the requirement in Article 5 that states parties undertake "to modify the social and cultural patterns of conduct of men and women" in order to eliminate stereotypes regarding inferiority or superiority with respect to men or women. It is apparent from their reports that CEDAW members see the connection between Articles 5 and 6 of the Convention. This link should be made more directly and more often. NGOs can assist in this process. When providing information on trafficking in a given state, and NGOs should consider illustrating the incidence of trafficking for prostitution as a manifestation of social and cultural patterns that are based on the idea of the inferiority of women and girls and on the stereotyped roles defined for them.

The following cases illustrate the need for such a conjunctive reading. In examining Tunisia's implementation of Article 5, Committee members first "praised efforts made to correct stereotypes through presenting a more positive image of women in school textbooks and through human rights education." CEDAW then used the opportunity to request more information "on violence against women of any kind, . . . in particular . . . violence against prostitutes and any other vulnerable groups." The government representative responded that because violence against women "had only recently become a subject of investigation, . . . it was difficult to obtain reliable statistical data because the victims only rarely reported such incidents to the competent authorities."

The link between violence against prostitute women and the need to challenge social and cultural patterns of prejudice was made in the CEDAW Committee's General Recommendation 19 on Violence Against Women, issued in 1993. That General Recommendation first states that "traditional attitudes . . . perpetuate widespread practices involving violence or coercion . . . These attitudes also contribute to the propagation of pornography and the depiction and other commercial exploitation of women as sexual objects, rather than as individuals. This in turn contributes to gender-based violence."

The General Recommendation next addresses the causes and effects of trafficking and exploitation of the prostitution of women by showing the link between trafficking for prostitution and violence against trafficked women. "Poverty and unemployment increase opportunities for trafficking in women," and new forms of sexual exploitation have emerged, such as sex tourism. "These practices are incompatible with the equal enjoyment of rights by women and with respect for their rights and dignity. They put women at special risk of violence and abuse." Poverty and unemployment not only increase opportunities for trafficking, but also "force many [females] into prostitution." Because their status may be unlawful, the General Recommendation notes, these women tend to be marginalized and thus are increasingly vulnerable to violence and need increased legal protection.

H. International Covenant on Economic, Social, and Cultural Rights

1. States Parties' Obligations

Although the International Covenant on Economic, Social and Cultural Rights (ICESCR) does not directly address trafficking for prostitution, it does contain many rights that are central to women's livelihood. When women and girls are deprived of certain rights in the Covenant, they become vulnerable to trafficking. The ICESCR requires "progressive" rather than immediate implementation of the rights it contains, based on the availability of resources. Nonetheless, the non-discrimination provision in Article 2(2) requires that any allocation of resources be made without discrimination on the basis of various grounds, including sex.

The Committee on Economic, Social and Cultural Rights was established by ECOSOC to monitor implementation of the ICESCR several years after the adoption of the Covenant. The Committee reviews states parties' reports, makes recommendations to states, and issues comments on individual states, in addition to issuing an annual report.

2. Enforcement—Review of States' Reports

A review of annual reports from 1987 through 1995 reveals that the Committee on Economic, Social and Cultural Rights has only once addressed trafficking for prostitution. It did so under Article 10, which addresses protection of the family, mothers and children. The Committee's 1990 examination of the Dominican Republic's report reflects a request for more information "on trafficking in children and child prostitution and the measures taken to combat them." Although the Dominican Republic, in responding to a separate question, stated that legislative measures had been taken to protect minors from exploitation, no information appears to have been provided in response to the request for specific information on trafficking and prostitution.

Recently, the Committee on Economic, Social and Cultural Rights has taken to examining implementation of the ICESCR in countries that have failed to submit reports, despite numerous requests. The Committee should be urged to include trafficking for prostitution among its subjects of inquiry when examining these and other reports.

3. Role for Nongovernmental Organizations

The Committee on Economic, Social and Cultural Rights can serve as a forum for bringing a government under international scrutiny for failure to take measures to stop trafficking for prostitution. NGOs should therefore share with the Committee their documentation in two areas: a state's failure to guarantee the rights in the Covenant without discrimination (Articles 2 and 3 of the Covenant); and a state's failure to protect children from economic and social exploitation and from harmful work (Article 10).

Trafficking for prostitution flourishes where gender discrimination hinders the exercise of one's right to food, health, education, or work. NGO input can strengthen the work of the Committee by making an explicit link between discrimination and trafficking in the information NGOs submit to the Committee. Furthermore, NGOs should emphasize that states cannot use the lack of resources as an excuse for failing to ensure these rights; the Covenant requires that existing resources be made available in a non-discriminatory manner.

NGOs should also focus on bringing to the Committee's attention situations where a state does not protect children "from economic and social exploitation" or from "employment in work harmful to their health or morals or dangerous to life or likely to hamper their normal development," as required under Article 10(3) of the ICESCR. This provision has been underutilized, but it provides an important opportunity to focus international attention on a government's failure to protect children from trafficking for prostitution.

I. Convention on the Rights of the Child

1. States Parties' Obligations

The substantive provisions of the Convention on the Rights of the Child (CRC), and its recognition of the need for coordinated efforts among intergovernmental and nongovernmental bodies, offer significant potential to help curb trafficking in children for prostitution. The CRC, which has achieved nearly universal ratification, contains several provisions applicable to trafficking in children for prostitution, particularly in its provisions regarding child labor and sexual exploitation.

Under Article 32, states parties "recognize the right of the child to be protected from economic exploitation and from performing any work that is likely to be hazardous or to interfere with the child's education, or to be harmful to the child's health or physical, mental, spiritual, moral or social development." To ensure implementation of this provision states parties must enact social and educational measures as well as legislative and administrative measures. States also "undertake to protect the child from all forms of sexual exploitation and sexual abuse," and to take "all appropriate national, bilateral and multilateral measures to prevent the abduction of, the sale of or traffic in children for any purpose or in any form." In addition, states parties undertake to "protect the child against all forms of exploitation prejudicial to any aspect of the child's welfare."

The CRC contains a number of economic and social rights that, if not ensured, can make children vulnerable to being trafficked. In Article 27, states parties recognize the right to "a standard of living adequate for the child's physical, mental, spiritual, moral and social development." In this context, states parties have an obligation, in cases of need, to provide assistance "particularly with regard to nutrition, clothing and housing." States parties also recognize the right to education (Articles 28 and 29) and the right of the child "to rest and leisure" (Article 31). In addition, states parties recognize the right of the child to "the enjoyment of the highest attainable standard of health" (Article 24).

The comprehensive approach to the well-being of children taken in the Convention on the Rights of the Child makes it a particularly useful substantive vehicle for activists in demanding government accountability for failure to reduce trafficking in children for prostitution. However, the primary mechanism for monitoring implementation of the rights in the Covenant is the state reporting procedure. As yet, there is no optional protocol such as that existing under the ICCPR. A limited optional protocol to allow for individual complaints has been proposed, but would apply only to children in situations of armed conflict. An optional protocol dealing with the sale of children, child prostitution, and child pornography has also been discussed. However, if the experience of attempting to achieve adoption of an optional protocol under the Women's Convention is any guide, proponents of such a protocol for the CRC will face an uphill struggle.

2. Enforcement—Review of States' Reports

A review of the 1993 and 1994 annual reports of the Committee on the Rights of the Child indicates that the Committee has twice taken the opportunity to raise concerns about trafficking in children when examining states' periodic reports. In reviewing Bolivia's report in 1994, for example, Committee members linked the deprivation of a number of rights in the Convention to trafficking and sexual exploitation. They noted that "vulnerable groups of children, including girl children, ... are particularly disadvantaged in their access to adequate health and educational facilities and are the primary victims of such abuses as sale and trafficking, child labour and sexual and other forms of exploitation."

That same year, the Committee also addressed trafficking in reviewing the report of Sweden. Committee members first expressed concern that "there seems to be a lack of information on children who are victims of sexual exploitation." In the "Concluding Observations," the Committee noted that "ratification of other international human rights instruments has a favourable influence on the promotion of the rights of the child," and stated in the mildest of terms that Sweden "might consider ratifying the Convention for the Suppression of the Traffic in Persons and of the Exploitation of the Prostitution of Others."

Since an estimated one million children are trafficked for prostitution each year, the CRC Committee should take every opportunity to ask governments what measures they have taken to stop the practice. In addition, NGOs and others should assist the CRC Committee's work by submitting information regarding trafficking in states that are about to be reviewed in the Committee's next session.

3. The Essential Role of Coordinated Efforts

A distinctive feature of the annual reports of the Committee on the Rights of the Child is the emphasis on the need for cooperative efforts among the various U.N. bodies, specialized agencies, and NGOs to achieve realization of the rights embodied in the CRC. In 1994, the Committee explored the "economic exploitation of the child," and provided an opportunity for the exchange of information and views among a range of bodies that deal with this issue. This session resulted in a decision to compile a dossier containing the statements made, as well as the basic documents adopted within the framework of the U.N. system relating to the economic exploitation of children. The Committee decided that the dossier, which would be produced and distributed in cooperation with the International Labour Organization, "should be brought to the attention of all states parties, U.N. organs and specialized agencies, financial institutions and development agencies, and other bodies competent in the field, including INTERPOL and the non-governmental organization community."

This multi-faceted approach is critical if trafficking of children for prostitution is to be curbed. One drawback to the treaty mechanisms described above is that the monitoring committee, in reviewing a state party's report, is limited to addressing that state's performance only. Trafficking that takes place across borders requires examination of at least two states at a time. By working with other intergovernmental and nongovernmental bodies, the Committee can prompt action on cross-border trafficking in children.

J. Benefits and Drawbacks of the Treaty Procedures; the Importance of NGOs

The ICCPR, Women's Convention, ICESCR, and CRC all contain periodic reporting mechanisms that NGOs and other activists can use to press governments to fulfill their treaty obligations and stop trafficking for prostitution.

NGOs are permitted to submit written "interventions" (statements) to the Committee on the Rights of the Child and the Committee on Economic, Social and Cultural Rights. Both Committees also allow oral statements to be made during their sessions, though in the Committee on the Rights of the Child such statements may not comment directly on the examination of a state report.

On an informal basis, prior to a session of any of the treaty bodies, NGOs may submit documentation relating to a state's report to the relevant Committee. This information may be taken into account by Committee members in assessing the information submitted by the state in its report, and in developing questions for the government representatives when the report is presented orally to the Committee. Some NGOs even propose questions to be asked of the government representatives. This should be done sufficiently in advance of the Committee's session so that the members have time to review the material submitted.

1. Benefits of the Treaty Procedures

Although the periodic reporting mechanism has certain drawbacks, its value should not be underestimated. Having to compile the information necessary to write the report requires a state to examine whether it has the legislation and enforcement mechanisms in place that fulfill its treaty obligations.

The reporting mechanism can also expose situations where a government has adequate legislation but inadequate enforcement. In their reports to the treaty bodies, states are required to report on both successful and unsuccessful enforcement measures.

An additional benefit of the reporting mechanism is that by presenting their report orally to the Committee, government representatives engage in a dialogue with Committee members. The question and answer period that follows an oral presentation can be of great value in emphasizing to the state its deficiencies in implementation or enforcement. As a result, some states have in fact changed their laws or implemented enforcement measures. The Human Rights Committee's reports also provide invaluable information to NGOs that are trying to pressure states to implement various treaty provisions.

Not all states parties file periodic reports with the relevant treaty body. The Committee on Economic, Social and Cultural Rights has begun reviewing the performance of states parties in the absence of a government report if after several requests, the state has failed to submit one. In taking this step, the Committee explained that "non-performance by a State party of its reporting obligations, in addition to constituting a breach of the Covenant, creates a severe obstacle to the fulfillment of the Committee's functions. Nevertheless, the Committee has to perform its supervisory role in such cases . . . ." In the absence of a government report, the Committee bases its observations on information from intergovernmental and NGO sources. Under the normal reporting procedures, "the constructive dialogue between a State party reporting and the Committee will provide an opportunity for the Government concerned to voice its own view, and to seek to refute such criticism and convince the Committee of the conformity of its policies with what is required by the Covenant. Non-submission of reports and non-appearance before the Committee deprives a Government of this possibility to set the record straight."

2. Drawbacks of the Treaty Procedures

Infrequency of monitoring is a significant drawback to the enforcement mechanisms established under the human rights treaties discussed above. Once the initial report is presented, subsequent reports are due only every four or five years thereafter. If a country's report has just been reviewed, an activist seeking to use the periodic reporting mechanism to pressure a given state party will have to wait several years before having the opportunity to bring a matter in that country to the relevant Committee's attention.

States also do not always provide complete and detailed reports on the extent to which they are complying with their treaty obligations, and at times do not submit reports at all. Furthermore, Committee members may lack the necessary information on a given state practice to ask sufficiently probing questions of state representatives. This makes the role of NGOs all the more important, for the information they provide can be of great value to the treaty bodies in reviewing state reports and in formulating questions for government representatives.

3. COSTS

JULIE PEARL—THE HIGHEST PAYING CUSTOMERS: AMERICA'S CITIES AND THE COSTS OF PROSTITUTION CONTROL

38 Hastings L.J. 769 (1987).

I. THE COSTS OF PROSTITUTION CONTROL

The author of this Note completed detailed cost analyses for sixteen of the nation's largest cities, which are divided into two size groups: those with populations exceeding one million (the "Big Six"), and those with populations between 500,000 and one million (the "Second Cities"). Predictably, the prevalence of both prostitution and related law enforcement efforts correlates positively to the size of a city's population. Over 85% of all prostitution arrests in this country are made in fifty-five cities, and a large percentage of those arrests occurs in the twenty-three largest cities. Prostitution is apparently not a major concern to law enforcement officials in most smaller cities. Those with 25,000 to 50,000 inhabitants, for example, reported an average of only three prostitution arrests in 1983. The arrest rate per 100,000 residents in the nation's fifty-four largest cities was twenty-three times higher.

A. *Expenditures of Public Funds*

In 1985, the cities in this study spent an average of approximately $7.5 million enforcing prostitution laws. This sum is more than some cities, such as Los Angeles, Dallas, Phoenix, San Diego, and New Orleans, spent on all health services and hospitals in 1982. Half of the cities studied spent more on prostitution control than on either education or public welfare. The estimated expenditures on prostitution arrests of all sixteen cities combined were over $120 million. Such expenditures fall into three categories: (1) police costs, (2) judicial costs, and (3) corrections costs.

(1) Police Costs

Police costs account for over 40% of all public funds expended to enforce prostitution laws. This figure is not surprising given the amount of police time required for each arrest. Officers working in pairs spend an average of twenty-one hours per arrest, which includes the time required to: (1) obtain a solicitation from, and make an arrest of, a suspected prostitute or customer; (2) transport the arrestee to the police station or detention center; (3) complete fingerprinting and identification processes; (4) write and file a report; and (5) testify in court. This fifth duty absorbs the majority of each arresting officer's twenty-one hours.

All vice officers interviewed said that prostitution arrests are far more difficult to make than civilians realize. Most arrests are accomplished either by the "decoy" method, in which male undercover officers pose as customers or, much less frequently, by having female officers pose as prostitutes. The officer may legally make the arrest only after the suspect has explicitly solicited the officer for the purpose of engaging in prostitution. The problem, according to the police, is that officers have previously arrested many prostitutes in a given area of the city; most of these prostitutes are now back on the same streets or in the same hotels, and they are all too familiar with the officers' faces and cars. San Francisco police, frustrated with these obstacles to arrest, recently gave one prostitute fifty-four citations over a three month period for "obstructing the sidewalk," resulting finally in a sixty-day jail sentence.

Moreover, when the former arrestees spot these officers, they warn nearby, unknowing prostitutes not to solicit. Vice squad police report that they are thus compelled to find new "subterfuges" and "sneaky" techniques. In Los Angeles, for example, vice officers commonly recruit police patrolmen to work undercover and hopefully unrecognized. Vice officers then "essentially have to walk through the arrests" with their colleagues, instructing them in the procedures for obtaining and filing arrests. Of course, this form of arrest requires extra police manhours.

Officers report that one of the most time-consuming and complicated aspects of arresting prostitutes is compliance with prohibitions on entrapment. Standards governing prostitution arrests require the officer to engage in a sufficiently detailed conversation with the suspect to receive explicit offers of a numerical fee, a particular service, and in some cities, a convenient location for the transaction. These same standards, however, restrict the officer in both the content and extent of his speech. As a Memphis vice sergeant laments, prostitutes "are getting very cautious. They know we have to be able to prove ... that she seriously offered explicit services, at a set price, to be performed at a stated place. She'll always make sure that she doesn't give us all three." Potential arrestees and vice officers thus engage in elaborate ruses, each trying to lure the other across the tenuous line into prohibited behavior.

Beyond the obvious costs associated with police employment are less apparent ancillary costs. Many of the vice squads contacted maintain expense accounts for the cash layouts required in prostitution arrests. For example, most vice decoys seek solicitations from within leased or rented automobiles, which must be changed every three to six months at premium leasing prices. Frequent changes in personal appearance are also necessary, and some dedicated decoys reportedly spend much time and money on wardrobes, hairstyles, and other means of disguise.

Even greater stealth and financial resources are required to arrest the "big fish"—those conspiring in the operation of escort services and other indoor prostitution rings. These businesses are usually too discreet to solicit over the telephone. Indeed, they will immediately ask for names and credit references, and they will call registries in other cities or take whatever action is necessary to ascertain a prospective customer's identity. An officer must therefore procure false identification and credit cards, then rent a hotel room and wait for the outcall prostitute to arrive. To convince the prostitute that he is an ordinary out-of-town customer, the officer will commonly obtain items to be strewn about the room, such as suitcases, airplane and luggage tickets, and toiletries.

Officers in Manhattan, however, report that businesses that have been established for at least a year will ask for a reference whenever a prospective customer calls. If a familiar name is not given, no escorts will be sent. In such circumstances, vice squads must resort to wiretapping and other expensive methods of arrest. In San Francisco and New Orleans, for example, some hotels allow vice patrolmen to plant video-taping equipment in rooms assigned to suspected outcall prostitutes and their customers.

Arrests of other indoor prostitutes are also time-consuming and potentially costly. For example, officers typically spend thirty to forty minutes in massage parlors before making an arrest. They must first undress, shower, receive a portion of the purchased massage, and then, "at some point ... she [the masseuse] will offer sexual services." In one instance, vice patrolmen in Houston, suspecting "modeling studios" of prostitution, ran a studio of their own. Although substantial police dollars were invested in the sting operation, it was aborted when a local judge ruled that the operation constituted entrapment. The Houston vice officers then began entering existing modeling studios as customers, "ten officers at a time, at $60 each, with no guarantee that we'd get solicited. In theory, we could spend $3000 or $4000 and not make a case."

In spite of the difficulties encountered in obtaining arrests, vice officers estimate that they spend most of their time in the postarrest process, rather than in the arrest itself. Once an arrest has been made, each officer spends an average of over sixteen hours fulfilling the remainder of his duties. These duties fall into two categories: (1) transporting arrestees to detention, fingerprinting, and filing reports; and (2) testifying in court. When officers indicated that they were either required to work in pairs or to provide corroborating testimony in court, the hours-per-arrest figures were doubled accordingly. Most arresting officers work night shifts and thus receive overtime pay for their daytime court appearances. Overtime pay therefore was included in the cost estimates, but not in the police manhour figures.

Once the total number of paid police hours spent per arrest was determined, it was necessary to multiply this figure by some indicia of financial costs to obtain a reasonable estimate of the actual expenditures on prostitution arrests. Wage rates alone would not accurately indicate total police costs, because they fail to include such extraneous expenses as automobile leasing, wire-tapping, and video and audio recording equipment. Therefore, the city's "hourly personnel value per police officer" was used. This figure is the product of a five-step calculation, beginning with total police expenditures in each city in 1985.

The analysis used here admittedly neglects other police costs. First, the cost of clerical assistance to arresting officers was not included in the calculation, because the number of administrative hours spent in each police department was indeterminable. Second, each city's total expenditures for 1985 prostitution control should reflect its number of related arrests, which were probably under-reported by vice officials in certain cities. Several department spokesmen suggested that a fair but indeterminable percentage of arrestees appearing in police statistics under headings of loitering, vagrancy, or "all other arrests" were actually "picked up for being prostitutes." The following estimates were based on the arrest figures reported or estimated by all officials interviewed.

Total police expenditures for the enforcement of
prostitution laws in all 16 cities in 1985: $53,155,688
Mean (per city) annual expenditures: $ 3,322,230
—Big Six Cities: $ 4,856,361
—Second Cities: $ 2,401,752

(2) Judicial Costs

The costs of prosecuting persons arrested for prostitution reflect the fact that most cases involve more than one court appearance. Many arrestees reportedly fail to procure legal counsel in time for their first court appearance, arraignment, which must then be rescheduled. The second court appearance, the initial trial date, is often continued for a variety of reasons. In Philadelphia, for example, many arrestees reportedly "shop around for a judge" at this point. The final appearance, at which sentencing is imposed, is likely to be the third time a given case has gone to court. The prosecution of an average prostitute thus requires nearly four hours of a court's full attention over a period of weeks or months. Moreover, since maintaining a house of prostitution is classified as a felony, prosecution of the "big fish" naturally consumes an even greater amount of judicial resources.

The most detailed study to date of judicial costs involved in prosecuting prostitution arrestees was conducted by the Boston University Law School Center for Criminal Justice. The study concentrated on the handling of prostitution cases by the Boston Municipal Court (BMC), which was found to typify that of nine cities visited by Center researchers. One-fourth of all criminal complaints heard by the BMC in 1972–73, exclusive of moving traffic violations, were prostitution charges. The Center report concluded: "Many of the court officers, administrators, and judges interviewed by our staff expressed the belief that if not for prostitution cases, the Second Session of the BMC, as it currently functions, would not be necessary."

The estimates of 1985 judicial costs of prostitution control presented here are based solely on personnel costs, because reliable data was not available for other judicial expenditures, such as overhead, courtroom supplies, and construction. An average "hourly personnel value per courtroom" in 1985 was calculated for the state in which each of the sixteen cities is situated. This figure was multiplied by an estimated average number of courtroom hours spent per prostitution arrestee in each city.

Estimated judicial personnel costs for prostitution cases in all 16 cities in 1985:	$35,627,496
Mean (per city) annual expenditures:	$ 2,226,719
—Big Six Cities:	$ 3,503,221
—Second Cities:	$ 1,460,817

(3) Correction Costs

An estimated 11% of convicted prostitutes in this country are sentenced to jail terms. Yet, in California, convicted prostitutes are estimated to account for at least 30% of the population in most women's jails; in some cities, such as New York, this figure exceeds 50%. These figures result because convicted prostitutes serve longer sentences than women convicted of most other misdemeanors.

Over a decade ago, the annual cost of incarcerating only four convicted prostitutes in Boston was almost $50,000. In 1977, San Francisco spent $433,000 to incarcerate 414 prostitutes. Correctional costs thus impose a substantial public burden, although they account in this analysis for little over 25% of all expenditures on prostitution control.

The following analysis derived estimates for these costs by multiplying the estimated number of days prostitutes spent in jail for each city in 1985 by the estimated daily jail expenditures per inmate in each city.

Estimated total corrections expenditures for prostitution convicts in all 16 cities in 1985:	$31,770,211
Mean (per city) annual expenditures:	$ 1,985,638
—Big Six Cities:	$ 3,526,826
—Second Cities:	$ 1,060,326

In sum, sixteen of our cities alone spent over $120 million in 1985 in their fight against contractual sex. To be sure, these expenditures annoy certain taxpayers; a strong majority of those polled in Boston, for example, would prefer alternatives to criminalized prostitution. Those in San Francisco—according to a police inspector there—are so opposed to the arrest of prostitutes that their district attorney declines to file cases on many arrestees for fear of losing too many court battles. Perhaps taxpayers would rather see their law enforcement dollars spent entirely on the deterrence of violent or property crime. With the $2.3 million New York City alone spent in 1985 controlling prostitution, the city could have purchased the entire 1982 police departments of Toledo, Tampa, Rochester, or St. Paul, or the fire departments of Atlanta, Honolulu, Indianapolis, Miami, or St. Louis.

The financial expenditures estimated above are transferable. The figures indicate in concrete terms a choice regarding tax dollars that could have been applied to a variety of alternatives. The decision as to whether other kinds of protection or services should be purchased at the price of prostitution control ultimately rests with citizens and legislators. It would be unwise to leave this decision to law enforcement agencies. Those charged with upholding prostitution laws, one vice supervisor remarks, are not as concerned with the manpower and financial costs involved: "The girls are back on the street before we are. We get paid by the hour, so we don't mind much, but if this were a business, we'd be bankrupt."

B. Decreased Protection from Other Crimes

As with all limited resources allocated to one cause in lieu of another, police, court, and correctional manhours spent enforcing prostitution laws may be subject to an opportunity-cost evaluation. Dozens of commentators in recent years have criticized prostitution laws on the ground that they divert law enforcement attention away from more "serious" crime. The devotion of criminal justice resources to prostitution cases may thus be measured in terms of lost opportunity costs if it can be established that: (1) an unacceptable amount of "serious" crime goes undeterred or unpunished; and (2) the resources currently absorbed by prostitution arrests could be channeled toward, and have some impact on, such crime.

Well over two million violent and property crimes were reported in 1985 to the police departments of the cities in this study. Eighty-three percent, or 1.9 million, of these reported offenses failed to result in arrest. For each of these nonarrest cases, police in these same cities last year spent nearly one hour enforcing prostitution laws. Law enforcement officers in San Francisco, for example, devoted ten hours to the arrest, transport, and prosecution of prostitution suspects for every local violent offense in which the perpetrator(s) evaded police apprehension. Cleveland officers spent eighteen hours—the equivalent of two workdays—on prostitution duty for every violent offense failing to yield an arrest. These manhours are thus expended at a time when 94% of respondents to a national poll insist that the police did not respond quickly enough to their calls for help.

There is no assurance that while police are arresting streetwalkers, they will also be patrolling for other crimes likely to occur in the area. First, police spokesmen report that prostitution arrests are generally the responsibility of vice officers, whose work is confined to activities falling under the vice crimes heading—typically including prostitution, drug, and gambling offenses. These officers have neither the time nor the responsibility to search for and arrest perpetrators of violent and property crimes.

Second, since almost all streetwalkers concentrate within one or two "red light" districts in each city, related police activity is limited to those few streets or clusters of city blocks. Although other crimes, such as assault, robbery, and pickpocketing, often occur in those same areas, every city studied has three or four nonprostitution areas in which the rates for these and other offenses is as high or higher. Officers on prostitution duty are thus not present in the vicinities where most of a city's crimes occur.

Third, police officers on prostitution duty generally do not work in public areas, where they might observe or deter other crimes. Police officials interviewed in the various cities agreed that over 90% of the officers' arrest-time is spent transporting prostitutes to detention and filling out the paperwork at the precinct. For every ten minutes a patrolman is on the street making an arrest, he spends fifteen to twenty minutes in transit and over two hours back at the police station. If an officer gathers together three or four streetwalkers within his first hour of duty, it is thus conceivable that he will spend the remainder of his shift at the station.

At least a third of the time spent making prostitution arrests—those of the "big fish"—is spent entirely off the streets; if they are not at the precinct station, officers are likely to be waiting in hotels, massage parlors, bars, or modeling studios. Add to this time spent indoors an average of twenty hours in court per arrest, then double the total figure—since officers generally work and testify in pairs—and it becomes evident that police on prostitution duty provide little—if any—protection against other street crime.

Vice officers are generally well-trained police employees whose skills would enable them to detect and curtail serious criminal activity. Some police officials interviewed stated that, on average, only 20% of their cities' entire police workforce is devoted to direct criminal law enforcement. Approximately 24% of all employees in municipal police departments are assigned to administrative positions or traffic control, and much of the general patrolmen's time is reportedly spent "providing services to people who are lost, locked out of their homes, or have stray cats." Of all police in the "operational" units, detectives and vice officers are generally the best trained in crime detection; the majority of traffic and general patrolmen are not apprenticed in undercover or surveillance work. Vice officers thus rank foremost among police employees who are not presently concerned with—but who would be very capable of—deterring violent and property crime, if their attention were directed toward it.

All of these factors increase the cost in terms of lost opportunity of enforcing prostitution laws. Such arrests consume an average of 1500 highly skilled police manhours weekly in each of the cities studied; the tiny fraction of these hours actually spent on the street is restricted to specific—and not necessarily the highest—crime areas. Meanwhile, eighty-three out of every one-hundred reported violent and property offenses never yield an arrest.

For some cities, such as Houston and New York, these numbers have assumed more than mere theoretical significance. Concerted efforts at prostitution control have been accompanied by an increase in assaultive crimes or a decrease in their clearance-by-arrest rate, or both. In 1975, Houston employed approximately two uniformed police officers and experienced seventy reported violent and property crimes for every one thousand citizens. While 11% of the police department's criminal investigative force handled prostitution cases exclusively, reported felonies increased and their rate of arrest decreased.

In Manhattan in 1978–79, the "Times Square Action Plan" succeeded in nearly doubling the prostitution arrest rate of the previous year. During that same period, and within the same midtown area, complaints of rape, robbery, burglary, and felonious assault rose by as much as 40%. A 30% increase in rape complaints was not accompanied by any increase in arrests; reported incidents of burglary rose by 22%, while the arrest rate plummeted 40%. For these results, the New York City Police Department deployed almost twice the number of patrol units used in Times Square a year earlier.

Faced with far more threatening crime, and the statistic that 90% of arrested prostitutes escape judicial sanction, one wonders why police departments devote so much of their resources to enforcing prostitution laws. A possible explanation is that prostitution cases raise the "closed by arrest rate" for total crime indices. Prostitution is one of the only offenses for which nearly 100% of "reported incidences" result in arrest. To the extent that total arrest rate indices are elevated by the inclusion of this high percentage for prostitution, they engender a false account of overall police protection. Few New York residents would be comforted by their state's 1981 breakdown: while twenty-four out of twenty-six reported prostitution cases were closed by arrest, only 5% of the claims for reported violent crimes yielded an arrest.

Another explanation commonly advanced for the amount of time dedicated to prostitution offenses is simply that police like the work. Prostitutes generally pose less danger to officers than persons arrested for other nighttime offenses or for assaultive crimes. Further, although the "decoy" method has been widely criticized and held by some courts to constitute entrapment, vice officers around the country prefer this approach; they speak at length of the newly leased cars, the clothes ("We've got to look like guys with money to burn."), and other aspects of their work. Although several officers interviewed volunteered statements concerning the homeliness of their cities' prostitutes, it is possible that many vice officers enjoy the time spent around women in massage parlors, modeling studios, and the like. There are undoubtedly far less pleasant ways for a law enforcement officer to spend his shift. Again, this explanation, if accurate, is unlikely to comfort the 94% of citizens surveyed nationwide who agreed that the police assistance they called for was not available soon enough.

Along with the opportunity costs of the present system in terms of police manhours, a complete analysis must account for the amount of judicial and correctional resources consumed in the enforcement of prostitution laws. These resources, too, are finite. It thus follows that prosecutorial services and jail space allocated to prostitution cases consume criminal justice resources that could be channeled toward other offenses. A year-long study in San Francisco in 1977, for example, concluded that 10% to 20% of the public defender's caseload and 10% of the district attorney's misdemeanor cases involved prostitution offenses.

All factors considered, prostitution laws clearly represent lost opportunities for the protection of society against other crimes. An unacceptably large amount of assaultive crime goes undeterred and unpunished, and the criminal justice resources currently devoted to prostitution control are sufficiently significant to have an impact on law enforcement efforts against those other crimes.

II.   WEIGHING THE COSTS OF ENFORCING PROSTITUTION LAWS: BENEFITS SOUGHT AND LAW ENFORCEMENT PRIORITIES

Responsible policy decisions on prostitution laws can only be reached by balancing the law enforcement costs against related considerations: the benefits the law seeks to attain by prohibiting prostitution, and the perceived priorities of all law enforcement efforts. Thus, the costs discussed above would most suitably—if not briefly—be considered in the context of the benefits they are intended to purchase and their relevance to the larger scheme of criminal justice objectives.

A.   Benefits Sought

In keeping with the general purpose of the criminal law, the stated purpose of prostitution laws is to benefit society, or to protect it from the harms associated with prostitution. Material harms have historically played a larger role than perceived moral harms in policy formation regarding prostitution. The Church in medieval Europe, for example, ceased its acceptance and regulation of prostitution when a syphilis epidemic took hundreds of lives. To this day, the spread of venereal disease remains a primary justification for our prostitution laws. Other material harms commonly linked to prostitution include organized crime and ancillary crime, such as narcotics use and robbery.

Church groups, feminists, lawyers, and neighborhood organizations alike have argued that laws against prostitution fail to alleviate the harms associated with the activity. These groups point first to the problem of venereal disease in this country, only 3% to 5% of which has been attributed to prostitutes by national health officials. Conceding that even a 5% figure threatens the public welfare, the proponents of decriminalization insist that criminalizing prostitution aggravates the problem because it inhibits some prostitutes from seeking frequent medical attention.

On similar grounds, those opposing prostitution laws have argued that the current legal approach does little to counter the problem of ancillary crime. The contention is generally that "if prostitution were not a crime, then those who consort with prostitutes and then become the victims of robberies and assaults might be more likely to report these crimes." To the extent that narcotics users, panderers, and other undesirables are associated with prostitution, the argument goes, they would be more effectively policed by a system of legalized prostitution, as illustrated by the Nevada and Western European experiences.

Whatever the strength of these and the competing arguments, the proffered benefits of prostitution laws must be examined in light of the tremendous burdens these laws impose on criminal justice resources. If it is true that criminalization fails adequately to address those harms associated with prostitution, then the minimal benefits obtained by the prohibition would indeed calibrate the costs discussed above as highly excessive. Although no study has pointed to a positive correlation between law enforcement efforts against prostitution and the reduction of related material harms, conclusive evidence of such results would serve to at least partially justify the costs.

B. Law Enforcement Priorities

Instinctively and logistically, we examine both the benefits and costs of all legal tenets with regard to our law enforcement priorities. Finite resources, particularly those allocated to the prevention of harm, often compel us to make "tragic choices." With limited manpower, police departments must attend to all of their communities' law enforcement needs.

The United States Justice Department recently commissioned researchers to conduct a voluminous nationwide survey on public perceptions of the severity of various crimes. Respondents were asked to rank 204 offenses, ranging from "a person plants a bomb in a public building" to "a person under sixteen years old plays hooky from school." Prostitution ranked number 174, immediately followed in perceived severity by "a store owner knowingly puts 'large' eggs into containers marked 'extra large'" and "a person makes an obscene phone call." Patronizing a prostitute ranked even lower, and both selling and buying sex were perceived as far less serious than a person cheating on his federal income tax return or calling in a false fire alarm.

Similarly, fewer than half of the adults polled in another national survey agreed with the statement: "Prostitutes do more harm than good." Although these polls are not conclusive of American attitudes toward prostitution, they strongly indicate that the activity is not seen as a major threat to society's physical welfare.

Of course, to say that a crime is lower in priority is not to say that laws prohibiting it are wholly without value. No legislature would repeal prohibitions of automobile theft simply because it is a less serious offense than homicide. The difference lies here: few will assert, as many do of prostitution, that an automobile theft causes no harm. The ambivalence toward whether the activity is harmful at all is the threshold that separates an activity such as prostitution from direct-victim crimes. This threshold test gains significance in the face of scarce police resources which a majority of Americans are unwilling to expand through additional taxes.

When citizens go under-protected from activity that threatens their lives or property, the choices made in the past must be reconsidered. Perhaps other laws, such as curfew or jaywalking restrictions, would be more acceptably repealed than prostitution laws. Few laws, however, are likely to have even a fraction of the impact that prostitution laws have on law enforcement resources. Even at present, when prostitution laws are so widely believed to exemplify a category of "under-enforced" legal provisions, the time criminal justice agents spend in their enforcement is demonstrably significant. These circumstances suggest that our decision to combat prostitution, which has required a substantial investment of scarce resources while ranking low among the public's priorities, should be reexamined if our law enforcement system is to serve its principal objectives.

Conclusion

Many Americans may never wish to condone prostitution, but the time has come to ask whether we can afford to keep it illegal. In the face of rising complaints of violent crime in virtually all major cities, the thousands of highly skilled vice officer manhours devoted weekly to prostitution represent tremendous opportunity costs. Such costs are evidenced by the experiences of New York City in 1979 and Houston in 1975: even the most vigorous police battles against prostitution yield Pyrrhic victories at best.

It is clear that many of the costs incurred in the enforcement of prostitution laws are inescapable. Measures designed to minimize the police hours involved could presumably reduce certain costs. Boston police, for example, streamline their prostitution arrest forms, and Los Angeles vice detectives now economize their court time by appearing on an on-call basis. Such revisions, however, would require strong administrative cooperation and widespread implementation to have any significant impact on the overall disinvestment of criminal justice resources.

Moreover, even when time-saving procedures have been instituted, the nature and sheer number of prostitution arrests continue to elevate enforcement costs. Given the prevailing judicial leniency toward prostitutes, police officers—who naturally seek the conviction and sentencing of arrestees—are compelled to arrest prostitutes repeatedly. Further, given the undercover preparation and subterfuge needed to make an arrest, the process of policing prostitution is inherently lengthy, particularly when compared to most other misdemeanors.

Most unfortunately, police on prostitution duty are seldom disposed to deter more assaultive crimes. Vice officers' efforts are restricted to specific offenses and city blocks, and over 90% of their time-per-arrest is spent indoors. Police indicate that the time they spend in hotel rooms and illicit houses awaiting solicitations is unavoidable; the laws charge police with apprehending prostitutes, and much prostitution in America is moving indoors.

The composite elements of prostitution control, in terms of both public fiscal expenditures and decreased protection from other crimes, appear highly disproportionate in light of the stated priorities of citizens and judges alike, and the apparently minimal benefits attained. With scarce police, judicial, and correctional services, Americans may soon have to choose between retaining prostitution laws and attending to more pressing law enforcement needs. A decision to reallocate our resources need not be a declaration of the acceptability of prostitution. Rather, it would be a well-founded statement concerning the proper use of criminal justice resources.

4. ALTERNATIVE MODELS OF REFORM

a. Zoning

Historically, many of the efforts to suppress prostitution have focused on controlling other "sexually themed" businesses, with policymakers reasoning that, if strip clubs and similar legal businesses can be contained through designated "red light districts" or other regulations, prostitution will be limited as well. Recently, however, that strategy has begun to break down.

DANIEL McDONALD—REGULATING SEXUALLY ORIENTED BUSINESSES: THE REGULATORY UNCERTAINTIES OF A "REGIME OF PROHIBITION BY INDIRECTION" AND THE OBSCENITY DOCTRINE'S COMMUNAL SOLUTION

1997 B.Y.U. L. Rev. 339.

II. Prohibition by Indirection: Regulation Through Zoning

A. The Zoning Framework

Just as "there is more than one way to skin a cat," there is more than one way to regulate sexually oriented businesses. In addition to obscenity prosecutions, such businesses have been regulated via zoning ordinances, licensing requirements, nuisance laws, and the federal Racketeer Influenced and Corrupt Organization (RICO) statute. The regulatory tool of choice, however, remains zoning ordinances. These ordinances generally take one of two approaches to regulating sexually oriented businesses. First, local governments may use zoning ordinances to concentrate adult business into a single area. This could be called the red-light-district approach. The second approach is to disperse adult businesses somewhat evenly throughout the community so as to avoid the creation of red-light districts. For purposes of this Comment, however, the zoning strategy used remains largely irrelevant since both present similar constitutional difficulties. Whether adult businesses are told they must locate in warehouse districts on the outskirts of town—where there is no pedestrian or vehicular traffic and, consequently, no clientele—or whether they are told to locate in a red-light district—where there is perhaps too much competition for clientele—adult businesses are likely to challenge any zoning restrictions placed upon them.

These challenges are most often based on the First Amendment, which provides that "Congress shall make no law ... abridging the freedom of speech" and has been made applicable to the States through the Due Process Clause of the Fourteenth Amendment. Because of these amendments, state and local governments cannot make laws abridging the freedom of speech. Adult businesses predictably contend that their services and products are a form of speech deserving constitutional protection against state and local regulation. So far, the Supreme Court has agreed. However, the amount of constitutional protection afforded depends largely on the purpose of the regulation as demonstrated by its effect on speech.

If the ordinance is predominately aimed at restricting the content of the speech itself, the ordinance will be placed under strict scrutiny by courts and will, almost presumptively, be declared invalid. Strict scrutiny requires the government to show that the content-based "regulation is a precisely drawn means of serving a compelling state interest." This type of judicial review has been described as "strict in theory, but fatal in fact" as nearly all such ordinances will be invalidated as violative of the Constitution. If, by contrast, the regulation seeks not to regulate the content of the speech itself but some other problem (e.g., rape or drug abuse) commonly associated with it, or in other words, if the regulation can be justified without regard to the content of the speech, the regulation can theoretically be deemed to make no reference to the content of the speech and is labeled "content neutral." Valid content-neutral regulation seeks only to restrict the "time, place or manner" in which the speech takes place and not the protected speech itself, thus making it constitutionally permissible. The critical distinction between an ordinance that is a content-based restriction and one that is not content-based seems to be whether the ordinance altogether bans the allegedly protected activity. If it does, then the ordinance will not be analyzed to determine whether it is a valid content-neutral time, place, and manner restriction but will be subjected to strict scrutiny.

The case of Young v. American Mini Theatres, Inc. is illustrative. There, the city of Detroit passed zoning ordinances that prohibited adult bookstores and adult theaters from being located within 1000 feet of any other similar business or 500 feet of a residential dwelling without the city's approval. The ordinances were based on findings that these types of businesses, when concentrated, had a blighting effect on surrounding neighborhoods. Various urban planning and real estate experts claimed that "the location of several such businesses in the same neighborhood tends to attract an undesirable quantity and quality of transients, adversely affects property values, causes an increase in crime, especially prostitution, and encourages residents and businesses to move elsewhere." A plurality of the Supreme Court upheld the ordinance as constituting a valid content-neutral time, place, and manner restriction because the ordinance was meant to "preserve the quality of urban life" by avoiding or mitigating the "secondary effects" of these businesses. The Court distinguished this situation, where the city was regulating only the effects of the businesses, from one in which the regulatory purpose was to suppress the businesses themselves.

Local governments frequently attempt to regulate sexually oriented businesses by the Young method of placing content-neutral restrictions upon them, since these restrictions are subjected to a lower level of constitutional scrutiny. To show that its regulation is content neutral and thus survive constitutional review through application of this lower level of scrutiny a governmental entity must show: (1) that the regulation was "designed to serve a substantial governmental interest" unrelated to the content of the speech; (2) that the regulation is narrowly tailored to serve that purpose; and (3) that the regulation does "not unreasonably limit alternative avenues of communication" for the speech that is incidentally burdened. If the government cannot show a substantial interest, the zoning scheme is prima facie invalid. Accordingly, the ultimate success of any such zoning scheme almost always turns upon whether the government has demonstrated the negative secondary effects these types of businesses have on a community. For all practical purposes, then, the premise underlying nearly all zoning of sexually oriented businesses is that these businesses generate negative secondary effects and that the government therefore has a substantial interest in imposing time, place, and manner restrictions upon them.

To show such a substantial interest, a city need not commission its own studies to demonstrate the blighting effects that adult businesses have had on their community. A city may "borrow" research from other jurisdictions that demonstrates the blighting effect adult businesses have on cities in general. Similarly, such businesses do not need to exist in a city before a city can enact an ordinance that regulates them. Such a content-neutral scheme was upheld in City of Renton v. Playtime Theatres, Inc. The Renton, Washington zoning ordinance prohibited "adult motion picture theaters from locating within 1,000 feet of any residential zone, single-or multiple-family dwelling, church, park, or school." The ordinance was enacted at a time when no adult businesses were located within the city. Therefore, whether Renton could justify such an ordinance on the Young rationale that such businesses generated negative secondary effects was at issue in the case. The Court held that "Renton was entitled to rely on the experiences of ... other cities" to show the negative secondary effects adult businesses generate because the First Amendment does not require a city, before enacting such an ordinance, to conduct new studies or produce evidence independent of that already generated by other cities, so long as whatever evidence the city relies upon is reasonably believed to be relevant to the problem that the city addresses.

The Young–Playtime Theatres method of regulating sexually oriented businesses has caught on. For example, a recent article by Barry K. Arrington, an attorney for the Coalition for Children and Families, announced that "fourteen studies from around the United States have documented a strong connection between sexually oriented businesses and increased levels of crime in an area." The article then provides an address and phone number for cities wishing to obtain the studies. Arrington notes, "In response to the findings of the surveys mentioned above, many communities have enacted ordinances imposing strict regulations on sex businesses," which have caused many "sexually oriented businesses [to close] or change operations." And in Utah, for example, several cities, including Salt Lake City, have recently sought to tighten their zoning restrictions on sexually oriented businesses.

Despite its apparent successes, this method of regulating sexually oriented businesses on the basis of the secondary effects they allegedly produce rests on an analytical foundation that will eventually crumble. This erosion of secondary effects analysis is inevitable for several reasons. First, the doctrinal premise of this mode of regulation, which is nothing more than a legal fiction, is paradoxically flawed and disingenuous. Second, even assuming the doctrinal soundness of secondary effects analysis, adult businesses may use their own factual settings to, figuratively-speaking, "call a city's bluff." They can do this by distinguishing their situation from the situations upon which a city's borrowed research is predicated or by demonstrating that the purported purposes of the regulation are not offended by the circumstances of their case. Third, emerging social research supported by large sums of money may rebut on a nationwide and case-by-case basis the presumption–"demonstrated" in most cases by the aforementioned "canned research" borrowed from other jurisdictions—that adult businesses generate negative secondary effects.

b. *Regulatory Decriminalization*

NICOLE BINGHAM—NEVADA SEX TRADE: A GAMBLE FOR THE WORKERS

10 Yale J.L. & Feminism 69 (1998).

IV. NEVADA REGULATION OF PROSTITUTION

When prostitution was illegal, the debate over whether it should be legal in the United States was mostly theoretical. In 1973, prostitution was no longer a crime per se in Nevada because local communities were allowed to legalize prostitution. While the debate over prostitution continues, little has been written about Nevada's regulatory system, and even less has been written about using the Nevada system as a model elsewhere in the United States. A look at legalized prostitution in Nevada in terms of prostitutes' rights and those who oppose prostitution is absent from the field of legal analysis or current social science research. This Article intends to explore that analysis and encourage subsequent discussion

The current existence of regulated prostitution in Nevada seems to reflect an attitude of general tolerance by Nevadans. Nevada, the thirty-sixth state to enter the union, is not widely populated and relies heavily on gaming, mining, agriculture, and tourism as its principal industries. Prostitution in this frontier state originally existed around mining camps, railroads, and cattle towns. Some attribute the local attitude to a sense of tradition that included brothels and did not consider them to be a threat to the community. According to Helen Reynolds:

> Brothels in operation today in Nevada are not the product of some new-found liberalism, or even libertarianism, but are a throw-back to an earlier time, a tradition that had not died out by the time legalized tolerance took the form of statewide statutes and local ordinances. In essence, the state and local laws merely reflect the general tenor of rural Nevada: prostitution has been around for a long time, the businesses of brothels seem to be fairly well controlled, and the houses serve some sort of social function.

Not everyone in Nevada welcomed the idea of allowing localities to choose whether or not to legalize prostitution. Some feared that it would draw unneeded attention to the gambling industry and allow organized crime to take over another "sinful" business.

A. Location of Brothels

The choice of location, particularly the proximity to a major roadway, railroad, large city, or resort town, seems to be important to the survival and prosperity of a brothel. The highways provide the brothels with a clientele of truck drivers, hunters, and other traveling men en route to the five surrounding states. The Cities of Elko and Winnemucca, both situated on Interstate 80, allow prostitution within the city limits, while in the rest of the county prostitution is prohibited in the unincorporated areas. The busiest brothels are those near to a large city such as Reno or Las Vegas or a resort town like Lake Tahoe. Since both Las Vegas and Reno prohibit prostitution within the city limits, the operation of a brothel near these cities has been very profitable. The location of a brothel may determine the financial success of the brothel owner, but does not necessarily mean that prostitutes are better off under a system of regulated prostitution.

B. State and Local Law

Prostitution may no longer be per se criminal in Nevada but that does not mean that Nevada grants legal status to prostitution in general. Prostitution and solicitation remain illegal, as do pandering and living from the earnings of a prostitute. An exception is made for prostitution and solicitation of prostitution if it occurs within a licensed house of prostitution under the Nevada Revised Statute 201.354. Article 19, Section 4 of the Nevada Constitution, which reserved the power of initiative and referendum to the people of each county or municipality, combined with Nevada Revised Statute 244.345, which allows counties with a certain population size to apply for a license to run a house of "ill fame or repute," better known as a house of prostitution, allow Nevada citizens to permit or prohibit prostitution at the county level.

The Supreme Court of Nevada, in Nye County v. Plankinton, held that Nevada Revised Statute 244.345 repealed the common-law rule that houses of prostitution constitute a nuisance per se. In Kuban v. McGimsey, the court rejected a constitutional challenge to a Lincoln County ordinance prohibiting prostitution within the county and found that such an ordinance is within the power reserved for the people of its county by the Nevada Constitution. While the court was upholding a local ordinance prohibiting prostitution, it confirmed that the right to decide this issue is up to the counties as long as counties permit only licensed brothels.

Since the choice whether to allow prostitution is left up to the counties themselves, there are variations among the local ordinances regarding prostitution. Currently, all seventeen county codes either permit and regulate or ban prostitution. Four counties prohibit prostitution (Carson City, Clark, Douglas, and Lincoln), six ban prostitution in the unincorporated areas of the county (Elko, Eureka, Humboldt, Pershing, Washoe, and White Pine), and seven counties permit prostitution in the county (Churchill, Esmeralda, Lander, Lyon, Mineral, Nye, and Storey).

There are also variations among counties in terms of the specific form of regulations within each county. Some county codes that allow prostitution have detailed rules concerning health, licensing, and other issues relating to prostitution. Nye County, for example, a rural county located in central Nevada, has a code that outlines a number of specific licensing requirements and restrictions. All houses of prostitution must display "one sign no larger than twenty-four square feet, to be located on the entrance of the house of prostitution and to contain the following words and no others: 'Brothel' or 'House of Prostitution' (name of the establishment)." This code not only has sign requirements, but also specifies that a licensed house of prostitution can have no more than three red exterior lights with a total wattage not exceeding two hundred watts per bulb. Nye County has the only code that mentions male prostitutes. Two other central Nevada counties, Mineral and Churchill, prohibit male employees in licensed houses of prostitution except for maintenance and repair work.

A Board of County Commissioners holds a significant amount of power to issue requirements and revoke licenses. Local sheriffs control unincorporated parts of a county, and public officials often have their own extralegal rules which they apply to prostitutes. Some of those rules involve regulating when prostitutes go into town, changing employment, or discouraging freelancing and promoting control over prostitutes. In addition to these rules, the madam who runs the individual brothel may have her own set of rules concerning procedure and conduct within the brothel. In incorporated towns, the local chief of police usually sets the rules, which are generally followed by the city council.

C. Health

The most heavily regulated area of prostitution is health. Both the Nevada Statutes and the Nevada Administrative Code require people engaged in prostitution to submit to HIV testing. A Nevada statute requires anyone who is arrested for violating Nevada Revised Statute 201.354, which prohibits engaging in prostitution or solicitation except in a licensed house of prostitution, to submit to a State Board of Health HIV test and receive the results. While this regulation may protect both the prostitute and the patron, it seems to be primarily concerned with keeping prostitution contained inside brothels. A person who engages in prostitution, including a prostitute in a licensed brothel, or solicitation after testing positive for exposure to HIV is guilty of a class B felony and will be punished by imprisonment for a minimum of two and a maximum of ten years, a fine of $10,000, or both under Nevada Revised Statute 201.358. This law is directed at anyone who continues to engage in prostitution or solicitation after testing positive for HIV. But the penalty of imprisonment will probably do little to protect a prostitute who works in a licensed brothel from being exposed to a customer, also known as a john, who is HIV positive and who either does not know it or who knows it but continues to frequent legal brothels.

In addition to these statutes, the Nevada Administrative Code establishes a number of regulations specifically targeted at prostitutes which require them to submit to invasive procedures. The Code requires a person seeking employment as a prostitute in a licensed house of prostitution to submit to a medical lab test for HIV, syphilis, and gonorrhea, monthly HIV and syphilis tests, and weekly gonorrhea and Chlamydia tests. The Code requires a person employed as a prostitute in a licensed house of prostitution to require a patron to use a latex prophylactic. In addition, the Code requires the person in charge of a licensed house of prostitution to post a health notice and to report the presence of a communicable disease to the health authority. While these regulations are meant to serve as protection, the question of who they are meant to protect remains open.

V. The Nevada Model in Terms of the Prostitution Debate

A. *Decriminalization v. Legalization*

Both those advocating the prostitution-as-work position and those advocating the prostitution-as-exploitation position agree that decriminalization, rather than legalization, is for the most part the correct approach. Legalization usually means some form of state-regulated prostitution, whereas decriminalization means the removal of laws prohibiting prostitution. Some opponents of prostitution advocate decriminalization for prostitutes but continued criminalization for pimps and johns. Even those who advocate this position agree that arresting prostitutes is an ineffective way to curb prostitution and secondarily victimizes women. Prostitution, with the exception of Nevada and a brief period of regulation in St. Louis, has not been regulated by legislation in the United States. State and local governments have spent thousands of taxpayer dollars in law enforcement efforts to eradicate it with little success. Theorists and supporters on both sides of the debate advocate decriminalization to prevent the frequent harassment, stigmatization, and violence perpetrated against prostitutes.

Prostitutes' rights organizations advocate decriminalization because of their basic belief that there is nothing wrong with prostitution, and that women who choose to engage in this type of work should have the same rights and protection as other workers. In the opinion of Priscilla Alexander, a co-founder of COYOTE:

> Decriminalization of prostitution and the regulation of pimping and pandering, it seems to me, offers the best chance for women who are involved in prostitution to gain some measure of control over their work. It would make it easier to prosecute those who abuse prostitutes, either physically or economically, because the voluntary, non-abusive situation would be left alone. Decriminalization allows for the possibility that the lives of prostitutes can become less dangerous.

Decriminalization would reduce the stigma attached to prostitution and prostitutes and allow them to better bargain for the rights and protection they deserve. Supporters of the prostitution-as-work perspective oppose legalization in the form of state enforced regulations unless they regulate third parties and improve the working conditions of prostitutes.

Kathleen Barry, a proponent of the prostitution-as-exploitation theory, also advocates the decriminalization of prostitution. In 1995, Barry revised her previous position on decriminalization from decriminalization for prostitutes and customers to decriminalization for only prostitutes and continued criminalization for customers.

> In the late 1970's, writing Female Sexual Slavery before a feminist movement developed to confront prostitution, I proposed decriminalization as the appropriate legal strategy to confront the sexual enslavement of women. Concerned with women's victimization by police under conditions where prostitution is criminalized, and with pimping that produces slavery of women in prostitution, I saw the urgent need to take the laws off prostitute women, as the abolitionists have argued, without promoting prostitution as the regulationists do. But at that time my proposal to decriminalize prostitution implicitly meant decriminalizing men who buy women's bodies. The error in proposing blanket decriminalization was that it decriminalizes the customers as well as the prostitute, leaving the customer, the direct perpetrator of sexual exploitation, virtually sanctioned.

Barry believes that this approach would render the customer, not the prostitute, the criminal. At the same time, she proposes that prostitutes be recognized as victims of sexual exploitation by the customer. Opponents of prostitution, such as Barry, reject the idea that decriminalization is necessary so that prostitution can be recognized as a valid form of work. In fact, Barry believes that using the term "sex work" is a sign of hopelessness when used by women in prostitution who would leave it if they were able. She states that "sex work language has been adopted out of despair, not because these women promote prostitution but because it seems impossible to conceive of any other way to treat prostitute women with dignity and respect than through normalizing their exploitation." Opponents of prostitution argue that prostitution is not inevitable and that the way to stop it is to provide prostitutes with resources to enable them to escape prostitution and sustain themselves economically.

Nevada uses a regulatory approach to prostitution rather than a decriminalization approach. Prostitution remains criminalized in Nevada, but local communities may permit a highly controlled and limited type of prostitution to exist in a limited geographical area. Under this model, the state enters into an area of regulating adult sexual relationships, an area that some question whether the state should regulate. State and local statutory systems are not a recognition of prostitution as a viable employment option for anyone who chooses it. Instead, these systems are an attempt to control an illegal activity that will not be eradicated despite the efforts of officials

Under Nevada's regulatory system, the "pimp/prostitute" relationship is redefined. It is clear that the only kind of prostitute who is legal and protected is the licensed brothel prostitute. Equally clear is that individual pimps controlling a number of prostitutes are replaced by a small number of legal brothel owners who are closely monitored by the government. The only legal pimps then become these limited numbers of brothel owners who have direct links with the local government. Some might consider this arrangement to mean that the state becomes the pimp by exploiting and abusing prostitutes through the system of licensed brothels. In any case, prostitutes are divided into two categories, licensed prostitutes who are legal, and all other prostitutes who are illegal. Therefore, non-licensed prostitutes do not gain anything from the regulatory system, since most prostitution remains illegal. Street prostitutes in the large cities are still more numerous than legal prostitutes in brothels, indicating that the regulatory scheme neither reduced prostitution nor brought the industry under state control.

B. Regulation or "Freedom" for Prostitutes

A regulatory system such as Nevada's provides the state with a controlled means to sell women's sexual services and eradicates choice for prostitutes themselves, rather than providing a way for prostitutes to gain a degree of control over their lives. The few references in articles about prostitution written either by prostitutes themselves or leading theorists, seem to confirm that being a licensed prostitute in one of the brothels in Nevada is not a liberating experience. Laura Anderson, a former brothel worker, states that the system results in mandatory exploitation. "Prostitutes are giving up too much autonomy, control, and choice over their work and lives. Because prostitutes are not allowed to work independently, or outside the brothel system, Nevada has essentially institutionalized third-party management with no other options." According to another prostitute who worked at the Mustang Ranch outside of Reno, it was "just like a prison."

Prostitutes under the brothel system are considered "independent contractors" and not full-time employees. Therefore, prostitutes do not gain the benefits of health care, vacation pay, retirement benefits, or any of the other benefits and rights many workers have. When a prostitute receives a license, she gives up some of her rights, including the right to freely travel when and wherever she wants, her right to refuse testing for sexually transmitted diseases, and her right to live and work where she wants. Prostitutes have little or no say in choosing their customers or the numbers of hours they work. A typical shift in a brothel is twelve to fourteen hours a day, every day for three weeks. A legal prostitute must share her earnings with the brothel, unlike the un-licensed prostitute who can try to work on her own and keep her earnings. By the time a prostitute is finished paying for all her expenses, her share of her earnings is about fifty percent. Each prostitute has to pay for room and board, maid services, supplies (including condoms), mandatory tipping for house employees, one dollar for each pair of panties washed, twenty dollars for the weekly venereal disease checkup, two dollars for each prescription, and any additional cost to have it filled. While a prostitute may be able to make a decent income if there is a steady stream of customers, it is clear that the brothel and the county benefit far more than the individual prostitute.

While legal prostitutes in Nevada may no longer suffer the stigma of being criminals, they are stigmatized by the licensing scheme and the widespread belief that prostitutes are the source of disease. Many prostitutes do not want to risk further stigmatization by going public as a prostitute and obtaining a license, or give up their freedom by working in a brothel, so the vast majority of prostitutes remain illegal. While legal prostitutes may not be stigmatized by arrests, they may suffer a similar stigma by being licensed. Just because something is not criminal does not necessarily remove the stigma of being considered an "other" woman or a source of "filth" and contagion. In fact, a significant part of the regulations passed surrounding prostitution concern the spread of disease.

Notes and Questions

1. The recent trajectory of prostitution as a political and legal issue in Western developed nations is puzzling in a number of respects. Concerns about prostitution and the victimization of female prostitutes range from exploitation by pimps (a major concern of Wolfenden) to international sex trafficking and involuntary servitude. No clear consensus has emerged on which types of criminal law policy changes would facilitate harm reduction with respect to those concerns. Is the amount of prostitution a high priority concern or a minor issue? Is the number of prostitutes the major cause for concern? Or, is there also social harm when citizens become customers? If not, shouldn't policy attempt to maximize the sexual reach of a small number of prostitutes? Or is it more important to discourage demand by

breaking down sex markets? In practice, what are the current policy priorities?

2. What would your priorities be in setting prostitution policy for a state legislature? For a local police department? Which level of government has the most influence on current policy in the United States—federal, state, or local government? Write a model code for the regulation of prostitution within either law or policy practice (or both).

3. What would be the likely impact of full decriminalization of prostitution on the amount of sexual services sold? On the number of men and women who commit acts of prostitution? On the risks assumed and harms experienced by prostitutes?

4. Does experience with limited experiments such as brothel decriminalization and regulation in Nevada reveal much about the impact of legalized commercial sex on illegal street prostitution? On the likely demand for other vice goods and services such as narcotics if made legally available under controlled conditions?

5. One major puzzle about prostitution as a candidate for law reform is the absence of legal change in most developed nations. Though the first topic of the Wolfenden Committee—sodomy—was struck from the criminal codes of developed nations in the half-century after 1953, the law regarding prostitution has stayed remarkably fixed on the premises and categories of mid-century England. Why is this?

One contrast with gambling is the smaller monetary gains associated with packaging the selling of sex. It is a labor-intensive trade without huge potential profits. It lacks the mass volume potential that generates profits in pornography. Is it the lack of financial benefit that holds back legal reform?

Or is it the lack of a powerful political constituency calling for reform? Certainly, that constituency is one feature of the gay rights movement in the late 20th century that is missing from the discourse about prostitution law reform.

There are two further explanations that relate to the limited appeal of prostitution law reform. The first is that there is no obvious crisis or cost in the current system in most nations and localities. The toleration and control of prostitutes by local law enforcement has no high costs or visible victims, and thus, there is also no obvious consensus that any particular reform would clearly be superior to the tolerable status quo.

Finally, the decentralized and law-enforcement-centered powers of the current system imply that any legislative change would have to reframe policy from above in many hundreds of policy jurisdictions.

Which are the more plausible explanations for the lack of legislative change? What, if anything, is likely to change in the United States, and when?

DAVID A.J. RICHARDS—BEYOND DECRIMINALIZATION

From "Commercial Sex and the Rights of the Person: A Moral Argument
for the Decriminalization of Prostitution." *University of
Pennsylvania Law Review* 127:1203–1214 (1979).

This Article has tried to establish that there are no good moral arguments for criminalizing consensual adult commercial sex, and that its punishment is a violation of the rights of the person. The criminalization of prostitution appears to be an illegitimate vindication of unjust social hatred and fear of autonomously sexual women and their rights to define and pursue their own vision of the good. Having given such reasons for decriminalizing prostitution, we are able to take a much less confining view of the legal treatment of prostitution. Let us briefly consider three alternatives: licensing; regulations of place, time, and methods; and no regulations at all. I assume throughout that per se criminal prohibitions of prostitution are repealed or otherwise invalidated.

A. LICENSING

The licensing of prostitutes is of ancient vintage, and was widespread in Europe until this century. The idea of licensing is that, in order to engage in commercial sex, one must secure a permit from the state that entails having one's name entered in a public record, various regulations of dress, price, and place of business and solicitation, and, in the widespread European practice, regular medical inspections for venereal disease. The European justification for licensing focused on alleged venereal disease prophylaxis. When these considerations were urged in Great Britain and the United States, they were successfully resisted by a constellation of powerful political forces, including purity reformers and feminists: The arguments of the feminists were of two kinds, the second of which is still made by contemporary feminists who urge decriminalization but condemn licensing: first, an attack on the double standard, urging that men be compelled to heed the same standards of chastity exacted from women; and second, the degrading nature of European licensing to women, including public records which made it difficult to leave the profession, various arbitrary regulations and demeaning inspections, and general failure to regulate brothels on terms fair to the prostitutes. Official European licensing schemes were ended, in large part, in response to international conventions that bound nations to end the "white slave trade" in women and girls that was alleged to be due largely to the demand for prostitutes occasioned by licensed brothels.

None of these arguments would be decisive against some form of licensing if there were good independent reasons for such licensing. First, the appeal to the double standard rests on an unexamined valuation of chastity that made sense in a sexually hypocritical era, but that makes little sense today when the answer to the double standard appears to be not equal chastity but equal sexual freedom. Second, the form of European licensing was arbitrarily demeaning to women because it was clearly designed not for the realistic protection of the rights of prostitutes but for the protection of their male customers at all costs. However, the excesses of licensing in Europe are not decisive of the merits of a licensing scheme that would accommodate the rights of the prostitutes. Such a scheme, for example, could ensure adequate and fair protection in their business dealings without making regulatory authorities the moralistic and often sadistically retributive police, and could keep records of prostitutes absolutely confidential, destroying them when the prostitute leaves the profession. Third, the "white slave trade" argument appears to have been a moralistic attack on commercial sex per se, overstating and distorting the facts. Often the trade consisted of consenting mature adults who wished to travel to a foreign country to be prostitutes, not of underage girls or bound-and-gagged women. Of course, there are moral objections to international traffic in compulsory adult or voluntary underage prostitution, but there are moral objections to prostitution itself in these forms. If this was the object of the "white slave" opponents, it should have been addressed as such, not in the form of hysterically overbroad arguments that trenched on the rights of mature adults to determine where and how they would live.

The problem with licensing is not that there are good arguments against it, but that there are no powerful arguments for it. The argument of prophylaxis of venereal disease appears to be weak, as there is no compelling evidence that licensing realistically advances this end. Less restrictive alternatives are available that would more rationally do so. For example, cheap and non-coercive medical inspections that prostitutes would have strong incentives to use could be made available. Adequate protection of the rights of prostitutes and customers would be secured by fair enforcement of existing criminal laws against force and fraud. Probably the best way to aid prostitutes to protect themselves from unfair business dealings with customers and pimps would be to provide legal facilities in the form of unions of prostitutes that would bring the force of collective organizational self-protection to this atomistic profession.

In general, licensing is an appropriate prerequisite to valid exercise of a service profession when there is a long professional education and when incompetence in providing the service will disastrously affect the interests of customers. Prostitution does not appear to satisfy either of these conditions, although arguably the development of specialized classes of prostitutes (for example, specialists in initiating virgin youth into sex or in certain kinds of sexual and psychological therapy) might at some point reasonably be subject to some form of licensing on the grounds that special training is needed and that important customer interests are thus furthered.

B.   REGULATIONS OF PLACE, TIME, AND METHOD

In continental Europe and England, regulations of place, time, and method take two different forms. First, in England, street solicitation for prostitution is forbidden, so that solicitation takes place through ambiguously worded advertisements placed in various journals or in certain well-known locations. A likely motive for the English form of regulation may have been the desire not that prostitution cease to be centered in the well-known London theatre and shopping district where it has familiarly been located, but that it cease to take the form of the obtrusive solicitation that was distressing to many theatre-goers and shoppers who could not conveniently avoid exposure to unwelcome solicitations. The English solution was to end such street solicitations entirely, requiring customers and prostitutes to seek one another out by more discreet means. In continental Europe, the form of regulation appears to be some form of zoning whereby solicitation is legal only in certain well-known districts of the urban centers. In West Germany, Hamburg's famous Eros Center was intended to centralize prostitutes in one building complex. Such businesslike centralization appears to be unappealing to customers and prostitutes alike, but prostitutes do tend to cluster in certain parts of town.

In the event of decriminalization in the United States, the English solution would clearly be appealing in a city like New York where prostitution tends to cluster in the theatre district and where absolute prohibitions on solicitation would obviate the problem of obtrusive solicitation of people who cannot conveniently avoid presence in the district on other business. As in London, there might be an interest in concentrating prostitution in this area while attacking the problem of obtrusive solicitation. However, first amendment considerations in the United States might make the English solution of absolute prohibitions on solicitation unconstitutional. A more precise solicitation statute would have to be drawn in order to accommodate the interests of prostitutes and customers and at the same time secure the rights of others not to be subject to obtrusive solicitations. Obviously, much further study must be made of this matter.

Alternatively, the continental European solution could be explored. Forms of regulatory zoning could limit solicitation to certain well-known parts of town little frequented by people on other business so that the interests of customers and prostitutes could be accommodated and obtrusive solicitations minimized. Zoning of the solicitation for prostitution may be an importantly different question from zoning of the prostitution itself. There may be no reasonable objections to the former; obtrusive solicitations are not protected by the rights of the prostitute or the customer, and zoning is one reasonable way to accommodate the rights of all concerned without violating the rights of any. There may also be just grounds for zoning the business of prostitution itself, but the justification seems of a different kind. If the business of a prostitute involves no obtrusive solicitation (assume a quite discreet call girl), the business cannot be zoned to one area on the ground of protecting the rights of people not to be obtrusively solicited. The considerations that might justify such zoning are the same that justify barring certain businesses from residential neighborhoods, namely, avoiding certain kinds of business-associated noises and disturbances. Prostitution, as a form of commercial service, may be zoned on grounds applied in an even-handed way to other businesses. But in addition to appropriate forms of zoning and solicitation regulations, consideration should be given to a limitation of commercial sex to brothels, as is currently the case in Nevada. Such regulations, which are another form of licensing, are problematic in the absence of effective regulations protecting the economic and social rights of prostitutes and forms of unionization which would assure some measure of equal bargaining power to prostitutes. The European history of such regulated brothels is a sorry one. Certainly, forms of brothel are not, in principle, illegitimate. But to require that brothels be the only form of legitimate commercial sex seems unwarranted.

C. Laissez-Faire

Finally, one may suggest a regime of laissez-faire. After decriminalization, there would be no licensing, nor any regulation, but only the application of existing criminal laws against force and fraud. The argument against forms of time, place, and manner regulation might suggest that such regulations are unnecessary. For all practical purposes, solicitations for prostitution occur in familiar locations where no reasonable person can claim surprise. Furthermore, the presence of prostitution is, on balance, one of the colorful amenities of life in large urban centers. It should not be hidden and isolated, but robustly accepted as what in fact it is: an inextricable part of urban life. In this view, forms of regulation are hypocritical and moralistic subterfuges of irresponsible politicians who seek to accomplish by isolation what they cannot legitimately achieve by prohibition. While these arguments for laissez-faire do understate the sound reasons for regulation, they raise a central question that we should discuss in conclusion: what are the general advantages of the availability of commercial sexual services?

Chapter 7

ALCOHOL

A. HISTORICAL BACKGROUND

RICHARD HAMM—SHAPING THE EIGHTEENTH AMENDMENT: TEMPERANCE, REFORM, LEGAL CULTURE, AND THE POLITY, 1880–1920

Chapel Hill: University of North Carolina Press (1995).

The American polity in the last quarter of the nineteenth century saw both the rebirth of the prohibition movement and the emergence of the manufacture and sale of liquor as one of the nation's leading industries. Conflict between the two was inevitable. But the ideas of the prohibition movement, the qualities and actions of the drys' opponents, and the nature of the polity channeled that conflict into certain courses. A radical temperance ideology with its allied Mosaic legal culture predominated within the temperance crusade in the last two decades of the century. The drys' ideology and legal notions made it difficult for them to achieve much success in the American polity dominated by formal and informal rules administered by political parties and courts. Yet the popularity of temperance allowed drys to establish beachhead prohibition states. The liquor industry, after failing to block the adoption of prohibition in these states, challenged the policy in the federal courts. These legal confrontations set the parameters for the next three decades of liquor law struggles.

As old as the republic, temperance was a quintessential American reform. At the time of the Revolution, some leading figures, most notably Benjamin Rush, advised Americans to moderate their consumption of liquor. The early agitators focused on the relatively new distilled spirits, advocating that people drink the less powerful fermented and brewed beverages. Their appeals to the citizenry had little effect. By the early nineteenth century per capita consumption of alcohol ran at least two times the modern average. Use of liquor pervaded American life. Most of the population, from youth to old age, consumed it, often at every meal from breakfast through supper. It was common practice to drink at every social event and even at work.

But the havoc that liquor worked in American life caused many to advocate temperance. Thus, in the early part of the nineteenth century, liquor lost its legitimate role in many parts of American society. The Second Great Awakening altered many middle-class Americans' view of alcoholic beverages. Going beyond the ideas of the earlier agitators, the new evangelicals saw liquor not as a necessary and benign part of life, but as an evil influence that threatened to weaken society by destroying individuals. They abstained from spirits themselves and sought to convince others to do so. In the 1840s the Washingtonians—a working-class temperance movement—emerged in the cities and spread across the nation. Members of this organization signed a temperance pledge not to drink any alcoholic liquors. In the next decade the pledge idea spread into the middle class, with the birth of other total-abstinence organizations. One of them, the Order of Good Templars, proclaimed their freedom from spirits by donning white ribbons and thus created the enduring symbol of the temperance movement. But moral suasion did not eliminate alcohol from American society, and this fact drove some temperance reformers to advocate legal means of controlling liquor.

One legal means, state prohibition of liquor, became the goal of many antialcohol reformers. Between 1851 and 1855 thirteen states adopted prohibition. The drys even proposed writing prohibitory clauses into state constitutions to assure that the policy would prevail. But in many states, court rulings undermined the effective enforcement of these laws; in two states the highest courts declared the measures unconstitutional. Furthermore, the rise of the Republican party, which avoided prohibition while promoting temperance, and the Civil War's effect of diverting the energies of the "moral reform forces" stopped, and then reversed, prohibition progress. By the end of the war, only five states maintained their prohibition laws; a decade later only Maine, New Hampshire, and Vermont continued as dry states with admittedly lax enforcement. This early antiliquor agitation shared parallels with other reforms.

The pattern of action shown by the temperance crusade in the early and middle nineteenth century corresponded roughly to the path followed by antigambling advocates. These reformers shared the drys' motivation, the goal of banning of a common social practice, and a similar decline during the sectional crisis. Before 1800 gambling was endemic in American society; indeed, colonial and early republic governments as well as private companies engaged in public works used lotteries extensively. In the early nineteenth century religious groups began to criticize lotteries, focusing on their abuses and urging people not to gamble. The Second Great Awakening added fuel to this antigambling movement and inspired it to urge the abolition of lotteries. Under this pressure, states began first to refuse licenses to new lotteries and then to ban them. By 1840 twelve states prohibited lotteries, and the movement put them on the defensive. But the war and Reconstruction slowed the campaign against lotteries, as they thrived in states where they were still legal and reappeared in some states where they had been outlawed as a means of raising revenue. The Louisiana State Lottery Company, created in 1868, became a powerhouse in that state's government and widely engaged in its trade against other states. Thus in the postwar period, reformers resumed their offensive against gambling.

The experience of temperance and antigambling reforms points to the fundamental fact that in this era, when moral reformers wished to accomplish something, they turned first to the state governments. For instance, another reform, the pure food movement, began at the state level. Lawyer George Thorndike Angell led the late-nineteenth-century pure food movement. Angell, who shared the religious values of the prohibitionists, came to the cause through his work against animal cruelty. His goal was to create an abolitionist-style crusade to purify the nation's food; he began his work at the state level. This common pattern underscores the decentralized nature of the American polity before the war. After the war, these early crusades reverberated in a changed American society.

The first temperance crusade made liquor drinking a public issue and changed Americans' drinking habits. Liquor lost its predominance as a drink for all occasions; when many had abandoned spirits, it became harder to include it in all activities. Thus, following the war, liquor consumption became centered in saloons. In 1873 about 100,000 of these establishments dotted the landscape. In 1890 cities with over 50,000 in population had a saloon for every 250 inhabitants. Besides their chief purpose of selling liquor, they served many important social functions on the frontiers and in the cities. But in doing so, they violated the most reasonable of restrictions, such as the prohibition on sales to minors, earning unsavory reputations. Nineteenth-century Americans sensitive to the liquor issue saw that drinking exacerbated certain illnesses, diverted income destined for subsistence, and led, in many cases, to violence and misery. They thought that banning liquor would alleviate, if not solve, these many social problems. These facts and arguments struck some Americans harder than others.

In the late nineteenth century, religious affiliation and ethnicity predisposed many to see prohibition as a viable method of controlling the general disorder in society, and others to perceive it as foolish and dangerous governmental meddling in people's lives. In particular, pietists, members of evangelical sects, including Baptists, Methodists, and Presbyterians, whose religions rested on the bedrock of conversation and good behavior, saw prohibition as a needed corrective to the nation's moral laxity and resulting social problems. Liturgicals—Catholics, Episcopalians, and German Lutherans, espousing religions that emphasized belief over action—did not find prohibition an appealing method of remedying social ills. Since religion followed ethnic lines, old-stock Americans—of English and Scottish heritage—and some Scandinavian immigrants and their children more often supported prohibition than the Irish, German, Italian, and Polish immigrants, along with their descendants. The settling of immigrants in the cities added urban and rural dimensions to the division between wet and dry. Thus a cluster of factors—religious ideology, ethnic tradition, and place of residence—combined to create two different worldviews, which found alcohol use either acceptable or abhorrent.

In the second half of the nineteenth century, despite the influx of immigrants and the collapse of state prohibition laws, temperance sentiment did not disappear. The temperance organizations, especially the Order of Good Templars and the newly founded National Temperance Society and Publication House (established in 1865) attempted to counteract the erosion of prohibitionist support. Their efforts centered on building favorable public opinion, chiefly through the publication of propaganda. Yet moral suasion did not forestall the repeal of state prohibition laws. So many drys determined to go beyond temperance tracts and speeches. From the rubble of the first, a second crusade emerged, becoming a national force in the 1880s. The revived temperance movement built a new structure on the antebellum reformers' foundation of moral suasion and legal remedies. New organizations, the National Prohibition party and the Woman's Christian Temperance Union, proposing programs more sweeping than the earlier reforms, dominated this second wave of temperance activity. Many drys blamed the earlier agitators' reversals on the political power of the liquor interests and entered politics to combat the influence of what they called the liquor traffic. In the wake of the organization of state prohibition parties in Michigan, Illinois, and Ohio, an 1869 convention called and attended by prominent prohibitionists launched the National Prohibition party. Dry distrust of the major parties, which largely ignored temperance reform, led to their forming a party dedicated to prohibition. They did so on their own terms; radical drys defined a political party idealistically as "an agreement of some number of people upon" public issues.

The formation of a new party underscores the difficulties the drys suffered in attempting to influence the polity to adopt their program. Other reformers of the period who shared similar origins, enunciated similar ideologies, and proposed abolishing other evils did not form political parties. They had no need to because the existing parties met their demands and they faced no organized opposition. For instance, the vice societies that sprang up in American cities in the 1870s—such as the New York Society for the Suppression of Vice and the Boston-based Watch and the Ward Society—remained societies and did not become political parties. Like the drys, members of these organizations, driven by religious and social values, sought to repress what they saw as a social evil. There was a close convergence between dry and vice-society ideas; for example, both movements believed, in the words of Anthony Comstock, that "private interests must be subservient to the general interests of the community" and that action was necessary "to prevent the moral diseases which lead to misery and crime." But the opponents of vice societies were "religious liberals and advocates of freedom of the press," which constituted a "small unheeded minority." Thus the existing parties acceded to the enactment and enforcement of stricter anti-obscenity laws; through reformers; agitation twenty-two states enacted general obscenity laws and another twenty-four banned birth control and abortion information. But the major parties rejected the prohibitionists, and given the constraints of the polity, they were forced to form their own party.

The Prohibition party emerged as the leading temperance organization in the 1870s and 1880s. Looking to what they perceived as the antislavery success of the 1850s, they believed that their efforts could destroy the current party system and give birth to a new political era dominated by a party favorable to prohibition. It never succeeded in its grandiose plan to reshape the party system. Its members came primarily from the temperance wing of the Republican party. While it failed to become a true national organization, it gained strength in the northeastern and midwestern states, traditional bastions of Republicanism. The party grew sporadically from the 1870s into 1890s, responding to state Republican organizations' stands on prohibition. Where the Republicans retreated on the issue, the Prohibition party gained votes, reaching its electoral zenith in 1892, when it gleaned over a quarter of a million votes. Its chief accomplishment was proselytizing; through its platforms and candidates the Prohibition party brought the liquor issue into the public eye. The party also took the lead in the articulating and refining of prohibitionist ideas and programs. But the party was never able to defeat the liquor interests in the political arena or curtail the sale of liquor.

After the war, the first temperance advocates to confront liquor sellers directly and demand a halt to alcohol sales were middle-class women of over four hundred midwestern villages, towns, and cities. In the winter of 1873–74 groups of women knelt in the snow before saloons and exhorted the proprietors and patrons to abandon "demon rum." The successes of these "women's crusades" in closing saloons and in capturing the nation's attention opened the eyes of many to the possibilities of direct action against the liquor interests. Overnight women organized temperance unions to channel female energy into the struggle. The next winter these local organizations federated into the National Women's Christian Temperance Union.

Paradoxically, building the WCTU organization diverted the women's energy from frontal assaults on liquor dealers. The women worked industriously, and in the 1880s the WCTU emerged as the nation's largest women's group. The WCTU's founders followed the pattern of trade unions in erecting an elaborate organizational structure. Each participating community had at least one union, formed under the authority of a state union. State organizations, while affiliated closely with the National WCTU, were in theory autonomous. In operation personality overcame these structural bonds.

The dynamic and charismatic Frances Willard, president of the National WCTU from 1879 to her death in 1898, dominated the formal organization and personally influenced the WCTU's rank and file as well as many other American women. Where Willard led they followed

Willard endorsed a "do everything" program that included women's suffrage, temperance education in schools, rights for laborers, and from 1884 to 1898 support of the Prohibition party. Since the lack of the franchise limited its political effectiveness, the WCTU's political program boiled down to lobbying legislators and circulating petitions. Thus, like the Prohibition party, the WCTU centered its efforts on turning public opinion against the liquor traffic.

The efforts of the Prohibition party and the WCTU in organizing and campaigning for prohibitionist candidates, along with their active programs of moral suasion, brought their message to the people. The extent of their activities was startling: John St. John, the 1884 Prohibitionist candidate for president, took to the lecture circuit in the late 1880s and by 1896 had delivered over 3,500 speeches. Frances Willard, Sallie Chapin, and other prominent white ribboners (members of the WCTU took the Templars' symbol as their own) kept a similar pace. During the late 1880s and early 1890s drys founded no fewer than three major weekly newspapers. By 1890 the party's papers (the *Voice* and the *Lever*) and the official WCTU newspaper (the *Union Signal*) had a combined subscribership of over 100,000. The success of these efforts in building public sentiment favorable to prohibition can be measured by the revival of agitation for state prohibition laws.

In 1875 just three prohibition states (Maine, New Hampshire, and Vermont) remained from the first temperance wave. By 1890 a second surge doubled the number of dry states, with Kansas, North Dakota, and South Dakota joining the fold. Iowa and Rhode Island also adopted prohibition but quickly repudiated the policy. Moreover, between 1880 and 1890, prohibition became a serious issue before the legislatures of at least fourteen other states. In some states, legislatures referred the issue to the public through referenda, and 46 percent of those voting in all the referenda held in that decade favored prohibition. Yet the widespread popularity of the cause did not transfer to the major temperance organizations. Most Americans considered the members of the Prohibition party and the WCTU to be extremists, and many denounced them as fanatics; the drys' ideology contributed to this negative impression of the movement.

A radical ideology dominated the national temperance organizations of the 1880s and 1890s. Radicals embraced an absolutist ideology and a crusading style. They followed the "radicalism of principle" and were "as constant in their devotion to the cause as the needle to the pole" because "the magnetism of right" directed them. For them, liquor, the embodiment of evil and sin, needed to be totally removed from society; they recognized no middle ground. Their views stemmed from the Christian heritage of come-outerism, combined with their perceptions that the liquor regulation programs of the 1870s and early 1880s had sorely failed to control demon rum. Support of total prohibition, rejection of all "halfway measures," hostility toward established party politics, and a conscious patterning of themselves on the abolitionists marked the philosophy and strategy of the radical prohibition movement.

The ancillary reforms supported by the radical prohibitionists revealed the extent of their radicalism. While not socialists or economic radicals, they advocated a host of other reforms. These reforms centered on the common theme of protecting the family, the key institution of Christian civilization, from the forces of corruption. For drys, threats to family order came under the rubric of "immoral influence" and spurred them to opposition. Thus they favored legislation prohibiting gambling, tobacco, and pornography; promoted uniform divorce laws; and engaged in near-hysterical denunciations of the Mormon Church. Likewise, prohibitionist support of trust busting, the eight-hour day, profit sharing, and other far-ranging changes in the economic structure during the late 1880s and early 1890s also grew from fears that untrammeled capitalism endangered the foundations of Christian civilization. In sum, prohibition radicals were social crusaders who only embraced absolutist positions. They regarded elimination of evil as the only acceptable solution.

Radical prohibitionists saw liquor as a national sin, requiring a national solution. Drawing on Calvinist theology, the *Union Signal* summarized this view: "The evil is a national evil, the sin of perpetuating it is a national sin; God deals with nations as nations, and accepts no action of isolated members as expiation for the nation's sin." This view separated drys from the mainstream of American public opinion. Most Americans agreed with the *New York Times'* assessment of temperance: "The liquor question can hardly be called a national question." The prophet of national prohibition was Republican senator Henry W. Blair of New Hampshire, whom the *Times* characterized as a political prohibitionist save in name. Blair repeatedly called for a national prohibition amendment implemented through congressional legislation because he feared that piecemeal state prohibition would not be sufficient to curb the national liquor traffic. He argued that, under the current Constitution, wet states would contaminate dry utopias and that no state alone could limit interstate and foreign importation of liquor. In a stand similar to that of the Garrisonian abolitionists, he called the organic law of the nation corrupt: "The constitution ... as it now is ... is a law for the unrestricted manufacture, sale, importation, exportation, and internal transportation of intoxicating liquors. It is the great legal fortress of intemperance in this country." Only by amendment, ceding part of the states' police powers to the national government, and subsequent legislation could national prohibition be achieved.

In the 1880s Blair's conceptions and arguments for a strong national policy against drink became the cornerstone of the Prohibition party; from the party they spread throughout the movement to become the credo of the radicals. By the end of the 1870s, the WCTU, the Prohibition party, and most drys had abandoned "compromise measures" in dealing with the liquor traffic. They had replaced the "little schemes and halfway measures" with one solution: total national constitutional prohibition of the manufacture and sale of liquor. The radicals believed that, besides the practical benefits of removing prohibition from the "vagaries of every election," a constitutional amendment elevated their policy to the "highest attainable degree" of authority. It invoked the "dignity and power" of the nation. In their view their position was "comprehensive and complete."

Temperance radicals renounced any measure but total prohibition. There could be "no compromise with wrong," and "separation from sin" was a necessity. They rejected regulation in all forms. For them there was "a law of gravitation in morals as well as nature," and any contact with sin led "steeply downward till the end is reached." Any other "palliative legislation" was "wrong in principle." The drys seriously wished to apply the scriptural passage "touch not the unclean thing" to state and federal regulation of liquor. They believed that governments should disassociate themselves from the liquor trade. Regulation merely created "a moneyed compromise on the part of government," conferring legitimacy on the alcohol industry. To make their point, drys cited other instances in which the government had renounced its association with evil. For example, New York lawyer Herbert Shattuck, after denouncing the liquor traffic as the worst evil of the day, causing more "pauperism and immorality" than "all other evils together," asked, "What shall be done about it?" He followed this query with a series of rhetorical questions: "What was done about slavery, and the lottery, and polygamy? What is the attitude of government toward all public evils?" Then he supplied radical answers: regulation was no solution, as it would not remove the evils "inherent in the business or in the liquor itself." Only prohibition would be the moral solution for society. Following this reasoning, the radicals objected to the federal liquor tax (see Chapter 3) and the state policies of high license and local option.

In the late 1880s and in the 1890s, the radical prohibitionists violently denounced the policy of high license. The high license program imposed exceptionally high license fees on wholesalers and retailers of liquor and also limited the number of such outlets. Ancillary provisions in most licensing legislation prohibited Sunday operations, sales to minors, and the employment of "immoral" persons. In the late 1870s and early 1880s, many prohibitionists supported the high license as a step in the proper direction. High license proponents contended that these restrictions assured a minimum of respectability in the liquor trade. The Republican party attempted to court the temperance vote by advocating high license, and in attempts to forestall prohibition the liquor manufacturers supported high license. As a result, the Republican party and the industry became identified with the policy. The rise of absolutist thinking and the dissatisfaction among temperance forces with the Republicans turned the movement against "seductive" high license.

The radicals based some of their opposition to high license on the liquor industry's support of it, but more important was its failure to lead to total prohibition. Their opposition centered in their abolitionist principles. The Prohibition party reduced its opposition to a banner in its 1888 convention: "No Evil can be Exterminated by Selling it the Right to Exist." Along the same lines, radicals responded to the claim "a license law is partial prohibition" with the rejoinder "a partial prohibition means a partial permission." High license was "nothing else than a recognition of the liquor dealers' claim" to legitimacy. It was "the monopoly of abomination," and it made the "community itself a rumseller." Indeed, "licensing the liquor traffic" lowered the "moral tone of the community." An article in the *Cyclopaedia of Temperance and Prohibition* on the ethics of licensing determined that it was in essence unethical. Establishing the saloon as an honest business, the radicals argued, only increased its evils. One sin would lead to others. They believed prostitution so endemic to high license establishments that they reduced their belief to a phrase: "Low license says, give me your son; high license says, give me your daughter also." The dry assumption that prostitution and high license went together was probably deepened by the attempts of urban reformers in the early 1870s to institute systems of regulated prostitution. Such attempts only made abolitionist reformers more suspicious of instituting any progress through regulation. In sum, the nature of high license was permissive, not restrictive, and therefore unworthy of prohibitionist support.

Similarly, the radical prohibitionists also attacked local option. A state local option law usually authorized the people of any township, county, city, or precinct to decide in a special election to allow liquor sales in their locality. In the 1870s and early 1880s drys supported this policy; their struggles and victories in local option campaigns—usually in this period framed in terms of granting or denying the local authority power to issue liquor licenses—helped define the movement. Ironically, what emerged was a radical movement, which, although it still used local option, found it tainted. Like high license, local option failed the critical criterion—absoluteness. According to the *Cyclopaedia of Temperance and Prohibition*, "Local option grew up as a kind of natural fungus upon the license system stock." It remained a "compromise measure" because it permitted the liquor traffic to flourish where localities voted wet. The survival of wet enclaves, especially in the cities, made the policy "too local" and "too optional" for the radicals. Their questioning of local option elections exposed the thinness of their commitment to majority rule. "No government ought to leave to the vicious, ignorant masses the option of deciding whether they shall have a traffic which makes them more ignorant and vicious," said the *Union Signal* in 1889. The radicals asserted that local option stripped the morality from law, substituting mere changeable majorities for God's "unchanging" and "all-pervading" law. Since compromise with sin was unthinkable, absolute prohibition, decreed by a higher law, was the only solution. The radicals, unlike drys still in the major political parties, contemplated "no other side—no alternative."

The radical prohibitionists' hostility toward party politics distinguished them from more moderate temperance advocates. They found that traditional party loyalty, which they labeled worship before "the mightiest God in the United States ... the party fetich," impeded temperance reform. The major parties were "hopelessly unwilling to adopt an adequate policy toward prohibition." Thus, many radicals joined or supported the Prohibition party. Its very nature guaranteed the party's radicalism, but the WCTU was not always so committed. From 1884 to 1898 the National WCTU endorsed temperance radicalism and the party, but this action provoked dissent and eventually split the organization. In an age of strong party loyalties, cutting the ties to major political parties symbolized the radical nature of the dry position.

The radicals vented their spleen on both parties. Most prohibition radicals saw no hope of instituting temperance reform under the auspices of the Democratic party. Its record was bad in the eyes of the prohibitionists; in the 1870s Democratic victories prompted the repeal of prohibitory legislation in five states. The *Cyclopaedia of Temperance and Prohibition*, while admitting the existence of a few local exceptions in the south, characterized the national Democratic party as the "special champion and protector of the liquor interests." The party existed as "the avowed and persevering opponent of prohibitory legislation." The radicals did not find the Republicans to be more congenial. In 1881 a temperance speaker asserted that the only difference between the two was that "Republicans drink wine at the Fifth Avenue Hotel, and Democrats 'bug juice' at the distilleries, the latter ending up in the station house and the former going home in coaches."

If anything, the radicals reserved their strongest venom for the Republicans. Typical of these attacks was a description of the 1892 Republican National Convention as "a period of the most stupendous debauchery known in all of the extended history of drunkenness." No gathering, not even a "brewers' congress ... has been more famous in its continued maudlin carousal than has characterized this national convention of the grand old party of temperance and reform." Republican Vice President Levi Morton's ownership of a restaurant with a liquor license earned him the prohibitionist epithet of "Rumseller Morton." Republican espousal of liquor regulation, not prohibition, angered the radicals. The Republicans' long association with reform and the Prohibition party's origins as a Republican splinter group deepened radical hostility. They guarded constantly against the allure of the old party. For example, the *Union Signal* asserted that the plank in the 1892 Republican platform expressing sympathy with temperance reform was meaningless "soundings of brass and tinkling cymbals."

In general, the major political parties dismissed prohibitionists as dangerous fanatics who advocated unrealistic plans: "they are people whose sentiments and emotions are too much for their reason." The Democrats—committed to limited government and localism and opposed to moral experiments—remained ideologically opposed to prohibition, and their large foreign-born constituency reinforced this view. The Democratic *Richmond Times* concluded that the prohibitionists' "single-idea party" was doomed to fail because "the majority of the voters will not join" a party that wished to eliminate "the habit" most voters practiced. The Democratic party also liked to attack the Republican party for its courting of the drys, tarring it as a proponent of what it labeled "sumptuary legislation."

The prohibition revival presented the Republicans with a dilemma. In brief, rejecting prohibition would alienate many of their supporters, while promoting it would anger the equally important German–American wing of their party and might rouse the electorate against them. In the 1880s divisions between wet and dry Republicans rent the party in traditional Republican strongholds. Afraid to act, they presented the issue to the people. The 1886 Republican platforms in ten states endorsed referenda on the question. In states that were already dry the Republican party stood on platforms favoring law enforcement, not prohibition. The party refused to support prohibition openly. Fearing the Prohibition party might erode their own electoral base, they worked to undercut the drys. For instance, during the 1888 campaign, Republicans obtained the subscription list of the *Voice* and mailed propaganda to the subscribers. In essence, both parties—in different ways—tried to make political hay from the prohibition issue without giving in to the radical prohibitionists.

Given the major parties' dominance of state and national legislatures, the radicals were unsuccessful in the legislative arena. For instance, neither the white ribboners nor the party played any role in the greatest victory for their cause in the 1880s, the adoption of constitutional prohibition by Kansas. Radicals exacerbated their difficulties by spending inordinate effort on lambasting the legislatures for public "carousals" or for allowing the sale of liquor in assembly buildings. They also mocked the actions taken by legislatures. "The Ohio Legislature has 'got its courage up to the sticking point'; and has actually prohibited the sale and use of—the toy pistol." Such attacks assured that radical dry programs would be poorly received by the professional politicians who controlled the legislatures. Thus while they bemoaned the political power of the liquor interests, the radicals undercut their ability to compete directly with the liquor lobby. Prohibitionist victories in the states came about primarily through the efforts of local drys who subverted Republican state parties to their own ends. The radical ideology of the national dry organizations proved more a hindrance than a help.

That they did not fare well before the policymakers did not upset the drys. The radicals comforted themselves with their conception of themselves as latter-day abolitionists, guardians of the truth that would eventually sweep the nation. They argued that "in the fifties it was the oppressed negro" who "aroused public sentiment" and that in the 1880s and 1890s it would be the "innocent victims of the liquor traffic" who would spark another purifying crusade. The attraction to antislavery was natural, as many temperance reformers of the antebellum period were sympathetic to abolition if not abolitionists. Similarly, the radicals portrayed the liquor industry as analogous to the slave power. "The liquor traffic is like the slave traffic. . . . It will not submit to restriction and legal supervisions; it is arrogant, defiant, and independent." Beyond reviving memories of past successes, this self-glorifying image emphasized the crusading nature of their movement.

In their accounts the drys blurred pure abolition with the political anti-slavery of the 1850s. This enabled them to claim Phillips, Garrison, and Lincoln as progenitors of their own crusade. It also justified their using the sectional crisis and Northern victory in the Civil War in their propaganda. A phrase in the Prohibition party's 1872 platform, "the abolition of those foul enormities, polygamy and the social evil," recalled the language of the 1856 Republican platform, which condemned "those twin relics of barbarism—polygamy and slavery." Every judicial setback for temperance became another "Dred Scot decision." the prohibitionists honored the Republican party "for its past" but believed it had failed to foster further reforms and therefore needed replacement. Just as the destruction of the Whigs had advanced the cause of antislavery, the radical prohibitionists argued that the collapse of the Republicans would promote prohibition. Most of all, the past provided powerful images of hope. In decrying the striking down of the Iowa prohibition constitutional amendment by the state supreme court, the state WCTU declared, "We had our Bull Run Disaster before we had vanquished Richmond." This type of retelling of history comforted the drys, assuring them that prohibition "will follow as inevitably as abolition came."

The prohibitionists attempted, by constant agitation, to bring about what they hoped was the inevitable. Beyond speeches, tracts, and newspapers they sought to spread the word by example. Radical drys devoted much time and energy to the creation of permanent temperance institutions—such as temperance hotels—and the founding of utopian prohibition communities. Their purpose was to convince the public of the benefits of temperance and prohibition. In the late nineteenth century various drys founded a number of temperance towns—Greely in Colorado, Palo Alto in California, Harvey near Chicago, and Vineland in New Jersey. But three other ventures were associated directly with national radical organizations: the Women's Temple in Chicago, Prohibition Park in Staten Island, and the dry town of Harriman, Tennessee. In each case the leaders of the Prohibition party and the WCTU directly promoted these schemes. These enterprises were a visible manifestation of the radical prohibition spirit.

In 1887 the Chicago and National WCTUs began planning the construction of a Chicago office building. Its name, the Women's Temple, revealed that this was more than another commercial structure. Drys conceived the Gothic-style, twelve-story building as a temperance response to the lavish structures erected by the liquor industry. Although its builders intended the Women's Temple to provided needed office space for the WCTU and anticipated its financial success, these were not its major purposes. To the officers, and especially to the rank and file, the Women's Temple became a tangible symbol of what women could accomplish outside the home. As one wrote, "My heart throbbed with delight that it was a woman's work that planned and completed such an undertaking." White ribboners showed their ardor for the undertaking by donating over one quarter of a million dollars to the Women's Temple. Beyond symbolizing woman in the public sphere, the WCTUs expected the Women's Temple to bring the message of prohibition and home protection into the financial capital of the Midwest. They missed few opportunities to proselytize. In 1890, at the laying of the cornerstone, 2000 children bearing banners marched through the Loop chanting, "Saloons, Saloons, Saloons must go." The building's auditorium, Willard Hall, was the physical incarnation of the dry women's desire to spread the word.

The leaders of the Prohibition party shared the proselytizing spirit of their sisters who planned the Women's Temple. On the Fourth of July 1888, they opened Prohibition Park on Staten Island. As conceived by the party's leaders, especially Issac K. Funk, the nature park and open air auditorium, "supplied by springs of pure water," were not another "money-making scheme" but rather "a grand enterprise to bless humanity by establishing an educational center to advance the cause of reform and prohibition." The promoters' vision quickly expanded as they decided to surround the park with a temperance town of summer homes. They sought to attract "New York business people" to what they advertised as a cross between Chautauqua and Ocean Grove. Like any real estate promoter, the radical prohibitionists lauded the park's ideal location, scenic beauty, superior transportation system, fine utilities, low taxes, and resale value. Initially their plans succeeded, and while they were trying to expand the park into a full-time prohibition community, they also decided to extend their real estate ventures.

Soon after the founding of Prohibition Park, many of its founders decided to establish an industrial town that would serve as a prohibition utopia. They intended to educate through action, proving that the "practical result of prohibition" was prosperity. They chose to build their dream town in east Tennessee, an area with abundant natural resources located in a state with a unique law that prohibited the sale liquor within four miles of a schoolhouse in unincorporated areas. This law would protected their venture in its infancy before it developed a government. In October 1889 they organized the East Tennessee Land Company. Within months they had purchased several thousand acres and laid out the town of Harriman. Once established, they key to guaranteeing prohibition in their town lay in the company's special restrictive title deeds. They required "every contract, deed or other conveyance to lease of real estate" to "contain a proviso" forbidding "the use of the property, or any building there on, for the purpose of making, storing, or selling intoxicating beverages." Advertised heavily in the prohibition press, this scheme enthralled drys. Prohibitionists and others flocked to the opening sale, and the company sold 573 lots for over $600,000. Subsequent sales and bond offers, while less spectacular, were also successful. These prohibition and industrial dreams flourished, and by July 1891 Harriman boasted several factories, fifty stores, three hundred dwellings, four churches, and two WCTUs. The creation of such experiments underscores the insular nature of the radical dry movement.

In general, the radical prohibitionists' isolation from the major political parties, their aping of the crusading style of the abolitionists, and their obsession with absolute purity compelled them to lead the temperance movement down the path of pure agitation. Their ideology did not make them effective manipulators of the parts of the polity controlled by the major political parties. And their legal culture made them equally maladroit in handling the legal environment.

B. PROHIBITION, ITS CAUSES, COSTS, AND AFTERMATH

As the previous selection indicated, the road to Prohibition was more complex than is often assumed today; as we shall see, its reality and legacy do not always match expectations either. Indeed, debates over exactly what Prohibition was—An attempt to implement social policy via the Constitution? A response to other impulses in American society?—have yet to be resolved.

DONALD BOUDREAUX AND A.C. PRITCHARD— THE PRICE OF PROHIBITION
36 Ariz. L. Rev. 1 (Spring 1994).

The standard account of alcohol prohibition in America focuses exclusively on ideology. Specifically, the story goes, vast numbers of citizens were so overcome with Progressive hubris that they set forth on a futile quest to mandate morality by banning the manufacture and sale of liquor. Within a few years, the folly of such moral legislation became transparent. Chastened by their experience, the American people abandoned their "noble experiment" in social engineering.

Public-choice theory offers a different vantage point from which to evaluate this standard account. Public-choice theory, consistent with other economic disciplines, focuses on self-interest—especially pecuniary self-interest—as the driving force behind political behavior and outcomes. Ideology carries little weight in typical public-choice analysis of legislation or regulation. Thus, a traditional public-choice explanation of prohibition and its repeal would eschew any reliance on ideological factors. A richer and more robust public-choice approach, however, can incorporate ideology in bringing economics to bear on the question of prohibition.

To put our general point simply, ideology matters to self-interested politicians when ideology matters to their constituents. Insofar as their constituents are willing to pay—in money and votes—for ideological legislation, politicians are willing to supply it. This approach recognizes that politicians protect their seats by seeking contributions and re-election votes in *two* conceptually distinct ways: (1) through taxation or regulation that redistributes wealth from politically ineffective groups to politically influential groups, or (2) through "social" legislation designed not so much to redistribute wealth, but, rather, to further ideological causes favored by well-organized interest groups. These two methods of securing votes are largely fungible; and indeed, in certain circumstances, they may well complement each other. If an organized interest group opposes a particular activity on ideological grounds, politicians who reduce that activity (or the appearance of that activity) through taxation or regulation will win the political support of this interest group. At the same time, politicians gain the support of other interest groups who have no ideological qualms with the activity but whose economic interests are served by the tax or regulation. Where the two methods conflict, however, economic theory predicts that politicians will trade off one against the other to maximize re-election chances.

Alcohol prohibition and its subsequent repeal offer a classic historical case of politicians' conflict between their desire to tax and regulate and their interest in serving well-organized ideological movements. Given that the temperance movement had been pressing for alcohol prohibition since the mid-nineteenth century, why did Congress wait until December 1917 to formally outlaw alcohol? And why did Congress repeal the prohibition amendment just fourteen years after its ratification?

In this Essay, we argue that the federal income tax played a central role, albeit behind the scenes, in the proposal and ratification of both the Eighteenth and the Twenty-first Amendments. The income tax proved a viable alternative to liquor taxation for raising revenue, thus making prohibition possible. To be sure, the ideology of voters and politicians mattered, but Congress could not afford the cost in foregone tax revenue (hence, foregone wealth redistribution) that an ideological vote for prohibition entailed until the income tax demonstrated its revenue-raising potential. The income tax's revenue prowess reduced the pain of an ideological vote for prohibition to a bearable level by filling in for foregone liquor tax revenues. Fourteen years later, that pain became unbearable: incomes dove precipitously and Congress unexpectedly found itself in need of an alternative revenue source. Thus, the quest for tax revenue—not any change in the nation's moral sense—drove prohibition's repeal.

I.   The Eighteenth Amendment

Prior to the advent of the modern income tax in 1913, the federal government relied mainly on liquor taxation and customs duties to generate revenues. Data from 1870 on (see Figure 1) show that customs duties and liquor taxes were the main revenue sources for the federal government until America entered World War I. Liquor taxes trailed only customs duties as the largest single source of revenues during the previous half-century, accounting for about a third of federal government revenues during the several decades leading up to W.W.I.

During the war, however, government revenues received through income taxation exceeded revenues extracted from any other single source for the first time. Figure 2 shows, for 1910 through 1920, the percentage of total federal government revenues derived from the taxation of incomes and profits. Income taxes went from supplying about 16% of the federal government's revenues in 1916 to supplying double that proportion in 1917. By 1918, as Figure 2 shows, the income tax supplied almost two-thirds of the revenue gathered by the federal government.

Income tax revenues accelerated most dramatically in 1918 (in terms of dollars raised), but the income tax had already demonstrated its prodigious revenue potential by 1917. The volume of 1917 receipts nearly tripled the 1916 level. More importantly, Congress passed in October 1917—two months before it successfully proposed the Eighteenth Amendment—the legislation that would yield 1918's enormous increase in income tax receipts. Congress predicted with considerable accuracy the amount of income tax receipts generated by the War Revenue Act of 1917. Congress believed the Act would raise $2.5 billion annually; and, indeed, the Act raised more than $2.3 billion in 1918.

By the fall of 1917, Congress saw the income tax as the chief source of federal government revenue. Consequently, the income tax's recognized ability to raise substantial government revenue reduced the cost to Congressmen of voting for prohibition in December 1917: liquor tax revenues lost as a result of prohibition (which went into effect on January 16, 1920) were trivial in comparison with the rapidly growing revenues derived from the individual and corporate income taxes. Thus, politicians had more than ample funds for the wealth redistributions necessary to secure re-election votes and contributions. By lowering the cost of voting for prohibition, the income tax tipped the balance in politicians' cost-benefit calculus in favor of voting dry. The temperance movement's long quest was seemingly brought to a triumphant conclusion.

II. THE TWENTY-FIRST AMENDMENT

In the immediate post-W.W.I period, Congressmen were finally able to satisfy the prohibitionists' social agenda without unduly hampering their ability to distribute tax revenues and, thus secure votes. Prohibition's costs increased not long afterward, however, and the Eighteenth Amendment was repealed in 1933. The conventional explanation of the Twenty-first Amendment's ratification emphasizes prohibition's unworkability: prohibition no longer reflected the sentiments of The People, and the federal government did not have the resources necessary to stamp out all alcohol distribution in the face of widespread defiance. While this explanation is plausible, it fails to adequately explain why Congress repealed the Eighteenth Amendment after such a short trial run, particularly in the light of the dearth of organized support for repeal during the 1920's. We submit that Congress proposed the Twenty-first Amendment in February 1933, not merely as a faithful agent in response to the wishes of the citizenry at large, nor as a faithful steward avoiding prohibition's high enforcement costs. Rather, in our view, Congress was attempting to overcome a sudden, unexpected, and substantial revenue shortfall that threatened wealth redistribution.

The Great Depression severely diminished individual and corporate incomes, and income tax revenues correspondingly plunged beginning in 1931. As Table 1 shows, in 1932—the year immediately prior to Congress's formal proposal of the Twenty-first Amendment—income tax receipts fell by well over a third from their level in 1931 and to almost half of their 1930 level. In 1933, income tax receipts were less than two-fifths of their 1930 level, and were at their lowest level since 1917 (when the income tax brought in just under $360 million). The income tax stream that had swelled so promisingly during Woodrow Wilson's second presidential term was, during the early 1930's, running dry.

Table 1

Year	Income Tax Receipts (1930)	Percent Change From Previous Year	Percent Change From 1930
1927	$2,139,416	+14	–
1928	$2,118,863	–1	–
1929	$2,271,649	+7	–
1930	$2,410,987	+6	–
1931	$2,039,515	–15	–15
1932	$1,291,879	–37	–46
1933	$962,361	–26	–60

Table 2 shows the correspondingly severe hit the Great Depression inflicted upon total federal government receipts. In both 1932 and 1933, total federal government receipts were reduced to approximately 60% of their 1930 level. The early years of the Depression greatly constrained Congress's ability to spend, and Congress now felt the fiscal strain caused by inability to tax liquor. The income tax, while an effective revenue raiser during the 1920's, did not suffice in 1933. With revenues plummeting, Congress searched for another source of income to fund its wealth redistributions.

Table 2

Year	Total Government Receipts (1930 $)	Percent Change From Previous Year	Percent Change From 1930
1927	$3,858,456	+8	–
1928	$3,801,490	–2	–
1929	$3,765,732	–1	–
1930	$4,057,884	+8	–
1931	$3,416,181	–16	–16
1932	$2,351,946	–31	–42
1933	$2,573,253	+9	–37

That search led the framers of the 1932 Democratic platform to call for repeal of the Eighteenth Amendment in order "to provide therefrom a proper and needed revenue." Jouett Shouse, president of the Association Against the Prohibition Amendment and a powerful figure in the Democratic party, predicted that repeal of the Eighteenth Amendment would generate, at a minimum, an additional one billion dollars in tax revenues. Facing the choice between taking corrective action to fill the revenue shortfall caused by lower income tax receipts or drastically curbing spending, Congress chose the former course. A prominent House leader in the fight for successful Congressional proposal of the Twenty-first Amendment admitted in 1934 that "if we [anti-prohibitionists] had not had the opportunity of using that argument, that repeal meant needed revenue for our Government, we would not have had repeal for at least ten years." As Figure 3 shows, the Twenty-first Amendment did indeed generate the anticipated higher liquor tax revenues. As a percentage of federal government revenues, liquor taxes jumped from 2% in 1933 to 9% in 1934 to 13% by 1936.

Liquor taxation was not a perfect substitute for income taxation; liquor taxes following repeal did not fully compensate for lost income tax revenues. Nevertheless, liquor taxation promised a sizable additional revenue stream to Congress, facing desperate times, to help cushion the spectacular decline in revenues caused by the Great Depression.

Congress had allies in this cause. Among the interest groups who supported the Twenty-first Amendment's ratification were organized labor in alliance with wealthy industrialists (such as Pierre and Irenee DuPont). Labor leaders and the very wealthy hoped that higher liquor taxes would reverse or restrain the expansion of income taxation.

In 1933, these interest-group demands were less costly for Congress to satisfy (compared to just a few years earlier) because, as shown in Table 1, the Depression substantially reduced the income tax's importance as a revenue raiser. Congress sacrificed less by reducing the rates of an income tax that raised only $2 billion annually compared with lowering the rates of an income tax that just a few years earlier raised double that amount.

Beginning in 1934, effective income tax rates did in fact decline for all tax-paying groups with net incomes of $20,000 or less. Although the typical income earner paid no taxes on his or her annual income during the 1930's, a significant number of unionized workers earned incomes high enough to be subject to federal income tax liability. For example, the median unionized worker in the building trades (of which there were nearly a half-million) earned an annual income in excess of $2,000 during all of the 1930s. Thus, many of these workers (depending on the number of exemptions) were subject to federal income tax liability for each year of this decade. Workers with incomes between $2,000 and $3,000 annually, and with a single exemption, saw their effective tax rate fall from 2% in 1933 to 1.6% for the years 1934 through 1939.

On the whole, then, income tax rates for persons owing taxes fell for all but the top earners. Thus, while the DuPonts and their peers failed to win lower income tax rates as a consequence of prohibition's repeal, the great majority of tax-paying Americans (including large numbers of unionized workers) had their income tax burden eased.

We do not assert that tax considerations were the only force behind the repeal of prohibition. Increased general sentiment across the nation favoring repeal no doubt helped grease the political wheel that carried the Twenty-first Amendment through to ratification. It is no coincidence, however, that Congress first acted to repeal the Eighteenth Amendment only after the severe revenue-reduction shock administrated by the Great Depression. General sentiment favoring a change in the law, even when combined with widespread disregard of the law, seldom spurs politicians into action. For a current example, consider the fact that laws against fornication and adultery remain on the books in several states. These laws are no longer enforced; they are flouted everywhere. It is plausible that a majority of Americans today would, if asked, favor repeal of these statutes. Nevertheless, many such statutes remain official law while large numbers of people violate these statutes with impunity. These laws remain on the books because insufficient organized pressure exists to repeal an unenforced law.

Economics explains this fact. Repealing statutes has its costs. These costs might be very low when a statute forbids widely practiced behavior generally regarded as harmless to society. But the benefits of repealing these statutes are nonexistent. Such statutes remain on the books by default, bothering few, if any, people.

Of course, it can be argued that there was popular pressure for repeal of the Eighteenth Amendment precisely because there were efforts to enforce prohibition. But it is doubtful that prohibition was enforced with sufficient vigor to impede seriously the ability of ordinary citizens to drink alcohol. Even if people felt that prohibition unduly hindered their alcohol consumption, Congress could accommodate such popular sentiment by not allocating resources for enforcement, much as the states today choose not to enforce existing laws against fornication and adultery. But this option would have done nothing for Congress's ability to redistribute wealth. Without first legalizing alcohol, Congress could not easily collect tax revenues from liquor production and sales. Openly collecting taxes on freely traded liquor without repealing the Eighteenth Amendment would have too blatantly flouted the Constitution. Such action by Congress would have been perceived as excessive and unnecessary, given that repeal was possible.

III.   CONCLUSION

As the cliché has it, money is the mother's milk of politics. Social agendas are likely to be given short shrift if they deprive Congress of the means to finance wealth redistributions. Desire for revenue drives politicians like no other motive. The evidence supports our contention that popular sentiment for repeal was less important in propelling the Twenty-first Amendment than was Congress's desire for increased revenues combined with interest-group pressures for lower income tax rates.

Our analysis of prohibition and its repeal has certain implications for current policy debates. Foes of the government's national war on drugs frequently couch their arguments in the futility of trying to proscribe the consensual sale and consumption of drugs: this is, of course, the conventional explanation for prohibition's repeal. But our analysis and common experience suggest that Congress is unlikely to repeal the drug laws simply because they do not achieve their publicly stated goal. Failure is by no means fatal to a social program when the government is running the show. As a strategic matter, we suggest that opponents of drug prohibition highlight the revenues that Congress could extract from a legalized trade in drugs. If our analysis is correct, money, not second thoughts about the war on drugs, will be the motive if and when Congress rethinks its policy.

DONALD HARRIS—THE CONCEPT OF STATE POWER UNDER THE TWENTY–FIRST AMENDMENT
40 Tenn. L. Rev. 465 (1973).

II.   THE PURPOSE OF THE TWENTY-FIRST AMENDMENT—A HISTORICAL ANALYSIS

That the states' powers to regulate intoxicating liquors are broad has never been questioned, even before ratification of the twenty-first amendment. In the first half of the nineteenth century, Chief Justice Taney stated:

> And if any State deems the retail and internal traffic in ardent spirits injurious to its citizens, and calculated to produce idleness, vice or debauchery, I see nothing in the constitution of the United States to prevent it from regulating and restraining the traffic, or from prohibiting it altogether, if it thinks proper.

About forty years later, the Court followed this dictum when, in *Mugler v. Kansas*, it held that a state could, without violating the Constitution, completely prohibit the manufacture and sale of intoxicating liquors.

Then in 1890, a bombshell was dropped from the Court's decision in *Leisy v. Hardin*. Leisy manufactured beer in Illinois and shipped it to an agent in Iowa who sold it there while still in sealed kegs. Pursuant to an Iowa statute that prohibited the sale of intoxicating liquor except for certain limited purposes, an Iowa constable seized some of the beer prior to its being sold. Leisy brought an action for its recovery, contending that the statute violated the commerce clause.

The Court noted that, though the power to regulate commerce among the states was a single unit vested in the United States Congress, it could be divided into two categories: (1) those subjects that do not require a general or uniform system of regulation and may be dealt with by the states until Congress otherwise directs; and (2) those subjects national in character that require uniform regulation and may be exercised only by the general government. Thus, when a power is necessarily exercised by Congress, and it remains silent, the only legitimate conclusion is that Congress intended that the power should not be affirmatively exercised.

The Court next decided that interstate commerce, consisting of transportation, purchase, sale and exchange of commodities (a term that the Court held to be descriptive of liquor), was national in character, and, therefore, since Congress had passed no law for its regulation, interstate commerce in intoxicating liquors apparently was to remain free and untrammelled. Having made this decision, the Court answered the question of when an item in interstate commerce became subject to state control. Relying on *Brown v. Maryland*, the Court held that when an item of interstate commerce is removed from its original package or is sold, it becomes part of the common mass of property and can be regulated by the state. Until that time, however, "in the absence of congressional permission to do so, the State had no power to interfere by seizure, or any other action, in prohibition of importation and sale by the foreign or non-resident importer." Notably, the Court did not rule the statute unconstitutional. It merely said that the state's police power could not be applied to liquors when they retained their characteristics as interstate commerce.

Leisy thus made state prevention of importation and consequent sale of intoxicants virtually impossible while the liquor remained in its original package. The power of Congress to regulate interstate commerce was thus exclusive with respect to intoxicating liquors, but the Court did indicate that the states would be allowed to exercise this power if Congress consented. Congress responded almost immediately by enacting the Wilson Act, otherwise known as the Original Package Act. It provided that upon arrival in a state, intoxicating liquor was subject to that state's laws, enacted in the exercise of its police power, to the same extent as if it had been produced within the state. The statute was held constitutional by the Supreme Court, but since it did not authorize a state to exercise any power over the transportation of intoxicants, state authority did not attach until after the receipt of the liquor within a state. Thus the Act was largely ineffective.

As a result of this deficiency, Congress passed the Webb–Kenyon Act:

> the shipment or transportation, in any manner or by any means whatsoever, of intoxicating liquor of any kind, from one State . . . into any other State . . . intended . . . to be received, possessed, sold, or in any manner used, either in the original package or otherwise, in violation of any law of such State . . . is hereby prohibited.

The constitutionality of this Act was attacked unsuccessfully in *Clark Distilling Co. v. Western Maryland Ry*. The two relevant questions dealt with by the Court in that case were whether Congress could lawfully enact the Webb–Kenyon Act and whether a state had the power to prohibit, within its borders, transportation of intoxicating liquor consistently with the exclusive power of Congress to regulate commerce.

In answering these questions, the Court relied heavily on In re *Rahrer*, the case that had upheld the Wilson Act. *Rahrer* may be summarized as recognizing that the states are instilled with an original authority to exercise the police power. By the adoption of the federal constitution, the ability of the states to act upon certain matters was said to be extinguished and the legislative will of the general government substituted. That division of powers is fixed by the constitution, and "Congress can neither delegate its own powers nor enlarge those of a state." This, however, does not mean that Congress could not enact the Wilson Act because in so doing it "has not attempted to delegate the power to regulate commerce, . . . or to grant a power not possessed by the States, or to adopt state laws. It has taken its own course, and made its own regulation . . . ." While the power to regulate commerce is solely in Congress, it is an essential part of that power to provide a regular means by which articles of commerce are introduced into the common "mass of property" of a state and thus become subject to its control. "No reason is perceived why, if Congress chooses to provide that certain designated subjects of interstate commerce shall be governed by a rule which divests them of that character at an earlier period of time than would otherwise be the case, it is not within its competency to do so." Congress, therefore, imparted no power to the state that it did not already possess but merely removed an impediment to the enforcement of state laws by allowing certain imported property to fall with the local jurisdiction immediately upon arrival within the state.

There is little doubt that this same rationale was applied in *Clark Distilling*. The Court noted that the purpose of the Webb–Kenyon Act "was to prevent the immunity characteristic of interstate commerce from being used to permit the receipt of liquor through such commerce in States contrary to their laws." It was also expressly stated that the "act did not simply forbid the introduction of liquor into a State for a prohibited use, but took the protection of interstate commerce away from all receipt and possession of liquor prohibited by state law." The *Clark Distilling* decision simply allowed the Congress to remove the impediment of interstate commerce at an earlier point than had been approved in *Rahrer*.

Neither the Wilson Act nor the Webb–Kenyon Act was considered to have transferred any power to the states, and effectuation of these statutes was based solely on the exercise by the several states of their police powers. Nor is there any indication in the decisions that impediments imposed by other provisions of the Constitution were removed by enactment of these laws. Rather, the states were left free to exercise their normal police powers changed only in that restrictions on those powers, imposed by the commerce clause, had been removed by an affirmative act of Congress.

Little more than two years after the decision in *Clark Distilling*, the eighteenth amendment was ratified, and prohibition became effective, thus foreclosing further litigation on the constitutionality of the Webb–Kenyon Act and rendering meaningless additional debate on the question of congressional power to enact such legislation. It seems clear, however, that the fact that a controversy had existed was in the minds of the legislators who proposed the twenty-first amendment for ratification.

Review of the legislative history of the proposed amendment leaves little doubt that section 2 was included to protect the dry states by making the Webb–Kenyon Act a permanent part of the Constitution. During debate on the floor of the Senate, it was repeatedly stated that, though the constitutionality of Webb–Kenyon had been upheld by a divided Supreme Court, future litigation might result in its being declared unconstitutional. Moreover, it was feared that, even if the Act continued to be considered constitutional, the states would be forced to rely indefinitely on the Congress to maintain the law. Repeal of the Webb–Kenyon and Wilson Acts would return the dry states to the mercy of the liquor industry under the doctrine espoused in *Leisy*.

Construing section 2 so as to permanently incorporate the Webb–Kenyon law into the Constitution would seem to make the construction given that Act in *Clark Distilling* equally applicable to the twenty-first amendment. So read, section 2 does not contain an affirmative grant of power but merely constitutionally removes the impediment of the congressional commerce power from the exercise by the states of their police powers in regard to intoxicating liquors.

This construction receives further support from a literal interpretation of section 2 of the amendment. It seems unlikely that language prohibiting the violation of state laws would be employed to express an affirmative grant of power. With no express grant of power in the amendment, the "laws" referred to therein must necessarily be derived from some other source, and the normal fountain of state authority is the police power with its traditional constitutional limitations.

Throughout the Senate debates preceding adoption of the resolution proposing the amendment, there is reference to the idea that the states alone should deal with the liquor problem. Control of liquor regulation by the individual states rather than by the federal government was, of course, the purpose of section 2 of the amendment. But some of the language referring to restoration to the states of "absolute control" over traffic in intoxicating liquors has been construed as giving to the states plenary powers apparently unlimited by constitutional restrictions. Such an interpretation gives this language too broad a meaning. When originally reported out of committee, the amendment contained a section 3, not present in the enacted amendment, that provided that Congress should have concurrent power with the states to regulate the sale of liquor to be consumed on the seller's premises. It was feared that this power, if retained by Congress, could be extended to all phases of liquor regulation and was therefore deleted from the proposed amendment. It was in response to the original section 3 and the retention by Congress of power to regulate liquor that references to "absolute control" by the states and similar language were used. Read in the proper context, this language cannot be taken to mean that the twenty-first amendment was intended to grant to the states powers unlimited by other constitutional provisions. Furthermore, to say that the twenty-first amendment granted powers in excess of those necessary to protect the health, welfare, morals, and safety of a state's citizens is unreasonable when fundamental constitutional rights are involved.

III. Judicial History of the Twenty-First Amendment

The first important case to interpret section 2 of the amendment was *State Board of Equalization v. Young's Market Co.* In that case, a constitutional challenge was made to a California license fee of $500 imposed on the privilege of importing beer into the state. The challenge was grounded on both the commerce and the equal protection clauses. The Court, employing reasoning that was to become the backbone of the amendment, said that since a state could, without violating the commerce clause, entirely prohibit importation of intoxicating beverages under the amendment's section 2, "surely the State may adopt a lesser degree of regulation than total prohibition." And if a state could totally exclude all importation of beer, could it not "instead of absolute exclusion, subject the foreign article to a heavy importation fee?" The Court concluded that the words of the amendment were "apt to confer upon the state the power to forbid all importations which do not comply with the conditions it prescribes." Thus, on its first opportunity to construe the amendment, the Court apparently interpreted it as affirmatively granting power to the states.

Consistent with this rationale was the Court's summary rejection of the equal protection argument, using the oft-quoted statement that a "classification recognized by the Twenty-first Amendment cannot be deemed forbidden by the Fourteenth." Furthermore, the Court refused to consider whether limitation of the language of the twenty-first was sanctioned by history, remarking that since "the language of the Amendment is clear, we do not discuss these matters." The Court did, however, state that its decision did not require a "declaration that the Amendment has, in respect to liquor, freed the States from all restrictions upon the police power to be found in other provisions of the Constitution."

In quick succession, the Court decided three other cases that served to solidify the strong position taken in *Young's Market*. In *Mahoney v. Joseph Triner Corp.*, a Minnesota statute prohibiting importation of certain liquor brands not registered with the United States patent office was upheld. The statute was challenged as an unreasonable regulation of liquor and as a violation of the equal protection clause. The Court held that under the twenty-first amendment, discrimination against imported liquors or between imported liquors was permissible and that the power of a state under the amendment was not limited to reasonable regulations of the liquor traffic. The reasonableness of the statute was therefore not considered.

The next two cases, *Indianapolis Brewing Co. v. Liquor Control Commission* and *Finch & Co. v. McKittrick*, involved retaliatory legislation enacted by Michigan and Missouri, respectively, that prohibited importing liquor manufactured in any state discriminating against the importation of liquor. In *Indianapolis Brewing*, the challengers contended that since the legislation was retaliatory, it was contrary to the purpose of the twenty-first amendment, because under it any state could punish another for conduct otherwise permitted under the rule applied in *Young's Market*. The Court, again without considering the purpose and history of the amendment, held that neither the commerce clause nor the fourteenth amendment was violated. Rather summarily, the Court concluded that "the right of a state to prohibit or regulate the importation of intoxicating liquor is not limited by the commerce clause," and "discrimination relating to importation of liquor is not prohibited by the equal protection clause."

In *Finch*, the challengers urged that, while the legislation did not relate to the protection of the public welfare, it was a weapon of economic retaliation and, therefore, not authorized by the twenty-first amendment. This argument was similarly rejected by the Court since the words of the amendment were "apt to confer upon the State the power to forbid all importations which do not comply with the conditions it prescribes."

While these cases seemingly held that, where the twenty-first amendment applies, the states' power to regulate intoxicating liquors is virtually unlimited, questions did arise concerning the jurisdictional limitations of the state power under the amendment. Essentially, this issue was answered by construction of the words "transportation or importation into any State . . . for delivery or use therein" contained in section 2 of the amendment.

The first case to consider this problem was *Collins v. Yosemite Park & Curry Co.* That decision involved the attempted application of licensing and regulatory provisions by California to the importation and sale of liquor for use within Yosemite National Park. The Court held that no transportation into California "for delivery or use therein" occurred since the delivery and use was in the Park where the United States, with a few unimportant exceptions, had exclusive jurisdiction. Thus, where transportation is merely "through" a state, as opposed to "into" a state for delivery or use therein, impliedly, the twenty-first amendment is not applicable. This distinction gradually became the standard for whether the state's power under the twenty-first amendment could be applied.

The next question concerned how much and what kind of power a state had over these "through" shipments of liquor. In *Duckworth v. Arkansas*, the Court upheld, under the state's police power, a statute requiring persons transporting liquor through the state to obtain a permit. In rejecting a challenge to this statute under the commerce clause, the Court noted the state's interest in preventing illegal diversion of liquor from "through" shipments into state channels. Thus it was unnecessary to decide whether the statute derived support from the twenty-first amendment. In a concurring opinion, Justice Jackson argued that the Court should have decided this issue rather than increasing the scope of a state's power to place restraints on national commerce. Justice Jackson's rationale was that since a state, under the twenty-first amendment, could exercise plenary power over shipments of liquor into the state, the amendment could be interpreted to authorize the state to exact some assurance that all liquor entering its territory either is imported for lawful delivery under its own laws or will pass through without diversion.

Another view of the "through shipment" problem was provided in *Carter v. Virginia*. A Virginia regulation required that persons transporting liquor "through" the state: (1) use the most direct route and carry a bill of lading showing the route it would travel; (2) post a $1,000 bond conditioned on lawful transportation; and (3) possess a bill of lading showing the true consignee who must have a legal right to receive the liquor at the stated destination. Responding to a challenge that the statute invaded the constitutional power of Congress under the commerce clause, the Court observed that the intoxicating liquors in question were intended for continuous shipment through Virginia. A question different from those considered under the twenty-first amendment was thus presented. The Court, however, upheld the statute under the state's police power "independently of the Twenty-first Amendment" in recognition of the state's interest in protecting itself from illicit diversion of the liquor traffic within its borders.

In a concurring opinion, Justice Frankfurter suggested that because of the twenty-first amendment and, indeed, under the power granted by it, the power of a state to regulate and control "through" shipments was as great as the state's power over "into" shipments. Recognizing that the regulations involved, if considered an exercise of the state's police power, would be struck down as violative of the commerce clause, Justice Frankfurter reasoned that because Virginia could prohibit importation of intoxicating liquors, it, a fortiori, had the authority to take whatever protective measures it decided were necessary to effectuate that power, including total prohibition of "through" shipments if it decided that other regulatory measures would be ineffective in stopping illicit diversion.

A further variation on the interrelationship of the police power and the twenty-first amendment was presented in *Ziffrin Inc. v. Reeves*. The appellant in that case was an Indiana corporation engaged in transporting whiskey from Kentucky distillers to consignees in Chicago. The Kentucky legislature enacted a comprehensive liquor control measure that, *inter alia*, required all persons transporting liquor within the state to obtain a transporter's license. Because the amendment was expressly made applicable to importation of liquor and appellant was involved in exportation, it was contended that the statute, as applied, must be considered an exercise of the state's police power that was subject to commerce clause limitations. A fair interpretation of the somewhat inconsistent opinion indicates that the statute was upheld as an exercise of the police power. By the Court's rationale, a state could, through the use of this power, totally prohibit the manufacture of intoxicants, and thus it necessarily included the exercise of a lesser degree of control. In *Ziffrin* the power was exercised by permitting "manufacture only upon condition that it be sold to an indicated class of customers and transported in definitely specified ways." The Court further indicated that these conditions were not unreasonable and were clearly appropriate for effectuating the policy of limiting traffic in order to minimize well known evils and secure payment of revenue. It is unclear from the opinion whether reasonableness and appropriateness are standards to be applied in such a situation or whether the authority to totally prohibit manufacture of intoxicants includes the power to subject it to any and all conditions prescribed by the state.

Still another limitation on the twenty-first amendment was suggested in *United States v. Frankfort Distilleries*. Defendants in the original action were producers, wholesalers and retailers charged with conspiring to fix retail prices of beverages sold in Colorado. The Court noted that 98% of the spiritous liquor and 80% of the wines consumed in Colorado were shipped into the state. One of the grounds on which defendants challenged the conviction was that the state's exclusive power to control the liquor traffic under the twenty-first amendment made the Sherman Act inapplicable. The Court disagreed and held that the twenty-first amendment did not give "the states plenary and exclusive power to regulate the conduct of persons doing an interstate liquor business outside their boundaries." Significantly, the decision did not actually prohibit the exercise of state power over the "conduct of persons doing an interstate liquor business outside their boundaries," nor did it make the application of federal regulations to interstate shipments of intoxicants always permissible. These omissions were apparent from the Court's caveat that this was not a case involving application of the Sherman Act to defeat announced policies of the state. The question of supremacy where state policy conflicted with the Sherman Act was expressly reserved.

Finally, two decisions in 1964 indicated that the Court might review the broad approval it had previously given state liquor regulation. The first of these, *Hostetter v. Idlewild Bon Voyage Liquor Corp.*, involved a corporation engaged in selling liquor to departing international airline passengers at a New York airport. The firm took orders from passengers who had boarding cards and tickets indicating their imminent departure. The liquor was not given immediately to the passengers but was placed aboard the aircraft and delivered upon arrival at the foreign destination. The beverages sold in this manner were purchased from wholesalers located outside the state. The New York State Liquor Authority informed the firm that such actions were both unlicensed and unlicensable under New York law. Idlewild sought an injunction to restrain the Liquor Authority from interfering with its business, contending that the New York statutes were repugnant to the commerce and supremacy clauses since the Bureau of Customs had approved Idlewild's business operations. The Court held that the state was not seeking to regulate or control passage through its territory for the purpose of preventing unlawful diversion into internal commerce. Consequently, it could not totally "prevent transactions carried on under the aegis of a law passed by Congress . . . to regulate commerce with foreign nations."

Two things are clear from the *Idlewild* opinion. First, a state may not totally prohibit transportation of intoxicants "through" its territory;

and second, the delivery or use contemplated by the twenty-first amendment is delivery or use by the ultimate consumer. It is not apparent, however, whether the federal control involved had any influence on the Court's decision except that it served to protect the state from illegal diversion. What is perhaps significant is the language used indicating that the Court made an accommodation between the twenty-first amendment and the commerce clause.

The second decision was *Department of Revenue v. James B. Beam Distilling Co.* A Kentucky law taxing all liquor shipped into the state was applied to a distributor who imported a brand of whiskey produced in Scotland and shipped through United States ports to the distributor's bonded warehouses in Kentucky. The liquor was subsequently sold to customers in domestic markets throughout the United States. The Court held the tax to be prohibited by the export-import clauses. Involved here, the Court pointed out, was "not the generalized authority given to Congress by the Commerce Clause, but a constitutional provision which flatly prohibits any State from imposing a tax on imports from abroad." Furthermore, the Court stated that nothing in the language or history of the twenty-first amendment leads to the concluson that it has completely repealed the export-import clause so far as intoxicants are concerned. It should be noted, however, that if the *Idlewild* interpretation of "delivery or use therein" as delivery to the ultimate consumer is applied to this case, the shipments could easily be designated as "through" shipments, and the state's power under the twenty-first amendment would be inapplicable. Though a portion of the shipments were probably delivered and used in Kentucky, the liquor involved was not designated for use in that state but was transported there for storage and subsequent distribution to customers in other jurisdictions. It is, of course, impossible to determine the result if the liquor had been imported exclusively for delivery and use within Kentucky.

Two years later, in *Joseph E. Seagram & Sons, Inc. v. Hostetter*, the Court appeared to reaffirm the accommodation language used in *Idlewild*. *Seagram* was an action for injunction and declaratory judgment against the enforcement of a New York statute requiring brand owners, their agents, and "related persons" to file price schedules for sales to wholesalers and retailers plus an affirmation that the prices charged were no higher than the lowest price at which sales were made anywhere in the United States. Persons other than brand owners, their agents, and "related persons" were required to make affirmations only as to other sales made by them. The statute was challenged as a violation of the commerce clause, the supremacy clause and the fourteenth amendment due process and equal protection clauses. The challengers contended that the statute would place an undue burden on interstate commerce because brand owners would be forced to raise prices in other states in order to maintain the New York price levels. The Court held that these effects were largely conjectural and, furthermore, that the "mere fact that state action may have repercussions beyond state lines is of not judicial significance so long as the action is not within that domain which the Constitution forbids."

In the same vein, another section, designed to bring wholesalers within the price requirements even though they took delivery outside the state, was upheld. There was no indication that the liquor authorities would require the filing of price schedules for sales unrelated to distribution of liquor within the state of New York. Thus, a state's power to regulate intrastate distribution of liquor under the twenty-first amendment may significantly affect transactions beyond its borders; but this fact does not exclude application of federal controls to such transactions. According to the Court, nothing in the twenty-first amendment would prevent enforcement of the Sherman Act against any attempt on the part of the brand owners to preserve their New York price level by conspiring to raise prices elsewhere.

The primary due process contention was that the statute was not aimed at promoting temperance and was unwise, impractical and oppressive. The Court decided, however, that it would not substitute its social and economic beliefs for the judgment of legislative bodies and that "nothing in the Twenty-first Amendment or any other part of the Constitution requires that state laws regulating the liquor business be motivated exclusively by a desire to promote temperance."

The equal protection argument was based on the arbitrariness of excepting consumer sales and private label brands from the price requirements and reducing the scope of the affirmation required with respect to sales made by those who were not "related persons." The Court held that these distinctions did not constitute invidious discrimination since the legislature could reasonably conclude that forcing a reduction of prices in those sales covered by the statute would result in reduced prices in the excepted sales as well.

While it might appear that *Seagram* is but another instance of the Court's giving its blanket approval to a state liquor regulation, it is perhaps significant that the Court applied, however arbitrarily, the traditional constitutional standards rather than summarily holding them inapplicable. Moreover, the idea of "accommodating" opposing state and federal interests seems to be present throughout the opinion, especially in the section dealing with the Sherman Act.

In what could be described as a continuation of the "accommodation" rationale, the Court in *Wisconsin v. Constantineau* held unconstitutional a Wisconsin statute providing for the public posting, without notice or hearing, of the names of persons who habitually engaged in excessive drinking. While recognizing the broad scope of state power over intoxicating liquors and especially over the evils described in the statute, Justice Douglas, speaking for a majority of the Court, felt that the private interests in preventing "such a stigma or badge of disgrace" were so great that the requirements of procedural due process must be met.

Additionally, the Court, in *Moose Lodge No. 107 v. Irvis* held that the state, by requiring private clubs to which it granted liquor licenses to comply with club by-laws, was engaged in unconstitutional state action insofar as it assisted such organizations in the enforcement of racially discriminatory provisions. Thus, application of state sanctions in the name of liquor regulation resulting in the enforcement of racial discrimination in private clubs was held to be violative of the equal protection clause.

This discernible trend toward an "accommodation" between state and federal interests in the regulation of intoxicating liquor has probably been halted by the Supreme Court's decision in *California v. LaRue*. It is not at all clear, however, that the state's power to deal with intoxicating liquors is now subject to no constitutional bounds. Because the problems presented in *LaRue* indicate a need for application of constitutional limitations, scrutiny of that decision is warranted.

IV. THE NEW ORDER

A majority of the Court in *California v. LaRue* upheld California regulations prohibiting certain sexually explicit acts or performances and films depicting such acts or performances in establishments licensed by the state to sell liquor by the drink. Conceding that some of the performances restricted by the regulations fell within the area of constitutionally protected speech, the *LaRue* majority, through Justice Rehnquist, felt the statutes should be considered, not as censorship of dramatic performances, but as rules relating to the issuance of liquor licenses. Viewed in this context, California was freed from the constitutional restrictions of decisions concerning obscenity and communicative conduct because of the state's broad authority under the twenty-first amendment. The regulations were, therefore, upheld as a rational exercise of the state's sweeping twenty-first amendment powers.

The activities that prompted the regulations involved in *LaRue* were described by the Court as follows:

> in licensed establishments where "topless" and "bottomless" dancers, nude entertainers, and films displaying sexual acts were shown, numerous incidents of legitimate concern to the Department had occurred. Customers were found engaging in oral copulation with women entertainers; customers engaged in public masturbation; and customers placed rolled currency either directly into the vagina of a female entertainer or on the bar in order that she might pick it up herself. Numerous other forms of contact between the mouths of male customers and the vaginal areas of female performers were reported to have occurred. Prostitution occurred in and around such licensed premises and involved some of the female dancers. Indecent exposure to young girls, attempted rape, rape itself, and assaults on police officers took place on or immediately adjacent to such premises.

In response to this conduct, regulations were promulgated to suppress such sexually explicit live performances and films. The rules: (1) prohibited topless waitresses and sexual contact between any persons on the premises; (2) prohibited nude entertainers, regulated the content of entertainment and required that certain entertainers perform on stage at least six feet from the nearest patron; (3) regulated the content of movies; and (4) prohibited any entertainment violative of a city or county ordinance.

Plaintiffs initially challenged all four rules, seeking a declaratory judgment of their constitutionality. At oral argument before a three-judge court in California, however, objections to the rules relating to the prohibition of topless waitresses and sexual contacts, compliance with local regulations, and the requirement that certain entertainers perform on a stage were withdrawn. The district court held that prohibiting the holding of liquor licenses in establishments where sexually explicit live performances and movies were shown without first applying the constitutional tests for obscenity was a violation of the first, fifth, and fourteenth amendments.

In this posture, the case was appealed to the United States Supreme Court. It is interesting to note that the rules to which objection was withdrawn would have prohibited most, if not all of the "incidents of legitimate concern to the Department" referred to by Justice Rehnquist. Rule 143.2, in addition to prohibiting topless waitresses, would have prohibited sexual activity between customers and employees and between customers and any other persons. The part of Rule 143.3 requiring certain performers to perform only on a stage six feet from the nearest patron would have prevented contact between customers and performers. Rule 143.5, requiring compliance with local ordinances and state obscenity laws, would be available to suppress performances adjudged to be obscene according to the established constitutional standards. Inclusion of these rather sordid details, however, apparently makes the decision more appealing. Furthermore, as pointed out by the district court, other legitimate state interests that were recognized in *Redrup v. New York*, were not involved. Minors were not allowed to view the entertainment; there was no pandering; and the entertainment was in no way forced upon unwilling individuals.

The state interest in suppressing the alleged criminal activity does not appear to support the censorship imposed. While it is perhaps true that prostitutes would be drawn to the type of establishment involved, as pointed out by Justice Marshall in his dissenting opinion, prostitution, assaults on police officers, and the other alleged criminal activity should be controlled by the imposition of criminal sanctions and not by a broad-scale attack on first amendment freedoms. While the incidents of indecent exposure and attempted and actual rape that purportedly occurred came closest to justifying the challenged state action, these too would seem to fall short of supporting the infringement of constitutional rights. The Report of the Commission on Obscenity and Pornography has largely discredited any empirical link between exposure to sex-related materials or entertainment and criminal activity.

Even if it is assumed, arguendo, that the combination of liquor and sexually explicit performances could have been a causative factor in past criminal activity, there are no adequate grounds for assuming that these crimes would not continue to occur under those new restrictions to which objection was withdrawn. Furthermore, the rules are potentially applicable to establishments and performances of a "more legitimate" variety to which such allegations would be absurd. Finally, applicable here as to those criminal activities discussed above, is the view that "among free men, the deterrents ordinarily to be applied to prevent crimes are education and punishment for violations of the law." Where first amendment rights are at stake, "the State must adopt the 'less restrictive alternative' unless it can make a compelling demonstration that the protected activity and criminal conduct are so closely linked that only through regulation of one can the other be stopped."

Given the now applicable restrictions to which objection was withdrawn in the lower federal court, there appears to be no requirement that the Court be shown a legitimate state interest justifying restraints on first amendment freedoms. The Court makes some rather futile efforts to classify the activities as "conduct" and, therefore, not within the area of freedoms protected by the first amendment. In the final analysis, however, the Court admits that the regulations address themselves to some performances within the limits of constitutional protection. Accordingly, except for the Court's interpretation of the twenty-first amendment, regulation of the performances would require a determination of obscenity under the prevailing constitutional standards.

Application of traditional first amendment limitations find the challenged regulations to be constitutionally defective. Since it is not the purpose of this comment to evaluate the first amendment ramifications of this decision, an extended discussion of those limitations applied by the courts is not appropriate. It is enough to recognize that a determination of obscenity is to be judicially made based on the work or performance taken as a whole, and, "when so viewed, must appeal to the prurient interest in sex, patently offend community standards relating to the depiction of sexual matters, and be utterly without redeeming social value."

The Court's view that some activities to which these regulations could be applied are within the area protected by the first amendment freedom of expression would ordinarily subject these rules to the constitutional limitation against overbreadth. This defect is made even more serious by the fact that in this litigation there were no "particularized facts" to which the regulations could be applied. Instead the state stipulated, apparently without reservation, that it would take disciplinary action against the licensees violating these rules. According to Justice Rehnquist, even though some of the performances deserved first amendment protection, "the critical fact is that California has not forbidden these performances across the board. It has merely proscribed such performances in establishments which it licenses to sell liquor by the drink.''

The power of government, both federal and state, to produce results that it can not constitutionally command by imposing unconstitutional conditions on the granting of benefits and privileges has frequently been condemned by the Supreme Court. This condemnation has been particularly notable in the area of first amendment freedoms. Recently, in *Perry v. Sinderman* the Court stated:

> For at least a quarter-century, this Court has made clear that even though a person has no "right" to a valuable governmental benefit and even though the government may deny him the benefit for any number of reasons, there are some reasons on which a government may not rely. It may not deny a benefit to a person on a basis that infringes his constitutionally protected interests—especially, his interest in freedom of speech. For if the government could deny a benefit to a person because of his constitutionally protected speech or associations, his exercise of those freedoms would in effect be penalized and inhibited. This would allow the government to "produce a result which it could not command directly." . . . . Such interference with constitutional rights is impermissible.

Since the state, in *LaRue*, conditioned the granting and holding of a liquor license on surrender by licensees of certain of their first amendment rights, the state's action would appear to be subject to this rationale. The Court, however, reasoned that the challenged regulations were to be considered, not in the context of censoring a dramatic performance, but in the context of licensing bars and nightclubs to sell liquor by the drink. So viewed, the state was held not to be limited by the confines of Supreme Court decisions on either obscenity or protected forms of communicative conduct because of the "broad sweep of the twenty-first amendment" and the "presumption" in favor of validity of state regulations that the twenty-first amendment requires.

While the Court interposed a caveat that future applications of the regulation may present constitutional questions, state authorities justifiably might view this decision as imparting virtually unlimited powers in the area of liquor regulation. Thus, future abuses will have to be corrected in the courts where a more suitable relationship between state power under the twenty-first amendment and other constitutional limitations await development. As one federal court has stated, "we must reconcile the power granted with the power prohibited." Since prior case law seems to provide inadequate authority as to the limitations on which state power in the area of liquor regulation may be based, more attention might possibly be given to the purposes considered in proposing the amendment.

Notes and Questions

1. Prohibition and its repeal is one of the most dramatic stories of compound legal change in the legal history of developed nations. But is it a

story with a moral, and if so, what is the central lesson to be learned? How would that lesson or lessons apply to the behaviors discussed in Chapters 2–6, supra?

2.   State-level alcohol prohibition was an important precursor to national prohibition. Ten states had prohibition by 1910, 21 by 1915 and 35 by 1919. What sorts of experience did these experiments in law reform produce? What was wrong with policy at the state level?

3.   What proportion of U.S. adults consumed alcohol in 1919? What were the attitudes of users to prohibition?

4.   It is estimated that alcohol consumption dropped 70% in the earliest period of prohibition and then increased to a level 30% below consumption prior to prohibition. Was the 70% figure a sign of policy success? Did a 30% decline represent a successful policy? What level would have made the experiment a success?

5.   How do the reductions in alcohol consumption compare with the deterrent effects of prohibitions on drugs, gambling and prostitution in recent years in the United States?

6.   What were the primary costs of prohibition of alcohol in the United States? Did corruption go down after repeal?

7.   If Boudreau and Pritchard are correct in arguing that federal revenue was the reason for prohibition's repeal, why didn't Congress legalize gambling as well?

8.   Why did few states prohibit alcohol after national prohibition's repeal?

C.   EVALUATING PROHIBITION

NATIONAL COMMISSION ON LAW OBSERVANCE AND ENFORCEMENT—REPORT ON THE ENFORCEMENT OF THE PROHIBITION LAWS OF THE UNITED STATES

January 7, 1931.

I.   THE EIGHTEENTH AMENDMENT AND THE NATIONAL PROHIBITION ACT

On December 18, 1917, the joint resolution was adopted by both houses with the required constitutional majority and was transmitted to the states for their consideration. On January 29, 1919, the Secretary of State, by proclamation, announced that on January 16th thirty-six states had ratified the amendment and therefore it had become a part of the Constitution. It was subsequently ratified by ten additional states. It became effective on January 16, 1920, as the Eighteenth Amendment to the Constitution, the pertinent sections of which are as follows:

"Sec. 1. After one year from the ratification of this article the manufacture, sale or transportation of intoxicating liquors within, the importation thereof into, or the exportation thereof from the United States and all territory subject to the jurisdiction thereof for beverage, purposes is hereby prohibited.

"Sec. 2. The Congress and the several states shall have concurrent power to enforce this article by appropriate legislation"

The absolute prohibitions of the Amendment extend only to the manufacture, sale, transportation, importation, or exportation of intoxicating liquors for beverage purposes. The Amendment does not prohibit the manufacture, sale, transportation, importation, or exportation of alcoholic liquors which are not intoxicating, or of intoxicating liquors for other than beverage purposes. It does not define intoxicating liquors or directly prohibit the purchase, possession by the purchaser, or use of any liquor, whether intoxicating or otherwise. The power to deal with these questions is vested in Congress under the provisions of Section 2 of the Amendment, or left to the several states.

In pursuance of this authority, in October, 1919 Congress passed the National Prohibition Act. In the title to this act three distinct purposes are stated: (1) to "prohibit intoxicating beverages," (2) to regulate the manufacture, production, use and sale of high proof spirits for other than beverage purposes, and (3) to "insure an ample supply of alcohol and promote its use in scientific research and in the development of fuel, dye and other lawful industries."

The law is divided into three titles. Title I deals with war-time prohibition and is not material to this inquiry; Title II with the prohibition of intoxicating beverages; and Title III with industrial alcohol.

By Section 3 of Title II it is declared that "all of the provisions of this Act shall be liberally construed to the end that the use of intoxicating liquor as a beverage may be prevented." This language has been criticized as extending the purpose of the Act beyond that of the Amendment of the Constitution. The criticism seems rather technical. The Amendment did not expressly prohibit the use of intoxicating liquors as a beverage, but without this use the things prohibited would not exist. On the other hand, if the direct prohibitions of the Amendment were effective there could be no use for beverage purposes except as to the limited simply on hand when the Amendment became operative. The direct and expressed purpose was to prohibit the sources and processes of supply; the ultimate purpose and, if successful, the inevitable effect was to prohibit and prevent the use of such liquor as a beverage.

It has been observed that the Eighteenth Amendment did not define intoxicating liquors which were prohibited for beverage purposes. In the absence of any definition this would, of course, mean liquors which were in fact intoxicating, a matter practically impossible of accurate determination, since it-would depend upon the amount and conditions of consumption, the physiology of the consumer, and other factors which vary in each case. The definition of this term to be effective must necessarily fix a somewhat arbitrary standard. It was left to the legislative discretion of Congress.

In Title II Section 2, of the National Prohibition Act, it was declared that the phrase "intoxicating liquors" should be construed to include alcohol, brandy, whisky, rum, gin, beer, ale, porter, and wine, and in addition thereto any spirituous, vinous, malt or fermented liquor, liquids and compounds. whether medicated, proprietary, patented or not, and by-whatever name called, "containing one-half of one per centum or more of alcohol by volume which are fit for use for beverage purposes."

The validity of the provision and the definition of alcoholic liquor therein were challenged in the courts and were sustained by the Supreme Court of the United States as being within the powers conferred upon Congress by the Amendment.

To this general limitation of less than one-half of one per cent alcoholic content by volume there is in the Act one exception as applied to manufacture.

This appears in Section 29 of Title II, which, after prescribing penalties for certain violations of the Act, including illegal manufacture and sale, declares that "the penalties provided in this Act against the manufacture of liquor without permit shall not apply to a person for manufacturing non-intoxicating cider and fruit juices exclusively for use in his home, but such cider or fruit juices shall not be sold or delivered except to persons having permits to manufacture vinegar."

History of Prohibition Enforcement Before the Bureau of Prohibition Act 1927

(a) Original Organization

The Amendment and the National Prohibition Act inaugurated one of the most extensive and sweeping efforts to change the social habits of an entire nation recorded in history. It Would naturally have been assumed that the enforcement of such a novel and sweeping reform in a democracy would have been undertaken cautiously, with a carefully selected and specially trained force adequately organized and compensated, accompanied by efforts to arouse to its support public sympathy and aid. No opportunity for such a course was allowed.

As already noted, it was necessary to leave the definition of intoxicating liquor to the legislature, and also necessary for the legislature to fix a somewhat arbitrary standard. Considerable public sentiment, was however, antagonized by the legislative fixing of the permissible content of alcohol at a percentage substantially below the possibility of intoxication. This gave offense to a number of people who perhaps did not give adequate consideration to the administrative difficulties which might be involved by permitting a larger alcoholic content. Instant compliance was necessarily required from the date the amendment became effective. Scant opportunity was allowed for the organization of a force to carry out the Congressional mandates. There was no time or opportunity for careful selection of personnel. The officials charged with the execution of the law realized grave difficulties in the task thus imposed upon them.

The Commissioner of Internal Revenue, in his Annual Report to the Secretary of the Treasury for the fiscal year ending June 30, 1919 made while the National Prohibition Act was pending in Congress, referred to the fact that that bill placed the responsibility for the enforcement of its provisions upon the Bureau of Internal Revenue of the Treasury Department, which already was burdened with the fiscal and revenue problems of the government. "Not to enforce prohibition thoroughly and effectively," said the Commissioner, "would reflect upon our form of government, and would bring into disrepute the reputation of the American people as law abiding citizens. No law can be effectively enforced except with the assistance and cooperation of the law-abiding element. The Bureau will accordingly put into operation at once the necessary organization to cooperate with the states and the public in the rigid enforcement of the prohibition law, and appeals to every law-abiding citizen for support. This contemplated end requires the closest cooperation between the Federal officers and all other law-enforcing officers, state, county, and municipal."

The Bureau naturally expects unreserved cooperation also from those moral agencies which are so vitally interested in the proper administration of this law. Such agencies include churches, civic organizations, educational societies, charitable and philanthropic societies. and other welfare bodies. The Bureau further expects cooperation and support from the law-abiding citizens of the United States who may have been opposed to the adoption of the Constitutional amendment and the law, which in pursuance of that amendment makes unlawful certain acts and privileges which were formerly not unlawful. Thus, it is the right of the Government officers charged with the enforcement of this law to expect the assistance and moral support of every citizen, in upholding the law, regardless of personal conviction.

If the cooperation thus referred to had been cordially given and the Bureau had been adequately and efficiently organized for the purpose of discharging the responsibilities laid upon it by the National Prohibition Act, it is probable that many problems of the character existing at the present time, would not have risen. As a matter of fact, very little cooperation was given by the agencies referred to and the organized bodies which had been instrumental in procuring the adoption of prohibition apparently abandoned all effort to convince the public of its advantages and placed all their reliance upon the power of the national government to enforce the law. The proponents of the law paid no heed to the admonition that "no law can be effectively enforced except with the assistance and cooperation of the law-abiding element." On the contrary, the passage of the act and its enforcement were urged with a spirit of intolerant zeal that awakened an equally intolerant opposition and the difficulties now being experienced in rallying public sentiment in support of the Eighteenth Amendment result largely from that spirit of intolerance.

On the passage of the law, the Bureau of Internal Revenue proceeded to organize departments under supervising Federal prohibition agents for the enforcement work and to create in each state an organization under a Federal prohibition director for the regulation and control of the

nonbeverage traffic in alcohol by a system of permits. The appointment
of prohibition directors and agents was not subject to the Civil Service
laws. The salaries of prohibition agents were too low to be attractive.
There has been much criticism of the character, intelligence and ability
of many of the force originally appointed and many of their successors,
and it is probably true that to their reputation for general unfitness may
be ascribed in large measure the public disfavor into which prohibition
fell. Allegations of corruption were freely made, and, in fact, a substantial number of prohibition agents and employees actually were indicted
and convicted of various crimes. The facts are given more in detail by the
Assistant Secretary of the Treasury in his testimony before the Senate
Committee hereinafter referred to.

When the new national administration came in, in 1921, a committee was appointed, consisting of two members of the cabinet and an
assistant secretary, who made a study of the subject, and recommended
the transfer of certain activities from one department to the other where
they appropriately belonged, including the transfer of the prohibition
enforcement unit to the Department of Justice. That transfer, which also
was recommended by this Commission in its preliminary report in
November 1929, was authorized by Congress and carried out in this
present year, 1930.

The organization set up under the Bureau of Internal Revenue was
headed by a Commissioner of Prohibition. The original appointee, served
from November 17, 1919, to June 11, 1921. His successor served until
May 20, 1927, but the latter's authority was curtailed on November 1,
1925 by the appointment of a Director of Prohibition with equal power,
who also served until May 20, 1927. On that date the offices were
reconsolidated and a new Commissioner appointed who served until July
1, 1930.

The Bureau of Internal Revenue charged with the enforcement of
prohibition as well as the Customs Bureau and the Coast Guard, were
directly under the supervision of an Assistant Secretary of the Treasury.
Five persons held that office between January 1920 and April 1925, and
for eight months there was a vacancy in the office and no Assistant
Secretary appears to have been especially charged with the supervision
of the prohibition forces or the coordination of the three services.

During the period prior to July, 1921, the enforcement and permissive features of the law were administered separately, with supervising
federal prohibition agents in charge of the former and state directors,
who were permitted to choose their own personnel, in charge of the
latter. During the short life of this system, an unusually large number of
supervising agents saw service as heads of the twelve departments into
which-the-country was divided. In July, 1921, the office of supervising
federal prohibition agent was abolished, and enforcement placed under
the state directors, 48 in number. The occupants of these positions were
constantly changing, and 184 men were in and out of these 48 positions
during the years 1921 to 1925, when the office was abolished. The

enforcement agents, inspectors and attorneys, as-was authorized in section 38 of the National Prohibition Act, were appointed without regard to the Civil Service rules. A force so constituted presented a situation conducive to bribery and official indifference to enforcement. It is common knowledge that large amounts of liquor were imported into the country or manufactured and sold, despite the law, with the connivance of agents of the law.

April 1, 1925, General Lincoln C. Andrews, a retired army officer was appointed Assistant Secretary of the Treasury and ascended to the supervision of Customs, Coast Guard and Prohibition. He reorganized the whole prohibition enforcement machinery, using the federal judicial district as the geographical unit, and grouping those units into districts. making in all twenty-four prohibition districts in each of which was placed an administrator, who was given the authority and was to be held responsible for the law's enforcement.

General Andrews, in a letter dated March 31, 1926, which was put in evidence at the hearing before the Senate Judiciary Committee, stated that 875 employees had been separated from the service for cause, from the commencement of prohibition to February 1, 1926 and of that number 658 separations had been effected since June 11, 1921. During substantially the same period, January 16, 1920 to March 30, 1926 148 officers and employees, including enforcement agents, inspectors, attorneys, clerks, etc., except-narcotic officers, were convicted on charges of criminality, including drunkenness and disorderly conduct.

While the number of convictions had in the federal courts for violation of provisions of the act, increased from 17,962 in the fiscal year ending June 30, 1921, to 37,018 in the fiscal year ending June 30, 1926, there was growing dissatisfaction with the results of the ad' ministration of the law, and an increasing volume of complaints against the service. These led to the introduction in Congress of a large variety of bills proposing amendments to the Eighteenth Amendment or to the National Prohibition Act and finally to demands for an investigation into the workings of the law.

Prohibition Enforcement Since 1927

The Bureau of Prohibition Act, 1927

Following the hearing before the Senate Committee, Congress, by act of March 3, 1927, known as "the Bureau of Prohibition Act" (44 Stats. 1381) created in the Department of the Treasury two bureaus a Bureau of Customs and a Bureau of Prohibition each under a commissioner; authorized the Secretary of the Treasury to appoint in each bureau one assistant commissioner, two deputy commissioners, one chief clerk, and such other officers and employees as he might deem necessary, and provided that the appointments should be subject to the provisions of the Civil Service laws and the salaries be fixed in accordance with the classification act of 1923. The Commissioner of Prohibition, with the approval of the Secretary of the Treasury, was authorized to appoint in the Bureau of Prohibition such employees in the field service as he might deem necessary, but it was expressly enacted that all appointments of such employees were to be made subject to the provisions of the Civil Service laws, notwithstanding the provisions of Section 38 of the National Prohibition Act. The term of office of any person who was transferred under this section to the Bureau of Prohibition, and who was not appointed subject to the provision of the Civil Service laws, was made to expire on the expiration of six months from the effective date of the Act, i.e, April 1, 1927.

From the time of enacting this law until the end of the year 1929, the tedious task of replacing men declared ineligible under the terms was taking place.

In April, 1927, the members of the force of the Bureau of Prohibition, exclusive of clerks in the field offices and clerks and administrative officials in the Washington headquarters (already serving under Civil Service regulations were subjected to examination to determine their eligibility to continue in the service). As a result, 41% of those of the force who took the examinations received therein passing marks by virtue of which they continued to hold their positions and 59% failed.

* * *

The foregoing statements are sufficient to indicate the nature, extent, and resources of the Governmental machinery which has been set up for the purpose of prohibition enforcement and the more important aspects of its administration. Viewed solely from the standpoint of the enforcement machinery and administration, it is obvious that the organization has passed through many vicissitudes and has been subject to conditions many of which have been prejudicial to effective service. How far these conditions were inherent in the nature and subject-matter of the undertaking and in the conditions under which it was inaugurated and has been developed and how far they might have been or may now be avoided is difficult of determination and opinions differ thereon. The Eighteenth Amendment represents the first effort in our history to extent directly by Constitutional provision the police control of the federal government to the personal habits and conduct of the individual. It was an experiment, the extent and difficulty of which was probably not appreciated. The government was without organization for or experience in the enforcement of a law of this character. In creating an organization for this purpose, it was necessary to proceed by the process of trial and error. The effort was subject to those limitations which are inseparable from all human and especially governmental activities.

II. THE PRESENT CONDITION AS TO OBSERVANCE AND ENFORCEMENT

Observance

There is a mass of information before us as to a general prevalence of drinking in homes, in clubs, and in hotels; of drinking parties given and attended by persons of high standing and respectability; of drinking by tourists at winter and summer resorts; and of drinking in connection with public dinners and at conventions. In the nature of the case it is not easy to get at the exact facts in such a connection, and conditions differ somewhat in different parts of the country and even to some extent from year to year. This is true likewise with respect to drinking by women and drinking by youth, as to which also there is a great mass of evidence. In weighing this evidence much allowance must be made for the effect of new standards of independence and individual self-assertion, changed ideas as to conduct generally, and the greater emphasis on freedom and the quest for excitement since the war. As to drinking among youth, the evidence is conflicting. Votes in colleges show an attitude of hostility to or contempt for the law on the part of those who are not unlikely to be leaders in the next generation. It is safe to say that a significant change has taken place in the social attitude toward drinking. This may be seen in the views and conduct of social leaders, business and professional men in the average community. It may be seen in the tolerance of conduct at social gatherings which would not have been possible a generation ago. It is reflected in a different way of regarding drunken youth, in a change in the class of excessive drinkers, and in the increased use of distilled liquor in places and connections where formerly it was banned. It is evident that, taking the country as a whole, people of wealth, businessmen and professional men, and their families, and, perhaps, the higher paid workingmen and their families, are drinking in large numbers in quite frank disregard of the declared policy of the National Prohibition Act.

There has been much discussion as to how the consumption of liquor today compares with that before prohibition. It will be necessary to go into that discussion later in considering the amount produced and imported in violation of law. So many purely speculative elements are involved in the making of any figures as to consumption today that in the present connection it is not worth while to make an elaborate review of the statistical material. But it may be remarked that the method of adding to the figures for the period before prohibition, in order to reach a basis of comparison, an annual increase in the proportion shown during the development of organized production and distribution is unsound. That rate of increase could not have gone on indefinitely into the future under any regime. The evidence as to Keely cures, as to arrests for drunkenness and the type of persons found drunk in public, as to deaths from causes attributable to alcohol, as to alcoholic insanity, as to hospital admissions for alcoholism, as to the change in the type of person treated for alcoholism, and as to drunken driving, while in each case subject to much criticism and raising many doubts, yet all seem to point in the same direction.

The Census Bureau figures for the year 1929 indicate a decline in the rate of deaths from alcoholism, and the figures on all the points referred to are still substantially below the pre-prohibition figures. Upon the whole, however, they indicate that after a brief period in the first years of the amendment there has been a steady increase in drinking.

To the serious effects of this attitude of disregard of the declared policy of the National Prohibition Act must be-added the bad effect on children and employees of what they see constantly in the conduct of otherwise law abiding persons. Such things and the effect on youth of the making of liquor in homes, in disregard of the policy, if not of the express provisions of the law, the effect on the families of workers of selling in homes, which obtains in many localities, and the effect on working people of the conspicuous newly acquired wealth of their neighbors who have engaged in bootlegging, are disquieting. This widespread and scarcely or not at all concealed contempt for the policy of the National Prohibition Act, and the effects of that contempt, must be weighed against the advantage of diminution (apparently lessening) of the amount in circulation.

These observations are not directed to a comparison between conditions before the Eighteenth Amendment and since, but only to changes taking place during the years since the adoption of the Amendment. The disquieting features above referred to should, of course, be weighed against the recognized fact that very large numbers of people have consistently observed the law.

III.   Bad Features of the Present Situation and Difficulties in the Way of Enforcement

Corruption

As to corruption it is sufficient to refer to the reported decisions of the courts during the past decade in all parts of the country, which reveal a succession of prosecutions for conspiracies, sometimes involving the police, prosecuting and administrative organizations of whole communities; to the flagrant corruption disclosed in connection with diversions of industrial alcohol and unlawful production of beer; to the record of federal prohibition administration as to which cases of corruption have been continuous and corruption has appeared in services which in the past had been above suspicion; to the records of state police organizations; to the revelations as to police corruption in every type of municipality, large and small, throughout the decade; to the conditions as to prosecution revealed in surveys of criminal justice in many parts of the land; to the evidence of connection between corrupt local politics and gangs and the organized unlawful liquor traffic, and of systematic collection of tribute from that traffic for corrupt political purposes. There have been other eras of corruption. Indeed, such eras are likely to follow wars. Also there was much corruption in connection with the regulation of the liquor traffic before prohibition. But the present regime of corruption in connection with the liquor traffic is operating in a new and larger field and is more extensive.

The Bad Start and Its Results

Too often during the early years of prohibition were arrests made and prosecutions instituted without sufficient evidence to justify them. In very many instances, unwarranted searches and seizures were made, which resulted in the refusal by Commissioners to issue warrants of arrest, or in the dismissal of the prosecution by the courts. In many instances, the character and appearance of the prohibition agents were such that the United States attorney had no confidence in the case and juries paid little attention to the witnesses. Thus some of the most important causes were lost to the Government. On the other hand, the prohibition agents were more concerned to secure a large number of arrests or seizures than to bring to the District Attorneys carefully prepared cases of actual importance. It is safe to say that the first seven years' experience in enforcing the law resulted in distrust of the prohibition forces by many of the United States attorneys and judges.

It must be said that enforcement of the National Prohibition Act made a bad start which has affected enforcement ever since. Many things contributed to this bad start.

(a) The Eighteenth Amendment was submitted and ratified during a great war. The National Prohibition Act was passed immediately thereafter. During a period of war the people readily yield questions of personal right to the strengthening of government and the increase of its powers. These periods are always characterized by a certain amount of emotionalism. This was especially true of the World War. These enlargements of governmental power, at the expense of individual rights are always followed by reactions against, the abuses of that power which inevitably occur. Periods following great wars are generally characterized by social discontent and unrest which frequently culminate in peaceful or violent revolutions. We have been passing through this secondary phase.

The Eighteenth Amendment and the National Prohibition Act came into existence, therefore, at the time best suited for their adoption and at the worst time for their enforcement. The general reaction against and resentment of the powers of government was inevitable. It could not fail to find expression in opposition to those laws which affected directly and sought in large measure to change the habits and conduct of the people. This attitude has been manifest in the non-observance and resistance to the enforcement of the prohibition laws.

The ratification of the Amendment was given by legislatures which were not in general elected with any reference to this subject. In many instances, as a result of old systems of apportionment. these legislative bodies were not regarded as truly representative of all elements of the community. When ratifications took place a considerable portion of the population were away in active military or other service. It may be doubted if under the conditions then prevailing the results would have been any different if these things had not been true yet these circumstances gave grounds for resentment which has been reflected in the public attitude toward the law and has thus raised additional obstacles to observance and enforcement.

(b) In the second place, the magnitude of the task was not appreciated. It seems to have been anticipated that the fact of the constitutional amendment and federal statute having put the federal government behind national prohibition would of itself operate largely to make the law effective. For a time, there appeared some warrant for this belief. For a time, uncertainty as to how far federal enforcement would prove able to go, lack of organization and experience on the part of law breakers, and perhaps some accumulated private stocks and uncertainty as to the demand and the profits involved, made violations cautious, relatively small in volume, and comparatively easy to handle. But soon after 1921 a marked chance took place. It became increasingly evident that violation was much easier and enforcement much more difficult than had been supposed. The means of enforcement provided proved increasingly inadequate. No thorough-going survey of the difficulties and consideration of how to meet them was undertaken, however, until violations had made such headway as to create a strong and growing public feeling of the futility of the law.

(c) A third cause was lack of experience of federal enforcement of a law of this sort. The subjects of federal penal legislation had been relatively few and either dealt with along well settled common law lines, or narrowly specialized. There was no federal police power and the use of federal powers for police purposes became important only in the present century. The existing federal machinery of law enforcement had not been set up for any such tasks and was ill adapted to those imposed upon it by the National Prohibition Act. But it was sought to adapt that machinery, or to let it find out how to adapt itself, without much prevision of the difficulties. Inadequate organization and equipment have resulted.

(d) A fourth cause which had serious incidental effects was the attempt to enforce the National Prohibition Act as something on another plane from the law generally; an assumption that it was of paramount importance and that constitutional guarantees and legal limitations on agencies of law enforcement and on administration must yield to the exigencies or convenience of enforcing it.

Some advocates of the law have constantly urged and are still urging disregard or abrogation of the guarantees of liberty and of sanctity of the home which had been deemed fundamental in our policy. In some states concurrent state enforcement made an especially bad start with respect to searches and seizures, undercover men, spies and informers; and by the public at large the distinction between federal and state enforcement officers was not easily made. Moreover, the federal field force as it was at first, was largely unfit by training, experience, or character to deal with so delicate a subject. High-handed methods, shootings and killings, even where justified, alienated thoughtful citizens, believers in law and order. Unfortunate public expressions by advocates of the law, approving killings and promiscuous shootings and lawless raids and seizures and deprecating the constitutional guarantees involved, aggravated this effect. Pressure for lawless enforcement, encouragement of bad methods and agencies of obtaining evidence, and crude methods of investigation and seizure on the part of incompetent or badly chosen agents started a current of adverse public opinion in many parts of the land.

(e) Another cause was the influence of politics. No doubt this influence of politics is inevitable in any connection where very large sums of money are to be made by manipulation of administration, and where control of patronage and through it of interference or noninterference with highly profitable activities may be made to yield huge funds for political organizations and as means to political power. In the enforcement of prohibition politics intervened decisively from the beginning, both in the selection of the personnel of the enforcing organization and in the details of operation. This political interference was particularly bad some years ago in connection with the permit system. When inquiry was made into large scale violations, when permits were sought by those not entitled to them, when attempt was made to revoke permits which had been abused, recourse was frequently had to local politicians to bring to bear political pressure whereby local enforcement activities were suspended or hampered or stopped. Nor was this the only source of interference. For some time over-zealous organizations, supporting the law, brought pressure to bear with respect to personnel and methods and even legislation which had unfortunate results. Only in the last few years has enforcement been reasonably emancipated from political interference.

(f) Constant changes in the statute and in the enforcing organization have also had an unfortunate effect. In eleven years the statute was amended or added to in important particulars four times. In that time the central organization as set up originally has twice been changed radically. In that same period the system of permits in connection with industrial alcohol has been changed three times. In consequence it may be claimed with good reason that administration of the law has not been as effective as it might have been.

(g) Another cause, which must not be overlooked, is lack of administrative technique in connection with the tribunals set up under the law. The National Prohibition Act gives to the supervisors of industrial alcohol powers of granting, renewing, and revoking permits-which may involve large investments and no inconsiderable businesses. Thus a system of administrative tribunals has been set up to pass on what may amount to very important property rights. The operation of administrative tribunals of all kinds, necessary as they obviously are, is giving serious concern, largely because of their lack of technique and lack of experience and the inherent difficulty of providing effective control. Perhaps nowhere are the results of this lack of technique more apparent than in connection with the administrative tribunals under the National Prohibition Act.

In some places administrative hearings with respect to permits are carried on as quasi-judicial proceedings, with the dignity of a court and with judicial methods. In others there is no settled procedure or systematic conduct of the proceedings, and in consequence there is want of uniformity, want of predictability, and often not a little dissatisfaction. In consequence there has been much variation in the attitude of the federal courts towards these tribunals. Where the courts have not supported or are not supporting the decisions of the administrators, it will be found as a rule, that the administrative tribunals in that particular locality are not, or until very recently were not, such in their personnel or in their procedure as to command judicial confidence. The evil that some of these tribunals did in the past lives after them in an unfortunate judicial attitude toward administration of the permit system in more than one important center.

(h) Another cause was lack of coordination of the several federal agencies actually or potentially concerned in enforcing prohibition, and consequent relative failure of cooperation until attention was given to this matter within the past few years.

Federal administration has always been more unified than that of the states. Yet friction and want of cooperation in law enforcement, as between different bureaus or services whose functions bear on the same fields or overlap, has been a common phenomenon which the exigencies of enforcing prohibition have merely made more prominent. Want of traditions of cooperation and departmental or bureau esprit de corps made it unlikely that services organized in different departments would cooperate heartily; and the services among which cooperation was to be promoted were distributed in the Department of the Treasury, the Department of Justice, the Department of Agriculture, and the Department of Labor. But even when the different agencies were in the same department, our traditions of independent individual administration led to habits or tendencies of non-cooperation among administrative bureaus. In some localities not long since there was often friction, and more often want of sympathetic common action between the customs authorities and the prohibition agents. There is evidence before us of "occasional co-operation" between the prohibition and the narcotic and immigration services as recently as a year ago. It is not much more than a year since a coordinator of the customs border patrol, coast guard and prohibition agencies was set up at one of the most important centers of importation of liquor in the United States. But for a decade those services were under one department.

When the services are organized in different departments, want of cooperation is even more to be expected. Before transfer of prohibition enforcement to the Department of Justice, there was not infrequent lack of cooperation between United States marshals and prohibition administrators. Within a year, in some places, there has been lack of cooperation between United States attorneys and prohibition administrators. Not long ago there was often much want of accord between them and even sometimes public disagreement. Recently there was want of cooperation between the prohibition administrator, or his agents, and agents of the Department of Agriculture in a section where enforcement is particularly difficult.

Thus enforcement has fallen short of what it should have been partly because of this tradition and these habits of non-cooperation between department and department, bureau and bureau, and service and service. But non-cooperative federal enforcement had gone on for a decade before much was done to co-ordinate the different federal activities and bring them into some unified system.

(i) Finally, enforcement was relied on in and of itself without any reinforcing activities to promote observance. After the passing of the National Prohibition Act, the educational activities toward a public opinion opposed to the use of intoxicating liquor gradually lost their impetus and largely became dormant. For a decade little or nothing has been done in this connection although such activities were peculiarly needed in an era of relaxing of standards of conduct and general free self-assertion. As a result too heavy a burden was put upon enforcement from the beginning and during the critical period in its history.

The State of Public Opinion

From the beginning ours has been a government of public opinion. We expect legislation to conform to public opinion, not public opinion to yield to legislation. Whether public opinion at a given time and on a given subject is right or wrong is not a question which according to American ideas may be settled by the words, "be it enacted." Hence it is futile to argue what public opinion throughout the land among all classes of the community ought to be in view of the Eighteenth Amendment and the achieved benefits of national prohibition. So long as state cooperation is required to make the amendment and the statute enforcing it effectual, adverse public opinion in some states and lukewarm public opinion with strong hostile elements in other states are obstinate facts which can not be coerced by any measures of enforcement tolerable under our polity. It is therefore a serious impairment of the legal order to have et national law upon the books theoretically governing the whole land and announcing a policy for the whole land which public opinion in many important centers will not enforce and in many others will not suffer to be enforced effectively. The injury to our legal and political institutions from such a situation must be weighed against the gains achieved by national prohibition. Means should be found of conserving the gains while adapting, or making it possible to adapt, legislation under the amendment to conditions and views of particular states.

Improved personnel and better training of federal enforcement agents under the present organization may well effect some change in public opinion, especially in localities where indignation has been aroused by crude or high handed methods formerly in vogue. But much of this indignation is due, to the conduct of state enforcement, which affects opinion as to enforcement generally. A change in the public attitude in such localities should follow an overhauling of state agencies.

We are not now concerned with the various theories as to prohibition, or with public opinion thereon, except as and to the extent that they are existing facts and causes affecting law observance and enforcement.

It is axiomatic that under any system of reasonably free government a law will be observed and may be enforced only where and to the extent that it reflects or is an expression of the general opinion of the normally law-abiding elements of the community. To the extent that this is the case, the law will be observed by the great body of the people and may reasonably be enforced as to the remainder.

The state of public opinion, certainly in many important portions of the country, presents a serious obstacle to the observance and enforcement of the national prohibition laws.

In view of the fact, however, that the prohibition movement received such large popular support and the Eighteenth Amendment was ratified by such overwhelming legislative majorities, inquiry naturally arises as to the causes of the present state of public opinion. There appear to be many causes, some arising out of the structure of the law the conditions to which it was to be applied, and the methods of its enforcement. Others, inherent in the principle of the act, may now be stated.

The movement against the liquor traffic and the use of intoxicating liquors for beverage purposes was originally a movement for temperance. The organizations which grew out of this movement and were potent in its development, were generally in their inception temperance organizations having as their immediate objectives the promotion of temperance in the use of alcoholic beverages and, as a means to this end, the abolition of the commercialized liquor traffic and the licensed saloon, which were the, obvious sources of existing abuses. In many of those states where prohibition laws were adopted and saloons abolished, provision was made for the legal acquisition of limited amounts of alcoholic liquors for beverage purposes. It was only when the Eighteenth Amendment was adopted that total abstinence was sought to be established by fiat of law throughout the territory of the United States or even in many of those states which had adopted limited prohibition laws.

There are obvious differences, both as to individual psychology and legal principle, between temperance and prohibition. Temperance assumes a moderate use of alcoholic beverages but seeks to prevent excess. Even though the ultimate objective may be total abstinence, it seeks to attain that objective by the most effective regulation possible and by the education of the individual to the avoidance of excess and gradual appreciation of the benefits of abstinence. To those holding this view, the field of legitimate governmental control over personal conduct is limited accordingly. Prohibition makes no distinction between moderate and excessive use. It is predicated upon the theory that any use of alcoholic liquors for beverage purposes, however, moderate and under any conditions, is antisocial and so injurious to the community as to justify legal restraint. To those who entertain this view the effort to enforce universal total abstinence by absolute legal mandate is logical. There is, therefore, a fundamental cleavage in principle between those who believe in temperance and those who believe in prohibition which it is difficult to reconcile under the traditional American attitude toward the law already discussed.

When the original temperance movement developed into one for prohibition, the immediate objective was the abolition of the commercialized liquor traffic and the legalized saloon. As between the alternatives of supporting prohibition or the saloon, those who favored the principle of temperance naturally supported prohibition; and, by a combination of the two groups, brought about the adoption of the Eighteenth Amendment and the National Prohibition Act.

When these measures became operative the situation was changed. The legalized liquor traffic and open saloon were abolished, and few desire their return. The question was no longer one between prohibition and the saloon but whether prohibition or the effort to enforce universal total abstinence by legal mandate was sound in principle or was the best and most effective method of dealing with the problem. On this question there was an immediate and inevitable cleavage between those who believed in prohibition and those who believed in temperance. Those who favored prohibition on principle naturally supported the law and demanded the most vigorous measures for its enforcement. Those who favored temperance on principle, while regarding the abolition of the legalized traffic and the saloon as a great and irrevocable step forward, yet looked upon the effort to require and enforce the total abstinence upon all the people, temperate and intemperate alike, by legal mandate, as unsound in principle and an unwarranted extension of governmental control over personal habits and conduct. They recognized and insisted upon the exercise of the right of the government to regulate and control the production, handling, and use of intoxicating liquors to the full extent necessary to prevent excessive use or other conduct which would be injurious to others or the community, but did not approve of the attempt to extend that power to the prevention of temperate use under conditions, not, in their view, injurious or antisocial. The abolition of the commercial traffic and the open saloon were so obviously steps in the right direction that for a time many of those holding this view acquiesced in the law or gave it passive support, but as its operations became more manifest and methods and efforts of enforcement developed, this acquiescence or indifference changed into non-observance or open hostility. Thus an ever widening difference was developed between those groups who by their united efforts for the abolition of the saloon had made possible the adoption of the Amendment and the National Prohibition Act.

Of course, there had been at all times a very substantial portion of the normally law-abiding people who had actively opposed the Eighteenth Amendment on principle. Many of these accepted and observed the law when once it was passed. When it became apparent that the results expected were not being realized, when the effects of the operations of the law and of the methods of enforcement which they deemed invasions of private rights became manifest, their opposition became aroused. This opposition was now, for reasons stated above, largely increased from the ranks of those who had formerly supported the law to get rid of the saloons, but felt that it went too far-who really favored the principle of temperance but did not favor prohibition. The cumulative result of these conditions was that from its inception to the present time the law has been to a constantly increasing degree deprived of that support in public opinion which was and inessential for its general observance or effective enforcement.

Economic Difficulties

Another type of difficulties are economic. Something has been said already of those involved in ease of production. The constant cheapening and simplification of production of alcohol and of alcoholic drinks, the improvement in quality of what may be made by illicit means the diffusion of knowledge as to how to produce liquor and the perfection of organization of unlawful manufacture and distribution have developed faster than the means of enforcement. But of even more significance is the margin of profit in smuggling liquor, in diversion of industrial alcohol, in illicit distilling and brewing, in bootlegging, and in the manufacture and sale of products of which the bulk goes into illicit or doubtfully lawful making of liquor. This profit makes possible systematic and organized violation of the National Prohibition Act on a large scale and offers rewards on a par with the most important legitimate industries. It makes lavish expenditure in corruption possible. It puts heavy temptation in the way of everyone engaged in enforcement or administration of the law. It affords a financial basis for organized crime.

Geographical Difficulties

A different type of difficulties may be called geographical. For one thing the proximity of sources of supply from the outside along almost 12,000 miles of Atlantic, Pacific and Gulf shore line, abounding in inlets, much of it adjacent to unoccupied tracts offering every facility to the smuggler, speaks for itself. But in addition the chief sources of supply from the outside are immediately accessible along nearly 3,000 miles of boundary on the Great Lakes and connecting rivers. Likewise we must take account of 3,700 miles of land boundaries. Our internal geography affords quite as much difficulty. Mountainous regions, such swamp areas as the Dismal Swamp and the Everglades islands in the great rivers such as the Mississippi, forested regions and barrens, are everywhere in relatively close proximity to cities affording steady and profitable markets for illicit liquor. Here also are the best of opportunities for unlawful manufacture.

Political Difficulties

What may be called political difficulties grow out of the limits of effective federal action in our polity, the need of state cooperation and the many factors operating against it, the tradition of politics and political interference in all administration, and the tendency to constant amendment of the law to be enforced.

It must be borne in mind that the federal government is one of limited powers. Except as granted to the United States or implied in those granted, all powers are jealously reserved to the state. Certain traditional lines of federal activity had become well developed and understood. Policing, except incidental to certain relatively narrow and specialized functions of the general government was not one of them. Importation, transportation across state lines, and the enforcement of excise tax laws were natural subjects of federal action. But prohibition of manufacture, distribution and sale within the states had always been solely within the scope of state action until the Eighteenth Amendment. This radical change in what had been our settled policy at once raised the question how far the federal government, as it was organized and had grown up under the Constitution, was adapted to exercise such a concurrent jurisdiction.

Nor was it merely that a radical change was made when the federal government was given jurisdiction over matters internal in the states. It was necessary also to adjust our federal polity to a conception of two sovereignties, each engaged independently in enforcing the same provision, so that, as it was supposed, wherever and whenever the one fell down the other might step in. Endeavor to bring about a nationally enforced universal total abstinence, instead of limiting the power devolved on the federal government to those features of the enforcement of the amendment which were naturally or traditionally of federal cognizance, invited difficulty at the outset. But difficulties inhered also in the conception of the amendment that nation and state were to act concurrently, each covering the whole of the same ground actually or potentially; each using its own governmental machinery at the same time with the other in enforcing provisions with respect to which each had a full jurisdiction.

There are four possibilities in such a situation (1) a strong, centralized, well-organized federal police; (2) full voluntary cooperation between state and nation; (3) a voluntary petition between state and nation in which each may be relied on to carry out zealously the part assigned to it, and (4) abdication of part, leaving to the states, if they care to exercise it full control over the field which the nation surrenders.

Attempts to bring about and maintain the requisite cooperation between national and state enforcement of prohibition encounter adverse public opinion in many important localities and are hampered by a bad tradition as to cooperation of state and federal governments and by irritation in communities which feel that the ideas of conduct and modes of life of other communities are being forced upon them.

We have a long tradition of independence of administrative officials and systematic decentralizing of administration. In consequence disinclination to cooperate has pervaded our whole polity, local, state, and federal; and for historical reasons since the Civil War there has been more or less latent, or even open, suspicion or jealousy of federal administrative agencies on the part of many of the states. Concurrent state and federal prohibition has shown us nothing new. It has repeated and recapitulated in a decade the experience of 140 years of administration of nation-wide laws in a government. In the beginnings of the federal government, it was believed that state officials and state tribunals could be made regularly available as the means of enforcing federal laws. It was soon necessary to set up a separate system of federal magistrates and federal enforcing agencies. We had no traditions of concerted action between independent governmental activities and it was not until the World War that we succeeded in developing a spirit of cooperation at least for the time being. In spite of that experience, the Eighteenth Amendment reverted to the policy of state enforcement of federal law, and again there has been not a little falling down of enforcement between concurrent agencies with diffused responsibility. The result was disappointing. Too frequently there has been a feeling, even in states which had prohibition laws before the National Prohibition Act, that enforcement of prohibition was now a federal concern with which the state need no longer trouble itself. Thus there has often been apathy or inaction on the part of state agencies even where local sentiment was strong for the law. It is true the good sense and energy of some prohibition directors and vigorous action on the art of some state executives have at times brought about a high degree of cooperation in more than one jurisdiction. Sometimes this cooperation is local and fitful, sometimes and in some places it is complete, and sometimes it is well organized and coordinated. But there are no guaranties of its continuance.

It seems now to be the policy of federal enforcement to make on its own motion a partition of the field, leaving all but interstate combinations and commercial manufacture to the state. This relinquishing of much of the field of concurrent jurisdiction, to be taken on by the states or not as they see fit, is a departure from the program of the Eighteenth Amendment.

All administration in the United States must struggle with a settled tradition of political interference. At the outset of enforcement of prohibition, the choice of enforcement agents was influenced for the worse both by politicians and by pressure of organizations. Positions in the enforcement organization were treated from the standpoint of patronage. Since the magnitude of the task could not have been appreciated, it was assumed that methods of filling federal administrative positions-which had on the whole sufficed as to other laws would suffice here. Thus the enforcement organization at first was not at all what the task called for. Moreover, political interference went beyond the filling of positions in the administrative organization. There was constant complaint of interference by politicians with the granting and revoking of permits, with efforts at enforcement and with the details of administration. Political interference has decreased, but as our institutions are organized and conducted, it will always be a menace to effectual enforcement.

Psychological Difficulties

A number of causes of resentment or irritation at the law or at features of its enforcement raise difficulties for national prohibition. A considerable part of the public were irritated at a constitutional "don't" in a matter where they saw no moral question. The statutory definition of "intoxicating" at a point clearly much below what is intoxicating in truth and fact, even if maintainable as a matter of legal power, was widely felt to be arbitrary and unnecessary. While there was general agreement that saloons were wisely eliminated, there was no general agreement on the universal regime of enforced total abstinence. In consequence many of the best citizens in every community, on whom we rely habitually for the upholding of law and order, are at most lukewarm as to the National Prohibition Act. Many who are normally law-abiding are led to an attitude hostile to the statute by a feeling that repression and interference with private conduct area carried too far. This is aggravated in many of the larger cities by a feeling that other parts of the land are seeking to impose ideas of conduct upon them and to mold city life to what are considered to be their provincial conceptions.

Other sources of resentment and irritation grow out of incidents of enforcement. In the nature of things it is easier to shut up the open drinking places and stop the sale of beer, which was drunk chiefly by working men, than to prevent the wealthy from having and using liquor in their homes and in their clubs. Naturally when the industrial benefits of prohibition are pointed out, laboring men resent the insistence of employers who drink that their employees be kept from temptation. It is easier to detect and apprehend small offenders than to reach the well organized larger operators. It is much easier to padlock a speakeasy than to close up a large hotel where important and influential and financial interests are involved. Thus the law may be made to appear as aimed at and enforced against the insignificant while the wealthy enjoy immunity. This feeling is reinforced when it is seen that the wealthy are generally able to procure pure liquors, where those with less means may run the risk of poisoning through the working over of denatured alcohol or, at best, must put up with cheap, crude, and even deleterious products. Moreover, searches of homes, especially under state laws, have necessarily seemed to bear more upon people of moderate means than upon those of wealth or influence. Resentment at crude methods of enforcement, unavoidable with the class of persons employed in the past and still often employed in state enforcement, disgust with informers, snoopers, and under-cover men unavoidably made use of if a universal total abstinence is to be brought about by law, and irritation at the inequalities of penalties, even in adjoining districts in the same locality and as between state and federal tribunals—something to be expected with respect to a law as to which opinions differ so widely—add to the burden under which enforcement must be conducted.

Resentment is aroused also by the government's collecting income tax from bootleggers and illicit manufacturers and distributors upon the proceeds of their unlawful business. This has been a convenient and effective way of striking at large operators who have not returned their true incomes. But it impresses many citizens as a legal recognition and even licensing of the business, and many who pay income taxes upon the proceeds of their legitimate activities feel strongly that illegitimate activities should be treated by the government as upon a different basis.

Any program of improvement should seek to obviate, or at least reduce to a minimum, these causes of resentment and irritation.

It will be perceived that some of them are due to differences of opinion as to total abstinence and could only be eliminated by bringing about a substantial unanimity on that subject throughout the land, or by conceding something to communities where public opinion is adverse thereto. Others are due largely to inherent features of all enforcement of law which have attracted special attention in connection with a matter of controversy. These may be met in part by improvements in the machinery of enforcement, by improvements in the general administration of criminal justice, and by unifying or reconciling public opinion, Still others are due to unfortunate but to no small extent remediable incidents of enforcement. Federal enforcement has been steadily improving in this respect. If state enforcement agencies in many jurisdictions could be similarly improved, the effect ought to be seen presently in a more favorable public opinion.

The Strain on Courts, Prosecuting Machinery, and Penal Institutions

Our federal organization of courts and of prosecution were ill adapted to the task imposed on them by the National Prohibition Act. Serious difficulties at this point soon became apparent and enforcement of national prohibition still wrestles with them. The program of concurrent federal and state enforcement imposes a heavy burden of what was in substance the work of police courts upon courts set up and hitherto employed chiefly for litigation of more than ordinary magnitude. In the first five years of national prohibition, the volume of liquor prosecutions in the federal courts had multiplied by seven and federal prosecutions under the Prohibition Act terminated in 1930 had become nearly eight times as many as the total number of all pending federal prosecutions in 1914. In a number of urban districts the enforcement agencies maintain that the only practicable way of meeting this situation with the existing machinery of federal courts and prosecutions is for the United States Attorneys to make bargains with defendants or their counsel whereby defendants plead quilt to minor offenses and escape with light penalties. Hence a disproportionate number of federal liquor prosecutions terminate in pleas of guilty: In the year ending June 30, 1930, over eight-ninths of the convictions were of this character. Since enactment of the Increased Penalties Act, 1929, prosecutors have proceeded by information for minor offenses in most cases, thus facilitating the bargain method of clearing the dockets. During the year ending June 30, 1930, whereas for the federal courts as a whole 41.4 per cent of the convictions resulted in sentences to some form of imprisonment, in three urban districts in which there was obvious congestion the percentages were 6.3, 3.9 and 5.0, respectively. The meagerness of the result in proportion to the effort shows the seriousness of the difficulty under which the enforcement of national prohibition has been laboring. But this is not all.

The bargain method of keeping up with the dockets which prevails of necessity in some of the most important jurisdictions of the country, plays into the hands of the organized illicit traffic by enabling it to reckon protection of its employees in the overhead. In some of our largest cities sentences have been almost uniformly to small fines or trivial imprisonment. Thus criminal prosecution, in view of the exigencies of disposing of so many cases in courts not organized for that purpose is a feeble deterrent. The most available methods of enforcement have come to be injunction proceedings and seizure and destruction of equipment and materials.

Lawyers everywhere deplore, as one of the most serious effects of prohibition, the change in the general attitude toward the federal courts. Formerly these tribunals were of exceptional dignity, and the efficiency and dispatch of their criminal business commanded wholesome fear and respect. The professional criminal, who sometimes had scanty respect for the state tribunals, was careful so to conduct himself as not to come within the jurisdiction of the federal courts. The effect of the huge volume of liquor prosecutions, which has come to these courts under prohibition, has inured their dignity, impaired their efficiency, and endangered the wholesome respect for them which once obtained. Instead of being impressive tribunals of superior jurisdiction, they have had to do the work of police courts and that work has been chiefly in the public eye. These deplorable conditions have been aggravated by the constant presence in about these courts of professional criminal lawyers and bail-bond agents, whose unethical and mercenary practices have detracted from these valued institutions.

Prosecutors, federal and state, have been affected no less than courts. They have been appointed and elected too often under pressure of organizations concerned only with prohibition, as if nothing else were to be considered in the conduct of criminal justice. Their work has been appraised solely in terms of their zeal in liquor cases. Under the pressure to make a record in such cases, it has not always been easy to keep up the right standards of forensic conduct and methods, and speeches such as had not been known in common law courts since the 17th century have become not uncommon in our criminal courts in the last decade. High-handed methods, unreasonable searches and seizures, lawless interference with personal and property rights, have had a bad effect on the work of prosecution at a time when the general condition of American administration of justice was imperatively demanding improvement.

Injurious effects upon the administrative machinery of the courts have been equally apparent. Instances of difficulty in procuring execution warrants by United States marshals, scandals in the carrying out of orders for the destruction of seized liquors, failure to serve orders in padlock injunction cases, and carrying on of illicit production and distribution under protection of a marshal or his assistants, in many places have brought the executive arm of the federal courts into disrespect, where until recently its efficiency was universally believed in. The procuring of permits, the giving of legal advice to beer rings and organizations of bootleggers and the acting as go-betweens between law-breakers and political organizations with a view to protection on one side and campaign contributions on the other, have made conspicuous a type of politician lawyer who had been absent from the federal courts in the past.

Nor have these bad effects been confined to the criminal side of the federal courts. There has been a general bad effect upon the whole administration of justice. There has been a tendency to appraise judges solely by their zeal in liquor prosecutions. In consequence the civil business of the court's has often been delayed or interfered with. Zealous organizations, dictating appointments, interfering with policies and seeking to direct the course of administering the law cooperating with other unfortunate conditions when the law took effect, brought about crude methods of enforcement. The gross inequalities of sentence made possible by the Increased Penalties Act, 1929, has added to the difficulties of the administration of criminal justice.

A policy, announced at one time, of dealing in the federal courts only with large-scale violations, with organized smuggling, diversion, and wholesale manufacture and transportation—leaving police cases to the state courts—was not generally successful for several reasons. Some states have no laws, and, in view of the clear implication of Section 2 of the Eighteenth Amendment, the federal government could not be expected to acquiesce in a general system of open violations in such states. Some states or localities, after the National Prohibition Act, began to leave all enforcement, or at least the brunt thereof, to the federal courts. In these states, too, the policy of Section 2 of the Amendment called for federal action. Moreover petty prosecutions often have an important place in a program of reaching larger violators. Before repeated offenders may be brought within the provisions of the statute as to second and subsequent offenses, it is necessary to prosecute them for a first time even if only for a relatively slight violation. Such prosecutions of small offenders may also be the means of inducing employees to confess and thus aid in detecting those who are behind them. Nor may we overlook the desire of federal agents and officials to make a record for liquor prosecutions and the difficulty of catching and convicting large-scale as compared with small-scale violators.

The operation of the National Prohibition Act has also thrown a greatly increased burden upon the federal penal institutions which seems bound to increase with any effective increase in enforcement. The reports of the Department of Justice show that the total federal long term prison population, i. e., prisoners serving sentences of more than a year, has risen from not more than 5,268 on June 30, 1921 to 14,115 on June 30, 1930. The number of long term prisoners confined in the five leading federal institutions on June 30, 1930 for violation of the National Prohibition Act and other national liquor laws was 4,296 out of a total of 12,332. The percentage of long term violators of the National Prohibition Act and other national liquor laws to total federal prisoners confined in the five leading federal institutions on June 30, 1930 was therefore something over one-third. This constituted by far the largest class of long term federal prisoners so confined, the next largest classes being made up of those sentenced for violation of the Dyer Act (the National Motor Vehicle Theft Act) and the Narcotic Acts, the percentage of whom on June 30, 1930 were, respectively, 13.2% and 22% of the total.

The figures above set out include only persons serving sentences of more than one year, and do not include the very large number of individuals confined in county jails and other institutions for violation of the National Prohibition Act under shorter sentences.

The recital of these figures is sufficient to indicate the gravity and difficulty of the problem from the, penal housing standpoint, which the effective enforcement of the National Prohibition Act presents.

How Far Are These Bad Features Necessarily Involved in National Prohibition?

As to the prevailing corruption, it has its foundation in the profit involved in violations of the National Prohibition Act. Hence it could be put an end to, or at least greatly reduced, by eliminating or reducing that profit. Also it could be materially reduced by better selection of personnel, both in the federal enforcing organization and in state police, administrative and prosecuting organizations. But it may be queried whether the profit in violation of the National Prohibition Act is likely to be eliminated or largely reduced so long as so many people and the people in so many localities are willing to pay considerable sums to obtain liquor, and so long as the money available for corruption is so wholly out of proportion to what is practicable in the way of salaries for those concerned with enforcement.

As to the state of public opinion, the way toward improvement is chiefly through education. Unhappily, since the National Prohibition Act the whole emphasis has been upon coercion rather than upon education. In addition many, at least, of the causes of resentment at national prohibition could be removed and thus a more favorable public attitude could be induced. On the other hand, it may be urged that it is too late to educate public opinion in those communities where a settled current adverse to national prohibition has set in. Also, care must be taken lest some of the changes in the law, necessary to remove what have become sources of irritation, may involve relaxation of enforcement so as to react unfavorably upon other features of the situation. The main difficulty will be to reconcile the population in our large urban centers to the policy announced in section three of the National Prohibition Act. How far this is possible is a matter of judgment on which opinions differ.

So also as to the profit involved in violations. How far as a practical matter this may be eliminated by more ample provision of machinery for enforcement and stimulating more complete cooperation in the enforcement of the law as it stands depends upon a judgment as to what may be achieved in places where there is hostile or lukewarm public opinion. At bottom, this question is linked to the preceding one.

The strain on federal courts and federal prosecuting machinery, grows out of the inadequacy of the organization of federal courts and of the federal prosecuting system to the task imposed upon it. To a degree, this inadequacy could be remedied. But it may be a question how far it is expedient to set up what would be in effect a system of federal police magistrates in order to enforce the National Prohibition Act in jurisdictions where the police will not deal with lesser violations to which the present federal judicial organization not adapted. If such violations are not prosecuted somewhere, either in state or in federal tribunals, there is to that extent nullification. While this bad feature of the present situation is not inherent in prohibition, it is closely connected with the question of cooperation between state and federal governments and of concurrent jurisdiction as contemplated by the Eighteenth Amendment, and what is done by way of remedy must depend upon the conclusions reached with respect to possibilities of cooperation.

Finally, with respect to the provision in Section 29 of Title 2 of the National Prohibition Act relation to home production of the bad or potentially bad, features of the present situation could be and ought to be eliminated by the simple process of making the provision in this respect uniform with those of the rest of the act. Removal of the anomalous provision in Section 29 would do away with what threatens to be a serious impairment of the legislatively announced policy of national prohibition.

IV.   THE DEGREE OF ENFORCEMENT DEMANDED

It is a truism that no laws are absolutely observed or enforced. A reasonable approximation to general observance and to full enforcement is the most we may expect. What, then, should be considered a reasonably practical enforcement of the National Prohibition Act? If we compare that Act with other laws, would not our measure be such an enforcement as operates on the whole as an effective deterrent and brings a high average of observance throughout the land?

If, with regard to any law, assuming a vigorous effort at enforcement the result is found to be that, notwithstanding enormous numbers of convictions, there is little deterrent effect and, after a decade of experience the volume of violations seems to increase steadily and the public attitude is increasingly indifferent or hostile, the question arises as to whether such a law is, in any proper sense, enforceable. Moreover, there is a difference in effect between failure of enforcement of such a law as the National Prohibition Act and lax or ineffective enforcement of other federal laws. The everyday work of police belongs to the states. The bulk of federal legislation has little or no relation to the general maintenance of law and order. Poor enforcement of the customs laws, for example, would chiefly affect the revenue and the particular businesses subjected to unlawful competition. But if the National Prohibition Act is not enforced, the collateral bad effects extend to every side of administration, police, and law and order. In view of the policy announced in section three of that Act, any large volume of intoxicating liquor continually in circulation shows a serious falling short of the goal, and is highly prejudicial to respect for law. The enforcement to be aimed at must be one operating as an effectual deterrent upon manufacture, importation, transportation, sale, and possession in every part of the land, resulting in a uniformly high observance of the announced purpose of the act everywhere; and restricting the liquor in general circulation to a relatively negligible amount.

X. Conclusions and Recommendations

1. The Commission is opposed to repeal of the Eighteenth Amendment.

2. The Commission is opposed to the restoration in any manner of the legalized saloon.

3. The Commission is opposed to the federal or state governments, as such, going into the liquor business.

4. The Commission is opposed to the proposal to modify the National Prohibition Act so as to permit manufacture and sale of light wines or beer.

5. The Commission is of opinion that the cooperation of the states is an essential element in the enforcement of the Eighteenth Amendment and the National Prohibition Act throughout the territory of the United States; that the support of public opinion in the several states is necessary in order to insure such cooperation.

6. The Commission is of opinion that prior to the enactment of the Bureau of Prohibition Act, 1927, the agencies for enforcement were badly organized and inadequate; that subsequent to that enactment there has been continued improvement in organization and effort for enforcement.

7. The Commission is of opinion that there is yet no adequate observance or enforcement.

8. The Commission is of opinion that the present organization for enforcement is still inadequate.

9. The Commission is of opinion that the federal appropriations for enforcement of the Eighteenth Amendment should be substantially increased and that the vigorous and better organized efforts which have gone on since the Bureau of Prohibition Act, 1927, should be furthered by certain improvements in the statutes and in the organization, personnel, and equipment of enforcement, so as to give to enforcement the greatest practicable efficiency.

10. Some of the Commission are not convinced that Prohibition under the Eighteenth Amendment is unenforceable and believe that a further trial should be made with the help of the recommended improvements, and that if after such trial effective enforcement is not secured there should be a revision of the Amendment. Others of the Commission are convinced that it has been demonstrated that Prohibition under the

Eighteenth Amendment is unenforceable and that the Amendment should be immediately revised, but recognizing that the process of amendment will require some time, they unite in the recommendations of Conclusion No. 9 for the improvement of the enforcement agencies.

11. All the Commission agree that if the Amendment is revised it should be made to read substantially as follows:

Section 1. The Congress shall have power to regulate or to prohibit the manufacture, traffic in or transportation of intoxicating liquors within, the importation thereof into and the exportation thereof from the United States and all territory subject to the jurisdiction thereof for beverage purposes.

12. The recommendations referred to in conclusion Number 9 are:

1. Removal of the, causes of irritation and resentment on the part of the medical profession by:

(a) Doing away with the statutory fixing of the amount which may be prescribed and the number of prescriptions;

(b) Abolition of the requirement of specifying the ailment for which liquor is prescribed upon a blank to go into the public files;

(c) Leaving as much as possible to regulations rather than fixing details by statute.

2. Removal of the anomalous provisions in Section 29, National Prohibition Act, as to cider and fruit juices by making some uniform regulation for a fixed alcoholic content.

3. Increase of the number of agents, storekeeper-gaugers, prohibition investigators, and special agents; increase in the personnel of the Customs Bureau and in the equipment of all enforcement organizations.

4. Enactment of a statute authorizing regulations permitting access to the premises and records of wholesale and retail dealers so as to make it possible to trace products of specially denatured alcohol to the ultimate consumer.

5. Enactment of legislation to prohibit independent denaturing plants.

6. The Commission is opposed to legislation allowing more latitude for federal searches and seizures.

7. The Commission renews the recommendation contained in its previous reports for codification of the National Prohibition Act and the acts supplemental to and in amendment thereof.

8. The Commission renews its recommendation of legislation for making procedure in the so-called padlock injunction cases more effective.

9. The Commission recommends legislation providing a mode of prosecuting petty offenses in the federal courts and modifying the

Increased Penalties Act of 1929, as set forth in the Chairman's letter to the Attorney General dated May 23, 1930, H. R. Rep. 1699.

There are differences of view among the members of the Commission as to certain of the conclusions stated and as to some matters included in or omitted from this report. The report is signed subject to individual reservation of the right to express these individual views in separate or supplemental reports to be annexed hereto.

Notes and Questions

1.   The Wickersham Commission was the first national blue ribbon commission on issues relating to crime and the administration of criminal justice. It reported in 1931, 12 years into the era of national prohibition and within two years of the 21st amendment and repeal. It was also the last national commission effort for more than three decades, until Lyndon Johnson created the President's Commission on Crime in the mid–1960s.

2.   Were there major issues about the impact of prohibition that the Commission missed? If not, what accounts for the absence of any argument for repeal of prohibition from members of the Commission? If the folly of alcohol prohibition is so obvious from the vantage point of seven decades after repeal, what accounts for the absence of a fundamental critique in 1931? Does this same kind of "stay-the-course conservative bias" inhibit discussion of modern criminal justice programs in areas such as drugs and gambling?

3.   Is the Wickersham Commission report a form of cost-benefit study? If not, would that form have changed its conclusions? What conditions might have persuaded the Commission to urge repeal?

4.   There have been presidential commissions in the United States on crime, on violence, on civil disorder and on pornography, but no national commissions on prostitution or on narcotics. Why? What explains the lack of a Wickersham-style inquiry in the late 1990s on the "war on drugs"? Should there be such an effort now?

D.   MODERN ALCOHOL POLICY

1.   MADD, SOBRIETY, AND DWI

ERIC GOUVIN—DRUNK DRIVING AND THE ALCOHOLIC OFFENDER: A NEW APPROACH TO AN OLD PROBLEM
12 Am. J. L. and Med. 99 (1986).

IV.   A NEW APPROACH TO THE ALCOHOLIC DWI OFFENDER

Several studies have demonstrated the extensive interrelation between alcohol abuse and drunk driving. One study has shown that almost two-thirds of those charged with DWI, and half the drivers involved in accidents after drinking, are either alcoholic or alcohol abusive. Since close to 66 percent of the DWI population suffers from alcohol problems, in contrast to a 10 percent incidence in the general population, there appears to be a significant correlation between alcohol abuse and DWI. Researchers generally agree that alcoholics and alcohol abusers are more likely to be involved in traffic accidents than light drinkers or non-drinkers. Therefore, it appears that drunk driving is symptomatic of the much bigger problem of alcoholism and alcohol abuse.

Virtually every state in the union has laws dealing with alcoholism. These state statutes either implicitly or explicitly recognize alcoholism as a treatable disease. At the same time, however, all of the states take a primarily criminal approach to the problem of drunk driving. The problem of DWI, however, seems to implicate medical issues beyond the scope of the criminal law.

Applying criminal sanctions to those not in control of their actions is both counterproductive and ineffective. Herbert Packer's comments concerning the crime of public intoxication apply with equal force to the failure of criminal sanctions to control drunk driving. In Packer's words, such a failure "provides a classic illustration of the twofold evil that results from misusing the criminal sanction: we burden the operations of the criminal process to no avail, and we delude ourselves into believing that we have thereby solved a social problem." Experience shows that public inebriation laws apparently did not affect the incidence of public drunkenness. Experience also shows that the problem of driving while intoxicated is apparently unaffected by the various criminal approaches designed to curtail it. The shortcomings of the criminal sanction in the DWI context are arguably the fault of states failing to recognize that the majority of DWI offenders have serious problems with alcohol abuse.

Because state laws relating to alcohol are internally inconsistent, getting to the root of the DWI problem appears difficult. If alcoholism is a disease under the public health code it should be treated as a disease in other areas of the law. Drafting a DWI law that is sensitive to the disease concept of alcoholism is potentially the most successful way to deal with the alcoholic DWI offender.

One such approach would be to require all DWI offenders to receive detoxification treatment, but this approach would be over-inclusive, since one-third of known DWI offenders are presumably in control of their drinking habits. These "social drinkers" should be able to conform their conduct to the dictates of the law. A criminal sanction is appropriate for these social drinkers who know the consequences of drinking and driving, but decide to drive anyway. To send social drinkers to a detoxification/rehabilitation program is an inappropriate medical response to a legal problem.

A second approach would be to impose a very severe criminal penalty on all DWI offenders. Although this might deter social drinkers, and although the general public might feel better having a "tough" drunk-driving law, it would do nothing to address the underlying drinking problems of two-thirds of the DWI offender class. Such a myopic approach would be inefficient in the long run.

A more reasonable approach would provide a mixture of punishment and treatment. This would entail testing all DWI offenders to determine their relationship with alcohol; if an offender is diagnosed alcoholic or alcohol abusive, he or she would be regarded as a person with a disease that affects driving ability. Disposition of the alcoholic DWI offender would be patterned after the way epileptic drivers are handled by the motor vehicle law. The alcoholic's license would be suspended until he could produce documented evidence from a doctor certified in the treatment of alcoholism that the offender's condition is being treated and that the offender is abstaining from alcohol. Furthermore, the law would require continued periodic documentation showing that the condition is under control in order to keep the driver's license in good standing. If an offender is diagnosed as a non-alcoholic, he would be sentenced with reasonable fines, community service, imprisonment, or a combination thereof. This new approach does not provide alcoholic DWI offenders with a complete excuse defense. Rather, it charges them with an affirmative duty to take care of their condition.

A. Diagnostic Problems

1. Separating Social Drinkers from Problem Drinkers

One criticism of this new approach is that it would be difficult to separate "problem drinkers" from "social drinkers." In the past fifteen years, the quality of alcoholism diagnosis and classification techniques has improved dramatically. As noted previously, alcohol consumption is defined along a continuum ranging from "healthy" to "chronic alcoholic." At the extremes, the diagnosis is accurate, but since most cases fall somewhere in the middle, professional judgment is required. The majority of police officers and judges do not possess the requisite medical expertise to diagnose alcoholism. In order to separate "alcoholics" from "non-alcoholics" for purposes of disposition under a disease concept DWI law, therefore, all offenders would be required to see a state-certified alcohol clinician for a diagnostic session. Although no one screening test has gained acceptance from all members of the alcohol research community, a clinician using a battery of tests can make a meaningful determination of the individual's relationship with alcohol. This determination would be passed along to the court for appropriate disposition. Several states currently require the screening of all DWI offenders for possible alcohol abuse problems. This is a step in the right direction, but it does not go far enough. Although an offender may be diagnosed alcoholic, judges in most states still have discretion to require treatment or impose a criminal sanction.

A judge should not have the discretion to impose only punishment, and no treatment, on a DWI offender diagnosed as alcoholic. If an offender is diagnosed as having a disease, an appropriate disposition should always include treatment, In some cases, a combination of treatment and punishment may be required, but the treatment aspect should not be omitted. For example, if an epileptic caused an accident because of an uncontrolled seizure, it would be unusual for a court to sentence that person without requiring him to either obtain treatment, or stop driving, or both. The same should hold true for alcoholic drivers. Under a coherent disease concept approach, the judge would have very limited discretion with regard to the alcoholic offender's punishment and treatment.

2. *Imposters*

Critics also raise the concern of an alcoholic posing as a "social drinker." If the balance between the punishment and treatment modes of disposition has been carefully struck, however, there will be no incentive for "social drinkers" to pose as "problem drinkers," or vice versa. A major goal of a mixed disposition approach is to overcome the notion that treatment means "letting the offender off easy." Although past and current court-ordered "treatment" programs have been called, with some justification, a "slap on the wrist," a true recovery program is an arduous journey which would not reward those seeking to avoid criminal sanctions with a pleasant hotel stay.

Differentiating between punishment and treatment is not always easy. The degree of unpleasantness or the severity of the disposition is not the defining characteristic. To use Herbert Packer's example, "thirty days in jail for disorderly conduct is much less unpleasant than a lifetime in the locked ward of a state mental hospital. Yet common usage will unhesitatingly classify the former as Punishment and the latter (perhaps not quite so unhesitatingly) as Treatment."

The ultimate goal of the disease concept DWI laws will be to treat the alcoholic offender as a sick individual even though he has committed an act which is a crime when committed by a "social drinker." The obvious parallel to the insanity defense is intentional. We do not punish insane offenders, but use the criminal justice system as a screening device to channel these individuals into the health care system. As with the treatment of the insane, alcoholism treatment should be designed to cure the truly ill, not coddle imposters.

B. *Treatment Problems*

Another difficulty with the proposed DWI approach involves how much treatment to require once an offender has been diagnosed as "alcoholic" or "alcohol abusive." As a practical matter, this determination largely depends on the attitude of the patient. If he is cooperative and motivated, progress will be his reward. If, however, the patient is recalcitrant and stubborn, it will take a longer time for him to start his recovery. Under a disease concept DWI law, the offender would have to remain under active treatment until an accredited alcohol clinician could certify that his alcoholism was under control, however long that might take.

No one is ever "cured" of alcoholism. Treatment after detoxification/rehabilitation, called "aftercare," is imperative. In the proposed disease concept DWI law, diagnosed alcoholic drivers would be handled as epileptic drivers are currently handled. An epileptic who is not in treatment, and is therefore not in control of his seizures, poses a serious public safety problem when he is behind the wheel of an automobile. Similarly, an alcoholic driver who is not in recovery, and therefore not in control of his drinking, also poses a serious public safety problem.

All states require epileptic drivers to produce evidence that they are in control of their seizures before they can receive a driver's license. These laws usually require proof of a long seizure-free period in order to establish that the epileptic is in control of his seizures. Additionally, most states require periodic reports from the epileptic's physician to certify that the epileptic is maintaining his treatment. The same requirements should apply to alcoholic drivers, since the broadly-worded driving laws used to reach epileptic drivers grant power to the commissioner of motor vehicles to deny a license to anyone who is medically unfit to drive. Often, the same laws that bar epileptics from driving specifically deny "habitual drunkards" the right to drive as well. Under a disease concept approach, a state could require treatment and an alcohol-free period of a year or more as a prerequisite for return of the driver's license and also require periodic certification from an accredited alcohol clinician that the alcoholic is continuing his treatment and receiving aftercare.

To fully implement this proposal, drivers who have been diagnosed alcoholic would have to be reported to a state's department of motor vehicles. Several states require epileptics, doctors, or others to report epileptic drivers to the state motor vehicle department. These reporting laws have come under attack from groups like the Epilepsy Foundation of America as being an invasion of the doctor/patient privilege and for tending to discourage some people from seeking treatment of their condition. These concerns could be met by applying the reporting requirement only to those cases where alcohol treatment is received pursuant to legal proceedings. Moreover, some courts have held that the state's interest in maintaining public safety is compelling enough to override the doctor/patient privilege.

Another controversial issue in the area of treatment is that requiring an offender to check into a treatment facility could amount to involuntary civil commitment. This problem could be avoided by not actually requiring treatment, but rather by making successful completion of a treatment program and continuing aftercare reports a condition for return of his license. The offender has the choice to either undergo treatment voluntarily and get his or her license back, or refuse treatment and give up the driving privilege.

1. Court Ordered Treatment Programs

There is a good deal of controversy as to the effectiveness of DWI rehabilitation programs. Much of the controversy surrounds a program adopted by the federal government in the 1970's called the Alcohol Safety Action Project (ASAP). ASAP had many components, including public education, driver training schools, increased enforcement, and required treatment programs. The most controversial component dealt with the identification and rehabilitation of problem drinkers. The federal government eventually set up pilot programs in thirty-five cities before funds ran out. The ASAP programs could not be adequately evaluated due to design flaws. However, anecdotal evidence and a methodologically suspect follow-up study pronounced the project ineffective.

The biggest problem with the follow-up study was an unstated belief that the goal of the ASAP programs was to reduce alcohol-related traffic fatalities. With that goal in mind, the study "proved" the ineffectiveness of the ASAP programs by finding no significant decrease in the incidence of fatal accidents involving alcohol after the programs were initiated. The study failed to note that in all alcohol-related highway fatalities, 96 percent of alcohol-impaired drivers had never been apprehended for drunk driving before the accident. To label a treatment program aimed at specific deterrence "ineffective" because individuals who have not gone through treatment have continued to engage in the offensive behavior, is simply not a valid criticism.

Alcoholism is a disease. People do not recover from a disease just because a new law has been passed. To evaluate the treatment approach, studies must focus on the effect of the treatment program on those who were treated. The goal of such studies would be to evaluate the public health consequences of more widespread treatment of alcoholism, rather than the treatment program's effect on safety.

Another study of ASAP evaluated its effect on recidivism. The study "provided no *overwhelming* evidence of program effectiveness as measured by reductions in crash or arrest recidivism" (emphasis added), although some reductions were reported. The report found that education programs had a small positive deterrent effect for social drinkers. Large impersonal lecture classes, however, had either no effect or a negative effect on deterring problem drinkers. A significant, but frequently overlooked finding of the report was that problem drinkers attending smaller, more personalized group therapy programs had lower re-arrest rates than those attending larger, more impersonal programs. The authors of the study, recognizing the methodological problems inherent in trying to evaluate the ASAP program, cautioned against placing too much emphasis on the findings of the evaluation reports.

The allegation that ASAP was ineffective in responding to the problem of alcoholic drivers is based on intrinsically flawed studies. These studies do not show that a treatment approach, like the one advocated in this Note, cannot work. Rather, they show that such a program must be evaluated in terms of its public health consequences and must treat alcoholics as individuals with a disease. The effectiveness of such a program has been neither proved nor disproved.

2. *Assuring Compliance With Treatment Programs*

Critics may argue that it would be extremely difficult to assure compliance with the treatment programs. However, it is constitutionally permissible for a state to impose criminal sanctions on an individual who fails to adhere to a medical program designed to protect public health and safety. As with the epileptic who fails to maintain his treatment, the state is justified in suspending the driver's license of the alcoholic driver who refuses treatment or returns to active alcoholism. If the driver continues to drive without a license, enforcement should be very strict. This two-stage disposition of the alcoholic offender is a carrot and stick approach. The initial treatment program is the carrot, but if that fails, the state may resort to the stick of criminal and civil penalties.

This resort to criminal sanctions against the alcoholic offender is not inconsistent with the proposed approach. The disease concept DWI law operates on the assumption that most offenders are unaware of their alcoholic status at the time of arrest. The diagnosis and court proceedings are medically and legally significant events that put the offender on notice that he is an alcoholic, not merely that he was driving while intoxicated. The sentence creates a duty on his part to take care of the condition. Therefore, punishment of an individual for failure to receive or maintain treatment for a known condition in order to protect public health and safety is not unconstitutional punishment for having the condition.

C. *Punishment Problems*

1. *Punishing "Social Drinkers"*

Critics are concerned with the disposition of the "social drinker" portion of the offender class and how to most effectively penalize that class. Popular thinking on this subject seems to be "the bigger the penalty, the better the deterrence." This simple formula, however, has not been confirmed by empirical data. Although most states that tough drunk driving laws do experience a short-term decline in the number of drunk driving related accidents, the effect is always just a short-term phenomenon. The key to deterrence lies in the enforcement of the laws. The chance of getting caught for DWI in the average American city has been estimated at one in 2000, which is less than the risk of getting in an automobile accident. This enforcement rate is so low that even the heaviest fine is deeply discounted, resulting in a small deterrent effect. Part of the answer to the drunk driving problem seems to lie in increasing the enforcement rate, or at least the perceived enforcement rate, for DWI. Still, that insight does not tell us how severe DWI penalties should be.

Our legal system requires that the penalty fit the crime. Judges sentence offenders in DWI cases. Some judges see the crime of DWI as so heinous that only a very great penalty will "pay" for it; other judges take a more lenient attitude. Despite these differences, judges in the same jurisdiction must strive to apply the law consistently and fairly.

The state may try to achieve the desired consistency through determinate sentencing. All violators would be treated exactly the same way. What this approach gains in consistency, it sacrifices in fairness. Often there are extenuating circumstances that call for a heavier or lighter penalty than the one mandated.

The disease concept DWI law would strive to ensure consistency, yet also allow flexibility. Under the proposed disease concept DWI law, if the findings of the clinician are not findings of fact but only recommendations, the court would retain its discretion to choose between treatment and punishment for the offenders. Presumably, some judges would sentence all offenders with a criminal sanction, thereby frustrating the goal of treating the medical problem of alcoholism, while other judges would sentence all offenders to treatment, thereby frustrating the goal of holding social drinkers responsible for their acts.

To avoid this problem, either the clinicians' findings must be binding on the court, or there must be a proper balance between the severity of punishment and the rigor of treatment so that judges will dispose of all cases properly. To achieve this balance, the treatment aspect of the law must be rigorous and lengthy enough to convince the "tough" judges (and juries) that the offender is not "getting off scot-free." In the proposed disease concept DWI law, the "treatment" option requires loss of license until documented successful treatment is achieved. Because the "treatment" disposition for the problem drinker may result in permanent loss of license, it is demanding enough "tough" judges would be willing to apply it. On the other hand, the criminal penalty for the social drinker must not be so onerous that lenient judges will be reluctant to apply it. A recurring problem with drunk driving laws is that the penalties are so severe that judges and juries hesitate to apply them.

Therefore, in the disease concept DWI law, the criminal sanctions would be marked by moderate fines, imprisonment, or community service. The treatment aspect would contain a serious alcoholism rehabilitation program (not just a driver's education program) with a rigorous aftercare component, requiring ongoing documentation of continued treatment.

2. Driver Culpability for Resultant Harm

Another argument against the disease concept approach is the problem of resultant harm caused by the drunk driver. The example often used is that of an innocent person killed by the alcoholic driver. A judge who is sensitive to public opinion will find it difficult to stick to the principles of culpability developed by H.L.A. Hart. Groups such as Mothers Against Drunk Drivers (MADD), Students Against Drunk Drivers (SADD) and Remove Intoxicated Drivers (RID) have done an excellent job in promoting public awareness of the drunk driving problem. Unfortunately, since the members of these groups usually have lost a loved one to a drunk driver, they have also done much to suffuse the issue with emotion. Emotionalism and the current penchant for "tough" punishment may unconsciously help society satisfy a need for cathartic retribution, but such primitive impulses are inappropriate in a culpability-based system of criminal justice.

As a logical matter, the problem of how to dispose of the alcoholic DWI offender in this situation is not difficult. The culpability of the alcoholic DWI offender must be evaluated just like any other defendant. If the court or jury determines that the offender had some degree of culpability, then he should be found guilty of some degree of homicide, ranging from vehicular homicide to murder. The mere presence of attendant harm does not make an offender more culpable. It would be appropriate in some cases to revoke the alcoholic defendant's license until successful completion of treatment, without criminal liability. This disposition would be appropriate if the court determined that the offender was involuntarily intoxicated. An argument can be made that a chronic alcoholic is involuntarily intoxicated, even though it appears that he has consumed alcohol voluntarily.

Many analysts determine the culpability of an intoxicated (not necessarily alcoholic) offender by determining the offender's culpability at the time of his first drink. This mens rea, or mental state, is then applied to the crime committed while the offender is intoxicated. While this analysis may be appropriate for the intoxicated offender, it does not work when dealing with the alcoholic offender. An alcoholic is an alcoholic whether he is dry or intoxicated. Determining an alcoholic's mens rea at the time of the first drink is meaningless. The compulsion w drink is as involuntary at the time of the first drink, as it is at the time of the tenth drink. An involuntary act has no mens rea. On the other hand, the social drinker is not compelled to drink. He has an identifiable mens rea at the time of the first drink, and is therefore appropriately subject to the criminal law in accordance with H.L.A. Hart's culpability principle.

The task of the criminal law is to determine the culpability of the offender. The problem of resultant harm is not the concern of the criminal law. Those aggrieved by a defendant's acts may proceed against him in a civil action if they desire compensation.

2. LIQUOR STORES, DISTRESSED NEIGHBORHOODS, AND POVERTY

BERNARD HARCOURT—THE COLLAPSE OF THE HARM PRINCIPLE
90 Journal of Criminal Law and Criminology 109 (1999).

In November 1998, fourteen neighborhoods in Chicago voted to shut down their liquor stores, bars, and lounges, and four more neighborhoods voted to close down specific taverns. Three additional liquor establishments were voted shut in February 1999. Along with the fourteen other neighborhoods that passed dry votes in 1996 and those that went dry right after Prohibition, to date more than 15% of Chicago has voted itself dry. The closures affect alcohol-related businesses, like liquor stores and bars, but do not restrict drinking in the privacy of one's home. The legal mechanism is an arcane 1933 "vote yourself dry" law, enacted at the time of the repeal of Prohibition, and amended by the state legislature in 1995.

Chicago's temperance movement reflects a fascinating development in the legal enforcement of morality. Instead of arguing about morals, the proponents of enforcement are talking about individual and social harms in contexts where, thirty years ago, the harm principle would have precluded regulation or prohibition. Chicago is a case on point. The closures are part of Mayor Richard Daley's campaign to revitalize neighborhoods. The campaign focuses on the harms that liquor-related businesses produce in a neighborhood, not on the morality or immorality of drinking. "People are voting for their pocketbook, for home values, for church, children and seniors," Mayor Daley is reported to have said. "This is a quality of life issue, not an attempt to impose prohibition."

A similar shift in justification is evident in a wide range of debates over the regulation or prohibition of activities that have traditionally been associated with moral offense—from prostitution and pornography, to loitering and drug use, to homosexual and heterosexual conduct. In a wide array of contexts, the proponents of regulation and prohibition have turned away from arguments based on morality, and turned instead to harm arguments. In New York City, for example, Mayor Rudolph Giuliani has implemented a policy of zero-tolerance toward quality-of-life offenses, and has vigorously enforced laws against public drinking, public urination, illegal peddling, squeegee solicitation, panhandling, prostitution, loitering, graffiti spraying, and turnstile jumping. According to Mayor Giuliani, aggressive enforcement of these laws is necessary to combat serious crime—murders and robberies—because minor disorderly offenses contribute causally to serious crime. The justification for the enforcement policy is the harms that the activities cause, not their immorality. "If a climate of disorder and lack of mutual respect is allowed to take root," Mayor Giuliani argues, "incidence of other, more serious antisocial behavior will increase ... Murder and graffiti are two vastly different crimes. But they are part of the same continuum. ..."

* * *

Alcohol Consumption and Harm

The traditional liberal position on alcohol consumption was always murky, in large part because of John Stuart Mill's writing on temperance. Relying on the harm and offense principles, Mill justified a wide and complex regulatory scheme directed at discouraging the use of alcohol. In addition to the prohibition on consuming excessive amounts of alcohol that could rightly be imposed on persons with prior convictions for drunken violence and on soldiers or policemen on duty, as well as the prohibition on public intoxication, Mill also approved of taxing the sale of alcohol and regulating the sale and consumption of liquor. Mill defended taxation on the ground that some taxation on consumption was inevitable and that it may as well be directed against disfavored consumption. "It is ... the duty of the State to consider, in the imposition of taxes, what commodities the consumers can best spare; and a fortiori, to select in preference those of which it deems the use, beyond a very moderate quantity, to be positively injurious." As a result, Mill concluded, "taxation ... of stimulants up to the point which produces the largest amount of revenue (supposing that the State needs all the revenue which it yields) is not only admissible, but to be approved of."

Mill also favored the regulation of alcohol-serving establishments, but opposed limiting the number of "beer and spirit houses." Because of its direct relevance to the contemporary Chicago temperance movement, I will quote his lengthy discussion verbatim:

> All places of public resort require the restraint of a police, and places of this kind peculiarly, because offenses against society are especially apt to originate there. It is, therefore, fit to confine the power of selling these commodities (at least for consumption on the spot) to persons of known or vouched-for respectability of conduct; to make such regulations respecting hours of opening and closing as may be requisite for public surveillance; and to withdraw the license if breaches of the peace repeatedly take place through the connivance or incapacity of the keeper of the house, or if it becomes a rendezvous for concocting and preparing offenses against the law. Any further restriction I do not conceive to be, in principle, justifiable. The limitation in number, for instance, of beer and spirit houses, for the express purpose of rendering them more difficult of access and diminishing the occasions of temptation, not only exposes all to an inconvenience because there are some by whom the facility would be abused, but is suited only to a state of society in which the laboring classes are avowedly treated as children or savages, and placed under an education of restraint, to fit them for future admission to the privileges of freedom. This is not the principle on which the laboring classes are professedly governed in any free country...

As this passage suggests, Mill opposed limiting the number of liquor establishments, but nevertheless justified significant regulations on the operation of bars and lounges. He justified these regulations because he perceived alcohol consumption as, in some sense, causally related to crime and the need for police expenditures.

Mill's position on alcohol consumption, then, was slightly inconsistent. In certain passages, Mill viewed the consumption of alcohol both as an offense, in the case of public intoxication, and as a harm that justified numerous regulations and, in some cases, prohibition. Mill justified taxing alcohol in order to make the cost of drinking prohibitive—especially, one would assume, among the less wealthy. In other passages, however, Mill opposed making access to alcohol more difficult because it would treat the laboring classes paternalistically. This seems inconsistent, or, at the very least, ambiguous.

In addition, Mill's discussion of alcohol consumption was somewhat at odds with his other applications of the harm principle in *On Liberty*. In the context of drinking, it seems, Mill failed to distinguish between harmful and harmless private consumption of alcohol. Surely the private consumption of alcohol in one's own home, even to excess, was not necessarily harmful from a Millian perspective. Certainly the private consumption of alcohol, even to excess, could not be viewed as more harmful than engaging in acts of prostitution. Why then would Mill justify taxing the sale of stimulants, but not regulating fornication?

The ambiguity in Mill's writings had a significant impact on the 1960s progressive position on drinking—a position which was equally murky. If anything, the progressive position rested on the offense principle. Drinking alcohol fit well within the framework of Hart's analysis of prostitution: the public manifestations should be prohibited in order to avoid any affront to public decency—"in order to protect the ordinary citizen, who is an unwilling witness of it in the streets, from something offensive." The justification for regulation was based on public offense, which explains why the matter of drinking generally fell under the rubric of "public decency." In Joel Feinberg's later work, Feinberg acknowledged one potential harm associated with drinking—specifically the risk of vehicular homicide and accidents—but nevertheless stressed the interests of the majority of innocent or harmless drinkers in being allowed to continue to drink.

Lord Devlin, in response to Hart, focused on the ambiguities of the progressive position. Devlin criticized the traditional liberal reliance, first, on the public-private distinction and, second, on the distinction between harmful and harmless private drinking. With regard to the latter, Devlin emphasized the harm that could be associated with private drinking and argued that there is no principled way to distinguish between harmless and harmful private drinking. According to Devlin, the determination of harm had to be made on a case-by-case basis and, as a result, there could be no principled opposition to complete prohibition if necessary. After an abbreviated discussion of harm, however, Devlin returned to his principal argument concerning legal moralism and his claim that shared morality is essential to social cohesion.

The debate over the regulation of alcohol consumption, then, had traditionally been fragmented. The progressive position was itself fractured. Mill had offered both harm and offense arguments in support of regulation. Later progressive thinkers focused increasingly on the offense argument, but nevertheless recognized potential harms. More conservative thinkers, like Devlin, capitalized on the ambiguity to argue about both harm and morality.

Today, however, the debate seems less fragmented, again, because contemporary proponents of regulation and prohibition have focused on the harm argument. The recent social and political movements in Chicago and New York City have zoomed-in on the specific causal relationship between liquor and harm. In Chicago, the new temperance movement has targeted liquor stores, bars and lounges because of the harm they are causing neighborhoods. The movement justifies closing businesses in order to revitalize neighborhoods, to cut down on crime, and to increase property value and commerce. Reverend Al Meeks, a Baptist minister and leader of the temperance movement, emphasizes that the closures are economic measures, and not moralistic measures. "We're trying to redevelop our community," Meeks explains. "This is not a return to Prohibition, we're not saying that people can't drink. We're not even saying that people can't buy alcohol... We're simply saying that on a commercial strip we need to have some immediate redevelopment." Chicago Mayor Richard Daley makes the same point. "This is a quality of life issue," Daley suggests, "not an attempt to impose prohibition."

The target is slightly different in New York City, but the focus is also on harm. Mayor Giuliani's policing initiative has targeted public drunks because of the harm they cause neighborhoods. The justification, again, is the broken windows argument, and the claim that small disorder causes serious crime. On the basis of this justification, the New York Police Department has cracked-down—and continues to crack-down—on "the squeegee pests; people urinating in public; people drinking in public; [and] illegal peddling."

The more intense focus on harm by contemporary proponents of legal regulation and prohibition has transformed the contemporary debate. It has undermined whatever remained of the harm principle in the context of alcohol consumption—already a thin fragment of a principle in the 1960s due to Mill's ambiguous writings on temperance. It has focused the debate on the different kinds of harm associated with liquor, ranging from the harms to commerce and community, to increased serious crime. And it has forced the participants in the debate to weigh harms, to value harms, and to compare harms. On these issues the harm principle itself offers no guidance.

Notes and Questions

1. What were the short-and long-term effects of repeal on alcohol consumption and its costs in the United States?

2. What would you guess to be the likely impact of repeal of laws against cocaine, marijuana, gambling, and prostitution in current circumstances in the United States?

3. What are the prospects of any renewed enthusiasm of national alcohol prohibition? For state-level alcohol prohibition?

4. Are the impacts of the repeal of alcohol prohibition a good model for any types of 21st century decriminalization of vice?

*

Index

References are to Pages

References are to Pages

References are to Pages

†